M000302005

BaseBall america®
2011 DIRECTORY

YOUR DEFINITIVE GUIDE TO THE GAME

Detailed Information On Baseball In All Leagues At All Levels

Majors

Minors

Independent

International

College

Amateur

BASEBALL AMERICA INC. · DURHAM, N.C.

baseballhall.org

Celebrate the Game...

Connect with Cooperstown.

**Preserving History.
Honoring Excellence.
Connecting Generations.**

BaseBall america
2011 DIRECTORY

Editor
JOSH LEVENTHAL

Assistant Editors
BEN BADLER, J.J. COOPER, AARON FITT,
CONOR GLASSEY, CASEY HULL, WILL LINGO, NATHAN RODE, JIM SHONERD

Database and Application Development
BRENT LEWIS

Photo Editor
NATHAN RODE

Design & Production
SARA HIATT MCDANIEL, TIFFANY SCHWARZ, LINWOOD WEBB

Programming & Technical Development
BRENT LEWIS

Cover Photo
DAVID SCHOFIELD

BaseBall america

PRESIDENT/PUBLISHER: LEE FOLGER
EDITORS IN CHIEF: WILL LINGO, JOHN MANUEL
EXECUTIVE EDITOR: JIM CALLIS
DESIGN & PRODUCTION DIRECTOR: SARA HIATT MCDANIEL
TECHNOLOGY MANAGER: BRENT LEWIS

©2011 BASEBALL AMERICA INC. NO PORTION OF THIS BOOK MAY BE REPRINTED OR REPRODUCED
WITHOUT THE WRITTEN CONSENT OF THE PUBLISHER. FOR ADDITIONAL COPIES, VISIT OUR WEBSITE AT
BASEBALLAMERICA.COM OR CALL 1-800-845-2726 TO ORDER. COST IS US $29.95, PLUS SHIPPING
AND HANDLING PER ORDER. EXPEDITED SHIPPING AVAILABLE.

DISTRIBUTED BY SIMON & SCHUSTER
ISBN-13: 978-1-932391-35-0

BaseballAmerica.com

From **A**BBOTT To **Z**IMMERMAN

J**IM** A**BBOTT**
1987 Golden Spikes Award Winner
1988 Olympic Gold Medalist

R**YAN** Z**IMMERMAN**
Washington Nationals 3B
2004 USA Baseball National Team

AND EVERYTHING IN BETWEEN...

 PHOTOS/VIDEO

 SHOP

 NEWS

 AUCTIONS

USABASEBALL.COM

TABLE OF CONTENTS

Dr. Pepper Ballpark, Frisco, Texas

JAMES GARNER

Major League Baseball			13
American League			15
National League			15

Arizona	16	Milwaukee	46
Atlanta	18	Minnesota	48
Baltimore	20	New York (NL)	50
Boston	22	New York (AL)	52
Chicago (NL)	24	Oakland	54
Chicago (AL)	26	Philadelphia	56
Cincinnati	28	Pittsburgh	58
Cleveland	30	St. Louis	60
Colorado	32	San Diego	62
Detroit	34	San Francisco	64
Florida	36	Seattle	66
Houston	38	Tampa Bay	68
Kansas City	40	Texas	70
Los Angeles (AL)	42	Toronto	72
Los Angeles (NL)	44	Washington	74

Media	76
General Information	81
Spring Training	85
Spring Training Schedules	244

MINOR LEAGUES

Minor League Baseball	90

International	92	Midwest	140
Pacific Coast	100	South Atlantic	148
Eastern	109	New York-Penn	156
Southern	116	Northwest	163
Texas	121	Appalachian	167
California	125	Pioneer	172
Carolina	130	Arizona	176
Florida State	134	Gulf Coast	176

INDEPENDENT LEAGUES

American Assoc.	178	Frontier	189
Atlantic	183	North American	194
Can-Am	186		

Minor League Schedules	204

OTHER LEAGUES & ORGANIZATIONS

International	198	High School	294
Winter	202	Youth	297
College	240	Adult	300
Amateur	280		

TRIPLE-A

Name Change: Omaha Royals become Omaha Storm Chasers
Ballpark: Omaha Storm Chasers—Werner Park.
Franchise Move: Portland Beavers (Pacific Coast) to Tucson Padres.
Affiliation Changes: Oklahoma City (Pacific Coast) from Rangers to Astros. Round Rock (Pacific Coast) from Astros to Rangers.

DOUBLE-A

Name Change: West Tenn Diamond Jaxx become Jackson Generals

HIGH CLASS A

Affiliation Changes: Bakersfield (California) from Rangers to Reds. Inland Empire (California) from Dodgers to Angels. Rancho Cucamonga (California) from Angels to Dodgers. Lynchurg (Carolina) from Reds to Braves. Myrtle Beach (Carolina) from Braves to Rangers.

LOW CLASS A

Affiliation Changes: Burlington (Midwest) from Royals to Athletics. Kane County (Midwest) from Athletics to Royals.

SHORT-SEASON

Affiliation Changes: Auburn (New York-Penn) from Blue Jays to Nationals. Vermont (New York-Penn) from Nationals to Athletics. Vancouver (Northwest) from Athletics to Blue Jays.

ROOKIE

Operator Change: Bluefield (Appalachian) from Orioles to Blue Jays.
New Affiliate: Arizona Diamondbacks join Arizona League.

NOW AVAILABLE

THE 2011 PROSPECT HANDBOOK

The 2011 Prospect Handbook is the definitive annual reference title on prospects. You find out the top 30 prospects for every organization in the game. If you order it from us, you'll also get a supplement that features an additional prospect for every team. You'll get a full scouting report and statistics for 30 additional players, just like the other 900 prospects that make the Prospect Handbook the best book of its kind.

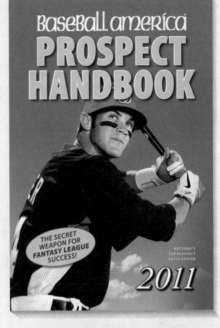

$32⁹⁵

BONUS SUPPLEMENT AVAILABLE ONLY FROM BASEBALL AMERICA

(800) 845-2726

Calls accepted Monday–Friday, 9 a.m.-5 p.m. ET.

BaseballAmerica.com/store

WISH YOU'D GOTTEN YOUR DIRECTORY SOONER?

Now if you order any of Baseball America's books and choose the Premium Shipping and Handling Option, your books will be shipped to you hot off the press via USPS Priority Mail. You'll get your books **FIRST**, before they hit the stores, giving you the fantasy league advantage or insider scoop you want.

Don't miss out: Pre-order next year's book **NOW!**

Map illustrations by Paul Trap

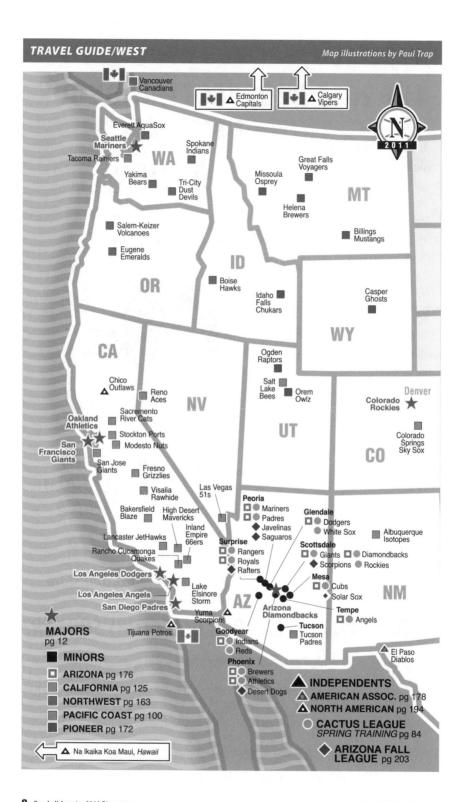

Vancouver
Canadians

Edmonton
Capitals

Calgary
Vipers

N
2011

Everett AquaSox

**Seattle
Mariners**

Tacoma Rainiers

Spokane
Indians

WA

Yakima
Bears

Tri-City
Dust
Devils

Missoula
Osprey

Great Falls
Voyagers

MT

Helena
Brewers

Salem-Keizer
Volcanoes

Billings
Mustangs

Eugene
Emeralds

ID

Boise
Hawks

OR

Idaho
Falls
Chukars

Casper
Ghosts

WY

Ogden
Raptors

Chico
Outlaws

Reno
Aces

Salt
Lake
Bees

Orem
Owlz

Denver

Colorado
Rockies

NV

Sacramento
River Cats

CA

**Oakland
Athletics**

Stockton Ports

Modesto Nuts

UT

CO

Colorado
Springs
Sky Sox

**San
Francisco
Giants**

San Jose
Giants

Fresno
Grizzlies

Visalia
Rawhide

Las Vegas
51s

Peoria
◻︎● Mariners
◻︎● Padres
◆ Javelinas
◆ Saguaros

Glendale
◻︎● Dodgers
● White Sox

Albuquerque
Isotopes

Bakersfield
Blaze

High Desert
Mavericks

Inland
Empire
66ers

Surprise
◻︎● Rangers
◻︎● Royals
◆ Rafters

Scottsdale
◻︎● Giants ◻︎● Diamondbacks
● Scorpions ● Rockies

Lancaster JetHawks

Rancho Cucamonga
Quakes

Los Angeles Dodgers

Los Angeles Angels

Mesa
◻︎● Cubs
◆ Solar Sox

NM

Lake
Elsinore
Storm

San Diego Padres

Yuma
Scorpions

AZ

**Arizona
Diamondbacks**

Tempe
◻︎● Angels

Tijuana Potros

★
MAJORS
pg 12

Goodyear
◻︎ Indians
◻︎ Reds

Tucson
● Tucson
Padres

El Paso
Diablos

Phoenix
◻︎● Brewers
◻︎● Athletics
◆ Desert Dogs

■ **MINORS**

◻︎ **ARIZONA** pg 176

■ **CALIFORNIA** pg 125

■ **NORTHWEST** pg 163

■ **PACIFIC COAST** pg 100

■ **PIONEER** pg 172

△ Na Ikaika Koa Maui, *Hawaii*

▲ **INDEPENDENTS**

▲ **AMERICAN ASSOC.** pg 178

△ **NORTH AMERICAN** pg 194

○ **CACTUS LEAGUE**
SPRING TRAINING pg 84

◆ **ARIZONA FALL
LEAGUE** pg 203

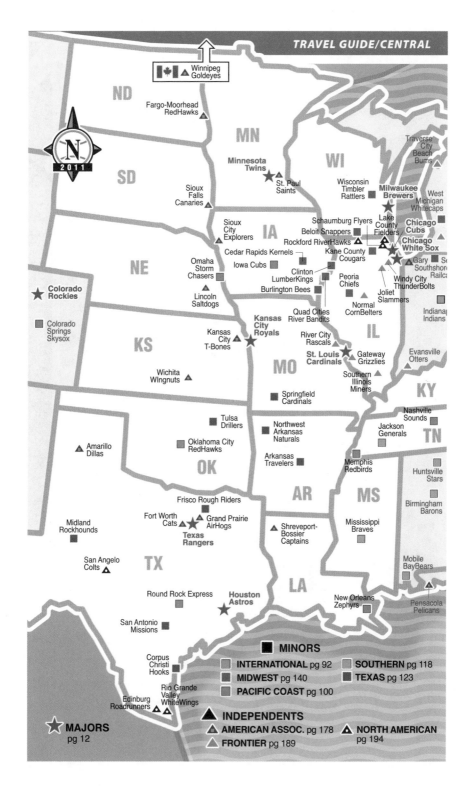

Winnipeg Goldeyes

ND

Fargo-Moorhead RedHawks

MN

Traverse City Beach Bums

SD

Minnesota Twins

St. Paul Saints

WI

Wisconsin Timber Rattlers

Milwaukee Brewers

West Michigan Whitecaps

Sioux Falls Canaries

Sioux City Explorers

IA

Schaumburg Flyers

Beloit Snappers

Lake County Fielders

Chicago Cubs

Rockford RiverHawks

Chicago White Sox

Cedar Rapids Kernels

Kane County Cougars

Gary Southshore Railca

Omaha Storm Chasers

Iowa Cubs

Clinton LumberKings

Windy City ThunderBolts

NE

Peoria Chiefs

Colorado Rockies

Lincoln Saltdogs

Burlington Bees

Joliet Slammers

Colorado Springs Skysox

Quad Cities River Bandits

Normal CornBelters

Indiana Indians

Kansas City Royals

KS

Kansas City T-Bones

River City Rascals

IL

Evansville Otters

Wichita WIngnuts

MO

St. Louis Cardinals

Gateway Grizzlies

Southern Illinois Miners

KY

Springfield Cardinals

Nashville Sounds

Tulsa Drillers

Northwest Arkansas Naturals

Jackson Generals

TN

Amarillo Dillas

Oklahoma City RedHawks

Arkansas Travelers

Memphis Redbirds

Huntsville Stars

OK

AR

MS

Birmingham Barons

Frisco Rough Riders

Midland Rockhounds

Fort Worth Cats

Grand Prairie AirHogs

Texas Rangers

Shreveport-Bossier Captains

Mississippi Braves

San Angelo Colts

TX

Mobile BayBears

Round Rock Express

Houston Astros

New Orleans Zephyrs

LA

Pensacola Pelicans

San Antonio Missions

Corpus Christi Hooks

MINORS

Rio Grande Valley WhiteWings

INTERNATIONAL pg 92

SOUTHERN pg 118

MIDWEST pg 140

TEXAS pg 123

PACIFIC COAST pg 100

Edinburg Roadrunners

INDEPENDENTS

★ **MAJORS** pg 12

AMERICAN ASSOC. pg 178

NORTH AMERICAN pg 194

FRONTIER pg 189

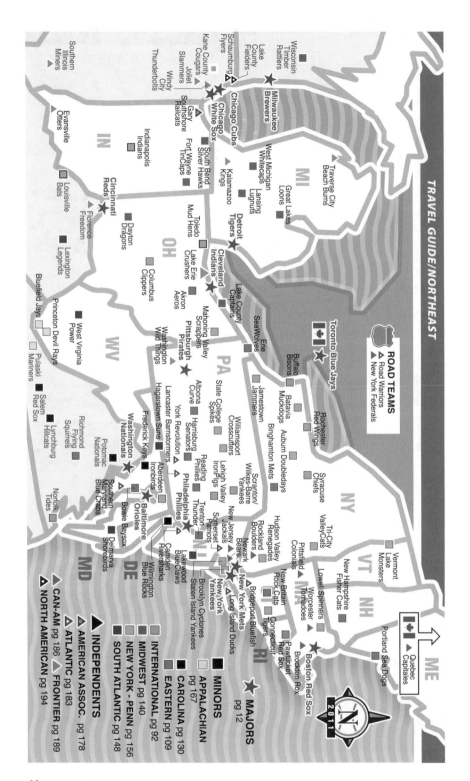

ROAD TEAMS
▲ Road Warriors
▲ New York Federals

Southern Illinois Miners
Wisconsin Timber Rattlers
Schaumburg Flyers
Kane County Cougars
Lake County Fielders
Joliet Slammers
Windy City Thunderbolts
Gary SouthShore Railcats
Chicago Cubs
Chicago White Sox
Milwaukee Brewers
West Michigan Whitecaps
Lansing Lugnuts
Great Lakes Loons
Traverse City Beach Bums
Evansville Otters
Indianapolis Indians
South Bend Silver Hawks
Fort Wayne TinCaps
Kalamazoo Kings
Detroit Tigers
Louisville Bats
Florence Freedom
Cincinnati Reds
Dayton Dragons
Toledo Mud Hens
Lake Erie Crushers
Cleveland Indians
Akron Aeros
Columbus Clippers
Lake County Captains
Lexington Legends
Bluefield Jays
Princeton Devil Rays
West Virginia Power
Pulaski Mariners
Salem Red Sox
Lynchburg Hillcats
Richmond Flying Squirrels
Norfolk Tides
Potomac Nationals
Washington Nationals
Frederick Keys
Hagerstown Suns
Mahoning Valley Scrappers
Pittsburgh Pirates
Washington Wild Things
Altoona Curve
State College Spikes
Harrisburg Senators
York Revolution
Lancaster Barnstormers
Reading Phillies
Lehigh Valley IronPigs
Williamsport Crosscutters
Jamestown Jammers
Batavia Muckdogs
Buffalo Bisons
Erie SeaWolves
Auburn Doubledays
Binghamton Mets
Scranton/Wilkes-Barre Yankees
Rochester Red Wings
Syracuse Chiefs
Toronto Blue Jays
Aberdeen IronBirds
Southern Maryland Blue Crabs
Bowie Baysox
Baltimore Orioles
Delmarva Shorebirds
Wilmington Blue Rocks
Camden Riversharks
Philadelphia Phillies
Trenton Thunder
Somerset Patriots
New Jersey Jackals
Newark Bears
Lakewood BlueClaws
Staten Island Yankees
Brooklyn Cyclones
New York Yankees
New York Mets
Long Island Ducks
Bridgeport Bluefish
Hudson Valley Renegades
Rockland Boulders
Tri-City ValleyCats
Pittsfield Colonials
New Britain Rock Cats
Connecticut Tigers
Vermont Lake Monsters
Lowell Spinners
New Hampshire Fisher Cats
Worcester Tornadoes
Pawtucket Red Sox
Brockton Rox
Boston Red Sox
Portland Sea Dogs
Quebec Capitales

ME
NH
VT
NY
MA
RI
CT
NJ
PA
MD
DE
WV
OH
IN
MI

Quebec Capitales

★ MAJORS pg 12

MINORS
■ APPALACHIAN pg 167
■ CAROLINA pg 130
■ EASTERN pg 109
■ INTERNATIONAL pg 92
■ MIDWEST pg 140
□ NEW YORK - PENN pg 156
□ SOUTH ATLANTIC pg 148

INDEPENDENTS
▲ AMERICAN ASSOC. pg 178
▲ ATLANTIC pg 183
▲ CAN-AM pg 186
▲ FRONTIER pg 189
▲ NORTH AMERICAN pg 194

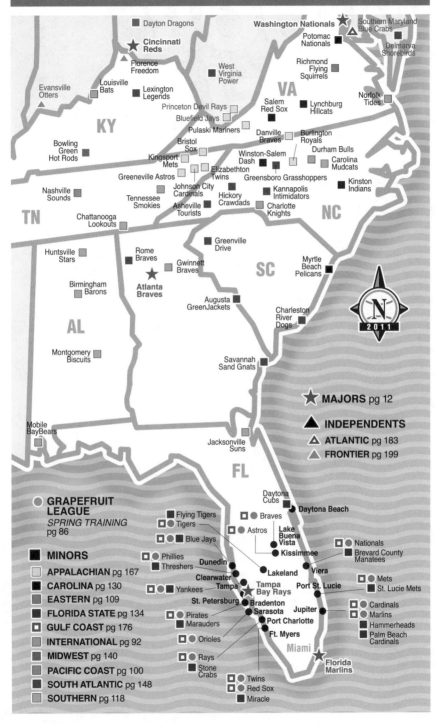

Dayton Dragons
Washington Nationals
Southern Maryland Blue Crabs
Cincinnati Reds
Potomac Nationals
Delmarva Shorebirds
Florence Freedom
West Virginia Power
Richmond Flying Squirrels
Evansville Otters
Louisville Bats
Lexington Legends
Salem Red Sox
Lynchburg Hillcats
Norfolk Tides
VA
KY
Princeton Devil Rays
Bluefield Jays
Bowling Green Hot Rods
Pulaski Mariners
Danville Braves
Burlington Royals
Durham Bulls
Bristol Sox
Kingsport Mets
Winston-Salem Dash
Carolina Mudcats
Nashville Sounds
Greeneville Astros
Elizabethton Twins
Greensboro Grasshoppers
Kinston Indians
Johnson City Cardinals
Kannapolis Intimidators
Tennessee Smokies
Hickory Crawdads
Asheville Tourists
Charlotte Knights
NC
TN
Chattanooga Lookouts
Huntsville Stars
Rome Braves
Greenville Drive
Gwinnett Braves
Myrtle Beach Pelicans
Birmingham Barons
Atlanta Braves
SC
Augusta GreenJackets
Charleston River Dogs
AL
Montgomery Biscuits
Savannah Sand Gnats
★ **MAJORS** pg 12

▲ **INDEPENDENTS**
Mobile BayBears
△ **ATLANTIC** pg 183
Jacksonville Suns
△ **FRONTIER** pg 199
FL

○ **GRAPEFRUIT LEAGUE**
SPRING TRAINING pg 86
Daytona Cubs
Daytona Beach
Flying Tigers
Braves
Tigers
Astros
Lake Buena Vista
■ **MINORS**
Blue Jays
Kissimmee
Nationals
Brevard County Manatees
☐ APPALACHIAN pg 167
Phillies
Viera
■ CAROLINA pg 130
Threshers
Dunedin
Lakeland
☐ EASTERN pg 109
Clearwater
Mets
■ FLORIDA STATE pg 134
Yankees
Tampa
Tampa Bay Rays
Port St. Lucie
St. Lucie Mets
☐ GULF COAST pg 176
St. Petersburg
Bradenton
☐ INTERNATIONAL pg 92
Pirates
Sarasota
Jupiter
Cardinals
■ MIDWEST pg 140
Marauders
Port Charlotte
Marlins
■ PACIFIC COAST pg 100
Orioles
Ft. Myers
Hammerheads
■ SOUTH ATLANTIC pg 148
Rays
Palm Beach Cardinals
☐ SOUTHERN pg 118
Stone Crabs
Miami
Twins
Florida Marlins
Red Sox
Miracle

MAJOR LEAGUES

MAJOR LEAGUE BASEBALL

Mailing Address: 245 Park Ave. New York, NY 10167.
Telephone: (212) 931-7800.
Website: www.mlb.com.
Commissioner: Allan H. "Bud" Selig.
Executive Vice President, Business: Tim Brosnan. **Executive VP, Labor Relations/Human Resources:** Robert Manfred. **Executive VP, Finance:** Jonathan Mariner. **Executive VP, Administration/Chief Information Officer/Interim Executive VP, Baseball Operations:** John McHale. **Executive VP, Baseball Development:** Jimmie Lee Solomon.

Bud Selig

BASEBALL OPERATIONS
Senior VP, Baseball Operations: Joe Garagiola Jr.
Senior VP, Baseball Operations: Frank Robinson.
VP, Baseball Operations/Administration: Ed Burns. **VP, International Baseball Operations:** Lou Melendez. **VP, Umpiring:** Mike Port. **VP, Youth/Facility Development:** Darrell Miller. **Senior Director, Major League Operations:** Roy Krasik. **Director, Minor League Operations:** Sylvia Lind.
Senior Manager, Baseball Operations: Jeff Pfeifer. **Manager, Dominican Operations:** Ronaldo Peralta. **Manager, Minor League Operations:** Fred Seymour. **Senior Specialist, On-Field Operations:** Darryl Hamilton.
Specialist, Amateur Player Administration: Chuck Fox. **Specialist, On-Field Operations:** Matt McKendry. **Specialist, Umpire Administration:** Cathy Davis. **Specialist, International Operations:** Joel Araujo.
Coordinator, Major League Operations: Gina Liento. **Coordinator, Minor League Operations:** Ben Baroody. **Supervisor, Umpiring:** Rich Rieker.
Director, Umpire Administration: Tom Lepperd. **Director, Umpire Medical Services:** Mark Letendre. **Umpiring Supervisors:** Cris Jones, Randy Marsh, Steve Palermo, Charlie Reliford, Larry Young.
Director, Arizona Fall League: Steve Cobb. **Director, Major League Scouting Bureau:** Frank Marcos. **Assistant Director, Scouting Bureau:** Rick Oliver.

Security
VP, Security/Facility Management: Earnell Lucas.
Director, Facility Operations: Linda Pantell. **Senior Manager, Facility Operations:** Bob Campbell. **Supervisor, Executive Offices Security Operations:** William Diaz. **Managing Director, Security:** John Skinner. **Supervisor, Executive Protection:** Charles Hargrove. **Security Analyst:** Christopher Ellis.
Coordinator, Security/Facility Management: Yenifer Nunez. **Assistant to VP, Security/Facility Management:** Danielle Beckom.

Investigations
Senior VP, Investigations: Dan Mullin.
VP, Investigations: George Hanna. **Manager, Investigations:** Nancy Zamudio.

Public Relations
Telephone: (212) 931-7878. **Fax:** (212) 949-5654.
Senior VP, Public Relations: Patrick Courtney.
VP, Business Public Relations: Matt Bourne.
Director, Media Relations: John Blundell. **Senior Project Manager, Baseball Information:** Rob Doelger. **Manager, Media Relations:** Michael Teevan. **Managers, Business Public Relations:** Jeff Heckelman, Daniel Queen. **Specialist, Media Relations:** Donald Muller. **Specialists, Business Public Relations:** Steven Arocho, Lauren Verrusio. **Coordinator, Business Public Relations:** Sarah Leer. **Senior Administrative Assistant:** Heather Flock. **Administrative Assistant:** Raquel Ramos.

Club Relations
Senior VP, Scheduling/Club Relations: Katy Feeney.
Senior Administrative Assistant, Scheduling/Club Relations: Raxel Concepcion. **Coordinator, Club Relations:** Bennett Shields. **Senior VP, Club Relations:** Phyllis Merhige. **Senior Administrative Assistant, Club Relations:** Angelica Cintron.

Licensing
Senior VP, Licensing: Howard Smith.
VP, Domestic Licensing: Steve Armus. **VP, Hard Goods:** Dan Weinberg.
Senior Director, Consumer Products, Retail Marketing: Adam Blinderman. **Director, Licensing/Minor Leagues:** Eliot Runyon. **Director, Gifts/Novelties:** Maureen Mason. **Director, Hard Goods:** Mike Napolitano. **Director, Non-Authentics:** Greg Sim. **Director, Authentic Collection:** Ryan Samuelson. **Senior Manager, Presence Marketing:** Robin Jaffe.

Publishing/Photographs
VP, Publishing/Photographs: Don Hintze.
Editorial Director: Mike McCormick. **Art Director, Publications:** Faith Rittenberg. **Director, MLB Photographs:** Rich

MAJOR LEAGUES

Pilling.

Special Events
Senior VP, Special Events: Marla Miller.
Senior Director, Special Events: Brian O'Gara. **Directors, Special Events:** Eileen Buser, Jacqueline Secaira-Cotto, Rob Capilli. **Managers, Special Events:** JB Hacking, Jennifer Jacobson.

Broadcasting
Senior VP, Broadcasting: Chris Tully.
VP, Broadcast Administration/Operations: Bernadette McDonald.
Senior Director, Broadcasting Business Affairs: Susanne Hilgefort. **Director, Broadcast Administration/Operations:** Chuck Torres.

Corporate Sales/Marketing
Senior VP, Corporate Sales/Marketing: Lou Koskovolis.
VP, Corporate Sales/Marketing: Jeremy Cohen.

Advertising
Senior VP/Chief Marketing Officer: Jacqueline Parkes.
Vice President, Research/Strategic Planning: Dan Derian. **Director, Research:** Marc Beck. **Vice President, Design Services:** Anne Occi.

Community Affairs
VP, Community Affairs: Tom Brasuell. **Director, Community Relations:** Celia Bobrowsky.

General Administration
Senior VP, Accounting/Treasurer: Bob Clark. **Senior VP/General Counsel, Labor Relations:** Dan Halem. **Senior VP/General Counsel, Business:** Ethan Orlinsky. **Senior VP/General Counsel, BOC:** Tom Ostertag. **Senior VP, Finance:** Kathleen Torres. **VP, Application Development:** Mike Morris. **VP, Deputy General Counsel:** Domna Candido.
Senior VP, Diversity/Strategic Alliances: Wendy Lewis. **VP, Human Resources:** Ray Scott. **VP/Deputy General Counsel:** Jennifer Simms. **VP, Operations/Tech Support:** Peter Surhoff. **Director, Baseball Assistance Team:** Joe Grippo. **VP, Office Operations:** Donna Hoder. **Senior Director, Quality Control:** Peggy O'Neill-Janosik. **VP, Recruitment:** John Quinones.
Director, Risk Management/Financial Reporting: Anthony Avitabile.
Senior Manager, Records: Mildred Delgado. **Director, Payroll/Pension:** Rich Hunt. **Director, Benefits/HRIS:** Diane Cuddy.

International
Mailing Address: 245 Park Ave., 31st Floor, New York, NY 10167. **Telephone:** (212) 931-7500. **Fax:** (212) 949-5795.
Senior VP, International Business Operations: Paul Archey.
VP, International Licensing: Denis Nolan. **VP/Executive Producer:** Russell Gabay.
Tournament Director, World Baseball Classic: James Pearce. **Director, International Licensing:** Josephine Fuzesi. **Director, International Marketing/Advertising:** Jacquelyn Walsh. **Vice President, International Broadcast Sales:** Frank Uddo. **Senior Director, International Sponsorship/Communications:** Dominick Balsamo. **VP/Managing Director, MLB Japan:** Jim Small. **Director, China Operations:** Michael Marone. **Director, Australian Operations:** Thomas Nicholson. **Director, European Operations:** Clive Russell.

MLB Western Operations
Office Address: 2415 East Camelback Rd., Suite 850, Phoenix, AZ 85016.
Telephone: (602) 281-7300. **Fax:** (602) 281-7313.
VP, Western Operations/Special Projects: Laurel Prieb.
Office Coordinator: Valerie Dietrich.

Major League Baseball Productions
Office Address: One MLB Network Plaza, Secaucus, NJ 07094-2403.
Telephone: (201) 751-8500. **Fax:** (201) 751-8568.
VP, Executive In Charge of Production: David Gavant. **VP, Programming/Business Affairs:** Elizabeth Scott. **Executive Producer:** David Check. **Senior Director, Operations:** Shannon Valine.
Coordinating Producer: Adam Schlackman. **Coordinating Producer, Field Production:** Robert Haddad.

Umpires
Lance Barksdale, Ted Barrett, Wally Bell, C.B. Bucknor, Mark Carlson, Gary Cederstrom, Eric Cooper, Derryl Cousins, Fieldin Culbreth, Phil Cuzzi, Kerwin Danley, Gary Darling, Bob Davidson, Gerry Davis, Dana DeMuth, Laz Diaz, Mike DiMuro, Rob Drake, Bruce Dreckman, Doug Eddings, Paul Emmel, Mike Everitt, Chad Fairchild, Andy Fletcher, Marty Foster, Greg Gibson, Brian Gorman, Chris Guccione, Tom Hallion, Angel Hernandez, Ed Hickox, John Hirschbeck, Bill Hohn, Sam Holbrook, James Hoye, Marvin Hudson, Dan Iassogna, Adrian Johnson, Jim Joyce, Jeff Kellogg, Ron Kulpa, Jerry Layne, Alfonso Marquez, Tim McClelland, Jerry Meals, Bill Miller, Paul Nauert, Jeff Nelson, Brian O'Nora, Tony Randazzo, Ed Rapuano, Jim Reynolds, Brian Runge, Paul Schrieber, Dale Scott, Tim Timmons, Tim Tschida, Larry Vanover, Mark Wegner, Bill Welke, Tim Welke, Hunter Wendelstedt, Joe West, Mike Winters, Jim Wolf.

Events
2011 All-Star Game: July 12 at Chase Field, Phoenix, AZ.
2011 World Series: TBD.

AMERICAN LEAGUE

Years League Active: 1901-.
2011 Opening Date: March 31. **Closing Date:** Sept. 28.
Regular Season: 162 games.
Division Structure: East—Baltimore, Boston, New York, Tampa Bay, Toronto. Central—Chicago, Cleveland, Detroit, Kansas City, Minnesota. West—Los Angeles, Oakland, Seattle, Texas.
Playoff Format: Three division champions and second-place team with best record meet in two best-of-five Division Series. Winners meet in best-of-seven League Championship Series.
All-Star Game: July 24, Chase Field, Arizona (National League vs American League).
Roster Limit: 25, through Aug. 31 when rosters expand to 40.
Brand of Baseball: Rawlings.
Statistician: MLB Advanced Media, 75 Ninth Ave., 5th Floor, New York, NY 10011.

STADIUM INFORMATION

Team	Stadium	Dimensions LF	CF	RF	Capacity	2010 Att.
Baltimore	Camden Yards	333	410	318	48,190	1,733,019
Boston	Fenway Park	310	390	302	36,525	3,046,445
Chicago	U.S. Cellular Field	330	400	335	40,615	2,194,378
Cleveland	Progressive Field	325	405	325	43,545	1,391,644
Detroit	Comerica Park	345	420	330	41,000	2,461,237
Kansas City	Kauffman Stadium	330	410	330	38,177	1,615,327
Los Angeles	Angel Stadium	333	404	333	45,050	3,250,814
Minnesota	Target Field	339	404	328	40,000	3,223,640
New York	Yankee Stadium	318	408	314	52,325	3,765,807
Oakland	McAfee Coliseum	330	400	367	34,077	1,418,391
Seattle	Safeco Field	331	405	326	47,447	2,085,630
Tampa Bay	Tropicana Field	315	404	322	41,315	1,864,999
Texas	Rangers Ballpark in Arlington	332	400	325	48,911	2,505,171
Toronto	Rogers Centre	328	400	328	49,539	1,625,555

NATIONAL LEAGUE

Years League Active: 1876-.
2011 Opening Date: March 31. **Closing Date:** Sept. 28.
Regular Season: 162 games.
Division Structure: East—Atlanta, Florida, New York, Philadelphia, Washington. Central—Chicago, Cincinnati, Houston, Milwaukee, Pittsburgh, St. Louis. West—Arizona, Colorado, Los Angeles, San Diego, San Francisco.
Playoff Format: Three division champions and second-place team with best record meet in two best-of-five Division Series. Winners meet in best-of-seven League Championship Series.
All-Star Game: July 24, Chase Field, Arizona (National League vs. American League).
Roster Limit: 25, through Aug. 31 when rosters expand to 40.
Brand of Baseball: Rawlings.
Statistician: MLB Advanced Media, 75 Ninth Ave., 5th Floor, New York, NY 10011.

STADIUM INFORMATION

Team	Stadium	Dimensions LF	CF	RF	Capacity	2010 Att.
Arizona	Chase Field	330	407	334	49,033	2,056,697
Atlanta	Turner Field	335	400	330	49,743	2,510,119
Chicago	Wrigley Field	355	400	353	41,160	3,062,973
Cincinnati	Great American Ball Park	328	404	325	42,319	2,060,551
Colorado	Coors Field	347	415	350	50,499	2,875,245
Florida	Sun Life Stadium	330	434	345	38,560	1,524,894
Houston	Minute Maid Park	315	435	326	40,976	2,331,490
Los Angeles	Dodger Stadium	330	395	330	56,000	3,562,320
Milwaukee	Miller Park	344	400	345	41,900	2,776,531
New York	Citi Field	335	408	330	42,000	2,559,738
Philadelphia	Citizens Bank Park	329	401	330	43,647	3,647,249
Pittsburgh	PNC Park	325	399	320	38,362	1,613,399
St. Louis	Busch Stadium	336	400	335	43,975	3,301,218
San Diego	PETCO Park	336	396	322	42,685	2,131,774
San Francisco	AT&T Park	339	399	309	41,503	3,037,443
Washington	Nationals Park	336	404	335	42,000	1,828,066

Arizona Diamondbacks

Office Address: Chase Field, 401 E. Jefferson St, Phoenix, AZ 85004.
Mailing Address: P.O. Box 2095, Phoenix, AZ 58001.
Telephone: (602) 462-6500. **Fax:** (602) 462-6599. **Website:** www.dbacks.com

Ownership
Managing General Partner: Ken Kendrick. **General Partners:** Mike Chipman, Jeff Royer.

BUSINESS OPERATIONS
President/CEO: Derrick Hall. **Executive Assistant to President/CEO:** Brooke Mitchell.
Special Assistants to President/CEO: Luis Gonzalez, Roland Hemond.

Broadcasting
Vice President, Broadcasting: Scott Geyer.

Corporate Partnerships/Marketing
Executive VP, Business Operations: Cullen Maxey.
Senior VP, Ticket Sales/Marketing: John Fisher. **VP, Business Development:** Jason Howard.
Senior Director, Marketing: Karina Bohn. **Brand Director:** Doug Alkire. **Senior Director, Corporate Partnerships:** Steve Mullins. **Director, Corporate Partnership Services:** Kerri White. **Senior Account Manager:** Tim Emory. **Director, Hispanic Sales/Marketing:** Julie Romero. **Director, Publications:** Greg Salvatore.

Ken Kendrick

Finance/Legal

Executive VP/CFO: Tom Harris. **Executive Assistant to Managing General Partner/CFO:** Sandy Cox. **VP, Finance:** Craig Bradley. **Senior VP/General Counsel:** Nona Lee. **Associate General Counsel:** Caleb Jay. **Legal Secretary:** Candace Kerege.

Community Affairs
VP, Corporate/Community Impact: Debbie Castaldo. **Director, Community Affairs:** Kristine Hedlund. **Manager, Community Programs:** Tara Trzinski.

Communications/Media Relations
Telephone: (602) 462-6519. **Fax:** (602) 462-6527.
VP, Communications: Shaun Rachau. **Manager, Player/Media Relations:** Casey Wilcox. **Coordinator, Player/Media Relations:** Morgan Ballard. **Coordinator, Communications:** Mallory Conger.

Stadium Operations
VP, Facility/Event Services: Russ Amaral. **Director, Security:** Sean Maguire. **Manager, Security:** Greg Green. **Director, Building Services:** Jim Hawkins. **Director, Engineering:** Jim White. **Director, Event Services:** Bryan White.

2011 SCHEDULE
Standard Game Times: 6:40 p.m.; Sun. 1:10.

APRIL		
1-3 . . . . at Colorado	13-15 . at Los Angeles (NL)	24-26 . . . . .at Detroit	12-14 . . . . .New York (NL)

APRIL
1-3 . . . . at Colorado
4-6 . . . . .at Chicago (NL)
8-10 . . . . Cincinnati
11-13 . . . . St. Louis
15-17 . . . . . San Francisco
19-21 . . . .at Cincinnati
22-24 . . . at New York (NL)
25-27 . . . . . .Philadelphia
28-30 . . . . . Chicago (NL)

MAY
1 . . . . Chicago (NL)
3-5 . . . . .Colorado
6-8 . . . . at San Diego
10-12 . . at San Francisco

13-15 . at Los Angeles (NL)
16-17 . . . . . . San Diego
18-19 . . . . Atlanta
20-22 . . . . . . Minnesota
24-26 . . . . . at Colorado
27-29 . . . . . .at Houston
30-31 . . . . Florida

JUNE
1 . . . . Florida
2-5 . . . . Washington
7-9 . . . . . . at Pittsburgh
10-13 . . . . . . .at Florida
14-16 . . . San Francisco
17-19 . . . . Chicago (AL)
21-23 . . . . .at Kansas City

24-26 . . . . . . .at Detroit
27-29 . . . . . Cleveland

JULY
1-3 . . . . .at Oakland
4-6 . . . . . at Milwaukee
7-10 . . . . . .at St. Louis
15-17 . . . Los Angeles (NL)
18-21 . . . . . .Milwaukee
22-24 . . . . . . .Colorado
26-28 . . . . . at San Diego
29-31 . at Los Angeles (NL)

AUGUST
1-3 . . . . at San Francisco
5-7 . . . . Los Angeles (NL)
8-11 . . . . Houston

12-14 . . . . .New York (NL)
16-18 . . . . at Philadelphia
19-21 . . . . at Atlanta
22-25 . . . . at Washington
26-28 . . . . San Diego
29-31 . . . . .Colorado

SEPTEMBER
2-4 . . . . . at San Francisco
5-7 . . . . . . at Colorado
8-11 . . . . San Diego
12-14 . at Los Angeles (NL)
16-18 . . . . . at San Diego
19-21 . . . . . . .Pittsburgh
23-25 . . . . . San Francisco
26-28 . . . Los Angeles (NL)

GENERAL INFORMATION
Stadium (year opened): Chase Field (1998).
Team Colors: Sedona Red, Sonoran Sand and Black.

Player Representative: Ian Kennedy.
Home Dugout: Third Base.
Playing Surface: Grass.

Event Coordinator: Stephanie Scheidler. **Head Groundskeeper:** Grant Trenbeath. **Official Scorer:** Rodney Johnson. **Manager, Spring Training Operations:** David Dunne.

Ticketing
Telephone: (602) 514-8400. **Fax:** (602) 462-4141.
Senior Director, Suite/Premium Services: Diney Ransford. **Director, Group/Suite Sales:** Scott Worden. **Assistant Director, Ticket Operations:** Luis Calderon. **Director, Ticket Development/Operations:** Kenny Farrell.

Travel, Clubhouse
Senior Director, Team Travel: Roger Riley. **Manager, Equipment/Visiting Clubhouse:** Bob Doty.

BASEBALL OPERATIONS
Telephone: (602) 462-6500. **Fax:** (602) 462-6425.
Executive Vice President/General Manager: Kevin Towers.
Assistant GM: Billy Ryan. **VP, Special Assistant to GM:** Bob Gebhard. **Assistant to GM/Major League Scout:** Bill Bryk. **Special Assistant to GM/Director, Latin America Operations:** Junior Noboa. **Director, Player Personnel:** Shiraz Rehman. **Director, Major League Scouting/Assistant to GM:** Ryan Isaac. **Baseball Operations Video Coordinator:** Jim Currigan. **Baseball Operations Assistant:** Sam Eaton.

Kevin Towers

Major League Staff
Manager: Kirk Gibson.
Coaches: Bench—Alan Trammell; Pitching—Charles Nagy; Batting—Don Baylor; First Base—Eric Young; Third Base—Matt Williams; Bullpen—Glenn Sherlock.

Medical, Training
Club Physicians: Dr. Michael Lee, Dr. Roger McCoy. **Head Trainer:** Ken Crenshaw.
Assistant Trainer: P.J. Mainville. **Strength/Conditioning Coordinator:** Nate Shaw.

Minor Leagues
Telephone: (602) 462-6500. **Fax:** (602) 462-6425.
Director, Player Development: Mike Bell.
Assistant Director, Player Development: Quinton McCracken. **Manager, Minor League Administration:** Susan Webner.
Coordinators: Chad Kreuter (field), Jeff Pico (pitching), Mel Stottlemyre, Jr. (short season pitching), Alan Cockrell (hitting), Tony Perezchica (infield), Joel Youngblood (outfield/baserunning), Bill Plummer (catching), Carlos Hernandez (short season catching), Hatuey Mendoza (Latin Liaison), Ryan DiPanfilo (medical), Jimmy Southard (assistant medical), Brett McCabe (strength), Jim Currigan (video), Bob Bensinger (complex), James Cameron and Ben Dorgan (clubhouse assistants).

Farm System

Class	Club (League)	Manager	Hitting Coach	Pitching Coach
Triple-A	Reno (PCL)	Brett Butler	Rick Burleson	Mike Parrott
Double-A	Mobile (SL)	Turner Ward	Alan Zinter	Dan Carlson
High A	Visalia (CAL)	Jason Hardtke	Andy Abad	Doug Drabek
Low A	South Bend (MWL)	Mark Haley	Bobby Smith	Wellington Cepeda
Short-season	Yakima (NWL)	Audo Vicente	Jacob Cruz	Doug Bochtler
Rookie	Missoula (PIO)	Hector de la Cruz	Andy Green	Gil Heredia
Rookie	Diamondbacks (AZL)	Kelly Stinnett	Abraham Nunez	Jeff Bajenaru

Scouting
Telephone: (602) 462-6518. **Fax:** (602) 462-6527.
Executive VP, Scouting/Player Development: Jerry Dipoto.
Director, Scouting: Ray Montgomery. **Director, Pro Scouting:** Mike Berger. **Director, Major League Scouting/Executive Assistant to GM:** Ryan Isaac. **Director, International Scouting:** Carlos Gomez. **Scouting Administrator:** Jennifer Blatt. **Scouting Coordinator:** Brendan Domaracki.
Director, Pacific Rim Operations: Mack Hayashi. **Special Assistant, Pacific Rim Operations:** Jim Marshall.
Major League Scouts: Bill Bryk, Special Asst. to GM (Schererville, IN); Todd Greene (Alpharetta, GA)
Pro Scouts: Joe Bohringer (De Kalb, IL); Mike Brown (Naples, FL) Pat Murtaugh (West Lafayette, IN), Mike Piatnik (Winter Haven, FL), Tom Romenesko (Santee, CA),Tim Schmidt (San Bernardino, CA), Mike Sgobba (Scottsdale, AZ),
Independent Leagues Coordinator: Mal Fichman (Boise, ID)
Regional Supervisors: Spencer Graham (San Dimas, CA), Greg Lonigro (Connellsville, PA), Steve McAllister (Chillicothe, IL), Howard McCullough (Greenville, NC);
Area Scouts: Shawn Barton (Reading, PA), John Bartsch (Rocklin, CA), Nathan Birtwell (Nashville, TN), Rodney Davis (Glendale, AZ), Denney Kyle (Carl Junction, MO), Todd Donovan (East Lyme, CT), Micah Franklin (Gilbert, AZ), Hal Kurtzman (Lake Balboa, CA), T.R. Lewis (Marietta, GA), Jeff Mousser (Huntington Beach, CA), James Mouton (Missouri City, TX), Donnie Reynolds (Portland, OR), Joe Robinson (St. Louis, MO), J.R. Salinas (Hutto, TX), Rick Short (Peoria, IL), Matt Smith (Surprise, AZ), George Swain (Wilmington, NC), Frankie Thon, Jr. (Miami, FL), Luke Wrenn (Lakeland, FL).
Part-Time Scouts: Homer Newlin (Tallahassee, FL), Steve Oleschuk (Verdun, Quebec).
International Scouts: Supervisor—Luis Baez (Santo Domingo, DR). Dominican Republic—Gabriel Berroa, José Ortiz, Rafael Mateo. Panama—José Díaz Perez. Nicaragua—Julio Sanchez. Colombia—Luis Gonzalez. Venezuela—Ubaldo Heredia, Marlon Urdaneta. Europe—Rene Saggiadi.

Atlanta Braves

Office Address: 755 Hank Aaron Dr, Atlanta, GA 30315.
Mailing Address: PO Box 4064, Atlanta, GA 30302.
Telephone: (404) 522-7630. **Website:** www.braves.com.

Ownership
Operated/Owned By: Liberty Media.
Chairman Emeritus: Bill Bartholomay. **Chairman/CEO:** Terry McGuirk.
President: John Schuerholz. **Senior Vice President:** Henry Aaron.

BUSINESS OPERATIONS
Executive Vice President, Business Operations: Mike Plant.
VP/General Counsel: Greg Heller.

Finance
Senior VP/Chief Financial Officer: Chip Moore.

Marketing, Sales
Executive VP, Sales/Marketing: Derek Schiller. **Executive Director, Marketing:** Gus Eurton.
Senior Director, Ticket Sales: Paul Adams. **Senior Director, Corporate Sales:** Jim Allen.

Media Relations/Public Relations
Telephone: (404) 614-1556. **Fax:** (404) 614-1391.
Director, Media Relations: Brad Hainje. **Director, Public Relations:** Beth Marshall.
Publications Manager: Andy Pressley. **Public Relations Manager:** Meagan Swingle. **Media Relations Manager:** Adrienne Midgley. **Media Relations Coordinator:** Jim Misudek.

Stadium Operations
Director, Stadium Operations/Security: Larry Bowman.
Field Director: Ed Mangan. **Director, Game Entertainment:** Scott Cunningham. **PA Announcer:** Casey Motter.
Official Scorers: Mike Stamus, Jack Wilkinson.

Ticketing
Telephone: (404) 577-9100. **Fax:** (404) 614-2480.
Director, Ticket Operations: Anthony Esposito.

Travel, Clubhouse
Director, Team Travel/Equipment Manager: Bill Acree.
Visiting Clubhouse Manager: John Holland.

Terry McGuirk

2011 SCHEDULE
Standard Game Times: 7:10 p.m.; Fri. 7:35; Sun. 1:35.

MARCH	6-8 . . . . . at Philadelphia	20-22 . . . . Toronto	12-14 . . . . . Chicago (NL)
31 . . . . . . at Washington	10-12 . . . . . Washington	24-26 . . . . . at San Diego	15-18 . . . . . San Francisco
	13-15 . . . . . . Philadelphia	27-29 . . . . at Seattle	19-21 . . . . Arizona
APRIL	16-17 . . . . Houston		22-25 . . . . at Chicago (NL)
2-3 . . . . . . at Washington	18-19 . . . . . . at Arizona	**JULY**	26-28 . . . at New York (NL)
4-7 . . . . at Milwaukee	20-22 . at Los Angeles (AL)	1-3 . . . . Baltimore	30-31 . . . . . . Washington
8-10 . . . . . . Philadelphia	24-25 . . . . . at Pittsburgh	4-7 . . . . Colorado	
12-14 . . . . Florida	27-29 . . . . . . Cincinnati	8-10 . . . . at Philadelphia	**SEPTEMBER**
15-17 . . . . New York (NL)	30-31 . . . . . . San Diego	15-17 . . . . . Washington	1 . . . . Washington
18-21 . at Los Angeles (NL)		18-21 . . . . . at Colorado	2-4 . . . . . Los Angeles (NL)
22-24 . . . at San Francisco	**JUNE**	22-24 . . . . . at Cincinnati	5-7 . . . . . at Philadelphia
25-27 . . . . at San Diego	1 . . . . San Diego	25-28 . . . . . . Pittsburgh	9-11 . . . . at St. Louis
29-30 . . . . St. Louis	3-5 . . . . at New York (NL)	29-31 . . . . Florida	12-14 . . . . Florida
	7-9 . . . . at Florida		16-18 . . . . New York (NL)
MAY	10-13 . . . . . at Houston	**AUGUST**	19-21 . . . . at Florida
1 . . . . St. Louis	14-16 . . . . New York (NL)	1-3 . . . . . at Washington	23-25 . . . . at Washington
2-5 . . . . Milwaukee	17-19 . . . . Texas	5-7 . . . . at New York (NL)	26-28 . . . . . Philadelphia
		8-10 . . . . at Florida	

GENERAL INFORMATION

Stadium (year opened): Turner Field (1997).
Team Colors: Red, white and blue.

Player Representative: Unavailable.
Home Dugout: First Base.
Playing Surface: Grass.

BASEBALL OPERATIONS

Telephone: (404) 522-7630. **Fax:** (404) 614-3308.
Executive VP/General Manager: Frank Wren.
Assistant GM: Bruce Manno. **Director, Baseball Administration:** John Coppolella. **Executive Assistants:** Annie Lee, Chris Rice.

Frank Wren

Major League Staff

Manager: Fredi Gonzalez
Coaches: Bench—Carlos Tosca; Pitching—Roger McDowell; Batting—Larry Parrish; First Base—Terry Pendleton; Third Base—Brian Snitker; Bullpen—Eddie Perez.

Medical, Training

Head Team Physician: Dr. **Norman Elliott.**
Trainer: Jeff Porter. **Assistant Trainer:** Jim Lovell. **Strength/Conditioning Coach:** Phil Falco.

Player Development

Telephone: (404) 522-7630. **Fax:** (404) 614-1350.
Director, Player Development: Kurt Kemp.
Assistant Director, Player Development: Ronnie Richardson. **Special Assistant to the GM, Player Development:** Jose Martinez. **Administrative Assistant:** Vickie Griffin.
Minor League Field Coordinator: Dave Trembley. **Pitching Coordinator:** Dave Wallace. **Hitting Coordinator:** Leon Roberts. **Roving Instructors:** Joe Breeden (catching), Lynn Jones (outfield/baserunning), Tommy Shields (infield), Luckie Dacosta (strength/conditioning), Matt Saitz (assistant strength/conditioning coach).

Farm System

Class	Club (League)	Manager	Coach	Pitching Coach
Triple-A	Gwinnett (IL)	Dave Brundage	Jamie Dismuke	Marty Reed
Double-A	Mississippi (SL)	Rocket Wheeler	Garey Ingram	Mike Alvarez
High A	Lynchburg (CL)	Luis Salazar	Bobby Moore	Derek Botelho
Low A	Rome (SAL)	Matt Walbeck	Carlos Mendez	Derrick Lewis
Rookie	Danville (APP)	Randy Ingle	D.J. Boston	Gabriel Luckert
Rookie	Braves (GCL)	Jonathan Schuerholz	Rick Albert	Vladimir Nunez
Rookie	Braves (DSL)	Jose Tartabull	Francisco Santiesteban	William Martinez

Scouting

Telephone: (404) 614-1359. **Fax:** (404) 614-1350.
Director, Scouting: Tony DeMacio. **Office Coordinator, Scouting:** Dixie Keller.
Advance Scout: Bob Johnson (University Park, FL). **Special Assistants to GM/Major League Scouts:** Dick Balderson (Englewood, CO), Dom Chiti (Auburndale, FL), Matt Carroll (Erdenheim, PA), Tim Conroy (Monroeville, PA), Jim Fregosi (Tarpon Springs, FL), Jeff Wren (Senoia, GA). **Professional Scouts:** Rod Gilbreath (Lilburn, GA), Lloyd Merritt (Myrtle Beach, SC), John Stewart (Granville, NY).
National Crosscheckers: John Flannery (Austin, TX), Deron Rombach (Mansfield, TX). **Regional Crosscheckers:** West—Tom Davis (Ripon, CA), Southwest—James "Bump" Merriweather (Glendale, AZ), East—Steve Fleming (Louisa, VA), Midwest—Terry R. Tripp (Harrisburg, IL), Southeast—Brian Bridges (Rome, GA).
Area Scouts: John Barron (Cameron, TX), Kevin Barry (Cream Ridge, NJ), Billy Best (Holly Spings, NC), Bill Bliss (Cincinnati, OH), Hugh Buchanan (Snellville, GA), Stu Cann (Bradley, IL), Brett Evert (Salem, OR), Ralph Garr (Richmond, TX), Buddy Hernandez (Orlando, FL), Brian Hunter (Lakewood, CA), Gene Kerns (Hagerstown, MD), Chris Knabenshue (Fort Collins, CO), Steve Leavitt (Huntington Beach, CA), Tim Moore (Sacramento, CA), Don Thomas (Geismar, LA), Terry C. Tripp (Raleigh, IL), Gerald Turner (Bedford, TX). **Part-Time Scouts:** Lew Graham (San Diego, CA), Dewayne Kitts (Moncks Corner, SC), Abraham Martinez (Santa Isabel, PR), Brendan Sagara (Wahiawa, HI), Lou Sanchez (Miami, FL).
Director, International Scouting: Johnny Almaraz. **Assistant Director, International Scouting/Operations:** Jose Martinez.
International Coordinators: Central American Supervisor—Luis Ortiz (San Antonio, TX), Eastern Rim—Phil Dale (Victoria, Australia).
International Area Supervisors: Matias Laureano (Dominican Republic), Hiroyuki Oya (Japan), Rolando Petit (Venezuela), Manuel Samaniego (Mexico). **Part-Time Scouts:** Eduardo Becerra (Venezuela), Neil Burke (Australia), Nehomar Caldera (Venezuela), Junior Carrion (Dominican Republic), Jeremy Chou (Taiwan), Carlos Garcia Roque (Colombia), Raul Gonzalez (Panama), Remmy Hernandez (Dominican Republic), Duk Lee (South Korea), Alfredo Molina (Ecuador), Rafael Motooka (Brazil), Manuel Paula (Dominican Republic), Nestor Perez (Spain), Jefferson Romero D'Lima (Venezuela), Eduardo Rosario (Venezuela), Miguel Theran (Colombia), Marvin Throneberry (Nicaragua), Carlos Torres (Venezuela).

April 2011

Baltimore Orioles

Office Address: 333 W. Camden St, Baltimore, MD 21201.
Telephone: (888) 848-BIRD. **Fax:** (410) 547-6272.
E-mail Address: birdmail@orioles.com. **Website:** www.orioles.com.

Ownership
Operated By: The Baltimore Orioles Limited Partnership Inc.
Chairman/CEO: Peter Angelos.

BUSINESS OPERATIONS
Executive Vice President: John Angelos. **VP/Special Liaison to Chairman:** Lou Kousouris.
General Legal Counsel: Russell Smouse. **Director, Human Resources:** Lisa Tolson. **Director, Information Systems:** James Kline.

Finance
Vice President/CFO: Robert Ames.

Public Relations/Communications
Telephone: (410) 547-6150. **Fax:** (410) 547-6272.
Director, Communications: Greg Bader. **Director, Public Relations:** Monica Barlow.
Manager, Media Relations: Jeff Lantz. **Coordinator, Baseball Information:** Jay Moskowitz.
Director, Promotion/Community Initiatives: Kristen Schultz.

Peter Angelos

Ballpark Operations
Director, Ballpark Operations: Ray Trifari.
Assistant Director, Ballpark Operations: Kevin Cummings. **Head Groundskeeper:** Nicole Sherry.
PA Announcer: David McGowan. **Official Scorers:** Jim Henneman, Marc Jacobsen.

Ticketing
Telephone: (888) 848-BIRD. **Fax:** (410) 547-6270.
Director, Sales/Fan Services: Neil Aloise. **Assistant Director, Sales:** Mark Hromalik. **Ticket Manager:** Audrey Brown.

Travel/Clubhouse
Coordinator, Team Travel: Kevin Buck.
Equipment Manager (Home): Jim Tyler. **Equipment Manager (Road):** Fred Tyler. **Umpires, Field Attendant:** Ernie Tyler.

2011 SCHEDULE
Standard Game Times: 7:05 p.m; Sun. 1:35

APRIL
1-3 . . . . . . at Tampa Bay
4 . . . . Detroit
6-7 . . . . Detroit
8-10 . . . . Texas
12-14 . . . at New York (AL)
15-17 . . . . .at Cleveland
18-21 . . . . . Minnesota
22-24 . . . .New York (AL)
26-28 . . . . Boston
29-30 . . . .at Chicago (AL)

MAY
1-2 . . . . . .at Chicago (AL)
3-5 . . . . . .at Kansas City
6-8 . . . . .Tampa Bay

10-12 . . . . Seattle
13-15 . . . . at Tampa Bay
16-17 . . . . .at Boston
18-19 . . . .New York (AL)
20-22 . . . . Washington
24-26 . . . . . Kansas City
27-29 . . . . . .at Oakland
30-31 . . . . . .at Seattle

JUNE
1 . . . . .at Seattle
3-5 . . . . .Toronto
6-8 . . . . Oakland
10-12 . . . . . . .Tampa Bay
14-16 . . . . . .at Toronto
17-19 . . . at Washington
20-22 . . . . at Pittsburgh

24-26 . . . . . . Cincinnati
28-30 . . . . St. Louis

JULY
1-3 . . . . at Atlanta
4-6 . . . . .at Texas
7-10 . . . . . . .at Boston
14-17 . . . . . . Cleveland
18-20 . . . . Boston
22-24 . . . Los Angeles (AL)
26-28 . . . . . . at Toronto
29-31 . . . at New York (AL)

AUGUST
2-4 . . . . . .at Kansas City
5-7 . . . . .Toronto
8-11 . . . . . . Chicago (AL)

12-14 . . . . Detroit
15-17 . . . . . . .at Oakland
19-21 . at Los Angeles (AL)
22-25 . . . . . at Minnesota
26-29 . . . .New York (AL)
30-31 . . . . .Toronto

SEPTEMBER
1 . . . . .Toronto
2-4 . . . . . . at Tampa Bay
5-7 . . . at New York (AL)
9-11 . . . . at Toronto
12-14 . . . . . . .Tampa Bay
16-18 . . . Los Angeles (AL)
19-21 . . . . . . .at Boston
22-25 . . . . . . .at Detroit
26-28 . . . . Boston

GENERAL INFORMATION
Stadium (year opened): Oriole Park at Camden Yards (1992).
Team Colors: Orange, black and white.

Player Representative: Unavailable.
Home Dugout: First Base.
Playing Surface: Grass.

BASEBALL OPERATIONS

Telephone: (410) 547-6121. **Fax:** (410) 547-6271.
President, Baseball Operations: Andy MacPhail.
Director, Baseball Operations: Matt Klentak.
Coordinator, Baseball Operations: June Napoli. **Player Information Analyst:** Ned Rice.
Baseball Operations Assistant: Mike Snyder.

Andy MacPhail

Major League Staff

Manager: Buck Showalter.
Coaches: Bench—Willie Randolph; Pitching—Mark Connor; Batting—Jim Presley; First Base—Wayne Kirby; Third Base—John Russell; Bullpen—Rick Adair.

Medical, Training

Club Physician: Dr. William Goldiner. **Club Physician, Orthopedics:** Dr. John Wilckens.
Head Athletic Trainer: Richie Bancells. **Assistant Athletic Trainer:** Brian Ebel. **Strength/Conditioning Coach:** Joe Hogarty. **Video Coordinator:** Michael Silverman.

Minor Leagues

Telephone: (410) 547-6120. **Fax:** (410) 547-6298.
Director, Player Development: John Stockstill. **Assistant Director, Player Development:** Tripp Norton. **Administrative Assistant, Player Development:** Maria Arellano. **Coordinator, Minor League Instruction:** Brian Graham. **Coordinator, Sarasota Operations:** Dave Schmidt. **Pitching Coordinator:** Alan Dunn. **Medical Coordinator:** Dave Walker. **Latin American Medical Coordinator:** Manny Lopez. **Strength/Conditioning Coordinator:** Ryan Driscoll. **Minor League Equipment Manager:** Jake Parker.
Roving Instructors: Mike Bordick (Offensive Instructor), Butch Davis (Outfield/Baserunning), Bobby Dickerson (Infield Coordinator), Denny Walling (Hitting), Don Werner (Catching).

Farm System

Class	Club (League)	Manager	Coach	Pitching Coach
Triple-A	Norfolk (IL)	Gary Allenson	Brad Komminsk	Mike Griffin
Double-A	Bowie (EL)	Gary Kendall	Denny Hocking/Einar Diaz	Kennie Steenstra
High A	Frederick (CL)	Orlando Gomez	Unavailable	Blaine Beatty
Low A	Delmarva (SAL)	Ryan Minor	Leo Gomez	Troy Mattes
Short-season	Aberdeen (NYP)	Unavailable	Cesar Devarez	Scott McGregor
Rookie	Orioles (GCL)	Ramon Sambo	Milt May/Jose Hernandez	Larry Jaster
Rookie	Orioles (DSL)	Miguel Jabalera	B. Adames/R. Lubo	R. Perez/D. Pascual

Professional Scouting

Telephone: (410) 547-6121. **Fax:** (410) 547-6298.
Director, Professional Scouting: Lee MacPhail IV.
Major League Advance Scout: Jim Thrift (Sarasota, FL). **Major League Scouts:** Dave Engle (San Diego, CA), Bruce Kison (Bradenton, FL). **Professional Scouts:** Chris Bourjos (Scottsdale, AZ), Todd Frohwirth (Waukesha, WI), Jim Howard (Clifton Park, NY), James Keller (Sacramento, CA), Ted Lekas (Brewster, MA), Gary Roenicke (Rough & Ready, CA), Fred Uhlman Sr. (Baltimore, MD).

Amateur Scouting

Telephone: (410) 547-6187. **Fax:** (410) 547-6298.
Director, Amateur Scouting: Joe Jordan. **Scouting Administrator:** Marcy Zerhusen.
National Crosschecker: Matt Reubel (Oklahoma City, OK). **Regional Crosscheckers:** East—Nick Presto (Palm Beach Gardens, FL), Dean Albany (Baltimore, MD), Central—Jim Richardson (Marlow, OK), West—David Blume (Elk Grove, CA).
Full-Time Scouts: Keith Connolly (Fair Haven, NJ), Adrian Dorsey (Florence, KY), Thom Dreier (Houston, TX), Christopher Gale (Raleigh, NC), John Gillette (Gilbert, AZ), Ernie Jacobs (Wichita, KS), David Jennings (Spanish Fort, AL), John Martin (Tampa, FL), Arthur McConnehead (Valdosta, GA), Rich Morales (Pacifica, CA), Mark Ralston (Carlsbad, CA), Bob Szymkowski (Chicago, IL), Scott Walter (Manhattan Beach, CA).

International Operations

Director, International Operations: David Stockstill.
Coordinator, Dominican Operations: Felipe Alou Jr.
International Scouts: Jesus Alfaro (Venezuela), Carlos Bernhardt (Dominican), Calvin Maduro (Caribbean), Ernst Meyer (Curacao), Salvador Ramirez (Dominican), Mike Snyder (Europe), Brett Ward (Australia)

Boston Red Sox

Office Address: Fenway Park, 4 Yawkey Way, Boston, MA 02215.
Telephone: (617) 226-6000. **Fax:** (617) 226-6416.
Website: www.redsox.com

Ownership
Principal Owner: John Henry. **Chairman:** Thomas C. Werner. **President/CEO:** Larry Lucchino.
Vice Chairmen: David Ginsberg, Phillip Morse.

BUSINESS OPERATIONS
EVP, Chief Operating Officer: Sam Kennedy. **EVP, Business Affairs:** Jonathan Gilula. **SVP, Fenway Affairs:** Larry Cancro. **Manager, Fenway Affairs:** Beth Krudys. **SVP, Boston Red Sox/Executive Director, Red Sox Foundation:** Meg Vaillancourt. **Executive Consultant:** Lou Gorman. **Director, Business Development:** Tim Zue. **Senior Advisor, Baseball Projects:** Jeremy Kapstein. **General Counsel, Fenway Sports Group, LLC:** Ed Weiss. **SVP/Assistant General Counsel:** Jennifer Flynn. **SVP/Special Counsel:** David Friedman. **VP/Club Counsel:** Elaine Weddington Steward.

Larry Lucchino

Finance/Human Resources/Information Technology
SVP/CFO: Steve Fitch. **Senior Advisor, Finance/Accounting:** Bob Furbush. **Controller:** Mark Solitro. **Director, Finance:** Ryan Oremus. **Payroll Administrator:** Mauricio Rosas. **Senior Manager, Accounting:** Cathy Fahy. **Senior Tax Accountant:** Erin Walsh. **Senior Accountant:** Mark Sirota. **Manager, Financial Planning/Analysis:** Ryan Scafidi. **VP, Human Resources/Office Administration:** Mary Sprong. **Human Resources Manager:** Patty Moseley. **Director, IT:** Steve Conley. **Senior Systems Analyst:** Randy George. **IT Manager:** Ryan Oreste.

Sales/Corporate Marketing/Fenway Enterprises
SVP, Corporate Sales/Fenway Enterprises: Joe Januszewski. **VP, Client Services:** Troup Parkinson. **Director, Client Services:** Marcell Bhangoo. **Senior Manager, Client Services:** Carole Alkins. **Manager, Suite Services:** Kim Cameron. **Manager, EMC/Dugout Services:** Erin Donovan.

Public Affairs/Media/Broadcasting/Marketing/Community Relations
SVP, Public Affairs/Marketing: Susan Goodenow. **Director, Media Relations:** Pam Ganley. **Manager, Media Relations:** Leah Tobin. **Managers, Public Affairs:** Mike Olano. **Manager, Photography:** Mike Ivins. **VP/Team Historian:** Dick Bresciani. **Director, Publications:** Debbie Matson. **Director, Marketing/Broadcast Services:** Colin Burch. **Manager, Marketing:** Ann Zeigler. **Senior Manager, Community Relations:** Sarah Stevenson.

Business/Ballpark Operations/Development
Director, Planning/Development: Paul Hanlon. **Director, Ballpark Operations:** Pete Nesbit. **Director, Concessions/Merchandise Operations:** Jeff Goldenberg. **Director, Grounds:** Dave Mellor. **Director Emeritus, Grounds:** Joe Mooney. **Assistant Director, Grounds:** Jason Griffeth. **Manager, Grounds:** Weston Appelfeller. **Facilities Superintendent:** Donnie Gardner. **Manager, Facilities Maintenance:** Glen McGlinchey. **Manager, Security/Emergency Services:** Mark Cacciatore. **Director, Florida Business Operations:** Katie Haas. **VP, Fan Services/Entertainment:** Sarah McKenna.

2011 SCHEDULE
Standard Game Times: 7:10 p.m.; Sun. 1:35

APRIL
1-3 . . . . .at Texas
5-7 . . . . . . .at Cleveland
8-10 . . . . .New York (AL)
11-13 . . . . . . .Tampa Bay
15-18 . . . . .Toronto
19-20 . . . . . .at Oakland
21-24 . at Los Angeles (AL)
26-28 . . . . . at Baltimore
29-30 . . . . Seattle

MAY
1 . . . . Seattle
2-5 . . . . Los Angeles (AL)
6-9 . . . . Minnesota
10-11 . . . . . . at Toronto

13-15 . . . at New York (AL)
16-17 . . . . . . Baltimore
18-19 . . . . Detroit
20-22 . . . . . Chicago (NL)
23-25 . . . . . .at Cleveland
26-29 . . . . . . .at Detroit
30-31 . . . . . Chicago (AL)

JUNE
1 . . . . Chicago (AL)
3-5 . . . . Oakland
7-9 . . . . at New York (AL)
10-12 . . . . . . at Toronto
14-16 . . . . . at Tampa Bay
17-19 . . . . . .Milwaukee
20-22 . . . . . . San Diego
24-26 . . . . . at Pittsburgh

28-30 . . . . at Philadelphia

JULY
1-3 . . . . .at Houston
4-6 . . . . .Toronto
7-10 . . . . Baltimore
15-17 . . . . . at Tampa Bay
18-20 . . . . . .at Baltimore
22-24 . . . . Seattle
25-28 . . . . . . Kansas City
29-31 . . . .at Chicago (AL)

AUGUST
1-4 . . . . Cleveland
5-7 . . . . . .New York (AL)
8-10 . . . . . at Minnesota
12-14 . . . . .at Seattle

16-17 . . . . . . .Tampa Bay
18-21 . . . .at Kansas City
22-25 . . . . .at Texas
26-28 . . . . Oakland
30-31 . . . .New York (AL)

SEPTEMBER
1 . . . . .New York (AL)
2-4 . . . . Texas
5-8 . . . . at Toronto
9-11 . . . . . at Tampa Bay
13-14 . . . . .Toronto
15-18 . . . . . . .Tampa Bay
19-21 . . . . Baltimore
23-25 . . at New York (AL)
26-28 . . . . . at Baltimore

GENERAL INFORMATION
Stadium (year opened): Fenway Park (1912).
Team Colors: Navy blue, red and white.

Player Representative: Unavailable.
Home Dugout: First Base.
Playing Surface: Grass.

Manager, Entertainment/Special Event Operations: Dan Lyons. Manager, Fan Services/Entertainment: Stephanie Maneikis. Senior Manager, Television Production: John Carter. Senior Manager, Video/Scoreboard Operations: Sarah Logan. PA Announcer: Carl Beane.

Ticketing Services/Operations
Telephone: 888-REDSOX6.
SVP, Ticketing: Ron Bumgarner. VP, Ticketing: Richard Beaton. Director, Ticketing: Naomi Calder. Assistant Director, Season Ticket Services: Joe Matthews. Manager, Ticket Operations: Gary Goldberg. Manager, Ticket Services: Jenean Rombola. Manager, Ticket Accounting: Sean Carragher. Manager, Ticket Fulfillment/Systems: Peter Fahey. Senior Manager, Premium Sales: Corey Bowdre. Manager, Premium Sales: William Droste.

BASEBALL OPERATIONS

Telephone: (617) 226-6000.
Executive VP/General Manager: Theo Epstein.
Senior VP/Assistant GM: Ben Cherington. Senior VP, International Scouting: Craig Shipley. Assistant to GM: Allard Baird. Special Assistant to GM: Dave Finley. Director, Baseball Operations: Brian O'Halloran. Director, Baseball Information Services: Tom Tippett. Assistant Director, Baseball Operations: Zack Scott. Assistant, Baseball Operations: Mike Murov. Software Developer: Shawn O'Rourke. Traveling Secretary: Jack McCormick. Executive Assistant: Erin Cox. Senior Advisor: Bill James.

Major League Staff
Manager: Terry Francona.
Coaches: Bench—DeMarlo Hale; Pitching—Curt Young; Batting—Dave Magadan; First Base—Ron Johnson; Third Base—Tim Bogar; Bullpen—Gary Tuck. Staff Assistants: Rob Leary, Ino Guerrero.

Theo Epstein

Medical/Training
Medical Director: Dr. Thomas Gill. Internist: Dr. Larry Ronan. Head Trainer/Assistant Director, Medical Services: Mike Reinold. Medical Operations Coordinator: Jim Rowe. Strength/Conditioning Coach: Dave Page.

Player Development
Telephone: (617) 226-6000.
Director, Player Development: Mike Hazen. Director, Minor League Operations: Raquel Ferreira. Assistant Director, Player Development: Ben Crockett. Assistant Director, Florida Baseball Operations: Ethan Faggett. Assistant Director, Latin American Operations: Eddie Romero. Field Coordinator: David Howard. Director, Dominican Academy: Jesus Alou. Latin American Field Coordinator: Jose Zapata. Latin American Pitching Coordinator: Goose Gregson. Strength/Conditioning Coordinator: Pat Sandora. Minor League Physical Therapist: Chip Simpson. Athletic Training Coordinator: Brad Pearson. Sports Psychology Coach: Bob Tewksbury. Coordinator, Player Development Programs: Duncan Webb. Roving Instructors: Andy Fox (infield), Chad Epperson (catching), Tom Goodwin (outfield/baserunning), Victor Rodriguez (hitting), Ralph Treuel (pitching).

Farm System

Class	Club (League)	Manager	Coach(es)	Pitching Coach
Triple-A	Pawtucket (IL)	Arnie Beyeler	Chili Davis	Rich Sauveur
Double-A	Portland (EL)	Kevin Boles	Dave Joppie	Bob Kipper
High A	Salem (CL)	Bruce Crabbe	Alex Ochoa	Kevin Walker
Low A	Greenville (SAL)	Billy McMillon	Luis Lopez	Dick Such
Short-season	Lowell (NYP)	Carlos Febles	Rich Gedman	Paul Abbott
Rookie	Red Sox (GCL)	George Lombard	U.L. Washington/D. Tomlin	Walter Miranda
Rookie	Red Sox (DSL)	Jose Zapata	N. Paulino/B. Alvarado	A. Telemaco/O. Lira

Scouting
Director, Amateur Scouting: Amiel Sawdaye. Assistant Director, Amateur Scouting: Gus Quattlebaum. Assistant Director, Professional Scouting: Jared Porter. Advance Scouting Coordinator: Steve Langone. Coordinator, Amateur Scouting: Jared Banner. Advance Scouts: Dana LeVangie (East Bridgewater, MA), Mike Cather (Roswell, GA). Special Assignment Scout: Mark Wasinger (El Paso, TX). Special Assignment Pitching Evaluator: Al Nipper (Chesterfield, MO).
Major League Scouts: Galen Carr (Burlington, VT), Kyle Evans (Boston, MA), Steve Peck (Scottsdale, AZ). Pro Scouts: Jaymie Bane (Parrish, FL), Nate Field (Denver, CO), Dave Klipstein (Roanoke, TX), John Lombardo (Grand Prairie, TX), Hal Morris (Palo Alto, CA). Consultants: Curtis Leskanic (Orlando, FL), Guy Mader (Tewksbury, MA), Joe McDonald (Lakeland, FL). National Crosschecker: Mike Rikard (Durham, NC). Regional Crosscheckers: East—Danny Haas (Ft. Myers, FL), Midwest—Fred Petersen (Horshoe Bay, TX), Tom Allison (Phoenix, AZ), West—Dan Madsen (Murrieta, CA). Area Scouts: Jon Adkins (Wayne, WV), Tom Battista (Thousand Oaks, CA), Quincy Boyd (Harrisburg, NC), Chris Calciano (Ocean View, DE), Matt Dorey (Houston, TX), Raymond Fagnant (East Granby, CT), Laz Gutierrez (Miramar, FL), Blair Henry (Naperville, IL), Tim Hyers (Loganville, GA), Matt Mahoney (Scottsdale, AZ), Chris Mears (Oklahoma City, OK), Edgar Perez (Vega Baja, PR), Pat Portugal (Seattle, WA), Chris Pritchett (Vancouver, BC), Demond Smith (Sacramento, CA), Jim Robinson (Arlington, TX), Anthony Turco (Tampa, FL), Danny Watkins (Tuscaloosa, AL), Jim Woodward (Claremont, CA).
Coordinator, Latin American Scouting/International Crosschecker: Todd Claus. Coordinator, Pacific Rim Scouting: Jon Deeble. Coordinator, European/Mexican Scouting: Mike Lord. Dominican Scouting Supervisor: Manny Nanita. International Scouts: Angel Escobar (Venezuela), Ernesto Gomez (Venezuela), John Kim (Korea), Louie Lin (Taiwan), Victor Rodriguez, Jr. (Dominican), Victor Torres (Dominican), Fernando Veracierto (Venezuela). International Consultants: Brian Farley (Europe), Jack Pierce (Mexico), Santiago Prada (Colombia), Antonio Simon (Curacao).

Chicago Cubs

Office Address: Wrigley Field, 1060 W. Addison St, Chicago, IL 60613.
Telephone: (773) 404-2827. **Fax:** (773) 404-4129.
E-mail Address: cubs@cubs.com. **Website:** www.cubs.com.

Ownership
Chairman: Tom Ricketts. **Board Members:** Laura Ricketts, Peter Ricketts, Todd Ricketts. **President:** Crane Kenney.

BUSINESS OPERATIONS
Phone: (773) 404-2827. **Fax:** (773) 404-4111.
Executive Vice President, Business Operations: Mark McGuire. **Executive VP/Chief Sales/Marketing Officer:** Wally Hayward. **Senior VP, Community Affairs/General Counsel:** Michael Lufrano. **VP/CFO:** John Griefenkamp. **VP, Business Development:** Alex Sugarman. **Executive Coordinator, Business Operations:** Sarah Poontong.

Tom Ricketts

Accounting/Human Resources
Director, Finance: Jodi Reischl. **Accounting Manager:** Mike Van Poucke. **Finance Manager:** Jaime Norton. **Manager, Distributions/Collections:** Theresa Bacholzky. **Senior Accountants:** Marian Greene, Aimee Sison. **Senior Director, Human Resources:** Jenifer Surma. **Employment Manager:** Marisol Widmayer. **Coordinator, Human Resources:** Danielle Alexa.

Event Operations/Security
Manager, Event Operations/Security: Mike Hill. **Manager, Event Operations/Security:** Julius Farrell. **Stadium Operations Manager:** Daniele Alexa. **Coordinator, Exterior Operations:** Mary Kusmirek. **Stadium Operations Management Assistant:** Russell Johnson. **Switchboard Operator/Receptionist:** Brenda Morgan.

Facility Management/Information Technology
Senior Director, Facility Management/Information Technology: Carl Rice. **Manager, IT:** Sean True.

Legal/Community Affairs
Assistant General Counsel: Lydia Wahlke. **Manager, Community Affairs:** Jill Lawlor. **Manager, Community Outreach/Grants/Donations:** Jennifer Dedes Nowak.

Marketing/Broadcasting
Managing Director, Corporate Partnerships: Samantha Coghill. **Director, Fan Experiences:** Jahaan Blake. **Director, Corporate Partnerships:** Michael Kirschner. **Assistant Director, Premium Seats/Services:** Andy Blackburn. **Manager, Mezzanine Suites:** Louis Artiaga. **Manager, Special Events/Player Relations/Entertainment:** Joe Rios.

Media Relations/Publications
Telephone: (773) 404-4191. **Fax:** (773) 404-4129.
Director, Media Relations: Peter Chase. **Assistant Director, Media Relations:** Jason Carr. **Coordinator, Media Relations:** Dani Holmes. **Assistant, Media Relations:** Dusty Harrington. **Public Relations/Marketing Specialist:** Kevin

2011 SCHEDULE
Standard Game Times: 1:20 p.m., 7:05.

APRIL		
1-3 . . . . Pittsburgh	13-15 . . . . . San Francisco	24-26 . . . . .at Kansas City
4-6. . . . . .Arizona	16-17 . . . . .at Cincinnati	28-30 . . . . San Francisco
8-10 . . . . . at Milwaukee	18-19 . . . . .at Florida	
11-13 . . . . .at Houston	20-22 . . . . .at Boston	**JULY**
15-17 . . . . . at Colorado	24-26 . . . .New York (NL)	1-3. . . . . . . Chicago (AL)
18-20 . . . . . San Diego	27-29 . . . . Pittsburgh	4-7. . . . . at Washington
22-24 . . . Los Angeles (NL)	30-31 . . . . Houston	8-10 . . . . . at Pittsburgh
25-27 . . . . . . .Colorado		14-17 . . . . Florida
28-30 . . . . at Arizona	**JUNE**	18-20 . . . . .Philadelphia
	1 . . . . Houston	22-24 . . . . Houston
MAY	3-5. . . . . .at St. Louis	26-28 . . . . . at Milwaukee
1 . . . . at Arizona	6-8. . . . . . .at Cincinnati	29-31 . . . . . . .at St. Louis
2-4. . . at Los Angeles (NL)	9-12 . . . . at Philadelphia	
6-8. . . . . Cincinnati	13-16 . . . . . . .Milwaukee	**AUGUST**
10-12 . . . . St. Louis	17-19 . . . .New York (AL)	1-4. . . . . . at Pittsburgh
	20-22 . . . at Chicago (AL)	5-7. . . . . Cincinnati
		8-10 . . . . Washington

12-14 . . . . at Atlanta	
15-17 . . . . . .at Houston	
19-21 . . . . St. Louis	
22-25 . . . . Atlanta	
26-28 . . . . at Milwaukee	
29-31 . . at San Francisco	
SEPTEMBER	
2-4. . . . . Pittsburgh	
5-7. . . . . Cincinnati	
9-11 . . . . at New York (NL)	
12-15 . . . . . .at Cincinnati	
16-18 . . . . Houston	
19-21 . . . . . .Milwaukee	
23-25 . . . . . . .at St. Louis	
26-28 . . . . at San Diego	

GENERAL INFORMATION
Stadium (year opened): Wrigley Field (1914).
Team Colors: Royal blue, red and white.
Player Representative: Unavailable.
Home Dugout: Third Base.
Playing Surface: Grass.

Saghy. **Director, Publications/Creative Services:** Lena McDonagh. **Manager, Editorial Projects:** Michael Huang. **Editorial Project Specialist:** Sean Ahmed. **Manager, Design/Production:** Juan Alberto Castillo. **Design/Creative Services Specialist:** Joaquin Castillo. **Team Photographer:** Stephen Green.

Ticket Operations
Telephone: (773) 404-2827. **Fax:** (773) 404-4014.
VP, Ticket Sales/Service: Colin Faulkner. **Director, Ticket Operations:** Frank Maloney. **Assistant Director, Ticket Sales:** Brian Garza. **Assistant Director, Ticket Services:** Joe Kirchen. **Vault Room Supervisor:** Cherie Blake. **Coordinator, Ticket Orders:** Jan Jotzat. **Coordinator, Ticket Sales:** Karry Kerness.

Game Day Operations
PA Announcers: Paul Friedman. **Umpires Room Attendant:** Tom Farinela. **Clubhouse Manager:** Tom Hellmann. **Visiting Clubhouse Manager:** Michael Burkhart. **Home Clubhouse Assistant:** Gary Stark.

BASEBALL OPERATIONS
Telephone: (773) 404-2827. **Fax:** (773) 404-4111.
Vice President/General Manager: Jim Hendry. **Assistant GM:** Randy Bush. **Director, Baseball Administration:** Scott Nelson. **Senior Advisors:** Billy Williams. **Assistant to GM:** Greg Maddux. **Special Assistants:** Gary Hughes, Ken Kravec, Dave Littlefield, Louie Eljaua. **Major League Scout:** Bill Harford. **Major League Advance Scout:** Brad Kelley. **Manager, Baseball Information:** Chuck Wasserstrom. **Manager, Statistical Analysis:** Ari Kaplan. **Traveling Secretary:** Jimmy Bank. **Executive Assistant to VP/GM:** Hayley DeWitte. Major League Video Coordinator: Naoto Masamoto. Japanese Interpreter/Media Assistant: Hiro Aoyama.

Major League Staff
Manager: Mike Quade.
Coaches: Pitching—Mark Riggins; Hitting—Rudy Jaramillo; Bench—Pat Listach; Third Base—Ivan DeJesus; First Base—Bob Dernier; Bullpen—Lester Strode; Staff Assistant—David Keller.

Jim Hendry

Medical/Training
Team Physician: Dr. Stephen Adams. **Team Orthopedist:** Dr. Stephen Gryzlo.
Orthopedic Consultant: Dr. Michael Schafer. **Director, Athletic Training:** Mark O'Neal. **Assistant Athletic Trainers:** Ed Halbur, Yoshi Nakazawa. **Major League Strength/Conditioning Coordinator:** Tim Buss.

Player Development
Telephone: (773) 404-4035. **Fax:** (773) 404-4147.
VP, Player Personnel: Oneri Fleita. **Manager, Player Development Administration:** Patti James. **Coordinator, Player Development/International Scouting:** Alex Suarez. **Baseball Operations Assistant:** Safdar Khan. **Field Coordinator:** Dave Bialas.
Coordinators: Dennis Lewallyn (pitching), Tom Beyers (hitting), Franklin Font (infield), Marty Pevey (catching), Lee Tinsley (outfield/baserunning), Carmelo Martinez (Latin American field coordinator). **Minor League Training Coordinator:** Justin Sharpe. **Assistant Training Coordinator:** Chuck Baughman. **Strength/Conditioning Coordinator:** Doug Jarrow. **Strength Coach:** Tyler Evans. **Equipment Manager:** Dana Noeltner.

Farm System
Class	Club (League)	Manager	Hitting Coach	Pitching Coach
Triple-A	Iowa (PCL)	Bill Dancy	Von Joshua	Mike Mason
Double-A	Tennessee (SL)	Brian Harper	Mariano Duncan	Marty Mason
High Class A	Daytona (FSL)	Buddy Bailey	Barbaro Garbey	Tom Pratt
Low Class A	Peoria (MWL)	Casey Kopitzke	Ricardo Medina	Jeff Fassero
Short-season	Boise (NWL)	Mark Johnson	Desi Wilson	David Rosario
Rookie	Cubs (AZL)	Juan Cabreja	Jason Dubois	Rick Tronerud/Frank Castillo
Rookie	Cubs I (DSL)	Manuel Collado	Alberto Garcia	Leo Hernandez
Rookie	Cubs II (DSL)	Yudith Ozorio	Leo Perez/F. Blanco	Anderson Tavares

Scouting
Telephone: (773) 404-2827. **Fax:** (773) 404-4147.
Director, Amateur/Professional Scouting: Tim Wilken (Dunedin, FL).
Director, International Scouting: Paul Weaver (Phoenix,AZ). **Special Assistant:** Steve Hinton (Mather, CA). **Senior Advisor:** Jim Crawford (Madison, MS). **Coordinator, Pro Scouting:** Jake Ciarrachi. **Administrative Assistant:** Patricia Honzik.
Pro Scouts: Mark Adair (Phoenix, AZ), Billy Blitzer (Brooklyn, New York), Tom Bourque (Cambridge, MA), Joe Housey (Hollywood, FL), Demie Mainieri (Ft. Lauderdale, FL), Mark Servais (LaCrosse, WI), Keith Stohr (Viera, FL), Richie Zisk (Lighthouse Point, FL). **Special Assignment Scout:** Bob Lofrano (Woodland Hills, CA). **National Crosschecker:** Sam Hughes (Atlanta, GA). **Crosscheckers:** East—Charles Aliano (Land O'Lakes, FL), Midwest—Steve Riha (Houston, TX), West—Tim Kissner (Kirkland, WA), Canadian/U.S./International: Ron Tostenson (El Dorado Hills, CA). **Area Scouts:** Tim Adkins (Huntington, WV), John Ceprini (Massapequa, NY), Tom Clark (Lake City, FL), Ramser Correa (Caguas, PR), Trey Forkerway (Houston, TX), Steve Fuller (Seal Beach, CA), Al Geddes (Canby, OR), Denny Henderson (Orange, CA), Keith Lockhart (Dacula, GA), Lazaro Llanes (Miami, FL), Steve McFarland (Scottsdale, AZ), Lukas McKnight (Safety Harbor, FL), Ty Nichols (Broken Arrow, OK), Keith Ryman (Jefferson City, TN), Rick Schroeder (Pleasanton, CA), Matt Sherman (Norwell, MA), Billy Swoope (Norfolk, VA), Stan Zielinski (Winfield, IL).
International Scouts: Hector Ortega (Venezuela), Jose Serra (Dominican Republic), Steve Wilson (Pacific Rim).

Chicago White Sox

Office Address: U.S. Cellular, Field, 333 W. 35th St., Chicago, IL 60616.
Telephone: (312) 674-1000. **Fax:** (312) 674-5116.
Website: www.whitesox.com.

Ownership

Chairman: Jerry Reinsdorf. **Vice Chairman:** Eddie Einhorn.
Board of Directors: Robert Judelson, Judd Malkin, Robert Mazer, Allan Muchin, Jay Pinsky, Larry Pogofsky, Lee Stern, Burton Ury, Charles Walsh.
Special Assistant to Chairman: Dennis Gilbert. **Assistant to Chairman:** Anita Fasano.

BUSINESS OPERATIONS

Executive Vice President: Howard Pizer.
Senior Director, Information Services: Don Brown. **Senior Director, Human Resources:** Moira Foy. **Administrators, Human Resources:** Leslie Gaggiano, J.J. Krane.

Finance

Senior VP, Administration/Finance: Tim Buzard. **Senior Director, Finance:** Bill Waters. **Accounting Manager:** Chris Taylor.

Marketing/Sales

Chief Marketing Officer/VP, Marketing: Brooks Boyer. **Senior Director, Business Development/Broadcasting:** Bob Grim. **Manager, Scoreboard Operations/Production:** Jeff Szynal. **Director, Game Operations:** Nichole Manning. **Manager, Game Operations:** Amy Sheridan. **Coordinator, Game Operations:** Dan Mielke.

Jerry Reinsdorf

Senior Director, Corporate Partnerships: Jim Muno. **Managers, Corporate Partnerships:** George McDoniel, Gail Tucker, Brad Dreher. **Manager, Client Services:** Stephanie Johnson. **Coordinator, Corporate Partnership Services:** Jorie Sax.
Director, Ticket Sales: Tom Sheridan. **Manager, Premium Seating Service:** Rob Boaz. **Senior Director, Community Relations:** Christine O'Reilly.
Director, Mass Communications: Maggie Luellen. **Manager, Design Services:** Gareth Breunlin. **Senior Coordinator, Design Services:** Matt Peterson. **Manager, Community Relations:** Danielle Disch. **Senior Coordinator, Community Relations:** Laina Myers. **Coordinators, Community Relations:** Stacy Tsihlopoulos, Dan Puente.

Media Relations

Telephone: (312) 674-5300. **Fax:** (312) 674-5116.
Senior VP, Communications: Scott Reifert.
Director, Media Relations: Bob Beghtol. **Director, Public Relations:** Lou Hernandez. **Assistant Director, Media Relations:** Pat O'Connell. **Coordinator, Public Relations:** Marty Maloney. **Coordinator, Media Relations/Services:** Ray Garcia.

2011 SCHEDULE

Standard Game Times: 7:10 p.m.; Sun. 1:10.

APRIL			
1-3 . . . . .at Cleveland	13-15 . . . . . .at Oakland	24-26 . . . . . Washington	12-14 . . . . . Kansas City
5-6 . . . . . .at Kansas City	16-17 . . . . Texas	28-30 . . . . . at Colorado	16-18 . . . . . . Cleveland
7-10 . . . . . . .Tampa Bay	18-19 . . . . . . Cleveland		19-21 . . . . Texas
11-13 . . . . Oakland	20-22 . . . Los Angeles (NL)	JULY	23-24 . at Los Angeles (AL)
15-17 . . Los Angeles (AL)	23-25 . . . . .at Texas	1-3 . . . . .at Chicago (NL)	26-28 . . . . .at Seattle
18-21 . . . . at Tampa Bay	26-29 . . . . . at Toronto	4-6 . . . . Kansas City	29-31 . . . . . .Minnesota
22-24 . . . . . . .at Detroit	30-31 . . . . .at Boston	7-10 . . . . . . .Minnesota	
25-28 . . at New York (AL)		15-17 . . . . . . .at Detroit	SEPTEMBER
29-30 . . . . . . Baltimore	JUNE	18-20 . . . .at Kansas City	2-4 . . . . .at Detroit
	1 . . . . .at Boston	22-24 . . . .at Cleveland	5-7 . . . . . . at Minnesota
MAY	3-5 . . . . Detroit	25-27 . . . . Detroit	8-11 . . . . Cleveland
1-2 . . . . Baltimore	6-8 . . . . Seattle	29-31 . . . . Boston	12-14 . . . . Detroit
3-4 . . . . .Minnesota	9-12 . . . . Oakland		15-18 . . . . .at Kansas City
6-8 . . . . .at Seattle	14-16 . . . at Minnesota	AUGUST	20-22 . . . . .at Cleveland
9-11 . . at Los Angeles (AL)	17-19 . . . . . at Arizona	1-4 . . . . . .New York (AL)	23-25 . . . . . Kansas City
	20-22 . . . . . Chicago (NL)	5-7 . . . . . . at Minnesota	26-28 . . . . .Toronto
		8-11 . . . . . . .at Baltimore	

GENERAL INFORMATION

Stadium (year opened): U.S. Cellular Field (1991).
Team Colors: Black, white and silver.

Player Representative: Unavailable.
Home Dugout: Third Base.
Playing Surface: Grass.

Stadium Operations
Senior VP, Stadium Operations: Terry Savarise. **Senior Director, Event Operations:** Troy Brown. **Senior Director, Guest Services/Diamond Suite Operations:** Julie Taylor. **Head Groundskeeper:** Roger Bossard. **PA Announcer:** Gene Honda. **Official Scorer:** Bob Rosenberg, Don Friske.

Ticketing
Telephone: (312) 674-1000. **Fax:** (312) 674-5102.
Director, Ticket Operations: Mike Mazza. **Manager, Ticket Accounting Administration:** Ken Wisz.

Travel/Clubhouse
Director, Team Travel: Ed Cassin.
Manager, White Sox Clubhouse: Vince Fresso. **Manager, Visiting Clubhouse:** Gabe Morell. **Manager, Umpires Clubhouse:** Joe McNamara Jr.

BASEBALL OPERATIONS

Ken Williams

Senior VP/General Manager: Ken Williams.
VP/Assistant GM: Rick Hahn. **Special Assistants:** Bill Scherrer, Dave Yoakum. **Executive Assistant to GM:** Nancy Nesnidal. **Director, Baseball Operations:** Dan Fabian. **Assistant Director, Baseball Operations:** Daniel Zien. **Special Assignment Scout:** Alan Regier.

Major League Staff
Manager: Ozzie Guillen.
Coaches: Bench—Joey Cora; Pitching—Don Cooper; Batting—Greg Walker; First Base—Harold Baines; Third Base—Jeff Cox; Bullpen—Juan Nieves.

Medical, Training
Senior Team Physician: Dr. **Charles Bush-Joseph.**
Head Athletic Trainer: Herm Schneider. **Assistant Athletic Trainer:** Brian Ball.
Director, Conditioning: Allen Thomas.

Player Development
Telephone: (312) 674-1000. **Fax:** (312) 674-5105.
Director, Player Development: Buddy Bell.
Senior Director, Minor League Operations: Grace Guerrero Zwit. **Assistant Director, Player Development/Scouting:** Del Matthews. **Senior Coordinator, Minor League Administration:** Kathy Potoski. **Manager, Clubhouse/Equipment:** Dan Flood.
Minor League Field Coordinator: Nick Capra. **Roving Instructors:** Daryl Boston (outfield), Kirk Champion (pitching), Everado Magallanes (infield), Jeff Manto (hitting), John Orton (catching), Dale Torborg (conditioning coordinator), Devon White (baserunning/bunting). **Latin Roving Instructor:** Jose Bautista. **Latin Cultural Coordinator:** Geronimo Mendoza. **Dominican Player Development/Scouting Supervisor:** Rafael Santana. **Coordinator, Minor League Trainers/Rehabilitation:** Scott Takao. **Coaching Assistant:** Tommy Thompson. **Dominican Coordinator:** Julio Valdez.

Farm System

Class	Club (League)	Manager	Coach	Pitching Coach
Triple-A	Charlotte (IL)	Joe McEwing	Timothy Laker	Richard Dotson
Double-A	Birmingham (SL)	Bobby Magallanes	Andy Tomberlin	J.R. Perdew
High A	Winston-Salem (CL)	Julio Vinas	Gary Ward	Bobby Thigpen
Low A	Kannapolis (SAL)	Tommy Thompson	Robert Sasser	Jose Bautista
Rookie	Bristol (APP)	Pete Rose Jr.	Greg Briley	Larry Owens
Rookie	Great Falls (PIO)	Ryan Newman	Charlie Poe	Brian Drahman
Rookie	White Sox (DSL)	Fermin Urbi	Domingo Michel	Efrain Valdez

Scouting
Telephone: (312) 674-1000. **Fax:** (312) 674-5105.
Pro Scouts: Joe Butler (Long Beach, CA), Gary Pellant (Chandler, AZ), Paul Provas (Arlington, TX), Daraka Shaheed (Vallejo, CA), Bill Young (Scottsdale, AZ), John Tumminia (Newburgh, NY), Dedrick Williams (Chicago, IL).
Director, Amateur Scouting: Doug Laumann (Florence, KY).
Assistant Director, Scouting/Player Development: J.J. Lally. **National Crosscheckers:** Nathan Durst (Sycamore, IL), Ed Pebley (Brigham City, UT). **Regional Crosscheckers:** East—Nick Hostetler (Union, KY), West—Derek Valenzuela (Temecula, CA). **Crosschecker:** Mike Shirley (Anderson, IN), **Advisor to Baseball Department:** Larry Monroe (Schaumburg, IL).
Area Scouts: Mike Baker (Santa Ana, CA), Kevin Burrell (Sharpsburg, GA), Alex Cosmidis (Raleigh, NC), Ryan Dorsey (Frederick, MD), Dan Durst (Rockford, IL), Phil Gulley (Morehead, KY), Warren Hughes (Mobile, AL), George Kachigian (Coronado, CA), John Kazanas (Phoenix, AZ), Jose Ortega (Fort Lauderdale, FL), Clay Overcash (Oologan, OK), Andrew Pinter (Raleigh, NC), Joe Siers (Wesley Chapel, FL), Keith Staab (College Station, TX), Adam Virchis (Modesto, CA), Gary Woods (Solvang, CA).
Part-Time Scouts: Tommy Butler (East Rancho Dominguez, CA), Karl Carswell (Kansas City, MO), Javier Centeno (Guaynabo, PR), John Doldoorian (Whitinsville, MA), Trent Eckstaine (Lemars, IA), Cade Griffis (Addison, TX), Jack Jolly (Murfreeboro, TN), Jason Morvant (Abbeville, LA), Glenn Murdock (Livonia, MI), Howard Nakagama (Salt Lake City, UT), Al Otto (Schaumburg, IL), Mike Paris (Boone, IA).
International Scouts: Marino DeLeon (Dominican Republic), Miguel Peguero (Dominican Republic), Guillermo Reyes (Dominican Republic), Amador Arias (Venezuela), Ehire Adrianza (Venezuela), Omar Sanchez (Venezuela).

Cincinnati Reds

Office Address: 100 Joe Nuxhall Way, Cincinnati, OH 45202.
Telephone: (513) 765-7000. **Fax:** (513) 765-7342.
Website: www.reds.com.

Ownership

Operated by: The Cincinnati Reds LLC.
President/CEO: Robert Castellini. **Chairman:** Joseph Williams Jr. **Vice Chairman/Treasurer:** Thomas Williams. **COO:** Phillip Castellini. **Executive Assistant to COO:** Diana Torry. **Secretary:** Christopher Fister.

BUSINESS OPERATIONS

Senior Vice President, Business Operations: Karen Forgus. **Senior Director, Business Development:** Lauren Werner. **Business Operations Assistant/Speakers Bureau:** Emily Chalfant. **Business/Broadcasting Administrator:** Ginny Kamp. **Special Events Manager:** Sally Greytak.

Finance/Administration

VP, Finance/CFO: Doug Healy. **VP/General Counsel:** James Marx. **Controller:** Bentley Viator. **Assistant to General Counsel/COO:** Teena Schweier. **Director, Human Resources:** Teddi Mangas-Coon. **Human Resources Generalist:** Sarah LaRue. **Benefits/Staffing Coordinator:** Allison Spurlock. **Director, Information Technology:** Brian Keys.

Sales

VP, Ticket Sales: John Davis. **Director, Client Services:** Craig Warman. **Ticket Development Manager:** Jodi Czanik. **Client Services Manager:** Nancy Bloss. **Director, Group Sales:** David Ziegler. **Group Sales Manager:** Ryan Niemeyer. **Suite/Premium Services Manager:** Shelly Volpenhein. **Premium Sales Manager:** Ryan Rizzo. **Season Sales Manager:** Chris Herrell. **Inside Sales Manager:** Mark Schueler.

Bob Castellini

Ticket Operations

Senior Director, Ticket Operations: John O'Brien. **Assistant Director, Ticket Operations:** Ken Ayer.

Media Relations

Director, Media Relations: Rob Butcher. **Assistant Directors, Media Relations:** Larry Herms, Jamie Ramsey.

Communications/Marketing

VP, Communications/Marketing: Ralph Mitchell. **Communications Manager:** Jarrod Rollins. **Design/Production Manager:** Jansen Dell. **Director, Promotional Events:** Zach Bonkowski. **Promotional Events Managers:** Kathryn Braun, Corey Hawthorne. **Public Relations Manager:** Michael Anderson. **Marketing Manager:** Lisa Braun.

Community Relations

Executive Director: Charley Frank. **Director, Community Relations:** Lorrie Platt. **Executive Director, Reds Hall of**

2011 SCHEDULE

Standard Game Times: 7:10 p.m.; Sun. 1:10

MARCH		
31 . . . . .Milwaukee		

APRIL		
2-3 . . . . .Milwaukee		
5-7 . . . . Houston		
8-10 . . . . at Arizona		
11-13 . . . at San Diego		
15-18 . . . . . Pittsburgh		
19-21 . . . . .Arizona		
22-24 . . . . .at St. Louis		
25-27 . . . . at Milwaukee		
29-30 . . . . Florida		

MAY		
1 . . . . Florida		
2-4 . . . . Houston		

6-8 . . . . . .at Chicago (NL)
9-11 . . . . . . .at Houston
13-15 . . . . . . St. Louis
16-17 . . . . . Chicago (NL)
18-19 . . . . . . Pittsburgh
20-22 . . . .at Cleveland
23-26 . . . . at Philadelphia
27-29 . . . . at Atlanta
30-31 . . . . . . .Milwaukee

JUNE		
1 . . . . .Milwaukee		
3-5 . . . . .Los Angeles (NL)		
6-8 . . . . . . .Chicago (NL)		
9-12 . . . at San Francisco		
13-15 . at Los Angeles (NL)		
17-19 . . . . .Toronto		

20-22 . . . .New York (AL)
24-26 . . . . .at Baltimore
27-29 . . . at Tampa Bay

JULY		
1-3 . . . . Cleveland		
4-6 . . . . .at St. Louis		
7-10 . . . . . at Milwaukee		
15-17 . . . . . . St. Louis		
18-20 . . . . . at Pittsburgh		
22-24 . . . . Atlanta		
25-28 . . . .New York (NL)		
29-31 . . . . .San Francisco		

AUGUST		
1-3 . . . . .at Houston		
5-7 . . . . .at Chicago (NL)		
8-11 . . . . .Colorado		

12-14 . . . . San Diego
16-18 . . . . at Washington
19-21 . . . . at Pittsburgh
23-25 . . . . .at Florida
26-28 . . . . . Washington
29-31 . . . . .Philadelphia

SEPTEMBER		
1 . . . . .Philadelphia		
2-4 . . . . .at St. Louis		
5-7 . . . . .at Chicago (NL)		
9-11 . . . . . at Colorado		
12-15 . . . . . Chicago (NL)		
16-18 . . . . . .Milwaukee		
19-21 . . . . Houston		
23-25 . . . . . at Pittsburgh		
26-28 . . . at New York (NL)		

GENERAL INFORMATION

Stadium (year opened): Great American Ball Park (2003).
Home Dugout: First Base.

Playing Surface: Grass.
Team Colors: Red, white and black.
Player Representative: Mike Leake.

Fame: Rick Walls. **Operations Manager/Chief Curator, Reds Hall of Fame:** Chris Eckes.

Corporate Sales
VP, Corporate Sales: Bill Reinberger.

Ballpark Operations
Vice President, Ballpark Operations: Declan Mullin.
Director, Ballpark Operations: Sean Brown. **Ballpark Operations Manager:** Colleen Rodenberg. **Ballpark Operations Superintendent:** Bob Harrison. **Guest Relations Manager:** Jan Koshover. **Manager, Technology Business Center:** Chris Campbell. **Director, Public Safety/Security:** Kenny Rowland. **Chief Engineer:** Roger Smith. **Head Groundskeeper:** Doug Gallant. **Assistant Groundskeeper:** Jon Phelps. **Grounds Supervisor:** Derrik Grubbs.

BASEBALL OPERATIONS
President, Baseball Operations/GM: Walt Jocketty.
VP/Assistant GM: Bob Miller. **VP, Scouting/Player Development/International Operations:** Bill Bavasi. **VP/Special Assistant:** Jerry Walker. **VP, Baseball Operations:** Dick Williams. **Special Assistants:** Eric Davis, Mario Soto. **Assistant Director, Baseball Operations:** Nick Krall. **Manager, Baseball Research/Analysis:** Sam Grossman. **Manager, Video Scouting:** Rob Coughlin. **Baseball Operations Assistant:** Stephanie Ben.

Medical/Training
Medical Director: Dr. Timothy Kremchek. **Head Athletic Trainer:** Paul Lessard.

Major League Staff
Manager: Dusty Baker.
Coaches: Bench—Chris Speier; Pitching—Bryan Price; Batting—Brook Jacoby; First Base—Billy Hatcher; Third Base—Mark Berry; Bullpen—Juan Lopez.

Player Development
Telephone: (513) 765-7700. **Fax:** (513) 765-7799.
Director, Minor League Administration: Lori Hudson. **Player Development Administrator:** Jeff Graupe. **Arizona Operations Manager:** Mike Saverino. **Assistant to Arizona Operations Manager:** Charlie Rodriguez. **Minor League Equipment Manager:** Jonathan Snyder.
Field Coordinator: Freddie Benavides. **Assistant Field Coordinator, Instruction:** Bill Doran. **Assistant Field Coordinator, Latin Focus:** Joel Noboa. **Coordinators:** Ronnie Ortegon (hitting), Mack Jenkins (pitching), Darren Bragg (outfield/baserunning), Pat Kelly (catching). **Strength/Conditioning Coordinator:** Matthew Krause. **Medical Coordinator:** Richard Stark. **Medical Administrator:** Patrick Serbus.
Strength/Conditioning Coordinator: Sean Marohn. **Rehab Coordinator/Physical Therapist:** Brad Epstein. **Strength/Conditioning Coaches:** Zach Gjestvang, Rigo Febles. **Director, Dominican Republic Academy:** Juan Peralta. **Director, Venezuela Academy:** Jose Fuentes.

Walt Jocketty

Farm System

Class	Club (League)	Manager	Coach	Pitching Coach
Triple-A	Louisville (IL)	Rick Sweet	Adrian Garrett	Ted Power
Double-A	Carolina (SL)	David Bell	Ryan Jackson	Tom Brown
High A	Bakersfield (CAL)	Ken Griffey	Tony Jaramillo	Rigo Beltran
Low A	Dayton (MWL)	Delino DeShields	Alex Pelaez	Tony Fossas
Rookie	Billings (PIO)	Pat Kelly	Eli Marrero	Bob Forsch
Rookie	Reds (AZL)	Jose Miguel Nieves	Jorge Orta	Tom Browning
Rookie	Reds (DSL)	Joel Noboa	Nilson Antiqua	Francisco Saneaux
Rookie	Reds (VSL)	Richard Paz	Unavailable	Jose Villa

Scouting
Senior Director, Amateur Scouting: Chris Buckley. **Assistant Director, Amateur Scouting. Senior Director, Pro/Global Scouting:** Terry Reynolds. **Special Assistant, Player Personnel:** Cam Bonifay. **Special Assistants:** J Harrison, Marty Maier, Mike Squires. **Major League Advance Scout:** Shawn Pender. **Professional Scouts:** Jeff Morris, John Morris, Steve Roadcap, Jeff Taylor, Dominic Viola.
National Crosscheckers: Wayne Britton (Waynesboro, VA), Mark McKnight (Tega Cay, SC), Mark Snipp (Humble, TX). **Crosschecker:** Jeff Barton (Gilbert, AZ). **Scouting Supervisors:** Tony Arias (Miami Lakes, FL), Rich Bordi (Rohnert Park, CA), Jeff Brookens (Chambersburg, PA), Bill Byckowski (Ontario, Canada), Clark Crist (Tucson, AZ), Rex De La Nuez (Burbank, CA), Jerry Flowers (Cypress, TX), Rick Ingalls (Long Beach, CA), Ben Jones (Alexandria, LA), Joe Katuska (Cincinnati, OH), Mike Keenan (Manhattan, KS), Brad Meador (Cincinnati, OH), Mike Misuraca (Murrieta, CA), John Poloni (Tarpon Springs, FL), Rick Sellers (Ft. Collins, CO), Lee Seras (Flanders, NJ), Perry Smith (Charlotte, NC), Andy Stack (Hartford, WI), Greg Zunino (Cape Coral, FL). **Part-Time Scouts:** Edwin Daub (Binghamton, N.Y.), Jim Grief (Paducha, KY), Bill Killian (Stanwood, MI), Denny Nagel (Cincinnati, OH), Marlon Styles (Cincinnati, OH), Mike Wallace (Escondido, CA), John Walsh (Windsor, CT), Roger Weberg (Bemidji, MN).
Director, Latin America Scouting: Tony Arias. **Assistant Director, Latin American Scouting:** Miguel Machado. **Director, Global Scouting:** Jim Stoeckel. **Scouting Coordinator, Dominican Republic:** Richard Jimenez. **International Scouts:** Jason Hewitt (Australia), Luke Prokopec (Australia), Geronimo Blnaco (Colombia), Carlos Batista (Dominican Republic), Edward Bens (Dominican Republic), Cesar Castro (Dominican Republic), Jose Manuel Pujols (Dominican Republic), Sal Varriale (Italy), Anibal Vega (Nicaragua), Anibal Reluz (Panama), Victor Oramas (Venezuela). **Consultants:** Nick Dempsey (South Africa), Evert-Jan't Hoen (The Netherlands).

Cleveland Indians

Office Address: Progressive Field, 2401 Ontario St, Cleveland, OH 44115.
Telephone: (216) 420-4200. **Fax:** (216) 420-4396.
Website: www.indians.com.

Ownership
Owner/CEO: Lawrence Dolan. **Chairman/Chief Executive Officer:** Paul Dolan.

BUSINESS OPERATIONS

President: Mark Shapiro. **Assistant to the President:** Andrew Miller. **Executive Administrative Assistant:** Marlene Lehky

Executive Vice President, Business: Dennis Lehman. **Executive Administrative Assistant, Business:** Dru Kosik.

Corporate Partnerships/Finance
Director, Corporate Partnerships: Ted Baugh. **Manager, New Business Development:** Sheff Webb. **Senior VP, Finance/CFO:** Ken Stefanov. **VP/General Counsel:** Joe Znidarsic. **Controller:** Sarah Taylor. **Director, Planning/Analysis/Reporting:** Rich Dorffer. **Manager, Accounting:** Karen Menzing. **Manager, Payroll Accounting:** Mary Forkapa.

Human Resources
VP, Human Resources/Diversity: Sara Lehrke. **Manager, Training/Development:** Mailynh Vu.

Larry Dolan

Technology Trainer: Jennifer Gibson. **Manager, Recruitment:** Crystal Basile. **Coordinator, Benefits:** Melissa Painter. **Senior VP, Sales/Marketing:** Vic Gregovits. **Director, Marketing:** Sanaa Julien. **Manager, Promotions:** Jason Kidik. **Manager, Productions:** Justin White. **Manager, Productions:** Annie Merovich. **Broadcast Engineer/Announcer:** Jim Rosenhaus. **Coordinator, Marketing/Copywriting:** Anne Madzelan. **Senior Director, Merchandising:** Kurt Schloss. **Merchandise Manager:** Karen Fox.

Public Relations/Communications
Telephone: (216) 420-4380. **Fax:** (216) 420-4396.
VP, Public Relations: Bob DiBiasio. **Director, Media Relations:** Bart Swain. **Manager, Media Relations/Administration:** Susie Giuliano. **Manager, Media Relations:** Jeff Sibel. **Assistant, Media Relations:** Matt Whewell. **Director, Communications/Creative Services:** Curtis Danburg. **Coordinator, Communications:** Danielle Cherry. **Coordinator, Digital Media:** Rob Campbell. **Team Photographer:** Dan Mendlik.

Ballpark Operations
VP, Ballpark Operations: Jim Folk.
Director, Facility Maintenance: Chris Donahoe. **Head Groundskeeper:** Brandon Koehnke. **Director, Ballpark Operations:** Jerry Crabb. **Assistant Director, Ballpark Operations:** Brad Mohr. **Assistant Director, Facility Maintenance:** Seth Cooper. **Coordinator, Game Day Staff:** Trevina Johnson. **Coordinator, Ballpark Services:** Steve Walters.

2011 SCHEDULE
Standard Game Times: 7:05 p.m.; Sun. 1:05.

APRIL
1-3 . . . . . . Chicago (AL)
5-7 . . . . Boston
8-10 . . . . .at Seattle
11-13 . at Los Angeles (AL)
15-17 . . . . . . Baltimore
18-21 . . . .at Kansas City
22-24 . . . . . at Minnesota
26-28 . . . . . Kansas City
29-30 . . . . Detroit

MAY
1 . . . . Detroit
3-5 . . . . .at Oakland
6-8 . . at Los Angeles (AL)
10-12 . . . . . .Tampa Bay

13-15 . . . . Seattle
16-17 . . . .at Kansas City
18-19 . . . .at Chicago (AL)
20-22 . . . . . . Cincinnati
23-25 . . . . Boston
27-29 . . . . at Tampa Bay
30-31 . . . . . at Toronto

JUNE
1 . . . . .at Toronto
2-5 . . . . Texas
6-8 . . . . .Minnesota
10-13 . . at New York (AL)
14-16 . . . . . . .at Detroit
17-19 . . . . . . Pittsburgh
20-22 . . . . . . .Colorado
24-26 . . at San Francisco

27-29 . . . . . at Arizona

JULY
1-3 . . . . . . .at Cincinnati
4-6 . . . . . .New York (AL)
7-10 . . . . .Toronto
14-17 . . . . . .at Baltimore
18-20 . . . . at Minnesota
22-24 . . . . Chicago (AL)
25-27 . . Los Angeles (AL)
29-31 . . . . . Kansas City

AUGUST
1-4 . . . . .at Boston
5-7 . . . . .at Texas
9-11 . . . . Detroit
12-14 . . . . . . Minnesota

16-18 . . . .at Chicago (AL)
19-21 . . . . . . .at Detroit
22-24 . . . . Seattle
26-28 . . . . . Kansas City
29-31 . . . . Oakland

SEPTEMBER
1 . . . . Oakland
2-4 . . . . . .at Kansas City
5-7 . . . . Detroit
8-11 . . . .at Chicago (AL)
13-15 . . . . . . .at Texas
16-18 . . . . at Minnesota
20-22 . . . . Chicago (AL)
23-25 . . . . . .Minnesota
26-28 . . . . . . .at Detroit

GENERAL INFORMATION
Stadium (year opened): Progressive Field (1994).
Team Colors: Navy blue, red and silver.

Player Representative: Justin Masterson.
Home Dugout: Third Base.
Playing Surface: Grass.

Information Systems
Senior Director, Information Systems: Dave Powell. **Manager, Systems Development:** Matt Tagliaferri. **Manager, End-User Support:** Dan Mendlik. **Network Manager:** Whitney Kuszmaul. **Programmer Analyst:** Plamen Kouzov.

Ticketing
Telephone: (216) 420-4487. **Fax:** (216) 420-4481.
Director, Ticket Services: Gene Connelly. **Manager, Ticket Services:** David Pike. **Manager, Ticket Office:** Ryan Beech. **Manager, Ticket Operations:** Andrea Zagger. **Senior Director, Tickets/Premium Sales:** Mike Mulhall. **Director, Fan Services:** Dave Murray.

Spring Training/Arizona Operations:
Manager, Arizona Operations: Ryan Lantz. **Manager, Home Clubhouse:** Fletcher Wilkes.
Director, Team Travel: Mike Seghi. **Home Clubhouse/Equipment Manager:** Tony Amato. **Manager, Video Operations:** Bob Chester. **Visiting Clubhouse Manager:** Willie Jenks.

BASEBALL OPERATIONS
Telephone: (216) 420-4200. **Fax:** (216) 420-4321.
Executive Vice President/General Manager: Chris Antonetti.
VP, Baseball Operations/Assistant GM: Mike Chernoff.
Director, Player Personnel: Steve Lubratich. **Director, Baseball Administration:** Wendy Hoppel. **Assistant Director, Baseball Operations:** Derek Falvey. **Manager, Baseball Research/Analytics:** Keith Woolner. **Assistant to the President:** Andrew Miller. **Assistant, Baseball Operations:** Meka Asonye. **Assistant Director, Professional Scouting:** Alex Eckelman. **Executive Administrative Assistant:** Marlene Lehky. **Administrative Assistant:** Barbara Lessman. **Sports Psychologist:** Dr. Charles Maher.

Chris Antonetti

Major League Staff
Manager: Manny Acta.
Coaches: Bench—Tim Tolman, Pitching—Tim Belcher, Hitting—Jon Nunnally, First Base—Sandy Alomar Jr., Third Base/Infield—Steve Smith, Bullpen—Scott Radinsky.
Assistants, Major League Staff: Armando Camacaro, Francisco Morales.

Medical, Training
Head Team Physician: Dr. Mark Schickendantz. **Director, Medical Services/Head Trainer:** Lonnie Soloff. **Assistant Athletic Trainers:** Rick Jameyson, Jeff Desjardins. **Strength/Conditioning Coach:** Joe Kessler.

Player Development
Telephone: (216) 420-4308. **Fax:** (216) 420-4321.
Vice President, Player Development: Ross Atkins.
Assistant, Player Development: Carter Hawkins. **Administrative Assistant:** Nilda Taffanelli. **Advisor, Player Development:** Johnny Goryl. **Director, Latin American Operations:** Ramon Pena. **Coordinators:** Travis Fryman (fielding), Dave Miller (pitching), Bruce Fields (hitting), Gary Thurman (outfield/baserunning), Ken Rowe (pitching advisor), David Wallace (catching), Jake Beiting (strength/conditioning), Julio Rangel (mental skills), Lino Diaz (cultural development). **Advisor, Latin America:** Minnie Mendoza.

Farm System

Class	Club	Manager	Coach	Pitching Coach
Triple-A	Columbus (IL)	Mike Sarbaugh	Lee May Jr.	Ruben Niebla
Double-A	Akron (EL)	Chris Tremie	Rouglas Odor	Tony Arnold
High A	Kinston (CL)	Aaron Holbert	Phil Clark	Mickey Callaway
Low A	Lake County (MWL)	Ted Kubiak	Jim Rickon	Jeff Harris
Short-season	Mahoning Valley (NYP)	David Wallace	Unavailable	Greg Hibbard
Rookie	Indians (AZL)	Anthony Medrano	Junior Betances	Dennis Malave
Rookie	Indians (DSL)	Wilfredo Tejada	G. Jabalera/C. Fermin	Mario Brito

Scouting
Telephone: (216) 420-4200. **Fax:** (216) 420-4321.
Vice President, Scouting Operations: John Mirabelli.
Director, Amateur Scouting: Brad Grant. **Assistant Director, Scouting:** Paul Gillispie. **Assistant Director, Professional Scouting:** Alex Eckelman. **Major League Scouts:** Dave Malpass (Huntington Beach, CA), Don Poplin (Norwood, NC), Chris Smith (Montgomery, TX). **Pro Scouts:** Doug Carpenter (North Palm Beach, FL), Jim Cuthbert (Summit, NJ), Steve Lyons (Lake Mary, FL).
National Crosschecker: Chuck Ricci (Greencastle, PA). **Regional Crosscheckers:** Scott Barnsby (Huntsville, AL), Paul Cogan (Rocklin, CA), Scott Meaney (Apex, NC), Derrick Ross (Lake Orion, MI). **Area Scouts:** Steve Abney (Lawrence, KS), Mark Allen (Houston, TX), Chuck Bartlett (Starkville, MS), Kevin Cullen (Dallas, TX), Byron Ewing (Goodyear, AZ), Don Lyle (Sacramento, CA), Bob Mayer (Somerset, PA), Junie Melendez (Lorain, OH), Les Pajari (Angora, MN), Vince Sagisi (Encino, CA), Jason Smith (Long Beach, CA), Mike Soper (Tampa, FL), Brad Tyler (Bishop, GA), Jack Uhey (Ridgefiled, WA), Brent Urcheck (Philadelphia, PA). **Latin America Crosschecker:** Cesar Geronimo (Aventura, FL).

Colorado Rockies

Office Address: 2001 Blake St., Denver, CO 80205.
Telephone: (303) 292-0200. **Fax:** (303) 312-2116.
Website: www.coloradorockies.com.

Ownership
Operated by: Colorado Rockies Baseball Club Ltd.
Owner/General Partner: Charles K. Monfort. **Owner/Chairman/Chief Executive Officer:** Richard L. Monfort. **Executive Assistant to the Owner/General Partner:** Patricia Penfold. **Executive Assistant to the Owner/Chairman/Chief Executive Officer:** Terry Douglass.

BUSINESS OPERATIONS
Executive Vice President/Chief Operating Officer: Greg Feasel. **Assistant to Executive VP/Chief Operating Officer:** Kim Olson. **VP, Human Resources:** Elizabeth Stecklein.

Finance
Executive VP/CFO/Legal Counsel: Hal Roth. **VP, Finance:** Michael Kent. **Senior Director, Purchasing:** Gary Lawrence. **Director, Accounting:** Phil Emerson.

Marketing/Sales
VP, Corporate Sales: Marcy Glasser. **Assistant to VP, Corporate Sales:** Jenny Roope. **Senior Account Executives, Corporate Sales:** Kari Anderson, Billy Witter. **Coordinators, Corporate Sales:** Amy Crawford, K`ari Ring. **Director, New Partner Development:** Brendan Falvey. **VP, Community/Retail Operations:** James P. Kellogg. **Assistant to VP, Community/Retail Operations:** Kelly Hall. **Managers, Community Affairs:** Dallas Davis, Antigone Vigil. **Manager, Community Fields Program/Club Historian:** Paul Parker. **Director, Retail Operations:** Aaron Heinrich. **Director, Information Systems:** Bill Stephani. **Director, Promotions/Special Events:** Jason Fleming. **Senior Director, Advertising/Marketing:** Jill Campbell.

Charles Monfort

Public Relations/Communications
Telephone: (303) 312-2325. **Fax:** (303) 312-2319.
VP, Communications/Public Relations: Jay Alves. **Assistant to VP, Communications/Public Relations:** Irma Castañeda. **Manager, Communications/Public Relations:** Nick Piburn. **Coordinator, Communications/Public Relations:** Mike Kennedy.

Ballpark Operations
VP, Ballpark Operations: Kevin Kahn. **Senior Director, Food Service Operations/Development:** Albert Valdes. **Manager, Ballpark Services:** Mary Beth Benner. **Senior Director, Guest Services:** Steven Burke. **Director, Security:** Don Lyon. **Senior Director, Engineering/Facilities:** James Wiener. **Director, Engineering:** Randy Carlill. **Director, Facilities:** Oly Olsen. **Head Groundskeeper:** Mark Razum. **Official Scorers:** Dave Einspahr, Dave Plati.

2011 SCHEDULE
Standard Game Times: 6:40 p.m.; Fri. 7:10; Sat. 6:10; Sun. 1:10.

APRIL		
1-3 . . . . Arizona	13-15 . . . . . . San Diego	24-26 . . . at New York (AL)
5-6 . . . . . Los Angeles (NL)	16-17 . . . . . San Francisco	28-30 . . . . . Chicago (AL)
7-10 . . . . . at Pittsburgh	18-19 . . . at Philadelphia	
11-14 . . . at New York (NL)	20-22 . . . . . at Milwaukee	**JULY**
15-17 . . . . . Chicago (NL)	24-26 . . . . Arizona	1-3 . . . . Kansas City
18-20 . . . . . San Francisco	27-29 . . . . St. Louis	4-7 . . . . at Atlanta
22-24 . . . . at Florida	30-31 . at Los Angeles (NL)	8-10 . . . . at Washington
25-27 . . . at Chicago (NL)		14-17 . . . . . . Milwaukee
29-30 . . . . Pittsburgh	**JUNE**	18-21 . . . . Atlanta
	1 . . . . at Los Angeles (NL)	22-24 . . . . . . at Arizona
MAY	3-5 . . . . . at San Francisco	25-27 . at Los Angeles (NL)
1 . . . . Pittsburgh	6-8 . . . . . . at San Diego	29-31 . . . . . at San Diego
3-5 . . . . at Arizona	9-12 . . . Los Angeles (NL)	
6-8 . . . . at San Francisco	13-15 . . . . . . San Diego	**AUGUST**
9-11 . . . . . New York (NL)	17-19 . . . . Detroit	1-3 . . . . Philadelphia
	20-22 . . . . . at Cleveland	4-7 . . . . Washington
		8-11 . . . . . .at Cincinnati

		SEPTEMBER
12-14 . . . . .at St. Louis		
15-17 . . . . Florida		
19-21 . . Los Angeles (NL)		
22-24 . . . . Houston		
26-28 . at Los Angeles (NL)		
29-31 . . . . . . at Arizona		
		2-4 . . . . . . at San Diego
		5-7 . . . . Arizona
		9-11 . . . . Cincinnati
		13-14 . . . . at Milwaukee
		15-18 . . . . San Francisco
		19-21 . . . . . . San Diego
		22-25 . . . . . .at Houston
		26-28 . . at San Francisco

GENERAL INFORMATION
Stadium (year opened): Coors Field (1995).   **Home Dugout:** First Base.
Team Colors: Purple, black and silver.   **Playing Surface:** Grass.
Player Representative: Troy Tulowitzki.

Ticketing
Telephone: (303) 762-5437, (800) 388-7625. **Fax:** (303) 312-2115.
VP, Ticket Operations/Sales/Services: Sue Ann McClaren. **Senior Director, Ticket Operations/Sales/Services:** Kevin Fenton. **Director, Ticket Operations/Finances:** Kent Hakes. **Assistant Director, Ticket Operations:** Scott Donaldson. **Manager, Ticket Operations:** Kevin Flood. **Manager, Ticket Services:** James Valdez. **Director, Season Tickets/Group Sales:** Jeff Benner. **Manager, Season Tickets:** Farrah Magee. **Director, Outbound Sales/Suites:** Matt Haddad. **Supervisor, Suites/Party Facilities:** Traci Sauerteig.

Travel/Clubhouse
Director, Major League Operations: Paul Egins.
Director, Clubhouse Operations: Keith Schulz. **Assistant Equipment Manager:** Joe Diaz. **Assistant Clubhouse Manager:** Mike Pontarelli. **Visiting Clubhouse Manager:** Alan Bossart.

BASEBALL OPERATIONS
Telephone: (303) 292-0200. **Fax:** (303) 312-2320.
Executive VP/Chief Baseball Officer/General Manager: Dan O'Dowd. **Assistant to Executive VP/Chief Baseball Officer/GM:** Adele Armagost. **Assistant GM/VP, Baseball Operations:** Bill Geivett. **Senior Director, Baseball Operations:** Jeff Bridich. **Assistant, Baseball Operations/General Counsel:** Zack Rosenthal. **Baseball Operations Assistants:** Walker Monfort, Kent McKendry. **Special Assistants to GM:** Pat Daugherty (Aurora, CO), Dave Holliday (Tulsa, OK), Marcel Lachemann (Penryn, CA).

Major League Staff
Manager: Jim Tracy.
Coaches: Bench—Tom Runnells; Pitching—Bob Apodaca; Hitting—Carney Lansford; First Base—Glenallen Hill; Third Base—Rich Dauer; Bullpen—Jim Wright; Major League Coach/Catching Instructor: Marv Foley; Bullpen Catcher—Pat Burgess; Strength/Conditioning—Brian Jordan; Video—Brian Jones.

Medical/Training
Senior Director, Medical Operations/Special Projects: Tom Probst. **Medical Director:** Dr. Thomas Noonan. **Club Physicians:** Dr. Allen Schreiber, Dr. Douglas Wyland. **Head Trainer:** Keith Dugger.

Dan O'Dowd

Player Development
Telephone: (303) 292-0200. **Fax:** (303) 312-2320.
Senior Director, Player Development: Marc Gustafson. **Assistant, Player Development:** Walter Sylvester. **Field Coordinator:** Ron Gideon.
Roving Instructors: Scott Fletcher (infield), Trenidad Hubbard (outfield/baserunning), Jim Johnson (hitting), Bo McLaughlin (pitching).
Special Assistant, Baseball Operations: Rick Mathews. **Senior Advisor, Player Development:** Bobby Knoop. **Strength/Conditioning Coordinator:** Gabe Bauer. **Mental Skills Coach:** Ronn Svetich. **Rehab Coordinator:** Scott Murayama. **Cultural Development Coordinator:** Daniel Pace. **Equipment Manager:** Jerry Bass.

Farm System

Class	Club (League)	Manager	Coach	Pitching Coach
Triple-A	Colorado Springs (PCL)	Stu Cole	Rene Lachemann	Doug Linton
Double-A	Tulsa (TL)	Duane Espy	Dave Hajek	Dave Schuler
High A	Modesto (CAL)	Jerry Weinstein	Kevin Riggs	Darryl Scott
Low A	Asheville (SAL)	Joe Mikulik	Lenn Sakata	Joey Eischen
Short-season	Tri-City (NWL)	Fred Ocasio	Anthony Sanders	Dave Burba
Rookie	Casper (PIO)	Tony Diaz	Jon Stone	Craig Bjornson
Rookie	Rockies (DSL)	Mauricio Gonzalez	F. Nunez/E. Jose	Edison Lora

Scouting
Telephone: (303) 292-0200. **Fax:** (303) 312-2320.
VP, Scouting: Bill Schmidt. **Assistant Director, Scouting:** Danny Montgomery. **Assistant Director, Scouting:** Zach Wilson. **Director, Pro Scouting:** Jon Weil.
Advance Scout: Chris Warren. **Pro Scouts:** Ty Coslow (Louisville, KY), Will George (Woolwich Township, NJ), Jack Gillis (Sarasota, FL), Mike Hamilton (Dallas, TX), Mike Paul (Tucson, AZ). **Special Assignment Scout:** Terry Wetzel (Overland Park, KS).
National Crosschecker: Mike Ericson (Phoenix, AZ). **Scouting Adviser:** Dave Snow (Seal Beach, CA).
Area Scouts: John Cedarburg (Fort Myers, FL), Scott Corman (Lexington, KY), Dar Cox (Frisco, TX), Jeff Edwards (Humble, TX), Chris Forbes (AZ), Mike Garlatti (Edison, NJ), Mark Germann (Atkins, IA), Matt Hattabaugh (Westminster, CA), Damon Iannelli (Brandon, MS), Jon Lukens (San Diego, CA), Alan Matthews (Atlanta, GA), Jay Matthews (Concord, NC), Jorge de Posada (Rio Piedras, PR), Jesse Retzlaff (Kirkland, WA), Ed Santa (Powell, OH), Gary Wilson (Sacramento, CA). **Part-Time Scouts:** Norm DeBriyn (Fayetteville, AR), Jeff Hipps (Millbrae, CA), Marc Johnson (Centennial, CO), Dave McQueen (Bossier City, LA), Greg Pullia (Plymouth, MA).
Senior Director, International Operations: Rolando Fernandez. **Manager, Dominican Operations:** Jhonathan Leyba. **Supervisor, Venezuelan Scouting:** Orlando Medina. **Manager, Pacific Rim Operations:** Ming Harbor. **International Scouts:** Phil Allen (Australia), Martin Cabrera (Dominican Republic), Claudino Hernandez (Panama), Carlos Gomez (Venezuela), Frank Roa (Dominican Republic), Chi-Sheng Tsai (Taiwan).

Detroit Tigers

Office Address: 2100 Woodward Ave, Detroit, MI 48201.
Telephone: (313) 471-2000. **Fax:** (313) 471-2138. **Website:** www.tigers.com

Ownership
Operated By: Detroit Tigers Inc. **Owner:** Michael Ilitch.
President/CEO/General Manager: David Dombrowski. **Special Assistants to President:** Al Kaline, Willie Horton.
Executive Assistant to President/CEO/GM: Marty Lyon. **Senior Vice President:** Jim Devellano.

BUSINESS OPERATIONS
Senior Vice President, Business Operations: Duane McLean.
Executive Assistant to Senior VP, Business Operations: Peggy Bacarella.

Finance
VP/CFO: Stephen Quinn. **Senior Director, Finance:** Kelli Kollman. **Director, Purchasing/Supplier Diversity:** DeAndre Berry. **Accounting Manager:** Sheila Robine. **Financial Analyst:** Kristin Jorgensen. **Accounts Payable Coordinator:** Debbi Sword. **Accounts Receivable Coordinator:** Sharon Szkarlat. **Administrative Assistant:** Tracy Rice. **Director, Human Resources:** Karen Gruca. **Director, Payroll Administration:** Maureen Kraatz. **Director, Information Technology:** Scott Wruble.

Public, Community Affairs
VP, Community/Public Affairs: Elaine Lewis. **Manager, Player Relations, Sports/Youth Programs:** Sam Abrams. **Director, Tigers Foundation:** Jordan Field. **Manager, Community Affairs:** Alexandrea Thrubis. **Community Affairs Coordinator:** Kristen Joe. **Administrative Assistant:** Audrey Zielinski.

Mike Ilitch

Sales, Marketing
VP, Corporate Partnerships/Ticket Sales: Steve Harms. **Senior Director, Corporate Sales:** Kurt Buhler. **Corporate Sales Managers:** Zach Wagner, John Wolski. **Sponsorship Services Manager:** Amy Peterson. **Sponsorship Services Coordinator:** Ashley Ransey. **VP, Marketing:** Ellen Hill Zeringue. **Director, Marketing:** Ron Wade. **Director, Promotions/In-Game Entertainment:** Eli Bayless. **Promotions Coordinator:** Jared Karner. **VP, Suite Sales/Services:** Scot Pett.

Media Relations, Communications
Telephone: (313) 471-2114. **Fax:** (313) 471-2138.
VP, Communications: Ron Colangelo. **Director, Baseball Media Relations:** Brian Britten. **Manager, Baseball Media Relations:** Rick Thompson. **Coordinator, Baseball Media Relations:** Aileen Villarreal. **Director, Broadcasting:** Molly Betensley.

Ballpark Operations
VP, Park Operations: Michael Healy. **Head Groundskeeper:** Heather Nabozny. **Assistant Groundskeeper:** Gail DeGennaro. **Senior Manager, Park Operations:** Ed Goward. **Manager, Event/Guest Services:** Jill Baran. **Park**

2011 SCHEDULE
Standard Game Times: 7:05 p.m.; Sun. 1:05.

MARCH		
31 . . . . . at New York (AL)		

APRIL
2-3 . . . . at New York (AL)
4 . . . . at Baltimore
6-7 . . . . at Baltimore
8-10 . . . . Kansas City
11-13 . . . . Texas
14-17 . . . . . . .at Oakland
18-20 . . . . .at Seattle
22-24 . . . . . Chicago (AL)
26-28 . . . . . . Seattle
29-30 . . . . . .at Cleveland

MAY
1 . . . . .at Cleveland

2-5 . . . . . .New York (AL)
6-9 . . . . at Toronto
10-11 . . . . . at Minnesota
13-15 . . . . . Kansas City
16-17 . . . . .Toronto
18-19 . . . . .at Boston
20-22 . . . . . at Pittsburgh
23-25 . . . . . . .Tampa Bay
26-29 . . . . Boston
30-31 . . . . . . Minnesota

JUNE
1 . . . . .Minnesota
3-5 . . . . . .at Chicago (AL)
6-8 . . . . .at Texas
9-12 . . . . Seattle
14-16 . . . . . . Cleveland

17-19 . . . . . at Colorado
20-22 . at Los Angeles (NL)
24-26 . . . . .Arizona
28-30 . . . . .New York (NL)

JULY
1-3 . . . . . . .San Francisco
4-6 . . . . . at Los Angeles
7-10 . . . . .at Kansas City
15-17 . . . . . Chicago (AL)
19-20 . . . . Oakland
21-24 . . . . . at Minnesota
25-27 . . . .at Chicago (AL)
28-31 . . Los Angeles (AL)

AUGUST
2-4 . . . . Texas
5-7 . . . . . .at Kansas City

9-11 . . . . . .at Cleveland
12-14 . . . . . .at Baltimore
15-17 . . . . . .Minnesota
19-21 . . . . . . Cleveland
22-25 . . . . at Tampa Bay
26-28 . . . . . at Minnesota
29-31 . . . . . Kansas City

SEPTEMBER
2-4 . . . . Chicago (AL)
5-7 . . . . . . .at Cleveland
9-11 . . . . Minnesota
12-14 . . . .at Chicago (AL)
15-18 . . . . . .at Oakland
20-21 . . . . .at Kansas City
22-25 . . . . . . Baltimore
26-28 . . . . . Cleveland

GENERAL INFORMATION
Stadium (year opened): Comerica Park (2000).
Team Colors: Navy blue, orange and white.

Player Representative: Unavailable.
Home Dugout: Third Base.
Playing Surface: Grass.

Operations Manager: Allan Carrise. **Scoreboard Operations Manager:** Robb Wilson. **Event Services Coordinator:** Rofeal Daniels.

Ticketing
Telephone: (313) 471-2255.
Director, Ticket Sales: Steve Fox. **Director, Group Sales:** Dwain Lewis. **Senior Director, Ticket Services:** Victor Gonzalez.

Travel, Clubhouse
Traveling Secretary: Bill Brown. **Manager, Home Clubhouse:** Jim Schmakel. **Assistant Manager, Visiting Clubhouse:** John Nelson. **Clubhouse Assistant:** Tyson Steele. **Baseball Video Operations:** Jeremy Kelch. **Assistant, Baseball Video Operations:** Andy Bjornstad, Tim Janicki.

BASEBALL OPERATIONS
Telephone: (313) 471-2000. **Fax:** (313) 471-2099.
General Manager: David Dombrowski.
VP/Assistant GM: Al Avila. **VP/Legal Counsel:** John Westhoff. **VP, Player Personnel:** Scott Reid. **Special Assistant:** Dick Egan. **Director, Baseball Operations:** Mike Smith. **Executive Assistant to President/GM:** Marty Lyon. **Executive Assistant:** Eileen Surma.

Major League Staff
Manager: Jim Leyland.
Coaches: Pitching—Rick Knapp; Batting—Lloyd McClendon; Infield—Rafael Belliard; First Base—Tom Brookens; Third Base—Gene Lamont; Bullpen—Jeff Jones.

Medical, Training
Director, Medical Services/Head Athletic Trainer: Kevin Rand. **Assistant Athletic Trainers:** Steve Carter, Doug Teter. **Strength/Conditioning Coach:** Javair Gillett. **Team Physicians:** Dr. Michael Workings, Dr. Stephen Lemos, Dr. Louis Saco (Florida). **Coordinator, Medical Services:** Gwen Keating.

Dave Dombrowski

Player Development
Telephone: (863) 413-4107. **Fax:** (863) 413-1954.
Director, Minor League Operations: Dan Lunetta. **Director, Player Development:** Mike Rojas. **Director, Minor League/Scouting Administration:** Cheryl Evans. **Director, Latin American Player Development:** Manny Crespo. **Minor League Operations Coordinator:** Avi Becher. **Administrative Assistant, Minor League Operations:** Marilyn Acevedo. **Minor League Field Coordinator:** Kevin Bradshaw. **Minor League Medical Coordinator:** Dustin Campbell. **Minor League Strength/Conditioning Coordinator:** Chris Walter. **Assistant Minor League Strength/Conditioning Coordinator:** Steve Chase.
Roving Instructors: Toby Harrah (hitting), Jon Matlack (pitching), Dave Owens (infield), Joe DePastino (catching), Gene Roof (outfield/baserunning), Brian Peterson (performance enhancement), Robert "Ghost" Frutchey (minor league clubhouse manager).

Farm System

Class	Club	Manager	Coach	Pitching Coach
Triple-A	Toledo (IL)	Phil Nevin	Leon Durham	A.J. Sager
Double-A	Erie (EL)	Chris Cron	Jerry Martin	Ray Burris
High A	Lakeland (FSL)	Dave Huppert	Larry Herndon	Joe Coleman
Low A	West Michigan (MWL)	Ernie Young	Ben Oglivie	Mark Johnson
Short-season	Connecticut (NYP)	Andrew Graham	Scott Dwyer	Jorge Cordova
Rookie	Tigers (GCL)	Basilio Cabrera	Mike Rabelo	Greg Sabat

Scouting
Telephone: (863) 413-4112. **Fax:** (863) 413-1954.
VP, Amateur Scouting/Special Assistant to GM: David Chadd. **Director, Amateur Scouting:** Scott Pleis. **Assistant Director, Amateur Scouting:** James Orr.
Major League Scouts: Eddie Bane (Encinitas, CA), Jim Olander (Vail, AZ), Mike Russell (Gulf Breeze, FL), Bruce Tanner (New Castle, PA), Jeff Wetherby (Wesley Chapel, FL).
National Crosscheckers: Ray Crone (Cedar Hill, TX), Tim Hallgren (Cape Girardeau, MO). **Regional Crosscheckers:** East—Murray Cook (Orlando, FL); Central—Tom Osowski (Franklin, WI); Midwest—Mike Hankins (Lee's Summit, MO); West—Tim McWilliam (San Diego, CA). **Area Scouts:** Bryson Barber (Pensacola, FL), Grant Brittain (Hickory, NC), Bill Buck (Manassas, VA), Rolando Casanova (Miami, FL), Scott Cerny (Rocklin, CA), Tim Grieve (New Braunfels, TX), Garrett Guest (Lockport, IL), Phil Huttmann (Pasadena, CA), Ryan Johnson (Oregon City, OR), Marty Miller (Chicago, IL), Steve Pack (San Marcos, CA), Brian Reid (Gilbert, AZ), Jim Rough (Sharpsburg, GA), Chris Wimmer (Yukon, OK), Harold Zonder (Louisville, KY).
Director, International Operations: Tom Moore. **Director, Latin American Development:** Manny Crespo. **Director, Latin American Scouting:** Miguel Garcia. **Coordinator, Pacific Rim Scouting:** Kevin Hooker. **Director, Dominican Operations:** Ramon Perez. **Coordinator, Dominican Academy:** Oliver Arias. **Venezuelan Scouting Supervisor:** Pedro Chavez. **Coordinator, Venezuelan Academy:** Oscar Garcia. **Scouting Assistant, International Operations:** Giovanni Hernandez.

Florida Marlins

Office Address: Sun Life Stadium, 2267 Dan Marino Blvd. **Miami, FL 33056.**
Telephone: (305) 626-7400. **Fax:** (305) 626-7302.
Website: www.marlins.com.

Ownership

Owner/CEO: Jeffrey Loria. **Vice Chairman:** Joel Mael.
President: David Samson. **Special Assistants to President:** Jeff Conine, Andre Dawson, Tony Perez. **Special Advisor to Owner:** Jack McKeon. **Executive Assistant to Owner/Vice Chairman/President:** Beth McConville.

BUSINESS OPERATIONS

Executive Vice President/CFO: Michel Bussiere. **Executive Assistant to the Executive VP/ CFO:** Lisa Milk. **Executive VP, Ballpark Development:** Claude Delorme. **Executive Assistant:** Ingrid Rodriguez. **Manager, Game Services:** Antonio Torres-Roman. **Coordinator, New Ballpark Development:** Karl Ebert.

Senior Director, Human Resources: Ana Hernandez. **Coordinator, Human Resources:** Brian Estes. **Administrator, Benefits:** Ruby Mattei. **Supervisor, Office Services:** Karl Heard. **Assistant, Office Services:** Donna Kirton. **Senior Receptionist:** Kathy Lanza. **Receptionist, New Ballpark:** Dianette Oliva.

Jeffrey Loria

Finance

Senior VP, Finance: Susan Jaison. **Controller:** Alina Trigo. **Administrator, Payroll:** Carolina Calderon. **Accountant:** Alina Quiros. **Coordinator, Accounts Payable:** Marva Alexander. **Coordinator, Finance:** Diana Jorge. **Assistant, Accounting:** Thomas Lundstedt. **Director, IT:** David Enriquez. **Manager, Technical Support:** David Kuan. **Network Engineer:** Ozzie Macias. **Manager, Telecommunications:** Sam Mora. **IT Technician:** Alexis Farres.

Marketing

Senior VP, Marketing: Sean Flynn. **Manager, Retail Operations:** Robyn Feinstein. **Director, Multicultural Marketing:** Juan Martinez. **Director, Marketing/Promotions:** Matt Britten. **Coordinator, Marketing:** Boris Menier. **Coordinator, Promotions:** Rafael Capdevila. **Coordinator, Marlins en Miami:** Danny Vargas.

Legal

Fax: 305-626-7371.
VP/General Counsel: Derek Jackson. **Associate Counsel:** Ashwin Krishnan. **Executive Assistant to VP/General Counsel:** A'kyra Hamilton.

Sales

VP, Business Development: Dale Hendricks. **Senior VP, Corporate Sales:** Brendan Cunningham. **Manager, Corporate Sales:** Tony Tome. **Corporate Sales Account Executive:** David Goldberg. **Coordinators, Corporate Sales:** Sheri Fanucci, Christina Portice. **Executive Assistant, Corporate Sales:** Judy Cavanagh. **Director, Customer Service:**

2011 SCHEDULE

Standard Game Times: 7:10 p.m.; Sun. 1:10

APRIL		
1-3 . . . . . . .New York (NL)	13-15 . . . . at Washington	28-30 . . . . . .at Oakland	15-17 . . . . . at Colorado
5-7 . . . . .Washington	16-17 . . . at New York (NL)		18-21 . . . . . at San Diego
8-10 . . . . . . .at Houston	18-19 . . . . . Chicago (NL)	**JULY**	23-25 . . . . Cincinnati
12-14 . . . . at Atlanta	20-22 . . . . . . .Tampa Bay	1-3 . . . . .at Texas	26-28 . . . . at Philadelphia
15-17 . . . . at Philadelphia	24-26 . . . at San Francisco	4-6 . . . . .Philadelphia	29-31 . . . at New York (NL)
19-21 . . . . .Pittsburgh	27-29 . at Los Angeles (NL)	7-10 . . . . Houston	
22-24 . . . . .Colorado	30-31 . . . . . . at Arizona	14-17 . . . .at Chicago (NL)	**SEPTEMBER**
25-27 . . . Los Angeles (NL)		19-21 . . . . . . San Diego	1 . . . . . . at New York (NL)
29-30 . . . . .at Cincinnati	**JUNE**	22-24 . . . . .New York (NL)	2-4 . . . . .Philadelphia
	1 . . . . at Arizona	26-28 . . . at Washington	5-7 . . . . . .New York (NL)
MAY	3-6 . . . . .Milwaukee	29-31 . . . . . . at Atlanta	9-11 . . . . . . at Pittsburgh
1 . . . . .at Cincinnati	7-9 . . . . Atlanta		12-14 . . . . at Atlanta
2-5 . . . . .at St. Louis	10-13 . . . . .Arizona	**AUGUST**	16-18 . . . . at Washington
6-8 . . . . . . .Washington	14-16 . . . . at Philadelphia	1-3 . . . . at New York (NL)	19-21 . . . . Atlanta
9-11 . . . . . .Philadelphia	17-19 . . . . at Tampa Bay	4-7 . . . . St. Louis	23-25 . . . . . at Milwaukee
	20-22 . . . Los Angeles (AL)	8-10 . . . . Atlanta	26-28 . . . . . .Washington
	24-26 . . . . Seattle	12-14 . . . . . San Francisco	

GENERAL INFORMATION

Stadium (year opened): Sun Life Stadium (1993).
Team Colors: Teal, black, white and silver.

Player Representative: Unavailable.
Home Dugout: First Base.
Playing Surface: Grass.

Spencer Linden. **Senior Account Executives, Group Sales/Special Events:** Mario Signorello, Bray LaDow. **Manager, Group Sales/Special Events:** Charles Sano. **Account Executives, Group Sales/Special Events:** Kathleen Massolio, Rahmel Fuller. **Senior Account Executives:** Anthony Jabara, Orestes Hernandez.

Media Relations, Communications

Telephone: (305) 626-7492. **Fax:** (305) 626-7302.
Senior VP, Communications/Broadcasting: P.J. Loyello. **Director, Media Relations:** Matthew Roebuck. **Manager, Media Relations:** Marty Sewell. **Administrative Assistant, Media Relations:** Maria Armella. **Director, Broadcasting:** Emmanuel Munoz. **Manager, Broadcasting:** Karen Deery. **Director, Business Communications:** Carolina Perrina. **Director, Community Outreach:** Angela Smith. **Manager, Player Relations:** Alex Morin. **Assistant, Community Outreach/Youth Baseball:** Juan Garciga. **Executive Director, Marlins Community Foundation:** Alfredo Mesa. **Director, Foundation Development:** Jennifer Dilliz.

In-Game Entertainment

Director, Game Presentation/Events: Larry Blocker. **Manager, Game Presentation/Events:** Eric Ramirez. **Director, Creative Services:** Alfred Hernandez. **Mascot:** John DeCicco. **PA Announcer:** Dick Sanford.

Travel, Clubhouse

Director, Team Travel: Manny Colon. **Equipment Manager:** John Silverman. **Visiting Clubhouse Manager:** Michael Rock Hughes. **Umpire Room Assistant:** Lou Assalone.

BASEBALL OPERATIONS

Telephone: 305-626-7400. **Fax:** 305-626-7433
President, Baseball Operations: Larry Beinfest.
VP/General Manager: Michael Hill. **Executive Assistant to the President, Baseball Operations/VP/GM:** Rita Filbert. **VP, Player Development/Scouting/Assistant GM:** Jim Fleming. **VP, Player Personnel/Assistant GM:** Dan Jennings. **Special Assistants to GM:** Orrin Freeman, Mark Wiley. **Director, Baseball Operations:** Mike Wickham. **Senior Director, Team Travel:** Bill Beck. **Director, Team Travel:** Manny Colon. **Video Coordinator:** Cullen McRae.

Larry Beinfest

Major League Staff

Manager: Edwin Rodriguez.
Coaches: Bench—Brandon Hyde; Pitching—Randy St. Claire; Hitting—John Mallee; First Base/Infield—Perry Hill; Third Base—Joe Espada; Bullpen—Reid Cornelius; Bullpen Coordinator—Jeff Urgelles.

Medical, Training

Head Trainer: Sean Cunningham. **Assistant Trainer:** Mike Kozak. **Director, Strength/Conditioning:** Paul Fournier.

Player Development

Director, Player Development: Brian Chattin. **Assistant Director, Player Development/International Operations:** Marc Lippman. **Supervisor, Player Development/Scouting:** Michael Youngberg.
Field Coordinator: John Pierson. **Coordinators:** Gene Basham (training/rehabilitation), Tarrik Brock (roving outfield/baserunning), Tim Cossins (roving catching), Jack Howell (roving hitting), Wayne Rosenthal (pitching), Tim Leiper (roving infield). **Minor League Equipment Manager:** Mark Brown.

Farm System

Class	Club (League)	Manager	Hitting Coach	Pitching Coach
Triple-A	New Orleans (PCL)	Greg Norton	Damon Minor	Charlie Corbell, Jr.
Double-A	Jacksonville (SL)	Andrew Barkett	Corey Hart	John Duffy
High A	Jupiter (FSL)	Ron Hassey	Frank Moore	Terry Abbott
Low A	Greensboro (SAL)	Andy Haines	Kevin Randel	William Glen
Short-season	Jamestown (NYP)	Dave Berg	Robert Bell	Blake McGinely
Rookie	Jupiter (GCL)	Jorge Hernandez	Angel Espada	Jeff Schwarz
Rookie	Marlins (DSL)	Ray Nunez	Luis Brito	Edison Santana

Scouting

Telephone: (561) 630-1816/Pro (561) 630-1809.
Director, Scouting: Stan Meek.
Assistant Director, Scouting: Gregg Leonard. **Assistant Director, Pro Scouting:** Dan Noffsinger. **Advance Scout:** Joel Moeller (San Clemente, CA).
Pro Scouts: Roger Jongewaard (Fallbrook, CA), Dave Roberts (Fort Worth, TX), Phil Rossi (Jessup, PA), Tommy Thompson (Greenville, NC), Pierre Arsenault (Pierrefonds, QC), Matt Kinzer (Fort Wayne, IN).
National Crosschecker: David Crowson (College Station, TX). **Regional Supervisors:** East—Matt Haas (Cincinnati, OH); Central—Ray Hayward (Norman, OK); West—Scott Goldby (Yuba City, CA); Canada—Steve Payne (Barrington, RI).
Area Scouts: Matt Anderson (Williamsport, PA), Carlos Berroa (Caguas, PR), Carmen Carcone (Canton, GA), Robby Corsaro (Victorville, CA), John Hughes (Walnut Creek, CA), Kevin Ibach (Arlington Heights, IL), Brian Kraft (Auburndale, FL), Joel Matthews (Concord, NC), Tim McDonnell (Westminster, CA), Gabe Sandy (Damascus, OR), Scott Stanley (Peoria, AZ), Steve Taylor (Shawnee, OK), Ryan Wardinsky (The Woodlands, TX), Mark Willoughby (Hammond, LA), Nick Zumsande (Fairfax, IA).
Director, International Operations: Albert Gonzalez. **Assistant Director, Player Development/International Operations:** Marc Lippman. **International Supervisors:** Sandy Nin (Santo Domingo, Dominican Republic), Wilmer Castillo (Maracay, VZ). **International Scouts:** Luis Cordoba (Panama), Alix Martinez (San Pedro de Macoris, DR), Hugo Martinez (Santiago, DR), Domingo Ortega (Santo Domingo, DR), Robin Ordonez (Zulia, VZ).

Houston Astros

Office Address: Minute Maid Park, Union Station, 501 Crawford, Suite 400, Houston, TX 77002.
Mailing Address: P.O. Box 288, Houston, TX 77001.
Telephone: (713) 259-8000. **Fax:** (713) 259-8981.
E-mail Address: fanfeedback@astros.mlb.com. **Website:** www.astros.com.

Ownership
Operated By: McLane Group LP. **Chairman/CEO:** Drayton McLane. **Board of Directors:** Drayton McLane, Bob McClaren, G.W. Sanford, Webster F. Stickney, Jr.

BUSINESS OPERATIONS
President, Business Operations: Pam Gardner. **Executive Assistant:** Eileen Colgin.
Senior Vice President, Finance/Administration: Jackie Traywick. **Senior Director, Risk Management:** Monica Rusch. **Controller:** Jonathan Germer. **Director, Treasury/Office Services:** Damian Babin. **Senior Accountant:** Monique Sam. **VP, Human Resources:** Larry Stokes. **Human Resources Manager:** Chanda Lawdermilk. **Director, Payroll/Employee Benefits:** Ruth Kelly. **Payroll Manager:** Jessica Horton. **Benefits Coordinator:** Cyndi Cook. **Director, Security:** Angel Zayas. **Receptionist:** Helen Washington. **Union Station Receptionist:** Heather Kuehn.
Senior VP, Premium Sponsorships: Jamie Hildreth. **VP, Sponsorships/Business Development:** John Sorrentino. **VP, Market Development:** Rosi Hernandez. **VP, Marketing/ Ticket Sales:** Jennifer Germer. **Director, Marketing:** Clint Pasche. **Director, Sponsorship Sales:** Shane Hildreth. **Manager, Marketing:** Chris Hunsaker. **Coordinator, Promotions/ Special Events:** Christie Miller. **Coordinator, Market Development:** Nicky Patriarca. **Graphics Designer:** Chris Garcia. **Assistant Director, Sponsorship Sales:** Clarence Estes. **Sponsorships Coordinators:** Melissa Garibay, Linda Pinsent.

Drayton McLane

Public Relations/Communications
Telephone: (713) 259-8900. **Fax:** (713) 259-8025.
Senior VP, Communications: Jay Lucas. **Director, Media Relations:** Gene Dias. **Assistant Director, Media Relations:** Sally Gunter. **Media Relations Coordinators:** Stephen Grande, MJ Trahan. **Senior Director, Digital Media:** Alyson Footer. **VP, Foundation Development:** Marian Harper. **Director, Community Affairs:** Shawn Bertani. **Director, Procurement:** Seth Courtney. **Director, Information Technology:** Steve Reese.

Stadium Operations
VP, Building Operations: Bobby Forrest. **VP, Special Events:** Kala Sorenson. **VP, Guest Services/Special Events:** Marty Price. **Director, Engineering/Maintenance:** David McKenzie. **Assistant Director, Building Operations:** Austin Malone. **Senior Director, Creative Services:** Kirby Kander. **Director, Ballpark Entertainment:** Brock Jessel. **Director, Broadcast Operations/Affiliate Relations:** Mike Cannon. **Director, Telecommunications/Executive Assistant:** Tracy Faucette. **Director, Guest Services:** Michael Kenny. **Assistant Director, Guest Services:** Cedrick Edwards. **Authentications Manager:** Mike Acosta. **Assistant Director, Special Events:** Jonathan Sterchy. **Assistant Sales Director, Special Events:**

2011 SCHEDULE
Standard Game Times: 7:05 p.m.; Sat. 6:05; Sun. 1:05.

APRIL			
1-3 . . . . . at Philadelphia	13-15 . . . . .New York (NL)	24-26 . . . . . .Tampa Bay	12-14 . at Los Angeles (NL)
5-7 . . . . . . .at Cincinnati	16-17 . . . . . . at Atlanta	28-30 . . . . Texas	15-17 . . . . . Chicago (NL)
8-10 . . . . Florida	18-19 . . . . . . .at St. Louis		19-21 . . . . San Francisco
11-13 . . . . . Chicago (NL)	20-22 . . . . . . at Toronto	**JULY**	22-24 . . . . . at Colorado
14-17 . . . . . . San Diego	23-25 . . . Los Angeles (NL)	1-3 . . . . Boston	25-28 . . at San Francisco
19-21 . . . at New York (NL)	27-29 . . . . .Arizona	4-6. . . . . . . at Pittsburgh	29-31 . . . . . . .Pittsburgh
22-24 . . . . . at Milwaukee	30-31 . . . .at Chicago (NL)	7-10 . . . . .at Florida	
26-28 . . . . St. Louis		15-17 . . . . . . .Pittsburgh	**SEPTEMBER**
29-30 . . . . . . .Milwaukee	**JUNE**	18-20 . . . . . Washington	2-4. . . . . . . .Milwaukee
	1 . . . . . .at Chicago (NL)	22-24 . . . .at Chicago (NL)	5-7 . . . . . at Pittsburgh
	2-5 . . . . . at San Diego	25-28 . . . . . .at St. Louis	9-11 . . . . at Washington
MAY	7-9 . . . . St. Louis	29-31 . . . . at Milwaukee	12-14 . . . . .Philadelphia
1 . . . . .Milwaukee	10-13 . . . . Atlanta		16-18 . . . .at Chicago (NL)
2-4 . . . . . . .at Cincinnati	14-16 . . . . . . Pittsburgh	**AUGUST**	19-21 . . . . .at Cincinnati
6-8 . . . . . . at Pittsburgh	17-19 . at Los Angeles (NL)	1-3 . . . . Cincinnati	22-25 . . . . .Colorado
9-11 . . . . Cincinnati	20-22 . . . . .at Texas	5-7 . . . . .Milwaukee	26-28 . . . . St. Louis
		8-11 . . . . at Arizona	

GENERAL INFORMATION
Stadium (year opened): Minute Maid Park (2000).
Team Colors: Brick red, sand and black.

Player Representative: Unavailable.
Home Dugout: First Base.
Playing Surface: Grass.

Katy Preisler. **Director, Major League Field Operations:** Dan Bergstrom. **First Assistant Groundskeeper:** Kyle Lewis. **Second Assistant Groundskeeper:** Joe Johannsen. Groundskeepers: Willie Berry, Eric Jaramillo. **PA Announcer:** Bob Ford.

Ticketing
Telephone: (713) 259-8500. **Fax:** (713) 259-8326.
Senior Director, Ticket Sales: Bill Goren. **Senior Director, Ticket Services:** Brooke Ellenberger. **Director, Ticket Operations:** Marcia Coronado. **Director, Box Office Operations:** Bill Cannon. **Manager, Premium Sales:** Clay Kowalski. **Manager, Ticket Systems/Customer Retention:** Jolene Sherman. **Senior Account Executive:** Brent Brousssard. **Manager, Ticket Sales:** Carl Grider. **Ticket Service Coordinator:** Kristen Lundgren. **Manager, Premium Sales:** Kelsey Matherne. **Administrative Assistant, Ticket Sales:** Joannie Cobb. **Ticket Production Coordinator:** Sandy Luna. **Ticket Office Clerk:** Yvonne Sims.

Travel/Clubhouse
Director, Team Travel: Barry Waters.
Equipment Manager: Dennis Liborio. **Assistant Equipment Manager:** Carl Schneider. **Visiting Clubhouse Manager:** Steve Perry. **Umpire/Clubhouse Assistant:** Chuck New. **Clubhouse Attendant:** David Burd.

BASEBALL OPERATIONS
Telephone: (713) 259-8000. **Fax:** (713) 259-8600.
President, Baseball Operations: Tal Smith.
General Manager: Ed Wade.
Assistant GM/Player Relations: David Gottfried. **Director, Baseball Research/Pro Scouting Coordinator:** Charlie Norton. **Executive Assistant:** Traci Dearing. **Video Coordinator:** Jim Summers.

Ed Wade

Major League Staff
Manager: Brad Mills.
Coaches: Bench—Al Pedrique; Pitching—Brad Arnsberg; Hitting—Mike Barnett; First Base—Bobby Meacham, Sr.; Third Base—Dave Clark; Bullpen—jamie Quirk.

Medical, Training
Medical Director: Dr. David Lintner. **Team Physicians:** Dr. Tom Mehlhoff, Dr. Jim Muntz.
Head Trainer: Nathan Lucero. **Assistant Trainer:** Rex Jones. **Strength/Conditioning Coach:** Dr. Gene Coleman.

Player Development
Telephone: (713) 259-8920. **Fax:** (713) 259-8600.
Director, Player Development: Fred Nelson. **Director, Florida Operations:** Jay Edmiston. **Coordinator, Player Development:** Allen Rowin. **Field Coordinator:** Paul Runge. **Minor League Coordinators:** Ty Van Burkleo (hitting), Jaime Garcia (pitching), Milt Thompson (outfield/baserunning), Danny Sheaffer (catching), Stubby Clapp (infield), Jamey Snodgrass (training/rehabilitation), Frank Renner (strength/conditioning).

Farm System

Class	Club	Manager	Hitting Coach	Pitching Coach
Triple-A	Oklahoma City (PCL)	Tony DeFrancesco	Keith Bodie	Burt Hooton
Double-A	Corpus Christi (TL)	Tom Lawless	John Moses	Don Alexander
High A	Lancaster (CAL)	Tom Spencer	Darryl Robinson	Travis Driskill
Low A	Lexington (SAL)	Rodney Linares	Joel Chimelis	Dave Borkowski
Short-season	Tri-City (NYP)	Stubby Clapp	Marc Bailey	Gary Ruby
Rookie	Greeneville (APP)	Omar Lopez	Josh Bonifay	Rick Aponte
Rookie	Astros (GCL)	Ed Romero	Edgar Alfonzo	H. Mercado/C. Taylor
Rookie	Astros (DSL)	Luis Martinez	Luis Mateo	Jose Martinez

Scouting
Telephone: (713) 259-8925. **Fax:** (713) 259-8600.
Assistant GM, Amateur Scouting: Bobby Heck. **Special Assistant to the GM, Latin America:** Felix Francisco. **Director, Major League Scouting:** Ricky Bennett. **Coordinator, Amateur Scouting:** Mike Burns. **Major League Scouts:** Jack Lind (Mesa, AZ), Paul Ricciarini (Pittsfield, MA), Ken Califano (Stafford, VA). **Special Assignment Scouts:** Gene DeBoer (Brandon, WI), Matt Galante (Staten Island, NY), Bob Skinner (San Diego, CA), Walt Matthews (Texarkana, TX). **Professional Scouts:** Hank Allen (Upper Marlboro, MD), Ruben Amaro Sr. (Weston, FL), Kenny Baugh (Houston, TX), Bob Rossi (Baton Rouge, LA), Josh Miller (Houston, TX), Tad Slowik (Arlington Heights, IL), Scipio Spinks (Missouri City, TX).
National Crosschecker: David Post (Canton, GA). **Regional Supervisors:** Midwest—Ralph Bratton (Dripping Springs, TX); West—Mark Ross (Tucson, AZ); East—Clarence Johns (Atlanta, GA). **Area Scouts:** J.D. Alleva (Charlotte, NC), Keith Bogan (Ridgeland, MS), Mike Brown (Chandler, AZ), Brad Budzinski (Huntington Beach, CA), Tim Costic (Stevenson Ranch, CA), Paul Gale (Keizer, OR), Joe Graham (Sacramento, CA), Troy Hoerner (Middleton, WI), John Kosciak (Milford, MA), Lincoln Martin (Douglasville, GA), Larry Pardo (Miami, FL), Rusty Pendergrass (Missouri City, TX), Jim Stevenson (Tulsa, OK), Everett Stull (Richmond, VA), Nick Venuto (Newton Falls, OH).
Senior Advising Scouts: Bob King (La Mesa, CA), Bob Poole (Redwood City, CA).
Part-Time Scouts: Ed Fastaia (Lake Ronkonkoma, NY), Tom McCormack (University City, MO), Joey Sola (Caguas, PR).
International Scouts: Venezuela—Daniel Acuna, Oscar Alvarado, Miguel Chacoa; Dominican Republic—Rafael Belen, Julio De La Cruz, Jose Lima, Francis Mojica, Jose Ortiz, Melvi Ortega; Colombia—Carlos Martinez; Europe—Mauro Mazzotti; Panama—Jose Luis Santos; Nicaragua—Leocadio Guevara; Curacao—Wellington Herrera.

Kansas City Royals

Office Address: One Royal Way, Kansas City, MO 64129.
Mailing Address: P.O. Box 419969, Kansas City, MO 64141.
Telephone: (816) 921-8000. **Fax:** (816) 924-0347. **Website:** www.royals.com

Ownership
Operated By: Kansas City Royals Baseball Club, Inc.
Chairman/CEO: David Glass. **President:** Dan Glass. **Board of Directors:** Ruth Glass, Don Glass, Dayna Martz, Julia Kauffman, Dale Rohr. **Executive Administrative Assistant (Executive Staff):** Ginger Salem.

BUSINESS OPERATIONS
Senior Vice President, Business Operations: Kevin Uhlich. **Executive Administrative Assistant:** Cindy Hamilton.

Hall of Fame
Director, Royals Hall of Fame: Curt Nelson.

Finance/Administration
VP, Finance/Administration: David Laverentz. **Director, Finance:** Adam Tyhurst. **Director, Renovation Accounting/Risk Management:** Patrick Fleischmann. **Senior Director, Payroll/Benefits/Human Resources:** Tom Pfannenstiel. **Senior Director, Information Systems:** Brian Himstedt. **Director, Information Systems Operations:** Scott Novak. **Senior Director, Ticket Operations:** Larry Chu. **Director, Ticket Operations:** Chris Darr.

David Glass

Communications/Broadcasting
VP, Communications/Broadcasting: Mike Swanson. **Director, Broadcast Services/Royals Alumni:** Fred White. **Director, Media Relations:** David Holtzman. **Coordinator, Media Services:** Dina Wathan. **Coordinator, Communications/Broadcasting:** Colby Curry.

Publicity/Community Relations
VP, Community Affairs/Publicity: Toby Cook. **Senior Director, Community Relations:** Ben Aken. **Senior Director, Publicity:** Lora Grosshans. **Senior Director, Royals Charities:** Joy Sedlacek. **Director, Community Outreach:** Betty Kaegel.

Ballpark Operations
VP, Ballpark Operations/Development: Bob Rice. **Director, Event Operations:** Renee VanLaningham. **Director, Fan Experience/Hospitality:** Carrie Bligh. **Director, Groundskeeping/Landscaping:** Trevor Vance. **Director, Ballpark Services:** Johnny Williams. **Director, Stadium Engineering/Maintenance:** Todd Burrow.

Marketing/Business Development
VP, Marketing/Business Development: Michael Bucek.

2011 SCHEDULE
Standard Game Times: 7:10 p.m.; Sat. 6:10; Sun. 1:10.

MARCH		
31 . . . . . Los Angeles (AL)		

APRIL
1-3 . . . . . Los Angeles (AL)
5-6 . . . . . . Chicago (AL)
8-10 . . . . .at Detroit
12-13 . . . . . at Minnesota
14-17 . . . . Seattle
18-21 . . . . . . Cleveland
22-24 . . . . . . .at Texas
26-28 . . . . .at Cleveland
29-30 . . . . . .Minnesota

MAY
1 . . . . .Minnesota
3-5 . . . . Baltimore

6-8 . . . . Oakland
10-12 . . . at New York (AL)
13-15 . . . . . . .at Detroit
16-17 . . . . . . Cleveland
18-19 . . . . Texas
20-22 . . . . St. Louis
24-26 . . . . .at Baltimore
27-29 . . . . . . .at Texas
30-31 . . . Los Angeles (AL)

JUNE
1 . . . . . . Los Angeles (AL)
2-5 . . . . .Minnesota
6-9 . . . . .Toronto
10-12 . at Los Angeles (AL)
14-16 . . . . . .at Oakland
17-19 . . . . . .at St. Louis

21-23 . . . . .Arizona
24-26 . . . . . Chicago (NL)
27-29 . . . at San Diego

JULY
1-3 . . . . .at Colorado
4-6 . . . . . .at Chicago (AL)
7-10 . . . . Detroit
14-17 . . . . . at Minnesota
18-20 . . . . Chicago (AL)
22-24 . . . . . . .Tampa Bay
25-28 . . . . . . .at Boston
29-31 . . . . .at Cleveland

AUGUST
2-4 . . . . Baltimore
5-7 . . . . Detroit

8-11 . . . . . at Tampa Bay
12-14 . . . .at Chicago (AL)
15-17 . . . .New York (AL)
18-21 . . . . Boston
23-25 . . . . . . at Toronto
26-28 . . . . .at Cleveland
29-31 . . . . . . .at Detroit

SEPTEMBER
2-4 . . . . Cleveland
5-7 . . . . .at Oakland
8-11 . . . . .at Seattle
13-14 . . . . . . .Minnesota
15-18 . . . . . Chicago (AL)
20-21 . . . . Detroit
23-25 . . .at Chicago (AL)
26-28 . . . . . at Minnesota

GENERAL INFORMATION
Stadium (year opened): Ewing M. Kauffman Stadium (1973).
Team Colors: Royal blue and white.

Player Representative: Unavailable.
Home Dugout: First Base.
Playing Surface: Grass.

Senior Director, Event Presentation/Production: Don Costante. Director, Event Presentation/Production: Chris DeRuyscher. Director, Online/Target Marketing: Erin Sleddens. Senior Director, Corporate Sponsorships/Broadcast Sales: Wes Engram. Senior Director, Client Services: Michele Kammerer. Director, Corporate Partnerships: Paul Kieffaber. Director, Special Event Sales: Ashley Berst.

Senior Director, Sales/Service: Steve Shiffman. Director, Sales: Theodore Hodges. Director, Ticket Services: Scott Wadsworth.

BASEBALL OPERATIONS

Telephone: (816) 921-8000. Fax: (816) 924-0347.

Senior VP, Baseball Operations/General Manager: Dayton Moore.

VP, Baseball Operations/Assistant GM: Dean Taylor. Assistant GM, Scouting/Player Development: J.J. Picollo. Senior Advisor to GM/Scouting/Player Development: Mike Arbuckle. Director, Baseball Administration: Jin Wong. Assistant to Baseball Operations: Mike Groopman. Baseball Operations Assistant: John Williams. Administrative Assistant to Baseball Operations: Emily Penning.

Dayton Moore

Manager, Arizona Operations: Nick Leto. Coordinator, Pro Scouting: Gene Watson. Senior Advisors: Art Stewart, Donnie Williams. Assistant to GM: Brian Murphy. Special Assistant to GM, International Operations: Rene Francisco. Special Assistant/Player Personnel: Louie Medina. VP, Baseball Operations: George Brett. Special Assistants to GM: Pat Jones, Rusty Kuntz, Bill Fischer, Mike Toomey. Team Travel: Jeff Davenport. Video Coordinator: Mark Topping.

Major League Staff

Manager: Ned Yost.

Coaches: Bench—John Gibbons; Pitching—Bob McClure; Batting—Kevin Seitzer; First Base—Doug Sisson; Third Base—Eddie Rodriguez; Bullpen—Steve Foster.

Medical/Training

Team Physician: Dr. Vincent Key. Athletic Trainer: Nick Kenney. Assistant Athletic Trainer: Kyle Turner.

Player Development

Telephone: (816) 921-8000. Fax: (816) 924-0347.

Director, Minor League Operations: Scott Sharp. Special Assistants: Jack Maloof (hitting), Chino Cadahia (instruction). Special Assistant to Player Development/Scouting: John Wathan. Coordinators: Tony Tijerina (field), Mark Davis (pitching), Glenn Hubbard (infield), Ryan Stoneberg (strength/conditioning), Tim Scheierman (rehab).

Farm System

Class	Club (League)	Manager	Hitting Coach	Pitching Coach
Triple-A	Omaha (PCL)	Mike Jirschele	Tommy Gregg	Doug Henry
Double-A	Northwest Arkansas (TL)	Brian Poldberg	Terry Bradshaw	Larry Carter
High A	Wilmington (CL)	Brian Rupp	Justin Gemoll	Steve Luebber
Low A	Kane County (MWL)	Vance Wilson	Damon Hollins	Jim Brower
Rookie	Idaho Falls (PIO)	Brian Buchanan	Omar Ramirez	Jerry Nyman
Rookie	Burlington (APP)	Nelson Liriano	Jon Williams	Bobby St. Pierre
Rookie	Royals (AZL)	Darryl Kennedy	A. David/J. Bruno	C. Martinez/C. Reyes
Rookie	Royals (DSL)	Jose Mejia	Larry Sutton	Rafael Roque

Scouting

Telephone: (816) 921-8000. Fax: (816) 924-0347.

Director, Scouting: Lonnie Goldberg.

Assistant, Scouting/Player Development: Kyle Vena. Manager, Scouting Operations: Linda Smith.

Major League Scouts: Charles Bolton (Indianapolis, IN), Matt Price (Atlanta, GA), Mike Pazik (Bethesda, MD). Advance Scout: Kelly Heath (Palm Harbor, FL).

National Supervisors: Paul Gibson (Center Moriches, NY), Junior Vizcaino (Raleigh, NC). Regional Supervisors: Gregg Kilby (Tampa, Florida), Dan Ontiveros (Laguna Niguel, CA), Sean Rooney (Pompton Lake, NJ), Mitch Webster (Kansas City, MO).

Area Scouts: Rich Amaral (Huntington Beach, CA), Jason Bryans (Windsor, Canada), Dennis Cardoza (Boyd, TX), Blake Davis (Plano, TX), Travis Ezi (Baton Rouge, LA), Casey Fahy (Apex, NC), Jim Farr (Williamsburg, VA), Sean Gibbs (Canton, GA), Colin Gonzales (Orlando, FL), Scott Groot (Mission Viejo, CA), Scott Melvin (Quincy, IL), Alex Mesa (Miami, FL), Ken Munoz (Scottsdale, AZ), Johnny Ramos (Carolina, PR), Scott Ramsay (Valley, WA), Brian Rhees (Live Oak, TX), Dennis Sheehan (Glasco, NY), Max Valencia (Chico, CA).

Latin America Supervisor: Orlando Estevez. International Scouts: Richard Castro (Venezuela), Alvin Cuevas (Dominican Republic), Alberto Garcia (Venezuela) Juan Indriago (Venezuela), Joelvis Gonzalez (Venezuela), Charlie Kim (Korea), Juan Lopez (Nicaragua), Nathan Miller (Taiwan), Rafael Miranda (Colombia), Fausto Morel (Dominican Republic), Ricardo Ortiz (Panama), Carlos Pascual (Special Assignments), Edis Perez (Dominican Republic), Hector Pineda (Dominican Republic), Rafael Vasquez (Dominican Republic), Franco Wawoe (Curacao).

Los Angeles Angels

Office Address: 2000 Gene Autry Way, Anaheim, CA 92806.
Mailing Address: P.O. Box 2000, Anaheim, CA 92803.
Telephone: (714) 940-2000. **Fax:** (714) 940-2205.
Website: www.angelsbaseball.com.

Ownership
Owner: Arte Moreno. **Chairman:** Dennis Kuhl. **President:** John Carpino.

BUSINESS OPERATIONS
Chief Financial Officer: Bill Beverage. **Vice President, Finance/Administration:** Molly Taylor Jolly. **Controller:** Cris Fisher. **Accountants:** Lorelei Largey, Kylie McManus, Jennifer Whynott. **Financial Analyst:** Jennifer Jeanblanc. **Assistant, Accounting:** Linda Chubak. **Director, Human Resources:** Jenny Price. **Benefits Coordinator:** Cecilia Schneider. **Human Resources Representative:** Arianna Fernandez. **Manager, Recruitment/Training:** Brittany Johnson. **Manager, Information Services:** Al Castro. **Senior Network Engineer:** Neil Farris. **Senior Customer Support Analyst:** David Yun. **Assistant Network Administrator:** Paramjit Singh. **Travel Account Manager:** Chantelle Ball.

Arte Moreno

Marketing/Corporate Sales
VP, Corporate Sales: Richard McClemmy. **Corporate Sales Account Executives:** Derek Ohta, Nicole Provansal, Jennifer Soliman, Rick Turner. **Senior Sponsorship Services Coordinator:** Maria Dinh. **Sponsorship Services Coordinators:** Bobby Kowan, Jackie Perkins.
VP, Marketing/Ticket Sales: Robert Alvarado. **Senior Marketing Manager:** Matt Artin. **Marketing Manager:** Ernie Prukner. **Promotions Representative:** John Rozak. **Marketing Coordinator/Graphic Designer:** Jeff Lee. **Ticket Sales Manager:** Tom DeTemple.
Director, Client Services: Brian Sanders. **Client Services Representatives:** Arthur Felix, Ashley Green, Justin Hallenbeck, Shawn Meyer, Alisa Moreno, Adrieanna Ryan, Matt Swanson. **Group Sales Account Executive:** Angel Rodriguez. **Premium Sales/Service Manager:** Brian Lawrence. **Ticket Sales Account Executives:** Clint Blevins, Jeff Leuenberger, Jasmin Matthews, Scott Tarlo. **Administrative Assistant, Marketing:** Monica Campanis.

Public/Media Relations/Communications
Telephone: (714) 940-2014. **Fax:** (714) 940-2205.
VP, Communications: Tim Mead. **Communications Manager:** Eric Kay. **Media Relations Representatives:** Jennifer Hoyer, Ryan Cavinder, Jonathon Ciani. **Community Relations Coordinator:** Lindsay McHolm. **Publications Manager:** Doug Ward. **Traveling Secretary:** Tom Taylor. **Club Photographers:** Debora Robinson, John Cordes, Bob Binder.

Ballpark Operations/Facilities
Director, Ballpark Operations: Sam Maida. **Director, Facility Services:** Mike McKay. **Event Manager:** Calvin Ching. **Maintenance Manager, Field/Ground:** Barney Lopas. **Assistant Manager, Facility Services:** Linda Fitzgerald.

2011 SCHEDULE
Standard Game Times: 7:05 p.m.; Sun. 12:35.

MARCH		
31 . . . . . . .at Kansas City	6-8. . . . . Cleveland	20-22 . . . . . . .at Florida
	9-11 . . . . . Chicago (AL)	24-26 . at Los Angeles (NL)
APRIL	13-15 . . . . .at Texas	27-29 . . . . . Washington
1-3 . . . . . .at Kansas City	16-17 . . . . . .at Oakland	
5-6. . . . . . at Tampa Bay	18-19 . . . . . .at Seattle	**JULY**
8-10 . . . . .Toronto	20-22 . . . . Atlanta	1-3 . . . . Los Angeles (NL)
11-13 . . . . . . Cleveland	23-26 . . . . Oakland	4-6. . . . . Detroit
15-17 . . . .at Chicago (AL)	27-29 . . . . at Minnesota	7-10 . . . . Seattle
18-20 . . . . . . .at Texas	30-31 . . . .at Kansas City	15-17 . . . . . .at Oakland
21-24 . . . . Boston		19-21 . . . . Texas
25-27 . . . . Oakland	**JUNE**	22-24 . . . . .at Baltimore
29-30 . . . . . at Tampa Bay	1 . . . . . . .at Kansas City	25-27 . . . . .at Cleveland
	3-5. . . . . .New York (AL)	28-31 . . . . . . .at Detroit
MAY	6-8. . . . . . . .Tampa Bay	
1 . . . . at Tampa Bay	10-12 . . . . . Kansas City	**AUGUST**
2-5. . . . . .at Boston	13-15 . . . . . . .at Seattle	2-4. . . . . .Minnesota
	17-19 . . at New York (NL)	5-7. . . . . Seattle
		9-11 . . . . at New York (AL)

12-14 . . . . . . at Toronto		
15-18 . . . . Texas		
19-21 . . . . . . Baltimore		
23-24 . . . . Chicago (AL)		
26-28 . . . . .at Texas		
29-31 . . . . .at Seattle		
SEPTEMBER		
1 . . . . .at Seattle		
2-4. . . . . .Minnesota		
5-7. . . . . Seattle		
9-11 . . . . .New York (AL)		
12-14 . . . . . .at Oakland		
16-18 . . . . .at Baltimore		
19-22 . . . . . . at Toronto		
23-25 . . . . Oakland		
26-28 . . . . Texas		

GENERAL INFORMATION
Stadium (year opened): Angel Stadium (1966).
Team Colors: Red, dark red, blue and silver.

Player Representative: Unavailable.
Home Dugout: Third Base.
Playing Surface: Grass.

BaseballAmerica.com

Purchasing Assistant: Suzanne Peters. **Receptionists:** Sandy Sanford, Margie Walsh.
Manager, Entertainment/Production: Peter Bull. **Producer, Video Operations:** David Tsuruda. **Associate Producer:** Danny Pitts. **Entertainment Supervisor:** Heather Capizzi. **PA Announcer:** David Courtney.

Ticketing
Manager, Ticket Operations: Sheila Brazelton. **Assistant Ticket Manager:** Susan Weiss. **Ticketing Supervisor:** Ryan Vance. **Ticketing Representatives:** Cyndi Nguyen, Clancy Holligan, Kim Weaver.

Travel/Clubhouse
Clubhouse Manager: Keith Tarter.
Assistant Clubhouse Manager: Shane Demmitt. **Visiting Clubhouse Manager:** Brian Harkins. **Senior Video Coordinator:** Diego Lopez. **Video Coordinator:** Ruben Montano.

BASEBALL OPERATIONS
General Manager: Tony Reagins.
Assistant GM: Ken Forsch. **Special Advisor:** Bill Stoneman. **Special Assistants to GM:** Gary Sutherland, Gary DiSarcina. **Manager, Baseball Operations:** Tory Hernandez.

Major League Staff
Manager: Mike Scioscia. **Coaches:** Bench—Rob Picciolo; Pitching—Mike Butcher; Batting—Mickey Hatcher; First Base—Alfredo Griffin; Third Base—Dino Ebel; Bullpen—Steve Soliz; Bullpen Catcher—Tom Gregorio.

Medical/Training
Medical Director: Dr. Lewis Yocum. **Team Physician:** Dr. Craig Milhouse. **Head Athletic Trainer:** Adam Nevala. **Athletic Trainer:** Rick Smith. **Assistant Athletic Trainer:** Adam Nevala. **Minor League Head Athletic Trainer:** Geoff Hostetter. **Strength/Conditioning Coach:** T.J. Harrington. **Director, Legal Affairs/Risk Management:** David Cohen. **Administrative Assistant, Trainers:** Chris Titchenal.

Tony Reagins

Player Development
Director, Player Development: Abe Flores.
Assistant, Player Development/Scouting: Justin Hollander. **Administrative Assistant:** Kathy Mair.
Administration Manager, Arizona: Eric Blum.
Field Coordinator/Hitting Instructor: Todd Takayoshi. **Roving Instructors:** Orlando Mercado (catching), Bill Lachemann (catching/special assignment), Bobby Mitchell (outfield/baserunning/bunting), Jeff Pickler (infield), Kernan Ronan (pitching).

Farm System

Class	Club	Manager	Coach	Pitching Coach
Triple-A	Salt Lake (PCL)	Keith Johnson	Jim Eppard	Erik Bennett
Double-A	Arkansas (TL)	Bill Mosiello	Francisco Matos	Brandon Emanuel
High A	Inland Empire (CAL)	Tom Gamboa	Damon Mashore	Dan Ricabal
Low A	Cedar Rapids (MWL)	Brent Del Chiaro	Mike Eylward	Trevor Wilson
Rookie	Orem (PIO)	Tom Kotchman	Nathan Haynes	Zeke Zimmerman
Rookie	Angels (AZL)	Ty Boykin	Dick Schofield	Jim Gott
Rookie	Angels (DSL)	Charlie Romero	Edgal Rodriguez	Santos Alcala

Scouting
Telephone: 714-940-2061. **Fax:** (714) 940-2203.
Director, Amateur Scouting: Ric Wilson. **Assistant, Scouting:** Kathy Mair.
Advance Scout: Willie Fraser.
Major League Scouts: Greg Morhardt (S. Windsor CT), Mike Pagliarulo (Winchester, MA), Rich Schlenker (Walnut Creek, CA), Jeff Schugel (Denver, CO), Brad Sloan (Brimfield, IL).
National Crosschecker: Jeff Malinoff (Lopez, WA). **Regional Supervisors:** Northeast—Jason Baker (Lynchburg, VA); Southeast—Chris McAlpin (Norman Park, GA); Midwest—Ron Marigny (Cypress, TX); West—Bo Hughes (Sherman Oaks, CA).
Area Scouts: Kenneth Brown (Hoover, AL), John Burden (Fairfield, OH), Tim Corcoran (Le Verne, CA), Bobby DeJardin (San Clemente, CA), Nick Gorneault (Springfield, MA), John Gracio (Mesa, AZ), Kevin Ham (Cypress, TX), Casey Harvie (Lake Stevens, WA), Tom Kotchman (Seminole, FL), Brandon McArthur (Kennesaw, GA), Joel Murrie (Evergreen, CO), Dan Radcliff (Palmyra, VA), Ralph Reyes (Miami, FL), Scott Richardson (Elk Grove, CA), Rudy Vasquez (San Antonio, TX), Rob Wilfong (San Dimas, CA).
Director, International Scouting: Marc Russo. **International Scouts:** Daniel MacLeith (Asia),Mario Mendoza (Mexico), Lebi Ochoa (Venezuela), Ralph Ramirez (Dominican Republic), Grant Weir (Australia).

Los Angeles Dodgers

Office Address: 1000 Elysian Park Ave, Los Angeles, CA 90090.
Telephone: (323) 224-1500. **Fax:** (323) 224-1269.
Website: www.dodgers.com

Ownership
Owner/Chairman: Frank McCourt.
Special Advisors to Chairman: Tommy Lasorda, Dr. Frank Jobe, Don Newcombe.

BUSINESS OPERATIONS
COO: Geoff Wharton. **Chief Revenue Officer:** Michael Young. **Senior Vice President/General Counsel:** Sam Fernandez. **CFO:** Peter Wilhelm. **Senior VP, Public Affairs:** Howard Sunkin.

Finance/Sales/Marketing/Partnerships
VP, Finance: Marlo Vandemore. **Senior Director, Ticket Sales:** David Siegel. **Director, Digital Marketing:** Josh Lukin. **Director, Corporate Partnerships:** Mike Fach. **Director, Partnership Administration:** Jenny Oh. **Director, Premium Sales/Services:** Antonio Morici.

Human Resources
Senior Director, Human Resources/Deputy General Counsel: Warren Leonard.
Director, Human Resources: Leonor Romero.

Communications
VP, Communications: Josh Rawitch. **Assistant Director, Public Relations:** Joe Jareck. **Assistant Director, Business/Multicultural PR:** Yvonne Carrasco. **Director, Publications:** Jorge Martin. **Manager, Public Relations:** Amy Summers. **Coordinator, Public Relations:** Jon Chapper.

Broadcasting:
VP, Broadcasting: Lauryn Lukin. **Director, Production:** Greg Taylor. **Director, Graphic Design:** Ross Yoshida.

Information Technology
Director, Information Technology: Ralph Esquibel.

Stadium Operations
VP, Stadium Operations: Francine Hughes. **Assistant Director, Turf/Grounds:** Eric Hansen. **PA Announcer:** Eric Smith. **Official Scorers:** Don Hartack, Ed Munson. **Organist:** Nancy Bea Hefley.

Ticketing
Telephone: (323) 224-1471. **Fax:** (323) 224-2609.
VP, Ticket Operations: Billy Hunter. **Director, Ticket Operations:** Seth Bluman.

Frank McCourt

2011 SCHEDULE
Standard Game Times: 7:10 p.m.; Sun. 1:10

MARCH		
31 . . . . San Francisco		

APRIL
1-3 . . . . San Francisco
5-6 . . . . at Colorado
8-10 . . . . . at San Diego
11-13 . . . at San Francisco
14-17 . . . . St. Louis
18-21 . . . . Atlanta
22-24 . . . . at Chicago (NL)
25-27 . . . . . . .at Florida
29-30 . . . . San Diego

MAY
1 . . . . San Diego
2-4 . . . . . . Chicago (NL)

6-8 . . . . . at New York (NL)
9-12 . . . . . . at Pittsburgh
13-15 . . . . Arizona
16-17 . . . . . . .Milwaukee
18-19 . . . San Francisco
20-22 . . . at Chicago (AL)
23-25 . . . . . . .at Houston
27-29 . . . . Florida
30-31 . . . . Colorado

JUNE
1 . . . . Colorado
3-5 . . . . . .at Cincinnati
6-8 . . . . . at Philadelphia
9-12 . . . . . . at Colorado
13-15 . . . . . . Cincinnati
17-19 . . . . Houston

20-22 . . . . Detroit
24-26 . . . Los Angeles (AL)
27-29 . . . . at Minnesota

JULY
1-3 . . . at Los Angeles (AL)
4-7 . . . . . .New York (NL)
8-10 . . . . San Diego
15-17 . . . . . . at Arizona
18-20 . . . at San Francisco
22-24 . . . . .Washington
25-27 . . . . . . .Colorado
29-31 . . . . Arizona

AUGUST
1-3 . . . . . . at San Diego
5-7 . . . . at Arizona

8-10 . . . . . .Philadelphia
12-14 . . . . Houston
15-18 . . . . at Milwaukee
19-21 . . . . . at Colorado
22-24 . . . . . . .at St. Louis
26-28 . . . . Colorado
29-31 . . . . San Diego

SEPTEMBER
2-4 . . . . at Atlanta
5-8 . . . . . at Washington
9-11 . . . . at San Francisco
12-14 . . . . Arizona
15-18 . . . . . . Pittsburgh
20-22 . . . . San Francisco
23-25 . . . . at San Diego
26-28 . . . . . . at Arizona

GENERAL INFORMATION
Stadium (year opened): Dodger Stadium (1962).
Team Colors: Dodger blue and white.

Player Representative: Clayton Kershaw.
Home Dugout: Third Base.
Playing Surface: Grass.

Travel, Clubhouse
Manager, Team Travel: Scott Akasaki. **Home Clubhouse Manager:** Mitch Poole. **Visiting Clubhouse Manager:** Jerry Turner. **Major League Interpreter:** Kenji Nimura. **Video Coordinator:** Chris Madden.

BASEBALL OPERATIONS

Ned Colletti

Telephone: (323) 224-1500. **Fax:** (323) 224-1463.
General Manager: Ned Colletti.
VP/Assistant GM: Kim Ng.
Special Assistants, Baseball Operations/Player Development: Bill Mueller, Aaron Sele, Mark Sweeney, Jose Vizcaino. **Director, Baseball Operations:** Ellen Harrigan. **Major League Video Coordinator:** Chris Madden. **Assistants, Baseball Operations:** Roman Barinas, Matt Marks, Jordan Peikin, Sebastian Saraceno, Will Sharp.

Major League Staff
Manager: Don Mattingly.
Coaches: Bench—Trey Hillman; Pitching—Rick Honeycutt; Hitting—Jeff Pentland; First Base—Davey Lopes; Third Base—Tim Wallach; Bullpen—Ken Howell.

Medical/Training
Director, Medical Services/Head Athletic Trainer: Stan Conte. **Assistant Athletic Trainers:** Todd Tomczyk, Nick Conte. **Strength/Conditioning Coach:** Brendon Huttmann. **Massage Therapist:** Ichiro Tani. **Head Team Physician:** Dr. Neal ElAttrache. **Minor League Strength/Conditioning Coordinator:** Mike Winkler. **Minor League Medical Coordinator:** Jim Young. **Minor League Rehab Coordinator:** Jeremiah Randall. **Minor League Athletic Trainers:** Greg Harrel (Albuquerque), Nancy Patterson (Chattanooga), Yosuke Nakajima (Rancho Cucamonga), Peter Houdek (Great Lakes), Lindsey Pyc (Ogden).

Player Development
Telephone: (323) 224-1500. **Fax:** (323) 224-1359.
Assistant GM, Player Development: De Jon Watson.
Senior Advisors to Player Development: PJ Carey, Gene Clines, Charlie Hough. **Assistant Director, Player Development:** Chris Haydock. **Coordinator, Minor League Administration:** Adriana Urzua. **Field Coordinator:** Bruce Hines. **Hitting Coordinator:** Eric Owens. **Pitching Coordinator:** Rafael Chaves. **Outfield/Baserunning Coordinator:** Rodney McCray. **Infield Coordinator:** Matt Martin. **Catching Coordinator:** Travis Barbary. **Campo Las Palmas Coordinator:** Henry Cruz. **Field Coordinator, Campo Las Palmas:** Antonio Bautista. **Coordinator, Instruction Camelback Ranch:** Jody Reed.

Farm System

Class	Club (League)	Manager	Coach	Pitching Coach
Triple-A	Albuquerque (PCL)	Lorenzo Bundy	John Valentin	Glenn Dishman
Double-A	Chattanooga (SL)	Carlos Subero	Franklin Stubbs	Chuck Crim
High A	Rancho Cucamonga (CAL)	Juan Bustabad	Michael Boughton	Hector Berrios
Low A	Great Lakes (MWL)	John Shoemaker	Lenny Harris	Kremlin Martinez
Rookie	Ogden (PIO)	Damon Berryhill	Johnny Washington	Bill Simas
Rookie	Dodgers (AZL)	Jody Reed	Leo Garcia	Matt Herges
Rookie	Dodgers (DSL)	Pedro Mega	E. Lopez/J. Martinez Hernandez	Alejandro Pena

Scouting
Assistant GM, Amateur/International Scouting: Logan White.
Global Crosschecker: Paul Fryer (Calabasas, CA). **Special Advisor, Amateur Scouting/National Crosschecker:** Gib Bodet (San Clemente, CA). **National Crosscheckers:** Larry Barton (Leona Valley, CA), John Green (Tucson, AZ). **Manager, Scouting/Travel Administration:** Jane Capobianco. **Coordinator, Scouting:** Trey Magnuson. **Eastern Regional Supervisor:** Gary Nickels (Naperville, IL). **Western Regional Supervisor:** Brian Stephenson (Chandler, AZ).
Area Scouts: Clint Bowers (The Woodlands, TX), Bobby Darwin (Corona, CA), Rich Delucia (Reading, PA), Scott Hennessey (Ponte Verde, FL), Orsino Hill (Sacramento, CA), Calvin Jones (Highland Village, TX), Henry Jones (Vancouver, WA), Lon Joyce (Spartanburg, SC), Marty Lamb (Nicholasville, KY), Scott Little (Cape Girardeau, MO), Dennis Moeller (Stevenson Ranch, CA), Matthew Paul (Slidell, LA), Clair Rierson (Wake Forest, NC), Chet Sergo (Stoughton, WI), Rob Sidwell (Windermere, FL), Tom Thomas (Phoenix, AZ).
Director, Pro Scouting/Special Advisor to the GM: Vance Lovelace.
Special Assistants to GM: Ken Bracey, Toney Howell, Rick Ragazzo.
Advance Scout: Wade Taylor. **Professional Scouts:** Bill Latham, Carl Loewenstine, Tydus Meadows, Ron Rizzi, John Sanders.
Senior Scouting Advisor: Ralph Avila.
Director, Asian Operations/Scouting: Acey Kohrogi. **Director, International/Minor League Relations:** Joseph Reaves. **Coordinator, Asian Operations:** Yayoi Sato. **Coordinator, International Scouting:** Manny Estrada. **International Scouts:** Wilton Guerrero (Dominican), Rafael Rijo (Dominican), Ezequiel Sepulveda (Dominican), Bienvenido Tavarez (Dominican), Gustavo Zapata (Central America), Rolando Chirino (Curacao), Keiichi Kojima (Japan), Byung-Hwan An (Korea), Mike Brito (Mexico), Elvio Jimenez (Venezuela), Camilo Pascual (Venezuela), Bernardino Torres (Venezuela), Oswaldo Villalobos (Venezuela), Francisco Cartaya (Venezuela). **Part Time Scouts:** Luis Faccio, Greg Goodwin, Artie Harris, Jimmy Johnston. **Scouting Consultant:** George Genovese.

Milwaukee Brewers

Office Address: Miller Park, One Brewers Way, Milwaukee, WI 53214.
Telephone: (414) 902-4400. **Fax:** (414) 902-4053.
Website: www.brewers.com.

Ownership
Operated By: Milwaukee Brewers Baseball Club.
Chairman/Principal Owner: Mark Attanasio.

BUSINESS OPERATIONS
Executive Vice President, Business Operations: Rick Schlesinger. **Executive VP, Finance/Administration:** Bob Quinn. **VP, General Counsel:** Marti Wronski. **Senior Director, Business Operations:** Teddy Werner. **Executive Assistant, Business Operations:** Adela Reeve. **Executive Assistant, Ownership Group:** Samantha Ernest.

Mark Attanasio

Finance/Accounting
VP/Controller: Joe Zidanic. **Director, Reporting/Special Projects:** Steve O'Connell.
Accounting Manager: Vicki Wise.
VP, Human Resources/Office Management: Sally Andrist. **Human Resources Generalist:** Zendy Hernandez.
Director, Network Services: Corey Kmichik. **Systems Support Specialist:** Adam Bauer.
Application Developer: Josh Krowiorz.

Marketing/Corporate Sponsorships
VP, Corporate Marketing: Tom Hecht. **Senior Director, Corporate Marketing:** Andrew Pauls. **Directors, Corporate Marketing:** Sarah Holbrook, Dave Tamburrino. **VP, Consumer Marketing:** Jim Bathey. **Senior Director, Marketing:** Kathy Schwab. **Director, Merchandise Branding:** Jill Aronoff. **Director, Corporate Suite Services:** Kristin Loeser.
VP, Broadcasting/Entertainment: Aleta Mercer. **Director, Audio/Video Productions:** Deron Anderson. **Manager, Entertainment/Broadcasting:** Andrew Olson. **Coordinator, Audio/Video Production:** Cory Wilson.

Media Relations/Communications
Telephone: (414) 902-4500. **Fax:** (414) 902-4053.
VP, Communications: Tyler Barnes. **Director, Media Relations:** Mike Vassallo. **Manager, Media Relations:** John Steinmiller. **Coordinator, Media Relations:** Ken Spindler.
Director, Community Relations: Katina Shaw. **Community Relations Assistant:** Erica Bowring. **Manager, Youth Outreach:** Larry Hisle. **Executive Director, Brewers Community Foundation:** Cecelia Gore.

Stadium Operations
Senior Director, Stadium Operations: Bob Hallas. **Senior Director, Event Services:** Matt Kenny. **Director, Grounds:** Gary Vanden Berg. **Supervisor, Warehouse:** Patrick Rogo. **VP, Brewers Enterprises:** Jason Hartlund. **Manager, Event Services:** Jennacy Cruz. **Receptionists:** Willa Oden, Jody McBee.

2011 SCHEDULE
Standard Game Times: 7:10 p.m.; Sun. 1:10.

MARCH		
31 . . . . .at Cincinnati	6-8. . . . . .at St. Louis	20-22 . . . . . .Tampa Bay	12-14 . . . . . . .Pittsburgh
APRIL	9-11 . . . . San Diego	24-26 . . . . . .Minnesota	15-18 . . . Los Angeles (NL)
2-3. . . . . . . .at Cincinnati	13-15 . . . . . . .Pittsburgh	28-30 . . . at New York (AL)	19-21 . . . at New York (NL)
4-7. . . . . Atlanta	16-17 . at Los Angeles (NL)	**JULY**	22-24 . . . . . at Pittsburgh
8-10 . . . . . Chicago (NL)	18-19 . . . . at San Diego	1-3. . . . . . at Minnesota	26-28 . . . . . Chicago (NL)
12-14 . . . . . at Pittsburgh	20-22 . . . . . . .Colorado	4-6. . . . . .Arizona	30-31 . . . . St. Louis
15-17 . . . at Washington	23-25 . . . . . Washington	7-10 . . . . Cincinnati	**SEPTEMBER**
18-20 . . . at Philadelphia	27-29 . . . San Francisco	14-17 . . . . . at Colorado	1 . . . . St. Louis
22-24 . . . . Houston	30-31 . . . . .at Cincinnati	18-21 . . . . . at Arizona	2-4. . . . . .at Houston
25-27 . . . . . . Cincinnati	**JUNE**	22-24 . . . at San Francisco	5-7. . . . . . . .at St. Louis
29-30 . . . . . .at Houston	1 . . . . .at Cincinnati	26-28 . . . . . Chicago (NL)	8-11 . . . . . .Philadelphia
MAY	3-6. . . . . .at Florida	29-31 . . . . Houston	13-14 . . . . . . .Colorado
1 . . . . .at Houston	7-9. . . . . .New York (NL)	**AUGUST**	16-18 . . . . .at Cincinnati
2-5. . . . . at Atlanta	10-12 . . . . St. Louis	1-3. . . . . St. Louis	19-21 . . . .at Chicago (NL)
	13-16 . . . .at Chicago (NL)	5-7. . . . . . . .at Houston	23-25 . . . . Florida
	17-19 . . . . .at Boston	9-11 . . . . .at St. Louis	26-28 . . . . . . .Pittsburgh

GENERAL INFORMATION
Stadium (year opened): Miller Park (2001).
Team Colors: Navy blue, gold and white.
Player Representative: Unavailable.

Home Dugout: First Base.
Playing Surface: Grass.

Ticketing
Telephone: (414) 902-4000. **Fax:** (414) 902-4100.
Director, Group Sales: Chris Barlow. **Director, Season Ticket Sales:** Billy Freiss. **Director, Ticket Operations:** Regis Bane. **Administrative Assistant:** Irene Bolton. **Assistant Director, Ticket Services:** Nancy Jorgensen. **Manager, Ticket Operations:** Chad Olson.

BASEBALL OPERATIONS
Telephone: (414) 902-4400. **Fax:** (414) 902-4515.
Executive VP/General Manager: Doug Melvin.
VP/Assistant GM: Gord Ash. **Special Assistant to GM/Baseball Operations:** Dan O'Brien.
Director, Baseball Operations: Tom Flanagan. **Director, Video Scouting/Baseball Research for Pro Scouting:** Karl Mueller. **Coordinator, Advance Scouting/Baseball Research:** Scott Campbell. **Manager/Coaching Assistant/Digital Media Coordinator:** Joe Crawford. **Senior Administrator, Baseball Operations:** Barb Stark.

Major League Staff
Manager: Ron Roenicke.
Coaches: Bench—Jerry Narron; Pitching—Rick Kranitz; Hitting—Dale Sveum; First Base—Garth Iorg; Third Base—Ed Sedar; Bullpen—Stan Kyles; Outfield Coach—John Shelby.

Medical, Training
Head Team Physician: Dr. William Raasch. **Head Athletic Trainer:** Roger Caplinger. **Assistant Athletic Trainer/Strength/Conditioning Coordinator:** Dan Wright. **Strength/Conditioning Specialist:** Josh Seligman.

Doug Melvin

Player Development
Special Assistant to GM/Director, Player Development: Reid Nichols (Phoenix, AZ).
Business Manager: Scott Martens. **Assistant Director, Player Development:** Tony Diggs. **Coordinator, Administration/Player Development:** Mark Mueller. **Field/Catching Coordinator:** Charlie Greene. **Coordinators:** Frank Neville (athletic training), Lee Tunnell (pitching), Darnell Coles (hitting). **Roving Instructors:** Bob Miscik (infield), Reggie Williams (outfield/baserunning).

Farm System

Class	Club (League)	Manager	Coach	Pitching Coach
Triple-A	Nashville (PCL)	Don Money	Sandy Guerrero	Rich Gale
Double-A	Huntsville (SL)	Mike Guerrero	Al Leboeuf	John Curtis
High A	Brevard County (FSL)	Unavailable	Dwayne Hosey	Fred Dabney
Low A	Wisconsin (MWL)	Matt Erickson	Dusty Rhodes	Chris Hook
Rookie	Helena (PIO)	Joe Ayrault	Ned Yost IV	Elvin Nina
Rookie	Brewers (AZL)	Tony Diggs	Kenny Dominguez	Steve Cline
Rookie	Brewers (DSL)	Nestor Corredor	Luis De Los Santos	Jose Nunez

Scouting
Telephone: (414) 902-4400. **Fax:** (414) 902-4059.
Special Assistant to GM/Pro Scouting/Player Personnel: Dick Groch (St. Claire, MI). **Director, Professional Scouting:** Zack Minasian. **Director, Amateur Scouting:** Bruce Seid. **Manager, Administration/Amateur Scouting:** Amanda Kropp. **Assistant Director, Baseball Research for Scouting:** Tod Johnson.
National Crosschecker: Joe Ferrone (Marine City, MI). **National Pitching Crosschecker:** Jim Rooney (Scottsdale, AZ). **Regional Supervisors:** West—Corey Rodriguez (Redondo Beach, CA); East—Doug Reynolds (Tallahassee, FL).
Pro Scouts: Lary Aaron (Atlanta, GA), Brad Del Barba (Ft. Mitchell, KY), Chris Bosio (Combined Locks, WI), Bryan Gale (Chicago, IL), Cory Melvin (Tampa, FL), Ben McLure (Hummelstown, PA), Tom Mooney (Pittsfield, MA), Marv Thompson (West Jordan, UT), Derek Watson (Charlotte, NC), Tom Wheeler (Martinez, CA), Leon Wurth (Paducah, KY).
Area Scouts: Drew Anderson (Cold Spring, MN), Josh Belovsky (Orange, CA), Jeremy Booth (Houston, TX), Tim Collinsworth (The Colony, TX), Mike Farrell (Indianapolis, IN), Brendan Hause (Scottsdale, AZ), Manolo Hernandez (Puerto Rico), Dan Huston (Thousand Oaks, CA), Harvey Kuenn, Jr. (New Berlin, WI), Marty Lehn (White Rock, British Columbia, Canada), Joe Mason (Millbrook, AL), Justin McCray (Davis, CA), Tim McIlvaine (Tampa, FL), Dan Nellum (Crofton, MD), Ryan Robinson (Tallahassee, FL), Brian Sankey (Yarmouth Port, MA), Charles Sullivan (Weston, FL), Shawn Whalen (Vancouver, WA).
Supervisor, Canada: Jay Lapp (London, Ontario, Canada).
Part-Time Scouts: John Bushart (West Hills, CA), Richard Colpaert (Shelby Township, MI), Don Fontana (Pittsburgh, PA), Joe Hodges (Rockwood, TN), Roger Janeway (Englewood, OH), Johnny Logan (Milwaukee, WI), J.P. Roy (Saint Nicolas, Quebec, Canada), Lee Seid (Las Vegas, NV), Brad Stoll (Lawrence, KS), Nathan Trosky (Carmel, CA).
Latin American Supervisor: Fernando Arango (Davie, FL). **Latin American Scouts:** Manny Batista (Dominican Republic/Venezuela/Puerto Rico), Freddy Torres (Venezuela), Rafael Espinal (Dominican Republic), Jose Guarache (Venezuela), Pedro Hernandez (Dominican Republic), Reinaldo Hidalgo (Venezuela), Juan Martinez (Dominican Republic).

Minnesota Twins

Office Address: Target Field, 1 Twins Way, Minneapolis, MN 55403.
Telephone: (612) 659-3400. **Fax:** 612-659-4025. **Website:** www.twinsbaseball.com.

Ownership
Operated By: The Minnesota Twins.
Chief Executive Officer: Jim Pohlad.
Chairman, Executive Committee: Howard Fox. **Executive Board:** James Pohlad, Robert Pohlad, William Pohlad, Dave St. Peter.

BUSINESS OPERATIONS

Jim Pohlad

President, Minnesota Twins: Dave St. Peter. **President, Twins Sports Inc.:** Jerry Bell. **Senior Vice President, Business Development:** Laura Day. **Senior VP, Business Administration/ CFO:** Kip Elliott.

Target Field
Executive Project Manager: Dick Strassburg. **Director, New Ballpark Development:** Scott O'Connell. **Manager, Project Finance/Accounting:** Dan Starkey.

Human Resources/Finance/Technology
VP, Human Resources/Diversity: Raenell Dorn. **Payroll Manager:** Lori Beasley. **Benefits Manager:** Leticia Silva. **Human Resources Generalist:** Holly Corbin.
Senior Director, Finance: Andy Weinstein. **Manager, Ticket Accounting:** Jerry McLaughlin. **Accountant:** Lyndsey Taylor. **Manager, Finance Planning/Analysis:** Amy Fong-Christianson. **Manager, Accounting:** Lori Windschitl. **Director, Purchasing:** Bud Hanley. **Administrative Assistant:** Ka Her. **Vice President, Technology:** John Avenson. **Director, Technology:** Wade Navratil. **Manager, Technology Infrastructure:** Tony Persio.

Marketing/Broadcasting
VP, Marketing: Patrick Klinger. **Senior Director, Advertising:** Nancy O'Brien. **Director, Event Marketing:** Heidi Sammon. **Promotions Manager:** Julie Rohloff. **Marketing Specialist:** Joe Pohlad. **Manager, Emerging Markets:** Miguel Ramos. **Director, Broadcasting/Game Presentation:** Andy Price. **Radio Network Producer:** Mark Genosky.

Corporate Partnerships
VP, Corporate Partnerships: Eric Curry. **Senior Manager, Client Services:** Bodie Forsling. **Manager, Corporate Client Services:** Katie Beaulieu. **Coordinator, Corporate Client Services:** Paulette Cheatham. **Coordinator, Traffic/ Service:** Amy Johnson.

Communications
Telephone: (612) 659-3475. **Fax:** (612) 659-3472.
Director, Baseball Communications: Mike Herman. **Senior Manager, Baseball Communications:** Dustin Morse. **Manager, Publications/Media Services:** Molly Gallatin. **Coordinator, Baseball Communications:** Mitch Hestad.

2011 SCHEDULE
Standard Game Times: 7:10 p.m.; Sun 1:10.

APRIL			
1-3 . . . . at Toronto	13-15 . . . . .Toronto	24-26 . . . . at Milwaukee	12-14 . . . . .at Cleveland
4-7 . . . . at New York (AL)	16-17 . . . . . . .at Seattle	27-29 . . . Los Angeles (NL)	15-17 . . . . .at Detroit
8-10 . . . . Oakland	18-19 . . . . . .at Oakland		18-21 . . . .New York (AL)
12-13 . . . . . . Kansas City	20-22 . . . . at Arizona	**JULY**	22-25 . . . . . Baltimore
14-17 . . . . at Tampa Bay	23-25 . . . . Seattle	1-3 . . . . .Milwaukee	26-28 . . . . Detroit
18-21 . . . .at Baltimore	27-29 . . . Los Angeles (AL)	4-6 . . . . .Tampa Bay	29-31 . . . .at Chicago (AL)
22-24 . . . . . . Cleveland	30-31 . . . . . . .at Detroit	7-10 . . . . .at Chicago (AL)	
26-28 . . . . .Tampa Bay		14-17 . . . . . Kansas City	**SEPTEMBER**
29-30 . . . .at Kansas City	**JUNE**	18-20 . . . . Cleveland	2-4 . . . at Los Angeles (AL)
	1 . . . . .at Detroit	21-24 . . . . Detroit	5-7 . . . . Chicago (AL)
MAY	2-5 . . . . . .at Kansas City	25-28 . . . . .at Texas	9-11 . . . . .at Detroit
1 . . . . .at Kansas City	6-8 . . . . . . .at Cleveland	29-31 . . . . . .at Oakland	13-14 . . . .at Kansas City
3-4 . . . . .at Chicago (AL)	9-12 . . . . Texas		16-18 . . . . . . Cleveland
6-9 . . . . .at Boston	14-16 . . . . Chicago (AL)	**AUGUST**	20-22 . . . . Seattle
10-11 . . . . Detroit	17-19 . . . . San Diego	2-4 . . at Los Angeles (AL)	23-25 . . . . .at Cleveland
	21-23 . . at San Francisco	5-7 . . . . . . Chicago (AL)	26-28 . . . . . Kansas City
		8-10 . . . . Boston	

GENERAL INFORMATION

Stadium (year opened): Target Field (2010). **Home Dugout:** First Base.
Team Colors: Red, navy blue and white. **Playing Surface:** Natural Grass.
Player Representative: Kevin Slowey.

Public Affairs
　　Executive Director, Public Affairs/Twins Community Fund: Kevin Smith. **Director, Community Affairs:** Bryan Donaldson. **Manager, Corporate Communications:** Chris Iles.

Ticket Sales/Service
　　Telephone: 1-800-33-TWINS. **Fax:** (612) 659-4030.
　　VP, Ticket Sales/Service: Steve Smith. **Director, Ticket Sales/Service:** Mike Clough. **Director, Suite/Premium Seat Sales/Service:** Scott O'Connell. **Senior Manager, Facility/Event Sales:** David Christie. **Manager, Season Ticket Sales/Service:** Eric Hudson. **Manager, Group Ticket Sales/Service:** Rob Malec. **Manager, Communications/Support:** Beth Vail. **Manager, Database Marketing:** Brandon Johnson.

Ticket Operations
　　Senior Director, Ticket Operations: Paul Froehle. **Senior Manager, Box Office:** Mike Stiles. **Supervisor, Box Office:** Robyn McQuillan. **Coordinator, Box Office Accounting:** Aaron Doepner. **Coordinator, Box Office Operations:** Nick Hetfeld.

Stadium Operations
　　VP, Operations: Matt Hoy. **Director, Stadium Operations:** Dave Horsman. **Manager, Stadium Operations:** Dan Smoliak. **Manager, Security:** Dick Dugan. **PA Announcer:** Adam Abrams. **Equipment Manager:** Rod McCormick. **Visitors Clubhouse:** Troy Matchan. **Manager, Major League Video:** Sean Harlin. **Head Groundskeeper:** Larry DiVito.

Bill Smith

BASEBALL OPERATIONS
　　Telephone: (612) 659-3485. **Fax:** (612) 659-4026.
　　Senior VP/General Manager: Bill Smith.
　　VP, Player Personnel: Mike Radcliff. **Assistant GM:** Rob Antony. **Senior Advisor:** Terry Ryan. **Special Assistants:** Joe McIlvaine, Tom Kelly. **Director, Baseball Operations:** Brad Steil. **Manager, Major League Administration:** Jack Goin. **Director, Team Travel:** Remzi Kiratli.

Major League Staff
　　Manager: Ron Gardenhire.
　　Coaches: Bench—Steve Liddle; Pitching—Rick Anderson; Batting—Joe Vavra; First Base—Jerry White; Third Base—Scott Ullger; Bullpen—Rick Stelmaszek.

Medical, Training
　　Club Physicians: Dr. Dan Buss, Dr. Vijay Eyunni, Dr. Tom Jetzer, Dr. John Steubs, Dr. Jon Hallberg, Dr. Gustavo Navarrete. **Head Trainer:** Rick McWane. **Assistant Trainer:** Dave Pruemer. **Strength/Conditioning Coach:** Perry Castellano.

Player Development
　　Telephone: (612) 659-3480. **Fax:** (612) 659-4026.
　　Director, Minor Leagues: Jim Rantz. **Manager, Minor League Administration:** Kate Townley. **Minor League Coordinators:** Joel Lepel (field), Eric Rasmussen (pitching), Bill Springman (hitting), Paul Molitor (infield/baserunning).

Farm System

Class	Club	Manager	Coach	Pitching Coach
Triple-A	Rochester (IL)	Tom Nieto	F. Rayford/R. Ingram	Bobby Cuellar
Double-A	New Britain (EL)	Jeff Smith	Tom Brunansky	Stu Cliburn
High A	Fort Myers (FSL)	Jake Mauer	Jim Dwyer	Steve Mintz
Low A	Beloit (MWL)	Nelson Prada	Tommy Watkins	Gary Lucas
Rookie	Elizabethton (APP)	Ray Smith	Jeff Reed	Jim Shellenback
Rookie	Twins (GCL)	Ramon Borrego	M. Cuyler/R. Hernandez	Ivan Arteaga
Rookie	Twins (DSL)	Jimmy Alvarez	Omar Rogers	Manuel Santana
Rookie	Twins (VSL)	Asdrubal Estrada	Unavailable	Luis Ramirez

Scouting
　　Telephone: (612) 659-3490. **Fax:** (612) 659-4026.
　　Director, Scouting: Deron Johnson.
　　Special Assignment Scouts: Tom Kelly, Joe McIlvaine. **Major League Scouts:** Ken Compton, Earl Frishman, Bob Hegman. **Coordinator, Professional Scouting:** Vern Followell. **Pro Scout:** Bill Milos. **Advance Scout:** Shaun McGinn.
　　Scouting Supervisors: East—Mark Quimuyog, West—Sean Johnson, Mideast—Tim O'Neil, Midwest—Mike Ruth.
　　Area Scouts: Trevor Brown (OR), Billy Corrigan (FL), JR DiMercurio (MO), Mike Eaglin (CA), Marty Esposito (TX), John Leavitt (CA), Hector Otero (FL), Jeff Pohl (IN), Jack Powell (TN), Greg Runser (TX), Elliott Strankman (CA), Ricky Taylor (NC), Jay Weitzel (PA), Ted Williams (AZ), John Wilson (NJ), Mark Wilson (MN), Earl Winn (KY).
　　Coordinator, International Scouting: Howard Norsetter. **Coordinator, Latin American Scouting:** Jose Marzan.
　　International Scouts—Full-Time: Cary Broder (Taiwan), Glenn Godwin (Europe, Africa), Fred Guerrero (Dominican Republic), David Kim (Pacific Rim), Jose Leon (Venezuela, Panama), Francisco Tejeda (Dominican Republic).
　　International Scouts—Part-Time: Vicente Arias (Dominican Republic), John Cortese (Italy), Eric Espinosa (Panama), Eurey Luis Haslen (Dominican Republic), Andy Johnson (Europe), Manuel Luciano (Dominican Republic), Nelson Meneses (Venezuela), Juan Padilla (Venezuela), Franklin Parra (Venezuela), Yan-Yu "Kenny" Su (Taiwan), Koji Takahashi (Japan), Pablo Torres (Venezuela), Lester Victoria (Curacao), Akihiro Yamaguchi (Japan).

New York Mets

Office Address: Citi Field, 126th Street, Flushing, NY 11368.
Telephone: (718) 507-6387. **Fax:** (718) 507-6395.
Website: www.mets.com, www.losmets.com.

Ownership
Operated By: Sterling Mets LP.
Chairman/Chief Executive Officer: Fred Wilpon. **President:** Saul Katz. **Chief Operating Officer:** Jeff Wilpon. **Board of Directors:** Fred Wilpon, Saul Katz, Jeff Wilpon, Richard Wilpon, Michael Katz, David Katz, Tom Osterman, Arthur Friedman, Steve Greenberg, Stuart Sucherman.

BUSINESS OPERATIONS
Executive Vice President, Business Operations: Dave Howard. **Executive VP/General Counsel:** David Cohen.

Finance
CFO: Mark Peskin. **VP/Controller:** Len Labita. **Assistant Controller/Director:** Rebecca Landau-Mahadeva. **Assistant Director/Controller:** Robert Gerbe.

Marketing, Sales
Senior VP, Marketing/Communications: David Newman. **Executive Director, Marketing Productions:** Tim Gunkel. **Senior Director, Marketing:** Tina Mannix. **Director, Broadcasting:** Lorraine Hamilton. **Director, Marketing Communications:** Jill Grabill. **Director, Community Outreach:** Jill Knee. **Senior VP, Corporate Sales/Services:** Paul Asencio. **Directors, Corporate Sales:** Pete Helfer, Matthew Soloff. **Director, Suite Sales/Services:** Patrick Jones.

Fred Wilpon

Media Relations
Telephone: (718) 565-4330. **Fax:** (718) 639-3619.
VP, Media Relations: Jay Horwitz. **Director, Media Relations:** Shannon Forde. **Director, Communications:** Danielle Parillo. **Manager, Media Relations:** Ethan Wilson. **Media Relations Coordinator:** Nicole Chayet. **Media Relations Assistant:** Jon Kerber.

Ballpark Operations
VP, Facilities: Karl Smolarz. **VP, Operations:** Pat McGovern. **Senior Director, Ballpark Operations:** Sue Lucchi. **Manager, Ballpark Operations:** Mike Dohnert. **Director, Field Operations:** Bill Deacon. **Executive Director, Information Technology:** Tom Festa. **Senior Director, IT:** Joe Milone. **Director, IT:** Robert Gradante. **PA Announcer:** Alex Anthony. **Official Scorers:** Howie Karpin, Jordan Sprechman, David Freeman, Billy Altman.

2011 SCHEDULE
Standard Game Times: 7:10 p.m.; Sun. 1:10.

APRIL
1-3 . . . . .at Florida
5-7 . . . . . at Philadelphia
8-10 . . . . . . Washington
11-14 . . . . Colorado
15-17 . . . . . . at Atlanta
19-21 . . . . . . Houston
22-24 . . . . Arizona
26-28 . . . at Washington
29-30 . . . . at Philadelphia

MAY
1 . . . . . . at Philadelphia
2-5 . . . . . . San Francisco
6-8 . . . . Los Angeles (NL)
9-11 . . . . . . at Colorado

13-15 . . . . . . .at Houston
16-17 . . . . Florida
18-19 . . . . . Washington
20-22 . . at New York (AL)
24-26 . . . .at Chicago (NL)
27-29 . . . . .Philadelphia
30-31 . . . . . . Pittsburgh

JUNE
1-2 . . . . Pittsburgh
3-5 . . . . Atlanta
7-9 . . . . at Milwaukee
10-13 . . . at Pittsburgh
14-16 . . . . . . at Atlanta
17-19 . . Los Angeles (AL)
21-23 . . . . Oakland
24-26 . . . . .at Texas

28-30 . . . . . . .at Detroit

JULY
1-3 . . . . . .New York (AL)
4-7 . . . at Los Angeles (NL)
8-10 . . . . at San Francisco
15-17 . . . . . .Philadelphia
19-21 . . . . . St. Louis
22-24 . . . . . . .at Florida
25-28 . . . .at Cincinnati
29-31 . . . . at Washington

AUGUST
1-3 . . . . Florida
5-7 . . . . Atlanta
8-11 . . . . San Diego
12-14 . . . . . . at Arizona

15-17 . . . . . at San Diego
19-21 . . . . . .Milwaukee
22-24 . . . at Philadelphia
26-28 . . . . Atlanta
29-31 . . . . Florida

SEPTEMBER
1 . . . . Florida
2-4 . . . . . at Washington
5-7 . . . . .at Florida
9-11 . . . . . Chicago (NL)
12-15 . . . . . Washington
16-18 . . . . . . at Atlanta
20-22 . . . . . .at St. Louis
23-25 . . . . .Philadelphia
26-28 . . . . . . Cincinnati

GENERAL INFORMATION
Stadium (year opened): Citi Field (2009).
Team Colors: Blue and orange.
Player Representative: Unavailable.

Home Dugout: First Base.
Playing Surface: Grass.

Ticketing
Telephone: (718) 507-8499. **Fax:** (718) 507-6369.
VP, Ticket Sales/Services: Leigh Castergine. **Executive Director, Ticket Sales/Services:** Joseph Barber. **Senior Director, Group Sales/Ticket Sales Services:** Tom Fersch. **Director, Season Ticket Account Services:** Jamie Ozure.

Venue Services
VP, Venue Services: Mike Landeen. **VP, Guest Experience:** Craig Marino.

Travel, Clubhouse
Clubhouse Manager: Kevin Keirst. **Assistant Equipment Manager:** Dave Berni. **Visiting Clubhouse Manager:** Tony Carullo. **Manager, Team Travel:** Brian Small. **Video Editor:** Joe Scarola, Sean Haggans.

BASEBALL OPERATIONS
Telephone: (718) 565-4339 Fax: (718) 507-6391.
General Manager: Sandy Alderson.
VP/Assistant GM: John Ricco. **Special Assistants to GM:** J.P. Ricciardi, Wayne Krivsky. **Executive Assistant to GM:** Diana Parra-Gonzalez. **Manager, Baseball Operations:** Adam Fisher. **Statistical Analyst:** Ben Baumer.

Major League Staff
Manager: Terry Collins.
Coaches: Bench—Ken Oberkfell; Pitching—Dan Warthen; Batting—Dave Hudgens; First Base—Mookie Wilson; Third Base—Chip Hale; Bullpen—Jon Debus.

Sandy Alderson

Medical, Training
Medical Director: Dr. David Altchek. **Physician:** Dr. Struan Coleman. **Trainer:** Ray Ramirez.

Player Development
Telephone: (718) 565-4302. **Fax:** (718) 205-7920.
VP, Scouting/Player Development: Paul DePodesta. **Director, Minor League Operations:** Adam Wogan. **Director, International Operations:** Rafael Perez. **Assistant Director, Minor League Operations:** Jon Miller. **Assistant, Player Development:** Michele Holmes. **Video Coordinator:** TJ Barra. **FL/GCL Administrator:** Ronny Reyes. **Field Coordinator:** Dick Scott.
Coordinator, Instruction/Infield: Kevin Morgan. **Hitting Coordinator:** Lamar Johnson. **Pitching Coordinator:** Rick Tomlin. **Catching Coordinator:** Bob Natal. **Outfield/Baserunning Coordinator:** Jack Voigt. **Rehab/Physical Therapist:** Dave Pearson. **Strength/Conditioning:** Jason Craig. **Rehab Pitching Coordinator:** Randy Niemann. **Senior Advisor:** Guy Conti. **Pitching Consultant:** Al Jackson. **Special Instructor:** Bobby Floyd. **Hitting Instructor:** Tom McCraw. **International Field Coordinator:** Rafael Landestoy. **International Catching Instructor:** Ozzie Virgil. International/Short-season Pitching Coordinator: Mark Brewer.

Farm System

Class	Club	Manager	Coach(es)	Pitching Coach
Triple-A	Buffalo (IL)	Tim Teufel	Mike Easler	Ricky Bones
Double-A	Binghamton (EL)	Wally Backman	Luis Natera	Marc Valdes
High A	St. Lucie (FSL)	Pedro Lopez	Joel Fuentes	Phil Regan
Low A	Savannah (SAL)	Ryan Ellis	B. Distefano/J. Carreno	Glenn Abbott
Short-season	Brooklyn (NYP)	Rich Donnelly	Bobby Malek	Frank Viola
Rookie	Kingsport (APP)	Frank Fultz	G. Greer/L. Rivera	Jonathan Hurst
Rookie	Mets (GCL)	Luis Rojas	Y. Garcia/J. Fuentes	Mark Brewer
Rookie	Mets 1 (DSL)	Jose Leger	M. Martinez/E. Chavez	Benjamin Marte
Rookie	Mets 2 (DSL)	Alberto Castillo	L. Hernandez/D. Davalillo	Francis Martinez

Scouting
Telephone: (718) 565-4311. **Fax:** (718) 205-7920.
VP, Scouting/Player Development: Paul DePodesta. **Director, Amateur Scouting:** Chad MacDonald. **Assistant, Amateur Scouting:** Elizabeth Gadsden. **Coordinator, Amateur Scouting:** Ian Levin. **Professional/International Scouting Assistant:** Diana Parra-Gonzalez. **Pro Scouts:** Mack Babitt (Richmond, CA), Jim D'Aloia (Lakewood, NJ), Roland Johnson (Newington, CT), David Keller (Phoenix, AZ), Bryan Lambe (N. Massapequa, NY), Harry Minor (Long Beach, CA), Isao O'Jimi (Japan), Roy Smith (Chicago, IL), Tom Tanous (Barrington, RI), Rudy Terrasas (Santa Fe, TX).
National Crosschecker: David Lakey (Kingwood, TX). **Regional Supervisors:** Southeast—Steve Barningham (Land O'Lakes, FL), West—Tim Fortugno (Elk Grove, CA), Northeast—Scott Hunter (Mount Laurel, NJ), Midwest—Mac Seibert (Cantonment, FL). **Area Supervisors:** Chris Becerra (Venice, CA), Erwin Bryant (Lexington, KY), Ray Corbett (College Station, TX), Steve Gossett (Fremont, NE), Jon Heuerman (Chandler, AZ), Larry Izzo, Jr. (Deer Park, NY), Tommy Jackson (Birmingham, AL), Fred Mazuca (Tustin, CA), Marlin McPhail (Irmo, SC), Steve Nichols (Mount Dora, FL), Les Parker (Hudson, FL), Claude Pelletier (St. Lazare, Quebec), Art Pontarelli (Lincoln, RI), Jim Reeves (Camas, WA), Junior Roman (San Sebastian, Puerto Rico), Max Semler (Allen, TX), Jim Thompson (Philadelphia, PA), Doug Thurman (San Jose, CA), Scott Trcka (Hobart, IN).
Director, International Operations: Rafael Perez. **Supervisor, Latin American Operations:** Ismael Cruz. **Area Supervisor, Venezuela:** Luis Marquez. **International Scouts:** Modesto Abreu (Dominican Republic), Imberwer Alvarez (Venezuela), Marciano Alvarez (Dominican Republic), Gerardo Cabrera (Dominican Republic), Carlos Capellan (Dominican Republic), Lionel Chatelle (Germany), Jose Contreras (Venezuela), Alexis DeLaCruz (Dominican Republic), Harold Herrera (Colombia), Gabriel Low (Mexico), Jose Mota (Venezuela), Daurys Nin (Dominican Republic), Clifford Nuitter (Venezuela), Jimmy Oliver (South Korea), Camilo Piña (Dominican Republic), Hector Rincones (Venezuela), Jose Sandy Rosario (Dominican Republic), Henry Sandoval (Venezuela), Alex Zapata (Panama).

New York Yankees

Office Address: Yankee Stadium, One East 161st Street, Bronx, NY 10451.
Telephone: (718) 293-4300. **Fax:** (718) 293-8431.
Website: www.yankees.com; www.yankeesbeisbol.com.

OWNERSHIP

Managing General Partner/Co-Chairperson: Harold Z. Steinbrenner.
General Partner/Co-Chairperson: Henry G. Steinbrenner. **General Partner/Vice Chairperson:** Jennifer Steinbrenner Swindal. **General Partner/Vice Chairperson:** Jessica Steinbrenner. **Vice Chairperson:** Joan Steinbrenner. **Senior Vice President:** Felix Lopez.

BUSINESS OPERATIONS

Harold Steinbrenner

President: Randy Levine, Esq.
COO: Lonn A. Trost, Esq.
Senior VP, Strategic Ventures: Marty Greenspun. **Senior VP, Chief Security Officer:** Sonny Hight. **Senior VP/Chief Financial Officer, Yankee Global Enterprises:** Anthony Bruno. **Senior VP, Corporate/Community Relations:** Brian Smith. **Senior VP, Corporate Sales/Sponsorship:** Michael Tusiani. **Senior VP, Marketing:** Deborah Tymon. **VP/Assistant GM:** Jean Afterman. **VP/CFO, Accounting:** Robert Brown. **CFO/VP, Financial Operations:** Scott Krug. **Deputy General Counsel/VP, Legal Affairs:** Alan Chang. **Controller:** Derrick Baio.

Business Development

Executive Director, Premium Sales: Troy Tutt.
Corporate Sales/Sponsorships
Directors, Corporate Sales/Sponsorships: Brian Calka. **Director, Sponsorship Services:** Nicole Arceneaux.

Communications/Media Relations

Telephone: (718) 579-4460. **Fax:** (718) 293-8414.
Director, Communications/Media Relations: Jason Zillo. **Managers, Media Relations:** Jason Latimer, Michael Margolis. **Coordinator, Media Relations:** Lauren Moran. **Assistants, Media Relations:** Kenny Leandry, Alexandra Trochanowski. **Administrative Assistant, Media Relations:** Dolores Hernandez.

Publications

Director, Publications: Alfred Santasiere III.

Office Operations

Senior Director, Technology: Mike Lane. **General Counsel:** Rachel M. Cohen, Esq. **Director, Creative Services:** Kara Mooney.

2011 SCHEDULE

Standard Game Times: 7:05 p.m.; Sat.-Sun. 1:05.

MARCH			
31 . . . . Detroit	6-8 . . . . .at Texas	20-22 . . . . .at Cincinnati	12-14 . . . . . .Tampa Bay
	10-12 . . . . . Kansas City	24-26 . . . . .Colorado	15-17 . . . .at Kansas City
APRIL	13-15 . . . . Boston	28-30 . . . . . . .Milwaukee	18-21 . . . . . at Minnesota
2-3 . . . . Detroit	16-17 . . . . at Tampa Bay		23-25 . . . . Oakland
4-7 . . . . .Minnesota	18-19 . . . . .at Baltimore	**JULY**	26-29 . . . . . at Baltimore
8-10 . . . . .at Boston	20-22 . . . . .New York (NL)	1-3 . . . . at New York (NL)	30-31 . . . . . . .at Boston
12-14 . . . . Baltimore	23-25 . . . . .Toronto	4-6 . . . . . . .at Cleveland	
15-17 . . . . Texas	27-29 . . . . . . .at Seattle	7-10 . . . . . . .Tampa Bay	**SEPTEMBER**
19-20 . . . . . . at Toronto	30-31 . . . . . .at Oakland	14-17 . . . . . . at Toronto	1 . . . . .at Boston
22-24 . . . .at Baltimore		18-21 . . . at Tampa Bay	2-4 . . . . .Toronto
25-28 . . . . . Chicago (AL)	**JUNE**	22-24 . . . . Oakland	5-7 . . . . Baltimore
29-30 . . . . .Toronto	1 . . . . .at Oakland	25-27 . . . . Seattle	9-11 . . at Los Angeles (AL)
	3-5 . . at Los Angeles (AL)	29-31 . . . . . Baltimore	12-14 . . . . .at Seattle
MAY	7-9 . . . . Boston		16-18 . . . . . . at Toronto
1 . . . . .Toronto	10-13 . . . . Cleveland	**AUGUST**	20-21 . . . . . . .Tampa Bay
2-5 . . . . .at Detroit	14-16 . . . . Texas	1-4 . . . . at Chicago (AL)	23-25 . . . . Boston
	17-19 . . . .at Chicago (NL)	5-7 . . . . .at Boston	26-28 . . . . . at Tampa Bay
		9-11 . . . . Los Angeles (AL)	

GENERAL INFORMATION

Stadium (year opened): Yankee Stadium (2009).
Team Colors: Navy blue and white.

Player Representative: Unavailable.
Home Dugout: First Base.
Playing Surface: Grass.

Scoreboard/Broadcasting
   Senior Director, Scoreboard/Broadcasting: Michael Bonner.

Security/Stadium Operations
   Executive Director, Stadium/Event Security: Todd Lechter. **Stadium Superintendent:** Pete Pullara. **Senior Director, Stadium Operations:** Doug Behar.

Ticket Operations
   Telephone: (718) 293-6000. **Fax:** (718) 293-4841.
   Senior Director, Ticket Operations: Irfan Kirimca. **Executive Director, Ticket Operations:** Kevin Dart.

BASEBALL OPERATIONS

   Telephone: (718) 293-4300. **Fax:** (718) 293-0015.
   Senior VP/General Manager: Brian Cashman.
   VP/Assistant GM: Jean Afterman, Esq. **Senior VP/Special Advisor:** Gene Michael. **Special Advisors:** Reggie Jackson, Yogi Berra. **Special Assistants:** Gordon Blakeley, Tino Martinez, Stump Merrill.
   Director, Quantitative Analysis: Michael Fishman. **Director, Mental Conditioning:** Chad Bohling. **Coordinator, Mental Conditioning:** Chris Passarella. **Assistant, Baseball Operations:** Steve Martone. **Systems Architect:** Brian Nicosia. **Research Assistant:** Jim Logue, Alex Rubin, David Grabiner. **Administrative Assistant:** Mary Pellino.

Major League Staff

Brian Cashman

   Manager: Joe Girardi.
   Coaches: Bench—Tony Pena; Pitching—Larry Rothschild; Batting—Kevin Long; First Base—Mick Kelleher; Third Base—Rob Thomson; Bullpen—Mike Harkey.

Medical/Training
   Team Physician, New York: Dr. Christopher Ahmad. **Senior Advisor, Orthopedics:** Stuart Hershon. **Team Physician, Tampa:** Dr. Andrew Boyer.
   Head Athletic Trainer: Gene Monahan. **Assistant Athletic Trainer:** Steve Donohue. **Strength/Conditioning Coordinator:** Dana Cavalea.

Player Development
   Telephone: (813) 875-7569. **Fax:** (813) 873-2302.
   Senior VP, Baseball Operations: Mark Newman. **VP, Player Personnel:** Billy Connors. **Director, Player Development:** Pat Roessler. **Assistant Director, Baseball Operations:** Eric Schmitt. **Administrative Assistant:** Jackie Williams. **Minor League Coordinators:** Nardi Contreras (pitching), James Rowson (hitting), Torre Tyson (defensive), Julio Mosquera (Catching), Jack Hubbard (outfield).

Farm System

Class	Club	Manager	Hitting Coach	Pitching Coach(s)/Coach
Triple-A	Scranton/WB (IL)	Dave Miley	Butch Wynegar	S. Aldred/F. Menechino
Double-A	Trenton (EL)	Tony Franklin	Julius Matos	T. Phelps/J. Pope
High A	Tampa (FSL)	Luis Sojo	Justin Turner	J. Ware/M. Garza
Low A	Charleston (SAL)	Aaron Ledesma	Gregg Colbrunn	C. Chantres/V. Valencia
Short-season	Staten Island (NYP)	Tom Slater	Ty Hawkins	D. Borrell/D. Valiente
Rookie	Tampa (GCL)	Carlos Mendoza	John Rodriguez	J. Rosado/G. Pavlick/B. Baisley
Rookie	Yankees I (DSL)	Raul Dominguez	Roy Gomez	W. Cordova/T. Olivares
Rookie	Yankees II (DSL)	Carlos Mota	Caonabo Cosme	J. Duran/R. Guillen/S. Encarnacion/R. Calderon

Scouting
   Telephone: (813) 875-7569. **Fax:** (813) 873-2302.
   VP, Amateur Scouting: Damon Oppenheimer. **Assistant Director, Amateur Scouting:** John Kremer.
   Senior Director, Pro Personnel: Billy Eppler. **Assistant, Professional Scouting:** Will Kuntz.
   Professional Scouts: Ron Brand (Plano, TX), Joe Caro (Tampa, FL), Jay Darnell (San Diego, CA), Gary Denbo (Tampa, FL), Bill Emslie (Tampa, FL), Dan Freed (Lexington, IL), Jalal Leach (Sacramento, CA), Bill Livesey (St. Petersburg, FL), Bill Mele (Boston, MA), Tim Naehring (Cincinnati, OH), Greg Orr (Sacramento, CA), Josh Paul (Tampa, FL), Kevin Reese (Sterling, VA), Rick Williams (Tampa, FL), Tom Wilson (Lake Havasu, AZ), Bob Miske (part-time, Amherst, NY). **Amateur Scouting, National Crosscheckers:** Brian Barber, Kendall Carter, Tim Kelly.
   Area Scouts: Mark Batchko (North Texas), Steve Boros (South Texas, KS), Andy Cannizaro (LA, MS), Jeff Deardorff (Clermont, FL), Mike Gibbons (Liberty Township, OH), Matt Hyde (Canton, MA.), David Keith (Anaheim, CA), Steve Kmetko (Phoenix, AZ), Steve Lemke (Geneva, IL), Scott Lovekamp (Lynchburg, VA), Carlos Marti (Miramar, FL), Tim McIntosh (Stockton, CA), Darryl Monroe (Decatur, GA), Jeff Patterson (Yorba Linda, CA), Cesar Presbott (Bronx, NY), Dennis Twombley (Redondo Beach, CA), D.J. Svihlik (Birmingham, AL), Mike Thurman (West Linn, OR).
   Director, International Scouting: Danny Rowland. **Assistant Director, International Operations:** Alex Cotto. **International Crosschecker:** Dennis Woody. **Coordinator, International Player Development:** Pat McMahon. **International Scouting Supervisors:** Victor Mata (Dominican Republic), Ricardo Final (Venezuela).
   Scouting Development Coaches: Argenis Paulino, Jonnathan Saturria.
   Dominican Scouts: Angel Ovalles, Juan Rosario, Jose Sabino, Raymond Sanchez. **Venezuelan Scouts:** Alan Atacho, Darwin Bracho, Jose Gavidia, Cesar Suarez. **International Scouts:** Chairon Isenia (Curacao), Jason Lee (Korea), Carlos Levy (Panama), Edgar Rodriguez (Nicaragua), Luis Sierra (Colombia), Lee Sigmen (Mexico), Ken Su (Pacific Rim), John Wadsworth (Australia).

Oakland Athletics

Office Address: 7000 Coliseum Way, Oakland, CA 94621.
Telephone: (510) 638-4900. **Fax:** (510) 562-1633. **Website:** www.oaklandathletics.com

Ownership
Co-Owner/Managing Partner: Lewis Wolff.

BUSINESS OPERATIONS
President: Michael Crowley. **Executive Assistant to President:** Carolyn Jones. **Assistant General Counsel:** Neil Kraetsch.

Finance/Administration
Vice President, Finance: Paul Wong. **Director, Finance:** Kasey Jarcik. **Payroll Manager:** Kathy Leviege. **Senior Accountant, Accounts Payable:** Isabelle Mahaffey.
Director, Human Resources: Kim Kubo. **Assistant, Human Resources:** Michaele Smith. **Director, Information Technology:** Nathan Hayes. **Systems Administrator:** David Frieberg. **Coordinator, Office Services:** Julie Vasconcellos. **Receptionist, Executive Offices:** Maggie Baptist.

Sales/Marketing
VP, Sales/Marketing: Jim Leahey. **Assistant, Sales/Marketing:** Breanne Pund. **Manager, Marketing/Advertising:** Zachary Glare. **Manager, Creative Services:** Mike Ono. **Senior Coordinator, Advertising:** Amy MacEwen. **Senior Director, Corporate Partnerships:** Darrin Gross. **Director, Partnership Services:** Franklin Lowe. **Corporate Account Managers:** Matthew Gallagher, Jill Golden, Meredith Hartery. **Manager, Promotions/Special Events:** Heather Rajeski. **Coordinator, Special Events:** Caroline Griggs. **Assistant, Special Events:** Sandy Karbel, Tim Sommer.

Public Relations/Communications
Telephone: (510) 563-2207. **Fax:** (510) 562-1633.
VP, Broadcasting/Communications: Ken Pries. **Manager, Broadcast Services:** Warren Chu. **Director, Public Relations:** Bob Rose. **Manager, Baseball Information:** Mike Selleck. **Manager, Media/Player Relations:** Kristy Fick. **Manager, Media Services:** Debbie Gallas. **Team Photographer:** Michael Zagaris.
Director, Community Relations: Detra Paige. **Coordinator, Community Relations:** Erik Farrell. **Senior Director, In-Stadium Entertainment:** Troy Smith. **Senior Director, Multimedia Services:** David Don.

Stadium Operations
VP, Stadium Operations: David Rinetti. **Director, Stadium Operations:** Paul LeVeau. **Head Groundskeeper:** Clay Wood. **Arizona Groundskeeper:** Chad Huss.

Ticket Operations
Executive Director, Ticket Sales/Operations: Steve Fanelli. **Director, Ticket Sales:** Brian DiTucci. **Coordinator, Sales/Ticket Operations:** Judy Del Rosario. **Manager, Premium Seating Sales:** Chris Van Dyne. **Manager, Group

Lew Wolff

2011 SCHEDULE
Standard Game Times: 7:05 p.m.; Sat./Sun. 1:05.

APRIL
1-3 . . . . Seattle
5-7 . . . . at Toronto
8-10 . . . . . at Minnesota
11-13 . . . at Chicago (AL)
14-17 . . . . Detroit
19-20 . . . . Boston
21-24 . . . . at Seattle
25-27 . at Los Angeles (AL)
29-30 . . . . Texas

MAY
1-2 . . . . Texas
3-5 . . . . Cleveland
6-8 . . . . . . at Kansas City
9-11 . . . . at Texas

13-15 . . . . . Chicago (AL)
16-17 . . . Los Angeles (AL)
18-19 . . . . Minnesota
20-22 . . . at San Francisco
23-26 . at Los Angeles (AL)
27-29 . . . . . . Baltimore
30-31 . . . . New York (AL)

JUNE
1 . . . . New York (AL)
3-5 . . . . at Boston
6-8 . . . . at Baltimore
9-12 . . . at Chicago (AL)
14-16 . . . . . Kansas City
17-19 . . . . San Francisco
21-23 . . at New York (NL)
24-26 . . . at Philadelphia

28-30 . . . . Florida

JULY
1-3 . . . . Arizona
4-6 . . . . Seattle
8-10 . . . . at Texas
15-17 . . . Los Angeles (AL)
19-20 . . . . at Detroit
22-24 . . at New York (AL)
25-28 . . . . . . Tampa Bay
29-31 . . . . . . Minnesota

AUGUST
1-3 . . . . at Seattle
5-7 . . . . . . at Tampa Bay
9-11 . . . . at Toronto
12-14 . . . . Texas

15-17 . . . . . . Baltimore
18-21 . . . . Toronto
23-25 . . at New York (AL)
26-28 . . . . at Boston
29-31 . . . . . at Cleveland

SEPTEMBER
1 . . . . at Cleveland
2-4 . . . . Seattle
5-7 . . . . Kansas City
9-11 . . . . at Texas
12-14 . . . Los Angeles (AL)
15-18 . . . . Detroit
20-22 . . . . Texas
23-25 . at Los Angeles (AL)
26-28 . . . . at Seattle

GENERAL INFORMATION
Stadium (year opened): McAfee Coliseum (1968).
Team Colors: Kelly green and gold.

Player Representative: Unavailable.
Home Dugout: Third Base.
Playing Surface: Grass.

Sales: Jessica Scott. **Manager, Inside Sales/CRM:** Aaron Dragomir. **Manager, Senior Account Premium Seating:** Parker Newton. **Manager, Senior Accounts:** Phil Chapman. .

Ticketing

Director, Ticket Sales: Josh Ziegenbusch. **Manager, Digital Ticketing Operations:** Travis LoDolce. **Manager, Ticket Operations:** David Adame. **Manager, Ticket Services:** Catherine Glazer. **Supervisor, Box Office:** Anthony Blue. **Director, Premium Seating Services:** Susie Weiss. **Assistant, Premium Seating Services:** Jason Hicks.

Travel/Clubhouse

Director, Team Travel: Mickey Morabito. **Equipment Manager:** Steve Vucinich. **Visitors Clubhouse:** Mike Thalblum. **Assistant Equipment Manager:** Brian Davis. **Umpires/Clubhouse Assistant:** Matt Weiss. **Clubhouse Assistant:** William Angel. **Supervisor, Arizona Clubhouse:** Jesse Sotomayor. **Manager, Arizona Clubhouse:** James Gibson. **Assistant Manager, Arizona Clubhouse:** Chad Yaconetti.

BASEBALL OPERATIONS

VP/General Manager: Billy Beane.
Assistant GM: David Forst. **Director, Player Personnel:** Billy Owens. **Special Assistant to GM:** Grady Fuson. **Executive Assistant:** Betty Shinoda. **Director, Baseball Administration:** Pamela Pitts. **Director, Baseball Operations:** Farhan Zaidi. **Video Coordinator:** Adam Rhoden. **Special Assistant to Baseball Operations:** Scott Hatteberg.

Billy Beane

Major League Staff

Manager: Bob Geren.
Coaches: Bench—Joel Skinner; Pitching—Ron Romanick; Batting—Gerald Perry; First Base—Tye Waller; Third Base—Mike Gallego; Bullpen—Rick Rodriguez.

Medical, Training

Head Athletic Trainer: Nick Paparesta. **Assistant Athletic Trainer:** Walt Horn. **Assistant Athletic Trainer:** Brian Schulman. **Director, Strength/Conditioning:** Bob Alejo. **Major League Massage Therapist:** Ozzie Lyles. **Coordinator, Medical Services:** Larry Davis. **Team Physicians:** Dr. Allan Pont, Dr. Elliott Schwartz. **Team Orthopedist:** Dr. Jon Dickinson. **Associate Team Orthopedist:** Dr. Will Workman. **Consulting Orthopedist:** Dr. Lewis Yocum. **Arizona Team Physicians:** Dr. Fred Dicke, Dr. Doug Freedberg.

Player Development

Telephone: (510) 638-4900. **Fax:** (510) 563-2376.
Director, Player Development: Keith Lieppman. **Director, Minor League Operations:** Ted Polakowski. **Administrative Assistant, Player Development:** Valerie Vander Heyden. **Minor League Roving Instructors:** Juan Navarrete (infield), Ron Plaza (infield), Gil Patterson (pitching), Greg Sparks (hitting). **Minor League Instructor:** Ruben Escalera. **Minor League Video Coordinator:** Mark Smith. **Minor League Medical Coordinator:** Jeff Collins. **Minor League Strength/Conditioning Coordinator:** Michael Henriques. **Minor League Strength/Conditioning Assistant Coordinator:** Thomas Shea. **Special Instructor, Pitching/Rehabilitation:** Garvin Alston. **Supervisor, Arizona Clubhouse:** Jesse Sotomayor. **Manager, Arizona Clubhouse:** James Gibson. **Staff, Arizona Clubhouse:** Chad Yaconetti.

Farm System

Class	Club (League)	Manager	Coach	Pitching Coach
Triple-A	Sacramento (PCL)	Darren Bush	Todd Steverson	Scott Emerson
Double-A	Midland (TL)	Steve Scarsone	Tim Garland	Don Schulze
High A	Stockton (CAL)	Webster Garrison	Brian McArn	Craig Lefferts
Low A	Burlington (MWL)	Aaron Nieckula	Haas Pratt	Jimmy Escalante
Short-season	Vermont (NYP)	Rick Magnante	Casey Myers	John Wasdin
Rookie	Athletics (AZL)	Marcus Jensen	Juan Dilone	Ariel Prieto
Rookie	Athletics (DSL)	Ruben Escalera	Rahdames Perez	David Brito

Scouting

Telephone: (510) 638-4900. **Fax:** (510) 563-2376.
Director, Scouting: Eric Kubota (Rocklin, CA).
Assistant Director, Scouting: Michael Holmes (Winston Salem, NC). **Director, Pro Scouting:** Chris Pittaro (Hamilton, NJ). **Coordinator, Scouting:** Sam Geaney. **National Crosschecker:** Ron Vaughn (Corona, CA). **Western Crosschecker:** Scott Kidd (Folsom, CA). **Midwest Crosschecker:** Steve Bowden (Oklahoma City, OK). **Pro Scouts:** Bryn Alderson (San Francisco, CA), Jeff Bittiger (Saylorsburg, PA), Will Schock (Oakland, CA), Steve Sharpe (Kansas City, MO), Craig Weissmann (San Diego, CA), Mike Ziegler (Orlando, FL).
Area Scouts: Neil Avent (Greensboro, NC), Yancy Ayres (Topeka, KS), Armann Brown (Texas City, TX), Marcus Cayenne (Nashville, TN), Jermaine Clark (Discovery Bay, CA), Jim Coffman (Portland, OR), Matt Higginson (Burlington, ON), Rick Magnante (Sherman Oaks, CA), Eric Martins (Diamond Bar, CA), Kevin Mello (Chicago, IL), Kelcey Mucker (Baton Rouge, LA), Matt Ranson (Kennesaw, GA), Marc Sauer (Cliffwood Beach, NJ), Trevor Schaffer (Belleair, FL), Jeremy Schied (San Tan Valley, AZ), Rich Sparks (Sterling Heights, MI), J.T. Stotts (Moorpark, CA).
Director, Latin American Operations: Raymond Abreu (Santo Domingo, DR). **Coordinator, International Operations/Baseball Operations Analyst:** Dan Kantrovitz (San Francisco, CA). **Coordinator, Latin American Scouting:** Julio Franco (Caracas, VZ).
International Scouts: Ruben Barradas (VZ), Juan Carlos De La Cruz (DR), Angel Eusebio (DR), Andri Garcia (VZ), Tom Gillespie (Europe), Adam Hislop (Taiwan), Lewis Kim (South Korea), Pablo Marmol (DR), Amaury Reyes (DR), Oswaldo Troconis (VZ), Juan Villanueva (VZ).

Philadelphia Phillies

August 2010

Office Address: Citizens Bank Park, One Citizens Bank Way, Philadelphia, PA 19148.
Telephone: (215) 463-6000. **Website:** www.phillies.com.

Ownership
Operated By: The Phillies.
President/CEO: David Montgomery. **Chairman:** Bill Giles.

BUSINESS OPERATIONS

David Montgomery

Vice President/General Counsel: Rick Strouse. **VP, Phillies Enterprises:** Richard Deats. **VP, Employee/Customer Services:** Kathy Killian. **Director, Ballpark Enterprises/Business Development:** Joe Giles. **Director, Information Systems:** Brian Lamoreaux. **Director, Employee Benefits/Services:** JoAnn Marano.

Ballpark Operations
Senior VP, Administration/Operations: Michael Stiles. **Director, Ballpark Operations:** Mike DiMuzio. **Director, Event Operations:** Eric Tobin. **Manager, Ballpark Operations/Security:** Sal DeAngelis. **Manager, Concessions Development:** Bruce Leith. **Head Groundskeeper:** Mike Boekholder. **PA Announcer:** Dan Baker. **Official Scorers:** Jay Dunn, Mike Maconi, Joseph Bellina.

Communications
Telephone: (215) 463-6000. **Fax:** (215) 389-3050.
VP, Communications: Bonnie Clark. **Director, Baseball Communications:** Greg Casterioto. **Coordinator, Baseball Communications:** Kevin Gregg. **Baseball Communications Assistant:** Craig Hughner. **Communications Assistant:** Deanna Sabec.

Finance
Senior VP, Business/Finance: Jerry Clothier. **VP/CFO:** John Nickolas. **Director, Payroll Services:** Karen Wright.

Marketing/Promotions
Senior VP, Marketing/Sales: David Buck. **Manager, Client Services/Alumni Relations:** Debbie Nocito. **Director, Corporate Partnership:** Rob MacPherson. **Director, Advertising Sales:** Brian Mahoney. **Managers, Advertising Sales:** Scott Nickle, Tom Sullivan. **Director, Marketing Programs/Events:** Kurt Funk. **Director, Entertainment:** Chris Long. **Manager, Broadcasting:** Rob Brooks. **Manager, Advertising/Internet Services:** Jo-Anne Levy-Lamoreaux.

Sales/Tickets
Telephone: (215) 463-1000. **Fax:** (215) 463-9878.
VP, Sales/Ticket Operations: John Weber. **Director, Ticket Department:** Dan Goroff. **Director, Ticket Technology/ Development:** Chris Pohl. **Director, Season Ticket Sales:** Derek Schuster. **Manager, Suite Sales/Services:** Tom Mashek. **Manager, Phone Center:** Phil Feather. **Manager, Season Ticket Services:** Mike Holdren.

2011 SCHEDULE
Standard Game Times: 7:05 p.m.; Sun. 1:35

APRIL		JULY	
1-3 . . . . Houston	13-15 . . . . . . at Atlanta	28-30 . . . . Boston	16-18 . . . . Arizona
5-7 . . . . . .New York (NL)	16-17 . . . . . .at St. Louis		19-21 . . . . at Washington
8-10 . . . . at Atlanta	18-19 . . . . . . .Colorado	1-3 . . . . at Toronto	22-24 . . . . .New York (NL)
12-14 . . . . at Washington	20-22 . . . . Texas	4-6 . . . . .at Florida	26-28 . . . . Florida
15-17 . . . . Florida	23-26 . . . . . . Cincinnati	8-10 . . . . Atlanta	29-31 . . . .at Cincinnati
18-20 . . . . . .Milwaukee	27-29 . . at New York (NL)	15-17 . . at New York (NL)	
21-24 . . . . at San Diego	30-31 . . . .at Washington	18-20 . . . .at Chicago (NL)	SEPTEMBER
25-27 . . . . . . at Arizona		22-25 . . . . . . San Diego	1 . . . . .at Cincinnati
29-30 . . . . .New York (NL)	JUNE	26-28 . . . . San Francisco	2-4 . . . . .at Florida
	1 . . . . . . at Washington	29-31 . . . . . . .Pittsburgh	5-7 . . . . Atlanta
MAY	3-5 . . . . . . at Pittsburgh		8-11 . . . . . . at Milwaukee
1 . . . . . . .New York (NL)	6-8 . . . Los Angeles (NL)	AUGUST	12-14 . . . . . .at Houston
3-5 . . . . Washington	9-12 . . . . . Chicago (NL)	1-3 . . . . at Colorado	16-19 . . . . St. Louis
6-8 . . . . Atlanta	14-16 . . . . Florida	4-7 . . . . at San Francisco	20-22 . . . . . Washington
9-11 . . . . .at Florida	17-19 . . . . . .at Seattle	8-10 . . at Los Angeles (NL)	23-25 . . at New York (NL)
	21-23 . . . . .at St. Louis	12-14 . . . . . .Washington	26-28 . . . . . . at Atlanta
	24-26 . . . . Oakland		

GENERAL INFORMATION

Stadium (year opened): Citizens Bank Park (2004).
Team Colors: Red, white and blue.

Player Representative: Unavailable.
Home Dugout: First Base.
Playing Surface: Natural Grass.

Travel/Clubhouse

Director, Team Travel/Clubhouse Services: Frank Coppenbarger.
Manager, Visiting Clubhouse: Kevin Steinhour. Manager, Home Clubhouse: Phil Sheridan. Manager, Equipment/ Umpire Services: Dan O'Rourke.

BASEBALL OPERATIONS

Senior VP/General Manager: Ruben Amaro Jr.
Assistant GM: Scott Proefrock. Assistant GM, Player Personnel: Benny Looper. Assistant GM, Player Development/Scouting: Chuck LaMar. Director, Baseball Administration: Susan Ingersoll Papaneri. Director, Professional Scouting: Mike Ondo. Baseball Information Analyst: Jay McLaughlin. Senior Advisor to GM: Dallas Green. Senior Advisor to the President/GM: Pat Gillick. Special Assistant to GM: Charley Kerfeld. Baseball Administration Representative: Chris Cashman. Administrative Assistant: Adele MacDonald.

Ruben Amaro, Jr.

Major League Staff

Manager: Charlie Manuel.
Coaches: Bench—Pete Mackanin; Pitching—Rich Dubee; Batting—Greg Gross; First Base— Sam Perlozzo; Third Base—Juan Samuel; Bullpen Coach—Mick Billmeyer; Bullpen Catcher— Jesus Tiamo.

Medical/Training

Director, Medical Services: Dr. Michael Ciccotti. Head Athletic Trainer: Scott Sheridan. Assistant Athletic Trainer: Mark Andersen. Strength/Conditioning Coordinator: Doug Lien. Employee Assistance Professional: Dickie Noles.

Player Development

Telephone: (215) 463-6000. Fax: (215) 755-9324.
Assistant GM, Player Personnel: Benny Looper. Assistant Directors, Minor League Operations: Steve Noworyta, Lee McDaniel. Administrative Assistant, Minor League Operations: Ray Robles. Director, Florida Operations: John Timberlake. Minor League Equipment Manager: Joe Cynar. Minor League Video Representative: Brett Gross.
Field Coordinator: Mike Compton. Coordinators: Brian Cammarota (trainer), Ernie Whitt (catching), Gorman Heimueller (pitching), Shawn Fcasni (conditioning), Steve Henderson (hitting), Donnie Sadler (outfield/baserunning), Doug Mansolino (infield).

Farm System

Class	Club(League)	Manager	Coach	Pitching Coach
Triple-A	Lehigh Valley (IL)	Ryne Sandberg	Sal Rende	Rod Nichols
Double-A	Reading (EL)	Mark Parent	Frank Cacciatore	Bob Milacki
High A	Clearwater (FSL)	Dusty Wathan	John Mizerock	Dave Lundquist
Low A	Lakewood (SAL)	Chris Truby	Greg Legg	Steve Schrenk
Short-season	Williamsport (NYP)	Mickey Morandini	Jorge Velandia	Lance Carter
Rookie	Clearwater (GCL)	Roly DeArmas	Kevin Jordan	Les Lancaster
Rookie	Phillies (DSL)	Manny Amador	L. Arzeno/C. Hernriquez	Cesar Mejia
Rookie	Phillies (VSL)	Rafael DeLima	S. Navas/ T. Aguilar	Les Straker

Scouting

Director, Scouting: Marti Wolever (Papillion, NE). Assistant Director, Scouting: Rob Holiday (Philadelphia, PA).
Coordinators, Scouting: Mike Ledna (Arlington Heights, IL), Bill Moore (Alta Loma, CA).
Regional Supervisors: Gene Schall (East/Harleysville, PA), Brian Kohlscheen (Central/Norman, OK), Darrell Conner (West/Riverside, CA).
Area Scouts: Shane Bowers (La Verne, CA), Steve Cohen (Spring, TX), Joey Davis (Ranco Murrieta, CA), Nate Dion (West Chester, OH), Mike Garcia (Moreno Valley CA), Brad Holland (Gilbert AZ), Eric Jacques (Bellevue, WA), Aaron Jersild (Atlanta, GA), Alan Marr (Sarasota, FL), Paul Murphy (Wilmington, DE), Demerius Pittman (Corona CA), Paul Scott (Rockwall, TX), David Seifert (Paw Paw, IL), Mike Stauffer (Ridgeland, MS), Eric Valent (Wernersville PA).
International Supervisor: Sal Agostinelli (Kings Park (NY).
International Scouts: Alex Agostino (Canada), Norman Anciani (Panama), Nathan Davison (Australia), Arnold Elles (Colombia), Tomas Herrera (Mexico), Joe Ko (Korea), Eric Jacques (Europe), Allan Lewis (Panama, Central America), Jesus Mendez (Venezuela), Manabu Noto (Japan), Koby Perez (Dominican Republic), Darryn Smith (South Africa).
Director, Major League Scouting: Gordon Lakey (Barker, TX). Special Assignment Scouts: Howie Frieling (Apex, NC), Dave Hollins (Orchard Park, NY). Major League Scout: Jim Fregosi Jr (Murrieta, CA). Advance Scout: Craig Colbert.
Professional Scouts: Sonny Bowers (Hewitt, TX), Dean Jongewaard (Fountain Valley, CA), Jesse Levis (Fort Washington, PA), Jon Mercurio (Coraopolis, PA), Roy Tanner (North Charleston, SC), Del Unser (Scottsdale, AZ), Dan Wright (Cave Springs, AR).

Pittsburgh Pirates

Office Address: PNC Park at North Shore, 115 Federal St, Pittsburgh, PA 15212.
Mailing Address: P.O. Box 7000, Pittsburgh, PA 15212.
Telephone: (412) 323-5000. **Fax:** (412) 325-4412. **Website:** www.pirates.com

Ownership

Chairman of the Board: Robert Nutting.
Board of Directors: Donald Beaver, G. Ogden Nutting, Robert Nutting, William Nutting, Duane Wittman.

BUSINESS OPERATIONS

President: Frank Coonelly.
Executive Vice President/CFO: Jim Plake. **Executive VP/General Manager, PNC Park:** Dennis DaPra. **Executive VP/Chief Marketing Officer:** Lou DePaoli. **Senior VP/General Counsel:** Larry Silverman.

Finance/Administration/Information Technology

Senior Director, Human Resources: Pam Nelson Minteer. **Senior Director, Information Technology:** Terry Zeigler. **Director, Employee Services:** Patti Mistick. **Director, Baseball Systems Development:** Dan Fox. **Manager, Ticket Accounting/Reporting:** Dave Wysocki.

Communications

Fax: (412) 325-4413.
Senior Director, Communications: Brian Warecki. **Director, Media Relations:** Jim Trdinich. **Director, Broadcasting:** Marc Garda. **Manager, Media Relations:** Dan Hart. **Manager, Business Communications:** Matt Nordby.

Community Relations

VP, Community/Public Affairs: Patty Paytas. **Director, Community Relations:** Michelle Mejia. **Manager, Diversity Initiatives:** Chaz Kellem.

Frank Coonelly

Marketing/Sales

Senior Director, Marketing/Special Events: Brian Chiera. **Senior Director, Corporate Partnerships:** Mike Egan. **Director, Alumni Affairs/Promotions/Licensing:** Joe Billetdeaux. **Director, Advertising/Creative Services:** Kiley Cauvel. **Director, Special Events:** Christine Serkoch. **Manager, Promotions:** Dan Millar. **Manager, In-Game Entertainment:** Eric Wolff. **Manager, Promotions/Licensing:** Megan Vizzini. **Manager, PNC Park Events:** Ann Elder. **Managers, Client Services:** Mike DeMars, Dana Geary.

Stadium Operations

Senior Director, Ballpark Operations: Chris Hunter. **Senior Director, Security/Contract Services:** Jeff Podobnik. **Manager, Security/Service Operations:** Mark Weaver. **Director, Field Operations:** Manny Lopez. **Operations Manager:** Ben Fortun. **Guest Relations Manager:** Melissa Cushey.

2011 SCHEDULE

Standard Game Times: 7:05 p.m.; Sun. 1:35.

APRIL
1-3 . . . . . .at Chicago (NL)
4-6 . . . . .at St. Louis
7-10 . . . . Colorado
12-14 . . . . .Milwaukee
15-18 . . . . .at Cincinnati
19-21 . . . . . . .at Florida
22-24 . . . . . Washington
26-28 . . . . San Francisco
29-30 . . . . . at Colorado

MAY
1 . . . . at Colorado
2-4 . . . . . . at San Diego
6-8 . . . . Houston
9-12 . . . . Los Angeles (NL)

13-15 . . . . . at Milwaukee
16-17 . . . . at Washington
18-19 . . . . .at Cincinnati
20-22 . . . . Detroit
24-25 . . . . Atlanta
27-29 . . . .at Chicago (NL)
30-31 . . . at New York (NL)

JUNE
1-2 . . . . at New York (NL)
3-5 . . . . .Philadelphia
7-9 . . . . Arizona
10-13 . . . . .New York (NL)
14-16 . . . . . .at Houston
17-19 . . . . .at Cleveland
20-22 . . . . Baltimore

24-26 . . . . Boston
28-30 . . . . at Toronto

JULY
1-3 . . . . . at Washington
4-6 . . . . Houston
8-10 . . . . . Chicago (NL)
15-17 . . . . . .at Houston
18-20 . . . . . . Cincinnati
22-24 . . . . St. Louis
25-28 . . . . . . at Atlanta
29-31 . . . . at Philadelphia

AUGUST
1-4 . . . . . . Chicago (NL)
5-7 . . . . San Diego
8-10 . . . . at San Francisco

12-14 . . . . . at Milwaukee
15-17 . . . . St. Louis
19-21 . . . . Cincinnati
22-24 . . . . . .Milwaukee
25-28 . . . . . .at St. Louis
29-31 . . . . . .at Houston

SEPTEMBER
2-4 . . . . . .at Chicago (NL)
5-7 . . . . Houston
9-11 . . . . Florida
12-14 . . . . St. Louis
15-18 . at Los Angeles (NL)
19-21 . . . . . . at Arizona
23-25 . . . . Cincinnati
26-28 . . . . . at Milwaukee

GENERAL INFORMATION

Stadium (year opened): PNC Park (2001).
Team Colors: Black and gold.
Player Representative: Paul Maholm.

Home Dugout: Third Base.
Playing Surface: Grass.

Ticketing
  Telephone: (800) 289-2827. **Fax:** (412) 325-4404.
  Senior Director, Ticket Sales/Services: Christopher Zaber. **Senior Director, Market Analytics/Business Development:** Jim Alexander. **Manager, CRM/Fan Database:** Mark Rudolph. **Director, Suite Sales/Service:** Terri Smith. **Director, Ticket New Business Development:** Jim Popovich. **Manager, Group Sales:** Justin Gurney. **Manager, Ticket Services/ Retention:** Raven Jemison. **Inside Sales Manager:** Travis Apple. **Manager, Ticket Operations:** Andrew Bragman.

BASEBALL OPERATIONS
  Senior VP/General Manager: Neal Huntington.
  Director, Player Personnel: Doug Strange. **Director, Baseball Operations:** Tyrone Brooks. **Director, Baseball Systems Development:** Dan Fox. **Assistant Director, Baseball Operations:** Kevan Graves. **Special Assistants to GM:** Jim Benedict, Larry Corrigan, Marc DelPiano, Jax Robertson, Pete Vuckovich. **Major League Scouts:** Mike Basso, Keith Champion, Bob Minor, Steve Williams. **Assistant, Baseball Operations:** Alex Langsam. **Video Coordinator:** Kevin Roach. **Video Advance Scout:** Simon Ferrer.

Neal Huntington

Major League Staff
  Manager: Clint Hurdle.
  Coaches: Bench—Jeff Banister; Pitching— Ray Searage; Hitting—Gregg Ritchie; First Base— Luis Silverio; Third Base—Nick Leyva; Bullpen—Euclides Rojas; Coach—Mark Strittmatter.

Medical/Training
  Medical Director: Dr Patrick DeMeo. **Team Physician:** Dr Edward Snell. **Head Athletic Trainer:** Brad Henderson. **Assistant Athletic Trainer:** Mike Sandoval. **Strength/Conditioning Coordinator:** Frank Velasquez. **Latin American Strength/Conditioning Coordinator:** Kiyoshi Momose. **Physical Therapist/Rehab Coordinator:** Erwin Valencia.

Player Development
  Director, Player Development: Kyle Stark.
  Coordinator, Instruction: Frank Kremblas. **Advisor, Player Development:** Brad Fischer. **Advisor, Latin American Operations:** Pablo Cruz. **Outfield/Baserunning Coordinator:** Kimera Bartee. **Pitching Coordinator:** Jim Benedict. **Assistant Pitching Coordinator:** Scott Mitchell. **Infield Coordinator:** Gary Green. **Hitting Coordinator:** Jeff Livesey. **Latin American Field Coordinator:** Luis Dorante. **Athletic Training Coordinator:** Carl Randolph. **Strength/Conditioning Coordinator:** Chris Sobonya. **Rehab Coordinator:** Marc Oceguera. **Mental Conditioning Coordinator:** Bernie Holliday. **Minor League Administrator:** Diane DePasquale. **Assistant, Player Development:** Brian Selman.

Farm System

Class	Club (League)	Manager	Coach(es)	Pitching Coach
Triple-A	Indianapolis (IL)	Dean Treanor	Jeff Branson	Tom Filer
Double-A	Altoona (EL)	P.J. Forbes	Brandon Moore	Wally Whitehurst
High A	Bradenton (FSL)	Carlos Garcia	Ryan Long	Mike Steele
Low A	West Virginia (SAL)	Gary Robinson	Dave Howard	Jeff Johnson
Short-season	State College (NYP)	Dave Turgeon	Edgar Varela	Justin Meccage
Rookie	Bradenton (GCL)	Tom Prince	W. Huyke/M. Lum	Miguel Bonilla
Rookie	Pirates (DSL)	Ramon Zapata	C. Beltre/Johe Acosta	Henry Corniel
Rookie	Pirates (VSL)	Osmin Melendez	I. Colmenares/J. Prieto	Dan Urbina

Scouting
  Fax: (412) 325-4414.
  Director, Scouting: Greg Smith. **Assistant Director, Scouting:** Joe Delli Carri. **Scouting Administrator:** Jim Asher.
  National Supervisors: Jack Bowen (Bethel Park, PA), Jimmy Lester (Columbus, GA).
  Regional Supervisors: Jesse Flores (Sacramento, CA), Rob Guzik (Latrobe, PA), Rodney Henderson (Lexington, KY), Everett Russell (Thibodaux, LA).
  Area Supervisors: Rick Allen (Agoura Hills, CA), Matt Bimeal (Baldwin City, KS), Larry Broadway (Glendale, AZ), Jerome Cochran (Slidell, LA), Jim Dedrick (Seattle, WA), Trevor Haley (Conroe, TX), Greg Hopkins (Beaverton, OR), Jerry Jordan (Kingsport, TN), Chris Kline (Northampton, MA), Mike Leuzinger (Canton, TX), Darren Mazeroski (Panama City Beach, FL), Rolando Pino (Pembroke Pines, FL), Greg Schilz (Atlanta, GA), Brian Tracy (Orange, CA), Matt Wondolowski (Washington D.C.), Anthony Wycklendt (Grafton, WI).
  Part-Time Scouts: Elmer Gray (Pittsburgh, PA), Enrique Hernandez (Puerto Rico), George Vranau (S. California), Sean Heffernan (Florence, SC).
  Director, Latin American Scouting: Rene Gayo.
  Full-Time Scouts: Orlando Covo (Colombia), Nelson Llenas (Dominican Republic), Rodolfo Petit (Venezuela), Marino Tejada (Dominican Republic), Cristino Valdez (Dominican Republic), Jesus Chino Valdez (Mexico).
  Part-Time Scouts: Marcos Briseno (Dominican Republic), Luis Campusano (Dominican Republic), Pablo Csorgi (Venezuela), Denny Diaz (Dominican Republic), Daniel Garcia (Colombia), Fernando Hernandez (Mexico), Jhoan Hidalgo (Venezuela), Jose Lavagnino (Mexico), Javier Magdaleno (Venezuela), Grimaldo Martinez (Mexico), Ezequiel Mora (Mexico), Juan Morales (Venezuela) Jose Pineda (Panama), Juan Pinto (Mexico), Francisco Valdez (Dominican Republic), Marc Van Zanten (Netherlands Antilles), Leon Taylor (Jamaica), Darryl Yrausquin (Aruba).
  International Scouts: Fu-Chun Chiang (Taiwan), Tony Harris (Australia), Tom Randolph (International).

St. Louis Cardinals

Office Address: 700 Clark Street, St. Louis MO 63102.
Telephone: (314) 345-9600. **Fax:** (314) 345-9523. **Website:** www.cardinals.com.

Ownership
Operated By: St. Louis Cardinals, LLC.
Chairman/Chief Executive Officer: William DeWitt, Jr.
Secretary: Fred Hanser. **Treasurer:** Andrew Baur. **President:** Bill DeWitt III. **Senior Administrative Assistant to Chairman:** Grace Pak. **Senior Administrative Assistant to President:** Julie Laningham.

BUSINESS OPERATIONS

Bill DeWitt III

Vice President, Event Services: Vicki Bryant. **Manager, Event Services:** Missy Tobey. **Director, Human Resources:** Christine Nelson. **Manager Employee Benefits:** Karen Brown.

Finance
Fax: (314) 345-9520.
Senior VP/Chief Financial Officer: Brad Wood. **Director, Finance:** Rex Carter.

Marketing/Sales
Fax: (314) 345-9529.
Senior VP, Sales/Marketing: Dan Farrell. **Administrative Assistant, VP Sales/Marketing:** Gail Ruhling. **VP, Corporate Marketing/Stadium Entertainment:** Thane van Breusegen. **Director Scoreboard Operantions/Senior Account Executive:** Tony Simokaitis. **Senior Account Executive, Corporate Sales:** Jeff Floerke.

Media Relations/Community Relations
Fax: (314) 345-9530.
Director, Media Relations: Brian Bartow. **Manager, Media Relations/New Media:** Melody Yount. **Director, Public Relations/Government Affairs:** Ron Watermon. **Director, Publications:** Steve Zesch. **Administrative Assistant:** Jama Fabry. **Director, Target Marketing:** Ted Savage. **Youth Baseball Commissioner, Cardinals Care:** Keith Brooks.

Stadium Operations
Fax: (314) 345-9535.
VP, Stadium Operations: Joe Abernathy. **Administrative Assistant:** Hope Baker. **Director, Stadium Operations:** Mike Bertani. **Director, Security/Special Services:** Joe Walsh. **Director, Quality Assurance/Guest Services:** Mike Ball. **Manager, Stadium Operations:** Cindy Richards. **Head Groundskeeper:** Bill Findley. **Assistant Head Groundskeeper:** Chad Casella. **PA Announcer:** John Ulett. **Official Scorers:** Gary Muller, Jeff Durbin, Mike Smith.

Ticketing
Fax: (314) 345-9522.
VP, Ticket Sales/Service: Joe Strohm. **Director, Ticket Services:** Rob Fasoldt. **Manager, Ticket Services:** Brady Bruhn.

2011 SCHEDULE
Standard Game Times: 7:15 p.m.; Sun. 1:15.

MARCH			
31 . . . . San Diego	6-8 . . . . .Milwaukee	21-23 . . . . .Philadelphia	12-14 . . . . .Colorado
	10-12 . . . .at Chicago (NL)	24-26 . . . . .Toronto	15-17 . . . . . at Pittsburgh
APRIL	13-15 . . . . .at Cincinnati	28-30 . . . . . .at Baltimore	19-21 . . . .at Chicago (NL)
2-3 . . . . San Diego	16-17 . . . . .Philadelphia		22-24 . . . Los Angeles (NL)
4-6 . . . . Pittsburgh	18-19 . . . . Houston	**JULY**	25-28 . . . . . . .Pittsburgh
8-10 . . . . at San Francisco	20-22 . . . .at Kansas City	1-3 . . . . . . at Tampa Bay	30-31 . . . . at Milwaukee
11-13 . . . . . . at Arizona	23-25 . . . . . at San Diego	4-6 . . . . Cincinnati	
14-17 . at Los Angeles (NL)	27-29 . . . . . at Colorado	7-10 . . . . Arizona	**SEPTEMBER**
19-21 . . . . . Washington	30-31 . . . . . San Francisco	15-17 . . . . .at Cincinnati	1 . . . . at Milwaukee
22-24 . . . . . . Cincinnati		19-21 . . . at New York (NL)	2-4 . . . . Cincinnati
26-28 . . . . . .at Houston	**JUNE**	22-24 . . . . at Pittsburgh	5-7 . . . . .Milwaukee
29-30 . . . . . . at Atlanta	1-2 . . . . . . San Francisco	25-28 . . . . Houston	9-11 . . . . Atlanta
	3-5 . . . . Chicago (NL)	29-31 . . . . Chicago (NL)	12-14 . . . . . at Pittsburgh
MAY	7-9 . . . . .at Houston		16-19 . . . . at Philadelphia
1 . . . . at Atlanta	10-12 . . . . . at Milwaukee	**AUGUST**	20-22 . . . . .New York (NL)
2-5 . . . . Florida	14-16 . . . . at Washington	1-3 . . . . . . at Milwaukee	23-25 . . . . . Chicago (NL)
	17-19 . . . . . . Kansas City	4-7 . . . . .at Florida	26-28 . . . . . . .at Houston
		9-11 . . . . . . .Milwaukee	

GENERAL INFORMATION
Stadium (year opened): Busch Stadium (2006).
Team Colors: Red and white.

Player Representative: Kyle McClellan.
Home Dugout: First Base.
Playing Surface: Grass.

Director, Ticket Development: Derek Thornburg. Manager, Premium Ticket Sales: Delores Scanlon. Manager, Season Ticket Sales/Services: Jamie Brickler. Manager, Ticket Technology: Jennifer Needham. Manager, All-Inclusive Tickets: Mary Clare Bena. Director, Fan Development/Alumni Relations: Martin Coco. Receptionist: Marilyn Mathews.

Travel, Clubhouse
Fax: (314) 345-9523.
Traveling Secretary: C.J. Cherre. Equipment Manager: Rip Rowan. Assistant Equipment Manager: Ernie Moore. Visiting Clubhouse Manger: Jerry Risch. Video Coordinator: Chad Blair.

BASEBALL OPERATIONS
Fax: (314) 345-9599.
VP, General Manager: John Mozeliak.
Assistant GM: Mike Girsch. Executive Assistant: Linda Brauer. Special Assistants to GM: Gary LaRocque, Mike Jorgensen, Matt Slater. Director, Major League Administration: Judy Carpenter-Barada. Director, International Operations: Moises Rodriguez. Director, Amateur Draft Analysis: Sig Mejdal. Manager, Amateur Scouting: Mike Elias. Manager, Baseball Information: Jeremy Cohen. Quantitative Analyst: Chris Correa. Baseball Operations Assistant: Tony Ferreira.

John Mozeliak

Player Development
Fax: (314) 345-9519.
VP, Amateur Scouting/Player Development: Jeff Luhnow. Farm Director: John Vuch. Minor League Field Coordinator: Mark DeJohn. Coordinators: Dyar Miller (pitching), Brent Strom (pitching instruction), Dann Bilardello (roving catching), Derrick May (hitting), Andrew McNally (minor league rehab), Rene Pena (strength/conditioning).
Minor League Equipment Manager: Buddy Bates.

Major League Staff
Telephone: (314) 345-9600.
Manager: Tony La Russa.
Coaches: Bench—Joe Pettini; Pitching—Dave Duncan; Batting—Mark McGwire; First Base—Dave McKay; Third Base—Jose Oquendo; Bullpen—Derek Lilliquist. Hitting Instructor: Mike Aldrete.

Medical/Training
Medical Advisor: Dr. George Paletta. Head Trainer: Greg Hauck. Assistant Trainer: Barry Weinberg. Assistant Trainer/Rehabilitation Coordinator: Adam Olsen.

Farm System

Class	Club (League)	Manager	Hitting Coach	Pitching Coach
Triple-A	Memphis (PCL)	Chris Maloney	Mark Budaska	Blaise Ilsley
Double-A	Springfield (TL)	Ron Warner	Phillip Wellman	Bryan Eversgerd
High A	Palm Beach (FSL)	Luis Aguayo	Jeff Albert	Dennis Martinez
Low A	Quad Cities (MWL)	Johnny Rodriquez	Joe Kruzel	Tim Leveque
Short-season	Batavia (NYP)	Dann Bilardello	Roger LaFrancois	Arthur Adams
Rookie	Johnson City (APP)	Mike Shildt	Ramon Ortiz	Doug White
Rookie	Cardinals (GCL)	Steve Turco	Oliver Marmol	Dernier Orozco
Rookie	Cardinals (DSL)	Claudio Almonte	Rene Rojas	Bill Villanueva
Rookie	Cardinals (VSL)	Unavailable	Unavailable	Unavailable

Scouting
Fax: (314) 345-9525.
Professional Scouts: Bruce Benedict (Atlanta, GA), Alan Benes (Town & Country, MO), Chuck Fick (Newbury Park, CA), Bill Gayton (San Diego, CA), Mike Jorgensen (Fenton, MO), Mike Juhl (Indian Trail, NC), Marty Keough (Scottsdale, AZ), Gary LaRocque (Greensboro, NC), Deric McKamey (Bluffton, OH), Joe Rigoli (Parsippany, NJ), Matt Slater (St. Louis, MO).
Crosscheckers: Joe Almaraz (San Antonio, TX), Mike Roberts (Hot Springs, AR), Roger Smith (Eastman, GA).
Area Supervisors: Matt Blood (Durham, NC), Nicholas Brannon (Newberry, SC), Jay Catalano (Joelton, TN), Mike Elias (Oakton, VA), Rob Fidler (Atlanta, GA), Ralph Garr, Jr. (Houston, TX), Charlie Gonzalez (Weston, FL), Kris Gross (Chicago, IL), Brian Hopkins (Brunswick, OH), Jeff Ishii (Chino, CA), Aaron Krawiec (Gilbert, AZ), Aaron Looper (Shawnee, OK), Sean Moran (Levittown, PA), Jamal Strong (Victorville, CA), Matt Swanson (Ripon, CA).
Part-Time Scouts: Alec Adame (Los Angeles, CA), Vince Bailey (Renton, WA), Manny Guerra (Las Vegas, NV), Jimmy Matthews (Athens, GA), Sam Pepper (So. Cal.), Juan Ramos (Carolina, Puerto Rico), John Ramirez (Springfield, MA).
Director, International Operations: Moises Rodriguez. Latin American Supervisor: Juan Mercado. Administrator. Administrator, Dominican Republic Operations: Aaron Rodriguez.
International Scouts: Domingo Garcia (Dominican Republic), Jose Gregorio Gonzalez (Venezuela), Carlos Heron (Panama), Carlos Lugo (Dominican Republic), Rene Rojas (Dominican Republic), Crysthiam Blanco (Nicaragua), Fermin Coronel (Curacao).

San Diego Padres

Office Address: PETCO Park, 100 Park Blvd, San Diego, CA 92101.
Mailing Address: P.O. Box 122000, San Diego, CA 92112.
Telephone: (619) 795-5000.
E-mail address: comments@padres.com. **Website:** www.padres.com.

Ownership
Operated By: Padres LP.
Chairman: John Moores. **Vice Chairmen/CEO:** Jeff Moorad.
President/COO: Tom Garfinkel.

BUSINESS OPERATIONS
Senior VP/General Counsel: Erik Greupner. **Executive VP/Senior Advisor:** Dave Winfield.
VP, Strategy/Business Analysis: John Abbamondi.

Finance/Administration/Information Technology
Executive VP/CFO: Fred Gerson. **VP, Information Technology:** John Winborn. **Controller/ Director, Finance:** Beth Bransford. **Executive Director, Human Resources:** Tamara Furman.

Media Relations/Community Relations
Telephone: (619) 795-5265. **Fax:** (619) 795-5266.
Director, Communications: Warren Miller. **Manager, Media Relations:** Bret Picciolo. **Manager, Communications:** Shana Wilson. **Assistant, Media Relations:** Josh Ishoo.
Director, Community Affairs/Padres Foundation: Sue Botos. **Manager, Community Affairs/Padres Foundation:** Nhu Tran.

Jeff Moorad

Brand Development/Entertainment/Partnerships/Marketing
Senior VP, Brand Development: Laura Broderick. **VP, Corporate Partnerships:** Tyler Epp. **VP, Creative Partnerships:** Dan Migala. **Director, Entertainment/Production:** Erik Meyer.
Manager, Marketing/Creative Services: Danny Palomino. **Coordinator, Advertising/Promotions:** Harrison Boyd.

Stadium Operations
Senior VP, Ballpark Operations: Brent Stehlik.
VP, Ballpark Operations: Mark Guglielmo. **VP, Non-Baseball Events:** Jeremy Horowitz.
Director, Event Operations: Ken Kawachi. **Director, Field/Landscape Maintenance:** Luke Yoder. **Director, Guest Services:** Kameron Durham. **PA Announcer:** Frank Anthony. **Official Scorers:** Bill Zavestoski, Jack Murray.

Ticketing
Telephone: (619) 795-5500. **Fax:** (619) 795-5034.
VP, Ticket Sales/Service: Jarrod Dillon.
Executive Director, Ticket Operations: Jim Kiersnowski. **Director, Season Ticket Sales:** Jonathan Tillman. **Director, Group Ticket Sales:** Amy Saxon.

2011 SCHEDULE
Standard Game Times: 7:05 p.m.; Sun. 1:05

MARCH			
31 . . . . .at St. Louis	6-8. . . . . .Arizona	20-22 . . . . .at Boston	8-11 . . . . at New York (NL)
APRIL	9-11 . . . . . at Milwaukee	24-26 . . . . Atlanta	12-14 . . . . . .at Cincinnati
2-3. . . . . .at St. Louis	13-15 . . . . . at Colorado	27-29 . . . . . Kansas City	15-17 . . . . .New York (NL)
5-6. . . . . .San Francisco	16-17 . . . . . . at Arizona		18-21 . . . . Florida
8-10 . . . . Los Angeles (NL)	18-19 . . . . . .Milwaukee	**JULY**	23-24 . . . at San Francisco
11-13 . . . . . . Cincinnati	20-22 . . . . Seattle	1-3. . . . . .at Seattle	26-28 . . . . at Arizona
14-17 . . . . . .at Houston	23-25 . . . . St. Louis	4-7. . . . at San Francisco	29-31 . at Los Angeles (NL)
18-20 . . .at Chicago (NL)	27-29 . . . . at Washington	8-10 . . at Los Angeles (NL)	
21-24 . . . . .Philadelphia	30-31 . . . . at Atlanta	14-17 . . . . .San Francisco	**SEPTEMBER**
25-27 . . . . Atlanta		19-21 . . . . . . .at Florida	2-4. . . . . .Colorado
29-30 . at Los Angeles (NL)	**JUNE**	22-25 . . . .at Philadelphia	5-7. . . . .San Francisco
	1 . . . . at Atlanta	26-28 . . . . . . .Arizona	8-11 . . . . . . .at Arizona
MAY	2-5. . . . . Houston	29-31 . . . . . . .Colorado	12-14 . . . at San Francisco
1 . . . . at Los Angeles (NL)	6-8. . . . . .Colorado		16-18 . . . . .Arizona
2-4. . . . . Pittsburgh	9-12 . . . . . .Washington	**AUGUST**	19-21 . . . . . at Colorado
	13-15 . . . . . at Colorado	1-3. . . . .Los Angeles (NL)	23-25 . . .Los Angeles (NL)
	17-19 . . . . . at Minnesota	5-7. . . . . . . at Pittsburgh	26-28 . . . . . Chicago (NL)

GENERAL INFORMATION
Stadium (year opened): Petco Park (2004).
Team Colors: Blue, white & Padres Sand

Player Representative: Heath Bell
Home Dugout: First Base.
Playing Surface: Grass.

Manager, Group Ticket Sales: Ryan Ross. **Manager, Inside Sales:** Robert Davis. **Director, Ticket Customer Services:** Laura Evans.

Travel, Clubhouse
 Director, Team Travel/Equipment Manager: Brian Prilaman. **Assistant Clubhouse Manager:** Tony Petricca. **Assistant to the Equipment Manager:** Spencer Dallin. **Visiting Clubhouse Manager:** David Bacharach.

BASEBALL OPERATIONS
 Telephone: (619) 795-5076. **Fax:** (619) 795-5361.
 Executive VP/General Manager: Jed Hoyer.
 Senior VP, Baseball Operations: Josh Byrnes. **VP/Assistant GM, Player Development/ Scouting:** Jason Mcleod. **VP/Assistant GM:** Fred Uhlman Jr. **VP, Pro Scouting:** AJ Hinch. **Special Assistant to GM:** Scott Bream. **Special Assistants to Baseball Operations:** Brad Ausmus, Mark Loretta. **Director, Baseball Operations:** Josh Stein. **Director, Player Personnel:** Chris Gwynn. **Director, Travel:** Brian Prilaman. **Assistant to the Director, Baseball Operations:** Alex Slater. **Developer, Baseball Operations:** Wells Oliver. **SR Quantitative Analyst:** Chris Long. **Video Coordinator, Clubhouse:** Mike Tompkins. **Executive Assistant to GM:** Julie Myers.

Jed Hoyer

Major League Staff
 Manager: Bud Black.
 Coaches: Bench—Rick Renteria; Pitching—Darren Balsley; Hitting—Randy Ready; First Base—Dave Roberts; Third Base—Glenn Hoffman; Bullpen—Darrel Akerfelds.

Medical/Training
 Club Physician: Scripps Clinic Medical Staff.
 Head Athletic Trainer: Todd Hutcheson. **Assistant Athletic Trainer:** Paul Navarro. **Strength/Conditioning Coach:** Jim Malone.

Player Development
 Telephone: (619) 795-5343. **Fax:** (619) 795-5036.
 VP, Scouting/Player Development: Jason McLeod.
 Director, Player Development/International Scouting: Randy Smith.
 Coordinator, Latin American Operations: Juan Lara. **Administrator, Dominican Republic Operations:** Cesar Rizik. **Manager, Minor Leagues:** Ilana Miller. **Roving Instructors:** Mike Couchee (pitching), Sean Berry (hitting), Randy Johnson (field coordinator), Glen Barker (outfield/baserunning) Gary Jones (infield), Jo Jo Tarantino (trainer coordinator), Dan Morrison (strength/conditioning), Ryan Bitzel (rehab).

Farm System

Class	Farm Club (League)	Manager	Coach	Pitching Coach
Triple-A	Tucson (PCL)	Terry Kennedy	Bob Skube	Steve Webber
Double-A	San Antonio (TL)	Doug Dascenzo	Tom Tornincasa	Jimmy Jones
High A	Lake Elsinore (CAL)	Carlos Leczano	Phil Plantier	Bronswell Patrick
Low A	Ft Wayne (MWL)	Shawn Wooten	Kory DeHaan	Willie Blair
Short-season	Eugene (NWL)	Pat Murphy	Chris Prieto	Dave Rajsich
Rookie	Padres (AZL)	Jim Gabella	Ivan Cruz	Nelson Cruz/Tim Worrell
Rookie	Padres (DSL)	Carlos Hernandez	Jose Mateo/Juan Rosario	Jose Amancio/Christian Reyes

Scouting
 Telephone: (619) 795-5362. **Fax:** (619) 795-5036.
 Director, Amateur Scouting: Jaron Madison.
 Director, Player Development/International Scouting: Randy Smith. **Assistant to the Director, Amateur Scouting:** Sam Ray.
 Major League Scouts: Ray Crone (Waxahachie, TX).
 Professional Scouts: John Vander Wal (Grand Rapids, MI), Van Smith (Belleville, IL), Joe Bochy (Plant City, FL), Jim Elliot (Winston Salem, NC), Al Hargesheimer (Arlington Heights, IL), Chris Young (Grand Rapids, MI). **Advance Scouts:** Scott Lonergan, Greg Olsen. **Special Assignment Scout:** Carmen Fusco (Mechanicsburg, PA), Kevin Jarvis (Franklin, TN). **National Supervisor:** Bob Filotei (Mobile, AL), Billy Gasparino (Venice, CA).
 Regional Supervisors: Pete DeYoung (La Jolla, CA), Tim Holt (Allen, TX), Chip Lawrence (Palmetto, FL), Sean Campbell (Franklin, TN).
 Amateur Scouts: Justin Baughman (Portland, OR), Willie Bosque (Winter Garden, FL), Adam Bourassa (Winston Salem, NC), Jim Bretz (South Windsor, CT), Mark Conner (Hendersonville, TN), Jeff Curtis (Arlington, TX), Lane Decker (Piedmont, OK), Kevin Ellis (Katy, TX), Josh Emmerick (Oceanside, CA), David Francia (Dickinson, AL), Noah Jackson (Mill Valley, CA), Dave Lottsfeldt (Castle Rock, CO), Brent Mayne (Costa Mesa, CA), Shane Monahan (Acworth, GA), Andrew Salvo (Manassas, VA), Jeff Stewart (Normal, IL). **Part-Time Scouts:** Robert Gutierrez (Carol City, FL), Hank Krause (Akron, IA), Willie Ronda (Las Lomas Rio Piedras, Puerto Rico), Cam Walker (Centerville, IA), Murray Zuk (Souris, Manitoba).
 Manager, Minor Leagues: Ilana Miller. **Coordinator, Latin American Scouting:** Felix Feliz. **Coordinator, Pacific Rim:** Trevor Schumm. **Supervisor, Venezuela:** Yfrain Linares. **Supervisor, Central America/Mexico:** Robert Rowley.
 International Scouts: Antonio Alejos (Venezuela), Milton Croes (Aruba), Marcial Del Valle (Colombia), Emenegildo Diaz (Dominican Republic), Elvin Jarquin (Nicaragua), Mayron Isenia (Curacao), Martin Jose (Dominican Republic), Victor Magdaleno (Venezuela), Ricardo Montenegro (Panama), Luis Prieto (Venezuela), Ysrael Rojas (Dominican Republic), Jose Salado (Dominican Republic).

San Francisco Giants

Office Address: AT&T Park, 24 Willie Mays Plaza, San Francisco, CA 94107.
Telephone: (415) 972-2000. **Fax:** (415) 947-2800. **Website:** sfgiants.com, sfgigantes.com.

Ownership
Operated by: San Francisco Baseball Associates L.P.
Chief Executive Officer: William H. Neukom. **Special Assistant:** Willie Mays. **Senior Advisor:** Willie McCovey.

BUSINESS OPERATIONS
President/Chief Operating Officer: Laurence M. Baer. **Senior VP/General Counsel:** Jack F. Bair. **Chief People Officer:** Leilani Gayles.

Finance
SVP/Chief Financial Officer: John F. Yee. **Senior VP/Chief Information Officer:** Bill Schlough. **Senior Director, Information Technology:** Ken Logan. **Senior VP, Facilities:** Alfonso G. Felder. **VP, Finance:** Lisa Pantages.

Marketing/Sales
Senior VP, Corporate Marketing: Mario Alioto. **VP, Corporate Sponsorship:** Jason Pearl. **Director, Special Events:** Valerie McGuire. **Senior VP, Consumer Marketing:** Tom McDonald. **Senior Director, Marketing/Entertainment:** Chris Gargano. **VP, Client Relations:** Annemarie Hastings. **VP, Sales:** Jeff Tucker. **Manager, Season Ticket Sales:** Craig Solomon. **General Manager, Retail:** Dave Martinez. **Director, Retail Operations:** Bonnie MacInnes.

Bill Neukom

Media Relations/Community Relations
Telephone: (415) 972-2445. **Fax:** (415) 947-2800.
Senior VP, Communications: Staci Slaughter. **Senior Director, Broadcast Services:** Maria Jacinto. **Senior Director, Media Relations:** Jim Moorehead. **Media Relations Manager:** Matt Chisholm. **Hispanic Media Relations Coordinator/Spanish Language Broadcaster:** Erwin Higueros. **Media Relations Assistant:** Eric Smith. **Vice President, Print Publications/Creative Services:** Nancy Donati. **Senior Director, Public Affairs/Community Relations:** Shana Daum. **Director, Photography/Archives:** Missy Mikulecky.

Ballpark Operations
Senior VP, Ballpark Operations: Jorge Costa. **VP, Guest Services:** Rick Mears. **Senior Director, Ballpark Operations:** Gene Telucci. **Senior Director, Security:** Tinie Roberson. **Head Groundskeeper:** Greg Elliott. **PA Announcer:** Renel Brooks-Moon. **Official Scorers:** Chuck Dybdal, Art Santo Domingo, Michael Duca, Dave Feldman.

Ticketing
Telephone: (415) 972-2000. **Fax:** (415) 972-2500.
Managing VP, Ticket Services/Client Relations: Russ Stanley. **Director, Ticket Services:** Devin Lutes. **Senior Ticket Accounting Manager:** Kem Easley. **Senior Ticket Operations Manager:** Anita Sprinkles. **Senior Box Office Manager:** Todd Pierce.

2011 SCHEDULE
Standard Game Times: 7:15 p.m.; Sun. 1:05

MARCH	6-8 . . . . .Colorado	21-23 . . . . . .Minnesota	8-10 . . . . . . .Pittsburgh
31 . . . at Los Angeles (NL)	10-12 . . . . .Arizona	24-26 . . . . . . .Cleveland	12-14 . . . . . . .at Florida
APRIL	13-15 . . . .at Chicago (NL)	28-30 . . . .at Chicago (NL)	15-18 . . . . at Atlanta
1-3. . . at Los Angeles (NL)	16-17 . . . . at Colorado	**JULY**	19-21 . . . . .at Houston
5-6. . . . . . . at San Diego	18-19 . at Los Angeles (NL)	1-3. . . . . .at Detroit	23-24 . . . . San Diego
8-10. . . . . St. Louis	20-22 . . . . Oakland	4-7. . . . . San Diego	25-28 . . . . Houston
11-13 . . . Los Angeles (NL)	24-26 . . . . Florida	8-10 . . . . .New York (NL)	29-31 . . . . . Chicago (NL)
15-17 . . . . . at Arizona	27-29 . . . . . at Milwaukee	14-17 . . . . at San Diego	**SEPTEMBER**
18-20 . . . . . at Colorado	30-31 . . . . . .at St. Louis	18-20 . . . Los Angeles (NL)	2-4. . . . . .Arizona
22-24 . . . . Atlanta	**JUNE**	22-24 . . . . . .Milwaukee	5-7. . . . . . at San Diego
26-28 . . . at Pittsburgh	1-2. . . . . . . .at St. Louis	26-28 . . . . at Philadelphia	9-11 . . . .Los Angeles (NL)
29-30 . . . . at Washington	3-5. . . . . .Colorado	29-31 . . . .at Cincinnati	12-14 . . . . . San Diego
	6-8. . . . . . . .Washington		15-18 . . . . . at Colorado
MAY	9-12 . . . . Cincinnati	**AUGUST**	20-22 . at Los Angeles (NL)
1-2. . . . . . at Washington	14-16 . . . . . at Arizona	1-3. . . . . .Arizona	23-25 . . . . . at Arizona
3-5. . . . .at New York (NL)	17-19 . . . . . .at Oakland	4-7. . . . . . . .Philadelphia	26-28 . . . . . . .Colorado

GENERAL INFORMATION
Stadium (year opened): AT&T Park (2000). **Home Dugout:** Third Base.
Team Colors: Black, orange and cream. **Playing Surface:** Grass.
Player Representative: Matt Cain.

Travel/Clubhouse
Coordinator, Team Travel: Michael King. **Coordinator, Organizational Travel:** Mike Scardino. **Giants Equipment Manager:** Miguel Murphy. **Visitors Clubhouse Manager:** Harvey Hodgerney. **Assistant Equipment Manager:** Ron Garcia.

BASEBALL OPERATIONS
Telephone: (415) 972-1922. **Fax:** (415) 947-2929.
Senior VP/General Manager: Brian R. Sabean.
VP, Player Personnel: Dick Tidrow. **VP, Baseball Operations:** Bobby Evans.
Special Assistant to the GM: Felipe Alou. **Special Assistant to the GM, Scouting:** John Barr.
Senior Advisor, Baseball Operations: Tony Siegle. **Senior Director, Baseball Operations/ Pro Scouting:** Jeremy Shelley. **Director, Minor League Operations/Quantitative Analysis:** Yeshayah Goldfarb. **Executive Assistant to the GM:** Karen Sweeney. **Coordinator, Video Operations:** Danny Martin.

Brian Sabean

Major League Staff
Manager: Bruce Bochy.
Coaches: Bench—Ron Wotus; Pitching—Dave Righetti; Hitting—Hensley Meulens; First Base—Roberto Kelly; Third Base—Tim Flannery; Bullpen—Mark Gardner, Bill Hayes.

Medical Training
Team Physicians: Dr. Robert Murray, Dr. Ken Akizuki, Dr. Anthony Saglimbeni.
Head Trainer: Dave Groeschner. **Assistant Trainers:** Mark Gruesbeck, Ben Potenziano.
Coordinator, Medical Administration: Chrissy Yuen.

Player Development
Director, Player Development: Fred Stanley.
Senior Consultant, Player Personnel: Jack Hiatt. **Special Assistants:** Joe Amalfitano, Jim Davenport. **Coordinator, Player Personnel Administration:** Clara Ho. **Minor League Operations Assistant:** Eric Flemming. **Director, Arizona Minor League Operations:** Alan Lee. **Arizona Minor League Operations Assistant:** Gabriel Alvarez. **Coordinator, Minor League Instruction:** Shane Turner. **Coordinator, Minor League Pitching:** Bert Bradley. **Coordinator, Minor League Hitting:** Bob Mariano. **Minor League Roving Instructors:** Lee Smith (pitching), Jose Alguacil (infield), Henry Cotto (baserunning/outfield), Kirt Manwaring (catching).

Farm System

Class	Farm Club (League)	Manager	Coach	Pitching Coach
Triple-A	Fresno (PCL)	Steve Decker	Russ Morman	Pat Rice
Double-A	Richmond (EL)	Dave Machemer	Ken Joyce	Ross Grimsley
High A	San Jose (CAL)	Andy Skeels	Gary Davenport	Brian Cooper
Low A	Augusta (SAL)	Lipso Nava	Jose Flores	Steve Kline
Short-season	Salem-Keizer (NWL)	Tom Trebelhorn	Ricky Ward	Jerry Cram
Rookie	Giants (AZL)	Mike Goff	Victor Torres	Marcos Garcia
Rookie	Giants (DSL)	Jesus Tavarez	Carlos Valderrama	Marcos Aguasvivas

Scouting
Telephone: (415) 972-2360. **Fax:** (415) 947-2929.
Special Assistant to GM, Scouting: John Barr (Haddonfield, NJ).
Senior Advisors, Scouting: Ed Creech (Moultrie, GA), Joe Lefebvre (Hookset, NH), Matt Nerland (Clayton, CA), Paul Turco Sr. (Sarasota, FL). **Coordinator, Amateur Scouting:** Doug Mapson (Chandler, AZ). **Scouting Assistant:** Adam Nieting.
Special Assignment Scout: Lee Elder (Evans, GA), Tom Korenek (Houston, TX), Darren Wittcke (Gresham, OR).
Major League Scouts: Steve Balboni (Murray Hill, NJ), Brian Johnson (Detroit, MI), Michael Kendall (Rancho Palos Verde, CA), Stan Saleski (Dayton, OH), Rudy Santin (Miami, FL), Tom Zimmer (Seminole, FL).
Senior Consultants, Scouting: Dick Cole (Costa Mesa, CA), Bo Osborne (Woodstock, CA). **Independent League:** Harry Stavrenos (Soquel, CA).
Supervisors: Northeast—John Castleberry (High Point, NC); Midwest—Arnold Brathwaite (Grand Prairie, TX); Southeast—Paul Turco, Jr. (Tampa, FL), West—Joe Strain (Englewood, CO).
Territorial Scouts: Northeast Region—Ray Callari (Cote St. Luc, Quebec), Kevin Christman (Noblesville, IN), John DiCarlo (Glenwood, NJ), Jeremy Cleveland (Oakton, VA), Glenn Tufts (Bridgewater, MA). Midwest Region—Lou Colletti (Elk Grove Village, IL), Daniel Murray (Prairie Village, KS), Todd Thomas (Dallas, TX), Hugh Walker (Jonesboro, AR). Southeast Region—Andrew Jefferson (Atlanta, GA), Ronnie Merrill (Tampa, FL), Mike Metcalf (Lakeland, FL). West Region—Brad Cameron (Los Alamitos, CA), Chuck Hensley (Erie, CO), Keith Snider (Stockton, CA), Matt Woodward (Vancouver, WA).
Part-Time Scouts: Bob Barth (Williamstown, NJ), Jim Chapman (Langley, BC), Felix Negron (Bayamon, PR), Tim Rock (Orlando, FL).
Director, Dominican Operations: Pablo Peguero. **Latin America Crosschecker:** Joe Salermo (Hallandale Beach, FL). **Venezuela Supervisor:** Ciro Villalobos. **Dominican Republic Scouting Coordinator:** Felix Peguero. **Coordinator, Pacific Rim Scouting:** John Cox. **Coordinator, Japan Operations:** Shun Kakazu.
International Scouts: Mateo Alou (Dominican Republic), Jonathan Arraiz (Venezuela), Jonathan Bautista (Dominican Republic), Phillip Elhage (Curacao/Bonaire/Aruba), Felix Fermin (Dominican Republic), Edgar Fernandez (Venezuela), Ricardo Heron (Panama), Juan Marquez (Venezuela), Sebastian Martinez (Venezuela), Daniel Mavarez (Colombia), Sandy Moreno (Nicaragua), Jim Patterson (Australia), Luis Pena (Mexico), Jesus Stephens (Dominican Republic).

Seattle Mariners

Office Address: 1250 First Avenue South, Seattle, WA 98134.
Mailing Address: P.O. Box 4100, Seattle, WA 98194.
Telephone: (206) 346-4000. **Fax:** (206) 346-4400.
Website: www.mariners.com.

Ownership

Board of Directors: Minoru Arakawa, John Ellis, Chris Larson, Howard Lincoln, Wayne Perry, Frank Shrontz.
Chair/CEO: Howard Lincoln.
President/Chief Operating Officer: Chuck Armstrong.

BUSINESS OPERATIONS

Chuck Armstrong

Finance

Executive Vice President, Finance/Ballpark Operations: Kevin Mather. **VP, Finance:** Tim Kornegay. **Controller:** Greg Massey. **VP, Human Resources:** Marianne Short.

Marketing, Sales

Executive VP, Business/Operations: Bob Aylward. **VP, Corporate Business/Community Relations:** Joe Chard. **Director, Corporate Business:** Ingrid Russell-Narcisse. **VP, Marketing:** Kevin Martinez. **Director, Marketing:** Gregg Greene. **Senior Director, Merchandise:** Jim La Shell.

VP, Sales: Frances Traisman. **Director, Group/Season Ticket Sales:** Bob Hellinger. **Director, Private Suite Sales:** Steve Camp. **Suite Sales:** Moose Clausen, Jill Dahlen.

Baseball Information/Communications

Telephone: (206) 346-4000. **Fax:** (206) 346-4400.
VP, Communications: Randy Adamack.
Director, Baseball Information: Tim Hevly. **Manager, Baseball Information:** Jeff Evans. **Coordinator, Baseball Information:** Kelly Munro. **Coordinator, Baseball Information:** Fernando Alcala.
Director, Public Information: Rebecca Hale. **Director, Graphic Design:** Carl Morton. **Director, Community Relations:** Gina Hasson. **Manager, Community Programs:** Sean Grindley.

Ticketing

Telephone: (206) 346-4001. **Fax:** (206) 346-4100.
Director, Ticketing/Parking Operations: Malcolm Rogel. **Director, Ticket Services:** Jennifer Sweigert. **Manager, Group/Suite Ticket Services:** Steve Belling. **Manager, Box Office:** Malcolm Rogel.

Stadium Operations

VP, Ballpark Operations: Scott Jenkins. **Senior Director, Safeco Field Operations:** Tony Pereira. **Director, Security:** Sly Servance. **Director, Events:** Jill Hashimoto.

2011 SCHEDULE

Standard Game Times: 7:10 p.m.; Sun. 1:10.

APRIL
1-3 . . . . .at Oakland
4-6 . . . . .at Texas
8-10 . . . . Cleveland
11-13 . . . . .Toronto
14-17 . . . .at Kansas City
18-20 . . . . Detroit
21-24 . . . . Oakland
26-28 . . . . . . .at Detroit
29-30 . . . . . . .at Boston

MAY
1 . . . . .at Boston
3-5 . . . . Texas
6-8 . . . . . . Chicago (AL)
10-12 . . . . .at Baltimore

13-15 . . . . .at Cleveland
16-17 . . . . . . .Minnesota
18-19 . . Los Angeles (AL)
20-22 . . . . at San Diego
23-25 . . . . at Minnesota
27-29 . . . .New York (AL)
30-31 . . . . . . Baltimore

JUNE
1 . . . . Baltimore
2-5 . . . . .Tampa Bay
6-8 . . . . .at Chicago (AL)
9-12 . . . . .at Detroit
13-15 . . Los Angeles (AL)
17-19 . . . . .Philadelphia
21-23 . . . . at Washington
24-26 . . . . .at Florida

27-29 . . . . Atlanta

JULY
1-3 . . . . San Diego
4-6 . . . . .at Oakland
7-10 . . at Los Angeles (AL)
14-17 . . . . Texas
19-21 . . . . . . at Toronto
22-24 . . . . . . .at Boston
25-27 . . . at New York (AL)
29-31 . . . . . . .Tampa Bay

AUGUST
1-3 . . . . Oakland
5-7 . . . at Los Angeles (AL)
8-10 . . . . .at Texas
12-14 . . . . Boston

15-17 . . . . .Toronto
19-21 . . . . at Tampa Bay
22-24 . . . . .at Cleveland
26-28 . . . . Chicago (AL)
29-31 . . . Los Angeles (AL)

SEPTEMBER
1 . . . . . . Los Angeles (AL)
2-4 . . . . .at Oakland
5-7 . . . at Los Angeles (AL)
8-11 . . . . Kansas City
12-14 . . . . .New York (AL)
16-18 . . . . Texas
20-22 . . . . . at Minnesota
23-25 . . . . .at Texas
26-28 . . . . Oakland

GENERAL INFORMATION

Stadium (year opened): Safeco Field (1999).
Team Colors: Northwest green, silver and navy blue.

Player Representative: Unavailable.
Home Dugout: First Base.
Playing Surface: Grass.

VP, Information Services: Dave Curry. **Director, PBX/Retail Systems:** Oliver Roy. **Director, Procurement:** Sandy Fielder.

Head Groundskeeper: Bob Christofferson. **Assistant Head Groundskeepers:** Tim Wilson, Leo Liebert. **PA Announcer:** Tom Hutyler. **Official Scorer:** Eric Radovich.

Travel, Clubhouse
Director, Team Travel: Ron Spellecy.
Clubhouse Manager: Ted Walsh. **Visiting Clubhouse Manager:** Henry Genzale. **Video Coordinator:** Carl Hamilton.

BASEBALL OPERATIONS
Executive VP/General Manager: Jack Zduriencik.
Assistant GM: Jeff Kingston. **Special Assistants:** Tony Blengino, John Boles, Ken Madeja. **Administrator, Baseball Operations:** Debbie Larsen.

Major League Staff
Manager: Eric Wedge.
Coaches: Bench—Robby Thompson; Pitching—Carl Willis; Batting—Chris Chambliss; First Base—Mike Brumley; Third Base—Jeff Datz; Bullpen—Jaime Navarro.

Medical, Training
Medical Director: Dr. Edward Khalfayan. **Club Physician:** Dr. Mitchel Storey. **Head Trainer:** Rick Griffin. **Assistant Trainers:** Rob Nodine, Takayoshi Morimoto. **Stength/Conditioning:** Allen Wirtala.

Jack Zduriencik

Player Development
Telephone: (206) 346-4316. **Fax:** (206) 346-4300.
Director, Minor League Operations: Pedro Grifol. **Director, Minor League/International Administration:** Hide Sueyoshi. **Administrator, Minor League Operations:** Jan Plein. **Assistant, Minor League Operations:** Casey Brett. **Coordinator, Minor League Instruction:** Andy Stankiewicz. **Supervisor, Athletic Training:** Chris Gorosics. **Coordinator, Rehab/Athletic Training:** Sean McQueeney. **Roving Instructors:** James Clifford/Danny Garcia (strength/conditioning), Darrin Garner (infield/baserunning), Roger Hansen (catching), Jose Castro/Rick Down (hitting), Rick Waits (pitching), John Tamargo (Latin America field coordinator), Nasusel Cabrera (Latin America pitching coordinator).

Farm System

Class	Club (League)	Manager	Coach	Pitching Coach
Triple-A	Tacoma (PCL)	Daren Brown	Alonzo Powell	Dwight Bernard
Double-A	Jackson (SL)	Jim Pankovits	Cory Snyder	Lance Painter
High A	High Desert (CAL)	Jose Moreno	Tommy Cruz	Tom Dettore
Low A	Clinton (MWL)	Eddie Menchaca	Terry Pollreisz	Rich Dorman
Short-season	Everett (NWL)	Scott Steinmann	Mike Kinkade	Andrew Lorraine
Rookie	Pulaski (APP)	Rob Mummau	Rafael Santo Domingo	Nasusel Cabrera
Rookie	Peoria (AZL)	Jesus Azuaje	A.Bottin/B.Johnson	Gary Wheelock
Rookie	Mariners (DSL)	Francisco Gerez	J.Guerrero/M.Pimentel	Danielin Acevedo
Rookie	Mariners (VSL)	Russell Vasquez	W.Oropeza/J.Umbria	Carlos Hernandez

Scouting
Telephone: (206) 346-4000. **Fax:** (206) 346-4300.
Director, Amateur Scouting: Tom McNamara. **Director. Scouting Administrator:** Hallie Larson.
Major League Scouts: John Boles (West Melbourne, FL), Bob Harrison (Long Beach, CA), Jordan Horne (Cincinnati, OH), Greg Hunter (Seattle, WA), Steve Jongewaard (Napa, CA), Bill Kearns (Milton, MA), John McMichen (Treasure Island, FL), Ken Madeja (Novi, MI), Bill Masse (Manchester, CT), Frank Mattox (Peoria, AZ), Joe Nigro (Staten Island, NY), Steve Pope (Asheville, NC), Duane Shaffer (Anaheim, CA), John Stearns (Port St. Lucie, FL), Woody Woodward (Palm Coast, FL).
National Crosschecker: Mike Cadahia (Miami Springs, FL).
Territorial Supervisors: West—Butch Baccala (Weimar, CA), North East—Alex Smith (Abingdon, MD), Southeast—Sean O'Connor (Cartersville, GA), Midwest—Mark Lummus (Cleburne,TX).
Area Supervisors: Dave Alexander (Lafayette, IN), Garrett Ball (Sandy Springs, GA), Jesse Kapellusch (Hays, KS), Devitt Moore (Gulfport, MS), Mike Moriarty (Edison, NJ), Rob Mummau (Stephens City, VA), Brian Nichols (Taunton, MA), Chris Pelekoudas (Goodyear, AZ), Stacey Pettis (Antioch, CA), John Ramey (Wildomar, CA), Alvin Rittman (Memphis, TN), Joe Ross (Kirkland, WA), Tony Russo (Fayetteville, NC), Noel Sevilla (Sunrise, FL), Bob Steinkamp (Beatrice, NE), Kyle Van Hook (Brenham, TX), Greg Whitworth (Los Angeles, CA), Brian Williams (Cincinnati, OH).
VP, International Operations: Bob Engle (Tampa, FL).
Coordinator, Special Projects International: Ted Heid (Glendale, AZ). **Special Assignment International:** Eugene Grimaldi (Paris, France). **Coordinator, Canada/Europe:** Wayne Norton (Port Moody, British Columbia). **Coordinator, Latin America:** Patrick Guerrero (Dominican Republic). **Administrative Director, Dominican Operations:** Martin Valerio. **Coordinator, Venezuelan Operations:** Emilio Carrasquel (Barquisimeto, Venezuela). Jamey Storvick (Taiwan), Pat Kelly (Australia), Luis Molina (Panama), Franklin Taveras, Jr. (Dominican Republic), Yasushi Yamamoto (Japan).

Tampa Bay Rays

Office Address: Tropicana Field, One Tropicana Drive, St. Petersburg, FL 33705.
Telephone: (727) 825-3137. **Fax:** (727) 825-3111. **Website:** www.raysbaseball.com.

Ownership
Principal Owner: Stuart Sternberg. **President:** Matt Silverman.

BUSINESS OPERATIONS
Senior Vice President, Administration/General Counsel: John Higgins. **Senior VP, Business Operations:** Brian Auld. **Senior VP/Chief Sales Officer:** Mark Fernandez. **Senior VP, Development/Business Affairs:** Michael Kalt. **VP, Development:** Melanie Lenz. **Director, Development:** William Walsh. **Senior Director, Procurement/Business Services:** Bill Wiener, Jr. **Director, Partner/VIP Relations:** Cass Halpin. **Senior Director, Information Technology:** Juan Ramirez. **Director, Human Resources:** Jennifer Tran.

Stuart Sternberg

Finance
VP, Finance: Rob Gagliardi. **Controller:** Patrick Smith.

Marketing/Community Relations
VP, Marketing/Community Relations: Tom Hoof. **Senior Director, Marketing:** Brian Killingsworth. **Senior Director, Community Relations:** Suzanne Murchland.

Communications/Broadcasting
Phone: (727) 825-3242.
VP, Communications: Rick Vaughn. **Director, Communications:** Dave Haller. **Senior Director, Broadcasting:** Larry McCabe. **Director, Radio Operations:** Rich Herrera.

Corporate Partnerships
Senior Director, Corporate Partnerships: Aaron Cohn. **Director, Corporate Partnerships:** Josh Bullock. **Director, Corporate Partnership Services:** Jason Wilmoth.

Ticket Sales
Phone: (888) FAN-RAYS.
VP, Sales/Service: Brian Richeson. **Senior Director, Group/Suite Sales:** Clark Beacom. **Director, Season Ticket Sales/Service:** Jeff Tanzer. **Director, Ticket Operations:** Robert Bennett. **Assistant Director, Ticket Operations:** Ken Mallory.

Stadium Operations
VP, Operations/Facilities: Rick Nafe. **Senior Director, Building Operations:** Scott Kelyman. **Director, Event Operations:** Tom Karac. **Director, Building Operations:** Chris Raineri. **Director, Audio/Visual Services:** Ron Golick. **Head Groundskeeper:** Dan Moeller. **VP, Branding/Fan Experience:** Darcy Raymond. **Director, In-Game Entertainment:**

2011 SCHEDULE
Standard Game Times: 7:10 p.m.; Sun. 1:40.

APRIL		
1-3 . . . . Baltimore	13-15 . . . . . . Baltimore	27-29 . . . . . . Cincinnati
5-6 . . . . Los Angeles (AL)	16-17 . . . . New York (AL)	**JULY**
7-10 . . . .at Chicago (AL)	18-19 . . . . . . at Toronto	1-3 . . . . St. Louis
11-13 . . . . .at Boston	20-22 . . . . . .at Florida	4-6 . . . . . . at Minnesota
14-17 . . . . . . Minnesota	23-25 . . . . . . .at Detroit	7-10 . . . at New York (AL)
18-21 . . . . Chicago (AL)	27-29 . . . . . . Cleveland	15-17 . . . . Boston
22-24 . . . . . . at Toronto	30-31 . . . . Texas	18-21 . . . .New York (AL)
26-28 . . . at Minnesota		22-24 . . . .at Kansas City
29-30 . . . Los Angeles (AL)	**JUNE**	25-28 . . . . . .at Oakland
	1 . . . . Texas	29-31 . . . . . . .at Seattle
MAY	2-5 . . . . .at Seattle	
1 . . . . . Los Angeles (AL)	6-8 . . . at Los Angeles (AL)	**AUGUST**
3-5 . . . . .Toronto	10-12 . . . . . .at Baltimore	2-4 . . . . .Toronto
6-8 . . . . .at Baltimore	14-16 . . . . Boston	5-7 . . . . Oakland
10-12 . . . . . .at Cleveland	17-19 . . . . . . Florida	8-11 . . . . Kansas City
	20-22 . . . . . at Milwaukee	12-14 . . . at New York (AL)
	24-26 . . . . . .at Houston	

16-17 . . . . .at Boston	
19-21 . . . . Seattle	
22-25 . . . . Detroit	
26-29 . . . . . . at Toronto	
30-31 . . . . .at Texas	
SEPTEMBER	
1 . . . . .at Texas	
2-4 . . . . Baltimore	
5-7 . . . . Texas	
9-11 . . . . Boston	
12-14 . . . . . . at Baltimore	
15-18 . . . . .at Boston	
20-21 . . . at New York (AL)	
23-25 . . . . .Toronto	
26-28 . . . .New York (AL)	

GENERAL INFORMATION
Stadium (year opened): Tropicana Field (1998).
Team Colors: Dark blue, light blue, yellow.

Player Representative: Evan Longoria.
Home Dugout: First Base.
Playing Surface: FieldTurf Duofilament.

Lou Costanza. **Director, Customer Service/Stadium Experience:** Eric Weisberg.

Travel, Clubhouse
  Director, Team Travel: Jeff Ziegler. **Equipment Manager, Home Clubhouse:** Chris Westmoreland. **Video Coordinator:** Chris Fernandez.

BASEBALL OPERATIONS
  Executive VP, Baseball Operations: Andrew Friedman. **Senior VP, Baseball Operations:** Gerry Hunsicker.
  Director, Baseball Operations: Dan Feinstein. **Director, Major League Administration:** Sandy Dengler. **Senior Baseball Advisor:** Don Zimmer.
  Architect, Baseball Systems: Brian Plexico. **Managers, Baseball Research/ Development:** James Click, Erik Neander. **Assistant, Baseball Operations:** Matt Hahn. **Developer, Baseball Systems:** Rob Naberhaus.

Andrew Friedman

Major League Staff
  Manager: Joe Maddon.
  Coaches: Bench—Dave Martinez; Pitching—Jim Hickey; Hitting—Derek Shelton; First Base—George Hendrick; Third Base—Tom Foley; Bullpen—Bobby Ramos; Assistant Pitching—Stan Boroski.

Medical/Training
  Medical Director: Dr. James Andrews. **Medical Team Physician:** Dr. Michael Reilly. **Orthopedic Team Physician:** Dr. Koco Eaton. **Head Athletic Trainer:** Ron Porterfield. **Assistant Athletic Trainers:** Paul Harker, Mark Vinson. **Strength/ Conditioning Coach:** Kevin Barr.

Player Development
  Telephone: (727) 825-3267. **Fax:** (727) 825-3493.
  Director, Minor League Operations: Mitch Lukevics. **Assistant Director, Minor League Operations:** Chaim Bloom. **Administrator, Player Development:** Giovanna Rodriguez.
  Field Coordinators: Jim Hoff, Bill Evers. **Minor League Coordinators:** Skeeter Barnes (outfield/baserunning), Dick Bosman (pitching), Steve Livesey (hitting), Jamie Nelson (catching), Matt Quatraro (hitting), Dewey Robinson (pitching), Lee Slagle (medical), Joel Smith (rehabilitation/athletic training), Trung Cao (strength/conditioning).
  Equipment Manager: Tim McKechney. **Assistant Equipment Manager:** Shane Rossetti.

Farm System

Class	Club (League)	Manager	Coach	Pitching Coach
Triple-A	Durham (IL)	Charlie Montoyo	Dave Myers	Neil Allen
Double-A	Montgomery (SL)	Billy Gardner Jr.	Ozzie Timmons	Bill Moloney
High A	Charlotte (FSL)	Jim Morrison	Joe Szekely	Steve Watson
Low A	Bowling Green (MWL)	Brady Williams	Manny Castillo	R.C. Lichtenstein
Short-season	Hudson Valley (NYP)	Jared Sandberg	Reinaldo Ruiz	Jack Giese
Rookie	Princeton (APP)	Michael Johns	Wuarnner Rincones	Marty DeMerritt
Rookie	Rays (GCL)	Joe Alvarez	D. DeMent/H. Torres	Darwin Peguero
Rookie	Rays (DSL)	Julio Zorrilla	A. DeFreites/R. Guerrero	Jose Gonzalez/Roberto Gil
Rookie	Rays (VSL)	Esteban Gonzalez	A. Freire/G. Omaña	J. Moncada/G. Melendez

SCOUTING
  Telephone: (727) 825-3241. **Fax:** (727) 825-3493.
  Director, Scouting: R.J. Harrison (Phoenix, AZ).
  Administrator, Scouting: Nancy Berry. **Assistant, Scouting/Minor League Operations:** Rob Metzler.
  Director, Pro Scouting: Matt Arnold. **Coordinator, Advance Scouting:** Mike Calitri. **Special Assignment Scouts:** Bart Braun (Vallejo, CA), Mike Cubbage (Keswick, VA), Larry Doughty (Leawood, KS). **Major League Scouts:** Bob Cluck (San Diego, CA), Gene Glynn (Weseca, MN), Jeff McAvoy (Palmer, MA).
  Professional Scouts: Gail Henley (La Verne, CA), Jason Karegeannes (Long Beach, CA), Brian Keegan (Matthews, NC), Jim Pransky (Davenport, IA).
  Pro/International Scout: Carlos Rodriguez (Miami, FL).
  National Crosscheckers: Jeff Cornell (Lee's Summit, MO), Tim Huff (Cave Creek, AZ). **East Coast Crosschecker:** Kevin Elfering (Wesley Chapel, FL).
  Midwest Crosschecker: Ken Stauffer (Katy, TX). **West Coast Crosschecker:** Fred Repke (Carson City, NV). **Scout Supervisors:** Tim Alexander (Jamesville, NY), James Bonnici (Birmingham, MI), Evan Brannon (St. Petersburg, FL), Tom Couston (Chicago, IL), Rickey Drexler (New Iberia, LA), Jayson Durocher (Phoenix, AZ), Brian Hickman (Broken Arrow, OK), Milt Hill (Cumming, GA), Paul Kirsch (Sherwood, OR), Brad Matthews (Concord, NC), Robbie Moen (El Segundo, CA), Brian Morrison (Fairfield, CA), Pat Murphy (Marble Falls, TX), Lou Wieben (Little Ferry, NJ), Jake Wilson (Ramona, CA).
  Part-Time Area Scouts: Brett Foley (Palm Harbor, FL), Jose Hernandez (Miami, FL), Jim Lief (Wellington, FL), Gil Martinez (San Juan, PR), Graig Merritt (Pitts Meadow, Canada), Casey Onaga (Aiea, HI), Jack Sharp (Dallas, TX), Donald Turley (Spring, TX).
  Director, International Operations: Carlos Alfonso (Naples, FL). **Director, Dominican Republic Operations:** Eddy Toledo. **Director, Venezuelan Operations:** Ronnie Blanco. **Pacific Rim Coordinator:** Tim Ireland. **Special Assistant, Baseball Operations:** Andres Reiner. **Assistant, International Operations:** Patrick Walters. **Consultant, International Operations:** John Gilmore. **International Scout:** Tateki Uchibori (Japan).

Texas Rangers

Office Address: 1000 Ballpark Way, Arlington, TX 76011.
Mailing Address: P.O. Box 90111, Arlington, TX 76011.
Telephone: (817) 273-5222. **Fax:** (817) 273-5110. **Website:** www.texasrangers.com.

Ownership
Managing Partner/CEO: Chuck Greenberg.
President: Nolan Ryan.

BUSINESS OPERATIONS

Chuck Greenberg

Chief Operationg Officer: Rick George. **Senior Executive Vice President:** Jim Sundberg.
Executive VP/Chief Financial Officer: Kellie Fischer.
Executive VP, Business Partnerships/Development: Joe Januszewski. **Executive VP, Ticket Sales/Marketing:** Todd Taylor. **Executive VP, Communications:** John Blake. **Executive VP, Ballpark/Event Operations:** Rob Matwick. **Senior VP:** Jay Miller. **Executive Assistant to CEO:** Karen Gallini. **Executive Assistant to President:** Courtney West. **Executive Assistant to COO/Finance:** Gabrielle Stokes. **Executive Assistant:** Leslie Dempsey.

Finance/Accounting
Assistant VP/Controller: Starr Pritchard. **Payroll Manager:** Donna Ebersole.

Human Resources/Legal/Information Technology
VP, Human Resources/Risk Management: Terry Turner. **Associate Counsel:** Kate Cassidy.
Managers, Human Resources: Shannon Abbott, Shelby Carpenter. **Assistant VP, Information Technology:** Mike Bullock. **Manager, IT Systems/Customer Service:** Fred Phillips.

Business/Event Operations
Senior Director, Customer Service: Donnie Pordash. **Director, Event Operations:** Danielle Cornwell. **Director, Parking/Security:** Mike Smith. **Assistant Director, Customer Service:** Taylore Scott.

Communications/Community Relations
Assistant VP, Player Relations: Taunee Paur Taylor. **Senior Director, Media Relations:** Rich Rice. **Senior Director, Broadcasting:** Angie Swint. **Manager, Media Relations/Publications:** Court Berry-Tripp. **Assistant Director, Player Relations:** Ashleigh Greathouse. **Coordinator, Media Relations:** Brian San Filippo. **Coordinator, Communications:** Amber Sims. **Assistant, Player Relations:** Becky Reed. **Executive Director, Foundation/Director, Hispanic Marketing:** Karin Morris. **Senior Director, Community Development:** Breon Davis.

Facilities
Assistant VP, Facilities Operations: Gib Searight. **Director, Grounds:** Dennis Klein.

Marketing/Game Presentation
Assistant VP, Marketing: Kelly Calvert. **Senior Creative Director, Graphic Design:** Rainer Uhlir. **Creative Director,**

2011 SCHEDULE
Standard Game Times: 7:05 p.m.; Sun. 2:05.

APRIL
1-3 . . . . Boston
4-6 . . . . Seattle
8-10 . . . . . . at Baltimore
11-13 . . . . at Detroit
15-17 . . at New York (AL)
18-20 . . . Los Angeles (AL)
22-24 . . . . . Kansas City
25-28 . . . . Toronto
29-30 . . . . . . at Oakland

MAY
1-2 . . . . at Oakland
3-5 . . . . at Seattle
6-8 . . . . . . New York (AL)
9-11 . . . . Oakland

13-15 . . . Los Angeles (AL)
16-17 . . . . at Chicago (AL)
18-19 . . . . at Kansas City
20-22 . . . at Philadelphia
23-25 . . . . . Chicago (AL)
27-29 . . . . . Kansas City
30-31 . . . . at Tampa Bay

JUNE
1 . . . . at Tampa Bay
2-5 . . . . at Cleveland
6-8 . . . . Detroit
9-12 . . . . . . at Minnesota
14-16 . . at New York (AL)
17-19 . . . . . at Atlanta
20-22 . . . . Houston
24-26 . . . . New York (NL)

28-30 . . . . . at Houston

JULY
1-3 . . . . Florida
4-6 . . . . Baltimore
8-10 . . . . Oakland
14-17 . . . . . . at Seattle
19-21 . at Los Angeles (AL)
22-24 . . . . Toronto
25-28 . . . . . Minnesota
29-31 . . . . . at Toronto

AUGUST
2-4 . . . . at Detroit
5-7 . . . . Cleveland
8-10 . . . . Seattle
12-14 . . . . . . at Oakland

15-18 . at Los Angeles (AL)
19-21 . . . . at Chicago (AL)
22-25 . . . . Boston
26-28 . . Los Angeles (AL)
30-31 . . . . . . Tampa Bay

SEPTEMBER
1 . . . . Tampa Bay
2-4 . . . . at Boston
5-7 . . . . . . at Tampa Bay
9-11 . . . . Oakland
13-15 . . . . . . Cleveland
16-18 . . . . . . at Seattle
20-22 . . . . . at Oakland
23-25 . . . . Seattle
26-28 . at Los Angeles (AL)

GENERAL INFORMATION
Stadium (year opened): Rangers
Ballpark in Arlington (1994).
Team Colors: Royal blue and red.

Player Representative: Unavailable.
Home Dugout: First Base.
Playing Surface: Grass.

Media: Rush Olson. **Vice President, In-Park Entertainment:** Chuck Morgan.

Merchandising
 Assistant VP, Merchandising: Diane Atkinson. **Director, Merchandising:** Stephen Moore.

Sponsorship/Ticket Sales/Ticket Operations
 VP, Corporate Sales: Jim Cochrane. **VP, Business Development:** Grady Raskin.
 Director, Sponsorship Sales: Guy Tomcheck. **VP, Suites Sales/Services:** Paige Farragut.

BASEBALL OPERATIONS
Telephone: (817) 273-5222. **Fax:** (817) 273-5285.
General Manager: Jon Daniels.
Assistant GM: Thad Levine. **Senior Advisor to the GM:** John Hart. **Senior Director, Baseball Operations:** Don Welke. **Senior Advisor to GM:** Tom Giordano. **Special Assistant, Baseball Operations:** Scott Littlefield. **Director, Baseball Operations:** Matt Vinnola. **Assistant, Baseball Operations:** Matt Klotsche. **Executive Assistant to GM:** Barbara Pappenfus.

Jon Daniels

Major League Staff
 Manager: Ron Washington.
 Coaches: Bench—Jackie Moore; Pitching—Mike Maddux; Hitting—Thad Bosley; First Base—Gary Pettis; Third Base—Dave Anderson; Bullpen—Andy Hawkins; Special Assignment Coach—Johnny Narron.

Medical, Training
 Team Physician: Dr. Keith Meister. **Team Internist:** Dr. David Hunter. **Spine Consultant:** Dr. Andrew Dossett. **Head Trainer/Medical Director:** Jamie Reed. **Assistant Trainers:** Kevin Harmon/Matt Lucero. **Director, Strength/Conditioning:** Jose Vazquez.

Player Development
 Telephone: (817) 273-5224. **Fax:** (817) 273-5285.
 Senior Director, Player Development: Scott Servais.
 Assistant Director, Player Development: Jake Krug. **Special Assistant, Player Development:** Harry Spilman. **Manager, Cultural Enhancement:** Bill McLaughlin. **Roving Instructors:** Mike Micucci (field coordinator), Danny Clark (pitching coordinator), Mike Boulanger (hitting coordinator), Luis Ortiz (hitting instructor), Keith Comstock (rehab pitching coordinator), Jayce Tingler (DR/AZ coordinator of instruction), Casey Candaele (special assignment coach), Napoleon Pichardo (strength/conditioning), Brian Bobier (medical coordinator), Dale Gilbert (rehab coordinator), Eduardo Tomas (DR strength/conditioning). **Player Development Administrator, Arizona Operations:** Mike LaCassa.
 Manager, Minor League Complex Operations: Chris Guth. **Assistant Equipment Manager:** Russ Oliver.

Farm System

Class	Club (League)	Manager	Coach	Pitching Coach
Triple-A	Round Rock (PCL)	Bobby Jones	S. Coolbaugh/S. Owen	Terry Clark
Double-A	Frisco (TL)	Steve Buechele	Brant Brown	Jeff Andrews
High A	Myrtle Beach (CL)	Jason Wood	Julio Garcia	Brad Holman
Low A	Hickory (SAL)	Bill Richardson	J. Hart/C. Ragsdale	Storm Davis
Short-season	Spokane (NWL)	Tim Hulett	J. Perez/B. Dayette	Dave Chavarria
Rookie	Rangers (AZL)	Hector Ortiz	O. Bernard	R. O'Malley/O. Marin
Rookie	Rangers (DSL)	Kenny Holmberg	A. Infante/R. Westman	P. Blanco/J. Jaimes

Scouting
 Telephone: (817) 273-5277. **Fax:** (817) 273-5285.
 Senior Director, Player Personnel: A.J. Preller.
 Director, Amateur Scouting: Kip Fagg. **Director, Pro Scouting:** Josh Boyd.
 Special Assistant, Scouting: Scott Littlefield.
 Manager, Amateur Scouting: Bobby Crook.
 Professional Scouts: Mike Anderson (Austin, TX), Russ Ardolina (Rockville, MD), Keith Boeck (Chandler, AZ), John Booher (Buda, TX), Scot Engler (Montgomery, IL), Greg Smith (Davenport, WA), Todd Walther (Dallas, TX), Mickey White (Sarasota, FL).
 Western Crosschecker: Kevin Bootay (Elk Grove, CA). **Central Crosschecker:** Mike Grouse (Olathe, KS). **Eastern Crosschecker:** Phil Geisler (Mount Horeb, WI).
 Area Scouts: Juan Alvarez (Miami, FL), Ryan Coe (Acworth, GA), Roger Coryell (Ypsilanti, MI), Jay Eddings (Sperry, OK), Steve Flores (Temecula, CA), Todd Guggiana (Long Beach, CA), Jay Heafner (Lakewood, NJ), Chris Kemp (Charlotte, NC), Derek Lee (Frankfurt, IL), Rick Matsko (Johnstown, PA), Mike McAbee (Euless, TX), Gary McGraw (Gaston, OR), Butch Metzger (Sacramento, CA), Andy Pratt (Peoria, AZ), Dustin Smith (Olathe, KS), Randy Taylor (Katy, TX), Frankie Thon (Guaynabo, Puerto Rico), Jeff Wood (Birmingham, AL).
 Video Scouting Assistants: Nick English (Pasadena, CA), Ross Fensermaker (Arlington, TX)
 Director, International Scouting: Mike Daly. **Director, Pacific Rim Operations:** Jim Colborn. **Coordinator, Pacific Rim Operations:** Joe Furukawa (Japan). **Dominican Program Coordinator:** Danilo Troncoso. **Manager, Korean Operations:** Curtis Jung. **Assistant International Operations:** Paul Kruger. **International Scouts:** Pedro Avila (Venezuela), Willy Espinal (Dominican Republic), Jose Fernandez (Florida), Daniel Floyd (West Australia), Chu Halabi (Aruba), Barry Holland (Australia), Gil Kim (Mexico), Bill McLaughlin (Mexico), Rodolfo Rosario (Dominican Republic), Joel Ronda (Puerto Rico), Rafic Saab (Venezuela), Hamilton Sarabia (Colombia), Eduardo Thomas (Panama), Hajime Watabe (Japan).

Toronto Blue Jays

Office/Mailing Address: 1 Blue Jays Way, Suite 3200, Toronto, Ontario M5V 1J1.
Telephone: (416) 341-1000. **Fax:** (416) 341-1250. **Website:** www.bluejays.com.

Ownership
Operated by: Toronto Blue Jays Baseball Club. **Principal Owner:** Rogers Communications Inc.

BUSINESS OPERATIONS

Vice Chairman, Rogers Communications: Phil Lind. **President, Rogers Media:** Keith Pelley.
President/CEO, Toronto Blue Jays/Rogers Centre: Paul Beeston.
Senior Vice President, Business Operations: Stephen R. Brooks. **VP, Special Projects:** Howard Starkman. **Executive Assistant to the President/CEO:** Sue Cannell.

Finance/Administration
Senior VP, Business Operations: Stephen R Brooks. **Executive Assistant:** Donna Kuzoff. **Controller:** Lynda Kolody. **Director, Payroll/Benefits:** Brenda Dimmer. **Director, Risk Management:** Suzanne Joncas. **Financial Business Managers:** Leslie Galant-Gardiner, Tanya Proctor. **Manager, Financial Planning:** Ciaran Keegan Manager. **Stadium Payroll:** Sharon Dykstra. **Manager, Ticket Receipts/Vault Services:** Joseph Roach. **Director, Human Resources:** Claudia Livadas. **Senior Manager, Human Resources:** Fiona Nugent. **Advisor, Human Resources:** Gurpreet Sing. **Director, Information Technology:** Mike Maybee. **Manager, Information Technology:** Anthony Miranda.

Paul Beeston

Marketing/Community Relations
VP, Marketing/Merchandising: Anthony Partipilo. **Executive Assistant, Marketing:** Maria Cresswell. **Director, Game Entertainment/Promotions:** Marnie Starkman. **Executive Director, Jays Care Foundation:** Danielle Silverstein. **Director, Business Development:** John Griffin. **Director, Strategic Marketing Partnerships:** Krista Semotiuk. **Senior Manager, Business Development:** Honsing Leung. **Senior Manager, Partnership Sales/Business Development:** Mark Palmer. **Manager, Corporate Partnership Marketing:** Stephanie Kay. **Manager, Sales Support:** Nicole MacKellar. **Coordinator, Corporate Partnerships:** Owen Welsh.

Communications
Telephone: (416) 341-1301/1302/1303. **Fax:** (416) 341-1250.
VP, Communications: Jay Stenhouse. **Manager, Baseball Information:** Mal Romanin. **Coordinator, Baseball Information:** Erik Grosman. **Coordinators:** Kendra Hunter, Sue Mallabon.

Stadium Operations
VP, Stadium Operations/Security: Mario Coutinho. **Executive Assistant:** June Sym. **Manager, Event Services:** Julie Minott. **Manager, Game Operations:** Karyn Gottschalk. **Operations Assistant:** Marion Farrell.

Ticket Operations
Director, Ticket Operations: Justin Hay. **Director, Ticket Services:** Sheila Stella. **Manager, Box Office:** Scott Hext.

2011 SCHEDULE
Standard Game Times: 7:07 p.m.; Sat/Sun: 1:07

APRIL		JULY	
1-3 . . . . Minnesota	13-15 . . . . . at Minnesota		15-17 . . . . .at Seattle
5-7 . . . . Oakland	16-17 . . . . .at Detroit	28-30 . . . . Pittsburgh	18-21 . . . . . . .at Oakland
8-10 . . at Los Angeles (AL)	18-19 . . . . . . .Tampa Bay	1-3 . . . . .Philadelphia	23-25 . . . . . Kansas City
11-13 . . . . .at Seattle	20-22 . . . . Houston	4-6 . . . . .at Boston	26-29 . . . . . .Tampa Bay
15-18 . . . . .at Boston	23-25 . . . at New York (AL)	7-10 . . . . . . .at Cleveland	30-31 . . . . .at Baltimore
19-20 . . . .New York (AL)	26-29 . . . . Chicago (AL)	14-17 . . . . .New York (AL)	
22-24 . . . . . .Tampa Bay	30-31 . . . . Cleveland	19-21 . . . . Seattle	SEPTEMBER
25-28 . . . . .at Texas		22-24 . . . . .at Texas	1 . . . . .at Baltimore
29-30 . . at New York (AL)	JUNE	26-28 . . . . . . Baltimore	2-4 . . . . at New York (AL)
	1 . . . . Cleveland	29-31 . . . . Texas	5-8 . . . . Boston
MAY	3-5 . . . . .at Baltimore		9-11 . . . . Baltimore
1 . . . . . at New York (AL)	6-9 . . . . . . .at Kansas City	AUGUST	13-14 . . . . .at Boston
3-5 . . . . . . at Tampa Bay	10-12 . . . . Boston	2-4 . . . . . . at Tampa Bay	16-18 . . . .New York (AL)
6-9 . . . . Detroit	14-16 . . . . . Baltimore	5-7 . . . . . . .at Baltimore	19-22 . . Los Angeles (AL)
10-11 . . . . Boston	17-19 . . . .at Cincinnati	9-11 . . . . Oakland	23-25 . . . . at Tampa Bay
	20-22 . . . . . . at Atlanta	12-14 . . . Los Angeles (AL)	26-28 . . . .at Chicago (AL)
	24-26 . . . . . .at St. Louis		

GENERAL INFORMATION
Stadium (year opened): Rogers Centre (1989).   **Home Dugout:** Third Base.
Playing Surface: Artificial.
Team Colors: Blue, silver, white and black.

Coordinators, Ticket Services: Sonia Privato, Lisa Simons. Coordinator, Ticket Operations: Eric Cowell.

Ticket Sales/Service
VP, Ticket Sales/Service: Jason Diplock. Executive Assistant: Stacey Jackson. Director, Premium Sales: Mike Hook. Director, Ticket Sales/Service: Franc Rota. Manager, Group Development: Ryan Gustavel. Manager, Premier Client Services: Erik Bobson. Manager, Ticket Sales: John Santana. Account Managers, Group Development: Andrew Haley, Paul Rabeau. Account Managers, Premium Sales: Mike Forty, Arlo Graham, Chris Schmidt. Coordinator, Premium Sales: Laura Attwell.

Travel/Clubhouse
Director, Team Travel/Clubhouse Operations: Mike Shaw. Equipment Manager: Jeff Ross. Clubhouse Manager: Kevin Malloy. Visiting Clubhouse Manager: Len Frejlich. Video Operations: Robert Baumander. Coordinator, Advance Scouting/Video: Brian Abraham.

BASEBALL OPERATIONS
Senior VP, Baseball Operations/General Manager: Alex Anthopoulos.
VP, Baseball Operations/Assistant GM: Tony LaCava. Assistant GM: Jay Sartori. Special Assistant to GM: Dana Brown. Consultant: Cito Gaston. Administrator, Baseball Operations: Heather Connolly. Baseball Information Analyst: Joe Sheehan. Executive Assistant to GM: Anna Coppola.

Major League Staff
Manager: John Farrell.
Coaches: Bench—Don Wakamatsu; Pitching—Bruce Walton; Hitting—Dwayne Murphy; First Base—Torey Lovullo; Third Base—Brian Butterfield; Bullpen—Pat Hentgen.

Medical, Training
Medical Advisor: Dr. Bernie Gosevitz. Team Physician: Dr. Ron Taylor.
Head Trainer: George Poulis. Assistant Trainer: Hap Hudson. Strength/Conditioning Coordinator: Bryan King. Director, Team Safety: Ron Sandelli.

Alex Anthopoulos

Player Development
Telephone: (727) 734-8007. Fax: (727) 734-8162.
Director, Minor League Operations: Charlie Wilson. Director, Employee Assistance Program: Ray Karesky. Minor League Field Coordinator: Doug Davis. Senior Advisor, Player Development: Mel Queen. Assistant, Latin American Administration: Blake Bentley. Coordinator, Minor League Administration: Joanna Nelson. Administrative Assistant: Kim Marsh. Roving Instructors: Anthony Iapoce (hitting), Mike Mordecai (infield), Rich Miller (outfield/baserunning), Dane Johnson (pitching), Rick Langford (rehab pitching), Minor League Coordinators: Mike Frostad (athletic training), Billy Wardlow (equipment), Donovan Santas (strength/conditioning).

Farm System

Class	Club (League)	Manager	Hitting Coach	Pitching Coach
Triple-A	Las Vegas (PCL)	Marty Brown	Chad Mottola	Tom Signore
Double-A	New Hampshire (EL)	Sal Fasano	Justin Mashore	Pete Walker
High A	Dunedin (FSL)	Clayton McCullough	Ralph Dickenson	Darold Knowles
Low A	Lansing (MWL)	Mike Redmond	John Tamargo Jr.	Vince Horsman
Short-season	Vancouver (NWL)	John Schneider	Dave Pano	Jim Czajkowski
Rookie	Bluefield (APP)	Dennis Holmberg	Kenny Graham	Antonio Caceres
Rookie	Blue Jays (GCL)	Omar Malave	P. Elliott/D. Solano	John Wesley
Rookie	Blue Jays (DSL)	Miguel Bernard	L. Rodriguez/O. Martinez	Oswald Peraza

Scouting
Telephone: (416) 341-1229. Fax: (416) 341-1245.
Director, Amateur Scouting: Andrew Tinnish. Director, Pro Scouting: Perry Minasian.
Assistant Director, Amateur Scouting: Ryan Mittleman. Coordinator, Professional Scouting: Harry Einbinder. Special Assignment Scout: Jon Lalonde. Major League Scouts: Jim Beattie, Russ Bove, Sal Butera, Ed Lynch. Professional Crosscheckers: Mike Mangan, Gary Rajsich. Pro Scouts: John Brickley, Tom Clark, Steve Connelly, Kimball Crossley, Bob Fontaine, Bob Hamelin, David May Jr., Wayne Morgan, Brian Parker, Marteese Robinson, Jim Skaalen, Steve Springer, Doug Witt, Calvin Minasian. National Crosscheckers: Dean Decillis, Marc Tramuta. Regional Crosscheckers: Matt Briggs, Tom Burns, Dan Cholowsky, Steve Miller, Tim Rooney. Area Scouts: Joey Aversa (Fountain Valley, CA), Darold Brown (Elk Grove, CA), Jon Bunnell (Overland Park, KS), Dan Cox (Santa Ana, CA), Blake Crosby (Gilbert, AZ), C.J. Ebarb (Friendswood, TX), Kevin Fox (La Mirada, CA), Ryan Fox (Yakima, WA), Bobby Gandolfo (Lansdale, PA), Joel Grampietro (Tampa, FL), John Hendricks (Mocksville, NC), Randy Kramer (Aptos, CA), Nick Manno (Brunswick, OH), Eric McQueen (Acworth, GA), Mike Medici (Naperville, IL), Nate Murrie (Bowling Green, KY), Matt O'Brien (Clermont, FL) Cliff Pastornicky (Birmingham, AL), Wes Penick (Clive, IA), Michael Pesce (New Hyde Park, NY), Jorge Rivera (Puerto Nuevo, PR), Rob St. Julien (Scott, LA), Darin Vaughan (Tulsa, OK), Michael Wagner (Addison, TX).
Canada Scouts: Don Cowan (Delta, BC), Jamie Lehman (Brampton, ON). Ambassadors, Canadian Amateur Baseball: Jim Fanning, Sean McCann.
Director, Latin American Operations: Marco Paddy. International Scouts: Miguel Bernard (San Pedro de Macoris, DR), Robinson Garces (Maracaibo, VZ), Pablo Leal (Maturin, VZ), Erick Medina (Cartagena, Columbia), Rafael Moncada (San Diego Valencia, VZ), Lorenzo Perez (Manoguayabo, DR), Hilario Soriano (Santo Domingo, DR), Domingo Toribio (San Pedro de Macoris, DR), Greg Wade (Queensland, Australia).

Washington Nationals

Office Address: 1500 South Capitol St. SE, Washington, DC 20003.
Telephone: (202) 640-7000. **Fax:** (202) 547-0025.
Website: www.nationals.com.

Ownership
Managing Principal Owner: Theodore Lerner.
Principal Owners: Annette Lerner, Mark Lerner, Marla Lerner Tanenbaum, Debra Lerner Cohen, Robert Tanenbaum, Edward Cohen, Judy Lenkin Lerner.

BUSINESS OPERATIONS

Ted Lerner

Chief Operating Officer, Lerner Sports: Alan Gottlieb. **COO:** Andrew Feffer. **Executive Vice President:** Bob Wolfe. **Vice President, Administration:** Elise Holman. **VP, Government/ Municipal Affairs:** Gregory McCarthy. **Executive Assistant to Executive VP:** Cheryl Rampy. **Marketing Project Manager/Executive Assistant to COO:** Britton Stackhouse Miller.

Business Affairs/Legal
Executive Director, Ballpark Enterprises/Guest Services: Catherine Silver. **Director, Ballpark Enterprises:** Heather Westrom. **Senior Manager, Ballpark Enterprises:** Maggie Gessner. **Manager, Foord Services/Retail Operations:** Jonathan Stahl. **VP/Managing Director, Corporate Partnerships/Business Development:** John Knebel. **Director, Partner Service:** Allison Grinham.
VP/General Counsel: Damon Jones. **Assistant Counsel:** Amy Inlander.

Finance/Human Resources
Chief Financial Officer: Lori Creasy. **Controller:** Ted Towne. **Director, Accounting:** Kelly Pitchford. **Senior Accountants:** Ross Hollander, Michael Page, Rachel Proctor. **Benefits Administrator:** Stephanie Giroux. **Coordinator, Human Resources:** Alan Gromest. **Assistant, Human Resources:** Ricardo Aponte, Jr.

Media Relations/Communications
Senior Director, Baseball Media Relations: John Dever. **Director, Baseball Media Relations:** Mike Gazda. **Coordinator, Baseball Media Relations:** Bill Gluvna. **VP/Managing Director, Communications/Brand Development:** Lara Potter. **Senior Manager New Media:** Chad Kurz. **Senior Manager, Communications:** Joanna Comfort.

Community Relations
Director, Community Relations: Israel Negron. **Coordinator, Community Relations:** Kyle Mann. **Community Relations Assistant for Military Affairs:** Rafael Delgado.

Marketing/Broadcasting
VP, Marketing/Broadcasting: John Guagliano. **Senior Director, Production/Entertainment:** Jacqueline Coleman. **Manager, Creative Services/Publications:** Daniel Kasper. **Manager, Consumer Marketing:** Scott Lewis. **Coordinator,**

2011 SCHEDULE
Standard Game Times: 7:05 p.m.; Sun. 1:35

MARCH	6-8. . . . . .at Florida	21-23 . . . . Seattle	12-14 . . . . at Philadelphia
31 . . . . Atlanta	10-12 . . . . . . at Atlanta	24-26 . . . .at Chicago (AL)	16-18 . . . . Cincinnati
	13-15 . . . . Florida	27-29 . at Los Angeles (AL)	19-21 . . . . .Philadelphia
APRIL	16-17 . . . . . . Pittsburgh		22-25 . . . . .Arizona
2-3. . . . . Atlanta	18-19 . . at New York (NL)	**JULY**	26-28 . . . .at Cincinnati
5-7. . . . . .at Florida	20-22 . . . . .at Baltimore	1-3. . . . . Pittsburgh	30-31 . . . . at Atlanta
8-10 . . . .at New York (NL)	23-25 . . . at Milwaukee	4-7. . . . . Chicago (NL)	
12-14 . . . . . .Philadelphia	27-29 . . . . . San Diego	8-10 . . . . .Colorado	**SEPTEMBER**
15-17 . . . . . .Milwaukee	30-31 . . . . .Philadelphia	15-17 . . . . . . at Atlanta	1 . . . . at Atlanta
19-21 . . . . . .at St. Louis		18-20 . . . . .at Houston	2-4. . . . . . .New York (NL)
22-24 . . . . at Pittsburgh	**JUNE**	22-24 . at Los Angeles (NL)	5-8. . . . .Los Angeles (NL)
26-28 . . . . .New York (NL)	1 . . . . .Philadelphia	26-28 . . . . Florida	9-11 . . . . Houston
29-30 . . . . San Francisco	2-5. . . . . . . at Arizona	29-31 . . . .New York (NL)	12-15 . . . at New York (NL)
	6-8. . . . at San Francisco		16-18 . . . . Florida
MAY	9-12 . . . . . at San Diego	**AUGUST**	20-22 . . . . at Philadelphia
1-2. . . . . . .San Francisco	14-16 . . . . St. Louis	1-3. . . . . Atlanta	23-25 . . . . Atlanta
3-5. . . . . at Philadelphia	17-19 . . . . . . Baltimore	4-7. . . . . . . at Colorado	26-28 . . . . . . .at Florida
		8-10 . . . . .at Chicago (NL)	

GENERAL INFORMATION
Stadium (year opened): Nationals Park (2008).
Team Colors: Red, white and blue.

Player Representative: Unavailable.
Home Dugout: First Base.
Playing Surface: Grass.

Promotions/Events: Adriana Villanueva. **Manager, Productions/Operations:** Dave Lundin. **Associate Producer:** Benjamin Smith. **Editor:** Mark Jackson.

Ticketing/Sales

VP/Managing Director, Sales/Client Services: Chris Gargani. **Director, Ticket Operations:** Derek Younger. **Manager, Ticket Services:** Andy Burns. **Manager, Box Office:** Tyler Hubbard. **Manager, Sales Development:** Rob Erwin. **Manager, Premium Sales:** Michael Shane.

Ballpark Operations

VP, Facilities: Frank Gambino. **Manager, Event Operations:** Adam Lasky. **Head Groundskeeper:** John Turnour. **Assistant Head Groundskeeper:** Mike Hrivnak. **Managers, Security:** Ronald Gordon, Reemberto Rodriguez. **Manager, Engineering Operations:** James Pantazis. **Director, Florida Operations:** Thomas Bell. **Manager, Florida Operations:** Jonathan Tosches.

BASEBALL OPERATIONS

Executive VP/General Manager: Mike Rizzo.
Assistant GM: Bryan Minniti. **Executive Assistant to GM:** Harolyn Cardozo. **Senior Advisor to GM:** Davey Johnson. **Senior Advisor to GM:** Phillip Rizzo. **Director, Baseball Operations:** Adam Cromie. **Director, Team Travel:** Rob McDonald. **Coordinator, Advance Scouting:** Erick Dalton. **Assistant, Advance Scouting:** Mike Mazur. **Analyst, Baseball Operations:** Sam Mondry-Cohen.

Major League Staff

Manager: Jim Riggleman.
Coaches: Bench—John McLaren; Pitching—Steve McCatty; Hitting—Rick Eckstein; First Base—Dan Radison; Third Base—Bo Porter; Bullpen—Jim Lett.

Mike Rizzo

Medical, Training

Team Medical Director: Dr. **Wiemi Duoghui. Head Trainer:** Lee Kuntz. **Assistant Trainer:** Mike McGowen. **Strength/Conditioning Coach:** John Philbin.

Player Development

Assistant GM/VP, Player Development: Bob Boone. **Senior Assistant, Player Development:** Pat Corrales. **Director, Player Development:** Doug Harris. **Director, Minor League Operations:** Mark Scialabba. **Director, Florida Operations:** Thomas Bell. **Dominican Republic Academy Administrator:** Fausto Severino. **Coordinator, Minor League Operations:** Ryan Thomas. **Coordinators:** Bobby Henley (field), Spin Williams (pitching), Rick Schu (hitting), Jeff Garber (infield), Tony Tarasco (outfield/baserunning), Gary Cathcart (coordinator), Mark Grater (rehab pitching), Steve Gober (medical/rehab), Landon Brandes (strength/conditioning). **Minor League Equipment/Clubhouse Manager:** John Mullin.

Farm System

Class	Club	Manager	Coach(es)	Pitching Coach
Triple-A	Syracuse (IL)	Randy Knorr	Jerry Browne	Greg Booker
Double-A	Harrisburg (EL)	Tony Beasley	Troy Gingrich	Randy Tomlin
High A	Potomac (CL)	Matt LeCroy	Mark Harris	Paul Menhart
Low A	Hagerstown (SAL)	Brian Daubach	Marlon Anderson	Chris Michalak
Short-season	Auburn (NYP)	Gary Cathcart	Luis Ordaz	Franklin Bravo
Rookie	Nationals (GCL)	Bobby Williams	S. Mendez/J. Poppert	Michael Tejera

Scouting

Assistant GM/VP, Player Personnel: Roy Clark. **Director, Amateur Scouting:** Kris Kline. **Director, Pro Scouting:** Bill Singer. **Director, Player Procurement:** Kasey McKeon. **Special Assistants to GM:** Jay Robertson, Chuck Cottier, Deric Ladnier, Bob Schaefer. **Assistant:** Eddie Longosz. **Pro Scout:** Mike Daughtry. **Crosscheckers:** Mark Baca (National/Western), Jimmy Gonzales (National/Mid Western Crosschecker), Jeff Zona (National/Eastern). **Area Supervisors:** Mike Alberts (Worcester, MA), Steve Arnieri (Barrington, IL), Fred Costello (Livermore, CA), Reed Dunn (Nashville, TN), Paul Faulk (Little River, SC), Ed Gustafson (Lubbock, TX), Craig Kornfeld (Santa Margarita, CA), Alex Morales (Wellington, FL), Tim Reynolds (Irvine, CA), Eric Robinson (Acworth, GA), Mitch Sokol (Phoenix, AZ), Paul Tinnell (Bradenton, FL), Tyler Wilt (Willis, TX).

Director, Latin American Operations: Johnny DiPuglia. **Dominican Republic Scouting Supervisor:** Moises De La Mota. **Venezuela Scouting Supervisor:** German Robles. **International Scout:** Modesto Ulloa (Dominican Republic) Part Time Scouts: Pablo Arias (Dominican Republic), Carlos Ulloa (Dominican Republic), Juan Garcia (Venezuela), Donatelli Salvador (Venezuela), Rafael Hernandez (Columbia), Wilbert Neuman (Curacao), Miguel Ruiz (Panama).

MEDIA
INFORMATION

LOCAL MEDIA INFORMATION

AMERICAN LEAGUE

BALTIMORE ORIOLES
Radio Announcers: Joe Angel, Fred Manfra. **Flagship Station:** TBD.
TV Announcers: Jim Hunter, Jim Palmer, Gary Thorne. **Flagship Station:** Mid-Atlantic Sports Network (MASN).

BOSTON RED SOX
Radio Announcers: Joe Castiglione, Dave O'Brien. **Flagship Station:** WEEI (850 AM).
TV Announcers: Don Orsillo, Jerry Remy. **Flagship Station:** New England Sports Network (regional cable).
Spanish Radio Announcers: Oscar Baez. **Flagship Station:** WWZN (1510 AM).

CHICAGO WHITE SOX
Radio Announcers: Ed Farmer, Darrin Jackson. **Flagship Station:** WSCR The Score 670-AM.
TV Announcers: Ken Harrelson, Steve Stone. **Flagship Stations:** WGN TV-9, WCIU-TV, Comcast SportsNet Chicago (regional cable).

CLEVELAND INDIANS
Radio Announcers: Tom Hamilton, Mike Hegan, Jim Rosenhaus. **Flagship Station:** WTAM 1100-AM.
TV Announcers: Rick Manning, Matt Underwood. **Flagship Station:** SportsTime Ohio.

DETROIT TIGERS
Radio Announcers: Dan Dickerson, Jim Price. **Flagship Station:** WXYT 1270-AM.
TV Announcers: Rod Allen, Mario Impemba. **Flagship Station:** Fox Sports Net Detroit (regional cable).

KANSAS CITY ROYALS
Radio Announcers: Denny Matthews, Bob Davis, Steve Stewart. **Kansas City affiliate:** KCSP 610-AM.
TV Announcers: Ryan Lefebvre, Frank White, Paul Splittorff, Joel Goldberg. **Flagship Station:** FOX Sports Kansas City.

LOS ANGELES ANGELS
Radio Announcers: Terry Smith, Jose Mota. **Spanish:** Rolando Nichols. **Flagship Station:** AM 830, ESPN Radio 710-AM, 1330 KWKW (Spanish).
TV Announcers: Victor Rojas, Mark Gubicza. **Flagship Stations:** FSN West (regional cable).

MINNESOTA TWINS
Radio Announcers: John Gordon, Dan Gladden, Jack Morris, Kris Atteberry. **Flagship Station:** ESPN-1500.
TV Announcers: Bert Blyleven, Dick Bremer. **Flagship Station:** Fox Sports North.

NEW YORK YANKEES
Radio Announcers: John Sterling, Suzyn Waldman.
Flagship Station: WCBS 880-AM.
Spanish Radio Announcers: Beto Villa, Francisco Rivera.
TV Announcers: John Flaherty, Michael Kay, Al Leiter, Paul O'Neill, Ken Singleton.
Flagship Station: YES Network (Yankees Entertainment & Sports).

OAKLAND ATHLETICS
Radio Announcers: Vince Cotroneo, Ray Fosse, Ken Korach. **Flagship Station:** XTRA 860-AM. **TV Announcers:** Ray Fosse, Glen Kuiper. **Flagship Stations:** Comcast Sports Net California.

SEATTLE MARINERS
TV/Radio Announcers: Mike Blowers, Rick Rizzs, Dave Simms.
Flagship Stations: KOMO 1000-AM (radio), FOX Sports Net Northwest (TV).

TAMPA BAY RAYS
Radio Announcers: Andy Freed, Dave Wills. **Flagship Station:** WDAE 620 AM.
TV Announcers: Brian Anderson, Dewayne Staats, Todd Kalas. **Flagship Station:** Sun Sports.

TEXAS RANGERS
Radio Announcers: Eric Nadel, Dave Barnett; Spanish—Eleno Ornelas, Jerry Romo. **Flagship Station:** KRLD 105.3 FM, 1080-AM, KFLC 1270-AM (Spanish).
TV Announcers: Josh Lewin, Tom Grieve. **Flagship Stations:** Fox Sports Southwest (regional cable).

TORONTO BLUE JAYS
Radio Announcers: Jerry Howarth, Alan Ashby, Mike Wilner. **Flagship Station:** SportsNet Radio Fan 590-AM.
TV Announcers: Jamie Campbell, Pat Tabler, Rance Mulliniks. **Flagship Station:** Rogers Sportsnet.

NATIONAL LEAGUE

ARIZONA DIAMONDBACKS
Radio Announcers: Greg Schulte, Tom Candiotti, Jeff Munn, Mike Fetters. **Spanish:** Miguel Quintana, Oscar Soria, Richard Saenz. **Flagship Stations:** KTAR 620-AM, ESPN DEPORTES 710-AM (Spanish).
TV Announcers: Daron Sutton, Mark Grace, Greg Schulte, Joe Garagiola. **Flagship Stations:** FOX Sports Arizona (regional cable).

ATLANTA BRAVES
Radio Announcers: Jim Powell and Don Sutton. **Flagship Station:** WCNN-AM 680 The Fan and WNNX-FM (100.5).
TV Announcers: FS South, SportSouth and Peachtree TV—Chip Caray and Joe Simpson. **Flagship Stations:** FS South and SportSouth (regional cable) and Peachtree TV (OTA).

CHICAGO CUBS
Radio Announcers: Pat Hughes. **Flagship Station:** WGN 720-AM.
TV Announcers: Len Kasper, Bob Brenly. **Flagship Stations:** WGN Channel 9 (national cable), Comcast Sports Net Chicago (regional cable), WCIU-TV Channel 26.

CINCINNATI REDS
Radio Announcers: Marty Brennaman, Thom Brennaman, Jeff Brantley, Jim Kelch. **Flagship Station:** WLW 700-AM.
TV Announcers: George Grande, Chris Welsh, Thom Brennaman, Jeff Brantley, Sean Casey. **Flagship Station:** Fox Sports Ohio (regional cable).

COLORADO ROCKIES
Radio Announcers: Jack Corrigan, Jerry Schemmel. **Flagship Station:** KOA 850-AM.
TV Announcers: Drew Goodman, George Frazier, Jeff Huson.

FLORIDA MARLINS
Radio Announcers: Dave Van Horne, Glenn Geffner. **Flagship Stations:** WAXY 790-AM, WAQI 710-AM (Spanish).
Spanish Radio Announcers: Felo Ramirez, Yiky Quintana.
TV Announcers: Tommy Hutton, Rich Waltz. **Spanish TV Announcers:** Cookie Rojas, Raul Striker Jr.
Flagship Stations: FSN Florida, Sun Sports (regional cable).

HOUSTON ASTROS
Radio Announcers: Brett Dolan, Milo Hamilton, Dave Raymond. **Spanish:** Alex Trevino, Francisco Romero. **Flagship Stations:** KTRH 740-AM, KLAT 1010-AM (Spanish).
TV Announcers: Bill Brown, Jim Deshaies. **Flagship Station:** Fox Sports Net.

LOS ANGELES DODGERS
Radio Announcers: Vin Scully, Rick Monday, Charley Steiner; Spanish: Jaime Jarrin, Fernando Valenzuela, Pepe Yniguez. **Flagship Stations:** KABC 790-AM, KTNQ 1020-AM (Spanish).
TV Announcers: Vin Scully, Steve Lyons, Eric Collins. **Flagship Stations:** KCAL 9, PRIME TICKET (regional cable).

MILWAUKEE BREWERS
Radio Announcers: Bob Uecker. **Flagship Station:** WTMJ 620-AM.
TV Announcers: Bill Schroeder, Brian Anderson. **Flagship Station:** Fox Sports Net North.

NEW YORK METS
Radio Announcers: Howie Rose, Wayne Hagin, Ed Coleman. **Flagship Station:** WFAN 660-AM. **TV Announcers:** Gary Cohen, Keith Hernandez, Ron Darling, Ralph Kiner, Kevin Burkhardt. **Flagship Stations:** PIX11-TV, Sports Net New York (regional cable).

PHILADELPHIA PHILLIES
Radio Announcers: Larry Andersen, Scott Franzke, Jim Jackson. **Flagship Stations:** WPHT 1210-AM.
TV Announcers: Tom McCarthy, Gary Matthews, Chris Wheeler. **Flagship Stations:** WPSG CW 57, Comcast SportsNet (regional cable).

PITTSBURGH PIRATES
Radio Announcers: Steve Blass, Greg Brown, Bob Walk, John Wehner. **Flagship Station:** WPGB 104.7 FM.
TV Announcers: Tim Neverett, Steve Blass, Greg Brown, Bob Walk, John Wehner. **Flagship Station:** Fox Sports Pittsburgh (regional cable).

ST. LOUIS CARDINALS
Radio Announcers: Mike Shannon, John Rooney. **Flagship Station:** KMOX 1120 AM.
TV Announcers: Rick Horton, Al Hrabosky, Dan McLaughlin. **Flagship Stations:** Fox Sports Midwest.

SAN DIEGO PADRES
Radio Announcers: Jerry Coleman, Ted Leitner, Andy Masur. **Flagship Station:** XX Sports Radio 1090-AM/ESPN 1700-AM.
TV Announcers: Dick Enberg, Mark Grant, Tony Gwynn, Mark Neely. **Flagship Station:** Channel 4 San Diego (cable).

SAN FRANCISCO GIANTS
Radio Announcers: Mike Krukow, Duane Kuiper, Jon Miller, Dave Flemming. **Spanish:** Tito Fuentes, Erwin Higueros. **Flagship Station:** KNBR 680-AM (English); KIQI-1010AM (Spanish).
TV Announcers: CSN Bay Area—Mike Krukow, Duane Kuiper; KNTV-NBC 11—Jon Miller, Mike Krukow, Duane Kuiper. **Flagship Stations:** KNTV-NBC 11, CSN Bay Area (regional cable).

WASHINGTON NATIONALS
Radio Announcers: Charlie Slowes, Dave Jageler. **Flagship Station:** Washington Post Radio (WFED 1500-AM, WWFD 820-AM, WWWT 107.7 FM).
TV Announcers: Bob Carpenter, F.P. Santangelo. **Flagship Station:** Mid-Atlantic Sports Network (MASN).

NATIONAL MEDIA INFORMATION

BASEBALL STATISTICS

ELIAS SPORTS BUREAU INC.
Official Major League Statistician
Mailing Address: 500 Fifth Ave., Suite 2140, New York, NY 10110. **Telephone:** (212) 869-1530. **Fax:** (212) 354-0980. **Website:** www.esb.com.
President: Seymour Siwoff.
Executive Vice President: Steve Hirdt. **Vice President:** Peter Hirdt. **Data Processing Manager:** Chris Thorn.

MAJOR LEAGUE BASEBALL ADVANCED MEDIA
Official Minor League Statistician
Mailing Address: 75 Ninth Ave., New York, NY 10011. **Telephone:** (212) 485-3444. **Fax:** (212) 485-3456.
Deputy Project Manager: Nathan Blackmon. **Senior Project Manager:** Sammy Arena. **Senior Editorial Producer:** Jason Ratliff. **Senior Manager, Statistics Operations:** Chris Lentine. **Senior Reporter:** Jonathan Mayo.

STATS Inc.
Mailing Address: 2775 Shermer Road, Northbrook, IL 60062. **Telephone:** (847) 583-2100. **Fax:** (847) 470-9140. **Website:** www.stats.com. **Email:** sales@stats.com. **Twitter:** twitter.com/STATSBiznews, twitter.com/STATS_MLB. **CEO:** Gary Walrath. **Executive Vice Presidents:** Steve Byrd, Robert Schur. **Senior Vice President, Sales:** Greg Kirkorsky. **Director, Sports Operations:** Allan Spear. **Manager, Baseball Operations:** Jeff Chernow.

TELEVISION NETWORKS

ESPN/ESPN2
Mailing Address, ESPN Connecticut: ESPN Plaza, Bristol, CT 06010. **Telephone:** (860) 766-2000. **Fax:** (860) 766-2213.
Mailing Address, ESPN New York Executive Offices: 77 W. 66th St., New York, NY, 10023. **Telephone:** (212) 456-7777. **Fax:** (212) 456-2930.
President, ESPN/ABC Sports: George Bodenheimer.
Executive Vice President, Administration: Ed Durso. **Executive VP, Content:** John Skipper. **Executive VP, Production:** Norby Williamson. **Senior VP, Programming/Acquisitions:** Len DeLuca. **VP, Programming:** Mike Ryan. **Senior VP/Executive Producer, Remote Production:** Jed Drake. **Senior Coordinating Producer, Remote Production:** Tim Scanlan. **Coordinating Producer, Event Production:** Matt Sandulli. **Senior VP/Managing Editor, Studio Production:** Mark Gross. **Senior Coordinating Producer, Baseball Tonight:** Jay Levy. **Senior VP, Operations:** Jodi Markley.

ESPN CLASSIC, ESPNEWS
Vice President, Programming/Acquisitions: John Papa. **Senior Coordinating Producer, ESPNEWS:** David Roberts.

ESPN INTERNATIONAL, ESPN DEPORTES
Executive VP/Managing Director, ESPN International: Russell Wolff.
Senior VP, ESPN Radio/ESPN Deportes: Traug Keller. **General Manager, ESPN Deportes:** Lino Garcia. **VP, International Production/Operations:** Chris Calcinari.

FOX SPORTS
Mailing Address, Los Angeles: Fox Network Center, Building 101, Fifth floor, 10201 West Pico Blvd., Los Angeles, CA 90035. **Telephone:** (310) 369-6000. **Fax:** (310) 969-6700.
Mailing Address, New York: 1211 Avenue of the Americas, 20th Floor, New York, NY 10036. **Telephone:** (212) 556-2500. **Fax:** (212) 354-6902. **Website:** www.foxsports.com.
Chairman/CEO, Fox Sports Television Group: David Hill. **President/Executive Producer:** Ed Goren. **COO:** Larry Jones. **Executive VP, Production/Coordinating Studio Producer:** Scott Ackerson. **Executive VP, Production/Field Operations:** Bill Brown. **Executive VP, Programming/Production:** George Greenberg. **Executive VP, Creative Director:** Gary Hartley. **Senior VP, Production:** Jack Simmons. **Senior VP, Field/Technical Opearations, MLB on Fox:** Jerry Steinberg. **Senior VP, Research/Programming:** Bill Wagner. **Coordinating Producer, MLB on Fox:** Pete Macheska. **Director, Game Production, MLB on Fox:** Jacob Ullman.
Senior VP, Communcations: Lou D'Ermilio. **VP, Communications:** Dan Bell. **Director, Communications:** Ileana Pena. **Publicists:** Eddie Motl, Bob Broderick.

MLB NETWORK
Mailing Address: 40 Hartz Way, Suite 10, Secaucus, NJ 07094. **Telephone:** (201) 520-6400.
President/CEO: Tony Petitti. **Executive VP, Advertising/Sales:** Bill Morningstar. **Senior VP, Marketing/Promotion:** Mary Beck. **Senior VP, Production:** John Entz. **Senior VP, Distribution, Affiliate Sales/Marketing:** Art Marquez. **Senior VP, Programming/Business Affairs:** Rob McGlarry. **Senior VP, Finance/Administration:** Tony Santomauro. **VP, Programming:** Andy Butters. **VP, Engineering/I.T.:** Mark Haden. **VP, Remote Production:** Susan Stone. **Director, Remote Operations:** Tom Guidice. **Director, Studio:** Karen Whritner. **VP, Business Public Relations, Major League Baseball:** Matt Bourne. **Specialist, Business Public Relations, Major League Baseball:** Lauren Verrusio.

TURNER SPORTS
Mailing Address: 1015 Techwood Drive, Atlanta, GA 30318. **Telephone:** (404) 827-1700. **Fax:** (404) 827-1339. **Website:** www.tbs.com.
President: David Levy. **Senior VP, Executive Producer:** Jeff Behnke. **Senior VP, Sports Marketing/Programming:**

Jennifer Storms. **Senior VP, Sports Production/New Media:** Lenny Daniels. **VP, Sports Program Planning:** John Vandegrift. **Executive VP, Turner Sports Ad Sales/Marketing:** Jon Diament. **VP, Production:** Howard Zalkowitz. **Senior VP, Public Relations:** Sal Petruzzi. **Senior Director, Public Relations:** Jeff Pomeroy.

FOX SPORTS NET
Mailing Address: 10201 W. Pico Blvd., Building 103, Los Angeles, CA 90035. **Telephone:** (310) 369-1000. **Fax:** (310) 969-6049.
President/CEO, Fox Sports Television Group: David Hill. **President, Fox National Cable Networks:** Bob Thompson. **President, Fox Regional Cable Sports Networks:** Randy Freer. **Executive VP, Production:** Doug Sellars. **Senior VP, Communicatioins:** Lou D'Ermilio. **Senior VP, LA News Resource Center:** Rick Jaffe.

OTHER TELEVISION NETWORKS

CBS SPORTS
Mailing Address: 51 W. 52nd St., New York, NY 10019. **Telephone:** (212) 975-5230. **Fax:** (212) 975-4063.
President: Sean McManus. **VPs, Programming:** Mike Aresco, Rob Correa. **VP, Communications:** Leslie Anne Wade.

CNN SPORTS
Mailing Address: One CNN Center, Atlanta, GA 30303. **Telephone:** (404) 878-1600. **Fax:** (404) 878-0011.
Vice President, Production: Jeffrey Green.

HBO SPORTS
Mailing Address: 1100 Avenue of the Americas, New York, NY 10036. **Telephone:** (212) 512-1000. **Fax:** (212) 512-1751.
President, HBO Sports: Ross Greenburg.

NBC SPORTS
Mailing Address: 30 Rockefeller Plaza, Suite 1558, New York, NY 10112. **Telephone:** (212) 664-2014. **Fax:** (212) 664-6365.
Chairman: Dick Ebersol. **President:** Ken Schanzer. **VP, Sports Communications:** Mike McCarley.

ROGERS SPORTSNET (Canada)
Mailing Address: 9 Channel Nine Court, Toronto, ON M1S 4B5. **Telephone:** (416) 332-5600. **Fax:** (416) 332-5629. **Website:** www.sportsnet.ca.
President, Rogers Media: Tony Viner. **President, Rogers Sportsnet:** Doug Beeforth. **Director, Communications/Promotions:** Dave Rashford.

THE SPORTS NETWORK (Canada)
Mailing Address: 9 Channel Nine Court, Toronto, ON M1S 4B5. **Telephone:** (416) 384-5000. **Fax:** (416) 332-4337. **Website:** www.tsn.ca. **Executive Producer:** Jim Marshall.

RADIO NETWORKS

ESPN RADIO
Address: ESPN Plaza, 935 Middle St., Bristol, CT 06010. **Telephone:** (860) 766-2000, (800) 999-9985. **Fax:** (860) 589-5523. **Website:** espnradio.espn.go.com/espnradio/index.
GM, ESPN Radio Network: Mo Davenport. **Senior Director, Operations:** Scott Masteller. **Senior Director, Operations/Events:** Keith Goralski. **Senior Director, Radio Content/Operations:** Peter Gianesini. **Senior Director, Marketing/Integration:** Freddy Rolon. **Executive Producer, Event Production:** John Martin. **Senior Director, Engineering:** Kevin Plumb. **Executive Director, Affiliate Relations:** Jim Roberts.

XM SATELLITE RADIO
Mailing Address: 1500 Eckington Place NE, Washington, DC 20002. **Telephone:** (202) 380-4000. **Fax:** 202-380-4500. **E-Mail Address:** mlb@xmradio.com. **Website:** www.xmradio.com.
President/Chief Conent Officer: Scott Greenstein. **Senior VP, Sports:** Steve Cohen. **Senior Director, MLB Programming:** Chuck Dickemann. **Senior Director, Communications/Sports Programming:** Andrew Fitzpatrick. **Executive Producer, MLB Home Plate:** Chris Eno.

SPORTING NEWS RADIO NETWORK
Mailing Address: 2800 28th Street, Suite #308, Santa Monica, CA 90405. **Telephone:** (800) 224-2004. **Producers Line:** (800) 224-2004. **Fax:** (480) 945-0177. **E-Mail Address formula:** first initial, last name@sportingnews.com. **Website:** www.sportingnewsradio.com.
President: Clancy Woods. **Senior VP, Business Development:** Shawn Pastor. **Senior Programming Manager:** Craig Larson.

SPORTS BYLINE USA
Mailing Address: 300 Broadway, Suite 8, San Francisco, CA 94133. **Telephone:** (415) 434-8300. **Guest Line:** (800) 358-4457. **Studio Line:** (800) 878-7529. **Fax:** (415) 391-2569. **E-Mail Address:** questions@sportsbyline.com. **Website:** www.sportsbyline.com. **President:** Darren Peck. **Executive Producer:** Ira Hankin.

GENERAL INFORMATION

MAJOR LEAGUE BASEBALL PLAYERS ASSOCIATION

Mailing Address: 12 E. 49th St., 24th Floor, New York, NY 10017. **Telephone:** (212) 826-0808. **Fax:** (212) 752-4378. **E-Mail Address:** feedback@mlbpa.org. **Website:** www.mlbplayers.com.

Year Founded: 1966.

Executive Director/General Counsel: Michael Weiner.

Chief Labor Counsel: David Prouty. **Senior Advisor:** Rick Shapiro. **Assistant General Counsels:** Doyle Pryor, Robert Lenaghan, Ian Penny, Timothy Slavin, Robert Guerra, Matt Nussbaum. **Special Counsel:** Steve Fehr.

Director, Player Relations: Tony Clark. **Chief Administrative Officer:** Martha Child. **Chief Financial Officer:** Marietta DiCamillo. **Special Assistants to the Executive Director:** Bobby Bonilla, Phil Bradley, Rick Helling, Stan Javier, Mike Myers, Steve Rogers. **Player Relations:** Allyne Price, Virginia Carballo, Leonor Barua. **Contract Administrator:** Cindy Abercrombie. **Director, Communications:** Greg Bouris. **Director, Player Trust:** Melissa Persaud. **Accounting Assistants:** Terri Hinkley, Yolanda Largo. **Program Coordinator:** Hillary Falk. **Administrative Assistants:** Aisha Hope, Melba Markowitz, Sharon O'Donnell, Lisa Pepin, Deirdre Sweeney. **Receptionist:** Rebecca Rivera.

General Manager, Licensing: Richard White. **Category Director, Interactive Media:** Michael Amin. **New Media Content Director:** Chris Dahl. **Category Director, Trading Cards/Collectibles/New Business Development:** Evan Kaplan. **Retail Development Director/Category Director, Apparel:** Nancy Willis. **Licensing Manager, Hard Goods/ Collectibles:** Tom Cerabino. **Business Services Manager:** Heather Gould. **Licensing Assistants:** Paul McNeill, Eric Rivera. **Licensing Assistant, Sponsorship:** Ed Cerulo. **Manager, Office Services:** Victor Lugo. **Executive Secretary/Licensing:** Sheila Peters.

Executive Board: Player representatives of the 30 major league clubs.

MLBPA Association Representatives: Curtis Granderson, Craig Counsell. **Alternate Association Representatives:** Dave Bush, Jeremy Guthrie.

MLBPA Pension Representatives: Chris Capuano, Aaron Heilman. **Alternate Pension Representatives:** Russ Ohlendorf, Kevin Slowey.

SCOUTING

MAJOR LEAGUE BASEBALL SCOUTING BUREAU

Mailing Address: 3500 Porsche Way, Suite 100, Ontario, CA 91764. **Telephone:** (909) 980-1881. **Fax:** (909) 980-7794. **Year Founded:** 1974.

Director: Frank Marcos. **Assistant Director:** Rick Oliver. **Office Coordinator:** Debbie Keedy. **Administrative Assistant:** Adam Cali.

Board of Directors: Ed Burns (Major League Baseball), Dave Dombrowski (Tigers), Bob Gebhard (Diamondbacks), Roland Hemond (Diamondbacks), Frank Marcos (MLBSB), Alex Anthopoulos (Blue Jays), Randy Smith (Padres), Art Stewart (Royals), Kevin Towers (Padres), Rene Francisco (Royals).

Scouts: Rick Arnold (Spring Mills, PA), Howard Bowens (Elk Grove, CA) Andy Campbell (Gilbert, AZ), Mike Childers (Lexington, KY), Craig Conklin (Cayucos, CA), Dan Dixon (Temecula, CA), Art Gardner (Walnut Grove, MS), Rusty Gerhardt (Overton, TX), Dennis Haren (San Diego, CA), Chris Heidt (Rockford, IL), Don Jacoby (Winter Haven, FL), Don Kohler (Asbury, NJ), Mike Larson (Waseca, MN), Johnny Martinez (Overland Park, KS), Steve Merriman (Grandville, MI), Paul Mirocke (Wesley Chapel, FL), Carl Moesche (Gresham, OR), Tim Osborne (Woodstock, GA), Charles Peterson (Pembina, ND), Gary Randall (Rock Hill, SC), Willie Romay (Miami Springs, FL), Kevin Saucier (Pensacola, FL), Harry Shelton (Ocoee, FL), Pat Shortt (South Hempstead, NY), Craig Smajstrla (Pearland, TX), Ed Sukla (Irvine, CA), Jim Walton (Shattuck, OK).

Supervisor, Canada: Walt Burrows (Brentwood Bay, B.C.). **Canadian Scouts:** Curtis Bailey (Red Deer, Alberta), Jason Chee-Aloy (Toronto, Ontario), Bill Green (Vancouver, B.C.), Andrew Halpenny (Winnipeg, Manitoba), Ian Jordan (Kirkland, Quebec), Ken Lenihan (Bedford, Nova Scotia), Chris Kemlo (Oshawa, Ontario), Ken Lenihan (Beford Nova Scotia), Todd Plaxton (Saskatoon, Saskatchewan), Jasmin Roy (Longueuil, Quebec), Bob Smyth (Ladysmith, B.C.), Tony Wylie (Anchorage, AK).

Supervisor, Puerto Rico: Pepito Centeno (Cidra, PR).

Video Technicians: Matt Barnicle (Long Beach, CA), Purvis Cowens (Las Vegas, NV), Wayne Mathis (Cuero, TX), Christie Wood (Raleigh, N.C.).

PROFESSIONAL BASEBALL SCOUTS FOUNDATION

Mailing Address: 5010 North Parkway Calabasas, Suite 201, Calabasas, CA 91302. **Telephone:** (818) 224-3906. **Fax:** (818) 267-5516. **Website:** www.probBaseballscouts.com.

SCOUT OF THE YEAR FOUNDATION

Mailing Address: P.O. Box 211585, West Palm Beach, FL 33421. **Telephone:** (561) 798-5897, (561) 818-4329. **Fax:** (561) 798-4644. **E-Mail Address:** bertmazur@aol.com.

President: Roberta Mazur. **Vice President:** Tracy Ringolsby. **Treasurer:** Ron Mazur II.

Board of Advisers: Pat Gillick, Roland Hemond, Gary Hughes, Tommy Lasorda.

Scout of the Year Program Advisory Board: Tony DeMacio, Joe Klein, Roland Hemond, Gary Hughes, Dan Jennings, Linda Pereira.

UMPIRES

JIM EVANS ACADEMY OF PROFESSIONAL UMPIRING
Mailing Address: 200 South Wilcox St., #508, Castle Rock, CO 80104. **Telephone:** (303) 290-7411. **E-Mail Address:** jeapu@umpireacademy.com. **Website:** www.umpireacademy.com.
Operator: Jim Evans.

PROFESSIONAL BASEBALL UMPIRE CORP
Street Address: 9550 16th Street North, St. Petersburg, FL 33716.
Mailing Address: P.O. Box A, St. Petersburg, FL 33731-1950.
Telephone: 727-822-6937. **Fax:** 727-821-5819.
President: Pat O'Conner.
Treasurer/VP, Administration: Tim Purpura. **Secretary/VP, Legal Affairs/General Counsel:** D Scott Poley. **Executive Director, PBUC:** Justin Klemm. **Chief of Instruction/PBUC Evaluator:** Mike Felt. **Field Evaluators/Instructors:** Jorge Bauza, Dusty Dellinger, Rich Garcia, Matt Hollowell, Larry Reveal, Darren Spagnardi. **Special Assistant, PBUC:** Lillian Patterson.

THE UMPIRE SCHOOL
Mailing Address: P.O. Box A, St. Petersburg, FL, 33731.
Telephone: (877) 799-UMPS. **Fax:** (727) 821-5819.
Email: info@therightcall.net. **Website:** www.therightcall.net.
Operator: MiLB Vero Beach.

WENDELSTEDT UMPIRE SCHOOL
Mailing Address: 88 S. St. Andrews Dr., Ormond Beach, FL 32174.
Telephone: 800-818-1690. **E-Mail Address:** admin@umpireschool.com. **Website:** www.umpireschool.com.

WORLD UMPIRES ASSOCIATION
Mailing Address: P.O. Box 394, Neenah, WI 54957. **Telephone:** (920) 969-1580. **Fax:** (920) 969-1892. **E-Mail Address:** worldumpiresassn@aol.com. **Website:** www.worldumpires.com.
Year Founded: 2000.
President: Joe West. **Vice President:** Tom Hallion. **Secretary/Treasurer:** Jerry Layne. **Labor Counsel:** Brian Lam. **Administrator:** Phil Janssen.

TRAINERS

PROFESSIONAL BASEBALL ATHLETIC TRAINERS SOCIETY
Mailing Address: 400 Colony Square, Suite 1750, 1201 Peachtree St., Atlanta, GA 30361. **Telephone:** (404) 875-4000, ext. **1. Fax:** (404) 892-8560. **E-Mail Address:** rmallernee@mallernee-branch.com. **Website:** www.pbats.com.
Year Founded: 1983.
President: Richie Bancells (Baltimore Orioles). **Secretary:** Mark O'Neal (Chicago Cubs). **Treasurer:** Jeff Porter (Atlanta Braves). **American League Head Athletic Trainer Representative:** Ron Porterfield (Tampa Bay Rays). **American League Assistant Athletic Trainer Representative:** Rob Nodine (Seattle Mariners). **National League Head Athletic Trainer Representative:** Roger Caplinger (Milwaukee Brewers). **National League Assistant Athletic Trainer Representative:** Mike Kozak (Florida Marlins). **Immediate Past President:** Jamie Reed (Texas Rangers)
General Counsel: Rollin Mallernee.

MUSEUMS

BABE RUTH BIRTHPLACE
Office Address: 216 Emory St., **Baltimore, MD 21230. Telephone:** (410) 727-1539. **Fax:** (410) 727-1652. **E-Mail Address:** info@baberuthmuseum.com. **Website:** www.baberuthmuseum.com.
Year Founded: 1973.
Executive Director: Mike Gibbons. **Curator:** Shawn Herne.
Museum Hours: April-September, 10 a.m.-6 p.m (10 a.m.-7:30 p.m. for Baltimore Orioles home games); October-March, Tuesday-Sunday, 10 a.m.-5 p.m. (10 a.m.-8 p.m. for Baltimore Ravens home games).

CANADIAN BASEBALL HALL OF FAME AND MUSEUM
Museum Address: 386 Church St., St. Marys, Ontario N4X 1C2. **Mailing Address:** P.O. Box 1838, St. Marys, Ontario N4X 1C2. **Telephone:** (519) 284-1838. **Fax:** (519) 284-1234. **E-Mail Address:** baseball@baseballhalloffame.ca.
Website: www.baseballhalloffame.ca.
Year Founded: 1983.
President/CEO: Tom Valcke. **Director, Operations:** Scott Crawford.
Museum Hours: May—weekends only; June 1-Oct. 8—Daily, 10:30-4p.m.

FIELD OF DREAMS MOVIE SITE
Address: 28995 Lansing Rd., Dyersville, IA 52040. **Telephone:** (563) 875-8404; (888) 875-8404. **Fax:** (563) 875-7253. **E-Mail Address:** info@fodmoviesite.com. **Website:** www.fieldofdreamsmoviesite.com. **Year Founded:** 1989. **Office/Business Manager:** Betty Boeckenstedt. **Hours:** April-November, 9 a.m.-6 p.m.

LITTLE LEAGUE BASEBALL MUSEUM
Office Address: 525 Route 15 S., Williamsport, PA 17701. **Mailing Address:** P.O. Box 3485, Williamsport, PA 17701. **Telephone:** (570) 326-3607. **Fax:** (570) 326-2267. **E-Mail Address:** museum@littleleague.org.
Website: www.littleleague.org/museum.

Year Founded: 1982.
Director: Janice Ogurcak. **Administrative Assistant:** Adam Thompson.
Museum Hours: Memorial Day-Labor Day, 10 a.m.-7 p.m. (Sun, noon-7 p.m.); Labor Day-Memorial Day, Mon, Thurs, Fri, 10 a.m.-5 p.m., Sat noon-5 p.m., Sun noon-4 p.m.

LOUISVILLE SLUGGER MUSEUM AND FACTORY
Office Address: 800 W. Main St., Louisville, KY 40202. **Telephone:** (502) 588-7228. **Fax:** (502) 585-1179.
Website: www.sluggermuseum.org.
Year Founded: 1996.
Executive Director: Anne Jewell.
Museum Hours: Mon-Sat, Jan. 2-Dec. 23, 9 a.m.-5 p.m,; Sun (April-November), noon-5 p.m.

NATIONAL BASEBALL HALL OF FAME AND MUSEUM
Address: 25 Main St., Cooperstown, NY 13326. **Telephone:** (888) 425-5633, (607) 547-7200. **FAX:** (607) 547-2044. **E-Mail Address:** info@baseballhalloffame.org. **Website:** www.baseballhall.org.
Year Founded: 1939.
Chairman: Jane Forbes Clark. **Vice Chairman:** Joe Morgan. **President:** Jeff Idelson.
Museum Hours: Memorial Day Weekend-The Day Before Labor Day, 9 a.m.-9 p.m.; remainder of year, 9 a.m.-5 p.m. Open daily except Thanksgiving, Christmas, New Year's Day.
2011 Hall of Fame Induction Ceremony: July 24, 1:30 p.m. ET, Cooperstown, NY.

NEGRO LEAGUES BASEBALL MUSEUM
Mailing Address: 1616 E. 18th St., Kansas City, MO 64108. **Telephone:** (816) 221-1920. **FAX:** (816) 221-8424. **E-Mail Address:** nlmuseum@hotmail.com. **Website:** www.nlbm.com.
Year Founded: 1990.
Interim President: Raymond Doswell. **Executive Director Emeritus:** Don Motley.
Museum Hours: Tues.-Sat. 9 a.m.-6 p.m.; Sun. noon-6 p.m. Closed Monday.

NOLAN RYAN FOUNDATION AND EXHIBIT CENTER
Mailing Address: 2925 S. Bypass 35, Alvin, TX 77511. **Telephone:** (281) 388-1134. **FAX:** (281) 388-1135. **Website:** www.nolanryanfoundation.org.
Hours: Mon.-Sat. 9 a.m.-4 p.m.

RESEARCH

SOCIETY FOR AMERICAN BASEBALL RESEARCH
Mailing Address: (until march 31, 2011): 812 Huron Rd. E., Suite 719, Cleveland, OH 44115. **Telephone:** (216) 575-0500. **Fax:** (216) 575-0502. **Website:** www.sabr.org.
Year Founded: 1971.
President: Andy McCue. **Vice President:** Bill Nowlin. **Secretary:** Vince Gennaro. **Treasurer:** F.X. Flinn. **Directors:** Gary Gillette, Tom Hufford, Paul Hirsch, Leslie Heaphy. **Executive Director:** Marc Appleman. **Web Content Editor/Producer:** Jacob Pomrenke.

ALUMNI ASSOCIATIONS

MAJOR LEAGUE BASEBALL PLAYERS ALUMNI ASSOCIATION
Mailing Address: 1631 Mesa Ave., Suite D, Colorado Springs, CO 80906. **Telephone:** (719) 477-1870. **Fax:** (719) 477-1875.
E-Mail Address: postoffice@mlbpaa.com. **Website:** www.baseballalumni.com.
Facebook: facebook.com/majorleaguebaseballplayersalumniassociation. **Twitter:** @MLBPAA.
Chief Executive Officer: Dan Foster (dan@mlbpaa.com). **Chief Operating Officer:** Geoffrey Hixson (geoff@mlbpaa.com). **Vice President, Legends Entertainment Group:** Chris Torgusen (chris@mlbpaa.com). **VP, Development:** Lance James (lmj@mlbpaa.com). **Director, Special Events:** Mike Groll (mikeg@mlbpaa.com). **Director, Administration:** Mary Russell Baucom (maryrussell@mlbpaa.com). **Special Events Coordinator:** Tyler Kourajian (tyler@mlbpaa.com). **Public Relations Coordinator:** Nikki Warner (Nikki@mlbpaa.com). **Membership Coordinator:** Andy Obringer (andy@mlbpaa.com). **Director, Memorabilia:** Matthew Hazzard (matt@mlbpaa.com). **Memorabilia Coordinators:** Billy Horn (bhorn@mlbpaa.com), Matt Tissi (mtissi@mlbpaa.com).
President: Brooks Robinson.
Board of Directors: Sandy Alderson, John Doherty, Denny Doyle, Brian Fisher, Jim "Mudcat" Grant, Rich Hand, Jim Hannan, Steve Rogers, Will Royster, Jim Sadowski, Jose Valdivielso, Fred Valentine. **Legal Counsel:** Sam Moore.

MINOR LEAGUE BASEBALL ALUMNI ASSOCIATION
Mailing Address: P.O. Box A, St. Petersburg, FL 33731. **Telephone:** (727) 822-6937. **Fax:** (727) 821-5819. **E-Mail Address:** alumni@minorleaguebaseball.com. **Website:** www.milb.com.
Manager, Exhibiton Services/Alumni Association: Noreen Brantner.

ASSOCIATION OF PROFESSIONAL BALL PLAYERS OF AMERICA
Mailing Address: 101 S. Kraemer Blvd. Suite 112. **Telephone:** (714) 528-2012. **Fax:** (714) 528-2037.
E-Mail Address: ballplayersassn@aol.com. **Website:** www.apbpa.org.
Year Founded: 1924.
President: Roland Hemond. **First Vice President:** Tal Smith. **Second VP:** Stephen Cobb. **Third VP:** Tony Siegle. **Secretary/Treasurer:** Dick Beverage. **Membership Services Administrator:** Jennifer Joost-Van Sant.
Directors: Tony Gwynn, Whitey Herzog, Tony La Russa, Tom Lasorda, Brooks Robinson, Nolan Ryan, Tom Seaver, James

Leyland, Mike Scioscia.

BASEBALL ASSISTANCE TEAM (BAT)
Mailing Address: 245 Park Ave., 34th Floor, New York, NY 10167.
Telephone: (212) 931-7822, **Fax:** (212) 949-5433.
Website: www.baseballassistanceteam.com.
Year Founded: 1986.
To Make a Donation: (866) 605-4594.
President: Ted Sizemore.
Vice Presidents: Bob Gibson (HOF), Frank Torre, Greg Wilcox.
Board of Directors: Ruben Amaro, Sr., Steve Garvey, Luis Gonzalez, Joe Morgan (HOF), Jim Pongracz, Robin Roberts (HOF), Octavio "Cookie" Rojas, Gary Thorne, Randy Winn.
Executive Director: Joseph Grippo. **Secretary:** Thomas Ostertag. **Treasurer:** Scott Stamp. **Consultant:** Sam McDowell. **Operations:** Dominique Correa, Erik Nilsen.

MINISTRY

Baseball Chapel
Mailing Address: P.O. Box 302, Springfield, PA 19064. **Telephone:** (610) 690-2477.
E-Mail Address: office@baseballchapel.org. **Website:** www.baseballchapel.org.
Year Founded: 1973.
President: Vince Nauss.
Hispanic Ministry: Cali Magallanes, Gio Llerena. **Director, Ministry Operations:** Rob Crose.
Staff Supervisor: Steve Sisco.
Board of Directors: Don Christensen, Greg Groh, Dave Howard, Vince Nauss, Bill Sampen, Walt Wiley.

TRADE/EMPLOYMENT

BASEBALL WINTER MEETINGS
Mailing Address: P.O. Box A, St. Petersburg, FL 33731. **Telephone:** (727) 822-6937. **Fax:** (727) 821-5819. **E-Mail Address:** BaseballWinterMeetings@milb.com. **Website:** www.baseballwintermeetings.com.
2011 Convention: Dec. 5-8, Hilton Anatole, Dallas, TX.

BASEBALL TRADE SHOW
Mailing Address: P.O. Box A, St. Petersburg, FL 33731. **Telephone:** (866) 926-6452. **Fax:** (727) 683-9865. **E-Mail Address:** tradeshow@milb.com. **Website:** www.baseballtradeshow.com.
Contact: Noreen Brantner, Sr. Asst. Director, Exhibition Services & Sponsorships.
2011 Show: Dec. 5-7, Hilton Anatole, Dallas, TX.

PROFESSIONAL BASEBALL EMPLOYMENT OPPORTUNITIES
Mailing Address: P.O. Box A, St. Petersburg, FL 33731-1950. **Telephone:** 866-WE-R-PBEO. **Fax:** 727-821-5819. **Website:** www.PBEO.com. **Email:** info@pbeo.com. **Contact:** Darryl Henderson.

BASEBALL CARD MANUFACTURERS

DONRUSS/PLAYOFF
Mailing Address: 2300 E. Randol Mill, Arlington, TX 76011. **Telephone:** (817) 983-0300. **Fax:** (817) 983-0400.
Website: www.donruss.com.
Marketing Manager: Scott Prusha.

GRANDSTAND CARDS
Mailing Address: 22647 Ventura Blvd., #192, Woodland Hills, CA 91364. **Telephone:** (818) 992-5642.
Fax: (818) 348-9122. **E-Mail Address:** gscards1@pacbell.net. **Website:** www.grandstandcards.com.

MULTIAD SPORTS
Mailing Address: 1720 W. Detweiller Dr., Peoria, IL 61615. **Telephone:** (800) 348-6485, ext. 5111. **Fax:** (309) 692-8378.
E-Mail Address: bjeske@multiad.com. **Website:** www.multiad.com/sports.

TOPPS
Mailing Address: One Whitehall St., New York, NY 10004. **Telephone:** (212) 376-0300. **Fax:** (212) 376-0573.
Website: www.topps.com.

UPPER DECK
Mailing Address: 5909 Sea Otter Place, Carlsbad, CA 92008. **Telephone:** (800) 873-7332. **Fax:** (760) 929-6548.
E-Mail Address: customer_service@upperdeck.com. **Website:** www.upperdeck.com.

SPRING TRAINING

CACTUS LEAGUE

ARIZONA DIAMONDBACKS

Major League Clubs
Complex Address: Salt River Fields at Talking Stick, 7555 N. Pima Road, Scottsdale, AZ 85256. **Telephone:** (480) 270-5800. **Seating Capacity:** 11,000. **Location:** Take exit 44 (Indian Bend Rd.) and turn west, proceeding for approximately a half mile. Turn right at Pima and the ballpark will be located on the right.

Minor League Clubs
Complex Address: Salt River Fields at Talking Stick, 7555 N. Pima Road, Scottsdale, AZ 85256. **Telephone:** (480) 270-5800.

CHICAGO CUBS

Major League Clubs
Major League Complex Address: HoHoKam Park, 1235 N. Center St., Mesa, AZ 85201. **Telephone:** (480) 668-0500. **Seating Capacity:** 12,632. **Location:** Main Street (U.S. Highway 60) to Center Street, north 1 1/2 miles on Center Street.
Hotel Address: Best Western Dobson Ranch Inn, 1666 S. Dobson Rd., Mesa, AZ 85202. **Telephone:** (480) 831-7000.

Minor League Clubs
Complex Address: Fitch Park, 160 E. Sixth Place, Mesa, AZ 85201. **Telephone:** (480) 668-0500. **Fax:** (480) 668-4501. **Hotel Address:** Best Western Mezona, 250 W. Main St., Mesa, AZ 85201. **Telephone:** (480) 834-9233.

CHICAGO WHITE SOX

Major League Clubs
Complex Address: Camelback Ranch—Glendale, 10710 West Camelback Road, Glendale, AZ 85037. **Telephone:** (623) 302-5200. **Seating Capacity:** 13,000.
Hotel Address: Comfort Suites Glendale, 9824 W. Camelback Rd., Glendale, AZ 85305. **Telephone:** (623) 271-9005.

Minor League Clubs
Complex Address: Same as major league club.

CINCINNATI REDS

Major League Clubs
Complex Address: Cincinnati Reds Player Development Complex, 3125 S. Wood Blvd., Goodyear, AZ 85338. (623) 932-6590. **Ballpark Address:** Goodyear Ballpark, 1933 S. Ballpark Way, Goodyear, AZ 85338. **(623) 882-3120**
Hotel Address: Marriott Residence Inn, 7350 N. Zanjero Blvd., Glendale. AZ 85305. **Telephone:** (623) 772-8900. **Fax:** (623) 772-8905.

Minor League Clubs
Complex Address: Same as major league club.

CLEVELAND INDIANS

Major League Clubs
Major League Complex Address: Cleveland Indians Player Development Complex, 2601 S. Wood Blvd., Goodyear, AZ 85338. **Telephone:** (623) 302-5678. **Fax:** (623) 302-5670. **Seating Capacity:** 8,000.
Hotel Address: Quality Inn, 950 North Dysart Road, Goodyear, AZ 85338. **Telephone:** (623) 932-9191. **Telephone:** (863) 294-4451.

Minor League Clubs
Complex Address/Hotel: Same as major league club.

COLORADO ROCKIES

Major League Clubs
Major League Complex Address: Salt River Fields at Talking Stick, 7555 N. Pima Rd., Scottsdale, AZ 85258. **Telephone:** (480) 270-5800. **Location:** From Loop 101 northbound, Take exit 44 (Indian Bend Rd.) and turn left, proceeding west for approximately a half mile. Turn right at Pima and the ballpark will be located on the right. From Loop 101 southbound, Take exit 43 (Via De Ventura) and turn right, proceeding west for a half mile. Turn left at the Via De Ventura entrance into the ballpark parking lot. **Hotel Address:** The Scottsdale Plaza Resort, 7200 North Scottsdale Road, Scottsdale, AZ 85253. **Telephone:** (480) 948-5000. **Fax:** (480) 951-5100.

Minor League Clubs
Complex/Hotel Address: Same as major league club.

KANSAS CITY ROYALS

Major League Clubs
Complex Address: Surprise Stadium, 15946 N. Bullard Ave., Surprise, AZ 85374. **Telephone:** (623) 222-2222. **Seating Capacity:** 10,700. **Location:** I-10 West to Route 101 North, 101 North to Bell Road, left on Bell for five miles, stadium on left.
Hotel Address: Wigwam Resort, 300 East Wigwam Blvd., Litchfield Park, Arizona 85340. **Telephone:** (623)-935-3811

Minor League Clubs
Complex: Same as major league club. **Hotel Address:** Comfort Hotel and Suites, 13337 W. Grand Ave., Surprise, AZ 85374. **Telephone:** (623) 583-3500.

LOS ANGELES ANGELS

Major League Clubs
Complex Address: Tempe Diablo Stadium, 2200 W. Alameda, Tempe, AZ 85282. **Telephone:** (480) 858-7500. **Fax:** (480) 438-7583. **Seating Capacity:** 9,558. **Location:** I-10 to exit 153B (48th Street), south one mile on 48th Street to Alameda Drive, left on Alameda.

Minor League Clubs
Complex Address: Tempe Diablo Minor League Complex, 2225 W. Westcourt Way, Tempe, AZ 85282. **Telephone:** (480) 858-7558. **Hotel Address:** Sheraton Phoenix Airport, 1600 South 52nd Street, Tempe, AZ 85281. **Telephone:** (480) 967-6600.

LOS ANGELES DODGERS

Major League Clubs
Complex Address: Camelback Ranch, 10710 West Camelback Rd., Phoenix, AZ 85037. **Seating Capacity:** 13,636.
Location: I-10 or I-17 to Loop 101 West or North, Take Exit 5, Camelback Road West to ballpark. **Telephone:** (623) 302-5000. **Hotel:** Unavailable.

Minor League Clubs
Complex/Hotel Address: Same as major league club.

MILWAUKEE BREWERS

Major League Clubs
Complex Address: Maryvale Baseball Park, 3600 N. 51st Ave., Phoenix, AZ 85031. **Telephone:** (623) 245-5555. **Seating Capacity:** 9,000. **Location:** I-10 to 51st Ave., north on 51st Ave.
Hotel Address: Staybridge Suites, 9340 West Cabella Drive, Glendale, AZ 85305. **Telephone:** (623) 842-0000

Minor League Teams
Complex Address: Maryvale Baseball Complex, 3805 N. 53rd Ave., Phoenix, AZ 85031. **Telephone:** (623) 245-5600. **Hotel Address:** Same as major league club.

OAKLAND ATHLETICS

Major League Clubs
Complex Address: Phoenix Municipal Stadium, 5999 E. Van Buren, Phoenix, AZ 85008. **Telephone:** (602) 225-9400. **Seating Capacity:** 8,500. **Location:** I-10 to exit 153 (48th Street), HoHoKam Expressway to Van Buren Street (U.S. Highway 60), right on Van Buren. **Hotel Address:** Doubletree Suites Hotel, 320 N. 44th St., Phoenix, AZ 85008. **Telephone:** (602) 225-0500.

Minor League Clubs
Complex Address: Papago Park Baseball Complex, 1802 N. 64th St., Phoenix, AZ 85008. **Telephone:** (480) 949-5951. **Hotel Address:** Crowne Plaza, 4300 E. Washington, Phoenix, AZ 85034. **Telephone:** (602) 273-7778.

SAN DIEGO PADRES

Major League Clubs
Complex Address: Peoria Sports Complex, 8131 W. Paradise Lane, Peoria, AZ 85382. **Telephone:** (623) 486-7000. **Fax:** (623) 486-7154. **Seating Capacity:** 10,000. **Location:** I-17 to Bell Road exit, west on Bell to 83rd Ave. **Hotel Address:** La Quinta Inns and Suites, 16321 N. 83rd Avenue Peoria, AZ 85382. **Telephone:** (623) 487-1900.

Minor League Teams
Complex/Hotel: Same as major league club.

SAN FRANCISCO GIANTS

Major League Clubs
Complex Address: Scottsdale Stadium, 7408 E. Osborn Rd., Scottsdale, AZ 85251. **Telephone:** (480) 990-7972. **Fax:** (480) 990-2643. **Seating Capacity:** 11,500. **Location:** Scottsdale Road to Osborne Road, east on Osborne 1/2 mile. **Hotel Address:** Hilton Garden Inn Scottsdale Old Town, 7324 East Indian School Rd., Scottsdale, AZ 85251. **Telephone:** (480) 481-0400.

Minor League Clubs
Complex Address: Giants Minor League Complex 8045 E. Camelback Road, Scottsdale, AZ 85251. **Telephone:** (480) 990-0052. **Fax:** (480) 990-2349.

SEATTLE MARINERS

Major League Clubs
Complex Address: Peoria Sports Complex (1993), 15707 N. 83rd Ave., Peoria, AZ 85382. **Telephone:** (623) 776-4800. **Fax:** (623) 776-4829. **Seating Capacity:** 11,000. **Location:** I-17 to Bell Road exit, west on Bell to 83rd Ave. **Hotel Address:** LaQuinta Inn & Suites, 16321 N. 83rd Ave., Peoria, AZ 85382. **Telephone:** (623) 487-1900.

Minor League Clubs
Complex Address: Peoria Sports Complex (1993), 15707 N. 83rd Ave., Peoria, AZ 85382. **Telephone:** (623) 776-4800. **Fax:** (623) 776-4828. **Hotel Address:** Hampton Inn, 8408 W. Paradise Lane, Peoria, AZ 85382. **Telephone:** (623) 486-9918.

TEXAS RANGERS

Major League Club
Complex Address: Surprise Stadium, 15754 N. Bullard Ave., Surprise, AZ 85374. **Telephone:** (623) 266-8100. **Seating Capacity:** 10,714. **Location:** I-10 West to Route 101 North, 101 North to Bell Road, left at Bell for seven miles, stadium on left. **Hotel Address:** Windmill Suites at Sun City West, 12545 W. Bell Rd., Surprise, AZ 85374. **Telephone:** (623) 583-0133.

Minor League Clubs
Complex Address: Same as major league club. **Hotel Address:** Hampton Inn, 2000 N. Litchfield Rd., Goodyear, AZ 85338. **Telephone:** (623) 536-1313; **Hotel Address:** Holiday Inn Express, 1313 N. Litchfield Rd., Goodyear, AZ 85338. **Telephone:** (623) 535-1313.

GRAPEFRUIT LEAGUE

ATLANTA BRAVES

Major League Clubs
Stadium Address: Champion Stadium at ESPN Wide World of Sports Complex, 700 S. Victory Way, Kissimmee, FL 34747. **Telephone:** (407) 939-1500. **Seating Capacity:** 9,500. **Location:** I-4 to exit 25B (Highway 192 West), follow signs to Magic Kingdom/Wide World of Sports Complex, right on Victory Way.
Hotel Address: World Center Marriott, World Center Drive, Orlando, FL 32821. **Telephone:** (407) 239-4200.

Minor League Clubs
Complex Address: Same as major league club. **Telephone:** (407) 939-2232. **Fax:** (407) 939-2225. **Address:** Marriot Village at Lake Buena Vista, 8623 Vineland Ave., Orlando, FL 32821. **Telephone:** (407) 938-9001.

BALTIMORE ORIOLES

Major League Clubs
Complex Address: Ed Smith Stadium, 2700 12th Street, Sarasota, FL 34237. **Telephone:** (941) 954-4101. **Fax:** (941) 365-1587. **Seating Capacity:** Unavailable. **Location:** I-75 to exit 210, West on Fruitville Road, right on Tuttle Avenue. **Hotel Address:** Homewood Suites by Hilton, 3470 Fruitville Road, Sarasota, FL 34237. **Telephone:** (941) 365-7300.

Minor League Clubs
Complex Address: Twin Lakes Park, 6700 Clark Rd., Sarasota, FL 34241. **Telephone:** (941) 923-1996. **Hotel Address:** Days Inn, 5774 Clark Rd., Sarasota, FL 34233. **Telephone:** (941) 921-7812. **Hotel Address:** AmericInn, 5931 Fruitville Rd., Sarasota, FL 34232. **Telephone:** (941) 342-8778.

BOSTON RED SOX

Major League Clubs
Complex Address: City of Palms Park, 2201 Edison Ave., Fort Myers, FL 33901. **Telephone:** (239) 334-4700. **Location:** I-75 to exit 138, four miles west to Fowler St., left on Fowler to Edison Ave., right on Edison Ave., park on right.

Minor League Clubs
Complex Address: Red Sox Player Development Complex, 4301 Edison Ave., Fort Myers, FL 33916. **Telephone:** (239) 334-4700.

DETROIT TIGERS

Major League Clubs
Complex Address: Joker Marchant Stadium, 2301 Lakeland Hills Blvd., Lakeland, FL 33805. **Telephone:** (863) 686-8075. **Seating Capacity:** 9,000. **Location:** I-4 to exit 19 (Lakeland Hills Boulevard). **Hotel Address:** Unavailable.

Minor League Clubs
Complex/Hotel Address: Tigertown, 2125 N. Lake Ave., Lakeland, FL 33805. **Telephone:** (863) 686-8075.

FLORIDA MARLINS

Major League Clubs
Complex Address: Roger Dean Stadium, 4751 Main St., Jupiter, FL 33458. **Telephone:** (561) 775-1818. **Telephone:** 561-799-1346.
Seating Capacity: 7,000.
Location: I-95 to exit 83, east on Donald Ross Road for one mile to Central Blvd, left at light, follow Central Boulevard to circle and take Main Street to Roger Dean Stadium.
Hotel Address: Hilton Garden Inn, 3505 Kyoto Gardens Dr., Palm Beach Gardens, FL 33410. **Telephone:** (561) 694-5833. **Fax:** (561) 694-5829.

Minor League Clubs
Complex Address: Same as major league club. **Hotel Address:** Same as Major League Club

HOUSTON ASTROS

Major League Clubs
Complex Address: Osceola County Stadium, 631 Heritage Park Way, Kissimmee, FL 34744. **Telephone:** (321) 697-3150. **Fax:** (321) 697-3195. **Seating Capacity:** 5,300. **Location:** From Florida Turnpike South, take exit 244, west on U.S. 192, right on Bill Beck Blvd.
Hotel Address: Reunion Resort & Club, 1000 Reunion Way, Reunion, Florida 34747. **Telephone:** 407-662-1000.

MINNESOTA TWINS

Major League Clubs
Complex Address: Lee County Sports Complex/Hammond Stadium, 14100 Six Mile Cypress Pkwy., Fort Myers, FL 33912. **Telephone:** (239) 533-7610. **Seating Capacity:** 7,905. **Location:** Exit 21 off I-75, west on Daniels Parkway, left on Six Mile Cypress Parkway.
Hotel Address: Hilton Garden Inn, 12600 University Drive, Fort Myers, FL 33907. **Telephone:** (239) 790-3500.

Minor League Clubs
Complex Address/Hotel: Same as major league club.

NEW YORK METS

Major League Clubs
Complex Address: Digital Domain Park, 525 NW Peacock Blvd., Port St. Lucie, FL 34986. **Telephone:** (772) 871-2100. **Seating Capacity:** 7,000. **Location:** Exit 121C (St. Lucie West Blvd) off I-95, east 1/4 mile, left onto NW Peacock.
Hotel Address: Hilton Hotel, 8542 Commerce Centre Drive, Port St. Lucie, FL 34986. **Telephone:** (772) 871-6850.

Minor League Clubs
Complex Address: Same as major league club. **Hotel Address:** Main Stay Suites, 8501 Champions Way, Port St. Lucie, FL 34986. **Telephone:** (772) 460-8882.

NEW YORK YANKEES

Major League Clubs

Complex Address: George M. Steinbrenner Field, One Steinbrenner Dr., Tampa, FL 33614. **Telephone:** (813) 879-2244. **Seating Capacity:** 11,076. **Hotel:** Unavailable.

Minor League Clubs

Complex Address: Yankees Player Development/Scouting Complex, 3102 N. Himes Ave., Tampa, FL 33607. **Telephone:** (813) 875-7569. **Hotel:** Unavailable.

PHILADELPHIA PHILLIES

Major League Clubs

Complex Address: Bright House Networks Field, 601 N. Old Coachman Rd., Clearwater, FL 33765. **Telephone:** (727) 467-4457. **Fax:** (727) 712-4498. **Seating Capacity:** 8,500. **Location:** Route 60 West, right on Old Coachman Road, ballpark on right after Drew Street.

Hotels: Holiday Inn Express, 2580 Gulf to Bay Blvd., Clearwater, FL 33765. **Telephone:** (727) 797-6300. La Quinta Inn, 21338 US 19 North, Clearwater, FL 33765. **Telephone:** (727) 799-1565.

Minor League Clubs

Complex Address: Carpenter Complex, 651 N. Old Coachman Rd., Clearwater, FL 33765. **Telephone:** (727) 799-0503. **Fax:** (727) 726-1793. **Hotel Addresses:** Hampton Inn, 21030 U.S. Highway 19 North, Clearwater, FL 34625. **Telephone:** (727) 797-8173. **Hotel Address:** Econolodge, 21252 U.S. Hwy. 19, Clearwater, FL 34625. **Telephone:** (727) 799-1569.

PITTSBURGH PIRATES

Major League Clubs

Stadium Address: McKechnie Field, 17th Ave. West and Ninth Street West, Bradenton, FL 34205. **Seating Capacity:** 6,562. **Location:** U.S. 41 to 17th Ave, west to 9th Street.

Complex/Hotel Address: Pirate City, 1701 27th St. E., Bradenton, FL 34208. **Telephone:** (941) 747-3031. **FAX:** (941) 747-9549.

Minor League Clubs

Complex/Hotel Address: Same as major league club.

ST. LOUIS CARDINALS

Major League Clubs

Complex Address: Roger Dean Stadium, 4795 University Dr., Jupiter, FL 33458. **Telephone:** (561) 775-1818. **Fax:** (561) 799-1380. **Seating Capacity:** 6,864. **Location:** I-95 to exit 58, east on Donald Ross Road for 1/4 mile.

Hotel Address: Embassy Suites, 4350 PGA Blvd., Palm Beach Gardens, FL 33410. **Telephone:** (561) 622-1000.

Minor League Clubs Complex: Same as major league club. **Hotel:** Double Tree Palm Beach Gardens.

TAMPA BAY RAYS

Major League Clubs

Stadium Address: Charlotte Sports Park, 2300 El Jobean Road, Port Charlotte, FL, 33948. **Telephone:** (888) 326-7297. **Seating Capacity:** 6,823. **Location:** I-75 to US-17 to US-41, turn left onto El Jobean Rd. **Hotel Address:** Unavailable.

Minor League Clubs

Complex/Hotel Address: Same as major league club.

TORONTO BLUE JAYS

Major League Clubs

Stadium Address: Florida Auto Exchange Stadium, 373 Douglas Ave., Dunedin, FL 34698. **Telephone:** (727) 734-8007. **Seating Capacity:** 5,509. **Location:** From I-275, north on Highway 19, left on Sunset Point Road for 4 miles, right on Douglas Avenue, stadium one mile on right.

Minor League Clubs

Complex Address: Bobby Mattick Training Center at Englebert Complex, 1700 Solon Ave., Dunedin, FL 34698. **Telephone:** (727) 743-8007. **Hotel Address:** Baymont Inn & Suites 26508 U.S. 19 North, Clearwater, FL 33761. **Telephone:** (727) 796-1234.

WASHINGTON NATIONALS

Major League Clubs

Complex Address: Space Coast Stadium, 5800 Stadium Pkwy., Viera, FL 32940. **Telephone:** (321) 633-9200. **Seating Capacity:** 8,100. **Location:** I-95 southbound to Fiske Blvd. (exit 74), south on Fiske/Stadium Parkway to stadium; I-95 northbound to State Road #509/Wickham Road (exit 73), left off exit, right on Lake Andrew Drive; turn right on Stadium Parkway, stadium is 1/2 mile on left.

Hotel Address: Melbourne Airport Hilton, 200 Rialto Place, Melbourne, FL 32901. **Telephone:** (321) 768-0200.

Minor League Clubs

Complex Address: Carl Barger Complex, 5600 Stadium Pkwy., Viera, FL 32940. **Telephone:** (321) 633-8119. **Hotel Address:** Imperial Hotel & Conference Center, 8298 N. Wickman Rd., Viera, FL 32940. **Telephone:** (321) 255-0077.

TEAM UP WITH A LEADER.
FOR OVER 80 YEARS.

GEAR UP WITH THE BEST.
FOR ALL YOUR BASEBALL NEEDS.

- **SHOES** NIKE • ADIDAS • MIZUNO • UNDER ARMOUR
  PITCHING TOES APPLIED ON PREMISES
- **GLOVES** FULL LINE OF PRO STOCK GLOVES
  WILSON • MIZUNO • RAWLINGS • NIKE • LOUISVILLE
- **PROTECTIVE GEAR** EVOSHIELD
- **PRO STOCK BATS**
- **UNDER ARMOUR**
- **BATTING GLOVES**
- **SLIDING SHORTS**
- **UNIFORMS**
- **HEADWEAR**
- **RADAR GUNS**
- **DRI-FIT CLOTHING**
- **TROPHIES**
- **& MORE**

FRANK'S
SPORT SHOP   *NEW YORK'S BEST SINCE 1922*

718**299-5223**   212**945-0020**   Fax 718**583-1652**

BaseBall america ®

MAJORS ◆ MINORS ◆ PROSPECTS ◆ DRAFT ◆ COLLEGE ◆ HIGH SCHOOL

BOOKS

CALL 800-845-2726 9 A.M. – 5 P.M., MONDAY-FRIDAY ET

CLICK BaseballAmerica.com/store

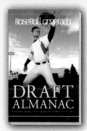

DRAFT ALMANAC

The only reference book of its kind, giving you a complete list of every player drafted since the draft's inception in 1965.

AVAILABLE NOW! $21.95

2011 ALMANAC

Major league news and stats, plus minor league stats, an overview of each organization's season, and a full draft.

AVAILABLE NOW! $23.95

2011 PROSPECT HANDBOOK

It's the definitive reference title on prospects, profiling the top 30 in each organization—900 reviews in all.

AVAILABLE NOW! $32.95

2011 SUPER REGISTER

The only book that lists career stats for every active player in the majors & minors in '10, more than 6,000 in all.

AVAILABLE NOW! $82.95

MAGAZINE

Every two weeks, Baseball America brings passionate fans and industry insiders the most complete coverage of the game. We've been around for over 29 years, bringing you baseball news you can't get anywhere else. Your subscription includes access to premium content at **BaseballAmerica.com**. Double issues count as two.

THREE MONTHS (6 ISSUES) $33.00   **ONE YEAR (26 ISSUES) $92.95**

SIX MONTHS (13 ISSUES) $57.95   **TWO YEARS (52 ISSUES) $137.90**

NEW! DIGITAL EDITION

It's the magazine on the go to click through, save stories, translaste them into multiple languages, and see photos bigger, better and in high resolution. Read back issues, or search for news about your favorite team or player.

ONE ISSUE $5.50

SIX MONTHS (13 ISSUES) $34.00

ONE YEAR (26 ISSUES) $44.00

WEBSITE

Visit **BaseballAmerica.com** for daily coverage and expansive draft coverage. Subscribers are entitled to premium Baseball America content you can't find anywhere else.

THREE MONTHS $27.00

SIX MONTHS $47.00

ONE YEAR $66.00

CLICK BaseballAmerica.com/subscribe

For international rates please visit our website

MINOR
LEAGUES

MINOR LEAGUE BASEBALL

NATIONAL ASSOCIATION OF PROFESSIONAL BASEBALL LEAGUES

MINOR LEAGUE BASEBALL ™

Street Address: 9550 16th Street North, St. Petersburg, FL 33716. **Mailing Address:** P.O. Box A, St. Petersburg, FL 33731-1950. **Telephone:** 727-822-6937. **Fax:** 727-821-5819. **Fax (Marketing):** 727-894-4227. **Fax (Licensing):** 727-825-3785. **President:** Pat O'Conner. **Vice President:** Stan Brand. **Executive VP/COO:** Tim Purpura. **Senior VP, Finance:** David Nunes; Senior VP, Legal Affairs/General Counsel: D. **Scott Poley. VP, Baseball/Business Operations:** Tim Brunswick. **VP, Business Development:** Tina Gust. **Special Counsel:** George Yund. **Executive Director, Communications:** Steve Densa. **Director, Security/Facility Operations:** John Skinner. **Assistant Director, Legal Affairs:** Louis Brown. **Manager, Baseball Operations/Executive Assistant to the President:** Mary Wooters.

MINOR LEAGUE BASEBALL DURHAM OPERATIONS OFFICE
Street Address: 539 Foster St., Durham, NC 27701. **Mailing Address:** PO Box 1371, Durham, NC 27702. **Telephone:** 919-530-8400. **Fax:** 919-530-8403. **Website:** www.durhamathleticpark. com. **General Manager, Durham Athletic Park:** Jill Rusinko.

MINOR LEAGUE BASEBALL VERO BEACH OPERATIONS OFFICE
Street Address: 4003 26th Street, Vero Beach FL 32961. **Mailing Address:** P.O. Box 2887, Vero Beach, FL 32961-2887. **Telephone:** 772-569-4900. **Fax:** 772-257-8560. **e-mail:** ccallan@milb.com. **VP, MiLB-Vero Beach:** Craig Callan. **Director, Athletics/Marketing:** Jeff Biddle. **Assistant to the VP:** Nancy Gollnick.

Pat O'Conner

AFFILIATED MEMBERS/COUNCIL OF LEAGUE PRESIDENTS

Triple-A

League	President	Telephone	Fax Number
International	Randy Mobley	(614) 791-9300	(614) 791-9009
Mexican	Plinio Escalante	011-52-555-557-1007	011-52-555-557-1007
Pacific Coast	Branch Rickey	(512) 310-2900	(512) 310-8300

Double-A

League	President	Telephone	Fax Number
Eastern	Joe McEacharn	(207) 761-2700	(207) 761-7064
Southern	Don Mincher	(770) 321-0400	(770) 321-0037
Texas	Tom Kayser	(210) 545-5297	(210) 545-5298

High Class A

League	President	Telephone	Fax Number
California	Charlie Blaney	(805) 985-8585	(805) 985-8580
Carolina	John Hopkins	(336) 691-9030	(336) 691-9070
Florida State	Chuck Murphy	(386) 252-7479	(386) 252-7495

Low Class A

League	President	Telephone	Fax Number
Midwest	George Spelius	(608) 364-1188	(608) 364-1913
South Atlantic	Eric Krupa	(727) 456-1240	(727) 499-6853

Short-Season

League	President	Telephone	Fax Number
New York-Penn	Ben Hayes	(727) 821-7000	(727) 822-3768
Northwest	Bob Richmond	(208) 429-1511	(208) 429-1525

Rookie Advanced

League	President	Telephone	Fax Number
Appalachian	Lee Landers	(704) 873-5300	(704) 873-4333
Pioneer	Jim McCurdy	(509) 456-7615	(509) 456-0136

Rookie

League	President	Telephone	Fax Number
Arizona	Bob Richmond	(208) 429-1511	(208) 429-1525
Dominican Summer	Orlando Diaz	(809) 532-3619	(809) 532-3619
Gulf Coast	Operated by MILB	(727) 456-1734	(727) 821-5819
Venezuela Summer	Saul Gonzalez	011-58-41-24-0321	011-58-41-24-0705

NATIONAL ASSOCIATION BOARD OF TRUSTEES

TRIPLE-A
At-large: Ken Young (Norfolk). **International League:** Mike Tamburro (Pawtucket). **Pacific Coast League:** Sam Bernabe, Chairman (Iowa). **Mexican League:** Cuauhtemoc Rodriguez (Quintana Roo).

DOUBLE-A
Eastern League: Joe Finley, (Trenton). **Southern League:** Frank Burke (Chattanooga). **Texas League:** Reid Ryan (Corpus Christi).

CLASS A
California League: Tom Volpe (Stockton). **Carolina League:** Chuck Greenberg (Myrtle Beach). **Florida State League:** Ken Carson, secretary (Dunedin). **Midwest League:** Dave Walker (Burlington). **South Atlantic League:** Chip Moore (Rome).

SHORT-SEASON
New York-Penn League: Bill Gladstone (Tri-City). **Northwest League:** Bobby Brett (Spokane).

ROOKIE
Appalachian League: Mitch Lukevics (Princeton). **Pioneer League:** Dave Baggott, vice chairman (Ogden). **Gulf Coast League:** Bill Smith (Twins).

PROFESSIONAL BASEBALL PROMOTION CORP
Street Address: 9550 16th Street North, St. Petersburg, FL 33716.
Mailing Address: P.O. Box A, St. Petersburg, FL 33731-1950.
Telephone: 727-822-6937. **Fax:** 727-821-5819. **Fax/Marketing:** 727-894-4227. **Fax/Licensing:** 727-825-3785.
President: Pat O'Conner.
Executive VP/COO: Tim Purpura. **Senior VP, Finance:** David Nunes. **Senior VP, Legal Affairs/General Counsel:** D. Scott Poley. **VP, Baseball/Business Operations:** Tim Brunswick. **VP, BIRCO/Business Services:** Brian Earle. **VP, Business Development:** Tina Gust. **VP, Sales/Marketing:** Rod Meadows. **Executive Director, Communications:** Steve Densa. **Director, Information Technology:** Rob Colamarino. **Director, Licensing:** Sandie Hebert. **Director, Business Development:** Scott Kravchuk. **Director, Security/Facility Operations:** John Skinner.
Senior Assistant Director, Event Services: Kelly Butler. **Senior Assistant Director, Exhibition Services/Sponsorships:** Noreen Brantner. **Assistant Director, Licensing:** Carrie Adams. **Assistant Director, Sales/Marketing:** Melissa Agee. **Assistant Director, Legal Affairs:** Louis Brown. **Assistant Director, Accounting:** James Dispanet. **GM, DAP/MiLB Charities:** Jill Rusinko. **Senior Account Manager:** Heather Raburn. **Manager, Accounting:** Jeff Carrier. **Manager, Sponsor Relations:** Nicole Ferro. **Contract Manager/Legal Assistant:** Jeannette Machicote. **Manager, Team Relations/Sponsorship Development:** Mary Marandi. **Manager, Creative Services:** Rusty Morris. **Trademark Manager:** Bryan Sayre. **Manager, Baseball Ops./Executive Assistant to President:** Mary Wooters. **Coordinator, Affiliate Programs:** Darryl Henderson. **Coordinator, Business Services:** Jessica Watts. **Assistant, Baseball Operations:** Andy Shultz. **Receptionist:** Sheryl Hamilton.

PROFESSIONAL BASEBALL UMPIRE CORP
Street Address: 9550 16th Street North, St. Petersburg, FL 33716.
Mailing Address: P.O. Box A, St. Petersburg, FL 33731-1950.
Telephone: 727-822-6937. **Fax:** 727-821-5819.
President: Pat O'Conner. **Treasurer/VP, Administration:** Tim Purpura. **Secretary/VP, Legal Affairs/General Counsel:** D. Scott Poley. **Executive Director, PBUC:** Justin Klemm. **Chief of Instruction/PBUC Evaluator:** Mike Felt. **Field Evaluators/Instructors:** Jorge Bauza, Dusty Dellinger, Rich Garcia, Matt Hollowell, Larry Reveal, Darren Spagnardi. **Special Assistant, PBUC:** Lillian Patterson.

GENERAL INFORMATION

Regular Season		All-Star Games					
	Teams	Games	Opening Day	Closing Day	Date	Host	
International	14	144	April 7	Sept. 5	*July 13	Salt Lake	
Pacific Coast	16	144	April 7	Sept. 5	*July 13	Salt Lake	
Eastern	12	142	April 7	Sept. 5	July 13	New Hampshire	
Southern	10	140	April 7	Sept. 5	June 21	Jackson	
Texas	8	140	April 7	Sept. 5	June 29	San Antonio	
California	10	140	April 7	Sept. 5	#June 21	Modesto	
Carolina	8	140	April 7	Sept. 5	#June 21	Modesto	
Florida State	12	140	April 7	Sept. 5	June 18	Clearwater	
Midwest	16	140	April 7	Sept. 5	June 21	Quad Cities	
South Atlantic	14	140	April 7	Sept. 5	June 21	Delmarva	
New York-Penn	14	76	June 17	Sept. 4	Aug. 16	Lowell	
Northwest	8	76	June 17	Sept. 3	None		
Appalachian	10	68	June 21	Aug. 30	None		
Pioneer	8	76	June 20	Sept. 8	None		
Arizona	13	56	June 20	Aug. 27	None		
Gulf Coast	15	56/60	June 20	Aug. 27	None		

*Triple-A All-Star Game. #California League vs. Carolina League

 # INTERNATIONAL LEAGUE

Office Address: 55 South High St., Suite 202, Dublin, Ohio 43017.
Telephone: (614) 791-9300. **Fax:** (614) 791-9009.
E-Mail Address: office@ilbaseball.com. **Website:** www.ilbaseball.com.
Years League Active: 1884-

President/Treasurer: Randy Mobley
Vice Presidents: Dave Rosenfield, Tex Simone.
Assistant to the President: Chris Sprague. **Corporate Secretary:** Max Schumacher.
Directors: North Johnson (Gwinnett), Don Beaver (Charlotte), Joe Finley (Lehigh Valley), George Habel (Durham), Joe Napoli (Toledo), Bob Rich Jr. (Buffalo), Dave Rosenfield (Norfolk), James Timlin (Scranton/Wilkes-Barre), Ken Schnacke (Columbus), Max Schumacher (Indianapolis), Naomi Silver (Rochester), John Simone (Syracuse), Mike Tamburro (Pawtucket), Gary Ulmer (Louisville).
Office Manager: Gretchen Addison.
Division Structure: North-Buffalo, Lehigh Valley, Pawtucket, Rochester, Scranton/Wilkes-Barre, Syracuse. West-Columbus, Indianapolis, Louisville, Toledo. South-Charlotte, Durham, Gwinnett, Norfolk.
Regular Season: 144 games. **2011 Opening Date:** April 7. **Closing Date:** Sept. 5.
All-Star Game: July 13 at Salt Lake City (IL vs. Pacific Coast League).

Randy Mobley

Playoff Format: South winner meets West winner in best of five series; wild card (non-division winner with best winning percentage) meets North winner in best of five series. Winners meet in best of five series for Governors' Cup championship.
Triple-A Championship Game: Sept. 20 (IL vs. Pacific Coast League).
Roster Limit: 24. **Player Eligibility:** No restrictions.
Official Baseball: Rawlings ROM-INT.
Umpires: Gerard Ascani (Tampa, FL), Lance Barrett (Burleson, TX), Craig Barron (Fayetteville, GA), Toby Basner (Snellville, GA), Karl Best (Richmond, VA), Travis Brown (Clearwater, FL), Kelvin Bultron (Canovanas, Puerto Rico), Fran Burke (Ridgewood, NJ), Jon Byrne (Thornlie, WA), Vic Carapazza (Palm Harbor, FL), John Conrad (Meriden, CT), Chris Conroy (North Adams, MA), Derek Crabill (Wonder Lake, IL), Mike Estabrook (Boynton Beach, FL), Manny Gonzalez (Valenica, Venezuela), Jeff Gosney (Lakeland, FL), Adam Hamari (Marquette, MI), Mark Lollo (New Lexington, OH), Brad Myers (Holland, OH), Alan Porter (Warminster, PA), David Rackley (League City, TX), D.J. Reyburn (Franklin, TX), Art Thigpen (Lakeland, FL), Chris Ward (Ashland, KY), Chad Whitson (Dublin, OH).

STADIUM INFORMATION

Club	Stadium	Opened	Dimensions			Capacity	2010 Att.
			LF	CF	RF		
Buffalo	Coca-Cola Field	1988	325	404	325	18,150	575,296
Charlotte	Knights Stadium	1990	325	400	325	10,002	305,842
Columbus	Huntington Park	2009	325	400	330	10,100	651,224
Durham	Durham Bulls Athletic Park	1995	305	400	327	10,000	500,073
Gwinnett	Coolray Field	2009	335	400	335	10,427	337,240
Indianapolis	Victory Field	1996	320	402	320	14,500	569,969
Lehigh Valley	Coca-Cola Park	2008	336	400	325	10,000	645,905
Louisville	Louisville Slugger Field	2000	325	400	340	13,131	613,020
Norfolk	Harbor Park	1993	333	410	318	12,067	392,752
Pawtucket	McCoy Stadium	1946	325	400	325	10,031	592,326
Rochester	Frontier Field	1997	335	402	325	10,840	462,004
Scranton/WB	PNC Field	1989	330	408	330	10,310	338,731
Syracuse	Alliance Bank Stadium	1997	330	400	330	11,671	416,382
Toledo	Fifth Third Field	2002	320	412	315	8,943	558,059

BUFFALO BISONS

Office Address: Coca-Cola Field, One James D. Griffin Plaza, Buffalo, NY 14203.
Telephone: (716) 846-2000. **Fax:** (716) 852-6530.
E-Mail address: info@bisons.com. **Website:** www.bisons.com.
Affiliation (3rd year): New York Mets (2009). **Years in League:** 1886-90, 1912-70, 1998-

OWNERSHIP, MANAGEMENT

Operated By: Rich Products Corp.
Principal Owner/President: Robert Rich Jr. **President, Rich Entertainment Group:** Melinda Rich. **President, Rich Baseball Operations:** Jon Dandes. **Vice President/Treasurer:** David Rich. **VP/Secretary:** William Gisel.
VP/General Manager: Mike Buczkowski. **VP, Finance:** Joseph Segarra. **Corporate Counsel:** Jill Bond, William Grieshober. **Director, Sales:** Anthony Sprague. **Director, Stadium Operations:** Tom Sciarrino. **Controller:** Kevin

Parkinson. **Senior Accountants:** Rita Clark, Nicole Hill. **Accountant:** Amy Delaney. **Director, Ticket Operations:** Mike Poreda. **Director, Public Relations:** Brad Bisbing. **Director, Game Day Entertainment/Promotions Coordinator:** Matt La Sota. **Sales Coordinators:** Rachel Osucha, Mike Simoncelli. **Account Executives:** Mark Gordon, Jim Harrington, Robert Kates, Geoff Lundquist, Burt Mirti, Frank Mooney, Amanda Sarver. **Manager, Merchandise:** Sara Bukas. **Manager, Office Services:** Margaret Russo. **Executive Assistant:** Tina Lesher. **Community Relations:** Gail Hodges. **Director, Food Services:** Robert Free. **Assistant Concessions Manager:** Roger Buczek. **Head Groundskeeper:** Chad Laurie. **Chief Engineer:** Pat Chella. **Home Clubhouse/Baseball Operations Coordinator:** Scott Lesher. **Visiting Clubhouse Manager:** Dan Brick.

FIELD STAFF
Manager: Tim Teufel. **Coach:** Mike Easler. **Pitching Coach:** Ricky Bones.

GAME INFORMATION
Radio Announcers: Ben Wagner, Duke McGuire. **No of Games Broadcast:** Home-72, Road-72. **Flagship Station:** WWKB-1520.

PA Announcer: Jason Mollica. **Official Scorers:** Kevin Lester, Jon Dare.

Stadium Name: Coca-Cola Field. **Location:** From north, take I-190 to Elm Street exit, left onto Swan Street. From east, take I-190 West to exit 51 (Route 33) to end, exit at Oak Street, right onto Swan Street. From west, take I-190 East, exit 53 to I-90 North, exit at Elm Street, left onto Swan Street. **Standard Game Times:** 7:05 p.m., Sun 1:05. **Ticket Price Range:** $5-18.

Visiting Club Hotel: Adams Mark Hotel, 120 Church St, Buffalo, NY 14202. **Telephone:** (716) 845-5100. Hyatt Hotel, 2 Fountain Plaza, Buffalo, NY 14202. **Telephone:** (716) 856-1234.

CHARLOTTE KNIGHTS

Office Address: 2280 Deerfield Dr., Fort Mill, SC 29715.
Telephone: (704) 357-8071. **Fax:** (704) 329-2155.
E-Mail address: knights@charlotteknights.com. **Website:** www.charlotteknights.com.
Affiliation (first year): Chicago White Sox (1999). **Years in League:** 1993-

OWNERSHIP, MANAGEMENT
Operated by: Knights Baseball, LLC.
Principal Owners: Don Beaver, Bill Allen.
Vice President/General Manager: Dan Rajkowski. **Director, Media Relations:** Patrick Stark. **Director, Broadcast Communications:** Matt Swierad. **VP, Sales:** Chris Semmens. **Director, Corporate Sales:** John Agresti. **Director, Stadium Operations:** Mark McKinnon. **Director, Merchandising:** Becka Leveille. **Business Manager:** Michael Sanger. **Ticket Sales Coordinator:** Tony Furr, Dave LaCroix, Matt Millward, Mac Simmons. **Ticket Office Manager:** Meredith Storrie. **Coordinator, Community/Team Relations:** Lindsey Roycraft. **Client Services Associate:** Patty Hunter. **Marketing/ Development:** Bill Walker. **Head Groundskeeper:** Eddie Busque. **Clubhouse Manager:** Dan Morphis. **Corporate Sales Account Executive:** Brett Butler. **Executive Assistant to VP/GM:** Julie Clark.

FIELD STAFF
Manager: Joe McEwing. **Coach:** Timothy Laker. **Pitching Coach:** Richard Dotson.

GAME INFORMATION
Radio Announcer: Mike Pacheco, Matt Swierad. **No. of Games Broadcast:** Home-72 Road-72. **Flagship Station:** WRHI 1340-AM/94.3-FM.

PA Announcer: Ken Conrad. **Official Scorers:** Sam Copeland, Bill Walker.

Stadium Name: Knights Stadium. **Location:** Exit 88 off I-77, east on Gold Hill Road. **Ticket Price Range:** $8-13.

Visiting Club Hotel: Comfort Suites, 10415 Centrum Parkway, Pineville, NC 28134. **Telephone:** 704-540-0559.

COLUMBUS CLIPPERS

Office Address: 330 Huntington Park Lane, Columbus, OH 43215.
Telephone: (614) 462-5250. **Fax:** (614) 462-3271. **Tickets:** (614) 462-2757.
E-Mail address: info@clippersbaseball.com. **Website:** www.clippersbaseball.com.
Affiliation (third year): Cleveland Indians (2009). **Years in League:** 1955-70, 1977-

OWNERSHIP, MANAGEMENT
Operated By: Columbus Baseball Team Inc.
Principal Owner: CBT Inc. **Board of Directors:** Steven Francis, Tom Fries, Wayne Harer, Thomas Katzenmeyer, David Leland, Cathy Lyttle, Robert Milbourne, Richard Smith, McCullough Williams.
President/General Manager: Ken Schnacke. **Assistant GM:** Mark Warren. **Director, Ballpark Operations:** Steve Dalin. **Assistant Director, Ballpark Operations:** Phil Colilla. **Director, Ticket Operations:** Scott Ziegler. **Assistant Director, Ticket Operations:** Eddie Langhenry. **Director, Marketing/Sales:** Mark Galuska. **Assistant Director, Marketing:** Ty Debevoise. **Assistant Directors, Sales:** Kyle Blizzard, Brittany McKittrick. **Director, Communications/Media/Team Historian:** Joe Santry. **Assistant Director, Media Relations:** Anthony Slosser. **Assistant Director, Communications:** Ben Leland. **Directors, Broadcasting:** Ryan Mitchell, Scott Leo. **Director, Merchandising:** Krista Oberlander. **Assistant Director, Merchandising:** Brandon Strull. **Director, Group Sales:** Ben Keller. **Assistant Directors, Group Sales:** Brett

Patton, Gabe Norris, Barry Keck. **Director, Multimedia:** Josh Glenn. **Assistant Director, Multimedia:** Yoshi Ando. **Director, Finance:** Bonnie Badgley. **Executive Assistant to the President/GM:** Ashley Alexander. **Office Manager:** Kelly Ryther. **Administrative Assistants:** Matt Hoffman, Shannon O'Boyle, Patrick Thompson. **Director, Sponsor Relationships:** Joyce Martin. **Director, Event Planning:** Micki Shier. **Assistant Director, Event Planning:** Sara Rudolph. **Director, Clubhouse Operations:** George Robinson. **Clubhouse Manager:** Matt Pruzinsky. **Ballpark Superintendent:** Gary Delozier. **Head Groundskeeper:** Wes Ganobcik. **Assistant Groundskeeper:** Cliff Biegler.

FIELD STAFF

Manager: Mike Sarbaugh. **Coach:** Lee May Jr. **Pitching Coach:** Ruben Niebla. **Trainer:** Michael Salazar. **Strength/ Conditioning Coach:** Todd Kubacki.

GAME INFORMATION

Radio Announcers: Ryan Mitchell, Scott Leo. **No of Games Broadcast:** Home-72, Road-72. **Flagship Station:** WMNI 920AM.

PA Announcer: Colin Smith. **Official Scorer:** Jim Habermehl, Ray Thomas.

Stadium Name: Huntington Park. **Location:** From north: South on I-71 to I-670 west. Exit at Neil Avenue. Turn left at intersection onto Neil Avenue. From south: North on I-71. Exit at Front St. (#100A). Turn left at intersection onto Front Street. Turn left onto Nationwide Blvd. From east: West on I-70. Exit at Fourth Street. Continue on Fulton Street to Front Street. Turn right onto Front Street. Turn left onto Nationwide Blvd. From west: East on I-70. Exit at Fourth Street. Continue on Fulton Street to Front Street. Turn right onto Front Street. Turn left onto Nationwide Blvd.

Ticket Price Range: $6-20.

Visiting Club Hotel: Crowne Plaza, 33 E. Nationwide Blvd., Columbus, OH 43215. **Telephone:** 877-348-2424. Drury Hotels Columbus Convention Center, 88 E. Nationwide Blvd., Columbus, OH 43215. **Telephone:** 614-221-7008. Hyatt Regency Downtown, 350 N. High St., Columbus, OH 43215. **Telephone:** 614-463-1234.

DURHAM BULLS

Office Address: 409 Blackwell St., Durham, NC 27701.
Mailing Address: P.O. Box 507, Durham, NC 27702.
Telephone: (919) 687-6500. **Fax:** (919) 687-6560.
Website: www.durhambulls.com
Affiliation (first year): Tampa Bay Rays (1998). **Years in League:** 1998-

OWNERSHIP, MANAGEMENT

Operated By: Capitol Broadcasting Company, Inc.

President, CEO: Jim Goodman. **Vice President:** George Habel.

General Manager: Mike Birling. **Assistant GM:** Jon Bishop. **Director, Corporate Partnerships:** Chris Overby. **Account Executives, Sponsorship:** Dustin Bass, Elizabeth Pritchett, Neil Solondz. **Coordinator, Sponsorship Services:** Molly Boyce. **Director, Media Relations/Promotions:** Matt DeMargel. **Coordinator, Multimedia:** John Blotzer Jr. **Coordinator, Mascot/Community Relations:** Nicholas Tennant. **Director, Ticket Operations:** Tim Seaton. **Manager, Premium Ticket Sales:** Mike Miller. **Ticket Sales Associates:** Caroline D'Englere, Jeff Gibbons, Nate Horowitz. **Manager, Group Ticket Sales:** Brian Simorka. **Coordinator, Special Events:** Mary Beth Warfford. **Box Office Sales:** Jerry Mach. **Director, Stadium Operations:** Josh Nance. **GM, Concessions:** Tammy Scott. **Assistant GM, Concessions:** Ralph Orona. **Head Groundskeeper:** Scott Strickland. **Manager, Business:** Rhonda Carlile. **Supervisor, Accounting:** Theresa Stocking. **Manager, Home Clubhouse:** Colin Saunders. **Manager, Visiting/Umpires Clubhouses:** Aaron Kuehner. **Team Ambassador:** Bill Law.

FIELD STAFF

Manager: Charlie Montoyo. **Coach:** Dave Myers. **Pitching Coach:** Neil Allen. **Trainer:** Lee Slagle.

GAME INFORMATION

Radio Announcers: Neil Solondz, Ken Tanner. **No. of Games Broadcast:** Home-72, Road-72. **Flagship Station:** 620-AM The Buzz, 99.9 FM the Fan.

PA Announcer: Tony Riggsbee. **Official Scorer:** Brent Belvin.

Stadium Name: Durham Bulls Athletic Park. **Location:** From Raleigh, I-40 West to Highway 147 North, exit 12B to Willard, two blocks on Willard to stadium. From I-85, Gregson Street exit to downtown, left on Chapel Hill Street, right on Mangum Street. **Standard Game Times:** 7:05 p.m., **Sunday 5:**05 p.m. **Ticket Price Range:** $7-9.

Visiting Club Hotel: Durham Marriot at the Civic Center, 201 Foster St., Durham, NC 27701. **Telephone:** (919) 768-6000.

GWINNETT BRAVES

Office Address: One Braves Ave, Lawrenceville, GA 30043.
Mailing Address: PO Box 490310, Lawrenceville, GA 30049.
Telephone: (678) 277-0300. **Fax:** (678) 277-0338.
E-Mail Address: gwinnettinfo@braves.com. **Website:** www.gwinnettbraves.com.
Affiliation (first year): Atlanta Braves (1966). **Years in League:** 1884, 1915-17, 1954-64, 1966-

OWNERSHIP, MANAGEMENT

General Manager: North Johnson. **Assistant GM:** Shari Massengil. **Office Manager:** Tyra Williams. **Manager, Stadium Operations:** Ryan Stoltenberg. **Manager, Field Maintenance:** Gerry Huppman. **Manager, Community Affairs:** Zayra Fosse. **Manager, Corporate/Group Sales:** Samantha Dunn. **Manager, Ticket Operations:** Mike Castle. **Manager, Marketing/Promotions:** Maggie Neil. **Coordinator, Marketing/Promotions:** Travis Orton. **Coordinator, Media Relations:** Nick Margiasso. **Coordinator, Stadium Operations:** Jonathan Blair. **Ticket/Corporate Sales Representatives:** Jerry Pennington, Lindsay Harmon, Paige Fleckenstien, Jordan Buck.

FIELD STAFF

Manager: Dave Brundage. **Coach:** Jamie Dismuke. **Pitching Coach:** Marty Reed. **Trainer:** Mike Graus.

GAME INFORMATION

Radio Announcers: Tony Schiavone, Judd Hickinbotham. **No of Games Broadcast:** Home-72 Road-72. **Flagship Station:** WDUN 550-AM.

PA Announcer: Jeff Bergmann. **Official Scorers:** Unavailable.

Stadium Name: Gwinnett Stadium. **Location:** I-85 (at Exit 115, S.R. **20 West) and I-985 (at Exit 4), follow signs to park. Ticket Price Range:** $5-30.

Visiting Club Hotel: Courtyard by Marriott Buford/Mall of Georgia, 1405 Mall of Georgia Boulevard, Buford, GA 30519. **Telephone:** (678) 215-8007.

INDIANAPOLIS INDIANS

Office Address: 501 W. Maryland Street, Indianapolis, IN 46225.
Telephone: (317) 269-3542. **Fax:** (317) 269-3541.
E-Mail address: indians@indyindians.com. **Website:** www.IndyIndians.com.
Affiliation (first year): Pittsburgh Pirates (2005). **Years in League:** 1963, 1998-

OWNERSHIP, MANAGEMENT

Operated By: Indians Inc.

President/Chairman of the Board: Max Schumacher.

Vice President/General Manager: Cal Burleson. **Assistant GM:** Randy Lewandowski. **Director, Special Projects:** Bruce Schumacher. **Director, Marketing/Communications:** Chris Herndon. **Director, Facilities:** Tim Hughes. **Director, Business Operations:** Brad Morris. **Director, Tickets:** Matt Guay. **Director, Corporate Partnerships:** Joel Zawacki. **Director, Merchandising:** Mark Schumacher. **Director, Broadcasting:** Howard Kellman. **Radio Broadcaster/Ticket Sales Executive:** Scott McCauley. **Media Relations Manager:** Brian Bosma. **Manager, Community Relations/Promotions:** Ryan Bowman. **Manager, Game Entertainment/Production:** Brian McLaughlin. **Marketing Manager:** Diana Nolting. **Merchandise Manager:** Missy Weaver. **Event Operations Manager:** Mark Anderson. **Stadium Operations Manager:** Steve Bray. **Stadium Maintenance Manager:** Allan Danehy.

Administrative Assistant: Angela Kendall. **Office Manager:** Julie Rumschlag. **Assistant Director, Facilities:** Bill Sampson. **Sponsorship Sales Account Executives:** Amanda Murray, Christina Toler. **Sponsorship Services Coordinator:** Keri Oberting. **Senior Ticket/Premium Services Manager:** Kerry Vick. **Ticket Sales Manager:** Chad Bohm. **Ticket Services Manager:** Bryan Spisak. **Ticket Sales Executives:** Ryan Barrett, Lauren Davis, Kyle Fisher, Jonathan Howard. **Media Relations Assistant:** Andrew Green. **Marketing Assistant:** Adam Pintar. **Community Relations/Promotions Assistant:** Kim Stoebick. **Merchandise Assistant:** Patrick Westrick. **Game Entertainment/Production Assistant:** Matt Houston. **Operations Assistant:** Ben Waivol. **Sponsorship Assistant:** Marc Porter. **Ticket Services Assistants:** Drew Donovan, Cory McConnaughhay, Marc Nelson. **Head Groundskeeper:** Joey Stevenson. **Assistant Groundskeeper:** Nick Averitt. **Home Clubhouse Manager:** Bob Martin. **Visiting Clubhouse Manager:** Jeremy Martin.

FIELD STAFF

Manager: Dean Treanor. **Coach:** Jeff Branson. **Pitching Coach:** Tom Filer. **Trainer:** Bryan Housand. **Strength/Conditioning Coach:** Chad Uihlein.

GAME INFORMATION

Radio Announcer: Howard Kellman, Scott McCauley. **No. of Games Broadcast:** Home-72, Road-72. **Flagship Station:** WNDE 1260-AM.

PA Announcer: David Pygman. **Official Scorers:** Bill McAfee, Gary Johnson, Kim Rogers, Bill Potter.

Stadium Name: Victory Field. **Location:** I-70 to West Street exit, north on West Street to ballpark; I-65 to Martin Luther King and West Street exit, south on West Street to ballpark. **Standard Game Times:** 7:05 p.m.; Wed. 1:05.; Fri 7:15; Sun 2:05. **Ticket Price Range:** $9-14.

Visiting Club Hotels: Courtyard by Marriott, 601 West Washington, Indianapolis, IN 46204. **Telephone:** (317) 822-9054.

LEHIGH VALLEY IRONPIGS

Office Address: 1050 IronPigs Way, Allentown, PA 18109.
Telephone: (610) 841-7447. **Fax:** (610) 841-1509.
E-Mail address: info@ironpigsbaseball.com. **Website:** www.ironpigsbaseball.com.
Affiliation (first year): Philadelphia Phillies (2008). **Years in League:** 2008-

OWNERSHIP, MANAGEMENT

Ownership: LV Baseball LP
President: Chuck Domino.
General Manager: Kurt Landes. **Assistant GM:** Howard Scharf. **Director, Media Relations:** Matt Provence. **Manager, Media Relations:** Jon Schaeffer. **Director, Community Relations:** Sarah Marten. **Director, Merchandise:** Adam Fondl. **Director, Ticket Sales:** Scott Hodge. **Director, Ticket Operations:** Amy Schoch. **Director, Group Sales:** Don Wilson. **Director, Marketing:** Ron Rushe. **Marketing Services Managers:** Erin Holt. **Alicia Marinelli. Director, Creative Services:** Matt Zidik. **Manager, Creative Services:** Tyler DeRouen. **Director, Promotions:** Lindsey Knupp. **Director, Special Events/Catering:** Mary Nixon. **Director, Concessions:** Alex Rivera. **Manager, Concessions:** Brock Hartranft. **Executive Chef:** Jan Giejda. **Controller:** Deb Landes. **Manager, Finance:** Michelle Perl.
Director, Stadium Operations: Garrett Fahrmann. **Stadium Operations Managers:** Paul Cashin, Jason Kiesel. **Marketing Managers:** Scott Evans, Brandon Greene, Rick Polster. **Manager, Ticket Operations:** Erin Owens. **Tickets/ Group Representatives:** Mark Anderson, Ryan Hines, Brad Ludwig, Alicia Rohrbach, Justin Scariato, Katie Ward. **Director, Field Operations:** Bill Butler. **Receptionist:** Pat Golden.

FIELD STAFF

Manager: Ryne Sandberg. **Hitting Coach:** Sal Rende. **Pitching Coach:** Rod Nichols. **Trainer:** Jason Kirkman. **Strength/ Conditioning:** Jason Meredith.

GAME INFORMATION

Radio Announcers: Matt Provence, Jon Schaeffer. **No. Games Broadcast:** 144 (72 Home; 72 Away). **Flagship Radio Station:** ESPN 1240/1320 AM. **Television Station:** TV2. **Television Announcers:** Mike Zambelli, Steve Degler, Matt Provence, Doug Heater. **No. Games Televised:** 72 Home. **PA Announcer:** Tim Chorones. **Official Scorers:** Jack Logic, David Sheriff. **Stadium Name:** Coca-Cola Park. **Location:** Take U.S. 22 to exit for Airport Road South. Head south, make right on American Parkway. Left into stadium. **Standard Game Times:** 7:05 p.m.; Sat 6:35; Sun 1:35 (April-June), 5:35 (July-August).
Visiting Club Hotel: Staybridge Suites Allentown Bethlehem Airport, 1787-A. **Airport Road, Allentown, PA 18019. Telephone:** 610-686-5002.

LOUISVILLE BATS

Office Address: 401 E. Main St, Louisville, KY 40202.
Telephone: (502) 212-2287. **Fax:** (502) 515-2255.
E-Mail address: info@batsbaseball.com. **Website:** www.batsbaseball.com.
Affiliation (first year): Cincinnati Reds (2000). **Years in League:** 1998-

OWNERSHIP, MANAGEMENT

Chariman: Dan Ulmer Jr. **Board of Directors:** Edward Glasscock, Gary Ulmer, Kenny Huber, Steve Trager, J. **Michael Brown.**
President/CEO: Gary Ulmer. **Vice President/General Manager:** Dale Owens. **Assistant GM/Director, Marketing:** Greg Galiette. **Director, Stadium Operations:** Scott Shoemaker. **Director, Ticket Sales:** James Breeding. **Director, Baseball Operations:** Earl Stubblefield. **Controller:** Michele Anderson. **Manager, Tickets:** George Veith. **Director, Ticket Operations:** Kyle Reh. **Director, Media/Public Relations:** Nick Evans. **Director, Group Sales:** Bryan McBride. **Director, Broadcasting:** Matt Andrews. **Director, Suite Level Services:** Kerri Ferrell. **Senior Account Executives:** Hal Norwood, Josh Hargreaves, Evan Patrick, Curtis Cunningham. **Assistant Director, Stadium Operations:** Randy Williams. **Graphic Designer:** Tony Brown. **Community Relations/Promotions Coordinator:** Sarah Nordman. **Account Executives:** Brad Wagner, Michael Harmon. **Groundskeeper:** Tom Nielsen. **Assistant Groundskeeper:** Eric Harshman.

FIELD STAFF

Manager: Rick Sweet. **Hitting Coach:** Adrian "Smokey" Garrett. **Pitching Coach:** Ted Power. **Trainer:** Tomas Vera.

GAME INFORMATION

Radio Announcers: Matt Andrews. **No. of Games Broadcast:** Home-72, Road-72. **Flagship Station:** WKRD 790-AM. **PA Announcer:** Charles Gazaway. **Official Scorer:** Dave Arnold. **Organist:** Bob Ramsey.
Stadium Name: Louisville Slugger Field. **Location:** I-64 and I-71 to I-65 South/North to Brook Street exit, right on Market Street, left on Jackson Street; stadium on Main Street between Jackson and Preston. **Ticket Price Range:** $6-11.
Visiting Club Hotel: Galt House Hotel, 140 North Fourth Street, Louisville, KY 40202. **Telephone:** (502) 589-5200.

NORFOLK TIDES

Office Address: 150 Park Ave, Norfolk, VA 23510.
Telephone: (757) 622-2222. **Fax:** (757) 624-9090.
E-Mail Address: receptionist@norfolktides.com. **Website:** www.norfolktides.com.
Affiliation (fifth year): Baltimore Orioles (2007). **Years in League:** 1969-

OWNERSHIP, MANAGEMENT

Operated By: Tides Baseball Club Inc.
President: Ken Young.
General Manager: Dave Rosenfield. **Assistant GM:** Ben Giancola. **Director, Business Development/Marketing:** Joe Pinto. **Business Manager:** Andrew Garrelts. **Director, Media Relations:** Justin Rosenberg. **Director, Community Relations:** Heather McKeating. **Director, Ticket Operations:** Gretchen Todd. **Director, Group Sales:** Stephanie Hierstein. **Director, Stadium Operations:** Mike Zeman. **Manager, Merchandising:** Ann Marie Piddisi. **Corporate Sponsorships, Promotions:** Jonathan Mensink, Mike Watkins. **Assistant Director, Stadium Operations:** Mike Cardwell. **Box Office Manager:** Linda Waisanen. **Ticket Office Assistant:** Sze Fong. **Administrative Assistant:** Lisa Cox. **Group/Corporate Sales:** Christina Dewey. **Head Groundskeeper:** Kenny Magner. **Assistant Groundskeeper:** Keith Collins. **Home Clubhouse Manager:** Kevin Casey. **Visiting Clubhouse Manager:** Mark Bunge. **Group Sales Interns:** Jeremy Cowen, Janelle Henry. **Media Relations Intern:** Ed Dilenno. **Stadium Operations Intern:** Matt Moyer.

FIELD STAFF

Manager: Gary Allenson. **Coach:** Brad Komminsk. **Pitching Coach:** Mike Griffin. **Trainer:** Mark Shires.

GAME INFORMATION

Radio Announcers: Pete Michaud, Tony Mercurio. **No. of Games Broadcast:** Home-72, Road-72. **Flagship Station:** ESPN 94.1 FM.
PA Announcers: Jack Ankerson. **Official Scorers:** Dave Lewis, Mike Holtzclaw.
Stadium Name: Harbor Park. **Location:** Exit 9, 11A or 11B off I-264, adjacent to the Elizabeth River in downtown Norfolk. **Ticket Price Range:** $9.50-13.
Visiting Club Hotel: Sheraton Waterside, 777 Waterside Dr, Norfolk, VA 23510. **Telephone:** (757) 622-6664.

PAWTUCKET RED SOX

Office Address: One Ben Mondor Way, Pawtucket, RI 02860.
Mailing Address: P.O. Box 2365, Pawtucket, RI 02861.
Telephone: (401) 724-7300. **Fax:** (401) 724-2140.
E-Mail Address: info@pawsox.com. **Website:** www.pawsox.com.
Affiliation (first year): Boston Red Sox (1973). **Years in League:** 1973-

OWNERSHIP, MANAGEMENT

Operated by: Pawtucket Red Sox Baseball Club, Inc.
President: Mike Tamburro.
Vice President/General Manager: Lou Schwechheimer. **VP, Chief Financial Officer:** Matt White. **VP, Sales/ Marketing:** Michael Gwynn. **VP, Stadium Operations:** Mick Tedesco. **VP, Public Relations:** Bill Wanless. **Director, Community Relations:** Jeff Bradley. **Manager, Sales:** Augusto Rojas. **Director, Merchandising:** Eric Petterson. **Director, Media Creation:** Kevin Galligan. **Director, Concession Services:** Jim Hogan. **Director, Corporate Sales:** Mike Abramson. **Director, Warehouse Operations:** Dave Johnson. **Assistant Director, Community Relations:** Becky Berta. **Director, Ticket Operations:** Kelly Bongiovanni. **Account Executives:** Shaun Dawson, Tom Linehan, Peter Sachs. **Field Superintendant:** Matt McKinnon. **Assistant Groundskeeper:** Kyle Carney. **Director, Security:** Rick Medeiros. **Director, Clubhouse Operations:** Carl Goodreau. **Executive Chef:** Ken Bowdish.

FIELD STAFF

Manager: Arnie Beyeler. **Coach:** Chili Davis. **Pitching Coach:** Rich Sauveur. **Trainer:** Jon Jochim.

GAME INFORMATION

Radio Announcer: Dan Hoard, Steve Hyder. **No. of Games Broadcast:** Home-72, Away-72. **Flagship Station:** WHJJ 920-AM.
PA Announcer: Scott Fraser. **Official Scorer:** Bruce Guindon.
Stadium Name: McCoy Stadium. **Location:** From north, 95 South to exit 2A in Massachusetts (Newport Ave.), follow Newport Ave. for 2 miles, right on Columbus Ave., follow one mile, stadium on right. From south, 95 North to exit 28 (School Street), right at bottom of exit ramp, through two sets of lights, left onto Pond Street, right on Columbus Ave., stadium entrance on left. From west (Worcester), 295 North to 95 South and follow directions from north. From east (Fall River), 195 West to 95 North and follow directions from south. **Standard Game Times:** 7 p.m.; Sat. 6, Sun. 1. **Ticket Price Range:** $6-10.
Visiting Club Hotel: Comfort Inn, 2 George St., Pawtucket, RI 02860. **Telephone:** (401) 723-6700.

ROCHESTER RED WINGS

Office Address: One Morrie Silver Way, Rochester, NY 14608.
Telephone: (585) 454-1001. **Fax:** (585) 454-1056, (585) 454-1057.
E-Mail Address: info@redwingsbaseball.com. **Website:** www.redwingsbaseball.com.
Affiliation (first year): Minnesota Twins (2003). **Years in League:** 1885-89, 1891-92, 1895-

OWNERSHIP, MANAGEMENT

Operated by: Rochester Community Baseball.
CEO/President: Naomi Silver. **Chairman:** Gary Larder.
General Manager: Dan Mason. **Assistant GM:** Will Rumbold. **Controller:** Darlene Giardina. **Head Groundskeeper:** Gene Buonomo. **Director, Media/Public Relations:** Chuck Hinkel. **Director, Corporate Development:** Nick Sciarratta. **Group/Picnic Director:** Parker Allen. **Director, Marketing:** Matt Cipro. **Director, Ticket Operations:** Rob Dermody. **Director, Production:** John Blotzer. **Director, Merchandising:** Barbara Moore. **Director, Human Resources:** Paula LoVerde. **Assistant Director, Group Sales:** Bob Craig. **Account Executives:** Danielle Barone, Eric Friedman, Derek Swanson. **Executive Secretary:** Ginny Colbert. **General Manager, Food Services:** Jeff Dodge. **Manager, Suites/Catering:** Pam Ford. **Catering Sales Manager:** Courtney Trawitz. **Manager, Concessions:** Jeff DeSantis. **Executive Chef:** Mark Feiock. **Warehouse Manager:** Mike Arbore. **Business Manager, Concessions:** Dave Bills. **Clubhouse Operations:** Terry Costello.

FIELD STAFF

Manager: Tom Nieto. **Coach:** Floyd Rayford. **Pitching Coach:** Bobby Cuellar. **Trainer:** Tony Leo.

GAME INFORMATION

Radio Announcers: Josh Whetzel. **No. of Games Broadcast:** Home-72, Away-72. **Flagship Stations:** WHTK 1280-AM, WYSL 1040-AM.
PA Announcer: Kevin Spears. **Official Scorer:** Warren Kozereski.
Stadium Name: Frontier Field. **Location:** I-490 East to exit 12 (Brown/Broad Street) and follow signs; I-490 West to exit 14 (Plymouth Ave) and follow signs. **Standard Game Times:** 7:05 p.m., Sun 1:35. **Ticket Price Range:** $6.50-10.50
Visiting Club Hotel: Rochester Plaza, 70 State St, Rochester, NY 14608. **Telephone:** (585) 546-3450.

SCRANTON/WILKES-BARRE
YANKEES

Office Address: 235 Montage Mountain Rd, Moosic, PA 18507.
Telephone: (570) 969-2255. **Fax:** (570) 963-6564.
E-Mail address: info@swbyankees.com. **Website:** www.swbyankees.com.
Affiliation (first year): New York Yankees (2007). **Years in League:** 1989-

OWNERSHIP, MANAGEMENT

Owned By: The Multi-Purpose Stadium Authority of Lackawanna County.
Operated By: SWB Yankees, LLC.
President: Kristen Rose. **Executive Vice President/General Manager:** Jeremy Ruby.
Senior Director, Marketing/Corporate Services: Katie Beekman. **Senior Sponsor Service Manager:** Kristina Knight. **Manager, Sponsor Service:** Amy Ott. **VP, Ticket Sales:** Doug Augis. **Manager, Ticket Operations:** Brian Modisett. **Manager, Corporate Marketing:** Jared Gigli. **Group Sales Coordinator:** Jake Winowich. **Group Sales Manager:** Bob McLane. **Director, Seasonal Sales Representatives:** Kelly Cusick, Allison Juchem, Matthew Kemp, Paul Migliorino. **Corporate Partnerships:** Mike Trudnak. **VP, Stadium Operations:** Curt Comoni. **Director, Facility Operations:** Joe Villano. **Director, Field Operations:** Steve Horne. **Operations Manager:** Rob Galdieri. **Director, Game Entertainment:** Barry Snyder. **VP, Accounting/Finance:** Paul Chilek. **Staff Accountant:** William Steiner. **Office Manager:** Kelly Byron. **Director, Merchandise:** Sarah Phillips. **Director, Media Relations/Broadcasting:** Mike Vander Woude.

FIELD STAFF

Manager: Dave Miley. **Hitting Coach:** Butch Wynegar. **Pitching Coach:** Scott Aldred. **Coach:** Frank Menechino. **Trainer:** Darren London. **Strength/Conditioning Coach:** Lee Tressel.

GAME INFORMATION

Radio Announcer: Mike Vander Woude. **No of Games Broadcast:** Home-72 Road-72. **Flagship Stations:** WICK 1400 AM/WYCK 1340 AM
PA Announcer: John Davies. **Official Scorers:** Dave Lauriha, Armand Rosamila.
Stadium Name: PNC Field. **Location:** I-81 to exit 182 (Davis Street/Montage Mountain Road), take Montage Mountain Road one mile to stadium. **Ticket Price Range:** $8-10.
Visiting Club Hotel: Radisson at Lackawanna Stadium, 700 Lackawanna Ave, Scranton, PA 18503. **Telephone:** (570) 342-8300.

SYRACUSE CHIEFS

Office Address: One Tex Simone Dr., **Syracuse, NY 13208.**
Telephone: (315) 474-7833. **Fax:** (315) 474-2658.
E-Mail Address: baseball@syracusechiefs.com. **Website:** www.syracusechiefs.com
Affiliation (third year): Washington Nationals (2009). **Years in League:** 1885-89, 1891-92, 1894-1901, 1918, 1920-27, 1934-55, 1961-

OWNERSHIP, MANAGEMENT

Operated by: Community Owned Baseball Club of Central New York, Inc. **Chairman:** Charles Rich. **President:** Ron Gersbacher. **Executive Vice President/COO:** Anthony "Tex" Simone. **General Manager:** John Simone. **Assistant GM/Director, Marketing/Promotions:** Mike Voutsinas. **Assistant GM, Business:** Don Lehtonen. **Director, Sales:** Paul Fairbanks. **Director, Group Sales:** Victor Gallucci. **Director, Broadcasting/Public Relations:** Jason Benetti. **Director, Merchandising:** Wendy Shoen. **Director, Ticket Office:** Josh Jones. **Coordinator, Group Sales:** Erin Shappell. **Coordinator, Diversity:** R. Otis Jennings. **Administrative Assistant:** Priscilla Venditti.
Turf Manager: Jon Stewart. **Team Historian:** Ron Gersbacher.

FIELD STAFF

Manager: Randy Knorr. **Coach:** Jerry Browne. **Pitching Coach:** Greg Booker. **Trainer:** Atushi Toriida. **Strength Coordinator:** Mike Warren.

GAME INFORMATION

Radio Announcer: Jason Benetti/Kevin Brown. **No. of Games Broadcast:** Home-72, Away-72. **Flagship Station:** The Score 1260 AM. **PA Announcer:** Brent Axe. **Official Scorer:** Tom Leo.
Stadium Name: Alliance Bank Stadium. **Location:** New York State Thruway to exit 36 (I-81 South), to 7th North Street exit, left on 7th North, right on Hiawatha Boulevard. **Standard Game Times:** 7 p.m., Sun 2/6. **Ticket Price Range:** $6-10.
Visiting Club Hotel: Ramada Inn, 1305 Buckley Rd., Syracuse, NY 13212. **Telephone:** (315) 457-8670.

TOLEDO MUD HENS

Office Address: 406 Washington St, Toledo, OH 43604.
Telephone: (419) 725-4367. **Fax:** (419) 725-4368.
E-Mail address: mudhens@mudhens.com. **Website:** www.mudhens.com.
Affiliation (first year): Detroit Tigers (1987). **Years in League:** 1889, 1965-

OWNERSHIP, MANAGEMENT

Operated By: Toledo Mud Hens Baseball Club, Inc.
Chairman of the Board: Michael Miller.
Vice President: David Huey. **Secretary/Treasurer:** Charles Bracken.
President/General Manager: Joseph Napoli.
Assistant GM/Director, Marketing/Advertising/Sales: Scott Jeffer. **Assistant GM/Director, Corporate Partnerships:** Neil Neukam. **Assistant GM, Ticket Sales/Operations:** Erik Ibsen. **Assistant GM, Food/Beverage:** Craig Nelson. **CFO:** Pam Alspach. **Manager, Promotions:** JaMay Edwards. **Director, Media/Public Relations:** Jason Griffin. **Director, Ticket Sales/Services:** Thomas Townley. **Accounting:** Sheri Kelly, Brian Leverenz. **Manager, Gameday Operations:** Greg Setola. **Manager, Community Relations:** Cheri Pastula. **Corporate Sales Associate:** Ed Sintic, Ryan Connors. **Season Ticket/Group Sales Associates:** Chris Hole, Mike Keedy, Frank Kristie, Kyle Moll, John Mulka. **Manager, Online Marketing:** Nathan Steinmetz. **Season Ticket Service Coordinator:** Jessica Aten. **Manager, Video Board Operations:** Mike Ramirez. **Graphic Designer:** Dan Royer. **Manager, Souvenir Sales:** Craig Katz. **Assistant Manager, Souvenir Sales:** Heidi Nafziger. **Manager, Ballpark Operations:** Ken Westenkirchner. **Office Manager:** Carol Hamilton. **Executive Assistant:** Tracy Evans. **Turf Manager:** Jake Tyler. **Assistant Turf Manager:** Kyle Leppelmeier. **Clubhouse Manager:** Joe Sarkisian. **Team Historian:** John Husman.

FIELD STAFF

Manager: Phil Nevin. **Coach:** Leon Durham. **Pitching Coach:** A.J. Sager. **Trainer:** Matt Rankin.

GAME INFORMATION

Radio Announcers: Jim Weber, Jason Griffin. **No of Games Broadcast:** Home-72 Road-72. **Flagship Station:** WCWA 1230 AM.
PA Announcer: Kevin Mullan. **Official Scorers:** Jeff Businger, Ron Klenfelter, Guy Lammers, Jay Wagner.
Stadium Name: Fifth Third Field. **Location:** From Ohio Turnpike 80/90, exit 54 (4A) to I-75 North, follow I-75 North to exit 201-B, left onto Erie Street, right onto Washington Street. From Detroit, I-75 South to exit 202-A, right onto Washington Street. From Dayton, I-75 North to exit 201-B, left onto Erie Street, right on Washington Street. From Ann Arbor, Route 23 South to I-475 East, I-475 east to I-75 South, I-75 South to exit 202-A, right onto Washington Street. **Ticket Price Range:** $9.
Visiting Club Hotel: Park Inn, 101 North Summit, Toledo, OH 43604. **Telephone:** (419) 241-3000.

PACIFIC COAST LEAGUE

Address: One Chisholm Trail, Suite 4200, Round Rock, Texas 78681.
Telephone: (512) 310-2900. **Fax:** (512) 310-8300.
E-Mail Address: office@pclbaseball.com. **Website:** www.pclbaseball.com.
President: Branch B. Rickey.

PACIFIC COAST LEAGUE

Vice President: Don Logan (Las Vegas).
Directors: Don Beaver (New Orleans), Sam Bernabe (Iowa), John Pontius (Memphis), Chris Cummings (Fresno), Dave Elmore (Colorado Springs), Kirby Schlegel (Tacoma), Don Logan (Las Vegas), George King (Round Rock), Greg Miller (Salt Lake), Bill Shea (Omaha), Art Matin (Oklahoma), Merritt Paulson (Portland), Alan Ledford (Sacramento), John Traub (Albuquerque), Frank Ward (Nashville), Stuart Katzoff (Reno).
Director, Business: Melanie Fiore. **Director, Baseball Operations:** Dwight Hall. **Media/Operations Assistant:** Chris Kutz.
Division Structure: American Conference—Northern: Iowa, Memphis, Nashville, Omaha. **Southern:** Albuquerque, New Orleans, Oklahoma, Round Rock. Pacific Conference—Northern: Colorado Springs, Reno, Salt Lake, Tacoma. Southern: Fresno, Las Vegas, Sacramento, Tucson.
Regular Season: 144 games. **2011 Opening Date:** April 7. **Closing Date:** Sept 5.
All-Star Game: July 13 at Salt Lake Bees, Salt Lake City, UT (PCL vs. International League).

Branch Rickey

Playoff Format: Pacific Conference/Northern winner meets Southern winner, and American Conference/Northern winner meets Southern winner in best-of-five semifinal series. Winners meet in best-of-five series for league championship.
Triple-A Championship Game: Sept 20 (PCL vs International League).
Roster Limit: 24. **Player Eligibility Rule:** No restrictions.
Brand of Baseball: Rawlings ROM.
Umpires: Dan Bellino (Crystal Lake, IL), Cory Blaser (Westminster, CO), Mark Buchanan (Phoenix, AZ), Darren Budahn (Milwaukee, WI), Angel Campos (San Bernadino, CA), Clint Fagan (Tomball, TX), Shaun Francis (Cohoes, NY), Tyler Funneman (Wildwood, IL), Take Hirabayashi (Edogawa, Tokyo, Japan), Mike Jarboe (La Crescenta, CA), Brian Knight (Helena, MT), Barry Larson (Hayden, ID), Eric Loveless (Layton, UT), Mike Lusky (Baldwin Park, CA), Jason Millsap (Bryan, TX), Michael Muchlinski (Ephrata, WA), Mark Ripperger (Carlsbad, CA), Dixon Stureman (Morgan Hill, CA), Todd Tichenor (Holcomb, KS), Chris Tiller (Bullard, TX), John Tumpane (Oak Lawn, IL).

STADIUM INFORMATION

Club	Stadium	Opened	LF	CF	RF	Capacity	2010 Att.
Albuquerque	Isotopes Park	2003	340	400	340	13,279	571,100
Colorado Springs	Security Service Field	1988	350	410	350	8,400	328,003
Fresno	Chukchansi Park	2002	324	402	335	12,500	481,606
Iowa	Principal Park	1992	335	400	335	11,000	536,872
Las Vegas	Cashman Field	1983	328	433	328	9,334	336,488
Memphis	AutoZone Park	2000	319	400	322	14,300	479,028
Nashville	Herschel Greer Stadium	1978	327	400	327	10,700	319,235
New Orleans	Zephyr Field	1997	333	405	332	10,000	380,538
Oklahoma City	AT&T Bricktown Ballpark	1998	325	400	325	11,455	381,343
Omaha	Werner Park	2011	310	402	315	9,023	406,276
Reno	Aces Ballpark	2009	339	410	340	9,100	447,701
Round Rock	The Dell Diamond	2000	330	400	325	10,000	596,985
Sacramento	Raley Field	2000	330	405	325	14,014	657,910
Salt Lake	Spring Mobile Ballpark	1994	345	420	315	15,500	510,484
Tacoma	Cheney Stadium	1960	325	425	325	7200	351,095
* Tucson	Kino Stadium	1998	340	405	340	11,500	N/A

* Team played in Portland in 2010

ALBUQUERQUE ISOTOPES

Office Address: 1601 Avenida Cesar Chavez SE, Albuquerque, NM 87106.
Telephone: (505) 924-2255. **Fax:** (505) 242-8899.
E-Mail address: info@albuquerquebaseball.com.
Website: www.albuquerquebaseball.com.
Affiliation (first year): Los Angeles Dodgers (2009). **Years in League:** 1972-2000, 2003-

OWNERSHIP, MANAGEMENT

President: Ken Young. **Secretary/Treasurer:** Emmett Hammond. **General Manager:** John Traub. **Assistant GM, Sales/Marketing:** Nick LoBue. **Director, Box Office/Retail Operations:** Chrissy Baines. **Director, Sales/Promotions:** Adam Beggs. **Director, Media Relations:** Steve Hurlbert. **Director, Stadium Operations:** Bobby Atencio. **Manager,**

Promotions/Marketing: Chris Holland. **Manager, Suite Relations:** Paul Hartenberger. **Manager, Creative Services:** Kris Shepard. **Season Ticket/Group Sales Representatives:** Eddie Enriquez, Jason Buchta, Quentin Andes, Alex Tainsh. **Director, Accounting:** Cynthia DiFrancesco. **Assistant Director, Retail Operations:** Kara Hayes. **Assistant Director, Box Office Operations:** Michelle Young.

Stadium Operations Assistant: Joe Fara. **Coordinator, Community Relations:** Ashley Belden. **Director, Field Operations:** Shawn Moore. **Assistant Director, Field Operations:** Casey Griffin. **Home Clubhouse Manager:** Tony Iliano, Visiting Clubhouse Manager: Rick Pollack. **Front Office Assistant:** Mark Otero. **GM, Ovations Foodservice:** Jay Satenspiel. **Assistant GM, Ovations Foodservice:** Bernie Tackett. **Catering Manager, Ovations Foodservice:** Karla Lewis. **Purchasing/Warehouse Director, Ovations Foodservice:** Matt Butler. **Office Manager, Ovations Foodservice:** Jamie Yoder.

FIELD STAFF

Manager: Lorenzo Bundy. **Coach:** John Valentin. **Pitching Coach:** Glenn Dishman. **Trainer:** Greg Harrel.

GAME INFORMATION

Radio Announcer: Robert Portnoy. **No. of Games Broadcast:** Home-72 Road-72. **Flagship Station:** KNML 610-AM. **PA Announcer:** Stu Walker. **Official Scorers:** Glen Rosales, Gary Herron. **Stadium Name:** Isotopes Park. **Location:** From 1-25, exit east on Avenida Cesar Chavez SE to University Boulevard; From I-40, exit south on University Boulevard SE to Avenida Cesar Chavez. **Standard Game Times:** 7:05 p.m., Sun 6:05. **Ticket Price Range:** $6-24.

Visiting Club Hotel: MCM Elegante, 2020 Menaul NE, Albuquerque, NM 87107. **Telephone:** (505) 884-2511.

COLORADO SPRINGS SKY SOX

Office Address: 4385 Tutt Blvd, Colorado Springs, CO 80922.
Telephone: (719) 597-1449. **Fax:** (719) 597-2491.
E-Mail address: info@skysox.com. **Website:** www.skysox.com.
Affiliation (first year): Colorado Rockies (1993). **Years in League:** 1988-

OWNERSHIP, MANAGEMENT

Operated By: Colorado Springs Sky Sox Inc.
Principal Owner: David Elmore.
President/General Manager: Tony Ensor. **Senior Vice President, Marketing:** Rai Henniger. **Assistant GM/Director, Public Relations:** Mike Hobson. **Assistant GM/Director, Corporate Sponsorships/Marketing:** Matt Person. **Director, Broadcast Operations:** Dan Karcher. **Accountant:** Kelly Hanlon. **Director, Ticket Sales:** Whitney Shellem. **Director, Stadium Operations:** Matt Pribbernow. **Director, Group Sales:** Keith Hodges. **Director, Community Relations:** Jon Eddy. **Graphics Manager:** Erin Eads. **Director, Promotions:** Wes Sharp. **Assistant Director, Group Sales:** Ryan Stos. **Groups Sales Managers:** Jim Rice, Geri Woessner. **Special Event Manager:** Brien Smith. **GM, Diamond Creations:** Don Giuliano. **Director, Catering:** Chris Evans. **Head Groundskeeper:** Steve DeLeon. **Administrative Assistant:** Marianne Paine. **Home Clubhouse Manager:** Ricky Grima. **Visiting Clubhouse Manager:** Steve Martin.

FIELD STAFF

Manager: Stu Cole. **Coach:** Rene Lachemann. **Pitching Coach:** Doug Linton. **Trainer:** Heath Townsend.

GAME INFORMATION

Radio Announcer: Dan Karcher. **No. of Games Broadcast:** Home-72 Road-72. **Flagship Station:** AM 1300 "The Sports Animal."
PA Announcer: Josh Howe. **Official Scorer:** Marty Grantz, Rich Wastler. **Stadium Name:** Security Service Field. **Location:** I-25 South to Woodmen Road exit, east on Woodmen to Powers Boulevard, right on Powers to Barnes Road. **Standard Game Times:** 7:05 p.m.; **Sun.** 1:05. **Ticket Price Range:** $5-12.
Visiting Club Hotel: Hilton Garden Inn, 1810 Briargate Parkway, Colorado Springs, CO 80920. **Telephone:** (719) 598-6866.

FRESNO GRIZZLIES

Office Address: 1800 Tulare St, Fresno, CA 93721.
Telephone: (559) 320-4487. **Fax:** (559) 264-0795.
E-Mail address: info@fresnogrizzlies.com. **Website:** www.fresnogrizzlies.com.
Affiliation (first year): San Francisco Giants (1998). **Years in League:** 1998-

OWNERSHIP, MANAGEMENT

Operated By: Fresno Baseball Club, LLC.
President: Chris Cummings. **Executive Vice President:** Brian Glover. **Chief Financial Officer:** SuSin Correa. **Director, Media/Public Relations:** Noah Frank. **Director, Marketing/Creative Services:** Walmer Medina. **Marketing/Promotions Manager:** Cody Turner. **Director, Strategic Alliances:** Michelle Sanchez. **Director, Community Relations:** Danielle Witt. **Coordinator, Community Relations:** Ryan Moran. **Director, Client Services:** Andrew Melrose. **Business Development Executive:** Jerry James. **Client Services Executive:** Veronica Morales.

Director, Sales: Derek Franks. **Group Sales Manager:** Freddie Dominguez, Jr. **Ticket Office Manager:** Pat Wallach. **Group Sales Account Executive:** Adam Gleich. **Account Executives:** Chris Curry, Andrew Milios, Kavi Kapur, Taylor

Woods. **Director, Stadium Operations:** Harvey Kawasaki. **Director, Event Operations:** Matt Studwell. **Manager, Event Operations:** Joe Castillo. **Manager, Operations:** Ira Calvin. **Head Groundskeeper:** David Jacinto. **Director, Human Resources:** Ashley Tennell. **Finance Manager:** Monica Delacerda. **Accounts Payable Clerk:** Brian Mehlman. **Team Store:** Megan O'Brien, Lalonnie Calderon. **Receptionist:** DeeAnn Hernandez. **GM, Ovations Concessions:** Tim Dickert.

FIELD STAFF

Manager: Steve Decker. **Coach:** Russ Morman. **Pitching Coach:** Pat Rice. **Athletic Trainer:** Anthony Reyes. **Strength/Conditioning Coach:** Carl Kochan.

GAME INFORMATION

Radio Announcer: Doug Greenwald. **No of Games Broadcast:** Home-72 Road-72. **Flagship Station:** 105.5 FM The Truth (Wilks Broadcasting).

Official Scorer: Darrell Copeland. **MLBAM Stringer:** Jim Nelson.

Stadium Name: Chukchansi Park. **Location:** 1800 Tulare St, Fresno, CA 93721. **Directions:** From 99 North, take Fresno Street exit, left on Fresno Street, left on Inyo or Tulare to stadium; From 99 South, take Fresno Street exit, left on Fresno Street, right on Broadway to H Street; From 41 North, take Van Ness exit toward Fresno, left on Van Ness, left on Inyo or Tulare, stadium is straight ahead; From 41 South, take Tulare exit, stadium is located at Tulare and H Streets, or take Van Ness exit, right on Van Ness, left on Inyo or Tulare, stadium is straight ahead. **Ticket Price Range:** $8-18.

Visiting Club Hotel: Holiday Inn Downtown Fresno, 1055 Van Ness, Fresno, CA 93721. **Telephone:** (888) 465-4329.

IOWA CUBS

Office Address: One Line Dr, Des Moines, IA 50309.
Telephone: (515) 243-6111. **Fax:** (515) 243-5152.
E-Mail address: info@iowacubs.com. **Website:** www.iowacubs.com
Affiliation (first year): Chicago Cubs (1981). **Years in League:** 1969-

OWNERSHIP, MANAGEMENT

Operated By: Raccoon Baseball Inc.

Chairman/Principal Owner: Michael Gartner. **Executive Vice President:** Michael Giudicessi.

President/General Manager: Sam Bernabe. **Shareholder:** Mike Gartner. **Vice President/Assistant GM:** Jim Nahas. **VP/CFO:** Sue Tollefson. **VP/Director, Broadcast Operations:** Deene Ehlis. **Media Relations Manager:** Andrea Breen. **Director, Logistics:** Scott Sailor. **Director, Ticket Operations:** Kenny Houser. **Director, Luxury Suites:** Brent Conkel. **Assistant Ticket Manager:** Mark Dempsey. **Stadium Operations Director:** Jeff Tilley. **Corporate Sales Executives:** Melanie Doser, Nate Teut, Randy Wehofer. **Corporate Relations:** Red Hollis. **Head Groundskeeper:** Chris Schlosser. **Director, Merchandise:** Rick Giudicessi. **Coordinator, Merchandise:** Holly Edwards. **Accountant:** Lori Auten. **Manager, Cub Club:** John Gordon. **Director, Information Systems:** Larry Schunk. **Landscape Coordinator:** Shari Kramer.

FIELD STAFF

Manager: Bill Dancy. **Coach:** Von Joshua. **Pitching Coach:** Mike Mason. **Trainer:** Matt Johnson.

GAME INFORMATION

Radio Announcers: Deene Ehlis, Randy Wehofer. **No. of Games Broadcast:** Home-72 Road-72. **Flagship Station:** AM 940 KPSZ.

PA Announcers: Geoff Conn, Mark Pierce, Corey Coon. **Official Scorers:** Dirk Brinkmeyer, Brian Gibson. **Stadium Name:** Principal Park. **Location:** I-80 or I-35 to I-235, to Third Street exit, south on Third Street, left on Line Drive. **Standard Game Times:** 7:05 p.m.; Sun 12:05/1:05. **Ticket Price Range:** $6-11.

Visiting Club Hotel: Embassy Suites, 101 East Locust St Des Moines, IA 50309. **Telephone:** (515) 244-1700.

LAS VEGAS 51S

Office Address: 850 Las Vegas Blvd North, Las Vegas, NV 89101. **Telephone:** (702) 386-7200. **Fax:** (702) 386-7214.

E-Mail address: info@lv51.com. **Website:** www.lv51.com/.
Affiliation (third year): Toronto Blue Jays (2009). **Years in League:** 1983-.

OWNERSHIP, MANAGEMENT

Operated By: Stevens Baseball Group.

Executive Director: Don Logan. **General Manager/VP, Marketing:** Chuck Johnson. **VP, Sales/Marketing:** Mike Hollister. **VP, Ticket Operations:** Mike Rodriguez. **VP, Operations/Security:** Nick Fitzenreider. **Director, Finance:** Drew Dondero. **Special Assistant to GM:** Bob Blum. **Controller:** Araxi Demirjian. **Director, Broadcasting:** Russ Langer. **Manager, Community Relations:** Larry Brown. **Manager, Baseball Administration:** Denise Korach. **Media Relations Director:** Jim Gemma. **Ticket Operations Assistant:** Michelle Taggart. **Administrative Assistants:** Jan Dillard, Pat Dressel. **Managers, Corporate Marketing:** Justin Dunbar, Adam Eisenberg, Erik Eisenberg, Melissa Harkavy. **Merchandise Coordinator:** Jason Weber. **Sponsorship Services Manager:** William Graham. **Operations Manager:** Chip Vespe.

FIELD STAFF

Manager: Marty Brown. **Coach:** Chad Mottola. **Pitching Coach:** Tom Signore. **Trainer:** Voon Chong. **Strength/**

Conditioning Coach: Rob Helmick.

GAME INFORMATION

Radio Announcer: Russ Langer. No. of Games Broadcast: Home-72 Road-72. Flagship Station: Fox Sports Radio 920-AM.

PA Announcer: Dan Bickmore. Official Scorers: Mark Wasik, Gary Arlitz.

Stadium Name: Cashman Field. Location: I-15 to US 95 exit (downtown), east to Las Vegas Boulevard North exit, one-half mile north to stadium. Standard Game Time: 7:05 p.m. Ticket Price Range: $10-14.

Visiting Club Hotel: Golden Nugget Hotel & Casino, 129 Fremont Street, Las Vegas, NV 89101. Telephone: (702) 385-7111.

MEMPHIS REDBIRDS

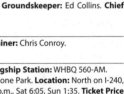

Office Address: 175 Toyota Plaza, Suite 300, Memphis, TN 38103.
Telephone: (901) 721-6000. Fax: (901) 842-1222.
Website: www.memphisredbirds.com
Affiliation (first year): St. Louis Cardinals (1998). Years in League: 1998-

OWNERSHIP, MANAGEMENT

Ownership: Memphis Redbirds Baseball Foundation, Inc.
Managed by: Global Spectrum.
General Manager: Ben Weiss. Assistant GM/Director, Sales: Derek Goldfarb. Director, Operations: Mark Anderson. Director, Finance: Art Davis. Director, Marketing: Adam Goldberg. Ticket Operations Manager: Travis Trumitch. Ticket Sales Manager: Jason Mott. Marketing Manager: Erin O'Donnell. Media Relations Manager: Jordan Marie Johnson. Community Relations Manager: Corey Gillum. Graphic Designer/Photographer: Allison Rhoades. Special Event Coordinator: Kellie Grabert. Corporate Sales Executives: Valerie Hight, Jody Sellers. Corporate Sales Coordinator: Leigh Eisenberg. Sales Coordinator: Jonathan Leshner. Ticket Sales Executives: Bryan Gore, Kyle Wicks, Keith Moor, Chris Coll. Staff Accountant: Cindy Neal. Office Coordinator: Linda Smith. Head Groundskeeper: Ed Collins. Chief Engineer: Danny Abbott. Maintenance: Spencer Shields.

FIELD STAFF

Manager: Chris Maloney. Coach: Mark Budaska. Pitching Coach: Blaise Ilsley. Trainer: Chris Conroy.

GAME INFORMATION

Radio Announcer: Steve Selby. No. of Games Broadcast: Home-72 Road-72. Flagship Station: WHBQ 560-AM.

PA Announcer: Unavailable. Official Scorer: JJ Guinozzo. Stadium Name: AutoZone Park. Location: North on I-240, exit at Union Avenue West, one and half mile to park. Standard Game Times: 7:05 p.m., Sat 6:05, Sun 1:35. Ticket Price Range: $5-17.

Visiting Club Hotel: Sleep Inn at Court Square, 40 N Front, Memphis, TN 38103. Telephone: (901) 522-9700.

NASHVILLE SOUNDS

Office Address: 534 Chestnut Street, Nashville, TN 37203.
Telephone: (615) 690-HITS. Fax: (615) 256-5684.
E-Mail address: info@nashvillesounds.com. Website: www.nashvillesounds.com
Affiliation (first year): Milwaukee Brewers (2005). Years in League: 1998-

OWNERSHIP, MANAGEMENT

Operated By: MFP Baseball.
Owners: Frank Ward, Steve Posner, Masahiro Honzawa.
Vice President/General Manager: Brad Tammen. Director, Operations/Communications: Doug Scopel. Director, Accounting: Barb Walker. Director, Community Relations: Heather Colvin. Manager, Sales/Sports Marketing: Drew Himsworth. Manager, Stadium Operations: Steven McKinney. Manager, Community Relations: Buddy Yelton. Manager, Ticketing: Eric Laue. Manager, Media Relations: Michael Whitty. Manager, Advertising/Marketing: Cliff McCardle. Manager, Merchandise: Janell Bullock. Senior Corporate Account Executive: Darren Feller. Manager, Sales: A.J. Rockwell. Account Executives: Carlton Recher, Kevin Samborski, Amanda Zuzik. Coordinator, Community Outreach: Michael Bigley. Coordinator, Stadium Operations: Mike Simonson. Coordinator, Accounts: Brandon Yerger. Office Manager: Sharon Ridley. Head Groundskeeper: Thomas Trotter. Assistant Groundskeeper: John Handzel. Clubhouse Managers: J.R. Rinaldi, Thomas Miller.

FIELD STAFF

Manager: Don Money. Coach: Sandy Guerrero. Pitching Coach: Rich Gale. Trainer: Dave Yeager. Strength/Conditioning Coach: Andrew Emmick.

GAME INFORMATION

Radio Announcer: Stu Paul. No of Games Broadcast: Home-72 Road-72. Flagship Station: WGFX 104.5 FM.

PA Announcers: Eric Berner, Jim Kiser. Official Scorers: Eric Jones, Trevor Garrett, Zack Blair, Robert Hernberger.

Stadium Name: Herschel Greer Stadium. Location: I-65 to Wedgewood exit, west to Eighth Avenue, right on Eighth to Chestnut Street, right on Chestnut. Standard Game Times: 7:05 p.m., Sat 6:35, Sun 2:05 (April-June 20), 6:35 (June

27-Sept). **Ticket Price Range:** $8-14.
  Visiting Club Hotel: Holiday Inn Vanderbilt, 2613 West End Ave, Nashville, TN 37203. **Telephone:** (615) 327-4707.

NEW ORLEANS ZEPHYRS

Office Address: 6000 Airline Dr, Metairie, LA 70003.
Telephone: (504) 734-5155. **Fax:** (504) 734-5118.
E-Mail address: zephyrs@zephyrsbaseball.com. **Website:** www.zephyrsbaseball.com.
Affiliation (first year): Florida Marlins (2009). **Years in League:** 1998-

OWNERSHIP, MANAGEMENT
  Managing Partner/President: Don Beaver.
  Executive Director/COO: Ron Maestri.
  Minority Owner/Vice President/General Counsel: Walter Leger.
  General Manager: Mike Schline. **VP, Sales/Marketing/Community Relations:** Jeff Booker. **Director, Finance/Accounting:** Donna Light. **Director, Broadcasting/Team Travel:** Tim Grubbs. **Color Analyst/Speakers Bureau:** Ron Swoboda. **Director, Media Relations:** Dave Sachs. **Director, Marketing/Suite Sales:** Katie Kelly. **Director, Promotions/Merchandise:** Jack Craig. **Director, Ticket Operations:** Kathy Kaleta. **Director, Community Relations:** Brandon Puls. **Director, Stadium Operations:** Chris Taylor. **Assistant, Stadium Operations:** Nathan McNair. **Director, Clubhouse:** Brett Herbert. **Director, Group Sales:** Trey Shields.
  Group Outings Coordinators: Katie Bonaccorso, Jimmy Coughlin, Jordan Price. **Head Groundskeeper:** Thomas Marks. **Assistant Groundskeeper:** Corey Cazaubon. **Maintenance Coordinator:** Craig Shaffer. **Receptionist:** Susan Hihar. **Director, Operations, Messina's Inc.:** George Messina. **Administrative Assistant, Messina's Inc.:** Priscilla Arbello. **Catering Manager, Messina's Inc.:** Darin Yuratich.

FIELD STAFF
  Manager: Greg Norton. **Coach:** Damon Minor. **Pitching Coach:** Charlie Corbell. **Trainer:** Steven Miller. **Strength/Conditioning:** Unavailable.

GAME INFORMATION
  Radio Announcers: Tim Grubbs, Ron Swoboda. **No. of Games Broadcast:** Home-72 Road-72. **Flagship Station:** WMTI 106.1 FM.
  PA Announcer: Doug Moreau. **Official Scorer:** JL Vangilder.
  Stadium Name: Zephyr Field. **Location:** I-10 West toward Baton Rouge, exit at Clearview Pkwy (exit 226) and continues south, right on Airline Drive (US 61 North) for 1 mile, stadium on left; From airport, take Airline Drive (US 61) east for 4 miles, stadium on right. **Standard Game Times:** 7 p.m., Sat 6, Sun 2 (April-May), 6 (June-Sept). **Ticket Price Range:** $6-10.
  Visiting Club Hotel: Best Western-St Christopher, 114 Magazine St, New Orleans, LA 70130. **Telephone:** (504) 648-0444.

OKLAHOMA CITY REDHAWKS

Office Address: 2 S. Mickey Mantle Dr., Oklahoma City, OK 73104.
Telephone: (405) 218-1000. **Fax:** (405) 218-1001.
E-Mail address: info@okcredhawks.com. **Website:** www.okcredhawks.com.
Affiliation (first year): Houston Astros (2011). **Years in League:** 1963-1968, 1998-

OWNERSHIP, MANAGEMENT
  Operated By: Oklahoma Baseball Club LLC.
  Principal Owner: Mandalay Baseball Properties.
  Executive Director: Michael Byrnes. **CFO:** Steve McEwen. **Director, Facility Operations:** Harlan Budde. **Director, Operations:** Mike Prange. **Ticket Operations Manager:** Armando Reyes. **Office Manager:** Kellie Mayberry. **Head Groundskeeper:** Monte McCoy.

FIELD STAFF
  Manager: Tony DeFrancesco. **Coach:** Keith Bodie. **Pitching Coach:** Burt Hooten. **Trainer:** Mike Freer.

GAME INFORMATION
  No. of Games Broadcast: Home-72 Road-72.
  Ballpark location: Near interchange of I-235 and I-40, take Lincoln exit off I-40 to Reno, west on Reno to ballpark. **Standard Game Times:** 7:05 p.m., Sun 4:05 (April-May), 7:05 (June-August). **Ticket Price Range:** $5-15.

OMAHA STORM CHASERS

Office Address: Werner Park, 12356 Ballpark Way, Papillion, NE 68046.
  Administrative Office Phone: (402) 734-2550. **Ticket Office Phone:** (402) 738-5100. **Fax:** (402) 734-7166. **E-mail Address:** info@omahastormchasers.com. **Website:** www.omahastormchasers.com.

Affiliation (first year): Kansas City Royals (1969). **Years in League:** 1998-

OWNERSHIP, MANAGEMENT

Operated by: Omaha Royals Limited Partnership and Omaha Storm Chasers Baseball Club.
Principal Owners: William Shea, Warren Buffett, Walter Scott.
President: Alan M Stein.
Vice President/General Manager: Martie J Cordaro. **Assistant GM:** Rob Crain. **Controller:** Laurie Schlender. **Director, Broadcasting:** Mark Nasser. **Director, Business Development:** Dave Endress. **Director, Merchandise:** Jason Kinney. **Director, Ticket Operations:** Paul Hammes. **Baseball Operations Manager:** James Jensen. **Group Sales Manager:** Danny Dunbar. **Media Relations Manager:** Mike Feigen. **Promotions Manager:** Ben Hemmen. **Ballpark Operations Manager:** Brett Myers. **Senior Ticket Sales Executive:** Andrea Stava. **Ticket Sales Executives:** Matthew Bradwell, Rustin Buysse. **Corporate Partnerships Executive:** Ben Kratz. **Ticket Operations:** Kaci Long. **Finance Assistant:** Drew Stauder. **Head Groundskeeper:** Mitch McClary.

FIELD STAFF

Manager: Mike Jirschele. **Coach:** Tommy Gregg. **Pitching Coach:** Doug Henry. **Athletic Trainer:** Dale Gilbert. **Strength Coach:** Nic Lively.

GAME INFORMATION

Radio Announcer: Mark Nasser. **No. of Games Broadcast:** Home-72, Away-72. **Flagship Station:** KOIL-AM 1180. **PA Announcers:** Bill Jensen, Craig Evans, Travis Justice, Jake Ryan. **Official Scores:** Frank Adkisson, Steve Pivovar, Ryan White.
Stadium Name (year opened): Werner Park (2011). **Location:** Hwy 370, just east of I-80 (exit 439).
Standard Game Times: 6:35 p.m. (April-May); 7:05 (June-Sept); Fri/Sat 7:05; Sun 2:05
Visiting Club Hotel: Courtyard Omaha La Vista, 12560 Westport Parkway, La Vista, NE 68128. **Telephone:** (402) 339-4900. **Fax:** (402) 339-4901.

RENO ACES

Office Address: 250 Evans Ave, Reno, NV 89501
Telephone: (775) 334-4700. **Fax:** (775) 334-4701. **Website:** www.renoaces.com
Affiliation (second year): Arizona Diamondbacks (2009). **Years in League:** 2009-.

OWNERSHIP, MANAGEMENT

President/Managing Partner: Stuart Katzoff.
Partners: Jerry Katzoff, Herb Simon.
Chief Financial Officer: Kevin Bower. **General Counsel:** Brett Beecham.
Executive Vice President, Business Operations: Justin Piper. **General Manager:** Rick Parr. **VP, Baseball Operations/ Communications:** TJ Lasita. **Director, Broadcasting:** Ryan Radtke. **Manager, Communications:** Zak Basch. **Senior Manager, Marketing Partnerships:** Brady Raggio. **Account Executive, Marketing Partnerships:** Amir Sanjar. **Director, Ticketing:** Brian Moss. **Account Executives, Group Tickets:** Jeff Kaminski, Amanda Belka. **Manager, Client Services:** Andrei Losche. **Client Services/Tickets:** Adam Kincaid.
Director, Ticket Operations: Charles Lucas. **Manager, Ticket Operations:** Brooke Noel. **Director, Marketing:** Brett McGinness. **Coordinator, Promotions:** Amanda Alling. **Coordinator, Mascot:** Bartholomew Piegdon. **Vice President, Ballpark Operations:** David Avila. **Director, Ballpark Operations:** Tara O'Connor. **Manager, Grounds:** Eric Blanton. **Director, Merchandise:** Jessica Berry. **Assistant Director, Merchandise:** Tonya Hunt-Gilbertson. **Controller:** Jerry Meyer. **Staff Accountant:** Matthew Molinari.

FIELD STAFF

Manager: Brett Butler. **Coach:** Rick Burleson. **Pitching Coach:** Mike Parrott. **Trainer:** James Ready. **Strength/ Conditioning Coordinator:** Josh Cuffe.

GAME INFORMATION

Radio Announcer: Ryan Radtke. **No. of Games Broadcast:** Home-72, Away-72. **Flagship Station:** Fox Sports 1450 AM.
PA Announcer: Mike Hagerty. **Official Scorers:** Steve Widmer, Chad Hartley, Jack Kuestermeyer.
Stadium Name: Aces Ballpark.
Location: From Carson City (south of Reno): 395 North to exit 66 (Mill Street), left at Mill Street, right at S Park Street, left at Kuenzli Street, right at East 2nd Street to ballpark. **From East:** I-80 West to exit 14 (Wells Avenue), left on Wells, right on Kuenzli, right at East 2nd Street.
Standard Game Times: 7:05 p.m., 6:05; Sun., **1:**05. **Ticket Price Range:** $6-30.
Visiting Club Hotel: Silver Legacy Resort Casino. **Telephone:** 775-325-7401.

ROUND ROCK EXPRESS

Office Address: 3400 East Palm Valley Blvd, Round Rock, TX 78665.
Telephone: (512) 255-2255. **Fax:** (512) 255-1558.
E-Mail Address: info@rrexpress.com. **Website:** www.roundrockexpress.com
Affiliation (first year): Houston Astros (2005). **Year in League:** 2005-

OWNERSHIP, MANAGEMENT

Operated By: Ryan Sanders Baseball, LP.
Principal Owners: Nolan Ryan, Reid Ryan, Reese Ryan, Don Sanders, Jay Miller, Eddie Maloney, Brad Sanders, Bret Sanders. **Executive VP, Ryan Sanders Baseball:** J.J. Gottsch. **Executive Assistants, Ryan Sanders Baseball:** Debbie Bowman, Kelly Looman.
President: Dave Fendrick. **Executive VP/General Manager:** George King. **VP, Corporate Sales:** Henry Green. **VP, Ticket Sales:** Gary Franke. **VP, Marketing:** Laura Fragoso. **VP, Business Development:** Gregg Miller. **Director, Communications/Baseball Operations:** Larry Little. **Director, Stadium Operations:** David Powers. **Controller:** Debbie Coughlin. **Director, United Heritage Center:** Scott Allen. **Director, Broadcasting:** Mike Capps. **Director, Merchandising:** Brooke Milam. **Director, Entertainment/Promotions:** Clint Musslewhite. **Director, Ticket Operations:** Ross Scott. **Director, Baseball Outreach:** Chris Almendarez. **Director, Stadium Maintenance:** Aurelio Martinez.
Senior Account Executive: Neil Moore. **Account Executives:** David Allen, Luke Crum. **Client Services Manager:** Molly Brinkmeyer. **Communications/Baseball Operations Manager:** Tim Jackson. **Retail Manager:** Debbie Goodman. **Corporate Sales Manager:** Brian Spieles. **Head Groundskeeper:** Garrett Reddehase. **Clubhouse Manager:** Kenny Bufton. **Communications Intern:** Zach Reed. **Maintenance Staff:** Raymond Alemon, Ofelia Gonzalez. **Event Staff Coordinator:** Randy Patterson. **Office Manager:** Wendy Abrahamsen.

FIELD STAFF

Manager: Bobby Jones. **Hitting Coach:** Scott Coolbaugh. **Pitching Coach:** Terry Clark. **Coach:** Spike Owen. **Trainer:** Jason Roberts.

GAME INFORMATION

Radio Announcers: Mike Capps, Jerry Grote. **No. of Games Broadcast:** Home—72, Road—72. **Flagship Station:** The Horn 104.9 FM ESPN Radio Austin. **PA Announcer:** Clint Musslewhite. **Official Scorer:** Tommy Tate. **Stadium Name:** The Dell Diamond.
Location: US Highway 79, 3.5 miles east of Interstate 35 (exit 253) or 1.5 miles west of Tollway 130.
Standard Game Times: 7:05 p.m., 6:05, 1:05. **Ticket Price Range:** $7-$14
Visiting Club Hotel: Hilton Garden Inn, 2310 North IH-35, Round Rock, TX 78681; (512) 341-8200

SACRAMENTO RIVER CATS

Office Address: 400 Ballpark Dr, West Sacramento, CA 95691.
Telephone: (916) 376-4700. **Fax:** (916) 376-4710.
E-Mail address: info@rivercats.com. **Website:** www.rivercats.com.
Affiliation (first year): Oakland Athletics (2000). **Years in League:** 1903, 1909-11, 1918-60, 1974-76, 2000-

OWNERSHIP, MANAGEMENT

Operated By: Sacramento River Cats Baseball Club, LLC.
Owner: Susan Savage. **President/General Manager/COO:** Alan Ledford. **General Counsel:** Matthew Re. **Senior Manager, Administrative Services:** Gay Caputo. **Executive VP/CFO:** Dan Vistica. **Director, Finance/IT/Accounting Services:** Jess Olivares. **Human Resources Manager:** Grace Bailey. **Accounting Clerk:** Madeline Strika. **Vice President, Business Operations:** Jeff Savage. **Senior Director, Operations:** Matt Thomas. **Head Groundskeeper:** Chris Ralston. **Manager, Sports Turf Management, Inc.:** Chris Martin. **Manager, Operations:** Mario Constancio. **Coordinator, Guest Services/Operations:** Shannon Roland. **Manager, Luxury Suites:** Ryan Von Sossan. **Manager, Corporate Partnerships:** Greg Coletti. **Account Executive:** Stacy Knight. **Manager, Client Services:** Kacie McDaniel. **Coordinator, Corporate Services:** Mitch Tom. **Sales/Service Assistant:** Andrew Shipp.
Manager, Merchandise: Rose Holland. **Coordinator, Website/Research:** Brent Savage. **Coordinator, Online Sales:** Megan Osgood. **Director, Ticket Sales:** Alex Zamansky. **Ticket Operations:** John Krivacic. **Manager, Ticket Services:** Matt Togami. **Manager, Inside Sales:** Chris Dreesman. **Manager, Season Tickets:** Christi Lorenson. **Senior Corporate Account Executives:** Bryan Iredell, Steve Gracio. **Corporate Account Executive:** Stuart Scally. **Senior Group Events Account Executives:** Melanie Levy, Ross Johnson. **Group Events Account Executives:** Kimberly Baptista, Emily Higginson. **Senior Director, Marketing/Events/Entertainment:** Jennifer Castleberry. **Manager, Communications:** Rebecca Brutlag. **Community Relations:** Tony Asaro. **Manager, Advertising:** Genene Chacon. **Producer, In-Game Entertainment:** Steven Lewandowski. **Coordinator, Multimedia/Graphic Design:** Mike Villarreal. **Graphic Designer:** Sara Molina. **Coordinators, Events/Entertainment:** Sara Wendt, Annalies van Stigt. **Coordinator, Day of Game Events:** Leslie Lindsey. **Mascot Coordinator:** Rhett Holland. **Coordinator, Media Relations/Interactive Media:** Nick Lozito.

FIELD STAFF

Manager: Darren Bush. **Coach:** Todd Steverson. **Pitching Coach:** Scott Emerson. **Trainer:** Brad LaRosa.

GAME INFORMATION
Radio Announcers: Johnny Doskow. **No. of Games Broadcast:** Home-72 Road-72. **Flagship Station:** Talk 650 KSTE
PA Announcer: Greg Lawson. **Official Scorers:** Brian Berger, Ryan Bjork, Mark Honbo.
Stadium Name: Raley Field. **Location:** I-5 to Business-80 West, exit at Jefferson Boulevard. **Standard Game Time:** 7:05
p.m. **Ticket Price Range:** $7-42
Visiting Club Hotel: Holiday Inn.

SALT LAKE BEES

Office Address: 77 W 1300 South, Salt Lake City, UT 84115.
Mailing Address: PO Box 4108, Salt Lake City, UT 84110.
Telephone: (801) 325-2337. **Fax:** (801) 485-6818.
E-Mail Address: info@slbees.com. **Website:** www.slbees.com.
Affiliation (first year): Los Angeles Angels of Anaheim (2001). **Years in League:** 1915-25, 1958-65, 1970-84, 1994-.

OWNERSHIP, MANAGEMENT
Operated by: Larry H Miller Baseball Inc.
Principal Owner: Gail Miller.
CEO, Larry H. Miller Group of Companies: Greg Miller.
President: Randy Rigby. **Executive Vice President/CFO:** Robert Hyde. **Senior VP:** Jim Olson. **VP/General Manager:**
Mark Amicone. **Senior VP, Broadcasting:** Chris Baum. **General Counsel:** Robert Tingey. **Controller:** McKay Smith.
Director, Corporate Travel: Judy Adams. **Senior VP, Communications:** Linda Luchetti. **Director, Broadcasting:**
Steve Klauke. **Communications Manager:** Hannah Lee. **Senior VP, Strategic Partnerships:** Mike Snarr. **VP, Corporate
Partnerships:** Greg Tanner. **VP, Marketing:** Craig Sanders. **VP, Ticket Sales:** Clay Jensen.
Director, Game Operations: Chance Fessler. **Director, Ticket Sales/Services:** Casey Patterson. **Director, Corporate
Partnerships:** Brian Prutch. **Box Office Manager:** Laura Russell. **Ticket/Group Sales Manager:** Brad Jacoway. **VP, Public
Safety:** Jim Bell. **Director, Public Safety:** Al Higham. **VP, Food Services:** Mark Stedman. **Director, Food Services:** Dave
Dalton. **Youth Programs Coordinator:** Nate Martinez. **Clubhouse Manager:** Eli Rice.

FIELD STAFF
Manager: Keith Johnson. **Coach:** Jim Eppard. **Pitching Coach:** Eric Bennett. **Trainer:** Brian Reinker.

GAME INFORMATION
Radio Announcer: Steve Klauke. **No. of Games Broadcast:** Home-72, Away-72. **Flagship Station:** ESPN 1230-AM.
PA Announcer: Jeff Reeves. **Official Scorers:** Howard Nakagama, Terry Harward.
Stadium name: Spring Mobile Ballpark. **Location:** I-15 North/South to 1300 South exit, east to ballpark at West
Temple. **Standard Game Times:** 7 p.m., **6:30** (April-May/August).
Ticket Price Range: $8-24.
Visiting Club Hotel: Sheraton City Centre, 150 W 500 South, Salt Lake City, UT 84101. **Telephone:** (801) 401-2000.

TACOMA RAINIERS

Stadium/Office Address: 2502 South Tyler St, Tacoma, WA 98405.
Telephone: (253) 752-7707. **Fax:** (253) 752-7135.
Website: www.tacomarainiers.com.
Affiliation: Seattle Mariners (1995). **Years in League:** 1904-1905, 1960-

OWNERSHIP, MANAGEMENT
Owners: Bob Schlegel, Kirby Schlegel, Nick Lachey.
President: Aaron Artman.
Director, Administration/Assistant to the President: Patti Stacy. **Vice President, Corporate Partnerships:** Kevin
Tiemann. **VP, Ticket Sales:** Chip Maxson. **General Manager, Food/Beverage:** Corey Brandt. **Creative Director:** Tony
Canepa. **Senior Director, Marketing/Community Development:** Annie Shultz. **Director, Corporate Partner Services:**
Audrey Berglund. **Director, Media Development/Events:** Alyson Jones. **Director, Game Entertainment:** Jessica
McDaniel. **Director, Facilities/Head Groundskeeper:** Ryan Schutt. **Director, Ticket Sales:** Shane Santman. **Director,
Operations:** Ashley Roth.
Ticket Operations Manager: Beth Dean. **Guest Services/Community Development Manager:** Mallory Beckingham.
Media Development Manager: Ben Spradling. **Publications/Marketing Coordinator:** Melissa Marchionna. **Suite
Services/Events Manager:** Nicole Strunks. **Controller:** Jacquie Sonnenfeld. **Accounting:** Elise Schorr. **Senior Corporate
Sales Managers:** Adam Baker, Brett Breece. **Corporate Sales Managers:** Sergio Magallanes, Jim Flavin. **Thomas
Knowlton. Senior Group Event Manager:** Nicole Eaton. **Group Event Manager:** Melissa Dingler. **Group Event
Coordinators:** Sarah Yelenich, Ryan Latham. **Home Clubhouse Manager:** Eddie Romprey.

FIELD STAFF
Manager: Daren Brown. **Coach:** Alonzo Powell. **Pitching Coach:** Dwight Bernard. **Trainer:** Tom Newberg. **Assistant
Trainer:** Jeremy Clipperton.

GAME INFORMATION
Radio Broadcaster: Mike Curto. **No. of Games Broadcast:** Home-72, Away-72. **Flagship Station:** KHHO 850-AM.

PA Announcer: Unavailable. **Official Scorekeeper:** Gary Brooks, Michael Jessee.

Stadium Name: Cheney Stadium. **Location:** From I-5, take exit 132 (Highway 16 West) for 1.2 miles to 19th Street East exit, right on Tyler St for 1/3 mile. **Standard Game Times:** 7 p.m., **Sun, 1:**35. **Ticket Price Range:** $7-$25.

Visiting Club Hotel: Hotel Murano, 1320 Broadway Plaza Tacoma, WA 98402. **Telephone:** (253) 238-8000.

TUCSON PADRES

Office Address: 2500 E Ajo Way, Tucson, AZ 85713.
Telephone: (520) 434-1367. **Fax:** (520) 434-1361.
Email address: info@tucsonpadres.com. **Website:** www.tucsonpadres.com.
Affiliation (first year): San Diego Padres (2011). **Years in League:** 1969-2008, 2011-

OWNERSHIP, MANAGEMENT

Operated By: Tucson Triple-A Baseball, LLC.

Vice President/General Manager: Mike Feder. **Senior Advisor:** Jack Donovan. **Business Manager/Director, Merchandising:** Pattie Feder. **Director, Operations:** Eric May. **Director, Game Day Operations:** Debbie Clark. **Director, Sales:** James Jensen. **Senior Account Executive:** Ray Depa. **Director, Inside Sales:** Sandy Davis. **Sports Marketing Specialist:** Ed Vosberg. **Director, Community Relations:** Crissy Ahmann-Perham. **Director, Broadcasting/Media Relations:** Tim Hagerty. **Home Clubhouse Manager:** T.J. Laidlaw. **Visiting Clubhouse Manager:** Cory McClelland.

FIELD STAFF

Manager: Terry Kennedy. **Coach:** Bob Skube. **Pitching Coach:** Steve Webber. **Trainer:** Wade Yamasaki.

GAME INFORMATION

Radio Announcer: Tim Hagerty. **No. of Games Broadcast:** Home-72 Road-72. **Flagship Station:** Tucsonpadres.com.
PA Announcer: Jonas Hunter. **Official Scorer:** Unavailable.
Stadium Name: Kino Stadium. **Location:** 2500 E. **Ajo Way. Tucson, AZ 85713.**
Standard Game Times: 7 p.m. Sun 6/7. **Ticket Price Range:** $5:50-$10.50.
Visiting Club Hotel: Unavailable.

EASTERN LEAGUE

Office Address: 30 Danforth St, Suite 208, Portland, ME 04101.
Telephone: (207) 761-2700. **Fax:** (207) 761-7064.
E-Mail Address: elpb@easternleague.com. **Website:** www.easternleague.com.
Years League Active: 1923-.
President/Treasurer: Joe McEacharn.

Vice President/Secretary: Charles Eshbach. **VP:** Chuck Domino. **Assistant to President:** Bill Rosario.

Directors: Greg Agganis (Akron), Rick Brenner (New Hampshire), Lou DiBella (Richmond), Bill Dowling (New Britain), Charles Eshbach (Portland), Joe Finley (Trenton), Bob Lozinak (Altoona), Art Matin (Erie), Michael Reinsdorf (Harrisburg), Brian Shallcross (Bowie), Craig Stein (Reading), Mike Urda (Binghamton).

Division Structure: Eastern—Binghamton, New Britain, New Hampshire, Portland, Reading, Trenton. Western—Akron, Altoona, Bowie, Erie, Harrisburg, Richmond.

Regular Season: 142 games. **2011 Opening Date:** April 7. **Closing Date:** Sept 5.

All-Star Game: July 13 at New Hampshire.

Playoff Format: Top two teams in each division meet in best-of-five series. Winners meet in best-of-five series for league championship.

Roster Limit: 24. **Player Eligibility Rule:** No restrictions. **Brand of Baseball:** Rawlings.

Joe McEacharn

Umpires: Joey Amaral (Columbia, MD), Joseph Born (Lafayette, IN), Matthew Cunningham (Indianapolis, IN), Andrew Dudones (Uniontown, OH), Christopher Graham (Courtice, Ontario), James Guyll (Fort Wayne, IN), Joseph Hannigan (Westmont, IL), Travis Hatch (Forrestfield, Australia), Thomas Honec (Harrisonburg, VA), Joel Hospodka (Omaha, NE), Patrick Mahoney (Pittsburg, CA), Benjamin May (Racine, WI), Jeffrey Morrow (Fenton, MO), Timothy Rosso (Saddle Brook, NJ), Jonathan Saphire (Centerville, OH), David Soucy (Brighton, MA), Christopher Vines (Kennesaw, GA), Thomas Woodring (Boulder, NV).

STADIUM INFORMATION

| Club | Stadium | Opened | Dimensions | | | Capacity | 2010 Att. |
			LF	CF	RF		
Akron	Canal Park	1997	331	400	337	9,447	261,563
Altoona	Blair County Ballpark	1999	325	405	325	7,210	286,321
Binghamton	NYSEG Stadium	1992	330	400	330	6,012	203,823
Bowie	Prince George's Stadium	1993	309	405	309	10,000	251,728
Erie	Jerry Uht Park	1995	312	400	328	6,000	218,748
Harrisburg	Commerce Bank Park	1987	335	400	335	6,000	294,325
New Britain	New Britain Stadium	1996	330	400	330	6,146	368,523
New Hampshire	MerchantsAuto.com Stadium	2005	326	400	306	6,500	386,102
Portland	Hadlock Field	1994	315	400	330	7,368	390,772
Reading	FirstEnergy Stadium	1951	330	400	330	9,000	456,466
Richmond	The Diamond	1985	330	402	330	9,560	463,842
Trenton	Mercer County Waterfront Park	1994	330	407	330	6,150	384,028

AKRON AEROS

Office Address: 300 S Main St, Akron, OH 44308.
Telephone: (330) 253-5151. **Fax:** (330) 253-3300.
E-Mail address: info@akronaeros.com. **Website:** www.akronaeros.com.
Affiliation (first year): Cleveland Indians (1989). **Years in League:** 1989-

OWNERSHIP, MANAGEMENT

Operated By: Akron Professional Baseball, Inc.

Principal Owners: Mike Agganis, Greg Agganis.

Executive Vice President/COO: Jim Pfander. **Executive VP/General Manager:** Jeff Auman. **Assistant GM, Media/Marketing:** Dan Foust. **Director, Finance:** Ken Fogel. **Director, Sales:** Greg Berry. **Manager, Sales:** Ben Muell. **Manager, Promotions:** Calvin Funkhouser. **Assistant Director, Ticket Sales/Box Office Manager:** Ross Swaldo. **Account Executive/Assistant Box Office Manager:** Brett Joyce. **Director, Group Sales:** Greg Berry. **Group Sales Representatives:** Mike Link, Nori Wieder. **Director, Merchandise:** Scott Riley. **Director, Food/Beverage:** Jason Kerton. **Assistant Director, Food/Beverage:** Nate Michel. **Coordinator, Suites/Picnics/Community Relations:** Nicole Blum. **Head Groundskeeper:** Matt Duncan. **Operations Assistant:** Steve Baer. **Office Manager/IT Specialist:** Arlene Spahn.

FIELD STAFF

Manager: Chris Tremie. **Coach:** Rouglas Odor. **Pitching Coach:** Tony Arnold. **Trainer:** Chad Wolfe.

GAME INFORMATION

Radio Announcers: Jim Clark. **No of Games Broadcast:** Home-71 Road-71. **Flagship Station:** Fox Sports Radio 1350-AM. **PA Announcer:** Joe Jastrzemski, Leonard Grabowski. **Official Scorer:** Eric Stasiowski, Bob Scott.

Stadium Name: Canal Park. **Location:** From I-76 East or I-77 South, exit onto Route 59 East, exit at Exchange/Cedar, right onto Cedar, left at Main Street; From I-76 West or I-77 North, exit at Main Street/Downtown, follow exit onto Broadway Street, left onto Exchange Street, right at Main Street. **Ticket Price Range:** $5-9.
Visiting Club Hotel: Akron City Centre, 20 W Mill St, Akron, OH 44308. **Telephone:** (330) 384-1500.

ALTOONA CURVE

Office Address: Blair County Ballpark, 1000 Park Avenue, Altoona, PA 16602.
Telephone: (814) 943-5400. **Fax:** (814) 942-9132.
E-Mail Address: frontoffice@altoonacurve.com. **Website:** www.altoonacurve.com.
Affiliation (first year): Pittsburgh Pirates (1999). **Years in League:** 1999-present.

OWNERSHIP, MANAGEMENT

Operated By: Lozinak Professional Baseball.
Managing Member: Bob Lozinak. **COO:** David Lozinak. **CFO:** Mike Lozinak. **Chief Administrative Officer:** Steve Lozinak. **General Manager:** Rob Egan. **Senior Advisor:** Sal Baglieri. **Assistant GM, Marketing/Promotions:** Matt Hoover. **Assistant GM, Sales:** Duane Miller. **Director, Communications:** Mike Passanisi. **Director, Community Relations:** Elsie Zengel. **Director, Merchandising:** Claire Martin. **Director, Ballpark Operations:** Kirk Stiffler. **Assistant Operations Manager:** Doug Mattern. **Director, Creative Services:** John Foreman. **Director, Mascot/Brand Development:** Bill Bettwy. **Senior Ticket Account Manager:** Mike Pence. **Ticket Sales Associates:** Chris Keefer, AJ Palazzi. **Administrative Assistant:** Carol Schmittle. **Sponsorship Sales Account Executive:** Chuck Griswold. **Manager, Concessions:** Glenn McComas. **Assistant Manager, Concessions:** Michelle Anna.

FIELD STAFF

Manager: P.J Forbes. **Coach:** Brandon Moore. **Pitching Coach:** Wally Whitehurst. **Trainer:** Mike Zalno. **Strength/ Conditioning:** Ricky White.

GAME INFORMATION

Radio Announcer: Mike Passanisi. **No. of Games Broadcast:** Home-71 Road-71. **Flagship Station:** ESPN Radio 1430 (WVAM-AM).
PA Announcer: Rich DeLeo. **Official Scorer:** Ted Beam, Dick Wagner.
Stadium Name: Blair County Ballpark. **Location:** Located just off the Frankstown Road Exit of I-99. **Standard Game Times:** 7 p.m., **6**:30 (April-May); Sun 6/2 (April-May). **Ticket Price Range:** $5-12.
Visiting Club Hotel: Ramada Altoona, Route 220 and Plank Road, Altoona, PA 16602. **Telephone:** (814) 946-1631.

BINGHAMTON METS

Office Address: 211 Henry St, Binghamton, NY 13901.
Mailing Address: PO Box 598, Binghamton, NY 13902.
Telephone: (607) 723-6387. **Fax:** (607) 723-7779.
E-Mail address: bmets@bmets.com. **Website:** www.bmets.com.
Affiliation (first year): New York Mets (1992). **Years in League:** 1923-37, 1940-63, 1966-68, 1992-

OWNERSHIP, MANAGEMENT

Principal Owners: Bill Maines, David Maines, George Scherer, Michael Urda.
General Manager: Jim Weed. **Director, Stadium Operations:** Richard Tylicki. **Director, Ticket Operations:** Casey Both. **Director, Video Productions:** Jon Cofer. **Director, Marketing:** Heith Tracy. **Special Event Coordinators:** Connor Gates, Erica Mincher, Bob Urda. **Scholastic Programs Coordinator:** Lou Ferraro. **Office Manager:** Amy Fancher. **Merchandising Manager:** Lisa Shattuck. **Director, Broadcast/Media Relations:** Matt McCabe. **Sports Turf Manager:** EJ Folli. **Home Clubhouse Manager:** Pete Stasio.

FIELD STAFF

Manager: Tim Teufel. **Coach:** Luis Natera. **Pitching Coach:** Marc Valdes.

GAME INFORMATION

Radio Announcer: Matt McCabe. **No. of Games Broadcast:** Home-71 Road-71. **Flagship Station:** WNBF 1290-AM.
PA Announcer: Unavailable. **Official Scorer:** Steve Kraly.
Stadium Name: NYSEG Stadium. **Location:** I-81 to exit 4S (Binghamton), Route 11 exit to Henry Street. **Standard Game Times:** 6:35, Fri-Sat 7:05, Day Games 1:05. **Ticket Price Range:** $9-11.
Visiting Club Hotel: Best Western, 569 Harry L Drive, Johnson City, NY 13790. **Telephone:** (607) 729-9194.

BOWIE BAYSOX

Office Address: Prince George's Stadium, 4101 NE Crain Hwy, Bowie, MD 20716.
Telephone: (301) 805-6000. **Fax:** (301) 464-4911.
E-Mail address: info@baysox.com. **Website:** www.baysox.com.
Affiliation (first year): Baltimore Orioles (1993). **Years in League:** 1993-

OWNERSHIP, MANAGEMENT

Owned By: Bowie Baysox Baseball Club LLC.
President: Ken Young.
General Manager: Brian Shallcross. **Assistant GM:** Phil Wrye. **Director, Marketing:** Brandan Kaiser. **Director, Field/Facility Operations:** Matt Parrott. **Director, Ticket Operations:** Charlene Fewer. **Director, Sponsorships:** Matt McLaughlin. **Promotions Manager:** Chris Rogers. **Communications Manager:** Tom Sedlacek. **Community Programs Manager:** Dana DeFilippo. **Account Executive:** Aaron Gunter. **Group Events Managers:** Vince Riggs. **Director, Gameday Personnel:** Darlene Mingioli. **Clubhouse Manager:** Andy Maalouf. **Visiting Clubhouse Manager:** Unavailable. **Bookkeeper:** Carol Terwilliger.

FIELD STAFF

Manager: Gary Kendall. **Coach:** Denny Hocking/Einar Diaz. **Pitching Coach:** Kennie Steenstra

GAME INFORMATION

Radio Announcer: Unavailable. **No. of Games Broadcast:** Unavailable. **Flagship Station:** Unavailable.
PA Announcer: Adrienne Roberson. **Official Scorer:** Bill Hay, Carl Smith, Peter O'Reilly.
Stadium Name: Prince George's Stadium. **Location:** 1/4 mile south of U.S. **50/RT. 301 Interchange in Bowie.**
Standard Game Times: 7:05 p.m; Sun 2:05 (April-May), 6:05 (June-Sept.). **Ticket Price Range:** $6-14.
Visiting Club Hotel: Best Western Annapolis, 2520 Riva Rd, Annapolis, MD 21401. **Telephone:** (410) 224-2800.

ERIE SEA WOLVES

Office Address: 110 E 10th St, Erie, PA 16501.
Telephone: (814) 456-1300. **Fax:** (814) 456-7520.
E-Mail address: seawolves@seawolves.com. **Website:** www.seawolves.com.
Affiliation (first year): Detroit Tigers (2001). **Years in League:** 1999-

OWNERSHIP, MANAGEMENT

Principal Owners: Mandalay Baseball Properties, LLC.
Team President/General Manager: John Frey. **Assistant GM, Sales:** Mike Uden. **Director, Ticket Sales:** Becky Obradovic. **Director, Media Relations/Broadcaster:** Greg Gania. **Director, Corporate Marketing:** Mark Pirrello. **Director, Operations/Concessions:** Brad Strobl. **Operations Manager:** Ryan Stephenson. **Ticket Operations Manager:** Cody Herrick. **Director, Special Events/Client Services:** Jason Vaughan. **Director, Entertainment:** Chris Norris

FIELD STAFF

Manager: Chris Cron. **Coach:** Jerry Martin. **Pitching Coach:** Ray Burris. **Trainer:** Chris McDonald.

GAME INFORMATION

Radio Announcer: Greg Gania. **No. of Games Broadcast:** Home-71 Road-71. **Flagship Station:** Fox Sports Radio WFNN 1330-AM.
PA Announcer: Bob Shreve. **Official Scorer:** Les Caldwell.
Stadium Name: Jerry Uht Park. **Location:** US 79 North to East 12th Street exit, left on State Street, right on 10th Street.
Standard Game Times: 7:05 p.m., 6:35 (April-May), Sun 1:05. **Ticket Price Range:** $5-12.
Visiting Club Hotel: Bel Aire Clarion Hotel, 2800 West 8th St Erie, PA 16505.

HARRISBURG SENATORS

Office Address: Metro Bank Park, City Island, Harrisburg, PA 17101.
Mailing Address: PO Box 15757, Harrisburg, PA 17105.
Telephone: (717) 231-4444. **Fax:** (717) 231-4445.
E-Mail address: information@senatorsbaseball.com. **Website:** www.senatorsbaseball.com.
Affiliation (first year): Washington Nationals (2005). **Years in League:** 1924-35, 1987-

OWNERSHIP, MANAGEMENT

Operated By: Senators Partners, LLC.
Chairman: Michael Reinsdorf.
CEO: Bill Davidson. **President:** Kevin Kulp.
General Manager: Randy Whitaker. **Assistant GM:** Aaron Margolis. **Accounting Manager:** Donna Demczak. **Senior Corporate Sales Executive:** Todd Matthews. **Director, Ticket Sales:** Denise Bell. **Senior Account Executives:** Jonathan Boles, Jessica Kauffman. **Ticket Sales Executive:** Daniel Haubert. **Director, Ticket Operations:** Dave Simpson. **Director, Merchandise:** Ann Marie Naumes. **Director, Stadium Operations:** Tim Foreman. **Head Groundskeeper:** Brandon Forsburg. **Stadium Operations Coordinator:** Ben Moyer. **Director, Broadcasting/Media Relations:** Terry Byrom. **Director, Community Relations:** Emily Winslow. **Director, Digital/New Media:** Ashley Grotte. **Ticket Sales Interns:** Andrew Madden, Patrick McGinley, Jaime Stambaugh. **Video Production Interns:** Richard Adragna, Sean Purcell. **Media Relations/Community Relations Intern:** Christy Buchar.

FIELD STAFF

Manager: Tony Beasley. **Coach:** Tony Gingrich. **Pitching Coach:** Randy Tomlin. **Trainer:** Jeff Allred.

GAME INFORMATION

Radio Announcer: Terry Byrom. **No. of Games Broadcast:** Home-71 Road-71. **Flagship Station:** 1460-AM.

PA Announcer: Chris Andre. **Official Scorers:** Terry Walters, Bruce Bashore. **Stadium Name:** Metro Bank Park. **Location:** I-83, exit 23 (Second Street) to Market Street, bridge to City Island. **Ticket Price Range:** $5-12.50.

Visiting Club Hotel: Park Inn Harrisburg West, 5401 Carlisle Pike, Mechanicsburg, PA 17050. **Telephone:** (800) 772-7829. **Visiting Team Workout Facility:** Gold's Gym, 3401 Hartzdale Dr, Camp Hill, PA 17011. **Telephone:** (717) 303-2070.

NEW BRITAIN ROCK CATS

Office Address: 230 John Karbonic Way, New Britain, CT 06051.
Mailing Address: PO Box 1718, New Britain, CT 06050.
Telephone: (860) 224-8383. **Fax:** (860) 225-6267.
E-Mail address: rockcats@rockcats.com. **Website:** www.rockcats.com.
Affiliation (first year): Minnesota Twins (1995). **Years in League:** 1983-

OWNERSHIP, MANAGEMENT

Operated By: Greater Hartford Sports Management, LLC.
Directors: William F Dowling, Coleman B Levy Esq.
President/CEO: William F Dowling. **Vice President:** Evan Levy. **Assistant GM:** Ricky Ferrell. **Director, Broadcasting:** Jeff Dooley. **Director, Ticket Operations:** Brendan O'Donnell. **Director, Group Sales:** Jonathan Lissitchuck. **Director, Promotions:** Kim Pizighelli. **Director, Media Relations:** Robert Dowling. **Corporate Sales/Hospitality:** Andres Levy. **Group Sales Manager:** Evan Paradis. **Marketing Coordinator:** Lori Soltis. **Corporate Sponsorship Manager:** Kate Baumann. **Director, Community Relations:** Amy Helbling. **Manager, Corporate Developement:** Steve Kunsey. **Controller:** Jim Bonfiglio. **Director, Stadium Operations:** Eric Fritz. **Client Service Coordinator:** Amanda Goldsmith. **Box Office Manager:** Josh Montinieri. **On-Site Manager, Concessionaire Centerplate:** Sheila Fagan.

FIELD STAFF

Manager: Jeff Smith. **Coach:** Tom Brunansky. **Pitching Coach:** Stu Cliburn. **Trainer:** Chad Jackson.

GAME INFORMATION

Radio Announcer: Jeff Dooley, Joe D'Ambrosio. **No. of Games Broadcast:** Home-71 Road-71. **Flagship Station:** WTIC 1080-AM/96.5-FM, WMRD 1150-AM.

PA Announcer: Don Steele. **Official Scorer:** Ed Smith.

Stadium Name: New Britain Stadium. **Location:** From I-84, take Route 72 East (exit 35 of Route 9 South (exit 39A), left at Ellis Street (exit 25), left at South Main Street, stadium one mile on right; From Route 91 or Route 5, take Route 9 North to Route 71 (exit 24), first exit. **Ticket Price Range:** $5-12.

Visiting Club Hotel: Holiday Inn Express, 120 Laning St, Southington, CT 06489. **Telephone:** (860) 276-0736.

NEW HAMPSHIRE
FISHER CATS

Office Address: 1 Line Dr, Manchester, NH 03101.
Telephone: (603) 641-2005. **Fax:** (603) 641-2055.
E-Mail address: info@nhfishercats.com. **Website:** www.nhfishercats.com.
Affiliation (first year): Toronto Blue Jays (2004). **Years in League:** 2004-

OWNERSHIP, MANAGEMENT

Operated By: Triple Play LLC.
Owner: Art Solomon.
President/General Manager: Rick Brenner. **Vice President:** John Willi. **VP, Business Operations:** Tim Restall. **VP, Sales:** Mike Ramshaw. **Corporate Controller:** Cindy Garron. **Executive Director, Public Affair/Marketing:** Danielle Matteau. **Executive Director, Ticket Sales:** Erik Lesniak. **Director, Stadium Operations:** Matt Moore. **Director, Sales:** Istvan Ats. **Director, Box Office Operations:** Tim Hough. **Director, Ticket Sales:** Joel Leroy. **Director, Group Sales:** Josh Hubbard. **Assistant Director, Marketing/Sales:** Liam Roberge. **Merchandise Manager:** Justin Stecz. **Production Manager:** Jake Dodge. **Media Relations Manager:** Matt Leite. **Head Turf Manager:** Shaun Meredith. **Ticket Sales Account Executives:** Gregg Tadgell, Billy Reardon, Mike Coziahr. **Box Office Assistant:** Matt Generaly. **Assistant Sports Turf Manager:** James Writer.

FIELD STAFF

Manager: Sal Fasano. **Coach:** Justin Mashore. **Pitching Coach:** Pete Walker. **Trainer:** Bob Tarpey.

GAME INFORMATION

Radio Announcer: Bob Lipman. **No. of Games Broadcast:** Home-71 Road-71. **Flagship Station:** WGIR 610-AM.

PA Announcer: Alex James. **Official Scorers:** Chick Smith, Lenny Parker, Greg Royce, Pete Dupuis, Chris Foley.

Stadium Name: Merchantsauto.com Stadium. **Location:** From I-93 North, take I-293 North to exit 5 (Granite Street), right on Granite Street, right on South Commercial Street, right on Line Drive. **Ticket Price Range:** $6-12.

Visiting Club Hotel: Comfort Inn, 298 Queen City Ave, Manchester, NH 03102. **Telephone:** (603) 668-2600.

PORTLAND SEA DOGS

Office Address: 271 Park Ave, Portland, ME 04102.
Mailing Address: PO Box 636, Portland, ME 04104.
Telephone: (207) 874-9300. **Fax:** (207) 780-0317.
E-Mail address: seadogs@seadogs.com. **Website:** www.seadogs.com.
Affiliation (first year): Boston Red Sox (2003). **Years in League:** 1994-

OWNERSHIP, MANAGEMENT

Operated By: Portland, Maine Baseball, Inc.
Founder/Chairman Emeritus: Daniel Burke. **Chairman:** Bill Burke.
Treasurer: Sally McNamara. **President:** Charles Eshbach. **Executive Vice President/General Manager:** Geoff Iacuessa. **Senior VP:** John Kameisha. **VP, Financial Affairs/Operations:** Jim Heffley. **Assistant GM, Media Relations:** Chris Cameron. **Director, Sales/Marketing/Promotions:** Liz Riley. **Director, Ticketing:** Dave Strong. **Director, Group Sales/Video Operations Manager:** Brian Murphy. **Sales Director, Ticketing:** Sarah Connolly. **Group Sales Manager:** Brayton Chase. **Director, Broadcasting:** Mike Antonellis. **Director, Food Services:** Mike Scorza. **Assistant Director, Food Services:** Greg Moyes. **Clubhouse Managers:** Craig Candage Sr, Mike Mestieri, Nick Fox. **Head Groundskeeper:** Rick Anderson.

FIELD STAFF

Manager: Kevin Boles. **Coach:** Dave Joppie. **Pitching Coach:** Bob Kipper. **Trainer:** Paul Buchheit.

GAME INFORMATION

Radio Announcer: Mike Antonellis. **No. of Games Broadcast:** Home-71 Road-71. **Flagship Station:** WBAE 1490-AM.
PA Announcer: Dean Rogers. **Official Scorer:** Thom Hinton.
Stadium Name: Hadlock Field. **Location:** From South, I-295 to exit 5, merge onto Congress Street, left at St John Street, merge right onto Park Ave; From North, I-295 to exit 6A, right onto Park Ave. **Ticket Price Range:** $4-9.
Visiting Club Hotel: Wyndham Hotel, 363 Maine Mall Rd, South Portland, ME 04106. **Telephone:** (207) 775-6161.

READING PHILLIES

Office Address: Route 61 South/1900 Centre Ave, Reading, PA 19605.
Mailing Address: PO Box 15050, Reading, PA 19612.
Telephone: (610) 375-8469. **Fax:** (610) 373-5868.
E-Mail Address: info@readingphillies.com. **Website:** www.readingphillies.com.
Affiliation (first year): Philadelphia Phillies (1967). **Years in League:** 1933-35, 1952-61, 1963-65, 1967-.

OWNERSHIP, MANAGEMENT

Operated By: E&J Baseball Club, Inc.
Principal Owner: Reading Baseball LP.
Managing Partner: Craig Stein.
General Manager: Scott Hunsicker. **Assistant GM:** Ashley Peterson. **Director, Stadium Operations/Concessions:** Andy Bortz. **Director, Sales:** Joe Bialek. **Director, Baseball Operations/Merchandise:** Kevin Sklenarik. **Director, PR/Media Relations:** Tommy Viola. **Director, Ticket Operations:** Mike Becker. **Director, Group Sales:** Mike Robinson. **Director, Fan Development/Staffing:** Chris McConney. **Controller:** Kristyne Haver. **Corporate Sales/Graphic Artist/ Game Entertainment:** Matt Jackson. **Assistant Director, Tickets:** Tim McGee. **Assistant Director, Groups:** Holly Frymyer. **Director, Community Relations:** Matt Hoffmaster. **Video Director:** Andy Kauffman. **Client Relationship Managers:** Curtis Burns, Jon Muldowney, Anthony Pignetti. **Operations/Concessions Assistant:** Tim Martino. **Head Groundskeeper:** Dan Douglas. **Office Manager:** Deneen Giesen. **Educational Programs/Youth Coordinator:** Todd Hunsicker.

FIELD STAFF

Manager: Mark Parent. **Coach:** Frank Cacciatore. **Pitching Coach:** Bob Milacki. **Trainer:** Chris Mudd.

GAME INFORMATION

Radio Announcers: Brian Seltzer. **No. of Games Broadcast:** Home-71, Away-71. **Flagship Station:** ESPN 1240-AM.
PA Announcer: Dave Bauman. **Official Scorers:** Paul Jones, Brian Kopetsky, Josh Leiboff, Dick Shute.
Stadium Name: FirstEnergy Stadium. **Location:** From east, take Pennsylvania Turnpike West to Morgantown exit, to 176 North, to 422 West, to Route 12 East, to Route 61 South exit; From west, take 422 East to Route 12 East, to Route 61 South exit; From north, take 222 South to Route 12 exit, to Route 61 South exit; From south, take 222 North to 422 West, to Route 12 East exit at Route 61 South. **Standard Game Times:** 7:05 p.m., 6:35 (April-May), Sun 1:05. **Ticket Price Range:** $6-11.
Visiting Club: Crowne Plaza Reading Hotel 1741 Papermill Road, Wyomissing, PA 19610. **Telephone:** (610) 376-3811.

RICHMOND FLYING SQUIRRELS

Office Address: 3001 N Boulevard, Richmond, VA 23230.
Telephone: (804) 359-3866. **Fax:** (804) 359-1373.
E-Mail address: info@squirrelsbaseball.com. **Website:** www.squirrelsbaseball.
com.
Affiliation (Second Year): San Francisco Giants (2009). **Years in League:** 2009-

OWNERSHIP, MANAGEMENT

Operated By: Navigators Baseball LP.
President/Managing Partner: Lou DiBella.
CEM: Chuck Domino. **Vice President/COO:** Todd "Parney" Parnell.
General Manager: Bill Papierniak. **Assistant GM:** Tom Denlinger. **Controller:** Faith Casey. **Assistant Controller:** Gail Olberg. **Director, Corporate Sales:** Ben Terry. **Corporate Sales Executives:** Mike Murphy, Jerrine Lee. **Director, Tickets:** Brendon Porter. **Box Office Manager:** Patrick Flower. **Ticket/Group Sales Specialist:** Dan Finerfrock. **Director, Broadcasting:** Jon Laaser. **Director, Media Relations:** Anthony Oppermann. **Director, Community Relations/Promotions:** Christina Shisler. **Coordinator, In-Game Entertainment:** Kellye Semonich. **Director, Group Sales:** Randy Atkinson. **Group Sales Executives:** Tara Gagnon, Amanda Schuman. **Suites/Group Sales Executive:** Elyse Holben. **Executive Director, Food/Beverage/Merchandise:** Ben Rothrock. **Director, Food/Beverage:** Justin Rink. **Assistant Director, Food/Beverage:** Clint Chamberlain. **Director, Catering:** Kurt Peter. **Director, Field Operations:** Steve Ruckman. **Director, Stadium Operations:** Tom White.

FIELD STAFF

Manager: Dave Machemer. **Coach:** Ken Joyce. **Pitching Coach:** Ross Grimsley.

GAME INFORMATION

Radio Announcers: Jon Laaser, Anthony Oppermann. **No. of Games Broadcast:** Home-71 Road-71. **Flagship Station:** Sports Radio 910 WRNL-AM. **PA Announcer:** Jimmy Barrett. **Official Scorer:** Scott Day. **Stadium Name:** The Diamond. **Capacity:** 9,560.
Location: Right off I-64 at the Boulevard exit.
Standard Game Times: 7:05 p.m., 6:35 (Sat), 5:05 (Sun).
Ticket Price Range: $7-11.
Visiting Club Hotel: Holiday Inn I-64 West End, 2000 Staples Mill Road, Richmond, VA 23230. **Telephone:** (804) 359-6061.

TRENTON THUNDER

Office Address: One Thunder Road, Trenton, NJ 08611.
Telephone: (609) 394-3300. **Fax:** (609) 394-9666.
E-Mail address: fun@trentonthunder.com. **Website:** www.trentonthunder.com.
Affiliation (first year): New York Yankees (2003). **Years in League:** 1994-

OWNERSHIP, MANAGEMENT

Operated By: Garden State Baseball, LLP.
General Manager/COO: Will Smith.
Senior Vice President, Corporate Sales/Sponsorships: Eric Lipsman. **Director, Ticket Operations:** Matt Pentima. **Director, Public Relations:** Bill Cook. **Director, Merchandising:** Joe Pappalardo. **VP, Operations:** Ryan Crammer. **Director, Food/Beverage:** Kevin O'Byrne. **Assistant Director, Food/Beverage:** Chris Champion. **Director, Community Relations:** Patience Purdy. **Director, Finance:** Catherine Gallagher. **VP, Business Development:** C.J. Johnson. **Office Manager:** Susanna Hall. **Production Manager:** Greg Lavin. **Corporate Partnerships Manager:** Marty Teller. **Baseball Operations/Accounting Manager:** Jeff Hurley. **Director, Broadcasting:** Jay Burnham.
Stadium Operations Manager: Steve Brokowsky. **Group Sales Managers:** Krysten Hardifer, Chad Heidel. **Group Sales Account Executives:** TJ Jahn, Nate Schneider. **Ticket Sales Account Executives:** Anna Rosenblatt, Bobby Picardo. **Ticket Sales Manager:** Erin Leigh. **Building Superintendent:** Scott Ribsam. **Home Clubhouse Manager:** Tom Kackley. **Visiting Clubhouse Manager:** Jim Billington. **Head Groundskeeper:** Ryan Hills. **Business Development Executives, Bill Hezel, Stephanie Fromm. Ticket Assistant:** Deana Ditri. **Merchandise Assistant:** Jennifer Murphy. **Broadcasting/ Media Relations Assistant:** Hank Fuerst. **Group Sales Coordinator:** Beth Ann Clyde. **Ticket Sales Interns:** Michael Medley, Caitlin Reardon.

FIELD STAFF

Manager: Tony Franklin. **Hitting Coach:** Julius Matos. **Pitching Coach:** Tommy Phelps. **Coach:** Justin Pope. **Trainer:** Tim Lentych. **Strength/Conditioning Coach:** Kaz Manabe.

GAME INFORMATION

Radio Announcer: Jay Burnham, Hank Fuerst. **No. of Games Broadcast:** Home-71 Road 71. **Flagship Station:** WTSR 91.3 FM.
PA Announcer: Unavailable. **Official Scorers:** Jay Dunn, Greg Zak.
Stadium Name: Samuel L Plumeri Sr Field at Mercer County Waterfront Park.
Location: From I-95, take Route 1 North to Route 29 South, stadium entrance just before tunnel; From NJ Turnpike, take Exit 7A and follow I-195 West, Road will become Rte 29, Follow through tunnel and ballpark is on left.
Standard Game Times: 7:05 p.m., Sat 1:05 (April), Sun 1:05.
Ticket Price Range: $9-13. **Visiting Club Hotel:** Unavailable.

SOUTHERN LEAGUE

Mailing Address: 2551 Roswell Rd, Suite 330, Marietta, GA 30062.
Telephone: (770) 321-0400. **Fax:** (770) 321-0037.
E-Mail Address: loriwebb@southernleague.com. **Website:** www.southernleague.com. **Years League Active:** 1964-.

President: Don Mincher. **Vice President:** Steve DeSalvo.

Directors: Peter Bragan Jr (Jacksonville), Steve Bryant (Carolina), Frank Burke (Chattanooga), Steve DeSalvo (Mississippi), Tom Dickson (Montgomery), Doug Kirchhofer (Tennessee), Jonathan Nelson (Birmingham), Miles Prentice (Huntsville), Bill Shanahan (Mobile), Reese Smith (Jackson).

VP, Operations: Lori Webb. **Media Relations Director:** Peter Webb.

Division Structure: North: Carolina, Chattanooga, Huntsville, Jackson, Tennessee. South: Birmingham, Jacksonville, Mississippi, Mobile, Montgomery.

Regular Season: 140 games (split schedule). **2011 Opening Date:** April 7. **Closing Date:** Sept 5.

All-Star Game: June 21, Jackson.

Playoff Format: First-half division winners meet second-half division winners in best-of-five series. Winners meet in best-of-five series for league championship.

Roster Limit: 24. **Player Eligibility Rule:** No restrictions.

Brand of Baseball: Rawlings.

Umpires: Jordan Baker, Sean Barber, Travis Carlson, Jason Cooksey, Blake Davis, Jordan Ferrell, Spencer Flynn, Brandon Henson, Anthony Johnson, Kolin Kline, Will Little, Marcus Pattillo, John Pierce, Brent Rice, and Chris Segal.

Don Mincher

STADIUM INFORMATION

Club	Stadium	Opened	Dimensions LF	CF	RF	Capacity	2010 Att.
Birmingham	Regions Park	1988	340	405	340	10,800	275,887
Carolina	Five County Stadium	1991	330	400	309	6,500	255,360
Chattanooga	AT&T Field	2000	325	400	330	6,362	217,469
Huntsville	Joe W. Davis Municipal Stadium	1985	345	405	330	10,488	91,237
Jackson	Pringles Park	1998	310	395	320	6,000	118,503
Jacksonville	Baseball Grounds of Jacksonville	2003	321	420	317	11,000	354,725
Mississippi	Trustmark Park	2005	335	402	332	7,416	178,138
Mobile	Hank Aaron Stadium	1997	325	400	310	6,000	201,628
Montgomery	Montgomery Riverwalk Stadium	2004	314	380	332	7,000	269,840
Tennessee	Smokies Park	2000	330	400	330	6,000	262,415

BIRMINGHAM BARONS

Office Address: 100 Ben Chapman Dr, Hoover, AL 35244.
Mailing Address: PO Box 360007, Birmingham, AL 35236.
Telephone: (205) 988-3200. **Fax:** (205) 988-9698.
E-Mail Address: barons@barons.com. **Website:** www.barons.com
Affiliation (first year): Chicago White Sox (1986). **Years in League:** 1964-65, 1967-75, 1981-

OWNERSHIP, MANAGEMENT

Principal Owners: Don Logan, Jeff Logan, Stan Logan.

General Manager: Jonathan Nelson. **Director, Stadium Operations:** James Young. **Director, Broadcasting:** Curt Bloom. **Director, Media Relations:** Adam C Nichols. **Director, Sales:** John Cook. **Director, Tickets:** Brandon Harms. **Director, Community Relations:** Shawn Pharo. **Director, Production:** Zane Davitz. **Manager, Operations:** David Madison. **Assistant, Sales/Marketing:** David Krakower. **Corporate Event Planners:** Dusty Lewis, Charlie Santiago. **General Manager, Grand Slam Catering:** Eric Crook. **Director, Catering:** Taylor Youngson. **Director, Concession:** Craig Spillman. **Office Manager:** Jennifer Dillard. **Accountants:** Jo Ann Bragan, Sammy Schillaci. **Head Groundskeeper:** Daniel Ruggiero.

FIELD STAFF

Manager: Bobby Magallanes. **Coach:** Andy Tomberlin. **Pitching Coach:** JR Pedrew. **Trainer:** Josh Fallin. **Strength/Conditioning:** Raymond Smith.

GAME INFORMATION

Radio Announcer: Curt Bloom. **No of Games Broadcast:** Home-70 Road-70. **Flagship Station:** Unavailable.

PA Announcer: Eddie Layne, Derek Scudder. **Official Scorer:** Unavailable. **Stadium Name:** Regions Park. **Location:** I-459 to Highway 150 (exit 10) in Hoover. **Standard Game Times:** 7:05 p.m., Sat 6:30, Sun 2:05 (first half), 5:05 (second half). **Ticket Price Range:** $7-12.

Visiting Club Hotel: Days Inn at the Galleria, 1800 Riverchase Dr, Birmingham, AL 35244. **Telephone:** (205) 985-7500.

CAROLINA MUDCATS

Office Address: 1501 NC Hwy 39, Zebulon, NC 27597.
Mailing Address: PO Drawer 1218, Zebulon, NC 27597.
Telephone: (919) 269-2287. **Fax:** (919) 269-4910.
E-Mail Address: muddy@carolinamudcats.com. **Website:** www.carolinamudcats.com.
Affiliation (first year): Cincinnati Reds (2009). **Years in League:** 1991-

OWNERSHIP, MANAGEMENT

Operated by: Carolina Mudcats Professional Baseball Club Inc.
Principal Owner: Steve Bryant.
General Manager: Joe Kremer. **Assistant GM:** Eric Gardner. **Office Manager:** Jackie DiPrimo. **Director, Stadium Operations:** Daniel Spence. **Stadium Operations:** Vinny Jones. **Director, Promotions/Marketing:** Sean Nickelsen. **Director, Food/Beverage:** Zia Torabian. **Director, Community Relations/Luxury Suites:** Macy Dykema. **Director, Merchandise:** Anne Allen. **Director, Video Operations/Multimedia Productions/Website:** Aaron Bayles. **Director, Tickets:** Brant Smith. **Director, Corporate Sales:** Ricky Ray. **Director, Group Sales:** Chris Signorelli. **Group Sales Associates:** Joshua Bridges, Drew Hemphill. **Director, Field Operations:** John Packer. **Social Networking/Promotions:** Matt Poloni

FIELD STAFF

Manager: David Bell. **Coach:** Ryan Jackson. **Pitching Coach:** Tom Brown. **Trainer:** Jimmy Mattocks.

GAME INFORMATION

Radio Announcers: Patrick Kinas, Joe Bourdow. **No. of Games Broadcast:** Home-70, Away-70. **Flagship Stations:** WRDU 106.1 FM, WRDU 106.1 HD2, Jammin 99.3 FM.
PA Announcer: Dave Slade. **Official Scorer:** John Hobgood.
Stadium Name: Five County Stadium. **Location:** From Raleigh, U.S. **64 East to 264 East, exit at Highway 39 in Zebulon. Standard Game Times:** 7:15 p.m., Sat 6:15, Sun 2. **Ticket Price Range:** $6-11.
Visiting Club Hotel: Hilton Garden Inn.

CHATTANOOGA LOOKOUTS

Office Address: 201 Power Alley, Chattanooga, TN 37402.
Mailing Address: PO Box 11002, Chattanooga, TN 37401.
Telephone: (423) 267-2208. **Fax:** (423) 267-4258.
E-Mail Address: lookouts@lookouts.com. **Website:** www.lookouts.com.
Affiliation (first year): Los Angeles Dodgers (2009). **Years in League:** 1964-65, 1976-

OWNERSHIP, MANAGEMENT

Operated By: Scenic City Baseball LLC.
Principal Owner: Daniel Burke, Frank Burke, Charles Eshbach.
President/General Manager: Frank Burke. **Vice President/Assistant GM:** John Maedel. **Director, Business Administration/Executive Assistant:** Debby Kennedy. **Director, Group Sales/Assistant Director, Concessions:** John Quirk. **Director, Group Sales/Assistant Director, Ticketing:** Gavin Cox. **Director, Merchandising/Marketing:** Chrysta Jorgensen. **Director, Media Relations:** Peter Intza. **Director, Ticketing Operations:** Luis Gonzalez. **Director, Concessions:** Steve Sullivan. **Director, Broadcasting:** Larry Ward. **Head Groundskeeper:** Joe Fitzgerald. **Director, Stadium Operations/Assistant Director, Broadcasting:** Will Poindexter. **Director, Business Administration/ Accounting:** Amy Leffew.

FIELD STAFF

Manager: Carlos Subero. **Coach:** Franklin Stubbs. **Pitching Coach:** Chuck Crim.

GAME INFORMATION

Radio Announcers: Larry Ward, Will Poindexter. **No. of Games Broadcast:** Home-70 Road-70. **Flagship Station:** 106.9 FM (WPLZ-HD2).
PA Announcer: John Maedel. **Official Scorers:** Wirt Gammon, Andy Paul.
Stadium Name: AT&T Field. **Location:** From I-24, take U.S. **27 North to exit 1C (4th Street), first left onto Chestnut Street, left onto Third Street. Ticket Price Range:** $4-8.
Visiting Club Hotel: Clarion Inn & Suites, 2345 Shallowford Rd, Chattanooga, TN 37412. **Telephone:** (423) 855-2898.

HUNTSVILLE STARS

Office Address: 3125 Leeman Ferry Rd, Huntsville, AL 35801.
Telephone: (256) 882-2562. **Fax:** (256) 880-0801.
E-Mail Address: info@huntsvillestars.com. **Website:** www.huntsvillestars.com.
Affiliation (first year): Milwaukee Brewers (1999). **Years in League:** 1985-

OWNERSHIP, MANAGEMENT

Operated By: Huntsville Stars LLC.
President: Miles Prentice.
General Manager: Buck Rogers. **Assistant GM:** Babs Rogers. **Director, Media Relations:** Jill Cacic. **Manager, Corporate Sales:** Ryan Edwards. **Manager, Group Sales:** Courtney White. **Office Manager:** Earl Grilliot. **Head Groundskeeper:** Kelly Rensel. **Director, Concessions:** Scott Tolmach.

FIELD STAFF

Manager: Mike Guerrero. **Coach:** Al LeBoeuf. **Pitching Coach:** John Curtis. **Athletic Trainer:** Aaron Hoback. **Strength/Conditioning Coach:** Jake Marx

GAME INFORMATION

PA Announcers: Stephanie Puttman. **Official Scorer:** Don Rizzardi.
Stadium Name: Joe W. **Davis Municipal Stadium. Location:** I-65 to I-565 East, south on Memorial Parkway to Drake Avenue exit, right on Don Mincher Drive. **Ticket Price Range:** $5-$20. **Visiting Club Hotel:** Holiday Inn, 401 Williams Avenue, Huntsville, AL, 35801. **Telephone:** 256-533-1400.

JACKSON GENERALS

Office Address: 4 Fun Place, Jackson, TN 38305.
Telephone: (731) 988-5299. **Fax:** (731) 988-5246.
E-Mail Address: fun@diamondjaxx.com. **Website:** www.diamondjaxx.com.
Affiliation (third year): Seattle Mariners (2007). **Years in League:** 1998-

OWNERSHIP, MANAGEMENT

Operated by: Jackson Baseball Club LP.
Chairman: David Freeman. **President:** Reese Smith.
General Manager: Tom Hanson. **Assistant GM:** Jason Compton. **Director, Security/Stadium Operations:** Robert Jones. **Accounting Manager:** Theresa Barnett. **Manager, Media Relations/Broadcasting:** Chris Harris. **Manager, Tickets/Merchandise:** Meghan O'Brien. **Turf Manager:** Tyler Brewer. **Manager, Catering/Concessions:** Kurt Brown. **Manager, Home Clubhouse:** C.J. **Fedewa. Manager, Visiting Clubhouse:** Bradley Arnold. **Community Relations/Sales Executive:** Jonna Sampson. **Media Relations/Publications Assistant:** Michael Young. **Accounting/Adminstrative Assistant:** Melissa Ferrell. **Sales Executive:** Dustin Smith. **Ticketing/Merchandise Assistant:** Kyle Nichols. **Ticketing/Merchandise Assistant:** Xan Stewart. **Sales Executive:** Nick Hall.

FIELD STAFF

Manager: Jim Pankovits. **Coach:** Cory Snyder. **Pitching Coach:** Lance Painter. **Trainer:** Matt Toth .

GAME INFORMATION

Radio Announcer: Chris Harris. **No. of Games Broadcast:** Home-70, Away-70. **Flagship Station:** WNWS 101.5 FM.
PA Announcer: Dan Reeves. **Official Scorer:** Unavailable.
Stadium Name: Pringles Park. **Location:** From I-40, take exit 85 South on FE Wright Drive, left onto Ridgecrest Road. **Standard Game Times:** 7:05 p.m., Sat 6:05, Sun 2:05. **Ticket Price Range:** $6-10.
Visiting Club Hotel: Doubletree Hotel, 1770 Hwy 45 Bypass, Jackson, TN 38305. **Telephone:** (731) 664-6900.

JACKSONVILLE SUNS

Office Address: 301 A Philip Randolph Blvd, Jacksonville, FL 32202.
Mailing Address: PO Box 4756, Jacksonville, FL 32201.
Telephone: (904) 358-2846. **Fax:** (904) 358-2845.
E-Mail Address: info@jaxsuns.com. **Website:** www.jaxsuns.com.
Affiliation (first year): Florida Marlins (2009). **Years In League:** 1970-

OWNERSHIP, MANAGEMENT

Operated by: Baseball Jax Inc.
Principal Owner/Chairman of the Board: Peter Bragan. **Sr. Madame Chairman:** Mary Frances Bragan.
President/General Manager: Peter Bragan Jr. **Assistant GM:** Chris Peters. **Director, Field Operations:** Ed Attalla. **Director, Merchandise:** Victoria Eure. **Director, Sales/Promotions:** Casey Nichols. **Director, Business Administration:** Barbara O'Berry. **Director, Video Services:** David Scheldorf. **Director, Group Sales:** January Putt Squyres. **Manager, Group Sales:** Lindsey Weeks. **Director, Ticket Operations:** Amy Delettre. **Manager, Stadium Operations:** JD Metrie.

Director, Community Relations: Sarah Foster. Manager, Media Relations/Website: Wesley Mitchell. General Manager, Ballpark Foods: Jamie Davis. Assistant GM, Ballpark Foods/Finance: Mitch Buska. Group Sales Associates: Teddy Foster, Jarrod Simmons. Interns: Antoine Lawrence, Sarah Ellis, Lindsey Powell. Executive Assistant: Theresa Viets.

FIELD STAFF
Manager: Andy Barkett. Coach: Corey Hart. Pitching Coach: John Duffy. Trainer: Dustin Luepker.

GAME INFORMATION
Radio Announcer: JP Shadrick. No. of Games Broadcast: Home-70, Away-70. Flagship Station: WFXJ 930-AM. PA Announcer: John Leard. Official Scorer: Jason Eliopulos. Press Box Assistant: Brian DeLettre.
Stadium Name: The Baseball Grounds of Jacksonville. Location: I-95 South to Martin Luther King Parkway exit, follow Gator Bowl Blvd around Alltel Stadium; I-95 North to Exit 347 (Emerson Street), go right to Hart Bridge Expressway, take Sports Complex exit, left at light to stop sign, take left and follow around Alltel Stadium; From Mathews Bridge, take A Philip Randolph exit, right on A Philip Randolph, straight to stadium. Standard Game Times: 7:05 p.m., Wed 1:05/7:05, Sun 3:05/5:05. Ticket Price Range: $7.50-22.50.
Visiting Club Hotel: Hyatt Regency Jacksonville Riverfront, 225 Coastline Dr., Jacksonville, FL 32202. Telephone: (904) 633-9095.

MISSISSIPPI BRAVES

Office Address: Trustmark Park, 1 Braves Way, Pearl, MS 39208.
Mailing Address: PO Box 97389, Pearl, MS 39288.
Telephone: (601) 932-8788. Fax: (601) 936-3567.
E-Mail Address: mississippi.braves@braves.com. Website: www.mississippibraves.com.
Affiliation (first year): Atlanta Braves (2005). Years in League: 2005-

OWNERSHIP, MANAGEMENT
Operated By: Atlanta National League Baseball Club Inc.
General Manager: Steve DeSalvo. Assistant GM: Jim Bishop. Ticket Manager: Nick Anderson. Merchandise Manager: Sarah Banta. Advertising/Design Manager: Brian Byrd. Sales Associate: Evan Perzel, Sean Guillotte, Jennifer Lyles, Tosha Taylor, Jake Smith. Head Chef: Tina Funches. Suites/Catering Manager: Debbie Herrington. Stadium Operations Manager: Matt McCoy. Promotions/Entertainment Manager: Brian Prochilo. Concessions Manager: Felicia Thompson. Office Administrator: Christy Shaw. Restaurant Manager: Gene Slaughter. Commissary Manager: James Davis. Director, Field/Facility Operations: Matt Taylor.

FIELD STAFF
Manager: Rocket Wheeler. Coach: Garey Ingram. Pitching Coach: Mike Alvarez. Trainer: Ricky Alcantara.

GAME INFORMATION
Radio Announcer: Ben Ingram. No. of Games Broadcast: Home-70 Road-70. Flagship Station: WYAB 103.9 FM. PA Announcer: Derrel Palmer. Official Scorer: Butch Raley. Stadium Name: Trustmark Park.
Location: I-20 to exit 48/Pearl (Pearson Road). Ticket Price Range: $5-12.
Visiting Club Hotel: Holiday Inn Trustmark Park, 110 Bass Pro Drive, Pearl, MS 39208. Telephone: (601) 939-5238.

MOBILE BAYBEARS

Office Address: Hank Aaron Stadium, 755 Bolling Bros Blvd, Mobile, AL 36606.
Telephone: (251) 479-2327. Fax: (251) 476-1147.
E-Mail Address: baybears@mobilebaybears.com. Website: www.mobilebaybears.com
Affiliation (first year): Arizona Diamondbacks (2007). Years in League: 1966, 1970, 1997-

OWNERSHIP, MANAGEMENT
Operated by: HWS Baseball Group.
Principal Owner: Mike Savit.
President/COO: Bill Shanahan. General Sales Manager: Jeff Long. Assistant General Manager, Finance: Betty Adams. Assistant GM, Promotions/Corporate Sales: Mike Callahan. Assistant GM, Stadium Operations: John Hilliard. Director, Community Relations/Director, Audio/Visual: Ari Rosenbaum. Director, Media Relations (team related): Wayne Randazzo. Director, Youth Programs/Media Relations (non-team related): JR Wittner. Director, Group Sales: Garrett Wolf. Sales Representative: John Golz. Concessions Manger: Tara Crawford. Box Office Manager: Adam Mettler. Director, Stadium Operations: John Harless. Clubhouse Manager: Hank Copley. Stadium Operations Assistant: Wade Vadakin. Internet Liaison/Team Chaplain: Lorin Barr.

FIELD STAFF
Manager: Turner Ward. Coach: Alan Zinter. Pitching Coach: Dan Carlson. Trainer: Joe Metz.

GAME INFORMATION
Radio Announcer: Wayne Randazzo. No. of Games Broadcast: Home-70, Away-70.
Flagship Station: 107.3 FMhd2, www.baybearsradio.com.
PA Announcer: Mike Callahan. Official Scorers: Unavailable.
Stadium Name: Hank Aaron Stadium. Location: I-65 to exit 1 (Government Blvd. East), right at Satchel Paige Drive,

right at Bolling Bros. Boulevard.

Standard Game Times: 7:05 p.m., Sun. 6:05, 2:05. **Ticket Price Range:** $5-15.
Visiting Club Hotel: Riverview Plaza, 64 S Water St, Mobile, AL 36602. **Telephone:** (251) 438-4000.

MONTGOMERY BISCUITS

Office Address: 200 Coosa St, Montgomery, AL 36104.
Telephone: (334) 323-2255. **Fax:** (334) 323-2225.
E-Mail address: info@biscuitsbaseball.com. **Website:** www.biscuitsbaseball.com.
Affiliation (first year): Tampa Bay Rays (2004). **Years in League:** 1965-1980, 2004-

OWNERSHIP, MANAGEMENT

Operated By: Montgomery Professional Baseball LLC.
Principal Owners: Tom Dickson, Sherrie Myers.
General Manager: Greg Rauch. **Assistant GM:** Marla Terranova Vickers. **Sales Director:** Scott Trible. **Group Sales Representatives:** Dan Boyd, Scott Reasoner. **Marketing Assistants:** Jackie Kampf, Jordan Mandelkorn. **Season Ticket Concierge:** Bob Rabon. **Sponsorship Service Representative:** Jonathan Vega. **Box Office Manager:** Devon Hasting. **Retail Manager:** Monte Meyers. **Director, Operations:** Steve Blackwell. **Head Groundskeeper:** Drew Ellis. **Director, Food/Beverage:** Travis Johnson. **Catering/Kitchen Manager:** Mike Smith. **Catering Coordinator:** Rene Ducote. **Director, Business Operations:** Linda Fast. **Assistant Business Manager:** Dewanna Croy. **Office Administrator:** Bill Sisk. **Concessions Manager:** Chase Elliott. **Sales Intern:** Ross Winkler.

FIELD STAFF

Manager: Billy Gardner Jr. **Coach:** Ozzie Timmons. **Pitching Coach:** Bill Moloney.

GAME INFORMATION

Radio Announcer: Joe Davis. **No of Games Broadcast:** Home-70 Road-70. **Flagship Station:** WLWI 1440-AM. **PA Announcer:** Rick Hendrick. **Official Scorer:** Kyle Kreutzer. **Stadium Name:** Montgomery Riverwalk Stadium.
Location: I-65 to exit 172, east on Herron Street, left on Coosa Street.
Ticket Price Range: $8-12. **Visiting Club Hotel:** Candlewood Suites.

TENNESSEE SMOKIES

Office Address: 3540 Line Drive, Kodak, TN 37764.
Telephone: (865) 865-2300. **Fax:** (865) 523-9913.
E-Mail Address: info@smokiesbaseball.com. **Website:** www.smokiesbaseball.com.
Affiliation (first year): Chicago Cubs (2007). **Years in League:** 1964-67, 1972-

OWNERSHIP, MANAGEMENT

Operated By: SPBC, LLC.
President: Doug Kirchhofer.
General Manager: Brian Cox. **Assistant GM:** Jeff Shoaf. **Director, Stadium Operations:** Bryan Webster. **Director, Community Relations:** Lauren Chesney. **Director, Food/Beverage:** Tony DaSilveira. **Director, Entertainment/Client Services:** Ryan Cox. **Director, Ticket/Retail Operations:** Robby Scheuermann. **Director, Field Operations:** Stuart Morris. **Director, Corporate Ticket Development:** Matt Strutner. **Senior Corporate Sales Executive:** Ken Franz. **Corporate Sales Executive:** Dan Blue. **Media Relations:** Adam Kline. **Video Production/Graphic Design Manager:** Tim Avery. **Group Sales Manager:** Rey Regenstreif-Harms. **Group Sales Representatives:** Baylor Love, Jeff Martin, Gabrielle Matus, Casey McDannald. **Business Manager:** Suzanne French. **Administrative Assistant:** Tolena Trout.

FIELD STAFF

Manager: Brian Harper. **Coach:** Mariano Duncan. **Pitching Coach:** Marty Mason. **Trainer:** Nick Frangella.

GAME INFORMATION

Radio Announcer: Mick Gillispie. **No. of Games Broadcast:** Home-70 Road-70. **Flagship Station:** WNML 99.1-FM/990-AM. **PA Announcer:** George Yardley. **Official Scorers:** Jack Tate, Jared Smith, Bernie Reimer.
Stadium Name: Smokies Park. **Location:** I-40 to exit 407, Highway 66 North. **Standard Game Times:** 7:15 p.m., Sat 6:15, Sun 2/5. **Ticket Price Range:** $5-10.
Visiting Club Hotel: Days Inn-Exit 407, 3402 Winfield Dunn Pkwy, Kodak, TN 37764. **Telephone:** (865) 933-4500.

BaseballAmerica.com

TEXAS LEAGUE

TEXAS LEAGUE™
OF PROFESSIONAL BASEBALL CLUBS

Mailing Address: 2442 Facet Oak, San Antonio, TX 78232.
Telephone: (210) 545-5297. **Fax:** (210) 545-5298.
E-Mail Address: texasleague@sbcglobal.net. **Website:** www.texas-league.com.
Years League Active: 1888-1890, 1892, 1895-1899, 1902-1942, 1946-.
President/Treasurer: Tom Kayser.
Vice Presidents: Monty Hoppel, Bill Valentine. **Corporate Secretary:** Mike Melega. **Assistant to the President:** Kevin Zeni.
Directors: Jon Dandes (Northwest Arkansas), Ken Schrom (Corpus Christi), William DeWitt III (Springfield), Dale Hubbard (Tulsa), Scott Sonju (Frisco), Miles Prentice (Midland), Russ Meeks (Arkansas), Burl Yarbrough (San Antonio).
Division Structure: North—Arkansas, Northwest Arkansas, Springfield, Tulsa. South—Corpus Christi, Frisco, Midland, San Antonio.
Regular Season: 140 games (split schedule). **2011 Opening Date:** April 7. **Closing Date:** Sept. 5. **All-Star Game:** June 29 at San Antonio.
Playoff Format: First-half division winners play second-half division winners in best-of-five series. Winners meet in best-of-five series for league championship.
Roster Limit: 24. **Player Eligibility Rule:** No restrictions.
Brand of Baseball: Rawlings.
Umpires: Allen Bailey (Big Spring, TX), Ryan Blakney (Wenatchee, WA), Seth Buckminster (Fort Worth, TX), Brian Hertzog (Lake Stevens, WA), Kellen Levy (Mesa, AZ), Brandon Misun (Oklahoma City, OK), Dan Oliver (Seattle, WA), Alex Ortiz (Los Angeles, CA), Stu Scheurwater (Regina, Saskatchewan, Canada), Adam Schwarz (Riverside, CA), Greg Stanzak (Surprise, AZ), Jimmy Volpi (Aurora, CO).

Tom Kayser

STADIUM INFORMATION

Club	Stadium	Opened	Dimensions LF	CF	RF	Capacity	2010 Att.
Arkansas	Dickey-Stephens Park	2007	332	413	330	10,000	326,066
Corpus Christi	Whataburger Field	2005	325	400	315	5,338	412,369
Frisco	Dr Pepper Ballpark	2003	335	409	335	10,216	562,380
Midland	Citibank Ballpark	2002	330	410	322	4,669	282,283
NW Arkansas	Arvest Ballpark	2008	325	400	325	6,500	320,523
San Antonio	Nelson W. Wolff Stadium	1994	310	402	340	6,200	289,113
Springfield	John Q. Hammons Field	2003	315	400	330	6,750	357,336
Tulsa	ONEOK Field	2010	330	400	307	7,833	408,183

ARKANSAS TRAVELERS

Office Address: Dickey-Stephens Park, 400 West Broadway, North Little Rock, AR 72114.
Mailing Address: PO Box 55066, Little Rock, AR 72215.
Telephone: (501) 664-1555. **Fax:** (501) 664-1834.
E-Mail address: travs@travs.com. **Website:** www.travs.com.
Affiliation (first year): Los Angeles Angels (2001). **Years in League:** 1966-

OWNERSHIP, MANAGEMENT
Ownership: Arkansas Travelers Baseball Club, Inc.
President: Russ Meeks.
General Manager: Pete Laven. **Assistant GM, Sales:** Paul Allen. **Assistant GM, Tickets:** David Kay. **Director, Broadcasting/Media Relations:** Phil Elson. **Director, Finance:** Ann McClure. **Director, Food/Beverage:** Billy Stinnette. **Director, In-Game Entertainment:** Tommy Adam. **Director, Merchandise:** Debra Wingfield. **Park Superintendent:** Greg Johnston. **Assistant Park Superintendent:** Reggie Temple. **Account Executive:** Brian Lyter. **Director, Media Production:** Jon Labello. **Office Manager:** Jared Schein.

FIELD STAFF
Manager: Bill Mosiello. **Coach:** Francisco Matos. **Pitching Coach:** Brandon Emanuel. **Trainer:** Dan Nickols.

GAME INFORMATION
Radio Announcers: Phil Elson, RJ Hawk. **No. of Games Broadcast:** Home-70 Road-70. **Flagship Station:** KARN 920 AM.
PA Announcer: Russ McKinney. **Official Scorers:** Tim Cooper, Mike Garrity, Todd Traub.
Stadium Name: Dickey-Stephens Park. **Location:** I-30 to Broadway exit, proceed west to ballpark, located at Broadway Avenue and the Broadway Bridge. **Standard Game Time:** 7:10 p.m. **Ticket Price Range:** $3-12.
Visiting Club Hotel: Hilton Little Rock, 925 S University Avenue, Little Rock, AR 72204. **Telephone:** (501) 664-5020. **Fax:** (501) 614-3803.

CORPUS CHRISTI HOOKS

Office Address: 734 East Port Ave, Corpus Christi, TX 78401.
Telephone: (361) 561-4665. **Fax:** (361) 561-4666.
E-Mail Address: info@cchooks.com. **Website:** www.cchooks.com.
Affiliation (first year): Houston Astros (2005). **Years in League:** 1958-59, 2005-

OWNERSHIP, MANAGEMENT

Operated By: Ryan-Sanders Baseball.
Principal Owners: Eddie Maloney, Reese Ryan, Reid Ryan, Nolan Ryan, Brad Sanders, Bret Sanders, Don Sanders. **CEO:** Reid Ryan. **CFO:** Reese Ryan. **Executive Vice President:** JJ Gottsch.
President: Ken Schrom. **General Manager:** Michael Wood. **VP, Sales:** Adam Nuse. **Director, Sponsor Services:** Elisa Macias. **Director, Retail:** Brooke Milam. **Controller:** Christy Lockard. **Director, Communications:** Matt Rogers. **Director, Broadcasting:** Matt Hicks. **Director, Stadium Operations:** Tina Athans. **Director, Group Sales:** Andy Steavens. **Director, Ballpark Entertainment:** Steve Richards. **Box Office Manager:** Spencer Moore. **Director, Season Ticket Services:** Bryan Mayhood. **Account Executives:** Jeff Mackor, Justin Sommer. **Field Superintendent:** Izzy Hinojosa. **Assistant Groundskeeper:** Josh Brewer. **Cleaning Manager:** Michael Shedd. **Maintenance Managers:** Leslie Hitt, Mark Rushton. **Community Relations Coordinator:** Gil Perez. **Game Day Staff Operations:** Matt Woodard. **Clubhouse Manager:** Brad Starr. **Media Relations Coordinator:** Michael Coffin. **Receptionists:** Abby Moore, Melissa Zimmer.

Field Staff

Manager: Tom Lawless. **Coach:** John Moses. **Pitching Coach:** Don Alexander. **Athletic Trainer:** Eric Montague.

GAME INFORMATION

Radio Announcers: Matt Hicks, Michael Coffin, Gene Kasprzyk. **No. of Games Broadcast:** Home-70 Road-70. **Flagship Station:** KKTX-AM 1360.
PA Announcer: Lon Gonzalez.
Stadium Name: Whataburger Field. **Location:** I-37 to end of interstate, left at Chaparral, left at Hirsh Ave. **Ticket Price Range:** $5-12.
Visiting Club Hotel: Omni Hotel, 900 N. Shoreline Dr., Corpus Christi, TX 78401. **Telephone:** (361) 886-3553.

FRISCO ROUGHRIDERS

Office Address: 7300 RoughRiders Trail, Frisco, TX 75034.
Telephone: (972) 731-9200. **Fax:** (972) 731-5355.
E-Mail Address: info@ridersbaseball.com. **Website:** www.ridersbaseball.com.
Affiliation (first year): Texas Rangers (2003). **Years in League:** 2003-

OWNERSHIP, MANAGEMENT

Operated by: Mandalay Baseball Properties.
President/General Manager: Scott Sonju. **Senior Vice President:** Billy Widner. **Accounting/HR Manager:** Dustin Alban. **VP, Partnerships/Communications:** Scott Burchett. **Director, Corporate Partnerships:** Steven Nelson. **Manager, Corporate Partnerships:** Mark Playko. **Partner/Event Services Coordinator:** Kristin Russell. **Partner Services Coordinators:** Matt Ratliff, David Kosydar. **Director, Community Development:** Michael Davidow. **Director, Ticket Sales:** Justin Ramquist. **Director, Ticket Operations:** Mac Amin. **Manager, Ticket Operations:** Jason Brayman. **Manager, Marketing/Special Events:** Gabrielle Ganz. **Senior Corporate Marketing Managers:** Matt Hernandez, Matt Korte, Eric Rowley. **Director, Game Entertainment:** Gabriel Wilhelm. **VP, Operations:** Michael Poole. **Director, Operations:** Scott Arnold. **Directors, Maintenance:** Alfonso Bailon, Gustavo Bailon. **Head Groundskeeper:** David Bicknell.

FIELD STAFF

Manager: Steve Buechele. **Coach:** Brant Brown. **Pitching Coach:** Jeff Andrews. **Trainer:** Carlos Olivas. **Strength/Conditioning:** Eric McMahon.

GAME INFORMATION

Broadcaster: Aaron Goldsmith. **No. of Games Broadcast:** Home-70, Away-70. **Flagship Station:** Unavailable.
PA Announcer: John Clemens. **Official Scorer:** Larry Bump.
Stadium Name: Dr Pepper Ballpark. **Location:** Dallas North Tollway to State Highway 121. **Standard Game Times:** 7 p.m., Sun 6.
Visiting Club Hotel: ExtendedStay Deluxe Plano, 2900 North Dallas Tollway. **Telephone:** (972) 378-9978.

MIDLAND ROCKHOUNDS

Office Address: 5514 Champions Dr., Midland, TX 79706.
Telephone: (432) 520-2255. **Fax:** (432) 520-8326.
Website: www.midlandrockhounds.org.
Affiliation (first year): Oakland Athletics (1999). **Years in League:** 1972-

OWNERSHIP, MANAGEMENT
Operated By: Midland Sports, Inc.
Principal Owners: Miles Prentice, Bob Richmond. **President:** Miles Prentice.
Executive Vice President: Bob Richmond. **General Manager:** Monty Hoppel. **Assistant GM:** Jeff VonHolle. **Assistant GM, Marketing/Tickets:** Jamie Richardson. **Assistant GM, Merchandise/Facilities:** Ray Fieldhouse. **Assistant GM, Media Relations:** Greg Bergman. **Director, Broadcasting/Publications:** Bob Hards. **Director, Business Operations:** Eloisa Galvan. **Director, Ticket Operations:** Michael Richardson. **Director, Group Sales:** Jeremy Lukas. **Head Groundskeeper:** Eric Ferland. **Office Manager:** Frances Warner. **Director, Game Entertainment/Promotions:** Anthony Orlando. **Assistant Groundskeeper:** Eric Campbell. **Marketing/Promotions Executive:** Ginny Gotcher. **Assistant Concessions Manager:** Reggie Donald. **Home Clubhouse Manager:** Rob Pelliccia. **Assistant Director, Stadium Operations:** Manabu Beppu. **Assistant Director, Community/Media Relations:** Brian Smith. **Sales/Operations Executive:** Alex Sanchez.

FIELD STAFF
Manager: Steve Scarsone. **Coach:** Tim Garland. **Pitching Coach:** Don Schulze. **Trainer:** Justin Whitehouse.

GAME INFORMATION
Radio Announcer: Bob Hards. **No. of Games Broadcast:** Home-70, Away-70. **Flagship Station:** Unavailable.
PA Announcer: Wes Coles. **Official Scorer:** Steve Marcum.
Stadium Name: Citibank Ballpark. **Location:** From I-20, exit Loop 250 North to Highway 191 intersection. **Standard Game Times:** 7 p.m., 6:30 (Mon-Wed), Sun 2 (April–May), 6 (June-Aug). **Ticket Price Range:** $5-9.
Visiting Club Hotel: Sleep Inn and Suites, 5612 Deauville Blvd, Midland, TX 79706. **Telephone:** (432) 694-4200.

NORTHWEST ARKANSAS
NATURALS

Office Address: 3000 S 56th Street, Springdale, AR 72762.
Telephone: (479) 927-4900. **Fax:** (479) 756-8088.
E-Mail Address: info@nwanaturals.com. **Website:** www.nwanaturals.com.
Affiliation (first year): Kansas City Royals (1995). **Years in League:** 1987-

OWNERSHIP, MANAGEMENT
Principal Owner: Rich Products Corp.
Chairman: Robert Rich Jr. **President, Rich Entertainment:** Melinda Rich. **President, Rich Baseball:** Jon Dandes.
General Manager: Eric Edelstein. **Assistant GM:** Justin Cole. **Business Manager:** Morgan Smith. **Marketing/PR Manager:** Frank Novak. **Stadium Operations Director:** George Sisson. **Field Turf Manager:** Monty Sowell. **Ticket Office Coordinator:** Shea Tedford. **Special Events Manager:** Kendra Carlson. **Broadcaster/Baseball Operations Coordinator:** Steven Davis. **Coordinator, Sales/Community Relations:** Amanda Potter. **Ticket Sales Coordinator:** Dustin Dethlefs. **Entertainment Coordinator:** Douglas Webb. **Account Executives:** Andrew Thaxton, Mark Zaiger, Brad Ziegler, Chelsea Smith, Sam Haugen. **Assistant Groundskeeper:** Kaleb Reynolds.

FIELD STAFF
Manager: Brian Poldberg. **Coach:** Terry Bradshaw. **Pitching Coach:** Larry Carter. **Trainer:** Dave Iannicca

GAME INFORMATION
Radio Announcers: Steven Davis. **No. of Games Broadcast:** Home-70, Away-70. **Flagship:** ESPN 92.1 The Ticket (KQSM-FM).
PA Announcer: Bill Rogers. **Official Scorer:** Chris Ledeker.
Stadium Name: Arvest Ballpark. **Location:** I-540 to US 412 West (Sunset Ave); Left on 56th St. **Ticket Price Range:** $6-12. **Standard Game Times:** 7 p.m.; Sun 2 (April/May), 6 (June-Sept), 6 (April 7, June 2, July 4).
Visiting Club Hotel: Holiday Inn Springdale; 1500 S 48th St, Springdale, AR 72762. **Telephone:** (479) 751-8300.

SAN ANTONIO MISSIONS

Office/Mailing Address: 5757 Highway 90 West, San Antonio, TX 78227.
Telephone: (210) 675-7275. **Fax:** (210) 670-0001. **E-Mail Address:** sainfo@samissions.com. **Website:** www.samissions.com.
Affiliation (first year): San Diego Padres (2007).
Years In Texas League: 1888, 1892, 1895-99, 1907-42, 1946-64, 1968-

OWNERSHIP, MANAGEMENT
Operated by: Elmore Sports Group.
Principal Owner: David Elmore.
President: Burl Yarbrough. **General Manager:** Dave Gasaway.
Assistant GMs: Mickey Holt, Jeff Long, Bill Gerlt. **GM, Diamond Concessions:** Sean Cavanagh. **Controller:** Ivan Molina. **Director, Broadcasting:** Roy Acuff. **Office Manager:** Delia Rodriguez. **Box Office Manager:** Tiffany Johnson. **Director, Operations:** John Hernandez. **Director, Group Sales:** George Levandoski. **Director, Public Relations:** Jim White. **Field Superintendent:** Karsten Blackwelder. **Assistant Field Superintendent:** Dan Looney.

Field Staff

Manager: Doug Dascenzo. **Coach:** Tom Tornicasa. **Pitching Coach:** Jimmy Jones. **Trainer:** Nathan Stewart.

Game Information

Radio Announcers: Roy Acuff, Mike Saeger. **No. of Games Broadcast:** Home-70, Away-70. **Flagship Station:** KKYX 680-AM. **PA Announcer:** Stan Kelly. **Official Scorer:** David Humphrey.

Stadium Name: Nelson W Wolff Stadium. **Location:** From I-10, I-35 or I-37, take US Hwy 90 West to Callaghan Road exit. **Standard Game Times:** 7:05 p.m., Sun 4:05/6:05.

Visiting Club Hotel: Holiday Inn Northwest/Sea World. **Telephone:** (210) 520-2508.

SPRINGFIELD CARDINALS

Office Address: 955 East Trafficway, Springfield, MO 65802.
Telephone: (417) 863-0395. **Fax:** (417) 863-0388.
E-Mail address: springfield@stlcardinals.com. **Website:** www.springfieldcardinals.com.
Affiliation (first year): St. Louis Cardinals (2005). **Years in League:** 2005-

OWNERSHIP, MANAGEMENT

Operated By: St. Louis Cardinals.

Vice President/General Manager: Matt Gifford. **VP, Baseball/Business Operations:** Scott Smulczenski. **VP, Sales:** Kim Inman. **VP, Facility Operations:** Bill Fischer. **Director, Ticket Operations:** Angela Deke. **Director, Sales/Marketing:** Dan Reiter. **Manager, Promotions/Productions:** Jacob Neimeyer. **Manager, Market Development:** Scott Bailes. **Manager, Stadium/Game Day Operations:** Aaron Lowrey. **Manager, Public Relations:** Jeff Levering. **Office/Guest Services Coordinator:** Christine Weyler. **Head Groundskeeper:** Brock Phipps. **Assistant Groundskeeper:** Derek Edwards.

FIELD STAFF

Manager: Ron Warner. **Coach:** Phillip Wellman. **Pitching Coach:** Bryan Eversgerd. **Trainer:** Jason Hall.

GAME INFORMATION

Radio Announcer: Jeff Levering. **No. of Games Broadcast:** Home-70 Road-70. **Flagship Station:** Unavailable.
PA Announcer: Kevin Howard. **Official Scorers:** Mark Stillwell, Tim Tourville.

Stadium Name: Hammons Field. **Location:** Highway 65 to Chestnut Expressway exit, west to National, south on National, west on Trafficway. **Standard Game Time:** 7:10 p.m. **Ticket Price Range:** $6-25.

Visiting Club Hotel: University Plaza Hotel, 333 John Q Hammons Parkway, Springfield, MO 65806. **Telephone:** (417) 864-7333.

TULSA DRILLERS

Office Address: 201 N. Elgin, Tulsa, OK 74120.
Telephone: (918) 744-5998. **Fax:** (918) 747-3267.
E-Mail Address: mail@tulsadrillers.com. **Website:** www.tulsadrillers.com.
Affiliation (first year): Colorado Rockies (2003). **Years in League:** 1933-42, 1946-65, 1977-

OWNERSHIP, MANAGEMENT

Operated By: Tulsa Baseball Inc.
Co-Chairmen: Dale Hubbard, Jeff Hubbard.

General Manager: Mike Melega. **Assistant GM:** Jason George. **Bookkeeper:** Cheryll Couey. **Executive Assistant:** Kara Biden. **Director, Stadium Operations:** Mark Hilliard. **Director, Media/Public Relations:** Brian Carroll. **Director, Ticket Operations:** Brandon Shiers. **Director, Marketing/Business Development:** Rob Gardenhire. **Director, Food Service:** Jason Wilson. **Director, Merchandise:** Tom Jones. **Manager, Group Ticket Sales:** Geoff Beaty. **Manager, Promotions:** Michael Taranto. **Manager, Video Productions:** David Ruckman. **Head Groundskeeper:** Gary Shepherd. **Assistant Manager, Group Sales:** Matt Larson. **Assistant Manager, Business Development:** Kevin Butcher. **Assistant Manager, Promotions:** Justin Gorski. **Assistant Bookkeeper:** Jenna Higgins. **Marketing Assistant:** Danielle Beck. **Ticket Office Assistant:** Erin Kostos. **Merchandise Assistant:** Lyndsay Larrivey. **Media/PR Assistant:** Kyle Rouvaldt. **Assistant Groundskeeper:** Logan Medlock. **Assistant Director, Food Service:** Shantel Lawson-Johnson. **Manager, Food Service:** Deanna Mierzwa. **Manager, Catering:** Carter Witt. **Team Photographer:** Rich Crimi.

FIELD STAFF

Manager: Duane Espy. **Coach:** Dave Hajek. **Pitching Coach:** Dave Schuler. **Trainer:** Austin O'Shea. **Strength Coach:** Al Sandoval.

GAME INFORMATION

Radio Announcer: Dennis Higgins. **No. of Games Broadcast:** Home-70 Road-70. **Flagship Station:** KTBZ 1430-AM.
PA Announcer: Kirk McAnany. **Official Scorers:** Bruce Howard, Duane DaPron, Larry Lewis, Barry Lewis.

Stadium Name: ONEOK Field. **Location:** Take I-244 to the Cincinnati/Detroit Exit (#6A); Go north on Detroit Ave, take a right onto John Hope Franklin Blvd, take a right on Elgin Ave. **Standard Game Times:** 7:05 p.m., Sun 2:05 (April-June 5)

Visiting Club Hotel: Southern Hills Marriott, 1902 E 71st St, Tulsa, OK 74136. **Telephone:** (918) 493-7000.

CALIFORNIA LEAGUE

Office Address: 3600 South Harbor Blvd, Suite 122, Oxnard, CA 93035.
Telephone: (805) 985-8585. **Fax:** (805) 985-8580.
Website: www.californialeague.com. **E-Mail:** info@californialeague.com.
Years League Active: 1941-1942, 1946-
President: Charlie Blaney.

Charlie Blaney

Vice President: Tom Volpe.

Directors: Bobby Brett (Rancho Cucamonga), Pete Carfagna (Lancaster), Dave Elmore (Inland Empire), DG Elmore (Bakersfield), Dave Heller (High Desert), Gary Jacobs (Lake Elsinore), Mike Savit (Modesto), Tom Seidler (Visalia), Tom Volpe (Stockton), Jim Weyermann (San Jose).

Director, Operations: Matt Blaney. **Director, Marketing:** Pete Thuresson. **Historian:** Chris Lampe. **Legal Counsel:** Jonathan Light. **CPA:** Jeff Hass.

Division Structure: North—Bakersfield, Modesto, San Jose, Stockton, Visalia. South—High Desert, Inland Empire, Lake Elsinore, Lancaster, Rancho Cucamonga.

Regular Season: 140 games (split schedule).

2011 Opening Date: April 7. **Closing Date:** Sept 5.

Playoff Format: Six teams. First-half winners in each division earn first-round bye; second-half winners meet wild cards with next best overall records in best-of-three quarterfinals. Winners meet first-half champions in best-of-five semifinals. Winners meet in best-of-five series for league championship.

All-Star Game: vs Carolina League, June 21 at Modesto.

Roster Limit: 25 active (35 under control).

Player Eligibility: No more than two players and one player/coach on active list may have more than six years experience.

Brand of Baseball: Rawlings.

Umpires: Matt Benham, Charles Billington, Johnathan Bostwick, Roger Craig, Ryan Goodman, Ryan Karle, Gabe Morales, Al Ruiz, Justin Sassaman, Brett Terry.

STADIUM INFORMATION

			Dimensions				
Club	**Stadium**	**Opened**	**LF**	**CF**	**RF**	**Capacity**	**2010 Att.**
Bakersfield	Sam Lynn Ballpark	1941	328	354	328	2,700	64,321
High Desert	Mavericks Stadium	1991	340	401	340	3,808	112,470
Inland Empire	Arrowhead Credit Union Park	1996	330	410	330	5,000	179,295
Lake Elsinore	The Diamond	1994	330	400	310	7,866	217,826
Lancaster	Clear Channel Stadium	1996	350	410	350	4,500	156,840
Modesto	John Thurman Field	1952	312	400	319	4,000	180,344
R. Cucamonga	The Epicenter	1993	335	400	335	6,615	150,687
San Jose	Municipal Stadium	1942	320	390	320	5,208	201,123
Stockton	Banner Island Ballpark	2005	300	399	326	5,200	200,662
Visalia	Recreation Ballpark	1946	320	405	320	2,468	108,681

BAKERSFIELD BLAZE

Office Address: 4009 Chester Ave, Bakersfield, CA 93301.
Mailing Address: PO Box 10031, Bakersfield, CA 93389.
Telephone: (661) 716-4487. **Fax:** (661) 322-6199.
E-Mail Address: blaze@bakersfieldblaze.com. **Website:** www.bakersfieldblaze.com.
Affiliation: Cincinnati Reds (2011). **Years In League:** 1941-42, 1946-75, 1978-79, 1982-

OWNERSHIP, MANAGEMENT

Principal Owner: Bakersfield Baseball Club LLC.

President: DG Elmore.

General Manager: Elizabeth Martin. **Assistant GMs:** Paul Rutherford, Philip Guiry. **Director, Food/Beverage:** Ryan Bigler. **Director, Operations/Grounds:** Jason Smith.

FIELD STAFF

Manager: Ken Griffey. **Coach:** Tony Jaramillo. **Pitching Coach:** Rigo Beltran. **Trainer:** Charles Leddon.

GAME INFORMATION

Radio: None.

PA Announcer: Mike Cushine. **Official Scorer:** Tim Wheeler.

Stadium Name: Sam Lynn Ballpark. **Location:** Highway 99 to California Avenue, east three miles to Chester Avenue, north two miles to stadium. **Standard Game Time:** 7:30 p.m. **Ticket Price Range:** $7-10.

Visiting Club Hotel: Four Points, 5101 California Ave Bakersfield, CA 93309. **Telephone:** (661) 862-7423.

HIGH DESERT MAVERICKS

Stadium/Office Address: 12000 Stadium Way, Adelanto, CA 92301.
Telephone: (760) 246-6287. **Fax:** (760) 246-3197.
E-Mail address: ejensen@hdmavs.com. **Website:** www.hdmavs.com.
Affiliation (first year): Seattle Mariners (2007). **Years in League:** 1991-

OWNERSHIP, MANAGEMENT
Operated By: Main Street California.
Vice President: Kirk Goodman. **General Manager:** Eric Jensen. **Director, Sponsorship/Promotions:** Jesse Zumbro. **Account Executive:** Ryan Kirkendoll. **Controller:** Robin Buckles.

FIELD STAFF
Manager: Jose Moreno. **Coach:** Tommy Cruz. **Pitching Coach:** Tom Dettore. **Athletic Trainer:** Eduardo Tamez.

GAME INFORMATION
Radio Announcer: None.
PA Announcer: Ernie Escajeda. **Official Scorer:** Daniel Gonzalez.
Stadium Name: Stater Bros Stadium. **Location:** I-15 North to Highway 395 to Adelanto Road. **Ticket Price Range:** $6-8.
Visiting Club Hotel: Motel 6, 9757 Cataba Rd, Hesperia, CA 92395. **Telephone:** (760) 947-0094.

INLAND EMPIRE 66ERS

Office Address: 280 South E St, San Bernardino, CA 92401.
Telephone: (909) 888-9922. **Fax:** (909) 888-5251.
Website: www.ie66ers.com.
Affiliation (first year): Los Angeles Angels of Anaheim (2011). **Years in League:** 1941, 1987-

OWNERSHIP, MANAGEMENT
Operated by: Inland Empire 66ers Baseball Club of San Bernardino.
Principal Owners: David Elmore, Donna Tuttle.
Owner/President: Dave Elmore. **Owner/Chairman:** Donna Tuttle. **Assistant General Managers:** Ryan English, Joe Hudson. **Vice President, Marketing:** Kevin Shaw. **CFO:** John Fonseca. **Director, Broadcasting/Media Relations:** Sam Farber. **Director, Group Sales:** Steve Pelle. **Corporate Groups Manager:** David May. **Director, Ticketing:** Joey Seymour. **Director, Promotions:** Matt Kowallis. **Graphics/Website Manager:** Robert Peters. **Administrative Assistant:** Angie Rodriguez. **Head Groundskeeper:** Jason Hilderbrand.

FIELD STAFF
Manager: Tom Gamboa. **Coach:** Damon Mashore. **Pitching Coach:** Dan Ricabal.

GAME INFORMATION
Radio Announcer: Sam Farber. **Flagship Station:** KCAA 1050-AM.
PA Announcer: JJ Gould. **Official Scorer:** Les Canterbury.
Stadium Name: Arrowhead Credit Union Park. **Location:** From south, I-215 to 2nd Street exit, east on 2nd, right on G Street; from north, I-215 to 3rd Street exit, left on Rialto, right on G Street. **Standard Game Times:** 7:05 p.m.; Sun 1:05 (April-June), 6:05 (July-Aug). **Ticket Price Range:** $5-10.
Visiting Club Hotel: Hilton San Bernardino, 285 East Hospitality Lane, San Bernardino, CA 92408. **Telephone:** (909) 889-0133.

LAKE ELSINORE STORM

Office Address: 500 Diamond Dr, Lake Elsinore, CA 92530.
Mailing Address: PO Box 535, Lake Elsinore, CA 92531.
Telephone: (951) 245-4487. **Fax:** (951) 245-0305.
E-Mail Address: info@stormbaseball.com. **Website:** www.stormbaseball.com.
Affiliation (first year): San Diego Padres (2001). **Years in League:** 1994-
Owners: Gary Jacobs, Len Simon.
President: Dave Oster. **Vice President/General Manager:** Chris Jones. **VP/GM, Events:** Bruce Kessman. **Assistant GM:** Tracy Kessman. **Director, Sales/Marketing:** Matt Thompson. **Director, Stadium Operations:** Matt Schaffner. **Director, Broadcasting:** Sean McCall. **Director, Media Relations/Advertising:** Steve Smaldone. **Director, Group Sales:** Raj Naranayan. **Director, Finance:** Deniise Emerson. **Group Sales Executive/In-Game Entertainment Supervisor:** Robert Gillett. **Senior Graphics/Animation Designer:** Mark Beskid. **Director, Ticketing:** JT Onyett. **Assistant Director, Ticketing:** Colt Riley. **Director, Mascot Operations:** Patrick Gardenier. **Director, Finance:** Rick Riegler. **Director, Marketing:** Courtney Kessler. **GM, Catering:** Arjun Suresh. **Executive Chef:** Steve Bearse. **Director, Food/Beverage:** Drew Garrison.

Finance Director, Catering: Christina Conlon. **Event Coordinator:** Michelle Priske. **Director, Grounds/Maintenance:** Peter Hayes. **Assistant Director, Grounds/Maintenance:** Rob Gladwell. **Maintenance Supervisor:** Jassiel Reza. **Office Manager:** Peggy Mitchell. **Clubhouse Manager:** Shawn Laidlaw.

FIELD STAFF

Manager: Carlos Lezcano. **Coach:** Phil Plantier. **Pitching Coach:** Bronswell Patrick. **Trainer:** Will Sinon.

GAME INFORMATION

Radio Announcer: Sean McCall. **No. of Games Broadcast:** Home-70 Road-70. **Flagship Station:** San Diego 1700-AM.

PA Announcer: Joe Martinez. **Official Scorer:** Lloyd Nixon.

Stadium Name: The Diamond. **Location:** From I-15, exit at Diamond Drive, west one mile to stadium. **Standard Game Times:** 7:05 p.m., Wed 6:05, Sun 2:05 (first half), 6:05 (second half). **Ticket Price Range:** $7-10.

Visiting Club Hotel: Lake Elsinore Hotel and Casino, 20930 Malaga St, Lake Elsniore, CA 92530. **Telephone:** (951) 674-3101.

LANCASTER JETHAWKS

Office Address: 45116 Valley Central Way, Lancaster, CA 93536.
Telephone: (661) 726-5400. **Fax:** (661) 726-5406.
E-Mail Address: info@jethawks.com. **Website:** www.jethawks.com.
Affiliation (first year): Houston Astros (2009). **Years in League:** 1996-

OWNERSHIP, MANAGEMENT

Operated By: Hawks Nest LLC.
President: Peter Carfagna. **Senior Vice President:** Pete Carfagna.
VP/General Manager: Larry Thornhill. **Assistant GM:** Derek Sharp. **Director, Stadium Operations:** John Laferney. **Director, Promotions/General Sales Manager:** Jeremy Castillo. **Director, Broadcasting/Media Relations:** Jeff Lasky. **Director, Community Relations:** Will Murphy. **Director, Food/Beverage:** Adam Fillenworth. **Director, Ticket Operations:** Will Murphy. **Media Manager/Program Director, CSN:** Will Thornhill. **Account Executives:** Albert Villalobos, Dale Billodeaux, Jenn Adamczyk.

FIELD STAFF

Manager: Tom Spencer. **Coach:** Darryl Robinson. **Pitching Coach:** Travis Driskill. **Trainer:** Bryan Baca.

GAME INFORMATION

Radio Announcers: Jeff Lasky, Scott Bluesiewicz. **No. of Games Broadcast:** Home-70, Away-70. **Flagship Station:** www.jethawks.com/CSN .

PA Announcer: Unavailable. **Official Scorer:** David Guenther.

Stadium Name: Clear Channel Stadium. **Location:** Highway 14 in Lancaster to Avenue I exit, west one block to stadium. **Standard Game Times:** 7 p.m., Sun 2 (April–June), 5 (July-Sept). **Ticket Price Range:** $6-12.

Visiting Club Hotel: Palmdale Hotel, 300 West Palmdale Blvd, Palmdale, CA 93551. **Telephone:** (661) 947-9593.

MODESTO NUTS

Office Address: 601 Neece Dr, Modesto, CA 95351.
Mailing Address: PO Box 883, Modesto, CA 95353.
Telephone: (209) 572-4487. **Fax:** (209) 572-4490.
E-Mail Address: fun@modestonuts.com. **Website:** www.modestonuts.com.
Affiliation (first year): Colorado Rockies (2005). **Years in League:** 1946-64, 1966-

OWNERSHIP, MANAGEMENT

Operated by: HWS Group IV.
Principal Owner: Mike Savit.
President: Bill Shanahan. **Vice President/GM:** Michael Gorrasi. **Assistant GM, Corporate Sponsorship/Sales:** Tyler Richardson. **Assistant GM, Operations:** Ed Mack. **Director, Tickets:** Zach Brockman. **Director, Marketing/Public Relations:** Christa Parr. **Director, Group Sales:** Eric Rauber. **Director, Stadium Operations:** Ryan Thomas. **Director, In-Game Production:** Randy Kulina. **Manager, Promotions:** Otoma Agnew. **Manager, Ticket Sales:** John Engelbrecht. **Manager, Ticket Sales:** Bradley Reynolds. **Manager, Group Sales:** Josh Rusnak. **Manager, Operations:** Wayne Loeblein, Jr.

FIELD STAFF

Manager: Jerry Weinstein. **Coach:** Kevin Riggs. **Pitching Coach:** Darryl Scott. **Trainer:** Chris Dovey.

GAME INFORMATION

Radio Announcer: Greg Young. **No. of Games Broadcast:** Home-50, Away-50. **Flagship Station:** KESP 970-AM.

PA Announcer: Unavailable. **Official Scorer:** Unavailable.

Stadium Name: John Thurman Field. **Location:** Highway 99 in southwest Modesto to Tuolomne Boulevard exit, west on Tuolomne for one block to Neece Drive, left for 1/4 mile to stadium. **Standard Game Times:** 7:05 p.m., Sun. 1:05. **Ticket Price Range:** $5-10.

Visiting Club Hotel: Clarion Inn, 1612 Sisk Rd, Modesto, CA 95350. **Telephone:** (209) 521-1612.

RANCHO CUCAMONGA
QUAKES

Office Address: 8408 Rochester Ave, Rancho Cucamonga, CA 91730.
Mailing Address: PO Box 4139, Rancho Cucamonga, CA 91729.
Telephone: (909) 481-5000. **Fax:** (909) 481-5005.
E-Mail Address: info@rcquakes.com. **Website:** www.rcquakes.com.
Affiliation (first year): Los Angeles Dodgers (2011). **Years in League:** 1993-

OWNERSHIP, MANAGEMENT
Operated By: Brett Sports & Entertainment.
Principal Owner: Bobby Brett.
President: Brent Miles. **Vice President/General Manager:** Grant Riddle. **VP, Tickets:** Monica Ortega. **Director, Group Sales:** Linda Rathfon. **Sports Marketing Consultants:** Ryan Millard, Andrew Zamarripa. **Director, Promotions:** AutumnRose Saenz. **Ticket Office Manager:** Rachel Barker. **Director, Season Tickets:** Jesse Robinson. **Group Sales Account Executives:** Kyle Burleson, Erik Fields, Jeremy Hansen. **Accounting Manager:** Amara McClellan. **Public Relations Manager/Voice of the Quakes:** Mike Lindskog. **Office Manager:** Shelley Scebbi.

FIELD STAFF
Manager: Juan Bustabad. **Coach:** Michael Boughton. **Pitching Coach:** Hector Berrios. **Trainer:** Yosuke Nakajima.

GAME INFORMATION
Radio Announcer: Mike Lindskog.
PA Announcer: Ernie Escajeda. **Official Scorer:** Ryan Wilson.
Stadium Name: The Epicenter. **Location:** I-10 to I-15 North, exit at Foothill Boulevard, left on Foothill, left on Rochester to Stadium. **Standard Game Times:** 7:05 p.m., 7:35 (home Fridays); Sun 2:05 (April-July), 5:05 (July-Sept). **Ticket Price Range:** $8-12.
Visiting Club Hotel: Best Western Heritage Inn, 8179 Spruce Ave, Rancho Cucamonga, CA 91730. **Telephone:** (909) 466-1111.

SAN JOSE GIANTS

Office Address: 588 E Alma Ave, San Jose, CA 95112.
Mailing Address: PO Box 21727, San Jose, CA 95151.
Telephone: (408) 297-1435. **Fax:** (408) 297-1453.
E-Mail Address: info@sjgiants.com. **Website:** www.sjgiants.com.
Affiliation (first year): San Francisco Giants (1988). **Years in League:** 1942, 1947-58, 1962-76, 1979-

OWNERSHIP, MANAGEMENT
Operated by: Progress Sports Management.
Principal Owners: San Francisco Giants, Heidi Stamas, Richard Beahrs.
President/CEO: Jim Weyermann.
Chief Operating Officer/General Manager: Mark Wilson. **Chief Marketing Officer:** Juliana Paoli. **VP, Operations/Assistant General Manager:** Zach Walter. **VP, Sales:** Ainslie Walter. **VP, Finance/Executive Director San Jose Giants Sports Foundation:** Cami Yuasa. **VP, Baseball Operations:** Lance Motch. **Director, Player Personnel:** Linda Pereira. **Director, Marketing:** Mandy Stone. **Director, Sales:** Taylor Haynes. **Director, Food/Beverage:** Will O'Sullivan. **Director, Broadcasting:** Joe Ritzo. **Finance/HR Manager:** Renee Ramirez. **Ticket Services Manager:** Kellen Minteer. **Ticket Sales Account Executive:** Tony Casalegno. **Foundation Projects Coordinator:** Cassandra Hofman. **Marketing/Merchandise Assistant:** Brad Brown. **Marketing Assistant:** Ben Guerrero.

FIELD STAFF
Manager: Andy Skeels. **Coach:** Gary Davenport. **Pitching Coach:** Brian Cooper. **Trainer:** LJ Petra. **Strength/Conditioning Coach:** Yousef Zamat.

GAME INFORMATION
Radio Announcers: Joe Ritzo, Rocky Koplik. **No. of Games Broadcast:** Home-70, Away-70. **Flagship:** www.sjgiants.com.
Television Announcers: Joe Ritzo, Dan Dibley, Rocky Koplik. **No. of Games Broadcast:** Home-20, Away-6. **Comcast Hometown Network Channel 104.**
PA Announcer: Russ Call. **Official Scorers:** Brian Burkett, Mike Hohler, Michael Melligan, Michael Duca.
Stadium Name: Municipal Stadium. **Location:** South on I-280, Take 10th/11th Street Exit, Turn right on 10th Street, Turn left on Alma Ave; North on I-280: Take the 10th/11th Street Exit, Turn left on 10th Street, Turn Left on Alma Ave.

Standard Game Times: 7 p.m., Sat 6, Sun 2 (5 after June 27). **Ticket Price Range:** $7-16.
Visiting Club Hotel: Pruneyard Plaza Hotel, 1995 S Bascom Ave, Campbell, CA 95008. **Telephone:** (408) 559-4300.

STOCKTON PORTS

Office Address: 404 W Fremont St, Stockton, CA 95203.
Telephone: (209) 644-1900. **Fax:** (209) 644-1931.
E-Mail Address: info@stocktonports.com. **Website:** www.stocktonports.com.
Affiliation (first year): Oakland Athletics (2005). **Years in League:** 1941, 1946-72, 1978-

OWNERSHIP, MANAGEMENT
Operated By: 7th Inning Stretch LLC.
President/General Manager: Pat Filippone. **Assistant GM:** Luke Reiff. **Director, Marketing:** Jeremy Neisser. **Director, Finance:** Terri Bailey. **Director, Corporate Sales:** Zach Sharkey. **Director, Business Development:** Tim Pasisz. **Inside Sales Manager:** John Watts. **Community Relations Manager:** Margaret Sacchet. **Stadium Operations Manager:** Bryan Meadows. **Ticket Office Manager:** Tim Pollack. **Media Relations Manager:** Allison Mandel. **Office Manager:** Charmie Hernandez. **Food/Beverage Service Provider:** Ovations.

FIELD STAFF
Manager: Webster Garrison. **Coach:** Brian McArn. **Pitching Coach:** Craig Lefferts. **Trainer:** Nathan Brooks.

GAME INFORMATION
Radio Announcer: Zack Bayrouty. **No of Games Broadcast:** Home-70, Away-70. **Flagship Station:** KWSX 1280 AM.
TV: Comcast Hometown Network, Channel 104, Regional Telecast
PA Announcer: Mike Conway. **Official Scorer:** Paul Muyskens.
Stadium Name: Banner Island Ballpark. **Location:** From I-5/99, take Crosstown Freeway (Highway 4) exit El Dorado Street, north on El Dorado to Fremont Street, left on Fremont.
Standard Game Times: 7:05 p.m., Sun 2:09 first half, 6:05 second half. **Ticket Price Range:** $6-$12.
Visiting Club Hotel: Hampton Inn Stockton, 5045 South State Route 99 East, Stockton, CA 95215. **Phone:** (209) 946-1234.

VISALIA RAWHIDE

Office Address: 300 N Giddings St, Visalia, CA 93291.
Telephone: (559) 732-4433. **Fax:** (559) 739-7732.
E-Mail Address: info@rawhidebaseball.com. **Website:** www.rawhide-baseball.com.
Affiliation (first year): Arizona Diamondbacks (2007). **Years in League:** 1946-62, 1968-75, 1977-

OWNERSHIP, MANAGEMENT
Operated By: Top of the Third Inc.
Principal Owners: Tom Seidler, Kevin O'Malley.
President/General Manager: Tom Seidler. **Assistant GM:** Jennifer Pendergraft. **Executive Assistant:** Kacey Conley. **Director, Food/Beverage Operations:** Chris Henstra.
Director, Ticketing: Mike Candela. **Assistant, Ticketing:** Adam Hayes. **Director, Broadcasting:** Donny Baarns. **Manager, Media Relations:** Mark Freeman. **Manager, Hispanic Marketing:** Mitch Retelny.
Head Groundskeeper: Brandon Benson. **Ballpark Operations Manager:** Dan Hargey. **Ballpark Operations Assistants:** Cody Gray, Charlie Bennett. **Group/Event Coordinators:** Amanda Shepley, Ben Baker. **Community Relations Coordinator:** Kathleen Decker. **Clubhouse Manager:** Ty Pendergraft. **Ballpark Operations:** Les Kissick.

FIELD STAFF
Manager: Jason Hardtke. **Coach:** Andy Abad. **Pitching Coach:** Doug Drabek. **Trainer:** Ben Fraser.

GAME INFORMATION
Radio Announcers: Donny Baarns, Mark Freeman. **No. of Games Broadcast:** Home-70, Away-70. **Flagship Station:** KJUG 1270-AM.
PA Announcer: Brian Anthony. **Official Scorer:** Harry Kargenian.
Stadium Name: Recreation Ballpark. **Location:** From Highway 99, take 198 East to Mooney Boulevard exit, left at second signal on Giddings; four blocks to ballpark. **Standard Game Times:** 7 p.m., Sun 2 (first half), 6 (second half).
Ticket Price Range: $5-20.
Visiting Club Hotel: Lamp Liter Inn, 3300 W Mineral King Ave, Visalia, CA 93291. **Telephone:** (559) 732-4511.

CAROLINA LEAGUE

Office Address: 1806 Pembroke Rd, Suite 2-B, Greensboro, NC 27408.
Mailing Address: same as street address
Telephone: (336) 691-9030. **Fax:** (336) 464-2737.
E-Mail Address: office@carolinaleague.com.
Website: www.carolinaleague.com

John Hopkins

Years League Active: 1945-.

President/Treasurer: John Hopkins.

Vice President: Art Silber (Potomac). **Corporate Secretary:** Ken Young (Frederick). **Directors:** Tim Zue (Salem), Rex Angel (Lynchburg), Chuck Greenberg (Myrtle Beach), Dave Ziedelis (Frederick), Steve Bryant (Kinston), Jack Minker (Wilmington), Billy Prim (Winston-Salem), Art Silber (Potomac).

Administrative Assistant: Marnee Larkins.

Division Structure: North—Frederick, Lynchburg, Potomac, Wilmington. South—Kinston, Myrtle Beach, Salem, Winston-Salem.

Regular Season: 140 games (split schedule). **2011 Opening Date:** April 8. **Closing Date:** Sept 5.

All-Star Game: June 21 at Modesto (Carolina League vs California League).

Playoff Format: First-half division winners play second-half division winners in best-of-five series; if a team wins both halves, it plays a wild card (team in that division with next-best second-half record). Division series winners meet in best-of-five series for Mills Cup.

Roster Limit: 25 active. **Player Eligibility Rule:** No age limit. No more than two players and one player/coach on active list may have six or more years of prior minor league service.

Brand of Baseball: Rawlings.

Umpires: John Bacon (Sherrodsville, OH), Guss Curtis (Lexington, KY), Luke Hamilton (Goshen, IN), Kiff Kinkead (Wilmington, NC), Shaun Lampe (Scottsdale, AZ), Nick Mahrley (Bartlett, IL), Thomas Newsom (King, NC), Mike Walsh (Old Bridge, NJ).

STADIUM INFORMATION

			Dimensions				
Club	**Stadium**	**Opened**	**LF**	**CF**	**RF**	**Capacity**	**2010 Att.**
Frederick	Harry Grove Stadium	1990	325	400	325	5,400	291,299
Kinston	Grainger Stadium	1949	335	390	335	4,100	118,741
Lynchburg	City Stadium	1939	325	390	325	4,000	152,161
Myrtle Beach	BB&T Coastal Field	1999	325	405	328	5,200	223,177
Potomac	Pfitzner Stadium	1984	315	400	315	6,000	205,279
Salem	Salem Memorial Stadium	1995	325	401	325	53,053	211,527
Wilmington	Frawley Stadium	1993	325	400	325	6,532	296,041
Winston-Salem	BB&T Ballpark	2010	315	399	323	5,500	312,313

FREDERICK KEYS

Office Address: 21 Stadium Dr, Frederick, MD 21703.
Telephone: (301) 662-0013. **Fax:** (301) 662-0018.
E-Mail address: info@frederickkeys.com. **Website:** www.frederickkeys.com.
Affiliation (first year): Baltimore Orioles (1989). **Years in League:** 1989-

OWNERSHIP, MANAGEMENT

Ownership: Maryland Baseball Holding LLC.

President: Ken Young. **General Manager:** Dave Ziedelis. **Assistant GM:** Branden McGee. **Director, Marketing/Public Relations:** Adam Pohl. **Director, Ticket Sales:** Jeff Wiggins. **Director, Sponsorship:** Christian Amorosi. **Creative Production Manager:** Paul Denillo. **Promotion Manager:** Brandon Apter. **Marketing Assistant:** Bridget McCabe. **Account Managers:** Matt Cherry, Matt Miller, Tyler Schlatter, Alan Tyson. **Box Office Manager:** Felicia Adamus. **Ticket Sales Assistant:** Greg Kozak. **Box Office Assistant:** Kevin Brown. **Head Groundskeeper:** Brannon Burks. **Office Manager:** Barb Freund. **Finance Manager:** Tami Hetrick. **General Manager, Ovations:** Anita Clarke. **Public Relations Assistant:** Tim Murray.

FIELD STAFF

Manager: Orlando Gomez. **Coach:** Unavailable. **Pitching Coach:** Blaine Beatty.

GAME INFORMATION

Radio Announcers: Adam Pohl, Tim Murray.

PA Announcer: Andy Redmond. **Official Scorers:** Bob Roberson, Dennis Hetrick, Dave Musil.

Stadium Name: Harry Grove Stadium. **Location:** From I-70, take exit 54 (Market Street), left at light; From I-270, take exit 32 (I-70 Baltimore/Hagerstown) towards Baltimore (I-70), to exit 54 at Market Street. **Ticket Price Range:** $8-11.

Visiting Club Hotel: Comfort Inn, 7300 Executive Way, Frederick, MD 21701. **Telephone:** (301) 668-7272.

KINSTON INDIANS

Office Address: 400 East Grainger Avenue, Kinston, NC 28501.
Mailing Address: PO Box 3542, Kinston, NC 28502.
Telephone: (252) 527-9111. **Fax:** (252) 527-0498.
E-Mail Address: info@kinstonindians.com. **Website:** www.kinstonindians.com.
Affiliation (first year): Cleveland Indians (1987). **Years in League:** 1956-57, 1962-74, 1978-

OWNERSHIP, MANAGEMENT
Operated by: Slugger Partners LP.
Principal Owner/Chairman: Cam McRae.
General Manager: Benjamin Jones. **Assistant GM:** Janell Bullock. **Director, Broadcasting/Public Relations:** Chris Hemeyer. **Head Groundskeeper:** Steven Watson. **Team Photographer:** Carl Kline.

FIELD STAFF
Manager: Aaron Holbert. **Coach:** Phil Clark. **Pitching Coach:** Mickey Callaway. **Trainer:** Jeremy Heller.

GAME INFORMATION
Radio Announcer: Chris Hemeyer. **No. of Games Broadcast:** Home-70, Away-70. **Flagship Station:** WWNB 1490 AM.
PA Announcer: Unavailable. **Official Scorer:** Steve Oliver.
Stadium Name: Grainger Stadium. **Location:** From west, take US 70 Business (Vernon Avenue), left on East Street; from east, take US 70 West, right on Highway 58, right on Vernon Avenue, right on East Street. **Standard Game Times:** 6:30 p.m., Sun 1:30. **Ticket Price Range:** $5-7.
Visiting Club Hotel: Hampton Inn, Highway 70 Bypass, Kinston NC 28504. **Telephone:** (252) 523-1400.

LYNCHBURG HILLCATS

Office Address: Lynchburg City Stadium, 3180 Fort Ave, Lynchburg, VA 24501.
Mailing Address: PO Box 10213, Lynchburg, VA 24506.
Telephone: (434) 528-1144. **Fax:** (434) 846-0768.
E-Mail address: info@lynchburg-hillcats.com. **Website:** www.lynchburg-hillcats.com.
Affiliation (first year): Atlanta Braves (2011). **Years in League:** 1966-

OWNERSHIP, MANAGEMENT
Operated By: Lynchburg Baseball Corp.
Chairman of the Board: Calvin Falwell.
President: C Rex Angel.
General Manager: Paul Sunwall. **Assistant GM:** Ronnie Roberts. **Head Groundskeeper/Sales:** Darren Johnson. **Director, Broadcasting/Publications:** Scott Bacon. **Director, Food/Beverage:** Tyree Kim. **Ticket Manager:** Zach Willis. **Director, Information Technology:** Andrew Chesser. **Office Manager:** Diane Tucker.

FIELD STAFF
Manager: Pat Kelly. **Coach:** Tony Jaramillo. **Pitching Coach:** Rigo Beltran. **Trainer:** Dale Nitzel. **Strength/Conditioning Coach:** Jake Dyskin.

GAME INFORMATION
Radio Announcer: Scott Bacon. **No. of Games Broadcast:** Home-70 Road-70. **Flagship Station:** WKDE 105.5-FM.
PA Announcer: Chuck Young. **Official Scorers:** Malcolm Haley, Chuck Young.
Stadium Name: Calvin Falwell Field at Lynchburg City Stadium. **Location:** US 29 Business South to Lynchburg City Stadium (exit 6); US 29 Business North to Lynchburg City Stadium (exit 4). **Ticket Price Range:** $5-9.
Visiting Club Hotel: Best Western, 2815 Candlers Mountain Rd, Lynchburg, VA 24502. **Telephone:** (434) 237-2986.

MYRTLE BEACH PELICANS

Office Address: 1251 21st Ave N, Myrtle Beach, SC 29577.
Telephone: (843) 918-6002. **Fax:** (843) 918-6001.
E-Mail Address: info@myrtlebeachpelicans.com. **Website:** www.myrtlebeachpelicans.com.
Affiliation (first year): Texas Rangers (2011). **Years in League:** 1999-

OWNERSHIP, MANAGEMENT
Operated By: Myrtle Beach Pelicans LP.
Managing Partner: Chuck Greenberg.
General Manager: Scott Brown. **Senior Director, Business Development:** Guy Schuman. **Senior Director, Finance:** Anne Frost. **Senior Director, Sports Turf Management/Ballpark Operations:** Chris Ball. **Director, Ticket Operations:** Josh Holley. **Director, Ticket Sales:** Denny Watson. **Corporate Sales Manager:** Junior Ramsey. **Group Sales Managers:**

Chris Herath, Corey Fetter. **Director, Broadcasting/Media Relations:** Tyler Maun. **Director, Marketing/Promotions:** Jen Borowski. **Director, Community Relations:** Julie Borshak. **Executive Producer, In-Game Entertainment:** Jake White. **Facility Operations Manager:** Mike Snow. **Director, Merchandising:** Dan Bailey. **Director, Food/Beverage:** Brad Leininger. **Clubhouse Manager:** Stan Hunter. **Visiting Clubhouse Manager:** Bob Leber. **Administrative Assistant:** Beth Freitas. **Accounting Assistant:** Karen Ulyicsni.

FIELD STAFF
Manager: Jason Wood. **Coach:** Julio Garcia. **Pitching Coach:** Brad Holman. **Athletic Trainer:** Jeff Bodenhamer. **Strength/Conditioning:** Ryan McNeal.

GAME INFORMATION
Radio Announcer: Tyler Maun. **No. of Games Broadcast:** Home-70, Road-70. **Flagship Station:** ESPN Radio The Team 93.9-FM/93.7-FM/1050-AM.
PA Announcer: Mike Browne. **Official Scorer:** Steve Walsh.
Stadium Name: BB&T Coastal Federal Field. **Location:** US Highway 17 Bypass to 21st Avenue North, 1/2 mile to stadium. **Standard Game Times:** 7:05 p.m.; Sun 3:05/6:05. **Ticket Price Range:** $7-13.
Visiting Club Hotel: Hampton Inn-Broadway at the Beach, 1140 Celebrity Circle, Myrtle Beach, SC 29577. **Telephone:** (843) 916-0600.

POTOMAC NATIONALS

Office Address: 7 County Complex Ct, Woodbridge, VA 22192.
Mailing Address: PO Box 2148, Woodbridge, VA 22195.
Telephone: (703) 590-2311. **Fax:** (703) 590-5716.
E-Mail Address: info@potomacnationals.com. **Website:** www.potomacnationals.com.
Affiliation (first year): Washington Nationals (2005). **Years in League:** 1978-

OWNERSHIP, MANAGEMENT
Operated By: Potomac Baseball LLC.
Principal Owner: Art Silber. **President:** Lani Silber Weiss.
General Manager: Josh Olerud. **Assistant GM, Stadium Operations:** Carter Buschman. **Director, Ticket Operations:** Michelle Metzgar. **Director, Corporate Sales:** Libby Huguley. **Director, Food Services:** Jim Johnson. **Director, Media Relations:** Will Flemming. **Group Sales Account Executive:** Andrew Stinson. **Corporate Sales Executive:** Travis Painter.

FIELD STAFF
Manager: Matt LeCroy. **Coach:** Mark Harris. **Pitching Coach:** Paul Menhart.

GAME INFORMATION
Radio Announcer: Will Flemming. **No. of Games Broadcast:** Home-70 Road-70. **Flagship:** www.potomacnationals.com.
Official Scorer: David Vincent, Ben Trittipoe.
Stadium Name: G Richard Pfitzner Stadium. **Location:** From I-95, take exit 158B and continue on Prince William Parkway for five miles, right into County Complex Court. **Standard Game Times:** 7:03 p.m.; Sat 6:35, Sun 1:05. **Ticket Price Range:** $7-14.
Visiting Club Hotel: Hampton Inn Gainesville-Haymarket, 7300 Atlas Walk Way, Gainesville, VA 22155. **Telephone:** (703) 753-1500.

SALEM RED SOX

Office Address: 1004 Texas St, Salem, VA 24153.
Mailing Address: PO Box 842, Salem, VA 24153.
Telephone: (540) 389-3333. **Fax:** (540) 389-9710.
E-Mail Address: info@salemsox.com. **Website:** www.salemsox.com.
Affiliation (first year): Boston Red Sox (2009). **Years in League:** 1968-

OWNERSHIP, MANAGEMENT
Operated By: Carolina Baseball LLC/Fenway Sports Group.
President: Sam Kennedy.
Vice President/General Manager: Todd Stephenson. **Senior Assistant GM:** Allen Lawrence. **Director, Ticketing:** Dennis Robarge. **Director, Media Relations:** Dave Cawley. **Director, Food/Beverage:** Giles Cochran. **Head Groundskeeper:** Tracy Schneweis. **Director, Marketing/Special Events:** Jeanne Boester. **Assistant Director, Group Sales:** Steven Elovich. **Food Service Manager:** Pete Morrison. **Broadcaster:** Evan Lepler. **Sales Coordinator:** Shea Maple. **Merchandise Manager:** Kristina Johnson. **Director, Finance:** Dinia Pease. **Clubhouse Manager:** Tom Wagner.

FIELD STAFF
Manager: Bruce Crabbe. **Coach:** Alex Ochoa. **Pitching Coach:** Kevin Walker. **Trainer:** Brandon Henry.

GAME INFORMATION
Radio Announcer: Evan Lepler. **No. of Games Broadcast:** Home-70 Road-70. **Flagship Station:** WFIR 960-AM.

PA Announcer: Travis Jenkins. **Official Scorer:** Billy Wells.

Stadium Name: Lewis-Gale Field at Salem Memorial Ballpark. **Location:** I-81 to exit 141 (Route 419), follow signs to Salem Civic Center Complex. **Standard Game Times:** 7:05 p.m.; Sat 6:05, Sun 4:05. **Ticket Price Range:** $7.50-10.

Visiting Club Hotel: Comfort Inn Airport, 5070 Valley View Blvd, Roanoke, VA 24012. **Telephone:** (540) 527-2020.

WILMINGTON BLUE ROCKS

Office Address: 801 Shipyard Dr, Wilmington, DE 19801.
Telephone: (302) 888-2015. **Fax:** (302) 888-2032.
E-Mail Address: info@bluerocks.com. **Website:** www.bluerocks.com.
Affiliation (first year): Kansas City Royals (2007). **Years in League:** 1993-Present

OWNERSHIP, MANAGEMENT

Operated by: Wilmington Blue Rocks LP.
Honorary President: Matt Minker. **President:** Tom Palmer. **General Manager:** Chris Kemple. **Assistant GM:** Andrew Layman. **Director, Broadcasting/Media Relations:** John Sadak. **Assistant Director, Broadcasting/Media Relations:** Matt Janus. **Director, Merchandise:** Jim Beck. **Assistant Director, Merchandise:** Jennifer Davis. **Director, Game Entertainment:** Kyle Love. **Game Entertainment Assistant:** Megan Holloway. **Director, Marketing:** Dave Arthur. **Marketing Assistants:** Marianne Marinella, Daniel Trimble.
Director, Community Affairs: Kevin Linton. **Community Relations Assistant:** Joe Rosensweet. **Director, Sales/Ticket Operations:** Jared Forma. **Ticket Manager:** Mike Miller. **Group Sales Associates:** Stefani DiChiara-Rash, Pat McVey. **Group Sales Assistant:** Greg Mathews. **Ticket Office Assistants:** Seth Kohler, Lindsey Ravior. **Director, Field Operations:** Steve Gold. **Director, Finance:** Joe Valenti. **Office Manager:** Elizabeth Kolodziej.

FIELD STAFF

Manager: Brian Rupp. **Coach:** Justin Gemoll. **Pitching Coach:** Steve Luebber. **Athletic Trainer:** Mark Stubblefield.

GAME INFORMATION

Radio Announcers: John Sadak, Matt Janus. **No. of Games Broadcast:** Home-70, Away-70. **Flagship Station:** 89.7 WGLS-FM.

PA Announcer: Kevin Linton. **Official Scorers:** Dick Shute, Adam Kamras.

Stadium Name: Judy Johnson Field at Daniel S Frawley Stadium. **Location:** I-95 North to Maryland Ave (exit 6), right on Maryland Ave, and through traffic light onto Martin Luther King Blvd, right at traffic light on Justison St, follow to Shipyard Dr; I-95 South to Maryland Ave (exit 6), left at fourth light on Martin Luther King Blvd, right at fourth light on Justison St, follow to Shipyard Dr. **Standard Game Times:** 7:05 p.m., 6:35 (April-May), Sat 6:05, Sun 1:35. **Ticket Price Range:** $4-10.

Visiting Club Hotel: Quality Inn-Skyways, 147 N DuPont Hwy, New Castle, DE 19720. **Telephone:** (302) 328-6666.

WINSTON-SALEM DASH

Office Address: 926 Brookstown Ave., **Winston-Salem, NC 27101.**
Stadium Address: 951 Ballpark Way, Winston-Salem, NC 27101.
Telephone: (336) 714-2287. **Fax:** (336) 714-2288.
Website: www.wsdash.com. **E-Mail Address:** info@wsdash.com.
Affiliation (first year): Chicago White Sox (1997). **Years in League:** 1945-present

OWNERSHIP, MANAGEMENT

Operated by: Sports Menagerie LLC. **Principal Owner:** Billy Prim. **President:** Geoff Lassiter. **VP/CFO:** Kurt Gehsmann. **VP, Baseball Operations:** Ryan Manuel. **VP, Ticket Sales:** Mike Thompson. **VP, Sponsorship Sales:** Josh Neelon. **VP, Sponsorship Services:** Gerri Brommer. **Director, Entertainment:** Trey Kalny. **Staff Accountant:** Irene Huo. **Sponsor Services Director:** Brandon Cathey. **Marketing Managers, Sponsor Services:** Kristen Farley, Jenna Anderson. **Creative Manager:** Caleb Pardick. **Box Office Manager:** Steve Young. **Box Office Assistant:** Tielor Robinson. **Season Ticket Sales Manager:** Chris Wood. **Outside Sales Representatives:** Geoff Burke, Darrell Southern, Darren Hill. **Group Sales Manager:** Brent Beam. **Group Sales Representatives:** Russell Parmele, Chris Loignon, Scott Byer. **Inside Sales Representative:** Sarah Baumann. **Sales Coordinator:** Nikki Caldwell. **Head Groundskeeper:** Doug Tanis. **Director, Stadium Operations:** Corey Bugno. **Director, Media Relations:** Alex Vispoli.

FIELD STAFF

Manager: Julio Vinas. **Coach:** Gary Ward. **Pitching Coach:** Bobby Thigpen. **Athletic Trainer:** Corey Barton. **Strength Coach:** Adam Tischler.

GAME INFORMATION

Radio Announcer: Alex Vispoli. **No. of Games Broadcast:** Home-70, Away-70. **Flagship Station:** www.wsdash.com.
PA Announcer: Cabell Philpott. **Official Scorer:** Bill Grainger, Steve Vrabel.
Stadium Name: BB&T Ballpark.
Stadium Location: I-40 Business to Peters Creek Parkway exit (exit 5A). **Standard Game Times:** 7 p.m.; Sun 2.
Visiting Club Hotel: Quality Inn at Hanes Mall, 2008 S Hawthorne Rd, Winston-Salem, NC 27103. **Telephone:** (336) 765-6670.

FLORIDA STATE LEAGUE

Office Address: 115 E Orange Ave Daytona Beach, FL 32114.
Mailing Address: PO Box 349, Daytona Beach, FL 32115.
Telephone: (386) 252-7479. **Fax:** (386) 252-7495.
E-Mail Address: fslbaseball@cfl.rr.com. **Website:** www.floridastateleague.com.
Years League Active: 1919-1927, 1936-1941, 1946-.

President/Treasurer: Chuck Murphy.

Executive Vice President: Ken Carson. **Vice Presidents:** North Division—Ken Carson. **South Division—Paul Taglieri. Corporate Secretary:** C David Hood.

Special Advisor: Ben J Hayes.

Directors: Joe Pinto (Jupiter/Palm Beach), Ken Carson (Dunedin), Jeff Eiseman (Port Charlotte), Marvin Goldklang (Fort Myers), Trevor Gooby (Bradenton), Ron Myers (Lakeland), Brady Ballard (Daytona), Kyle Smith (Brevard County), Vance Smith (Tampa), Paul Taglieri (St. Lucie), John Timberlake (Clearwater).

Office Manager: Laura LeCras.

Division Structure: North—Brevard County, Clearwater, Daytona, Dunedin, Lakeland, Tampa. South—Fort Myers, Jupiter, Palm Beach, Port Charlotte, St. Lucie, Bradenton.

Regular Season: 140 games (split schedule). **2011 Opening Date:** April 7. **Closing Date:** Sept. 4.

Chuck Murphy

All-Star Game: June 18 at Clearwater

Playoff Format: First-half division winners meet second-half winners in best-of-three series. Winners meet in best-of-five series for league championship.

Roster Limit: 25. **Player Eligibility Rule:** No age limit. No more than two players and one player-coach on active list may have six or more years of prior minor league service.

Brand of Baseball: Rawlings.

Umpires: Jonathan Bailey (Mableton, GA), Brian De Brauwere (Hummelstown, PA), Ramon De Jesus (Santo Domingo, DR), Ian R Fazio (Tavernier, FL), Blake Felter (St Louis, MO), Brett Houseman (Dayton, OH), Matthew Jones (Newtown, PA), Nicolas Lentz (Holland, MI), Matthew McCoy (Tallahassee, FL), Derek Mollica (Lake Worth, FL), Jose Rivera (San Juan, PR), William Thornewell III (Austin, TX).

STADIUM INFORMATION

Club	Stadium	Opened	Dimensions LF	CF	RF	Capacity	2010 Att.
Bradenton	McKechnie Field	1923	335	400	335	6,602	51,856
Brevard County	Space Coast Stadium	1994	340	404	340	7,500	89,729
Charlotte	Charlotte Sports Park	2009	343	413	343	5,028	171,450
Clearwater	Bright House Field	2004	330	400	330	8,500	172,726
Daytona	Jackie Robinson Ballpark	1930	317	400	325	4,000	150,157
Dunedin	Dunedin Stadium	1977	335	400	327	5,509	36,892
Fort Myers	Hammond Stadium	1991	330	405	330	7,500	112,733
Jupiter	Roger Dean Stadium	1998	330	400	325	6,871	67,614
Lakeland	Joker Marchant Stadium	1966	340	420	340	7,100	64,010
Palm Beach	Roger Dean Stadium	1998	330	400	325	6,871	64,767
St. Lucie	Digital Domain Park	1988	338	410	338	7,500	100,921
Tampa	Steinbrenner Field	1996	318	408	314	10,386	99,736

BRADENTON MARAUDERS

Mailing Address: 1701 27th Street East, Bradenton, FL 34208.
Telephone: (941) 747-3031. **Fax:** (941) 747-9442.
E-Mail Address: MaraudersInfo@pirates.com. **Website:** www.BradentonMarauders.com
Affiliation (first year): Pittsburgh Pirates (2010). **Years in League (Bradenton):** 1919-20, 1923-24, 1926.

OWNERSHIP, MANAGEMENT

Operated By: Pittsburgh Associates.

Director, Florida Operations: Trevor Gooby. **Manager, Florida Operations:** AJ Grant. **Concessions Manager:** Terry Pajka. **Manager, Sales/Marketing:** Rachelle Madrigal. **Coordinator, Sales/Marketing:** Stacy Morgan. **Coordinator, Stadium Operations:** James Ammons. **Coordinator, Ticket Operations:** Justin Kristich. **Head Groundskeeper:** Victor Madrigal.

FIELD STAFF

Manager: Carlos Garcia. **Coach:** Ryan Long. **Pitching Coach:** Mike Steele. **Athletic Trainer:** Keito Homma. **Strength/Conditioning Coach:** James Gonzalez.

GAME INFORMATION
Radio: None.
PA Announcer: Art Ross. **Official Scorer:** Unavailable.
Stadium Name: McKechnie Field. **Location:** I-75 to exit 220 (220B from I-75N) to SR 64 West/Manatee Ave, Left onto 9th St West, McKechnie Field on the left. **Standard Game Times:** 7 p.m.; Tues 6, Sun 5. **Ticket Price Range:** $5-7.
Visiting Club Hotel: Courtyard by Marriott Bradenton Sarasota Waterfront, 100 Riverfront Drive West, Bradenton, FL 34205. **Telephone:** (941) 747-3727.

BREVARD COUNTY MANATEES

Office Address: 5800 Stadium Pkwy, Suite 101, Viera, FL 32940.
Telephone: (321) 633-9200. **Fax:** (321) 633-4418.
E-Mail Address: info@spacecoaststadium.com. **Website:** www.manateesbaseball.com.
Affiliation (first year): Milwaukee Brewers (2005). **Years in League:** 1994-

OWNERSHIP, MANAGEMENT
Operated By: Central Florida Baseball Group LLC.
Chairman: Dr Tom Winters. **Vice Chairman:** Dwight Titus. **President:** Charlie Baumann.
General Manager: Kyle Smith. **Business Operations Manager:** Kelley Wheeler. **Director, Group Sales/Community Relations:** Stephanie Webber. **Ticket Operations/Corporate Sales Manager:** Benjamin Wein. **Clubhouse Managers:** Ryan McDonald. **Head Groundskeeper:** Doug Lopas. **Team Chaplains:** Donnie Legg, Abraham Medina.

FIELD STAFF
Manager: Unavailable. **Coach:** Dwayne Hosey. **Pitching Coach:** Fred Dabney.

GAME INFORMATION
PA Announcer: JC Meyerholz. **Radio:** None.
Official Scorer: Eric Valenstein.
Stadium Name: Space Coast Stadium. **Location:** I-95 North to Wickham Rd (exit 191), left onto Wickham, right at traffic circle onto Lake Andrew Drive for 1 1/2 miles through the Brevard County government office complex to the four-way stop, right on Stadium Parkway, Space Coast Stadium 1/2 mile on the left; I-95 South to Rockledge exit (exit 195), left onto Stadium Parkway, Space Coast Stadium is 3 miles on right. **Standard Game Times:** 7 pm., Sat 7, Sun. 1. **Ticket Price Range:** $7.
Visiting Club Hotel: Holiday Inn Hotel & Conference Center, 8928 N Wickham Rd, Viera, FL 32940. **Telephone:** (321) 255-0077.

CHARLOTTE STONE CRABS

Office Address: 2300 El Jobean Rd, Port Charlotte, FL 33948.
Mailing Address: 2300 El Jobean Rd, Building A, Port Charlotte, FL 33948.
Telephone: (941) 206-4487. **Fax:** (941) 206-3599.
E-Mail Address: info@stonecrabsbaseball.com. **Website:** www.stonecrabsbaseball.com.
Affiliation (first year): Tampa Bay Rays (2009). **Years in League:** 2009-

OWNERSHIP, MANAGEMENT
Operated By: Ripken Baseball.
General Manager: Joe Hart. **Director/Assistant GM, Food/Beverage/Operations:** Nick Barkley. **Director, Stadium Operations:** Sean Sawyer. **Box Office Manager:** Chris Sprunger. **Assistant GM, Sales:** Patrick McMaster. **Account Representatives:** Eric Schmidlkofer, Rob Coons, Scott Allen, Joe Mandele. **Full Charge Bookkeeper:** Tamera Figueroa. **Accounting Clerk:** Sue Denny.

FIELD STAFF
Manager: Jim Morrison. **Coach:** Joe Szekely. **Pitching Coach:** Steve Watson.

GAME INFORMATION
PA Announcer: Josh Grant. **Official Scorer:** Unavailable.
Stadium Name: Charlotte Sports Park. **Location:** I-75 to Exit 179, turn left onto Toldeo Blade Blvd then right on El Jobean Rd. **Ticket Price Range:** $6-11.
Visiting Club Hotel: Days Inn, 1941 Tamiami Trail, Port Charlotte, FL 33948. **Telephone:** 941-627-8900.

CLEARWATER THRESHERS

Office Address: 601 N Old Coachman Rd, Clearwater, FL 33765.
Telephone: (727) 712-4300. **Fax:** (727) 712-4498.
Website: www.threshersbaseball.com.
Affiliation (first year): Philadelphia Phillies (1985). **Years in League:** 1985-

OWNERSHIP, MANAGEMENT

Operated by: Philadelphia Phillies.
Chairman: Bill Giles. **President:** David Montgomery.
Director, Florida Operations/General Manager: John Timberlake. **Assistant Director, Minor League Operations:** Lee McDaniel. **Business Manager:** Dianne Gonzalez. **Assistant GM/Director, Sales:** Dan McDonough. **Assistant GM/Ticketing:** Jason Adams. **Office Administration:** DeDe Angelillis. **Manager, Group Sales:** Dan Madden. **Assistant Manager, Group Sales:** Bobby Mitchell. **Manager, Ballpark Operations:** Jerry Warren. **Operations Assistant:** Sean McCarthy. **Coordinator, Facility Maintenance:** Cory Sipe. **Manager, Special Events:** Doug Kemp. **Manager, Community Relations/Promotions:** Amanda Warner. **Clubhouse Manager:** Mark Meschede. **Manager, Food/Beverage:** Brad Dudash. **Assistant, Food/Beverage:** Craig Glover. **Ticket Office Manager:** Mike Nash. **Group Sales Assistant:** Michelle Finley. **Operations Assistant:** Sean McCarthy. **Coordinator, Audio/Video:** Nic Repper. **Interns:** John Kerstetter.

FIELD STAFF

Manager: Dusty Wathan. **Coach:** John Mizerock. **Pitching Coach:** Dave Lundquist.

GAME INFORMATION

Radio: None.
PA Announcer: Don Guckian. **Official Scorer:** Larry Wiederecht.
Stadium Name: Bright House Field. **Location:** US 19 North and Drew Street in Clearwater. **Standard Game Times:** 7 p.m., Fri/Sat 6:30; Sun 1. **Ticket Price Range:** $5-9.
Visiting Club Hotel: Unavailable.

DAYTONA CUBS

Office Address: 105 E Orange Ave, Daytona Beach, FL 32114.
Telephone: (386) 257-3172. **Fax:** (386) 257-3382.
E-Mail Address: info@daytonacubs.com. **Website:** www.daytonacubs.com.
Affiliation (first year): Chicago Cubs (1993). **Years in League:** 1920-24, 1928, 1936-41, 1946-73, 1977-87, 1993-

OWNERSHIP, MANAGEMENT

Operated By: Big Game Florida LLC.
Principal Owner/President: Andrew Rayburn.
General Manager: Brady Ballard. **Assistant GM:** Josh Lawther. **Director, Broadcasting/Media Relations:** Robbie Aaron. **Director, Stadium Operations:** JR Laub. **Director, Tickets:** Amanda Earnest. **Director, Sales:** Clint Cure. **Director, Corporate Accounts:** Mike Sandler. **Manager, Special Events/Community Relations:** Janelle Yonkovitch. **Director, Groups/Merchandise:** Jim Jaworski. **Manager, Group Sales:** Jason Wilford. **Office Manager:** Tammy Devine.

FIELD STAFF

Manager: Buddy Bailey. **Coach:** Barbaro Garbey. **Pitching Coach:** Tom Pratt. **Trainer:** Peter Fagan.

GAME INFORMATION

Radio Announcer: Robbie Aaron. **No. of Games Broadcast:** Home-70, Road-70. **Flagship Station:** AM-1340 WROD.
PA Announcer: Tim Lecras. **Official Scorer:** Don Roberts.
Stadium Name: Jackie Robinson Ballpark. **Location:** I-95 to International Speedway Blvd Exit (Route 92), east to Beach Street, south to Magnolia Ave east to ballpark; A1A North/South to Orange Ave west to ballpark. **Standard Game Time:** 7:05 p.m. **Ticket Price Range:** $6-12.
Visiting Club Hotel: Acapulco Hotel & Resort, 2505 S Atlantic Ave Daytona Beach Shores, FL 32218. **Telephone:** (386) 761-2210.

DUNEDIN BLUE JAYS

Office Address: 373 Douglas Ave Dunedin, FL 34698.
Telephone: (727) 733-9302. **Fax:** (727) 734-7661.
E-Mail Address: dunedin@bluejays.com. **Website:** www.dunedinbluejays.com.
Affiliation (first year): Toronto Blue Jays (1987). **Years in League:** 1978-79, 1987-

OWNERSHIP, MANAGEMENT

Operated by: Toronto Blue Jays.
Director/General Manager, Florida Operations: Shelby Miller. **Assistant GM:** Janette Donoghue. **Senior Consultant:** Ken Carson. **Office Manager:** Karen Howell. **Manager, Group Sales/Community Relations:** Kathi Wiegand. **Supervisor, Ticket Operations:** Garrett Konrad. **Account Manager, Sales:** Kevin Schildt. **Community Relations Coordinator:** Morgan Bell. **Communications Coordinator:** Craig Durham. **Ticket Operations Coordinator:** Jonathon Valdez. **Administration Assistant/Receptionist:** Michelle Smith. **Clubhouse Manager:** Jeff Pink. **Clubhouse Assistant:** Nate Barker. **Head Superintendent:** Patrick Skunda. **Grounds Crew Supervisor:** Matt Johnson.

FIELD STAFF

Manager: Clayton McCullough. **Coach:** Ralph Dickenson. **Pitching Coach:** Darold Knowles. **Trainer:** Dan McIntosh.

GAME INFORMATION

Radio: None.
PA Announcer: Alan Wilcox. **Official Scorer:** Josh Huff.
Stadium Name: Florida Auto Exchange Stadium. **Location:** From I-275, north on Highway 19, left on Sunset Point Rd for 4 ½ miles, right on Douglas Ave stadium is ½ mile on right. **Standard Game Times:** 7 p.m.; Sun 1. **Ticket Price Range:** $6.
Visiting Club Hotel: Comfort Inn Countryside, 26508 US 19 N, Clearwater, FL 33761. **Telephone:** (727) 796-1234.

FORT MYERS MIRACLE

Office Address: 14400 Six Mile Cypress Pkwy, Fort Myers, FL 33912.
Telephone: (239) 768-4210. **Fax:** (239) 768-4211.
E-Mail Address: miracle@miraclebaseball.com.
Website: www.miraclebaseball.com.
Affiliation (first year): Minnesota Twins (1993). **Years in League:** 1926, 1978-87, 1991-

OWNERSHIP, MANAGEMENT

Operated By: Greater Miami Baseball Club LP.
Principal Owner/Chairman: Marvin Goldklang. **Executive Advisor To The Chairman:** Mike Veeck. **Executive Vice President/General Manager:** Steve Gliner. **VP/Assistant GM:** Andrew Seymour. **Senior Director, Corporate Sales/Marketing:** Terry Simon. **Senior Director, Business Operations:** Suzanne Reaves. **Director, Media Relations/Promotions:** Gary Sharp. **Director, Food/Beverage:** Nick Bilski. **Manager, Tickets:** Andy Rielly. **Community Relations Coordinator:** Joy Donahue. **Food/Beverage Assistant:** Phillip Busch. **Account Executive:** Sean Kelly. **Director, Broadcasting/Account Executive:** Alex Margulies. **Customer Relations Associate:** Nicole Greer. **Administrative Assistant/Operations:** Ryan Olsen. **Head Groundskeeper:** Keith Blasingim. **Clubhouse Manager:** TJ Weil.

FIELD STAFF

Manager: Jake Mauer. **Coach:** Jim Dwyer. **Pitching Coach:** Steve Mintz. **Trainer:** Larry Bennese.

GAME INFORMATION

Radio Announcer: Alex Margulies. **No. of Games Broadcast:** Home-70, Road-70. **Internet Broadcasts:** www.miracle-baseball.com.
PA Announcer: Gary Sharp. **Official Scorer:** Scott Pedersen.
Stadium Name: William H Hammond Stadium. **Location:** Exit 131 off I-75, west on Daniels Parkway, left on Six Mile Cypress Parkway. **Standard Game Times:** 7:05 p.m., Sat. 6:05; Sun 1:05. **Ticket Price Range:** $5-8.50.
Visiting Club Hotel: Fairfield Inn by Marriot, 7090 Cypress Terrace, Fort Myers, FL 33907. **Telephone:** (239) 437-5600.

JUPITER HAMMERHEADS

Office Address: 4751 Main Street, Jupiter, FL 33458.
Telephone: (561) 775-1818. **Fax:** (561) 691-6886.
E-Mail Address: f.desk@rogerdeanstadium.com
Website: www.jupiterhammerheads.com.
Affiliation (first year): Florida Marlins (2002). **Years in League:** 1998-

OWNERSHIP, MANAGEMENT

Owned By: Florida Marlins.
Operated By: Jupiter Stadium, LTD.
General Manager, Jupiter Stadium, LTD: Unavailable. **Executive Assistant:** Carol McAteer. **GM, Jupiter Hammerheads:** Mike Bauer. **Corporate Partnership Manager:** Judy Gibson. **Merchandise Manager:** Lauren Gurley. **Ticket Manager:** Amanda Avila. **Assistant Ticket Manager:** Jason Cantone. **Ticket Sales/Promotions Director:** Lisa Fegley. **Stadium/Event Operations Manager:** Bryan Knapp. **Assistant Building Manager:** Walter Herrera. **Grounds Director:** Jordan Treadway. **Accounting Director:** John McCahan. **Office Manager:** David Vago.

FIELD STAFF

Manager: Ron Hassey. **Coach:** Frank Moore. **Pitching Coach:** Terry Abbott.

GAME INFORMATION

Radio: None. **PA Announcers:** John Frost, Dick Sanford, Lou Palmer. **Official Scorer:** Brennan McDonald.
Stadium Name: Roger Dean Stadium. **Location:** I-95 to exit 83, east on Donald Ross Road for 1/4 mile.
Standard Game Times: 6:30 p.m., Sun 5. **Ticket Price Range:** $6.50-8.50.
Visiting Club Hotel: Comfort Inn & Suites Jupiter, 6752 West Indiantown Rd, Jupiter, FL 33458. **Telephone:** (561) 745-7997.

LAKELAND FLYING TIGERS

Office Address: 2125 N Lake Ave, Lakeland, FL 33805.
Mailing Address: 2125 N Lake Ave, Lakeland, FL 33805.
Telephone: (863) 686-8075. **Fax:** (863) 688-9589.
Website: www.lakelandflyingtigers.com
Affiliation (first year): Detroit Tigers (1967). **Years in League:** 1919-26, 1953-55, 1960, 1962-64, 1967-.

OWNERSHIP, MANAGEMENT
Owned By: Detroit Tigers, Inc.
Principal Owner: Mike Ilitch. **President:** David Dombrowski. **Director, Florida Operations:** Ron Myers.
General Manager: Zach Burek. **Manager, Administration/Operations:** Shannon Follett. **Ticket Manager:** Ryan Eason. **Group Sales Manager:** Dan Lauer. **Executive Chef:** Tom Mackinnon. **Receptionist:** Maria Walls.

FIELD STAFF
Manager: Dave Huppert. **Coach:** Larry Herndon. **Pitching Coach:** Joe Coleman.

GAME INFORMATION
Radio: None.
PA Announcers: Shari Szabo. **Official Scorer:** Sandy Shaw.
Stadium Name: Joker Marchant Stadium. **Location:** Exit 33 on I-4 to 33 South, 1.5 miles on left. **Standard Game Times:** 7 pm, Sat 6, Sun 1. **Ticket Price Range:** $4-6.
Visiting Club Hotel: Lakeland Hotel & Conference Center, 3260 US Highway 98 North, Lakeland, FL 33805. **Telephone:** (863) 688-8080.

PALM BEACH CARDINALS

Office Address: 4751 Main Street, Jupiter, FL 33458.
Telephone: (561) 775-1818. **Fax:** (561) 691-6886.
E-Mail address: f.desk@rogerdeanstadium.com.
Website: www.palmbeachcardinals.com.
Affiliation (first year): St. Louis Cardinals (2003). **Years in League:** 2003-

OWNERSHIP, MANAGEMENT
Owned By: St. Louis Cardinals.
Operated By: Jupiter Stadium LTD.
General Manager, Jupiter Stadium, LTD: Unavailable. **Executive Assistant:** Carol McAteer. **GM, Palm Beach Cardinals:** Mike Bauer. **Corporate Partnership Manager:** Judy Gibson. **Merchandise Manager:** Lauren Gurley. **Ticket Manager:** Amanda Avila. **Assistant Ticket Manager:** Jason Cantone. **Ticket Sales/Promotions Director:** Lisa Fegley. **Stadium/Event Operations Manager:** Bryan Knapp. **Assistant Building Manager:** Walter Herrera. **Grounds Director:** Jordan Treadway. **Accounting Director:** John McCahan. **Office Manager:** David Vago.

FIELD STAFF
Manager: Luis Aguayo. **Coach:** Jeff Albert. **Pitching Coach:** Dennis Martinez.

GAME INFORMATION
Radio: None. **PA Announcers:** John Frost, Dick Sanford, Lou Palmer.
Official Scorer: Lou Villano.
Stadium Name: Roger Dean Stadium. **Location:** I-95 to exit 83, east on Donald Ross Road for 1/4 mile.
Standard Game Times: 6:30 p.m.; Sun 5. **Ticket Price Range:** $6.50-8.50.
Visiting Club Hotel: Comfort Inn & Suites Jupiter, 6752 West Indiantown Rd, Jupiter, FL 33458. **Telephone:** (561) 745-7997.

ST. LUCIE METS

Office Address: 525 NW Peacock Blvd, Port St Lucie, FL 34986.
Telephone: (772) 871-2100. **Fax:** (772) 878-9802.
Website: www.DigitalDomainPark.com
Affiliation (first year): New York Mets (1988). **Years in League:** 1988-

OWNERSHIP, MANAGEMENT
Operated by: Sterling Mets LP.
Chairman/CEO: Fred Wilpon. **President:** Saul Katz. **Senior Executive Vice President/COO:** Jeff Wilpon.
Director, Florida Operations/General Manager: Paul Taglieri. **Assistant Director, Florida Operations/Assistant GM:** Traer Van Allen. **Manager, Food/Beverage Operations:** Brian Paupeck. **Manager, Sales/Ballpark Operations:** Ryan Strickland. **Manager, Group Sales/Community Relations:** Katie Hatch. **Executive Assistant:** Cynthia Malaspino. **Staff Accountant:** Paula Andreozzi. **Manager, Media Relations:** Matt Gagnon. **Manager, Ticketing/Merchandise:** Clinton

Van Allen. **Head Groundskeeper:** Tommy Bowes. **Clubhouse Manager:** Jack Brenner.

FIELD STAFF

Manager: Pedro Lopez. **Coach:** Joel Fuentes. **Pitching Coach:** Phil Regan.

GAME INFORMATION

Radio: None.
PA Announcer: Matt Gagnon. **Official Scorer:** Bob Adams.
Stadium Name: Digital Domain Park. **Location:** Exit 121 (St. Lucie West Blvd) off I-95, east 1/2 mile, left on NW Peacock Blvd. **Standard Game Times:** 6:30 p.m.; Sun 1. **Ticket Price Range:** $4-8.
Visiting Club Hotel: SpringHill Suites, 2000 NW Courtyard Circle, Port St. Lucie, FL 34986. **Telephone:** (772) 871-2929.

TAMPA YANKEES

Office Address: One Steinbrenner Dr, Tampa, FL 33614.
Telephone: (813) 875-7753. **Fax:** (813) 673-3174.
E-Mail Address: vsmith@yankees.com. **Website:** tybaseball.com.
Affiliation (first year): New York Yankees (1994). **Years in League:** 1919-27, 1957-1988, 1994-

OWNERSHIP, MANAGEMENT

Operated by: New York Yankees LP.
Principal Owner: George Steinbrenner.
General Manager: Vance Smith. **Assistant GM:** Matt Gess. **Business Operations:** Julie Kremer. **Director, Sales/Marketing:** Howard Grosswirth. **Director, Ticket Sales:** Brian Valdez. **Head Groundskeeper:** Ritchie Anderson.

FIELD STAFF

Manager: Luis Sojo. **Hitting Coach:** Justin Turner. **Pitching Coach:** Jeff Ware. **Coach:** Mario Garza. **Trainer:** Scott DiFrancesco. **Strength/Conditioning:** Jay Signorelli.

GAME INFORMATION

Radio: None.
PA Announcer: Unavailable. **Official Scorer:** Unavailable.
Stadium Name: Steinbrenner Field. **Location:** I-275 to Martin Luther King, west on Martin Luther King to Dale Mabry. **Standard Game Times:** 7 p.m., Sat. 6, Sun. 1. **Ticket Price Range:** $4-6.
Visiting Club Hotel: Sheraton Suites Tampa Airport, 4400 W Cypress St Tampa, FL 33607. **Telephone:** (813) 873-8675.

MIDWEST LEAGUE

Office Address: 1118 Cranston Rd., Beloit, WI 53511.
Mailing Address: PO Box 936, Beloit, WI 53512.
Telephone: (608) 364-1188. **Fax:** (608) 364-1913.
E-Mail Address: mwl@midwestleague.com. **Website:** www.midwestleague.com.

Years League Active: 1947-.
President, Treasurer: George H. Spelius.
Vice Presidents: Ed Larson, Richard A. Nussbaum II. **Legal Counsel/Secretary:** Richard A. Nussbaum II.

Directors: Gary Keoppel (Cedar Rapids), Peter Carfagna (Lake County), Lew Chamberlin (West Michigan), Dennis Conerton (Beloit), Tom Dickson (Lansing), Jason Freier (Fort Wayne), David Heller (Quad Cities), Joe Kernan (South Bend), Gary Mayse (Dayton), Paul Schnack (Clinton), Art Solomon (Bowling Green), William Stavropoulos (Great Lakes), Rocky Vonachen (Peoria), Dave Walker (Burlington), Mike Woleben (Kane County), Rob Zerjav (Wisconsin).

League Administrator: Holly Voss.
Division Structure: East—Bowling Green, Dayton, Fort Wayne, Lake County, Lansing, South Bend, Great Lakes, West Michigan. West—Beloit, Burlington, Cedar Rapids, Clinton, Kane County, Peoria, Quad Cities, Wisconsin.

Regular Season: 140 games (split schedule). **2011 Opening Date:** April 7. **Closing Date:** Sept 5.

All-Star Game: June 21 at Quad Cities (Davenport, Iowa).

Playoff Format: Eight teams qualify. First-half and second-half division winners and wild-card teams meet in best-of-three quarterfinal series. Winners meet in best-of-three series for division championships. Division champions meet in best-of-five final for league championship.

Roster Limit: 25 active. **Player Eligibility Rule:** No age limit. No more than two players and one player-coach on active list may have more than five years experience.

Brand of Baseball: Rawlings ROM-MID.
Umpires: Unavailable.

George Spelius

STADIUM INFORMATION

Club	Stadium	Opened	Dimensions LF	CF	RF	Capacity	2010 Att.
Beloit	Pohlman Field	1982	325	380	325	3,500	73,440
Bowling Green	Bowling Green Ballpark	2009	312	401	325	4,559	235,412
Burlington	Community Field	1947	338	403	318	3,200	60,508
Cedar Rapids	Veterans Memorial Stadium	2000	315	400	325	5,300	173,210
Clinton	Alliant Energy Field	1937	335	390	325	4,000	123,553
Dayton	Fifth Third Field	2000	338	402	338	7,230	597,433
Fort Wayne	Parkview Field	2009	336	400	318	8,100	404,942
Great Lakes	Dow Diamond	2007	332	400	325	5,200	263,878
Kane County	Philip B. Elfstrom Stadium	1991	335	400	335	7,400	430,831
Lake County	Classic Park	2003	320	400	320	7,273	287,935
Lansing	Cooley Law School Stadium	1996	305	412	305	11,000	360,510
Peoria	O'Brien Field	2002	310	400	310	7,500	203,558
Quad Cities	Modern Woodmen Park	1931	343	400	318	4,024	224,128
South Bend	Coveleski Regional Stadium	1987	336	405	336	5,000	129,599
West Michigan	Fifth Third Ballpark	1994	317	402	327	10,051	371,575
Wisconsin	Fox Cities Stadium	1995	325	400	325	5,500	244,331

BELOIT SNAPPERS

Office Address: 2301 Skyline Dr, Beloit, WI 53511.
Mailing Address: PO Box 855, Beloit, WI 53512.
Telephone: (608) 362-2272. **Fax:** (608) 362-0418.
E-Mail Address: snappy@snappersbaseball.com.
Website: www.snappersbaseball.com.
Affiliation (first year): Minnesota Twins (2005). **Years in League:** 1982-.

OWNERSHIP, MANAGEMENT

Operated by: Beloit Professional Baseball Association Inc.
Chairman: Dennis Conerton. **President:** Perry Folts.
General Manager: Jeff Vohs. **Assistant GM:** Matt Bosen. **Corporate Sales/Promotions:** Matt Glocke. **Director, Media/Community Relations/Marketing:** Justin Waters. **Director, Food/Beverage:** Will Shelton. **Head Groundskeeper:** Eric Williams.

FIELD STAFF

Manager: Nelson Prada. **Coach:** Tommy Watkins. **Pitching Coach:** Gary Lucas. **Trainer:** Alan Rail.

GAME INFORMATION

Radio Announcer: Andrew Liebetrau. **No. of Games Broadcast:** 25. **Flagship Station:** 1380-AM ESPN. **PA Announcer:** Justin Waters. **Official Scorer:** Unavailable. **Stadium Name:** Pohlman Field. **Location:** I-90 to exit 185-A, right at Cranston Road for 1 1/2 miles; I-43 to Wisconsin 81 to Cranston Road, right at Cranston for 1 1/2 miles. **Standard Game Times:** 7 p.m., 6:30 (April-May); Sun 2. **Ticket Price Range:** $6-8. **Visiting Club Hotel:** Econo Lodge, 2956 Milwaukee Rd, Beloit, WI 53511. **Telephone:** (608) 364-4000.

BOWLING GREEN HOT RODS

Office Address: Bowling Green Ballpark, 300 8th Avenue, Bowling Green, KY 42101. **Telephone:** (270) 901-2121. **Fax:** (270) 901-2165. **E-Mail Address:** fun@bghotrods.com. **Website:** www.bghotrods.com. **Affiliation (first year):** Tampa Bay Rays (2009). **Years in League:** 2010-

OWNERSHIP, MANAGEMENT

Ownership: Operated by DSF Sports **Owner:** Art Solomon. **President, DSF Sports:** Rick Brenner. **Vice President, DSF Sports:** John Willi. **President:** Brad Taylor. **General Manager:** Ryan Gates. **Assistant GM, Operations:** Ken Clary. **Controller:** Sally Lancaster. **Ticket Sales Manager:** Keith Hetzer. **Director, Broadcast/Media Relations:** Tom Gauthier. **Director, Merchandise:** Kyle Hanrahan. **Head Turf Manager:** Ray Sayre. **Production Manager:** Atlee McHeffey. **Ticket Operations Manager:** Julie Harrigan. **Account Executives:** Matt Davisson, Adam Smedberg. **Office Manager:** Jennifer Johnson.

FIELD STAFF

Manager: Brady Williams. **Coach:** Manny Castillo. **Pitching Coach:** RC Lichtenstein. **Trainer:** Unavailable.

GAME INFORMATION

Radio Announcer: Tom Gauthier. **No. of Games Broadcast:** Home-70, Away-70. **Flagship Station:** WBGN 1340-AM. **PA Announcer:** Chris Kelly. **Official Scorer:** Chad Young. **Stadium Name:** Bowling Green Ballpark. **Location:** From I-65, take Exit 26 (KY-234/Cemetery Road) into Bowling Green for 3.0 miles, Left onto College Street for 0.2 miles, Right onto 8th Avenue. **Standard Game Times:** 6:35 p.m. (April, Aug), 7:05 (May-July); Fri 7:05; Sat 7:05; Sun 2:05. **Ticket Price Range:** $5-10. **Visiting Club Hotel:** Candlewood Suites, 540 Wall Street, Bowling Green, KY 42104. **Telephone:** (270) 843-5505.

BURLINGTON BEES

Office Address: 2712 Mt. Pleasant St, Burlington, IA 52601. **Mailing Address:** PO Box 824, Burlington, IA 52601. **Telephone:** (319) 754-5705. **Fax:** (319) 754-5882. **E-Mail Address:** staff@gobees.com. **Website:** www.gobees.com. **Affiliation (first year):** Oakland Athletics (2011). **Years in League:** 1962-

OWNERSHIP, MANAGEMENT

Operated By: Burlington Baseball Association Inc. **President:** Dave Walker. **General Manager:** Chuck Brockett. **Assistant GM, Sales/Marketing:** Jared Schjei. **Director, Group Outings:** Whitney Henderson. **Groundskeeper:** TJ Brewer.

FIELD STAFF

Manager: Aaron Nieckula. **Coach:** Haas Pratt. **Pitching Coach:** Jimmy Escalante. **Athletic Trainer:** Brian Thorson.

GAME INFORMATION

Radio Announcer: Unavailable. **No. of Games Broadcast:** Home-70, Away-70. **Flagship Station:** NewsRadio KBUR 1490-AM. **PA Announcer:** Nathan McCoy. **Official Scorer:** Ted Gutman. **Stadium Name:** Community Field. **Location:** From US 34, take US 61 North to Mt. Pleasant Street, east 1/8 mile. **Standard Game Times:** 6:30 p.m., Sun 2. **Ticket Price Range:** $4-8. **Visiting Club Hotel:** Pzazz Best Western FunCity, 3001 Winegard Dr, Burlington, IA 52601. **Telephone:** (319) 753-2223.

CEDAR RAPIDS KERNELS

Office Address: 950 Rockford Rd SW, Cedar Rapids, IA 52404.
Mailing Address: P.O. Box 2001, Cedar Rapids, IA 52406.
Telephone: (319) 363-3887. **Fax:** (319) 363-5631. **E-Mail Address:** kernels@kernels.com. **Website:** www.kernels.com.
Affiliation (first year): Los Angeles Angels (1993). **Years in League:** 1962-

OWNERSHIP, MANAGEMENT

Operated by: Cedar Rapids Ball Club Inc.
President: Gary Keoppel.
General Manager: Doug Nelson. **Assistant GM:** Scott Wilson. **Radio Broadcaster/Sales:** Morgan Hawk. **IT/Communications Manager:** Andrew Pantini. **Sports Turf Manager:** Jesse Roeder. **Director, Ticket/Group Sales:** Andrea Murphy. **Director, Finance:** Charlie Patrick. **Entertainment/Community Relations Manager:** Brandon Clemens. **Stadium Operations Manager:** Seth Dohrn. **Director, Corporate Sales/Marketing:** Jessica Fergesen. **Corporate Sales Executive:** Wes Cooling. **Director, Food/Beverage:** Debra Maier. **Receptionist:** Marcia Moran.

FIELD STAFF

Manager: Brent Del Chiaro. **Coach:** Mike Eylward. **Pitching Coach:** Trevor Wilson. **Trainer:** Eric Munson.

GAME INFORMATION

Radio Announcer: Morgan Hawk. **No. of Games Broadcast:** Home-70, Away-70. **Flagship Station:** KMRY 1450-AM.
PA Announcer: Dale Brodt. **Official Scorer:** Unavailable.
Stadium Name: Veterans Memorial Stadium. **Location:** From I-380 North, take the Wilson Ave exit, turn left on Wilson Ave. After the railroad tracks, turn right on Rockford Road. Proceed .8 miles, stadium is on left. From I-380 South, exit at First Avenue. Proceed to Eighth Avenue (first stop sign) and turn left. Stadium entrance is .1 miles on right (before tennis courts). **Standard Game Times:** 6:35 p.m., Sat-Sun: 2:05. **Ticket Price Range:** $7-10.
Visiting Club Hotel: Best Western Cooper's Mill, 100 F Ave NW, Cedar Rapids, IA 52405. **Telephone:** (319) 366-5323.

CLINTON LUMBERKINGS

Office Address: Alliant Energy Field, 537 Ball Park Drive, Clinton, IA 52732.
Mailing Address: PO Box 1295, Clinton, IA 52733.
Telephone: (563) 242-0727. **Fax:** (563) 242-1433.
E-Mail Address: lumberkings@lumberkings.com. **Website:** www.lumberkings.com.
Affiliation (first year): Seattle Mariners (2009). **Years in League:** 1956-

OWNERSHIP, MANAGEMENT

Operated By: Clinton Baseball Club Inc.
President: Paul Schnack.
General Manager: Ted Tornow. **Assistant GM:** Nate Kreinbrink. **Director, Broadcasting/Media Relations:** Dave Lezotte. **Director, Operations:** Mitch Butz. **Stadium/Sportsturf Manager:** Dustin Krogman. **Accountant:** Ryan Marcum. **Assistant Director, Operations:** Morty Kriner. **Director, Facility Compliance:** Tom Whaley. **Office Procurement Manager:** Les Moore. **Clubhouse Manager:** Tyler Hildreth.

FIELD STAFF

Manager: Eddie Menchaca. **Coach:** Terry Pollreisz. **Pitching Coach:** Rich Dorman. **Trainer:** Jacob Naas.

GAME INFORMATION

Radio Announcer: Dave Lezotte. **No. of Games Broadcast:** Home-70, Away-70. **Flagship Station:** KCLN 1390-AM.
PA Announcer: Brad Seward. **Official Scorers:** Jared Lueders, J Robert Willey.
Stadium Name: Alliant Energy Field. **Location:** Highway 67 North to Sixth Avenue North, right on Sixth, cross railroad tracks, stadium on right. **Standard Game Times:** 6:30 p.m. (April-May, Aug 17-Sept), 7 (June-Aug 12); Sat 6, Sun 2. **Ticket Price Range:** $5-8.
Visiting Club Hotel: Super 8, 1711 Lincoln Way, Clinton IA 52732. **Telephone:** 563-242-8870

DAYTON DRAGONS

Office Address: Fifth Third Field, 220 N Patterson Blvd, Dayton, OH 45402.
Mailing Address: PO 2107, Dayton, OH 45401.
Telephone: (937) 228-2287. **Fax:** (937) 228-2284.
E-Mail Address: dragons@daytondragons.com. **Website:** www.daytondragons.com.
Affiliation (first year): Cincinnati Reds (2000). **Years in League:** 2000-

OWNERSHIP, MANAGEMENT

Operated By: Dayton Professional Baseball Club LLC/Mandalay Baseball Properties, LLC. **Owners:** Mandalay Baseball Properties LLC, Earvin "Magic" Johnson, Archie Griffin.

President: Robert Murphy.

Executive Vice President: Eric Deutsch. **Executive VP/General Manager:** Gary Mayse. **VP, Accounting/Finance:** Mark Schlein. **VP, Corporate Partnerships:** Jeff Webb. **VP, Ticket Sales:** Jeff Stewart. **VP, Sponsor Services:** Brad Eaton.

Director, Media Relations: Tom Nichols. **Director, Operations:** Andrew Ottmar. **Director, Entertainment:** Kaitlin Rohrer. **Director, Marketing:** Jim Francis.

Senior Marketing Managers: Brandy Abney, Laura Rose, Clint Taylor. **Marketing Managers:** Brian Botos, Dean Freson, Lindsey Huerter. **Director, Ticket Sales:** Andrew Aldenderfer. **Director, Group Sales:** Mike Vujea. **Ticketing Coordinator:** Chris Fogle. **Corporate Marketing Managers:** Sean Allen, Viterio Jones, Nick Kuchey, Phil Salwan. **Event Operations Manager:** Chad Adams. **Senior Operations Director:** Joe Eaglowski. **Facilities Operations Manager:** Joe Elking. **Baseball Operations Manager:** John Wallace. **Entertainment Assistant:** Sam Blaine. **Office Manager/ Executive Assistant to the President:** Leslie Stuck. **Staff Accountant:** Dorothy Day. **Administrative Assistant:** Lisa Rike. **Administrative Secretary:** Barbara Van Schaik. **Head Groundskeeper:** Unavailable.

FIELD STAFF

Manager: Delino Deshields. **Coach:** Alex Pelaez. **Pitching Coach:** Tony Fossas. **Trainer:** Tyler Steele.

GAME INFORMATION

Radio Announcers: Tom Nichols, Mike Couzens. **No. of Games Broadcast:** Home-70, Away-70. **Flagship Station:** WONE 980 AM.

PA Announcers: Ben Oburn, Kim Parker. **Official Scorers:** Matt Lindsay, Tom Harner, Mike Lucas.

Stadium Name: Fifth Third Field. **Location:** I-75 South to downtown Dayton, left at First Street; I-75 North, right at First Street exit. **Ticket Price Range:** $7.00-$13.75.

Visiting Club Hotel: Comfort Inn, 7125 Miller Lane, Dayton, OH 45414. **Phone:** (937) 890-9995. **Fax:** (937) 890-9995.

FORT WAYNE TINCAPS

Office Address: 1301 Ewing St. Fort Wayne, IN 46802.

Telephone: (260) 482-6400. **Fax:** (260) 471-4678.

E-Mail Address: info@tincaps.com. **Website:** www.tincaps.com.

Affiliation (first year): San Diego Padres (1999). **Years in League:** 1993-.

OWNERSHIP, MANAGEMENT

Operated By: Hardball Capital.

Owners: Jason Freier, Chris Schoen.

President/General Manager: Mike Nutter. **Vice President/Assistant GM, Sales/Finance:** Brian Schackow. **VP/Senior Assistant GM, Corporate Partnerships:** David Lorenz. **VP/Assistant GM, Marketing/Entertainment/Promotions:** Michael Limmer. **Director, Group Sales:** Brad Shank. **Assistant Director, Group Sales:** Jared Parcell. **Director, Ticketing:** Pat Ventura. **Assistant Director, Ticketing:** Paige Salway. **Director, Food/Beverage:** Bill Lehn. **Culinary Director:** Scott Kammerer. **Manager, Catering:** Brandon Tinkle. **Food/Beverage Operations Manager:** Dan Krleski. **Coordinators, Special Events:** Holly Raney, Jen Walters. **Director, Facilities:** Tim Burkhart. **Assistant Director, Facilities:** Chris Watson. **Assistant Director, Maintenance:** Donald Miller. **Head Groundskeeper:** Keith Winter. **Creative Director:** Tony DesPlaines. **Manager, Video Production:** Jeff Greer. **Managers, Ticket Sales:** Tyler Baker, Brent Harring, Penny Wascovich, Justin Shurley, Erik Lose. **Manager, Corporate Partnerships:** Chris Snyder. **Director, Broadcasting:** Dan Watson. **Office Manager:** Cathy Tinney. **Manager, Merchandise:** Karen Schieber. **Manager, Promotions:** Abby Naas.

FIELD STAFF

Manager: Shawn Wooten. **Coach:** Kory DeHaan. **Pitching Coach:** Willie Blair. **Trainer:** Dan Turner.

GAME INFORMATION

Radio Announcers: Dan Watson, Mike Maahs. **No. of Games Broadcast:** Home-70, Away-70. **Flagship Station:** WKJG 1380-AM. **PA Announcers:** Jared Parcell, Jim Shovlin. **Official Scorers:** Rich Tavierne, Bill Salyer, Bill Scott.

Stadium Name: Parkview Field. **Location:** Downtown Fort Wayne off of Jefferson Blvd. **Ticket Price Range:** $5-12.50.

Visiting Club Hotel: Downtown Courtyard by Marriott, 1150 S Harrison Street, Fort Wayne, IN 46802. **Telephone:** (260) 490-3629.

GREAT LAKES LOONS

Office Address: 825 East Main St, Midland, MI 48640.

Mailing Address: 825 East Main St, Midland, MI 48640.

Telephone: (989) 837-2255. **Fax:** (989) 837-8780.

E-Mail Address: info@loons.com. **Website:** www.loons.com.

Affiliation (fifth year): Los Angeles Dodgers (2007). **Years in League:** 2007-.

OWNERSHIP, MANAGEMENT

Operated By: Michigan Baseball Operations.

Stadium Ownership: Michigan Baseball Foundation.

Founder/Foundation President: William Stavropoulos.

President/General Manager: Paul Barbeau.

Vice President, Corporate Partnerships/Event Operations: Scott Litle. VP, Facilities/Operations: Matt McQuaid. VP, Finance: Tammy Brinkman. VP, Marketing/Entertainment: Chris Mundhenk. GM, ESPN 100.9-FM: Jerry O'Donnell. GM, Dow Diamond Events: Dave Gomola. Assistant GM, Business Operations (Loons)/Director, Programs/Fund Development (MBF): Patti Tuma. Assistant GM, Production/Entertainment: Chris Lones. Assistant GM, Retail Operations/Guest Services: Ann Craig. Assistant GM, Ticket Sales: Lance LeFevre.

Director, Accounting: Jamie Start. Director, Corporate Partnerships: Emily Schafer. Director, Food, Beverage/Catering: Alyson Schafer. Director, Group Sales: Tiffany Seward. Director, Programming (ESPN 100.9-FM): Brad Golder. Director, Promotions: Linda Lones. Director, Sales (ESPN 100.9-FM): Jay Arons. Director, Ticket Operations: Heather Jones.

Assistant to MBF President: Marge Parker. Corporate Account Executive: Kevin Schunk. Account Executive: Marcelle Smith. Group Sales Manager: Jessica Olpere. Communications Manager: Alex Wassel. Traffic Manager: Robin Gover. Payroll Assistant: Cindy Munro. Catering Coordinator: Seleena Carpenter. Executive Chef: Jenny Coleman. Retail Manager: Jenean Clarkson. Stadium Operations Manager: Charlie Dijak. Head, Grounds: Matt Ellis. Grounds Crew Supervisor: Dan Jennings.

FIELD STAFF

Manager: John Shoemaker. Coach: Lenny Harris. Pitching Coach: Kremlin Martinez.

GAME INFORMATION

Radio Announcer: Brad Golder. No. of Games Broadcast: Home-70, Away-70. Flagship Station: ESPN 100.9-FM WLUN.

PA Announcer: Jerry O'Donnell. Official Scorers: Terry Wilczek, Larry Loiselle.

Stadium Name: Dow Diamond. Location: I-75 to US-10 W, Take the M-20/US-10 Business exit on the left toward downtown Midland, Merge onto US-10 W/MI-20 W (also known as Indian Street), Turn left onto State Street, The entrance to the stadium is at the intersection of Ellsworth and State Streets.

Standard Game Times: 6:05 p.m. (April), 7:05 (May-Sept.), Sun. 2:05.

Ticket Price Range: $6-9.

Visiting Club Hotel: Holiday Inn, 810 Cinema Dr, Midland, MI 48642. Telephone: (989) 794-8500.

KANE COUNTY COUGARS

Office Address: 34W002 Cherry Lane, Geneva, IL 60134.
Telephone: (630) 232-8811. Fax: (630) 232-8815.
E-Mail Address: info@kanecountycougars.com. Website: www.kccougars.com.
Affiliation (first year): Kansas City Royals (2011). Years in League: 1991-

OWNERSHIP, MANAGEMENT

Operated By: Cougars Baseball Partnership.

Managing Partners: Mike Woleben, Mike Murtaugh.

Assistant GM/Sales Director: Curtis Haug. Assistant GM, Media/Promotions: Jeff Ney. Concessions Supervisor: Jon Williams. Personnel Manager: Robin Hull. Senior Ticket Sales Representative: Alex Miller. Director, Ticket Operations: Erin Wiencek. Box Office Manager: Rob Koskosky. Ticket Operations: Paul Quillia, Heather Mills, Jenni Brechtel. Director, Community Relation Programming: Amy Mason. Media Relations Coordinator: Shawn Touney. Manager, Advertising Placement: Bill Baker. Design/Graphics: Emmet Broderick. Webmaster/PA Announcer: Kevin Sullivan. Radio Announcer: Jeff Hem. Controller: Doug Czurylo. Finance/Accounting Manager: Lance Buhmann. Director, Security: Dan Klinkhamer. Stadium Operations/Account Executive: Mike Klafehn. Director, Food/Beverage: Mike Koski. Stadium Maintenance Supervisor: Jeff Snyder. Head Groundskeeper: Levi Manche.

FIELD STAFF

Manager: Vance Wilson. Coach: Damon Hollins. Pitching Coach: Jim Brower. Trainer: James Stone.

GAME INFORMATION

Radio Announcer: Jeff Hem. No. of Games Broadcast: Home-70, Away-70. Flagship Station: WBIG 1280-AM.

PA Announcer: Kevin Sullivan. Official Scorer: Bill Baker.

Stadium Name: Philip B. Elfstrom Stadium. Location: From east or west, I-88 (Ronald Reagan Memorial Tollway) to Farnsworth Avenue North exit, north five miles to Cherry Lane, left into stadium complex; from northwest, I-90 (Jane Addams Memorial Tollway) to Randall Road South exit, south to Fabyan Parkway, east to Kirk Road, north to Cherry Lane, left into stadium complex. Standard Game Times: 6:30 p.m., Sat 6, Sun 1. Ticket Price Range: $8-14.

Visiting Club Hotel: Best Western Naperville, 1617 Naperville Rd, Naperville, IL 60563. Telephone: (630) 505-0200.

LAKE COUNTY CAPTAINS

Office Address: Classic Park, 35300 Vine Street, Eastlake, OH 44095-3142.
Telephone: (440) 975-8085. Fax: (440) 975-8958.
E-Mail Address: bseymour@captainsbaseball.com. Website: www.captains-baseball.com.
Affiliation (first year): Cleveland Indians (2003). Years in League: 2010-

OWNERSHIP, MANAGEMENT

Operated By: Cascia, LLC.
Owners: Peter and Rita Carfagna, Ray and Katie Murphy.
Chairman/Secretary/Treasurer: Peter Carfagna. **Vice Chairman:** Rita Carfagna. **Vice President:** Ray Murphy. **Senior VP:** Pete E Carfagna. **VP, General Manager:** Brad Seymour. **Assistant GM, Sales:** Neil Stein. **Senior Director, Media/Community Relations:** Craig Deas. **Director, Promotions:** Jake Schrum. **Director, Captains Concessions:** John Klein. **Manager, Stadium Operations:** Josh Porter. **Director, Turf Management/Stadium Operations:** Jared Olson. **Director, Finance:** Rob Demko. **Manager, Ticket Operations/Merchandise:** Jen Yorko. **Manager, Group Sales:** Amy Gladieux. **Director, Special Projects:** Bill Levy. **Senior Ticket Sales Account Excutive:** Andrew Grover. **Ticket Sales Account Executives:** Josh Berger, David Kodish, Dan Torf. **Office Assistant:** Jim Carfagna.

FIELD STAFF

Manager: Ted Kubiak. **Coach:** Jim Rickon. **Pitching Coach:** Jeff Harris.

GAME INFORMATION

Radio Announcer: Craig Deas. **No. of Games Broadcast:** Home-70, Away-70. **Flagship Station:** WELW 1330-AM.
PA Announcer: Ray Milavec. **Official Scorer:** Glen Blabolil.
Stadium Name: Classic Park. **Location:** From Ohio State Route 2 East, exit at Ohio 91, go left and the stadium is 1/4 mile north on your right. From Ohio State Route 90 East, exit at Ohio 91, go right and the stadium in approximately five miles north on your right. **Standard Game Times:** 7 p.m., Sat 1 (April), 7 (May-Sept), Sun 1.
Visiting Club Hotel: Comfort Inn & Suites, 7701 Reynolds Road, Mentor, OH 44060. **Telephone:** (440) 951-7333.

LANSING LUGNUTS

Office Address: 505 E Michigan Ave, Lansing, MI 48912.
Telephone: (517) 485-4500. **Fax:** (517) 485-4518.
E-Mail Address: info@lansinglugnuts.com. **Website:** www.lansinglugnuts.com.
Affiliation (first year): Toronto Blue Jays (2005). **Years in League:** 1996-

OWNERSHIP, MANAGEMENT

Operated By: Take Me Out to the Ballgame LLC.
Principal Owners: Tom Dickson, Sherrie Myers.
General Manager: Pat Day. **Assistant GM:** Nick Grueser. **Director, Sales:** Nick Brzezinski. **Corporate Account Executives:** Scott Tenney, Kohl Tyrrell. **Group Sales Representatives:** Chris Arth, Eric Beadle, Adam Wood. **Box Office Manager:** Brian Burita. **Season Ticket Concierge:** David Link. **Retail Manager:** Matt Hicks. **Director, Stadium Operations:** Matt Anderson. **Stadium Operations Supervisor:** Dennis Busse. **Director, Food/Beverage:** Brett Telder. **Assistant Director, Food/Beverage:** Mike Koski. **Director, Marketing:** Julia Janssen. **Marketing Assistant:** Lauren Truax. **Sponsorship Service Representatives:** Michaela McAnany, Mia Trimboli. **Business Manager:** Heather Viele. **Assistant Business Manager:** Travis Pohl. **Administrative Assistant:** Angela Sees.

FIELD STAFF

Manager: Mike Redmond. **Coach:** John Tamargo, Jr. **Pitching Coach:** Vince Horsman. **Trainer:** James Gardiner.

GAME INFORMATION

Radio Announcer: Jesse Goldberg-Strassler. **No of Games Broadcast:** Home-70, Away-70. **Flagship Station:** WQTX 92.1-FM.
PA Announcer: Joe Warrick. **Official Scorers:** Seth Van Hoven, Tim Zeko.
Stadium Name: Cooley Law School Stadium. **Location:** I-96 East/West to US 496, exit at Larch Street, north of Larch, stadium on left. **Ticket Price Range:** $8-10.
Visiting Club Hotel: Lexington Lansing Grand Hotel, 925 South Creyts Road, Lansing MI 48917. **Telephone:** (517) 323-7100.

PEORIA CHIEFS

Office Address: 730 SW Jefferson, Peoria, IL 61605.
Telephone: (309) 680-4000. **Fax:** (309) 680-4080.
E-Mail Address: feedback@chiefsnet.com. **Website:** www.peoriachiefs.com.
Affiliation (first year): Chicago Cubs (2005). **Years in League:** 1983-

OWNERSHIP, MANAGEMENT

Operated By: Peoria Chiefs Community Baseball Club LLC.
President: Rocky Vonachen. **Vice President/General Manager:** Ralph Converse. **VP, Corporate Sales:** Josh Morin. **Director, Ticket Sales:** Eric Obalil. **Broadcast/Media Manager:** Nathan Baliva. **Manager, Box Office:** Ryan Sivori. **Entertainment/Events Manager:** Megan Miller. **Director, Guest Services/Account Executive:** John Kramer. **Account Executives:** Justin Hopper, Mike Schulte, Kevin Hall. **Director, Food/Beverage:** Austin Sagolla.

FIELD STAFF

Manager: Casey Kopitzke. **Coach:** Ricardo Medina. **Pitching Coach:** Jeff Fassero. **Trainer:** AJ Larson.

GAME INFORMATION

Radio Announcer: Nathan Baliva. **No. of Games Broadcast:** Home-70, Away-70. **Flagship Station:** Unavailable
PA Announcer: Unavailable. **Official Scorer:** Unavailable.
Stadium Name: O'Brien Field. **Location:** From South/East, I-74 to exit 93 (Jefferson Street), continue one mile, stadium is one block on left; From North/West, I-74 to Glen Oak Exit, Turn right on Glendale which turns into Kumpf Blvd, Turn right on Jefferson, stadium on left. **Standard Game Times:** 7 p.m., 6:30 (April-May, after Aug 24), Sat 6:30, Sun 1.
Ticket Price Range: $7-11.
Visiting Club Hotel: Jameson Inn & Suites, 4112 N Brandywine Drive, Peoria, IL 61614. **Telephone:** 309-685-5226.

QUAD CITIES RIVER BANDITS

Office Address: 209 S Gaines St, Davenport, IA 52802.
Telephone: (563) 322-6348. **Fax:** (563) 324-3109.
E-Mail Address: bandit@riverbandits.com. **Website:** www.riverbandits.com.
Affiliation (first year): St Louis Cardinals (2005). **Years in League:** 1960-.

OWNERSHIP, MANAGEMENT

Operated by: Main Street Iowa LLC, David Heller, Bob Herrfeldt.
Vice President/General Manager: Kirk Goodman.
Assistant GMs: Stefanie Brown, Jamie Jarrett. **VP, Sales:** Shawn Brown. **Director, Media Relations:** Tommy Thrall. **Director, Group Sales:** Matt Tangen. **Director, Baseball Operations:** Bob Evans. **Director, Stadium Operations/ Head Groundskeeper:** Kyle Brudos. **Director, Ticket Operations:** Blake Huckaby. **Director, Special Events:** Andrea Nolan. **Manager, Production:** Andrew Demsky. **Manager, Marketing/Promotions:** Shelley Heward. **Manager, Community Relations/Merchandise:** Whitney Campbell. **Account Executive:** Mickey Kirk. **Director, Food/Beverage:** Ben Blankenship. **Executive Chef:** Patrick Glackin.

FIELD STAFF

Manager: Johnny Rodriguez. **Coach:** Joe Kruzel. **Pitching Coach:** Tim Leveque. **Trainer:** Eric Bauer.

GAME INFORMATION

Radio: None.
PA Announcer: Scott Werling. **Official Scorer:** Jim Tappa.
Stadium Name: Modern Woodmen Park. **Location:** From I-74, take Grant Street exit left, west onto River Drive, left on South Gaines Street; from I-80, take Brady Street exit south, right on River Drive, left on South Gaines Street. **Standard Game Times:** 7 p.m.,
Sat: 6, Sun: 1 (April-May, Aug-Sept), 5 (June-July). **Ticket Price Range:** $5-12.
Visiting Club Hotel: Clarion Hotel, 5202 Brady St, Davenport, IA 52806. **Telephone:** (563) 391-1230.

SOUTH BEND
SILVER HAWKS

Office Address: 501 W South St, South Bend, IN 46601.
Mailing Address: PO Box 4218, South Bend, IN 46634.
Telephone: (574) 235-9988. **Fax:** (574) 235-9950.
E-Mail Address: hawks@silverhawks.com. **Website:** www.silverhawks.com.
Affiliation (first year): Arizona Diamondbacks (1997). **Years in League:** 1988-.

OWNERSHIP, MANAGEMENT

Operated By: South Bend Professional Baseball Club LLC.
President: Joe Kernan.
Vice President/General Manager: Lynn Kachmarik. **Assistant GM, Operations:** Peter Argueta. **Director, Finance:** Cheryl Carlson. **Director, Sales/Marketing:** Nicolle Meyer. **Director, Group/Corporate Partnerships:** James McAvoy. **Director, Merchandise:** Jeff Scholfield. **Director, Production:** Todd Edwards. **Assistant Director, Marketing/ Promotions:** Emily Riggs. **Assistant Director, Marketing/Media/Broadcasting:** Owen Serey. **Group Partnership Executives:** Dan Loding, Andrew Bowen, Robbie Lightfoot. **Head Groundskeeper:** Joel Reinebold.

FIELD STAFF

Manager: Mark Haley. **Coach:** Bobby Smith. **Pitching Coach:** Wellington Cepeda. **Trainer:** Brian Czachowski. **Strength Coach:** Jason Mitchell.

GAME INFORMATION

Radio Announcer: Owen Serey. **Flagship Station:** WDND 1620-AM ESPN Radio.
Stadium Name: Stanley Coveleski Regional Stadium. **Location:** I-80/90 toll road to exit 77, take US 31/33 south to South Bend to downtown (Main Street), to Western Avenue, right on Western, left on Taylor. **Ticket Price Range:** $6-8.
Visiting Club Hotel: Ramada Plaza Hotel 213 W Washington, South Bend, IN 46601. **Telephone:** (574) 232-3941.

WEST MICHIGAN
WHITECAPS

Office Address: 4500 West River Dr, Comstock Park, MI 49321.
Mailing Address: PO Box 428, Comstock Park, MI 49321.
Telephone: (616) 784-4131. **Fax:** (616) 784-4911.
E-Mail Address: playball@whitecaps-baseball.com. **Website:** www.whitecapsbaseball.com.
Affiliation (first year): Detroit Tigers (1997). **Years in League:** 1994-

OWNERSHIP, MANAGEMENT

Operated By: Whitecaps Professional Baseball Corp.
Principal Owners: Denny Baxter, Lew Chamberlin.
President: Scott Lane. **Vice President, Whitecaps Professional Baseball:** Jim Jarecki. **VP, Sales:** Steve McCarthy.
Manager, Facility Events: Dan Glowinski. **Manager, Operations:** Craig Yust. **Director, Food/Beverage:** Matt Timon.
Community Relations Coordinator: Anna Petersen. **Director, Marketing/Media:** Mickey Graham. **Promotions/Multi-Media Manager:** Brian Oropallo. **Box Office Manager:** Meghan Brennan. **Groundskeeper:** Greg Salyer. **Manager, Facility Maintenance:** John Passarelli. **Director, Ticket Sales:** Chad Sayen.

FIELD STAFF

Manager: Ernie Young. **Coach:** Ben Olgivie. **Pitching Coach:** Mark Saunders. **Trainer:** Corey Tremble.

GAME INFORMATION

Radio Announcers: Ben Chiswick, Dan Elve. **No. of Games Broadcast:** Home-70, Away-70. **Flagship Station:** WBBL 107.3-FM.
PA Announcers: Mike Newell, Bob Wells. **Official Scorers:** Mike Dean, Don Thomas.
Stadium Name: Fifth Third Ballpark. **Location:** US 131 North from Grand Rapids to exit 91 (West River Drive). **Ticket Price Range:** $6-13.
Visiting Club Hotel: Holiday Inn Express-GR North, 358 River Ridge Dr NW, Walker, MI 49544. **Telephone:** (616) 647-4100.

WISCONSIN TIMBER RATTLERS

Office Address: 2400 N Casaloma Dr, Appleton, WI 54913.
Mailing Address: PO Box 7464, Appleton, WI 54912.
Telephone: (920) 733-4152. **Fax:** (920) 733-8032.
E-Mail Address: info@timberrattlers.com. **Website:** www.timberrattlers.com.
Affiliation (first year): Milwaukee Brewers (2009). **Years in League:** 1962-

OWNERSHIP, MANAGEMENT

Operated By: Appleton Baseball Club, Inc.
Chairman: Alan Stewart.
President/General Manager: Rob Zerjav. **Assistant GM/Director, Ticket Sales:** Aaron Hahn. **Controller:** Cathy Spanbauer. **Vice President, Marketing:** Angie Ceranski. **Director, Media Relations:** Chris Mehring. **Director, Food/Beverage:** Ryan Grossman. **Director, Stadium Operations:** Ron Kaiser. **Director, Community Relations:** Dayna Baitinger. **Corporate Partnerships:** Ryan Cunniff, Brett Nagan. **Merchandise Manager:** Jay Gruszynski. **Box Office Manager:** Ryan Moede. **Group Sales:** Brandon Goebel, Chumley Hodgson, Seth Merrill. **Graphic Designer/Marketing Assistant:** Ann Mollica. **Production Manager/Marketing Assistant:** Cameron Wengrzyn. **Team Operations/Clubhouse Manager:** Seth Hatley. **Office Manager:** Mary Robinson. **Groundskeeper:** Eddie Warczak.

FIELD STAFF

Manager: Matt Erickson. **Coach:** Dusty Rhodes. **Pitching Coach:** Chris Hook. **Trainer:** Jeff Paxson.

GAME INFORMATION

Radio Announcer: Chris Mehring. **No. of Games Broadcast:** Home-70, Away-70. **Flagship Station:** WNAM 1280-AM.
PA Announcer: Joe Dotterweich. **Official Scorer:** Jay Grusznski.
Stadium Name: Time Warner Cable Field at Fox Cities Stadium. **Location:** Highway 41 to Highway 15 (00) exit, west to Casaloma Drive, left to stadium. **Standard Game Times:** 7:05 p.m., 6:35 (April-May); Sat 6:35; Sun 1:05. **Ticket Price Range:** $5-10.
Visiting Club Hotel: Microtel Inn & Suites, 321 Metro Dr, Appleton, WI 54913. **Telephone:** (920) 997-3121.

SOUTH ATLANTIC LEAGUE

Office Address: 111 Second Avenue NE, Suite 335, St Petersburg, FL 33701.
Telephone: (727) 456-1240. **Fax:** (727) 499-6853.
E-Mail Address: office@saloffice.com. **Website:** www.southatlanticleague.com.
Years League Active: 1904-1964, 1979-.
President/Secretary/Treasurer: Eric Krupa.
First Vice President: Chip Moore (Rome). **Second Vice President:** Craig Brown (Greenville).
Directors: Don Beaver (Hickory), Cooper Brantley (Greensboro), Craig Brown (Greenville), Brian DeWine (Asheville), Jeff Eiseman (Augusta), Joseph Finley (Lakewood), Jason Freier (Savannah), Marvin Goldklang (Charleston), Alan Levin (West Virginia), Chip Moore (Rome), Bruce Quinn (Hagerstown), Brad Smith (Kannapolis), Alan Stein (Lexington), Tom Volpe (Delmarva).
Division Structure: North—Delmarva, Greensboro, Hagerstown, Hickory, Kannapolis, Lakewood, West Virginia. South—Asheville, Augusta, Charleston, Greenville, Lexington, Rome, Savannah.
Regular Season: 140 games (split schedule). **2011 Opening Date:** April 7. **Closing Date:** Sept. 5.

Eric Krupa

All-Star Game: June 21 at Delmarva.
Playoff Format: First-half and second-half division winners meet in best-of-three semifinal series. Winners meet in best-of-five series for league championship.
Roster Limit: 25 active. **Player Eligibility Rule:** No age limit. No more than two players and one player-coach on active list may have more than five years of experience.
Brand of Baseball: Rawlings.
Umpires: Joshua Clark (McDonough, GA), Garrett Corl (Port Matilda, PA), Jose Esteras (Hialeah, FL), Bryan Fields (Dallas, TX), Ramon Hernandez (Columbia, MO), Aaron Larsen (Tomah, WI), Benjamin Leake (Roswell, GA), Shane Livensparger (Ponte Vedra Beach, FL), Roberto Ortiz (Caguas, PR), Lawrence Reeves (Elizabeth City, NC), Aaron Reynolds (Columbia, MO), Jeremy Riggs (Suffolk, VA), Aaron Roberts (Moose Jaw, SK, Canada), Carlos Torres (Acarigua Portuguesa, Venezuela).

STADIUM INFORMATION

| Club | Stadium | Opened | Dimensions | | | Capacity | 2010 Att. |
			LF	CF	RF		
Asheville	McCormick Field	1992	326	373	297	4,000	160,023
Augusta	Lake Olmstead Stadium	1995	330	400	330	4,322	201,760
Charleston	Joseph P. Riley Jr. Ballpark	1997	306	386	336	5,800	269,023
Delmarva	Arthur W. Perdue Stadium	1996	309	402	309	5,200	221,051
Greensboro	NewBridge Bank Park	2005	322	400	320	7,599	379,511
Greenville	Fluor Field	2006	310	400	302	5,000	337,918
Hagerstown	Municipal Stadium	1931	335	400	330	4,600	135,799
Hickory	L.P. Frans Stadium	1993	330	401	330	5,062	140,789
Kannapolis	Fieldcrest Cannon Stadium	1995	330	400	310	4,700	123,828
Lakewood	FirstEnergy Park	2001	325	400	325	6,588	431,954
Lexington	Applebee's Park	2001	320	401	318	6,033	336,168
Rome	State Mutual Stadium	2003	335	400	330	5,100	193,061
Savannah	Historic Grayson Stadium	1941	290	410	310	8,000	120,426
West Virginia	Appalachian Power Park	2005	330	400	320	4,300	172,344

ASHEVILLE TOURISTS

Office Address: McCormick Field, 30 Buchanan Place, Asheville, NC 28801.
Telephone: (828) 258-0428. **Fax:** (828) 258-0320.
E-Mail Address: info@theashevilletourists.com. **Website:** www.theashevilletourists.com.
Affiliation (first year): Colorado Rockies (1994). **Years in League:** 1976-

OWNERSHIP, MANAGEMENT

Operated By: DeWine Seeds Silver Dollar Baseball LLC.
President: Brian DeWine.
General Manager: Larry Hawkins. **Assistant GM:** Chris Smith. **Box Office Manager:** Patrick Spence. **Office Manager:** Ryan Straney. **Merchandise/Promotions Manager:** Jon Clemmons. **Director, Broadcasting:** Doug Maurer. **Group Sales Manager:** Matt Riley. **Group Sales Representatives:** Danielle Hanula, Jamie Shand. **Outside Sales Representative:** Bob Jones. **Operations Manager:** Nick Cataldi. **Director, Food/Beverage:** Craig Phillips. **Publications/Website:** Bill Ballew.

FIELD STAFF

Manager: Joe Mikulik. **Coach:** Lenn Sakata. **Pitching Coach:** Joey Eischen. **Trainer:** Billy Whitehead.

GAME INFORMATION

Radio Announcer: Doug Maurer. **No. of Games Broadcast:** Home-70, Away-70. **Flagship Station:** WRES 100.7-FM.
PA Announcer: Rick Diggler. **Official Scorers:** Mike Gore, Jim Baker.
Stadium Name: McCormick Field. **Location:** I-240 to Charlotte Street South exit, south one mile on Charlotte, left on McCormick Place. **Ticket Price Range:** $6-11.
Visiting Club Hotel: Quality Inn, 1 Skyline Drive, Arden, NC 28704. **Telephone:** (828) 684-6688.

AUGUSTA GREENJACKETS

Office Address: 78 Milledge Rd., Augusta, GA 30904.
Mailing Address: PO Box 3746 Hill Station, Augusta, GA 30914.
Telephone: (706) 736-7889. **Fax:** (706) 736-1122.
E-Mail Address: info@greenjacketsbaseball.com. **Website:** www.greenjacketsbaseball.com.
Affiliation (first year): San Francisco Giants (2005). **Years in League:** 1988-.

OWNERSHIP, MANAGEMENT

Owners: Baseball Enterprises, LCC.
Operated By: Ripken Professional Baseball.
General Manager: Nick Brown. **Director, Stadium Operations:** David Ryther, Jr. **Director, Game Entertainment/ Marketing:** Lauren Christie. **Ticket Sales Manager:** Andy Beuster. **Corporate Partnership Manager:** Jonathan Pribble.
Box Office Manager: Brian Marshall. **Account Executives:** Joe Reeder, Dan Szatkowski, Zach Lecker, Marissa Ponzi, Gabe Gadson. **Bookkeeper:** Debbie Brown.

FIELD STAFF

Manager: Lipso Nava. **Coach:** Jose Flores. **Pitching Coach:** Steve Kline. **Trainer:** David Getsoff.

GAME INFORMATION

Radio Announcer: Eric Little. **No. of Games Broadcast:** Home-70, Away-70. **Flagship Station:** WRDW 1630-AM.
PA Announcer: Scott Skadan. **Official Scorer:** Ted Miller.
Stadium Name: Lake Olmstead Stadium. **Location:** I-20 to Washington Road exit, east to Broad Street exit, left on Milledge Road. **Standard Game Times:** 7:05 p.m.; Sun 2:05/5:35. **Ticket Price Range:** $7-12.
Visiting Club Hotel: Baymont Inn & Suites, 629 Northwest Frontage Road, Augusta, GA 30907. **Telephone:** (706) 855-6060.

CHARLESTON RIVERDOGS

Office Address: 360 Fishburne St, Charleston, SC 29403.
Mailing Address: PO Box 20849, Charleston, SC 29413.
Telephone: (843) 723-7241. **Fax:** (843) 723-2641.
E-Mail Address: admin@riverdogs.com. **Website:** www.riverdogs.com.
Affiliation (first year): New York Yankees (2005). **Years in League:** 1973-78, 1980-.

OWNERSHIP, MANAGEMENT

Operated by: The Goldklang Group/South Carolina Baseball Club LP.
Chairman: Marv Goldklang. **President:** Mike Veeck. **Director of Fun:** Bill Murray.
Co-Owners: Dr Gene Budig, Al Phillips, Peter Freund.
Executive Vice President/General Manager: Dave Echols. **Assistant GMs:** Andy Lange, Harold Craw. **Director, Promotions:** Noel Blaha. **Director, Media Relations:** Andy Solomon. **Business Manager:** Dale Stickney. **Director, Special Events:** Melissa McCants. **Sales Managers:** Jake Terrell, Mike Petrini. **Office Manager:** Kristal Lessington. **Director, Community Relations:** Sarah Ward. **Box Office Manager:** David Cullins. **Director, Merchandise:** Mike DeAntonio. **Head Groundskeeper:** Mike Williams. **Clubhouse Manager:** Vinnie Colangelo.

FIELD STAFF

Manager: Aaron Ledesma. **Coach:** Greg Colbrunn. **Pitching Coach:** Carlos Chantres. **First-Base Coach:** Victor Valencia. **Trainer:** Lee Meyer. **Strength/Conditioning Coach:** Mike Kicia

GAME INFORMATION

Radio Announcer: Danny Reed. **No. of Games Broadcast:** Home-70, Away-70. **Flagship Station:** WTMZ 910-AM.
PA Announcer: Ken Carrington. **Official Scorer:** Chuck Manka.
Stadium Name: Joseph P Riley Jr Ballpark. **Location:** From US 17, take Lockwood Drive North, right on Fishburne Street. **Standard Game Times:** 7:05 p.m., Sun 5:05. **Ticket Price Range:** $5-15.
Visiting Club Hotel: Best Western, 146 Lockwood Dr, Charleston, SC 29403.Telephone: (843) 722-4000.

DELMARVA SHOREBIRDS

Office Address: 6400 Hobbs Rd, Salisbury, MD 21804.
Mailing Address: PO Box 1557, Salisbury, MD 21802.
Telephone: (410) 219-3112. **Fax:** (410) 219-9164.
E-Mail Address: information@theshorebirds.com. **Website:** www.theshorebirds.com.
Affiliation (first year): Baltimore Orioles (1997). **Years in League:** 1996-.

OWNERSHIP, MANAGEMENT

Operated By: 7th Inning Stretch, LLP.
Directors: Tom Volpe, Pat Filippone.
General Manager: Chris Bitters.
Assistant GM: Jimmy Sweet. **Director, Community Relations/Marketing:** Shawn Schoolcraft. **Director, Ticket Sales:** David Bledsoe. **Group Sales Manager:** Sam Ward. **Senior Ticket Sales Executive:** Brandon Berns. **Ticket Sales Account Executive:** Mike Steinhice. **Director, Stadium Operations:** Aaron Becker. **Head Groundskeeper:** Dave Super. **Director, Broadcasting/Graphic Design:** Bret Lasky. **Corporate Sales/Special Events Executive:** Stephanie Cohn. **Accounting Manager:** Gail Potts. **Office Manager:** Audrey Vane.

FIELD STAFF

Manager: Ryan Minor. **Coach:** Leo Gomez. **Pitching Coach:** Troy Mattes.

GAME INFORMATION

Radio Announcer: Bret Lasky. **No of Games Broadcast:** Home-70, Away-70. **Flagship Station:** Unavailable.
PA Announcer: Unavailable. **Official Scorer:** Gary Hicks.
Stadium Name: Arthur W Perdue Stadium. **Location:** From US 50 East, right on Hobbs Road; From US 50 West, left on Hobbs Road. **Standard Game Times:** 7:05 p.m. **Ticket Price Range:** $4-12.
Visiting Club Hotel: Unavailable

GREENSBORO GRASSHOPPERS

Office Address: 408 Bellemeade St, Greensboro, NC 27401.
Telephone: (336) 268-2255. **Fax:** (336) 273-7350.
E-Mail Address: info@gsohoppers.com. **Website:** www.gsohoppers.com.
Affiliation (first year): Florida Marlins (2003). **Years in League:** 1979-.

OWNERSHIP, MANAGEMENT

Operated By: Greensboro Baseball LLC.
Principal Owners: Cooper Brantley, Wes Elingburg, Len White.
President/General Manager: Donald Moore.
Vice President, Baseball Operations: Katie Dannemiller. **CFO:** Jimmy Kesler. **Assistant GM/Head Groundskeeper:** Jake Holloway. **Assistant GM, Sales/Marketing:** Tim Vangel. **Director, Ticket Sales:** Erich Dietz. **Director, Community/ Event Development:** Laura Damico. **Director, Production/Entertainment:** Shawn Russell. **Director, Creative Services:** Amanda Williams. **Director, Merchandise:** Yunhui Bradshaw. **Executive Director, Business Development:** John Redhead. **Group Sales Associates:** Travis Kerstetter, Todd Olson. **Sales Associate:** Rosalee Brewer. **Assistant Director, Stadium Operations:** Chad Green. **Assistant Groundskeeper:** Kaid Musgrave.

FIELD STAFF

Manager: Andy Haines. **Coach:** Kevin Randel. **Pitching Coach:** Willie Glen. **Trainer:** Masa Fujimoto.

GAME INFORMATION

Radio Announcer: Andy Durham. **No. of Games Broadcast:** Home-70, Away-0. **Flagship Station:** WPET 950-AM.
PA Announcer: Jim Scott. **Official Scorer:** Paul Wirth.
Stadium Name: NewBridge Bank Park. **Location:** From I-85, take Highway 220 South (exit 36) to Coliseum Blvd, continue on Edgeworth Street, ballpark at corner of Edgeworth and Bellemeade Streets. **Standard Game Times:** 7 p.m., Sun 4. **Ticket Price Range:** $6-9.
Visiting Club Hotel: Continental Inn & Suites 6102 Landmark Center Boulevard, Greensboro, NC 27407. **Telephone:** (336) 553-2763.

GREENVILLE DRIVE

Office Address: 945 South Main St, Greenville, SC 29601.
Telephone: (864) 240-4500. **Fax:** (864) 240-4501.
E-Mail Address: info@greenvilledrive.com. **Website:** www.greenvilledrive.com.
Affiliation (first year): Boston Red Sox (2005). **Years in League:** 2005-

OWNERSHIP, MANAGEMENT
Operated By: Greenville Drive, LLC.
Co-Owner/President: Craig Brown.
Co-Owners: Roy Bostock, Paul Raether.
General Manager: Mike deMaine. **Senior Vice President:** Nate Lipscomb. **VP, Finance:** Cathy Boortz. **VP, Ticket Sales:** Brad Sexton. **Senior Director, Marketing/Media Services:** Eric Jarinko. **Director, Food/Beverage:** Larry Mattson. **Director, Merchandise:** Kelly Trnka. **Director, Game Entertainment:** Jon Eckert. **Sponsor/Event Services Manager:** Samantha Lussier. **Partner Services Manager:** Jennifer Brown. **Production Manager:** Sam LoBosco. **Box Office Manager:** Ryan Miller. **Special Projects Manager:** Samantha Bauer. **Concessions Manager:** Michael Rennison. **Account Executives:** Jeff Chiappini, Brendan Jones, Ashley Peden. **Head Groundskeeper:** Greg Burgess. **Assistant Groundskeeper:** Ross Groenevelt. **General Accountant:** Connie Pynne.

FIELD STAFF
Manager: Billy McMillon. **Coach:** Luis Lopez. **Pitching Coach:** Dick Such. **Head Trainer:** David Herrera.

GAME INFORMATION
Radio Announcer: Unavailable.
No. of Games Broadcast: Home-70, Away-0. **Flagship Station:** www.greenvilledrive.com.
PA Announcer: Chris Lee. **Official Scorer:** Sanford Rogers.
Stadium Name: Fluor Field. **Location:** From south: I-85N to exit 42 toward downtown Greenville, turn left onto Augusta Road, stadium is two miles on the left. **From north:** I-85S to I-385 toward Greenville, turn left onto Church Street, turn right onto University Ridge. **Standard Game Times:** 7 p.m., Sun 4. **Ticket Price Range:** $5-8.
Visiting Club Hotel: Hampton Inn Greenville-Haywood, 246 Congaree Road, Greenville, SC 29607. **Telephone:** (864) 288-1200.

HAGERSTOWN SUNS

HAGERSTOWN SUNS

Office Address: 274 E Memorial Blvd, Hagerstown, MD 21740.
Telephone: (301) 791-6266. **Fax:** (301) 791-6066.
E-Mail Address: info@hagerstownsuns.com. **Website:** www.hagerstownsuns.com.
Affiliation (first year): Washington Nationals (2007). **Years in League:** 1993-

OWNERSHIP, MANAGEMENT
Principal Owner/Operated by: Hagerstown Baseball LLC.
President: Bruce Quinn. **General Manager:** Bill Farley.
Director, Media Relations/Broadcasting: Bryan Holland. **Director, Marketing/Community Relations:** Sara Grasmon. **Director, Entertainment:** Rechelle Bischoff. **Director, Operations:** Tony Iovieno. **Corporate Sales Executive:** Chris Vierling. **Group Sales Executive:** Josh Mastin. **Ticket Sales Executive:** Ben Scheffel. **Head Groundskeeper:** Brian Eiche. **Clubhouse Manager:** Michael Jech.

FIELD STAFF
Manager: Brian Daubach. **Coach:** Marlon Anderson. **Pitching Coach:** Chris Michalak. **Trainer:** Jon Kotredes.

GAME INFORMATION
Radio Announcer: Bryan Holland. **No. of Games Broadcast:** Home-70, Away-70. **Flagship Station:** Unavailable.
PA Announcer: Danny Grove. **Official Scorer:** Will Kauffman.
Stadium Name: Municipal Stadium. **Location:** Exit 32B (US 40 West) on I-70 West, left at Eastern Boulevard; Exit 6A (US 40 East) on I-81, right at Eastern Boulevard. **Standard Game Times:** 6:35 p.m. (April-May); 7:05 (June-Sept); Sun. 4:05 (April-Aug). **Ticket Price Range:** $8-11.
Visiting Club Hotel: Clarion Hotel, 901 Dual Highway, Hagerstown, MD, 21740.

HICKORY CRAWDADS

Office Address: 2500 Clement Blvd NW, Hickory, NC 28601.
Mailing Address: PO Box 1268, Hickory, NC 28603.
Telephone: (828) 322-3000. **Fax:** (828) 322-6137.
E-Mail Address: crawdad@hickorycrawdads.com. **Website:** www.hickorycrawdads.com.
Affiliation (first year): Texas Rangers (2009). **Years in League:** 1952, 1960, 1993-

OWNERSHIP, MANAGEMENT
Operated by: Hickory Baseball Inc.
Principal Owners: Don Beaver, Luther Beaver, Charles Young.
President: Don Beaver. **General Manager:** Mark Seaman.
Assistant GM: Charlie Downs. **Director, Promotions:** Jonathan Mercier. **Director, Broadcasting/Media Relations:** Andrew Buchbinder. **Business Manager:** Donna White. **Head Groundskeeper:** Andrew Tallent. **Clubhouse Manager:** Chris Ackerman. **Director, Group Sales:** Kathryn Bobel. **Director, Ticket Operations/Merchandising:** Douglas Locascio. **Group Sales Assistants:** Megan Meade, Ryan Chenoweth. **Media Relations Assistant:** Alexander Leopold. **Concessions Assistant:** Stephen O'Berg. **Promotions Assistant:** Jared Weymier. **Stadium Operations Assistant:** Derek Bonner.

FIELD STAFF
Manager: Bill Richardson. **Coach:** Jason Hart. **Pitching Coach:** Storm Davis. **Coach:** Corey Ragsdale. **Trainer:** Jacob Newburn. **Strength/Conditioning:** Anthony Miller.

GAME INFORMATION
Radio Announcer: Andrew Buchbinder. **No. of Games Broadcast:** Home-70, Away-70. **Flagship Station:** WMNC 92.1-FM.
PA Announcers: Ralph Mangum, Jason Savage. **Official Scorer:** Mark Parker.
Stadium Name: L.P Frans Stadium. **Location:** I-40 to exit 123 (Lenoir North), 321 North to Clement Blvd, left for 1/2 mile. **Standard Game Times:** 7 p.m., Sun. 5.
Visiting Club Hotel: Crowne Plaza, 1385 Lenior-Rhyne Boulevard SE, Hickory, NC 28602. **Telephone:** (828) 323-1000.

KANNAPOLIS INTIMIDATORS

Office Address: 2888 Moose Rd, Kannapolis, NC 28083.
Mailing Address: PO Box 64, Kannapolis, NC 28082.
Telephone: (704) 932-3267. **Fax:** (704) 938-7040.
E-Mail Address: info@intimidatorsbaseball.com.
Website: www.intimidatorsbaseball.com.
Affiliation (first year): Chicago White Sox (2001). **Years in League:** 1995-

OWNERSHIP, MANAGEMENT
Operated by: Smith Family Baseball Inc.
President: Brad Smith.
Vice President: Tim Mueller. **General Manager:** Randy Long. **Head Groundskeeper/Director, Stadium Operations:** Billy Ball. **Director, Ticket Sales:** Jason Bright. **Director, Group Sales:** Greg Pizzuto. **Director, Broadcasting/Media Relations/Sales Executive:** Josh Feldman. **Food/Beverage Manager:** Mark Harley. **Intern:** Blair Hooper.

FIELD STAFF
Manager: Tommy Thompson. **Coach:** Rob Sasser. **Pitching Coach:** Jose Bautista. **Trainer:** Scott Johnson. **Strength/Conditioning Coach:** Jeremie Imbus.

GAME INFORMATION
Radio Announcer: Josh Feldman. **No. of Games Broadcast:** Home-70, Away-0. **Flagship Station:** www.intimidatorsbaseball.com.
PA Announcer: Sean Fox. **Official Scorer:** Unavailable.
Stadium Name: Fieldcrest Cannon Stadium. **Location:** Exit 63 on I-85, west on Lane Street to Stadium Drive. **Standard Game Times:** 7:05 p.m., Sun. 5:05. **Ticket Price Range:** $5-$9.
Visiting Club Hotel: Fairfield Inn by Marriott, 3033 Cloverleaf Pkwy, Kannapolis, NC 28083. **Telephone:** (704) 795-4888.

LAKEWOOD BLUECLAWS

Office Address: 2 Stadium Way, Lakewood, NJ 08701.
Telephone: (732) 901-7000. **Fax:** (732) 901-3967.
Email Address: info@blueclaws.com. **Website:** www.blueclaws.com.
Affiliation (first year): Philadelphia Phillies (2001). **Years in League:** 2001-

OWNERSHIP, MANAGEMENT

Operated By: American Baseball Company, LLC.
President: Joseph Finley. **Partners:** Joseph Caruso, Lewis Eisenberg, Joseph Plumeri, Craig Stein.
General Manager: Geoff Brown. **Assistant GM, Operations:** Brandon Marano. **Assistant GM, Sales:** Rich Mozingo.
Controller: Bob Halsey. **Director, Marketing:** Mike Ryan. **Director, Promotions:** Hal Hansen. **Director, Community Relations:** Jim DeAngelis. **Director, Business Development:** Dan DeYoung. **Director, Group Sales:** Jim McNamara. **Director, New Client Development:** Mike Van Hise. **Director, Ticket Operations:** Rebecca Ramos. **Director, Ticket Sales:** Joe Harrington. **Director, Special Events:** Steve Farago. **Director, Inside Sales:** Lisa Carone. **Director, Food/Beverage Services:** Chris Tafrow. **Executive Chef:** Sandy Cohen.
Front Office Manager: Jaimie Smith. **Media/Public Relations Manager:** Greg Giombarrese. **Group Sales Manager:** Ross Pibal. **Ticket Sales Manager:** Rob Vota. **Regional Sales Managers:** Casey Coppinger, Kevin Fenstermacher, Whitney Goulish. **Corporate Sales Manager:** Joe Pilon. **Merchandise Manager:** Garret Streisel. **Marketing Manager:** Amy DeMichele. **Ticket Sales Coordinator:** Kevin Kay. **Clubhouse Manager:** Russ Schaffer. **Head Groundskeeper:** Ryan Radcliffe.

Field Staff

Manager: Chris Truby. **Coach:** Greg Legg. **Pitching Coach:** Steve Schrenk. **Trainer:** Mickey Kozack.

Game Information

Radio Announcers: Greg Giombarrese, Sean Houston. **No. of Games Broadcast:** Home-70, Away-70. **Flagship Station:** WOBM 1160-AM.
PA Announcers: Kevin Clark, Mike Gavin. **Official Scorer:** Joe Bellina.
Stadium Name: FirstEnergy Park. **Location:** Route 70 to New Hampshire Ave, north on New Hampshire for 2 1/2 miles to ballpark. **Standard Game Times:** 7:05 p.m., 6:35 (April-May); Sun 1:05, 5:05 (July-Aug). **Ticket Prices:** $7-11.
Visiting Team Hotel: Quality Inn of Toms River, 815 Route 37 West, Toms River, NJ 08755. **Telephone:** (732) 341-3400.

LEXINGTON LEGENDS

Office Address: 207 Legends Lane, Lexington, KY 40505.
Telephone: (859) 252-4487. **Fax:** (859) 252-0747.
E-Mail Address: webmaster@lexingtonlegends.com. **Website:** www.lexington-legends.com.
Affiliation (first year): Houston Astros (2001). **Years in League:** 2001-

OWNERSHIP, MANAGEMENT

Operated By: Ivy Walls Management Co.
Principal Owner: Bill Shea. **President/COO:** Alan Stein.
General Manager: Andy Shea. **Vice President, Facilities:** Gary Durbin. **Director, Stadium Operations/Human Resource Manager:** Shannon Kidd. **Business Manager:** Jeff Black. **Staff Accountant:** Tina Wright. **Director, Marketing:** Seth Poteat. **Box Office Manager:** David Barry. **Director, Ticket Operations:** Adam English. **Director, Broadcasting/Media Relations:** Keith Elkins. **Account Executive:** Ron Borkowski. **Group Sales Director:** Justin Ball. **Senior Sales Executive:** Kyle Krebs. **Office Manager/Community Relations:** Stephanie Fish. **Promotions Coordinator:** Lauren Shrader. **Head Groundskeeper:** Blake Anderson. **Facility Specialist:** Steve Moore.

FIELD STAFF

Manager: Rodney Linares. **Coach:** Joel Chimelis. **Pitching Coach:** Dave Borkowski. **Trainer:** Grant Hufford.

GAME INFORMATION

Radio Announcer: Keith Elkins. **No of Games Broadcast:** Home-70, Away-70. **Flagship Station:** WLXG 1300-AM.
PA Announcer: Unavailable. **Official Scorer:** Travis Weber.
Stadium Name: Applebee's Park. **Location:** From I-64/75, take exit 113, right onto North Broadway toward downtown Lexington for 1.2 miles, past New Circle Road (Highway 4), right into stadium, located adjacent to Northland Shopping Center. **Standard Game Times:** 7:05 p.m., Sun. 2:05 (April-May), 5:05 (June-Aug). **Ticket Price Range:** $4-$22.
Visiting Club Hotel: Ramada Inn and Conference Center, 2143 N Broadway, Lexington, KY 40505. **Telephone:** (859) 299-1261.

ROME BRAVES

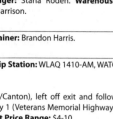

Office Address: State Mutual Stadium, 755 Braves Blvd, Rome, GA 30161.
Mailing Address: PO Box 1915, Rome, GA 30162-1915.
Telephone: (706) 368-9388. **Fax:** (706) 368-6525.
E-Mail Address: rome.braves@braves.com. **Website:** www.romebraves.com.
Affiliation (first year): Atlanta Braves (2003). **Years in League:** 2003-.

OWNERSHIP, MANAGEMENT
Operated By: Atlanta National League Baseball Club Inc.
General Manager: Michael Dunn. **Assistant GM:** Jim Jones. **Director, Stadium Operations:** Eric Allman. **Director, Ticket Manager:** Doug Bryller. **Director, Director, Culinary Services:** Dave Atwood. **Food/Beverage Director:** Brad Smith. **Special Projects Manager:** Erin White. **Administrative Manager:** Libby Simons. **Account Representatives:** John Layng, David Lembeck. **Head Groundskeeper:** Mike Geiger. **Retail Manager:** Starla Roden. **Warehouse Operations Manager:** Terry Morgan. **Neighborhood Outreach Coordinator:** Laura Harrison.

FIELD STAFF
Manager: Matt Walbeck. **Coach:** Carlos Mendez. **Pitching Coach:** Derrick Lewis. **Trainer:** Brandon Harris.

GAME INFORMATION
Radio Announcer: JB Smith. **No. of Games Broadcast:** Home-70, Away-70. **Flagship Station:** WLAQ 1410-AM, WATG 95.7 FM.
PA Announcer: Unavailable. **Official Scorers:** Jim O'Hara, Lyndon Huckaby.
Stadium Name: State Mutual Stadium. **Location:** I-75 North to exit 190 (Rome/Canton), left off exit and follow Highway 411/Highway 20 to Rome, right at intersection on Highway 411 and Highway 1 (Veterans Memorial Highway), stadium is at intersection of Veterans Memorial Highway and Riverside Parkway. **Ticket Price Range:** $4-10.
Visiting Club Hotel: Days Inn, 840 Turner McCall Blvd, Rome, GA 30161. **Telephone:** (706) 295-0400.

SAVANNAH SAND GNATS

Office Address: 1401 E Victory Dr, Savannah, GA 31404.
Mailing Address: PO Box 3783, Savannah, GA 31414.
Telephone: (912) 351-9150. **Fax:** (912) 352-9722.
E-Mail Address: info@sandgnats.com. **Website:** www.sandgnats.com.
Affiliation (first year): New York Mets (2007). **Years in League:** 1904-1915, 1936-1960, 1962, 1984-

OWNERSHIP, MANAGEMENT
Operated By: Savannah Professional Baseball, LLC.
President: John Katz.
Vice President, Business Operations: Jeremy Auker. **VP, Food/Beverage:** Scott Burton. **Public Affairs, Special Events/Merchandise Manager:** Ryan Kirwan. **Stadium Operations Manager:** Evan Christian. **Ticketing/Accounting Manager:** Darryl Aldridge. **Group Sales Manager:** Chase Polhemus. **Director, Broadcasting/Communications:** Toby Hyde. **Head Groundskeeper:** Andy Rock.

FIELD STAFF
Manager: Ryan Ellis. **Coach:** B Distefano/J Carreno. **Pitching Coach:** Glenn Abbott.

GAME INFORMATION
Radio Announcer: Toby Hyde. **No. of Games Broadcast:** Home-70, Away-0. **Flagship Station:** WBMQ 960-AM.
PA Announcer: Unavailable. **Official Scorer:** Michael MacEachern.
Stadium Name: Historic Grayson Stadium. **Location:** I-16 to 37th Street exit, left on 37th, right on Abercorn Street, left on Victory Drive; From I-95 to exit 16, east on 204, right on Victory Drive, Stadium is on right in Daffin Park. **Standard Game Times:** 7:05 p.m., Sun 2:05. **Ticket Price Range:** $7-10.
Visiting Club Hotel: Unavailable.

WEST VIRGINIA POWER

Office Address: 601 Morris St, Suite 201, Charleston, WV 25301.
Telephone: (304) 344-2287. **Fax:** (304) 344-0083.
E-Mail Address: info@wvpower.com. **Website:** www.wvpower.com.
Affiliation (third year): Pittsburgh Pirates (2009). **Years in League:** 1987-

OWNERSHIP, MANAGEMENT

Operated By: Palisades Baseball.
Principal Owner: Alan Levin.
Executive Vice President: Andy Milovich. **Assistant General Manager, Operations:** Jeremy Taylor. **Director/Assistant GM, Marketing:** Kristin Call. **VP, Sales:** Joe Payne. **Director, Food/Beverage:** Jeff Meehan. **Assistant Director, Food/Beverage:** Keegan McDonalds. **Accountant:** Kim Cook. **Box Office Manager:** Joseph Turley. **Director, Media Relations/Broadcaster:** Adam Marco. **Event Planner:** Kevin Buffalino. **Event Planner:** Derrick Crump. **Groundskeeper:** Brent Szarka. **Receptionist:** Terri Byrd.

FIELD STAFF

Manager: Gary Robinson. **Coach:** Dave Howard. **Pitching Coach:** Jeff Johnson. **Trainer:** Unavailable.

GAME INFORMATION

Radio Announcer: Adam Marco. **No. of Games Broadcast:** Home-70, Away-70. **Flagship Station:** WSWW 1490-AM.
PA Announcer: Unavailable. **Official Scorer:** Unavailable.
Stadium Name: Appalachian Power Park. **Location:** I-77 South to Capitol Street exit, left on Lee Street, left on Brooks Street. **Standard Game Times:** 7:05 p.m., Sun 2:05. **Ticket Price Range:** $6-8.
Visiting Club Hotel: Ramada Charleston, 400 Second Avenue SW, South Charleston, WV 25303. **Telephone:** (304) 744-4641.

NEW YORK-PENN LEAGUE

Mailing Address: 6161 MLK Street North, Suite 205, St. Petersburg, FL 33703.
Telephone: (727) 289-7112. **Fax:** (727) 683-9691.
Website: www.newyork-pennleague.com.
Years League Active: 1939–

President: Ben J Hayes.

President Emeritus: Robert F Julian. **Treasurer:** Jon Dandes (Jamestown). **Secretary:** Doug Estes

Directors: Tim Bawmann (Lowell), Steve Cohen (Brooklyn), Jon Dandes (Jamestown), Jeff Eiseman (Aberdeen), Tom Ganey (Auburn), Bill Gladstone (Tri-City), Jeff Goldklang (Hudson Valley), Chuck Greenberg (State College), Kyle Bostick (Vermont), Michael Savit (Mahoning Valley), E. Miles Prentice (Connecticut), Naomi Silver (Batavia), Art Matin (Staten Island), Paul Velte (Williamsport).

League Historian: Charles Wride.

Division Structure: McNamara—Aberdeen, Brooklyn, Hudson Valley, Staten Island. Pinckney—Auburn, Batavia, Jamestown, Mahoning Valley, State College, Williamsport. Stedler—Lowell, Connecticut, Tri-City, Vermont.

Regular Season: 76 games. **2011 Opening Date:** June 17. **Closing Date:** Sept 4. **All-Star Game:** Aug 16 at Lowell. **Playoff Format:** Division winners and wild-card team meet in best-of-three semifinals. Winners meet in best-of-three series for league championship.

Roster Limit: 30 active, but only 25 may be in uniform and eligible to play in any given game. **Player Eligibility Rule:** No more than four players 23 or older; no more than three players on active list may have four or more years of prior service. **Brand of Baseball:** Rawlings. **Umpires:** Unavailable.

Ben Hayes

STADIUM INFORMATION

Club	Stadium	Opened	LF	CF	RF	Capacity	2010 Att.
Aberdeen	Ripken Stadium	2002	310	400	310	6,000	242,258
Auburn	Falcon Park	1995	330	400	330	2,800	56,810
Batavia	Dwyer Stadium	1996	325	400	325	2,600	36,601
Brooklyn	KeySpan Park	2001	315	412	325	7,500	264,441
Connecticut	Dodd Stadium	1995	309	401	309	6,270	50,511
Hudson Valley	Dutchess Stadium	1994	325	400	325	4,494	158,932
Jamestown	Russell E. Diethrick Jr. Park	1941	335	410	353	3,324	44,895
Lowell	Edward LeLacheur Park	1998	337	400	301	4,842	201,512
Mahoning Valley	Eastwood Field	1999	335	405	335	6,000	114,556
State College	Medlar Field at Lubrano Park	2006	325	399	320	5,412	140.927
Staten Island	Richmond County Bank Ballpark	2001	325	400	325	6,500	209,018
Tri-City	Joseph L. Bruno Stadium	2002	325	400	325	5,000	155,315
Vermont	Centennial Field	1922	323	405	330	4,000	88,340
Williamsport	Bowman Field	1923	345	405	350	4,200	65,639

ABERDEEN IRONBIRDS

Office Address: 873 Long Drive, Aberdeen, MD 21001.
Telephone: (410) 297-9292. **Fax:** (410) 297-6653.
E-Mail Address: info@ironbirdsbaseball.com. **Website:** www.ironbirdsbaseball.com.
Affiliation (tenth year): Baltimore Orioles (2002). **Years in League:** 2002-

OWNERSHIP, MANAGEMENT

Operated By: Ripken Professional Baseball LLC.

Principal Owner: Cal Ripken Jr. **Co-Owner/Executive Vice President:** Bill Ripken. **VP:** Jeff Eiseman.

General Manager: Aaron Moszer. **Assistant GMs:** Jenna Raglani, Kari Rumfield. **Director, Ticket Operations:** Brad Cox. **Director, Retail Merchandising:** Don Eney. **Video Production Manager:** Jason Vaughn. **Manager, Facilities:** Steve Fairbaugh. **Head Groundskeeper:** Chris Walsh.

FIELD STAFF

Manager: Unavailable. **Coach:** Cesar Devarez. **Pitching Coach:** Scott McGregor.

GAME INFORMATION
Radio Announcer: Towney Godfrey. No. of Games Broadcast: Home-38, Away-38. Flagship Station: Unavailable. PA Announcer: Jay Szech. Official Scorer: Joe Stetka.
Stadium Name: Ripken Stadium. Location: I-95 to exit 85 (Route 22), west on 22 West, right onto Long Drive. Ticket Price Range: $7-16.

AUBURN DOUBLEDAYS

Office Address: 130 N Division St, Auburn, NY 13021.
Telephone: (315) 255-2489. Fax: (315) 255-2675.
E-Mail Address: ddays@auburndoubledays.com. Website: www.auburndoubledays. com.
Affiliation (first year): Washington Nationals (2011). Years in League: 1958-80, 1982-

OWNERSHIP, MANAGEMENT
Operated by: Auburn Community Non-Profit Baseball Association Inc.
CEO: Tom Ganey. General Manager: Kyle Schoonover.

FIELD STAFF
Manager: Gary Cathcart. Coach: Luis Ordaz. Pitching Coach: Franklin Bravo.

GAME INFORMATION
Radio Announcer: Unavailable. No of Games Broadcast: Home-38 Away-38. Flagship Station: WIN 89.1 FM.
PA Announcer: Unavailable. Official Scorer: Unavailable.
Stadium Name: Falcon Park. Location: I-90 to exit 40, right on Route 34 for 8 miles to York Street, right on York, left on North Division Street. Standard Game Times: 7 p.m., Sun 6. Ticket Price Range: $5-8.
Visiting Club Hotel: Inn at the Fingerlakes, 12 Seminary Ave, Auburn, NY 13021. Telephone: (315) 253-5000.

BATAVIA MUCKDOGS

Office Address: Dwyer Stadium, 299 Bank St, Batavia, NY 14020.
Telephone: (585) 343-5454. Fax: (585) 343-5620.
E-Mail Address: info@muckdogs.com. Website: www.muckdogs.com.
Affiliation (first year): St. Louis Cardinals (2007). Years in League: 1939-53, 1957-59, 1961-

OWNERSHIP, MANAGEMENT
Operated By: Red Wings Management, LLC.
General Manager: Travis Sick. Assistant GM: Mike Ewing. Director, Stadium Operations: Don Rock. Director, Merchandise: Barbara Moore. Clubhouse Manager: Tony Pecora.

FIELD STAFF
Manager: Dann Bilardelo. Coach: Roger LaFrancois. Pitching Coach: Arthur "Ace" Adams. Trainer: Mike Petrarca.

GAME INFORMATION
Radio Announcer: Unavailable. No. of Games Broadcast: Home-38 Away-20.
Flagship Station: WBTA 1490-AM. PA Announcer: Unavailable. Official Scorer: Greg Parks.
Stadium Name: Dwyer Stadium.
Location: I-90 to exit 48, left on Route 98 South, left on Richmond Avenue, left on Bank Street.
Standard Game Times: 7:05 p.m., Sun 1:05, 5:05. Ticket Price Range: $5.50-7.50.
Visiting Club Hotel: Days Inn of Batavia, 200 Oak St, Batavia, NY 14020. Telephone: (585) 343-1440.

BROOKLYN CYCLONES

Office Address: 1904 Surf Ave, Brooklyn, NY 11224.
Telephone: (718) 449-8497. Fax: (718) 449-6368.
E-Mail Address: info@brooklyncyclones.com. Website: www.brooklyncyclones.com.
Affiliation (first year): New York Mets (2001). Years in League: 2001-

OWNERSHIP, MANAGEMENT
Chairman, CEO: Fred Wilpon.
President: Saul Katz. COO: Jeff Wilpon.
General Manager: Steve Cohen. Assistant GM: Kevin Mahoney. Director, Communications: Billy Harner. Director, New Business Development: Gary J. Perone. Marketing Assistant/Promotions Manager: Alexa Atria. Graphics Manager: Kevin Jimenez. Operations Manager: Vladimir Lipsman. Manager, Ticket Operations: Ian McFate. Head Groundskeeper: Kevin Ponte. Senior Accountant: Sharif Soliman. Account Executives: Brian Berman, Greg Conway, Danny Diaz, Randy, Randy Lauwasser, Jake McCalister, Miguel Montano, Ricky Viola. Staff Accountant: Tatiana Isdith.

Administrative Assistant, Community Relations: Sharon Lundy-Ross.

FIELD STAFF

Manager: Rich Donnelly. **Coach:** Bobby Malek. **Pitching Coach:** Frank Viola.

GAME INFORMATION

Radio Announcer: Warner Fusselle. **No. of Games Broadcast:** Home-38, Away-38. **Flagship Station:** WKRB 90.3-FM. **PA Announcer:** Unavailable. **Official Scorer:** Unavailable.

Stadium Name: MCU Park. **Location:** Belt Parkway to Cropsey Ave South, continue on Cropsey until it becomes West 17th St, continue to Surf Ave, stadium on south side of Surf Ave; By subway, west/south to Stillwell Ave./Coney Island station. **Ticket Price Range:** $8-17.

Visiting Club Hotel: Holiday Inn Express, 279 Butler Street, Brooklyn, NY 11217. **Telephone:** (718) 855-9600.

CONNECTICUT TIGERS

Office Address: 14 Stott Avenue, Norwich, CT 06360.
Mailing Address: 14 Stott Avenue, Norwich, CT 06360.
Telephone: (860) 887-7962. **Fax:** (860) 886-5996.
E-Mail Address: info@cttigers.com. **Website:** www.cttigers.com.
Affiliation (first year): Detroit Tigers (1999). **Years in League:** 1966-

OWNERSHIP, MANAGEMENT

Operated By: Oneonta Athletic Corp.
President: Miles Prentice. **General Manager:** Andrew Weber. **Assistant GM:** Eric Knighton. **Vice President, Operations:** CJ Knudsen. **Director, Community Relations/Promotions:** Dave Schermerhorn. **Director, Concessions/Merchandise:** Heather Bartlett. **Director, Facilities/Turf Management:** Bryan Barkley. **Director, Business Development/Client Relations:** Matt Deltenre.

FIELD STAFF

Manager: Andrew Graham. **Coach:** Scott Dwyer. **Pitching Coach:** Jorge Cordova. **Trainer:** TJ Obergefell.

GAME INFORMATION

Radio: Eric Knighton.
PA Announcer: Ed Weyant. **Official Scorer:** Chris Cote.
Stadium Name: Dodd Stadium. **Location:** Exit 82 off I-395. **Standard Game Times:** 7:05 p.m., Sun 1:05. **Ticket Price Range:** $7-20.
Visiting Club Hotel: Holiday Inn, 10 Laura Boulevard, Norwich, CT 06360. **Telephone:** (860) 889-5201.

HUDSON VALLEY RENEGADES

Office Address: Dutchess Stadium, 1500 Route 9D, Wappingers Falls, NY 12590.
Mailing Address: PO Box 661, Fishkill, NY 12524.
Telephone: (845) 838-0094. **Fax:** (845) 838-0014.
E-Mail Address: gadesinfo@hvrenegades.com. **Website:** www.hvrenegades.com.
Affiliation (first year): Tampa Bay Rays (1996). **Years in League:** 1994-.

OWNERSHIP, MANAGEMENT

Operated by: Keystone Professional Baseball Club Inc.
Principal Owner: Marv Goldklang. **President:** Jeff Goldklang.
General Manager: Eben Yager. **Assistant GM:** Corey Whitted. **Sales Manager:** Joe Ausanio. **Director, Media Relations:** Rick Kubitschek. **Director, Community Relations:** Kaitlin Lambert. **Director, Ticket Sales:** Kristen Huss. **Group Sales Manager:** Corinne Adams. **Sales Account Executive:** Sean Kammerer. **Community Relations Specialist:** Bob Outer. **Director, Business Operations:** Vicky DeFreese. **Director, Pitch for Kids:** Rick Zolzer. **Director, New Technology:** Andy Wilmert. **Director, Promotions:** Kevin McGuire. **Director, Stadium Operations:** Tom Hubmaster.

FIELD STAFF

Manager: Jared Sandberg. **Coach:** Reinaldo Ruiz. **Pitching Coach:** Jack Giese. **Trainer:** Andrew Hauser.

GAME INFORMATION

Radio Announcer: Jacob Wilkins. **No. of Games Broadcast:** Home-38, Away-38. **Flagship Stations:** WBNR 1260-AM/WLNA 1420-AM.
PA Announcer: Rick Zolzer. **Official Scorers:** Unavailable.
Stadium Name: Dutchess Stadium. **Location:** I-84 to exit 11 (Route 9D North), north one mile to stadium.
Standard Game Times: 7:05 p.m., **Sun.** 5:05.
Visiting Club Hotel: Ramada Inn, 20 Schuyler Blvd and Route 9, Fishkill, NY 12524. **Telephone:** (845) 896-4995.

JAMESTOWN JAMMERS

Office Address: 485 Falconer St, Jamestown, NY 14701.
Mailing Address: PO Box 638, Jamestown, NY 14702.
Telephone: (716) 664-0915. **Fax:** (716) 664-4175.
E-Mail Address: email@jamestownjammers.com. **Website:** www.jamestownjammers.com.
Affiliation (first year): Florida Marlins (2002). **Years in League:** 1939-57, 1961-73, 1977-.

OWNERSHIP, MANAGEMENT
Operated By: Rich Baseball Operations.
President: Robert Rich Jr. **Chief Operating Officer:** Jonathon Dandes.
General Manager: Matthew Drayer. **Sales/Operations Manager:** John Pogorzelski. **Director, Head Groundskeeper:** Josh Waid.

FIELD STAFF
Manager: David Berg. **Coach:** Robert Bell. **Pitching Coach:** Blake McGinley. **Trainer:** Patrick Amorelli.

GAME INFORMATION
Radio: Unavailable.
PA Announcer: Dan Scotchmer. **Official Scorer:** Rim Riggs, Scott Eddy.
Stadium Name: Russell E Diethrick Jr Park. **Location:** From I-90, south on Route 60, left on Buffalo Street, left on Falconer Street. **Standard Game Times:** 7:05 p.m., Sun 6:05. **Ticket Price Range:** $5-7.
Visiting Club Hotel: Red Roof Inn, 1980 Main St., Falconer, NY 14733. **Telephone:** (716) 665-3670.

LOWELL SPINNERS

Office Address: 450 Aiken St, Lowell, MA 01854.
Telephone: (978) 459-2255. **Fax:** (978) 459-1674.
E-Mail Address: generalinfo@lowellspinners.com. **Website:** www.lowellspinners.com.
Affiliation (first year): Boston Red Sox (1996). **Years in League:** 1996-

OWNERSHIP, MANAGEMENT
Operated By: Diamond Action Inc.
Owner/CEO: Drew Weber.
President/General Manager: Tim Bawmann. **VP, Business Operations:** Brian Lindsay. **VP/Controller:** Patricia Harbour. **VP, Corporate Communications:** Jon Goode. **VP, Stadium Operations:** Dan Beaulieu. **Director, Facility Management:** Gareth Markey. **Director, Media Relations:** Jon Boswell. **Director, Merchandising:** Jeff Cohen. **VP, Group Ticketing:** Jon Healy. **Director, Ticket Operations:** Justin Williams. **Director, Game Day Entertainment:** Matt Steinberg. **Administrative Assistant:** Kyle Coffman. **Head Groundskeeper:** Jeff Paolino. **Director, Creative Services:** Jarrod FitzGerald. **Clubhouse Manager:** Del Christman.

FIELD STAFF
Manager: Carlos Febles. **Coach:** Rich Gedman. **Pitching Coach:** Paul Abbott. **Trainer:** Mauricio Elizondo.

GAME INFORMATION
Radio Announcer: Ken Cail. **No. of Games Broadcast:** Home-38 Away-38. **Flagship Station:** WCAP 980-AM.
PA Announcer: George Brown. **Official Scorers:** David Rourke.
Stadium Name: Edward A. **LeLacheur Park. Location:** From Route 495 and 3, take exit 35C (Lowell Connector), follow connector to exit 5B (Thorndike Street) onto Dutton Street, left onto Father Morrissette Boulevard, right on Aiken Street. **Standard Game Times:** 7:05 p.m., Sat-Sun 5:05. **Ticket Price Range:** $5-10.
Visiting Club Hotel: Radisson of Chelmsford, 10 Independence Dr, Chelmsford, MA 01879. **Telephone:** (978) 356-0800.

MAHONING VALLEY
SCRAPPERS

Office Address: 111 Eastwood Mall Blvd, Niles, OH 44446.
Mailing Address: 111 Eastwood Mall Blvd, Niles, OH 44446.
Telephone: (330) 505-0000. **Fax:** (303) 505-9696.
E-Mail Address: info@mvscrappers.com. **Website:** www.mvscrappers.com.
Affiliation (first year): Cleveland Indians (1999). **Years in League:** 1999-

OWNERSHIP, MANAGEMENT
Operated By: HWS Baseball Group.
Managing General Partner: Michael Savit.

General Manager: Jordan Taylor. **Assistant GM, Business Operations:** Debbie Primmer. **Director, Corporate Sales:** Matt Thompson. **Box Office Manager:** Stephanie Fife. **Director, Stadium Operations:** Brad Hooser. **Director, Entertainment/Promotions:** Heather Sahli. **Director, Group Sales:** Mark Libs. **Account Executive:** Chris Sumner. **Head Groundskeeper:** Matt Rollins.

FIELD STAFF

Manager: Dave Wallace. **Coach:** Unavailable. **Pitching Coach:** Greg Hibbard.

GAME INFORMATION

Radio Announcer: Unavailable. **No. of Games Broadcast:** Home-38, Away-38. **Flagship Station:** Unavailable. **PA Announcer:** Unavailable. **Official Scorer:** Craig Antush.
Stadium Name: Eastwood Field. **Location:** I-80 to 11 North to 82 West to 46 South; stadium located behind Eastwood Mall. **Ticket Price Range:** $5-11.
Visiting Club Hotel: Days Inn & Suites, 1615 Liberty St, Girard, OH 44429. **Telephone:** (330) 759-9820.

STATE COLLEGE SPIKES

Office Address: 112 Medlar Field, Lubrano Park, University Park, PA 16802.
Telephone: (814) 272-1711. **Fax:** (814) 272-1718.
Website: www.statecollegespikes.com.
Affiliation (first year): Pittsburgh Pirates (2007). **Years in League:** 2006-.

OWNERSHIP, MANAGEMENT

Operated By: Spikes Baseball LP.
Chairman/Managing Partner: Chuck Greenberg.
Executive Vice President: Rick Janac. **General Manager:** Jason Dambach.
Assistant GM: Chris Phillips. **Director, Ticket Sales:** Scott Walker. **Director, Promotions/Community Relations:** David Wells. **Director, Ballpark Operations:** Dan Petrazzolo. **Accounting Manager:** Karen Mahon. **Accounting/Box Office Assistant:** Ashley McGarvey. **Concessions Manager:** Unavailable. **Senior Premium Sales Manager:** Greg Huff. **Ticket Account Executives:** Kris McDonough, Will West. **Sports Turf Manager:** Matt Neri.

FIELD STAFF

Manager: Dave Turgeon. **Coach:** Edgar Varela. **Pitching Coach:** Justin Meccage. **Trainer:** Thomas Pribyl.

GAME INFORMATION

Radio Announcers: Steve Jones, Unavailable. **No of Games Broadcast:** Home-38 Road-38. **Flagship Station:** WZWW 95.3-FM.
PA Announcer: Jeff Brown. **Official Scorer:** Dave Baker, John Dixon.
Stadium Name: Medlar Field at Lubrano Park. **Location:** From west, US 322 to Mount Nittany Expressway, I-80 to exit 158 (old exit 23/Milesburg), follow Route 150 South to Route 26 South; From east, I-80 to exit 161 (old exit 24/Bellefonte) to Route 26 South or US 220/I-99 South. **Standard Game Times:** 7:05 p.m., Sun. 6:05. **Ticket Price Range:** $6-14.
Visiting Club Hotel: Ramada Conference Center State College, 1450 Atherton St, State College, PA 16801. **Telephone:** (814) 238-3001.

STATEN ISLAND YANKEES

Stadium Address: 75 Richmond Terrace, Staten Island, NY 10301.
Telephone: (718) 720-9265. **Fax:** (718) 273-5763.
Website: www.siyanks.com.
Affiliation (first year): New York Yankees (1999). **Years in League:** 1999-.

OWNERSHIP, MANAGEMENT

Operated by: Mandalay Baseball Properties.
Principal Owners: Staten Island Minor League Holdings LLC.
President: Joseph Ricciutti.
Executive Vice President/General Manager: Jane Rogers. **VP, Ticket Sales:** Jason Cohen. **Director, Ticket Operations:** Matt Gulino. **Director, Entertainment:** Mike d'Amboise. **Director, Sponsor Services:** Heidi Silber. **Manager, Sponsor Services:** Tak Mihara. **Marketing Coordinator:** John McCutchan. **Senior Corporate Marketing Manager:** Domenick Loccisano. **Group Sales Coordinators:** Thomas Sheridan, John DeLuca, Evan Doyle. **Customer Account Managers:** Tom Conway, Stephanie DiMuro. **Groundskeeper:** Ryan Woodley.

FIELD STAFF

Manager: Josh Paul. **Coach:** Ty Hawkins. **Coach:** Justin Pope. **Pitching Coach:** Pat Daneker. **Trainer:** Lee Myers.

GAME INFORMATION

Radio Announcer: Unavailable. **No. of Games Broadcast:** Home-38, Away-38. **Flagship Station:** Unavailable. **PA Announcer:** Unavailable. **Official Scorer:** Unavailable.

BaseballAmerica.com

Stadium Name: Richmond County Bank Ballpark at St George. **Location:** From I-95, take exit 13E (1-278 and Staten Island), cross Goethals Bridge, stay on I-278 East and take last exit before Verrazano Narrows Bridge, north on Father Cappodanno Boulevard, which turns into Bay Street, which goes to ferry terminal; ballpark next to Staten Island Ferry Terminal. **Standard Game Times:** 7 p.m., Sun 2. **Ticket Price Range:** $9-11.
Visiting Club Hotel: The Navy Lodge, 408 North Path Rd, Staten Island, NY 10305. **Telephone:** (718) 442-0413.

TRI-CITY VALLEYCATS

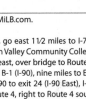

Office Address: Joseph L Bruno Stadium, 80 Vandenburg Ave, Troy, NY 12180.
Mailing Address: PO Box 694, Troy, NY 12181.
Telephone: (518) 629-2287. **Fax:** (518) 629-2299.
E-Mail Address: info@tcvalleycats.com. **Website:** www.tcvalleycats.com.
Affiliation (first year): Houston Astros (2001). **Years in League:** 2002-

OWNERSHIP, MANAGEMENT
Operated By: Tri-City ValleyCats Inc.
Principal Owners: Martin Barr, John Burton, William Gladstone, Rick Murphy, Alfred Roberts, Stephen Siegel.
President: William Gladstone.
Vice President/General Manager: Rick Murphy. **Assistant GM:** Matt Callahan. **Fan Development Manager:** Michelle Skinner. **Stadium Operations Manager:** Keith Sweeney. **Community Relations Manager:** Ryan Burke. **Media Relations Manager:** Chris Chenes. **Business Development Manager:** Joel Pagliaro. **Account Executives:** Chris Dawson, Kyle Wheeler. **Food/Beverage Coordinator:** Gian Rafaniello. **Box Office Manager:** Jessica Kaszeta. **Consultant:** Don McCormick. **Bookkeeper:** Gene Gleason.

FIELD STAFF
Manager: Stubby Clapp. **Coach:** Mark Bailey. **Pitching Coach:** Gary Ruby. **Trainer:** Kevin Ortega.

GAME INFORMATION
Radio Announcer: Evan Valenti. **No. of Games Broadcast:** Home-38. **Flagship Station:** MiLB.com.
PA Announcer: Anthony Pettograsso. **Official Scorer:** Kevin Whitaker.
Stadium Name: Joseph L Bruno Stadium. **Location:** From north, I-87 to exit 7 (Route 7), go east 1 1/2 miles to I-787 South, to Route 378 East, go over bridge to Route 4, right to Route 4 South, one mile to Hudson Valley Community College campus on left; From south, I-87 to exit 23 (I-787), I-787 north six miles to exit for Route 378 east, over bridge to Route 4, right to Route 4 South, one mile to campus on left; From east, Massachusetts Turnpike to exit B-1 (I-90), nine miles to Exit 8 (Defreestville), left off ramp to Route 4 North, five miles to campus on right; From west, I-90 to exit 24 (I-90 East), I-90 East for six miles to I-787 North (Troy), 2.2 miles to exit for Route 378 East, over bridge to Route 4, right to Route 4 south for one mile to campus on left. **Standard Game Times:** 7 p.m., Sun 5. **Ticket Price Range:** $5-10.
Visiting Club Hotel: Hilton Garden Inn, 235 Hoosick Street, Troy, NY 12180.

VERMONT LAKE MONSTERS

Office Address: 1 King Street Ferry Dock, Burlington, VT 05401.
Telephone: (802) 655-4200. **Fax:** (802) 655-5660.
E-Mail Address: info@vermontlakemonsters.com. **Website:** www.vermontlakemonsters.com.
Affiliation (first year): Oakland Athletics (2011). **Years in League:** 1994-

OWNERSHIP, MANAGEMENT
Operated by: Vermont Expos Inc.
Principal Owner/President: Ray Pecor.
General Manager: Nate Cloutier. **Assistant GM:** Joe Doud. **Accounts Manager/Merchandise Director:** Kate Echo. **Director, Community Relations/Promotions:** Emily McDonald. **Director, Ticket Operations:** Unavailable. **Director, Media Relations:** Paul Stanfield. **Clubhouse Operations:** Phil Schelzo.

FIELD STAFF
Manager: Rick Magnante. **Coach:** Casey Myers. **Pitching Coach:** John Wasdin.

GAME INFORMATION
Radio Announcers: Rob Ryan. **No. of Games Broadcast:** Home-38, Away-12. **Flagship Station:** Champ 101.3 FM.
PA Announcer: Rich Haskell. **Official Scorer:** Bruce Bosley.
Stadium Name: Centennial Field. **Location:** I-89 to exit 14W, right on East Avenue for one mile, right at Colchester Avenue. **Standard Game Times:** 7:05 p.m., Sat 6:05, Sun 1:05.
Ticket Price Range: $5-8.
Visiting Club Hotel: Comfort Inn & Suites, 5 Dorset St, South Burlington, VT 05403. **Telephone:** (802) 863-5541.

WILLIAMSPORT CROSSCUTTERS

Office Address: Bowman Field, 1700 W Fourth St, Williamsport, PA 17701.
Mailing Address: PO Box 3173, Williamsport, PA 17701.
Telephone: (570) 326-3389. **Fax:** (570) 326-3494.
E-Mail Address: mail@crosscutters.com. **Website:** www.crosscutters.com.
Affiliation (first year): Philadelphia Phillies (2007). **Years in League:** 1968-72, 1994-

OWNERSHIP, MANAGEMENT

Operated By: Geneva Cubs Baseball Inc.
Principal Owners: Paul Velte, John Schreyer.
President: Paul Velte. **Executive Vice President:** John Schreyer.
VP/General Manager: Doug Estes. **VP, Marketing/Public Relations:** Gabe Sinicropi. **Director, Concessions:** Bill Gehron. **Director, Ticket Operations/Community Relations:** Sarah Budd. **Director, Partner Services:** Pam Long. **Head Groundskeeper:** Brian McLaughlin.

FIELD STAFF

Manager: Mickey Morandini. **Coach:** Jorge Velandia. **Pitching Coach:** Lance Carter.

GAME INFORMATION

Radio Announcer: Todd Bartley. **No. of Games Broadcast:** Home-38, Away-38. **Flagship Station:** WLYC 1050-AM, 104.1-FM.
PA Announcer: Rob Thomas. **Official Scorer:** Ken Myers.
Stadium Name: Bowman Field. **Location:** From south, Route 15 to Maynard Street, right on Maynard, left on Fourth Street for one mile; From north, Route 15 to Fourth Street, left on Fourth. **Ticket Price Range:** $4.50-7.50
Visiting Club Hotel: Best Western, 1840 E Third St, Williamsport, PA 17701. **Telephone:** (570) 326-1981.

NORTHWEST LEAGUE

Office Address: 620 W Franklin St, Boise, ID 83702.
Mailing Address: PO Box 1645, Boise, ID 83701.
Telephone: (208) 429-1511. **Fax:** (208) 429-1525.
E-Mail Address: bobrichmond@qwestoffice.net. **Website:** www.northwestleague.com.
Years League Active: 1954-.
President/Treasurer: Bob Richmond.
Vice President: Todd Rahr (Boise). **Corporate Secretary:** Jerry Walker (Salem-Keizer).
Directors: Bob Beban (Eugene), Bobby Brett (Spokane), Tom Volpe (Everett), Jake Kerr (Vancouver), Mike McMurray (Yakima), Brent Miles (Tri-City), Jerry Walker (Salem-Keizer), Neil Leibman (Boise). **Administrative Assistant:** Rob Richmond.
Division Structure: East—Boise, Spokane, Tri-City, Yakima. West—Eugene, Everett, Salem-Keizer, Vancouver.
Regular Season: 76 games (split schedule). **2011 Opening Date:** June 17. **Closing Date:** Sept. 3.
Playoff Format: First-half division winners meet second-half division winners in best-of-three series. Winners meet in best-of-three series for league championship.

Bob Richmond

All-Star Game: None.
Roster Limit: 30 active, 35 under control. **Player Eligibility Rule:** No more than three players on active list may have four or more years of prior service.
Brand of Baseball: Rawlings.
Umpires: Unavailable.

STADIUM INFORMATION

Club	Stadium	Opened	Dimensions			Capacity	2010 Att.
			LF	CF	RF		
Boise	Memorial Stadium	1989	355	400	335	4,500	105,671
Eugene	PK Park	2010	335	400	325	4,000	107,561
Everett	Everett Memorial Stadium	1984	330	395	330	3,682	90,079
Salem-Keizer	Volcanoes Stadium	1997	325	400	325	4,100	96,219
Spokane	Avista Stadium	1958	335	398	335	7,162	175,287
Tri-City	Dust Devils Stadium	1995	335	400	335	3,700	84,921
Vancouver	Nat Bailey Stadium	1951	335	395	335	6,500	154,592
Yakima	Yakima County Stadium	1993	295	406	295	3,000	70,695

BOISE HAWKS

Office Address: 5600 N. Glenwood St. Boise, ID 83714.
Telephone: (208) 322-5000. **Fax:** (208) 322-6846.
Website: www.boisehawks.com.
Affiliation (first year): Chicago Cubs (2001). **Years in League:** 1975-76, 1978, 1987-

OWNERSHIP, MANAGEMENT
Operated by: Boise Baseball LLC.
CEO: Neil Leibman.
President/General Manager: Todd Rahr. **Assistant GM/Director, Business Operations:** Dina Duncan. **Director, Sales:** Andy Simon. **Director, Brand/Creative Services:** Kelly Kerkvliet. **Director, Marketing/Media Relations/Events:** Kristen Nimmo. **Ticket Operations Manager:** Greg Marconi. **Ticket Sales Account Executive:** Katie Leonick. **Web/Digital Content:** Ken Hyde. **Stadium Operations:** Todd Rahr.

FIELD STAFF
Manager: Mark Johnson. **Coach:** Desi Wilson. **Pitching Coach:** David Rosario. **Trainer:** Bob Grimes.

GAME INFORMATION
Radio Announcer: Mike Safford. **No. of Games Broadcast:** Home-38, Away-38. **Flagship Station:** KTIK 1350-AM.
PA Announcer: Unavailable. **Official Scorer:** Unavailable.
Stadium Name: Memorial Stadium. **Location:** I-84 to Cole Road, north to Western Idaho Fairgrounds at 5600 North Glenwood Street. **Standard Game Time:** 7:15 p.m. **Ticket Price Range:** $6-$12.
Visiting Club Hotel: Owyhee Plaza Hotel, 1109 Main St, Boise, ID 83702. **Telephone:** (208) 343-4611.

EUGENE EMERALDS

Office Address: 2760 Martin Luther King Jr Blvd, Eugene, OR 97401.
Mailing Address: PO Box 5566, Eugene, OR 97405.
Telephone: (541) 342-5367. **Fax:** (541) 342-6089. **E-Mail Address:** info@emeraldsbaseball.com. **Website:** www.emeraldsbaseball.com.
Affiliation (first year): San Diego Padres (2001). **Years in League:** 1955-68, 1974-

OWNERSHIP, MANAGEMENT
Operated By: Elmore Sports Group Ltd.
Principal Owner: David Elmore.
General Manager: Allan Benavides. **Assistant GM:** Sarah Heth. **Director, Corporate Sales:** Matt Dompe. **Food/Beverage Director:** Kelly Hallquest. **Director, Tickets Sales:** Ruli Garcia. **Director, Corporate Events:** Travis Anderson. **Director, Media Relations:** Onalee Carson. **Director, Mascot Operations:** Teigh Bowen. **Events Manager:** Drew Pryse. **Accountant:** Andy Hoedt.

FIELD STAFF
Manager: Pat Murphy. **Coach:** Chris Prieto. **Pitching Coach:** Dave Rajsich. **Trainer:** Zach Jones.

GAME INFORMATION
Radio Announcer: Chris Fisher. **No. of Games Broadcast:** Home-38, Away-38. **Flagship Station:** 95.3 "The Score".
PA Announcer: Matt Dompe. **Official Scorer:** George McPherson.
Stadium Name: PK Park, 2760 Martin Luther King Jr Blvd. **Standard Game Time:** 7:05 p.m., Sun 1:05. **Ticket Price Range:** $6-12.
Visiting Club Hotel: Valley River Inn, 1000 Valley River Way, Eugene, OR 97401. **Telephone:** (541) 743-1000.

EVERETT AQUASOX

Mailing Address: 3802 Broadway, Everett, WA 98201.
Telephone: (425) 258-3673. **Fax:** (425) 258-3675.
E-Mail Address: aquasox@aquasox.com. **Website:** www.aquasox.com.
Affiliation (first year): Seattle Mariners (1995). **Years in League:** 1984-

OWNERSHIP, MANAGEMENT
Operated by: 7th Inning Stretch, LLC
Directors: Tom Volpe, Pat Filippone.
Executive Vice President: Tom Backemeyer. **VP, Corporate Sponsorships:** Brian Sloan. **VP, Tickets:** Rick Dooley. **Director, Corporate Partnerships/Broadcasting:** Pat Dillon. **Director, Food/Beverage:** Todd Holterhoff. **Director, Accounting/Player Housing:** Teresa Sarsted. **Director, Community Relations:** Katie Crawford. **Manager, Ticket Operations:** Ryan Pearman. **Account Executive:** Alex Dadisman. **Coordinator, Ticket Sales:** Katie Nefzger. **Head Groundskeeper:** Brian Burroughs.

FIELD STAFF
Manager: Scott Steinmann. **Coach:** Mike Kinkade. **Pitching Coach:** Andrew Lorraine.

GAME INFORMATION
Radio Announcer: Pat Dillon. **No. of Games Broadcast:** Home-38, Away-38. **Flagship Station:** KRKO 1380-AM.
PA Announcer: Tom Lafferty. **Official Scorer:** Pat Castro.
Stadium Name: Everett Memorial Stadium. **Location:** I-5, exit 192. **Standard Game Times:** 7:05 p.m., Sun 1:05. **Ticket Price Range:** $7-15.
Visiting Club Hotel: Holiday Inn, Downtown Everett, 3105 Pine St, Everett, WA 98201. **Telephone:** (425) 339-2000.

SALEM-KEIZER VOLCANOES

Street Address: 6700 Field of Dreams Way NE, Keizer, OR 97303.
Mailing Address: PO Box 20936, Keizer, OR 97307.
Telephone: (503) 390-2225. **Fax:** (503) 390-2227.
E-Mail Address: probasebal@aol.com. **Website:** www.volcanoesbaseball.com.
Affiliation (first year): San Francisco Giants (1997). **Years in League:** 1997-

OWNERSHIP, MANAGEMENT
Operated By: Sports Enterprises Inc.
Principal Owners: Jerry Walker, Bill Tucker.
President/General Manager: Jerry Walker. **Vice President, Operations:** Rick Nelson. **Corporate Sponsorships:** Jerry Howard. **Media Relations:** Rick Nelson. **Director, Ticket Office Operations:** Bea Howard.

FIELD STAFF
Manager: Tom Trebelhorn. **Coach:** Ricky Ward. **Pitching Coach:** Jerry Cram.

GAME INFORMATION
Radio Announcer: Matt Pedersen. **No. of Games Broadcast:** Home-38, Away-38. **Flagship Station:** KBZY AM-1490. **PA Announcer:** Michael Trevino. **Official Scorer:** Scott Sepich. **Stadium Name:** Volcanoes Stadium. **Location:** I-5 to exit 260 (Chemawa Road), west one block to Stadium Way NE, north six blocks to stadium. **Standard Game Times:** 6:35 p.m., Fri-Sat 7:05, Sun 5:05. **Ticket Price Range:** $7-11. **Visiting Club Hotel:** Comfort Suites, 630 Hawthorne Ave SE, Salem, OR 97301. **Telephone:** (503) 585-9705.

SPOKANE INDIANS

Office Address: Avista Stadium, 602 N Havana, Spokane, WA 99202.
Mailing Address: PO Box 4758, Spokane, WA 99220.
Telephone: (509) 535-2922. **Fax:** (509) 534-5368.
E-Mail Address: mail@spokaneindiansbaseball.com.
Website: www.spokaneindiansbaseball.com.
Affiliation (first year): Texas Rangers (2003). **Years in League:** 1972, 1983-

OWNERSHIP, MANAGEMENT
Operated By: Longball Inc.
Principal Owner: Bobby Brett. **Senior Advisor:** Andrew Billig.
Vice President/General Manager: Chris Duff. **Senior VP:** Otto Klein. **VP, Tickets:** Josh Roys. **Assistant GM:** Lesley DeHart. **Director, Sponsorships/Operations:** Rob Allyn. **Director, Promotions:** Dimitri Perera. **Director, Group Sales:** Sean Minty. **Group Sales Coordinator:** Nick Gaebe. **Director, Concessions/Hospitality:** Ryan Jordan. **CFO:** Greg Sloan. **Accounting:** Dawnelle Shaw. **Head Groundskeeper:** Adam Farrell. **Assistant Director, Stadium Operations:** Larry Blumer.

FIELD STAFF
Manager: Tim Hulett. **Coaches:** Josue Perez, Brian Dayette. **Pitching Coach:** Dave Chavarria.

GAME INFORMATION
Radio Announcer: Mike Boyle. **No. of Games Broadcast:** Home-38, Away-38. **Flagship Station:** 1510 KGA. **PA Announcer:** Unavailable. **Official Scorer:** Unavailable. **Stadium Name:** Avista Stadium at the Spokane Fair and Expo Center. **Location:** From west, I-90 to exit 283B (Thor/Freya), east on Third Avenue, left onto Havana; From east, I-90 to Broadway exit, right onto Broadway, left onto Havana. **Standard Game Time:** 6:30 p.m. **Ticket Price Range:** $4-9. **Visiting Club Hotel:** Mirabeau Park Hotel & Convention Center, N 1100 Sullivan Rd, Spokane, WA 99037. **Telephone:** (509) 924-9000.

TRI-CITY DUST DEVILS

Office Address: 6200 Burden Blvd, Pasco, WA 99301.
Telephone: (509) 544-8789. **Fax:** (509) 547-9570.
E-Mail Address: info@dustdevilsbaseball.com. **Website:** www.dustdevilsbaseball.com.
Affiliation (first year): Colorado Rockies (2001). **Years in League:** 1955-1974, 1983-1986, 2001-.

OWNERSHIP, MANAGEMENT
Operated by: Northwest Baseball Ventures.
Principal Owners: George Brett, Hoshino Dreams Corp, Brent Miles.
President: Brent Miles. **Vice President/General Manager:** Derrel Ebert. **VP, Business Operations:** Tim Gittel. **Assistant GM, Sponsorships:** Kelli Foos. **Assistant GM, Tickets:** Dennis da Silva. **Director, Group Sales:** Dan O'Neill. **Sponsorships Coordinator:** Lauren Coombs. **Group Sales Coordinator:** Anne Brenner. **Account Executives:** Nick Jutila, Patrick Covert. **Director, Concessions:** Katie Mulhausen. **Stadium Operations Coordinator:** Pat Dorer. **Media Relations Coordinator:** Heath Harshman. **Head Groundskeeper:** Michael Angel.

FIELD STAFF
Manager: Freddie Ocasio. **Coach:** Anthony Sanders. **Pitching Coach:** Dave Burba. **Trainer:** Andy Stover.

GAME INFORMATION
Radio Announcer: Unavailable. **No. of Games Broadcast:** Home-38, Away-38. **Flagship Station:** Newstalk 870 AM KFLD. **PA Announcer:** Patrick Harvey. **Official Scorers:** Tony Wise, Scott Tylinski. **Stadium Name:** Gesa Stadium. **Location:** I-182 to exit 9 (Road 68), north to Burden Blvd, right to stadium. **Standard Game Time:** 7:15 p.m. **Ticket Price Range:** $5-9. **Visiting Club Hotel:** Red Lion Hotel-Columbia Center, 1101 N Columbia Center Blvd, Kennewick, WA 99336. **Telephone:** (509) 783-0611.

VANCOUVER CANADIANS

Office Address: Scotiabank Field at Nat Bailey Stadium, 4601 Ontario St, Vancouver, British Columbia V5V 3H4.
Telephone: (604) 872-5232. **Fax:** (604) 872-1714.
E-Mail Address: staff@canadiansbaseball.com. **Website:** www.canadiansbaseball.com.
Affiliation (first year): Toronto Blue Jays (2011). **Years in League:** 2000-

OWNERSHIP, MANAGEMENT

Operated by: Vancouver Canadians Professional Baseball LLP.
Principal Owners: Jake Kerr, Jeff Mooney. **President:** Andy Dunn.
General Manager: Jason Takefman. **Assistant GMs:** Rob Fai, JC Fraser. **VP, Sales/Marketing:** Graham Wall. **Director, Sales/Marketing Services:** Cynthia Wildman. **Director, Ticket Operations:** Allan Bailey. **Director, Group Sales/Community Relations:** Spiro Khouri; Coordinator, Sales/Promotion: Grace Kim. **Coordinator, Sales/Community Relations, Jeff Holloway. Groundskeepers:** Tom Archibald, Trevor Sheffield, Teppei Fujino. **Financial Controller:** Cara Ferguson.

FIELD STAFF

Manager: John Schneider. **Coach:** Dave Pano. **Pitching Coach:** Jim Czajkowski.

GAME INFORMATION

Radio Announcer: Rob Fai. **No. of Games Broadcast:** Home-38, Away-38. **Flagship Station:** The Team 1040-AM.
PA Announcer: Don Andrews. **Official Scorer:** Unavailable.
Stadium Name: Nat Bailey Stadium. **Location:** From downtown, take Cambie Street Bridge, left on East 25th Ave./King Edward Ave, right on Main Street, right on 33rd Ave, right on Ontario St to stadium; From south, take Highway 99 to Oak Street, right on 41st Ave, left on Main Street to 33rd Ave, right on Ontario St to stadium. **Standard Game Times:** 7:05 p.m., Sun 1:05. **Ticket Price Range:** $9-20.
Visiting Club Hotel: Accent Inns, 10551 Edwards Dr, Richmond, BC V6X 3L8. **Telephone:** (604) 273-3311.

YAKIMA BEARS

Office Address: 17 N 3rd Street, Suite 101, Yakima, WA 98901.
Mailing Address: PO Box 483, Yakima, WA 98907.
Telephone: (509) 457-5151. **Fax:** (509) 457-9909.
E-Mail Address: info@yakimabears.com. **Website:** www.yakimabears.com.
Affiliation (first year): Arizona Diamondbacks (2001). **Years in League:** 1955-66, 1990-

OWNERSHIP, MANAGEMENT

Operated by: Short Season LLC.
Managing Partners: Mike McMurray, Mike Ellis, Josh Weinman, Myron Levin, Mike Ormsby.
President: Mike McMurray.
General Manager: KL Wombacher. **Assistant GM, Sales:** Aaron Arndt. **Chief Financial Officer:** Laura McMurray. **Director, Ballpark Operations:** Jared Jacobs. **Director, Ticket Operations:** Ryan Coffey. **Director, Group Sales:** Luke Moedritzer. **Director, Merchandise:** Lauren Wombacher. **Head Groundskeeper:** Ronnie Ross. **Director, Media Relations/Broadcasting:** Drew Bontadelli. **Receptionist:** Lucy Mattingly.

FIELD STAFF

Manager: Audo Vicente. **Coach:** Jacob Cruz. **Pitching Coach:** Doug Bochtler. **Trainer:** Unavailable.

GAME INFORMATION

Radio Announcer: Drew Bontadelli. **No. of Games Broadcast:** Home-38, Away-38. **Flagship Station:** KUTI 1460-AM.
PA Announcer: Todd Lyons. **Official Scorer:** Unavailable.
Stadium Name: Yakima County Stadium. **Location:** I-82 to exit 34 (Nob Hill Boulevard), west to Fair Avenue, right on Fair, right on Pacific Avenue. **Standard Game Times:** 7:05 p.m., Sun 5:35 p.m. **Ticket Price Range:** $4.50-$9.50.
Visiting Club Hotel: Best Western Ahtanum Inn, 2408 Rudkin Rd, Union Gap, WA 98903. **Telephone:** (509) 248-9700.

APPALACHIAN LEAGUE

APPALACHIAN LEAGUE
of professional baseball clubs

ROOKIE ADVANCED

Mailing Address: 283 Deerchase Circle, Statesville, NC 28625.
Telephone: (704) 873-5300. **Fax:** (704) 873-4333.
E-Mail Address: applg@hughes.net. **Website:** www.appyleague.com.
Years League Active: 1921-25, 1937-55, 1957-.
President/Treasurer: Lee Landers. **Corporate Secretary:** Jim Holland (Princeton).
Directors: Fred Nelson (Greeneville), Pedro Grifol (Pulaski), Mitch Lukevics (Princeton), Scott Sharp (Burlington), Buddy Bell (Bristol), Charlie Wilson (Bluefield), John Vuch (Johnson City), Kurt Kemp (Danville), Adam Wogan (Kingsport), Jim Rantz (Elizabethton).
League Administrator: Bobbi Landers.
Division Structure: East—Bluefield, Burlington, Danville, Princeton, Pulaski. **West**—Bristol, Elizabethton, Greeneville, Johnson City, Kingsport.
Regular Season: 68 games. **2011 Opening Date:** June 21. **Closing Date:** Aug. 30.
All-Star Game: None.
Playoff Format: First round (best of three): East winner versus West 2nd place; West winner versus East 2nd place. Winners meet in best of three for league championship.
Roster Limit: 30 active, 35 under control. **Player Eligibility Rule:** No more than two years of prior minor league service.
Brand of Baseball: Rawlings.
Umpires: Unavailable

Lee Landers

STADIUM INFORMATION

Club	Stadium	Opened	LF	CF	RF	Capacity	2010 Att.
				Dimensions			
Bluefield	Bowen Field	1939	335	400	335	2,250	22,868
Bristol	DeVault Memorial Stadium	1969	325	400	310	2,000	22,019
Burlington	Burlington Athletic Stadium	1960	335	410	335	3,000	30,273
Danville	Dan Daniel Memorial Park	1993	330	400	330	2,588	30,615
Elizabethton	Joe O'Brien Field	1974	335	414	326	1,500	24,668
Greeneville	Pioneer Park	2004	331	400	331	2,400	47,321
Johnson City	Howard Johnson Field	1956	320	410	320	2,500	24,049
Kingsport	Hunter Wright Stadium	1995	330	410	330	2,500	28,822
Princeton	Hunnicutt Field	1988	330	396	330	1,950	26,946
Pulaski	Calfee Park	1935	335	405	310	2,500	32,348

BLUEFIELD BLUE JAYS

Office Address: Stadium Drive, Bluefield, WV 24701.
Mailing Address: P.O. Box 356, Bluefield, WV 24701.
Telephone: (276) 326-1326. **Fax:** (276) 326-1318.
E-Mail Address: babybirds1@comcast.net. **Website:** www.minorleaguebaseball.com/index.jsp?sid=t517.
Affiliation (first year): Toronto Blue Jays (2011). **Years in League:** 1946-55, 1957-

OWNERSHIP, MANAGEMENT
Operated By: Adam Shaffer.
Director: Charlie Wilson (Toronto Blue Jays).
Vice President: Cecil Smith. **Secretary:** M.K. Burton. **Counsel:** David Kersey.
President: George McGonagle. **General Manager:** Jim Pettus. **Director, Creative Services:** Katherine Ward. **Director, Field Operations/Grounds:** Mike White.

FIELD STAFF
Manager: Dennis Holmberg. **Coach:** Kenny Graham. **Pitching Coach:** Antonio Caceres.

GAME INFORMATION
Radio Announcer: Buford Early. **No. of Games Broadcast:** Home-34 Road-34. **Flagship Station:** WHIS 1440-AM/WTZE 1470-AM.
PA Announcer: Buford Early. **Official Scorer:** Unavailable.
Stadium Name: Bowen Field. **Location:** I-77 to Bluefield exit 1, Route 290 to Route 460 West, fourth light right onto Leatherwood Lane, left at first light, past Chevron station and turn right, stadium 1/4 mile on left. **Ticket Price Range:** $3.50.
Visiting Club Hotel: Holiday Inn Bluefield, 3350 Big Laurel Highway. U.S. 460, Bluefield, WV 24701. **Telephone:** (304) 325-6170.

BRISTOL WHITE SOX

Ballpark Location: 1501 Euclid Ave., Bristol, VA 24201.
Mailing Address: P.O. Box 1434, Bristol, VA 24203.
Telephone: (276) 206-9946. **Fax:** (276) 669-7686.
E-Mail Address: brisox@btes.tv. **Website:** www.bristolsox.com.
Affiliation (first year): Chicago White Sox (1995). **Years in League:** 1921-25, 1940-55, 1969-

OWNERSHIP, MANAGEMENT

Owned by: Chicago White Sox.
Operated by: Bristol Baseball Inc.
Director: Buddy Bell (Chicago White Sox).
President: Mahlon Luttrell. **Vice Presidents:** Lynn Armstrong, Perry Hustad.
General Manager: Mahlon Luttrell. **Treasurer:** Dorothy Cox. **Secretary:** Tim Johnston.

FIELD STAFF

Manager: Pete Rose Jr. **Coach:** Greg Briley. **Pitching Coach:** Larry Owens. **Trainer:** Kevin Pillifant. **Conditioning Coach:** Ibrahim Rivera.

GAME INFORMATION

Radio: Internet broadcast through milb.com.
PA Announcer: Chuck Necessary. **Official Scorer:** Perry Hustad.
Stadium Name: DeVault Memorial Stadium. **Location:** I-81 to exit 3 onto Commonwealth Ave., right on Euclid Ave. for ½ mile. **Standard Game Time:** 7 p.m. **Ticket Price Range:** $3-6.
Visiting Club Hotel: Holiday Inn, 3005 Linden Drive Bristol VA 24202. **Telephone:** (276) 466-4100.

BURLINGTON ROYALS

Office Address: 1450 Graham St., Burlington, NC 27217.
Mailing Address: P.O. Box 1143, Burlington, NC 27216.
Telephone: (336) 222-0223. **Fax:** (336) 226-2498.
E-Mail Address: info@burlingtonroyals.com. **Website:** www.burlingtonroyals.com.
Affiliation (first year): Kansas City Royals (2007). **Years in League:** 1986-

OWNERSHIP, MANAGEMENT

Operated by: Burlington Baseball Club Inc.
Director: Scott Sharp (Kansas City Royals).
President: Miles Wolff. **Vice President:** Dan Moushon.
General Manager: Steve Brice. **Assistant GM:** Ben Abzug. **Director, Stadium Operations:** Mike Thompson.

FIELD STAFF

Manager: Nelson Liriano. **Coach:** Jon Williams. **Pitching Coach:** Bobby St. Pierre.

GAME INFORMATION

Radio Announcer: Unavailable. **No. of Games Broadcast:** Home-34, Away-4. **Flagship:** www.burlingtonroyals.com.
PA Announcer: Unavailable. **Official Scorer:** Unavailable.
Stadium Name: Burlington Athletic Stadium. **Location:** I-40/85 to exit 145, north on Route 100 (Maple Avenue) for 1½ miles, right on Mebane Street for 1½ miles, right on Beaumont, left on Graham. **Standard Game Time:** 7 p.m. **Ticket Price Range:** $4-8.

DANVILLE BRAVES

Office Address: Dan Daniel Memorial Park, 302 River Park Dr., Danville, VA 24540.
Mailing Address: P.O. Box 378, Danville, VA 24543.
Telephone: (434) 797-3792. **Fax:** (434) 797-3799.
E-Mail Address: info@dbraves.com. **Website:** www.dbraves.com.
Affiliation (first year): Atlanta Braves (1993). **Years in League:** 1993-

OWNERSHIP, MANAGEMENT

Operated by: Atlanta National League Baseball Club Inc. **Director:** Kurt Kemp (Atlanta Braves). **General Manager:** David Cross. **Assistant GM:** Bob Kitzmiller. **Operations Manager:** Brandon Bennett. **Head Groundskeeper:** Jon Hall.

FIELD STAFF

Manager: Randy Ingle. **Coach:** DJ Boston. **Pitching Coach:** Gabe Luckert. **Athletic Trainer:** Colin Myers.

GAME INFORMATION

Radio Announcer: Nick Pierce. **No. of Games Broadcast:** Home-Unavailable, Away-Unavailable. **Flagship Station:** Unavailable.

PA Announcer: Jay Stephens. **Official Scorer:** Mark Bowman.
Stadium Name: American Legion Field Post 325 Field at Dan Daniel Memorial Park. **Location:** U.S. 29 Bypass to River Park Drive/Dan Daniel Memorial Park exit; follow signs to park. **Standard Game Times:** 7 p.m., Sun. 4. **Ticket Price Range:** $4-7.
Visiting Club Hotel: Innkeeper-West, 3020 Riverside Dr., Danville, VA 24541. **Telephone:** (434) 799-1202.

ELIZABETHTON TWINS

Office Address: 300 West Mill Street, Elizabethton, TN 37643.
Stadium Address: 208 N. Holly Lane, Elizabethton, TN 37643.
Mailing Address: 136 S. Sycamore St., Elizabethton, TN 37643.
Telephone: (423) 547-6441. **Fax:** (423) 547-6442.
E-Mail Address: etwins@cityofelizabethton.org.
Website: www.elizabethtontwins.com.
Affiliation (first year): Minnesota Twins (1974). **Years in League:** 1937-42, 1945-51, 1974-

OWNERSHIP, MANAGEMENT
Operator: City of Elizabethton.
Director: Jim Rantz (Minnesota Twins).
President: Harold Mains.
General Manager: Mike Mains. **Clubhouse Operations/Head Groundskeeper:** David McQueen.

FIELD STAFF
Manager: Ray Smith. **Coach:** Jeff Reed. **Pitching Coach:** Jim Shellenback. **Trainer:** Ryan Headwall.

GAME INFORMATION
Radio Announcer: Unavailable. **No. of Games Broadcast:** Home-34, Away-6. **Flagship Station:** WBEJ 1240-AM.
PA Announcer: Tom Banks. **Official Scorer:** Bill Crow.
Stadium Name: Joe O'Brien Field. **Location:** I-81 to Highway I-26, exit at Highway 321/67, left on Holly Lane.
Standard Game Time: 7 p.m. **Ticket Price Range:** $3-5.
Visiting Club Hotel: Holiday Inn, 101 W. Springbrook Dr., Johnson City, TN 37601. **Telephone:** (423) 282-4611.

GREENEVILLE ASTROS

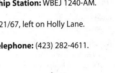

Office Address: 135 Shiloh Road, Greeneville, TN 37743.
Mailing Address: PO Box 5192, Greeneville, TN 37743.
Telephone: (423) 638-0411. **Fax:** (423) 638-9450.
E-Mail Address: info@greenevilleastros.com. **Website:** www.greenevilleastros.com.
Affiliation (first year): Houston Astros (2004). **Years in League:** 2004-

OWNERSHIP, MANAGEMENT
Operated by: Houston Astros Baseball Club.
Director: Fred Nelson (Houston Astros).
General Manager: David Lane. **Assistant GM:** Hunter Reed. **Head Groundskeeper:** Tyler Mittlesteadt. **Clubhouse Operations:** Unavailable.

FIELD STAFF
Manager: Omar Lopez. **Pitching Coach:** Rick Aponte. **Coach:** Josh Bonifay. **Trainer:** Michael Rendon.

GAME INFORMATION
Radio: None.
PA Announcer: Bobby Rader. **Official Scorer:** Johnny Painter.
Stadium Name: Howard Johnson Field at Cardinal Park. **Location:** I-181 to exit 32, left on East Main, through light onto Legion Street. **Standard Game Time:** 7 p.m. **Ticket Price Range:** $3-7.
Visiting Club Hotel: Jameson Inn.

JOHNSON CITY CARDINALS

Office Address: 111 Legion St, Johnson City, TN 37601.
Mailing Address: PO Box 179, Johnson City, TN 37605.
Telephone: (423) 461-4866. **Fax:** (423) 461-4864.
E-Mail Address: info@jccardinals.com. **Website:** www.jccardinals.com.
Affiliation (first year): St. Louis Cardinals (1975). **Years in League:** 1911-13, 1921-24, 1937-55, 1957-61, 1964-

OWNERSHIP, MANAGEMENT
Operated by: Johnson City Sports Foundation Inc.
President: Mark Fox (JCSF).

Director: John Vuch (St. Louis Cardinals). **General Manager:** Chuck Arnold.
Assistant GM: Sean Salemme.

FIELD STAFF

Manager: Mike Shildt. **Coach:** Ramon Ortiz. **Pitching Coach:** Doug White.

GAME INFORMATION

Radio: None.
PA Announcer: Unavailable. **Official Scorer:** Gene Renfro.
Stadium Name: Howard Johnson Field at Cardinal Park. **Location:** I-26 to exit 23, left on East Main, through light onto Legion Street. **Standard Game Time:** 7 p.m. **Ticket Price Range:** $3-5.
Visiting Club Hotel: Holiday Inn, 101 W Springbrook Dr., **Johnson City, TN 37601. Telephone:** (423) 282-4611.

KINGSPORT METS

Office Address: 800 Granby Rd, Kingsport, TN 37660.
Mailing Address: P.O. Box 1128, Kingsport, TN 37662.
Telephone: (423) 378-3744. **Fax:** (423) 392-8538.
E-Mail Address: info@kmets.com. **Website:** www.kmets.com.
Affiliation (first year): New York Mets (1980). **Years in League:** 1921-25, 1938-52, 1957, 1960-63, 1969-82, 1984-

OWNERSHIP, MANAGEMENT

Operated By: S&H Baseball LLC.
Director: Adam Wogan (New York Mets).
President: Rick Spivey. **Vice President:** Steve Harville. **VP/General Manager:** Roman Stout. **Accountant:** Bob Dingus.
Director, Concessions: Teresa Haywood. **Head Groundskeeper:** Josh Warner. **Clubhouse Manager:** Travis Baker.

Field Staff

Manager: Frank Fultz. **Coach:** George Greer. **Pitching Coach:** Jonathan Hurst.

GAME INFORMATION

Radio: None.
PA Announcer: Don Spivey. **Official Scorer:** Eddie Durham.
Stadium Name: Hunter Wright Stadium. **Location:** I-81 to I-181 North, exit 1 (Stone Drive), left on West Stone Drive (U.S. 11W), right on Granby Road. **Ticket Price Range:** $2-5.
Visiting Club Hotel: The Jameson Inn, 3004 Bays Mountain Plaza, Kingsport, TN 37660. **Telephone:** (423) 282-4611.

PRINCETON RAYS

Office Address: 205 Old Bluefield Rd, Princeton, WV 24740.
Mailing Address: P.O. Box 5646, Princeton, WV 24740.
Telephone: (304) 487-2000. **Fax:** (304) 487-8762.
E-Mail Address: princetonrays@frontier.com. **Website:** www.princetonrays.net.
Affiliation (first year): Tampa Bay Rays (1997). **Years in League:** 1988-

OWNERSHIP, MANAGEMENT

Operated By: Princeton Baseball Association Inc.
Director: Mitch Lukevics (Tampa Bay Rays). **President:** Mori Williams.
General Manager: Jim Holland. **Director, Stadium Operations:** Mick Bayle. **Official Scorer:** Bob Redd. **Head, Security/Ticket Sales:** Ken Wallace. **Graphic Designer:** Warren Hypes. **Administrative Assistant:** Tommy Thomason.
Chaplain: Craig Stout.

FIELD STAFF

Manager: Michael Johns. **Coach:** Wuarnner Rincones. **Pitching Coach:** Marty DeMerritt.

GAME INFORMATION

Radio Announcer: Kyle Cooper. **No. of Games Broadcast:** Home-34, Away-34. **Flagship Station:** WMTD 102.3-FM.
PA Announcer: Unavailable. **Official Scorer:** Bob Redd.
Stadium Name: Hunnicutt Field. **Location:** Exit 9 off I-77, U.S. 460 West to downtown exit, left on Stafford Drive, stadium located behind Mercer County Technical Education Center. **Standard Game Times:** 7 p.m., Sun 3. **Ticket Price Range:** $4-6.

Visiting Club Hotel: Days Inn, I-77 and Ambrose Lane, Princeton, WV 24740. **Telephone:** (304) 425-8100.

PULASKI MARINERS

Mailing Address: P.O. Box 676, Pulaski, VA 24301.
Telephone: (540) 980-1070. **Fax:** (540) 980-1850.
E-Mail Address: info@pulaskimariners.net
Affiliation (first year): Seattle Mariners (2008). **Years in League:** 1946-50, 1952-55, 1957-58, 1969-77, 1982-92, 1997-2006, 2008-

OWNERSHIP, MANAGEMENT
Operated By: Pulaski Baseball Inc.
Director: Pedro Grifol (Seattle Mariners).
President/General Manager: Tom Compton.

FIELD STAFF
Manager: Rob Mummau. **Coach:** Rafael Santo Domingo. **Pitching Coach:** Nasusel Cabrera.

GAME INFORMATION
Radio: None.
PA Announcer: Unavailable. **Official Scorer:** Charles Altizer.
Stadium Name: Calfee Park. **Location:** Interstate 81 to Exit 89-B (Route 11), north to Pulaski, right on Pierce Avenue.
Standard Game Times: 7 p.m.
Ticket Price Range: $4-6.
Visiting Club Hotel: Comfort Inn, 4424 Cleburne Blvd, Dublin, Virginia. **Telephone:** (540) 674-1100.

PIONEER LEAGUE

ROOKIE LEAGUE

Office Address: 1003 E Trent Ave #140, Spokane, WA 99202.
Mailing Address: P.O. Box 2564, Spokane, WA 99220.
Telephone: (509) 456-7615. **Fax:** (509) 456-0136.
E-Mail Address: fanmail@pioneerleague.com. **Website:** www.pioneerleague.com.
Years League Active: 1939-42, 1946-.
President/Secretary/Treasurer: Jim McCurdy.
Vice President: Mike Ellis (Missoula).
Directors: Dave Baggott (Ogden), Mike Ellis (Missoula), D.G. Elmore (Helena), Kevin Greene (Idaho Falls), Michael Baker (Casper), Jeff Katofsky (Orem), Vinny Purpura (Great Falls), Jim Iverson (Billings).
Administrative Assistant: Teryl MacDonald. **Assistant to the President:** Mary Ann McCurdy.
Division Structure: North—Billings, Great Falls, Helena, Missoula. **South**—Casper, Idaho Falls, Ogden, Orem.
Regular Season: 76 games (split schedule). **2011 Opening Date:** June 20. **Closing Date:** Sept. 8.
Playoff Format: First-half division winners meet second-half division winners in best-of-three series. Winners meet in best-of-three series for league championship.
All-Star Game: None.
Roster Limit: 35 active, 30 dressed for each game. **Player Eligibility Rule:** No more than 17 players 21 and older, provided that no more than two are 23 or older (age limits waived). No player on active list may have three or more years of prior minor league service.
Brand of Baseball: Rawlings.
Umpires: Unavailable.

Jim McCurdy

STADIUM INFORMATION

Club	Stadium	Opened	Dimensions LF	CF	RF	Capacity	2010 Att.
Billings	Dehler Park	2008	329	410	350	3,071	101,516
Casper	Mike Lansing Field	2002	355	400	345	2,500	57,120
Great Falls	Centene Stadium at Legion Park	1956	335	414	335	3,800	66,106
Helena	Kindrick Field	1939	335	400	325	1,700	31,962
Idaho Falls	Melaleuca Field	1976	340	400	350	3,400	91,551
Missoula	Ogren Park at Allegiance Field	2004	309	398	287	3,500	87,345
Ogden	Lindquist Field	1997	335	396	334	5,000	132,799
Orem	Home of the Owlz	2005	305	408	312	4,500	81,229

BILLINGS MUSTANGS

Office Address: Dehler Park, 2611 9th Avenue North, Billings, MT 59101.
Mailing Address: PO Box 1553, Billings, MT 59103.
Telephone: (406) 252-1241. **Fax:** (406) 252-2968.
E-Mail Address: mustangs@billingsmustangs.com. **Website:** www.billingsmustangs.com .
Affiliation (first year): Cincinnati Reds (1974). **Years in League:** 1948-63, 1969-

OWNERSHIP, MANAGEMENT

Operated By: Billings Pioneer Baseball Club Inc.
President: Woody Hahn.
General Manager: Gary Roller. **Assistant GM:** Matt Bender. **Director, Stadium Operations:** Chris Marshall. **Director, Food/Beverage:** Curt Prchal. **Director, Broadcasting:** Unavailable. **Director, Field Maintenance:** John Barta. **Director, Clubhouse Operations:** Dixie Davis.

FIELD STAFF

Manager: Pat Kelly. **Coach:** Eli Marrero. **Pitching Coach:** Bob Forsch. **Strength Coach:** Rigo Febles. **Trainer:** Clete Sigwart.

GAME INFORMATION

Radio Announcer: Unavailable. **No. of Games Broadcast:** Home-38, Away-38. **Flagship Station:** ESPN Billings KQBL 105.1 FM.
PA Announcer: Kyle Riley. **Official Scorer:** Phil Sites.
Stadium Name: Dehler Park. **Location:** I-90 to Exit 450, north on 27th Street North to 9th Avenue North. **Standard Game Times:** 7:05 p.m., Sun 4:05 p.m. **Ticket Price Range:** $3-9. **Visiting Club Hotel:** Unavailable.

CASPER GHOSTS

Office Address: 330 Kati Lane, Casper, WY 82601.
Mailing Address: P.O. Box 1293, Casper, WY 82602.
Telephone: (307) 232-1111. **Fax:** (307) 265-7867.
E-Mail Address: cmaxwell@ghostsbaseball.com.
Website: www.ghostsbaseball.com.
Affiliation (first year): Colorado Rockies (2001). **Years in League:** 2001-

OWNERSHIP, MANAGEMENT
Operated by: Casper Ghosts Baseball.
Principal Owner/Senior Vice President: Michael Baker.
Executive Director: Tim Ray.
General Manager: Chris Maxwell. **Office Manager:** Marlyn Black. **Assistant General Manager:** Phil Choler. **Director, Ticket/Merchandise Sales:** Melissa Domol.

FIELD STAFF
Manager: Tony Diaz. **Coach:** Jonathan Stone. **Pitching Coach:** Craig Bjornson. **Trainer:** Josh Guterman.

GAME INFORMATION
Radio Announcer: Unavailable. **No. of Games Broadcast:** Home-38, Away-38. **Flagship Station:** Unavailable.
PA Announcer: Chris Maxwell. **Official Scorer:** Kelly O'Brien.
Stadium Name: Mike Lansing Field. **Location:** I-25 to Poplar Street exit, north on Poplar Street, right into Crossroads Park. **Standard Game Times:** 7:05 p.m., Sun. 4:05. **Ticket Price Range:** $7.50-9.
Visiting Club Hotel: La Quinta, 300 F St., Casper, WY 82601. **Telephone:** (307) 265-1200.

GREAT FALLS VOYAGERS

Office Address: 1015 25th St. N, Great Falls, MT 59401.
Mailing Address: 1015 25th St. N, Great Falls, MT 59401.
Telephone: (406) 452-5311. **Fax:** (406) 454-0811.
E-Mail Address: voyagers@gfvoyagers.com. **Website:** www.gfvoyagers.com.
Affiliation (first year): Chicago White Sox (2003). **Years in League:** 1948-1963, 1969-

OWNERSHIP, MANAGEMENT
Operated By: Great Falls Baseball Club, Inc.
President: Vinney Purpura. **General Manager:** Kattie Swartz. **Assistant GM:** Dave Wellenzohn. **Sales Manager:** Scott Reasoner. **Head Groundskeeper:** Billy Chafin. **Office Manager:** Janet Stone.

FIELD STAFF
Manager: Ryan Newman. **Coach:** Charlie Poe. **Pitching Coach:** Brian Drahman.

GAME INFORMATION
Radio Announcer: Jared Sandler. **No. of Games Broadcast:** Home-38, Away-38. **Flagship Station:** KMON 560-AM.
PA Announcer: Lance DeHaan. **Official Scorer:** Mike Lewis.
Stadium Name: Centene Stadium located at Legion Park. **Location:** From I-15 to exit 281 (10th Ave. S), left on 26th, left on Eighth Ave. North, right on 25th, ballpark on right, past railroad tracks. **Ticket Price Range:** $5-8.
Visiting Club Hotel: Mid Town Motel, 526 Second Ave. N. Great Falls, MT 59401. **Telephone:** (406) 453-2411.

HELENA BREWERS

Office Address: 1300 N. Ewing, Helena, MT 59601.
Mailing Address: P.O. Box 6756, Helena, MT 59604.
Telephone: (406) 495-0500. **Fax:** (406) 495-0900.
E-Mail Address: info@helenabrewers.net. **Website:** www.helenabrewers.net.
Affiliation (first year): Milwaukee Brewers (2003). **Years in League:** 1978-2000, 2003-

OWNERSHIP, MANAGEMENT
Operated by: Helena Baseball Club LLC.
Principal Owner: D.G. Elmore.
General Manager: Paul Fetz. **Assistant GM:** Nick Bowsher. **Director, Hospitality:** Emma Moore. **Director, Broadcasting/Media Relations:** Steve Wendt.

FIELD STAFF
Manager: Joe Ayrault. **Coach:** Ned Yost IV. **Pitching Coach:** Elvin Nina. **Trainer:** Jimmy Gentry.

GAME INFORMATION
Radio Announcer: Unavailable. **No. of Games Broadcast:** Home-38, Away-38. **Flagship Station:** KCAP 1340-AM.

PA Announcer: Randy Bowsher. **Official Scorers:** Kevin Higgens, Craig Struble, Jim Shope, Andrew Gideon. **Stadium Name:** Kindrick Field. **Location:** Cedar Street exit off I-15, west to Last Chance Gulch, left at Memorial Park. **Standard Game Time:** 7:05 p.m., Sun 1:05. **Ticket Price Range:** $6-9. **Visiting Club Hotel:** Red Lion Colonial. **Telephone:** 406-443-2100.

IDAHO FALLS CHUKARS

Office Address: 568 W Elva, Idaho Falls, ID 83402.
Mailing Address: PO 2183, Idaho, ID 83403.
Telephone: (208) 522-8363. **Fax:** (208) 522-9858.
E-Mail Address: chukars@ifchukars.com. **Website:** www.ifchukars.com.
Affiliation (first year): Kansas City Royals (2004). **Years in League:** 1940-42, 1946-

OWNERSHIP, MANAGEMENT

Operated By: The Elmore Sports Group.
Principal Owner: David Elmore.
President/General Manager: Kevin Greene. **Assistant GM, Merchandise:** Andrew Daugherty. **Account Manager/Food Service Specialist:** Paul Henderson. **Head Groundskeeper:** Steve Reuteman. **Clubhouse Manager:** Jared Troescher.

FIELD STAFF

Manager: Brian Buchanan. **Coach:** Omar Ramirez. **Pitching Coach:** Jerry Nyman. **Trainer:** Masa Koyanagi.

GAME INFORMATION

Radio Announcers: John Balginy, Aaron Cox. **No. of Games Broadcast:** Home-38 Road-38. **Flagship Station:** KUPI 980-AM.
Official Scorer: John Balginy.
Stadium Name: Melaleuca Field. **Location:** I-15 to West Broadway exit, left onto Memorial Drive, right on Mound Avenue, 1⁄4 mile to stadium. **Standard Game Times:** 7:15 p.m., Sun 4. **Ticket Price Range:** $6-9.
Visiting Club Hotel: Guesthouse Inn & Suites, 850 Lindsay Blvd, Idaho Falls, ID 83402. **Telephone:** (208) 522-6260.

MISSOULA OSPREY

Office Address: 412 W Alder St, Missoula, MT 59802.
Telephone: (406) 543-3300. **Fax:** (406) 543-9463.
E-Mail Address: info@missoulaosprey.com. **Website:** www.missoulaosprey.com.
Affiliation (first year): Arizona Diamondbacks (1999). **Years in League:** 1956-60, 1999-

OWNERSHIP, MANAGEMENT

Operated By: Mountain Baseball LLC.
President: Mike Ellis. **Vice President:** Judy Ellis.
Executive VP: Matt Ellis. **VP, Finance/Merchandising:** Shelly Ellis. **General Manager/Operations:** Jared Amoss. **GM, Sales/Marketing:** Jeff Griffin. **Director, Stadium Operations:** Byron Dike. **Director, Ticket Operations/Office Manager:** Nola Hunter.

FIELD STAFF

Manager: Hector De La Cruz. **Coach:** Andy Green. **Pitching Coach:** Gil Heredia. **Strength/Conditioning:** Mike Schofield. **Trainer:** Scott Barringer.

GAME INFORMATION

Radio Announcer: Ben Catley. **No. of Games Broadcast:** Home-38, Away-38. **Flagship Station:** KMPT 930-AM.
PA Announcer: Dan Stromme. **Official Scorer:** Dan Hunter, David Kinsey.
Stadium Name: Ogren Park at Allegiance Field. **Location:** 700 Cregg Lane. **Directions:** Take Orange Street to Cregg Lane, west on Cregg Lane, stadium west of McCormick Park. **Standard Game Times:** 7:05 p.m., Sun 5:05. **Ticket Price Range:** $6-12.
Visiting Club Hotel: Mountain Valley Inn, 420 W. Broadway, Missoula, Mt. 59802. **Telephone:** (406) 728-4500

OGDEN RAPTORS

Office Address: 2330 Lincoln Ave, Ogden, UT 84401.
Telephone: (801) 393-2400. **Fax:** (801) 393-2473.
E-Mail Address: homerun@ogden-raptors.com. **Website:** www.ogden-raptors.com.
Affiliation (first year): Los Angeles Dodgers (2003). **Years in League:** 1939-42, 1946-55, 1966-74, 1994-

OWNERSHIP, MANAGEMENT

Operated By: Ogden Professional Baseball, Inc.

Principal Owners: Dave Baggott, John Lindquist. **Chairman, President:** Dave Baggott.
General Manager: Joey Stein. **VP/Director, Marketing:** John Stein. **Broadcaster/Media Relations:** Eric Knighton. **Director, Merchandise:** Gerri Kopinski. **Public Relations:** Pete Diamond. **Groundskeeper:** Kenny Kopinski. **Assistant Groundkeeper:** Bob Richardson. **Assistant Food Director:** Louise Hillard. **Clubhouse Manager:** Kirby Hoover. **Director, Press Box:** Brandon Kunimura.

FIELD STAFF

Manager: Damon Berryhill. **Coach:** Juhnny Washington. **Pitching Coach:** Chuck Crim. **Trainer:** Robert Dyson. **Strength/Conditioning:** Adam Wagner.

GAME INFORMATION

Radio Announcer: Jake Kelman. **No. of Games Broadcast:** Home-38, Away-38. **Flagship Station:** 1490 AM KOGN. **PA Announcer:** Pete Diamond. **Official Scorer:** Dennis Kunimura.
Stadium Name: Lindquist Field. **Location:** I-15 North to 21th Street exit, east to Lincoln Avenue, south three blocks to park. **Standard Game Times:** 7 p.m., Sun 1. **Ticket Price Range:** $6-9.
Visiting Club Hotel: Hotel Ben Lomond, 2510 Washington Blvd., Ogden, UT 84401. **Telephone:** (801) 627-1900.

OREM OWLZ

Office Address: 970 W. University Parkway, Orem, UT 84058.
Telephone: (801) 377-2255. **Fax:** (801) 377-2345.
E-Mail Address: fan@oremowlz.com. **Website:** www.oremowlz.com.
Affiliation (first year): Los Angeles Angels (2001). **Years in League:** 2001-

OWNERSHIP, MANAGEMENT

Operated By: Bery Bery Gud To Me LLC.
Principal Owner: Jeff Katofsky.
General Manager: Jason Badell. **Assistant GM:** Brett Crane. **Director, Promotions/Community Relations:** Jillian Dingee. **IT Manager:** Julie Hatch. **Clubhouse Manager:** Casey Brailsford.

FIELD STAFF

Manager: Tom Kotchman. **Coach:** Nathan Haynes. **Pitching Coach:** Zeke Zimmerman. **Trainer:** Mike Dart. **Strength/Conditioning:** Matt Hill.

GAME INFORMATION

Radio Announcer: Matt Gittins. **No. of Games Broadcast:** Home-38, Away-38. **Flagship Station:** Unavailable.
PA Announcer: Lincoln Fillmore. **Official Scorer:** Unavailable.
Stadium Name: Home of the Owlz. **Location:** Exit 269 (University Parkway) off I-15 at Utah Valley University campus. **Ticket Price Range:** $4-9.
Visiting Club Hotel: Provo Days Inn, 1675 N. 200 West, Provo, UT 84604. **Telephone:** (801) 375-8600.

ARIZONA LEAGUE

Office Address: 620 W. Franklin St., Boise, ID 83702.
Mailing Address: P.O. Box 1645, Boise, ID 83701.
Telephone: (208) 429-1511. **Fax:** (208) 429-1525. **E-Mail Address:** bobrichmond@qwestoffice.net
Years League Active: 1988-.
President/Treasurer: Bob Richmond.
Vice President: Oneri Fleita (Cubs). **Corporate Secretary:** Ted Polakowski (Athletics).
Administrative Assistant: Rob Richmond.
Division Structure: East/Central/West divisions.
Regular Season: 56 games. Aug 30 semifinal games; Aug 31 championship. **2011 Opening Date:** June 20.
Closing Date: Aug. 27.
Standard Game Times: 7 p.m.
Playoff Format: Team with best record plays wildcard in one-game playoff on Aug 30; other two divisions play one-game playoff. Winners play for League championship on Aug 31.
All-Star Game: None.
Roster Limit: 35 active. **Player Eligibility Rule:** No player may have three or more years of prior Minor League Service.
Brand of Baseball: Rawlings.

`Clubs	Playing Site	Manager	Coach	Pitching Coach
Angels	Angels complex, Tempe	Ty Boykin	Dick Schofield	Jim Gott
Athletics	Papago Park Baseball Complex, Phoenix	Marcus Jensen	Juan Dilone	Ariel Prieto
Brewers	Maryvale Baseball Complex, Phoenix	Tony Diggs	Kenny Dominguez	Steve Cline
Cubs	Fitch Park, Mesa	Juan Cabreja	Jason Dubois	R. Tronerud/F. Castillo
D-backs	Salt River Fields at Talking Stick	Kelly Stinnett	Abraham Nunez	Jeff Bajenaru
Dodgers	Camelback Ranch, Glendale	Jody Reed	Leo Garcia	Matt Herges
Giants	Giants complex, Scottsdale	Mike Goff	Victor Torres	Marcos Garcia
Indians	Goodyear Ballpark	Anthony Medrano	Junior Betances	Dennis Malave
Mariners	Peoria Sports Complex	Jesus Azuaje	A. Bottin/B. Johnson	Gary Wheelock
Padres	Peoria Sports Complex	Jim Gabella	Ivan Cruz	N. Cruz/T. Worrell
Rangers	Surprise Recreation Campus	Jayce Tingler	H. Ortiz/O. Bernard	R. O'Malley/J. Jaimes
Reds	Goodyear Ballpark	Jose Miguel Nieves	Jorge Orta	Tom Browning
Royals	Surprise Recreation Campus	Darryl Kennedy	A. David/J. Bruno	C. Reyes/C. Martinez

GULF COAST LEAGUE

Operated By: Minor League Baseball.
Office Address: 9550 16th Street North, St. Petersburg, FL 33716.
Telephone: 727-456-1734. **Fax:** 727-821-5819.
Website: www.milb.com. **E-mail Address:** gcl@milb.com.
Executive Vice President/COO: Tim Purpura. **Vice President, Baseball/Business Operations:** Tim Brunswick. **Baseball Operations Assistant:** Andy Shultz.
2011 Opening Date: June 20. **Closing Date:** August 27. **Regular Season:** 56/60 games.
Divisional Alignment: East—Astros, Cardinals, Marlins, Mets, Nationals. North—Blue Jays, Braves, Phillies, Pirates, Tigers, Yankees. South—Orioles, Rays, Red Sox, Twins.
Playoff Format: The division winner with the best record plays the wild card; the other two division winners meet in a one-game playoff. The winners meet in a best-of-three series.
All-Star Game: None. **Roster Limit:** 35 active, only 30 of whom may be in uniform and eligible to play in any given game. At least 10 must be pitchers as of July 1.
Player Eligibility Rule: No player may have three or more years of prior minor league service.
Brand of Baseball: Rawlings. **Statistician:** Major League Baseball Advanced Media

Clubs	Playing Site	Manager	Coach(es)	Pitching Coach
Astros	Astros complex, Kissimmee	Ed Romero	Edgar Alfonzo	H. Mercado/C. Taylor
Blue Jays	Mattick Training Center, Dunedin	Omar Malave	P. Elliott/D. Solano	John Wesley
Braves	Disney's Wide World of Sports, Orlando	Jonathan Schuerholz	Rick Albert	Vladimir Nunez
Cardinals	Cardinals complex, Jupiter	Steve Turco	Oliver Marmol	Dernier Orozco
Marlins	Roger Dean complex, Jupiter	Jorge Hernandez	Angel Espada	Jeff Schwarz
Mets	St. Lucie Sports Complex, St. Lucie	Luis Rojas	Y. Garcia/J. Fuentes	Mark Brewer
Nationals	Carl Barger Baseball Complex, Melbourne	Bobby Williams	S. Mendez/J. Poppert	Miguel Tejera
Orioles	Twin Lakes Park, Sarasota	Ramon Sambo	M. May/J. Hernandez	Larry Jaster
Phillies	Carpenter Complex, Clearwater	Roly DeArmas	Kevin Jordan	Les Lancaster
Pirates	Pirate City Complex, Bradenton	Tom Prince	W. Huyke/M. Lum	Miguel Bonilla
Rays	Charlotte County Complex, Port Charlotte	Joe Alvarez	D. DeMent/H. Torres	Darwin Peguero
Red Sox	Red Sox complex	George Lombard	U. Washington/D. Tomlin	Walter Miranda
Tigers	Tigertown, Lakeland	Basilio Cabrera	Mike Rabelo	Greg Sabat
Twins	Lee County Complex, Fort Myers	Ramon Borrego	M. Cuyler/R. Hernandez	Ivan Arteaga
Yankees	Yankee complex, Tampa	Carlos Mendoza	John Rodriguez	J.Rosado/G.Pavlick

INDEPENDENT LEAGUES

AMERICAN ASSOCIATION

Office Address: 1415 Hwy 54 West, Suite 210, Durham, NC 27707.
Telephone: (919) 401-8150. **Fax:** (919) 401-8152. **Website:** www.americanassociationbaseball.com.
Year Founded: 2005.
Commissioner: Miles Wolff. **President:** Dan Moushon.
Administrative Assistant: Jason Deans. **Director, Umpires:** Kevin Winn.
Division Structure: North Division—Fargo-Moorhead RedHawks, Sioux Falls Pheasants, St. Paul Saints, Winnipeg Goldeyes. Central Division—Gary SouthShore RailCats, Kansas City T-Bones, Lincoln Saltdogs, Sioux City Explorers, Wichita Wingnuts. South Division—Amarillo Sox, El Paso Diablos, Fort Worth Cats, Grand Prairie AirHogs, Shreveport-Bossier Captains.
Regular Season: 100 games. **2011 Opening Date:** May 12. **2011 Closing Date:** Aug 30.
Playoff Format: Three division winners and one wild card play in best-of-five series. Winners play for best-of-five American Association Championship.
Roster Limit: 22. **Eligibility Rule:** Minimum of four first-year players; maximum of four veterans.
Brand of Baseball: Rawlings.
Statistician: Pointstreak.com, 602-1595 16th Avenue, Richmond Hill, ON Canada L4B 3N9.

STADIUM INFORMATION

Club	Stadium	Opened	Dimensions LF	CF	RF	Capacity	2010 Att.
#Amarillo	Potter Co. Memorial Stadium	1949	355	429	355	7,500	143,795
El Paso	Cohen Stadium	1990	340	410	340	9,725	179,452
&Fargo-Moorhead	Newman Outdoor Field	1996	314	408	318	4,513	183,145
Fort Worth	LaGrave Field	2002	325	400	335	5,100	122,062
&Gary SouthShore	U.S. Steel Yard	2002	320	400	335	6,139	166,366
Grand Prairie	QuikTrip Park at Grand Prairie	2008	330	400	330	5,445	124,539
&Kansas City	Community America Ballpark	2003	300	396	328	6,537	264,368
Lincoln	Haymarket Park	2001	335	395	325	4,500	163,676
St. Paul	Midway Field	1982	320	400	320	6,069	237,994
Shreveport-Bossier	Fair Grounds Field	1986	330	400	330	4,500	71,468
Sioux City	Lewis and Clark Park	1993	330	400	330	3,630	56,428
Sioux Falls	Sioux Falls Stadium	1964	312	410	312	4,029	86,518
Wichita	Lawrence-Dumont Stadium	1934	344	401	312	6,055	134,773
&Winnipeg	Shaw Park	1999	325	400	325	7,481	271,399

\# - Operated in United League in 2010
& - Operated in Northern League in 2010

AMARILLO SOX

Office Address: 801 S Polk St, Amarillo, TX 79106.
Telephone: (806) 242-4653. **Fax:** (806) 322-1839.
E-mail Address: vulture4246@yahoo.com. **Website:** www.amarillosox.com.
VP/General Manager: Mark Lee. **Assistant GM:** Jaylin Henderson. **Director, Publication/Sales:** Ben Miller.
Manager: John Harris.

GAME INFORMATION
Internet Broadcaster: Ben Miller.
Stadium Name: Potter County Memorial Stadium. **Location:** Take Exit 72B toward Grand St, turn left on Grand St., turn left onto SE 3rd Ave.
Standard Game Times: 7:05 p.m., **Sun 6:**05.

EL PASO DIABLOS

Office Address: 9700 Gateway North Blvd, El Paso, TX 79924.
Telephone: (915) 755-2000. **Fax:** (915) 757-0681.
E-mail Address: info@diablos.com. **Website:** www.diablos.com.
Managing Partner: Mark Schuster. Ventura Sports Group, LLC.
General Manager: Matt LaBranche. **Business Manager:** Pat Hofman. **Director, Corporate Sponsorships:** Bernie Ricono. **Manager, Media/Community Relations:** Lizette Espinosa. **Box Office Manager:** Steve Martinez. **Marketing/Promotions Manager:** Henry Quintana III. **Senior Account Executive:** Donna Blair. **Ticket Sales Coordinator:** Adam Diaz. **Account Executives:** Victor Reta, Christine Aranda, Valerie Ortiz, Priscilla Pinon.
Manager: Jorge Alvarez. **Coaches:** Andy Torres, Jerry Verastegui, Albenis Machado.

GAME INFORMATION

Radio Announcer: Nick Vlietstra. **Games Broadcast:** 100. **Flagship Station:** 1380-AM. **Webcast Address:** www.diablos.com.

Stadium Name: Cohen Stadium. **Location:** I-10 to U.S.54 (Patriot Freeway), east to Diana exit to Gateway North Boulevard.

Standard Game Times: 7:05 p.m., Sun 6:05.

FARGO-MOORHEAD
REDHAWKS

Office Address: 1515 15th Ave N, Fargo, ND 58102.
Telephone: (701) 235-6161. **Fax:** (701) 297-9247.
E-Mail Address: redhawks@fmredhawks.com. **Website:** www.fmredhawks.com.
Operated by: Fargo Baseball LLC.
President: Bruce Thom. **Chief Executive Officer:** Brad Thom.
General Manager: Josh Buchholz. **Senior Accountant:** Sue Wild. **Director, Promotions:** Eric Jorgenson. **Director, Ticket Sales:** Michael Larson. **Director, Community Relations/Group Events:** Karl Hoium. **Director, Food/Beverage:** Sean Kiernan. **Director, Field/Stadium Operations:** Matt Wallace.
Manager/Director, Player Procurement: Doug Simunic. **Player Procurement Consultant:** Jeff Bittiger. **Pitching Coach:** Steve Montgomery. **Coach:** Bucky Burgau. **Trainer:** Mike Bogenreif. **Clubhouse Operations:** Matt Gastecki.

GAME INFORMATION

Radio Announcer: Scott Miller. **No. of Games Broadcast:** Home-50, Away-50. **Flagship Station:** 740-AM The FAN.

Stadium Name: Newman Outdoor Field. **Location:** I-29 North to exit 67, right on 19th Ave North, right on Albrecht Boulevard.

Standard Game Times: 7:02 p.m., Sat 6, Sun 1.

Visiting Club Hotel: Howard Johnson Inn, 301 3rd Ave N, Fargo, ND 58102. **Telephone:** (701) 232-8850.

FORT WORTH CATS

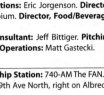

Office Address: 301 NE Sixth St, Fort Worth, TX 76164.
Telephone: (817) 332-2287. **Fax:** (817) 870-4961.
E-Mail Address: info@fwcats.com. **Website:** www.fwcats.com.
Principal Owner/CEO: Carl Bell. **General Manager:** Dick Smith. **Operations Consultant:** Steven Brubaker. **Director, Media/Public Relations:** Bric Shelton. **Director, Ticket Sales:** Corey Troxell. **Sponsorship/Corporate Sales:** Tim Trout. **Community Relations/Merchandise:** Rachel Taft. **Bookkeeper:** Heather Wiginton. **Field Operations:** Jeff Martin.
Manager: Stan Hough. **Coaches:** Lance Brown; Mike Bascik, Sr. **Clubhouse Manager:** Randy Christian.

GAME INFORMATION

Stadium Name: LaGrave Field. **Location:** One mile north of downtown Fort Worth; From I-30, take I-35 North to North Side Drive exit, left (west) off exit to Main Street, left (south) on Main, left (east) onto NE Sixth Street.

Standard Game Times: 7:05 p.m., Sun 6:05.

GARY SOUTHSHORE RAILCATS

Office Address: One Stadium Plaza, Gary, IN 46402.
Telephone: (219) 882-2255. **Fax:** (219) 882-2259.
E-Mail Address: info@railcatsbaseball.com. **Website:** www.railcatsbaseball.com.
Operated by: PLS Holdings.
Owner/CEO: Pat Salvi. **Owner:** Lindy Salvi.
President/General Manager: Andy Viano. **Chief Financial Officer:** Becky Kremer. **Director, Sales/Ticketing:** Alan Bowman. **Director, Stadium Operations:** Nick Lampasona. **Director, Marketing/Promotions:** Natalie Kirby. **Manager, Merchandise:** Laura Blakeley. **Manager, Community Relations:** Radley Robinson. **Manager, Box Office:** Adam Harris. **Manager, Group Sales:** Aaron Pineda. **Account Executives:** Nikki Kimbrough, Chanelle Yarber. **Head Groundskeeper:** Blake Bostelman. **Graphic Designer:** Domonic Edwards. **Executive Assistant:** Arcella Moxley. **Stadium Maintenance:** Stephanie Tavorn.
Manager: Greg Tagert. **Coaches:** Jamie Bennett, Mick Curran.

GAME INFORMATION
No. of Games Broadcast: Home-50, Away-50. **Flagship Station:** WLPR 89.1-FM.
Stadium Name: US Steel Yard. **Location:** I-80/94 to Broadway Exit (Exit 10), north on Broadway to Fifth Avenue, east one block to stadium.
Standard Game Times: 7:10 p.m., Sat 6:10, Sun 2:10.

GRAND PRAIRIE AIRHOGS

Office Address: 1600 Lone Star Parkway, Grand Prairie, TX 75050.
Telephone: (972) 504-9383. **Fax:** (972) 504-2288.
Website: www.airhogsbaseball.com.
Operated By: Ventura Sports Group, LLC.
Assistant General Manager, Sales/Marketing: Matt Barry. **Ticket Sales Manager:** J Willms. **Finance Manager:** Trista Earlston. **Business Development:** Karen Lucchesi. **Food/Beverage:** Sodexo. **CFO:** John Keel.
Manager: Pete Incaviglia.

GAME INFORMATION
Stadium Name: QuikTrip Park at Grand Prairie. **Location:** From I-30, take Beltline Road exit going north, take Lone Star Park entrance towards the stadium.
Standard Game Times: 7:05, Sun 6:05.
Visiting Club Hotel: Elegante Hotel and Suites, 2330 West Northwest Highway, Dallas, TX 75220. **Telephone:** (214) 351-4477.

KANSAS CITY T-BONES

Office Address: 1800 Village West Parkway Kansas City, KS 66111.
Telephone: (913) 328-2255. **Fax:** (913) 328-5652.
E-mail Address: batterup@tbonesbaseball.com.
Website: www.tbonesbaseball.com.
Operated By: T-Bones Baseball Club, LLC; Ehlert Development.
Owner/President: John Ehlert. **Vice President:** Adam Ehlert.
VP/General Manager: Chris Browne. **VP/Corporate Partnerships:** Scott Steckly. **Assistant GM, Group Sales:** Eric Marshall. **Director, Media Relations/Press Box:** Stan Duitsman. **Director, Promotions:** Emily Hoskins. **Director, Ticket Operations/Box Office Manager:** Kurt Sieker. **Director, Broadcasting:** Brian Bruce. **Operations Manager:** Rylan D. Brody. **Bookkeeper:** Sherrie Stover. **Account Executives:** Jason Young, Ryan Thayer.
Manager: Tim Doherty. **Coaches:** Damian Rolls, Caleb Balbuena. **Trainer:** Josh Adams.

GAME INFORMATION
Radio Announcer: Brian Bruce. **No. of Games Broadcast:** Home-50, Away-50. **Flagship Station:** WDAF 1660-AM.
Stadium Name: Community America Ballpark. **Location:** State Avenue West off I-435 and State Avenue. **Standard Game Times:** 7:05 p.m., Sun 5:05.
Visiting Club Hotel: Hyatt Regency Crown Center, 2345 McGee Street, Kansas City, MO, 64108. **Telephone:** (816) 421-1234.

LINCOLN SALTDOGS

Office Address: 403 Line Drive Circle, Suite A, Lincoln, NE 68508.
Telephone: (402) 474-2255. **Fax:** (402) 474-2254.
E-Mail Address: info@saltdogs.com. **Website:** www.saltdogs.com.
Owner: Jim Abel. **President:** Charlie Meyer.
Vice President/General Manager: Tim Utrup. **Assistant GM/Director, Sales/Marketing:** Bret Beer. **Director, Broadcasting/Communications:** Jason Van Arkel. **Director, Merchandising/Promotions:** Anne Duchek. **Director, Season Tickets/Ticket Packages:** Toby Antonson. **Director, Stadium Operations:** Dave Aschwege. **Assistant Director, Stadium Operations:** Jeff Koncaba. **Office Manager:** Alicia Oakeson. **Athletic Turf Manager:** Josh Klute. **Assistant Turf Managers:** J.J. Borecky, Jen Roeber.
Manager: Marty Scott. **Coaches:** Chris Miyake, Jarrett Gardner.

GAME INFORMATION
Radio Announcer: Jason Van Arkel. **No. of Games Broadcast:** 100. **Flagship Station:** KFOR 1240-AM. **Webcast Address:** www.kfor1240.com.
Stadium Name: Haymarket Park. **Location:** I-80 to Cornhusker Highway West, left on First Street, right on Sun Valley Boulevard, left on Line Drive. **Standard Game Times:** 7:05 p.m., **Sun** 5:05.
Visiting Club Hotel: Country Inn & Suites, 5353 N. 27th, Lincoln, NE 68521. **Telephone:** (402) 476-5353.

ST. PAUL SAINTS

Office Address: 1771 Energy Park Dr, St Paul, MN 55108.
Telephone: (651) 644-3517. **Fax:** (651) 644-1627.
E-Mail Address: funisgood@saintsbaseball.com. **Website:** www.saintsbaseball.com.

Principal Owners: Marv Goldklang, Mike Veeck, Bill Murray. **Chairman:** Marv Goldklang. **President:** Mike Veeck.
Executive Vice President/General Manager: Derek Sharrer. **Executive VP:** Tom Whaley. **Assistant GM:** Dan Lehv.
VP, Customer Service/Community Partnerships: Annie Huidekoper. **Director, Corporate Partnerships:** Chris Schwab.
Director, Broadcast/Media Relations: Sean Aronson. **Group/Season Ticket Sales Manager:** Erin Luethi. **Coordinator Corporate Sponsorships/Special Events:** Erin Kohles. **Box Office Manager:** Joshua Hauser.
Manager, Technology/Ticket Sales Representative: Chelsey Wentz. **Promotions Coordinator/Ticket Sales Representative:** Brian Kaufenberg. **Ticket Sales Representative:** Chuck Richards. **Director, Food/Beverage:** Curtis Nachtsheim. **Business Manager:** Leesa Anderson. **Office Manager:** Gina Kray. **Stadium Operations:** Bob Klepperich.
Groundskeeper: Connie Rudolph.
Manager: George Tsamis. **Coaches:** Lamarr Rogers, Jason Verdugo, TJ Wiesner.

GAME INFORMATION
Radio Announcer: Sean Aronson. **No. of Games Broadcast:** 100. **Flagship Station:** Relevant Radio 1330-AM.
Webcast Address: www.saintsbaseball.com.
Stadium Name: Midway Stadium. **Location:** From I-94, take Snelling Avenue North exit, west onto Energy Park Drive.
Standard Game Times: 7:05 p.m., **Sun** 1:05.
Visiting Club Hotel: Sheraton St. Paul Woodbury, 676 Bielenberg Drive, Woodbury, MN55125.
Telephone: (651)209-3280.

SHREVEPORT-BOSSIER
CAPTAINS

Office Address: 2901 Pershing Blvd, Shreveport, LA 71109.
Telephone: (318) 636-5555. **Fax:** (318) 636-5670.
Website: www.sbcaptains.com.
Owner: Gary Elliston. **President:** Scott Berry.
Vice President/General Manager: Craig Brasfield. **Assistant GM:** Chet Carey. **Director, Stadium Operations:** Wiley Clark. **Business Manager/Director, Merchandise:** Carrie Brasfield. **Head Manager:** Ricky VanAsselberg. **Coaches:** B.J. Litchfield, Darien Dukes.

GAME INFORMATION
No. of Games Broadcast: 100. **Webcast Address:** www.sbcaptains.com.
Stadium Name: Fair Grounds Field. **Location:** Hearne Avenue (US 171) exit off I-20 at Louisiana State Fairgrounds.
Standard Game Times: 7:05 p.m., Sun 6:05.
Visiting Club Hotel: Holiday Inn Shreveport West, 5555 Financial Plaza, Shreveport, LA 71129.
Telephone: (318) 688-3000.

SIOUX CITY EXPLORERS

Office Address: 3400 Line Drive, Sioux City, IA 51106.
Telephone: (712) 277-9467. **Fax:** (712) 277-9406.
E-Mail Address: promotions@xsbaseball.com. **Website:** www.xsbaseball.com.
President: John Roost.
General Manager: Shane M Tritz. **Assistant GM:** Ashley Schoenrock. **Office Manager:** Julie Stringer.
Field Manager: Stan Cliburn. **Coaches:** Bobby Post, Alex Llanos.

GAME INFORMATION
Radio Announcer: Dave Nitz. **No. of Games Broadcast:** 100.
Flagship Station: KSCJ 1360-AM. **Webcast Address:** www.xsbaseball.com.
Stadium Name: Lewis and Clark Park. **Location:** I-29 to Singing Hills Blvd, North, right on Line Drive.
Standard Game Times: 7:05 p.m., Sun 6:05.
Visiting Club Hotel: Clarion Hotel & Conference Center, 707 Fourth Street Sioux City, IA, 51101.
Telephone: (712) 277-4101.

SIOUX FALLS PHEASANTS

Office Address: 1001 N West Ave, Sioux Falls, SD 57104.
Telephone: (605) 333-0179. **Fax:** (605) 333-0139.
E-Mail Address: info@sfpheasants.com. **Website:** www.sfpheasants.com.
Operated by: Sioux Falls Sports, LLC.
   Director, Baseball Operations: Adam Peterman. **Director, Stadium Operations:** Larry McKenney. **Office/Ticketing Manager:** Wendy Loria. **VP, Media/Public Relations:** Jim Olander. **VP, Corporate Operations:** Tim Barth.
   Manager: Steve Shirley.

GAME INFORMATION
   Stadium Name: Sioux Falls Stadium. **Location:** I-29 to Russell Street, east one mile, right on West Avenue.
   Standard Game Times: 7:05 p.m., Sat 6:05, Sun 2:05/5:05.

WICHITA WINGNUTS

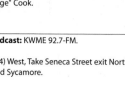

Office Address: 300 South Sycamore, Wichita, KS 67213.
Telephone: (316) 264-6887. **Fax:** (316) 264-2129.
Website: www.wichitawingnuts.com.
Owners: Steve Ruud, Dan Waller, Gary Austerman, Nick Easter, Nate Robertson.
President/General Manager: Josh Robertson. **Assistant GM/Director, Corporate Sales:** Ben Keiter. **Assistant GM/Director, Ticket Sales:** Jeremy Mock. **Special Assistant to GM:** Brian Holman. **Director, Broadcast:** Steve Schuster. **Director, Finance:** Kay Brown. **Director, Stadium Operations:** Jeff Kline. **Crew Chief, Stadium Operations:** Scott Taylor. **Tournament Director, NBC World Series:** Jerry Taylor. **Operations Manager, NBC World Series:** Casey Walkup. **Group Sales Manager:** Brian Turner. **Game Day Personnel/Merchandise Manager:** Caitlin Smith.
   Clubhouse Manager: Brad Brungardt. **Assistant Clubhouse Manager:** Bill "Sarge" Cook.
   Manager: Kevin Hooper. **Coaches:** Luke Robertson, Jose Amado, Brian Rose.

GAME INFORMATION
   Radio Announcer: Steve Schuster. **No. of Games Broadcast:** 100. **Games Broadcast:** KWME 92.7-FM.
   Webcast Address: www.wichitawingnuts.com.
   Stadium Name: Lawrence-Dumont Stadium. **Location:** 135 North to Kellogg (54) West, Take Seneca Street exit North to Maple, Go East on Maple to Sycamore, Stadium is located on corner of Maple and Sycamore.
   Standard Game Times: 7:05 p.m., Sun 5:05.
   Visiting Club Hotel: North Rock Suites, 7856 E 36th St, N, Wichita, KS, 67226. **Telephone:** (316) 634-2303.

WINNIPEG GOLDEYES

Office Address: One Portage Ave E, Winnipeg, Manitoba R3B 3N3.
Telephone: (204) 982-2273. **Fax:** (204) 982-2274.
E-Mail Address: goldeyes@goldeyes.com. **Website:** www.goldeyes.com.
Operated by: Winnipeg Goldeyes Baseball Club Inc.
Principal Owner/President: Sam Katz.
   General Manager: Andrew Collier. **Assistant GM:** Regan Katz. **Media Relations Manager:** Scott Unger. **Administrative Assistant:** Bonnie Benson. **Chief Financial Officer:** Jason McRae-King. **Controller:** Judy Jones. **Director, Sales/Marketing:** Dan Chase. **Sales/Marketing Coordinator:** Angela Sanche. **Account Representatives:** Blake Schultz, Paul Edmonds, Dennis McLean, Scott Taylor. **Promotions Coordinator:** Sarah Kyrylchuk. **Box Office Manager:** Kevin Arnst. **Retail Manager:** Megan Tucker. Facility Manager/Head Groundskeeper: Don Ferguson.
   Manager/Director, Player Procurement: Rick Forney. **Coaches:** Tom Vaeth, Brendan Sagara. **Trainer:** Shane Zdebiak. **Clubhouse Manager:** Jamie Samson.

GAME INFORMATION
   Radio Announcer: Paul Edmonds. **No. of Games Broadcast:** Home-50, Road-50. **Flagship Station:** Sports Radio 1290-AM.
   Television Announcers: Scott Taylor, Ken Wiebe, Jim Toth. **No. of Games Telecast:** Home-24, Away-0. **Station:** Shaw TV Channel 9.
   Stadium Name: Shaw Park. **Location:** North on Pembina Highway to Broadway, East on Broadway to Main Street, North on Main Street to Water Avenue, East on Water Avenue to Westbrook Street, North on Westbrook Street to Lombard Avenue, East on Lombard Avenue to Mill Street, South on Mill Street to ballpark.
   Standard Game Times: 7:00 p.m., Sat 6, Sun 1:30.
   Visiting Club Hotel: The Radisson Hotel Winnipeg Downtown, 288 Portage Ave, Winnipeg, Manitoba R3C 0B8. **Telephone:** (204) 956-0410.

ATLANTIC LEAGUE

Mailing Address: 401 N Delaware Ave Camden, NJ 08102.
Telephone: (856) 541-9400. **Fax:** (856) 541-9410.
E-Mail Address: info@atlanticleague.com. **Website:** www.atlanticleague.com.
Year Founded: 1998.
Chief Executive Officer/Founder: Frank Boulton. **Vice Presidents:** Peter Kirk, Steven Kalafer.
Executive Director: Joe Klein.
Directors: Frank Boulton (Long Island, Bridgeport, Newark), Steve Kalafer (Somerset), Peter Kirk (Lancaster, York, Southern Maryland), Frank Boulton/Peter Kirk (Camden).
Latin Coordinator: Ellie Rodriguez. **Director, Baseball Administration:** Patty MacLuckie.
Division Structure: Liberty—Bridgeport, Camden, Long Island, Southern Maryland. Freedom—Lancaster, Road Warriors, Somerset, York.
Regular Season: 140 games (split-schedule).
2011 Opening Date: April 29. **Closing Date:** Sept. 18.
All-Star Game: July 12 at York.
Playoff Format: First-half division winners meet second-half winners in best of five series. Winners meet in best-of-five final for league championship.
Roster Limit: 25. Teams may keep 27 players from start of season until May 31, 2011.
Eligibility Rule: No restrictions.
Brand of Baseball: Rawlings.
Statistician: Pointstreak.com. **Address:** 602-1595 16th Avenue, Richmond Hill, ON, Canada L4B 3N9.

STADIUM INFORMATION

Club	Stadium	Opened	LF	CF	RF	Capacity	2010 Att.
Bridgeport	The Ballpark at Harbor Yard	1998	325	405	325	5,300	160,653
Camden	Campbell's Field	2001	325	405	325	6,425	246,039
Lancaster	Clipper Magazine Stadium	2005	372	400	300	6,000	327,467
Long Island	Citibank Park	2000	325	400	325	6,002	410,619
Somerset	Commerce Bank Ballpark	1999	317	402	315	6,100	369,466
So. Maryland	Regency Stadium	2008	305	400	320	6,000	240,777
York	Sovereign Bank Stadium	2007	300	400	325	5,000	278,410

(Dimensions headers: LF, CF, RF)

BRIDGEPORT BLUEFISH

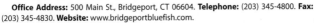

Office Address: 500 Main St., Bridgeport, CT 06604. **Telephone:** (203) 345-4800. **Fax:** (203) 345-4830. **Website:** www.bridgeportbluefish.com.
Operated by: Past Time Partners, LLC.
Principal Owner/CEO, Past Time Partners: Frank Boulton. **Senior VP, Past Time Partners:** Mike Pfaff. **Partners, Past Time Partners:** Tony Rosenthal, Fred Heyman, Jeff Serkes.
General Manager: Robert Goughan. **Business Manager:** Mary Jayne Wells. **Public Relations Director:** Paul Herrmann. **Community Relations Coordinator:** Marilyn Guarino. **Facilities Coordinator:** Tom Yario. **Promotions Coordinator:** Tim Carr. **Head Groundskeeper:** Don Lemieux. **Broadcast Coordinator:** Perry Miles. **Merchandise Coordinator:** Bobby Aanonsen. **Ticket Sales Coordinator:** Dan Cunningham. **Account Executive/Operation Assistant:** Jim Foltz. **Ticket Sales Coordinator:** Nicole Salcito.
Manager: Willie Upshaw. **Coach:** Unavailable. **Pitching Coach:** Unavailable. **Trainer:** Ericka Ventura.

GAME INFORMATION

Radio Announcer: Perry Miles. **No. of Games Broadcast:** 124 (webcast). **Flagship Station:** Unavailable. **PA Announcer:** Bill Jensen. **Official Scorer:** Chuck Sadowski.
Stadium Name: The Ballpark at Harbor Yard. **Location:** I-95 to exit 27, Route 8/25 to exit 1. **Standard Game Times:** 7:05 p.m., Sun 2:05.
Visiting Club Hotel: Holiday Inn Bridgeport, 1070 Main St, Bridgeport, CT 06604. **Telephone:** (203) 334-1234.

CAMDEN RIVERSHARKS

Office Address: 401 N Delaware Ave, Camden, NJ 08102.
Telephone: (856) 963-2600. **Fax:** (856) 963-8534.
E-Mail Address: riversharks@riversharks.com. **Website:** www.riversharks.com.
Operated by: Camden Baseball, LLC.
Principal Owners: Frank Boulton, Peter Kirk. **President:** Jon Danos. **Controller:** Emily Merrill. **General Manager:** Adam Lorber. **Director, Group Events:** Bob Nehring. **Group Account Managers:** Mark Schieber, Lindsay Rosenberg. **Group Sales Manager:** Brian Frankowski. **Director, Finance/Ticketing:** Sean Maher. **Corporate Partnerships Manager:** Drew Nelson. **Corporate Partnerships Manager:** Aaron Moss. **Corporate

Partnerships Manager: Kristin Segers. **Marketing Manager:** Gina DiDomenicis. **Creative Services Manager:** Meaghan Rhoades. **Community Relations Manager:** Sean Armstrong. **Group Sales Assistants:** Kimberly Perno, Brian Henninger, Ross Anderson. **Public Relations Assistant:** Sarah Wasser. **Ticket Office Assistant:** Dana Rommel. **Stadium Operations Manager:** Frank Slavinski. **Stadium Operations Assistant:** Nick Razler. **Office Manager:** Dolores Rozier. **Legends Hospitality Assistant General Manager:** Harry Smith.

Director, Baseball Operations: Jeff Scott. **Manager:** Von Hayes. **Pitching Coach:** Jeff Scott.

GAME INFORMATION

Radio: www.riversharks.com. **Riversharks Broadcaster:** Tim Saunders

PA Announcer: Kevin Casey. **Official Scorer:** Dick Shute. **Stadium Name:** Campbell's Field.

Location: From Philadelphia, right on Sixth Street, right after Ben Franklin Bridge toll booth, right on Cooper Street until it ends at Delaware Ave. From Camden, I-676 to exit 5B, follow signs to field. **Standard Game Times:** 7:05 p.m., Sat 5:35, Sun 1:05. Gates open one hour prior to game time.

Visiting Club Hotel: Holiday Inn, Route 70 and Sayer Avenue, Cherry Hill, NJ 08002. **Telephone:** (856) 663-5300; Extended Stay America, 1653 E State Highway 70, Cherry Hill, NJ 08002. **Telephone:** (856) 616-1200.

LANCASTER BARNSTORMERS

Office Address: 650 North Prince St., **Lancaster, PA 17603.**

Telephone: (717) 509-4487. **FAX:** (717) 509-4486.

E-Mail Address: info@lancasterbarnstormers.com. **Website:** www.lancasterbarnstormers.com.

Operated by: Lancaster Barnstormers Baseball Club, LLC.

Principal Owners: Opening Day Partners.

President: Jon Danos.

Vice President, Business Development: Mark Wilson. **Controller:** Emily Merrill. **General Manager:** Vince Bulik. **Assistant GM:** Kristen Simon. **Director, Stadium Operations:** Don Pryer. **Director, Finance:** Jackie Zanghi. **Creative Services Manager:** Tom Gorman. **Ticket Services Manager:** Maureen Wheeler. **Stadium Operations Manager:** Ed Snyder. **Public Relations Manager:** Pamela Denlinger. **Marketing Manager:** Bryan Shaffer. **Director, Business Development:** Bob Ford. Director, Events/Entertainment: Brian Radle. **Group Events Coordinators:** Christopher Burton, Jennifer Dougherty, Josh Kirchner, John Warnick. **Administrative Assistant:** Liz Welch.

Manager: Butch Hobson. **Pitching Coach:** Marty Janzen. **Hitting Coach:** Lance Burkhart. **Trainer:** Unavailable.

GAME INFORMATION

Radio Announcer: Dave Collins. **No. of Games Broadcast:** Home-72, Away-54. **Flagship Station:** WLPA 1490-AM. **PA Announcer:** John Witwer. **Official Scorer:** Joel Schreiner.

Stadium Name: Clipper Magazine Stadium. **Location:** From Route 30, take Fruitville Pike or Harrisburg Pike toward downtown Lancaster, stadium at intersection of Prince Street and Harrisburg Pike. **Standard Game Times:** 7 p.m., 6:30, 1:30. **Visiting Team Hotel:** Unavailable.

LONG ISLAND DUCKS

Mailing Address: 3 Court House Dr, Central Islip, NY 11722.

Telephone: (631) 940-3825. **Fax:** (631) 940-3800.

E-Mail Address: info@liducks.com. **Website:** www.liducks.com.

Operated by: Long Island Ducks Professional Baseball, LLC.

Principal Owner/CEO: Frank Boulton. **Owners:** Bud Harrelson, Tony Rosenthal, Seth Waugh.

President/General Manager: Michael Pfaff. **Assistant GMs:** Doug Cohen, Alex Scannella. **Director, Group Sales:** John Wolff. **Director, Administration:** Gerry Anderson. **Director, Merchandise/Operations:** Anthony Barberio. **Manager, Box Office:** Ben Harper. **Director, Marketing/Entertainment:** Rob Lyons. **Manager, Media Relations:** Casey Lynn. **Merchandise/Client Services Coordinator:** Stephen Malone. **Operations Coordinator:** Tim LaMare. **Manager, Ticket Sales:** Brad Kallman. **Manager, Community Relations:** Chris Gee. **Coordinator, Administration:** Megan Gordon. **Account Executives:** Jay Randle, Chris Rufle. **Head Groundskeeper:** Brad Keith. **Clubhouse Manager:** Rich Jensen. **Ticket Assistant:** Chris Lukas. **Group Sales Assistant:** Lauren Brady.

Manager: Kevin Baez. **Coach:** Jay Loviglio. **Trainers:** Tony Amin, Adam Lewis, Dorothy Pitchford.

GAME INFORMATION

Radio Announcers: Chris King, Casey Lynn, David Weiss. **No. of Games Broadcast:** 126 on www.liducks.com. **Flagship Station:** Unavailable. **PA Announcer:** Bob Ottone. **Official Scorers:** Unavailable

Stadium Name: Bethpage Ballpark. **Location:** Southern State Parkway east to Carleton Avenue North (exit 43 A), right onto Courthouse Drive, stadium behind federal courthouse complex. **Standard Game Times:** 7:05 p.m., Sun 1:35/5:05.

Visiting Club Hotel: Holiday Inn, Long Island Islip Airport, 3845 Veterans Memorial Highway, Ronkonkoma NY 11779. **Telephone:** (631) 585-9500.

SOMERSET PATRIOTS

Office Address: One Patriots Park, Bridgewater, NJ 08807.
Telephone: (908) 252-0700. **Fax:** (908) 252-0776.
Website: www.somersetpatriots.com.
Operated by: Somerset Patriots Baseball Club, LLC.
Principal Owners: Steve Kalafer, Jack Cust, Byron Brisby, Don Miller. **Chairman:** Steve Kalafer.
President/General Manager: Patrick McVerry. **Senior Vice President, Marketing:** Dave Marek. **VP/Assistant GM:** Rob Lukachyk. **VP, Public Relations:** Marc Russinoff. **VP, Ticketing:** Bryan Iwicki. **Head Groundskeeper:** Dan Purner. **Director, Group Sales:** Matt Kopas. **Director, Sales:** Kevin Forrester. **Director, Operations:** Tim Ur. **Director, Merchandise:** Rob Crossman. **Corporate Sales Manager:** Jen Dikdan. **Community Relations Manager:** Brian Cahill. **Group Sales Managers:** Tom Gibat, Anthony Lugara. **Ticket Sales Manager:** Ken Greco. **Account Executive:** Deanna Liotard. **Executive Assistant to GM:** Michele DaCosta. **Controller:** Ron Schulz. **Accountant:** Stephanie Diez. **Receptionist:** Lorraine Ott. **GM, Centerplate:** Mike McDermott.
Manager: Sparky Lyle. **Director, Player Personnel/Pitching Coach:** Brett Jodie. **Hitting Coach:** Travis Anderson. **Trainer:** Ryan McMahon.

GAME INFORMATION
Radio Announcer: Adam Amin. **No. of Games Broadcast:** Home-72, Away-54. **Flagship Station:** WCTC 1450-AM. **PA Announcer:** Paul Spychala. **Official Scorer:** John Nolan.
Stadium Name: TD Bank Ballpark. **Location:** Route 287 North to exit 13B/Route 287 South to exit 13 (Somerville Route 28 West); follow signs to ballpark. **Standard Game Times:** 7:05 p.m., Sun, 1:35. **Visiting Club Hotel:** Unavailable.

SOUTHERN MARYLAND
BLUE CRABS

Office Address: 11765 St Linus Dr, Waldorf, MD 20602.
Telephone: 301-638-9788. **Fax:** 301-638-9788.
E-Mail address: info@somdbluecrabs.com. **Website:** www.somdbluecrabs.com.
Principal Owners: Opening Day Partners LLC, Brooks Robinson.
Chairman: Peter Kirk. **President:** Jon Danos. **Controller:** Emily Merrill.
General Manager: Keith Lupton. **Director, Finance:** Sheree Ebron. **Director, Group Sales:** Kyle Knichel. **Sales Account Executives:** Casey Eliff, Matthew Ammerman, Stefanie Harms. **Director, Sales:** Candace Gick. **Director, Creative Services:** Chris Deines. **Marketing Manager:** Courtney Freeland. **Director, Ticketing:** Josh Cockerham. **Stadium Operations:** Matt Myers. **GM, Centerplate Concessions/Merchandise:** Darren Hubbard. **Centerplate Chef:** Scott Fowler. **Head Groundskeeper:** Kevin Moses.
Manager: Patrick Osborn. **Hitting Coach:** Jeremy Owens (player/coach).

GAME INFORMATION
Radio: All Home and Away Games, www.somdbluecrabs.com. **Stadium:** Regency Furniture Stadium. **Standard Game Times:** 7:05 p.m., Sat 6:35, Sun 2:05/5:05.

YORK REVOLUTION

Office Address: 5 Brooks Robinson Way, York, PA 17401.
Telephone: (717) 801-4487. **FAX:** (717) 801-4499.
E-mail Address: info@yorkrevolution.com. **Website:** www.yorkrevolution.com.
Operated by: York Professional Baseball Club, LLC.
Principal Owners: Opening Day Partners.
President/General Manager: Eric Menzer. **VP, Business Development:** Neil Fortier. **Finance Manager:** Lori Brunson. **Assistant GM, Business Operations:** John Gibson. **Director, Ticketing:** Cindy Burkholder. **Box Office Manager:** Caleb Farkas. **Client Services Coordinator:** Brittney Sanders. **Corporate Partnerships Associates:** Stephen Linebaugh, Lindsay Kirk, Mike Chatburn, Kaylee Swanson, Karen Luciano. **Head Groundskeeper:** Brandon Putman. **Promotions/Communications Manager:** Paul Braverman. **Stadium Operations Manager:** Ryan Long. **Centerplate General Manager:** Rob Wilson. **Chef:** Tiffany Eger.
Director, Baseball Operations: Michael Kirk. **Manager:** Andy Etchebarren. **Pitching Coach:** Mark Mason. **Infield Coach:** Enohel Polanco.

GAME INFORMATION
Radio Announcer: Darrell Henry. **No. of Games Broadcast:** 126. **Flagship Station:** WOYK 1350 AM. **PA Announcer:** Chris DePatto, Ron Ruman. **Official Scorer:** Brian Wisler. **Stadium Name:** Sovereign Bank Stadium. **Location:** Take Route 30 West to North George Street, Turn left onto North George Street, Follow that straight for four lights, Sovereign Bank Stadium is on left. **Standard Game Times:** 6:30 p.m., Sun 1. (April, May, Sept), 5 (June, July, August).
Visiting Club Hotel: The Yorktowne Hotel, 48 E Market St York, PA 17401. **Telephone:** 717-848-1111.

CAN-AM LEAGUE

Office Address: 1415 Hwy 54 West, Suite 210, Durham, NC 27707.
Telephone: (919) 401-8150. **Fax:** (919) 401-8152. **Website:** www.canamleague.com. **Year Founded:** 2004.
Commissioner: Miles Wolff. **President:** Dan Moushon.
Administrative Assistant: Jason Deans. **Director, Umpires:** Kevin Winn.
Division Structure: None.
Regular Season: 94 games (split schedule). **2011 Opening Date:** May 26.
2011 Closing Date: September 5.
Playoff Format: Winners of each half play vs two teams with next-best overall records. Winners meet in a best-of-5 championship series with the final three games at the team with the best overall record.
Roster Limit: 22. **Eligibility Rule:** Minimum of five first-year players; maximum of four veterans.
Brand of Baseball: Rawlings.
Statistician: Pointstreak.com. **Address:** 602-1595 16th Avenue, Richmond Hill, ON, Canada L4B 3N9.

STADIUM INFORMATION

| Club | Stadium | Opened | Dimensions | | | Capacity | 2010 Att. |
			LF	CF	RF		
Brockton	Campanelli Stadium	2002	340	404	320	4,750	100,092
#Newark	Bears & Eagles Riverfront Stadium	1999	302	394	323	6,200	117,985
New Jersey	Yogi Berra Stadium	1998	308	398	308	3,784	86,014
Pittsfield	Wahconah Park	1919	334	374	333	4,500	29,485
Quebec	Stade Municipal	1938	315	385	315	4,800	147,978
Rockland	Ramapo Ballpark	2011	323	403	313	4,750	
Worcester	Hanover Insurance Park-Fitton Field	1905	361	417	307	3,000	88,499

#Operated in Atlantic League in 2010
Rockland is new for 2011

BROCKTON ROX

Office Address: One Feinberg Way, Brockton, MA 02301.
Telephone: (508) 559-7000. **Fax:** (508) 587-2802.
E-Mail: roxfun@brocktonrox.com. **Website:** www.brocktonrox.com.
Principal Owner: Van Schley. **CEO:** Chris Carminucci. **Executive Vice President:** Michael Canina. **Legal Counsel:** Jack Yunits.
Assistant General Managers: Hoffman Wolff, Tom Healy. **Accountant:** Jim Holmes. **Director, Community Relations:** Terri Kuskoski. **Groundskeeper:** Tom Hassett.
Manager: Bill Buckner. **Coach:** Dan McNamara.

GAME INFORMATION

Stadium Name: Campanelli Stadium. **Location:** Route 24 North/South to Route 123 east, stadium is two miles on right.
Standard Game Times: 7:05 p.m., Sun 1:05 (May/June/September) 5:05 (July/August).
Visiting Club Hotel: Courtyard by Marriott Stoughton, 200 Technology Center Drive, Stoughton MA 02072. **Telephone:** (781) 297-7000.

NEWARK BEARS

Office Address: 450 Broad St., **Newark, NJ 07102.**
Telephone: (973) 848-1000. **Fax:** (973) 621-0095
Website: www.newarkbears.com
Operated by: Thomas Cetnar, Owner, CEO.
Chief Administrative Officer: Shelley Garrett.
General Manager: Adam Shubsda. **Assistant General Manager:** Samantha Cetnar. **Vice President, Operations:** Sakinah Abdul-Hakeem. **VP, Tickets:** Patrick Quinn. **VP, Public Relations:** Jim Hague. **Director, Sales:** Bridgette Berra. **Director, Stadium Operations:** Alex Krohn.
Manager: Tim Raines. **Coach:** Ron Karkovice.

GAME INFORMATION

Radio Announcer: Jim Hague. **No. Of Games Broadcast:** Home-54, Away-40. **Flagship Station:** All-In Internet Broadcasting.
Stadium Name: Bears & Eagles Riverfront Stadium. **Location:** Garden State Parkway North/South to exit 145 (280 East), to exit 15; New Jersey Turnpike North/South to 280 West, to exit 15A.
Standard Game Times: 11:05 a.m./5:35 p.m. (Mon/Tues), 11:05 a.m. (Wed), 5:35 (Thurs), 6:35 (Fri), 6:35 (Sat), 1:05 (Sun).
Visiting Club Hotel: Best Western, Robert Treat Hotel, 50 Park Place, Newark, NJ, 07102-4398. **Telephone:** (973) 622-1000.

NEW JERSEY JACKALS

Office Address: One Hall Dr, Little Falls, NJ 07424.
Telephone: (973) 746-7434. **Fax:** (973) 655-8006.
E-Mail Address: info@jackals.com. **Website:** www.jackals.com.
Operated by: Floyd Hall Enterprises, LLC.
Chairman: Floyd Hall. **President:** Greg Lockard.
General Manager: Larry Hall. **Business Manager:** Jennifer Fertig. **Director, Operations:** Pierson Van Raalte. **Director, Sales:** Sue Beck. **Group Sales Representative:** Jordan Cascino. **Facilities Manager:** Aldo Licitra. **Concessions Manager:** Michelle Guarino. **Clubhouse Manager:** Wally Brackett.
Manager: Joe Calfapietra. **Coaches:** Ed Ott, Ani Ramos.

GAME INFORMATION
Announcer (Webcast): Cody Chrusciel. **No. of Games Broadcast:** 94. **Webcast Address:** www.jackals.com.
Stadium Name: Yogi Berra Stadium. **Location:** Route 80 or Garden State Parkway to Route 46, take Valley Road exit to Montclair State University. **Standard Game Times:** 7:05 p.m., Sat 6:35, Sun 2:05.
Visiting Club Hotel: Ramada Inn, 130 Rte 10 West, East Hanover, NJ 07936. **Telephone:** (973) 386-5622.

PITTSFIELD COLONIALS

Office Address: 2 South Street, Pittsfield, MA 01201.
Operated By: Boston Baseball All-Stars, LLC.
Principal Owner: Buddy Lewis.
Chairman: Robert Seaman.
General Manager: Jamie Keefe. **Assistant to the GM/Administrative Assistant:** Amanda Iozzo. **Director, Fun/Entertainment/Director, Community Relations:** Heather Cachat. **Assistant to the GM/Director, Stadium Operations:** Nick Avanzato. **Director, Public Relations/Play-by-Play Announcer:** Chad Cooper.
Manager/Baseball Operations: Jamie Keefe. **Director, Player Procurement:** Kevin Tuve.

GAME INFORMATION
Stadium Name: Wahconah Park. **Location:** From the west: 295-E to 41-N to 20-E to Pittsfield, left on Route 7, right on North Street, left on Wahconah Street; From the east: Massachusetts Turnpike exit 2 to Route 7, right on North Street, left on Wahconah Street.
Standard Game Times: 7 p.m., Sun, 2:00.

QUEBEC CAPITALES

Office Address: 100 Rue du Cardinal Maurice-Roy, Quebec City, QC G1K8Z1.
Telephone: (418) 521-2255. **Fax:** (418) 521-2266.
E-Mail Address: baseball@capitalesdequebec.com. **Website:** www.capitalesdequebec.com.
Owner: Jean Tremblay
President: Michel Laplante.
General Manager: Alex Harvey. **Assistant GM:** Julie Lefrancois. **Media/Marketing Director:** Pier-Luc Nappert. **Assistant, Media/Marketing:** Marc-Antoine Gariἐpy.
Manager: Patrick Scalabrini.

GAME INFORMATION
Radio Announcers: Jacques Doucet, Francois Paquet. **No. of Games Broadcast:** 94. **Flagship Station:** Quebec 800-AM. **Webcast Address:** www.info800.ca.
Stadium Name: Stade Municipal de Quebec. **Location:** Highway 40 to Highway 173 (Centre-Ville) exit 2 to Parc Victoria.
Standard Game Times: 7:05 p.m., 1:05.
Visiting Club Hotel: Le Clarendon 57 rue Sainte-Anne, QuÈbec, QC, G1R 3X4, (418) 692-2480.

ROCKLAND BOULDERS

Mailing Address: PO Box 354, Suffern, NY 10901.
Website: www.rocklandboulders.com .
President: Ken Lehner. **Executive Vice President:** Shawn Reilly. **Counsel:** Jonathan Fine.

GAME INFORMATION
Stadium Name: Ramapo Ballpark. **Location:** Take Exit 12 towards Route 45, make left at stop sign on Conklin Road, make left on Route 45, turn right on Pomona Road, take 1st right on Firemanís Memorial Drive.
Standard Game Times: 7:05 p.m., Sun 5:05.

WORCESTER TORNADOES

Office Address: 303 Main St, Worcester, MA 01613.
Telephone: (508) 792-2288. Fax: (506) 926-3662.
E-Mail Address: info@worcestertornadoes.com. Website: www.worcestertornadoes.com.
General Manager: Jorg Bassiacos. Executive VP: Lev Shellenberger. Director, Communications: Mike Tetler. Senior Account Executive: Sarah Farley. Account Executives: Tim Jones, Mike Nicholas, Erik Taber.
Manager: Ed Riley. Coach: Chip Plante. Director, Player Personnel: Brad Michals.

GAME INFORMATION
No. of Games Broadcast: 94. Webcast Address: www.worcestertornadoes.com.
Stadium Name: Hanover Insurance Park at Fitton Field. Location: I-290 to exit 11 College Square, right on College Street, left on Fitton Avenue.
Standard Game Times: 7:05 p.m., Sun 4:05.
Visiting Club Hotel: Quality Inn & Suites, 50 Oriol Drive, Worcester, MA 01605. Telephone: (508) 852-2800. Fax: (508) 852-4605.

FRONTIER LEAGUE

Office Address: 2041 Goose Lake Rd Suite 2A, Sauget, Il 62206.
Mailing Address: Same as above.
Telephone: (618) 215-4134. **Fax:** (618) 332-2115.
E-Mail Address: office@frontierleague.com. **Website:** www.frontierleague.com.
Year Founded: 1993.
Commissioner: Bill Lee.
President: Rich Sauget (Gateway). **Vice Presidents:** Clint Brown (Florence) Stu Williams (Washington). **Secretary:** Erik Haag (Southern Illinois). **Treasurer:** Bob Wolfe. **Deputy Commissioner:** Steve Tahsler. **Directors:** Tim Birtsas (Oakland County), Clint Brown (Florence), Bill Bussing (Evansville), Steven Edelson (Lake Erie), Erik Haag (Southern Illinois), Chris Hanners (Chillicothe), Steve Malliet (River City/Normal), Alan Oremus (Joliet), Bill Wright (Kalamazoo), Rich Sauget (Gateway), Mike Stranczek (Windy City), Stu Williams (Washington), Leslye Wuerfel (Traverse City).
Division Structure: Eastó Joliet, Kalamazoo, Lake Erie, Traverse City, Washington, Windy City WestóEvansville, Florence, Gateway, Normal, River City, Southern Illinois.
Regular Season: 96 games. **2011 Opening Date:** May 19. **Closing Date:** Sept. 4.
All-Star Game: July 13 at Lake Erie.
Playoff Format: Top 2 teams in each Division will meet in best-of-five semifinal series. Winners meet in best-of-five series for league championship.
Roster Limit: 24. **Eligibility Rule:** Minimum of eleven Rookie 1 or Rookie 2 players. No player may be 27 prior to Jan. 1 of current season with the exeption of one player that may not be 30 years of age prior to Jan. 1 of the current season.
Brand of Baseball: Wilson.
Statistician: Pointstreak, 602-1595 16th Avenue, Richmond Hill, ONT L4B 3N9.

STADIUM INFORMATION

Club	Stadium	Opened	Dimensions			Capacity	2010 Att.
			LF	CF	RF		
Evansville	Bosse Field	1915	315	415	315	5,181	110,711
Florence	Florence Freedom Field	2004	325	395	325	4,200	112,844
Gateway	GCS Ballpark	2002	318	395	325	5,500	186,147
Joliet	Silver Cross Field	2002	330	400	327	4,616	
Kalamazoo	Homer Stryker Field	1995	306	400	330	4,806	56,342
Lake Erie	All-Pro Freight Stadium	2009	325	400	325	5,000	159,580
Normal	The Corn Crib		356	400	344	7,000	132,309
River City	T.R. Hughes Ballpark	1999	320	382	299	4,989	113,431
So. Illinois	Rent One Park	2007	325	400	330	4,500	204,181
Traverse City	Wuerfel Park	2006	320	400	320	4,600	204,440
Washington	CONSOL Energy Park	2002	325	400	325	3,200	116,722
Windy City	Standard Bank Stadium	1999	335	390	335	2,598	92,240

EVANSVILLE OTTERS

Mailing Address: 1701 N. Main St., Evansville, IN 47711.
Telephone: (812) 435-8686.
Operated by: Evansville Baseball, LLC.
President: Bill Bussing.
Senior Vice President: Pat Rayburn. **General Manager:** Liam Miller. **Accounting Manager:** Casie Williams. **Director, Sales/Revenue Development:** Joel Padfield. **Manager/Director, Baseball Operations:** Andy McCauley.

GAME INFORMATION
Radio Announcer: Unavailable. **No. of Games Broadcast:** Home-48, Away-48. **Flagship Station:** WUEV 91.5-FM. **PA Announcer:** Unavailable. **Official Scorer:** Kevin Cope.
Stadium Name: Bosse Field. **Location:** US 41 to Lloyd Expressway West (IN-62), Main St Exit, Right on Main St, ahead 1 mile to Bosse Field. **Standard Game Times:** 6:35 p.m., Sun, 1:05/4:35.
Visiting Club Hotel: Unavailable.

FLORENCE FREEDOM

Office Address: 7950 Freedom Way, Florence, KY 41042.
Telephone: (859) 594-4487. **Fax:** (859) 594-3194.
E-Mail Address: info@florencefreedom.com.
Website: www.florencefreedom.com.
Operated by: Canterbury Baseball, LLC.
President: Clint Brown. **Vice President, Operations:** Matt Resar. **Director, Community Relations:** Kim Brown.

Stadium Operations Manager: Stephen Mace. Director, Ticket Sales: Elizabeth Quatman. Media Relations Manager: Megan Smith. Promotions Manager: Kevin Schwab. Box Office Manager: Dana White. Director, Broadcasting/ Amateur Baseball: Matt Friedman.
   Baseball Operations/Manager: Fran Riordan. Pitching Coach: Wes Crawford. Trainer: Chris Unkraut.

GAME INFORMATION

Flagship Station: 1160 AM. Radio Broadcaster: Matt Friedman. PA Announcer: Kevin Schwab. Official Scorer: Unavailable.
   Stadium: Freedom Park. Location: I-71/75 South to exit 180, left onto US 42, right on Freedom Way; I-71/75 North to exit 180.
   Standard Game Times: 7:05 p.m., Sat/Sun 6:05.
   Visiting Club Hotel: Wildwood Inn.

GATEWAY GRIZZLIES

Mailing Address: 2301 Grizzlie Bear Blvd, Sauget, IL 62206
Telephone: (618) 337-3000. FAX: (618) 332-3625.
E-Mail Address: info@gatewaygrizzlies.com. Website: www.gatewaygrizzlies.com.
Operated by: Gateway Baseball, LLC.
Managing Officer: Richard Sauget. General Manager: Steven Gomric. Director, Stadium Operations: Brent Pownall. Director, Corporate Sales: C.J. Hendrickson. Media Relations Director/Events Manager: Jeff O'Neill. Director, Group Sales: Jason Murphy. Director, Sales: Craig Dohm. Assistant Director, Stadium Operations: Josh LeMasters. Director, Marketing: Monica Rodriguez. Director, Merchandise: Lauren Jones. Head Groundskeeper: Ben Young. Broadcaster: Adam Young. Director, Promotions: Katie Patton.
   Manager: Phil Warren. Pitching Coach: Randy Martz. Hitting Coach: Darin Kinsolving. Defensive Coach: Zach Borowiak. Trainer: Geof Manzo. Clubhouse Manager: Chris Majerchin.

GAME INFORMATION

Radio Announcer: Adam Young. No of Games Broadcast: Home-48, Away-48. Flagship Station: 590-AM KFNS. PA Announcer: Tom Calhoun. Official Scorer: Garen Vartanian.
   Stadium Name: GCS Ballpark. Location: I-255 at exit 15 (Mousette Lane). Standard Game Times: 7:05 p.m., Sun 6:05/3:05.
   Visiting Club Hotel: Ramada Inn, 6900 N. Illinois St., Fairview Heights, IL 62208. Telephone: (618) 632-4747.

JOLIET SLAMMERS

Office Address: 1 Mayor Art Schultz Dr., Joliet, IL 60432.
Telephone: (815)722-2287. Fax: (815) 726-4304.
E-Mail Address: info@jolietslammers.com. Website: www.jolietslammers.com.
Operated by: Steel City Baseball, LLC.
Owner: J Alan Oremus.
President: Bill Waliewski. Executive Vice President/General Manager: John Dittrich. VP/Baseball Operations: Ron Biga. VP/Stadium Operations: Paul Rathje. Office/Business Manager: Lois Dittrich. Director, Sales: Dan DeCaprio. Director, Community Relations/Promotions: Kelli Drechsel. Director, Special Projects: Ken Miller. Stadium Operations: Jim Domabyl.
   Manager: Bart Zeller. Coach: Ron Biga. Pitching Coach: Unavailable. Clubhouse Manager: Unavailable. Trainer: Unavailable.

GAME INFORMATION

Radio Announcer: Unavailable. No. of Games Broadcast: Home-48, Away-48. Flagship Station: WJOL (1340 AM). PA. Announcer: Unavailable. Official Scorer: Dave Laketa.
   Stadium Name: Silver Cross Field. Location: Corner of Mayor Art Schultz Drive and Jefferson Street in downtown Joliet. Standard Game Times: 7:05 p.m. Visiting Club Hotel: Unavailable.

KALAMAZOO KINGS

Mailing Address: 251 Mills Street, Kalamazoo, MI 49048.
Telephone: 269-388-3826 Fax: 269-388-8333.
Website: www.kalamazookings.com.
Operated by: Team Kalamazoo, LLC.
Owners: Bill Wright, Mike Seelye, Pat Seelye, Ed Bernard, Scott Hocevar, Joe Rosenhagen.
General Manager: Ryan LaPorte. Concessionaire: EMA Enterprises.
Field Manager: TBD.

GAME INFORMATION

Radio Announcer: Mike McCann. Games broadcast: Home 48, Away 48. Flagship station: www.Ustream.tv. PA

Announcer: Jim Lefler. **Official Scorer:** Jason Zerban.

Stadium Name: Homer Stryker Field. **Directions:** I-94 to Sprinkle Road (exit 80), north on Sprinkle Road, left at Business Loop I-94, left on Kings Highway, right on Mills Street. **Standard Game Times:** 7:05 p.m., Sun 1:05 p.m.

Visiting Club Hotel: Red Roof Inn, 5425 W Michigan Ave, Kalamazoo, MI 49009. **Phone:** 269-375-7400

LAKE ERIE CRUSHERS

Mailing Address: 2009 Baseball Blvd, Avon, OH, 44011.
Telephone: (440) 934-3636. **Fax:** (440) 934-2458.
E-Mail Address: info@lakeeriecrushers.com. **Website:** www.lakeeriecrushers.com.
Operated by: Avon Pro Baseball LLC.
Managing Officer: Steven Edelson.
General Manager: Ryan Gates. **Assistant GM, Operations:** Paul Siegwarth. **Director, Marketing:** Daniel Helm.
Accountant: Lisa Rueber. **Box Office Manager:** Kelly Dolan. **Director, Group Sales:** Derek Stapinski. **Outside Events Coordinator:** Amy Focareto. **Director, Concessions/Catering:** Kevin Dailey. **Account Executives:** Brittany Kachingwe, Michael Keefe.
Manager: John Massarelli. **Pitching Coach:** Chris Steinborn. **Hitting Coach:** Dave Schaub.

GAME INFORMATION
Stadium Name: All Pro Freight Stadium. **Location:** Intersection of I-90 and Colorado Ave, Avon, OH.
Standard Game Times: 7:05 p.m.; Sun 5:05.

NORMAL CORNBELTERS

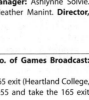

Mailing Address: 1000 West Raab Road, Normal, IL 61761.
Telephone: (309) 454-2255(BALL). **Fax:** (309) 454-2287(BATS).
Ownership: Normal Baseball Group.
President: Steve Malliet. **Assistant General Manager/Vice President, Corporate Partnerships:** Kyle Kreger. **Corporate Partnerships Manager:** Alexandra Singer. **VP, Fan Experiences:** Zach Ziler. **Box Office Director/Fan Experiences Manager:** David Sowa. **Director, Fan Experiences:** Joe Rejc. **Fan Experiences Managers:** Nate Elrod, Kyle Rose. **Public/Media Relations Manager:** Ashlynne Solvie. **Community Relations/Baseball Operations Manager:** Jon Young. **Business Manager:** Heather Manint. **Director, Stadium Operations:** Alex Totura.
Field Manager: Hal Lanier. **Pitching Coach:** Brook Carey.

GAME INFORMATION
Radio Announcer: Unavailable. **Flagship Station:** WJBC 1230 AM, WHOW 95.9 FM. **No. of Games Broadcast:** Home—48, Away—48.
Stadium Name: The Corn Crib. **Location:** From I-55 North, Go south on I-55 and take the 165 exit (Heartland College, Turn left at light, Turn right on Raab Road to ballpark on right; From south, go north on I-55 and take the 165 exit (Heartland); Merge onto Route 51 (Main street); Turn right on Raab Road to ballpark on right.
Standard Game Times: 7 p.m., Aug 6.
Visiting Club Hotel: The Chateau Bloomington Hotel & Conference Center.

RIVER CITY RASCALS

Office Address: 900 TR Hughes Blvd, Fallon, MO 63366.
Telephone: (636) 240-2287. **Fax:** (636) 240-7313.
E-Mail Address: info@rivercityrascals.com. **Website:** www.rivercityrascals.com.
Operated by: PS and J Professional Baseball Club LLC. **Owners:** Tim Hoeksema, Jan Hoeksema, Fred Stratton, Anne Stratton, Pam Malliet, Steve Malliet, Michael Veeck, Greg Wendt.
President: John Kuhn. **Vice President/General Manager:** Chris Franklin. **Business Manager:** Michelle Stuckey. **Director, Corporate Sales:** Zach Prehn. **Ticket Sales Representative:** Aaron Smith. **Director, Media Relations/ Broadcasting:** Jason Troop. **Executive Assistant:** Courtney Oakley. **Promotions Coordinator:** Abby Matusiak.
Team Manager: Steve Brook. **Assistant Coach:** Mike Breyman. **Bench Coach:** Dave Garcia.

GAME INFORMATION
Radio Announcer: Jason Troop. **No. of Games Broadcast:** Home-48, Away-48. **Flagship Station:** FM-94.1 PA Announcer: Randy Moehlman. **Official Scorer:** Logan Stuckey.
Stadium Name: T.R. Hughes Ballpark. **Location:** I-70 to exit 219, north on TR Hughes Road, follow signs to ballpark. **Standard Game Times:** 7:05 p.m., Sun 6:05.
Visiting Club Hotel: Hilton Garden Inn, 2310 Technology Drive, OíFallon, MO 63368, (636) 625-2700.

SOUTHERN ILLINOIS MINERS

Office Address: Rent One Park, 1000 Miners Drive, Marion, IL 62959.
Telephone: (618) 998-8499. **Fax:** (618) 969-8550.
E-Mail Address: info@southernillinoisminers.com. **Website:** www.southernillinoisminers.com.
Operated by: Southern Illinois Baseball Group.
Vice President: Erik Haag. **General Manager:** Tim Arseneau. **Assistant GM:** Billy Richards. **Director, Ticket Operations:** Billy Leitner. **Manager, Client Services/Marketing Coordinator:** Terra Brenner. **Director, Media Relations/Broadcasting:** Scott Gierman. **Director, Finance:** Cathy Perry. **Director, Stadium Operations:** Billy Peterman. **Operations/Clubhouse Manager:** Jeff Pink. **Director, Group Sales:** Dennis Watson. **Account Executives:** Ryan Schmidt, Andrew Bowlby.
Manager: Mike Pinto. **Pitching Coach:** Bart Zeller. **Hitting Coach:** Ralph Santana.

GAME INFORMATION
Radio Announcer: Scott Gierman. **No. of Games Broadcast:** 96. **Flagship Station:** 97.7 WHET-FM.
Stadium Name: Rent One Park. **Location:** US 57 to Route 13 East, right at Halfway Road to Fairmont Dr. **Standard Game Times:** 7:05 p.m., Sun 5:05.
Visiting Club Hotel: Econo Lodge, 1806 Bittle Place, Marion, IL 62959.

TRAVERSE CITY BEACH BUMS

Office Address: 333 Stadium Dr, Traverse City, MI 49684.
Telephone: (231) 943-0100. **Fax (231) 943-0900.**
E-Mail Address: info@tcbeachbums.com. **Website:** www.traversecitybeachbums.com.
Operated by: Traverse City Beach Bums, LLC.
Managing Partners: John Wuerfel, Leslye Wuerfel, Jason Wuerfel.
President/CEO: John Wuerfel. **Member/CFO:** Leslye Wuerfel. **Vice President/Director, Baseball Operations:** Jason Wuerfel. **General Manager:** Jeremy Crum. **Director, Concessions:** Tom Goethel III.
Manager: Gregg Langbehn. **Hitting Coach:** Jason Wuerfel. **Infield Coach:** Matt Pulley. **Clubhouse Manager:** Denny Dame. **Trainer:** Jennifer Scamehorn.

GAME INFORMATION
No. of Games Broadcast: Home-48, Away-48. **Flagship Stations:** WLDR 101.9-FM; **PA Announcer:** Tim Moeggenberg.
Official Scorer: Kris Herman
Stadium Name: Wuerfel Park. **Location:** 3 miles south of the Grand Traverse Mall just off US-31 and M-37 in Chums Village, Stadium is visible from the highway (Or north of US 31 and M-37 Chums Corner intersection), Turn-west on Chums Village Drive, north on Village Park Drive, right on Stadium Drive.
Standard Game Times: 7:05 p.m., Sun 5:05.
Visiting Club Hotel: Days Inn & Suites of Traverse City.

WASHINGTON WILD THINGS

Office Address: One Washington Federal Way, Washington, PA 15301.
Telephone: (724) 250-9555. **Fax:** (724) 250-2333.
E-Mail Address: info@washingtonwildthings.com.
Website: www.washingtonwildthings.com.
Owned by: Sports Facility, LLC. **Operated by:** Washington Frontier League Baseball, LLC.
Managing Director: Todd Marlin. **President/Chief Executive Officer:** Jeff Coury. **Director, Marketing:** Christine Blaine. **Director. Stadium Operations:** Steve Zavacky. **Public Relations:** Lauren Hindman. **Corporate Partnership Manager:** Jim Gibson. **Ticket Operations/Sponsorship Manager:** Dave Wojtkowski. **Merchandise Manager:** Kate Billings. **Ticket Account Executives:** Ashley Brush, Carissa Diethorn. **Business Manager:** Tammy Pirone.
Manager: Darin Everson. **Pitching Coach:** Mark Dewey; **Coach:** Bob Bozzuto.

GAME INFORMATION
Radio Announcer: Randy Gore. **No. of Games Broadcast:** Home-48, Away-48. **Flagship Station:** WJPA 95.3-FM.
Official Scorer: Unavailable.
Stadium Name: CONSOL Energy Park. **Location:** I-70 to exit 15 (Chestnut Street), right on Chestnut Street to Washington Crown Center Mall, right at mall entrance, right on to Mall Drive to stadium. **Standard Game Times:** 7:05 p.m., **Sun 6:**35.
Visiting Club Hotel: Unavailable.

WINDY CITY THUNDERBOLTS

Office Address: 14011 South Kenton Ave, Crestwood, IL 60445-2252.
Telephone: (708) 489-2255. **Fax:** (708) 489-2999.
E-Mail Address: info@wcthunderbolts.com. **Website:** www.wcthunderbolts.com.
Owned by: Crestwood Professional Baseball, LLC.
General Manager: Mike Lucas. **Director, Food/Beverage:** Adam Schwarzenpraub. **Director, Community Relations:** Kathy Jermal. **Director, Operations/Head Groundskeeper:** Mike VerSchave.
Field Manager: Mike Kashirsky. **Pitching Coach:** Corey Domel.

GAME INFORMATION

Radio Announcers: Unavailable. **No. of Games Broadcast:** 96. **Flagship Station:** WXAV, 88.3 FM. **PA Announcer:** Unavailable. **Official Scorer:** Jason Caollins.
Stadium Name: Standard Bank Stadium. **Location:** I-294 to S Cicero Ave, exit (Route 50), south for 1 1/2 miles, left at Midlothian Turnpike, right on Kenton Ave.; I-57 to 147th Street, west on 147th to Cicero, north on Cicero, right on Midlothian Turnpike, right on Kenton. **Standard Game Times:** 7:05 p.m., Sun 6:05.
Visiting Club Hotel: Georgioís Comfort Inn, 8800 W 159th St, Orland Park, IL 60462. **Telephone:** (708) 403-1100. **Fax:** (708) 403-1105.

NORTH AMERICAN LEAGUE

Office Address: 6111 Bollinger Canyon Road, Suite 580, San Ramon, CA 94583.
Telephone: (925) 302-7378. **Fax:** (925) 302-7375.
E-Mail Address: info@northamericanleague.com. **Website:** www.northamericanleague.com.
Founded: 2011.
CEO: Kevin Outcalt. **Executive Director, Operations:** Harry Stavrenos.
Division Structure: West--Edmonton, Calgary, Chico, Maui, Yuma, Henderson. **East--Schaumburg, Rockford, Lake County, San Angelo, Harlingen, Edinburg.Regular Season:** 96 games.
Regular Season: 96 games.
2011 Opening Date: May 25. **Closing Date:** Sep 5.
Playoff Format: Top six teams to meet in a double-elimination tournament from Sept 8-11. Site is to be determined.
Roster Limit: 22.
Eligibility Rules: No minimum number of rookies, age limit of 31 as of Jan 1 unless player has major league, Triple-A, Double-A, top foreign or recent Golden, Northern or United League experience.
All-Star Game: Prospects showcase game on July 19.
Statistician: Pointstreak, www.pointstreak.com.

CALGARY VIPERS

Address: 2255 Crowchild Trail NW, Calgary, Alberta, Canada T2M4S7.
Telephone: (403) 277-2255
E-Mail Address: johnconrad@calgaryvipers.com. **Website:** www.calgaryvipers.com.
President/Chief Operating Officer: John Conrad. **Facilities Director:** Matt Horan.
Accountant: John Kirkbride. **Director, Absolute Baseball Academy:** Neil Gidney. **Media Relations:** Patrick Haas.
Administrative Assistance: Melissa Davies.
Manager: Morgan Burkhart. **Coach:** Unavailable. **Pitching Coach:** Unavailable.

GAME INFORMATION

Radio Announcer: Patrick Haas. **No. of Games Broadcast:** Home-46 Away-46. **Flagship Station:** AM 770 CHQR. **PA Announcer:** Kramer. **Official Scorer:** Darcy Leitz/Gord Siminon.
Stadium Name: Foothills Athletic Park. **Standard Game Times:** 6:05 pm, Sat 5:05, Sun 1:35.
Visiting Club Hotel: Best Western Village Park.

CHICO OUTLAWS

Office Address: 313 Walnut St, Suite 110, Chico, CA 95928
Telephone: (530) 345-3210.
E-Mail Address: mmarshall@goldenbaseball.com. **Website:** www.chicooutlawsbaseball.com.
Owner: Diamond Sports & Entertainment. **General Manager/Field Manager:** Mike Marshall.

GAME INFORMATION

Radio Announcer: Unavailable. **No. of Games Broadcast:** Home-45, Away-45. **Flagship Station:** Unavailable.
PA Announcer: Shelly Rogers. **Official Scorer:** Unavailable.
Stadium Name: Nettleton Stadium. **Location:** California 99 North to California 32 West/East Eighth Street, right on ain Street, left on West First Street; stadium at 400 West First Street. **Standard Game Times:** 7:05 pm, Sun 1:05.
Visiting Club Hotel: Unavailable.

EDINBURG ROADRUNNERS

Office Address: 920 North Sugar Road, Edinburg, TX 78541.
Telephone: 956-380-4446. **Fax:** 956-380-4344.
E-Mail Address: roadrunners2009@gmail.com. **Website:** www.roadrunnerball.com.
General Manager: Doug Leary. **Director, Sales/Marketing:** Jeremy Martin. **Ticket Manager:** Jesse Gonzalez.
Account Executive: Rudy Rodriguez. **Office Manager:** Alejandra Cobos. **Stadium Opertations:** Estella De La Cruz.
Merchandise Manager: Elva Garza. **Manager/Director, Player Personnel:** Vince Moore.

GAME INFORMATION

Radio Announcer: Danny Elizondo. **No. of Games Broadcast:** 90. **Website:** www.roadrunnerball.com.
PA Announcer: Seve Lara. **Official Scorer:** Rey Silva.
Stadium: Edinburg Stadium. **Standard Game Time:** 7:05 pm, Sun 6:05.

EDMONTON CAPITALS

Ballpark Address: 10233-96 Avenue, Edmonton, Alberta, Canada T5K 0A5.
Administration Address: 11230 110 Street, Edmonton, Alberta, Canada T5G 3H7.
Telephone: (780) 414-GOAL (4685).
E-Mail Address: capsinfo@capsbaseball.ca. **Website:** www.capsbaseball.ca. **Facebook:** www.facebook.com/EdmCapitals. **Twitter:** www.twitter.com/edmcapitals.
Owner: Katz Baseball Corporation.
Governor: Patrick LaForge. **Alternate Governor:** Darryl Boessenkool.
Director, Baseball Operations: Gord Gerlach.
Manager: Orv Franchuk. **Hitting Coach:** Gord Gerlach. **Pitching Coach:** Mark Randall.
Director, Business Operations: Matt McPhee. **Manager, Communications:** Ryan Frankson.

HENDERSON ROADRUNNERS

Address: 700 College Drive, Henderson, NV.
Telephone: (702) 715-5320
E-Mail Address: info@hendersonroadrunners.com Website: www.hendersonroadrunners.com
Owner: Diamond Sports & Entertainment.
General Manager/President: Alan Mintz.
Manager: Unavailable. **Coach:** Unavailable. **Pitching Coach:** Unavailable.

GAME INFORMATION
Radio Announcer: N/A. **No. of Games Broadcast:** Home-48 Away-48. **Flagship Station:** Unavailable.

LAKE COUNTY FIELDERS

Office Address: 1665 Green Bay Road, Zion, IL 60099.
Telephone: (847) 731-8000. **Website:** www.fieldersbaseball.com.
Operated by: Grand Slam Sports & Entertainment, LLC.
Owner: Kevin Costner.
Managing Partner/President: Rich Ehrenreich.
Executive VP: Rick Rungaitis. **VP, Sales/Business Development:** Avery Robbins. **Director, Stadium/Baseball Operations:** Andrew Lieber. **Director, Group Sales:** Ron Poe. **Graphics/Publications Manager:** Davi Marx. **Manager, Community Relations/Promotions:** Kelly Wells. **Inside Sales Representatives:** Dennis Widdows, Sean Clement. **Field Agent:** Scott Murphy.
Manager: Tim Johnson. **Coach:** Unavailable. **Pitching Coach:** Unavailable.

GAME INFORMATION
Radio Announcer: Dominic Fortini. **No. of Games broadcast:** Home-46, Away-46. **Flagship Station:** WKRS 1220-AM.
Stadium Name: Fielders Stadium.
Location: From the North (Wisconsin): Green Bay Rd (Rt 131) South, NW corner of Green Bay Rd and Rosecrans (Rt 173); From the South: I-94N or US41 (Skokie Hwy) N to Rt 173 (Rosecrans), East on Rt 173 to Green Bay Rd (Rt 131); From the East: Rt 173 West to Green Bay Rd (Rt 131); From the West: Rt 173 (Rosecrans) East to Green Bay Rd (Rt 131).
Standard Game Times: 7 pm; Sat 6:30; Sun 1; DH 11:30 am, 7 pm.

NA IKAIKA KOA MAUI

Address: 700 Halia Nakoa Street, Wailuku, Maui, HI.
Telephone: (808)270-7389.
Website: www.nakoaikaikamaui.com.
Owners: Leroy Pettigrew, Harris E Tulchin, Robert J Young.
Managing Members: Harris E Tulchin, Robert J Young.

Account Executive/Assistant to the Managing Members: Louis Friedlander. **Account Executives:** Trina Maddela, Mark Okano.

Manager: Garry Templeton. **Coach:** Unavailable. **Pitching Coach:** Unavailable.

GAME INFORMATION
Stadium Name: Iron Maehara Stadium. **Location:** 700 Halia Nakoa Street, Wailuku, HI. **Maui.**

Standard Game Times: 7:05 pm, Sun 1:05.

RIO GRANDE VALLEY
WHITEWINGS

Office Address: 1216 Fair Park Blvd, Harlingen, TX 78550. **Telephone:** (956) 423-WING (9464). **Fax:** (956) 423-9466. **E-mail Address:** cdirksen@whitewingsbaseball.com. **Website:** www.whitewingsbaseball.com.

General Manager: Cory Dirksen. **Director, Sales/Marketing:** Stephanie Bierbaum. **Director, Communications:** Jonah Goldberg. **Director, Group Sales:** Christina Dirksen. **Business Mamager:** Beverly Woodward. **Account Executive:** Glenn Payne.

Manager: Eddie Dennis. **Hitting Coach:** Eric Gonzalez.

GAME INFORMATION
Radio Announcer: Unavailable. **No. of Games Broadcast:** 96. **Website:** www.white-wingsbaseball.com.

Stadium: Harlingen Field. **Standard Game Time:** 7:05 pm.

ROCKFORD RIVERHAWKS

Office Address: 4503 Interstate Blvd, Loves Park, IL 61111.

Telephone: (815) 885-2255. **Fax:** (815) 885-2204.

Website: www.rockfordriverhawks.com.

Owners: Dennis Arouca, Kurt Carlson, Dave Ciarrachi, Brian McClure. **Managing Partner:** Dave Ciarrachi.

General Manager: Brad Sholes. **Director, Broadcasting/Media Relations:** Bill Czaja. **Director, Tickets/Finance:** Brad Sholes. **Director, Operations:** Chris Daleo. **Director, Group Sales:** Jeff Olerud.

Manager: Bob Koopmann. **Coaches:** JD Arndt, Sam Knaack, Spiro Lempesis, Ralph Riske.

GAME INFORMATION
Radio Announcer: Bill Czaja. **No. of Games Broadcast:** 96. **Flagship Station:** WTJK1380-AM.

Stadium Name: Road Ranger Stadium. **Location:** I-90 (Jane Addams Tollway) to Riverside Boulevard exit (automatic toll booth), east to Interstate Drive, left on Interstate Drive. **Standard Game Times:** 7:05 pm, Sat 6:05, Sun 4:05.

SAN ANGELO COLTS

Office Address: 1600 University, San Angelo, TX 76951.

Telephone: (325) 942-6587. **Fax:** (325) 947-9480.

E-mail Address: mbabcock@sanangelocolts.com. **Website:** www.sanangelocolts.com.

General Manager: Mike Babcock.

Head Groundskeeper: Drew Caraway. **Director, Sales:** Mike Clark. **Director, Broadcasting/Media Relations:** Ira Liebman. **Director, Ticketing/Office Manager:** Lea Self.

Manager/Director, Player Personnel: Doc Edwards. **Trainer:** Mark Duncan.

GAME INFORMATION
Radio Announcer: Ira Liebman. **No. of Games Broadcast:** 100. **Flagship Station:** KKSA-1260 AM. **PA Announcer:** John Flynt. **Official Scorer:** Dave Augustine.

Standard Game Time: 7:05 pm.

Visiting Club Hotel: Days Inn.

SCHAUMBURG FLYERS

Office Address: 1999 S Springinsguth Rd, Schaumburg, IL 60193.

Telephone: (847) 891-2255. Fax: (847) 891-6441.

E-Mail Address: info@flyersbaseball.com. Website: www.flyersbaseball.com.

Principal Owners: Richard Ehrenreich, John Hughes, Mike Conley. Managing Partner: Richard Ehrenreich.

Executive Director: Scott Boor. Director, Business Development: Joseph Wright.
Director, Stadium Operations: Bryan Boehm. Ticket Manager: Dave Lesch. Head
Groundskeeper: Michele Pickering. Director, Accounting: Charlene Lynn. Account
Executive: Ray Gross. Maintenance Manager: Bruce Sholin.

Manager: Chad Parker.

GAME INFORMATION

Radio Announcer: Unavailable. PA Announcer: Unavailable.

Stadium Name: Alexian Field. Location: From north, I-290 to Elgin-OíHare Expressway (Thorndale), west on expressway to Irving Park Road exit, left on Springinsguth under expressway, stadium on left; From south, US 20 West (Lake Street) to Elgin-OíHare Expressway (Thorndale), east on expressway, south on Springinsguth Road.

Standard Game Times: 7 pm, Sat 6:45, Sun 1.

YUMA SCORPIONS

Address: 1280 W Desert Sun Dr, Yuma, AZ 85366.

Telephone: (928) 257-4700.

Website: www.yumascorpions.com.

GAME INFORMATION

Stadium Name: Desert Sun Stadium. Location: From I-8, take Fourth Avenue or 16th Street exit to Avenue A.

INTERNATIONAL

AMERICAS

MEXICO
MEXICAN LEAGUE

Member, National Association
NOTE: The Mexican League is a member of the National Association of Professional Baseball Leagues and has a Triple-A classification. However, its member clubs operate largely independent of the 30 major league teams, and for that reason the league is listed in the international section.

Address: Av. Insurgentes Sur #797 3er. piso. Col. Napoles. C.P. 03810, Benito Juarez, Mexico, D.F. **Telephone:** 52-55-5557-1007. **Fax:** 52-55-5395-2454. **E-Mail Address:** oficina@lmb.com.mx. **Website:** www.lmb.com.mx.

Years League Active: 1955-.
President: Plinio Escalante Bolio. **Operations Manager:** Nestor Alba Brito.

Division Structure: Madero—Chihuahua, Laguna, Mexico, Monclova, Monterrey, Nuevo Laredo, Reynosa, Saltillo. Hidalgo—Campeche, Minatitlan, Oaxaca, Puebla, Quintana Roo, Tabasco, Veracruz, Yucatan.

Regular Season: 110 games (split-schedule). **2010 Opening Date:** March 25. **Closing Date:** July 30.

All-Star Game: June 7, site unavailable.

Playoff Format: Eight teams qualify, including first- and second-half division winners plus wild-card teams with best overall records. Quarterfinals, semifinals and finals are all best of seven series.

Roster Limit: 28. **Roster Limit, Imports:** 6.

CAMPECHE PIRATES
Office Address: Calle Filiberto Qui Farfan No. 2, Col. Camino Real, CP 24020, Campeche, Campeche. **Telephone:** (52) 981-827-4759. **Fax:** (52) 981-8274767. **E-Mail Address:** piratas@prodigy.net.mx. **Website:** www.piratasdecampeche.com.mx.

President: Gabriel Escalante Castillo. **General Manager:** Maria del Socorro Morales.
Manager: Hector Estrada.

CHIHUAHUA GOLDENS
Office Address: Blvd. Juan Pablo II No. 4506, Col. Aeropuerto CP 31380. **Telephone:** (52) 614-459-0317. **Fax:** (52) 614-459-0336. **E-Mail Address:** icampos@doraslmb.com. **Website:** www.doradoslmb.com.

President: Mario Rodriguez. **General Manager:** Iram Campos Lara.
Manager: Arturo de Freitas.

LAGUNA COWBOYS
Office Address: Juan Gutenberg s/n, Col. Centro, CP 27000, Torreon, Coahuila. **Telephone:** (52) 871-718-5515. **Fax:** (52) 871-717-4335. **E-Mail Address:** unionlag@prodigy.net.mx. **Website:** www.clubvaqueroslaguna.com.

President: Carlos Gomez del Campo. **General Manager:** Carlos de la Garza.
Manager: Derek Bryant.

MEXICO CITY RED DEVILS
Office Address: Av. Cuauhtemoc #451-101, Col. Narvarte, CP 03020, Mexico DF. **Telephone:** (52) 555-639-8722. **Fax:** (52) 555-639-9722. **E-Mail Address:** diablos@sportsya.com. **Website:** www.diablos.com.mx.

President: Roberto Mansur Galán. **General Manager:** Eduardo de la Cerda.
Manager: Daniel Fernandez.

MONCLOVA STEELERS
Office Address: Cuauhtemoc #299, Col. Ciudad Deportiva, CP 25750, Monclova, Coahuila. **Telephone:** (52) 866-636-2650. **Fax:** (52) 866-636-2688. **E-Mail Address:** acererosdelnorte@prodigy.net.mx. **Website:** www.acereros.com.mx.

President: Donaciano Garza Gutierrez. **General Manager:** Victor Favela Lopez.
Manager: Francisco Rodriguez.

MONTERREY SULTANS
Office Address: Av. Manuel Barragan s/n, Estadio Monterrey, Apartado Postal 870, Monterrey, Nuevo Leon, CP 66460. **Telephone:** (52) 81-8351-0209. **Fax:** (52) 81-8351-8022. **E-Mail Address:** sultanes@sultanes.com.mx. **Website:** www.sultanes.com.mx.

President: José Maiz García. **General Manager:** Roberto Magdaleno Ramírez.
Manager: Felix Fermin.

NUEVO LAREDO OWLS
Office Address: Av. Santos Degollado 235-G, Col. Independencia, CP 88020, Nuevo Laredo, Tamaulipas. **Telephone:** (52) 867-712-2299. **Fax:** (52) 867-712-0736. **E-Mail Address:** tecolotes@globalpc.net. **Website:** www.tecolotesdenuevolaredo.com.

President: Victor Lozano Rendon. **General Manager:** Ruben Estrada Ordonez.
Manager: Gerardo Sanchez.

OAXACA WARRIORS
Office Address: M. Bravo 417 Col. Centro 68000, Oaxaca, Oaxaca. **Telephone:** (52) 951-515-5522. **Fax:** (52) 951-515-4966. **E-Mail Address:** oaxacaguerreros@gmail.com. **Website:** www.guerrerosdeoaxaca.com.mx.

President: Avellá Villa Vicente Pérez. **General Manager:** Lic Spindola Guillermo Morales.
Manager: Eddy Diaz.

MINATITLAN OILERS
Office Address: Av. Avila Camacho esquina con H. Colegio Militar, Estadio 18 de Marzo de 1938, Col. De los Maestros, CP 96849, Minatitlan, Veracruz. **Telephone:** (52) 951-515-5522. **Fax:** (52) 951-515-4966. **E-Mail Address:** webmaster@petrolerosdeminatitlan.com.mx. **Website:** www.petrolerosdeminatitlan.com.mx.

Manager: Andres Mora.

PUEBLA PARROTS
Office Address: Calz. Zaragoza S/N, Unidad Deportiva 5 de Mayo, Col. Maravillas, CP 72220, Puebla, Puebla. **Telephone:** (52) 222-222-2116. **Fax:** (52) 222-222-2117. **E-Mail Address:** oficina@pericosdepuebla.com.mx. **Website:** www.pericosdepuebla.com.mx.

President: Rafael Moreno Valle Sanchez. **General Manager:** Edgar Ramirez.
Manager: Alfonso Jimenez.

QUINTANA ROO TIGERS
Office Address: Av. Mayapan Mz. 4 Lt. 1 Super Mz. 21, CP 77500, Cancun, Quintana Roo. **Telephone:** (52) 998-887-3108. **Fax:** (52) 998-887-1313. **E-Mail Address:** tigres@tigrescapitalinos.com.mx. **Website:** www.tigresqr.com.

President: Cuauhtémoc Rodriguez. **General Manager:** Francisco Minjarez.
Manager: Matias Carrillo.

SALTILLO SARAPE MAKERS
Office Address: Blvd. Nazario Ortiz Esquina con Blvd. Jesus Sanchez, CP 25280, Saltillo, Coahuila. **Telephone:**

(52) 844-416-9455. **Fax:** (52) 844-439-1330. **E-Mail Address:** aley@grupoley.com. **Website:** www.saraperos.com.mx.

President: Alvaro Ley Lopez. **General Manager:** Eduardo Valenzuela Guajardo.

Manager: Orlando Sanchez.

TABASCO OLMECS

Office Address: Explanada de la Ciudad Deportiva, Parque de Beisbol Centenario del 27 de Febrero, Col. Atasta de Serra, CP 86100, Villahermosa, Tabasco. **Telephone:** (52) 993-352-2787. **Fax:** (52) 993-352-2788. **E-Mail Address:** olmecastab@prodigy.net.mx. **Website:** www.olmecasdetabasco.com.mx.

President: Raul Gonzalez Rodriguez. **General Manager:** Luis Guzman Ramos.

Manager: Luis de los Santos.

REYNOSA BRONCOS

Office Address: Paris 511, Esq. **c/** Tiburcio Garza Zamora Altos, Locales 6 y 7, Col Beatty, Reynosa, Tamps. **Telephone:** (52) 922-3462. **Fax:** (52) 925-7118. **E-Mail Address:** broncosdereynosa@gmail.com. **Website:** www.broncosreynosa.com.

Manager: Homar Rojas.

VERACRUZ RED EAGLES

Office Address: Av. Jacarandas S/N, Esquina España, Fraccionamiento Virginia, CP 94294, Boca del Rio, Veracruz. **Telephone:** (52) 229-935-5004. **Fax:** (229) 935-5008. **E-Mail Address:** rojosdelaguila@terra.com.mx. **Website:** www.aguiladeveracruz.com.

President: Jose Antonio Mansur Beltran. **General Manager:** Carlos Nahun Hernandez.

Manager: Enrique Reyes.

YUCATAN LIONS

Office Address: Calle 50 #406-B, Entre 35 y 37, Col. Jesus Carranza, CP 97109, Merida, Yucatán. **Telephone:** (52) 999-926-3022. **Fax:** (52) 999-926-3631. **E-Mail Addresses:** leones@prodigy.net.mx. **Website:** www.leonesdeyucatan.com.mx.

President: Ricalde Gustavo Durán. **General Manager:** Jose Rivero.

Manager: Lino Rivera.

MEXICAN ACADEMY

Rookie Classification

Mailing Address: Angel Pola No. 16, Col. Periodista, CP 11220, Mexico, D.F. **Telephone:** (52) 555-557-1007. **Fax:** (52) 555-395-2454. **E-Mail Address:** mbl@prodigy.net.mx. **Website:** www.academialmb.com.

Member Clubs: Celaya, Guanajuato, Queretaro, Salamanca.

Director General: Raul Martinez. **Administration:** Pela Villalobos.

Regular Season: 50 games. **2008 Opening Date:** Oct. 9. **Closing Date:** Dec. 21.

DOMINICAN REPUBLIC

DOMINICAN SUMMER LEAGUE

Member, National Association
Rookie Classification
Mailing Address: Calle Segunda No. 64, Reparto Antilla, Santo Domingo, Dominican Republic. **Telephone/Fax:** (809) 532-3619. **Website:** www.dominicansummerleague.com. **E-Mail Address:** ligadeverano@codetel.net.do.

Years League Active: 1985-.

President: Orlando Diaz.

Member Clubs/Division Structure: Boca Chica North—Blue Jays, Brewers/Orioles (shared team), Cubs 2, Dodgers, Giants, Marlins, Mets, Pirates, Rays, Red Sox, Royals, Yankees 1. Santo Domingo North—Athletics, Cardinals, Mariners, Phillies. Boca Chica Baseball City—Cubs 1, Diamondbacks, Indians, Nationals, Orioles, Padres, Reds, Rockies, Tigers, Twins, White Sox, Yankees 2. San Pedro de Macoris—Angels, Astros, Braves, Rangers 1, Rangers 2.

Regular Season: 72 games. **2010 Opening Date:** June 3. **Closing Date:** Aug. 20.

Playoff Format: Six teams qualify for playoffs, including four division winners and two wild-card teams. Teams with two best records receive a bye to the semifinals; four other playoff teams play best-of-three series. Winners advance to best-of-three semifinals. Winners advance to best-of-five championship series.

Roster Limit: 35 active. **Player Eligibility Rule:** No player may have four or more years of prior minor league service. Draft-eligible players may not participate in the DSL or VSL, with the exception of two players from Puerto Rico. No age limits apply.

VENEZUELA

VENEZUELAN SUMMER LEAGUE

Member, National Association
Rookie Classification
Mailing Address: Torre Movilnet, Oficina 10, Piso 9, Valencia, Carabobo, Venezuela. **Telephone:** (58) 241-823-8101. **Fax:** (58) 241-824-3340. **Website:** www.vsl.com.ve.

Years League Active: 1997-.

Administrator: Saul Gonzalez. **Coordinator:** Ramon Feriera.

Participating Organizations: Cardinals, Mariners, Mets, Phillies, Pirates, Rays, Tigers.

Regular Season: 70 games. **2010 Opening Date:** May 17. **Closing Date:** Aug. 27.

Playoffs: Best-of-three series between top two teams in regular season.

Roster Limit: 35 active. **Player Eligibility Rule:** No player may have four or more years of prior minor league service. Draft-eligible players may not participate in the DSL or VSL, with the exception of two players from Puerto Rico. No age limits apply.

ASIA

CHINA

CHINA BASEBALL LEAGUE

Mailing Address: 5, Tiyuguan Road, Beijing 100763, China. **Telephone:** (86) 10-6716-9082. **Fax:** (86) 10-6716-2993. **E-Mail Address:** cga_cra@263.net.

Years League Active: 2002-.

Chairman: Hu Jian Guo. **Vice Chairmen:** Tom McCarthy, Shen Wei. **Executive Director:** Yang Jie. **General Manager, Marketing/Promotion:** Lin Xiao Wu.

Member Clubs: Beijing Tigers, Guangdong Leopards, Henan Elephants, Jiangsu Hopestars, Shanghai Golden Eagles, Sichuan Dragons, Tianjin Lions.

Regular Season: 28 games.

Playoff Format: Top two teams meet in one-game championship.

JAPAN

NIPPON PROFESSIONAL BASEBALL

Mailing Address: Imperial Tower, 14F, 1-1-1 Uchisaiwai-cho, Chiyoda-ku, Tokyo 100-0011. **Telephone:** 03-3502-0022. **Fax:** 03-3502-0140. **Website:** www.npb.or.jp, www.npb.or.jp/eng

Commissioner: Ryozo Kato.

Executive Secretary: Kunio Shimoda. **Director, Administration:** Atsushi Ihara. **Director, Baseball Operations:** Nobby Ito. **Directors, Public Relations:** Minoru Hirata, Katsuhisa Matsuzaki.

Director, Central League Operations: Kazunori Ogaki. **Director, Pacific League Operations:** Shiromitsu Hanai.

Japan Series: Best-of-seven series between Central and Pacific League champions, begins Oct. 29 at home of Pacific League club.

All-Star Series: July 22 at Nagoya Dome; July 23 at Tokyo Dome; July 24 at QVC Marine Field, Chiba.

Roster Limit: 70 per organization (one major league club, one minor league club). Major league club is permitted to register 28 players at a time, though just 25 may be available for each game.

Roster Limit, Imports: Four in majors (no more than three position players or pitchers); unlimited in minors.

CENTRAL LEAGUE

Regular Season: 144 games.

2011 Opening Date: March 25. **Closing Date:** Sept. 25, with makeup games played until Oct. 10.

Playoff Format: Second-place team meets third-place team in best-of-three series. Winner meets first-place team in best-of-seven series to determine representative in Japan Series (first-place team has one-game advantage to begin series).

CHUNICHI DRAGONS

Mailing Address: Chunichi Bldg. 6F, 4-1-1 Sakae, Naka-ku, Nagoya 460-0008. **Telephone:** 052-261-8811. **Fax:** 052-263-7696.

Chairman: Bungo Shirai. **President:** Junnosuke Nishikawa. **General Manager:** Norihito Nishwaki. **Field Manager:** Hiromitsu Ochiai.

2011 Foreign Players: Tony Blanco, Felix Carrasco, Joel Guzman, Maximo Nelson, Chen Wei Yin.

HANSHIN TIGERS

Mailing Address: 2-33 Koshien-cho, Nishinomiya-shi, Hyogo-ken 663-8152. **Telephone:** 0798-46-1515. **Fax:** 0798-46-3555.

Chairman: Shinya Sakai. **President:** Nobuo Minami. **Field Manager:** Akinobu Mayumi.

2011 Foreign Players: Craig Brazell, Cheng Kai Un, Randy Messenger, Matt Murton, Jason Standridge.

HIROSHIMA TOYO CARP

Mailing Address: 2-3-1 Minami Kaniya, Minami-ku, Hiroshima 732-8501. **Telephone:** 082-554-1000. **Fax:** 082-568-1190.

President: Hajime Matsuda. **General Manager:** Kiyoaki Suzuki. **Field Manager:** Kenjiro Nomura.

2011 Foreign Players: Giancarlo Alvarado, Bryan Bullington, Dennis Sarfate, Mike Schultz, Dioni Soriano, Chad Tracy.

TOKYO YAKULT SWALLOWS

Mailing Address: Shimbashi MCV Bldg. 5F, 5-13-5 Shimbashi, Minato-ku, Tokyo 105-0004. **Telephone:** 03-5470-8915. **Fax:** 03-5470-8916.

Chairman: Sumiya Hori. **President:** Tadashi Suzuki. **General Manager:** Junsei Atarashi. **Field Manager:** Junji Ogawa.

2011 Foreign Players: Wladimir Balentien, Tony Barnette, Aaron Guiel, Lim Chang Yong, Josh Whitesell.

YOKOHAMA BAYSTARS

Mailing Address: Kannai Arai Bldg, 7F, 1-8 Onoe-cho, Naka-ku, Yokohama 231-0015. **Telephone:** 045-681-0811. **Fax:** 045-661-2500.

Chairman: Kiyoshi Wakabayashi. **President:** Takao Kaji. **Field Manager:** Takao Obana.

2011 Foreign Players: Clayton Hamilton, Brent Leach, Brandon Mann, Brett Harper, Terrmel Sledge.

YOMIURI GIANTS

Mailing Address: Otemachi Nomura Bldg., 7F, 2-1-1 Otemachi, Chiyoda-ku, Tokyo 100-8151. **Telephone:** 03-3246-7733. **Fax:** 03-3246-2726.

Chairman: Takuo Takihana. **President:** Tsunekazu Momoi. **General Manager:** Hidetoshi Kiyotake. **Field Manager:** Tatsunori Hara.

2011 Foreign Players: Jonathan Albaladejo, Brian Bannister, Fan Tsu Lon, Dicky Gonzalez, Seth Greisinger, Lin Yi Hao, Alex Ramirez, Levi Romero, Rusty Ryal, Carlos Torres. **Coach:** John Turney.

PACIFIC LEAGUE

Regular Season: 144 games.

2011 Opening Date: March 25. **Closing Date:** Oct. 4, with makeup games played until Oct. 10.

Playoff Format: Second-place team meets third-place team in best-of-three series. Winner meets first-place team in best-of-seven series to determine league's representative in Japan Series (first-place team has one-game advantage to begin series).

CHIBA LOTTE MARINES

Mailing Address: 1 Mihama, Mihama-ku, Chiba-shi, Chiba-ken 261-8587. **Telephone:** 03-5682-6341.

Chairman: Takeo Shigemitsu. **President:** Ryuzo Setoyama. **Field Manager:** Norifumi Nishimura.

2011 Foreign Players: Kim Tae Hyun, Bob McCrory, Bill Murphy, Hayden Penn.

FUKUOKA SOFTBANK HAWKS

Mailing Address: Fukuoka Yahoo! Japan Dome, Hawks Town, Chuo-ku, Fukuoka 810-0065. **Telephone:** 092-847-1006. **Fax:** 092-844-4600.

Owner: Masayoshi Son. **Chairman:** Sadaharu Oh. **President:** Kazuhiko Kasai. **Field Manager:** Koji Akiyama.

2011 Foreign Players: Alex Cabrera, Brian Falkenborg, D.J. Houlton, Lee Boem Ho, Anthony Lerew, Jose Ortiz, Yang Yao-hsun.

HOKKAIDO NIPPON HAM FIGHTERS

Mailing Address: 1 Hitsujigaoka, Toyohira-ku, Sapporo 062-8655. **Telephone:** 011-857-3939. **Fax:** 011-857-3900.

Chairman: Hiroji Okoso. **President:** Junichi Fujii. **General Manager:** Masao Yamada. **Field Manager:** Masataka Nashida.

2010 Foreign Players: Micah Hoffpauir, Bobby Keppel, Wirfin Obispo, Brian Wolfe.

ORIX BUFFALOES

Mailing Address: 3-Kita-2-30 Chiyozaki, Nishi-ku, Osaka 550-0023. **Telephone:** 06-6586-0221. **Fax:** 06-6586-0240.

Chairman: Yoshihiko Miyauchi. **President:** Hiroaki Nishina. **General Manager:** Yoshio Murayama. **Field Manager:** Akinobu Okada.

2011 Foreign Players: Aarom Baldiris, Francisco Caraballo, Alfredo Figaro, Mike Hessman, Lee Seung Yeop, Evan MacLane, Park Chan Ho.

SAITAMA SEIBU LIONS

Mailing Address: 2135 Kami-Yamaguchi, Tokorozawa-

shi, Saitama-ken 359-1189. **Telephone:** 04-2924-1155. **Fax:** 04-2928-1919.

President: Shinji Kobayashi. **Field Manager:** Hisanobu Watanabe.

2011 Foreign Players: Dee Brown, Jose Fernandez, Alex Graman, Hsu Ming-chieh, Brian Sikorski.

TOHOKU RAKUTEN GOLDEN EAGLES

Mailing Address: 2-11-6 Miyagino, Miyagino-ku, Sendai-shi, Miyagi-ken 983-0045. **Telephone:** 022-298-5300. **Fax:** 022-298-5360.

Chairman: Hiroshi Mikitani. **President:** Toru Shimada. **Field Manager:** Senichi Hoshino.

2011 Foreign Players: Kelvin Jimenez, Kim Byung Hyun, Juan Morillo, Darrell Rasner, Randy Ruiz.

KOREA
KOREA BASEBALL ORGANIZATION

Mailing Address: 946-16 Dokokdong, Kangnam-gu, Seoul, Korea. **Telephone:** (02) 3460-4600. **Fax:** (02) 3460-4639.

Years League Active: 1982-.

Website: www.koreabaseball.com.

Commissioner: Shin Sang-woo. **Secretary General:** Ha Il-sung. **Deputy Secretary General:** Lee Sang-il.

Member Clubs: Doosan Bears, Hanwha Eagles, Kia Tigers, LG Twins, Lotte Giants, Samsung Lions, Seoul Heroes, SK Wyverns.

Regular Season: 133 games. **2010 Opening Date:** April 4.

Playoffs: Third- and fourth-place teams meet in best-of-three series; winner advances to meet second-place team in best-of-five series; winner meets first-place team in best-of-seven Korean Series for league championship.

Roster Limit: 26 active through Sept. 1, when rosters expand to 31. **Imports:** Two active.

TAIWAN
CHINESE PROFESSIONAL BASEBALL LEAGUE

Mailing Address: 2F, No. 32, Pateh Road, Sec. 3, Taipei, Taiwan 10559. **Telephone:** 886-2-2577-6992. **Fax:** 886-2-2577-2606. **Website:** www.cpbl.com.tw.

Years League Active: 1990-.

Commissioner: Shou-Po Chao. **Secretary General:** Wen-pin Lee. **International Affairs:** Richard Wang. **E-Mail Address:** richard.wang@cpbl.com.tw.

Member Clubs: Brother Elephants, Uni Lions, Sinon Bulls, La New Bears.

Regular Season: 100 games. **2010 Opening Date:** March 28.

Playoffs: Second- and third-place teams meet in best-of-five series; winner advances to meet first-place team in best-of-seven championship series.

Import Rule: Only three import players may be active, and only two may be on the field at the same time.

EUROPE

NETHERLANDS
DUTCH MAJOR LEAGUE

Mailing Address: Koninklijke Nederlandse Baseball en Softball Bond (Royal Dutch Baseball and Softball Association), Postbus 2650, 3430 GB Nieuwegein, Holland. **Telephone:** 31-30-751-3650. **FAX:** 31-30-751-3651. **Website:** www.knbsb.nl.

Member Clubs: ADO, Amsterdam Pirates, HCAW, Hoofddorp Pioniers, Kinheim, Neptunus, Sparta/Feyenoord, UVV.

President: Bob Bergkamp.

ITALY
SERIE A

Mailing Address: Federazione Italiana Baseball Softball, Viale Tiziano 74, 00196 Roma, Italy. **Telephone:** 39-06-32297201. **FAX:** 39-06-36858201. **Website:** www.fibs.it.

Member Clubs: Bologna, Godo, Grosseto, Nettuno, Parma, Paterno, Rimini, San Marino.

President: Riccardo Fraccari.

WINTER BASEBALL

CARIBBEAN BASEBALL CONFEDERATION

Mailing Address: Frank Feliz Miranda No. 1 Naco, Santo Domingo, Dominican Republic. **Telephone:** (809) 381-2643. **Fax:** (809) 565-4654. **Website:** www.ebeisbol.com.

Commissioner: Juan Francisco Puello. **Secretary:** Benny Agosto.

Member Countries: Colombia, Dominican Republic, Mexico, Nicaragua, Puerto Rico, Venezuela (Colombia and Nicaragua do not play in the Caribbean Series).

2011 Caribbean Series: Dominican Republic, February.

DOMINICAN LEAGUE

Office Address: Estadio Quisqueya, 2da. Planta, Ens. La Fe, Santo Domingo, Dominican Republic. **Telephone:** (809) 567-6371. **Fax:** (809) 567-5720. **E-Mail Address:**

ligadom@hotmail.com. **Website:** www.lidom.com.

Years League Active: 1951-.

President: Leonardo Matos Berrido. **Vice President:** Jose Rafael Alvarez Sanchez. **Administrator:** Marcos Rodríguez. **Public Relations Director:** Jorge Torres.

Member Clubs: Aguilas Cibaenas, Estrellas de Oriente, Gigantes del Cibao, Leones del Escogido, Tigres del Licey, Toros del Este.

Regular Season: 50 games. **2010 Opening Date:** Oct. 16.

Playoff Format: Top four teams meet in 18-game round-robin. Top two teams advance to best-of-nine series for league championship. Winner advances to Caribbean Series.

Roster Limit: 30. **Imports:** 7.

MEXICAN PACIFIC LEAGUE

Mailing Address: Blvd. Solidaridad No. 335, Plaza las Palmas, Edificio A, Nivel 1, Local 4, Hermosillo, Sonora,

Mexico CP 83246. **Telephone:** (52) 662-310-9714. **Fax:** (52) 662-310-9715. **E-Mail Address:** ligadelpacifico@ligadel-pacifico.com.mx. **Website:** www.ligadelpacifico.com.mx.
Years League Active: 1958-.
President: Omar Canizales. **Administration:** Vanessa Palacios. **Sports Manager:** Dennis Gonzalez Oviel.
Member Clubs: Culiacan Tomateros, Guasave Algodoneros, Hermosillo Naranjeros, Los Mochis Caneros, Mazatlan Venados, Mexicali Aguilas, Navojoa Mayos, Obregon Yaquis.
Regular Season: 68 games. **2010 Opening Date:** Oct. 16.
Playoff Format: Six teams advance to best-of-seven quarterfinals. Three winners and losing team with best record advance to best-of-seven semifinals. Winners meet in best-of-seven series for league championship. Winner advances to Caribbean Series.
Roster Limit: 30. **Imports:** 5.

PUERTO RICAN LEAGUE

Office Address: Avenida Munoz Rivera 1056, Edificio First Federal, Suite 501, Rio Piedras, PR 00925. **Mailing Address:** P.O. Box 191852, San Juan, PR 00019. **Telephone:** (787) 765-6285, 765-7285. **Fax:** (787) 767-3028. **Website:** www.puertoricobaseballleague.com.
Years League Active: 1938-2007; 2008-
President: Joaquin Monserrate Matienzo. **Executive Director:** Benny Agosto.
Member Clubs: Arecibo Lobos, Caguas Criollos, Carolina Gigantes, Mayaguez Indios, Ponce Leones.
Regular Season: 42 games. **2010 Opening Date:** Nov. 11.
Playoff Format: Top four teams meet in best-of-seven semifinal series. Winners meet in best-of-nine series for league championship. Winner advances to Caribbean Series.
Roster Limit: 30. **Imports:** 5.

VENEZUELAN LEAGUE

Mailing Address: Avenida Casanova, Centro Comercial "El Recreo," Torre Sur, Piso 3, Oficinas 6 y 7, Sabana Grande, Caracas, Venezuela. **Telephone:** (58) 212-761-6408. **Fax:** (58) 212-761-7661. **Website:** www.lvbp.com.
Years League Active: 1946-.
President: Jose Grasso Vecchio. **Vice Presidents:** Rafael Chaverogazdik, Gustavo Massiani. **General Manager:** Domingo Alvarez.
Member Clubs: Anzoategui Caribes, Aragua Tigres, Caracas Leones, La Guaira Tiburones, Lara Cardenales, Magallanes Navegantes, Margarita Bravos, Zulia Aguilas.
Regular Season: 64 games. **2010 Opening Date:** Oct. 18.
Playoff Format: Top two teams in each division, plus a wild-card team, meet in 16-game round-robin series. Top two finishers meet in best-of-seven series for league championship. Winner advances to Caribbean Series.
Roster Limit: 26. **Imports:** 7.

COLOMBIAN LEAGUE

Office/Mailing Address: Unavailable. **Telephone:** Unavailable. **Website:** www.teamrenteria.com.
Member Clubs: Barranquilla, Cartagena, Monteria,
Sincelejo.
Regular season: 65 games. **2010 Opening Date:** Oct. 28.
Playoff Format: Top two teams meet in best-of-seven finals for league championship.

NICARAGUAN LEAGUE

Office Address/Mailing Address: Canal 2 TV, Casa #26, Managua, Nicaragua. **Telephone:** 505-2266-3645. **Website:** www.lnbp.com.ni.
Commissioner: Noel Urcuyo Baez. **General Manager:** Azalea Salmeron. **Marketing Director:** Jessica Market.
Member Clubs: Chinandega, Granada, Leon, Managua.
Regular Season: 40 games. **2010 Opening Date:** Dec. 1.
Playoff Format: Top two teams meet in best-of-seven finals for league championship.

AUSTRALIA

AUSTRALIAN BASEBALL LEAGUE

Mailing Address: 1 Palm Meadows Drive, Carrara, QLD, 4211, Australia. **Telephone:** 61-7-5510-6819. **Fax:** 61-7-5510-6855. **E-Mail Address:** admin@ableague.com.au. **Website:** www.theabl.com.
CEO: Peter Wermuth. **Operations Manager:** Ben Foster.
Teams: Adelaide, Brisbane, Canberra, Melbourne, Perth, Sydney.
Playoff Format: First-place team plays second-place team in major semifinal; third-place team plays fourth-place team in minor semifinal, both best of three series. Loser of major semifinal plays winner of minor semifinal in best of three series. Winner of that series plays winner of major semifinal in best of three series for league championship.

DOMESTIC LEAGUE

ARIZONA FALL LEAGUE

Mailing Address: 2415 E. Camelback Road, Suite 850, Phoenix, AZ 85016. **Telephone:** (602) 281-7250. **Fax:** (602) 281-7313. **E-Mail Address:** afl@mlb.com. **Website:** www.mlb.com.
Years League Active: 1992-.
Operated by: Major League Baseball.
Executive Director: Steve Cobb. **Seasonal Assistant:** Joan McGrath.
Teams: Mesa Solar Sox, Peoria Javelinas, Peoria Saguaros, Phoenix Desert Dogs, Scottsdale Scorpions, Surprise Rafters.
2010 Opening Date: Unavailable. Play usually opens in mid-October.
Playoff Format: Division champions meet in one-game championship.
Roster Limit: 30. Players with less than one year of major league service are eligible, with one foreign player and one player below the Double-A level allowed per team.

MINOR LEAGUE SCHEDULES

TRIPLE-A

INTERNATIONAL LEAGUE

BUFFALO

APRIL	
7-8	Syracuse
9-12	Pawtucket
13-15	at Scranton/Wilkes-Barre
16-17	at Pawtucket
18-21	Rochester
22-25	Lehigh Valley
26-29	at Rochester
30	at Lehigh Valley

MAY	
1-3	at Lehigh Valley
5-8	Louisville
9-12	Scranton/Wilkes-Barre
13-16	at Louisville
17-20	at Indianapolis
21-24	Charlotte
26-29	Gwinnett
30-31	at Charlotte

JUNE	
1-2	at Charlotte
3-6	at Gwinnett
7-10	Indianapolis
11-14	Columbus
16-19	at Norfolk
20-23	at Durham
24-27	Norfolk
28-30	Lehigh Valley

JULY	
1	Lehigh Valley
2-3	Syracuse
4-5	at Syracuse
6-8	at Scranton/Wilkes-Barre
9-10	at Pawtucket
14-15	Rochester
16-17	at Rochester
18-21	at Syracuse
22-25	Pawtucket
26-29	Scranton/Wilkes-Barre
30-31	at Lehigh Valley

AUGUST	
1-2	at Rochester
4-7	at Pawtucket
8-9	at Syracuse
10-11	Syracuse
13-15	Durham
16-19	Toledo
20-23	at Columbus
24-27	at Toledo
28-29	Rochester
31	Syracuse

SEPTEMBER	
1	Syracuse
2-3	at Lehigh Valley
4-5	Scranton/Wilkes-Barre

CHARLOTTE

APRIL	
7-10	Norfolk
11-13	Durham
14-15	at Gwinnett
16-18	at Norfolk
19-22	at Durham
23-25	Gwinnett
26-29	Scranton/Wilkes-Barre
30	Columbus

MAY	
1-3	Columbus
5-8	at Toledo
9-12	at Columbus
13-16	Rochester
17-20	Toledo
21-24	at Buffalo
26-29	at Syracuse
30-31	Buffalo

JUNE	
1-2	Buffalo
3-6	Lehigh Valley
7-10	at Scranton/Wilkes-Barre
11-14	at Pawtucket
16-19	Syracuse
20-23	at Rochester
24-27	at Lehigh Valley
28-30	Durham

JULY	
1	Durham
2-3	at Norfolk
4-5	Norfolk
6-7	Gwinnett
8-10	at Gwinnett
14-17	Louisville
18-21	at Indianapolis
22-25	at Louisville
26-29	Indianapolis
30-31	at Durham

AUGUST	
2-3	Durham
4-5	Gwinnett
6-7	at Gwinnett
8-11	Pawtucket
12-15	Norfolk
16-19	at Norfolk
20-21	Gwinnett
22-23	at Gwinnett
25-28	at Durham
29-30	at Norfolk
31	Durham

SEPTEMBER	
1	Durham
2-3	Gwinnett
4-5	at Gwinnett

COLUMBUS

APRIL	
7-10	at Indianapolis
11-12	at Louisville
14-15	at Toledo
16-18	Toledo
19-22	Louisville
23-25	Indianapolis
26-29	at Gwinnett
30	at Charlotte

MAY	
1-3	at Charlotte
5-8	Lehigh Valley
9-12	Charlotte
13-16	at Indianapolis
17-20	at Pawtucket
21-24	Durham
26-29	at Norfolk
30-31	at Durham

DURHAM

JUNE	
1-2	at Durham
3-4	at Louisville
5-6	Louisville
7-10	Rochester
11-14	at Buffalo
16-19	at Scranton/Wilkes-Barre
20-21	Toledo
22-23	at Toledo
24-27	Gwinnett
28-29	Toledo
30	at Toledo

JULY	
1	at Toledo
2-3	Louisville
4-6	at Louisville
7-8	Toledo
9-10	at Toledo
14-17	Indianapolis
18-21	Scranton/Wilkes-Barre

APRIL	
7-10	at Gwinnett
11-13	at Charlotte
14-15	Norfolk
16-18	Gwinnett
19-22	Charlotte
23-25	at Norfolk
26-29	at Louisville
30	at Indianapolis

MAY	
1-3	at Indianapolis
5-8	Syracuse
9-12	Indianapolis
13-16	at Syracuse
17-20	Louisville
21-24	at Columbus
26-29	at Toledo
30-31	Columbus

JUNE	
1-2	Columbus
3-6	Pawtucket
7-10	at Lehigh Valley
11-14	Norfolk
16-19	at Gwinnett
20-23	Buffalo
24-27	Scranton/Wilkes-Barre
28-30	at Charlotte

22-25	at Lehigh Valley
26-29	at Syracuse
30-31	Norfolk

AUGUST	
1-2	Norfolk
4-7	Syracuse
8-9	at Louisville
10-11	Indianapolis
12-15	at Rochester
16-19	at Pawtucket
20-23	Buffalo
24-25	at Indianapolis
26-27	Indianapolis
28-29	Louisville
30-31	at Louisville

SEPTEMBER	
2-3	Toledo
4-5	at Toledo

JULY	
1	at Charlotte
2-3	Gwinnett
4-5	at Gwinnett
6-8	Norfolk
9-10	at Norfolk
14-17	at Pawtucket
18-21	at Rochester
22-25	Toledo
26-29	Gwinnett
30-31	Charlotte

AUGUST	
2-3	at Charlotte
4-7	Lehigh Valley
8-11	Rochester
12-15	at Buffalo
16-19	at Scranton/Wilkes-Barre
20-21	at Norfolk
23-24	Norfolk
25-28	Charlotte
29-30	Gwinnett
31	at Charlotte

SEPTEMBER	
1	at Charlotte
2-5	at Norfolk

GWINNETT

APRIL	
7-10	Durham
11-13	Norfolk
14-15	Charlotte
16-18	at Durham
19-22	at Norfolk
23-25	at Charlotte
26-29	Columbus
30	Scranton/Wilkes-Barre

MAY	
1-3	Scranton/Wilkes-Barre
5-8	at Rochester
9-12	at Pawtucket
13-16	Toledo
17-20	Rochester
21-24	at Lehigh Valley
26-29	at Buffalo
30-31	Lehigh Valley

JUNE	
1-2	Lehigh Valley
3-6	Buffalo
7-10	at Toledo
11-14	at Indianapolis
16-19	Durham
20-23	Syracuse
24-27	at Columbus
28-30	at Louisville

JULY	
1	at Louisville
2-3	at Durham
4-5	Durham
6-7	at Charlotte
8-10	Charlotte
14-17	Norfolk
18-21	Louisville
22-25	at Norfolk
26-29	at Durham
30-31	Indianapolis

AUGUST
1-2 . . . . . . .Indianapolis
4-5 . . . . . . at Charlotte
6-7 . . . . . . .Charlotte
8-11 at Scranton/Wilkes-Barre
12-15 . . . . . Pawtucket
16-19 . . . . . at Syracuse
20-21 . . . . at Charlotte
22-23 . . . . . .Charlotte

INDIANAPOLIS

APRIL
7-10 . . . . . . Columbus
11-12 . . . . . . Toledo
13-15 . . . . .Louisville
16-18 . . . . .Louisville
19-22 . . . . .at Toledo
23-25 . . . . at Columbus
26-29 . . . . . Norfolk
30 . . . . Durham

MAY
1-3 . . . . . . Durham
5-8 . . . . . at Norfolk
9-12 . . . . .at Durham
13-16 . . . . Columbus
17-20 . . . . . Buffalo
21-24 at Scranton/Wilkes-Barre
26-29 . . . . at Pawtucket
30-31 . Scranton/Wilkes-Barre

JUNE
1-2 . . Scranton/Wilkes-Barre
3-6 . . . . . . Syracuse
7-10 . . . . .at Buffalo
11-14 . . . . .Gwinnett
16-19 . . . . .at Rochester
20-23 . . at Lehigh Valley
24-27 . . . . Pawtucket
28-30 . . . . . at Syracuse

JULY
1 . . . . at Syracuse
2-3 . . . . . . .at Toledo
4-6 . . . . Toledo
7-8 . . . . . at Louisville
9-10 . . . . . .Louisville
14-17 . . . . at Columbus
18-21 . . . . .Charlotte
22-25 . . . . . Rochester
26-29 . . . . at Charlotte
30-31 . . . . at Gwinnett

AUGUST
1-2 . . . . . at Gwinnett
4-7 . . . . . . Toledo
8-9 . . . . . .at Toledo
10-11 . . . at Columbus
12-15 . . . at Louisville
16-19 . . . . .Louisville
20-23 . . . Lehigh Valley
24-25 . . . . Columbus
26-27 . . . at Columbus
28-29 . . . . .at Toledo
30-31 . . . . . Toledo

SEPTEMBER
2-3 . . . . . . .Louisville
4-5 . . . . . at Louisville

LEHIGH VALLEY

APRIL
7-8 . . Scranton/Wilkes-Barre
9-12 . . . . . . Syracuse
13-15 . . . . .at Rochester
16-17 . . . . . at Syracuse
18-21 . Scranton/Wilkes-Barre
22-25 . . . . .at Buffalo
26-29 . . . . . Pawtucket
30 . . . . Buffalo

MAY
1-3 . . . . . . Buffalo
5-8 . . . . at Columbus
9-12 . . . . . at Toledo
13-16 . . . . . Norwich
17-20 at Scranton/Wilkes-Barre
21-24 . . . . .Gwinnett
26-29 . . . . Rochester
30-31 . . . . at Gwinnett

JUNE
1-2 . . . . . at Gwinnett
3-6 . . . . at Charlotte
7-10 . . . . . . Durham
11-14 . . . . .Louisville
16-19 . . at Pawtucket
20-23 . . . . .Indianapolis
24-27 . . . .Charlotte
28-30 . . . .at Buffalo

JULY
1 . . . . .at Buffalo
2-3 . . . . Rochester
4-5 . at Scranton/Wilkes-Barre
6-8 . . . . . .at Rochester
9-10 . . . . at Syracuse
14-15 . . . . . Syracuse
16-17 . . . . at Syracuse
18-21 . . . at Pawtucket
22-25 . . . . . Columbus
26-29 . . . . . Pawtucket
30-31 . . . . . Buffalo

AUGUST
1-2 . at Scranton/Wilkes-Barre
4-7 . . . . .at Durham
8-11 . . . . . at Norfolk
12-15 . . . . . Toledo
16-17 . . . . Rochester
18-19 . . . .at Rochester
20-23 . . . at Indianapolis
24-27 . . . . at Louisville
28-29 . . . . . Syracuse
30-31 . Scranton/Wilkes-Barre

SEPTEMBER
2-3 . . . . Buffalo
4-5 . . . . . . at Syracuse

LOUISVILLE

APRIL
7-10 . . . . Toledo
11-12 . . . . . . Columbus
13-15 . . . . at Indianapolis
16-18 . . . . .Indianapolis
19-22 . . . . at Columbus
23-25 . . . . . . .at Toledo
26-29 . . . . . Durham
30 . . . . Norfolk

MAY
1-3 . . . . Norfolk
5-8 . . . . . .at Buffalo
9-12 . . .at Rochester
13-16 . . . . . . Buffalo
17-20 . . . . . at Durham
21-24 . . . . at Norfolk
26-29 . Scranton/Wilkes-Barre
30-31 . . . . . Syracuse

JUNE
1-2 . . . . . . Syracuse
3-4 . . . . . . Columbus
5-6 . . . . at Columbus
7-10 . . . . . at Syracuse
11-14 . . at Lehigh Valley
16-19 . . . . . Toledo
20-23 . . . . Pawtucket
24-27 . . . . .at Toledo
28-30 . . . . .Gwinnett

JULY
1 . . . . .Gwinnett

NORFOLK

APRIL
7-10 . . . . at Charlotte
11-13 . . . . at Gwinnett
14-15 . . . . .at Durham
16-18 . . . . .Charlotte
19-22 . . . . .Gwinnett
23-25 . . . . . Durham
26-29 . . . at Indianapolis
30 . . . . . . at Louisville

MAY
1-3 . . . . . . at Louisville
5-8 . . . . . .Indianapolis
9-12 . . . . . Syracuse
13-16 . . . at Lehigh Valley
17-20 . . . . at Syracuse
21-24 . . . . .Louisville
26-29 . . . . Columbus
30-31 . . . at Pawtucket

JUNE
1-2 . . . . . at Pawtucket
3-6 . . . . . .at Rochester
7-10 . . . . Pawtucket
11-14 . . . at Durham
16-19 . . . . . Buffalo
20-23 at Scranton/Wilkes-Barre
24-27 . . . . .at Buffalo
28-30 . Scranton/Wilkes-Barre

JULY
1 . . . Scranton/Wilkes-Barre
2-3 . . . . .Charlotte
4-5 . . . . . at Charlotte
6-8 . . . . . .at Durham
9-10 . . . . . . Durham
14-17 . . . . at Gwinnett
18-21 . . . . . Toledo
22-25 . . . . .Gwinnett
26-29 . . . . . .at Toledo
30-31 . . . . at Columbus

AUGUST
1-2 . . . . . at Columbus
4-7 . . . . Rochester
8-11 . . . . Lehigh Valley
12-15 . . . at Charlotte
16-19 . . . . . .Charlotte
20-21 . . . . . Durham
23-24 . . . . .at Durham
25-28 . . . at Gwinnett
29-30 . . . . .Charlotte
31 . . . . .Gwinnett

SEPTEMBER
1 . . . . .Gwinnett
2-5 . . . . Durham

PAWTUCKET

APRIL
7-8 . . . . Rochester
9-12 . . . . . .at Buffalo
13-15 . . . at Syracuse
16-17 . . . . . Buffalo
18-21 . . . . Syracuse
22-25 . . .at Rochester
26-29 . . at Lehigh Valley
30 . . . . Toledo

MAY
1-3 . . . . Toledo
5-8 . at Scranton/Wilkes-Barre
9-12 . . . . .Gwinnett
13-16 . Scranton/Wilkes-Barre
17-20 . . . at Columbus
21-24 . . . . .at Toledo
26-29 . . . .Indianapolis
30-31 . . . . . Norfolk

JUNE
1-2 . . . . Norfolk
3-6 . . . . . .at Durham
7-10 . . . . at Norfolk
11-14 . . . . .Charlotte
16-19 . . . Lehigh Valley
20-23 . . . at Louisville
24-27 . . at Indianapolis
28-30 . . . . Rochester

JULY
1 . . . . Rochester
2-3 . . Scranton/Wilkes-Barre
4-5 . . . . .at Rochester
6-8 . . . . . at Syracuse
9-10 . . . . . . Buffalo
14-17 . . . . . Durham
18-21 . . . Lehigh Valley
22-25 . . . . .at Buffalo

26-29 . . . . at Lehigh Valley
30-31 . . . . .Louisville

AUGUST
1-2 . . . . .Louisville
4-7 . . . . Buffalo
8-11 . . . . at Charlotte
12-15 . . . . . . at Gwinnett
16-19 . . . . Columbus

ROCHESTER

APRIL
7-8 . . . . at Pawtucket
9-12 . . Scranton/Wilkes-Barre
13-15 . . . . . Lehigh Valley
16-17 at Scranton/Wilkes-Barre
18-21 . . . . .at Buffalo
22-25 . . . . . . Pawtucket
26-29 . . . . Buffalo
30 . . . . at Syracuse

MAY
1-3 . . . . at Syracuse
5-8 . . . . .Gwinnett
9-12 . . . . .Louisville
13-16 . . . . . at Charlotte
17-20 . . . . . at Gwinnett
21-24 . . . . Syracuse
26-29 . . at Lehigh Valley
30-31 . . . . Toledo

JUNE
1-2 . . . . Toledo
3-6 . . . . Norfolk
7-10 . . . . . at Columbus
11-14 . . . . at Toledo
16-19 . . . . . Indianapolis
20-23 . . . . . . .Charlotte
24-25 . . . . . at Syracuse
26-27 . . . . . . Syracuse
28-30 . . . . . at Pawtucket

SCRANTON/WILKES-BARRE

APRIL
7-8 . . . . . at Lehigh Valley
9-12 . . . . . . .at Rochester
13-15 . . . . Buffalo
16-17 . . . . Rochester
18-21 . . . . at Lehigh Valley
22-25 . . . . Syracuse
26-29 . . . . . at Charlotte
30 . . . . at Gwinnett

MAY
1-3 . . . . .Gwinnett
5-8 . . . . Pawtucket
9-12 . . . . .at Buffalo
13-16 . . . . at Pawtucket
17-20 . . . . . Lehigh Valley
21-24 . . . . .Indianapolis
26-29 . . . . . at Louisville
30-31 . . . at Indianapolis

JUNE
1-2 . . . . .Indianapolis
3-6 . . . . Toledo
7-10 . . . . .Charlotte
11-14 . . . . at Syracuse
16-19 . . . . . Columbus
20-23 . . . . Norfolk
24-27 . . . . . . .at Durham

SYRACUSE

APRIL
7-8 . . . . .at Buffalo
9-12 . . . . at Lehigh Valley

20-23 . . . . Syracuse
24-25 . . . . . . at Syracuse
26-29 at Scranton/Wilkes-Barre
30-31 . . . . . .at Rochester

SEPTEMBER
2-3 . . . Scranton/Wilkes-Barre
4-5 . . . . Rochester

JULY
1 . . . . at Pawtucket
2-3 . . . . . at Lehigh Valley
4-5 . . . . Pawtucket
6-8 . . . . . . Lehigh Valley
9-10 at Scranton/Wilkes-Barre
14-15 . . . . . . .at Buffalo
16-17 . . . . Buffalo
18-21 . . . . . . Durham
22-25 . . . . at Indianapolis
26-29 . . . . at Louisville
30-31 . Scranton/Wilkes-Barre

AUGUST
1-2 . . . . Buffalo
4-7 . . . . at Norfolk
8-11 . . . . . .at Durham
12-15 . . . . Columbus
16-17 . . . at Lehigh Valley
18-19 . . . . . Lehigh Valley
20-21 Scranton/Wilkes-Barre
22-25 at Scranton/Wilkes-Barre
26-27 . . . . . at Syracuse
28-29 . . . . . . .at Buffalo
30-31 . . . . . . Pawtucket

SEPTEMBER
2-3 . . . . Syracuse
4-5 . . . . at Pawtucket

28-30 . . . . . . at Norfolk

JULY
1 . . . . at Norfolk
2-3 . . . . . at Pawtucket
4-5 . . . . . . Lehigh Valley
6-8 . . . . Buffalo
9-10 . . . . Rochester
14-17 . . . . .at Toledo
18-21 . . . . at Columbus
22-25 . . . . . Syracuse
26-29 . . . . . .at Buffalo
30-31 . . . . .at Rochester

AUGUST
1-2 . . . . . . Lehigh Valley
4-7 . . . . .Louisville
8-11 . . . . .Gwinnett
12-15 . . . . at Syracuse
16-19 . . . . . . Durham
20-21 . . . . . .at Rochester
22-25 . . . . . . Rochester
26-29 . . . . . Pawtucket
30-31 . . . . at Lehigh Valley

SEPTEMBER
2-3 . . . . at Pawtucket
4-5 . . . . .at Buffalo

22-25 at Scranton/Wilkes-Barre
26-29 . . . . Toledo
30 . . . . Rochester

MAY
1-3 . . . . Rochester
5-8 . . . . .at Durham
9-12 . . . . at Norfolk
13-16 . . . . . . Durham
17-20 . . . . Norfolk
21-24 . . . . . .at Rochester
26-29 . . . . . .Charlotte
30-31 . . . . . at Louisville

JUNE
1-2 . . . . . . at Louisville
3-6 . . . . . at Indianapolis
7-10 . . . . . . .Louisville
11-14 . Scranton/Wilkes-Barre
16-19 . . . . . at Charlotte
20-23 . . . . . at Gwinnett
24-25 . . . . . . Rochester
26-27 . . . . . at Rochester
28-30 . . . . .Indianapolis

JULY
1 . . . . .Indianapolis
2-3 . . . . .at Buffalo

TOLEDO

APRIL
7-10 . . . . at Louisville
11-12 . . . at Indianapolis
14-15 . . . . Columbus
16-18 . . . . at Columbus
19-22 . . . . .Indianapolis
23-25 . . . . . . .Louisville
26-29 . . . . . at Syracuse
30 . . . . . . at Pawtucket

MAY
1-3 . . . . . . at Pawtucket
5-8 . . . . .Charlotte
9-12 . . . . . Lehigh Valley
13-16 . . . . . . at Gwinnett
17-20 . . . . . at Charlotte
21-24 . . . . . Pawtucket
26-29 . . . . . . Durham
30-31 . . . . . .at Rochester

JUNE
1-2 . . . . .at Rochester
3-6 at Scranton Wilkes/Barre
7-10 . . . . .Gwinnett
11-14 . . . . . Rochester
16-19 . . . . at Louisville
20-21 . . . . . at Columbus
22-23 . . . . . Columbus
24-27 . . . . . . .Louisville
28-29 . . . . at Columbus

4-5 . . . . Buffalo
6-8 . . . . Pawtucket
9-10 . . . . . Lehigh Valley
14-15 . . . . at Lehigh Valley
16-17 . . . . . Lehigh Valley
18-21 . . . . Buffalo
22-25 at Scranton/Wilkes-Barre
26-29 . . . . Columbus
30-31 . . . . .at Toledo

AUGUST
1-2 . . . . .at Toledo
4-7 . . . . . at Columbus
8-9 . . . . Buffalo
10-11 . . . . .at Buffalo
12-15 . Scranton/Wilkes-Barre
16-19 . . . . .Gwinnett
20-23 . . . . at Pawtucket
24-25 . . . . . Pawtucket
26-27 . . . . . . Rochester
28-29 . . . at Lehigh Valley
31 . . . . .at Buffalo

SEPTEMBER
1 . . . . at Buffalo
2-3 . . . . .at Rochester
4-5 . . . . . . Lehigh Valley

30 . . . . Columbus

JULY
1 . . . . Columbus
2-3 . . . . . . .Indianapolis
4-6 . . . . . at Indianapolis
7-8 . . . . . . at Columbus
9-10 . . . . Columbus
14-17 . Scranton/Wilkes-Barre
18-21 . . . . . . at Norfolk
22-25 . . . . . .at Durham
26-29 . . . . Norfolk
30-31 . . . . Syracuse

AUGUST
1-2 . . . . Syracuse
4-7 . . . . . at Indianapolis
8-9 . . . . . . .Indianapolis
10-11 . . . . . . .Louisville
12-15 . . . at Lehigh Valley
16-19 . . . . . .at Buffalo
20-21 . . . . . . .Louisville
22-23 . . . . at Louisville
24-27 . . . . Buffalo
28-29 . . . . .Indianapolis
30-31 . . . at Indianapolis

SEPTEMBER
2-3 . . . . at Columbus
4-5 . . . . Columbus

PACIFIC COAST LEAGUE

ALBUQUERQUE

APRIL
7-10 . . . . Omaha
11-14 . . . . .Iowa
15-18 . . at Oklahoma City
19-22 . . . . at Iowa
23-26 . . . . New Orleans
28-30 . . . . . . at Nashville

MAY
1 . . . . at Nashville
2-5 . . . . Omaha
6-9 . . . . .Memphis
10-13 . . . . . .at Las Vegas
14-17 . . . . .at Tucson

19-22 . . . . Reno
23-26 . . Colorado Springs
27-30 . . . .at New Orleans
31 . . . . at Memphis

JUNE
1-3 . . . . at Memphis
4-7 . . . . . . at Round Rock
9-12 . . . . .Nashville
13-16 . . at Oklahoma City
17-20 . . . . .Iowa
21-24 . . . . Oklahoma City
25-28 . . . . at Iowa
30 . . . . at Omaha

JULY
1-3	at Omaha
4-6	Round Rock
7-10	Nashville
14-17	at Nashville
18-21	Oklahoma City
22-25	New Orleans
26-29	at Omaha
30-31	at New Orleans

AUGUST
1-2	at New Orleans

COLORADO SPRINGS

APRIL
7-10	Tucson
11-14	Reno
15-18	at Reno
19-22	at Tacoma
23-26	Las Vegas
28-30	at Tucson

MAY
1	at Tucson
2-5	Fresno
6-9	at Sacramento
10-13	Iowa
14-17	Omaha
19-22	at Round Rock
23-26	at Albuquerque
27-30	Fresno
31	at Fresno

JUNE
1-3	at Fresno
4-7	Sacramento
9-12	Reno
13-16	at Las Vegas
17-20	Tucson
21-24	at Tacoma

FRESNO

APRIL
7-10	Las Vegas
11-14	Tacoma
15-18	at Las Vegas
19-22	at Tucson
23-26	Reno
28-30	at Salt Lake

MAY
1	at Salt Lake
2-5	at Colorado Springs
6-9	Tucson
10-13	at Nashville
14-17	at Memphis
19-22	New Orleans
23-26	Oklahoma City
27-30	at Colorado Springs
31	Colorado Springs

JUNE
1-3	Colorado Springs
4-7	Las Vegas
9-12	at Salt Lake
13-16	Tacoma
17-20	at Sacramento
21-24	Salt lake

IOWA

APRIL
7-10	at Round Rock
11-14	at Albuquerque
15-18	Memphis
19-22	Albuquerque
23-26	at Memphis

3-6	Tacoma
7-10	Salt Lake
12-15	at Fresno
16-19	at Sacramento
20-23	Memphis
24-28	Round Rock
29-31	at Memphis

SEPTEMBER
1	at Memphis
2-5	at Round Rock

25-28	at Salt Lake
30	at Las Vegas

JULY
1-3	at Las Vegas
4-6	Tacoma
7-10	Salt Lake
14-17	at Reno
18-21	Las Vegas
22-25	at Fresno
26-29	at Tucson
30-31	at Sacramento

AUGUST
1-2	at Sacramento
3-6	Nashville
7-10	Memphis
12-15	at Oklahoma City
16-19	at New Orleans
20-23	Salt Lake
24-28	Tacoma
29-31	at Salt Lake

SEPTEMBER
1	at Salt Lake
2-5	Sacramento

25-28	at Tucson
30	at Tacoma

JULY
1-3	at Tacoma
4-6	Sacramento
8-10	Tucson
14-17	at Sacramento
18-21	at Reno
22-25	Colorado Springs
26-29	Salt Lake
30-31	Reno

AUGUST
1-2	Reno
3-6	at Iowa
7-10	at Omaha
12-15	Albuquerque
16-19	Round Rock
20-23	at Las Vegas
24-28	Sacramento
29-31	at Reno

SEPTEMBER
1	at Reno
2-5	at Tacoma

28-30	at Omaha

MAY
1	at Omaha
2-5	Round Rock
6-9	New Orleans
10-13	at Colorado Springs

14-17	at Reno
19-22	Tucson
23-26	Las Vegas
27-30	at Round Rock
31	at Nashville

JUNE
1-3	at Nashville
4-7	Omaha
9-12	Round Rock
13-16	at Omaha
17-20	at Albuquerque
21-24	Memphis
25-28	Albuquerque
30	New Orleans

JULY
1-3	New Orleans
4-6	at Oklahoma City
7-10	at New Orleans

LAS VEGAS

APRIL
7-10	at Fresno
11-14	at Sacramento
15-18	Fresno
19-22	Salt Lake
23-26	at Colorado Springs
28-30	Sacramento

MAY
1	Sacramento
2-5	Reno
6-9	at Tacoma
10-13	Albuquerque
14-17	Round Rock
19-22	at Omaha
23-26	at Iowa
27-30	Tacoma
31	Tucson

JUNE
1-3	Tucson
4-7	at Fresno
9-12	at Tucson
13-16	Colorado Springs
17-20	Reno
21-24	at Reno

MEMPHIS

APRIL
7-10	Oklahoma City
11-14	New Orleans
15-18	at Iowa
19-22	at Omaha
23-26	Iowa
28-30	Round Rock

MAY
1	Round Rock
2-5	at New Orleans
6-9	at Albuquerque
10-13	Sacramento
14-17	Fresno
19-22	at Tacoma
23-26	at Salt Lake
27-30	Omaha
31	Albuquerque

JUNE
1-3	Albuquerque
4-7	at Oklahoma City
9-12	at New Orleans
13-16	New Orleans
17-20	Nashville
21-24	at Iowa

14-17	Oklahoma City
18-21	Nashville
22-25	at Nashville
26-29	at New Orleans
30-31	at Memphis

AUGUST
1-2	at Memphis
3-6	Fresno
7-10	Sacramento
12-15	at Tacoma
16-19	at Salt Lake
20-23	Oklahoma City
24-28	at Oklahoma City
29-31	Nashville

SEPTEMBER
1	Nashville
2-5	Omaha

25-28	Tacoma
30	Colorado Springs

JULY
1-3	Colorado Springs
4-6	at Salt Lake
7-9	Sacramento
14-17	at Tucson
18-21	at Colorado Springs
22-25	Tucson
26-29	at Reno
30-31	at Tacoma

AUGUST
1-2	at Tacoma
3-6	Oklahoma City
7-10	New Orleans
12-15	at Nashville
16-19	at Memphis
20-23	Fresno
24-28	at Salt Lake
29-31	at Sacramento

SEPTEMBER
1	at Sacramento
2-5	Salt Lake

25-28	at Omaha
30	Oklahoma City

JULY
1-3	Oklahoma City
4-6	at Nashville
7-10	at Round Rock
14-17	Round Rock
18-21	Omaha
22-25	at Oklahoma City
26-29	at Round Rock
30-31	Iowa

AUGUST
1-2	Iowa
3-6	at Reno
7-10	at Colorado Springs
12-15	Tucson
16-19	Las Vegas
20-23	at Albuquerque
24-28	at Nashville
29-31	Albuquerque

SEPTEMBER
1	Albuquerque
2-5	Nashville

NASHVILLE

APRIL
7-10 . . . . . . New Orleans
11-14 . . . . Oklahoma City
15-18 . . . . at Omaha
19-22 . . . . at New Orleans
23-26 . . . . Omaha
28-30 . . . . . Albuquerque

MAY
1 . . . . Albuquerque
2-5 . . . . at Oklahoma City
6-9 . . . . at Round Rock
10-13 . . . . Fresno
14-17 . . . . . . Sacramento
19-22 . . . . . at Salt Lake
23-26 . . . . at Tacoma
27-30 . . . Oklahoma City
31 . . . . Iowa

JUNE
1-3 . . . . Iowa
4-7 . . . at New Orleans
9-12 . . . . at Albuquerque
13-16 . . . . . Round Rock
17-20 . . . . at Memphis
21-24 . . . . Omaha

25-28 . . . . . New Orleans
30 . . . . . . at Round Rock

JULY
1-3 . . . . . at Round Rock
4-6 . . . . Memphis
7-10 . . . . at Albuquerque
14-17 . . . . Albuquerque
18-21 . . . . at Iowa
22-25 . . . . Iowa
26-29 . . at Oklahoma City
30-31 . . . . . Round Rock

AUGUST
1-2 . . . . Round Rock
3-6 . . at Colorado Springs
7-10 . . . . at Reno
12-15 . . . . . . Las Vegas
16-19 . . . . Tucson
20-23 . . . . . at Omaha
24-28 . . . . . . Memphis
29-31 . . . . at Iowa

SEPTEMBER
1 . . . . at Iowa
2-5 . . . . . at Memphis

NEW ORLEANS

APRIL
7-10 . . . . at Nashville
11-14 . . . . . at Memphis
15-18 . . . . . Round Rock
19-22 . . . . . . Nashville
23-26 . . . . at Albuquerque
28-30 . . . . Oklahoma City

MAY
1 . . . . . Oklahoma City
2-5 . . . . Memphis
6-9 . . . . . at Iowa
10-13 . . . . . . Salt Lake
14-17 . . . . Tacoma
19-22 . . . at Fresno
23-26 . . . . at Sacramento
27-30 . . . . Albuquerque
31 . . . . at Omaha

JUNE
1-3 . . . . at Omaha
4-7 . . . . Nashville
9-12 . . . . . . Memphis
13-16 . . . at Memphis
17-20 . . at Oklahoma City
21-24 . . . . . Round Rock

25-28 . . . . . at Nashville
30 . . . . at Iowa

JULY
1-3 . . . . at Iowa
4-6 . . . . Omaha
7-10 . . . . Iowa
14-17 . . . . . at Omaha
18-21 . . at Round Rock
22-25 . . at Albuquerque
26-29 . . . . Iowa
30-31 . . . Albuquerque

AUGUST
1-2 . . . . . Albuquerque
3-6 . . . . . . at Tucson
7-10 . . . . at Las Vegas
12-15 . . . . Reno
16-19 . . Colorado Springs
20-23 . . at Round Rock
24-28 . . . . . . Omaha
29-31 . . . Oklahoma City

SEPTEMBER
1 . . . . . . Oklahoma City
2-5 . . . . at Oklahoma City

OKLAHOMA CITY

APRIL
7-10 . . . . . . at Memphis
11-14 . . . . . at Nashville
15-18 . . . . . Albuquerque
19-22 . . . . . Round Rock
23-26 . . . at Round Rock
28-30 . . at New Orleans

MAY
1 . . . . . at New Orleans
2-5 . . . . Nashville
6-9 . . . . . . at Omaha
10-13 . . . . Tacoma
14-17 . . . . Salt Lake
19-22 . . . at Sacramento
23-26 . . . . at Fresno
27-30 . . . . at Nashville
31 . . . . . . Round Rock

JUNE
1-3 . . . . . . Round Rock
4-7 . . . . Memphis
9-12 . . . . . . at Omaha
13-16 . . . . Albuquerque
17-20 . . . . New Orleans
21-24 . . at Albuquerque
25-28 . . . . at Round Rock
30 . . . . at Memphis

JULY
1-3 . . . . . . at Memphis
4-6 . . . . Iowa
7-10 . . . . Omaha
14-17 . . . . . . at Iowa
18-21 . . . at Albuquerque
22-25 . . . . . . Memphis
26-29 . . . . . Nashville
30-31 . . . . Omaha

OMAHA

APRIL
7-10 . . . . at Albuquerque
11-14 . . . . at Round Rock
15-18 . . . . . Nashville
19-22 . . . . . Memphis
23-26 . . . at Nashville
28-30 . . . . Iowa

MAY
1 . . . . Iowa
2-5 . . . . . Albuquerque
6-9 . . . . Oklahoma City
10-13 . . . . . at Reno
14-17 . at Colorado Springs
19-22 . . . . . Las Vegas
23-26 . . . . . . Tucson
27-30 . . . . at Memphis
31 . . . . . New Orleans

JUNE
1-3 . . . . . . New Orleans
4-7 . . . . at Iowa
9-12 . . . . Oklahoma City
13-16 . . . . Iowa
17-20 . . . at Round Rock
21-24 . . . . . at Nashville

25-28 . . . . Memphis
30 . . . . Albuquerque

JULY
1-3 . . . . . Albuquerque
4-6 . . . at New Orleans
7-10 . . . at Oklahoma City
14-17 . . . New Orleans
18-21 . . . at Memphis
22-25 . . . . Round Rock
26-29 . . . Albuquerque
30-31 . . at Oklahoma City

AUGUST
1-2 . . . . at Oklahoma City
3-6 . . . . Sacramento
7-10 . . . . Fresno
12-15 . . . . . at Salt Lake
16-19 . . . . . at Tacoma
20-23 . . . . . . Nashville
24-28 . . at New Orleans
29-31 . . . . Round Rock

SEPTEMBER
1 . . . . Round Rock
2-5 . . . . at Iowa

RENO

APRIL
7-10 . . . . . at Salt Lake
11-14 . at Colorado Springs
15-18 . . Colorado Springs
19-22 . . . . Sacramento
23-26 . . . . . at Fresno
28-30 . . . Tacoma

MAY
1 . . . . Tacoma
2-5 . . . . . . at Las Vegas
6-9 . . . . . at Salt Lake
10-13 . . . . . . Omaha
14-17 . . . . Iowa
19-22 . . . at Albuquerque
23-26 . . at Round Rock
27-30 . . . . Sacramento
31 . . . . . . at Tacoma

JUNE
1-3 . . . . . . at Tacoma
4-7 . . . . Salt Lake
9-12 . . at Colorado Springs
13-16 . . . . . Tucson
17-20 . . . . . at Las Vegas
21-24 . . . . . Las Vegas

25-28 . . . at Sacramento
30 . . . . Salt Lake

JULY
1-3 . . . . Salt Lake
4-6 . . . . . . at Tucson
7-10 . . . . . at Tacoma
14-17 . . . Colorado Springs
18-21 . . . . . Fresno
22-25 . . . at Sacramento
26-29 . . . .Las Vegas
30-31 . . . . at Fresno

AUGUST
1-2 . . . . at Fresno
3-6 . . . . Memphis
7-10 . . . . Nashville
12-15 . . at New Orleans
16-19 . . . Oklahoma City
20-23 . . . . Tacoma
24-28 . . . at Tucson
29-31 . . . . Fresno

SEPTEMBER
1 . . . . Fresno
2-5 . . . . Tucson

ROUND ROCK

APRIL
7-10 . . . . Iowa
11-14 . . . . . . Omaha
15-18 . . . . at New Orleans
19-22 . . at Oklahoma City
23-26 . . . Oklahoma City
28-30 . . . . . at Memphis

MAY
1 . . . . at Memphis
2-5 . . . . at Iowa
6-9 . . . . Nashville

10-13 . . . . at Tucson
14-17 . . . . at Las Vegas
19-22 . . .Colorado Springs
23-26 . . . . .Reno
27-30 . . . . Iowa
31 . . .at Oklahoma City

JUNE
1-3 . . . . . at Oklahoma City
4-7 . . . . . . Albuquerque
9-12 . . . . . . at Iowa
13-16 . . . . . at Nashville

17-20 . . . . Omaha
21-24 . . . . . at New Orleans
25-28 . . . . . Oklahoma City
30 . . . . Nashville

JULY

1-3 . . . . .Nashville
4-6 . . . . at Albuquerque
7-10 . . . . .Memphis
14-17 . . . . . . at Memphis
18-21 . . . . . New Orleans
22-25 . . . . at Omaha
26-29 . . . . . . .Memphis
30-31 . . . . . . at Nashville

SACRAMENTO

APRIL

7-10 . . . . Tacoma
11-14 . . . . .Las Vegas
15-18 . . . . . . at Tacoma
19-22 . . . . at Reno
23-26 . . . . Tucson
28-30 . . . . at Las Vegas

MAY

1 . . . . at Las Vegas
2-5 . . . . Salt Lake
6-9 . . .Colorado Springs
10-13 . . . . . at Memphis
14-17 . . . . at Nashville
19-22 . . . . Oklahoma City
23-26 . . . .New Orleans
27-30 . . . . at Reno
31 . . . . Salt Lake

JUNE

1-3 . . . . Salt Lake
4-7 . . at Colorado Springs
9-12 . . . . .Tacoma
13-16 . . . . . at Salt Lake
17-20 . . . . . . .Fresno
21-24 . . . . . . .at Tucson

SALT LAKE

APRIL

7-10 . . . . .Reno
11-14 . . . . Tucson
15-18 . . . . . .at Tucson
19-22 . . . . at Las Vegas
23-26 . . . . .Tacoma
28-30 . . . . .Fresno

MAY

1 . . . . .Fresno
2-5 . . . . . . at Sacramento
6-9 . . . . .Reno
10-13 . . . . at New Orleans
14-17 . . .at Oklahoma City
19-22 . . . . Nashville
23-26 . . . . . .Memphis
27-30 . . . . . .at Tucson
31 . . . . . . at Sacramento

AUGUST

1-2 . . . . at Nashville
3-6 . . . . Salt Lake
7-10 . . . . .Tacoma
12-15 . . . . at Sacramento
16-19 . . . . .at Fresno
20-23 . . . . New Orleans
24-28 . . . at Albuquerque
29-31 . . . . at Omaha

SEPTEMBER

1 . . . . at Omaha
2-5 . . . . . . Albuquerque

25-28 . . . . .Reno
30 . . . . Tucson

JULY

1-3 . . . . Tucson
4-6 . . . . .at Fresno
7-9 . . . . . at Las Vegas
14-17 . . . . .Fresno
18-21 . . . . at Salt Lake
22-25 . . . . .Reno
26-29 . . . . . at Tacoma
30-31 . . .Colorado Springs

AUGUST

1-2 . . . . .Colorado Springs
3-6 . . . . at Omaha
7-10 . . . . at Iowa
12-15 . . . . . Round Rock
16-19 . . . . . Albuquerque
20-23 . . . . .at Tucson
24-28 . . . . . . at Fresno
29-31 . . . . .Las Vegas

SEPTEMBER

1 . . . . .Las Vegas
2-5 . . . . at Colorado Springs

AUGUST

1-2 . . . . Tucson
3-6 . . . . . at Round Rock
7-10 . . . . at Albuquerque
12-15 . . . . Omaha
16-19 . . . . .Iowa

TACOMA

APRIL

7-10 . . . . . at Sacramento
11-14 . . . . .at Fresno
15-18 . . . . . Sacramento
19-22 . . Colorado Springs
23-26 . . . . at Salt Lake
28-30 . . . . .at Reno

MAY

1 . . . . .at Reno
2-5 . . . . Tucson
6-9 . . . . .Las Vegas
10-13 . . at Oklahoma City
14-17 . . . .at New Orleans
19-22 . . . . .Memphis
23-26 . . . . . . Nashville
27-30 . . . . at Las Vegas
31 . . . . Reno

JUNE

1-3 . . . . Reno
4-7 . . . . .at Tucson
9-12 . . . . at Sacramento
13-16 . . . . . . .at Fresno
17-20 . . . . . Salt Lake
21-24 . . . Colorado Springs

TUCSON

APRIL

7-10 . . .at Colorado Springs
11-14 . . . . at Salt Lake
15-18 . . . . . Salt Lake
19-22 . . . . Fresno
23-26 . . . . . at Sacramento
28-30 . . . . Colorado Springs

MAY

1 . . . . Colorado Springs
2-5 . . . . at Tacoma
6-9 . . . . .at Fresno
10-13 . . . . . Round Rock
14-17 . . . . . Albuquerque
19-22 . . . . at Iowa
23-26 . . . . . at Omaha
27-30 . . . . . Salt Lake
31 . . . . .at Las Vegas

JUNE

1-3 . . . . . . .at Las Vegas
4-7 . . . . .Tacoma
9-12 . . . . .Las Vegas
13-16 . . . . .at Reno
17-20 . . at Colorado Springs
21-24 . . . . . . Sacramento

20-23 . .at Colorado Springs
24-28 . . . . . . .Las Vegas
29-31 . . . Colorado Springs

SEPTEMBER

1 . . . . . Colorado Springs
2-5 . . . . .at Las Vegas

25-28 . . . . . . at Las Vegas
30 . . . . Fresno

JULY

1-3 . . . . Fresno
4-6 . . . .at Colorado Springs
7-10 . . . . Reno
14-17 . . . . . Salt Lake
18-21 . . . . .at Tucson
22-25 . . . . . at Salt Lake
26-29 . . . Sacramento
30-31 . . . . .Las Vegas

AUGUST

1-2 . . . . .Las Vegas
3-6 . . . . . at Albuquerque
7-10 . . . . . at Round Rock
12-15 . . . . .Iowa
16-19 . . . . Omaha
20-23 . . . . .at Reno
24-28 . .at Colorado Springs
29-31 . . . . Tucson

SEPTEMBER

1 . . . . Tucson
2-5 . . . . Fresno

25-28 . . . . Fresno
30 . . . . . . at Sacramento

JULY

1-3 . . . . . . at Sacramento
4-6 . . . . Reno
7-10 . . . . .at Fresno
14-17 . . . . . . .Las Vegas
18-21 . . . . .Tacoma
22-25 . . . . at Las Vegas
26-29 . . . Colorado Springs
30-31 . . . . at Salt Lake

AUGUST

1-2 . . . . at Salt Lake
3-6 . . . . New Orleans
7-10 . . . . . Oklahoma City
12-15 . . . . at Memphis
16-19 . . . . . at Nashville
20-23 . . . . . Sacramento
24-28 . . . . Reno
29-31 . . . . . . at Tacoma

SEPTEMBER

1 . . . . at Tacoma
2-5 . . . . .at Reno

DOUBLE-A

EASTERN LEAGUE

AKRON AEROS

APRIL

6 . . . . at Columbus
7-10 . . . . . .Binghamton
11-13 . . . . .Altoona
14-17 . . . . . . .at Reading

18-20 . . . . at Bowie
21-23 . . . . Reading
25-28 . . . . Bowie
29-30 . . . at Binghamton

MAY

1 . . . . at Binghamton
2-5 . . . . at Altoona
6-8 . . . . .Trenton
9-11 . . . . .at Erie
12-15 . . . . at Bowie
17-19 . . . . .Altoona
20-22 . . . . . at Altoona
23-26 . . . . . Harrisburg
27-30 . . . . . Richmond

31 . . . . .at Reading

JUNE

1-2 . . . . .at Reading
3-5 . . . . .Binghamton
7-9 . . . . . .at New Britain
10-12 . . . . at Harrisburg
14-16 . . . . New Hampshire
17-19 . . . . Portland
21-23 . . . . at Binghamton
24-26 . . . . Reading

27-29 . . . . .Bowie	
30 . . . . .at Erie	

JULY
1-3. . . . . .at Erie
4-7. . . . . at Altoona
8-11 . . . . Erie
14-17 . . . at Harrisburg
18-20 . . . . .Altoona
21-24 . . . . .at Erie
25-27 . . . . .Trenton
28-31 . . . . Erie

ALTOONA CURVE

APRIL
7-10 . . . . .at Erie
11-13 . . . . at Akron
14-17 . . . . Richmond
18-20 . . . . .Harrisburg
21-23 . . . . at Richmond
25-28 . . . at Harrisburg
29-30 . . . . Erie

MAY
1 . . . . Erie
2-5. . . . . Akron
6-8. . . . . at Richmond
9-11 . . . . . at Harrisburg
12-15 . . . . Erie
17-19 . . . . at Akron
20-22 . . . . Akron
23-26 . . . . .Bowie
27-30 . . . . at Binghamton
31 . . . . .Trenton

JUNE
1-2. . . . . . . at Trenton
3-5. . . . . Portland
7-9. . . . . Erie
10-12 . . . . . . .at Reading
14-16 . . . . . . New Britain
17-19 . . . . . .Harrisburg
21-23 . . .at New Hampshire

BINGHAMTON METS

APRIL
7-10 . . . . at Akron
11-13 . . . . .at Erie
14-17 . . . . New Hampshire
18-20 . . . . Portland
21-23 . . .at New Hampshire
25-28 . . . . at Portland
29-30 . . . . .Akron

MAY
1 . . . . .Akron
2-5. . . . . Erie
6-8. . . .at New Hampshire
9-11 . . . . New Britain
12-15 . . . . . at Trenton
17-19 . .at New Hampshire
20-22 . . . . . .Harrisburg
23-26 . . . at New Britain
27-30 . . . . .Altoona
31 . . . . Erie

JUNE
1-2. . . . . Erie
3-5. . . . . . . at Akron
7-9. . . . . . . .Harrisburg
10-12 . . . . . at Trenton
14-16 . . . . . at Richmond
17-19 . . . . . . .Trenton
21-23 . . . . .Akron

24-26 . . . . . at Harrisburg
27-29 . . . . Reading
30 . . . . at Trenton

JULY
1-3. . . . . at Trenton
4-7. . . . . Akron
8-11 . . . . .Bowie
14-17 . . . . . . .at Erie
18-20 . . . . at Akron
21-24 . . . . . New Britain
25-27 . . . .at Reading
28-31 . . . .at Portland

AUGUST
2-4. . . . . . . .Binghamton
5-7. . . . . .Trenton
9-11 . . . . . .at New Britain
12-14 . . . . Reading
16-18 . . . . New Hampshire
19-21 . . . . . .at Reading
22-24 . . . . . . Richmond
25-28 . . . at Binghamton
29-31 . . . . . . at Bowie

SEPTEMBER
1 . . . . at Bowie
2-5. . . . . Richmond

24-26 . . . . at Bowie
27-29 . . . . .at Erie
30 . . . . .Bowie

JULY
1-3. . . . . .Bowie
4-7. . . . . Portland
8-11 . . . . . at New Britain
14-17 . . . New Hampshire
18-20 . . . . . at Portland
21-24 . . . .at Reading
25-27 . . . . . . Portland
28-31 . . . at Harrisburg

AUGUST
2-4. . . . . at Altoona
5-7. . . . . Reading
9-11 . . . . . . .at Trenton
12-14 . . . . . . Richmond
16-18 . . . . . New Britain
19-21 . . . . . at Portland
22-24 . . . . Erie
25-28 . . . . . . .Altoona
29-31 . . . . .at Erie

SEPTEMBER
1 . . . . .at Erie
2-5. . . . . Reading

BOWIE BAYSOX

APRIL
7-10 . . . . . . at Harrisburg
11-13 . . . . at Richmond
14-17 . . . . Erie
18-20 . . . . Akron
21-23 . . . . .at Erie
25-28 . . . . . at Akron
29-30 . . . . Richmond

MAY
1 . . . . Richmond
2-5. . . . . .Harrisburg
6-8. . . . . .at Erie
9-11 . . . . Richmond
12-15 . . . . .Akron
17-19 . . . . at Richmond
20-22 . . . . Erie
23-26 . . . . at Altoona
27-30 . . . at Harrisburg
31 . . . . Richmond

JUNE
1-2. . . . . Richmond
3-5. . . . . . . New Britain
7-9. . .at New Hampshire
10-12 . . . .at Portland
14-16 . . . . . . Reading
17-19 . . . . . at Richmond
21-23 . . . .at New Britain

24-26 . . . . . .Binghamton
27-29 . . . . at Akron
30 . . . . . . at Binghamton

JULY
1-3. . . . . . at Binghamton
4-7. . . . . Reading
8-11 . . . . . . at Altoona
14-17 . . . . . . Richmond
18-20 . . . at Harrisburg
21-24 . . . . . . .Trenton
25-27 . . . . . Harrisburg
28-31 . . .at New Britain

AUGUST
2-4. . . . . Portland
5-7. . . . . New Hampshire
9-11 . . . . .at Reading
12-14 . . . . . New Britain
16-18 . . . . at Richmond
19-21 . . . . . at Trenton
22-24 . . . . Akron
25-28 . . . . .at Erie
29-31 . . . . .Altoona

SEPTEMBER
1 . . . . .Altoona
2-5. . . . . Erie

ERIE SEAWOLVES

APRIL
7-10 . . . . .Altoona
11-13 . . . . . .Binghamton
14-17 . . . . . . at Bowie
18-19 . . . . .at Reading
21-23 . . . . .Bowie
25-28 . . . . . Reading
29-30 . . . . at Altoona

MAY
1 . . . . at Altoona
2-5. . . . . at Binghamton
6-8. . . . . .Bowie
9-11 . . . . .Akron
12-15 . . . . at Altoona
17-19 . . . . . . .Trenton
20-22 . . . . . . at Bowie
23-26 . . . . at Richmond
27-30 . . . . . . Reading
31 . . . . . . at Binghamton

JUNE
1-2. . . . . at Binghamton
3-5. . . . . . . .Harrisburg
7-9. . . . . . .at Altoona
10-12 . . .at New Britain
14-16 . . . . . Portland
17-19 . . . . New Hampshire
20-23 . . . . . . .at Reading

24-26 . . . . . at Richmond
27-29 . . . . .Binghamton
30 . . . . Akron

JULY
1-3. . . . . Akron
4-7. . . . . . at Harrisburg
8-11 . . . . at Akron
14-17 . . . . . . .Altoona
18-20 . . . . . at Trenton
21-24 . . . . Akron
25-27 . . . . . . Richmond
28-31 . . . . . at Akron

AUGUST
2-4. . . . . . . New Britain
5-7. . . . . . . .Harrisburg
9-11 . . .at New Hampshire
12-14 . . . . . .at Portland
16-18 . . . . .Trenton
19-21 . . . . at Harrisburg
22-24 . . . at Binghamton
25-28 . . . . .Bowie
29-31 . . . . . .Binghamton

SEPTEMBER
1 . . . . .Binghamton
2-5. . . . . . . at Bowie

HARRISBURG SENATORS

APRIL
7-10 . . . . .Bowie
11-13 . . . . . New Britain
14-17 . . . . . at Trenton
18-20 . . . . at Altoona
21-23 . . . . . . .Trenton
25-28 . . . . . .Altoona
29-30 . . . .at New Britain

MAY
1 . . . . . . .at New Britain
2-5. . . . . at Bowie
6-8. . . . . Reading

9-11 . . . . .Altoona
12-15 . . . . . at Richmond
17-19 . . . . . New Britain
20-22 . . . at Binghamton
23-26 . . . . . . at Akron
27-30 . . . . .Bowie
31 . . . . . New Hampshire

JUNE
1-2. . . . . New Hampshire
3-5. . . . . .at Erie
7-9. . . . . at Binghamton
10-12 . . . . Akron

14-16 . . . . at Trenton
17-19 . . . . at Altoona
21-23 . . . . Richmond
24-26 . . . . .Altoona
27-29 . . . . . at Richmond
30 . . . . . . .at New Britain

JULY

1-3 . . . . . . .at New Britain
4-7 . . . . Erie
8-11 . . . . . . at Richmond
14-17 . . . . Akron
18-20 . . . . Bowie
21-24 . . . . . . at Richmond
25-27 . . . . at Bowie

NEW BRITAIN ROCK CATS

APRIL

7-10 . . . . . . at Richmond
11-13 . . . . . at Harrisburg
14-17 . . . . Portland
18-20 . . . New Hampshire
21-23 . . . . . . .at Portland
25-28 . . .at New Hampshire
29-30 . . . . . . Harrisburg

MAY

1 . . . . Harrisburg
2-5 . . . . Richmond
6-8 . . . . .at Portland
9-11 . . . . . at Binghamton
12-15 . . . . Portland
17-19 . . . . . at Harrisburg
20-22 . . . New Hampshire
23-26 . . . . . . .Binghamton
27-30 . . .at New Hampshire
31 . . . . Portland

JUNE

1-2 . . . . Portland
3-5 . . . . . . at Bowie
7-9 . . . . Akron
10-12 . . . . Erie
14-16 . . . . . . at Altoona
17-19 . . . . at Reading

21-23 . . . . Bowie
24-26 . . . . Trenton
27-29 . . . . .at Portland
30 . . . . Harrisburg

JULY

1-3 . . . . Harrisburg
4-7 . . . .at New Hampshire
8-11 . . . . . . .Binghamton
14-17 . . . . . . .at Portland
18-20 . . . . . . Richmond
21-24 . . . . . . at Altoona
25-27 . . . New Hampshire
28-31 . . . . Bowie

AUGUST

2-4 . . . . .at Erie
5-7 . . . . . . at Akron
9-11 . . . . .Altoona
12-14 . . . . . . at Bowie
16-18 . . . . at Binghamton
19-21 . . . New Hampshire
22-24 . . . . . Reading
25-28 . . . . at Trenton
29-31 . . . . at Richmond

SEPTEMBER

1 . . . . at Richmond
2-5 . . . . .Trenton

NEW HAMPSHIRE FISHER CATS

APRIL

7-10 . . . . .Trenton
11-13 . . . . Reading
14-17 . . . . at Binghamton
18-20 . . . . .at New Britain
21-23 . . . . . . .Binghamton
25-28 . . . . . New Britain
29-30 . . . . at Trenton

MAY

1 . . . . at Trenton
2-5 . . . . .at Reading
6-8 . . . . . . .Binghamton
9-11 . . . . Portland
12-15 . . . . . .at Reading
17-19 . . . . . .Binghamton
20-22 . . . . .at New Britain
23-26 . . . . . .at Portland
27-30 . . . . . New Britain
31 . . . . . . at Harrisburg

JUNE

1-2 . . . . at Harrisburg
3-5 . . . . at Trenton
7-9 . . . . .Bowie
10-12 . . . . Richmond
14-16 . . . . at Akron
17-19 . . . . .at Erie

21-23 . . . . .Altoona
24-26 . . . . Portland
27-29 . . . . at Trenton
30 . . . . .at Portland

JULY

1-3 . . . . .at Portland
4-7 . . . . New Britain
8-11 . . . . Portland
14-17 . . . . at Binghamton
18-20 . . . . Reading
21-24 . . . . Portland
25-27 . . . .at New Britain
28-31 . . . . Reading

AUGUST

2-4 . . . . at Richmond
5-7 . . . . at Bowie
9-11 . . . . Erie
12-14 . . . . Akron
16-18 . . . . . . at Altoona
19-21 . . . . .at New Britain
22-24 . . . . .Trenton
25-28 . . . . . Harrisburg
29-31 . . . . at Trenton

SEPTEMBER

1 . . . . at Trenton
2-5 . . . . .at Portland

PORTLAND SEA DOGS

APRIL

7-10 . . . . Reading
11-13 . . . . .Trenton
14-17 . . . .at New Britain
18-20 . . . at Binghamton
21-23 . . . . New Britain
25-28 . . . . .Binghamton
29-30 . . . . . .at Reading

MAY

1 . . . . .at Reading
2-5 . . . . at Trenton
6-8 . . . . New Britain
9-11 . . . .at New Hampshire
12-15 . . . .at New Hampshire
17-19 . . . . Reading
20-22 . . . . . at Trenton
23-26 . . . New Britain
27-30 . . . . .Trenton
31 . . . .at New Britain

JUNE

1-2 . . . . . .at New Britain
3-5 . . . . at Altoona
7-9 . . . . Richmond
10-12 . . . . Bowie
14-16 . . . . . . .at Erie
17-19 . . . . . at Akron
21-23 . . . . . . .Trenton

24-26 . . .at New Hampshire
27-29 . . . . . . New Britain
30 . . . . . New Hampshire

JULY

1-3 . . . . . . New Hampshire
4-7 . . . . . at Binghamton
8-11 . . . .at New Hampshire
14-17 . . . . . . New Britain
18-20 . . . . . . .Binghamton
21-24 . . .at New Hampshire
25-27 . . . at Binghamton
28-31 . . . . .Altoona

AUGUST

2-4 . . . . at Bowie
5-7 . . . . at Richmond
9-11 . . . . Akron
12-14 . . . . Erie
16-18 . . . . . .at Reading
19-21 . . . . . . .Binghamton
22-24 . . . . . . Harrisburg
25-28 . . . . . at Reading
29-31 . . . . at Harrisburg

SEPTEMBER

1 . . . . at Harrisburg
2-5 . . . . . New Hampshire

READING PHILLIES

APRIL

7-10 . . . .at Portland
11-13 . . .at New Hampshire
14-17 . . . . Akron
18-19 . . . . Erie
21-23 . . . . . . at Akron
25-28 . . . . . . .at Erie
29-30 . . . . Portland

MAY

1 . . . . Portland
2-5 . . . . . New Hampshire
6-8 . . . . at Harrisburg
9-11 . . . . at Trenton
12-15 . . . . . New Hampshire
17-19 . . . . . .at Portland
20-22 . . . . Richmond
24-26 . . . . . . .Trenton
27-30 . . . . . . .at Erie
31 . . . . Akron

JUNE

1-2 . . . . Akron
3-5 . . . . . . at Richmond
6-9 . . . . .Trenton
10-12 . . . . .Altoona
14-16 . . . . . . at Bowie
17-19 . . . . . New Britain
20-23 . . . . Erie

24-26 . . . . at Akron
27-29 . . . . . . at Altoona
30 . . . . Richmond

JULY

1-3 . . . . Richmond
4-7 . . . . at Bowie
8-11 . . . . .Trenton
14-17 . . . . . . at Trenton
18-20 . . .at New Hampshire
21-24 . . . . . . .Binghamton
25-27 . . . . .Altoona
28-31 . . .at New Hampshire

AUGUST

2-4 . . . . Harrisburg
5-7 . . . . . at Binghamton
9-11 . . . . Bowie
12-14 . . . . . at Altoona
16-18 . . . . Portland
19-21 . . . . .Altoona
22-24 . . . . .at New Britain
25-28 . . . . . Portland
29-31 . . . . . at Akron

SEPTEMBER

1 . . . . at Akron
2-5 . . . . . . at Binghamton

RICHMOND FLYING SQUIRRELS

APRIL

7-10 . . . . . New Britain
11-13 . . . . . . .Bowie
14-17 . . . . at Altoona
18-20 . . . at Trenton
21-23 . . . . . .Altoona
25-28 . . . . . .Trenton
29-30 . . . . . at Bowie

MAY

1 . . . . at Bowie
2-5 . . . . . . .at New Britain
6-8 . . . . .Altoona

9-11 . . . . at Bowie
12-15 . . . . Harrisburg
17-19 . . . . .Bowie
20-22 . . . . . . .at Reading
23-26 . . . . Erie
27-30 . . . . . . at Akron
31 . . . . at Bowie

JUNE

1-2 . . . . at Bowie
3-5 . . . . Reading
7-9 . . . . .at Portland
10-12 . . .at New Hampshire

14-16 . . . . . .Binghamton
17-19 . . . . .Bowie
21-23 . . . . . at Harrisburg
24-26 . . . . Erie
27-29 . . . . Harrisburg
30 . . . . .at Reading

JULY
1-3 . . . . .at Reading
4-7 . . . . .Trenton
8-11 . . . . Harrisburg
14-17 . . . . at Bowie
18-20 . . . .at New Britain
21-24 . . . . Harrisburg
25-27 . . . . at Trenton

TRENTON THUNDER

APRIL
7-10 . . . .at New Hampshire
11-13 . . . . . . .at Portland
14-17 . . . . Harrisburg
18-20 . . . . Richmond
21-23 . . . . . at Harrisburg
25-28 . . . . at Richmond
29-30 . . . New Hampshire

MAY
1 . . . . . . New Hampshire
2-5 . . . . Portland
6-8 . . . . at Akron
9-11 . . . . Reading
12-15 . . . . . .Binghamton
17-19 . . . . at Erie
20-22 . . . . Portland
24-26 . . . . . .at Reading
27-30 . . . . . .at Portland
31 . . . . .Altoona

JUNE
1-2 . . . . .Altoona
3-5 . . . . . New Hampshire
6-9 . . . . . . .at Reading
10-12 . . . . . .Binghamton
14-16 . . . . Harrisburg
17-19 . . . . at Binghamton

SOUTHERN LEAGUE

BIRMINGHAM BARONS

APRIL
7-11 . . . . .at Montgomery
13-17 . . . . . Chattanooga
18-22 . . . . . .Mississippi
23-27 . . . . . .at Huntsville
28-30 . . . . Mobile

MAY
1-2 . . . . Mobile
3-7 . . . . at Jackson
9-13 . . . . Carolina
14-18 . . . . . Montgomery
19-23 . . . at Jacksonville
25-29 . . . . at Carolina
30-31 . . . . Chattanooga

JUNE
1-3 . . . . . . Chattanooga
4-8 . . . . at Jacksonville
9-13 . . . . . . Mobile
15-19 . . . . . .at Huntsville
23-27 . . . . Tennessee

CAROLINA MUDCATS

APRIL
7-11 . . . . Mobile
13-17 . . . . . .at Huntsville

AUGUST
2-4 . . . . New Hampshire
5-7 . . . . Portland
9-11 . . . . . at Harrisburg
12-14 . . . . at Binghamton
16-18 . . . . Bowie
19-21 . . . . Akron
22-24 . . . . at Altoona
25-28 . . . . . at Akron
29-31 . . . . New Britain

SEPTEMBER
1 . . . . New Britain
2-5 . . . . at Altoona

21-23 . . . . . .at Portland
24-26 . . . .at New Britain
27-29 . . . New Hampshire
30 . . . . .Altoona

JULY
1-3 . . . . .Altoona
4-7 . . . . . . at Richmond
8-11 . . . . . .at Reading
14-17 . . . . Reading
18-20 . . . . Erie
21-24 . . . . . at Bowie
25-27 . . . . . at Akron
28-31 . . . . . . Richmond

AUGUST
2-4 . . . . Akron
5-7 . . . . at Altoona
9-11 . . . . . . .Binghamton
12-14 . . . at Harrisburg
16-18 . . . . .at Erie
19-21 . . . . Bowie
22-24 . . .at New Hampshire
25-28 . . . . New Britain
29-31 . . . . New Hampshire

SEPTEMBER
1 . . . . . . New Hampshire
2-5 . . . . . . .at New Britain

28-30 . . . . . at Jacksonville

JULY
1-3 . . . . . at Jacksonville
4-7 . . . . Mobile
8-11 . . . . . . at Jackson
13-18 . . . . . Jacksonville
20-24 . . . . . . .at Mobile
26-30 . . . . . . Huntsville
31 . . . . at Tennessee

AUGUST
1-4 . . . . . at Tennessee
5-9 . . . . .Jackson
10-14 . . . .at Chattanooga
16-20 . . . . . Montgomery
21-25 . . . . . .at Huntsville
26-30 . . . at Mississippi

SEPTEMBER
1-5 . . . . Tennessee

18-22 . . . . . . Tennessee
23-27 . . . . . Chattanooga
28-30 . . . . . at Tennessee

MAY
1-2 . . . . . . at Tennessee
3-7 . . . . . . Montgomery
9-13 . . . . at Birmingham
14-18 . . . . . .at Mobile
20-24 . . . . Chattanooga
25-29 . . . . .Birmingham
30-31 . . . at Jacksonville

JUNE
1-3 . . . . . at Jacksonville
4-8 . . . .at Chattanooga
9-13 . . . . . . Tennessee
15-18 . . . . . at Jackson
23-27 . . . . . . Huntsville
28-30 . . . . at Tennessee

JULY
1-3 . . . . at Tennessee

CHATTANOOGA LOOKOUTS

APRIL
7-11 . . . . Tennessee
13-17 . . . . at Birmingham
18-22 . . . . . . Huntsville
23-27 . . . .at Carolina
28-30 . . . . . . .Jackson

MAY
1-2 . . . . .Jackson
3-7 . . . . .Mississippi
9-13 . . . . at Montgomery
14-18 . . . . . . Tennessee
20-24 . . . .at Carolina
25-29 . . . . . Huntsville
30-31 . . . at Birmingham

JUNE
1-3 . . . . . at Birmingham
4-8 . . . . Carolina
9-13 . . . . . at Mississippi
15-19 . . . . . at Tennessee
23-27 . . . . . . Jacksonville

HUNTSVILLE STARS

April
7-11 . . . . . at Jacksonville
13-17 . . . . Carolina
18-22 . . . .at Chattanooga
23-27 . . . . . . .Birmingham
28-30 . . . . . at Mississippi

MAY
1-2 . . . . . at Mississippi
3-7 . . . . . . Jacksonville
9-13 . . . . . at Tennessee
14-18 . . . . . at Jackson
19-23 . . . . . Montgomery
25-29 . . . . Chattanooga
30-31 . . . . . Tennessee

JUNE
1-3 . . . . . . Tennessee
4-8 . . . . . . .at Mobile
9-13 . . . . . . .Jackson
15-19 . . . . .Birmingham
23-27 . . . . .at Carolina

JACKSON GENERALS

APRIL
7-11 . . . . . . at Mississippi
13-17 . . . . . Jacksonville
18-22 . . . . at Montgomery
23-27 . . . . Mobile
28-30 . . . .at Chattanooga

4-7 . . . . Jacksonville
8-11 . . . . . .at Huntsville
13-18 . . . . .Jackson
20-24 . . . . at Tennessee
26-30 . . . . . Jacksonville
31 . . . . .at Huntsville

AUGUST
1-4 . . . . . . .at Huntsville
5-9 . . . . . . at Mississippi
11-15 . . . . . Montgomery
16-20 . . . .at Chattanooga
21-25 . . . . . Jacksonville
26-30 . . . .at Montgomery

SEPTEMBER
1-5 . . . . .Mississippi

28-30 . . . . . . at Jackson

JULY
1-3 . . . . at Jackson
4-7 . . . . Huntsville
8-11 . . . . . . at Tennessee
13-18 . . . . Mobile
20-24 . . . .at Huntsville
26-30 . . . . .Jackson
31 . . . . .at Mobile

AUGUST
1-4 . . . . .at Mobile
5-9 . . . . . at Jacksonville
10-14 . . . . . .Birmingham
16-20 . . . . . . Carolina
21-25 . . . . at Tennessee
26-30 . . . . . . .at Mobile

SEPTEMBER
1-5 . . . . Montgomery

29-30 . . . . . . .Mississippi

JULY
1-3 . . . . .Mississippi
4-7 . . . .at Chattanooga
8-11 . . . . Carolina
13-18 . . . . at Montgomery
20-24 . . . . . Chattanooga
26-30 . . . at Birmingham
31 . . . . Carolina

AUGUST
1-4 . . . . Carolina
5-9 . . . . Tennessee
. . . .
11-15 . . . . . . at Jackson
16-20 . . . . at Mississippi
21-25 . . . . . .Birmingham
26-30 . . . at Jackson

SEPTEMBER
1-5 . . . . Mobile

MAY
1-2 . . . .at Chattanooga
3-7 . . . . . . .Birmingham
9-13 . . . . . at Huntsville
14-18 . . . . Huntsville
19-23 . . . . . .Mississippi
25-29 . . . . . . .at Mobile
30-31 . . . . . Montgomery

JUNE
1-3 . . . . Montgomery
4-8 . . . . at Tennessee
9-13 . . . . . . .at Huntsville
15-18 . . . . Carolina
23-27 . . . .at Montgomery
28-30 . . . . . Chattanooga

JULY
1-3 . . . . . . Chattanooga
4-7 . . . . . . at Mississippi
8-11 . . . . . . .Birmingham
13-18 . . . . . . at Carolina

JACKSONVILLE SUNS

APRIL
7-11 . . . . Huntsville
13-17 . . . . at Jackson
18-22 . . . . . .at Mobile
23-27 . . . . Tennessee
28-30 . . . . at Montgomery

MAY
1-2 . . . . . at Montgomery
3-7 . . . . . . .at Huntsville
9-13 . . . . Mobile
14-18 . . . . at Mississippi
19-23 . . . . .Birmingham
25-29 . . . . at Montgomery
30-31 . . . . Carolina

JUNE
1-3 . . . . Carolina
4-8 . . . . . .Birmingham
9-13 . . . . at Montgomery
15-19 . . . . .Mississippi
23-27 . . . .at Chattanooga

MISSISSIPPI BRAVES

APRIL
7-11 . . . . .Jackson
13-17 . . . . .at Mobile
18-22 . . . . at Birmingham
23-27 . . . . . Montgomery
28-30 . . . . . Huntsville

MAY
1-2 . . . . Huntsville
3-7 . . . . . .at Chattanooga
9-13 . . . . .Jackson
14-18 . . . . . Jacksonville
19-23 . . . . at Jackson
24-28 . . . . at Tennessee
30-31 . . . . Mobile

JUNE
1-3 . . . . Mobile
4-8 . . . . .at Montgomery
9-13 . . . . . . Chattanooga
15-19 . . . at Jacksonville

MOBILE BAYBEARS

APRIL
7-11 . . . . .at Carolina
13-17 . . . . . .Mississippi
18-22 . . . . . Jacksonville
23-27 . . . . . at Jackson
28-30 . . . . . at Birmingham

MAY
1-2 . . . . . at Birmingham
3-7 . . . . Tennessee
9-13 . . . . at Jacksonville
14-18 . . . . Carolina
19-23 . . . . at Tennessee
25-29 . . . . . . .Jackson

20-23 . . . . . Montgomery
26-30 . . . .at Chattanooga
31 . . . . .Mississippi

AUGUST
1-4 . . . . .Mississippi
5-9 . . . . . at Birmingham
11-15 . . . . Huntsville
16-20 . . . . Tennessee
21-25 . . . . . .at Mobile
26-30 . . . . . . Huntsville

SEPTEMBER
1-5 . . . . . . at Jacksonville

28-30 . . . . . .Birmingham

JULY
1-3 . . . . .Birmingham
4-7 . . . . .at Carolina
8-11 . . . . Montgomery
13-18 . . . at Birmingham
20-24 . . . . . . .Mississippi
26-30 . . . . . . .at Carolina
31 . . . . Montgomery

AUGUST
1-4 . . . . Montgomery
5-9 . . . . . . Chattanooga
10-14 . . . . . at Tennessee
16-20 . . . . Mobile
21-25 . . . . . .at Carolina
26-30 . . . . at Tennessee

SEPTEMBER
1-5 . . . . .Jackson

23-27 . . . . Mobile
29-30 . . . . . .at Huntsville

JULY
1-3 . . . . .at Huntsville
4-7 . . . . .Jackson
8-11 . . . . .at Mobile
13-18 . . . . Tennessee
20-24 . . . . at Jacksonville
26-30 . . . . Mobile
31 . . . . at Jackson

AUGUST
1-4 . . . . at Jackson
5-9 . . . . Carolina
10-14 . . . . . .at Mobile
16-20 . . . . . . Huntsville
21-25 . . . .at Montgomery
26-30 . . . . .Birmingham

SEPTEMBER
1-5 . . . . .at Carolina

MONTGOMERY BISCUITS

APRIL
7-11 . . . . . . .Birmingham
13-17 . . . . . . at Tennessee
18-22 . . . . .Jackson
23-27 . . . . at Mississippi
28-30 . . . . . . Jacksonville

MAY
1-2 . . . . . . Jacksonville
3-7 . . . . .at Carolina
9-13 . . . . . Chattanooga
14-18 . . . . at Birmingham
19-23 . . . . .at Huntsville
25-29 . . . . . Jacksonville
30-31 . . . . . at Jackson

JUNE
1-3 . . . . at Jackson
4-8 . . . . .Mississippi
9-13 . . . . . Jacksonville
15-19 . . . . . . .at Mobile
23-27 . . . . . . .Jackson

TENNESSEE SMOKIES

APRIL
7-11 . . . . .at Chattanooga
13-17 . . . . . Montgomery
18-22 . . . . . . at Carolina
23-27 . . . . at Jacksonville
28-30 . . . . Carolina

MAY
1-2 . . . . Carolina
3-7 . . . . .at Mobile
9-13 . . . . Huntsville
14-18 . . . .at Chattanooga
19-23 . . . . Mobile
24-28 . . . . . .Mississippi
30-31 . . . .at Huntsville

JUNE
1-3 . . . . . . .at Huntsville
4-8 . . . . .Jackson
9-13 . . . . at Carolina
15-19 . . . . Chattanooga

28-30 . . . . . . .at Mobile

JULY
1-3 . . . . .at Mobile
4-7 . . . . Tennessee
8-11 . . . . . . at Jacksonville
13-18 . . . . . Huntsville
20-23 . . . . . at Jackson
26-30 . . . . . . Tennessee
31 . . . . at Jacksonville

AUGUST
1-4 . . . . . . at Jacksonville
5-9 . . . . Mobile
11-15 . . . . .at Carolina
16-20 . . . . at Birmingham
21-25 . . . . . . .Mississippi
26-30 . . . . Carolina

SEPTEMBER
1-5 . . . . . .at Chattanooga

23-27 . . . . at Birmingham
28-30 . . . . Carolina

JULY
1-3 . . . . Carolina
4-7 . . . . . .at Montgomery
8-11 . . . . . Chattanooga
13-18 . . . . at Mississippi
20-24 . . . . Carolina
26-30 . . . .at Montgomery
31 . . . . .Birmingham

AUGUST
1-4 . . . . .Birmingham
5-9 . . . . . . .at Huntsville
10-14 . . . . . Jacksonville
16-20 . . . . . at Jackson
21-25 . . . . Chattanooga
26-30 . . . . Jacksonville

SEPTEMBER
1-5 . . . . . . at Birmingham

TEXAS LEAGUE

ARKANSAS TRAVELERS

APRIL
7-9 . . . . .at Midland
10-12 . . . . at Frisco
14-16 . . . . Midland
17-19 . . . . Frisco
21-24 at Northwest Arkansas
25-28 . . . . .Tulsa
29-30 . .Northwest Arkansas

MAY
1-2 . . .Northwest Arkansas
3-6 . . . . at Tulsa
7-10 . . . . at Springfield
12-15 . . . . .Tulsa
16-19 . . . . . .Springfield
20-23 at Northwest Arkansas
25-27 . . . . . .San Antonio

28-30 . . . . . .Corpus Christi

JUNE
1-3 . . . . . . at San Antonio
4-6 . . . . . at Corpus Christi
8-11 . .Northwest Arkansas
12-15 . . . . . . .Springfield
16-19 . . . . at Tulsa
20-23 . . . . at Springfield
24-27 . Northwest Arkansas
30 . . . . .at Midland

JULY
1-2 . . . . .at Midland
3-5 . . . . at Frisco
7-9 . . . . Midland
10-12 . . . . Frisco
14-17 . . . . . . at Tulsa

18-21 . .Northwest Arkansas
22-25 . . . . at Tulsa
26-28 . . . . at Springfield
29-31 . . . . .Tulsa

AUGUST
1 . . . . .Tulsa
2-4 . . . . .Springfield
5-8 . . at Northwest Arkansas
10-12 . . . . .Corpus Christi

CORPUS CHRISTI HOOKS

APRIL
7-9 . . . . at Tulsa
10-12 at Northwest Arkansas
14-16 . . . . .Tulsa
17-19 . .Northwest Arkansas
21-24 . . . . at Frisco
25-28 . . . . . . at Midland
29-30 . . . . Frisco

MAY
1-2 . . . . Frisco
3-6 . . . . Midland
7-10 . . . . . at San Antonio
12-15 . . . . . . at Midland
16-19 . . . . . .San Antonio
20-23 . . . . Midland
25-27 . . . . at Springfield
28-30 . . . . . . at Arkansas

JUNE
1-3 . . . . .Springfield
4-6 . . . . Arkansas
8-11 . . . . .at Midland
12-15 . . . at San Antonio
16-19 . . . . Frisco
20-23 . . . . . .San Antonio
24-27 . . . . Frisco
30 . . . . at Tulsa

FRISCO ROUGHRIDERS

APRIL
7-9 . . . . .Springfield
10-12 . . . . . . Arkansas
14-16 . . . . . at Springfield
17-19 . . . . . at Arkansas
21-24 . . . .Corpus Christi
25-28 . . . at San Antonio
29-30 . . . at Corpus Christi

MAY
1-2 . . . . at Corpus Christi
3-6 . . . . .San Antonio
7-10 . . . . . . .at Midland
12-15 . . . . .Corpus Christi
16-19 . . . . . Midland
20-23 . . . at San Antonio
25-27 . .Northwest Arkansas
28-30 . . . . .Tulsa

JUNE
1-3 . . at Northwest Arkansas
4-6 . . . . at Tulsa
8-11 . . . . . . .San Antonio
12-15 . . . . . .at Midland
16-19 . . . at Corpus Christi
20-23 . . . . . Midland
24-27 . . . at Corpus Christi

MIDLAND ROCKHOUNDS

APRIL
7-9 . . . . Arkansas
10-12 . . . . . .Springfield
14-16 . . . . . at Arkansas
17-19 . . . . . at Springfield

13-15 . . . . . .San Antonio
17-19 . . . at Corpus Christi
20-22 . . . . at San Antonio
23-26 . . . . .Tulsa
27-29 . . . . . . .Springfield
30-31 at Northwest Arkansas

SEPTEMBER
1-2 . at Northwest Arkansas
3-5 . . . . at Springfield

JULY
1-2 . . . . at Tulsa
3-5 . . at Northwest Arkansas
7-9 . . . . .Tulsa
10-12 . .Northwest Arkansas
14-17 . . . . at Frisco
18-21 . . . . Midland
22-25 . . . . at Frisco
26-28 . . . . .San Antonio
29-31 . . . .at Midland

AUGUST
1 . . . . .at Midland
2-4 . . . . . at San Antonio
5-8 . . . . Midland
10-12 . . . . at Arkansas
13-15 . . . at Springfield
17-19 . . . . . Arkansas
20-22 . . . . . .Springfield
23-26 . . . . .at Midland
27-29 . . . . .San Antonio
30-31 . . . . Frisco

SEPTEMBER
1-2 . . . . Frisco
3-5 . . . . . . at San Antonio

30 . . . . .Springfield

JULY
1-2 . . . . .Springfield
3-5 . . . . Arkansas
7-9 . . . . . . at Springfield
10-12 . . . . . at Arkansas
14-17 . . . . .Corpus Christi
18-21 . . . . at San Antonio
22-25 . . . . .Corpus Christi
26-28 . . . . . Midland
29-31 . . . . at San Antonio

AUGUST
1 . . . . at San Antonio
2-4 . . . . .at Midland
5-8 . . . . .San Antonio
10-12 . .Northwest Arkansas
13-15 . . . . .Tulsa
17-19 at Northwest Arkansas
20-22 . . . . at Tulsa
23-26 . . . . . .San Antonio
27-29 . . . . . . .at Midland
30-31 . . . at Corpus Christi

SEPTEMBER
1-2 . . . . at Corpus Christi
3-5 . . . . Midland

21-24 . . . . . .San Antonio
25-28 . . . . .Corpus Christi
29-30 . . . . at San Antonio

MAY
1-2 . . . . . . at San Antonio

3-6 . . . . . at Corpus Christi
7-10 . . . . Frisco
12-15 . . . . . .San Antonio
16-19 . . . . . . at Frisco
20-23 . . . at Corpus Christi
25-27 . . . . .Tulsa
28-30 . .Northwest Arkansas

JUNE
1-3 . . . . at Tulsa
4-6 . . at Northwest Arkansas
8-11 . . . . . .Corpus Christi
12-15 . . . . Frisco
16-19 . . . at San Antonio
20-23 . . . . at Frisco
24-27 . . . at San Antonio
30 . . . . Arkansas

JULY
1-2 . . . . Arkansas
3-5 . . . . .Springfield
7-9 . . . . . . at Arkansas

NORTHWEST ARKANSAS NATURALS

APRIL
7-9 . . . . .San Antonio
10-12 . . . .Corpus Christi
14-16 . . . . at San Antonio
17-19 . . . at Corpus Christi
21-24 . . . . Arkansas
25-28 . . . at Springfield
29-30 . . . . at Arkansas

MAY
1-2 . . . . . . at Arkansas
3-6 . . . . .Springfield
7-10 . . . . .Tulsa
12-15 . . . at Springfield
16-19 . . . . . . at Tulsa
20-23 . . . . . Arkansas
25-27 . . . . . at Frisco
28-30 . . . . . .at Midland

JUNE
1-3 . . . . Frisco
4-6 . . . . Midland
8-11 . . . . . . at Arkansas
12-15 . . . . .Tulsa
16-19 . . . . . .Springfield
20-23 . . . . . at Tulsa
24-27 . . . . at Arkansas

SAN ANTONIO MISSIONS

APRIL
7-9 . at Northwest Arkansas
10-12 . . . . . . at Tulsa
14-16 . .Northwest Arkansas
17-19 . . . . .Tulsa
. . . .
21-24 . . . . . . .at Midland
25-28 . . . . Frisco
29-30 . . . . . . Midland

MAY
1-2 . . . . Midland
3-6 . . . . at Frisco
7-10 . . . . . .Corpus Christi
12-15 . . . . .at Midland
16-19 . . . at Corpus Christi
20-23 . . . . Frisco
25-27 . . . . . at Arkansas
28-30 . . . . . at Springfield

JUNE
1-3 . . . . Arkansas
4-6 . . . . .Springfield
8-11 . . . . at Frisco
12-15 . . . . .Corpus Christi
16-19 . . . . Midland

10-12 . . . . . at Springfield
14-17 . . . . . .San Antonio
18-21 . . . at Corpus Christi
22-25 . . . . . .San Antonio
26-28 . . . . at Frisco
29-31 . . . . .Corpus Christi

AUGUST
1 . . . . .Corpus Christi
2-4 . . . . Frisco
5-8 . . . at Corpus Christi
10-12 . . . . .Tulsa
13-15 . .Northwest Arkansas
17-19 . . . . at Tulsa
20-22 at Northwest Arkansas
23-26 . . . . .Corpus Christi
27-29 . . . . Frisco
30-31 . . . at San Antonio

SEPTEMBER
1-2 . . . . . at San Antonio
3-5 . . . . at Frisco

30 . . . . .San Antonio

JULY
1-2 . . . . .San Antonio
3-5 . . . . . . .Corpus Christi
7-9 . . . at San Antonio
10-12 . . at Corpus Christi
14-17 . . . . . .Springfield
18-21 . . . . at Arkansas
22-25 . . . . . .Springfield
26-28 . . . . .Tulsa
29-31 . . . at Springfield

AUGUST
1 . . . . at Springfield
2-4 . . . . at Tulsa
5-8 . . . . Arkansas
10-12 . . . . at Frisco
13-15 . . .at Midland
17-19 . . . . . Frisco
20-22 . . . . . Midland
23-26 . . . at Springfield
27-29 . . . . .Tulsa
30-31 . . . . . Arkansas

SEPTEMBER
1-2 . . . . Arkansas
3-5 . . . . at Tulsa

20-23 . . . . at Corpus Christi
24-27 . . . . . . Midland
30 . . at Northwest Arkansas

JULY
1-2 . . at Northwest Arkansas
3-5 . . . . at Tulsa
7-9 . . .Northwest Arkansas
10-12 . . . . .Tulsa
14-17 . . . . . . .at Midland
18-21 . . . . Frisco
22-25 . . . . . .at Midland
26-28 . . . at Corpus Christi
29-31 . . . . Frisco

AUGUST
1 . . . . Frisco
2-4 . . . . . .Corpus Christi
5-8 . . . . at Frisco
10-12 . . . . . at Springfield
13-15 . . . . . . at Arkansas
17-19 . . . . . .Springfield
20-22 . . . . . Arkansas
23-26 . . . . at Frisco
27-29 . . . at Corpus Christi
30-31 . . . . Midland

SEPTEMBER
1-2 . . . . Midland

3-5 . . . . .Corpus Christi

SPRINGFIELD CARDINALS

APRIL	
7-9 . . . . at Frisco	30 . . . . at Frisco
10-12 . . . . .at Midland	**JULY**
14-16 . . . . Frisco	1-2 . . . . at Frisco
17-19 . . . . Midland	3-5 . . . . .at Midland
21-24 . . . . at Tulsa	7-9 . . . . Frisco
25-28 . .Northwest Arkansas	10-12 . . . . Midland
29-30 . . . . Tulsa	14-17 at Northwest Arkansas
MAY	18-21 . . . . Tulsa
1-2. . . . . Tulsa	22-25 at Northwest Arkansas
3-6. . at Northwest Arkansas	26-28 . . . . Arkansas
7-10 . . . . Arkansas	29-31 . .Northwest Arkansas
12-15 . .Northwest Arkansas	**AUGUST**
16-19 . . . . at Arkansas	1 . . . . .Northwest Arkansas
20-23 . . . . at Tulsa	2-4 . . . . at Arkansas
25-27 . . . . .Corpus Christi	5-8 . . . . at Tulsa
28-30 . . . . . . .San Antonio	10-12 . . . . . .San Antonio
JUNE	13-15 . . . . .Corpus Christi
1-3 . . . . at Corpus Christi	17-19 . . . . at San Antonio
4-6. . . . . . at San Antonio	20-22 . . at Corpus Christi
8-11 . . . . Tulsa	23-26 . .Northwest Arkansas
12-15 . . . . . at Arkansas	27-29 . . . . . . at Arkansas
16-19 at Northwest Arkansas	30-31 . . . . at Tulsa
20-23 . . . . Arkansas	**SEPTEMBER**
24-27 . . . . Tulsa	1-2 . . . . .at Tulsa
	3-5 . . . . Arkansas

TULSA DRILLERS

APRIL	
7-9 . . . . .Corpus Christi	30 . . . . . . .Corpus Christi
. . . .	**JULY**
10-12 . . . . . . .San Antonio	1-2 . . . . .Corpus Christi
14-16 . . at Corpus Christi	3-5 . . . . San Antonio
17-19 . . at San Antonio	7-9 . . . at Corpus Christi
21-24 . . . . . . .Springfield	10-12 . . . at San Antonio
25-28 . . . . . at Arkansas	14-17 . . . . Arkansas
29-30 . . . at Springfield	18-21 . . . . at Springfield
MAY	22-25 . . . . Arkansas
1-2 . . . . . at Springfield	26-28 at Northwest Arkansas
3-6. . . . . Arkansas	29-31 . . . . at Springfield
7-10 . at Northwest Arkansas	**AUGUST**
12-15 . . . . . at Arkansas	1 . . . . at Arkansas
16-19 . .Northwest Arkansas	2-4 . . . .Northwest Arkansas
20-23 . . . . . . .Springfield	5-8 . . . . .Springfield
25-27 . . . . . .at Midland	10-12 . . . . .at Midland
28-30 . . . . . . at Frisco	13-15 . . . . . . at Frisco
JUNE	17-19 . . . . Midland
1-3. . . . . Midland	20-22 . . . . Frisco
4-6. . . . . Frisco	23-26 . . . . . at Arkansas
8-11 . . . . at Springfield	27-29 at Northwest Arkansas
12-15 at Northwest Arkansas	30-31 . . . . . . .Springfield
16-19 . . . . Arkansas	**SEPTEMBER**
20-23 . .Northwest Arkansas	1-2 . . . . .Springfield
24-27 . . . . . at Springfield	3-5 . . . .Northwest Arkansas

HIGH CLASS A

CALIFORNIA LEAGUE

BAKERSFIELD

APRIL		
7-10 . . . . at Visalia	27-30 . . . . . . at Stockton	
11-13 . . . . . . at Modesto	**JULY**	
14-16 . . . . .Inland Empire	1-3 . . . . .Inland Empire	
17-20 . . . . . . Modesto	4-6. . . . . at Lancaster	
21-23 . . . . at Inland Empire	7-10 . . . . . . .at San Jose	
25-28 . . . . Visalia	12-15 . . . . . . Stockton	
29-30 . . . . at Stockton	16-18 . . . . at High Desert	
MAY	20-22 . . . . . . San Jose	
1 . . . . at Stockton	23-25 . . . . . at Stockton	
2-5. . . . . .at Lake Elsinore	27-30 . . . . . at Modesto	
6-8. . . . . San Jose	31 . . . . .Lancaster	
10-13 . . . . . . at Visalia	**AUGUST**	
14-16 . . . . Modesto	1-2 . . . . .Lancaster	
17-20 . . . . . Stockton	3-6 . . . . Lake Elsinore	
21-23 . . . . . at Modesto	7-9 . . . . . . .at San Jose	
25-28 . . . . . . San Jose	11-14 at Rancho Cucamonga	
29-31 . . . . .Visalia	15-17 . . . . .Visalia	
JUNE	18-21 . . . . Lake Elsinore	
1-4. . . . . at Stockton	23-25 at Rancho Cucamonga	
5-7 . . .Rancho Cucamonga	26-29 . . . . at High Desert	
9-12 . . . . Stockton	30-31 . . . . San Jose	
13-15 . . . . . . .at San Jose	**SEPTEMBER**	
16-19 . . . . at Visalia	1 . . . . San Jose	
23-26 . . . . Modesto	2-5 . . . . High Desert	

HIGH DESERT

APRIL	MAY
7-10 . . . . . . .at Lancaster	1 . . . .Rancho Cucamonga
11-13 . . . . at Inland Empire	2-5 . . . . at Modesto
14-16 . . . . . Lake Elsinore	6-8. . at Rancho Cucamonga
17-20 . . . . . .Lancaster	10-13 . . . . . Lake Elsinore
21-23 . . . . .at Lake Elsinore	14-16 . .Rancho Cucamonga
25-28 . . . . . Inland Empire	17-20 . . . . . at Lancaster
29-30 . .Rancho Cucamonga	21-23 . . . . at Visalia

25-28 . . . . Modesto	27-29 . . . at Inland Empire
29-31 . . . . .Lancaster	30 . . . . . . .Inland Empire
JUNE	31 . . . . . .at Lake Elsinore
1-4. . at Rancho Cucamonga	**AUGUST**
5-7 . . . . . . .Inland Empire	1-2 . . . . . .at Lake Elsinore
9-12 . . . . . . Lake Elsinore	3-6 . . . . San Jose
13-15 . . . . . . at Stockton	7-9 . . . . at Modesto
16-19 . . .at Lake Elsinore	11-14 . . . . Stockton
23-26 . . . . .Visalia	15 . . . . . at Inland Empire
27-30 . . . . at Lancaster	16-17 . . . . .Inland Empire
JULY	19-22 . . . . .at San Jose
1-3. . at Rancho Cucamonga	23-25 . . . . . . at Visalia
4-6. . . . . Stockton	26-29 . . . . . . .Bakersfield
7-10 . . . . at Inland Empire	30-31 . .Rancho Cucamonga
12-15 . . . . .Lancaster	**SEPTEMBER**
16-18 . . . . . . .Bakersfield	1 . . . . . .Rancho Cucamonga
20-22 . . . . . .at Lancaster	2-5 . . . . . . at Bakersfield
23-25 . . . . Modesto	

INLAND EMPIRE

APRIL	JUNE
7-10 . . .Rancho Cucamonga	1-4. . . . . .at Lake Elsinore
11-13 . . . . . . High Desert	5-7 . . . . . . at High Desert
14-16 . . . . at Bakersfield	9-12 . . . . .Lancaster
17-20 . . . . . .at San Jose	13-15 at Rancho Cucamonga
21-23 . . . . . .Bakersfield	16-19 . . . . . .at Lancaster
25-28 . . . at High Desert	23-26 . . . . . Lake Elsinore
29-30 . . . . .Lancaster	27-30 . . . . at Visalia
MAY	**JULY**
1 . . . . .Lancaster	1-3 . . . . . . at Bakersfield
2-5. . . . . Stockton	4-6. . . . . .Visalia
6-8. . . . . . . at Lancaster	7-10 . . . . . . High Desert
10-13 . .Rancho Cucamonga	12-15 . . . . . . at Modesto
14-15 . . . . .Visalia	16-18 . . . . . .at San jose
17-20 . . . at Inland Empire	20-22 . . . . . Lake Elsinore
21-23 at Rancho Cucamonga	23-25 at Rancho Cucamonga
25-28 . . . . . Lake Elsinore	27-29 . . . . . High Desert
29-31 . . . . Modesto	30 . . . . . . at High Desert
	31 . . . . San Jose

AUGUST
1-2 . . . . San Jose
3-6 . . . . at Lancaster
7-9 . . . . . Lake Elsinore
11-14 . . . . at Visalia
15 . . . . High Desert
16-17 . . . . at High Desert

LAKE ELSINORE

APRIL
7-10 . . . . San Jose
11-13 . .Rancho Cucamonga
14-16 . . . at High Desert
17-20 at Rancho Cucamonga
21-23 . . . . . . High Desert
25-28 . . . . . at Stockton
29-30 . . . . . . .at San Jose
MAY
1 . . . . .at San Jose
2-5 . . . . .Bakersfield
6-8 . . . . Stockton
10-13 . . . at High Desert
14-16 . . . . at Lancaster
17-20 . . . . .Inland Empire
21-23 . . . . .Lancaster
25-28 . . at Inland Empire
29-31 at Rancho Cucamonga
JUNE
1-4 . . . . . . .Inland Empire
5-7 . . . . . at Lancaster
9-12 . . . . at High Desert
13-15 . . . . . . .Lancaster
16-19 . . . . . High Desert
23-26 . . . at Inland Empire
27-29 . Rancho Cucamonga

LANCASTER

APRIL
7-10 . . . . High Desert
11-13 . . . . . . San Jose
14-16 at Rancho Cucamonga
17-20 . . . . at High Desert
21-23 . . . . . Stockton
25-28 at Rancho Cucamonga
29-30 . . . . at Inland Empire
MAY
1 . . . . . . at Inland Empire
2-5 . . . Rancho Cucamonga
6-8 . . . . . . .Inland Empire
10-13 . . . . . .at San Jose
14-16 . . . . . Lake Elsinore
17-20 . . . . . High Desert
21-23 . . . .at Lake Elsinore
25-28 . .Rancho Cucamonga
29-31 . . . . at High Desert
JUNE
1-4 . . . . at Modesto
5-7 . . . . Lake Elsinore
9-12 . . . . at Inland Empire
13-15 . .at Lake Elsinore
16-19 . . . . .Inland Empire
23-26 at Rancho Cucamonga

MODESTO

APRIL
7-10 . . . . Stockton
11-13 . . . . . . .Bakersfield
14-16 . . . . . at Stockton
17-20 . . . at Bakersfield
21-23 . Rancho Cucamonga
25-28 . . . . . . .at San Jose

18-21 . .Rancho Cucamonga
23-25 . . . . . . .Lancaster
26-29 . . . . . . at Stockton
30-31 . . . . .at Lake Elsinore
SEPTEMBER
1 . . . . . . .at Lake Elsinore
2-5 . . . . Stockton

30 . . at Rancho Cucamonga
JULY
1-3 . . . . at Visalia
4-6 . . . .Rancho Cucamonga
7-10 . . . . .Visalia
12-14 at Rancho Cucamonga
15 . . .Rancho Cucamonga
16-18 . . . . . . .Lancaster
20-22 . . . . at Inland Empire
23-25 . . . . at Lancaster
27-30 . Rancho Cucamonga
31 . . . . High Desert
AUGUST
1-2 . . . . High Desert
3-6 . . . . . . at Bakersfield
7-9 . . . . at Inland Empire
11-14 . . . . Modesto
15-17 . . . . . San Jose
18-21 . . . . . at Bakersfield
22-24 . . . . . at Modesto
26-28 . . . . .Lancaster
29-31 . . . . .Inland Empire
SEPTEMBER
1 . . . . .Inland Empire
2-5 . . . . at Lancaster

27-30 . . . . . . High Desert
JULY
1-3 . . . . at Modesto
4-6 . . . . .Bakersfield
7-10 . .Rancho Cucamonga
12-15 . . . at High Desert
16-18 . . . .at Lake Elsinore
20-22 . . . . . High Desert
23-25 . . . . . Lake Elsinore
27-30 . .Rancho Cucamonga
31 . . . . High Desert
AUGUST
1-2 . . . . High Desert
3-6 . . . . . . at Bakersfield
7-9 . . . . at Inland Empire
11-14 . . . . Modesto
15-17 . . . . . San Jose
18-21 . . . . . at Bakersfield
22-24 . . . . . at Modesto
26-28 . . . . .Lancaster
29-31 . . . . .Inland Empire
SEPTEMBER
1 . . . . .Inland Empire
2-5 . . . . at Lancaster

17-20 . . . . San Jose
21-23 . . . . . . .Bakersfield
25-28 . . . . at High Desert
29-31 . . . at Inland Empire
JUNE
1-4 . . . . .Lancaster
5-7 . . . . at Visalia
9-12 . . . . San Jose
13-15 . . . . .Visalia
16-19 . . . . . . .at San Jose
23-26 . . . . at Bakersfield
27-30 . . . . San Jose
JULY
1-3 . . . . .Lancaster
4-6 . . . . . . .at San Jose
7-10 . . . . . . at Stockton
12-15 . . . . .Inland Empire
16-18 at Rancho Cucamonga

RANCHO CUCAMONGA

APRIL
7-10 . . . .at Inland Empire
11-13 . . .at Lake Elsinore
14-16 . . . . . .Lancaster
17-20 . . . . Lake Elsinore
21-23 . . . . . at Modesto
25-28 . . . . . .Lancaster
29-30 . . . at High Desert
MAY
1 . . . . at High Desert
2-5 . . . . . . at Lancaster
6-8 . . . . High Desert
10-13 . . . at Inland Empire
14-16 . . . at High Desert
17-20 . . . . .Visalia
21-23 . . . . .Inland Empire
25-28 . . . . at Lancaster
29-31 . . . . . Lake Elsinore
JUNE
1-4 . . . . High Desert
5-7 . . . . . at Bakersfield
9-12 . . . . .Visalia
13-15 . . . . .Inland Empire
16-19 . . . . . at Stockton
23-26 . . . . . . .Lancaster
27-39 . . .at Lake Elsinore

SAN JOSE

APRIL
7-10 . . . . .at Lake Elsinore
11-13 . . . . . .at Lancaster
14-16 . . . . .Visalia
17-20 . . . . .Inland Empire
21-23 . . . . . . at Visalia
25-28 . . . . Modesto
29-30 . . . . . Lake Elsinore
MAY
1 . . . . Lake Elsinore
2-5 . . . . at Visalia
6-8 . . . . . . at Bakersfield
10-13 . . . . . . .Lancaster
14-16 . . . . Stockton
17-20 . . . . . at Modesto
21-23 . . . . . at Stockton
25-28 . . . . at Bakersfield
29-31 . . . . Stockton
JUNE
1-4 . . . . .Visalia
5-7 . . . . at Stockton
9-12 . . . . . . at Modesto
13-15 . . . . . .Bakersfield
16-19 . . . . Modesto
23-26 . . . . Stockton

20-22 . . . . Stockton
23-25 . . . . at High Desert
27-30 . . . . . . .Bakersfield
31 . . . . Stockton
AUGUST
1-2 . . . . Stockton
3-6 . . at Rancho Cucamonga
7-9 . . . . High Desert
11-14 . . . .at Lake Elsinore
15-17 . . . . . at Lancaster
18-21 . . . . .Visalia
22-24 . . . . . Lake Elsinore
26-29 . . . . . . at Visalia
30-31 . . . . at Stockton
SEPTEMBER
1 . . . . at Stockton
2-5 . . . . .Visalia

30 . . . . Lake Elsinore
JULY
1-3 . . . . High Desert
4-6 . . . . . .at Lake Elsinore
7-10 . . . . . at Lancaster
12-14 . . . . . Lake Elsinore
15 . . . . at Lake Elsinore
16-18 . . . . Modesto
20-22 . . . . . . at Visalia
23-25 . . . . .Inland Empire
27-30 . . .at Lake Elsinore
31 . . . . at Visalia
AUGUST
1-2 . . . . at Visalia
3-6 . . . . Modesto
7-9 . . . . . . at Stockton
11-14 . . . . . .Bakersfield
15-17 . . . . . . Stockton
18-21 . . . . at Inland Empire
23-25 . . . . . .Bakersfield
26-29 . . . . . . San Jose
30-31 . . . at High Desert
SEPTEMBER
1 . . . . at High Desert
2-5 . . . . at San Jose

27-30 . . . . at Modesto
JULY
1-3 . . . . at Stockton
4-6 . . . . Modesto
7-10 . . . . . . .Bakersfield
12-15 . . . . . . at Visalia
16-18 . . . . .Inland Empire
20-22 . . . . . at Bakersfield
23-25 . . . . .Visalia
27-30 . . . . . . .Lancaster
31 . . . . . at Inland Empire
AUGUST
1-2 . . . . . .at Inland Empire
3-6 . . . . . at High Desert
7-9 . . . . .Bakersfield
11-14 . . . . . . .at Lancaster
15-17 . . . .at Lake Elsinore
19-22 . . . . . . High Desert
23-25 . . . . Stockton
26-29 at Rancho Cucamonga
30-31 . . . at Bakersfield
SEPTEMBER
1 . . . . at Bakersfield
2-5 . . . .Rancho Cucamonga

STOCKTON

APRIL
7-10 . . . . at Modesto
11-13 . . . . at Visalia
14-16 . . . . Modesto
17-20 . . . . .Visalia
21-23 . . . . . . at Lancaster
25-28 . . . . . Lake Elsinore
29-30 . . . . . . .Bakersfield

MAY
1 . . . . .Bakersfield
2-5 . . . . at Inland Empire
6-8 . . . . . at Lake Elsinore
10-13 . . . . Modesto
14-16 . . . . . . at San Jose
17-20 . . . . at Bakersfield
21-23 . . . . San Jose
25-28 . . . . . . at Visalia
29-31 . . . . . at San Jose

JUNE
1-4 . . . . .Bakersfield
5-7 . . . . at San Jose
9-12 . . . . at Bakersfield
13-15 . . . . . . High Desert
16-19 . Rancho Cucamonga
23-26 . . . . . at San Jose

JULY
27-30 . . . . . . .Bakersfield
1-3 . . . . San Jose
4-6 . . . at High Desert
7-10 . . . . Modesto
12-15 . . . . . at Bakersfield
16-18 . . . . .Visalia
20-22 . . . at Modesto
23-25 . . . . .Bakersfield
27-30 . . . . . . at Visalia
31 . . . . at Modesto

AUGUST
1-2 . . . . at Modesto
3-6 . . . . .Visalia
7-9 . . . Rancho Cucamonga
11-14 . . . . at High Desert
15-17 at Rancho Cucamonga
18-21 . . . . Lancaster
23-25 . . . . . at San Jose
26-29 . . . . .Inland Empire
30-31 . . . . Modesto

SEPTEMBER
1 . . . . Modesto
2-5 . . . . . at Inland Empire

VISALIA

APRIL
7-10 . . . . .Bakersfield
11-13 . . . . Stockton
14-16 . . . . . at San Jose
17-20 . . . . . at Stockton
21-23 . . . . San Jose
25-28 . . . . at Bakersfield
29-30 . . . . Modesto

MAY
1 . . . . Modesto
2-5 . . . . San Jose
6-8 . . . . at Modesto
10-13 . . . . . . .Bakersfield
14-16 . . . at Inland Empire
17-20 at Rancho Cucamonga
21-23 . . . . . High Desert
25-28 . . . . Stockton
29-31 . . . at Bakersfield

JUNE
1-4 . . . . at San Jose
5-7 . . . . Modesto
9-12 . at Rancho Cucamonga
13-15 . . . . . at Modesto
16-19 . . . . .Bakersfield
23-26 . . . . . at High Desert

JULY
27-30 . . . . .Inland Empire
1-3 . . . . Lake Elsinore
4-6 . . . . at Inland Empire
7-10 . . . .at Lake Elsinore
12-15 . . . . San Jose
16-18 . . . at Stockton
20-22 . .Rancho Cucamonga
23-25 . . . . . at San Jose
27-30 . . . . Stockton
31 . . . Rancho Cucamonga

AUGUST
1-2 . . . .Rancho Cucamonga
3-6 . . . . at Stockton
7-9 . . . . .Lancaster
11-14 . . . . .Inland Empire
15-17 . . . . . at Bakersfield
18-21 . . . . . . at Modesto
23-25 . . . . . High Desert
26-29 . . . . . . Modesto
30-31 . . . . . at Lancaster

SEPTEMBER
1 . . . . .at Lancaster
2-5 . . . . at Modesto

CAROLINA LEAGUE

FREDERICK

APRIL
8-10 . . . . at Salem
12-14 . . . . . Myrtle Beach
15-17 . . . . Salem
18-20 . . . at Potomac
21-24 . . . . . .Lynchburg
25-28 . . . at Winston-Salem
29-30 . . . .at Myrtle Beach

MAY
1 . . . . . . .at Myrtle Beach
2-4 . . . . . . Winston-Salem
5-8 . . . . Wilmington
10-12 . . . at Lynchburg
13-15 . . . . at Kinston

16-19 . . . . Potomac
20-22 . . . . Kinston
23-25 . . .at Wilmington
27-29 . . . . at Salem
30-31 . . . . . Myrtle Beach

JUNE
1-2 . . . . . Myrtle Beach
3-5 . . . . Salem
6-9 . . . . at Potomac
10-12 . . . . . . .Lynchburg
13-15 . . . at Winston-Salem
16-19 . . .at Myrtle Beach
23-25 . . . . Winston-Salem
26-28 . . . Wilmington

29-30 . . . . . at Lynchburg

JULY
1 . . . . . at Lynchburg
2-4 . . . . at Kinston
6-8 . . . . Potomac
9-11 . . . . Kinston
13-16 . . . .at Wilmington
17-20 . . . . at Salem
22-24 . . . Myrtle Beach
25-28 . . . . Salem
29-31 . . . at Potomac

KINSTON

APRIL
8-10 . . . . Winston-Salem
11-13 . . . . . Wilmington
15-17 . . at Winston-Salem
18-20 . . . .at Wilmington
21-24 . . . Myrtle Beach
25-28 . . . . . Wilmington
29-30 . . . . at Lynchburg

MAY
1 . . . . at Lynchburg
2-4 . . . . at Salem
5-8 . . . . Potomac
10-12 . . .at Myrtle Beach
13-15 . . . . Frederick
16-19 . . . . .Lynchburg
20-22 . . . at Frederick
23-25 . . . at Potomac
26-28 . . . Winston-Salem
30-31 . . . Wilmington

JUNE
1-2 . . . . . Wilmington
3-5 . . . . at Winston-Salem
6-9 . . . . . .at Wilmington
10-12 . . . . Myrtle Beach
13-15 . . . . Salem
16-19 . . . . . at Lynchburg

23-25 . . . . at Salem
26-28 . . . . Potomac
29-30 . . .at Myrtle Beach

JULY
1 . . . . . . .at Myrtle Beach
2-4 . . . . .Frederick
6-8 . . . . .Lynchburg
9-11 . . . . . . at Frederick
13-16 . . . . . at Potomac
17-20 . . . Winston-Salem
22-24 . . . . Wilmington
25-28 . . . at Winston-Salem
29-31 . . . . . .at Wilmington

AUGUST
2-4 . . . . . Myrtle beach
5-7 . . . . Salem
8-10 . . . . at Lynchburg
11-14 . . . . . . at Salem
15-17 . . . . Potomac
18-21 . . .at Myrtle Beach
22-25 . . . . at Frederick
26-28 . . . . .Lynchburg
30-31 . . . . Frederick

SEPTEMBER
1-2 . . . . Frederick
3-5 . . . . at Potomac

LYNCHBURG

APRIL
8-10 . . . . at Potomac
12-14 . . . . at Salem
15-17 . . . Myrtle beach
18-19 . . . . Salem
20 . . . . at Salem
21-24 . . . . . at Frederick
25-28 . . . . . Wilmington
29-30 . . . . Kinston

MAY
1 . . . . Kinston
2-4 . . . . . .at Wilmington
5-8 . . . at Winston-Salem
10-12 . . . . . . .Frederick
13-15 . . .at Myrtle Beach
16-19 . . . . . . at Kinston
20-22 . . . . Potomac
23-25 . . . Winston-Salem
27-29 . . . at Potomac
30-31 . . . . at Salem

JUNE
1 . . . . at Salem
2 . . . . Salem
3-5 . . . Myrtle beach
6-9 . . . . Salem
10-12 . . . . . . at Frederick
13-15 . . . . . . Wilmington

16-19 . . . . Kinston
23-25 . . .at Wilmington
26-28 . . . at Winston-Salem
29-30 . . . . . . .Frederick

JULY
1 . . . . .Frederick
2-5 . . . . Myrtle Beach
6-8 . . . . at Kinston
9-11 . . . . Potomac
13-16 . . . Winston-Salem
17-20 . . . . . at Potomac
21-23 . . . . . . at Salem
25-28 . . .at Myrtle Beach
29-31 . . . . Salem

AUGUST
2-4 . . . . at Frederick
5-7 . . . . . Wilmington
8-10 . . . . Kinston
11-14 . . . .at Wilmington
15-17 . . at Winston-Salem
18-21 . . . . Frederick
23-25 . . .at Myrtle Beach
26-28 . . . . . at Kinston
30-31 . . . . Potomac

SEPTEMBER
1-2 . . . . Potomac
3-5 . . . . . . Winston-Salem

MYRTLE BEACH

APRIL
8-10 . . . . Wilmington	23-25 . . . . Potomac
12-14 . . . . . . at Frederick	26-28 . . . . at Salem
15-17 . . . . . at Lynchburg	29-30 . . . . Kinston
18-20 . . . . Winston-Salem	
21-24 . . . . at Kinston	**JULY**
25-28 . . . . Potomac	1 . . . . Kinston
29-30 . . . . Frederick	2-5 . . . . . . at Lynchburg

MAY
1 . . . . Frederick	6-8 . . . at Winston-Salem
2-4 . . . . at Potomac	9-11 . . . . .at Wilmington
5-8 . . . . at Salem	13-16 . . . . Salem
10-12 . . . . Kinston	18-21 . . . . . . Wilmington
13-15 . . . . Lynchburg	22-24 . . . . . at Frederick
16-19 . . . at Winston-Salem	25-28 . . . . . . Lynchburg
20-22 . . . .at Wilmington	29-31 . . . . Winston-Salem
24-26 . . . . Salem	
27-29 . . . . . . Wilmington	**AUGUST**
30-31 . . . . . . at Frederick	2-4 . . . . at Kinston

JUNE
1-2 . . . . at Frederick	5-7 . . . . Potomac
3-5 . . . . . at Lynchburg	8-10 . . . . Frederick
6-9 . . . . Winston-Salem	11-14 . . . . . at Potomac
10-12 . . . . . . at Kinston	15-17 . . . . . . at Salem
13-15 . . . . . at Potomac	18-21 . . . . Kinston
16-19 . . . . Frederick	23-25 . . . . . . Lynchburg
	26-28 . . . at Winston-Salem
	29-31 . . . . .at Wilmington
	SEPTEMBER
	1 . . . . .at Wilmington
	3-5 . . . . Salem

POTOMAC

APRIL
8-10 . . . . Lynchburg	23-25 . . . .at Myrtle Beach
11-13 . . . . Winston-Salem	26-28 . . . . . . at Kinston
15-17 . . . .at Wilmington	29-30 . . . Winston-Salem
18-20 . . . . Frederick	
21-24 . . . . at Salem	**JULY**
25-28 . . . .at Myrtle Beach	1 . . . . . . Winston-Salem
29-30 . . . . at Salem	2-5 . . . . Wilmington

MAY
1 . . . . at Salem	6-8 . . . . . . at Frederick
2-4 . . . . . . Myrtle Beach	9-11 . . . . . at Lynchburg
5-8 . . . . at Kinston	13-16 . . . . Kinston
9-11 . . . at Winston-Salem	17-20 . . . . . . Lynchburg
13-15 . . . . . . Wilmington	22-24 . . . at Winston-Salem
16-19 . . . . . at Frederick	25-28 . . . .at Wilmington
20-22 . . . . at Lynchburg	29-31 . . . . Frederick
23-25 . . . . Kinston	
27-29 . . . . Lynchburg	**AUGUST**
30-31 . . . at Winston-Salem	2-4 . . . . at Salem

JUNE
1-2 . . . . at Winston-Salem	5-7 . . . . . .at Myrtle Beach
3-5 . . . . . .at Wilmington	8-10 . . . . Salem
6-9 . . . . Frederick	11-14 . . . . . Myrtle Beach
10-12 . . . . Salem	15-17 . . . . . . at Kinston
13-15 . . . . Myrtle Beach	18-21 . . . Winston-Salem
16-19 . . . . Salem	23-25 . . . . . . Wilmington
	26-28 . . . . . at Frederick
	30-31 . . . . . at Lynchburg
	SEPTEMBER
	1-2 . . . . at Lynchburg
	3-5 . . . . Kinston

SALEM

APRIL
8-10 . . . . Frederick	10-12 . . . .at Wilmington
12-14 . . . . . . Lynchburg	13-15 . . . Winston-Salem
15-17 . . . . . at Frederick	16-19 . . . . . Wilmington
18-19 . . . . . at Lynchburg	20-22 . . at Winston-Salem
20 . . . . Lynchburg	24-26 . . . .at Myrtle Beach
21-24 . . . . Potomac	27-29 . . . . Frederick
25-28 . . . . . at Kinston	30-31 . . . . . . Lynchburg
29-30 . . . . Potomac	
	JUNE
MAY	1 . . . . Lynchburg
1 . . . . Potomac	2 . . . . . . at Lynchburg
2-4 . . . . Kinston	3-5 . . . . . . at Frederick
5-8 . . . . . . Myrtle Beach	6-9 . . . . . . at Lynchburg
	10-12 . . . . . at Potomac
	13-15 . . . . . . at Kinston

WILMINGTON

APRIL
8-10 . . . . .at Myrtle Beach	23-25 . . . . Lynchburg
11-13 . . . . . . at Kinston	26-28 . . . . . at Frederick
15-17 . . . . Potomac	29-30 . . . . Salem
18-20 . . . . Kinston	
21-24 . . at Winston-Salem	**JULY**
25-28 . . . . at Lynchburg	1 . . . . Salem
29-30 . . . . Winston-Salem	2-5 . . . . at Potomac

MAY
1 . . . . . . Winston-Salem	6-8 . . . . at Salem
2-4 . . . . Lynchburg	9-11 . . . . . . Myrtle Beach
5-8 . . . . at Frederick	13-16 . . . . Frederick
10-12 . . . . Salem	18-21 . . . . .at Myrtle Beach
13-15 . . . . . at Potomac	22-24 . . . . . . at Kinston
16-19 . . . . . . at Salem	25-28 . . . . Potomac
20-22 . . . Myrtle Beach	29-31 . . . . Kinston
23-25 . . . . . Frederick	
27-29 . . . .at Myrtle Beach	**AUGUST**
30-31 . . . . . . at Kinston	2-4 . . . . at Winston-Salem

JUNE
1-2 . . . . at Kinston	5-7 . . . . . . at Lynchburg
3-5 . . . . Potomac	8-10 . . . . Winston-Salem
6-9 . . . . Kinston	11-14 . . . . . . Lynchburg
10-12 . . at Winston-Salem	15-17 . . . . . at Frederick
13-15 . . . at Lynchburg	18-21 . . . . Salem
16-19 . . . Winston-Salem	23-25 . . . . . at Potomac
	26-28 . . . . . . at Salem
	39-31 . . . . Myrtle Beach
	SEPTEMBER
	1 . . . . Myrtle Beach
	3-5 . . . . Frederick

WINSTON-SALEM

APRIL
8-10 . . . . at Kinston	23-25 . . . . . . at Frederick
11-13 . . . . . . at Potomac	26-28 . . . . . . Lynchburg
15-17 . . . . Kinston	29-30 . . . . . at Potomac
18-20 . . . .at Myrtle Beach	
21-24 . . . . . Wilmington	**JULY**
25-28 . . . . . Frederick	1 . . . . at Potomac
29-30 . . . . at Wilmington	2-5 . . . . Salem

MAY
1 . . . . at Wilmington	6-8 . . . . . . Myrtle Beach
2-4 . . . . at Frederick	9-11 . . . . at Salem
5-8 . . . . Lynchburg	13-16 . . . . . at Lynchburg
9-11 . . . . Potomac	17-20 . . . . . . at Kinston
13-15 . . . . . at Salem	22-24 . . . . . . Potomac
16-19 . . . . Myrtle Beach	25-28 . . . . Kinston
20-22 . . . . Salem	29-31 . . . .at Myrtle Beach
23-25 . . . . at Lynchburg	
26-28 . . . . . at Kinston	**AUGUST**
30-31 . . . . . . Potomac	2-4 . . . . . . Wilmington

JUNE
1-2 . . . . Potomac	5-7 . . . . Frederick
3-5 . . . . Kinston	8-10 . . . . . at Wilmington
6-9 . . . . .at Myrtle Beach	11-14 . . . . at Frederick
10-12 . . . . . Wilmington	15-17 . . . . . Lynchburg
13-15 . . . . . Frederick	18-21 . . . . . at Potomac
16-19 . . . at Wilmington	22-25 . . . . . . at Salem
	26-28 . . . . Myrtle Beach
	31 . . . . Salem
	SEPTEMBER
	1-2 . . . . Salem
	3-5 . . . . . . at Lynchburg

FLORIDA STATE LEAGUE

BRADENTON

APRIL
7 . . . . at Charlotte
8 . . . . .Charlotte
9 . . . . at Charlotte
10 . . . . .Charlotte
11-13 . . . . Jupiter
14-16 . . . . Fort Myers
17-19 . . . . . . .at Jupiter
20-22 . . . . . at Fort Myers
23-25 . . . . . . Palm Beach
26-27 . . . . St. Lucie
28-29 . . . . . . .at St. Lucie
30 . . . . . . .at Palm Beach

MAY
1-2. . . . . . . .at Palm Beach
4-5. . . . . St. Lucie
6 . . . . at Charlotte
7 . . . . .Charlotte
8 . . . . at Charlotte
10-13 . . . . .at Tampa
14-17 . . . . . . .Clearwater
18-21 . . . . Dunedin
22-25 . . . . . . at Lakeland
26-29 . . . . . . .at Daytona
31 . . . . . .Brevard County

JUNE
1-3. . . . . . .Brevard County
4 . . . . .Charlotte
5-6. . . . . at Charlotte
8-10 . . . . .at Jupiter
11 . . . . Fort Myers
12-13 . . . . . at Fort Myers
14 . . . . at Charlotte
15 . . . . .Charlotte

16 . . . . at Charlotte
20-22 . . . . Jupiter
23 . . . . at Fort Myers
24-25 . . . . . . .Fort Myers
26-27 . . . . . . .at St. Lucie
28 . . . . St. Lucie
29-30 . . . . . . Palm Beach

JULY
1 . . . . Palm Beach
2-3. . . . . St. Lucie
4-7. . . . . . .at Palm Beach
8-11 . . . . Lakeland
13-16 . . . . . . at Dunedin
17-20 . . . . Daytona
21-24 . . . . Tampa
25-28 . . . . . at Clearwater
29-31 . . . at Brevard County

AUGUST
1 . . . . at Brevard County
3-5. . . . . .Fort Myers
6-8. . . . . Jupiter
9-11 . . . . . . at Fort Myers
12-14 . . . . . . .at Jupiter
16 . . . . .Charlotte
17 . . . . at Charlotte
18 . . . . .Charlotte
19-21 . . . . . . .at St. Lucie
23-25 . . . . . Palm Beach
26-27 . . . . . . at St. Lucie
28-29 . . . . . . St. Lucie
30-31 . . . . .at Palm Beach

SEPTEMBER
1-2. . . . . .Charlotte
3 . . . . at Charlotte
4 . . . . .Charlotte

BREVARD COUNTY

APRIL
7 . . . . Daytona
8-9. . . . . .at Daytona
10 . . . . Daytona
11-13 . . . . .at Tampa
14-16 . . . . . .Clearwater
17-19 . . . . Tampa
20-22 . . . . at Clearwater
23-26 . . . . at Lakeland
27-29 . . . . . . Dunedin
30 . . . . Lakeland

MAY
1-2. . . . . Lakeland
3-5. . . . . at Dunedin
6-7. . . . . Daytona
9 . . . . .at Daytona
10-13 . . . . .Charlotte
14-15 . . . . . . St. Lucie
16-17 . . . . . .at St. Lucie
18-21 . . . . . at Fort Myers
22-25 . . . . . Palm Beach
26-29 . . . . . . Jupiter
31 . . . . . at Bradenton

JUNE
1-3. . . . . . . at Bradenton
4 . . . . .at Daytona
5 . . . . Daytona
6 . . . . .at Daytona
8-9. . . . . Dunedin
10 . . . . . . at Dunedin
11-13 . . . . at Lakeland
14 . . . . Daytona
15 . . . . . . .at Daytona
16 . . . . Daytona

20-21 . . . . . . at Dunedin
22 . . . . Dunedin
23-25 . . . . . . Lakeland
26-28 . . . . Tampa
29-30 . . . . . at Clearwater

JULY
1 . . . . at Clearwater
2-3. . . . . .at Tampa
4-7. . . . . . . .Clearwater
8-11 . . . . Fort Myers
13-16 . . . . . . .at Jupiter
17-20 . . . . .at Palm Beach
21-22 . . . . . . St. Lucie
23-24 . . . . . .at St. Lucie
25-28 . . . . at Charlotte
29-31 . . . . . Bradenton

AUGUST
1 . . . . Bradenton
3-5. . . . . Dunedin
6 . . . . at Lakeland
7-8. . . . . Lakeland
9-11 . . . . . . at Dunedin
12-13 . . . . . at Lakeland
14 . . . . Lakeland
16-17 . . . . . . Daytona
18 . . . . . .at Daytona
19-21 . . . . Tampa
23-25 . . . . at Clearwater
26-29 . . . . . at Tampa
30-31 . . . . .Clearwater

SEPTEMBER
1-2. . . . . .at Daytona
3 . . . . Daytona
4 . . . . .at Daytona

CHARLOTTE

APRIL
7 . . . . Bradenton
8 . . . . at Bradenton
9 . . . . at Bradenton
10 . . . . at Bradenton
11-13 . . . .at Palm Beach
14-16 . . . . . .at St. Lucie
17-19 . . . . . . Palm beach
20-22 . . . . St. Lucie
23-26 . . . . at Fort Myers
27-29 . . . . Jupiter
30 . . . . Fort Myers

MAY
1-2. . . . . Fort Myers
3-5. . . . . . . .at Jupiter
6 . . . . Bradenton
7 . . . . at Bradenton
8 . . . . Bradenton
10-13 . . . at Brevard County
14-17 . . . . Lakeland
18-21 . . . . at Clearwater
22-25 . . . . . at Dunedin
26-29 . . . . Tampa
31 . . . . Daytona

JUNE
1-3. . . . . Daytona
4 . . . . at Bradenton
5-6. . . . . Bradenton
8-9. . . . . St. Lucie
10 . . . . .at St. Lucie
11-13 . . . .at Palm Beach
14 . . . . Bradenton
15 . . . . at Bradenton
16 . . . . Bradenton
20-21 . . . . . .at St. Lucie

22 . . . . St. Lucie
23-25 . . . . . Palm Beach
26 . . . . Fort Myers
27-28 . . . . at Fort Myers
29-30 . . . . . . .at Jupiter

JULY
1 . . . . .at Jupiter
2-3. . . . . . . at Fort Myers
4-7. . . . . Jupiter
8-11 . . . . .at Daytona
13-16 . . . . . . .Clearwater
17-20 . . . . . at Lakeland
21-24 . . . . Dunedin
25-28 . . . .Brevard County
29-31 . . . . . . .at Tampa

AUGUST
1 . . . . .at Tampa
3-5. . . . . Palm beach
6 . . . . .at St. Lucie
7-8. . . . . St. Lucie
9-11 . . . . . . .at Palm Beach
12-13 . . . . . .at St. Lucie
14 . . . . St. Lucie
16 . . . . at Bradenton
17 . . . . at Bradenton
18 . . . . at Bradenton
19-21 . . . . . . .Fort Myers
23-25 . . . . . . .at Jupiter
26-27 . . . . . .Fort Myers
28-29 . . . . at Fort Myers
30-31 . . . . Jupiter

SEPTEMBER
1-2. . . . . . . at Bradenton
3 . . . . Bradenton
4 . . . . at Bradenton

CLEARWATER

APRIL
7 . . . . at Dunedin
8 . . . . Dunedin
9 . . . . at Dunedin
10 . . . . Dunedin
11-13 . . . . .at Daytona
14-16 . . . at Brevard County
17-19 . . . . . . Daytona
20-22 . . . .Brevard County
23-26 . . . . . . .at Tampa
27-28 . . . . . . Lakeland
29 . . . . . . at Lakeland
30 . . . . Tampa

MAY
1-2. . . . . Tampa
3 . . . . Lakeland
4-5. . . . . . at Lakeland
6-7. . . . . Dunedin
9 . . . . at Dunedin
10-13 . . . . Palm Beach
14-17 . . . . at Bradenton
18-21 . . . . . .Charlotte
22-25 . . . . . .at Jupiter
26-29 . . . at Fort Myers
31 . . . . St. Lucie

JUNE
1-3. . . . . St. Lucie
4-6. . . . . Dunedin
7 . . . . Tampa
9-10 . . . . .at Tampa
11-13 . . . . .at Daytona

14-16 . . . . . . at Dunedin
20-21 . . . . . . Tampa
22 . . . . .at Tampa
23-25 . . . . . . Daytona
26-28 . . . . . . at Lakeland
29-30 . . . . .Brevard County

JULY
1-3. . . . . Lakeland
4-7. . . . . at Brevard County
8-11 . . . . Jupiter
13-16 . . . . at Charlotte
17-20 . . . . . .at St. Lucie
21-24 . . . . . Fort Myers
25-28 . . . . . . Bradenton
29-31 . . . . .at Palm Beach

AUGUST
1 . . . . .at Palm Beach
2-5. . . . . Tampa
6-8. . . . . Daytona
9-11 . . . . .at Tampa
12-14 . . . . . .at Daytona
16-17 . . . . . . Dunedin
18 . . . . . . at Dunedin
19-21 . . . . at Lakeland
23-25 . . . . .Brevard County
26-29 . . . . . Lakeland
30-31 . . . at Brevard County

SEPTEMBER
1-3. . . . . at Dunedin
4 . . . . Dunedin

DAYTONA

APRIL
7 . . . . . at Brevard County
8-9 . . . . . .Brevard County
10 . . . . at Brevard County
11-13 . . . . . .Clearwater
14-16 . . . . . . at Lakeland
17-19 . . . . . at Clearwater
20-21 . . . . .Lakeland
22 . . . . at Lakeland
23-25 . . . . . at Dunedin
27-29 . . . . Tampa
30 . . . . Dunedin

MAY
1-2 . . . . Dunedin
3-5 . . . . .at Tampa
6-7 . . . . at Brevard County
9 . . . . . .Brevard County
10-13 . . . . . . .at Jupiter
14-17 . . . . . . .Fort Myers
18-21 . . .at Palm Beach
22-25 . . . . St. Lucie
26-29 . . . . Bradenton
31 . . . . at Charlotte

JUNE
1-3 . . . . . . at Charlotte
4 . . . . . . .Brevard County
5 . . . . at Brevard County
6 . . . . . .Brevard County
8-9 . . . . Lakeland
10 . . . . at Lakeland
11-13 . . . . . . .Clearwater
14 . . . . at Brevard County
15 . . . . .Brevard County

DUNEDIN

APRIL
7 . . . . .Clearwater
8 . . . . at Clearwater
9 . . . . .Clearwater
10 . . . . at Clearwater
11-13 . . . . Lakeland
14-16 . . . . Tampa
17-19 . . . . at Lakeland
20-22 . . . . . at Tampa
23-25 . . . . Daytona
27-29 . . . at Brevard County

MAY
1-2 . . . . .at Daytona
3-5 . . . . . .Brevard County
6-7 . . . . at Clearwater
9 . . . . .Clearwater
10-13 . . . . . . at Fort Myers
14-17 . . . . . . Jupiter
18-21 . . . . at Bradenton
22-25 . . . . . . .Charlotte
26-29 . . . . at St. Lucie
31 . . . . . Palm Beach

JUNE
1-3 . . . . Palm Beach
4-6 . . . . at Clearwater
8-9 . . . . at Brevard County
10 . . . . . .Brevard County
11-13 . . . . Tampa
14-16 . . . . . . .Clearwater
20-21 . . . . .Brevard County

FORT MYERS

APRIL
7-8 . . . . .at Jupiter
9-10 . . . . Jupiter
11-13 . . . . . . St. Lucie

16 . . . . . at Brevard County
20 . . . . at Lakeland
21-22 . . . . Lakeland
23-25 . . . . at Clearwater
26-28 . . . . Dunedin
29-30 . . . . . . at Tampa

JULY
1 . . . . .at Tampa
2-3 . . . . at Dunedin
4-7 . . . . Tampa
8-11 . . . . .Charlotte
13-16 . . . at Fort Myers
17-20 . . . . at Bradenton
21-24 . . . . Palm Beach
25-28 . . . .at St. Lucie
29-31 . . . . . . Jupiter

AUGUST
1 . . . . Jupiter
3-5 . . . . .Lakeland
6-8 . . . . at Clearwater
9-11 . . . . . at Lakeland
12-14 . . . . . .Clearwater
16-17 . . . at Brevard County
18 . . . . . .Brevard County
19-21 . . . . . . Dunedin
23-25 . . . .at Tampa
26-29 . . . . at Dunedin
30-31 . . . . Tampa

SEPTEMBER
1-2 . . . . . .Brevard County
3 . . . . . . at Brevard County
4 . . . . . . .Brevard County

---

22 . . . . . at Brevard County
23-25 . . . . .at Tampa
26-28 . . . . . .at Daytona
29-30 . . . . . Lakeland

JULY
1 . . . . Lakeland
2-3 . . . . Daytona
4-7 . . . . at Lakeland
8-11 . . . . . .at Palm Beach
13-16 . . . . . . Bradenton
17-20 . . . . . . Fort Myers
21-24 . . . . . at Charlotte
25-28 . . . . .at Jupiter
29-31 . . . . . . St. Lucie

AUGUST
1 . . . . St. Lucie
3-5 . . . . at Brevard County
6-8 . . . . .at Tampa
9-11 . . . . .Brevard County
12-14 . . . . Tampa
16-17 . . . . at Clearwater
18 . . . . .Clearwater
19-21 . . . . . .at Daytona
23-25 . . . . Lakeland
26-29 . . . . . . Daytona
30-31 . . . . . at Lakeland

SEPTEMBER
1-3 . . . . .Clearwater
4 . . . . . . at Clearwater

JUPITER

APRIL
7-8 . . . . .Fort Myers
9-10 . . . . at Fort Myers
11-13 . . . . at Bradenton
14 . . . . .at Palm Beach
15-16 . . . . Palm Beach
17-19 . . . . . Bradenton
20-22 . . . . .at Palm Beach
23-25 . . . . . St. Lucie
27-29 . . . . at Charlotte
30 . . . . .at St. Lucie

MAY
1-2 . . . . . . .at St. Lucie
3-5 . . . . .Charlotte
6-7 . . . . . at Fort Myers
9 . . . . Fort Myers
10-13 . . . . . . Daytona
14-17 . . . . . at Dunedin
18-21 . . . . at Lakeland
22-25 . . . . .Clearwater
26-29 . . . at Brevard County
31 . . . . Tampa

JUNE
1-3 . . . . Tampa
4-6 . . . . at Fort Myers
8-10 . . . . . Bradenton
11-13 . . . .at St. Lucie
14-16 . . . . . Fort Myers
20-22 . . . . at Bradenton
23-25 . . . . . St. Lucie
26 . . . . . . .at Palm Beach
27 . . . . . . Palm Beach

LAKELAND

APRIL
7 . . . . Tampa
8 . . . . .at Tampa
9 . . . . Tampa
10 . . . . .at Tampa
11-13 . . . . . at Dunedin
14-16 . . . . Dayton
17-19 . . . . . . Dunedin
20-21 . . . . at Dayton
22 . . . . Dayton
23-26 . . . . .Brevard County
27-28 . . . . . at Clearwater

27-29 . . . . .at Palm Beach
30 . . . . at Charlotte

MAY
1-2 . . . . at Charlotte
3-5 . . . . . Palm Beach
6-7 . . . . Jupiter
9 . . . . .at Jupiter
10-13 . . . . Dunedin
14-17 . . . .at Daytona
18-21 . . . . .Brevard County
22-25 . . . . . .at Tampa
26-29 . . . . . .Clearwater
31 . . . . at Lakeland

JUNE
1-3 . . . . . . at Lakeland
4-6 . . . . Jupiter
8-10 . . . . . Palm Beach
11 . . . . . . at Bradenton
12-13 . . . . . . Bradenton
14-16 . . . . . .at Jupiter
20-22 . . .at Palm Beach
23 . . . . Bradenton
24-25 . . . . at Bradenton
26 . . . . . . at Charlotte
27-28 . . . . . .Charlotte
29-30 . . . . . St. Lucie

JULY
1 . . . . St. Lucie
2-3 . . . . .Charlotte
4-7 . . . . .at St. Lucie
8-11 . . . at Brevard County
13-16 . . . . . . Daytona
17-20 . . . . at Dunedin
21-24 . . . at Clearwater
25-28 . . . . . . Tampa
29-31 . . . . . . .Lakeland

AUGUST
1 . . . . .Lakeland
3-5 . . . . . . at Bradenton
6-8 . . . . .at Palm Beach
9-11 . . . . Bradenton
12-14 . . . . Palm Beach
16-17 . . . . .at Jupiter
18 . . . . Jupiter
19-21 . . . . at Charlotte
23-25 . . . . . . St. Lucie
26-27 . . . . at Charlotte
28-29 . . . . . .Charlotte
30-31 . . . .at St. Lucie

SEPTEMBER
1-2 . . . . Jupiter
3-4 . . . . .at Jupiter

---

28 . . . . . .at Palm Beach
29-30 . . . . .Charlotte

JULY
1 . . . . .Charlotte
2-3 . . . . . Palm Beach
4-7 . . . . at Charlotte
8-11 . . . at Clearwater
13-16 . . . .Brevard County
17-20 . . . . . . at Tampa
21-24 . . . . . Lakeland
25-28 . . . . . . Dunedin
29-31 . . . . . .at Daytona

AUGUST
1 . . . . .at Daytona
3-5 . . . . . . St. Lucie
6-8 . . . . . at Bradenton
9-11 . . . . at St. Lucie
12-14 . . . . . Bradenton
16-17 . . . . . Fort Myers
18 . . . . . at Fort Myers
19 . . . .at Palm Beach
20 . . . . . Palm Beach
21 . . . .at Palm Beach
23-25 . . . . . . .Charlotte
26 . . . .at Palm Beach
27-29 . . . . Palm Beach
30-31 . . . at Charlotte

SEPTEMBER
1-2 . . . . . . at Fort Myers
3-4 . . . . . . Fort Myers

---

29 . . . . .Clearwater
30 . . . . at Brevard County

MAY
1-2 . . . . at Brevard County
3 . . . . . . at Clearwater
4-6 . . . . . .Clearwater
7-9 . . . . .at Tampa
10-13 . . . . . .at St. Lucie
14-17 . . . . at Charlotte
18-21 . . . . . Jupiter
22-25 . . . . Bradenton

26-29 . . . . . at Palm Beach
31 . . . . Fort Myers

JUNE
1-3 . . . . Fort Myers
4 . . . . Tampa
5 . . . . at Tampa
6 . . . . Tampa
8-9 . . . . . . at Dayton
10 . . . . Dayton
11-13 . . . . Brevard County
14 . . . . Tampa
15-16 . . . . at Tampa
20 . . . . Dayton
21-22 . . . . at Dayton
23-25 . . at Brevard County
26-28 . . . . Clearwater
29-30 . . . . . at Dunedin

JULY
1 . . . . at Dunedin
2-3 . . . . . at Clearwater
4-7 . . . . . . Dunedin
8-11 . . . . at Bradenton
13-16 . . . . St. Lucie

PALM BEACH

17-20 . . . . Charlotte
21-24 . . . . . . at Jupiter
25-28 . . . . . Palm Beach
29-31 . . . . at Fort Myers

AUGUST
1 . . . . at Fort Myers
3-5 . . . . . . at Dayton
6 . . . . . Brevard County
7-8 . . . . at Brevard County
9-11 . . . . Dayton
12-13 . . . Brevard County
14 . . . . at Brevard County
16 . . . . at Tampa
17-18 . . . . . . Tampa
19-21 . . . . Clearwater
23-25 . . . . at Dunedin
26-29 . . . at Clearwater
30-31 . . . . . Dunedin

SEPTEMBER
1 . . . . at Tampa
2 . . . . Tampa
3 . . . . at Tampa
4 . . . . Tampa

23-25 . . . . at Jupiter
26-27 . . . . . at Bradenton
28-29 . . . . . . Bradenton
30 . . . . Jupiter

MAY
1-2 . . . . Jupiter
4-7 . . . . . at Palm Beach
9 . . . . Palm Beach
10-13 . . . . . . Lakeland
14-15 . . at Brevard County
16-17 . . . Brevard County
18-21 . . . . . at Tampa
22-25 . . . at Daytona
26-29 . . . . . Dunedin
31 . . . . . at Clearwater

JUNE
1-3 . . . . . . at Clearwater
4-6 . . . . . at Palm Beach
8-9 . . . . . . at Charlotte
10 . . . . Charlotte
11-13 . . . . . Jupiter
14-16 . . . . Palm Beach
20-21 . . . . . Charlotte
22 . . . . . . at Charlotte
23-25 . . . . . at Jupiter
26-27 . . . . Bradenton
28 . . . . . at Bradenton
29-30 . . . . at Fort Myers

TAMPA

APRIL
7 . . . . at Lakeland
8 . . . . Lakeland
9 . . . . at Lakeland
10 . . . . Lakeland
11-13 . . . . Brevard County
14-16 . . . . . at Dunedin
17-19 . . at Brevard County
20-22 . . . . . Dunedin
23-26 . . . . . Clearwater
27-29 . . . . at Daytona
30 . . . . . . at Clearwater

MAY
1-2 . . . . . . at Clearwater
3-5 . . . . Daytona
6 . . . . at Lakeland
7-9 . . . . Lakeland
10-13 . . . . . Bradenton
14-17 . . . at Palm Beach
18-21 . . . . . . St. Lucie
22-25 . . . . . Fort Myers
26-29 . . . . at Charlotte
31 . . . . at Jupiter

JUNE
1-3 . . . . at Jupiter
4 . . . . at Lakeland
5 . . . . at Lakeland
6 . . . . at Lakeland
7 . . . . . . at Clearwater
9-10 . . . . . Clearwater
11-13 . . . . at Dunedin
14 . . . . . . at Lakeland
15-16 . . . . . Lakeland

JULY
1 . . . . at Fort Myers
2-3 . . . . . . at Bradenton
4-7 . . . . Fort Myers
8-11 . . . . Tampa
13-16 . . . . . at Lakeland
17-20 . . . . . Clearwater
21-22 . . at Brevard County
23-24 . . . Brevard County
25-28 . . . . . Daytona
29-31 . . . . at Dunedin

AUGUST
1 . . . . at Dunedin
3-5 . . . . at Jupiter
6 . . . . Charlotte
7-8 . . . . . . at Charlotte
9-11 . . . . . . Jupiter
12-13 . . . . Charlotte
14 . . . . . . at Charlotte
16-17 . . . . Palm Beach
18 . . . . at Palm Beach
19-21 . . . . . Bradenton
23-25 . . . at Fort Myers
26-27 . . . . Bradenton
28-29 . . . at Bradenton
30-31 . . . . Fort Myers

SEPTEMBER
1-2 . . . . . . at Palm Beach
3-4 . . . . Palm Beach

20-21 . . . . . at Clearwater
22 . . . . Clearwater
23-25 . . . . . Dunedin
26-28 . . at Brevard County
29-30 . . . . . Daytona

JULY
1 . . . . Daytona
2-3 . . . . . Brevard County
4-7 . . . . . . at Daytona
8-11 . . . . . at St. Lucie
13-16 . . . . Palm Beach
17-20 . . . . . . Jupiter
21-24 . . . . at Bradenton
25-28 . . . at Fort Myers
29-31 . . . . . Charlotte

AUGUST
1 . . . . Charlotte
2-5 . . . . . at Clearwater
6-8 . . . . Dunedin
9-11 . . . . . Clearwater
12-14 . . . . at Dunedin
16 . . . . Lakeland
17-18 . . . . at Lakeland
19-21 . . at Brevard County
23-25 . . . . . Daytona
26-29 . . . Brevard County
30-31 . . . . at Daytona

SEPTEMBER
1 . . . . Lakeland
2 . . . . at Lakeland
3 . . . . Lakeland
4 . . . . at Lakeland

PALM BEACH

APRIL
7-8 . . . . at St. Lucie
9-10 . . . . . . St. Lucie
11-13 . . . . . . Charlotte
14 . . . . Jupiter
15-16 . . . . . at Jupiter
17-20 . . . . at Charlotte
20-22 . . . . . . Jupiter
23-25 . . . at Bradenton
27-29 . . . . . Fort Myers
30 . . . . Bradenton

MAY
1-2 . . . . Bradenton
3-5 . . . . . at Fort Myers
6-7 . . . . St. Lucie
9 . . . . . . at St. Lucie
10-13 . . . . at Clearwater
14-17 . . . . . . Tampa
18-21 . . . . . Daytona
22-25 . . at Brevard County
26-29 . . . . . Lakeland
31 . . . . . . at Dunedin

JUNE
1-3 . . . . . . at Dunedin
4-6 . . . . St. Lucie
8-10 . . . . . at Fort Myers
11-13 . . . . Charlotte
14-16 . . . . at St. Lucie
20-22 . . . . Fort Myers
23-25 . . . at Charlotte
26 . . . . Jupiter

27 . . . . at Jupiter
28 . . . . Jupiter
29-30 . . . . . at Bradenton

JULY
1 . . . . at Bradenton
2-3 . . . . at Jupiter
4-7 . . . . Bradenton
8-11 . . . . Dunedin
13-16 . . . . . . at Tampa
17-20 . . . Brevard County
21-24 . . . . . at Daytona
25-28 . . . . . at Lakeland
29-31 . . . . Clearwater

AUGUST
1 . . . . Clearwater
3-5 . . . . . . at Charlotte
6-8 . . . . . . Fort Myers
9-11 . . . . . . Charlotte
12-14 . . . . at Fort Myers
16-17 . . . . at St. Lucie
18 . . . . St. Lucie
19 . . . . Jupiter
20 . . . . at Jupiter
21 . . . . Jupiter
23-25 . . . . at Bradenton
26 . . . . Jupiter
27-29 . . . . . at Jupiter
30-31 . . . . . Bradenton

SEPTEMBER
1-2 . . . . St. Lucie
3-4 . . . . . . at St. Lucie

ST. LUCIE

APRIL
7-8 . . . . . Palm Beach
9-10 . . . . . at Palm Beach

11-13 . . . . at Fort Myers
14-16 . . . . . Charlotte
17-19 . . . . . Fort Myers
20-22 . . . . at Charlotte

LOW CLASS A

MIDWEST LEAGUE

BELOIT

APRIL
7-10 . . . . . at Quad Cities
11-14 . . . . Clinton
15-17 . . . . . Cedar Rapids

18-20 . . . . . at Wisconsin
21-23 . . . . at Peoria
25-27 . . . . . . Burlington
28-30 . . . . Peoria

MAY
1-3 . . . . at Clinton

4-6 . . . . Wisconsin
7-9 . . . . . at Cedar Rapids
10-12 . . . . at Kane County
13-15 . . . . . Quad Cities
17-19 . . . . . at Wisconsin
20-23 . . . . . Kane County
24-26 . . . . . . Burlington

27-30 . . . . at Clinton
31 . . . . at Dayton

JUNE
1-2. . . . . at Dayton
3-5. . . . . at Bowling Green
7-9. . . . . Fort Wayne
10-12 . . . . . .Lake County
14-16 . . . . . Cedar Rapids
17-19 . . . . at Burlington
24-26 . . . . . Cedar Rapids
27-29 . . . .at Kane County
30 . . .at Kane County

JULY
1-2. . . . . .at Kane County
3-5. . . . . Wisconsin
6-8. . . . . at Peoria
9-11 . . . . Clinton
13-15 . . . . . South Bend
16-18 . . . . West Michigan

BOWLING GREEN

APRIL
7-10 . . . . at Dayton
11-14 . . . . . Fort Wayne
15-17 . . . . .Lake County
18-20 . . . . . at Dayton
21-23 . . . at Lake County
25-27 . . . . South Bend
28-30 . . . . . Great Lakes

MAY
1-3. . . . . Dayton
4-6. . . . at Lake County
7-9. . . . . .at Great Lakes
10-12 . . . at Fort Wayne
13-15 . . . . South Bend
17-19 . . . West Michigan
20-23 . . . . . at Lansing
24-26 . . .at West Michigan
27-30 . . . . Lansing
31 . . . . Wisconsin

JUNE
1-2. . . . . Wisconsin
3-5. . . . . Beloit
7-9. . . . . .at Kane County
10-12 . . . . . . at Clinton
14-16 . . . . West Michigan
17-19 . . . . at South Bend
24-26 . . . . Dayton
27-29 . . . .at Great Lakes

BURLINGTON

APRIL
7-10 . . . . at Clinton
11-14 . . . . .Peoria
15-17 . . . .at Quad Cities
18-20 . . .at Kane County
21-23 . . . . . Wisconsin
25-27 . . . . at Beloit
28-30 . . . . . Kane County

MAY
1-3. . . . . .Peoria
4-6. . . . .at Cedar Rapids
7-9. . . . . . at Clinton
10-12 . . . . at Peoria
13-15 . . . . Cedar Rapids
17-19 . . . . . Clinton
20-23 . . . .at Wisconsin
24-26 . . . . at Beloit
27-30 . . . . Quad Cities
31 . . . . . .at Great Lakes

JUNE
1-2. . . . . .at Great Lakes
3-5. . . . . . at Lansing

20-22 . . . .at Great Lakes
23-25 . . . . . . at Lansing
27-29 . . . at Burlington
30-31 . . . .at Cedar Rapids

AUGUST
1 . . . . . . .at Cedar Rapids
2-5. . . . . . . Kane County
6-9. . . . . . . Quad Cities
10-12 . . . .at Wisconsin
13-15 . . . . .Burlington
17-19 . . .at Kane County
20-23 . . .at Quad Cities
24-26 . . . . .Burlington
27-30 . . . . at Clinton
31 . . . . .Peoria

SEPTEMBER
1-2. . . . . .Peoria
3-5. . . . . . . Wisconsin

30 . . . . at Dayton

JULY
1-2. . . . . . . at Dayton
3-5. . . . . . . Great Lakes
6-8. . . . . . .Lake County
9-11 . . . .at West Michigan
13-15 . . .at Cedar Rapids
16-18 . . . . .at Quad Cities
20-22 . . . . . Burlington
23-25 . . . . . .Peoria
27-29 . . . at Lake County
30-31 . . . . . . Dayton

AUGUST
1 . . . . Dayton
2-5. . . . . . . Fort Wayne
6-9. . . . . at South Bend
10-12 . . . .at Fort Wayne
13-15 . . . . South Bend
17-19 . . . . . .Lansing
20-23 . . .at Great Lakes
24-26 . . . . . at Lansing
27-30 . . . . Great Lakes
31 . . . . Dayton

SEPTEMBER
1-2. . . . . Dayton
3-5. . . . . at Lake County

7-9. . . . . . . South Bend
10-12 . . . . West Michigan
14-16 . . . . Kane County
17-19 . . . . Beloit
24-26 . . . . . at Clinton
27-29 . . . . Kane County
30 . . . . .Peoria

JULY
1-2. . . . . .Peoria
3-5. . . . . .at Cedar Rapids
6-8. . . . . . . Quad Cities
9-11 . . . .at Kane County
13-15 . . . . Fort Wayne
16-18 . . . . .Lake County
20-22 . . . at Bowling Green
23-25 . . . . at Dayton
27-29 . . . . Beloit
30-31 . . . . .at Wisconsin

AUGUST
1 . . . . .at Wisconsin
2-5. . . . . at Peoria
6-9. . . . . Clinton

10-12 . . . . .at Quad Cities
13-15 . . . . . at Beloit
17-19 . . . . . Cedar Rapids
20-23 . . . . . . Wisconsin
24-26 . . . . . at Beloit

CEDAR RAPIDS

APRIL
7-10 . . . . at Peoria
11-14 . . . . . . Wisconsin
15-17 . . . . . at Beloit
18-20 . . . . . at Clinton
21-23 . . . . . Quad Cities
25-27 . . . . Kane County
28-30 . . . .at Quad Cities

MAY
1-3. . . . . .at Kane County
4-6. . . . . . . .Burlington
7-9. . . . . Beloit
10-12 . . . .at Wisconsin
13-15 . . . . at Burlington
17-19 . . . . Kane County
20-23 . . . .at Quad Cities
24-26 . . . . . . Clinton
27-30 . . . . .Peoria
31 . . . . . at South Bend

JUNE
1-2. . . . . . at South Bend
3-5. . . .at West Michigan
7-9. . . . . . . Great Lakes
10-12 . . . . . .Lansing
14-16 . . . . . . at Beloit
17-19 . . . . . Wisconsin
24-26 . . . . . at Beloit
27-29 . . . . .at Quad Cities

CLINTON

APRIL
7-10 . . . . . . .Burlington
11-14 . . . . . . at Beloit
15-17 . . . . Kane County
18-20 . . . . Cedar Rapids
21-23 . . . .at Kane County
25-27 . . . . . . .Peoria
28-30 . . . .at Wisconsin

MAY
1-3. . . . . Beloit
4-6. . . . . at Peoria
7-9. . . . . . . .Burlington
10-12 . . . .at Quad Cities
13-15 . . . . . Wisconsin
17-19 . . . . at Burlington
20-23 . . . . . . at Peoria
24-26 . . .at Cedar Rapids
27-30 . . . . Beloit
31 . . . . .at Fort Wayne

JUNE
1-2. . . . . at Fort Wayne
3-5. . . . . at Lake County
7-9. . . . . Dayton
10-12 . . . . Bowling Green
14-16 . . . . Quad Cities
17-19 . . .at Kane County
24-26 . . . . .Burlington
27-29 . . . . Beloit

DAYTON

APRIL
7-10 . . . . . Bowling Green
11-14 . . . . at Lake County
15-17 . . . . at Lansing

27-30 . . . . .at Quad Cities
31 . . . . Wisconsin

SEPTEMBER
1-2. . . . . Wisconsin
3-5. . . . . . . Cedar Rapids

30 . . . . Wisconsin

JULY
1-2. . . . . Wisconsin
3-5. . . . . . . .Burlington
6-8. . . . . . . at Clinton
9-11 . . . . .Peoria
13-15 . . . . Bowling Green
16-18 . . . . Dayton
20-22 . . . .at Fort Wayne
23-25 . . . . at Lake County
27-29 . . . .at Kane County
30-31 . . . . Beloit

AUGUST
1 . . . . Beloit
2-5. . . . . . . Quad Cities
6-9. . . . . . . at Peoria
10-12 . . . . . at Clinton
13-15 . . . . Kane County
17-19 . . . . at Burlington
20-23 . . . . . . .Peoria
24-26 . . . . Clinton
27-30 . . . .at Wisconsin
31 . . . . Kansas City

SEPTEMBER
1-2. . . . . . . Kansas City
3-5. . . . . . at Burlington

30 . . . . . . .at Quad Cities

JULY
1-2. . . . . . .at Quad Cities
3-5. . . . . . . at Peoria
6-8. . . . . Cedar Rapids
9-11 . . . . . . at Beloit
13-15 . . . . . . Great Lakes
16-18 . . . . .Lansing
20-22 . . . . at South Bend
23-25 . . .at West Michigan
27-29 . . . . . Wisconsin
30-31 . . . . . . .Peoria

AUGUST
1 . . . . .Peoria
2-5. . . . . . .at Wisconsin
6-9. . . . . . at Burlington
10-12 . . . . . Cedar Rapids
13-15 . . . . . at Peoria
17-19 . . . . Quad Cities
20-23 . . . . . Kane County
24-26 . . .at Cedar Rapids
27-30 . . . . Beloit
31 . . . . . . .at Quad Cities

SEPTEMBER
1-2. . . . . .at Quad Cities
3-5. . . . . .at Kane County

18-20 . . . . . Bowling Green
21-23 . . . . .at Great Lakes
25-27 . . . . West Michigan
28-30 . . . . . . Fort Wayne

MAY
1-3 . . . . . at Bowling Green
4-6 . . . . South Bend
7-9 . . . . .at West Michigan
10-12 . . . . .Lake County
13-15 . . . . .at Fort Wayne
17-19 . . . . . . Great Lakes
20-23 . . . . .Lake County
24-26 . . . . .at Great Lakes
27-30 . . . . . at South Bend
31 . . . . Beloit

JUNE
1-2 . . . . Beloit
3-5 . . . . Wisconsin
7-9 . . . . at Clinton
10-12 . . . .at Kane County
14-16 . . . .at Fort Wayne
17-19 . . . . .Lansing
24-26 . . . at Bowling Green
27-29 . . . . .Lansing
30 . . . . . . Bowling Green

JULY
1-2 . . . . . . Bowling Green

3-5 . . . . . . at South Bend
6-8 . . . . . .at Fort Wayne
9-11 . . . . South Bend
13-15 . . . .at Quad Cities
16-18 . . . .at Cedar Rapids
20-22 . . . . .Peoria
23-25 . . . . Burlington
27-29 . . . . Fort Wayne
30-31 . . . at Bowling Green

AUGUST
1 . . . . . . at Bowling Green
2-5 . . . . . . West Michigan
6-9 . . . . . . at Lake County
10-12 . . .at West Michigan
13-15 . . . . . .Lake County
17-19 . . . . . . Great Lakes
20-23 . . . . at Lansing
24-26 . . . . .at Great Lakes
27-30 . . . . . West Michigan
31 . . . . at Bowling Green

SEPTEMBER
1-2 . . . . . at Bowling Green
3-5 . . . . .Lansing

FORT WAYNE

APRIL
7-10 . . . . South Bend
11-14 . . . at Bowling Green
15-17 . . . . . . Great Lakes
18-20 . . . at West Michigan
21-23 . . . . at South Bend
25-27 . . . . . .Lake County
28-30 . . . . . . at Dayton

MAY
1-3 . . . . . . West Michigan
4-6 . . . . .Lansing
7-9 . . . . at South Bend
10-12 . . . . Bowling Green
13-15 . . . . Dayton
17-19 . . . .at Lake County
20-23 . . at West Michigan
24-26 . . . . . . at Lansing
27-30 . . . . . . Great Lakes
31 . . . . Clinton

JUNE
1-2 . . . . Clinton
3-5 . . . . Kane County
7-9 . . . . at Beloit
10-12 . . . . . .at Wisconsin
14-16 . . . . Dayton
17-19 . . . .at Great Lakes
24-26 . . . . . .Lake County
27-29 . . . . at Lake County

GREAT LAKES

APRIL
7-10 . . . . . . .Lake County
11-14 . . .at West Michigan
15-17 . . . . .at Fort Wayne
18-20 . . . . . South Bend
21-23 . . . . Dayton
25-27 . . . . . . at Lansing
28-30 . . . at Bowling Green

MAY
1-3 . . . . . . at South Bend
4-6 . . . . . . West Michigan
7-9 . . . . . . Bowling Green
10-12 . . . . .Lansing
13-15 . . . . . at Lansing
17-19 . . . . . . at Dayton
20-23 . . . . South Bend
24-26 . . . . Dayton
27-30 . . . . .at Fort Wayne

30 . . . . . at West Michigan

JULY
1-2 . . . . at West Michigan
3-5 . . . . . . West Michigan
6-8 . . . . Dayton
9-11 . . . . .at Great Lakes
13-15 . . . . at Burlington
16-18 . . . . . . at Peoria
20-22 . . . . . Cedar Rapids
23-25 . . . . Quad Cities
27-29 . . . . . at Dayton
30-31 . . . . . . Great Lakes

AUGUST
1 . . . . .Great Lakes
2-5 . . . . at Bowling Green
6-9 . . . . .Lansing
10-12 . . . . Bowling Green
13-15 . . . . . . at Lansing
17-19 . . . . West Michigan
20-23 . . . at Lake County
24-26 . . . . at South Bend
27-30 . . . . .Lansing
31 . . . . South Bend

SEPTEMBER
1-2 . . . . South Bend
3-5 . . . . at West Michigan

31 . . . . Burlington

JUNE
1-2 . . . . Burlington
3-5 . . . . .Peoria
7-9 . . . .at Cedar Rapids
10-12 . . . . .at Quad Cities
14-16 . . . . at Lake County
17-19 . . . . Fort Wayne
24-26 . . . . . . at Lansing
27-29 . . . . Bowling Green
30 . . . . .Lansing

JULY
1-2 . . . . .Lansing
3-5 . . . . at Bowling Green
6-8 . . . . . at South Bend
9-11 . . . . Fort Wayne
13-15 . . . . at Clinton
16-18 . . . .at Kane County

20-22 . . . . Beloit
23-25 . . . . Wisconsin
27-29 . . . . . . South Bend
30-31 . . . at Fort Wayne

AUGUST
1 . . . . .at Fort Wayne
2-5 . . . . .Lake County
6-9 . . . . .at West Michigan
10-12 . . . at Lake County

KANE COUNTY

APRIL
7-10 . . . . . . .at Wisconsin
11-14 . . . . . . Quad Cities
15-17 . . . . . . at Clinton
18-20 . . . . . .Burlington
21-23 . . . . Clinton
25-27 . . .at Cedar Rapids
28-30 . . . . at Burlington

MAY
1-3 . . . . . . Cedar Rapids
4-6 . . . . Quad Cities
7-9 . . . . at Peoria
10-12 . . . . Beloit
13-15 . . . . .Peoria
17-19 . . .at Cedar Rapids
20-23 . . . . . . at Beloit
24-26 . . .at Quad Cities
27-30 . . . . . Wisconsin
31 . . . . . . at Lake County

JUNE
1-2 . . . . . at Lake County
3-5 . . . .at Fort Wayne
7-9 . . . Bowling Green
10-12 . . . . Dayton
14-16 . . . at Burlington
17-19 . . . . Clinton
24-26 . . . . . . at Peoria
27-29 . . . at Burlington

LAKE COUNTY

APRIL
7-10 . . . . .at Great Lakes
11-14 . . . . Dayton
15-17 . . at Bowling Green
18-20 . . . . .Lansing
21-23 . . . . Bowling Green
25-27 . . . .at Fort Wayne
28-30 . . . . South Bend

MAY
1-3 . . . . at Lansing
4-6 . . . . . . Bowling Green
7-9 . . . . at Lansing
10-12 . . . . at Dayton
13-15 . . . . West Michigan
17-19 . . . . . . Fort Wayne
20-23 . . . . . . at Dayton
24-26 . . . . at South Bend
27-30 . . . . West Michigan
31 . . . . Kane County

JUNE
1-2 . . . . . . Kane County
3-5 . . . . Clinton
7-9 . . . .at Wisconsin
10-12 . . . . at Beloit
14-16 . . . . . . Great Lakes
17-19 . . .at West Michigan
24-26 . . . .at Fort Wayne

13-15 . . . . West Michigan
17-19 . . . . . . at Dayton
20-23 . . . . Bowling Green
24-26 . . . . Dayton
27-30 . . . at Bowling Green
31 . . . . at Lansing

SEPTEMBER
1-2 . . . . at Lansing
3-5 . . . . South Bend

30 . . . . Beloit

JULY
1-2 . . . . Beloit
3-5 . . . . Quad Cities
6-8 . . . . .at Wisconsin
9-11 . . . . Burlington
13-15 . . . . .Lansing
16-18 . . . . . . Great Lakes
20-22 . . . at West Michigan
23-25 . . . at South Bend
27-29 . . . . . Cedar Rapids
30-31 . . .at Quad Cities

AUGUST
1 . . . . .at Quad Cities
2-5 . . . . at Beloit
6-9 . . . . Wisconsin
10-12 . . . . .Peoria
13-15 . . .at Cedar Rapids
17-19 . . . . Beloit
20-23 . . . . . . at Clinton
24-26 . . . .at Wisconsin
27-30 . . . . .Peoria
31 . . . . . .at Cedar Rapids

SEPTEMBER
1-2 . . . . . .at Cedar Rapids
3-5 . . . . Clinton

27-29 . . . . Fort Wayne
30 . . . . South Bend

JULY
1-2 . . . . South Bend
3-5 . . . . at Lansing
6-8 . . . . . at Bowling Green
9-11 . . . . .Lansing
13-15 . . . . at Peoria
16-18 . . . . . . at Burlington
20-22 . . . . . Quad Cities
23-25 . . . . . Cedar Rapids
27-29 . . . . . Bowling Green
30-31 . . . . . . at Lansing

AUGUST
1 . . . . at Lansing
2-5 . . . . .at Great Lakes
6-9 . . . . Dayton
10-12 . . . . . Great Lakes
13-15 . . . . . . at Dayton
17-19 . . . . at South Bend
20-23 . . . . . Fort Wayne
24-26 . . . .at West Michigan
27-30 . . . . at South Bend
31 . . . . . West Michigan

SEPTEMBER
1-2 . . . . . . West Michigan
3-5 . . . . . . Bowling Green

LANSING

APRIL
7-9 . . . . . . West Michigan
10 . . . . . .at West Michigan
11-14 . . . . . at South Bend
15-17 . . . . Dayton
18-20 . . . at Lake County
21-23 . . .at West Michigan
25-27 . . . . . Great Lakes
28 . . . . . . West Michigan
29-30 . . .at West Michigan

MAY
1-3 . . . . . . .Lake County
4-6 . . . . . at Fort Wayne
7-9 . . . . . . .Lake County
10-12 . . . . .at Great Lakes
13-15 . . . . . Great Lakes
17-19 . . . . at South Bend
20-23 . . . . Bowling Green
24-26 . . . . . . Fort Wayne
27-30 . . . at Bowling Green
31 . . . . .Peoria

JUNE
1-2 . . . . .Peoria
3-5 . . . . Burlington
7-9 . . . . . . .at Quad Cities
10-12 . . . .at Cedar Rapids
14-16 . . . . . . South Bend
17-19 . . . . . . at Dayton

JUNE
24-26 . . . . . . Great Lakes
27-29 . . . . at Dayton
30 . . . . . . .at Great Lakes

JULY
1-2 . . . . . . .at Great Lakes
3-5 . . . . . .Lake County
6-8 . . . . . West Michigan
9-11 . . . . at Lake County
13-15 . . . .at Kane County
16-18 . . . . . . at Clinton
20-22 . . . . . . Wisconsin
23-25 . . . . Beloit
27-29 . . .at West Michigan
30-31 . . . . . .Lake County

AUGUST
1 . . . . .Lake County
2-5 . . . . . . South Bend
6-9 . . . . . .at Fort Wayne
10-12 . . . . at South Bend
13-15 . . . . . . Fort Wayne
17-19 . . . at Bowling Green
20-23 . . . . Dayton
24-26 . . . . Bowling Green
27-30 . . . .at Fort Wayne
31 . . . . Great Lakes

SEPTEMBER
1-2 . . . . Great Lakes
3-5 . . . . at Dayton

PEORIA

APRIL
7-10 . . . . . . Cedar Rapids
11-14 . . . . . at Burlington
15-17 . . . . .at Wisconsin
18-20 . . .at Quad Cities
21-23 . . . . Beloit
25-27 . . . . at Clinton
28-30 . . . . . at Beloit

MAY
1-3 . . . . . . at Burlington
4-6 . . . .
7-9 . . . . . . Kane County
10-12 . . . . . Burlington
13-15 . . .at Kane County
17-19 . . . . Quad Cities
20-23 . . . . Clinton
24-26 . . . . . . Wisconsin
27-30 . . .at Cedar Rapids
31 . . . . at Lansing

JUNE
1-2 . . . . at Lansing
3-5 . . . . . .at Great Lakes
7-9 . . . . . West Michigan
10-12 . . . . South Bend
14-16 . . . . . . Wisconsin
17-19 . . . .at Quad Cities
24-26 . . . . . Kane County

QUAD CITIES

APRIL
7-10 . . . . Beloit
11-14 . . .at Kane County
15-17 . . . . .Burlington
18-20 . . . . .Peoria
21-23 . . .at Cedar Rapids
25-27 . . .at Wisconsin
28-30 . . . . . Cedar Rapids

MAY
1-3 . . . . Wisconsin

27-29 . . . . .at Wisconsin
30 . . . . . . at Burlington

JULY
1-2 . . . . . . at Burlington
3-5 . . . . Clinton
6-8 . . . . Beloit
9-11 . . . . .at Cedar Rapids
13-15 . . . .Lake County
16-18 . . . . . . Fort Wayne
20-22 . . . . . . at Dayton
23-25 . . . at Bowling Green
27-29 . . .at Quad Cities
30-31 . . . . at Clinton

AUGUST
1 . . . . at Clinton
2-5 . . . . Burlington
6-9 . . . . Cedar Rapids
10-12 . . . .at Kane County
13-15 . . . . Clinton
17-19 . . . . . . Wisconsin
20-23 . . . .at Cedar Rapids
24-26 . . . . Quad Cities
27-30 . . . .at Kane County
31 . . . . at Beloit

SEPTEMBER
1-2 . . . . at Beloit
3-5 . . . . Quad Cities

MAY
4-6 . . . . . .at Kane County
7-9 . . . . . . .at Wisconsin
10-12 . . . . . at Clinton
13-15 . . . . . at Beloit
17-19 . . . . . at Peoria
20-23 . . . . Cedar Rapids
24-26 . . . . Kane County
27-30 . . . . at Burlington
31 . . . .at West Michigan

JUNE
1-2 . . . . . . .at West Michigan
3-5 . . . . . . at South Bend
7-9 . . . . .Lansing
10-12 . . . . . Great Lakes
14-16 . . . . . . at Clinton
17-19 . . . . .Peoria
24-26 . . . . .at Wisconsin
27-29 . . . . Cedar Rapids
30 . . . . Clinton

JULY
1-2 . . . . Clinton
3-5 . . . . .at Kane County
6-8 . . . . . . at Burlington
9-11 . . . . . . Wisconsin
13-15 . . . . Dayton
16-18 . . . . Bowling Green
20-22 . . . at Lake County

SOUTH BEND

APRIL
7-10 . . . . . .at Fort Wayne
11-14 . . . . .Lansing
15-17 . . . . West Michigan
18-20 . . .at Great Lakes
21-23 . . . . Fort Wayne
25-27 . . . at Bowling Green
28-30 . . . at Lake County

MAY
1-3 . . . . Great Lakes
4-6 . . . . at Dayton
7-9 . . . . Fort Wayne
10-12 . . .at West Michigan
13-15 . . . at Bowling Green
17-19 . . . . .Lansing
20-23 . . . . .at Great Lakes
24-26 . . . . .Lake County
27-30 . . . . Dayton
31 . . . . Cedar Rapids

JUNE
1-2 . . . . Cedar Rapids
3-5 . . . . Quad Cities
7-9 . . . . . at Burlington
10-12 . . . . . . at Peoria
14-16 . . . . . at Lansing
17-19 . . . . Bowling Green
24-26 . . . . . West Michigan

27-29 . . .at West Michigan
30 . . . . . . at Lake County

JULY
1-2 . . . . . at Lake County
3-5 . . . . Dayton
6-8 . . . . . . Great Lakes
9-11 . . . . . . at Dayton
13-15 . . . . . . at Beloit
16-18 . . . . . .at Wisconsin
20-22 . . . . Clinton
23-25 . . . . . Kane County
27-29 . . .at Great Lakes
30-31 . . . . . West Michigan

AUGUST
1 . . . . West Michigan
2-5 . . . . at Lansing
6-9 . . . . . . Bowling Green
10-12 . . . . .Lansing
13-15 . . . at Bowling Green
17-19 . . . . .Lake County
20-23 . . .at West Michigan
24-26 . . . . . Fort Wayne
27-30 . . . .Lake County
31 . . . . at Fort Wayne

SEPTEMBER
1-2 . . . . . .at Fort Wayne
3-5 . . . . . . .at Great Lakes

WEST MICHIGAN

APRIL
7-9 . . . . at Lansing
10 . . . . .Lansing
11-14 . . . . . Great Lakes
15-17 . . . . at South Bend
18-20 . . . . . . Fort Wayne
. . . .
21-23 . . . . .Lansing
25-27 . . . . . at Dayton
28 . . . . at Lansing
29-30 . . . . .Lansing

MAY
1-3 . . . . . . .at Fort Wayne
4-6 . . . . .at Great Lakes
7-9 . . . . Dayton
10-12 . . . . . South Bend
13-15 . . . . at Lake County
17-19 . . . at Bowling Green
20-23 . . . . . . Fort Wayne
24-26 . . . . Bowling Green
27-30 . . . .at Lake County
31 . . . . Quad Cities

JUNE
1-2 . . . . Quad Cities

3-5 . . . . Cedar Rapids
7-9 . . . . at Burlington
10-12 . . . at Burlington
14-16 . . . at Bowling Green
17-19 . . . .Lake County
24-26 . . . . at South Bend
27-29 . . . . . South Bend
30 . . . . Fort Wayne

JULY
1-2 . . . . Fort Wayne
3-5 . . . . . .at Fort Wayne
6-8 . . . . at Lansing
9-11 . . . . . Bowling Green
13-15 . . . .at Wisconsin
16-18 . . . . . at Beloit
20-22 . . . . Kane County
23-25 . . . . Clinton
27-29 . . . . .Lansing
30-31 . . . at South Bend

AUGUST
1 . . . . at South Bend
2-5 . . . . at Dayton
6-9 . . . . Great Lakes
10-12 . . . . Dayton

13-15 . . . . . .at Great Lakes
17-19 . . . . . .at Fort Wayne
20-23 . . . . . . South Bend
24-26 . . . . . .Lake County
27-30 . . . . . . at Dayton

WISCONSIN

APRIL
7-10 . . . . . . Kane County
11-14 . . . .at Cedar Rapids
15-17 . . . . .Peoria
18-20 . . . . Beloit
21-23 . . . . . at Burlington
25-27 . . . . . Quad Cities
28-30 . . . . Clinton

MAY
1-3 . . . . . . .at Quad Cities
4-6 . . . . at Beloit
7-9 . . . . . . Quad Cities
10-12 . . . . . Cedar Rapids
13-15 . . . . . . at Clinton
17-19 . . . . Beloit
20-23 . . . . . . Burlington
24-26 . . . . . . at Peoria
27-30 . . . .at Kane County
31 . . . . . at Bowling Green

JUNE
1-2 . . . . at Bowling Green
3-5 . . . . at Dayton
7-9 . . . . .Lake County
10-12 . . . . . Fort Wayne
14-16 . . . . . . at Peoria
17-19 . . .at Cedar Rapids
24-26 . . . . . . Quad Cities
27-29 . . . . Peoria

31 . . . . at Lake County

SEPTEMBER
1-2 . . . . . at Lake County
3-5 . . . . Fort Wayne

30 . . . . . .at Cedar Rapids

JULY
1-2 . . . . . .at Cedar Rapids
3-5 . . . . at Beloit
6-8 . . . . . . Kane County
9-11 . . . .at Quad Cities
13-15 . . . . . West Michigan
16-18 . . . . . . South Bend
20-22 . . . . . . at Lansing
23-25 . . . .at Great Lakes
27-29 . . . . . at Clinton
30-31 . . . . . . .Burlington

AUGUST
1 . . . . Burlington
2-5 . . . . Clinton
6-9 . . . .at Kane County
10-12 . . . . Beloit
13-15 . . . . . Quad Cities
17-19 . . . . . . at Peoria
20-23 . . . . . at Burlington
24-26 . . . . . Kane County
27-30 . . . . Cedar Rapids
31 . . . . at Burlington

SEPTEMBER
1-2 . . . . . at Burlington
3-5 . . . . . . at Beloit

SOUTH ATLANTIC LEAGUE

ASHEVILLE

APRIL
7-10 . . . . at Hickory
11-14 . . . .at West Virginia
15-18 . . . . . . Lexington
19-23 . . . . . . Lakewood
25-29 . . . . . . at Rome
30 . . . . .at Greenville

MAY
1-3 . . . . . . .at Greenville
5-8 . . . . Delmarva
9-12 . . . . . . Greenville
13-16 . . . . . .at Lexington
17-19 . . . . Rome
20-23 . . . . . . Lexington
25-28 . . . . at Hagerstown
29-31 . . . . .at Greenville

JUNE
1-4 . . . . Augusta
5-7 . . . . Savannah
9-11 . . . . . . at Charleston
12-15 . . . . . . .Hickory
16-19 . . . . . .at Augusta

23-26 . . . . Rome
27-30 . . . . . .at Greenville

JULY
1-3 . . . . . at Kannapolis
4-6 . . . . Greenville
7-10 . . . . Augusta
12-15 . . . . . . at Delmarva
16-18 . . . . at Greensboro
20-22 . . . . . .Kannapolis
23-26 . . . . . Greensboro
28-31 . . . . at Kannapolis

AUGUST
1-4 . . . . .Charleston
5-8 . . . . .Hickory
10-13 . . . . at Rome
14-17 . . . . . .at Savannah
18-21 . . . . Rome
22-25 . . . . .at Lexington
26-30 . . . . . .Hagerstown

SEPTEMBER
1-5 . . . . . at Charlestown

AUGUSTA

APRIL
7-10 . . . . . .at Greenville
11-14 . . . . . . at Rome
15-18 . . . . . West Virginia
19-23 . . . . Delmarva
25-29 . . . . . . at Hickory
30 . . . . .at Lexington

MAY
1-3 . . . . .at Lexington
5-8 . . . . West Virginia
9-12 . . . . Rome
13-16 . . . . at Hickory
17-19 . . . . Greenville
20-23 . . . . . at Charleston
25-28 . . . . Savannah

29-31 . . . . at Rome

JUNE
1-4 . . . . at Asheville
5-7 . . . . .Charleston
9-11 . . . . . . .at Savannah
12-15 . . . . . . Lexington
16-19 . . . . Asheville
23-26 . . . . . at Savannah
27-30 . . . . . . .Charleston

JULY
1-3 . . . . Savannah
4-6 . . . . . at Charleston
7-10 . . . . . at Asheville
12-15 . . . . Hagerstown
16-18 . . . . . Savannah

CHARLESTON

APRIL
7-10 . . . .at Lexington
11-14 . . . .at Greenville
15-18 . . . . Rome
19-23 . . . . Greenville
25-29 . . . . at Lakewood
30 . . . . .at Delmarva

MAY
1-3 . . . . .at Delmarva
5-8 . . . . Lakewood
9-12 . . . . . West Virginia
13-16 . . . .at Greenville
17-19 . . . . . . Savannah
20-23 . . . . . . Augusta
25-28 . . . . . at Hickory
29-31 . . . .at Savannah

JUNE
1-4 . . . . Rome
5-7 . . . . .at Augusta
9-11 . . . . Asheville
12-15 . . . . . . Greenville
16-19 . . . . . at Hickory

20-22 . . . . . at Hagerstown
23-26 . . . . at Lakewood
28-31 . . . . .Hickory

AUGUST
1-4 . . . . .at Savannah
5-8 . . . . Rome
10-13 . . . . .at Lexington
14-17 . . . . at Greensboro
18-21 . . . . . . .Charleston
22-25 . . . . . .Kannapolis
26-30 . . . . . .at Greenville

SEPTEMBER
1-5 . . . . Rome

23-26 . . . . . .Kannapolis
27-30 . . . . . . .at Augusta

JULY
1-3 . . . . at Rome
4-6 . . . . Augusta
7-10 . . . . Delmarva
12-15 . . . . at Greensboro
16-18 . . . . .at West Virginia
20-22 . . . . Lexington
23-26 . . . . . West Virginia
28-31 . . . . .at Greenville

AUGUST
1-4 . . . . at Asheville
5-8 . . . . Savannah
10-13 . . . . .at West Virginia
14-17 . . . . .Hickory
18-21 . . . . . .at Augusta
22-25 . . . . . Greenville
26-30 . . . . .at Savannah

SEPTEMBER
1-5 . . . . .Asheville

DELMARVA

APRIL
7-10 . . . . . . Greensboro
11-14 . . . . . .Kannapolis
15-18 . . . . at Greensboro
19-23 . . . . . .at Augusta
25-29 . . . . . . Savannah
30 . . . . .Charleston

MAY
1-3 . . . . .Charleston
5-8 . . . . at Asheville
9-12 . . . . . at Hagerstown
13-16 . . . . . Greensboro
17-19 . . . . . . Lakewood
20-23 . . . .at Kannapolis
25-28 . . . . . West Virginia
29-31 . . . . . at Lakewood

JUNE
1-4 . . . . .Hickory
5-7 . . . . .at West Virginia
9-11 . . . . . .Hagerstown
12-15 . . . . .at Kannapolis
16-19 . . . . . at Hagerstown

23-26 . . . . . at Lakewood
27-30 . . . . . . Greensboro

JULY
1-3 . . . . Lakewood
4-6 . . . . at Hickory
7-10 . . . . . at Charleston
12-15 . . . . Asheville
16-18 . . . . . . .Hickory
20-22 . . . . . . at Rome
23-26 . . . . . . at Hickory
28-31 . . . . . .Hagerstown

AUGUST
1-4 . . . . Lakewood
5-8 . . . . . . .at Kannapolis
10-13 . . . . . .Hagerstown
14-17 . . . . . at Lakewood
18-21 . . . .at West Virginia
22-25 . . . . Lakewood
26-30 . . . . at Greensboro

SEPTEMBER
1-5 . . . . West Virginia

GREENSBORO

APRIL
7-10 . . . . . .at Delmarva
11-14 . . . . at Lakewood
15-18 . . . . . . Delmarva
19-23 . . . . .Rome
25-29 . . . . . at Greenville

30 . . . . . .at West Virginia

MAY
1-3 . . . . . .at West Virginia
5-8 . . . . .Hickory
9-12 . . . . Lakewood

13-16 . . . . . . at Delmarva	12-15 . . . . Charleston
17-19 . . . . at Hickory	16-18 . . . . Asheville
20-23 . . . . Hagerstown	20-22 . . . . at Hickory
25-28 . . . . . at Lakewood	23-26 . . . . . . at Asheville
29-31 . . . . Lexington	28-31 . . . . Savannah

JUNE	AUGUST
1-4 . . . . Lakewood	1-4 . . . . . at West Virginia
5-7 . . . . . at Hagerstown	5-8 . . . . . . at Hagerstown
9-11 . . . . . . .Kannapolis	10-13 . . . . . . Lakewood
12-15 . . . . West Virginia	14-17 . . . . Augusta
16-19 . . . . at Kannapolis	18-21 . . . . at Lakewood
23-26 . . . . . . Hagerstown	22-25 . . . . West Virginia
27-30 . . . . . at Delmarva	26-30 . . . . . . Delmarva

JULY	SEPTEMBER
1-3 . . . . .at West Virginia	1-5 . . . . . . at Kannapolis
4-6 . . . . .Kannapolis	
7-10 . . . . . . at Savannah	

GREENVILLE

APRIL	
7-10 . . . . Augusta	23-26 . . . . . .at Lexington
11-14 . . . . . . .Charleston	27-30 . . . . . . Asheville
15-18 . . . . . at Savannah	
19-23 . . at Charleston	JULY
25-29 . . . . . Greensboro	1-3 . . . . .Hickory
30 . . . . Asheville	4-6 . . . . at Asheville

MAY	7-10 . . . . at Rome
1-3 . . . . Asheville	12-15 . . . . . . Lakewood
5-8 . . . . . . at Kannapolis	16-18 . . . . Rome
9-12 . . . . . at Asheville	20-22 . . . . at Lakewood
13-16 . . . . .Charleston	23-26 . . . at Hagerstown
17-19 . . . . . .at Augusta	28-31 . . . . . . .Charleston
20-23 . . . . . .at Savannah	
25-28 . . . . . .Kannapolis	AUGUST
29-31 . . . . . Asheville	1-4 . . . . at Rome

JUNE	5-8 . . . . Lexington
1-4 . . . . at Hagerstown	10-13 . . . at Savannah
5-7 . . . . . . Lexington	14-17 . . . . Rome
9-11 . . . . . . at Rome	18-21 . . . . . . Savannah
12-15 . . . . at Charleston	22-25 . . . at Charleston
16-19 . . . . . Savannah	26-30 . . . . Augusta

	SEPTEMBER
	1-5 . . . . at Hickory

HAGERSTOWN

APRIL	
7-10 . . . . at Rome	23-26 . . . . at Greensboro
11-14 . . . . . .at Lexington	27-30 . . . . Lakewood
15-18 . . . . . . Lakewood	
19-23 . . . . .Hickory	JULY
25-29 . . . .at West Virginia	1-3 . . . . Lexington
30 . . . . at Rome	4-6 . . . . at Lakewood

MAY	7-10 . . . . . West Virginia
1-3 . . . . at Rome	12-15 . . . . . .at Augusta
5-8 . . . . Lexington	16-18 . . . . . .at Lexington
9-12 . . . . Delmarva	20-22 . . . . . . Augusta
13-16 . . . . at Lakewood	23-26 . . . . . . Greenville
17-19 . . . . . .Kannapolis	28-31 . . . . .at Delmarva
20-23 . . . . at Greensboro	
25-28 . . . . . Asheville	AUGUST
29-31 . . . . at Kannapolis	1-4 . . . . at Hickory

JUNE	5-8 . . . . Greensboro
1-4 . . . . Greenville	10-13 . . . . at Delmarva
5-7 . . . . . . Greensboro	14-17 . . . . . . Lexington
9-11 . . . . . .at Delmarva	18-21 . . . . at Kannapolis
12-15 . . . . at Lakewood	22-25 . . . . Hickory
16-19 . . . . . . Delmarva	26-30 . . . . . at Asheville

	SEPTEMBER
	1-5 . . . . Lakewood

HICKORY

APRIL	
7-10 . . . . Asheville	19-23 . . . . at Hagerstown
11-14 . . . . . . Savannah	25-29 . . . . Augusta
15-18 . . . . . at Kannapolis	30 . . . . .Kannapolis

MAY	4-6 . . . . .Delmarva
1-3 . . . . .Kannapolis	7-10 . . . . Lexington
5-8 . . . . .at Greensboro	12-15 . . . at West Virginia
9-12 . . . . . .at Savannah	16-18 . . . . at Delmarva
13-16 . . . . . . Augusta	20-22 . . . . . Greensboro
17-19 . . . . . Greensboro	23-26 . . . . . . .Delmarva
20-23 . . . . . at Rome	28-31 . . . . . .at Augusta
25-28 . . . . .Charleston	
29-31 . . . .at West Virginia	AUGUST

JUNE	1-4 . . . . Hagerstown
1-4 . . . . at Delmarva	5-8 . . . . . . at Asheville
5-7 . . . . Lakewood	10-13 . . . . . . .Kannapolis
9-11 . . . . . .at Lexington	14-17 . . . . at Charleston
12-15 . . . . . at Asheville	18-21 . . . . . . Lexington
16-19 . . . . . .Charleston	22-25 . . . . at Hagerstown
23-26 . . . . . West Virginia	26-30 . . . . . . Lakewood
27-30 . . . . . at Kannapolis	

JULY	SEPTEMBER
1-3 . . . . . . .at Greenville	1-5 . . . . Greenville

KANNAPOLIS

APRIL	
7-10 . . . . . . at Lakewood	23-26 . . . . . at Charleston
11-14 . . . . .at Delmarva	27-30 . . . . . . .Hickory
15-18 . . . . . . .Hickory	
19-23 . . . . West Virginia	JULY
25-29 . . . . .at Lexington	1-3 . . . . Asheville
30 . . . . at Hickory	4-6 . . . . . at Greensboro

MAY	7-10 . . . . . . at Lakewood
1-3 . . . . at Hickory	12-15 . . . . Rome
5-8 . . . . Greenville	16-18 . . . . . . Lakewood
9-12 . . . . Lexington	20-22 . . . . . at Asheville
13-16 . . . .at West Virginia	23-26 . . . . . . at Rome
17-19 . . . . at Hagerstown	28-31 . . . . Asheville
20-23 . . . . . Delmarva	
25-28 . . . .at Greenville	AUGUST
29-31 . . . . . Hagerstown	1-4 . . . . .at Lexington

JUNE	5-8 . . . . Delmarva
1-4 . . . . .at Savannah	10-13 . . . . . . at Hickory
5-7 . . . . Rome	14-17 . . . . West Virginia
9-11 . . . . . at Greensboro	18-21 . . . . . Hagerstown
12-15 . . . . . . Delmarva	22-25 . . . . . .at Augusta
16-19 . . . . . Greensboro	26-30 . . . . . . at Rome

	SEPTEMBER
	1-5 . . . . Greensboro

LAKEWOOD

APRIL	
7-10 . . . . .Kannapolis	23-26 . . . . . . Delmarva
11-14 . . . . . . Greensboro	27-30 . . . . at Hagerstown
15-18 . . . . at Hagerstown	
19-23 . . . . at Asheville	JULY
25-29 . . . . .Charleston	1-3 . . . . at Delmarva
30 . . . . Savannah	4-6 . . . . Hagerstown

MAY	7-10 . . . . .Kannapolis
1-3 . . . . Savannah	12-15 . . . . .at Greenville
5-8 . . . . . . at Charleston	16-18 . . . . at Kannapolis
9-12 . . . . at Greensboro	20-22 . . . . . Greenville
13-16 . . . . .Hagerstown	23-26 . . . . . . Augusta
17-19 . . . . . at Delmarva	28-31 . . . .at West Virginia
20-23 . . . .at West Virginia	
25-28 . . . . Greensboro	AUGUST
29-31 . . . . . . Delmarva	1-4 . . . . at Delmarva

JUNE	5-8 . . . . . . West Virginia
1-4 . . . . . at Greensboro	10-13 . . . . at Greensboro
5-7 . . . . at Hickory	14-17 . . . . Delmarva
9-11 . . . . . West Virginia	18-21 . . . . . . Greensboro
12-15 . . . . .Hagerstown	22-25 . . . . at Delmarva
16-19 . . . .at West Virginia	26-30 . . . . . . .Hickory

	SEPTEMBER
	1-5 . . . . . . at Hagerstown

LEXINGTON LEGENDS

APRIL	
7-10 . . . . .Charleston	11-14 . . . . . .Hagerstown
	15-18 . . . . . . at Asheville

19-23 . . . . . .at Savannah
25-29 . . . . . .Kannapolis
30 . . . . Augusta

MAY
1-3 . . . . Augusta
5-8 . . . . . at Hagerstown
9-12 . . . . . .at Kannapolis
13-16 . . . . Asheville
17-19 . . . . West Virginia
20-23 . . . . . at Asheville
25-28 . . . . Rome
29-31 . . . at Greensboro

JUNE
1-4 . . . . West Virginia
5-7 . . . . . .at Greenville
9-11 . . . . . . .Hickory
12-15 . . . . . .at Augusta
16-19 . . . . . . at Rome
23-26 . . . . . . Greenville
27-39 . . . .at West Virginia

ROME

APRIL
7-10 . . . . . . .Hagerstown
11-14 . . . . Augusta
15-18 . . . . at Charleston
19-23 . . . . at Greensboro
25-29 . . . . Asheville
30 . . . . .Hagerstown

MAY
1-3 . . . . .Hagerstown
5-8 . . . . .at Savannah
9-12 . . . . . .at Augusta
13-16 . . . . Savannah
17-19 . . . . at Asheville
20-23 . . . . . . .Hickory
25-28 . . . . . .at Lexington
29-31 . . . . . . Augusta

JUNE
1-4 . . . . at Charleston
5-7 . . . . . .at Kannapolis
9-11 . . . . Greenville
12-15 . . . . .at Savannah
16-19 . . . . . . Lexington

23-26 . . . . . . at Asheville
27-30 . . . . Savannah

JULY
1-3 . . . . .Charleston
4-6 . . . . . . .at Savannah
7-10 . . . . . . Greenville
12-15 . . . at Kannapolis
16-18 . . . .at Greenville
20-22 . . . . . . Delmarva
23-26 . . . . . .Kannapolis
28-31 . . . . .at Lexington

AUGUST
1-4 . . . . Greenville
5-8 . . . . .at Augusta
10-13 . . . . Asheville
14-17 . . . .at Greenville
18-21 . . . . at Asheville
22-25 . . . . . . Savannah
26-30 . . . . . .Kannapolis

SEPTEMBER
1-5 . . . . .at Augusta

SAVANNAH

APRIL
7-10 . . . . .at West Virginia
11-14 . . . . at Hickory
15-18 . . . . . . Greenville
19-23 . . . . . . Lexington
25-29 . . . at Delmarva
30 . . . . at Lakewood

MAY
1-3 . . . . at Lakewood
5-8 . . . . Rome
9-12 . . . . .Hickory
12-16 . . . . at Rome
17-19 . . . at Charleston
20-23 . . . . . . Greenville
25-28 . . . . . .at Augusta
29-31 . . . .Charleston

JUNE
1-4 . . . . .Kannapolis
5-7 . . . . at Asheville
9-11 . . . . Augusta
12-15 . . . . Rome
16-19 . . . . .at Greenville

23-26 . . . . Augusta
27-30 . . . . at Rome

JULY
1-3 . . . . .at Augusta
4-6 . . . . Rome
7-10 . . . . Greensboro
12-15 . . . . .at Lexington
16-18 . . . . .at Augusta
20-22 . . . . . West Virginia
23-26 . . . . . . Lexington
28-31 . . . at Greensboro

AUGUST
1-4 . . . . Augusta
5-8 . . . . . at Charleston
10-13 . . . . . Greenville
14-17 . . . . . . Asheville
18-21 . . . .at Greenville
22-25 . . . . . at Rome
26-30 . . . . . . .Charleston

SEPTEMBER
1-5 . . . . .at Lexington

WEST VIRGINIA

APRIL
7-10 . . . . Savannah
11-14 . . . . . . Asheville
15-18 . . . . . .at Augusta
19-23 . . . .at Kannapolis
25-29 . . . .Hagerstown
30 . . . . Greensboro

MAY
1-3 . . . . Greensboro
5-8 . . . . .at Augusta
9-12 . . . at Charleston
13-16 . . . . . .Kannapolis
17-19 . . . .at Lexington
20-23 . . . . . . Lakewood
25-28 . . . . at Delmarva
29-31 . . . . . . .Hickory

JUNE
1-4 . . . . .at Lexington
5-7 . . . . Delmarva
9-11 . . . . . . at Lakewood
12-15 . . . . at Greensboro
16-19 . . . . Lakewood

23-26 . . . . . . at Hickory
27-30 . . . . Lexington

JULY
1-3 . . . . Greensboro
4-6 . . . . . . at Lexington
7-10 . . . . . at Hagerstown
12-15 . . . . . . .Hickory
16-18 . . . . . .Charleston
20-22 . . . . . .at Savannah
23-26 . . . at Charleston
28-31 . . . . . . Lakewood

AUGUST
1-4 . . . . Greensboro
5-8 . . . . . at Lakewood
10-13 . . . . .Charleston
14-17 . . . . at Kannapolis
18-21 . . . . . Delmarva
22-25 . . . . at Greensboro
26-30 . . . . . . Lexington

SEPTEMBER
1-5 . . . . .at Delmarva

SHORT SEASON

NEW YORK-PENN LEAGUE

ABERDEEN

JUNE
17-19 . . . . . Hudson Valley
20-22 . . . . at Brooklyn
23-25 . . . . . . Staten Island
26-28 . . . . Brooklyn
29-30 . . . .at Staten Island

JULY
1 . . . . .at Staten Island
2-3 . . . . .at Hudson Valley
4-5 . . . . . . Hudson Valley
6-8 . . . . .Lowell
9-11 . . . . .at Tri-City
13-15 . . . . Vermont
16-18 . . . . . .at Vermont
19-20 . . . . Brooklyn
21-22 . . . . . . at Brooklyn

23-25 . . . . Batavia
27-29 . . . . . .at Jamestown
30-31 . . . .Mahoning Valley

AUGUST
1 . . . . .Mahoning Valley
2-4 . . . . .at Lowell
5-6 . . . . . .at Hudson Valley
7-8 . . . . . . Hudson Valley
9-11 . . . . . at State College
12-14 . . . . . . Williamsport
17-19 . . . . . . at Auburn
20-22 . . . . . at Connecticut
23-25 . . . . . .Connecticut
26-27 . . . . . Staten Island
28-29 . . . .at Staten Island
30-31 . . . . Tri-City

SEPTEMBER
1 . . . . Tri-City

AUBURN

JUNE
17 . . . . at Batavia
18 . . . . Batavia
19 . . . . at Batavia
20-22 . . . . at State College
23-25 . . . .Mahoning Valley
26-28 . . . . .Williamsport
29-30 . . . at Williamsport

JULY
1 . . . . at Williamsport
2-3 . . . . at State College
4-5 . . . . . . State College
6-8 . . . . . .at Jamestown
9-11 . . . . Jamestown
13-15 . . . . . . at Brooklyn

2-4 . . . . . .at Hudson Valley

SEPTEMBER
1 . . . . Tri-City

16 . . . . Batavia
17 . . . . at Batavia
18 . . . . Batavia
19-20 . . . .at Williamsport
21-22 . . . . . .Williamsport
23-25 . . . . . .at Lowell
27-29 . . . .Hudson Valley
30-31 . . . . .at Tri-City

AUGUST
1 . . . . .at Tri-City
2-4 . . . . .Connecticut
5-6 . . . at Mahoning Valley
7-8 . . . . . Mahoning Valley
9-11 . . . . Vermont
12-14 . . . .at Staten Island

17-19 . . . . Aberdeen
20-22 . . . . . State College
23-25 . . at Mahoning Valley
26 . . . . Batavia
27 . . . . at Batavia
28 . . . . Batavia

BATAVIA

JUNE
17 . . . . Auburn
18 . . . . at Auburn
19 . . . . Auburn
20-22 . . at Mahoning Valley
23-25 . . . . at Williamsport
26-28 . . . . . Jamestown
29-30 . . .at Jamestown
JULY
1 . . . . . .at Jamestown
2-3 . . . at Mahoning Valley
4-5 . . . . . Mahoning Valley
6-8 . . . . State College
9-11 . . . . at State College
13-15 . . . . Tri-City
16 . . . . at Auburn
17 . . . . Auburn
18 . . . . at Auburn
19-20 . . .at Jamestown
21-22 . . . . . Jamestown
23-25 . . . . . .at Aberdeen
27-29 . . . . . Staten Island

BROOKLYN

JUNE
17 . . . . . .at Staten Island
18-19 . . . . Staten Island
20-22 . . . . . . Aberdeen
23-24 . . . at Hudson Valley
25 . . . . . .Hudson Valley
26-28 . . . .at Aberdeen
29 . . . . . .Hudson Valley
30 . . . . at Hudson Valley
JULY
1 . . . . . .at Hudson Valley
2 . . . . . .at Staten Island
3 . . . . Staten Island
4-5 . . . . . .at Staten Island
6-8 . . . . Vermont
9-11 . . . . at Connecticut
13-15 . . . . Auburn
16-18 . . . . .Lowell
19-20 . . . . . .at Aberdeen
21-22 . . . . Aberdeen
23-25 . . . . at State College
27-29 . . . . . Connecticut

CONNECTICUT

JUNE
17-19 . . . . .at Lowell
20-22 . . . . Tri-City
23-25 . . . .at Vermont
26-28 . . . .at Tri-City
29-30 . . . . Vermont
JULY
1 . . . . Vermont
2-3 . . . . .Lowell
4-5 . . . . at Lowell
6-8 . . . . . .at Staten Island
9-11 . . . . Brooklyn
13-15 . . at Mahoning Valley
16-18 . . . at Hudson Valley
19-20 . . . . .at Tri-City

29-30 . . . . .at Jamestown
31 . . . . Jamestown
SEPTEMBER
1 . . . . Jamestown
2 . . . . Batavia
3-4 . . . . at Batavia

30-31 . . . . . at Connecticut
AUGUST
1 . . . . at Connecticut
2-4 . . . . . at Hudson Valley
5-6 . . . . .Williamsport
7-8 . . . . .at Williamsport
9-11 . . . . Brooklyn
12-14 . . . . Vermont
17-19 . . . . . . at Lowell
20-22 . . . . Mahoning Valley
23-25 . . . . .Williamsport
26 . . . . at Auburn
27 . . . . Auburn
28 . . . . at Auburn
29-30 . . . . . State College
31 . . . . . . at State College
SEPTEMBER
1 . . . . . . at State College
2 . . . . at Auburn
3-4 . . . . Auburn

30-31 . . . . . . .at Vermont
AUGUST
1 . . . . .at Vermont
2-4 . . . . .Williamsport
5 . . . . . .at Staten Island
6 . . . . Staten Island
7 . . . . . . .at Staten Island
8 . . . . Staten Island
9-11 . . . . at Batavia
12-14 . . at Mahoning Valley
17-19 . . . . . Jamestown
20-22 . . . . Tri-City
23-25 . . . . . .at Tri-City
26 . . . . . .Hudson Valley
27 . . . at Hudson Valley
28-29 . . . .Hudson Valley
30-31 . . . . . . at Lowell
SEPTEMBER
1 . . . . .at Lowell
2 . . . . Staten Island
3 . . . . . . .at Staten Island
4 . . . . Staten Island

21-22 . . . . Tri-City
23-25 . . . . .Williamsport
27-29 . . . . . at Brooklyn
30-31 . . . . Batavia
AUGUST
1 . . . . Batavia
2-4 . . . . at Auburn
5-6 . . . . at Lowell
7-8 . . . . .Lowell
9-11 . . . . Jamestown
12-14 . . . . at State College
17-19 . . . . . Staten Island
20-22 . . . . Aberdeen
23-25 . . . . .at Aberdeen
26-27 . . . . Vermont

28-29 . . . . . .at Vermont
30-31 . . . . .Hudson Valley

HUDSON VALLEY

JUNE
17-19 . . . . . .at Aberdeen
20 . . . . Staten Island
21 . . . . .at Staten Island
22 . . . . . . Staten Island
23-24 . . . . Brooklyn
25 . . . . at Brooklyn
26-27 . . .at Staten Island
28 . . . . . . Staten Island
29 . . . . . . at Brooklyn
30 . . . . Brooklyn
JULY
1 . . . . Brooklyn
2-3 . . . . Aberdeen
4-5 . . . . . . .at Aberdeen
6-8 . . . . Tri-City
9-11 . . . . at Lowell
13-15 . . . . .at Jamestown
16-18 . . . .Connecticut
19-20 . . . . Staten Island
21-22 . . . .at Staten Island

JAMESTOWN

JUNE
17-19 . . at Mahoning Valley
20-22 . . . . . Williamsport
23-25 . . . . . State College
26-28 . . . . . at Batavia
29-30 . . . . . . Batavia
JULY
1 . . . . Batavia
2-3 . . . . . . .Williamsport
4-5 . . . . at Williamsport
6-8 . . . . .Auburn
9-11 . . . . at Auburn
13-15 . . . . Hudson Valley
16-18 . . . Mahoning Valley
19-20 . . . . Batavia
21-22 . . . . . at Batavia
23-25 . . . . . . .at Vermont

LOWELL

JUNE
17-19 . . . . .Connecticut
20-22 . . . . . .at Vermont
23-25 . . . . . .at Tri-City
26-28 . . . . . . Vermont
29-30 . . . . Tri-City
JULY
1 . . . . Tri-City
2-3 . . . . . at Connecticut
4-5 . . . . .Connecticut
6-8 . . . . . . .at Aberdeen
9-11 . . . . .Hudson Valley
13-15 . . . . . .Williamsport
16-18 . . . . . at Brooklyn
19-20 . . . . . . Vermont
21-22 . . . . .at Vermont
23-25 . . . . . . .Auburn
27-29 . . at Mahoning Valley

MAHONING VALLEY

JUNE
17-19 . . . . . . Jamestown
20-22 . . . . Batavia

SEPTEMBER
1 . . . . .Hudson Valley
2-4 . . . . .Lowell

23-25 . . . . Mahoning Valley
27-29 . . . . at Auburn
30-31 . . . . . at Williamsport
AUGUST
1 . . . . . . .at Williamsport
2-4 . . . . Batavia
5-6 . . . . Aberdeen
7-8 . . . . .at Aberdeen
9-11 . . . . .Lowell
12-14 . . . . . .at Tri-City
17-19 . . . . . State College
20-22 . . . . . .at Vermont
23-25 . . . . Vermont
26 . . . . at Brooklyn
27 . . . . Brooklyn
28-29 . . . . . . at Brooklyn
30-31 . . . . at Connecticut
SEPTEMBER
1 . . . . .Connecticut
2-4 . . . . Aberdeen

27-29 . . . . Aberdeen
30-31 . . . .at Staten Island
AUGUST
1 . . . . .at Staten Island
2-4 . . . . Tri-City
5-6 . . . . at State College
7-8 . . . . . State College
9-11 . . . . at Connecticut
12-14 . . . . . . .Lowell
17-19 . . . . at Brooklyn
20-22 . . . .at Williamsport
23-25 . . . at State College
26-28 . . at Mahoning Valley
29-30 . . . . .Auburn
31 . . . . at Auburn
SEPTEMBER
2-4 . . . . . Mahoning Valley

30-31 . . . . at State College
AUGUST
1 . . . . . . at State College
2-4 . . . . Aberdeen
5-6 . . . . . . .Connecticut
7-8 . . . . . . at Connecticut
9-11 . . . . .at Hudson Valley
12-14 . . . .at Jamestown
17-19 . . . . Batavia
20-22 . . . . . Staten Island
23-25 . . . .at Staten Island
26-27 . . . . Tri-City
28-29 . . . . . .at Tri-City
30-31 . . . . Brooklyn
SEPTEMBER
1 . . . . Brooklyn
2-4 . . . . . . at Connecticut

23-25 . . . . at Auburn
26-28 . . . . . State College
29-30 . . . . at State College

JULY

1 . . . at State College
2-3 . . . Batavia
4-5 . . . at Batavia
6-8 . . . Williamsport
9-11 . . . at Williamsport
13-15 . . . Connecticut
16-18 . . . at Jamestown
19-20 . . . State College
21-22 . . . at State College
23-25 . . . at Hudson Valley
27-29 . . . Lowell
30-31 . . . at Aberdeen

AUGUST

1 . . . at Aberdeen
2-4 . . . Staten Island
5-6 . . . Auburn
7-8 . . . at Auburn
9-11 . . . at Tri-City
12-14 . . . Brooklyn
17-19 . . . at Vermont
20-22 . . . at Batavia
23-25 . . . Auburn
26-28 . . . Jamestown
29-30 . . . at Williamsport
31 . . . Williamsport

SEPTEMBER

1 . . . Williamsport
2-4 . . . at Jamestown

STATE COLLEGE

JUNE

17-18 . . . at Williamsport
19 . . . Williamsport
20-22 . . . Auburn
23-25 . . . at Jamestown
26-28 . . . at Mahoning Valley
29-30 . . . Mahoning Valley

JULY

1 . . . Mahoning Valley
2-3 . . . Auburn
4-5 . . . at Auburn
6-8 . . . at Batavia
9-11 . . . Batavia
13-15 . . . at Staten Island
16 . . . at Williamsport
17-18 . . . Williamsport
19-20 . . . at Mahoning Valley
21-22 . . . Mahoning Valley
23-25 . . . Brooklyn
27-29 . . . at Tri-City
30-31 . . . Lowell

AUGUST

1 . . . Lowell
2-4 . . . at Vermont
5-6 . . . Jamestown
7-8 . . . at Jamestown
9-11 . . . Aberdeen
12-14 . . . Connecticut
17-19 . . . at Hudson Valley
20-22 . . . at Auburn
23-25 . . . Jamestown
26-28 . . . Williamsport
29-30 . . . at Batavia
31 . . . Batavia

SEPTEMBER

1 . . . Batavia
2-4 . . . at Williamsport

STATEN ISLAND

JUNE

17 . . . Brooklyn
18-19 . . . at Brooklyn
20 . . . at Hudson Valley
21 . . . Hudson Valley
22 . . . at Hudson Valley
23-25 . . . at Aberdeen
26-27 . . . Hudson Valley
28 . . . at Hudson Valley
29-30 . . . Aberdeen

JULY

1 . . . Aberdeen
2 . . . Brooklyn
3 . . . at Brooklyn
4-5 . . . Brooklyn
6-8 . . . Connecticut
9-11 . . . at Vermont
13-15 . . . State College
16-18 . . . at Tri-City
19-20 . . . at Hudson Valley
21-22 . . . Hudson Valley
23-25 . . . Tri-City
27-29 . . . at Batavia
30-31 . . . Jamestown

AUGUST

1 . . . Jamestown
2-4 . . . at Mahoning Valley
5 . . . Brooklyn
6 . . . at Brooklyn
7 . . . Brooklyn
8 . . . at Brooklyn
9-11 . . . at Williamsport
12-14 . . . Auburn
17-19 . . . at Connecticut
20-22 . . . at Lowell
23-25 . . . Lowell
26-27 . . . at Aberdeen
28-29 . . . Aberdeen
30-31 . . . Vermont

SEPTEMBER

1 . . . Vermont
2 . . . at Brooklyn
3 . . . Brooklyn
4 . . . at Brooklyn

TRI-CITY

JUNE

17-19 . . . Vermont
20-22 . . . Connecticut
23-25 . . . Lowell
26-28 . . . Connecticut
29-30 . . . at Lowell

JULY

1 . . . at Lowell
2-3 . . . at Vermont
4-5 . . . Vermont
6-8 . . . at Hudson Valley
9-11 . . . Aberdeen
13-15 . . . at Batavia
16-18 . . . Staten Island
19-20 . . . Connecticut
21-22 . . . at Connecticut
23-25 . . . at Staten Island
27-29 . . . State College
30-31 . . . Auburn

AUGUST

1 . . . Auburn
2-4 . . . at Jamestown
5-6 . . . Vermont
7-8 . . . at Vermont
9-11 . . . Mahoning Valley
12-14 . . . Hudson Valley
17-19 . . . at Williamsport
20-22 . . . at Brooklyn
23-25 . . . Brooklyn
26-27 . . . at Lowell
28-29 . . . Lowell
30-31 . . . at Aberdeen

SEPTEMBER

1 . . . at Aberdeen
2-4 . . . at Vermont

VERMONT

JUNE

17-19 . . . at Tri-City
20-22 . . . Lowell
23-25 . . . Connecticut
26-28 . . . at Lowell
29-30 . . . at Connecticut

JULY

1 . . . at Connecticut
2-3 . . . Tri-City
4-5 . . . at Tri-City
6-8 . . . at Brooklyn
9-11 . . . Staten Island
13-15 . . . at Aberdeen
16-18 . . . Aberdeen
19-20 . . . at Lowell
21-22 . . . Lowell
23-25 . . . Jamestown
27-29 . . . at Williamsport
30-31 . . . Brooklyn

AUGUST

1 . . . Brooklyn
2-4 . . . State College
5-6 . . . at Tri-City
7-8 . . . Tri-City
9-11 . . . at Auburn
12-14 . . . at Batavia
17-19 . . . Mahoning Valley
20-22 . . . Hudson Valley
23-25 . . . at Hudson Valley
26-27 . . . at Connecticut
28-29 . . . Connecticut
30-31 . . . at Staten Island

SEPTEMBER

1 . . . at Staten Island
2-4 . . . Tri-City

WILLIAMSPORT

JUNE

17-18 . . . State College
19 . . . at State College
20-22 . . . at Jamestown
23-25 . . . Batavia
26-28 . . . at Auburn
29-30 . . . Auburn

JULY

1 . . . Auburn
2-3 . . . at Jamestown
4-5 . . . Jamestown
6-8 . . . at Mahoning Valley
9-11 . . . Mahoning Valley
13-15 . . . at Lowell
16 . . . State College
17-18 . . . at State College
19-20 . . . Auburn
21-22 . . . at Auburn
23-25 . . . at Connecticut
27-29 . . . Vermont
30-31 . . . Hudson Valley

AUGUST

1 . . . Hudson Valley
2-4 . . . at Brooklyn
5-6 . . . at Batavia
7-8 . . . Batavia
9-11 . . . Staten Island
12-14 . . . at Aberdeen
17-19 . . . Tri-City
20-22 . . . Jamestown
23-25 . . . at Batavia
26-28 . . . at State College
29-30 . . . Mahoning Valley
31 . . . at Mahoning Valley

SEPTEMBER

1 . . . at Mahoning Valley
2-4 . . . State College

NORTHWEST LEAGUE

BOISE

JUNE

17-21 . . . at Eugene
22-24 . . . Tri-City
25-27 . . . Spokane
28-30 . . . at Tri-City

JULY

1-3 . . . at Yakima
4-6 . . . Yakima
7-11 . . . Everett
13-17 . . . at Vancouver
18-20 . . . at Spokane
21-23 . . . Yakima
24-26 . . . Spokane
27-31 . . . at Everett

AUGUST

2-6 . . . Salem-Keizer
7-9 . . . Tri-City
10-14 . . . Eugene
15-17 . . . Tri-City
18-20 . . . at Spokane
21-23 . . . at Yakima
24-28 . . . at Salem Keizer
30-31 . . . Vancouver

SEPTEMBER

1-3 . . . Vancouver

EUGENE

JUNE	
17-21	Boise
22-24	at Salem-Keizer
25-27	at Everett
28-30	Salem-Keizer

JULY	
1-3	at Vancouver
4-6	Vancouver
7-11	Yakima
13-17	at Tri-City
18-20	Vancouver
21-23	Vancouver
24-26	Everett

27-31	at Spokane

AUGUST	
2-6	Tri-City
7-9	at Salem-Keizer
10-14	at Boise
15-17	Everett
18-20	Salem-Keizer
21-23	at Everett
24-28	Spokane
30-31	at Yakima

SEPTEMBER	
1-3	at Yakima

EVERETT

JUNE	
17-21	at Tri-City
22-24	Vancouver
25-27	Eugene
28-30	at Vancouver

JULY	
1-3	at Salem-Keizer
4-6	Salem-Keizer
7-11	at Boise
13-17	Spokane
18-20	at Salem-Keizer
21-23	Salem-Keizer
24-26	at Eugene

27-31	Boise

AUGUST	
2-6	at Yakima
7-9	Vancouver
10-14	Tri-City
15-17	at Eugene
18-20	at Vancouver
21-23	Eugene
24-28	Yakima
30-31	at Spokane

SEPTEMBER	
1-3	at Spokane

SALEM-KEIZER

JUNE	
17-21	at Spokane
22-24	Eugene
25-27	Vancouver
28-30	at Eugene

JULY	
1-3	Everett
4-6	at Everett
7-11	Tri-City
13-17	at Yakima
18-20	Everett
21-23	at Everett
24-26	at Vancouver

27-31	Yakima

AUGUST	
2-6	at Boise
7-9	Eugene
10-14	Spokane
15-17	at Vancouver
18-20	at Eugene
21-23	Vancouver
24-28	Boise
30-31	at Tri-City

SEPTEMBER	
1-3	at Tri-City

SPOKANE

JUNE	
17-21	Salem-Keizer
22-24	at Yakima
25-27	at Boise
28-30	Yakima

JULY	
1-3	at Tri-City
4-6	Tri-City
7-11	Vancouver
13-17	at Everett

18-20	Boise
21-23	Tri-City
24-26	at Boise
27-31	Eugene

AUGUST	
2-6	at Vancouver
7-9	Yakima
10-14	at Salem-Keizer

TRI-CITY

JUNE	
17-21	Everett
22-24	at Boise
25-27	at Yakima
28-30	Boise

JULY	
1-3	Spokane
4-6	at Spokane
7-11	at Salem-Keizer
13-17	Eugene
18-20	Yakima
21-23	at Spokane
24-26	at Yakima

27-31	Vancouver

AUGUST	
2-6	at Eugene
7-9	Boise
10-14	at Everett
15-17	at Boise
18-20	Yakima
21-23	Spokane
24-28	at Vancouver
30-31	Salem-Keizer

SEPTEMBER	
1-3	Salem-Keizer

VANCOUVER

JUNE	
17-21	Yakima
22-24	at Everett
25-27	at Salem-Keizer
28-30	Everett

JULY	
1-3	Eugene
4-6	at Eugene
7-11	at Spokane
13-17	Boise
18-20	Eugene
21-23	at Eugene
24-26	Salem-Keizer

27-31	at Tri-City

AUGUST	
2-6	Spokane
7-9	at Everett
10-14	at Yakima
15-17	Salem-Keizer
18-20	Everett
21-23	at Salem-Keizer
24-28	Tri-City
30-31	at Boise

SEPTEMBER	
1-3	at Boise

YAKIMA

JUNE	
17-21	at Vancouver
22-24	Spokane
25-27	Tri-City
28-30	at Spokane

JULY	
1-3	Boise
4-6	at Boise
7-11	at Eugene
13-17	Salem-Keizer
18-20	at Tri-City
21-23	at Boise
24-26	Tri-City

27-31	at Salem-Keizer

AUGUST	
2-6	Everett
7-9	at Spokane
10-14	Vancouver
15-17	Spokane
18-20	at Tri-City
21-23	Boise
24-28	at Everett
30-31	Eugene

SEPTEMBER	
1-3	Eugene

ROOKIE

APPALACHIAN LEAGUE

BLUEFIELD

JUNE	
21-23	at Elizabethton
24-26	Danville
27-29	Bristol
30	at Princeton

JULY	
1-3	at Princeton
4	Princeton
5-7	Johnson City

8-10	at Danville
12-14	at Bristol
15-17	Kingsport
18-20	Burlington
21-23	at Pulaski
24-26	Princeton
27-29	at Burlington
30-31	at Kingsport

AUGUST	
1	at Kingsport
3-5	Greeneville
6-8	at Johnson City
9-11	Princeton
12-14	at Pulaski

16-18	Burlington
19-21	Pulaski
22-24	at Greeneville
25-27	Elizabethton
28-30	at Danville

BRISTOL

JUNE	
21-23	Greeneville
24-26	at Kingsport
27-29	at Bluefield

30	Burlington

JULY	
1-3	Pulaski

4-7 . . . . .at Pulaski
8-10 . . . . . . at Burlington
12-14 . . . . Bluefield
15-17 . . . . Pulaski
18-20 . . . .at Elizabethton
21-23 . . . . .at Greeneville
24-26 . . . . Kingsport
28-30 . . . .at Johnson City
31 . . . . Danville

BURLINGTON

JUNE	
21-23 . . . . . at Princeton	24-26 . . . . . .Elizabethton
24-26 . . . . at Elizabethton	27-29 . . . . Bluefield
27-29 . . . . Pulaski	30-31 . . . . .at Pulaski
30 . . . . at Bristol	

JULY		AUGUST	
1-3 . . . . at Danville	1 . . . . .at Pulaski
4 . . . . .Danville	3-5 . . . . Pulaski
5-7 . . . . .Princeton	6-8 . . . . Kingsport
8-10 . . . . Bristol	9-11 . . . . . at Greeneville
12-14 . . . . . at Princeton	12-14 . . . . .Danville
15-17 . . . . . . .Danville	16-18 . . . . . at Bluefield
18-20 . . . . at Bluefield	19-21 . . . . .at Kingsport
21-23 . . . . at Danville	22-24 . . . . Johnson City
	25-27 . . . . . Greeneville
	28-30 . . . .at Johnson City

DANVILLE

JUNE		24-26 . . . . Pulaski
21-23 . . . . .at Pulaski	28-30 . . . at Elizabethton
24-26 . . . . . . at Bluefield	31 . . . . at Bristol
27-29 . . . . . . .Princeton	
30 . . . . Greeneville	

JULY		AUGUST	
1-2 . . . . Greeneville	1-2 . . . . at Bristol
3 . . . . Burlington	3-5 . . . . at Princeton
4-7 . . . . . at Greeneville	6-8 . . . . .Bristol
8-10 . . . . Bluefield	9-11 . . . . . .Elizabethton
12-14 . . . . . . Kingsport	12-14 . . . . at Burlington
15-17 . . . . at Burlington	16-18 . . . . . .Princeton
18-20 . . . . . . .at Pulaski	19-21 . . .at Johnson City
21-23 . . . . . Burlington	22-24 . . . . .at Kingsport
	25-27 . . . Johnson City
	28-30 . . . . . Bluefield

ELIZABETHTON

JUNE		21-23 . . . . . at Princeton
21-23 . . . . Bluefield	24-26 . . . . . at Burlington
24-26 . . . . . . Burlington	28-30 . . . . . .Danville
27-29 . . . .at Johnson City	31 . . . . . . Johnson City
30 . . . . Kingsport	

JULY		AUGUST	
1-2 . . . . Kingsport	1-2 . . . . . Johnson City
3 . . . . Greeneville	3-5 . . . . . .at Kingsport
4 . . . . . .at Greeneville	6-8 . . . . .at Pulaski
5-7 . . . .at Kingsport	9-11 . . . . . . at Danville
8-10 . . . . . . Greeneville	12-14 . . . . Johnson City
12-14 . . . . Pulaski	16-18 . . . . .Bristol
15-17 . . . . at Greeneville	19-21 . . . at Greeneville
18-20 . . . . .Bristol	22-24 . . . . . . at Bristol
	25-27 . . . . at Bluefield
	28-30 . . . . . . .Princeton

GREENEVILLE

JUNE		15-17 . . . . . .Elizabethton
21-23 . . . . at Bristol	18-20 . . . . .at Kingsport
24-26 . . . . . Johnson City	21-23 . . . . .Bristol
27-29 . . . . Kingsport	24-26 . . . .at Johnson City
30 . . . . .at Danville	27-29 . . . . Kingsport
	30-31 . . . . .Princeton

JULY		AUGUST	
1-2 . . . . at Danville	1 . . . . .Princeton
3 . . . . at Elizabethton	3-5 . . . . at Bluefield
4 . . . . .Elizabethton	6-8 . . . . at Princeton
5-7 . . . . .Danville	9-11 . . . . Burlington
8-10 . . . . at Elizabethton	12-14 . . . . at Bristol
12-14 . . .at Johnson City	

16-18 . . . . .at Pulaski
19-21 . . . . .Elizabethton
22-24 . . . . Bluefield

JOHNSON CITY

JUNE		24-26 . . . . . . Greeneville
21 . . . . Kingsport	28-30 . . . . .Bristol
22-23 . . . . . at Kingsport	31 . . . . . . at Elizabethton
24-26 . . . . .at Greeneville	
27-29 . . . . .Elizabethton	AUGUST
30 . . . . Pulaski	1-2 . . . . . .at Elizabethton

JULY		3-5 . . . . at Bristol
1-2 . . . . Pulaski	6-8 . . . . Bluefield
3 . . . . Kingsport	9-11 . . . . .Bristol
4 . . . . .at Kingsport	12-14 . . . . at Elizabethton
5-7 . . . . . . at Bluefield	16 . . . . .at Kingsport
8-10 . . . . . . .at Pulaski	17-18 . . . . . . Kingsport
12-14 . . . . . Greeneville	19-21 . . . . .Danville
15-17 . . . . . .Princeton	22-24 . . . . at Burlington
18-20 . . . . at Princeton	25-27 . . . . .at Danville
21-23 . . . . .at Kingsport	28-30 . . . . . Burlington

KINGSPORT

JUNE		24-26 . . . . at Bristol
21 . . . . . .at Johnson City	27-29 . . . . .at Greeneville
22-23 . . . . . Johnson City	30-31 . . . . Bluefield
24-26 . . . . .Bristol	
27-29 . . . . .at Greeneville	AUGUST
30 . . . . . . at Elizabethton	1 . . . . Bluefield

JULY		3-5 . . . . .Elizabethton
1-2 . . . . . at Elizabethton	6-8 . . . . . . at Burlington
3 . . . . . .at Johnson City	9-11 . . . . Pulaski
4 . . . . . . Johnson City	12-14 . . . . . at Princeton
5-7 . . . . . . .Elizabethton	16 . . . . Johnson City
8-10 . . . . . . .Princeton	17-18 . . . .at Johnson City
12-14 . . . . . at Danville	19-21 . . . . . . Burlington
15-17 . . . . at Bluefield	22-24 . . . . .Danville
18-20 . . . . . Greeneville	25-27 . . . . . .at Pulaski
21-23 . . . . . Johnson City	28-30 . . . . . at Bristol

PRINCETON

JUNE		24-26 . . . . . . at Bluefield
21-23 . . . . . . Burlington	27-29 . . . . Pulaski
24-26 . . . . . . .at Pulaski	30-31 . . . .at Greeneville
27-29 . . . . . .at Danville	
30 . . . . Bluefield	AUGUST

JULY		1 . . . . .at Greeneville
1-3 . . . . Bluefield	3-5 . . . . .Danville
4 . . . . at Bluefield	6-8 . . . . Greeneville
5-7 . . . . . . at Burlington	9-11 . . . . . . at Bluefield
8-10 . . . . .at Kingsport	12-14 . . . . . . Kingsport
12-14 . . . . . . Burlington	16-18 . . . . . at Danville
15-17 . . . .at Johnson City	19-21 . . . . . . at Bristol
18-20 . . . . Johnson City	22-24 . . . . Pulaski
21-23 . . . . .Elizabethton	25-27 . . . . .Bristol
	28-30 . . . . .at Elizabethton

PULASKI

JUNE		24-26 . . . . . . at Danville
21-23 . . . . .Danville	27-29 . . . . . at Princeton
24-26 . . . . .Princeton	30-31 . . . . Burlington
27-29 . . . . at Burlington	
30 . . . . . .at Johnson City	AUGUST

JULY		1 . . . . Burlington
1-2 . . . . . .at Johnson City	3-5 . . . . . . at Burlington
3 . . . . at Bristol	6-8 . . . . .Elizabethton
4-7 . . . . .Bristol	9-11 . . . . . . .at Kingsport
8-10 . . . . . Johnson City	12-14 . . . . Bluefield
12-14 . . . at Elizabethton	16-18 . . . . . . Greeneville
15-17 . . . . . . at Bristol	19-21 . . . . at Bluefield
18-20 . . . . . . .Danville	22-24 . . . . at Princeton
21-23 . . . . Bluefield	25-27 . . . . Kingsport
	28-30 . . . .at Greeneville

PIONEER LEAGUE

BILLINGS

JUNE	
20-23	Great Falls
24-26	at Helena
27-28	at Missoula
29-30	Helena

JULY	
1	Helena
2-4	Missoula
5-8	at Great Falls
9-11	at Missoula
13-15	Orem
16-19	Ogden
21-24	at Orem
25-27	at Ogden
29-31	Helena

AUGUST	
1-2	Missoula
3-5	at Missoula
6-7	at Great Falls
8-9	at Helena
10-13	Great Falls
15-18	at Idaho Falls
19-21	at Casper
22-24	Idaho Falls
25-28	Casper
30-31	at Helena

SEPTEMBER	
1	at Helena
2-3	at Great Falls
4-6	Missoula
7-8	Helena

CASPER

JUNE	
20-23	at Orem
24-27	at Ogden
28-30	Idaho Falls

JULY	
1	Idaho Falls
2-4	Orem
5-7	at Idaho Falls
8-11	at Ogden
13-15	Missoula
16-19	Helena
21-24	at Missoula
25-27	at Helena
29-31	Orem

AUGUST	
1-2	at Idaho Falls
3-4	Ogden
5-8	Idaho Falls
9-11	at Idaho Falls
12-13	at Orem
15-18	Great Falls
19-21	Billings
22-24	at Great Falls
25-28	at Billings
30-31	Ogden

SEPTEMBER	
1-2	Ogden
3-4	Orem
5-6	at Orem
7-8	Ogden

GREAT FALLS

JUNE	
20-23	at Billings
24-26	Missoula
27-28	at Helena
29-30	at Missoula

JULY	
1	at Missoula
2-4	Helena
5-8	Billings
9-11	at Helena
13-15	Ogden
15-19	Orem
21-24	at Ogden
25-27	at Orem
29-31	Missoula

AUGUST	
1-2	Helena
3-5	at Helena
6-7	Billings
8-9	Missoula
10-13	at Billings
15-18	at Casper
19-21	at Idaho Falls
22-24	Casper
25-28	Idaho Falls
30-31	at Missoula

SEPTEMBER	
1	at Missoula
2-3	Billings
4-6	Helena
7-8	at Missoula

HELENA

JUNE	
20-21	Missoula
22-23	at Missoula
24-26	Billings
27-28	Great Falls
29-30	at Billings

JULY	
1	at Billings
2-4	at Great Falls
5-6	Missoula
7-8	at Missoula
9-11	Great Falls
13-15	at Idaho Falls
16-19	at Casper
21-24	Idaho Falls
25-27	Casper
29-31	at Billings

AUGUST	
1-2	at Great Falls
3-5	Great Falls
6-7	at Missoula
8-9	Billings
10-11	Missoula
12-13	at Missoula

IDAHO FALLS

JUNE	
20-21	Ogden
22-23	at Ogden
24-27	Orem
28-30	at Casper

JULY	
1	at Casper
2-4	Ogden
5-7	Casper
8-11	at Orem
13-15	Helena
16-19	Missoula
21-24	at Helena
25-27	at Missoula
29-31	Ogden

AUGUST	
1-2	Casper
3-4	at Orem
5-8	at Casper
9-11	Casper
12-13	at Ogden
15-18	Billings
19-21	Great Falls
22-24	at Billings
25-28	at Great Falls
30-31	Orem

SEPTEMBER	
1-2	Orem
3-6	at Ogden
7-8	at Orem

MISSOULA

JUNE	
20-21	at Helena
22-23	Helena
24-26	at Great Falls
27-28	Billings
29-30	Great Falls

JULY	
1	Great Falls
2-4	at Billings
5-6	at Helena
7-8	Helena
9-11	Billings
13-15	at Casper
16-19	at Idaho Falls
21-24	Casper
25-27	Idaho Falls
29-31	at Great Falls

AUGUST	
1-2	at Billings
3-5	Billings
6-7	Helena
8-9	at Great Falls
10-11	at Helena
12-13	Helena
15-18	Orem
19-21	Ogden
22-24	at Orem
26-28	at Ogden
30-31	Great Falls

SEPTEMBER	
1	Great Falls
2-3	at Helena
4-6	at Billings
7-8	Great Falls

OGDEN

JUNE	
20-21	at Idaho Falls
22-23	Idaho Falls
24-27	Casper
28-30	at Orem

JULY	
1	at Orem
2-4	at Idaho Falls
5-7	Orem
8-11	Casper
13-15	at Great Falls
16-19	at Billings
21-24	Great Falls
25-27	Billings
29-31	at Idaho Falls

AUGUST	
1-2	Orem
3-4	at Casper
5-8	at Casper
9-11	Orem
12-13	Idaho Falls
15-18	at Helena
19-21	at Missoula
22-24	Helena
25-28	Missoula
30-31	at Casper

SEPTEMBER	
1-2	at Casper
3-6	Idaho Falls
7-8	at Casper

OREM

JUNE	
20-23	Casper
24-27	at Idaho Falls
28-30	Ogden

JULY	
1	Ogden
2-4	at Casper
5-7	at Ogden
8-11	Idaho Falls
13-15	at Billings

16-19	at Great Falls
21-24	Billings
25-27	Great Falls
29-31	at Casper

AUGUST	
1-2	at Ogden
3-4	Idaho Falls
5-8	Ogden
9-11	at Ogden
12-13	Casper

15-18 . . . . . . at Missoula	
19-21 . . . . .at Helena	
22-24 . . . . Missoula	
25-28 . . . . Helena	
30-31 . . . . . at Idaho Falls	

ARIZONA LEAGUE

ANGELS

JUNE			
20 . . . . A's	25 . . . . Mariners
21 . . . . Indians	27 . . . . .Giants
24 . . . . Giants	30 . . . . A's
26 . . . . .Brewers	**AUGUST**
30 . . . . Padres	1 . . . . .Reds
JULY	5 . . . . .Royals
2 . . . . .Royals	7 . . . . .Cubs
5 . . . . .Cubs	9 . . . . Dodgers
6 . . . . . . Diamondbacks	12 . . . . Padres
10 . . . . Mariners	14 . . . . .Rangers
13 . . . . Dodgers	15 . . . . .Cubs
15 . . . . A's	19 . . . . . Diamondbacks
17 . . . . .Reds	22 . . . . .Giants
20 . . . . . Diamondbacks	24 . . . . . Diamondbacks
22 . . . . Indians	25 . . . . A's

ATHLETICS

JUNE			
21 . . . . .Cubs	25 . . . . Dodgers
22 . . . . .Brewers	28 . . . . .Royals
26 . . . . Indians	31 . . . . Padres
27 . . . . . Diamondbacks	**AUGUST**
30 . . . . .Rangers	2 . . . . .Brewers
JULY	5 . . . . Mariners
2 . . . . Padres	6 . . . . .Giants
5 . . . . .Giants	10 . . . . .Reds
6 . . . . .Reds	12 . . . . . Diamondbacks
11 . . . . Angels	15 . . . . .Rangers
13 . . . Diamondbacks	16 . . . . .Giants
16 . . . . .Cubs	19 . . . . Indians
18 . . . . .Giants	20 . . . . Angels
22 . . . . Mariners	26 . . . . .Cubs
23 . . . . Angels	27 . . . . . Diamondbacks

BREWERS

JUNE			
21 . . . . Dodgers	28 . . . . Angels
24 . . . . . . Diamondbacks	30 . . . . .Reds
28 . . . . .Reds	**AUGUST**
29 . . . . A's	1 . . . . A's
JULY	4 . . . . .Reds
3 . . . . .Cubs	8 . . . . . . Diamondbacks
4 . . . . Indians	9 . . . . Indians
6 . . . . Dodgers	11 . . . . Dodgers
9 . . . . Angels	13 . . . . .Royals
11 . . . . Mariners	18 . . . . Padres
13 . . . . Padres	19 . . . . .Reds
19 . . . . .Royals	22 . . . . .Rangers
20 . . . . Indians	24 . . . . Indians
23 . . . . .Cubs	26 . . . . Mariners
25 . . . . .Giants	27 . . . . Dodgers

CUBS

JUNE		JULY	
20 . . . . .Giants	1 . . . . A's
22 . . . . . . Diamondbacks	7 . . . . .Giants
25 . . . . Indians	8 . . . . .Brewers
27 . . . . Angels	10 . . . . Padres
30 . . . . .Royals	13 . . . . .Rangers
	18 . . . . Dodgers

SEPTEMBER	
1-2 . . . . at Idaho Falls
3-4 . . . . .at Casper
5-6 . . . . Casper
7-8 . . . . Idaho Falls

19 . . . . Mariners	8 . . . . Dodgers
22 . . . . .Reds	10 . . . . .Rangers
24 . . . . Indians	11 . . . . Angels
27 . . . . A's	16 . . . . .Reds
28 . . . Diamondbacks	17 . . . . A's
31 . . . . .Royals	21 . . . . Mariners
AUGUST	22 . . . . . . Diamondbacks
2 . . . . Angels	25 . . . . .Giants
6 . . . . .Brewers	28 . . . . . Diamondbacks

DIAMONDBACKS

JUNE			
21 . . . . .Giants	25 . . . . Padres
23 . . . . Padres	27 . . . . Mariners
26 . . . . Mariners	29 . . . . Dodgers
28 . . . . .Cubs	**AUGUST**
JULY	3 . . . . .Cubs
1 . . . . Angels	4 . . . . A's
2 . . . . .Brewers	7 . . . . .Royals
7 . . . . A's	9 . . . . .Rangers
8 . . . . Indians	13 . . . . Indians
14 . . . . .Royals	14 . . . . .Giants
15 . . . . .Giants	16 . . . . Angels
17 . . . . .Brewers	18 . . . . .Reds
18 . . . . .Rangers	21 . . . . A's
24 . . . . Dodgers	23 . . . . .Cubs
	26 . . . . .Giants
	29 . . . . Angels

DODGERS

JUNE			
22 . . . . .Rangers	27 . . . . .Reds
23 . . . . .Reds	28 . . . . Padres
26 . . . . .Cubs	**AUGUST**
29 . . . . . Diamondbacks	1 . . . . .Giants
JULY	4 . . . . Indians
1 . . . . .Brewers	6 . . . . . . Diamondbacks
3 . . . . .Royals	7 . . . . .Brewers
7 . . . . Angels	12 . . . . .Brewers
9 . . . . Indians	13 . . . . Padres
11 . . . . .Reds	17 . . . . Angels
14 . . . . Mariners	19 . . . . .Royals
17 . . . . Indians	22 . . . . A's
20 . . . . A's	23 . . . . Indians
22 . . . . .Brewers	28 . . . . .Rangers
23 . . . . .Giants	29 . . . . .Reds

GIANTS

JUNE			
22 . . . . Angels	28 . . . . .Rangers
25 . . . . .Rangers	30 . . . . . . Diamondbacks
27 . . . . .Brewers	**AUGUST**
JULY	2 . . . . Dodgers
1 . . . . Mariners	4 . . . . Angels
2 . . . . Dodgers	5 . . . . .Cubs
4 . . . . Padres	10 . . . . Indians
6 . . . . .Cubs	11 . . . . Mariners
9 . . . . .Reds	15 . . . . .Reds
11 . . . . .Cubs	17 . . . . .Brewers
16 . . . . Angels	19 . . . . Padres
17 . . . . A's	21 . . . . Angels
21 . . . . A's	24 . . . . A's
22 . . . . . . Diamondbacks	27 . . . . .Cubs
26 . . . . .Royals	29 . . . . A's

INDIANS

JUNE			
20 . . . . .Reds	30 . . . . .Giants
23 . . . . .Brewers	**JULY**
24 . . . . A's	3 . . . . Mariners
28 . . . . Dodgers	5 . . . . .Rangers
	10 . . . . .Royals

11 . . . . . . Diamondbacks
14 . . . . Reds
15 . . . . Dodgers
19 . . . . . . Diamondbacks
21 . . . . Cubs
26 . . . . Padres
27 . . . . Brewers
30 . . . . Rangers

AUGUST
1 . . . . Cubs
3 . . . . Dodgers

MARINERS

JUNE
20 . . . . Padres
24 . . . . Royals
25 . . . . Reds
29 . . . . Angels
30 . . . . Reds

JULY
4 . . . . Dodgers
6 . . . . Indians
8 . . . . Rangers
9 . . . . A's
15 . . . . Padres
17 . . . . Cubs
20 . . . . Royals
21 . . . . . . Rangers
24 . . . . . . Brewers

PADRES

JUNE
22 . . . . Royals
25 . . . . Angels
27 . . . . . . Dodgers
29 . . . . Giants

JULY
3 . . . . . . Diamondbacks
5 . . . . . . Mariners
7 . . . . . . Rangers
9 . . . . Royals
14 . . . . Cubs
16 . . . . . . Mariners
18 . . . . . . Brewers
20 . . . . Reds
23 . . . . . . Rangers
24 . . . . Royals

RANGERS

JUNE
20 . . . . Royals
23 . . . . . . Mariners
24 . . . . . . Dodgers
28 . . . . Padres
29 . . . . Indians

JULY
2 . . . . Cubs
4 . . . . Angels
9 . . . . . Diamondbacks
10 . . . . A's
14 . . . . . . Brewers
16 . . . . Royals
19 . . . . Padres
20 . . . . Giants
24 . . . . Reds

REDS

JUNE
21 . . . . . . Mariners

---

6 . . . . Mariners
8 . . . . Reds
11 . . . . A's
15 . . . . Royals
16 . . . . . . Brewers
20 . . . . Giants
21 . . . . . . Dodgers
25 . . . . Reds
26 . . . . Angels
29 . . . . . . Brewers

26 . . . . Angels
31 . . . . Giants

AUGUST
1 . . . . . Diamondbacks
3 . . . . Royals
4 . . . . . . Rangers
9 . . . . A's
10 . . . . Padres
14 . . . . . . Brewers
16 . . . . . . Dodgers
18 . . . . Cubs
20 . . . . . . Rangers
24 . . . . Royals
25 . . . . Padres
28 . . . . Indians

29 . . . . Indians
30 . . . . . . Dodgers

AUGUST
2 . . . . . Diamondbacks
5 . . . . Indians
7 . . . . Giants
8 . . . . . . Mariners
14 . . . . A's
15 . . . . . . Mariners
17 . . . . . . Rangers
20 . . . . Cubs
23 . . . . Reds
24 . . . . . . Rangers
27 . . . . Angels
28 . . . . Royals

26 . . . . Cubs
29 . . . . . . Mariners
31 . . . . Angels

AUGUST
3 . . . . Padres
5 . . . . Reds
7 . . . . A's
8 . . . . Royals
12 . . . . Giants
13 . . . . . . Mariners
18 . . . . . . Dodgers
19 . . . . . . Mariners
23 . . . . . . Brewers
25 . . . . Royals
29 . . . . Padres

24 . . . . Padres
26 . . . . Giants
29 . . . . Royals

JULY
1 . . . . Indians
3 . . . . Rangers
4 . . . . . Diamondbacks
8 . . . . Dodgers
10 . . . . Giants
15 . . . . . . Brewers
16 . . . . Indians
19 . . . . . . Dodgers
21 . . . . Angels
25 . . . . . . Rangers
26 . . . . A's
29 . . . . Cubs

ROYALS

JUNE
23 . . . . Cubs
25 . . . . A's
27 . . . . . . Rangers
28 . . . . . . Mariners

JULY
4 . . . . A's
5 . . . . Reds
7 . . . . Brewers
8 . . . . Padres
13 . . . . Giants
15 . . . . . . Rangers
18 . . . . Angels
21 . . . . Padres
23 . . . . . Diamondbacks

GULF COAST LEAGUE

ASTROS

JUNE
21 . . . . . . Cardinals
25 . . . . Marlins
27 . . . . Mets
29 . . . . . . Nationals

JULY
1 . . . . . . Cardinals
5 . . . . Marlins
7 . . . . Mets
9 . . . . . . Nationals
11 . . . . . . Cardinals
15 . . . . Marlins
17 . . . . Mets
19 . . . . . . Nationals
21 . . . . . . Cardinals

BLUE JAYS

JUNE
20 . . . . Pirates
23 . . . . . . Yankees
24 . . . . Tigers
28 . . . . Braves
29 . . . . . . Phillies

JULY
2 . . . . Pirates
4 . . . . . . Yankees
7 . . . . Tigers
8 . . . . Braves
12 . . . . . . Phillies
13 . . . . Pirates
16 . . . . . . Yankees
18 . . . . Tigers
21 . . . . Braves
22 . . . . . . Phillies

---

31 . . . . Indians

AUGUST
3 . . . . Brewers
6 . . . . Angels
9 . . . . Padres
11 . . . . . Diamondbacks
13 . . . . Cubs
14 . . . . Indians
20 . . . . Royals
21 . . . . . . Brewers
24 . . . . . . Dodgers
26 . . . . . . Dodgers
28 . . . . . . Brewers

25 . . . . Indians
29 . . . . . . Brewers
30 . . . . . . Mariners

AUGUST
2 . . . . . . Rangers
4 . . . . Padres
9 . . . . Giants
10 . . . . Angels
12 . . . . Cubs
14 . . . . . . Dodgers
17 . . . . . Diamondbacks
18 . . . . Indians
22 . . . . Padres
23 . . . . . . Mariners
27 . . . . . . Rangers
29 . . . . . . Mariners

25 . . . . Marlins
27 . . . . Mets
29 . . . . . . Nationals
31 . . . . . . Cardinals

AUGUST
4 . . . . Marlins
6 . . . . Mets
8 . . . . . . Nationals
10 . . . . . . Cardinals
14 . . . . Marlins
16 . . . . Mets
18 . . . . . . Nationals
20 . . . . . . Cardinals
24 . . . . Marlins
26 . . . . Mets

BLUE JAYS

26 . . . . Pirates
27 . . . . . . Yankees
30 . . . . Tigers

AUGUST
1 . . . . Braves
4 . . . . . . Phillies
5 . . . . Pirates
9 . . . . . . Yankees
10 . . . . Tigers
13 . . . . Braves
15 . . . . . . Phillies
18 . . . . Pirates
19 . . . . . . Yankees
23 . . . . Tigers
24 . . . . Braves
27 . . . . . . Phillies

BRAVES

JUNE	
21	Yankees
23	Phillies
25	Pirates
27	Blue Jays
30	Tigers

JULY	
1	Yankees
4	Phillies
6	Pirates
9	Blue Jays
11	Tigers
14	Yankees
16	Phillies
19	Pirates
20	Blue Jays
23	Tigers

25	Yankees
27	Phillies
29	Pirates

AUGUST	
2	Blue Jays
3	Tigers
6	Yankees
9	Phillies
11	Pirates
12	Blue Jays
16	Tigers
17	Yankees
19	Phillies
22	Pirates
25	Blue Jays
26	Tigers

CARDINALS

JUNE	
22	Marlins
23	Nationals
26	Astros
29	Mets

JULY	
2	Marlins
3	Nationals
6	Astros
9	Mets
12	Marlins
13	Nationals
16	Astros
19	Mets
22	Marlins

23	Nationals
26	Astros
29	Mets

AUGUST	
1	Marlins
2	Nationals
5	Astros
8	Mets
11	Marlins
12	Nationals
15	Astros
18	Mets
21	Marlins
22	Nationals
25	Astros

MARLINS

JUNE	
20	Astros
23	Mets
26	Nationals
27	Cardinals
30	Astros

JULY	
3	Mets
6	Nationals
7	Cardinals
10	Astros
13	Mets
16	Nationals
17	Cardinals
20	Astros
23	Mets

26	Nationals
27	Cardinals
30	Astros

AUGUST	
2	Mets
5	Nationals
6	Cardinals
9	Astros
12	Mets
15	Nationals
16	Cardinals
19	Astros
22	Mets
25	Nationals
26	Cardinals

METS

JUNE	
22	Astros
24	Cardinals
25	Nationals
28	Marlins

JULY	
2	Astros
4	Cardinals
5	Nationals
8	Marlins
12	Astros
14	Cardinals
15	Nationals
18	Marlins
22	Astros

24	Cardinals
25	Nationals
28	Marlins

AUGUST	
1	Astros
3	Cardinals
4	Nationals
7	Marlins
11	Astros
13	Cardinals
14	Nationals
17	Marlins
21	Astros
23	Cardinals
24	Nationals
27	Marlins

NATIONALS

JUNE	
20	Mets
21	Marlins
24	Astros
28	Cardinals
30	Mets

JULY	
1	Marlins
4	Astros
8	Cardinals
10	Mets
11	Marlins
14	Astros
18	Cardinals
20	Mets
21	Marlins

24	Astros
28	Cardinals
30	Mets
31	Marlins

AUGUST	
3	Astros
7	Cardinals
9	Mets
10	Marlins
13	Astros
17	Cardinals
19	Mets
20	Marlins
23	Astros
27	Cardinals

ORIOLES

JUNE	
21	Twins
23	Red Sox
24	Rays
27	Twins
29	Red Sox

JULY	
2	Rays
4	Red Sox
7	Twins
8	Rays
13	Twins
15	Red Sox
16	Rays
19	Twins
21	Red Sox
22	Rays

25	Twins
27	Red Sox
30	Rays

AUGUST	
2	Red Sox
4	Twins
5	Rays
8	Red Sox
10	Twins
13	Rays
16	Twins
18	Red Sox
19	Rays
23	Red Sox
25	Twins
27	Rays

PHILLIES

JUNE	
21	Tigers
22	Braves
25	Yankees
27	Pirates
30	Blue Jays

JULY	
1	Tigers
5	Braves
6	Yankees
9	Pirates
11	Blue Jays
14	Tigers
15	Braves
19	Yankees
20	Pirates
23	Blue Jays

25	Tigers
28	Braves
29	Yankees

AUGUST	
2	Pirates
3	Blue Jays
6	Tigers
8	Braves
11	Yankees
12	Pirates
16	Blue Jays
17	Tigers
20	Braves
22	Yankees
25	Pirates
26	Blue Jays

PIRATES

JUNE	
21	Blue Jays
23	Tigers
24	Braves
28	Phillies
30	Yankees

JULY	
1	Blue Jays
4	Tigers
7	Braves
8	Phillies
11	Yankees
14	Blue Jays

16	Tigers
18	Braves
21	Phillies
23	Yankees
25	Blue Jays
27	Tigers
30	Braves

AUGUST	
1	Phillies
3	Yankees
6	Blue Jays
9	Tigers
10	Braves

13 . . . . Phillies
16 . . . . .Yankees
17 . . . . Blue Jays
19 . . . . Tigers

23 . . . . .Braves
24 . . . . Phillies
26 . . . . .Yankees

RAYS

JUNE	
20 . . . . .Red Sox	23 . . . . Orioles
22 . . . . Twins	26 . . . . .Red Sox
25 . . . . Orioles	28 . . . . Twins
28 . . . . .Red Sox	29 . . . . Orioles
30 . . . . Twins	**AUGUST**
JULY	1 . . . . Twins
1 . . . . Orioles	3 . . . . .Red Sox
5 . . . . Twins	6 . . . . Orioles
6 . . . . .Red Sox	9 . . . . Twins
9 . . . . Orioles	11 . . . . .Red Sox
11 . . . . Twins	12 . . . . Orioles
12 . . . . Orioles	15 . . . . .Red Sox
13 . . . . .Red Sox	17 . . . . Twins
18 . . . . .Red Sox	20 . . . . Orioles
20 . . . . Twins	22 . . . . Twins
	25 . . . . .Red Sox
	26 . . . . Orioles

RED SOX

JUNE	
21 . . . . Rays	25 . . . . Rays
22 . . . . Orioles	28 . . . . Orioles
25 . . . . Twins	29 . . . . Twins
27 . . . . Rays	**AUGUST**
30 . . . . Orioles	1 . . . . Orioles
JULY	4 . . . . Rays
1 . . . . Twins	6 . . . . Twins
5 . . . . Orioles	9 . . . . Orioles
7 . . . . Rays	10 . . . . Rays
9 . . . . Twins	12 . . . . Twins
11 . . . . Orioles	16 . . . . Rays
12 . . . . Twins	17 . . . . Orioles
14 . . . . Rays	20 . . . . Twins
19 . . . . Rays	22 . . . . Orioles
20 . . . . Orioles	24 . . . . Rays
23 . . . . Twins	26 . . . . Twins

TIGERS

JUNE	
20 . . . . Phillies	29 . . . . .Braves
22 . . . . Pirates	**JULY**
25 . . . . Blue Jays	2 . . . . Phillies
28 . . . . .Yankees	5 . . . . Pirates
	6 . . . . Blue Jays

8 . . . . .Yankees
12 . . . . .Braves
13 . . . . Phillies
15 . . . . Pirates
19 . . . . Blue Jays
21 . . . . .Yankees
22 . . . . .Braves
26 . . . . Phillies
28 . . . . Pirates
29 . . . . Blue Jays
AUGUST
1 . . . . .Yankees

TWINS

JUNE	
20 . . . . Orioles	26 . . . . Orioles
23 . . . . Rays	27 . . . . Rays
24 . . . . .Red Sox	30 . . . . .Red Sox
28 . . . . Orioles	**AUGUST**
29 . . . . Rays	2 . . . . Rays
JULY	3 . . . . Orioles
2 . . . . .Red Sox	5 . . . . .Red Sox
4 . . . . Rays	8 . . . . Rays
6 . . . . Orioles	11 . . . . Orioles
8 . . . . .Red Sox	13 . . . . .Red Sox
14 . . . . Orioles	15 . . . . Orioles
15 . . . . Rays	18 . . . . Rays
16 . . . . .Red Sox	19 . . . . .Red Sox
18 . . . . Orioles	23 . . . . Rays
21 . . . . Rays	24 . . . . Orioles
22 . . . . .Red Sox	27 . . . . .Red Sox

YANKEES

JUNE	
20 . . . . .Braves	26 . . . . .Braves
22 . . . . Blue Jays	28 . . . . Blue Jays
24 . . . . Phillies	30 . . . . Phillies
27 . . . . Tigers	**AUGUST**
29 . . . . Pirates	2 . . . . Tigers
JULY	4 . . . . Pirates
2 . . . . .Braves	5 . . . . .Braves
5 . . . . Blue Jays	8 . . . . Blue Jays
7 . . . . Phillies	10 . . . . Phillies
9 . . . . Tigers	12 . . . . Tigers
12 . . . . Pirates	15 . . . . Pirates
13 . . . . .Braves	18 . . . . .Braves
15 . . . . Blue Jays	20 . . . . Blue Jays
18 . . . . Phillies	23 . . . . Phillies
20 . . . . Tigers	25 . . . . Tigers
22 . . . . Pirates	27 . . . . Pirates

INDEPENDENT

AMERICAN ASSOCIATION HOME GAMES ONLY

AMARILLO SOX

MAY	JULY
12-15 . . . . Wichita	3-5 . . . . Shreveport-Bossier
20-22 . . Shreveport-Bossier	7-10 . . . . . . Grand Prairie
24-26 . . . . . . Sioux Falls	11-13 . . . . El Paso
30-31 . . . . St. Paul	22-24 . . . . . Grand Prairie
JUNE	25-27 . . . . Fort Worth
1-2 . . . . St. Paul	**AUGUST**
10-12 . . . . Fort Worth	8-11 . . . . El Paso
13-15 . . . . El Paso	19-21 . . . . . . Kansas City
16-19 . . . . Wichita	
24-26 . . Shreveport-Bossier	

EL PASO DIABLOS

MAY	JULY
12-15 . . . . . . Kansas City	2-5 . . . . Lincoln
16-18 . . . . Amarillo	14-17 . . . . Fort Worth
23-26 . . Shreveport-Bossier	19-21 . . . . . Grand Prairie
27-28 . . . . Amarillo	**AUGUST**
JUNE	2-4 . . . . Shreveport-Bossier
6-9 . . . . Fort Worth	5-7 . . . . Fort Worth
10-12 . . . . . Grand Prairie	15-17 . . . . Amarillo
21-23 . . . . Amarillo	19-21 . . . . . Grand Prairie
	27-30 . . . . Wichita

FARGO-MOORHEAD

MAY	
16-18 . . . . St. Paul	
23-26 . . . . Winnipeg	
27-29 . . . . . . Sioux City	

JUNE	
3-5 . . . . Lincoln	
13-15 . . . . Gary	
16-19 . . . . . . Sioux Falls	
24-26 . . . . Sioux City	

JULY	
7-10 . . . . Winnipeg	
14-17 . . . . . . Kansas City	
19-21 . . . . Lincoln	

AUGUST	
2-4 . . . . Wichita	
5-7 . . . . Sioux Falls	
12-14 . . . . St. Paul	
16-18 . . . . . . Sioux City	
27-30 . . . . . . Kansas City	

FORT WORTH CATS

MAY	
12-15 . . . . Sioux City	
16-18 . . . . Wichita	
27-28 . . . . . . Sioux Falls	

JUNE	
3-5 . . . . Amarillo	
13-15 . . . . Grand Prairie	
27-20 . . . . Amarillo	

JULY	
2 . . . . Grand Prairie	
4 . . . . Grand Prairie	

| 6-9 . . . . Shreveport-Bossier |
| 18-20 . . . . Gary |
| 22-24 . . Shreveport-Bossier |
| 28-30 . . . . El Paso |

AUGUST	
1-3 . . . . Lincoln	
12-14 . . . . Amarillo	
15-16 . . . . . Grand Prairie	
23-26 . . . . El Paso	
27-30 . . Shreveport-Bossier	

GARY SOUTH SHORE

MAY	
20-22 . . . . Fargo-Moorhead	
23-25 . . . . Wichita	

JUNE	
3-5 . . . . Winnipeg	
6-9 . . . . Sioux City	
16-19 . . . . St. Paul	
21-23 . . . Fargo-Moorhead	

JULY	
2-5 . . . . Sioux Falls	
11-13 . . . . Sioux City	
22-24 . . . Fargo-Moorhead	
25-27 . . . . . . Sioux Falls	

AUGUST	
5-7 . . . . Kansas City	
21-17 . . Shreveport-Bossier	
23-26 . . . . Lincoln	
27-30 . . . . St. Paul	

GRAND PRAIRIE

MAY	
12-15 . . . . Gary	
16-18 . . . . Lincoln	
27-29 . . Shreveport-Bossier	

JUNE	
3-5 . . . . St. Paul	
6-8 . . . . Amarillo	
16-19 . . . . El Paso	
24-26 . . . . El Paso	
27-30 . . Shreveport-Bossier	

JULY	
1 . . . . Fort Worth	
3 . . . . Fort Worth	
11-13 . . . . Fort Worth	
15-17 . . . . Wichita	
29-31 . . . . Lincoln	

AUGUST	
1-4 . . . . Amarillo	
12-14 . . . . El Paso	
17-18 . . . . Fort Worth	
27-29 . . . . Amarillo	

KANSAS CITY

MAY	
6 . . . . Wichita	
7-8 . . . . Lincoln	
17-19 . . . . Gary	
20-22 . . . . . Grand Prairie	
27-29 . . . . St. Paul	
30-31 . . . . . Grand Prairie	

JUNE	
1-2 . . . . . . Grand Prairie	
7-9 . . . . Fargo-Moorhead	
17-19 . . . . . . Winnipeg	
24-26 . . . . . . Fort Worth	

| 28-30 . . . . . . Winnipeg |

JULY	
3-4 . . . . Wichita	
7-10 . . . . El Paso	
18-20 . . . . Amarillo	
29-30 . . . . Wichita	

AUGUST	
2-4 . . . . Sioux City	
8-11 . . . . . Grand Prairie	
12-14 . . . . Lincoln	
23-26 . . . . . . Sioux Falls	

LINCOLN

MAY	
24-26 . . . . . . Kansas City	
27-29 . . . . Wichita	

JUNE	
6-9 . . . . Winnipeg	
10-12 . . Shreveport-Bossier	
16-19 . . . . . . Sioux City	
20-22 . . . . St. Paul	
27-30 . . . . Gary	

JULY	
11-13 . . . . . . Kansas City	
14-17 . . . . Amarillo	
22-24 . . . . . . Kansas City	
25-27 . . . . El Paso	

AUGUST	
5-7 . . . . . . Grand Prairie	
8-11 . . . . Fargo-Moorhead	
16-18 . . . . . . Sioux Falls	
19-21 . . . . Winnipeg	

ST. PAUL

MAY	
12-15 . . . . . . Sioux Falls	
20-22 . . . . Winnipeg	
23-25 . . . . . . Fort Worth	

JUNE	
10-12 . . . . Gary	
13-15 . . . . Lincoln	
24-26 . . . . Wichita	
28-30 . . . . Fargo-Moorhead	

JULY	
1 . . . . Fargo-Moorhead	
7-10 . . . . Gary	
11-13 . . . . Winnipeg	
22-24 . . . . . . Sioux City	
25-27 . . . . . . Kansas City	

AUGUST	
5-7 . . . . Winnipeg	
8-11 . . . . Wichita	
19-21 . . . Fargo-Moorhead	
23-26 . . . . Sioux City	

SHREVEPORT-BOSSIER

MAY	
12 . . . . Lincoln	
14-15 . . . . Lincoln	
16-17 . . . . . . Sioux City	
30-31 . . . . El Paso	

JUNE	
1-4 . . . . El Paso	
6-8 . . . . St. Paul	
17-19 . . . . . . Fort Worth	
20-22 . . . . . Grand Prairie	

JULY	
1-2 . . . . Amarillo	
15-17 . . . . Gary	
18-20 . . . . Wichita	
26-28 . . . . . Grand Prairie	
29-31 . . . . Amarillo	

AUGUST	
5-7 . . . . Amarillo	
9-11 . . . . Fort Worth	
19-22 . . . . Fort Worth	
23-26 . . . . . Grand Prairie	

SIOUX CITY

MAY	
20-22 . . . . . . Forth Worth	
23-25 . . . . . Grand Prairie	
30-31 . . . . Gary	

JUNE	
1-2 . . . . Gary	
3-5 . . . . Sioux Falls	
13-15 . . . . . . Kansas City	
20-22 . . . . . . Winnipeg	
29-30 . . . . . . Sioux Falls	

JULY	
2-5 . . . . . Fargo-Moorhead	
8 . . . . Sioux Falls	
14-17 . . . . St. Paul	
25-27 . . . . Winnipeg	
29-31 . . . . Gary	

AUGUST	
5-7 . . . . Wichita	
8-11 . . . . Gary	
19-21 . . . . . . Sioux Falls	
27-30 . . . . Lincoln	

SIOUX FALLS

MAY	
16-19 . . . . Winnipeg	
20-22 . . . . Lincoln	
30-31 . . . . Lincoln	

JUNE	
1-2 . . . . Lincoln	
7-9 . . . . Wichita	
10-12 . . . Fargo-Moorhead	
20-23 . . . . . Kansas City	
24-26 . . . . Gary	
28 . . . . Sioux City	

JULY	
1 . . . . Sioux City	
7 . . . . Sioux City	
9 . . . . Sioux City	
11-13 . . . . Fargo-Moorhead	
18-20 . . . . St. Paul	
22-24 . . . . Winnipeg	
28-30 . . . . Fargo-Moorhead	

AUGUST	
1-3 . . . . St. Paul	
12-14 . . . . . . Sioux City	
27-30 . . . . Winnipeg	

WICHITA

MAY	
20-22	El Paso
30-31	Fort Worth

JUNE	
1-2	Fort Worth
3-5	Kansas City
10-12	Sioux City
13-15	Shreveport-Bossier
21-23	Fort Worth
27-30	El Paso

JULY	
1-2	Kansas City
6	Kansas City
7-9	Lincoln
10-13	Shreveport-Bossier
22-24	El Paso
25-27	Fargo-Moorhead
28	Kansas City

AUGUST	
16-18	Kansas City
19-21	Gary
23-26	Amarillo

WINNIPEG

MAY	
12-15	Fargo-Moorhead
27-29	Gary
30-31	Fargo-Moorhead

JUNE	
1	Fargo-Moorhead
10-12	Kansas City
13-15	Sioux Falls
24-26	Lincoln

JULY	
2-5	St. Paul
14-17	Sioux Falls
19-21	Sioux City
29-31	St. Paul

AUGUST	
1-3	Gary
8-11	Sioux Falls
12-14	Wichita
15-17	St. Paul
23-26	Fargo-Moorhead

ATLANTIC LEAGUE HOME GAMES ONLY

BRIDGEPORT

APRIL	
29-30	Long Island

MAY	
1	Long Island
4-5	Road Warriors
11-12	York
20-22	Lancaster
27-30	York
31	Somerset

JUNE	
1-2	Somerset
10-12	Long Island
14-16	Road Warriors
17-19	Camden
21-23	Somerset
28-30	Southern Maryland

JULY	
1-3	Lancaster
8-11	Road Warriors
18-20	Camden
24-26	Somerset
27-29	York

AUGUST	
3-5	Road Warriors
6-8	Southern Maryland
12-14	Road Warriors
16-18	Camden
25-27	Southern Maryland
28-30	Lancaster

SEPTEMBER	
7-9	Long Island
10-11	Road Warriors

CAMDEN

MAY	
3-5	Long Island
6-7	York
13-15	Somerset
17-19	Bridgeport
20-22	Road Warriors
31	Lancaster

JUNE	
1-2	Lancaster
3-5	Bridgeport
7-9	Road Warriors
14-16	Southern Maryland
24-26	Road Warriors

JULY	
5-7	Lancaster
8-10	Southern Maryland
22-23	Road Warriors
24-26	Long Island
27-29	Southern Maryland

AUGUST	
6-8	Road Warriors
9-11	York
19-21	Long Island
22-24	Road Warriors
25-27	Somerset
31	Lancaster

SEPTEMBER	
1-2	Lancaster
3-5	Bridgeport
7-9	York
16-18	Somerset

LANCASTER

APRIL	
29-30	Road Warriors

MAY	
1	Road Warriors
4-5	Southern Maryland
10-12	Camden
13-15	Bridgeport
18-19	Somerset
26	York

JUNE	
3-6	Southern Maryland
7-9	Long Island
10-12	Road Warriors
14-16	Long Island
24-27	Somerset
28-30	Road Warriors

JULY	
8-10	York
15-17	Bridgeport
21-23	Bridgeport
24-26	York
30-31	Camden

AUGUST	
1	Camden
9-11	Somerset
12-14	Long Island
16-17	York
25-27	Road Warriors

SEPTEMBER	
3-5	Southern Maryland
7-9	Road Warriors
13-15	Camden
16-18	Road Warriors

LONG ISLAND

MAY	
6-7	Bridgeport
10-12	Southern Maryland
13-15	Road Warriors
25-26	Camden
27-29	Lancaster
30	Road Warriors

JUNE	
1-2	Road Warriors
3-5	Somerset
17-19	Road Warriors
20-23	Camden
28-30	York

JULY	
8-10	Somerset
15-17	Road Warriors

18-20	Southern Maryland
21-23	York
27-29	Lancaster
30-31	Road Warriors

AUGUST	
1	Road Warriors
6-8	Lancaster
9-11	Bridgeport
16-18	Road Warriors
22-24	Southern Maryland
25-27	York
28-30	Somerset

SEPTEMBER	
10-11	Camden
16-18	Bridgeport

ROAD WARRIORS

APRIL	
29-30	at Lancaster

MAY	
1	at Lancaster
4-5	at Bridgeport
6-8	at Southern Maryland
10-12	at Somerset
13-15	at Long Island
17-19	at York
20-22	at Camden
24-26	at Southern Maryland
27-29	at Somerset
30	at Long Island

JUNE	
1-2	at Long Island
3-5	at York
7-9	at Camden
10-12	at Lancaster
14-16	at Bridgeport
17-19	at Long Island
20-23	at York
24-26	at Camden
28-30	at Lancaster

JULY	
1-3	at Southern Maryland
4-6	at Somerset

8-11	at Bridgeport
15-17	at Long Island
18-20	at York
22-23	at Camden
24-26	at Southern Maryland
27-29	at Somerset
30-31	at Long Island

AUGUST	
1	at Long Island
3-5	at Bridgeport
6-8	at Camden
9-11	at Southern Maryland
12-14	at Bridgeport
16-18	at Long Island
19-21	at York
22-24	at Camden
25-27	at Lancaster
28-30	at Southern Maryland
31	at Somerset

SEPTEMBER	
1-2	at Somerset
3-5	at York
7-9	at Lancaster
10-11	at Bridgeport
13-15	at Somerset
16-18	at Lancaster

SOMERSET

MAY	
6-8 . . . . .Lancaster	
10-12 . . . . . .Road Warriors	
20-22 . . Southern Maryland	
24-26 . . . . . . .Bridgeport	
27-29 . . . . .Road Warriors	

JUNE	
10-12 . . . . Camden	
14-16 . . . . York	
17-19 . . Southern Maryland	
28-30 . . . . Camden	

JULY	
1-3 . . . . Long Island	
4-6 . . . . . . .Road Warriors	
15-17 . . . . Camden	
18-20 . . . . .Lancaster	

27-29 . . . . .Road Warriors
30-31 . . . . .Bridgeport

AUGUST
1 . . . . .Bridgeport
3-5 . . . . Long Island
12-14 . . . . York
16-18 . . Southern Maryland
19-21 . . . . .Bridgeport
23-24 . . . . .Lancaster
31 . . . . .Road Warriors

SEPTEMBER
1-2 . . . . . . .Road Warriors
3-5 . . . . Long Island
10-12 . . . . York
13-15 . . . . .Road Warriors

SOUTHERN MARYLAND

APRIL	
29-30 . . . . .Somerset	

MAY	
1 . . . . .Somerset	
6-8 . . . . . .Road Warriors	
17-19 . . . . . . Long Island	
24-26 . . . . .Road Warriors	
27-29 . . . . Camden	
31 . . . . York	

JUNE	
1-2 . . . . York	
7-9 . . . . .Bridgeport	
10-12 . . . . York	
21-23 . . . . .Lancaster	
24-26 . . . . . . Long Island	

JULY	
1-3 . . . . . . .Road Warriors	

4-6 . . . . .Bridgeport
15-17 . . . . York
21-23 . . . . .Somerset
24-26 . . . . .Road Warriors

AUGUST
3-5 . . . . Camden
9-11 . . . . . .Road Warriors
12-14 . . . . Camden
19-21 . . . . .Lancaster
28-30 . . . . .Road Warriors
31 . . . . .Bridgeport

SEPTEMBER
1-2 . . . . .Bridgeport
7-9 . . . . .Somerset
10-12 . . . . .Lancaster
13-15 . . . . . . Long Island

YORK

APRIL	
29-30 . . . . Camden	

MAY	
1 . . . . Camden	
4-5 . . . . .Somerset	
13-15 . . Southern Maryland	
18-19 . . . . .Road Warriors	
20-22 . . . . . . Long Island	
25 . . . . .Lancaster	

JUNE	
3-5 . . . . . .Road Warriors	
6-9 . . . . .Somerset	
17-19 . . . . .Lancaster	
20-23 . . . . .Road Warriors	
24-26 . . . . . . .Bridgeport	

JULY	
1-3 . . . . Camden	

4-6 . . . . Long Island
9 . . . . .Lancaster
18-20 . . . . .Road Warriors
30-31 . . Southern Maryland

AUGUST
1 . . . . . Southern Maryland
3-5 . . . . .Lancaster
6-8 . . . . .Somerset
18 . . . . .Lancaster
19-21 . . . . .Road Warriors
22-24 . . . . .Bridgeport
28-30 . . . . Camden
31 . . . . Long Island

SEPTEMBER
1-2 . . . . Long Island
3-5 . . . . . . .Road Warriors
13-15 . . . . .Bridgeport
16-18 . . Southern Maryland

CAN-AM LEAGUE

HOME GAMES ONLY

BROCKTON

MAY	
26-29 . . . . Worcester	
30-31 . . . . .Quebec	

JUNE	
1 . . . . .Quebec	
10-12 . . . . Newark	
14-16 . . . . .Rockland	

24-26 . . . . . . New Jersey
28-30 . . . . .New York

JULY
1 . . . . .New York
6-9 . . . . .New York
10-12 . . . . Pittsfield
17-20 . . . . .New York
22-24 . . . . .Newark

NEWARK

AUGUST	
1-3 . . . . .New York	
4-7 . . . . .Rockland	
15-18 . . . . .Quebec	
19-21 . . . . Worcester	

30-31 . . . . Pittsfield
SEPTEMBER
1 . . . . Pittsfield
2-4 . . . . New Jersey

MAY	
26-28 . . . . .Rockland	
29 . . . . New Jersey	

June	
2-6 . . . . .New York	
7-8 . . . . . . New Jersey	
17-19 . . . . .Brockton	
20-23 . . . . Worcester	
28-30 . . . . Pittsfield	

JULY	
1 . . . . Pittsfield	
5 . . . . .Rockland	
11-13 . . . . .New York	

14-16 . . . . .Quebec
17-20 . . . . Worcester
25-28 . . . . . .New York
29-31 . . . . .Brockton

AUGUST
1-3 . . . . Pittsfield
12-14 . . . . .Quebec
19-21 . . . . . . .New York
23-25 . . . . . New Jersey

SEPTEMBER
2-3 . . . . .Rockland

NEW JERSEY

MAY	
31 . . . . Newark	

JUNE	
1 . . . . Newark	
3-6 . . . . .Rockland	
9 . . . . Newark	
10-12 . . . . Worcester	
13-16 . . . . Pittsfield	
20-23 . . . . . . .New York	
28-30 . . . . .Quebec	

JULY	
1 . . . . .Quebec	
2-4 . . . . .New York	
14-16 . . . . Brockton	

20 . . . . .Rockland
21-24 . . . . . .New York
29-31 . . . . Pittsfield

AUGUST
1-3 . . . . .Quebec
12-14 . . . . Worcester
16-18 . . . . . . .New York
19 . . . . .Rockland
21 . . . . .Rockland
26-29 . . . . Brockton
30-31 . . . . .Newark

SEPTEMBER
1 . . . . .Newark

PITTSFIELD

MAY	
26-28 . . . . . New Jersey	
29-31 . . . . . . .Rockland	

JUNE	
1 . . . . .Rockland	
7-9 . . . . Worcester	
10-12 . . . . .New York	
17-19 . . . . .New York	
20-23 . . . . .Quebec	

JULY	
2-4 . . . . Brockton	

7-9 . . . . Newark
17-20 . . . . .Quebec
25-28 . . . . . . .Rockland

AUGUST
5-8 . . . . New Jersey
9-11 . . . . .New York
12-14 . . . . Brockton
23-25 . . . . . . Worcester
26-28 . . . . Newark

SEPTEMBER
2-5 . . . . .New York

QUEBEC

MAY	
26-29 . . . . . . .New York	

JUNE	
2-5 . . . . Pittsfield	
7-9 . . . . Brockton	
14-16 . . . . .New York	
24-26 . . . . Newark	

JULY	
2-4 . . . . Worcester	
6-9 . . . . . . New Jersey	
11-13 . . . . .Rockland	

22-24 . . . . .Rockland
25-28 . . . . Brockton

AUGUST
4-7 . . . . Newark
9-11 . . . . . New Jersey
19-21 . . . . Pittsfield
23-25 . . . . . . .New York
30-31 . . . . . . .New York

SEPTEMBER
1 . . . . .New York
2-5 . . . . Worcester

ROCKLAND

JUNE	
10-12 . . . . .Quebec	

17-19 . . . . . . New Jersey
20-23 . . . . Brockton

24-27 . . . . .New York

JULY
2-4 . . . . .Newark
6-9 . . . . Worcester
10 . . . . .New York
14-16 . . . . Pittsfield
17-19 . . . . . . New Jersey
29-31 . . . . .Quebec

AUGUST
1-3 . . . . Worcester
9-11 . . . . Newark
12-14 . . . . . . .New York
15-18 . . . . Pittsfield
20 . . . . New Jersey
23-25 . . . . Brockton
26-28 . . . . . . .New York

SEPTEMBER
4-5 . . . . Newark

WORCESTER

MAY
30-31 . . . . New York

JUNE
1 . . . . New York
2-5 . . . . Brockton
13-15 . . . . Newark
17-19 . . . . Quebec
24-26 . . . . . . Pittsfield
28-30 . . . . . . Rockland

JULY
1 . . . . .Rockland
10-12 . . . . . . New Jersey

14-16 . . . . New York
22-24 . . . . Pittsfield
25-28 . . . . . . New Jersey
29-31 . . . . New York

AUGUST
4-7 . . . . .New York
9-11 . . . . Brockton
15-18 . . . . Newark
26-28 . . . . Quebec
30-31 . . . . Rockland

SEPTEMBER
1 . . . . .Rockland

FRONTIER LEAGUE   HOME GAMES ONLY

EVANSVILLE

MAY
20-22 . . . . Florence
27-29 . . . . Gateway

JUNE
7-9 . . . . .Windy City
10-12 . . . . Joliet
19-20 . . . . . . .River City
25-26 . . . . Southern Illinois

JULY
5-7 . . . . Traverse City
8-10 . . . . .Kalamazoo

15-17 . . . . Normal
24-25 . . . . Southern Illinois
27-29 . . . . Gateway
30-31 . . . . .River City

AUGUST
9-11 . . . . Washington
12-14 . . . . Lake Erie
23-25 . . . . Florence
30-31 . . . . Normal

SEPTEMBER
1 . . . . Normal

FLORENCE

MAY
24-26 . . . . Normal
27-29 . . . . .River City

JUNE
7-9 . . . . Joliet
10-12 . . . . . .Windy City
19-21 . . . . Southern Illinois
29-30 . . . . . . .Kalamazoo

JULY
1 . . . . .Kalamazoo
8-10 . . . . . . Traverse City
18-20 . . . . Evansville

21-23 . . . . Gateway
24-26 . . . . Normal

AUGUST
2-4 . . . . Lake Erie
5-7 . . . . Washington
16-18 . . . . . . Evansville
19-21 . . . . Southern Illinois
26-28 . . . . . .River City
30-31 . . . . Gateway

SEPTEMBER
1 . . . . Gateway

GATEWAY

MAY
10 . . . . . . Southern Illinois
15 . . . . .River City
20-22 . . . . Southern Illinois
31 . . . . Traverse City

JUNE
1-2 . . . . Traverse City
3-5 . . . . .Kalamazoo
13-15 . . . . Normal
16-18 . . . . Florence
22-24 . . . . . . Evansville

JULY
2-4 . . . . Washington

5-7 . . . . Lake Erie
15-17 . . . . Florence
24-26 . . . . . . .River City

AUGUST
2-4 . . . . Joliet
5-7 . . . . .Windy City
16-18 . . . . Southern Illinois
19-21 . . . . Normal
26-28 . . . . . . Evansville

SEPTEMBER
2-4 . . . . .River City

JOLIET

MAY
19-21 . . . . . . Washington
24-26 . . . . . at Windy City
27-29 . . . . at Lake Erie
31 . . . . Florence

JUNE
1-2 . . . . Florence
3-5 . . . . Evansville
7-9 . . . . .at Florence
10-12 . . . . . at Evansville
13-15 . . . . . . Washington
16-18 . . . at Traverse City
19-21 . . . . . . .Kalamazoo
22-24 . . . . . Windy City
25-27 . . . at Kalamazoo
29-30 . . at Southern Illinois

JULY
1 . . . . at Southern Illinois
2-4 . . . . Normal
5-7 . . . . . . Southern Illinois
8-10 . . . . . . at Normal

15-17 . . . . . .Kalamazoo
18-20 . . . . at Windy City
21-23 . . . . . . Lake Erie
24-26 . . . . at Traverse City
27-29 . . . . at Lake Erie
30-31 . . . . Traverse City

AUGUST
1 . . . . Traverse City
2-5 . . . . at Gateway
6-7 . . . . . . at River City
9-11 . . . . Gateway
12-14 . . . . . .River City
16-18 . . . . Normal
19-21 . . . . Traverse City
23-25 . . . . . . Lake Erie
26-28 . . . . at Washington
30-31 . . . .Windy City

SEPTEMBER
1 . . . . .Windy City
2-4 . . . . . . at Kalamazoo

KALAMAZOO

MAY
21-22 . . . . . Traverse City
24-26 . . . . . . Lake Erie

JUNE
7-9 . . . . .River City
10-12 . . . . . . Gateway
16-18 . . . . . Lake Erie
25-27 . . . . Joliet

JULY
2-4 . . . . Evansville
5-7 . . . . Florence

21-23 . . . . . . Washington
24-26 . . . . . . Windy City

AUGUST
2-4 . . . . . Southern Illinois
5-7 . . . . Normal
16-18 . . . . . Windy City
19-21 . . . . . Washington
30-31 . . . . Traverse City

SEPTEMBER
1 . . . . Traverse City
2-4 . . . . Joliet

LAKE ERIE

MAY
27-29 . . . . Joliet
31 . . . . Normal

JUNE
1-2 . . . . Normal
10-12 . . . . Southern Illinois
13-15 . . . . . Traverse City
19-21 . . . . . .Windy City
22-24 . . . . Traverse City
29-30 . . . . . . Gateway

JULY
1 . . . . Gateway
2-4 . . . . .River City

18-20 . . . . . .Kalamazoo
27-29 . . . . . . Joliet
30-31 . . . . Washington

AUGUST
1 . . . . Washington
5-7 . . . . Evansville
9-11 . . . . . . Florence
19-21 . . . . . .Windy City
26-28 . . . . .Kalamazoo
30-31 . . . . Washington

SEPTEMBER
1 . . . . Washington

NORMAL

MAY
27-29 . . . . Southern Illinois

JUNE
3-5 . . . . Washington
7-9 . . . . Lake Erie
16-18 . . . . . Evansville
19-21 . . . . . Gateway
25-27 . . . . . Florence

JULY
5-7 . . . . . . .Windy City
8-10 . . . . Joliet

18-20 . . . . . . .River City
21-23 . . . . . . Evansville
30-31 . . . . . . Gateway

AUGUST
1 . . . . Gateway
9-11 . . . . . Traverse City
12-14 . . . . .Kalamazoo
23-25 . . . . .River City
26-28 . . . . Southern Illinois

SEPTEMBER
2-4 . . . . Florence

RIVER CITY

MAY	
10 . . . . Normal	
14 . . . . Gateway	
20-22 . . . . Normal	
24-26 . . . . Gateway	
31 . . . . .Kalamazoo	

JUNE	
1-2. . . . . .Kalamazoo	
3-5. . . . . . . Traverse City	
13-15 . . . . Evansville	
22-24 . . . . Florence	
25-27 . . . . Gateway	

JULY	
5-7. . . . . . . Washington	
8-10 . . . . Lake Erie	
21-23 . . . . . . Southern Illinois	
27-29 . . . . Florence	

AUGUST	
2-4. . . . . .Windy City	
5-7. . . . . Joliet	
16-18 . . . . Normal	
19-21 . . . . Evansville	
30-31 . . . . . . Southern Illinois	

SEPTEMBER	
1 . . . . . . Southern Illinois	

SOUTHERN ILLINOIS MINERS

MAY	
11 . . . . Gateway	
17 . . . . Evansville	
24-26 . . . . Evansville	
31 . . . . Washington	

JUNE	
1-2. . . . . Washington	
3-5. . . . . Lake Erie	
13-15 . . . . Florence	
16-18 . . . . .River City	
22-24 . . . . Normal	
29-30 . . . . Joliet	

JULY	
1 . . . . Joliet	
2-4. . . . . .Windy City	
15-17 . . . . .River City	
18-20 . . . . Gateway	
27-29 . . . . Normal	
30-31 . . . . Florence	

AUGUST	
1 . . . . Florence	
9-11 . . . . .Kalamazoo	
12-14 . . . . . . Traverse City	
23-25 . . . . Gateway	

SEPTEMBER	
2-4. . . . . Evansville	

TRAVERSE CITY

MAY	
27-29 . . . . . . .Kalamazoo	

JUNE	
7-9. . . . . Gateway	
10-12 . . . . .River City	
16-18 . . . . Joliet	
19-21 . . . . . . Washington	

JULY	
1 . . . . Evansville	
2-4. . . . . Florence	
15-17 . . . . . . .Windy City	
18-20 . . . . . . Washington	
24-26 . . . . Joliet	

AUGUST	
2-4. . . . . Normal	
5-7. . . . . Southern Illinois	
16-18 . . . . Lake Erie	
23-25 . . . . . . .Kalamazoo	
26-28 . . . . . . .Windy City	

SEPTEMBER	
2-4. . . . . Lake Erie	

WASHINGTON

MAY	
24-26 . . . . . Traverse City	
27-29 . . . . . .Windy City	

JUNE	
7-9. . . . . Southern Illinois	
10-12 . . . . Normal	
16-18 . . . . . .Windy City	
22-24 . . . . . .Kalamazoo	
25 . . . . . . Traverse City	
27 . . . . . . Traverse City	
29-30 . . . . . . .River City	

JULY	
1 . . . . .River City	
8-10 . . . . Gateway	
15-17 . . . . Lake Erie	
24-26 . . . . Lake Erie	
27-29 . . . . . . .Kalamazoo	

AUGUST	
2-4. . . . . Evansville	
12-14 . . . . Florence	
16-18 . . . . Joliet	
26-28 . . . . Joliet	

WINDY CITY

MAY	
19-21 . . . . . . Lake Erie	
24-26 . . . . Joliet	
31 . . . . Evansville	

JUNE	
1-2. . . . . Evansville	
3-5. . . . . Florence	

(cont.)	
13-15 . . . . . . .Kalamazoo	
25-27 . . . . Lake Erie	
29-30 . . . . Normal	

JULY	
1 . . . . Normal	
9-10 . . . . Southern Illinois	
18-20 . . . . Joliet	

21-23 . . . . . Traverse City
27-29 . . . . Traverse City
30-31 . . . . . .Kalamazoo

AUGUST
1 . . . . .Kalamazoo
9-11 . . . . .River City

12-14 . . . . Gateway
24-25 . . . . . . Washington

SEPTEMBER
2-4. . . . . Washington

N. AMERICAN LEAGUE   HOME GAMES ONLY

CALGARY VIPERS

JUNE	
4-7. . . . . . . Edmonton	
9-12. . . . . Chico	
14-17 . . . . . . .Henderson	
23-26 . . . . Yuma	
28-30 . . . . .Maui	

JULY	
1 . . . . .Maui	
12-14 . . . . Edmonton	

20-22 . . . . Edmonton
23-27 . . . . .Maui
28-31 . . . . . . .Henderson

AUGUST
12-14 . . . . Chico
16 . . . . Chico
17-21 . . . . Yuma
22-24 . . . . . Edmonton

CHICO OUTLAWS

JUNE	
18-21 . . . . Calgary	
23-26 . . . . . Schaumburg	

JULY	
2-6. . . . . Edmonton	
8-11 . . . . Calgary	
19-22 . . . . .Maui	
23-26 . . . . Yuma	

AUGUST
8-10 . . . . Edmonton
22-25 . . . . .Maui
30-31 . . . . . . .Henderson

SEPTEMBER
1-2. . . . . .Henderson
3-5. . . . . Yuma

EDINBURG ROADRUNNERS

MAY	
25-28 . . . Rio Grande Valley	
29-31 . . . . . . San Angelo	

JUNE	
1 . . . . San Angelo	
20-23 . . . . .Maui	
24-27 . . . Rio Grande Valley	

JULY	
3-6. . . . . San Angelo	
13-16 . . . . Rockford	
21-22 . . . Rio Grande Valley	

26-27 . . . Rio Grande Valley
30-31 . . . Rio Grande Valley

AUGUST
5-7. . . . Rio Grande Valley
9-11 . . . . Rio Grande Valley
12-15 . . . .Lake County
21-23 . . . . Rockford
25-26 . . . Rio Grande Valley
31 . . . . . Rio Grande Valley

SEPTEMBER
1 . . . . . . Rio Grande Valley

EDMONTON CAPITALS

MAY	
31 . . . . Calgary	

JUNE	
1-3. . . . . Calgary	
9-13. . . . . . . .Henderson	
14-17 . . . . Chico	
23-26 . . . . . . .Henderson	
28-30 . . . . Yuma	

JULY	
1 . . . . Yuma	

15-18 . . . . Calgary
23-24 . . . . .Henderson
26-27 . . . . . . .Henderson
28-31 . . . . .Maui

AUGUST
11-14 . . . . Yuma
16 . . . . Yuma
18-21 . . . . Chico
25-28 . . . . Calgary

HENDERSON ROADRUNNERS

MAY	
25-28 . . . . Edmonton	
29-31 . . . . Yuma	

JUNE	
1 . . . . Yuma	
3-5. . . . . Chico	
18-21 . . . . . Schaumburg	

28-30 . . . . Chico

JULY
1 . . . . Chico
13-17 . . . . .Maui
18-22 . . . . Yuma

AUGUST
2-6. . . . . San Angelo

8-9 . . . . Yuma
26-29 . . . . .Maui

LAKE COUNTY FIELDERS

JUNE	
2-5 . . . . Schaumburg
8-9 . . . . Rockford
10-13 . . . . Edinburgh
17-20 . . . . Rockford
26-27 . . . . Rockford
29-30 . . . . . . Schaumburg

JULY	
3-6 . . . . Rio Grande Valley

MAUI NA KOA IKAIKA

MAY	
25-28 . . . . Chico
30-31 . . . . Chico

JUNE	
1 . . . . Chico
3-7 . . . . Yuma
9-11 . . . . Yuma

JULY	
4-6 . . . . .Henderson

RIO GRANDE VALLEY WHITEWINGS

MAY	
29-31 . . . . . .Lake County

JUNE	
6-9 . . . . San Angelo
15-18 . . . . .Maui
20-23 . . . . . . San Angelo

JULY	
13-16 . . . . . . San Angelo
17-20 . . . . Rockford

ROCKFORD RIVERHAWKS

MAY	
26-29 . . . . . Schaumburg

JUNE	
2-5 . . . . Edinburgh
7 . . . . .Lake County
15-16 . . . . . .Lake County
22-25 . . . . . .Lake County
29-30 . . . Rio Grande Valley

JULY	
1-2 . . . . . Rio Grande Valley

7-8 . . . . Rockford
13-15 . . . . . Schaumburg
19-21 . . . . . Schaumburg
27-28 . . . . Chico

AUGUST	
1-2 . . . . Schaumburg
17-20 . . . . . Schaumburg
25-28 . . . . . Schaumburg
2-5 . . . . San Angelo

8-11 . . . . . . .Henderson

AUGUST	
2-6 . . . . Calgary
8-10 . . . . Calgary
12-15 . . . . . .Henderson
17-20 . . . . . .Henderson
30-31 . . . . . . Edmonton

SEPTEMBER	
1-5 . . . . Edmonton

23-24 . . . . Edinburgh
28-29 . . . . Edinburgh

AUGUST	
1-4 . . . . Edinburgh
12-15 . . . . . San Angelo
17-20 . . . . Rockford
27-30 . . . . Edinburgh

SEPTEMBER	
2-5 . . . . Edinburgh

3-6 . . . . Schaumburg
9-11 . . . . . . .Lake County
30-31 . . . . Chico

AUGUST	
1-2 . . . . Chico
3-6 . . . . .Lake County
7 . . . . Schaumburg
11-15 . . . . . Schaumburg
25-28 . . . . . . San Angelo
29-31 . . . . . .Lake County

SAN ANGELO COLTS

MAY	
25-28 . . . . . .Lake County

JUNE	
2-5 . . . . Rio Grande Valley
10-13 . . . Rio Grande Valley
15-18 . . . . Edinburgh
24-25 . . . . .Maui
27 . . . . .Maui
29-30 . . . . Edinburgh

SCHAUMBURG FLYERS

MAY	
30-31 . . . . Rockford
June
1 . . . . Rockford
6-9 . . . . Edinburgh
10-13 . . . . Rockford

JULY	
1-2 . . . . . .Lake County
7-10 . . . . . . .Rio Grande
16-18 . . . . . .Lake County
22-24 . . . . . .Lake County

YUMA SCORPIONS

MAY	
25-28 . . . . Calgary

JUNE	
15-17 . . . . . Schaumburg
18-21 . . . . Edmonton

JULY	
2-6 . . . . Calgary
8-11 . . . . Edmonton
14-16 . . . . Chico

JULY	
1-2 . . . . Edinburgh
7-10 . . . . Edinburgh
17-20 . . . . Edinburgh
21-24 . . . . Rockford

AUGUST	
8-11 . . . . . . .Lake County
17-20 . . . . Edinburgh
21-23 . . . Rio Grande Valley

26-29 . . . . Rockford
30-31 . . . . . .Lake County

AUGUST	
3-6 . . . . Chico
8-10 . . . . Rockford
21-24 . . . . . .Lake County
29-31 . . . . . . San Angelo

SEPTEMBER	
1 . . . . San Angelo
2-5 . . . . Rockford

27-31 . . . . San Angelo

AUGUST	
2-6 . . . . Edmonton
22-25 . . . . . . .Henderson
26-28 . . . . Chico
30-31 . . . . Calgary

SEPTEMBER	
1-2 . . . . Calgary

SPRING TRAINING SCHEDULES

ARIZONA CACTUS LEAGUE

ARIZONA DIAMONDBACKS

FEBRUARY	
25 . . . . . at San Francisco	12 . . . . at Milwaukee
26 . . . . .Colorado	12 . . . . at Colorado
27 . . . . .San Francisco	13 . . . . Chicago (NL)
28 . . . . .Colorado	15 . . . . .San Francisco
MARCH	16 . . . . . .Los Angeles (AL)
1 . . . . at Colorado	17 . . . . at Los Angeles (NL)
2 . . . . Seattle	18 . . . . at Seattle
2 . . . . . . at San Francisco	19 . . . . Cincinnati
3 . . . . at San Diego	20 . . . . at Cleveland
4 . . . . San Diego	20 . . . . at Oakland
5 . . . . Texas	21 . . . . .Los Angeles (AL)
6 . . . . at Los Angeles (AL)	22 . . . . Cleveland
7 . . . . . at Kansas City	23 . . . . at Texas
7 . . . . . . Chicago (AL)	24 . . . . Oakland
8 . . . . . . at Cleveland	25 . . . . .at Chicago (AL)
9 . . . . Milwaukee	26 . . . . . . Kansas City
10 . . . . . Chicago (AL)	27 . . . . . at Cincinnati
11 . . . . at Los Angeles (AL)	28 . . . . Texas
	29 . . . . . .at Chicago (NL)

CHICAGO CUBS

FEBRUARY	
27 . . . . Oakland	13 . . . . .Los Angeles (NL)
28 . . . . Milwaukee	13 . . . . at Arizona
MARCH	14 . . . . at Seattle
1 . . . . . . at San Francisco	15 . . . . at Oakland
2 . . . . .at Milwaukee	15 . . . . .Colorado
3 . . . . Texas	17 . . . . at Oakland
4 . . . . at Kansas City	18 . . . . Cincinnati
5 . . . . . . San Diego	19 . . . . . . at San Diego
6 . . . . . . at Cincinnati	20 . . . . . .San Francisco
6 . . . . .Los Angeles (NL)	21 . . . at Los Angeles (AL)
7 . . . . .Los Angeles (AL)	22 . . at Los Angeles (NL)
8 . . . . at Colorado	23 . . . . Oakland
9 . . . . Kansas City	24 . . . . Chicago (AL)
10 . . . . Cleveland	25 . . . . Seattle
11 . . . . . .at Chicago (AL)	26 . . . . at Texas
12 . . . . Cincinnati	27 . . . . .Colorado
12 . . . . Cincinnati	28 . . . . . . at Cleveland
	29 . . . . .Arizona

CHICAGO WHITE SOX

FEBRUARY	
28 . . . . at Los Angeles (NL)	13 . . . . at Los Angeles (NL)
MARCH	14 . . . . San Diego
1 . . . . Milwaukee	16 . . . . . . .San Francisco
2 . . . . at Cincinnati	17 . . . . . . .at Milwaukee
3 . . . . Seattle	17 . . . . at Colorado
4 . . . . at Los Angeles (AL)	18 . . . . Oakland
5 . . . . . . at Cleveland	19 . . . . at Oakland
6 . . . . . . Kansas City	20 . . . . .Los Angeles (NL)
7 . . . . at Arizona	21 . . . . . . at San Diego
7 . . . . Cleveland	22 . . . . at Seattle
8 . . . . .Colorado	23 . . . . .Los Angeles (NL)
9 . . . . . . at San Francisco	24 . . . . .at Chicago (NL)
10 . . . . at Texas	25 . . . . .Arizona
10 . . . . at Arizona	26 . . . . .Los Angeles (AL)
11 . . . . Chicago (NL)	27 . . . . . . .at Milwaukee
12 . . . . Texas	28 . . . . Cincinnati
	29 . . . . . . at Kansas City
	30 . . . . at WS

CINCINNATI REDS

FEBRUARY	
27 . . . . at Cleveland	13 . . . . .Los Angeles (AL)
28 . . . . Cleveland	14 . . . . at Colorado
MARCH	16 . . . . Kansas City
1 . . . . at Los Angeles (AL)	17 . . . . Cleveland
1 . . . . at Oakland	18 . . . .at Chicago (NL)
2 . . . . Chicago (AL)	19 . . . . .Colorado
3 . . . . . .Los Angeles (NL)	19 . . . . at Arizona
4 . . . . at Seattle	20 . . . . . . .at Milwaukee
5 . . . . at Los Angeles (NL)	21 . . . . Seattle
6 . . . . . Chicago (NL)	22 . . . . Oakland
7 . . . . Milwaukee	23 . . . . . at San Diego
8 . . . . at Kansas City	24 . . . . Texas
9 . . . . at San Diego	25 . . . . San Diego
10 . . . . .San Francisco	26 . . . . at San Francisco
11 . . . . . . at Texas	27 . . . . .Arizona
12 . . . . .at Chicago (NL)	28 . . . . .at Chicago (AL)
12 . . . . .at Chicago (NL)	29 . . . . . at Cleveland

CLEVELAND INDIANS

FEBRUARY	
27 . . . . Cincinnati	13 . . . . at San Diego
28 . . . . at Cincinnati	14 . . . . Oakland
MARCH	15 . . . . Milwaukee
1 . . . . . .Los Angeles (NL)	17 . . . . . . at Cincinnati
2 . . . . at Oakland	18 . . . . . at Kansas City
3 . . . . at Texas	18 . . . . Texas
4 . . . . .Colorado	19 . . . at Los Angeles (AL)
5 . . . . . . Chicago (AL)	20 . . . . .Arizona
5 . . . . . . at Seattle	21 . . . . . at Kansas City
6 . . . . . at Colorado	22 . . . . at Arizona
7 . . . .at Chicago (AL)	23 . . . . Kansas City
8 . . . . .Arizona	24 . . . . at San Francisco
9 . . . . San Diego	25 . . . . . .at Milwaukee
10 . . . .at Chicago (AL)	26 . . . . . . .San Francisco
11 . . . . Seattle	27 . . . at Los Angeles (NL)
12 . . . . .Los Angeles (AL)	28 . . . . Chicago (NL)
	29 . . . . Cincinnati
	30 . . . . at Colorado

COLORADO ROCKIES

FEBRUARY	
26 . . . . at Arizona	13 . . . . at Oakland
28 . . . . at Arizona	14 . . . . Cincinnati
MARCH	15 . . . .at Chicago (AL)
1 . . . . .Arizona	16 . . . . at Texas
2 . . . . at San Diego	17 . . . . Chicago (AL)
3 . . . . .San Francisco	18 . . . . Milwaukee
4 . . . . . . at Cleveland	19 . . . . . . at Cincinnati
5 . . . . at Kansas City	20 . . . . .Los Angeles (AL)
6 . . . . Cleveland	21 . . . . at San Francisco
7 . . . . .Los Angeles (NL)	23 . . . . Seattle
8 . . . . .at Chicago (AL)	24 . . . at Los Angeles (NL)
8 . . . . . . Chicago (NL)	25 . . . . Texas
9 . . . . at Los Angeles (AL)	26 . . . . at Oakland
10 . . . . . . at Milwaukee	27 . . . . .at Chicago (NL)
11 . . . . . . Kansas City	27 . . . . Oakland
12 . . . . San Diego	28 . . . . at Seattle
12 . . . . .Arizona	29 . . . . Seattle
	30 . . . . .at Tulsa

KANSAS CITY ROYALS

FEBRUARY
27 . . . . at Texas
28 . . . . at Texas

MARCH
1 . . . . San Diego
2 . . . . at Los Angeles (NL)
3 . . . . at Los Angeles (AL)
4 . . . . Chicago (NL)
5 . . . . .Colorado
6 . . . . .at Chicago (AL)
7 . . . . .Arizona
7 . . . . . . at San Diego
8 . . . . Cincinnati
9 . . . . . .at Chicago (NL)
10 . . . at Los Angeles (AL)
10 . . . . at Oakland
11 . . . . at Colorado

12 . . . . .Los Angeles (NL)
13 . . . . . . .at Milwaukee
15 . . . . Oakland
16 . . . . at Cincinnati
17 . . . . Seattle
18 . . . . Cleveland
19 . . . . . at San Francisco
20 . . . . Texas
21 . . . . Cleveland
22 . . . . .Los Angeles (AL)
23 . . . . at Cleveland
24 . . . . at Seattle
25 . . . . . . .San Francisco
26 . . . . at Arizona
27 . . . . . . .San Francisco
28 . . . . Milwaukee
29 . . . . Chicago (AL)

LOS ANGELES DODGERS

FEBRUARY
26 . . . . at Los Angeles (AL)
26 . . . . . at San Francisco
27 . . . .Los Angeles (AL)
28 . . . . . . Chicago (AL)

MARCH
1 . . . . at Cleveland
2 . . . . Kansas City
3 . . . . at Cincinnati
4 . . . . .San Francisco
5 . . . . Cincinnati
6 . . . . . .at Chicago (NL)
7 . . . . at Colorado
8 . . . . .at Milwaukee
9 . . . . Seattle
10 . . . . .San Diego
11 . . . . at Oakland
12 . . . . . at Kansas City
12 . . . . . at San Francisco

13 . . . . Chicago (AL)
13 . . . . . .at Chicago (NL)
14 . . . . at Texas
15 . . . . Texas
17 . . . . .Arizona
18 . . . . . at San Francisco
19 . . . . Milwaukee
20 . . . . . .at Chicago (AL)
21 . . . . Oakland
21 . . . . at Arizona
22 . . . . Chicago (NL)
23 . . . . . .at Chicago (AL)
24 . . . . .Colorado
25 . . . . at Seattle
26 . . . . . . at San Diego
27 . . . . Cleveland
28 . . . . .Los Angeles (AL)
29 . . . at Los Angeles (AL)
30 . . . . Seattle

MILWAUKEE BREWERS

FEBRUARY
28 . . . . . .at Chicago (NL)
28 . . . . . . .San Francisco

MARCH
1 . . . . . . .at Chicago (NL)
2 . . . . Chicago (NL)
3 . . . . Oakland
4 . . . . at San Francisco
5 . . . . .Los Angeles
6 . . . . at Oakland
6 . . . . at Texas
7 . . . . at Cincinnati
8 . . . .Los Angeles (NL)
9 . . . . . . .at Arizona
10 . . . . .Colorado
11 . . . . Oakland
12 . . . . .Arizona

13 . . . . Kansas City
14 . . . . . at San Francisco
15 . . . . at Cleveland
16 . . . . at Seattle
17 . . . . Chicago (AL)
18 . . . . at Colorado
19 . . . at Los Angeles (NL)
20 . . . . Cincinnati
21 . . . . Texas
22 . . . . San Diego
24 . . . at Los Angeles (AL)
25 . . . . Cleveland
26 . . . . Seattle
27 . . . . Chicago (AL)
28 . . . . . . at Kansas City
28 . . . . San Diego
29 . . . . at San Diego

OAKLAND ATHLETICS

FEBRUARY
27 . . . . . .at Chicago (NL)
28 . . . . at Los Angeles (AL)

MARCH
1 . . . . Cincinnati
2 . . . . Cleveland
3 . . . . .at Milwaukee
4 . . . . Texas
5 . . . . . . .San Francisco
6 . . . . Milwaukee
6 . . . . . . at San Diego
7 . . . . Seattle
8 . . . . San Diego
9 . . . . at Texas
10 . . . . . . Kansas City
11 . . . . .Los Angeles (NL)
11 . . . . . . .at Milwaukee
12 . . . . at Seattle
13 . . . . .Colorado

14 . . . . at Cleveland
15 . . . . Chicago (NL)
15 . . . . . . at Kansas City
17 . . . . Chicago (NL)
18 . . . . . .at Chicago (AL)
19 . . . . Chicago (AL)
20 . . . . .Arizona
20 . . . . . at San Francisco
21 . . . . . . at Los Angeles
22 . . . . at Cincinnati
23 . . . . . .at Chicago (NL)
24 . . . . at Arizona
25 . . . . . .Los Angeles (AL)
26 . . . . .Colorado
27 . . . . at Colorado
28 . . . . . . at San Francisco
29 . . . . . . .San Francisco
30 . . . . . at San Francisco

LOS ANGELES ANGELS

FEBRUARY
26 . . . . .Los Angeles (NL)
27 . . . at Los Angeles (NL)
28 . . . . Oakland

MARCH
1 . . . . Cincinnati
2 . . . . at Texas
3 . . . . Kansas City
4 . . . . Chicago (AL)
5 . . . . .at Milwaukee
6 . . . .`.Arizona
7 . . . . .at Chicago (NL)
8 . . . . Texas
9 . . . . .Colorado
10 . . . . at Seattle
10 . . . . . at Kansas City
11 . . . . .Arizona
12 . . . . at Cleveland
13 . . . . at Cincinnati

13 . . . . Seattle
15 . . . . at San Diego
16 . . . . at Arizona
17 . . . . at San Francisco
18 . . . . San Diego
19 . . . . Cleveland
20 . . . . at Colorado
21 . . . . Chicago (NL)
22 . . . . . at Kansas City
23 . . . . . . .San Francisco
24 . . . . Milwaukee
25 . . . . at Oakland
26 . . . . . .at Chicago (AL)
27 . . . . San Diego
28 . . . at Los Angeles (NL)
29 . . . . .Los Angeles (NL)
31 . . . . . . at Kansas City

SAN DIEGO PADRES

FEBRUARY
27 . . . . at Seattle
28 . . . . Seattle

MARCH
1 . . . . at Kansas City
2 . . . . .Colorado
3 . . . . .Arizona
4 . . . . at Arizona
5 . . . . . .at Chicago (NL)
6 . . . . Oakland
7 . . . . Kansas City
8 . . . . at Oakland
9 . . . . Cincinnati
9 . . . . at Cleveland
10 . . . . at Los Angeles (NL)
11 . . . . . . .San Francisco
12 . . . . at Colorado

13 . . . . Cleveland
14 . . . . . .at Chicago (AL)
15 . . . . . .Los Angeles (AL)
17 . . . . Texas
18 . . . at Los Angeles (AL)
19 . . . . Chicago (NL)
20 . . . . at Seattle
21 . . . . Chicago (AL)
22 . . . . .at Milwaukee
23 . . . . Cincinnati
24 . . . . at Texas
25 . . . . at Cincinnati
26 . . . . .Los Angeles (NL)
27 . . . at Los Angeles (AL)
28 . . . . . . .at Milwaukee
29 . . . . Milwaukee

SAN FRANCISCO GIANTS

FEBRUARY
25 . . . . .Arizona
26 . . . . .Los Angeles (NL)
27 . . . . at Arizona
28 . . . . at Milwaukee

MARCH
1 . . . . Chicago (NL)
2 . . . . .Arizona
3 . . . . at Colorado
4 . . . . Milwaukee
4 . . . at Los Angeles (NL)
5 . . . . at Oakland
6 . . . . Seattle
7 . . . . Texas
8 . . . . at Seattle
9 . . . . Chicago (AL)
10 . . . . . . at Cincinnati
11 . . . . . . at San Diego
12 . . . . .Los Angeles (NL)

13 . . . . at Texas
14 . . . . Milwaukee
15 . . . . at Arizona
16 . . . . .at Chicago (AL)
17 . . . . .Los Angeles (AL)
18 . . . .Los Angeles (NL)
19 . . . . Kansas City
20 . . . . Oakland
20 . . . .at Chicago (NL)
21 . . . . .Colorado
23 . . . at Los Angeles (AL)
24 . . . . Cleveland
25 . . . . . . at Kansas City
26 . . . . Cincinnati
26 . . . . . . at Cleveland
27 . . . . . . at Kansas City
28 . . . . Oakland
29 . . . . at Oakland
30 . . . . Oakland

SEATTLE MARINERS

FEBRUARY
27 . . . . San Diego
28 . . . . . . at San Diego

MARCH
1 . . . . Texas
2 . . . . at Arizona
3 . . . . . .at Chicago (AL)
4 . . . . Cincinnati
5 . . . . Cleveland
6 . . . . . at San Francisco
7 . . . . at Oakland
8 . . . . .San Francisco
9 . . . at Los Angeles (NL)
10 . . . . .Los Angeles (AL)
11 . . . . at Cleveland
12 . . . . Oakland
13 . . . . at Los Angeles (AL)

14 . . . . Chicago (NL)
16 . . . . Milwaukee
17 . . . . . . at Kansas City
18 . . . . .Arizona
19 . . . . at Texas
20 . . . . .San Diego
21 . . . . . at Cincinnati
22 . . . . . Chicago (AL)
23 . . . . . . at Colorado
24 . . . . . . Kansas City
25 . . . .at Chicago (NL)
25 . . . .Los Angeles (NL)
26 . . . . at Milwaukee
27 . . . . Texas
28 . . . . .Colorado
29 . . . . . . at Colorado
30 . . at Los Angeles (NL)

TEXAS RANGERS

FEBRUARY
27 . . . . Kansas City
28 . . . . Kansas City

MARCH
1 . . . . at Seattle
2 . . . . . .Los Angeles (AL)
3 . . . . Cleveland
3 . . . .at Chicago (NL)
4 . . . . at Oakland
5 . . . . at Arizona
6 . . . . Milwaukee
7 . . . . at San Francisco
8 . . at Los Angeles (AL)
9 . . . . Oakland
10 . . . . . . Chicago (AL)
11 . . . . Cincinnati
12 . . . . . .at Chicago (AL)
13 . . . . . . .San Francisco

14 . . . . .Los Angeles (NL)
15 . . . at Los Angeles (NL)
16 . . . . .Colorado
17 . . . . . . at San Diego
18 . . . . . . at Cleveland
19 . . . . Seattle
20 . . . . . at Kansas City
21 . . . . . .at Milwaukee
23 . . . . .Arizona
24 . . . . . at Cincinnati
24 . . . . . . .San Diego
25 . . . . . . at Colorado
26 . . . . . . Chicago (NL)
27 . . . . at Seattle
28 . . . . at Arizona
29 . . . . at CCU
30 . . . . at RR

FLORIDA GRAPEFRUIT LEAGUE

ATLANTA BRAVES

FEBRUARY
26 . . .at New York (NL)
27 . . . . New York (NL)
28 . . . . Houston

MARCH
1 . . . . at Houston
2 . . . . at Boston
3 . . . . Detroit
4 . . . . at Washington
4 . . . . Toronto
5 . . . . . . New York (NL)
6 . . . . at Washington
7 . . . . at Florida
8 . . . . . New York (AL)
9 . . . . St. Louis
10 . . . . St. Louis
11 . . . at New York (AL)
12 . . . . New York (NL)
13 . . . . Houston

14 . . . . .at St. Louis
15 . . . . .at St. Louis
16 . . . . Boston
17 . . . . .Washington
18 . . . . .at New York (NL)
19 . . . . at Detroit
19 . . . . New York (NL)
20 . . . . Houston
21 . . .at New York (NL)
23 . . . . Florida
24 . . . . at Toronto
25 . . .at Philadelphia
25 . . . . Detroit
26 . . .at New York (NL)
27 . . . . Philadelphia
28 . . . . .Washington
29 . . . . .Minnesota
30 . . . . .Minnesota

BALTIMORE ORIOLES

FEBRUARY
28 . . . . . . at Pittsburgh

MARCH
1 . . . . Tampa Bay
2 . . . .at Philadelphia
3 . . . . .Minnesota
4 . . . . at Detroit
5 . . . . Boston
6 . . . . . at Minnesota
7 . . . . at Boston
7 . . . . . New York (AL)
8 . . .at Philadelphia
9 . . . . .Minnesota
9 . . . . at Boston
10 . . . . . . at Pittsburgh
11 . . . . . . Philadelphia
12 . . . . . . at Houston
13 . . . . Detroit

14 . . . . .Pittsburgh
15 . . . . Houston
16 . . . . .at New York (AL)
17 . . . . . at Pittsburgh
18 . . . . . . .Minnesota
19 . . . . . . Philadelphia
20 . . . . . . at Tampa Bay
22 . . . . . New York (AL)
23 . . . . . at Minnesota
24 . . . . .Pittsburgh
25 . . . . . at Minnesota
26 . . . . . at Tampa Bay
27 . . . . at Toronto
27 . . . . Boston
28 . . . . Detroit
29 . . . . Toronto

BOSTON RED SOX

FEBRUARY
26 . . . . .BC
26 . . . . .NEU
27 . . . . . . at Minnesota
28 . . . . .Minnesota

MARCH
1 . . . . at Minnesota
2 . . . . .Atlanta
3 . . . . Philadelphia
4 . . . .at New York (AL)
5 . . . . .at Baltimore
5 . . . . Florida
6 . . .at New York (NL)
7 . . . . Baltimore
8 . . . . . . .at St. Louis
9 . . . . Baltimore
10 . . . . . . at Tampa Bay
11 . . . . . . at Minnesota
12 . . . . Florida

13 . . . . . . at Pittsburgh
14 . . . . . New York (AL)
15 . . . . . . at Detroit
16 . . . . at Atlanta
17 . . . . . New York (NL)
18 . . . . Detroit
18 . . . . . at Tampa Bay
19 . . . . . at Pittsburgh
20 . . . . St. Louis
21 . . . .at Philadelphia
22 . . . . . Tampa Bay
24 . . . . . . at Florida
25 . . . . Toronto
26 . . . . . . .Minnesota
27 . . . . . . at Baltimore
28 . . . . . . at Toronto
29 . . . . . . Tampa Bay
30 . . . . . . at Houston
31 . . . . . . at Houston

DETROIT TIGERS

FEBRUARY
25 . . . . FSO
26 . . . . at Toronto
27 . . . . Toronto
28 . . . . . . New York (AL)

MARCH
1 . . . . .at Philadelphia
1 . . . . Toronto
2 . . . . Houston
3 . . . . at Atlanta
4 . . . . Baltimore
5 . . . . at Houston
5 . . . . at Toronto
6 . . . . Philadelphia
7 . . . . .at New York (NL)
8 . . . . Florida
9 . . . . Philadelphia
10 . . . . at Florida

11 . . . . .at St. Louis
12 . . . . Toronto
13 . . . . .at Baltimore
13 . . . . Houston
14 . . . . . at Washington
15 . . . . Boston
16 . . . . St. Louis
17 . . . . .Minnesota
18 . . . . at Boston
19 . . . . Atlanta
20 . . . . . at Washington
21 . . . . . . at Houston
22 . . . . . . New York (NL)
24 . . . . .Washington
25 . . . . at Atlanta
26 . . . . Philadelphia
27 . . . . . . at Houston
28 . . . . .at Baltimore
29 . . . . . at New York (AL)

FLORIDA MARLINS

FEBRUARY
27 . . . . Miami
28 . . . . .at St. Louis

MARCH
1 . . . . St. Louis
2 . . . . at Washington
3 . . . . at Houston
4 . . . . New York (NL)
5 . . . . at Boston
6 . . . . St. Louis
7 . . . . Atlanta
8 . . . . at Detroit
9 . . . . .Washington
10 . . . . . . New York (NL)
10 . . . . Detroit
11 . . . . .at New York (NL)
12 . . . . at Boston
13 . . . . .Washington

14 . . . . at Minnesota
15 . . . . . . at Tampa Bay
16 . . . . Tampa Bay
17 . . . . .at St. Louis
18 . . . . Houston
19 . . . . .at St. Louis
20 . . . . . . New York (NL)
22 . . . . .Minnesota
23 . . . . at Atlanta
24 . . . . Boston
25 . . . . New York (NL)
26 . . . . St. Louis
27 . . . . . at Washington
28 . . . . .at St. Louis
28 . . . . .at New York (NL)
29 . . . . St. Louis
30 . . . . . at New York (NL)

HOUSTON ASTROS

FEBRUARY
28 . . . . at Atlanta

MARCH
1 . . . . Atlanta
2 . . . . at Detroit
2 . . . . .at New York (AL)
3 . . . . Florida
4 . . . . St. Louis
5 . . . . Detroit
5 . . . . .at St. Louis
6 . . . . . . New York (AL)
7 . . . . . . at Washington
8 . . . . . . New York (NL)
9 . . . . .at New York (NL)
10 . . . . .Washington
11 . . . . . at Washington
12 . . . . Baltimore
13 . . . . at Atlanta
13 . . . . at Detroit

14 . . . . Philadelphia
15 . . . . .at Baltimore
16 . . . . .Washington
18 . . . . at Florida
19 . . . . St. Louis
20 . . . . at Atlanta
20 . . . . .Pittsburgh
21 . . . . Detroit
22 . . . . . . at Washington
23 . . . . at Pittsburgh
24 . . . . Tampa Bay
25 . . . .at New York (AL)
26 . . . . .Washington
27 . . . . Detroit
28 . . . . .at Philadelphia
29 . . . at Oklahoma City
30 . . . . Boston
31 . . . . Boston

MINNESOTA TWINS

FEBRUARY
27 . . . . Boston
28 . . . . at Boston

MARCH
1 . . . . Boston
2 . . . . at Pittsburgh
3 . . . . .at Baltimore
4 . . . . Tampa Bay
5 . . . . . at Tampa Bay
6 . . . . Baltimore
7 . . . . St. Louis
8 . . . . .Pittsburgh
9 . . . . .at Baltimore
10 . . . . Toronto
11 . . . . Boston
12 . . . . . . .at St. Louis
13 . . . .at New York (AL)

13 . . . . Philadelphia
14 . . . . Florida
16 . . . . . New York (NL)
17 . . . . . . at Detroit
18 . . . . .at Baltimore
19 . . . . Tampa Bay
20 . . . . at Toronto
21 . . . . . . at Pittsburgh
22 . . . . at Florida
23 . . . . Baltimore
24 . . . . . .at Philadelphia
25 . . . . Baltimore
26 . . . . . . at Boston
27 . . . . . New York (AL)
28 . . . . .Pittsburgh
29 . . . . . . at Atlanta
30 . . . . . . at Atlanta

NEW YORK METS

FEBRUARY
26 . . . . Atlanta
27 . . . . Michigan
27 . . . . at Atlanta
28 . . . . .Washington

MARCH
1 . . . . at Washington
2 . . . . .at St. Louis
3 . . . . St. Louis
4 . . . . at Florida
5 . . . . at Atlanta
6 . . . . Boston
7 . . . . Detroit
8 . . . . . . at Houston
8 . . . . .Washington
9 . . . . Houston
10 . . . . . . at Florida
10 . . . . . at Washington
11 . . . . Florida

12 . . . . at Atlanta
13 . . . . St. Louis
15 . . . . .Washington
16 . . . . . . at Minnesota
17 . . . . . at Boston
18 . . . . Atlanta
19 . . . . . . at Atlanta
19 . . . . . . .Washington
20 . . . . . . at Florida
21 . . . . Atlanta
22 . . . . at Detroit
23 . . . . . . .at St. Louis
24 . . . . St. Louis
25 . . . . . at Florida
26 . . . . Atlanta
27 . . . . . . .at St. Louis
28 . . . . Florida
29 . . . . . at Washington
30 . . . . Florida

NEW YORK YANKEES

FEBRUARY
26 . . . . Philadelphia
27 . . . . . .at Philadelphia
28 . . . . at Detroit

MARCH
1 . . . . at Pittsburgh
2 . . . . Houston
3 . . . . . . at Tampa Bay
4 . . . . Boston
5 . . . . .Washington
6 . . . . . . at Houston
7 . . . . Philadelphia
7 . . . . . .at Baltimore
8 . . . . . . at Atlanta
9 . . . . .Pittsburgh
10 . . . . . .at Philadelphia
11 . . . . Atlanta

11 . . . . .at Toronto
12 . . . . . at Washington
13 . . . . . . .Minnesota
14 . . . . . . at Boston
16 . . . . Baltimore
17 . . . . . . Tampa Bay
18 . . . . . . at Toronto
19 . . . . Toronto
20 . . . . .at Philadelphia
21 . . . . . .at Tampa Bay
22 . . . . . .at Baltimore
23 . . . . Toronto
25 . . . . Houston
26 . . . . . . .Pittsburgh
27 . . . . .at Minnesota
28 . . . . . . Tampa Bay
29 . . . . Detroit

PHILADELPHIA PHILLIES

FEBRUARY
26 ..... at New York (AL)
27 ..... New York (AL)
28 ..... at Toronto

MARCH
1 ..... Detroit
2 ..... Baltimore
3 ..... at Boston
4 ..... at Pittsburgh
5 ..... Pittsburgh
6 ..... at Detroit
6 ..... Tampa Bay
7 ..... at New York (AL)
8 ..... Baltimore
9 ..... at Detroit
10 ..... New York (AL)
11 ..... at Baltimore
12 ..... at Pittsburgh
12 ..... Tampa Bay
13 ..... at Minnesota
14 ..... at Houston
15 ..... at Toronto
17 ..... Toronto
18 ..... Pittsburgh
19 ..... at Baltimore
20 ..... New York (AL)
21 ..... Boston
22 ..... at Toronto
23 ..... at Tampa Bay
24 ..... Minnesota
25 ..... Atlanta
26 ..... at Detroit
26 ..... Toronto
27 ..... at Atlanta
28 ..... Houston
29 ..... Pittsburgh
30 ..... Pittsburgh

PITTSBURGH PIRATES

FEBRUARY
25 ..... MCC
26 ..... at Tampa Bay
27 ..... Tampa Bay
28 ..... Baltimore
28 ..... at Tampa Bay

MARCH
1 ..... New York (AL)
2 ..... Minnesota
3 ..... at Toronto
4 ..... Philadelphia
5 ..... at Philadelphia
6 ..... Toronto
7 ..... Tampa Bay
8 ..... at Minnesota
9 ..... at New York (AL)
10 ..... Baltimore
11 ..... at Tampa Bay
12 ..... Philadelphia
12 ..... at Toronto
13 ..... Boston
14 ..... at Baltimore
16 ..... Toronto
17 ..... Baltimore
18 ..... at Philadelphia
19 ..... Boston
20 ..... at Houston
21 ..... Minnesota
23 ..... Houston
24 ..... at Baltimore
25 ..... at Tampa Bay
26 ..... at New York (AL)
27 ..... Tampa Bay
28 ..... at Minnesota
29 ..... at Philadelphia
30 ..... at Philadelphia

ST. LOUIS CARDINALS

FEBRUARY
28 ..... Florida

MARCH
1 ..... at Florida
2 ..... New York (NL)
3 ..... Washington
3 ..... at New York (NL)
4 ..... at Houston
5 ..... Houston
6 ..... at Florida
7 ..... at Minnesota
8 ..... Boston
9 ..... at Atlanta
10 ..... at Atlanta
11 ..... Detroit
12 ..... Minnesota
13 ..... at New York (NL)
14 ..... Atlanta
15 ..... Atlanta
16 ..... at Detroit
17 ..... Florida
18 ..... at Washington
19 ..... Florida
19 ..... at Houston
20 ..... at Boston
21 ..... Washington
23 ..... New York (NL)
24 ..... at New York (NL)
25 ..... at Washington
26 ..... at Florida
27 ..... New York (NL)
28 ..... Florida
29 ..... at Florida
29 ..... at Springfield

TAMPA BAY RAYS

FEBRUARY
26 ..... Pittsburgh
27 ..... at Pittsburgh
28 ..... Pittsburgh

MARCH
1 ..... at Baltimore
2 ..... at Toronto
3 ..... New York (AL)
4 ..... at Minnesota
5 ..... Minnesota
6 ..... at Philadelphia
7 ..... at Pittsburgh
8 ..... Toronto
9 ..... Toronto
10 ..... Boston
11 ..... Pittsburgh
12 ..... at Philadelphia
13 ..... at Toronto
15 ..... Florida
16 ..... at Florida
17 ..... at New York (AL)
18 ..... Boston
19 ..... at Minnesota
20 ..... Baltimore
21 ..... New York (AL)
22 ..... at Boston
23 ..... Philadelphia
24 ..... at Houston
25 ..... Pittsburgh
26 ..... Baltimore
27 ..... at Pittsburgh
28 ..... at New York (AL)
29 ..... at Boston
30 ..... Toronto

TORONTO BLUE JAYS

FEBRUARY
26 ..... Detroit
27 ..... at Detroit
28 ..... Philadelphia

MARCH
1 ..... at Detroit
2 ..... Tampa Bay
3 ..... Pittsburgh
4 ..... at Atlanta
5 ..... Detroit
6 ..... at Pittsburgh
8 ..... at Tampa Bay
9 ..... at Tampa Bay
10 ..... at Minnesota
11 ..... New York (AL)
12 ..... Pittsburgh
12 ..... at Detroit
13 ..... Tampa Bay
15 ..... Philadelphia
16 ..... at Pittsburgh
17 ..... at Philadelphia
18 ..... New York (AL)
19 ..... at New York (AL)
20 ..... Minnesota
22 ..... Philadelphia
23 ..... at New York (AL)
24 ..... Atlanta
25 ..... at Boston
26 ..... at Philadelphia
27 ..... Baltimore
28 ..... Boston
29 ..... at Baltimore
30 ..... at Tampa Bay

WASHINGTON NATIONALS

FEBRUARY
28 ..... at New York (NL)

MARCH
1 ..... New York (NL)
2 ..... Florida
3 ..... at St. Louis
4 ..... Atlanta
5 ..... at New York (NL)
6 ..... Atlanta
7 ..... Houston
8 ..... at New York (NL)
9 ..... at Florida
10 ..... New York (NL)
10 ..... at Houston
11 ..... Houston
12 ..... New York (AL)
13 ..... at Florida
14 ..... Detroit
15 ..... at New York (NL)
16 ..... at Houston
17 ..... at Atlanta
18 ..... St. Louis
19 ..... at New York (NL)
20 ..... Detroit
21 ..... at St. Louis
22 ..... Houston
24 ..... at Detroit
25 ..... St. Louis
26 ..... at Houston
27 ..... Florida
28 ..... at Atlanta
29 ..... New York (NL)

COLLEGE

COLLEGE ORGANIZATIONS

NATIONAL COLLEGIATE ATHLETIC ASSOCIATION

Mailing Address: PO Box 6222, Indianapolis, IN 46206. **Telephone:** (317) 917-6222. **Fax:** (317) 917-6826 (championships), 917-6710 (baseball). **E-Mail Addresses:** dpoppe@ncaa.org (Dennis Poppe), rbuhr@ncaa.org (Randy Buhr), dleech@ncaa.org (Damani Leech), jham-ilton@ncaa.org (JD Hamilton), ctolliver@ncaa.org (Chad Tolliver), ryurk@ncaa.org (Russ Yurk), aholman@ncaa.org (Anthony Holman).

Websites: www.ncaa.org, www.ncaa.com.

President: Dr. Mark Emmert.

Vice President, Division I Baseball/Football: Dennis Poppe. **Director, Baseball:** Damani Leech. **Associate Director, Championships:** Randy Buhr. **Coordinator, Division I Baseball/Football:** Chad Tolliver. **Division II Assistant Director, Championships:** Russ Yurk. **Division III Associate Director, Championships:** Anthony Holman. **Media Contact, Division I College World Series:** JD Hamilton. **Contacts, Statistics:** Sean Straziscar, Jeff Williams.

Chairman, Division I Baseball Committee: Tim Weiser (Deputy Commissioner, Big 12 Conference). **Division I Baseball Committee:** John Anderson (Head Coach, Minnesota); Dennis Farrell (Commissioner, Big West Conference); Larry Gallo Jr (Senior Associate Athletic Director, North Carolina); John Hardt (Athletic Director, Bucknell); Kyle Kallander (Commissioner, Big South Conference); Mark LaBarbera (Athletic Director, Valparaiso); Chris Monasch (Athletics Director, St. John's); Gary Overton (Assistant Athletics Director, East Carolina); Bobby Staub (Athletic Director, Louisiana-Monroe).

Chairman, Division II Baseball Committee: Jeff Schaly (Assistant Athletic Director, Lynn University). **Chairman, Division III Baseball Committee:** Jack McKiernan (Associate Athletic Director, Kean).

2012 National Convention: Jan. 11-14 at Indianapolis

2011 CHAMPIONSHIP TOURNAMENTS

NCAA DIVISION I
65th College World Series . . . . .Omaha, June 18-28/29
Super Regionals (8) . . . . .Campus sites, June 10-13
Regionals (16). . . . . .Campus sites, June 3-6

NCAA DIVISION II
44th annual World Series . . . USA Baseball National Training Complex, Cary, N.C., May 28-June 4.
Regionals (8) . . . . Campus sites, May 19-23.

NCAA DIVISION III
36th annual World Series . . . . . Appleton, Wis., May 27-31
Regionals (8) . . . . Campus sites, May 18-22

NATIONAL ASSOCIATION OF INTERCOLLEGIATE ATHLETICS

Mailing Address: 1200 Grand Blvd, Kansas City, MO 64106. **Telephone:** (816) 595-8000. **Fax:** (816) 595-8200. **E-Mail Address:** cwaller@naia.org. **Website:** www.naia.org.

President/CEO: Jim Carr.

Manager, Championship Sports: Scott McClure. **Director, Sports Information:** Chad Waller. **President, Coaches Association:** Kirk Kelley.

2011 CHAMPIONSHIP TOURNAMENT

Opening round: May 13-16, campus locations.

Avista-NAIA World Series: May 27-June 3, Lewiston, Idaho.

NATIONAL JUNIOR COLLEGE ATHLETIC ASSOCIATION

Mailing Address: 1631 Mesa Ave, Suite B, Colorado Springs, CO 80906. **Telephone:** (719) 590-9788. **Fax:** (719) 590-7324. **E-Mail Address:** mkrug@njcaa.org. **Website:** www.njcaa.org.

Executive Director: Mary Ellen Leicht.

Director, Division I Baseball Tournament: Jamie Hamilton. **Director, Division II Baseball Tournament:** Billy Mayberry. **Director, Division III Baseball Tournament:** Tim Drain. **Director, Media Relations:** Mark Krug.

2011 CHAMPIONSHIP TOURNAMENTS

DIVISION I
World Series. . . . . Grand Junction, Colo., May 28-June 4

DIVISION II
World Series. . . . . Enid, Okla., May 28-June 4

DIVISION III
World Series. . . . . .Tyler, Texas, May 21-27

CALIFORNIA COMMUNITY COLLEGE COMMISSION ON ATHLETICS

Mailing Address: 2017 O St., Sacramento, CA 95811-5211. **Telephone:** (916) 444-1600. **Fax:** (916) 444-2616. **E-Mail Addresses:** ccarter@cccaasports.org, jboggs@ cccaasports.org. **Website:** www.cccaasports.org.

Executive Director: Carlyle Carter.

Director, Member Services: Debra Wheeler. **Assistant Director, Sports Information/Communications:** Jason Boggs.

2011 CHAMPIONSHIP TOURNAMENT

State Championship . . . . Bakersfield, Calif., May 20-22

NORTHWEST ATHLETIC ASSOCIATION OF COMMUNITY COLLEGES

Mailing Address: Clark College TGB 121, 1933 Fort Vancouver Way, Vancouver, WA 98663-3598. **Telephone:** (360) 992-2833. **Fax:** (360) 696-6210. **E-Mail Address:** nwaacc@clark.edu. **Website:** www.nwaacc.org.

Executive Director: Dick McClain.

Executive Assistant: Carol Hardin. **Director, Marketing:** Charles Warner. **Sports Information Director:** Tracy Swisher.

2011 CHAMPIONSHIP TOURNAMENT

NWAACC Championship. . . . . Lower Columbia CC, Longview, Wash., May 26-30

AMERICAN BASEBALL COACHES ASSOCIATION

Office Address: 108 S University Ave, Suite 3, Mount Pleasant, MI 48858-2327. **Telephone:** (989) 775-3300. **Fax:** (989) 775-3600. **E-Mail Address:** abca@abca.org. **Website:** www.abca.org.

Executive Director: Dave Keilitz.

Assistant to Executive Director: Betty Rulong. **Membership/Convention Coordinator:** Nick Phillips. **Assistant Coordinator:** Juahn Clark.

Chairman: Jack Kaiser. **President:** Joe Roberts (Armstrong Atlantic State, Ga.).

2012 National Convention: Jan. 5-9 at Hilton and Marriott Hotels in Anaheim, Calif.

NCAA DIVISION I CONFERENCES

AMERICA EAST CONFERENCE

Mailing Address: 215 First Street, Suite 140, Cambridge, MA 02142. **Telephone:** (617) 695-6369. **Fax:** (617) 695-6380. **E-Mail Address:** hanna@americaeast. com. **Website:** www.americaeast.com.

Baseball Members (First Year): Albany (2002), Binghamton (2002), Hartford (1990), Maine (1990), Maryland-Baltimore County (2004), Stony Brook (2002).

Associate Director, Communications: Leslie Hanna.

2011 Tournament: Four teams, double-elimination. May 25-28 at highest-seeded team.

ATLANTIC COAST CONFERENCE

Office Address: 4512 Weybridge Lane, Greensboro, NC 27407. **Mailing Address:** PO Drawer ACC, Greensboro, NC 27417. **Telephone:** (336) 851-6062. **Fax:** (336) 854-8797. **E-Mail Address:** sphillips@theacc.org. **Website:** www.theacc.com.

Baseball Members (First Year): Boston College (2006), Clemson (1954), Duke (1954), Florida State (1992), Georgia Tech (1980), Maryland (1954), Miami (2005), North Carolina (1954), North Carolina State (1954), Virginia (1955), Virginia Tech (2005), Wake Forest (1954).

Assistant Director, Communications: Steve Phillips.

2011 Tournament: Eight teams, group play. May 26-29 at Durham Bulls Athletic Park, Durham, N.C.

ATLANTIC SUN CONFERENCE

Mailing Address: 3370 Vineville Ave., Suite 108-B, Macon, GA 31204. **Telephone:** (478) 474-3394. **Fax:** (478) 474-4272. **E-Mail Addresses:** emoyer@atlanticsun.org. **Website:** www.atlanticsun.org.

Baseball Members (First Year): Belmont (2002), Campbell (1995), East Tennessee State (2006), Florida Gulf Coast (2008), Jacksonville (1999), Kennesaw State (2006), Lipscomb (2004), Mercer (1979), North Florida (2006), South Carolina-Upstate (2008), Stetson (1986).

Director, Communications: Eric Moyer.

2011 Tournament: Six teams, double-elimination. May 25-28 at Nashville (Lipscomb).

ATLANTIC 10 CONFERENCE

Mailing Address: 11827 Canon Blvd., Suite 200, Newport News, VA 23606. **Telephone:** (757) 706-3059. **Fax:** (757) 706-3042. **E-Mail Address:** mkristofak@atlantic10.org. **Website:** www.atlantic10.org.

Baseball Members (First Year): Charlotte (2006), Dayton (1996), Fordham (1996), George Washington (1977), LaSalle (1996), Massachusetts (1977), Rhode Island (1981), Richmond (2002), St. Bonaventure (1980), Saint Joseph's (1983), Saint Louis (2006), Temple (1983), Xavier (1996).

Commissioner: Bernadette V. McGlade. **Director, Communications:** Jason Leturmy. **Assistant Director, Communications/Baseball Contact:** Melissa Kristofak.

2011 Tournament: Six teams, double elimination. May 25-28 at Campbell's Field, Camden, N.J.

BIG EAST CONFERENCE

Mailing Address: 16 Park Row West, Providence, RI 02903. **Telephone:** (401) 453-0660. **Fax:** (401) 751-8540. **E-Mail Address:** csullivan@bigeast.org. **Website:** www.bigeast.org.

Baseball Members (First Year): Cincinnati (2006), Connecticut (1985), Georgetown (1985), Louisville (2006), Notre Dame (1996), Pittsburgh (1985), Rutgers (1996), St. John's (1985), Seton Hall (1985), South Florida (2006),

Villanova (1985), West Virginia (1996).

Director, Communications: Chuck Sullivan.

2011 Tournament: Eight teams, double-elimination. May 26-29 at Clearwater, Fla.

BIG SOUTH CONFERENCE

Mailing Address: 7233 Pineville-Matthews Rd., Suite 100, Charlotte, NC 28226. **Telephone:** (704) 341-7990. **Fax:** (704) 341-7991. **E-Mail Address:** marks@bigsouth. org. **Website:** www.bigsouthsports.com.

Baseball Members (First Year): Charleston Southern (1983), Coastal Carolina (1983), Gardner-Webb (2009), High Point (1999), Liberty (1991), UNC Asheville (1985), Presbyterian (2009), Radford (1983), Virginia Military Institute (2004), Winthrop (1983).

Assistant Commissioner, Public Relations: Mark Simpson.

2011 Tournament: Eight teams, single-elimination in first round followed by six-team double-elimination. May 24-28 at Lexington, Va. (Virginia Military Institute).

BIG TEN CONFERENCE

Mailing Address: 1500 W Higgins Rd, Park Ridge, IL 60068. **Telephone:** (847) 696-1010. **Fax:** (847) 696-1110. **E-Mail Addresses:** vtodryk@bigten.org. **Website:** www. bigten.org.

Baseball Members (First Year): Illinois (1896), Indiana (1906), Iowa (1906), Michigan (1896), Michigan State (1950), Minnesota (1906), Northwestern (1898), Ohio State (1913), Penn State (1992), Purdue (1906).

Associate Director, Communications: Valerie Todryk Krebs.

2011 Tournament: Six teams, double-elimination. May 25-28 at Huntington Park in Columbus, Ohio.

BIG 12 CONFERENCE

Mailing Address: 400 E. John Carpenter Freeway, Irving, TX 75062. **Telephone:** (469) 524-1000. **E-Mail Address:** carmen@big12sports.com. **Website:** www.big-12sports.com.

Baseball Members (First Year): Baylor (1997), Kansas (1997), Kansas State (1997), Missouri (1997), Nebraska (1997), Oklahoma (1997), Oklahoma State (1997), Texas (1997), Texas A&M (1997), Texas Tech (1997).

Assistant Director, Communications: Carmen Branch.

2011 Tournament: Double-elimination division play. May 25-29 at RedHawks Ballpark, Oklahoma City.

BIG WEST CONFERENCE

Mailing Address: 2 Corporate Park, Suite 206, Irvine, CA 92606. **Telephone:** (949) 261-2525. **Fax:** (949) 261-2528. **E-Mail Address:** jstcyr@bigwest.org. **Website:** www.bigwest.org.

Baseball Members (First Year): Cal Poly (1997), UC Davis (2008), UC Irvine (2002), UC Riverside (2002), UC Santa Barbara (1970), Cal State Fullerton (1975), Cal State Northridge (2001), Long Beach State (1970), Pacific (1972).

Associate Information Director: Julie St. Cyr.

2011 Tournament: None.

COLONIAL ATHLETIC ASSOCIATION

Mailing Address: 8625 Patterson Ave., Richmond, VA 23229. **Telephone:** (804) 754-1616. **Fax:** (804) 754-1830. **E-Mail Address:** rwashburn@caasports.com. **Website:** www.caasports.com.

Baseball Members (First Year): Delaware (2002), George Mason (1986), Georgia State (2006), Hofstra (2002), James Madison (1986), UNC Wilmington (1986),

Northeastern (2006), Old Dominion (1992), Towson (2002), Virginia Commonwealth (1996), William & Mary (1986).

Associate Commissioner/Communications: Rob Washburn.

2011 Tournament: Four teams, double-elimination. May 26-28 at Wilmington, N.C. (UNC Wilmington).

CONFERENCE USA

Mailing Address: 5201 N. O'Connor Blvd., Suite 300, Irving, TX 75039. **Telephone:** (214) 774-1300. **Fax:** (214) 496-0055. **E-Mail Address:** rdanderson@c-usa.org. **Website:** www.conferenceusa.com.

Baseball Members (First Year): East Carolina (2002), Houston (1997), Marshall (2006), Memphis (1996), Rice (2006), Southern Miss (1996), Tulane (1996), UAB (1996), UCF (2006),.

Assistant Commissioner, Baseball Operations: Russell Anderson.

2011 Tournament: Eight-team, two-division pool play. May 25-28 at Pearl, Miss. (Southern Mississippi).

GREAT WEST CONFERENCE

Mailing Address: PO Box 9344, Naperville, IL 60567. **Telephone:** (630) 428-4492. **Fax:** (630) 548-0705. **E-Mail Address:** martin@gwconference.org. **Website:** www.greatwestconference.org.

Baseball Members (First Year): Chicago State (2010), Houston Baptist (2010), New Jersey Tech (2010), New York Tech (2010), North Dakota (2010), Northern Colorado (2010), Texas-Pan American (2010), Utah Valley (2010).

Director, Media Relations: Jacque Cottrell. **Assistant Director, Media Relations:** Cliff Martin.

2011 Tournament: Eight teams, double-elimination, May 24-28 at Grand Forks, N.D.

HORIZON LEAGUE

Mailing Address: 201 S. Capitol Ave., Suite 500, Indianapolis, IN 46225. **Telephone:** (317) 237-5604. **Fax:** (317) 237-5620. **E-Mail Address:** kmurphy@horizon-league.org. **Website:** www.horizonleague.org.

Baseball Members (First Year): Butler (1979), Cleveland State (1994), Illinois-Chicago (1994), Wisconsin-Milwaukee (1994), Valparaiso (2008), Wright State (1994), Youngstown State (2002).

Communications Assistant: Kristy Murphy.

2011 Tournament: Six teams, double-elimination. May 25-28 at Dayton, Ohio (Wright State).

IVY LEAGUE

Mailing Address: 228 Alexander Rd., Second Floor, Princeton, NJ 08544. **Telephone:** (609) 258-6426. **Fax:** (609) 258-1690. **E-Mail Address:** sarah@ivyleaguesports.com. **Website:** www.ivyleaguesports.com.

Baseball Members (First Year): Rolfe—Brown (1948), Dartmouth (1930), Harvard (1948), Yale (1930). Gehrig—Columbia (1930), Cornell (1930), Pennsylvania (1930), Princeton (1930).

Assistant Director, Communications: Sarah Finney.

2011 Tournament: Best-of-three series between division champions. May 7-8 at team with best overall record.

METRO ATLANTIC ATHLETIC CONFERENCE

Mailing Address: 712 Amboy Ave., Edison, NJ 08837. **Telephone:** (732) 738-5455. **Fax:** (732) 738-8366. **E-Mail Address:** jill.skotarczak@maac.org. **Website:** www.maac-sports.com.

Baseball Members (First Year): Canisius (1990), Fairfield (1982), Iona (1982), Manhattan (1982), Marist (1998), Niagara (1990), Rider (1998), St. Peter's (1982), Siena (1990).

Assistant Commissioner, Media Relations: Jill Skotarczak.

2011 Tournament: Four teams, double-elimination. May 25-29 at Waterfront Park, Trenton, N.J.

MID-AMERICAN CONFERENCE

Mailing Address: 24 Public Square, 15th Floor, Cleveland, OH 44113. **Telephone:** (216) 566-4622. **Fax:** (216) 858-9622. **E-Mail Address:** jguy@mac-sports.com. **Website:** www.mac-sports.com.

Baseball Members (First Year): Akron (1992), Ball State (1973), Bowling Green State (1952), Buffalo (2001), Central Michigan (1971), Eastern Michigan (1971), Kent State (1951), Miami (1947), Northern Illinois (1997), Ohio (1946). Toledo (1950), Western Michigan (1947).

Director, Communications: Jeremy Guy.

2011 Tournament: Eight teams (top three in each division and two teams with the next-best overall records, regardless of division), double-elimination. May 25-28 at VA Memorial Stadium (Chillicothe, Ohio).

MID-EASTERN ATHLETIC CONFERENCE

Mailing Address: 2730 Ellsmere Avenue, Norfolk, VA 23513. **Telephone:** (757) 951-2055. **Fax:** (757) 951-2077. **E-Mail Address:** rashids@themeac.com; porterp@themeac.com. **Website:** www.meacsports.com.

Baseball Members (First Year): Bethune-Cookman (1979), Coppin State (1985), Delaware State (1970), Florida A&M (1979), Maryland Eastern Shore (1970), Norfolk State (1998), North Carolina A&T (1970).

Assistant Director, Media Relations/Baseball Contact: Sahar Abdur-Rashid.

2011 Tournament: Six teams, double-elimination. May 19-22 at Daytona Beach, Fla. (Bethune-Cookman).

MISSOURI VALLEY CONFERENCE

Mailing Address: 1818 Chouteau Ave, St. Louis, MO 63103. **Telephone:** (314) 444-4300. **Fax:** (314) 421-3505. **E-Mail Address:** kbriscoe@mvc.org. **Website:** www.mvc-sports.com.

Baseball Members (First Year): Bradley (1955), Creighton (1976), Evansville (1994), Illinois State (1980), Indiana State (1976), Missouri State (1990), Southern Illinois (1974), Wichita State (1945).

Assistant Director, Communications: Kelli Briscoe.

2011 Tournament: Eight-team tournament with two four-team brackets mirroring the format of the College World Series, with the winners of each four-team bracket meeting in a single championship game. May 24-28 at TD Ameritrade Park Omaha (Creighton).

MOUNTAIN WEST CONFERENCE

Mailing Address: 15455 Gleneagle Dr., Suite 200, Colorado Springs, CO 80921. **Telephone:** (719) 488-4050. **Fax:** (719) 487-7241. **E-Mail Address:** kmelcher@themwc.com. **Website:** www.themwc.com.

Baseball Members (First Year): Air Force (2000), BYU (2000), UNLV (2000), New Mexico (2000), San Diego State (2000), TCU (2006), Utah (2000).

Director, Communications: Kim Melcher.

2011 Tournament: Six teams, double-elimination. May 24-28 at San Diego (San Diego State).

NORTHEAST CONFERENCE

Mailing Address: 399 Campus Drive, Somerset, NJ 08873. **Telephone:** (732) 469-0440. **Fax:** (732) 469-0744. **E-Mail Address:** rventre@northeastconference.org. **Website:** www.northeastconference.org.

Baseball Members (First Year): Bryant (2010), Central Connecticut State (1999), Fairleigh Dickinson (1981), Long

Island (1981), Monmouth (1985), Mount St. Mary's (1989), Quinnipiac (1999), Sacred Heart (2000), Wagner (1981).

Associate Commissioner: Ralph Ventre.

2011 Tournament: Four teams, double-elimination. May 19-21. **Site:** Norwich, Conn.

OHIO VALLEY CONFERENCE

Mailing Address: 215 Centerview Dr., Suite 115, Brentwood, TN 37027. **Telephone:** (615) 371-1698. **Fax:** (615) 371-1788. **E-Mail Address:** kschwartz@ovc.org. **Website:** www.ovcsports.com.

Baseball Members (First Year): Austin Peay State (1962), Eastern Illinois (1996), Eastern Kentucky (1948), Jacksonville State (2003), Morehead State (1948), Murray State (1948), Southeast Missouri State (1991), Tennessee-Martin (1992), Tennessee Tech (1949).

Assistant Commissioner: Kyle Schwartz.

2011 Tournament: Six teams, double-elimination. May 25-29 at Jackson, Tenn.

PACIFIC-10 CONFERENCE

Mailing Address: 1350 Treat Blvd., Suite 500. **Telephone:** (925) 932-4411. **Fax:** (925) 932-4601. **E-Mail Address:** ayee@pac-10.org. **Website:** www.pac-10.org.

Baseball Members (First Year): Arizona (1979), Arizona State (1979), California (1916), UCLA (1928), Oregon (1916-1981, 2009) Oregon State (1916), Southern California (1923), Stanford (1918), Washington (1916), Washington State (1919).

Public Relations Contact: Allison Yee.

2011 Tournament: None.

PATRIOT LEAGUE

Mailing Address: 3773 Corporate Pkwy, Suite 190, Center Valley, PA 18034. **Telephone:** (610) 289-1963. **Fax:** (610) 289-1951. **E-Mail Address:** mdougherty@patriot-league.com. **Website:** www.patriotleague.org.

Baseball Members (First Year): Army (1993), Bucknell (1991), Holy Cross (1991), Lafayette (1991), Lehigh (1991), Navy (1993).

Director, Media Relations: Matt Dougherty.

2011 Tournament: Four teams, May 14-15 and May 21-22 at site of higher seeds.

SOUTHEASTERN CONFERENCE

Mailing Address: 2201 Richard Arrington Blvd. N., Birmingham, AL 35203. **Telephone:** (205) 458-3000. **Fax:** (205) 458-3030. **E-Mail Address:** cdunlap@sec.org. **Website:** www.secsports.com.

Baseball Members (First Year): East—Florida (1933), Georgia (1933), Kentucky (1933), South Carolina (1933), Tennessee (1933), Vanderbilt (1933). West—Alabama (1933), Arkansas (1992), Auburn (1933), Louisiana State (1933), Mississippi (1933), Mississippi State (1933).

Associate Director, Media Relations: Chuck Dunlap.

2011 Tournament: Eight teams, modified double-elimination. May 25-29 at Hoover, Ala.

SOUTHERN CONFERENCE

Mailing Address: 702 N. Pine St., Spartanburg, SC 29303. **Telephone:** (864) 591-5100. **Fax:** (864) 591-4282. **E-Mail Address:** jcaskey@socon.org. **Website:** www.soconsports.com.

Baseball Members (First Year): Appalachian State (1971), College of Charleston (1998), The Citadel (1936), Davidson (1991), Elon (2004), Furman (1936), Georgia Southern (1991), UNC Greensboro (1997), Samford (2009), Western Carolina (1976), Wofford (1997).

Media Relations: Jonathan Caskey.

2011 Tournament: Eight teams, double-elimination.

May 25-29 at Joseph P. Riley Jr. Park, Charleston, S.C.

SOUTHLAND CONFERENCE

Mailing Address: 2600 Network Blvd., Suite 150, Frisco, Texas 75034. **Telephone:** (972) 422-9500. **Fax:** (972) 422-9225. **E-Mail Address:** tlamb@southland.org. **Website:** www.southland.org.

Baseball Members (First Year): Central Arkansas (2007), Lamar (1999), McNeese State (1973), Nicholls State (1992), Northwestern State (1988), Sam Houston State (1988), Southeastern Louisiana (1998), Stephen F. Austin (2006), Texas-Arlington (1964), Texas-San Antonio (1992), Texas A&M-Corpus Christi (2007), Texas State (1988).

Baseball Contact/Assistant Commissioner: Todd Lamb.

2011 Tournament: Two four-team brackets, double-elimination. May 25-28 at San Marcos, Texas (Texas State).

SOUTHWESTERN ATHLETIC CONFERENCE

Mailing Address: 2101 6th Avenue North, Suite 700, Birmingham, AL 35203. **Telephone:** (205) 251-7573. **Fax:** (205) 297-9820. **E-Mail Address:** t.galbraith@swac.org. **Website:** www.swac.org.

Baseball Members (First Year): East—Alabama A&M (2000), Alabama State (1982), Alcorn State (1962), Jackson State (1958), Mississippi Valley State (1968). West—Arkansas-Pine Bluff (1999), Grambling State (1958), Prairie View A&M (1920), Southern (1934), Texas Southern (1954).

Assistant Commissioner, Communications: Tom Galbraith.

2011 Tournament: Eight teams, double-elimination. May 18-22 at Shreveport, La.

SUMMIT LEAGUE

Mailing Address: 340 W Butterfield Rd, Suite 3-D, Elmhurst, IL 60126. **Telephone:** (630) 516-0661. **Fax:** (630) 516-0673. **E-Mail Address:** mette@thesummitleague.org. **Website:** www.thesummitleague.org.

Baseball Members (First Year): Centenary (2004), IPFW (2008), North Dakota State (2008), Oakland (2000), Oral Roberts (1998), South Dakota State (2008), Southern Utah (2000), Western Illinois (1984).

Associate Director, Communications (baseball contact): Greg Mette.

2011 Tournament: Four teams, double-elimination. May 26-28 at Sioux Falls, S.D. (South Dakota State).

SUN BELT CONFERENCE

Mailing Address: 601 Poydras St, Suite 2355, New Orleans, LA 70130. **Telephone:** (504) 299-9066. **Fax:** (504) 299-9068. **E-Mail Address:** nunez@sunbeltsports.org. **Website:** www.sunbeltsports.org.

Baseball Members (First Year): Arkansas-Little Rock (1991), Arkansas State (1991), Florida Atlantic (2007), Florida International (1999), Louisiana-Lafayette (1991), Louisiana-Monroe (2007), Middle Tennessee (2001), South Alabama (1976), Troy (2006), Western Kentucky (1982).

Director, Media Relations: Keith Nunez.

2011 Tournament: Eight-team, two-division pool play. May 25-29 at Monroe, La. (Louisiana-Monroe).

WEST COAST CONFERENCE

Mailing Address: 1111 Bayhill Dr, Suite 405, San Bruno, CA 94066. **Telephone:** (650) 873-8622. **Fax:** (650) 873-7846. **E-Mail Addresses:** jtourial@westcoast.org. **Website:** www.wccsports.com.

Baseball Members (First Year): Gonzaga (1996), Loyola Marymount (1968), Pepperdine (1968), Portland (1996), Saint Mary's (1968), San Diego (1979), San Francisco

(1968), Santa Clara (1968).

Director, Communications: Jeff Tourial. **Associate Director, Communications:** James Vega.

2011 Tournament: None.

WESTERN ATHLETIC CONFERENCE

Mailing Address: 9250 East Costilla Ave, Suite 300, Englewood, CO 80112. **Telephone:** (303) 799-9221. **Fax:** (303) 799-3888. **E-Mail Address:** jerickson@wac.org. **Website:** www.wacsports.com.

Baseball Members (First Year): Fresno State (1993), Hawaii (1980), Louisiana Tech (2002), Nevada (2001), New Mexico State (2006), Sacramento State (2006), San Jose State (1997).

Commissioner: Karl Benson. **Senior Associate Commissioner:** Jeff Hurd. **Director, Sports Information:** Jason Erickson.

2011 Tournament: Six teams, double elimination. May 25-29 at Hohokam Stadium, Mesa, Ariz.

NCAA DIVISION I TEAMS
*Recruiting coordinator

AIR FORCE FALCONS

Conference: Mountain West.

Mailing Address: 2169 Field House Drive, USAF Academy, CO 80840. **Website:** goairforcefalcons.com.

Head Coach: Mike Kazlausky. **Assistant Coaches:** Toby Bicknell, Tim Dixon. **Telephone:** (719) 333-0835. **Baseball SID:** Nick Arseniak. **Telephone:** (719) 333-9251. **Fax:** (719) 333-3798.

Home Field: Falcon Field. **Seating Capacity:** 1,000. **Outfield Dimension:** LF—349, CF—400, RF—316. **Press Box Telephone:** (719) 333-3472.

AKRON ZIPS

Conference: Mid-American (East).

Mailing Address: University of Akron, Rhodes Arena, Akron, OH 44325. **Website:** www.GoZips.com.

Head Coach: Pat Bangtson. **Assistant Coaches:** *Greg Cypret, Kurt Davidson. **Telephone:** (330) 972-7290. **Baseball SID:** Rita Chinyere. **Telephone:** (330) 972-7171. **Fax:** (330) 374-8844.

Home Field: Lee R Jackson Field. **Seating Capacity:** 1,500. **Outfield Dimension:** LF—330, CF—400, RF—330. **Press Box Telephone:** (330) 972-8896.

ALABAMA CRIMSON TIDE

Conference: Southeastern (West).

Mailing Address: Coleman Coliseum Rm 170, 1201 Coliseum Blvd, Tuscaloosa, AL 35487. **Website:** www.rolltide.com.

Head Coach: Mitch Gaspard. **Assistant Coaches:** *Dax Norris, Andy Phillips. **Telephone:** (205) 348-4029. **Baseball SID:** Rich Davi. **Telephone:** (205) 348-3550. **Fax:** (205) 348-6084.

Home Field: Sewell-Thomas Stadium. **Seating Capacity:** 6,571. **Outfield Dimensions:** LF—335, CF—400, RF—325. **Press Box Telephone:** (205) 348-4927.

ALABAMA A&M BULLDOGS

Conference: Southwestern Athletic.

Mailing Address: 4900 Meridian Street, Huntsville, AL 35762. **Website:** www.aamusports.com.

Head Coach: Ed McCann. **Assistant Coach:** Michael Tompkins. **Telephone:** (256) 372-4004. **Baseball SID:** Brandon Willis. **Telephone:** (256) 372-4005. **Fax:** (256) 372-5919.

Home Field: Bulldog Field. **Seating Capacity:** 500. **Outfield Dimensions:** LF—330, CF—404, RF—329.

ALABAMA STATE HORNETS

Conference: Southwestern Athletic.

Mailing Address: 915 S. Jackson St, Montgomery, AL 36106. **Website:** www.bamastatesports.com.

Head Coach: Larry Watkins. **Assistant Coach:** Anthony Macon. **Telephone:** (334) 229-4228. **Baseball SID:** Darrell Orand. **Telephone:** (334) 229-5215. **Fax:** (334) 262-2971.

Home Field: Paterson Field. **Seating Capacity:** 7,000. **Outfield Dimensions:** LF—330, CF—380, RF—330.

ALABAMA-BIRMINGHAM BLAZERS

Conference: Conference USA.

Mailing Address: 1530 3rd Ave S, Birmingham, AL 35294. **Website:** www.uabsports.com.

Head Coach: Brian Shoop. **Assistant Coaches:** Josh Hopper, *Perry Roth. **Telephone:** (205) 934-5181. **Baseball SID:** Tyson Mathews. **Telephone:** (205) 996-2576. **Fax:** (205) 934-7505.

Home Field: Young Memorial Field. **Seating Capacity:** 1,000. **Outfield Dimensions:** LF—330, CF—400, RF—330. **Press Box Telephone:** (205) 934-0200.

ALBANY GREAT DANES

Conference: America East.

Mailing Address: 1400 Washington Ave, PE Bldg 123, Albany, NY 12222. **Website:** www.ualbanysports.com.

Head Coach: Jon Mueller. **Assistant Coaches:** Garett Baron, *Drew Pearce. **Telephone:** (518) 442-3014. **Baseball SID:** Brianna LaBrecque. **Telephone:** (518) 442-5733. **Fax:** (518) 442-3139.

Home Field: Varsity Field. **Seating Capacity:** 1,000. **Outfield Dimension:** LF—345, CF—375, RF—325.

ALCORN STATE BRAVES

Conference: Southwestern Athletic.

Mailing Address: 1000 ASU Drive, Alcorn State, MS 39096. **Website:** www.alcornsports.com.

Head Coach: Barret Rey. **Assistant Coaches:** David Gomez, Kevin Vital. **Telephone:** (601) 877-6500. **Baseball SID:** LaToya Shields. **Telephone:** (601) 877-6509. **Fax:** (601) 877-3821.

APPALACHIAN STATE MOUNTAINEERS

Conference: Southern.

Mailing Address: Appalachian State University Box 32025, Boone, NC 28608. **Website:** www.goasu.com.

Head Coach: Chris Pollard. **Assistant Coaches:** *Josh Jordan, Chris Moore. **Telephone:** (828) 262-6097. **Baseball SID:** Mike Flynn. **Telephone:** (828) 262-2845. **Fax:** (828) 262-6106.

Home Field: Beaver Field at Jim and Bettie Smith Stadium. **Seating Capacity:** 1,000. **Outfield Dimension:** LF—330, CF—400, RF—330. **Press Box Telephone:** (828) 262-2016.

ARIZONA WILDCATS

Conference: Pacific-10.

Mailing Address: 1 National Championship Dr, Tucson, AZ 85721. **Website:** www.arizonaathletics.com.

Head Coach: Andy Lopez. **Assistant Coaches:** Shaun Cole, *Mark Wasikowski. **Telephone:** (520) 621-4102. **Baseball SID:** Blair Willis. **Telephone:** (520) 621-0914. **Fax:** (520) 621-2681.

Home Field: Jerry Kindall Field at Frank Sancet Stadium. **Seating Capacity:** 6,000. **Outfield Dimensions:** LF—360, CF—400, RF—360. **Press Box Telephone:** (520) 621-4440.

ARIZONA STATE SUN DEVILS

Conference: Pacific-10.
Mailing Address: 500 East Veteran's Way Tempe, AZ 85287. **Website:** www.TheSunDevils.com.
Head Coach: Tim Esmay. **Assistant Coaches:** *Travis Jewett, Ken Knutson. **Telephone:** (480) 965-3677. **Baseball SID:** Randy Policar. **Telephone:** (480) 965-6594. **Fax:** (480) 965-5408.
Home Field: Packard Stadium. **Seating Capacity:** 3,879. **Outfield Dimensions:** LF—338, CF—395, RF—338. **Press Box Telephone:** (480) 727-7253.

ARKANSAS RAZORBACKS

Conference: Southeastern (West).
Mailing Address: 131 Barnhill Arena, Fayetteville, AR, 72701. **Website:** www.arkansasrazorbacks.com.
Head Coach: Dave Van Horn. **Assistant Coaches:** *Todd Butler, Dave Jorn. **Telephone:** (479) 575-3655. **Baseball SID:** Chad Crunk. **Telephone:** (479) 575-2753. **Fax:** (479) 575-7481.
Home Field: Baum Stadium. **Seating Capacity:** 10,737. **Outfield Dimensions:** LF—320, CF—400, RF—320. **Press Box Telephone:** (479) 575-4141.

ARKANSAS STATE RED WOLVES

Conference: Sun Belt.
Mailing Address: PO Box 1000, State University, AR 72467. **Website:** www.astateredwolves.com.
Head Coach: Tommy Raffo. **Assistant Coaches:** *Chris Cook, Justin Meccage. **Telephone:** (870) 972-2700. **Baseball SID:** Van Provence. **Telephone:** (870) 972-3547. **Fax:** (870) 972-3367.
Home Field: Tomlinson Stadium Kell Field. **Seating Capacity:** 1500. **Outfield Dimensions:** LF—335, CF—400, RF—335. **Press Box Telephone:** (870) 972-3383.

ARKANSAS-LITTLE ROCK TROJANS

Conference: Sun Belt.
Mailing Address: 2801 S University Ave, Little Rock, AR 72204. **Website:** www.ualrtrojans.com.
Head Coach: Scott Norwood. **Assistant Coaches:** Jeremy Haworth, *Brandon Rowan. **Telephone:** (501) 663-8095. **Baseball SID:** Joe Angiola. **Telephone:** (501) 569-3449. **Fax:** (501) 683-7002. **Home Field:** Gary Hogan Field. **Seating Capacity:** 1,000. **Outfield Dimension:** LF—330, CF—400, RF—325. **Press Box Telephone:** (501) 351-1060.

ARKANSAS-PINE BLUFF GOLDEN LIONS

Conference: Southwestern Athletic.
Mailing Address: 1200 N University Dr, Mail Slot 4949, Pine Bluff, AR 71601. **Website:** www.uapblionsroar.com.
Head Coach: Carlos James. **Assistant Coaches:** *Marc MacMillan, Kevin Tucker. **Telephone:** (870) 575-8995. **Baseball SID:** Andrew Roberts. **Telephone:** (870) 575-7949. **Fax:** (870) 575-7880.
Home Field: Torii Hunter Baseball Complex. **Seating Capacity:** 2,500. **Outfield Dimension:** LF—330, CF—400, RF—330.

ARMY BLACK KNIGHTS

Conference: Patriot.
Mailing Address: 639 Howard Rd, West Point, NY 10996. **Website:** www.goarmysports.com.
Head Coach: Joe Sottolano. **Assistant Coaches:** Anthony DeCicco, *Matt Reid. **Telephone:** (845) 938-3712. **Baseball SID:** Bob Beretta. **Telephone:** (845) 938-6416. **Fax:** (845) 446-2556.
Home Field: Doubleday Field. **Seating Capacity:** 9,791.

Outfield Dimensions: LF—296, CF—390, RF—312.

AUBURN TIGERS

Conference: Southeastern (West).
Mailing Address: 351 South Donahue Drive, Auburn, AL 36830. **Website:** www.auburntigers.com.
Head Coach: John Pawlowski. **Assistant Coaches:** *Scott Foxhall, Link Jarrett. **Telephone:** (334) 844-4975. **Baseball SID:** Dan Froehlich. **Telephone:** (344) 844-9803. **Fax:** (334) 844-9807.
Home Field: Plainsman Park. **Seating Capacity:** 4,096. **Outfield Dimension:** LF—315, CF—385, RF—331. **Press Box Telephone:** (334) 844-4138.

AUSTIN PEAY STATE GOVERNORS

Conference: Ohio Valley.
Mailing Address: Dept of Intercollegiate Athletics, PO Box 4515, Clarksville, TN 37044. **Website:** www.lets-gopeay.com.
Head Coach: Gary McClure. **Assistant Coaches:** Derrick Dunbar, *Joel Mangrum. **Telephone:** (931) 221-6266. **Baseball SID:** Cody Bush. **Telephone:** (931) 221-7561. **Fax:** (931) 221-7389.
Home Field: Raymond C Hand. **Seating Capacity:** 3,000. **Outfield Dimensions:** LF—319, CF—405, RF—320.

BALL STATE CARDINALS

Conference: Mid-American (West).
Mailing Address: HP 245, Muncie, IN 47306. **Website:** www.ballstatesports.com.
Head Coach: Alex Marconi. **Assistant Coaches:** Pete Milas, *Jeremy Plexico. **Telephone:** (765) 285-1425. **Baseball SID:** Matt McCollester. **Telephone:** (765) 285-8242 Fax: (765) 285-8929.
Home Field: Ball Diamond. **Seating Capacity:** 2,000. **Outfield Dimensions:** LF—330, CF—400, RF—330.

BAYLOR BEARS

Conference: Big 12 (South).
Mailing Address: 1612 S University Parks Dr, Waco, TX 76712. **Website:** www.baylorbears.com.
Head Coach: Steve Smith. **Assistant Coaches:** Steve Johnigan, *Mitch Thompson. **Telephone:** (254) 710-3097. **Baseball SID:** David Kaye. **Telephone:** (254) 710-4389. **Fax:** (254) 710-1369.
Home Field: Baylor Ballpark. **Seating Capacity:** 5,000. **Outfield Dimensions:** LF—330, CF—400, RF—330. **Press Box Telephone:** (254) 754-5546.

BELMONT BRUINS

Conference: Atlantic Sun.
Mailing Address: 1900 Belmont Blvd, Nashville, TN 37212. **Website:** www.belmontbruins.com.
Head Coach: Dave Jarvis. **Assistant Coaches:** *Matt Barnett, Scott Hall. **Telephone:** (615) 460-6166. **Baseball SID:** Dan Forcella. **Telephone:** (615) 460-8023. **Fax:** (615) 460-5584.
Home Field: Shelby Park. **Seating Capacity:** 1,000. **Outfield Dimension:** LF—327, CF—400, RF—327.

BETHUNE-COOKMAN WILDCATS

Conference: Mid-Eastern Athletic.
Mailing Address: 640 Dr Mary McLeod Bethune Blvd, Daytona Beach, FL 32114. **Website:** www.bccathletics.com.
Head Coach: Mervyl Melendez. **Assistant Coaches:** Drew Clark, *Jose Vazquez. **Telephone:** (386) 481-2224. **Baseball SID:** Michael Stambaugh. **Telephone:** (386) 481-2278. **Fax:** (386) 481-2238.

Home Field: Jackie Robinson. **Seating Capacity:** 5,000. **Outfield Dimensions:** LF—325, CF—400, RF—325.

BINGHAMTON BEARCATS

Conference: America East.
Mailing Address: Binghamton University, Events Center Office #110, Binghamton, NY, 13902. **Website:** www.bubearcats.com.
Head Coach: Tim Sinicki. **Assistant Coaches:** Ed Folli, *Ryan Hurba. **Telephone:** (607) 777-2525. **Baseball SID:** John Hartrick. **Telephone:** (607) 777-6800. **Fax:** (607) 777-4597.
Home Field: Varsity Field. **Seating Capacity:** Unavailable. **Outfield Dimension:** LF—315, CF—390, RF—315.

BOSTON COLLEGE EAGLES

Conference: Atlantic Coast (Atlantic).
Mailing Address: 140 Commonwealth Ave, Chestnut Hill, MA 02467. **Website:** bceagles.cstv.com.
Head Coach: Mike Gambino. **Assistant Coaches:** Steve Englert, *Scott Friedholm. **Telephone:** (617) 552-2674. **Baseball SID:** Matt Lynch. **Telephone:** (617) 552-2193. **Fax:** (617) 552-4903.
Home Field: Shea Field. **Seating Capacity:** 1,000. **Outfield Dimensions:** LF—330, CF—410, RF—318.

BOWLING GREEN STATE FALCONS

Conference: Missouri Valley.
Mailing Address: 201 Doyt Perry Stadium East, Bowling Green, OH 43403. **Website:** www.bgsufalcons.com.
Head Coach: Danny Schmitz. **Assistant Coaches:** *Rick Blanc, Spencer Schmitz. **Telephone:** (419) 372-7065. **Baseball SID:** Ryan Gasser. **Telephone:** (419) 372-7105. **Fax:** (419) 372-6015.
Home Field: Warren E Steller. **Seating Capacity:** 1,100. **Outfield Dimensions:** LF—345, CF—400, RF—345. **Press Box Telephone:** (419) 372-1234.

BRADLEY BRAVES

Conference: Missouri Valley.
Mailing Address: 1501 W. Bradley Ave, Peoria, IL 61625. **Website:** www.bubraves.com.
Head Coach: Elvis Dominguez. **Assistant Coaches:** *John Corbin, Sean Lyons. **Telephone:** (309) 677-2684. **Baseball SID:** Bobby Parker. **Telephone:** (309) 677-2624. **Fax:** (309) 677-2626.
Home Field: O'Brien Stadium. **Seating Capacity:** 7,500. **Outfield Dimensions:** LF—310, CF—400, RF—310. **Press Box Telephone:** (309) 256-4302.

BRIGHAM YOUNG COUGARS

Conference: Mountain West.
Mailing Address: 30 SFH, BYU, Provo, UT 84602. **Website:** www.byucougars.com.
Head Coach: Vance Law. **Assistant Coaches:** Bobby Applegate, *Ryan Roberts. **Telephone:** (801) 422-5049. **Baseball SID:** Ralph Zobell. **Telephone:** (801) 422-9769. **Fax:** (801) 422-0633.
Home Field: Larry H Miller Field. **Seating Capacity:** 2,204. **Outfield Dimensions:** LF—345, CF—400, RF—345. **Press Box Telephone:** (801) 422-4041.

BROWN BEARS

Conference: Ivy League (Rolfe).
Mailing Address: 235 Hope St, Providence, RI 02912. **Website:** www.brownbears.com.
Head Coach: Marek Drabinski. **Assistant Coaches:** Brian Murphy, *Mike O'Malley. **Telephone:** (401) 863-3090. **Baseball SID:** Mike Gambardella. **Telephone:** (401)

863-6069. **Fax:** (401) 863-1436.
Home Field: Murray Stadium. **Seating Capacity:** 1,000. **Outfield Dimension:** LF—340, CF—405, RF—330. **Press Box Telephone:** (401) 863-9427.

BRYANT BULLDOGS

Conference: Northeast.
Mailing Address: 1150 Douglas Pike, Smithfield RI 02917. **Website:** www.bryantbulldogs.com.
Head Coach: Steve Owens. **Assistant Coaches:** Kevin Cobb, Ryan Fecteau. **Telephone:** (401) 232-6397. **Baseball SID:** Eric Peterson. **Telephone:** (401)-232-6558. **Fax:** (401) 232-6361.
Home Field: The Bryant University Baseball Complex. **Seating Capacity:** Unavailable. **Outfield Dimensions:** LF—330, CF—400, RF—330.

BUCKNELL BISON

Conference: Patriot.
Mailing Address: Bucknell University, Moore Ave, Lewisburg, PA 17837. **Website:** www.bucknellbison.com.
Head Coach: Gene Depew. **Assistant Coaches:** Jim Gulden, Scott Heather. **Telephone:** (570) 577-3593. **Baseball SID:** Todd Merriett. **Telephone:** (570) 577-3488. **Fax:** Fax: (570) 577-1660.
Home Field: Depew Field. **Seating Capacity:** 500. **Outfield Dimensions:** LF—330, CF—400, RF—330.

BUFFALO BULLS

Conference: Mid-American (East).
Mailing Address: University at Buffalo, Division of Athletics, 175 Alumni Arena, Buffalo, NY 14260. **Website:** www.buffalobulls.com.
Head Coach: Ron Torgalski. **Assistant Coaches:** *Jim Koerner, Steve Ziroli. **Telephone:** (716) 645-6834. **Baseball SID:** Joe Kepler. **Telephone:** (716) 645-5523. **Fax:** (716) 645-6840.
Home Field: Amherst Audubon Field. **Seating Capacity:** 500. **Outfield Dimensions:** LF—330, CF—400, RF—330. **Press Box Telephone:** (716) 867-1908.

BUTLER BULLDOGS

Conference: Horizon.
Mailing Address: 510 W 49th Street, Indianapolis, IN 46208. **Website:** www.butlersports.com.
Head Coach: Steve Farley. **Assistant Coaches:** Jeff Thomas, *Matt Tyner. **Telephone:** (317) 940-9721. **Baseball SID:** Josh Rattray. **Telephone:** (317) 940-9994. **Fax:** (317) 940-9808.
Home Field: Bulldog Park. **Seating Capacity:** 500. **Outfield Dimension:** LF—330, CF—400, RF—330. **Press Box Telephone:** (317) 945-8943.

CALIFORNIA GOLDEN BEARS

Conference: Pacific-10.
Mailing Address: Haas Pavilion, Berkeley, CA 94720. **Website:** www.calbears.com.
Head Coach: David Esquer. **Assistant Coaches:** Tony Arnerich, *Dan Hubbs. **Telephone:** (510) 642-9026. **Baseball SID:** Scott Ball. **Telephone:** (510) 643-1741. **Fax:** (510) 643-7778.
Home Field: Evans Diamond. **Seating Capacity:** 2,500. **Outfield Dimensions:** LF—320, CF—395, RF—320. **Press Box Telephone:** (510) 642-3098.

UC DAVIS AGGIES

Conference: Big West.
Mailing Address: Hickey Gym 119, One Shields Ave, Davis, CA 95616. **Website:** ucdavisaggies.com.
Head Coach: Rex Peters. **Assistant Coaches:** *Tony

Schifano, Matt Vaughn. **Telephone:** (530) 752-7513. **Baseball SID:** Wes Collins. **Telephone:** (530) 752-3505. **Fax:** (530) 754-5674.
    Home Field: Dobbins Stadium. **Seating Capacity:** 3,500. **Outfield Dimension:** LF—310, CF—410, RF—310. **Press Box Telephone:** (530) 752-3673.

UC IRVINE ANTEATERS

Conference: Big West.
    Mailing Address: UC Irvine Athletics, 903 W Peltason Drive, Irvine, CA 92697. **Website:** www.ucirvinesports.com.
    Head Coach: Mike Gillespie. **Assistant Coaches:** Jason Dietrich, *Pat Shine. **Telephone:** (949) 824-4292. **Baseball SID:** Fumi Kimura. **Telephone:** (949) 824-9474. **Fax:** (949) 824-5260.
    Home Field: Anteater Ballpark. **Seating Capacity:** 3,200. **Outfield Dimensions:** LF—335, CF—405, RF—335. **Press Box Telephone:** (949) 824-9905.

UCLA BRUINS

Conference: Pacific-10.
    Mailing Address: JD Morgan Center, 325 Westwood Plaza, Los Angeles, CA 90095. **Website:** www.uclabruins.com.
    Head Coach: John Savage. **Assistant Coaches:** TJ Bruce, *Rick Vanderhook. **Telephone:** (310) 794-2470. **Baseball SID:** Alex Timiraos. **Telephone:** (310) 206-4008. **Fax:** (310) 825-8664.
    Home Field: Jackie Robinson Stadium. **Seating Capacity:** 1,550. **Outfield Dimensions:** LF—330, CF—395, RF—330. **Press Box Telephone:** (310) 794-8213.

UC RIVERSIDE HIGHLANDERS

Conference: Big West.
    Mailing Address: Dept of Athletics, UC Riverside, 900 University Ave, Riverside, CA 92521. **Website:** www.gohighlanders.com.
    Head Coach: Doug Smith. **Assistant Coaches:** Randy Betten, *Nathan Choate. **Telephone:** (951) 827-5441. **Baseball SID:** John Maxwell. **Telephone:** (951) 827-5438. **Fax:** (951) 827-3569.
    Home Field: Riverside Sports Complex. **Seating Capacity:** 2,500. **Outfield Dimensions:** LF—330, CF—400, RF—330.

UC SANTA BARBARA GAUCHOS

Conference: Big West.
    Mailing Address: ICA Building, UC Santa Barbara, CA 93106-5200. **Website:** www.ucsbgauchos.com.
    Head Coach: Bob Brontsema. **Assistant Coaches:** Jason Lefkowitz, *Tom Myers. **Telephone:** (805) 893-3690. **Baseball SID:** Matt Hurst. **Telephone:** (805) 893-8603. **Fax:** (805) 893-5477.
    Home Field: Caesar Uysaka Stadium. **Seating Capacity:** 1,000. **Outfield Dimensions:** LF—335, CF—400, RF—335. **Press Box Telephone:** (805) 893-4671.

CAL POLY MUSTANGS

Conference: Big West.
    Mailing Address: 1 Grand Avenue, San Luis Obispo, CA 93407-0388. **Website:** www.GoPoly.com.
    Head Coach: Larry Lee. **Assistant Coaches:** Jason Kelly, *Teddy Warrecker. **Telephone:** (805) 756-6367. **Baseball SID:** Eric Burdick. **Telephone:** (805) 756-6550. **Fax:** (805) 756-2650.
    Home Field: Baggett Stadium. **Seating Capacity:** 1,734. **Outfield Dimensions:** LF—335, CF—405, RF—335. **Press Box Telephone:** (805) 756-7456.

CAL STATE FULLERTON TITANS

Conference: Big West.
    Mailing Address: 800 N State College, Fullerton, CA 92834. **Website:** www.fullertontitans.com.
    Head Coach: Dave Serrano. **Assistant Coaches:** *Greg Bergeron, Gregg Wallis. **Telephone:** (657) 278-3780. **Baseball SID:** Mike Greenlee. **Telephone:** (657) 278-3081. **Fax:** (657) 278-3141.
    Home Field: Goodwin Field. **Seating Capacity:** 3,500. **Outfield Dimensions:** LF—330, CF—400, RF—330. **Press Box Telephone:** (657) 278-5327.

CAL STATE NORTHRIDGE MATADORS

Conference: Big West.
    Mailing Address: 18111 Nordhoff Street, Northridge, CA 91330. **Website:** www. **gomatadors.cstv.com.**
    Head Coach: Matt Curtis. **Assistant Coaches:** *Shaun Larkin, Tim Leary. **Telephone:** (818) 677-7055. **Baseball SID:** Eric Bankston. **Telephone:** (818) 677-3860. **Fax:** (818) 677-4950.
    Home Field: Matador Field. **Seating Capacity:** 1,000. **Outfield Dimensions:** LF—325, CF—400, RF—325. **Press Box Telephone:** (818) 677-4292.

CAMPBELL FIGHTING CAMELS

Conference: Atlantic Sun.
    Mailing Address: PO Box 10, Buies Creek, NC 27506. **Website:** www.gocamels.com.
    Head Coach: Greg Goff. **Assistant Coaches:** *Justin Haire, Rick McCarty. **Telephone:** (910) 893-1354. **Baseball SID:** Jason Williams. **Telephone:** (910) 814-4367. **Fax:** (910) 893-1330.
    Home Field: Taylor Field. **Seating Capacity:** 500. **Outfield Dimensions:** LF—337, CF—395, RF—328. **Press Box Telephone:** (910) 228-6908.

CANISIUS GOLDEN GRIFFINS

Conference: Metro Atlantic.
    Mailing Address: 2001 Main St, Buffalo, NY 14208. **Website:** www.gogriffs.com.
    Head Coach: Mike McRae. **Assistant Coaches:** Ryan Asis, *Matt Mazurek. **Telephone:** (716) 888-3207. **Baseball SID:** Matt Lozar. **Telephone:** (716) 888-3756. **Fax:** (716) 888-8444.
    Home Field: Demske Sports Complex. **Seating Capacity:** 1,000. **Outfield Dimension:** LF—310, CF—400, RF—310. **Press Box Telephone:** (440) 477-3777.

CENTENARY GENTS

Conference: Summit.
    Mailing Address: 2911 Centenary Blvd, Shreveport, LA 71104. **Website:** www.gocentenary.com.
    Head Coach: Mike Diaz. **Assistant Coaches:** Austin Jones, Jason Stephens. **Telephone:** (318) 869-5298. **Baseball SID:** Allison McClain. **Telephone:** (318) 869-5092. **Fax:** (318) 869-5145.

CENTRAL ARKANSAS BEARS

Conference: Southland.
    Mailing Address: 2401 College Ave, Conway, AR 72034. **Website:** www.ucasports.com..
    Head Coach: Allen Gum. **Assistant Coaches:** *Dallas Black, Wes Johnson. **Telephone:** (501) 450-3147. **Baseball SID:** Steve East. **Telephone:** (501) 450-5743. **Fax:** (501) 450-5740.
    Home Field: Bear Stadium. **Seating Capacity:** 2,000. **Outfield Dimension:** LF—320, CF—400, RF—320. **Press Box Telephone:** (501) 450-5972.

CENTRAL CONNECTICUT STATE BLUE DEVILS

Conference: Northeast.
Mailing Address: 16151 Stanley St, New Britain, CT 06050. **Website:** www.ccsubluedevils.com.
Head Coach: Charlie Hickey. **Telephone:** (860) 832-3074. **Baseball SID:** Tom Pincince. **Telephone:** (860) 832-3089. **Fax:** (860) 832-3754.
Assistant Coaches: *Pat Hall, James Ziogas. **Telephone:** (860) 832-3075.
Home Field: Balf Savin Baseball Field. **Seating Capacity:** Unavailable.
Outfield Dimensions: LF—330, CF—400, RF—310.

CENTRAL FLORIDA KNIGHTS

Conference: Conference USA.
Mailing Address: 4000 Central Florida Blvd, Bldg 39, Room 109, Orlando, FL 32816. **Website:** www.ucfathletics.com.
Head Coach: Terry Rooney. **Assistant Coaches:** *Cliff Godwin, Jeff Palumbo. **Telephone:** (407) 823-0140. **Baseball SID:** Brian Ormiston. **Telephone:** (407) 823-2409. **Fax:** (407) 823-5266.
Home Field: Jay Bergman Field. **Seating Capacity:** 2,230. **Outfield Dimensions:** LF—320, CF—390, RF—320. **Press Box Telephone:** (407) 823-4487.

CENTRAL MICHIGAN CHIPPEWAS

Conference: Mid-American (West).
Mailing Address: Suite 120 Rose Center, Mt Pleasant, MI 48859. **Website:** www.cmuchippewas.com.
Head Coach: Steve Jaksa. **Assistant Coach:** Brett Haring, *Jeff Opalewski. **Telephone:** (989) 774-2051. **Baseball SID:** Mike Boseak. **Telephone:** (989) 774-1763. **Fax:** (989) 774-5391.
Home Field: Theunissen Stadium. **Seating Capacity:** 2,046. **Outfield Dimension:** LF—330, CF—400, RF—330. **Press Box Telephone:** (989) 774-3594.

COLLEGE OF CHARLESTON COUGARS

Conference: Southern.
Mailing Address: 66 George Street, Charleston, SC 29424. **Website:** www.cofcsports.com.
Head Coach: Monte Lee. **Assistant Coaches:** Matt Heath, *Chris Morris. **Telephone:** (843) 953-5916. **Baseball SID:** Simon Whitaker. **Telephone:** (843) 953-3683. **Fax:** (843) 953-6534.
Home Field: Patriots Point. **Seating Capacity:** 1,500. **Outfield Dimensions:** LF—310, CF—400, RF—320. **Press Box Telephone:** (843) 953-9141.

CHARLESTON SOUTHERN BUCCANEERS

Conference: Big South.
Mailing Address: 9200 University Blvd, N Charleston, SC 29405. **Website:** www.csusports.com.
Head Coach: Stuart Lake. **Assistant Coaches:** *Charles Assey, Sid Fallaw. **Telephone:** (843) 863-7591. **Baseball SID:** Ashley Bailey. **Telephone:** (843) 863-7688. **Fax:** (843) 863-7676.
Home Field: CSU Ballpark. **Seating Capacity:** 1,500. **Outfield Dimensions:** LF—330, CF—400, RF—330. **Press Box Telephone:** (843) 863-7591.

CHARLOTTE 49ERS

Conference: Atlantic 10.
Mailing Address: 9201 University City Blvd Charlotte, NC 28223. **Website:** www.charlotte49ers.com.
Head Coach: Loren Hibbs. **Assistant Coaches:** *Brandon Hall, Kris Rochelle. **Telephone:** (704) 687-3933. **Baseball SID:** Ryan Rose. **Telephone:** (704) 687-6312. **Fax:**

(704) 687-4918.
Home Field: Robert and Mariam Hayes Stadium. **Seating Capacity:** 1,100/3,200. **Outfield Dimensions:** LF—335, CF—390, RF—335. **Press Box Telephone:** (704) 687-5959.

CHICAGO STATE COUGARS

Conference: Great West.
Mailing Address: 9501 S King Dr, Chicago, IL 60628. **Website:** www.csu.edu/athletics.
Head Coach: Michael Caston. **Assistant Coach:** *Neal Frendling. **Telephone:** (773) 995-3659. **Baseball SID:** Corey Miggins. **Telephone:** (773) 995-2217. **Fax:** (773) 995-3656.
Home Field: Gwendolyn Brooks Field. **Seating Capacity:** 2,000. **Outfield Dimensions:** LF—310, CF—400, RF—310.

CINCINNATI BEARCATS

Conference: Big East.
Mailing Address: University of Cincinnati, 2751 O'Varsity Way, Suite 860, Richard E Lindner Center, Cincinnati, Ohio 45221. **Website:** gobearcats.com.
Head Coach: Brian Cleary. **Assistant Coaches:** *J.D. Heilmann, Greg Mamula. **Telephone:** (513) 556-1577. **Baseball SID:** Jeff Geiser. **Telephone:** (513) 556-0618. **Fax:** (513) 556-0619.
Home Field: Marge Schott Stadium. **Seating Capacity:** 3,085. **Outfield Dimensions:** LF—325, CF—400, RF—325. **Press Box Telephone:** (513) 556-9645.

THE CITADEL BULLDOGS

Conference: Big South.
Mailing Address: 171 Moultrie Street, Charleston, SC 29409. **Website:** www.citadelsports.com.
Head Coach: Fred Jordan. **Assistant Coaches:** *David Beckley, Randy Carlson. **Telephone:** (843) 953-5901. **Baseball SID:** Ben Waring. **Telephone:** (843) 953-5120. **Fax:** (843) 953-6727.
Home Field: Joseph P Riley, Jr Park. **Seating Capacity:** 6,000. **Outfield Dimensions:** LF—305, CF—398, RF—337. **Press Box Telephone:** (843) 965-4151.

CLEMSON TIGERS

Conference: Atlantic Coast (Atlantic).
Mailing Address: PO Box 31, Clemson, SC 29633. **Website:** clemsontigers.com.
Head Coach: Jack Leggett. **Assistant Coaches:** *Bradley LeCroy, Dan Pepicelli. **Telephone:** (864) 656-1947. **Baseball SID:** Brian Hennessy. **Telephone:** (864) 656-1921. **Fax:** (864) 656-0299.
Home Field: Doug Kingsmore Stadium. **Seating Capacity:** 6,346. **Outfield Dimensions:** LF—320, CF—400, RF—330. **Press Box Telephone:** (864) 656-7731.

CLEVELAND STATE VIKINGS

Conference: Horizon.
Mailing Address: 2000 Prospect Ave, Cleveland, Ohio 44114. **Website:** www.csuvikings.com.
Head Coach: Kevin Kocks. **Assistant Coaches:** Shane Davis, *Rob Henry. **Telephone:** (216) 687-4822. **Baseball SID:** Dan Carr. **Telephone:** (216) 687-4818. **Fax:** (216) 523-7257.
Home Field: All-Pro Freight Stadium. **Seating Capacity:** 5,000. **Outfield Dimensions:** LF—325 feet, CF—400 feet, RF—325 feet.

COASTAL CAROLINA CHANTICLEERS

Conference: Big South.
Mailing Address: PO Box 261954, Conway, SC 29528.

Website: www.GoCCUSports.com.
Head Coach: Gary Gilmore. **Assistant Coaches:** Brendan Dougherty, *Kevin Schnall. **Telephone:** (843) 349-2820. **Baseball SID:** Mike Cawood. **Telephone:** (843) 349-2822. **Fax:** (843) 349-2819.
Home Field: Watson Stadium/Vrooman Field. **Seating Capacity:** 2,000. **Outfield Dimensions:** LF—320, CF—390, RF—325. **Press Box Telephone:** (843) 421-8244.

COLUMBIA LIONS

Conference: Ivy League (Gehrig).
Mailing Address: 3030 Broadway, Mail Code 1901, New York, NY 10027. **Website:** www.gocolumbialions.com.
Head Coach: Brett Boretti. **Assistant Coaches:** *Pete Maki, Jay Quinn. **Telephone:** (212) 854-8448. **Baseball SID:** Peter McHugh. **Telephone:** (212) 854-7064. **Fax:** (212) 854-8168.
Home Field: Robertson Field. **Seating Capacity:** 300. **Outfield Dimension:** LF—330, CF—350, RF—325. **Press Box Telephone:** (917) 678-3621.

CONNECTICUT HUSKIES

Conference: Big East.
Mailing Address: 2095 Hillside Road, Storrs, CT 06268. **Website:** www.UConnHuskies.com.
Head Coach: Jim Penders. **Assistant Coaches:** *Justin Blood, Steven Malinowski. **Telephone:** (860) 486-4089. **Baseball SID:** Kristen DeCarli. **Telephone:** (860) 486-3531. **Fax:** (860) 486-5085.
Home Field: J.O. Christian Field. **Seating Capacity:** 2,000. **Outfield Dimensions:** LF—337, CF—400, RF—325. **Press Box Telephone:** (860) 486-2018.

COPPIN STATE

Conference: Mid-Eastern Athletic.
Mailing Address: 2500 W North Ave, Baltimore, MD 21216. **Website:** www.coppinstatesports.com.
Head Coach: Sherman Reed. **Assistant Coach:** Greg Beckman. **Telephone:** (410) 951-3723. **Baseball SID:** Roger McAfee. **Telephone:** (410) 951-3729. **Fax:** (410) 951-3717.
Home Field: Joe Cannon Stadium. **Seating Capacity:** 2,000. **Outfield Dimension:** 310, CF—400, RF—310.

CORNELL BIG RED

Conference: Ivy League (Rolfe).
Mailing Address: Cornell Baseball, Teagle Hall, Campus Rd, Ithaca, NY 14853. **Website:** www.cornellbigred.com.
Head Coach: Bill Walkenbach. **Assistant Coaches:** Tom Ford, *Scott Marsh. **Telephone:** (607) 255-3812. **Baseball SID:** Kevin Zeise. **Telephone:** (607) 255-5627. **Fax:** (607) 255-9791.
Home Field: David F Hoy Field. **Seating Capacity:** 1,000. **Outfield Dimensions:** LF—315, CF—405, RF—325.

CREIGHTON BLUEJAYS

Conference: Missouri Valley.
Mailing Address: 2500 California Ave, Omaha, NE 68178. **Website:** www.gocreighton.com.
Head Coach: Ed Servais. **Assistant Coaches:** Craig Moore, *Rob Smith. **Telephone:** (402) 280-2483. **Baseball SID:** Shannon Pivovar. **Telephone:** (402) 280-5801. **Fax:** (402) 280-2495.
Home Field: Creighton Sports Complex. **Seating Capacity:** 1,000. **Outfield Dimensions:** LF—335, CF—408, RF—335. **Press Box Telephone:** (402) 280-1676.

DALLAS BAPTIST PATRIOTS

Conference: Independent.
Mailing Address: 3000 Mountain Creek Pkwy, Dallas, TX 75211. **Website:** www.dbu.edu/athletics.
Head Coach: Dan Heefner. **Assistant Coaches:** *Nate Frieling, Bob Keller. **Telephone:** (214) 333-5324. **Baseball SID:** Matt Williams. **Telephone:** (214) 333-5324. **Fax:** (214) 333-5306.
Home Field: Patriot Field. **Seating Capacity:** 1,520. **Outfield Dimensions:** LF—330, CF—390, RF—330. **Press Box Telephone:** (214) 333-5542.

DARTMOUTH BIG GREEN

Conference: Ivy League (Rolfe).
Mailing Address: 6083 Alumni Gym, Hanover, NH 03755. **Website:** www.dartmouthsports.com.
Head Coach: Bob Whalen. **Assistant Coaches:** Jonathan Anderson, *Nicholas Enriquez. **Telephone:** (603) 646-2477. **Baseball SID:** Rick Bender. **Telephone:** (603) 646-1030. **Fax:** (603) 646-1286.
Home Field: Rolfe Field at Biondi Park. **Seating Capacity:** 2,000. **Outfield Dimension:** LF—325, CF—402, RF—340. **Press Box Telephone:** (603) 646-6937.

DAVIDSON WILDCATS

Conference: Southern.
Mailing Address: Box 7158 Davidson College, Davidson, NC 28035. **Website:** www.davidsonwildcats.com.
Head Coach: Dick Cooke. **Assistant Coaches:** Tod Gross, *Mike Zandler. **Telephone:** (704) 894-2368. **Baseball SID:** Lauren Biggers. **Telephone:** (704) 894-2815. **Fax:** (704) 894-2636.
Home Field: Wilson Field. **Seating Capacity:** 700. **Outfield Dimensions:** LF—320, CF—385, RF—325. **Press Box Telephone:** (704) 894-2740.

DAYTON FLYERS

Conference: Atlantic 10.
Mailing Address: 300 College Park Ave, Dayton, OH 45469. **Website:** www.daytonflyers.com.
Head Coach: Tony Vittorio. **Assistant Coaches:** Terry Bell, *Todd Linklater, Matt Talarico. **Telephone:** (937) 229-4456. **Baseball SID:** Brian Karst. **Telephone:** (937) 229-4431. **Fax:** (937) 229-4461.
Home Field: Time Warner Cable Stadium. **Seating Capacity:** 2,000. **Outfield Dimensions:** LF—330, CF—400, RF—330. **Press Box Telephone:** (937) 229-2255.

DELAWARE FIGHTIN' BLUE HENS

Conference: Colonial Athletic.
Mailing Address: 116 Delaware Field House, Newark, DE 19716. **Website:** www.bluehens.com.
Head Coach: Jim Sherman. **Assistant Coaches:** *Dan Hammer, Mike Ranson. **Telephone:** (302) 831-8596. **Baseball SID:** Dan Lauletta. **Telephone:** (302) 831-6439. **Fax:** (302) 831-8653.
Home Field: Bob Hannah Stadium. **Seating Capacity:** 1,300. **Outfield Dimensions:** LF—330, CF—400, RF—330.

DELAWARE STATE HORNETS

Conference: Mid-Eastern Athletic.
Mailing Address: 1200 N Dupont Hwy, Dover, DE 19901. **Website:** www.dsuhornets.com.
Head Coach: JP Blandin. **Assistant Coaches:** Michael August, Scott Shockley. **Telephone:** (302) 857-6035. **Baseball SID:** Dennis Jones. **Telephone:** (302) 857-6068. **Fax:** (302) 857-6069.

DUKE BLUE DEVILS

Conference: Atlantic Coast (Coastal).
Mailing Address: 118 Cameron Indoor Stadium, Durham, NC 27708. **Website:** www.goduke.com.
Head Coach: Sean McNally. **Assistant Coaches:** Sean Snedeker, *Edwin Thompson. **Telephone:** (919) 668-0255. **Baseball SID:** Chris Cook. **Telephone:** (919) 684-8708. **Fax:** (919) 684-2489.
Home Field: Durham Bulls Athletic Park. **Seating Capacity:** 10,000. **Outfield Dimensions:** LF—330, CF—400, RF—330. **Press Box Telephone:** (919) 812-7141.

EAST CAROLINA PIRATES

Conference: Conference USA.
Mailing Address: 102 Clark-LeClair Stadium, Greenville, NC 27858. **Website:** www.ecupirates.com.
Head Coach: Billy Godwin. **Assistant Coaches:** Dan Rozsel, *Nick Schnabel. **Telephone:** (252) 737-1985. **Baseball SID:** Malcolm Gray. **Telephone:** (252) 737-4523. **Fax:** (252) 737-4528.
Home Field: Clark-LeClair Stadium. **Seating Capacity:** 5,000. **Outfield Dimensions:** LF—320, CF—400, RF—320. **Press Box Telephone:** (252) 328-0068.

EAST TENNESSEE STATE BUCCANEERS

Conference: Atlantic Sun.
Mailing Address: PO Box 70707, Johnson City, TN 37614. **Website:** www.etsubucs.com.
Head Coach: Tony Skole. **Assistant Coaches:** Reid Casey, *Clay Greene. **Telephone:** (423) 439-4496. **Baseball SID:** Jeff Schneider. **Telephone:** (423) 439-5612. **Fax:** (423) 439-6138.
Home Field: Cardinal Park. **Seating Capacity:** 2,000. **Outfield Dimensions:** LF—325, CF—430, RF—320. **Press Box Telephone:** (423) 741-5297.

EASTERN ILLINOIS PANTHERS

Conference: Ohio Valley.
Mailing Address: 600 Lincoln Ave, Charleston, IL 61920. **Website:** www.EIUpanthers.com.
Head Coach: Jim Schmitz. **Assistant Coaches:** James Conrad, *Skylar Meade. **Telephone:** (217) 581-2522. **Baseball SID:** Rich Moser. **Telephone:** (217) 581-7480. **Fax:** (217)-581-6434.
Home Field: Coaches Stadium. **Seating Capacity:** 600. **Outfield Dimensions:** LF—340, CF—380, RF—340.

EASTERN KENTUCKY COLONELS

Conference: Ohio Valley.
Mailing Address: 521 Lancaster Ave, Richmond, KY 40475. **Website:** www.ekusports.com.
Head Coach: Jason Stein. **Assistant Coaches:** *Jerry Edwards, John Peterson. **Telephone:** (859) 622-2128. **Baseball SID:** Steve Fohl. **Telephone:** (859) 622-1253. **Fax:** (859) 622-5108.
Home Field: Turkey Hughes Field. **Seating Capacity:** 1,000. **Outfield Dimensions:** LF—330, CF—415, RF—340. **Press Box Telephone:** (859) 200-1958.

EASTERN MICHIGAN EAGLES

Conference: Mid-American (West).
Mailing Address: 200 Bowen Field House, Ypsilanti, MI 48197. **Website:** www.emueagles.com.
Head Coach: Jay Alexander. **Assistant Coaches:** Aaron Hepner, *Andrew Maki. **Telephone:** (734) 487-0315. **Baseball SID:** Lucas Pattarozzi. **Telephone:** (734) 487-0317. **Fax:** (734) 485-3840.
Home Field: Oestrike Stadium. **Seating Capacity:** 1,200. **Outfield Dimensions:** LF—330, CF—390, RF—370. **Press Box Telephone:** (734) 481-9328.

ELON PHOENIX

Conference: Southern.
Mailing Address: 2500 Campus Box, 100 Campus Drive, Elon, NC 27244. **Website:** www.elonphoenix.com.
Head Coach: Mike Kennedy. **Assistant Coaches:** Robbie Huffstetler, *Greg Starbuck. **Telephone:** (336) 278-6741. **Baseball SID:** Chris Rash. **Telephone:** (336) 278-6712. **Fax:** (336) 278-6768.
Home Field: Latham Park. **Seating Capacity:** 2,000. **Outfield Dimensions:** LF—327, CF—385, RF—328. **Press Box Telephone:** (336) 278-6788.

EVANSVILLE PURPLE ACES

Conference: Missouri Valley.
Mailing Address: 1800 Lincoln Ave, Evansville, IN 47722. **Website:** www.gopurpleaces.com.
Head Coach: Wes Carroll. **Assistant Coaches:** Josh Reynolds, *Marc Wagner. **Telephone:** (812) 488-2059. **Baseball SID:** Lizzie Barlow. **Telephone:** (812) 488-1152. **Fax:** (812) 488-2090.
Home Field: Charles H Braun Stadium. **Seating Capacity:** 1,200. **Outfield Dimensions:** LF—330, CF—400, RF—330. **Press Box Telephone:** (812) 479-2587.

FAIRFIELD STAGS

Conference: Metro Atlantic.
Mailing Address: 1073 North Benson Rd, Fairfield, CT 06824. **Website:** www.fairfieldstags.com.
Head Coach: John Slosar. **Assistant Coaches:** Bill Currier, *Adam Taraska. **Telephone:** (203) 254-4000, ext 2605. **Baseball SID:** Kelly McCarthy. **Telephone:** (203) 254-4000 ext. **2877. Fax:** (203) 254-4117.
Home Field: Alumni Baseball Diamond. **Seating Capacity:** Unavailable. **Outfield Dimension:** LF—330, CF—400, RF—330.

FAIRLEIGH-DICKINSON KNIGHTS

Conference: Northeast.
Mailing Address: 1000 River Road, Teaneck, NJ 07666. **Website:** www.fduknights.com.
Head Coach: Gary Puccio. **Assistant Coaches:** Enver Lopez, *Justin McKay. **Telephone:** (201) 692-2245. **Baseball SID:** Chris Strauch. **Telephone:** (201) 692-2204. **Fax:** (201) 692-9361.
Home Field: Namoli Family Baseball Complex. **Seating Capacity:** 500. **Outfield Dimensions:** LF—321, CF—375, RF—327.

FLORIDA GATORS

Conference: Southeastern.
Mailing Address: University Athletic Association, PO Box 14485, Gainesville, FL 32604. **Website:** www.GatorZone.com.
Head Coach: Kevin O'Sullivan. **Assistant Coaches:** *Craig Bell, Brad Weitzel. **Telephone:** (352) 375-4457. **Baseball SID:** John Hines. **Telephone:** (352) 375-4683, ext 6130. **Fax:** (352) 375-4809.
Home Field: Alfred A McKethan Stadium. **Seating Capacity:** 5,550. **Outfield Dimensions:** LF—329, CF—400, RF—325.

FLORIDA A&M RATTLERS

Conference: Mid-Eastern Athletic.
Mailing Address: 1835 Wahnish Way, Tallahassee, FL 32307. **Website:** www.famu.edu/athletics.
Head Coach: Brett Richardson. **Assistant Coaches:** Unavailable. **Telephone:** (850) 599-3202. **Baseball SID:** Ronnie Johnson. **Telephone:** (850) 599-3736. **Fax:** (850) 599-3206. **Telephone:** (850) 599-3202.

FLORIDA ATLANTIC OWLS

Conference: Sun Belt.
Mailing Address: 777 Glades Rd, Boca Raton, FL 33431.
Website: www.fausports.com.
Head Coach: John McCormack. **Assistant Coaches:** *Jason Jackson, Ben Sanderson. **Telephone:** (561) 297-1055. **Baseball SID:** Jered Smith. **Telephone:** (561) 756-0653. **Fax:** (561) 297-0142.
Home Field: FAU Stadium. **Seating Capacity:** 2,500. **Outfield Dimension:** LF—330, CF—400, RF—330. **Press Box Telephone:** (561) 297-3455.

FLORIDA GULF COAST EAGLES

Conference: Atlantic Sun.
Mailing Address: 10501 FGCU Blvd S, Fort Myers, FL 33965-6566. **Website:** www.fgcuathletics.com.
Head Coach: Dave Tollett. **Assistant Coaches:** Forrest Martin, *Rusty McKee. **Telephone:** (239) 590-7051. **Baseball SID:** Patrick Pierson. **Telephone:** (239) 590-7061. **Fax:** (239) 590-7014.
Home Field: Swanson Stadium. **Seating Capacity:** 1,500. **Outfield Dimensions:** LF—330, CF—400, RF—330.

FLORIDA INTERNATIONAL PANTHERS

Conference: Sun Belt.
Mailing Address: 11200 SW 8th St, Miami, FL 33199. **Website:** www.fiusports.com.
Head Coach: Turtle Thomas. **Assistant Coaches:** *Sean Allen, Frank Damas. **Telephone:** (305) 348-3144. **Baseball SID:** Mat Ratner. **Telephone:** (305) 348-1496. **Fax:** (305) 348-2963.
Home Field: FIU Stadium. **Seating Capacity:** 2,500. **Outfield Dimensions:** LF—325, CF—400, RF—325. **Press Box Telephone:** (561) 441-8057.

FLORIDA STATE SEMINOLES

Conference: Atlantic Coast (Atlantic).
Mailing Address: PO Box 2195, Tallahassee, FL 32316. **Website:** www.seminoles.com.
Head Coach: Mike Martin. **Assistant Coaches:** Mike Martin Jr, *Jamey Shouppe. **Telephone:** (850) 644-1073. **Baseball SID:** Bob Thomas. **Telephone:** (850) 644-0615. **Fax:** (850) 644-7213.
Home Field: Dick Howser Stadium at Mike Martin Field. **Seating Capacity:** 6,700. **Outfield Dimensions:** LF—340, CF—400, RF—320.

FORDHAM RAMS

Conference: Atlantic 10.
Mailing Address: 441 East Fordham Rd, Bronx, NY 10458. **Website:** www.fordhamsports.com.
Head Coach: Nick Restaino. **Assistant Coaches:** Trevor Brown, Jerry DeFabbia. **Telephone:** (718) 817-4292. **Baseball SID:** Scott Kwiatkowski. **Telephone:** (718) 817-4219. **Fax:** (718) 817-4244.
Home Field: Houlihan Park at Jack Coffey Field. **Seating Capacity:** 1,000. **Outfield Dimensions:** LF—338, CF—400, RF—338. **Press Box Telephone:** (718) 817-0773.

FRESNO STATE BULLDOGS

Conference: Western Athletic.
Mailing Address: 1620E Bulldog Lane, OF 87, Fresno, CA 93740. **Website:** www.gobulldogs.com.
Head Coach: Mike Batesole. **Assistant Coaches:** Steve Rousey, *Pat Waer. **Telephone:** (559) 278-2178. **Baseball SID:** Theresa Kurtz. **Telephone:** (559) 278-2509. **Fax:** (559) 278-4689.
Home Field: Beiden Field. **Seating Capacity:** 3,575.

Outfield Dimensions: LF—330, CF—400, RF—330. **Press Box Telephone:** (559) 278-7678.

FURMAN PALADINS

Conference: Southern.
Mailing Address: 3300 Poinsett Highway, Greenville, SC 29613. **Website:** www.furmanpaladins.com.
Head Coach: Ron Smith. **Assistant Coaches:** Britt Reames, Jeff Whitfield. **Telephone:** (864) 294-2146. **Baseball SID:** Hunter Reid. **Telephone:** (864) 294-2061. **Fax:** (864) 294-3061.
Home field: Latham Baseball Stadium. **Seating Capacity:** 2,000. **Outfield Dimensions:** LF—330, CF—393, RF—330.

GARDNER-WEBB RUNNIN' BULLDOGS

Conference: Atlantic Sun.
Mailing Address: PO Box 877 Boiling Springs, NC 28017. **Website:** www.gwusports.com.
Head Coach: Rusty Stroupe. **Assistant Coaches:** Jason Burke, *Kent Cox. **Telephone:** (704) 406-4421. **Baseball SID:** Marc Rabb. **Telephone:** (704) 406-4355. **Fax:** (704) 406-4739.
Home Field: Moss Stadium. **Seating Capacity:** 600. **Outfield Dimensions:** LF—330, CF—390, RF—330.

GEORGE MASON PATRIOTS

Conference: Colonial Athletic.
Mailing Address: 4400 University Drive, Fairfax VA, 22030-4444. **Website:** www.gomason.com.
Head Coach: Bill Brown. **Assistant Coaches:** *Steve Hay, Lucas Jones. **Telephone:** (703) 993-3282. **Baseball SID:** Richard Coco. **Telephone:** (703) 993-3264. **Fax:** (703) 993-3259.
Home Field: Spuhler Field. **Seating Capacity:** 900. **Outfield Dimensions:** LF—320, CF—400, RF—320.

GEORGE WASHINGTON COLONIALS

Conference: Atlantic 10.
Mailing Address: 600 22nd Street NW, Washington, DC 20052. **Website:** www.gwsports.cstv.com.
Head Coach: Steve Mrowka. **Assistant Coaches:** Tim Brown, Jon Greenwich. **Telephone:** (202) 994-7399. **Baseball SID:** Dan DiVeglio. **Telephone:** (202) 994-0339. **Fax:** (202) 994-2713.
Home Field: Barcroft Park. **Seating Capacity:** 1,000. **Outfield Dimensions:** LF—321, CF—370, RF—321.

GEORGETOWN HOYAS

Conference: Big East.
Mailing Address: Georgetown Baseball Office, 3700 O St NW, Washington, DC 20057. **Website:** www.guhoyas.com.
Head Coach: Pete Wilk. **Assistant Coaches:** *Curtis Brown, Matt Kirby. **Telephone:** (202) 687-2462. **Baseball SID:** Mike Carey. **Telephone:** (202) 687-2475. **Fax:** (202) 687-2491.
Home Field: Shirley Povich Field. **Seating Capacity:** 1,500. **Outfield Dimensions:** LF—330, CF—375, RF—330. **Press Box Telephone:** (267) 304-2440.

GEORGIA BULLDOGS

Conference: Southeastern (East).
Mailing Address: PO Box 1472, Athens, GA 30603-1472. **Website:** www.georgiadogs.com.
Head Coach: David Perno. **Assistant Coaches:** *Jason Eller, Allen Osborne. **Telephone:** (706) 542-7971. **Baseball SID:** Christopher Lakos. **Telephone:** (706) 542-7994. **Fax:** (706) 542-7993.
Home Field: Foley Field. **Seating Capacity:** 3,291.

Outfield Dimensions: LF—350, CF—404, RF—314. **Press Box Telephone:** (706) 542-6161.

GEORGIA SOUTHERN EAGLES

Conference: Southern.
Mailing Address: PO Box 8095, Statesboro GA 30460.
Website: www.georgiasoutherneagles.com.
Head Coach: Rodney Hennon. **Assistant Coaches:** BJ Green, *Mike Tidick. **Telephone:** (912) 478-7360. **Baseball SID:** Rose Carter. **Telephone:** (912) 478-0352. **Fax:** (912) 478-1063.
Home Field: JI Clements Stadium. **Seating Capacity:** 3,000. **Outfield Dimension:** LF—325, CF—385, RF—325. **Press Box Telephone:** (912) 478-5764.

GEORGIA STATE PANTHERS

Conference: Colonial Athletic.
Mailing Address: 125 Decatur Street, Suite 201, Atlanta, GA 30309. **Website:** www.georgiastatesports.com.
Head Coach: Greg Frady. **Assistant Coaches:** Jason Arnold, *Brad Stromdahl. **Telephone:** (404) 413-4077. **Baseball SID:** Mike Holmes. **Telephone:** (404) 259-9716. **Fax:** (404) 413-4035.
Home Field: The Field at Panthersville. **Seating Capacity:** 1,000. **Outfield Dimensions:** LF—334, CF—385, RF—338. **Press Box Telephone:** (404) 241-9850.

GEORGIA TECH Yellow Jackets
Conference: Atlantic Coast (Coastal).
Mailing Address: 150 Bobby Dodd Way, Atlanta, GA 30332. **Website:** www.ramblinwreck.com.
Head Coach: Danny Hall. **Assistant Coaches:** Tom Kinkelaar, *Bryan Prince. **Telephone:** (404) 894-5471. **Baseball SID:** Mike Huff. **Telephone:** (404) 385-2959. **Fax:** (404) 894-1248.
Home Field: Russ Chandler Stadium. **Seating Capacity:** 4,157. **Outfield Dimensions:** LF—328, CF—400, RF—334. **Press Box Telephone:** (404) 894-3167.

GONZAGA BULLDOGS

Conference: West Coast.
Mailing Address: 502 E Boone Ave, Spokane, WA 99258. **Website:** www.gozags.com.
Head Coach: Mark Machtolf. **Assistant Coaches:** Steve Bennett, *Danny Evans. **Telephone:** (509) 313-4209. **Baseball SID:** Richard Hoskin. **Telephone:** (509) 313-4227. **Fax:** (509) 313-5730.
Home Field: Patterson Baseball Complex and Washington Trust Field. **Seating Capacity:** 3,000. **Outfield Dimensions:** LF—328, CF—398, RF—328. **Press Box Telephone:** (509) 279-1005.

GRAMBLING STATE TIGERS

Conference: Southwestern Athletic.
Mailing Address: PO Box 868, Grambling, LA 71245. **Website:** www.gsutigers.com.
Head Coach: James Cooper. **Assistant Coaches:** David Pierre, Joshua Scott. **Telephone:** (318) 274-6204. **Baseball SID:** Roderick Mosley. **Telephone:** (318) 274-6562.

HARTFORD HAWKS

Conference: America East.
Mailing Address: Sports Center, 200 Bloomfield Ave, West Hartford, CT 06117. **Website:** www.hartfordhawks.com.
Head Coach: Jeff Calcaterra. **Assistant Coaches:** Inaki Ormaechea, *Jerry Shank. **Telephone:** (860) 768-5760. **Baseball SID:** Sam Angell. **Telephone:** (860) 768-4620. **Fax:** (860) 68-5047.
Home Field: Fiondella Field. **Seating Capacity:** 1,500. **Outfield Dimensions:** LF—325, CF—400, RF—325.

HARVARD CRIMSON

Conference: Ivy League (Rolfe).
Mailing Address: 65 North Harvard St, Boston, MA 02163. **Website:** www.gocrimson.com.
Head Coach: Joe Walsh. **Assistant Coaches:** Morgan Brown, *Tom Lo Ricco. **Telephone:** (617) 495-2629. **Baseball SID:** Kurt Svoboda. **Telephone:** (617) 495-2206. **Fax:** (617) 495-2130.
Home Field: O'Donnell Field. **Seating Capacity:** 1,600. **Outfield Dimensions:** LF—335, CF—415, RF—335.

HAWAII Rainbows
Conference: Western Athletic.
Mailing Address: 1337 Lower Campus Rd, Honolulu, HI 96822. **Website:** www.hawaiiathletics.com.
Head Coach: Mike Trapasso. **Assistant Coaches:** *Chad Konishi, Rusty McNamara. **Telephone:** (808) 956-6247. **Baseball SID:** Derek Inouchi. **Telephone:** (808) 956-4478. **Fax:** (808) 956-4470.
Home Field: Les Murakami Stadium. **Seating Capacity:** 4,312. **Outfield Dimensions:** LF—325, CF—385, RF—325.

HIGH POINT PANTHERS

Conference: Big South.
Mailing Address: 833 Montlieu Ave, High Point, NC 27262. **Website:** www.highpointpanthers.com.
Head Coach: Craig Cozart. **Assistant Coaches:** *Bryan Peters, Rich Wallace. **Telephone:** (336) 841-9190. **Baseball SID:** Erika Carrubba. **Telephone:** (336) 841-4640. **Fax:** (336) 841-9182.
Home Field: Williard Stadium. **Seating Capacity:** 550. **Outfield Dimensions:** LF—350, CF—400, RF—330. **Press Box Telephone:** (336) 841-9192.

HOFSTRA PRIDE

Conference: Colonial Athletic.
Mailing Address: 1000 Hempstead Turnpike, Hempstead, NY 11549. **Website:** www.gohofstra.com.
Head Coach: Patrick Anderson. **Assistant Coaches:** James Lally, *John Russo. **Telephone:** (516) 463-5065. **Baseball SID:** Len Skoros. **Telephone:** (516) 463-4602. **Fax:** (516) 463-5033.
Home Field: University Field. **Seating Capacity:** 600. **Outfield Dimensions:** LF—331, CF—380, RF—340. **Press Box Telephone:** (516) 463-1896.

HOLY CROSS CRUSADERS

Conference: Patriot.
Mailing Address: One College St, Worcester MA, 01610. **Website:** www.goholycross.com.
Head Coach: Greg DiCenzo. **Assistant Coaches:** *Jeff Kane, Ron Rakowski. **Telephone:** (508) 793-2753. **Baseball SID:** Meredith Cook. **Telephone:** (508) 793-2780. **Fax:** (508) 793-2309.
Home Field: Hanover Insurance Park at Fitton Field. **Seating Capacity:** 3,000. **Outfield Dimensions:** LF—332, CF—385, RF—313.

HOUSTON COUGARS

Conference: Conference USA.
Mailing Address: 3100 Cullen Blvd, Houston, TX 77204. **Website:** www.UHCougars.com.
Head Coach: Todd Whitting. **Assistant Coaches:** *Trip Couch, Jack Cressend. **Telephone:** (713) 743-9416. **Baseball SID:** Jamie Zarda. **Telephone:** (713) 743-9406. **Fax:** (713) 743-9411.
Home Field: Cougar Field. **Seating Capacity:** 4,000. **Outfield Dimensions:** LF—330, CF—390, RF—330. **Press Box Telephone:** (713) 743-0840.

HOUSTON BAPTIST HUSKIES

Conference: Great West.
Mailing Address: 7502 Fondren Rd, Houston TX 77074.
Website: www.hbuhuskies.com.
Head Coach: Jared Moon. **Assistant Coaches:** *Xavier Hernandez, Russell Stockton. **Telephone:** (281) 649-3332. **Baseball SID:** Russ Reneau. **Telephone:** (281) 649-3098. **Fax:** (281) 649-3496.
Home Field: Husky Field. **Seating Capacity:** 500. **Outfield Dimensions:** LF—330, CF—400, RF—330. **Press Box Telephone:** (281) 649-3126.

ILLINOIS FIGHTING ILLINI

Conference: Big Ten.
Mailing Address: 1700 S Fourth St, Champaign, IL 61820. **Website:** www.fightingillini.com.
Head Coach: Dan Hartleb. **Assistant Coaches:** *Eric Snider, Ken Westray. **Telephone:** (217) 244-8144. **Baseball SID:** Ben Taylor. **Telephone:** (217) 244-5045. **Fax:** (217) 333-5540.
Home Field: Illinois Field. **Seating Capacity:** 1,500. **Outfield Dimension:** LF—330, CF—400, RF—330. **Press Box Telephone:** (217) 333-1227.

ILLINOIS STATE REDBIRDS

Conference: Missouri Valley.
Mailing Address: Illinois State Athletic Media Relations, 202 Horton Field House, Normal, IL 61671. **Website:** www.GoRedbirds.com.
Head Coach: Mark Kingston. **Assistant Coaches:** *Bo Durkac, Bill Mohl. **Telephone:** (309) 438-5709. **Baseball SID:** John Twork. **Telephone:** (309) 438-5746. **Fax:** (309) 438-5634.
Home Field: Duffy Bass Field. **Seating Capacity:** 1,000. **Outfield Dimensions:** LF—330, CF—400, RF—330.

ILLINOIS-CHICAGO FLAMES

Conference: Horizon.
Mailing Address: 839 West Roosevelt Rd, MC 195), Chicago, IL 60608. **Website:** www.uicflames.cstv.com.
Head Coach: Mike Dee. **Assistant Coaches:** *John Flood, Sean McDermott. **Telephone:** (312) 996-8645. **Baseball SID:** Dan Yopchick. **Telephone:** (312) 996-5881. **Fax:** (312) 996-8349.
Home Field: Les Miller Field. **Seating Capacity:** 1,100. **Outfield Dimensions:** LF—330, CF—401, RF—330. **Press Box Telephone:** (312) 355-1190.

INDIANA HOOSIERS

Conference: Big Ten.
Mailing Address: 1001 E 17th St, Bloomington, IN 47408. **Website:** www.iuhoosiers.com.
Head Coach: Tracy Smith. **Assistant Coaches:** Ben Greenspan, *Ty Neal. **Telephone:** (812) 855-8240. **Baseball SID:** Kyle Kuhlman. **Telephone:** (812) 855-4770. **Fax:** (812) 855-9401.
Home Field: Sembower Field. **Seating Capacity:** 2,250. **Outfield Dimensions:** LF—333, CF—395, RF—333. **Press Box Telephone:** (812) 855-4787.

INDIANA STATE SYCAMORES

Conference: Missouri Valley.
Mailing Address: ISU Arena, 401 N 4th St, Terre Haute, IN 47809. **Website:** www.gosycamores.com.
Head Coach: Rick Heller. **Assistant Coaches:** *Tyler Herbst, Brian Smiley. **Telephone:** (812) 237-4051. **Baseball SID:** Danny Pfrank. **Telephone:** (812) 237-4159. **Fax:** (812) 237-4157.
Home Field: Bob Warn Field at Sycamore Stadium.

Seating Capacity: 1,000. **Outfield Dimensions:** LF—340, CF—402, RF—340.

IONA GAELS

Conference: Metro Atlantic.
Mailing Address: 715 North Ave, New Rochelle, NY 10801. **Website:** www.icgaels.com.
Head Coach: Pat Carey. **Assistant Coaches:** Rob DiToma, James LaSala. **Telephone:** (914) 633-2319. **Baseball SID:** Brian Beyrer. **Telephone:** (914) 633-2334. **Fax:** (914) 633-2072.
Home Field: Salesian Field. **Seating Capacity:** 450. **Outfield Dimension:** LF—301, CF—401, RF—320. **Press Box Telephone:** (914) 497-3136.

IOWA HAWKEYES

Conference: Big Ten.
Mailing Address: 232 Carver Hawkeye Arena, Iowa City, IA 52242. **Website:** www.hawkeyesports.com.
Head Coach: Jack Dahm. **Assistant Coaches:** *Ryan Brownlee, Chris Maliszewski. **Telephone:** (319) 335-9743. **Baseball SID:** Matt Weitzel. **Telephone:** (319) 335-9411. **Fax:** (319) 335-9417.
Home Field: Duane Banks Field. **Seating Capacity:** 1,000. **Outfield Dimensions:** LF—329, CF—395, RF—329. **Press Box Telephone:** (319) 335-9520.

IPFW MASTODONS

Conference: Summit.
Mailing Address: 2101 E Coliseum Blvd, Fort Wayne, IN 46805. **Website:** www.gomastodons.com.
Head Coach: Bobby Pierce. **Assistant Coaches:** *Grant Birely, Alex Rinearson. **Telephone:** (260) 481-5480. **Baseball SID:** Rudy Yovich. **Telephone:** (260) 481-6646. **Fax:** (260) 481-6002.
Home Field: Mastodon Field. **Seating Capacity:** 500. **Outfield Dimensions:** LF—335, CF—400, RF—335. **Press Box Telephone:** (260) 402-6599.

JACKSON STATE TIGERS

Conference: Southwestern Athletic.
Mailing Address: JSU Box 18060, Jackson, MS 39217-0660. **Website:** www.jsutigers.com.
Head Coach: Omar Johnson. **Assistant Coach:** Ryan Goodwin. **Telephone:** (601) 979-3930. **Baseball SID:** Wesley Peteron. **Telephone:** (601) 979-2274. **Fax:** (601) 979-2000.
Home Field: Robert "Bob" Braddy Sr Field. **Seating Capacity:** 800. **Outfield Dimension:** LF—325, CF—400, RF—325.

JACKSONVILLE DOLPHINS

Conference: Atlantic Sun.
Mailing Address: 2800 University Blvd N, Jacksonville, FL 32211. **Website:** www.judolphins.com.
Head Coach: Terry Alexander. **Assistant Coaches:** *Tim Montez, Tommy Murphy. **Telephone:** (904) 256-7425. **Baseball SID:** Josh Ellis. **Telephone:** (904) 256-7402. **Fax:** (904) 256-7424.
Home Field: John Sessions Stadium. **Seating Capacity:** 3,000. **Outfield Dimensions:** LF—340, CF—405, RF—340. **Press Box Telephone:** (904) 256-7444.

JACKSONVILLE STATE GAMECOCKS

Conference: Ohio Valley.
Mailing Address: 700 Pelham Road North, Jacksonville, AL 36265. **Website:** www.jsugamecocksports.com.
Head Coach: Jim Case. **Assistant Coaches:** *Steve Gillispie, Travis Janssen. **Telephone:** (256) 782-5367. **Baseball SID:** Greg Seitz. **Telephone:** (256) 782-5279.

Fax: (256) 782-5958.
Home Field: Rudy Abbott Field. **Seating Capacity:** 1,500. **Outfield Dimensions:** LF—330, CF—400, RF—330. **Press Box Telephone:** (256) 782-5533.

JAMES MADISON DUKES

Conference: Colonial Athletic.
Mailing Address: 395 South High St, MSC 6925, Memorial Hall, Harrisonburg, VA 22807. **Website:** www.jmusports.com.
Head Coach: Spanky McFarland. **Assistant Coaches:** *Jay Sullenger, Ted White. **Telephone:** (540) 568-5510. **Baseball SID:** Kevin Warner. **Telephone:** (540) 568-6154. **Fax:** (540) 568-3703.
Home Field: Veterans Memorial Park. **Seating Capacity:** 1,200. **Outfield Dimension:** LF—340, CF—400, RF—320. **Press Box Telephone:** (540) 568-6545.

KANSAS JAYHAWKS

Conference: Big 12.
Mailing Address: Allen Fieldhouse, 1651 Naismith Dr, Lawrence, KS 66045. **Website:** www.kuathletics.com.
Head Coach: Ritch Price. **Assistant Coaches:** Ryan Graves. **Telephone:** (785) 864-7907. **Baseball SID:** Mike Cummings. **Telephone:** (785) 864-3575. **Fax:** (785) 864-7944.
Home Field: Hoglund Ballpark. **Seating Capacity:** 2,500. **Outfield Dimensions:** LF—330, CF—400, RF—330. **Press Box Telephone:** (785) 864-4037.

KANSAS STATE WILDCATS

Conference: Big 12.
Mailing Address: 1800 College Ave, Manhattan, KS 66502. **Website:** www.kstatesports.com.
Head Coach: Brad Hill. **Assistant Coaches:** Josh Reynolds, *John Szefc. **Telephone:** (785) 532-3926. **Baseball SID:** Ryan Lackey. **Telephone:** (785) 532-7708. **Fax:** (785) 532-6093.
Home Field: Tointon Family Stadium. **Seating Capacity:** 2,331. **Outfield Dimensions:** LF—340, CF—400, RF—325. **Press Box Telephone:** (785) 532-5801.

KENNESAW STATE OWLS

Conference: Atlantic Sun.
Mailing Address: 1000 Chastain Rd, Kennesaw, GA 30144. **Website:** ksuowls.com.
Head Coach: Mike Sansing. **Assistant Coaches:** Kevin Erminio, *Derrick Tucker. **Telephone:** (770) 423-6264. **Baseball SID:** Mark Toma. **Telephone:** (770) 499-23217. **Fax:** (770) 423-6555.
Home Field: Stillwell Stadium. **Seating Capacity:** 1,065. **Outfield Dimension:** LF—331, CF—400, RF—330. **Press Box Telephone:**

KENT STATE GOLDEN FLASHES

Conference: Mid-American (East).
Mailing Address: 234 MAC Center, Kent, OH 44242. **Website:** www.kentstatesports.com.
Head Coach: Scott Stricklin. **Assistant Coaches:** Mike Birkbeck, *Scott Daeley. **Telephone:** (330) 672-8432. **Baseball SID:** Mike Ashcraft. **Telephone:** (330) 672-2110. **Fax:** (330) 672-2112.
Home Field: Schoonover Stadium. **Seating Capacity:** 1,000. **Outfield Dimensions:** LF—320, CF—415, RF—325. **Press Box Telephone:** (330) 672-3696.

KENTUCKY WILDCATS

Conference: Southeastern (East).
Mailing Address: Joe Craft Center, 338 Lexington Ave, Lexington, KY 40506. **Website:** www.ukathletics.com.

Head Coach: Gary Henderson. **Assistant Coaches:** *Brad Bohannon, Brian Green. **Telephone:** (859) 257-8502. **Baseball SID:** Brent Ingram. **Telephone:** (859) 257-8504. **Fax:** (859) 323-4310.
Home Field: Cliff Hagan Stadium. **Seating Capacity:** 3,000. **Outfield Dimensions:** LF—340, CF—390, RF—310. **Press Box Telephone:** (859) 257-9011.

LA SALLE EXPLORERS

Conference: Atlantic 10.
Mailing Address: 1900 Olney Avenue, Philadelphia, PA 19141. **Website:** www.goexplorers.com.
Head Coach: Mike Lake. **Assistant Coaches:** Bob File, *Toby Fisher. **Telephone:** (215) 951-1995. **Baseball SID:** Kevin Bonner. **Telephone:** (215) 951-1513. **Fax:** (215) 951-1694.
Home Field: Hank DeVincent Field. **Seating Capacity:** 1,000. **Outfield Dimensions:** LF—305, CF—410, RF—321.

LAFAYETTE LEOPARDS

Conference: Patriot. **Mailing Address:** Kirby Sports Center, Pierce & Hamilton Streets, Easton, PA 18042. **Website:** www.goleopards.com.
Head Coach: Joe Kinney. **Assistant Coaches:** *Greg Durrah, Brandt Godshalk. **Telephone:** (610) 330-5471. **Baseball SID:** Drew Kingsley. **Telephone:** (610) 330-5897. **Fax:** (610) 330-5702.
Home Field: Kamine Stadium. **Seating Capacity:** 500. **Outfield Dimension:** LF—332, CF—403, RF—335.

LAMAR CARDINALS

Conference: Southland.
Mailing Address: PO Box 10066, Beaumont, TX 77710. **Website:** lamarcardinals.com.
Head Coach: Jim Gilligan. **Assistant Coaches:** Scott Hatten, *Jim Ricklefson. **Telephone:** (409) 880-8315. **Baseball SID:** Rush Wood. **Telephone:** (409) 880-7845. **Fax:** (409) 880-2338.
Home Field: Vincent-Beck Stadium. **Seating Capacity:** 3,500. **Outfield Dimensions:** LF—325, CF—380, RF—325. **Press Box Telephone:** (409) 880-8327.

LE MOYNE DOLPHINS

Conference: Independent.
Mailing Address: 1419 Salt Springs Road, Syracuse, NY 13214. **Website:** www.lemoynedolphins.com.
Head Coach: Scott Cassidy. **Assistant Coaches:** *Scott Landers, Matt Nandin.
Telephone: (315) 445-4415. **Baseball SID:** Kevin McNeil. **Telephone:** (315) 445-4412. **Fax:** (315) 445-4678.
Home Field: Dick Rockwell Field. **Seating Capacity:** 2,500. **Outfield Dimensions:** LF—314 CF—375, RF—337.

LEHIGH MOUNTAIN HAWKS

Conference: Patriot.
Mailing Address: 641 Taylor St, Bethlehem, PA 18015. **Website:** www.lehighsports.com.
Head Coach: Sean Leary. **Assistant Coaches:** John Bisco, *Brian Hirschberg. **Telephone:** (610) 758-4315. **Baseball SID:** Justin LaFleur. **Telephone:** (610) 758-6631. **Fax:** (610) 758-4407.
Home Field: Lehigh Field. **Seating Capacity:** 250. **Outfield Dimension:** LF—320, CF—400, RF—320.

LIBERTY FLAMES

Conference: Big South.
Mailing Address: 1971 University Blvd, Lynchburg, VA 24502. **Website:** www.libertyflames.com.
Head Coach: Jim Toman. **Assistant Coaches:** *Jason

Murray, Garrett Quinn. **Telephone:** (434) 582-2305. **Baseball SID:** Ryan Bomberger. **Telephone:** (434) 582-2605. **Fax:** (434) 582-2076.

Home Field: Worthington Stadium. **Seating Capacity:** 1,000. **Outfield Dimensions:** LF—335, CF—400, RF—335. **Press Box Telephone:** (434) 582-2914.

LIPSCOMB BISONS

Conference: Atlantic Sun.
Mailing Address: 1 University Park Dr, Nashville, TN 37204. **Website:** www.lipscombsports.com.
Head Coach: Jeff Forehand. **Assistant Coaches:** *Chris Collins, Tyler Shrout. **Telephone:** (615) 966-5716. **Baseball SID:** Mark McGee. **Telephone:** (615) 966-5990. **Fax:** (615) 966-1806.
Home Field: Dugan Field. **Seating Capacity:** 1,500. **Outfield Dimension:** LF—330, CF—405, RF—330. **Press Box Telephone:** (615) 479-3794.

LONG BEACH STATE DIRTBAGS

Conference: Big West.
Mailing Address: 1250 Bellflower Blvd, Long Beach, CA 90840. **Website:** www.longbeachstate.com.
Head Coach: Troy Buckley. **Assistant Coaches:** Shawn Gilbert, *Jesse Zepeda. **Telephone:** (562) 985-4661. **Baseball SID:** Roger Kirk. **Telephone:** (562) 985-7565. **Fax:** (562) 985-1549.
Home Field: Blair Field. **Seating Capacity:** 3,000. **Outfield Dimensions:** LF—348, CF—400, RF—348. **Press Box Telephone:** (562) 505-0975.

LONG ISLAND BLACKBIRDS

Conference: Northeast.
Mailing Address: 1 University Plaza, Brooklyn, NY 11201. **Website:** www.liuathletics.com.
Head Coach: Don Maines. **Assistant Coaches:** *Craig Noto, Dan Pirillo. **Telephone:** (718) 488-1538. **Baseball SID:** Shawn Sweeney. **Telephone:** (718) 488-1307. **Fax:** (718) 488-3302.
Home Field: LIU Field. **Seating Capacity:** 500. **Outfield Dimension:** LF—315, CF—416, RF—315.

LONGWOOD LANCERS

Conference: Independent.
Mailing Address: 201 High St, Farmville, VA 23909. **Website:** www.longwoodlancers.com.
Head Coach: Buddy Bolding. **Assistant Coaches:** Brian McCullough, *Brett Mooney. **Telephone:** (434) 395-2352. **Baseball SID:** Greg Prouty. **Telephone:** (434) 395-2097. **Fax:** (434) 395-2568.
Home Field: Charles Buddy Bolding Stadium. **Seating Capacity:** 500. **Outfield Dimension:** LF—335, CF—400, RF—335. **Press Box Telephone:** (434) 395-2710.

LOUISIANA STATE FIGHTING TIGERS

Conference: Southeastern (West).
Mailing Address: PO Box 25095, Baton Rouge, LA 70894. **Website:** www.LSUsports.net.
Head Coach: Paul Mainieri. **Assistant Coaches:** *David Grewe, Javi Sanchez. **Telephone:** (225) 578-4148. **Baseball SID:** Bill Franques. **Telephone:** (225) 578-8226. **Fax:** (225) 578-1861.
Home Field: Alex Box Stadium. **Seating Capacity:** 10,150. **Outfield Dimensions:** LF—330, CF—405, RF—330. **Press Box Telephone:** (225) 578-4149.

LOUISIANA TECH BULLDOGS

Conference: Western Athletic.
Mailing Address: Thomas Assembly Center, Room 161, Ruston, LA, 71270. **Website:** www.latechsports.com.

Head Coach: Wade Simoneaux. **Assistant Coaches:** Fran Andermann, *Brian Rountree. **Telephone:** (318) 257-5318. **Baseball SID:** Austin Staton. **Telephone:** (318) 257-5071. **Fax:** (318) 257-3757.
Home Field: JC Love Field at Pat Patterson Park. **Seating Capacity:** 3,000. **Outfield Dimensions:** LF—315, CF—385, RF—325. **Press Box Telephone:** (318) 257-3144.

LOUISIANA-LAFAYETTE RAGIN' CAJUNS

Conference: Sun Belt.
Mailing Address: 201 Reinhardt Dr, Lafayette, LA 70506. **Website:** www.ragincajuns.com.
Head Coach: Tony Robichaux. **Assistant Coaches:** Anthony Babineaux, *Mike Trahan. **Telephone:** (337) 428-6189. **Baseball SID:** Matt Hebert. **Telephone:** (337) 482-6330. **Fax:** (337) 482-6529.
Home Field: ML "Tigue" Moore Field. **Seating Capacity:** 3,600. **Outfield Dimensions:** LF—330, CF—400, RF—300. **Press Box Telephone:** (337) 851-2255.

LOUISIANA-MONROE WARHAWKS

Conference: Sun Belt.
Mailing Address: 308 Warhawk Way, Monroe, LA 71209. **Website:** www.ulmwarhawks.com.
Head Coach: Jeff Schexnaider. **Assistant Coaches:** *Cory Barton, Lantz Wheeler. **Telephone:** (318) 342-3591. **Baseball SID:** Adam Prendergast. **Telephone:** (318) 342-5463.
Home Field: Warhawk Field. **Seating Capacity:** 1,800. **Outfield Dimension:** LF—330, CF—400, RF—330. **Press Box Telephone:** (318) 342-5476.

LOUISVILLE CARDINALS

Conference: Big East.
Mailing Address: 215 Central Ave, Louisville, KY 40292. **Website:** www.UofLSports.com.
Head Coach: Dan McDonnell. **Assistant Coaches:** *Chris Lemonis, Roger Williams. **Telephone:** (502) 852-0103. **Baseball SID:** Garett Wall. **Telephone:** (502) 852-3088. **Fax:** (502) 852-7401.
Home Field: Jim Patterson Stadium. **Seating Capacity:** 2,500. **Outfield Dimensions:** LF—330, CF—402, RF—330. **Press Box Telephone:** (502) 852-3700.

LOYOLA MARYMOUNT LIONS

Conference: West Coast.
Mailing Address: 1 LMU Drive, Leavy Suite G, Los Angeles California, 90045. **Website:** lmulions.com.
Head Coach: Jason Gill. **Assistant Coaches:** Ted Silva, *Bryant Ward. **Telephone:** (310) 338-2949. **Baseball SID:** Tyler Geivett. **Telephone:** (310) 338-7638. **Fax:** (310) 338-2703.
Home Field: Page Stadium. **Seating Capacity:** 600. **Outfield Dimensions:** LF—326, CF—413, RF—330. **Press Box Telephone:** (310) 338-3046.

MAINE BLACK BEARS

Conference: America East.
Mailing Address: 5747 Memorial Gym, Orono, ME 04469. **Website:** www.goblackbears.com.
Head Coach: Stephen Trimper. **Assistant Coaches:** Billy Cather, *Jason Spaulding. **Telephone:** (207) 581-1098. **Baseball SID:** Laura Reed. **Telephone:** (207) 581-3646. **Fax:** (207) 581-3297.
Home Field: Mahaney Diamond. **Seating Capacity:** 4,000. **Outfield Dimensions:** LF—330, CF—400, RF—330. **Press Box Telephone:** (207) 581-1049.

MANHATTAN JASPERS

Conference: Metro Atlantic.
Mailing Address: 4513 Manhattan College Pkwy, Riverdale, NY 10471. **Website:** www.gojaspers.com.
Head Coach: Kevin Leighton. **Assistant Coaches:** Ryan Darcy, Rene Ruiz. **Telephone:** (718) 862-7936. **Baseball SID:** Stephen Dombroski. **Telephone:** (718) 862-7228. **Fax:** (718) 862-8020.
Home Field: Van Cortlandt Park. **Seating Capacity:** 500. **Outfield Dimension:** LF—320, CF—398, RF—320.

MARIST RED FOXES

Conference: Metro Atlantic.
Mailing Address: 3399 North Road, Poughkeepsie, NY 12601. **Website:** www.goredfoxes.com.
Head Coach: Chris Tracz. **Assistant Coaches:** *Joe Michalski, Thomas Seay. **Telephone:** (845) 575-3699, ext 2570. **Baseball SID:** Mike Ferraro. **Telephone:** (845) 575-3699, ext 3321.
Home Field: McCann Baseball Field. **Seating Capacity:** 350. **Outfield Dimension:** LF—337, CF—414, RF—330.

MARSHALL THUNDERING HERD

Conference: Conference USA.
Mailing Address: 2001 3rd Ave, Huntington, WV 25715. **Website:** www.herdzone.com.
Head Coach: Jeff Waggoner. **Assistant Coaches:** Tim Donnelly, *Joe Renner. **Telephone:** (304) 696-6454. **Baseball SID:** Ben Warnick. **Telephone:** (304) 696-4662. **Fax:** (304) 696-2325.
Home Field: Appalachian Power Park. **Seating Capacity:** 4,500. **Outfield Dimension:** LF—330, CF—400, RF—320.

MARYLAND TERRAPINS

Conference: Atlantic Coast (Atlantic).
Mailing Address: 1 Terrapin Tr, College Park, MD 20742. **Website:** umterps.com.
Head Coach: Erik Bakich. **Assistant Coaches:** *Dan Burton, Sean Kenny. **Telephone:** (301) 314-1845. **Baseball SID:** Justin Moore. **Telephone:** (301) 314-7068. **Fax:** (301) 314-9094.
Home Field: Bob Turtle Smith Stadium. **Seating Capacity:** 2500. **Outfield Dimensions:** LF—320, CF—380, RF—320. **Press Box Telephone:** (270) 316-3748.

MARYLAND-BALTIMORE COUNTY RETRIEVERS

Conference: America East.
Mailing Address: 1000 Hilltop Circle, Baltimore, MD 21250. **Website:** www.umbcretrievers.com.
Head Coach: John Jancuska. **Assistant Coaches:** *Bob Mumma, Tim O'Brien. **Telephone:** (410) 455-2239. **Baseball SID:** Tom Fenstermaker. **Telephone:** (410) 455-1530. **Fax:** (410) 455-3994.
Home Field: Baseballfactory Field at UMBC. **Seating Capacity:** 1,000. **Outfield Dimension:** LF—330, CF—360, RF—340.

MARYLAND-EASTERN SHORE HAWKS

Conference: Mid-Eastern.
Mailing Address: William P. **Hytche Athletic Center, One Backbone Rd, Princess Anne, MD 21853.** **Website:** www.umeshawks.com.
Head Coach: Will Gardner. **Assistant Coaches:** Eric Armstrong, Robbie Bailey. **Telephone:** (410) 651-8158. **Baseball SID:** Stan Bradley. **Telephone:** (410) 651-7888. **Fax:** (410) 651-7514.
Home Field: Hawk Stadium. **Seating Capacity:** 1,000. **Outfield Dimension:** LF—340, CF—400, RF—340.

MASSACHUSETTS MINUTEMEN

Conference: Atlantic 10.
Mailing Address: 131 Commonwealth Ave, Amherst, MA 01003. **Website:** umassathletics.com.
Head Coach: Mike Stone. **Assistant Coaches:** Ryan Franczek, *Mike Sweeney. **Telephone:** (413) 545-3120. **Baseball SID:** Jillian Jakuba. **Telephone:** (413) 577-0053. **Fax:** (413) 545-1404.
Home Field: Earl Lorden Field. **Seating Capacity:** Unavailable. **Outfield Dimension:** LF—330, CF—400, RF—330. **Press Box Telephone:** (413) 420-3116.

MCNEESE STATE COWBOYS

Conference: Southland.
Mailing Address: 615 Bienville Street, Lake Charles, LA 70607. **Website:** mcneesesports.com.
Head Coach: Terry Burrows. **Assistant Coaches:** *Bubbs Merrill, Clay Van Hook. **Telephone:** (337) 475-5484. **Baseball SID:** Louis Bonnette. **Telephone:** (337) 475-5207. **Fax:** (337) 475-5202.
Home Field: Cowboy Diamond. **Seating Capacity:** 2,000. **Outfield Dimension:** LF—330, CF—400, RF—330. **Press Box Telephone:** (337) 475-8007.

MEMPHIS TIGERS

Conference: Conference USA.
Mailing Address: 570 Normal, Memphis, TN 38152. **Website:** www.gotigersgo.com.
Head Coach: Daron Schoenrock. **Assistant Coaches:** Fred Corral, *Jerry Zulli. **Telephone:** (901) 678-4137. **Baseball SID:** Jason Redd. **Telephone:** (901) 678-4640. **Fax:** (901) 678-4134.
Home Field: FedEx Park. **Seating Capacity:** 2,000. **Outfield Dimension:** LF—318, CF—380, RF—317.

MERCER BEARS

Conference: Atlantic Sun.
Mailing Address: 1400 Coleman Ave, Macon, GA 31207. **Website:** www.mercerbears.com.
Head Coach: Craig Gibson. **Assistant Coaches:** Justin Holmes, *Brent Shade. **Telephone:** (478) 301-2396. **Baseball SID:** Jason Farhadi. **Telephone:** (478) 301-5218. **Fax:** (478) 301-5350.
Home Field: Claude Smith Field. **Seating Capacity:** 500. **Outfield Dimensions:** LF—330, CF—400, RF—320. **Press Box Telephone:** (478) 301-2339.

MIAMI HURRICANES

Conference: Atlantic Coast (Coastal).
Mailing Address: 6201 San Amaro Dr, Coral Gables, FL 33146 **Website:** www.hurricanesports.com.
Head Coach: Jim Morris. **Assistant Coaches:** *JD Arteaga, Joe Mercadante. **Telephone:** (305) 284-4171. **Baseball SID:** Bryan Harvey. **Telephone:** (305) 284-3249. **Fax:** (305) 284-2807.
Home Field: Alex Rodriguez Park. **Seating Capacity:** 5,000. **Outfield Dimensions:** LF—330, CF—400, RF—330. **Press Box Telephone:** (305) 284-8192.

MIAMI (OHIO) REDHAWKS

Conference: Mid-American (East).
Mailing Address: 120 Withrow Court, Oxford, OH 45056. **Website:** www.muredhawks.com.
Head Coach: Dan Simonds. **Assistant Coaches:** *Ben Bachmann, Jeremy Ison. **Telephone:** (513) 529-6631. **Baseball SID:** Jim Stephan. **Telephone:** (513) 529-4330. **Fax:** (513) 529-6729.
Home Field: McKie Field at Hayden Park. **Seating Capacity:** 1,000. **Outfield Dimensions:** LF—332, CF—

400, RF—343. **Press Box Telephone:** Press Box Telephone: (513) 529-4331.

MICHIGAN WOLVERINES

Conference: Big Ten.
Mailing Address: 1114 S State St, Ann Arbor, MI 48104. **Website:** www.mgoblue.com.
Head Coach: Rich Maloney. **Assistant Coaches:** *Matt Husted, Matt White. **Telephone:** (734) 647-4555. **Baseball SID:** Kent Reichert. **Telephone:** (734) 647-1726. **Fax:** (734) 647-1188.
Home Field: Wilpon Complex/Ray Fisher Stadium. **Seating Capacity:** 3,500. **Outfield Dimensions:** LF—312, CF—395, RF—320. **Press Box Telephone:** (734) 647-1283.

MICHIGAN STATE SPARTANS

Conference: Big Ten.
Mailing Address: 304 Jenison Field House, East Lansing, MI 48824. **Website:** msuspartans.com.
Head Coach: Jake Boss. **Assistant Coaches:** Graham Sikes, *Mark Van Ameyde. **Telephone:** (517) 353-0816. **Baseball SID:** Ben Phlegar. **Telephone:** (517) 355-2271. **Fax:** (517) 353-9636.
Home Field: McLane Baseball Stadium at Kobs Field. **Seating Capacity:** 2,500. **Outfield Dimensions:** LF—340, CF—400, RF—301. **Press Box Telephone:** (517) 353-3009.

MIDDLE TENNESSEE STATE BLUE RAIDERS

Conference: Sun Belt.
Mailing Address: MTSU Box 90, Murfreesboro, TN 37132. **Website:** www.goblueraiders.com.
Head Coach: Steve Peterson. **Assistant Coaches:** *Jim McGuire, Mike McLaury. **Telephone:** (615) 898-2984. **Baseball SID:** Jessica Stauffacher. **Telephone:** (615) 904-8115. **Fax:** (615) 898-5626.
Home Field: Reese Smith Jr. **Field. Seating Capacity:** 2,100. **Outfield Dimensions:** LF—330, CF—390, RF—330. **Press Box Telephone:** (615) 898-2117.

MINNESOTA GOLDEN GOPHERS

Conference: Big Ten.
Mailing Address: 516 15th Avenue SE, Minneapolis, MN 55455. **Website:** www.gophersports.com.
Head Coach: John Anderson. **Assistant Coaches:** *Rob Fornasiere, Todd Oakes. **Telephone:** (612) 625-4057. **Baseball SID:** Steve Geller. **Telephone:** (612) 624-9396. **Fax:** (612) 625-0359.
Home Field: Metrodome. **Seating Capacity:** 48,000. **Outfield Dimensions:** LF—340, CF—408, RF—327. **Press Box Telephone:** (612) 210-2380.

MISSISSIPPI REBELS

Conference: Southeastern (West).
Mailing Address: Ole Miss Baseball Office, University Place, University, MS 38677. **Website:** www.OleMissSports.com.
Head Coach: Mike Bianco. **Assistant Coaches:** *Carl Lafferty, Matt Mossberg. **Telephone:** (662) 915-6643. **Baseball SID:** Bill Bunting. **Telephone:** (662) 915-1083. **Fax:** (662) 915-7006.
Home Field: Oxford-University Stadium. **Seating Capacity:** 10,323. **Outfield Dimensions:** LF—330, CF—390, RF—330. **Press Box Telephone:** (662) 915-7858.

MISSISSIPPI STATE BULLDOGS

Conference: Southeastern (West).
Mailing Address: Box 5327, Mississippi State, MS 39762. **Website:** www.mstateathletics.com.

Head Coach: John Cohen. **Assistant Coaches:** Lane Burroughs, *Butch Thompson. **Telephone:** (662) 325-3597. **Baseball SID:** Joe Dier. **Telephone:** (662) 325-8040. **Fax:** (662) 325-3600.
Home Field: Dudy Noble Field/Polk-DeMent Stadium. **Seating Capacity:** 15,000. **Outfield Dimensions:** LF—330, CF—390, RF—326. **Press Box Telephone:** (662) 325-3776.

MISSISSIPPI VALLEY STATE DELTA DEVILS

Conference: Southwestern Athletic.
Mailing Address: 14000 Highway 82 West, #7246, Itta Bena, MS 38941. **Website:** www.mvsu.edu/athletics.
Head Coach: Doug Shanks. **Assistant Coach:** Aaron Stevens. **Telephone:** (662) 254-3834. **Baseball SID:** William Bright Jr. **Telephone:** (662) 254-3011. **Fax:** (662) 254-3639.

MISSOURI TIGERS

Conference: Big 12.
Mailing Address: 100 MATC, Columbia, MO 65211. **Website:** mutigers.com.
Head Coach: Tim Jamieson. **Assistant Coaches:** Matt Hobbs, *Kerrick Jackson. **Telephone:** (573) 882-0731. **Baseball SID:** Josh Murray. **Telephone:** (573) 882-0711.
Home Field: Taylor Stadium. **Seating Capacity:** 2,500. **Outfield Dimensions:** LF—330, CF—400, RF—340. **Press Box Telephone:** (573) 884-8912.

MISSOURI STATE BEARS

Conference: Missouri Valley.
Mailing Address: 901 S National Ave, Springfield, MO 65897. **Website:** www.missouristatebears.com.
Head Coach: Keith Guttin. **Assistant Coaches:** *Paul Evans, Brent Thomas. **Telephone:** (417) 836-4497. **Baseball SID:** Ben Adamson. **Telephone:** (417) 836-4584. **Fax:** Fax: (417) 836-4868.
Home Field: Hammons Field. **Seating Capacity:** 8,000. **Outfield Dimensions:** LF—315, CF—400, RF—330. **Press Box Telephone:** Press Box Telephone: (417) 863-0395, ext 3070.

MONMOUTH HAWKS

Conference: Northeast.
Mailing Address: 400 Cedar Ave, West Long Branch, NJ 07764. **Website:** www.gomuhawks.com.
Head Coach: Dean Ehehalt. **Assistant Coaches:** Jimmy Belanger, *Karl Nonemaker. **Telephone:** (732) 263-5186. **Baseball SID:** Jarred Weiss. **Telephone:** (732) 263-5557. **Fax:** (732) 571-3535.
Home Field: MU Baseball Field. **Seating Capacity:** 500. **Outfield Dimensions:** LF—325, CF—395, RF—325. **Press Box Telephone:** (732) 263-5401.

MOREHEAD STATE EAGLES

Conference: Ohio Valley.
Mailing Address: Allen Field, Morehead, KY 40351. **Website:** www.msueagles.com.
Head Coach: Jay Sorg. **Assistant Coaches:** Dillion Lawson, *Jason Neal. **Telephone:** (606) 783-2882. **Baseball SID:** Drew Dickerson. **Telephone:** (606) 783-2500. **Fax:** (606) 783-5035.
Home Field: Allen Field. **Seating Capacity:** 1,500. **Outfield Dimension:** LF—320, CF—370, RF—310.

MOUNT ST. MARY'S MOUNTAINEERS

Conference: Northeast.
Mailing Address: 16300 Old Emmitsburg Rd, Emmitsburg, MD 21727. **Website:** www.mountathletics.com.

Head Coach: Scott Thomson. Assistant Coach: Greg White. Telephone: (301) 447-3806. Baseball SID: Mark Vandergrift. Telephone: (301) 447-5384. Fax: (301) 447-5300.

MURRAY STATE THOROUGHBREDS

Conference: Ohio Valley.
Mailing Address: 217 Stewart Stadium, Murray, KY, 42071. Website: goracers.com.
Head Coach: Rob McDonald. Assistant Coaches: *Chris Cole, Dan Skirka. Telephone: (270) 809-4892. Baseball SID: John Brush. Telephone: (270) 809-7044. Fax: (270) 809-6814.
Home Field: Reagan Field. Seating Capacity: 800. Outfield Dimensions: LF—330, CF—400, RF—330. Press Box Telephone: (270) 809-5650.

NAVY MIDSHIPMEN

Conference: Patriot.
Mailing Address: 566 Brownson Rd, Annapolis, MD 21402. Website: navysports.com.
Head Coach: Paul Kostacopoulos. Assistant Coaches: Ryan Mau, *Matt Reynolds. Telephone: (410) 293-5571. Baseball SID: Jeff Barnes. Telephone: (410) 293-8771. Fax: (410) 293-8954.
Home Field: Max Bishop Stadium. Seating Capacity: 1,500. Outfield Dimensions: LF—323, CF—397, RF—304. Press Box Telephone: (410) 293-5430.

NEBRASKA CORNHUSKERS

Conference: Big 12.
Mailing Address: 403 Line Drive Circle, Lincoln, NE, 68588. Website: huskers.com.
Head Coach: Mike Anderson. Assistant Coaches: *Dave Bingham, Eric Newman. Telephone: (402) 472-2269. Baseball SID: Brandon Gries. Telephone: (402) 472-7781. Fax: (402) 472-2005.
Home Field: Hawks Field. Seating Capacity: 8,500. Outfield Dimensions: LF—335, CF—400, RF—325. Press Box Telephone: (402) 434-6861.

NEVADA WOLF PACK

Conference: Western Athletic.
Mailing Address: 1664 N Virginia St, Legacy Hall 264, Reno, NV 89557. Website: www.nevadawolfpack.com.
Head Coach: Gary Powers. Assistant Coaches: Buddy Gouldsmith, *Chris Pfatenhauer. Telephone: (775) 682-6978. Baseball SID: Jack Kuestermeyer. Telephone: (775) 682-6984. Fax: (775) 784-4386.
Home Field: Peccole Park. Seating Capacity: 3,000. Outfield Dimensions: LF—340, CF—401, RF—340. Press Box Telephone: (775) 784-1585.

NEVADA-LAS VEGAS REBELS

Conference: Mountain West.
Mailing Address: 4505 S Maryland Parkway, Las Vegas, NV 89154. Website: www.unlvrebels.com.
Head Coach: Tim Chambers. Assistant Coaches: Kevin Higgins, Stan Stolte. Telephone: (702) 895-3499. Baseball SID: Paul Pancoe. Telephone: (702) 895-3764. Fax: (702) 895-0989.
Home Field: Earl E Wilson Stadium. Seating Capacity: 3,000. Outfield Dimension: LF—335, CF—400, RF—335. Press Box Telephone: (702) 895-1595.

NEW JERSEY TECH HIGHLANDERS

Conference: Great West.
Mailing Address: University Heights, Newark, NJ 07102-1982. Website: www.njithighlanders.com.
Head Coach: Mike Cole. Assistant Coaches: Brian

Guiliana, Trevor Marcotte. Telephone: (973) 596-5827. Baseball SID: Tim Camp. Telephone: (973) 596-8461. Fax: (973) 596-8295.

NEW MEXICO LOBOS

Conference: Mountain West.
Mailing Address: Colleen J. Maloof Administration Building, MSC04 2680, 1 University of New Mexico, Albuquerque, NM 87131-0001. Website: golobos.com.
Head Coach: Ray Birmingham. Assistant Coaches: *Ken Jacome, David Martinez. Telephone: (505) 925-5720. Baseball SID: Taylor Stern. Telephone: (505) 925-5520. Fax: (505) 925-5734.
Home Field: Isotopes Park. Seating Capacity: 12,000. Outfield Dimensions: LF—340, CF—400, RF—340. Press Box Telephone: (505) 222-4093.

NEW MEXICO STATE AGGIES

Conference: Western Athletic.
Mailing Address: Regents Row Athletics Complex, MSC 3145, 1 Regents Row, Las Cruces, NM 88001-8001. Website: nmstatesports.com.
Head Coach: Rocky Ward. Assistant Coaches: *Chase Tidwell, Gary Ward. Telephone: (575) 646-5813. Baseball SID: Eddie Morelos. Telephone: (575) 646-1885. Fax: (575) 646-2099.
Home Field: Presley Askew Field. Seating Capacity: 1,000. Outfield Dimensions: LF—345, CF—400, RF—345. Press Box Telephone: (575) 646-5700.

NEW YORK TECH BEARS

Conference: Great West.
Mailing Address: Sports Complex, Northern Blvd, Old Westbury, NY 11568-8000. Website: www.nyit.edu/athletics.
Head Coach: Bob Hirschfield. Assistant Coaches: *Michael Caulfield, Ronald McKay. Telephone: (516) 686-7513. Baseball SID: Sabrina Polidoro. Telephone: (516) 686-7504. Fax: (516) 686-1219.
Home Field: President's Field. Seating Capacity: 500. Outfield Dimensions: LF—315, CF—421, RF—315. Press Box Telephone: (516) 686-7886.

NIAGARA PURPLE EAGLES

Conference: Metro Atlantic.
Mailing Address: PO Box 2009, UL Gallagher Ctr, Niagara University, NY 14109. Website: www.purpleeagles.com.
Head Coach: Rob McCoy. Assistant Coaches: *Eric Peterson, Jeff Ziemecki. Telephone: (716) 286-7361. Baseball SID: Derrick Thornton. Telephone: (716) 286-8588. Fax: (716) 286-8582.
Home Field: Sal Maglie Stadium. Seating Capacity: 2,500. Outfield Dimensions: LF—320, CF—408, RF—330.

NICHOLLS STATE COLONELS

Conference: Southland.
Mailing Address: PO Box 2032, Thibodaux, LA 70310. Website: geauxcolonels.com.
Head Coach: Chip Durham. Assistant Coaches: Chris Prothro, Seth Thibodeaux. Telephone: (985) 448-4808. Baseball SID: Charlie Gillingham. Telephone: (985) 448-4282. Fax: (985) 448-4814.
Home Field: Ray Didier Field. Seating Capacity: 3,000. Outfield Dimension: LF—340, CF—400, RF—330.

NORFOLK STATE SPARTANS

Conference: Mid-Eastern Athletic.
Mailing Address: 700 Park Ave, Norfolk, VA 23504.

Website: www.nsuspartans.com.
Head Coach: Claudell Clark. **Assistant Coach:** AJ Corbin, Quentin Jones. **Telephone:** (757) 823-8196. **Baseball SID:** Matt Michalec. **Telephone:** (757) 823-2628. **Fax:** (757) 823-8218.
Home Field: Marty L Miller Field. **Seating Capacity:** 1,500. **Outfield Dimension:** LF—330, CF—404, RF—318. **Press Box Telephone:** (757) 823-8196.

NORTH CAROLINA TAR HEELS

Conference: Atlantic Coast (Coastal).
Mailing Address: PO Box 2126, Chapel Hill, NC 27515. **Website:** tarheelblue.com.
Head Coach: Mike Fox. **Assistant Coaches:** Scott Forbes, *Scott Jackson. **Telephone:** (919) 962-2351. **Baseball SID:** Dave Schmidt. **Telephone:** (919) 962-0084. **Fax:** (919) 962-7002.
Home Field: Bryson Field at Boshamer Stadium. **Seating Capacity:** 4,000. **Outfield Dimensions:** LF—335, CF—400, RF—340. **Press Box Telephone:** (919) 962-3509.

NORTH CAROLINA A&T AGGIES

Conference: Mid-Eastern Athletic.
Mailing Address: 1601 E Market St, Greensboro, NC 27411-0001. **Website:** www.ncataggies.com.
Head Coach: Keith Shumate. **Assistant Coach:** Austin Love. **Telephone:** (336) 285-4272. **Baseball SID:** Brian Holloway. **Telephone:** (336) 334-7141. **Fax:** (336) 334-7181.
Home Field: War Memorial Stadium. **Seating Capacity:** 2,500. **Outfield Dimension:** LF—327, CF—400, RF—327.

NORTH CAROLINA CENTRAL EAGLES

Conference: Independent.
Mailing Address: 1801 Fayetteville St, Durham, NC 27707. **Website:** www.nccueaglepride.com.
Head Coach: Henry White. **Assistant Coaches:** Chris Smith, Ken Valentine. **Telephone:** (919) 530-6723. **Baseball SID:** Reah Nicholson. **Telephone:** (919) 530-6892. **Fax:** (919) 530-5426.
Home Field: Durham Athletic Park. **Seating Capacity:** 5,000. **Outfield Dimension:** LF—330, CF—405, RF—305.

NORTH CAROLINA STATE WOLFPACK

Conference: Atlantic Coast (Atlantic).
Mailing Address: 1081 Varsity Drive, Raleigh, NC 27695. **Website:** gopack.com.
Head Coach: Elliott Avent. **Assistant Coaches:** Chris Hart, *Tom Holliday. **Telephone:** (919) 515-3613. **Baseball SID:** Bruce Winkworth. **Telephone:** (919) 515-1182. **Fax:** (919) 515-3624.
Home Field: Doak Field at Dail Park. **Seating Capacity:** 3,000. **Outfield Dimensions:** LF—320, CF—400, RF—330. **Press Box Telephone:** (919) 819-3035.

UNC ASHEVILLE BULLDOGS

Conference: Big South.
Mailing Address: One University Heights, Justice Center CPO #2600, Asheville, NC 28804. **Website:** www.uncabulldogs.com.
Head Coach: Tom Smith. **Assistant Coaches:** *Aaron Rembert, Kenny Smith. **Telephone:** (828) 251-6920. **Baseball SID:** Mike Gore. **Telephone:** (828) 251-6923. **Fax:** (828) 251-6386.
Home Field: McCormick Field. **Seating Capacity:** 4,000. **Outfield Dimension:** LF—326, CF—370, RF—297. **Press Box Telephone:** (828) 254-5125.

UNC GREENSBORO SPARTANS

Conference: Southern.
Mailing Address: 1400 Spring Garden St, Greensboro, NC 27412. **Website:** www.uncgspartans.com.
Head Coach: Mike Gaski. **Assistant Coaches:** *Jamie Athas, Jarrett Santos. **Telephone:** (336) 334-3247. **Baseball SID:** David Percival. **Telephone:** (336) 334-5615. **Fax:** (336) 334-3182.
Home Field: UNCG Baseball Stadium. **Seating Capacity:** 3,500. **Outfield Dimensions:** LF—340, CF—405, RF—340. **Press Box Telephone:** (336) 334-3885.

UNC WILMINGTON SEAHAWKS

Conference: Colonial Athletic.
Mailing Address: 601 South College Road, Wilmington, NC 28403. **Website:** www.uncwsports.com.
Head Coach: Mark Scalf. **Assistant Coaches:** *Randy Hood, Jason Howell. **Telephone:** (910) 962-3570. **Baseball SID:** Tom Riordan. **Telephone:** (910) 962-4099. **Fax:** (910) 962-3001.
Home Field: Brooks Field. **Seating Capacity:** 3,500. **Outfield Dimensions:** LF—340, CF—380, RF—340. **Press Box Telephone:** (910) 395-4151.

NORTH DAKOTA FIGHTING SIOUX

Conference: Great West.
Mailing Address: Hyslop Sports Center Rm 120, 2751 2nd Ave N, Stop 9013, Grand Forks, ND 58202. **Website:** www.fightingsioux.com.
Head Coach: Jeff Dodson. **Assistant Coaches:** Brian DeVillers, *JC Field. **Telephone:** (701) 777-4038. **Baseball SID:** Ryan Powell. **Telephone:** (701) 777-2986. **Fax:** (701) 777-2285.
Home Field: Kraft Field. **Seating Capacity:** 2,000. **Outfield Dimensions:** LF—330, CF—410, RF—330.

NORTH DAKOTA STATE BISON

Conference: Summit.
Mailing Address: NDSU Dept 1200, PO Box 6050, Fargo, ND 58108-6050. **Website:** www.gobison.com.
Head Coach: Tod Brown. **Assistant Coaches:** Jake Angier, *David Pearson. **Telephone:** (701) 231-8853. **Baseball SID:** Ryan Perreault. **(701) 231-8331. Fax:** (701) 231-8022.
Home Field: Newman Outdoor Field. **Seating Capacity:** 4,513. **Outfield Dimension:** LF—318, CF—408, RF—314. **Press Box Telephone:** (701) 235-5204.

NORTH FLORIDA OSPREYS

Conference: Atlantic Sun.
Mailing Address: 1 UNF Drive, Jacksonville, FL 32224. **Website:** www.unfospreys.com.
Head Coach: Smoke Laval. **Assistant Coaches:** *Judd Loveland, Tim Parenton. **Telephone:** (904) 620-1556. **Baseball SID:** Chris Whitehead. **Telephone:** (904) 620-4029. **Fax:** (904) 620-2821.
Home Field: Harmon Stadium. **Seating Capacity:** 1,000. **Outfield Dimension:** LF—325, CF—400, RF—325. **Press Box Telephone:** (904) 620-1557.

NORTHEASTERN HUSKIES

Conference: Colonial Athletic.
Mailing Address: 219 Cabot, 360 Huntington Ave, Boston MA 02115. **Website:** www.gonu.com.
Head Coach: Neil McPhee. **Assistant Coaches:** *Mike Glavine, Jamie Pinzino. **Telephone:** (617) 373-3657. **Baseball SID:** Jack Grinold. **Telephone:** (617) 373-2691. **Fax:** (617) 373-3152.
Home Field: Friedman Diamond. **Seating Capacity:**

3,000. **Outfield Dimensions:** LF—325, CF—420, RF—338.

NORTHERN COLORADO BEARS

Conference: Great West.
Mailing Address: 270 Butler-Hancock Sports Pavilion, Greeley, CO 80639. **Website:** uncbears.com.
Head Coach: Carl Iwasaki. **Assistant Coaches:** Anthony Everman, *Gabe Ribas. **Telephone:** (970) 351-1714. **Baseball SID:** Heather Kennedy. **Telephone:** (970) 351-1065. **Fax:** (970) 351-2018.
Home Field: Jackson Field. **Seating Capacity:** 2,500. **Outfield Dimensions:** LF—348, CF—416, RF—356. **Press Box Telephone:** (970) 978-0675.

NORTHERN ILLINOIS HUSKIES

Conference: Mid-American (West).
Mailing Address: Intercollegiate Athletics Convocation Center, 1525 W Lincoln Hwy, DeKalb, IL 60115. **Website:** niuhuskies.com.
Head Coach: Ed Mathey. **Assistant Coaches:** *Steven Joslyn, Ray Napientek. **Telephone:** (815) 753-2225. **Baseball SID:** Zach Peters. **Telephone:** (815) 753-9572. **Fax:** (815) 753-7700.
Home Field: Ralph McKinzie Field. **Seating Capacity:** 2,000. **Outfield Dimensions:** LF—312, CF—395, RF—322. **Press Box Telephone:** (815) 753-8094.

NORTHWESTERN WILDCATS

Conference: Southland.
Mailing Address: 1501 Central St, Evanston, IL 60208. **Website:** nusports.com.
Head Coach: Paul Stevens. **Assistant Coaches:** *Jon Mikrut, Tim Stoddard. **Telephone:** (847) 491-4652. **Baseball SID:** Nick Brilowski. **Telephone:** (847) 467-3831. **Fax:** (847) 491-8818.
Home Field: Rocky Miller Park. **Seating Capacity:** 1,000. **Outfield Dimensions:** LF—330, CF—400, RF—320. **Press Box Telephone:** (847) 491-4200.

NORTHWESTERN STATE DEMONS

Conference: Southland.
Mailing Address: Athletic Fieldhouse, Natchitoches, LA 71497. **Website:** www.nsudemons.com.
Head Coach: JP Davis. **Assistant Coaches:** *Jeff McCannon, Philip Miller. **Telephone:** (318) 357-4139. **Baseball SID:** Matthew Bonnette. **Telephone:** (318) 357-6469. **Fax:** (318) 357-4515.
Home Field: Brown Stroud Field. **Seating Capacity:** 1,200. **Outfield Dimension:** LF—320, CF—400, RF—330. **Press Box Telephone:** (318) 357-4606.

NOTRE DAME FIGHTING IRISH

Conference: Big East.
Mailing Address: 202 Joyce Center, Notre Dame, IN 46556. **Website:** und.com.
Head Coach: Mik Aoki. **Assistant Coaches:** *Joe Hastings, Jesse Woods. **Telephone:** (574) 631-8466. **Baseball SID:** Michael Bertsch. **Telephone:** (574) 631-8642. **Fax:** (574) 631-7941.
Home Field: Frank Eck Stadium. **Seating Capacity:** 2,500. **Outfield Dimensions:** LF—330, CF—400, RF—330. **Press Box Telephone:** (574) 631-9018.

OAKLAND GOLDEN GRIZZLIES

Conference: Summit.
Mailing Address: 2200 N Squirrel Road, Rochester, MI 48309. **Website:** www.ougrizzlies.com.
Head Coach: John Musachio. **Assistant Coach:** *Matt Plante. **Telephone:** (248) 370-4059. **Baseball SID:** Scott

Dunford. **Telephone:** (248) 370-3123. **Fax:** (248) 370-4056.
Home Field: OU Baseball Field. **Seating Capacity:** 500. **Outfield Dimensions:** LF—333, CF—380, RF—338. **Press Box Telephone:** (248) 688-7646.

OHIO BOBCATS

Conference: Mid-American (East).
Mailing Address: N117 Convocation Center, Athens, OH 45701. **Website:** www.ohiobobcats.com.
Head Coach: Joe Carbone. **Assistant Coaches:** Scott Malinowski, *Andrew See. **Telephone:** (740) 593-1180. **Baseball SID:** Jason Corriher. **Telephone:** (740) 593-1298. **Fax:** (740) 597-1838.
Home Field: Bob Wren Stadium. **Seating Capacity:** 4,000. **Outfield Dimension:** LF—340, CF—405, RF—340. **Press Box Telephone:** (740) 593-0526.

OHIO STATE BUCKEYES

Conference: Big Ten.
Mailing Address: 650 Borror Drive, Suite 250, Columbus, Ohio 43210. **Website:** www.ohiostatebuckeyes.com.
Head Coach: Greg Beals. **Assistant Coaches:** Chris Holick, *Mike Stafford. **Telephone:** (614) 292-1075. **Baseball SID:** Brett Rybak. **Telephone:** (614) 688-0343. **Fax:** (614) 292-8547.
Home Field: Bill Davis Stadium. **Seating Capacity:** 4,450. **Outfield Dimension:** LF—330, CF—400, RF—330. **Press Box Telephone:** (614) 292-0021.

OKLAHOMA SOONERS

Conference: Big 12.
Mailing Address: 401 Imhoff, Norman, OK 73019. **Website:** www.soonersports.com.
Head Coach: Sunny Golloway. **Assistant Coaches:** Mike Bell, *Tim Tadlock. **Telephone:** (405) 325-8354. **Baseball SID:** Craig Moran. **Telephone:** (405) 325-6449. **Fax:** (405) 325-7623.
Home Field: L Dale Mitchell Park. **Seating Capacity:** 2,700. **Outfield Dimensions:** LF—335, CF—411, RF—335. **Press Box Telephone:** (405) 325-8363.

OKLAHOMA STATE COWBOYS

Conference: Big 12.
Mailing Address: 220 Athletics Center, Stillwater, OK 74078. **Website:** www.okstate.com.
Head Coach: Frank Anderson. **Assistant Coaches:** Greg Evans, *Billy Jones. **Telephone:** (405) 744-5849. **Baseball SID:** Wade McWhorter. **Telephone:** (405) 744-7853. **Fax:** (405) 744-7754.
Home Field: Allie P Reynolds Stadium. **Seating Capacity:** 4,000. **Outfield Dimensions:** LF—330, CF—398, RF—330. **Press Box Telephone:** (405) 744-5757.

OLD DOMINION MONARCHS

Conference: Colonial Athletic.
Mailing Address: Athletic Admin Bldg, Norfolk, VA 23529-0201. **Website:** www.odusports.com.
Head Coach: Nate Goulet. **Assistant Coaches:** Tim Lavigne, Tag Montague. **Telephone:** (757) 683-4230. **Baseball SID:** Carol Hudson. **Telephone:** (757) 683-3372. **Fax:** (757) 683-3119.
Home Field: Bud Metheny Complex. **Seating Capacity:** 2,500. **Outfield Dimension:** LF—325, CF—395, RF—325. **Press Box Telephone:** (757) 683-5036.

ORAL ROBERTS GOLDEN EAGLES

Conference: Summit.
Mailing Address: 7777 S Lewis Ave, Tulsa OK 74171.

Website: www.orugoldeneagles.com.
Head Coach: Rob Walton. **Assistant Coaches:** Ryan Folmar, *Ryan Neill. **Telephone:** (918) 495-7130. **Baseball SID:** Chris Blevin. **Telephone:** (918) 495-7205. **Fax:** (918) 495-7123.
Home Field: JL Johnson. **Seating Capacity:** 2,400. **Outfield Dimensions:** LF—330, CF—400, RF—330. **Press Box Telephone:** (918) 495-7165.

OREGON DUCKS

Conference: Pacific-10.
Mailing Address: 2727 Leo Harris Parkway, Eugene, OR 97401. **Website:** www.goducks.com.
Head Coach: George Horton. **Assistant Coaches:** *Andrew Checketts, Mike Kirby. **Telephone:** (541) 346-5235. **Baseball SID:** Andria Wenzel. **Telephone:** (541) 346-0962. **Fax:** (541) 346-5449.
Home Field: PK Park. **Seating Capacity:** 4,000. **Outfield Dimensions:** LF—335, CF—400, RF—325. **Press Box Telephone:** (541) 346-6309.

OREGON STATE BEAVERS

Conference: Pacific-10.
Mailing Address: 114 Gill Coliseum, Corvallis, OR 97333. **Website:** www.osubeavers.com.
Head Coach: Pat Casey. **Assistant Coaches:** Pat Bailey, *Marty Lees. **Telephone:** (541) 737-0598. **Baseball SID:** Hank Hager. **Telephone:** (541) 737-7472. **Fax:** (541) 737-3072.
Home Field: Goss Stadium. **Seating Capacity:** 3,248. **Outfield Dimensions:** LF—330, CF—400, RF—330. **Press Box Telephone:** (541) 737-7475.

PACIFIC TIGERS

Conference: Big West.
Mailing Address: 3601 Pacific Ave, Stockton CA 95211. **Website:** pacifictigers.com.
Head Coach: Ed Sprague. **Assistant Coaches:** *Don Barbara, Mike Mccormick. **Telephone:** (209) 946-2709. **Baseball SID:** Kevin Wilinson. **Telephone:** (209) 946-2479. **Fax:** (209) 946-2757.
Home Field: Klein Family Field. **Seating Capacity:** 1,500. **Outfield Dimensions:** LF—317, CF—405, RF—325. **Press Box Telephone:** (209) 946-2722.

PENNSYLVANIA QUAKERS

Conference: Ivy League (Gehrig).
Mailing Address: 235 S 33rd St, Philadelphia, PA 19104. **Website:** www.pennathletics.com.
Head Coach: John Cole. **Assistant Coaches:** John Cross, *John Yurkow. **Telephone:** (215) 898-6282. **Baseball SID:** Ben Stockwell. **Telephone:** (215) 898-6128. **Fax:** (215) 898-1747.
Home Field: Meiklejohn Stadium. **Seating Capacity:** 900. **Outfield Dimensions:** LF—325, CF—380, RF—355.

PENN STATE NITTANY LIONS

Conference: Big Ten.
Mailing Address: 112 Bryce Jordan Center, University Park, PA 16802. **Website:** www.GoPSUsports.com.
Head Coach: Robbie Wine. **Assistant Coaches:** Jason Bell, *Eric Folmar. **Telephone:** (814) 863-0239. **Baseball SID:** Justin Lefleur. **Telephone:** (814) 865-1757. **Fax:** (814) 863-3165.
Home Field: Medlar Field at Lubrano Park. **Seating Capacity:** 5,406. **Outfield Dimension:** LF—325, CF—399, RF—320.

PEPPERDINE WAVES

Conference: West Coast.
Mailing Address: 24255 Pacific Coast Highway, Malibu, CA 90263. **Website:** www.PepperdineSports.com.
Head Coach: Steve Rodriguez. **Assistant Coaches:** Rick Hirtensteiner, *Jon Strauss. **Telephone:** (310) 506-4371. **Baseball SID:** Chris Macaluso. **Telephone:** (310) 506-4333. **Fax:** (310) 506-4322.
Home Field: Eddy D Field Stadium. **Seating Capacity:** 2,000. **Outfield Dimensions:** LF—325, CF—400, RF—325. **Press Box Telephone:** (310) 506-4598.

PITTSBURGH PANTHERS

Conference: Big East.
Mailing Address: 3719 Terrace Street, Pittsburgh, PA 15261. **Website:** pittsburghpanthers.com.
Head Coach: Joe Jordano. **Assistant Coaches:** Tom Lipari, *Danny Lopaze. **Telephone:** (412) 648-8206. **Baseball SID:** Mendy Nestor. **Telephone:** (412) 648-8240. **Fax:** (412) 648-8248.
Home Field: Petersen Sports Complex. **Seating Capacity:** 900. **Outfield Dimensions:** LF—330, CF—405, RF—330. **Press Box Telephone:** (412) 849-9470.

PORTLAND PILOTS

Conference: West Coast.
Mailing Address: 5000 North Willamette Blvd, Portland, OR 97203. **Website:** www.portlandpilots.com.
Head Coach: Chris Sperry. **Assistant Coaches:** Tucker Brack, *Larry Casian. **Telephone:** (503) 943-7745. **Baseball SID:** Adam Linnman. **Telephone:** (503) 943-7731. **Fax:** (503) 943-7242.
Home Field: Joe Etzel Field. **Seating Capacity:** 1,000. **Outfield Dimension:** LF—350, CF—390, RF—340.

PRAIRIE VIEW A&M PANTHERS

Conference: Southwestern Athletic.
Mailing Address: PO Box 519 MS 1500, Prairie View, TX 77446. **Website:** sports.pvamu.edu.
Head Coach: Waskyla Cullivan. **Assistant Coach:** *Byron Carter. **Telephone:** (936) 261-9121. **Baseball SID:** Reginald Rouzan. **Telephone:** (936) 261-9106. **Fax:** (936) 261-9159.

PRESBYTERIAN BLUE HOSE

Conference: Big South.
Mailing Address: 105 Ashland Ave, Clinton, SC 29325. **Website:** www.gobluehose.com.
Head Coach: Elton Pollock. **Assistant Coaches:** Josh Davis, Chris Edwards. **Telephone:** (864) 833-8236. **Baseball SID:** AJ Henderson. **Telephone:** (864) 833-8252. **Fax:** (864) 833-8323.
Home Field: Baseball Complex. **Seating Capacity:** 500. **Outfield Dimension:** LF—325, CF—400, RF—325.

PRINCETON TIGERS

Conference: Ivy League (Gehrig).
Mailing Address: Jadwin Gymnasium, Princeton, NJ 08544. **Website:** www.GoPrincetonTigers.com.
Head Coach: Scott Bradley. **Assistant Coaches:** *Lloyd Brewer, Han Coogan. **Telephone:** (609) 258-5059. **Baseball SID:** Yariv Amir. **Telephone:** (609) 258-5701. **Fax:** (609) 258-2399.
Home Field: Clarke Field. **Seating Capacity:** 500. **Outfield Dimensions:** LF—335, CF—400, RF—325. **Press Box Telephone:** (609) 462-0248.

PURDUE BOILERMAKERS

Conference: Big Ten.
Mailing Address: Mollenkopf Athletic Center, 1225 Northwestern Ave, West Lafayette, IN 47907. **Website:** purduesports.com.
Head Coach: Doug Schreiber. **Assistant Coaches:** Jeff Duncan, *Ryan Sawyers. **Telephone:** (765) 494-3998. **Baseball SID:** Ben Turner. **Telephone:** (765) 494-3198. **Fax:** (765) 494-5447.
Home Field: Lambert Field. **Seating Capacity:** 1,100. **Outfield Dimensions:** LF—340, CF—408, RF—340. **Press Box Telephone:** (217) 549-7965.

QUINNIPIAC BOBCATS

Conference: Northeast.
Mailing Address: 275 Mount Carmel Ave, Hamden, CT 06518. **Website:** quinnipiacbobcats.com.
Head Coach: *Dan Gooley. **Assistant Coaches:** Tim Binkoski, Marc Stonaha. **Telephone:** (203) 582-8966. **Baseball SID:** Ken Sweeten. **Telephone:** (203) 582-8625. **Fax:** (203) 582-5385.
Home Field: Quinnipiac Field. **Seating Capacity:** 1,000. **Outfield Dimension:** LF—340, CF—400, RF—340. **Press Box Telephone:** (203) 859-8529.

RADFORD Highlanders
Conference: Big South.
Mailing Address: Radford University Athletics, PO Box 6913, Radford, VA 24142. **Website:** www.ruhighlanders. com.
Head Coach: Joe Raccuia. **Assistant Coaches:** *Brian Anderson, Kyle Werman. **Telephone:** (540) 831-5881. **Baseball SID:** Patrick Reed. **Telephone:** (540) 831-5211. **Fax:** (540) 831-6095.
Home Field: Radford Baseball Field. **Seating Capacity:** 1,000. **Outfield Dimensions:** LF—330, CF—400, RF—330. **Press Box Telephone:** (540) 257-1159.

RHODE ISLAND RAMS

Conference: Atlantic 10.
Mailing Address: 3 Keaney Rd, Suite One, Kingston, RI 02881. **Website:** gorhody.com.
Head Coach: Jim Foster. **Assistant Coaches:** *Steve Breitbach, Eric Cirella. **Telephone:** (401) 874-4550. **Baseball SID:** Jodi Pontbriand. **Telephone:** (401) 874-5356. **Fax:** (401) 874-5354.
Home Field: Bill Beck Field. **Seating Capacity:** Unavailable. **Outfield Dimensions:** LF—330, CF—400, RF—330.

RICE OWLS

Conference: Conference USA.
Mailing Address: 6100 Main St, MS 547, Houston, TX 77251. **Website:** www.riceowls.com.
Head Coach: Wayne Graham. **Assistant Coaches:** *David Pierce, *Mike Taylor. **Telephone:** (713) 348-8864. **Baseball SID:** John Sullivan. **Telephone:** (713) 348-5636. **Fax:** (713) 348-6019.
Home Field: Reckling Park. **Seating Capacity:** 5,368. **Outfield Dimensions:** LF—330, CF—400, RF—330. **Press Box Telephone:** (713) 348-4931.

RICHMOND SPIDERS

Conference: Atlantic 10.
Mailing Address: The Robins Center, Richmond, VA 23173. **Website:** RichmondSpiders.com.
Head Coach: Mark McQueen. **Assistant Coaches:** Chad Oxendine, *Ryan Wheeler. **Telephone:** (804) 289-8391. **Baseball SID:** Mike DeGeorge. **Telephone:** (804) 287-6313. **Fax:** (804) 289-8820.

Home Field: Pitt Field. **Seating Capacity:** 600. **Outfield Dimension:** LF—320, CF—380, RF—320. **Press Box Telephone:** (804) 289-8714.

RIDER BRONCS

Conference: Metro Atlantic.
Mailing Address: 2083 Lawrenceville Rd, Lawrenceville, NJ 08648. **Website:** www.gobroncs.com.
Head Coach: Barry Davis. **Assistant Coaches:** Jaime Steward, Tim Reilly. **Telephone:** (609) 896-5055. **Baseball SID:** Bud Focht. **Telephone:** (609) 896-7264. **Fax:** (609) 896-0341.
Home Field: Sonny Pittaro Field. **Seating Capacity:** 1,000. **Outfield Dimensions:** LF—330, CF—405, RF—330.

RUTGERS SCARLET KNIGHTS

Conference: Big East.
Mailing Address: 83 Rockafeller Road, Piscataway, NJ 08844. **Website:** www.scarletknights.com.
Head Coach: Fred Hill. **Assistant Coaches:** *Darren Fenster, Rick Freeman. **Telephone:** (732) 445-7834. **Baseball SID:** Doug Drabik. **Telephone:** (732) 445-7884. **Fax:** (732) 445-3063.
Home Field: Bainton Field. **Seating Capacity:** 1,500. **Outfield Dimensions:** LF—330, CF—410, RF—320. **Press Box Telephone:** (732) 921-1067.

SACRAMENTO STATE HORNETS

Conference: Western Athletic.
Mailing Address: 6000 J Street, Sacramento, CA 95819. **Website:** www.hornetsports.com.
Head Coach: Reggie Christiansen. **Assistant Coaches:** Thad Johnson, *Tommy Nicholson. **Telephone:** (916) 278-4036. **Baseball SID:** Joe Waltasti. **Telephone:** (916) 278-6896. **Fax:** (916) 278-5429.
Home Field: Hornet Field. **Seating Capacity:** 1,200. **Outfield Dimensions:** LF—333, CF—400, RF—333. **Press Box Telephone:** (209) 210-8858.

SACRED HEART PIONEERS.

Conference: Northeast.
Mailing Address: 5151 Park Ave, Fairfield, CT 06825. **Website:** www.sacredheartpioneers.com.
Head Coach: Nick Giaguinto. **Assistant Coaches:** Wayne Mazzoni, Tyler Kavanaugh. **Telephone:** (203) 365-7632. **Baseball SID:** Randy Brochu. **Telephone:** (203) 396-8127. **Fax:** (203) 371-7889.
Home Field: Ballpark at Harbor Yard. **Seating Capacity:** 5,300. **Outfield Dimensions:** LF—325, CF—405, RF—325.

ST. BONAVENTURE BONNIES

Conference: Atlantic 10.
Mailing Address: PO Box G, Reilly Center, St. Bonaventure, NY 14778. **Website:** gobonnies.com.
Head Coach: Larry Sudbrook. **Assistant Coaches:** Nick LaBella, Cory Sudbrook. **Telephone:** (716) 375-2641. **Baseball SID:** Jason MacBain. **Telephone:** (716) 375-4019. **Fax:** (716) 375-2383.
Home Field: Fred Handler Park. **Seating Capacity:** Unavailable. **Outfield Dimensions:** LF—330, CF—402, RF—330.

ST. JOHN'S RED STORM

Conference: Big East.
Mailing Address: 8000 Utopia Parkway, Queens, NY 11439. **Website:** www.redstormsports.com.
Head Coach: Ed Blankmeyer. **Assistant Coaches:** Scott Brown, *Mike Hampton. **Telephone:** (718) 990-6148.

Baseball SID: Tim Brown. Telephone: (718) 990-1521. Fax: (718) 969-8468.
Home Field: Kaiser Stadium. Seating Capacity: 3,500. Outfield Dimensions: LF—325, CF—400, RF—325. Press Box Telephone: (718) 990-2724.

ST. JOSEPH'S HAWKS

Conference: Atlantic 10.
Mailing Address: 5600 City Ave, Philadelphia, PA 19131. Website: sjuhawks.com.
Head Coach: Fritz Hamburg. Assistant Coaches: *Jake Gill, Greg Manco. Telephone: (610) 660-1718. Baseball SID: Joe Greenwich. Telephone: (610) 660-1738. Fax: (610) 660-1724.
Home Field: Campbell's Field. Seating Capacity: 6,425. Outfield Dimension: LF—325, CF—405, RF—325.

SAINT LOUIS BILLIKENS

Conference: Atlantic 10.
Mailing Address: 3330 Laclede Ave, St. Louis, MO 63103. Website: www.slubillikens.com.
Head Coach: Darin Hendrickson. Assistant Coaches: Will Bradley, *Kevin Moulder. Telephone: (314) 977-3172. Baseball SID: Chuck Yahng. Telephone: (314) 977-2524. Fax: (314) 977-3178.
Home Field: The Billiken Sports Center. Seating Capacity: 500. Outfield Dimensions: LF—330, CF—403, RF—330. Press Box Telephone: (314) 808-4868.

ST. MARY'S GAELS

Conference: West Coast.
Mailing Address: 1928 Saint Mary's Rd, Moraga, CA 94575. Website: www.smcgaels.com.
Head Coach: Jedd Soto. Assistant Coaches: *Lloyd Acosta, Gape Zappin. Telephone: (925) 631-4637. Baseball SID: Rich Davi. Telephone: (925) 631-4402. Fax: (925) 631-4405.
Home Field: Louis Guisto Field. Seating Capacity: 1,000. Outfield Dimension: LF—340, CF—400, RF—340. Press Box Telephone: (925) 376-3906.

ST. PETER'S PEACOCKS

Conference: Metro Atlantic.
Mailing Address: 2641 Kennedy Blvd, Jersey City, NJ 07306. Website: www.spc.edu.
Head Coach: Derek England. Assistant Coaches: Pedro Adorno, Joe Romano. Telephone: (201) 761-7319. Baseball SID: Scott Johnson. Telephone: (201) 761-7315. Fax: (201) 761-7317.

SAM HOUSTON STATE BEARKATS

Conference: Southland.
Mailing Address: PO Box 2268, Huntsville, TX 77341. Website: gobearkats.com.
Head Coach: Mark Johnson. Assistant Coaches: Chris Berry, *Jim Blair. Telephone: (936) 294-1731. Baseball SID: Paul Ridings. Telephone: (936) 294-1764. Fax: (936) 294-3538.
Home Field: Don Sanders Stadium. Seating Capacity: 1,163. Outfield Dimensions: LF—330, CF—400, RF—330.

SAMFORD BULLDOGS

Conference: Southern.
Mailing Address: Samford Athletics, 800 Lakeshore Drive, Birmingham, AL 35229. Website: samfordsports.cstv.com.
Head Coach: Casey Dunn. Assistant Coaches: *Tony David, Mick Fieldbinder. Telephone: (205) 726-2134. Baseball SID: Joey Mullins. Telephone: (205) 726-2799.

Fax: (205) 726-2132.
Home Field: Joe Lee Griffin Field. Seating Capacity: 1,500. Outfield Dimensions: LF—336, CF—390, RF—338. Press Box Telephone: (205) 726-4167.

SAN DIEGO TOREROS

Conference: West Coast.
Mailing Address: 5998 Alcala Park, San Diego, CA 92110. Website: usdtoreros.cstv.com.
Head Coach: Rich Hill. Assistant Coaches: *Jay Johnson, Tyler Kincaid. Telephone: (619) 260-5953. Baseball SID: Chris Loucks. Telephone: (619) 260-7930. Fax: (619) 260-2213.
Home Field: Cunningham Stadium. Seating Capacity: 1,500. Outfield Dimensions: LF—309, CF—395, RF—329. Press Box Telephone: (619) 260-8829.

SAN DIEGO STATE AZTECS

Conference: Mountain West.
Mailing Address: 5302 55th Street, Suite 3014, San Diego, CA 92182. Website: www.goaztecs.com.
Head Coach: Tony Gwynn. Assistant Coaches: Mark Martinez, *Eric Valenzuela. Telephone: (619) 594-6889. Baseball SID: Dave Kuhn. Telephone: (619) 594-5242. Fax: (619) 582-6541.
Home Field: Tony Gwynn Stadium. Seating Capacity: 3,000. Outfield Dimensions: LF—340, CF—410, RF—340. Press Box Telephone: (619) 594-4186.

SAN FRANCISCO DONS

Conference: West Coast.
Mailing Address: 2130 Fulton Street, San Francisco, CA 94117. Website: www.usfdons.com.
Head Coach: Nino Giarratano. Assistant Coaches: Greg Moore, *Troy Nakamura. Telephone: (415) 422-2934. Baseball SID: Stacy Hicklin. Telephone: (415) 422-6161. Fax: (415) 422-2510.
Home Field: Benedetti Diamond. Seating Capacity: 1,000. Outfield Dimensions: LF—335, CF—415, RF—312. Press Box Telephone: (415) 422-2919.

SAN JOSE STATE SPARTANS

Conference: Western Athletic.
Mailing Address: One Washington Square, San Jose, Ca 95192-0062. Website: www.sjsuspartans.com.
Head Coach: Sam Piraro. Assistant Coaches: Tom Kunis, *Jeff Pritchard. Telephone: (408) 924-1255. Baseball SID: Richard Stern. Telephone: (408) 924-1208. Fax: (408) 924-1291.
Home Field: Municipal Stadium. Seating Capacity: 5,200. Outfield Dimensions: LF—365, CF—390, RF—365. Press Box Telephone: (408) 924-7276.

SANTA CLARA BRONCOS

Conference: West Coast.
Mailing Address: 500 El Camino Real, Santa Clara, CA 95053. Website: www.santaclarabroncos.com.
Head Coach: Mark O'Brien. Assistant Coaches: Chad Baum, *Mike Zirelli. Telephone: (408) 554-4680. Baseball SID: Julie Juarez. Telephone: (408) 554-4670. Fax: (408) 554-6942.
Home Field: Schott Stadium. Seating Capacity: 1,500. Outfield Dimensions: LF—340, CF—402, RF—335. Press Box Telephone: (408) 554-5587.

SAVANNAH STATE TIGERS

Conference: Independent.
Mailing Address: 3219 College St, Savannah, GA 31404. Website: www.ssuathletics.com.
Head Coach: Carlton Hardy. Assistant Coach: Joel

Crisler. **Telephone:** (912) 356-2801. **Baseball SID:** Opio Mashariki. **Telephone:** (912) 356-2446. **Fax:** (912) 353-5287.

SEATTLE REDHAWKS

Conference: Independent.
Mailing Address: 901 12th Avenue, PO Box 222000, Seattle, WA, 98122. **Website:** www.goseattleu.com.
Head Coach: Donny Harrel. **Assistant Coaches:** *Casey Powell, Dave Wainhouse. **Telephone:** (206) 398-4399. **Baseball SID:** Jason Behenna. **Telephone:** (206) 296-5915. **Fax:** (206) 296-2154.
Home Field: Bannerwood Park. **Seating Capacity:** 1,200. **Outfield Dimensions:** LF—320, CF—405, RF—320.

SETON HALL PIRATES

Conference: Big East.
Mailing Address: 400 South Orange Ave, South Orange, NJ 07079. **Website:** www.shupirates.com.
Head Coach: Rob Sheppard. **Assistant Coaches:** Phil Cundari, Jim Duffy. **Telephone:** (973) 761-9557. **Baseball SID:** Joe Montefusco. **Telephone:** (973) 761-9493. **Fax:** (073) 761-9061.
Home Field: Owen T Carroll Field. **Seating Capacity:** 1,000. **Outfield Dimension:** LF—315, CF—401, RF—330. **Press Box Telephone:** (973) 670-2752.

SIENA SAINTS

Conference: Metro Atlantic.
Mailing Address: 515 Loudon Rd, Loudonville, New York 12211. **Website:** www.sienasaints.com.
Head Coach: Tony Rossi. **Assistant Coaches:** Keith Glasser, *Jimmy Jackson. **Telephone:** (518) 786-5044. **Baseball SID:** Jason Rich. **Telephone:** (518) 783-2411. **Fax:** (518) 783-2992.
Home Field: Siena Field. **Seating Capacity:** 500. **Outfield Dimension:** LF—300, CF—400, RF—325.

SOUTH ALABAMA JAGUARS

Conference: Sun Belt.
Mailing Address: 1209 Mitchell Center, Mobile, AL 36688. **Website:** www.usajaguars.com.
Head Coach: Steve Kittrell. **Assistant Coaches:** *Mark Calvi, Seth VonBehren. **Telephone:** (251) 461-1397. **Baseball SID:** Charlie Nichols. **Telephone:** (251) 414-8017. **Fax:** (251) 460-7297.
Home Field: Stanky Field. **Seating Capacity:** 4,000. **Outfield Dimensions:** LF—330, CF—400, RF—330. **Press Box Telephone:** (251) 461-1842.

SOUTH CAROLINA GAMECOCKS

Conference: Southeastern (East).
Mailing Address: Carolina Stadium, 431 Williams Street, Columbia, SC 29201. **Website:** www.gamecocksonline.com.
Head Coach: Ray Tanner. **Assistant Coaches:** *Chad Holbrook, Jerry Meyers. **Telephone:** (803) 777-0116. **Baseball SID:** Andrew Kitick. **Telephone:** (803) 777-5257. **Fax:** (803) 777-2967.
Home Field: Carolina Stadium. **Seating Capacity:** 8,242 (standing room included). **Outfield Dimensions:** LF—325, CF—390, RF—325. **Press Box Telephone:** (803) 777-6648.

SOUTH CAROLINA-UPSTATE SPARTANS

Conference: Atlantic Sun.
Mailing Address: 800 University Way, Spartanburg, SC 29303. **Website:** upstatespartans.com.
Head Coach: Matt Fincher. **Assistant Coaches:** *Grant

Rembert, Jim Kais. **Telephone:** (864) 503-5135. **Baseball SID:** Joe Guistina. **Telephone:** (864) 503-5152. **Fax:** (864) 503-5127.
Home Field: Harley Park. **Seating Capacity:** 500. **Outfield Dimension:** LF—325, CF—402, RF—325. **Press Box Telephone:** (864) 503-5058.

SOUTH DAKOTA STATE JACKRABBITS

Conference: Summit.
Mailing Address: 2820 HPER Center, Brookings, SD 57007. **Website:** gojacks.com.
Head Coach: Ritchie Price. **Assistant Coaches:** Jason Laws, Tyler Oakes. **Telephone:** (605) 688-5027. **Baseball SID:** Jason Hove. **Telephone:** (605) 688-4623. **Fax:** (605) 688-5999.
Home Field: Erv Huether Field. **Seating Capacity:** 400. **Outfield Dimension:** LF—330, CF—400, RF—330. **Press Box Telephone:** (605) 695-1827.

SOUTH FLORIDA BULLS

Conference: Big East.
Mailing Address: 4202 E Fowler Ave, ATH 100, Tampa, FL 33620. **Website:** www.GoUSFBulls.com.
Head Coach: Lelo Prado. **Assistant Coaches:** Chris Heintz, Chuck Hernandez. **Telephone:** (813) 974-2504. **Baseball SID:** Brad Borghetti. **Telephone:** (813) 974-4029. **Fax:** (813) 974-4029.
Home Field: Red McEwen Field. **Seating Capacity:** 1,500. **Outfield Dimension:** LF—375, CF—400, RF—375. **Press Box Telephone:** (813) 410-1194.

SOUTHEAST MISSOURI STATE REDHAWKS

Conference: Ohio Valley.
Mailing Address: 1221 Broadway, Cape Girardeau, MO 63701. **Website:** gosoutheast.com.
Head Coach: Mark Hogan. **Assistant Coaches:** *Steve Bieser, Chris Cafalone. **Telephone:** (573) 986-6002. **Baseball SID:** Bo Bunton. **Telephone:** (573) 651-2294. **Fax:** (573) 651-2810.
Home Field: Capaha Park. **Seating Capacity:** 2,000. **Outfield Dimensions:** LF—335, CF—400, RF—335. **Press Box Telephone:** (573) 651-9139.

SOUTHEASTERN LOUISIANA LIONS

Conference: Southland.
Mailing Address: 800 Galloway Dr, Hammond, LA 70402. **Website:** www.lionsports.net.
Head Coach: Jay Artigues. **Assistant Coaches:** *Justin Hill, Matt Riser. **Telephone:** (985) 549-3566. **Baseball SID:** Matt Sullivan. **Telephone:** (985) 549-2142. **Fax:** (985) 549-3495.
Home Field: Pat Kenelly Diamond at Alumni Field. **Seating Capacity:** 2,500. **Outfield Dimensions:** LF—330, CF—400, RF—330. **Press Box Telephone:** (985) 549-2431.

SOUTHERN JAGUARS

Conference: Southwestern Athletic.
Mailing Address: Baseball Office, FG Clark Center, Harding Blvd, Baton Rouge, LA 70813. **Website:** gojag-sports.com.
Head Coach: Roger Cador. **Assistant Coach:** *Fernando Puebla. **Telephone:** (225) 771-2513. **Baseball SID:** Kevin Manns. **Telephone:** (225) 771-2601. **Fax:** (225) 771-4400.
Home Field: Lee-Hines Field. **Seating Capacity:** 1,500. **Outfield Dimension:** LF—360, CF—395, RF—325.

SOUTHERN CALIFORNIA TROJANS

Conference: Pacific-10.
Mailing Address: Dedeaux Field, 1021 Childs Way, Los

Angeles, CA 90089-0731. **Website:** usctrojans.com.

Head Coach: Frank Cruz. **Assistant Coaches:** Gabe Alvarez, *Doyle Wilson. **Telephone:** (213) 740-5762. **Baseball SID:** Jason Pommier. **Telephone:** (213) 740-3807. **Fax:** (213) 740-7584.

Home Field: Dedeaux Field. **Seating Capacity:** 2,500. **Outfield Dimension:** LF—335, CF—395, RF—335. **Press Box Telephone:** (213) 748 3449.

SOUTHERN ILLINOIS SALUKIS

Conference: Missouri Valley.

Mailing Address: Saluki Baseball Clubhouse, Mail Code 6702, Carbondale, IL 62901. **Website:** siusalukis.com.

Head Coach: Ken Henderson. **Assistant Coach:** *PJ Finigan. **Telephone:** (618) 453-3794. **Baseball SID:** Jason Clay. **Telephone:** (618) 453-5470. **Fax:** (618) 453-2648.

Home Field: Abe Martin Field. **Seating Capacity:** 2,000. **Outfield Dimensions:** LF—340, CF—390, RF—340. **Press Box Telephone:** (618) 453-3794.

SOUTHERN ILLINOIS-EDWARDSVILLE COUGARS

Conference: Independent.

Mailing Address: Box 1129, Edwardsville, IL 62026. **Website:** www.siuecougars.com.

Head Coach: Gary Collins. **Assistant Coaches:** Danny Jackson, *Tony Stoecklin. **Telephone:** (618) 650-2872. **Baseball SID:** Joe Pott. **Telephone:** (618) 650-2860. **Fax:** (618) 650-2296.

Home Field: Roy Lee Field at Simmons Cooper Complex. **Seating Capacity:** 750. **Outfield Dimensions:** LF—330, CF—390, RF—330.

SOUTHERN MISSISSIPPI GOLDEN EAGLES

Conference: Conference USA.

Mailing Address: 118 College Dr, #5161, Hattiesburg, MS 39401. **Website:** www.southernmiss.com.

Head Coach: Scott Berry. **Assistant Coaches:** *Chad Caillet, Michael Federico. **Telephone:** (601) 266-5017. **Baseball SID:** Jack Duggan. **(601) 266-5332. Fax:** (601) 266-4507.

Home Field: Pete Taylor Park. **Seating Capacity:** 6,600. **Outfield Dimension:** LF—340, CF—400, RF—340. **Press Box Telephone:** (601) 266-5684.

SOUTHERN UTAH THUNDERBIRDS

Conference: Summit.

Mailing Address: 351 West University Blvd, Cedar City, UT 84720. **Website:** www.suutbirds.com.

Head Coach: David Eldredge. **Assistant Coaches:** Chase Hudson, Dustin Wittwer. **Telephone:** (435) 327-0452. **Baseball SID:** Kyle Cottam. **Telephone:** (435) 586-7752. **Fax:** (435) 586-5444.

Home Field: Thunderbird Park. **Seating Capacity:** 500. **Outfield Dimension:** LF—345, CF—410, RF—330.

STANFORD CARDINAL

Conference: Pacific-10.

Mailing Address: 641 E Campus Dr, Stanford, CA 94305. **Website:** gostanford.com.

Head Coach: Mark Marquess. **Assistant Coaches:** Rusty Filter, *Dean Stotz. **Telephone:** (650) 723-4528. **Baseball SID:** Niall Adler. **Telephone:** (650) 725-2959. **Fax:** (650) 725-2957.

Home Field: Klein Field at Sunken Diamond. **Seating Capacity:** 4,000. **Outfield Dimension:** LF—335, CF—400, RF—335. **Press Box Telephone:** (650) 723-4629.

STEPHEN F. AUSTIN STATE LUMBERJACKS

Conference: Southland.

Mailing Address: PO Box 13010, SFA Station,

Nacogdoches, TX 75962. **Website:** www.sfajacks.com.

Head Coach: Johnny Cardenas. **Assistant Coaches:** *Chris Connally, Chad Massengale. **Telephone:** (936) 468-5982. **Baseball SID:** Ben Rikard. **Telephone:** (936) 468-5801. **Fax:** (936) 468-4593.

Home Field: Jaycees Field. **Seating Capacity:** 1,000. **Outfield Dimension:** LF—330, CF—400, RF—300. **Press Box Telephone:** (936) 559-8344.

STETSON HATTERS

Conference: Atlantic Sun.

Mailing Address: Department of Athletics, 421 N Woodland Blvd, Unit 8359, DeLand, FL, 32723. **Website:** www.gohatters.com.

Head Coach: Pete Dunn. **Assistant Coaches:** *Mark Leavitt, Chris Roberts. **Telephone:** (386) 822-8730. **Baseball SID:** Dean Watson. **Telephone:** (386) 822-8130. **Fax:** (386) 822-7486.

Home Field: Melching Field at Conrad Park. **Seating Capacity:** 2,500. **Outfield Dimensions:** LF—335, CF—403, RF—325. **Press Box Telephone:** (386) 736-7360.

STONY BROOK SEAWOLVES

Conference: America East.

Mailing Address: Stony Brook University, Indoor Sports Complex, Stony Brook, NY, 11794-3500. **Website:** goseawolves.cstv.com.

Head Coach: Matt Senk. **Assistant Coaches:** Mike Marron, *Joe Pennucci. **Telephone:** (631) 632-9226. **Baseball SID:** Jeremy Cohen. **Telephone:** (631) 632-6328. **Fax:** (631) 632-8841.

Home Field: Joe Nathan Field. **Seating Capacity:** 1,000. **Outfield Dimensions:** LF—330, CF—390, RF—330. **Press Box Telephone:** (860) 690-3482.

TEMPLE OWLS

Conference: Atlantic Sun.

Mailing Address: 1700 North Broad Street, Philadelphia, PA 19122. **Website:** www.owlsports.com.

Head Coach: Rob Valli. **Assistant Coaches:** Joe Agnello, Sean Cashman, *Tim Perry. **Telephone:** (215) 204-8639. **Baseball SID:** Alex Samuelian. **Telephone:** (215) 204-7445. **Fax:** (215) 933-5257.

Home Field: Skip Wilson Field. **Seating Capacity:** 1,000. **Outfield Dimensions:** LF—330, CF—400, RF—330. **Press Box Telephone:** (609) 969-0975.

TENNESSEE VOLUNTEERS

Conference: Southeastern (East).

Mailing Address: 1511 Pat Summitt Dr, Knoxville, TN 37996. **Website:** www.UTsports.com.

Head Coach: Todd Raleigh. **Assistant Coaches:** Jason Beverlin. ***Ash Lawson. **Telephone:** (865) 974-2057. **Baseball SID:** Cameron Harris. **Telephone:** (865) 974-8876. **Fax:** (865) 974-8875.

Home Field: Lindsey Nelson Stadium. **Seating Capacity:** 3,800. **Outfield Dimensions:** LF—320, CF—390, RF—320. **Press Box Telephone:** (865) 974-3376.

TENNESSEE TECH GOLDEN EAGLES

Conference: Ohio Valley.

Mailing Address: 1100 McGee Blvd, Cookeville, TN 38505. **Website:** www.ttusports.com.

Head Coach: Matt Bragga. **Telephone:** (931) 372-3925. **Baseball SID:** Kate Nicewicz. **Telephone:** (931) 372-3293. **Fax:** (931) 372-3114.

Assistant Coaches: Larry Bragga, *Donnie Suttles. **Telephone:** (931) 372-3853.

Home Field: Bush Stadium, Averitt Express Baseball Complex. **Seating Capacity:** 1,100. **Outfield Dimensions:**

LF—331, CF—405, RF—329.

TENNESSEE-MARTIN SKYHAWKS

Conference: Ohio Valley.
Mailing Address: 1037 Elam Center, Martin, TN 38238.
Website: www.utmsports.com.
Head Coach: Victor "Bubba" Cates. **Assistant Coaches:** Trevor Berryhill, *Brad Goss. **Telephone:** (731) 881-7337. **Baseball SID:** Joe Lofaro. **Telephone:** (731) 881-7632. **Fax:** (731) 881-7624.
Home Field: Skyhawk Field. **Seating Capacity:** 300. **Outfield Dimension:** LF—330, CF—385, RF—330.

TEXAS LONGHORNS

Conference: Big 12.
Mailing Address: 2100 San Jacinto Boulevard, 327 Bellmont Hall, Austin, TX 78712. **Website:** www.TexasSports.com.
Head Coach: Augie Garrido. **Assistant Coaches:** *Tommy Harmon, Skip Johnson. **Telephone:** (512) 471-1404. **Baseball SID:** Thomas Dick. **Telephone:** (512) 471-6039. **Fax:** (512) 471-6040.
Home Field: UFCU Disch Falk Field. **Seating Capacity:** 6,876. **Outfield Dimension:** LF—340, CF—400, RF—320.

TEXAS A&M AGGIES

Conference: Big 12.
Mailing Address: PO Box 30017, College Station, TX 77842-3017. **Website:** AggieAthletics.com.
Head Coach: Rob Childress. **Assistant Coaches:** Andy Sawyers, *Justin Seely. **Telephone:** (979) 845-4810. **Baseball SID:** Adam Quisenberry. **Telephone:** (979) 845-4810. **Fax:** (979) 845-6825.
Home Field: Olsen Field. **Seating Capacity:** 7,053. **Outfield Dimensions:** LF—330, CF—400, RF—330. **Press Box Telephone:** (979) 458-3604.

TEXAS A&M-CORPUS CHRISTI ISLANDERS

Conference: Southland.
Mailing Address: 6300 Ocean Drive, Unit 5719, Corpus Christi TX 78412. **Website:** www.goislanders.com.
Head Coach: Scott Malone. **Assistant Coaches:** *Chris Ramirez, Marty Smith. **Telephone:** (361) 825-3413. **Baseball SID:** Matt Brady. **Telephone:** (812) 825-3410. **Fax:** (361) 825-3218.
Home Field: Whataburger Field. **Seating Capacity:** 8,000. **Outfield Dimension:** LF—327, CF—400, RF—315. **Press Box Telephone:** (361) 561-4665.

TEXAS CHRISTIAN HORNED FROGS

Conference: Mountain West.
Mailing Address: 2900 Stadium Dr, Fort Worth, TX 76129. **Website:** www.gofrogs.com.
Head Coach: Jim Schlossnagle. **Assistant Coaches:** Randy Mazey, *Tony Vitello. **Telephone:** (817) 257-5354. **Baseball SID:** Brandie Davidson. **Telephone:** (817) 257-7479. **Fax:** (817) 257-7964.
Home Field: Lupton Stadium. **Seating Capacity:** 4,500. **Outfield Dimensions:** LF—330, CF—400, RF—330. **Press Box Telephone:** (817) 257-7966.

TEXAS SOUTHERN TIGERS

Conference: Southwestern Athletic.
Mailing Address: H&PE Building, Room 111, 3100 Cleburne Ave, Houston, TX 77004. **Website:** www.tsu.edu/athletics.
Head Coach: Michael Robertson. **Assistant Coaches:** *Marqus Johnson. **Telephone:** (713) 313-4315. **Baseball SID:** Rodney Bush. **Telephone:** (713) 313-7603. **Fax:** (713) 313-1045.

TEXAS STATE BOBCATS

Conference: Southland.
Mailing Address: 601 University Drive, San Marcos, TX 78666. **Website:** txstatebobcats.com.
Head Coach: Ty Harrington. **Assistant Coaches:** Jeremy Fikac, *Derek Matlock. **Telephone:** (512) 245-3383. **Baseball SID:** Steve Appelhans. **Telephone:** (512) 245-4387. **Fax:** (512) 245-8387.
Home Field: Bobcat Baseball Stadium. **Seating Capacity:** 2,000. **Outfield Dimensions:** LF—330, CF—405, RF—330.

TEXAS TECH RED RAIDERS

Conference: Big 12.
Mailing Address: Box 43021, 6th and Boston Ave, Lubbock, TX 79409. **Website:** www.texastech.com.
Head Coach: Dan Spencer. **Assistant Coaches:** Jim Horner, *Trent Petrie. **Telephone:** (806) 742-3355. **Baseball SID:** Blayne Beal. **Telephone:** (806) 742-2770. **Fax:** (806) 742-1970.
Home Field: Dan Law Field. **Seating Capacity:** 5,026. **Outfield Dimension:** LF—330, CF—405, RF—330. **Press Box Telephone:** (806) 742-3688.

TEXAS-ARLINGTON MAVERICKS

Conference: Southland.
Mailing Address: 1309 West Mitchell Street, Arlington, TX 76019. **Website:** utamavs.com.
Head Coach: Darin Thomas. **Assistant Coaches:** KJ Hendricks, *Jay Sirianni. **Telephone:** (817) 272-2542. **Baseball SID:** Scott Lacefield. **Telephone:** (817) 272-2239. **Fax:** (817) 272-5037.
Home Field: Clay Gould Ballpark. **Seating Capacity:** 1,600. **Outfield Dimension:** LF—330, CF—400, RF—330. **Press Box Telephone:** (817) 462-4225.

TEXAS-PAN AMERICAN BRONCS

Conference: Independent.
Mailing Address: 1201 W University Drive, Edinburg, TX 78539. **Website:** utpabroncs.com.
Head Coach: Manny Mantrana. **Assistant Coaches:** Robert Lopez, Norbert Lopez. **Telephone:** (956) 665-2234. **Baseball SID:** Rebecca Sweat. **Telephone:** (956) 381-2240. **Fax:** (956) 381-2261.
Home Field: Edinburg Baseball Stadium. **Seating Capacity:** 4,000. **Outfield Dimension:** Unavailable.

TEXAS-SAN ANTONIO ROADRUNNERS

Conference: Southland.
Mailing Address: One UTSA Circle, San Antonio, TX 78249. **Website:** www.goutsa.com.
Head Coach: Sherman Corbett. **Assistant Coaches:** Brett Lawler, *Jason Marshall. **Telephone:** (210) 458-4805. **Baseball SID:** Tony Baldwin. **Telephone:** (210) 458-6460. **Fax:** (210) 458-4569.
Home Field: Roadrunner Field. **Seating Capacity:** 800. **Outfield Dimensions:** LF—335, CF—405, RF—340. **Press Box Telephone:** (210) 458-4612.

TOLEDO ROCKETS

Conference: Mid-American (West).
Mailing Address: 2801 West Bancroft Street, Toledo, OH 43606. **Website:** utrockets.com.
Head Coach: Cory Mee. **Assistant Coaches:** *Josh Bradford, Nick McIntyre. **Telephone:** (419) 530-6263. **Baseball SID:** Brian DeBenedictis. **Telephone:** (419) 530-4919. **Fax:** (419) 530-4428.
Home Field: Scott Park. **Seating Capacity:** 1,000. **Outfield Dimensions:** LF—330′, CF—400′, RF—330′. **Press**

Box Telephone: (419) 530-3089.

TOWSON TIGERS

Conference: Colonial Athletic.
Mailing Address: 8000 York Road, Towson, MD 21252-0001. **Website:** www.towsontigers.com.
Head Coach: Mike Gottlieb. **Assistant Coaches:** Lance Mauck, *Scott Roane. **Telephone:** (410) 704-3775. **Baseball SID:** Dan O'Connell. **Telephone:** (410) 704-3102. **Fax:** (410) 704-3861.
Home Field: John B Schuerholz Park. **Seating Capacity:** 1,200. **Outfield Dimension:** LF—312, CF—424, RF—302. **Press Box Telephone:** (410) 704-5810.

TROY TROJANS

Conference: Sun Belt.
Mailing Address: 5000 Veterans Stadium Drive, Troy, AL 36082. **Website:** www.TroyTrojans.com.
Head Coach: Bobby Pierce. **Assistant Coaches:** Brad Phillips, *Mark Smartt. **Telephone:** (334) 670-3489. **Baseball SID:** Ricky Hazel. **Telephone:** (334) 670-3832. **Fax:** (334) 670-5665.
Home Field: Riddle-Pace Field. **Seating Capacity:** 2,000. **Outfield Dimensions:** LF—340, CF—400, RF—310. **Press Box Telephone:** (334) 670-5701.

TULANE GREEN WAVE

Conference: Conference USA.
Mailing Address: James Wilson Center, New Orleans, LA 70118. **Website:** www.TulaneGreenWave.com.
Head Coach: Rick Jones. **Assistant Coaches:** *Chad Sutter, Jake Gautreau. **Telephone:** (504) 862-8238. **Baseball SID:** Greg Campbell. **Telephone:** (504) 314-7271. **Fax:** (504) 862-8569.
Home Field: Greer Field at Turchin Stadium. **Seating Capacity:** 5,000. **Outfield Dimensions:** LF—330, CF—400, RF—330.

UTAH UTES

Conference: Mountain West.
Mailing Address: 1825 E South Campus Dr, Salt Lake City, Utah 84112. **Website:** utahutes.com.
Head Coach: Bill Kinneberg. **Assistant Coaches:** *Mike Crawford, Bryan Kinneberg. **Telephone:** (801) 581-3526. **Baseball SID:** Brooke Frederickson. **Telephone:** (801) 581-8302. **Fax:** (801) 581-4358.
Home Field: Spring Mobile Ballpark. **Seating Capacity:** 15,000. **Outfield Dimensions:** LF—320, CF—410, RF—315.

UTAH VALLEY WOLVERINES

Conference: Independent.
Mailing Address: 800 W University Parkway, Orem, UT 84058. **Website:** www.WolverineGreen.com.
Head Coach: Eric Madsen. **Assistant Coaches:** *Dave Carter, Mike Martin. **Telephone:** (801) 863-6509. **Baseball SID:** Clint Burgi. **Telephone:** (801) 863-8644. **Fax:** (801) 863-8813.
Home Field: Brent Brown Ballpark. **Seating Capacity:** 5,000. **Outfield Dimension:** LF—312, CF—408, RF—315. **Press Box Telephone:** (801) 362-1548.

VALPARAISO CRUSADERS

Conference: Horizon.
Mailing Address: 1009 Union St, Valparaiso, IN 46383. **Website:** www.valpoathletics.com.
Head Coach: Tracy Woodson. **Assistant Coaches:** Adam Piotrowicz, *Brian Schmack. **Telephone:** (219) 464-5239. **Baseball SID:** Ryan Wronkowicz. **Telephone:** (219) 464-5232. **Fax:** (219) 464-5762.

Home Field: Emory G Bauer Field. **Seating Capacity:** 500. **Outfield Dimension:** LF—330, CF—400, RF—330. **Press Box Telephone:** (219) 464-6006.

VANDERBILT COMMODORES

Conference: Southeastern (East).
Mailing Address: 2601 Jess Neely Drive, Nashville, TN 37212. **Website:** www.vucommodores.com.
Head Coach: Tim Corbin. **Assistant Coaches:** *Josh Holliday, Derek Johnson. **Telephone:** (615) 322-3716. **Baseball SID:** Kyle Parkinson. **Telephone:** (615) 343-0020. **Fax:** (615) 343-7064.
Home Field: Hawkins Field. **Seating Capacity:** 3,700. **Outfield Dimensions:** LF—310, CF—400, RF—330. **Press Box Telephone:** (615) 320-0436.

VILLANOVA WILDCATS

Conference: Big East.
Mailing Address: 800 E Lancaster Avenue, Jake Nevin Field House, Villanova, PA 19085. **Website:** villanova.com.
Head Coach: Joe Godri. **Assistant Coaches:** *Jim Carone, Dave Miller. **Telephone:** (610) 519-4926. **Baseball SID:** David Berman. **Telephone:** (610) 519-4122. **Fax:** (610) 519-7323.
Home Field: Villanova Ballpark at Plymouth. **Seating Capacity:** 750. **Outfield Dimensions:** LF—330, CF—405, RF—330. **Press Box Telephone:** (860) 490-6398.

VIRGINIA CAVALIERS

Conference: Atlantic Coast (Coastal).
Mailing Address: PO Box 400853, Charlottesville, VA 22904-4853. **Website:** www.virginiasports.com.
Head Coach: Brian O'Connor. **Assistant Coaches:** Karl Kuhn, *Kevin McMullan. **Telephone:** (434) 982-4932. **Baseball SID:** Andy Fledderjohann. **Telephone:** (434) 982-5131. **Fax:** (434) 982-5525.
Home Field: Davenport Field. **Seating Capacity:** 4,825. **Outfield Dimensions:** LF—335, CF—408, RF—335. **Press Box Telephone:** (434) 244-4071.

VIRGINIA COMMONWEALTH RAMS

Conference: Colonial Athletic.
Mailing Address: 1300 W Broad Street, Richmond, VA 23284. **Website:** www.vcuathletics.com.
Head Coach: Paul Keyes. **Assistant Coaches:** *Shawn Stiffler, Cory Whitby. **Telephone:** (804) 828-4820. **Baseball SID:** Mitchell Moore. **Telephone:** (804) 828-8496. **Fax:** (804) 828-4938.
Home Field: The Diamond. **Seating Capacity:** 12,134. **Outfield Dimension:** LF—330, CF—402, RF—330. **Press Box Telephone:** (302) 593-0115.

VIRGINIA MILITARY INSTITUTE KEYDETS

Conference: Big South.
Mailing Address: Cameron Hall, VMI, Lexington, VA 24450. **Website:** www.VMIKeydets.com.
Head Coach: Marlin Ikenberry. **Assistant Coaches:** *Jonathan Hadra, Daniel Latham. **Telephone:** (540) 464-7609. **Baseball SID:** Brad Salois. **Telephone:** (540) 464-7015. **Fax:** (540) 464-7583.
Home Field: Gray-Minor Stadium. **Seating Capacity:** 1,400. **Outfield Dimensions:** LF—330, CF—395, RF—330. **Press Box Telephone:** (540) 460-6920.

VIRGINIA TECH HOKIES

Conference: Atlantic Coast (Coastal).
Mailing Address: 460 Jamerson Athletic Center, Blacksburg, VA 24061-0502. **Website:** www.hokiesports.com.
Head Coach: Pete Hughes. **Assistant Coaches:** Mike

Kunigonis, *Patrick Mason. **Telephone:** (540) 231-3671. **Baseball SID:** Marc Mullen. **Telephone:** (540) 231-1894. **Fax:** (540) 231-6984.
    Home Field: English Field. **Seating Capacity:** 4,000. **Outfield Dimensions:** LF—330, CF—400, RF—330. **Press Box Telephone:** (540) 231-8974.

WAGNER SEAHAWKS

    Conference: Northeast.
    Mailing Address: Spiro Sports Center, One Campus Rd, Staten Island, NY 10301. **Website:** wagnerathletics.com.
    Head Coach: Joe Litterio. **Assistant Coaches:** Mike Consolmagno, Billy Malloy. **Telephone:** (718) 390-3154. **Baseball SID:** Kevin Ross. **Telephone:** (718) 390-3215. **Fax:** (718) 420-4015.
    Home Field: Richmond County Bank Ballpark. **Seating Capacity:** 6,900. **Outfield Dimension:** LF—320, CF—390, RF—318. **Press Box Telephone:** (716) 969-6126.

WAKE FOREST DEMON DEACONS

    Conference: Atlantic Coast (Atlantic).
    Mailing Address: 1834 Wake Forest Road, Winston-Salem, NC 27106. **Website:** wakeforestsports.com.
    Head Coach: Tom Walter. **Assistant Coaches:** Bill Cilento, *Dennis Healy. **Telephone:** (336) 758-5570. **Baseball SID:** Steven Wright. **Telephone:** (336) 758-4120. **Fax:** (336) 758-5140.
    Home Field: Wake Forest Baseball Park. **Seating Capacity:** 6,000. **Outfield Dimensions:** LF—300, CF—400, RF—310. **Press Box Telephone:** (336) 759-7373.

WASHINGTON HUSKIES

    Conference: Pacific-10.
    Mailing Address: Graves Annex Box 354080, Seattle, WA 98195-4080. **Website:** www.gohuskies.com.
    Head Coach: Lindsay Meggs. **Assistant Coaches:** Dave Dangler, *Dave Nakama. **Telephone:** (206) 543-9365. **Baseball SID:** Jeff Bechthold. **Telephone:** (206) 685-7910. **Fax:** (206) 543-5000.
    Home Field: Husky Ballpark. **Seating Capacity:** 1,500. **Outfield Dimension:** LF—327, CF—395, RF—317. **Press Box Telephone:** (206) 685-1994.

WASHINGTON STATE COUGARS

    Conference: Pacific-10.
    Mailing Address: 195 Bohler Athletic Complex, Pullman, WA 99164-1602. **Website:** wsucougars.cstv.com.
    Head Coach: Donnie Marbut. **Assistant Coaches:** *Spencer Allen, Gregg Swenson. **Telephone:** (509) 335-0332. **Baseball SID:** Craig Lawson. **Telephone:** (509) 335-0265. **Fax:** (206) 543-5000.
    Home Field: Bailey-Brayton Field. **Seating Capacity:** 3,500. **Outfield Dimensions:** LF—330, CF—400, RF—330. **Press Box Telephone:** (509) 335-8291.

WEST VIRGINIA MOUNTAINEERS

    Conference: Big East.
    Mailing Address: PO Box 0877, Morgantown, WV 26505. **Website:** www.msnsportsnet.com.
    Head Coach: Greg Van Zant. **Assistant Coaches:** *Pat Sherald, Jake Weghorst. **Telephone:** (304) 293-9881. **Baseball SID:** Shannon McNamara. **Telephone:** (304) 293-2821. **Fax:** (304) 293-4105.
    Home Field: Hawley Field. **Seating Capacity:** 1,500. **Outfield Dimension:** LF—325, CF—390, RF—325. **Press Box Telephone:** (304) 293-5988.

WESTERN CAROLINA CATAMOUNTS

    Conference: Southern.
    Mailing Address: Ramsey Center, Cullowhee, NC 28723. **Website:** catamountsports.com.
    Head Coach: Bobby Moranda. **Assistant Coaches:** *Alan Beck, David Haverstick. **Telephone:** (828) 227-2021. **Baseball SID:** Daniel Hooker. **Telephone:** (828) 227-2339. **Fax:** (828) 227-7688.
    Home Field: Childress Field at Hennon Stadium. **Seating Capacity:** 1,200. **Outfield Dimensions:** LF—325, CF—390, RF—325. **Press Box Telephone:** (828) 227-7020.

WESTERN ILLINOIS FIGHTING LEATHERNECKS

    Conference: Summit.
    Mailing Address: 1 University Circle, Macomb, IL 61455. **Website:** www.wiuathletics.com.
    Head Coach: Mike Villano. **Assistant Coaches:** *Todd Coryell, Cooper Stewart. **Telephone:** (309) 298-1521. **Baseball SID:** Cameron Weidenthaler. **Telephone:** (309) 298-1133. **Fax:** (309) 298-1960.
    Home Field: Alfred D Boyer Stadium. **Seating Capacity:** 500. **Outfield Dimensions:** LF—330, CF—400, RF—330. **Press Box Telephone:** (309) 298-1190.

WESTERN KENTUCKY HILLTOPPERS

    Conference: Sun Belt.
    Mailing Address: 1605 Avenue of Champions, Bowling Green, KY 42101. **Website:** www.wkusports.com.
    Head Coach: Chris Finwood. **Assistant Coaches:** *Blake Allen, Matt Myers. **Telephone:** (270) 745-2493. **Baseball SID:** Melissa Anderson. **Telephone:** (270) 745-3756. **Fax:** (270) 745-3444.
    Home Field: Nick Denes Field. **Seating Capacity:** 1,500. **Outfield Dimensions:** LF—330, CF—400, RF—330. **Press Box Telephone:** (270) 745-6941.

WESTERN MICHIGAN BRONCOS

    Conference: Mid-American (West).
    Mailing Address: 1903 West Michigan Ave, Kalamazoo, MI 49008. **Website:** www.wmubroncos.com.
    Head Coach: Billy Gernon. **Assistant Coaches:** *Brent Alwine, Blaine McFerrin. **Telephone:** (269) 276-3205. **Baseball SID:** Kristin Keirns. **Telephone:** (269) 387-4123. **Fax:** (269) 387-4139.
    Home Field: Hyames Field. **Seating Capacity:** 3,500. **Outfield Dimensions:** LF—325, CF—395, RF—320. **Press Box Telephone:** (269) 387-8210.

WICHITA STATE SHOCKERS

    Conference: Missouri Valley.
    Mailing Address: 1845 Fairmount, Campus Box 18, Wichita, KS 67260-0018. **Website:** www.goshockers.com.
    Head Coach: Gene Stephenson. **Assistant Coaches:** *Brent Kemnitz, Jim Thomas. **Telephone:** (316) 978-3636. **Baseball SID:** Tami Cutler. **Telephone:** (316) 978-5559. **Fax:** (316) 978-3336.
    Home Field: Eck Stadium/Tyler Field. **Seating Capacity:** 7,851. **Outfield Dimensions:** LF—330, CF—390, RF—330. **Press Box Telephone:** (316) 978-3390.

WILLIAM & MARY TRIBE

    Conference: Colonial Athletic.
    Mailing Address: PO Box 399, Williamsburg, VA 23187. **Website:** www.tribeathletics.com.
    Head Coach: Frank Leoni. **Assistant Coaches:** Kyle Padgett, *Jad Prachniak. **Telephone:** (757) 221-3399. **Baseball SID:** Scott Burns. **Telephone:** (757) 221-3344. **Fax:** (757) 221-2989.
    Home Field: Plumeri Park. **Seating Capacity:** 1,200. **Outfield Dimension:** LF—330, CF—400, RF—330. **Press Box Telephone:** (757) 221-3562.

WINTHROP EAGLES

Conference: Big South.
Mailing Address: 1162 Eden Terrace Road, Rock Hill, SC 29733. **Website:** www.winthropeagles.com.
Head Coach: Tom Riginos. **Assistant Coaches:** Clint Chrysler, *Mike McGuire. **Telephone:** (803) 323-6235. **Baseball SID:** Wes Herring. **Telephone:** (803) 323-6067. **Fax:** (803) 323-4965.
Home Field: Winthrop Ballpark. **Seating Capacity:** 5,000. **Outfield Dimensions:** LF—325, CF—390, RF—325. **Press Box Telephone:** (803) 323-2155.

WISCONSIN-MILWAUKEE PANTHERS

Conference: Horizon.
Mailing Address: 3409 N Downer Ave, Milwaukee, WI 53201. **Website:** uwmpanthers.com.
Head Coach: Scott Doffek. **Assistant Coaches:** Cory Bigler, Mike Goetz. **Telephone:** (414) 229-5670. **Baseball SID:** Chris Zills. **Telephone:** (414) 229-4593. **Fax:** (414) 229-6759.
Home Field: Henry Aaron Field. **Seating Capacity:** Unavailable. **Outfield Dimensions:** LF—320, CF—390, RF—320. **Press Box Telephone:** (414) 750-2090.

WOFFORD TERRIERS

Conference: Southern.
Mailing Address: 429 N Church Street, Spartanburg, SC 29303. **Website:** athletics.wofford.edu.
Head Coach: Todd Interdonato. **Assistant Coaches:** *Dusty Blake. **Telephone:** (864) 597-4497. **Baseball SID:** Brent Williamson. **Telephone:** (864) 597-4093. **Fax:** (864) 597-4129.
Home Field: Russell C King Field. **Seating Capacity:** 2,500. **Outfield Dimension:** LF—325, CF—395, RF—325. **Press Box Telephone:** (864) 597-4478.

WRIGHT STATE RAIDERS

Conference: Horizon.
Mailing Address: 3640 Colonel Glenn Hwy, Dayton, OH 45435. **Website:** wsuraiders.cstv.com.
Head Coach: Rob Cooper. **Assistant Coaches:** *Greg

Lovelady, Ross Oeder. **Telephone:** Telephone: (937) 775-3667. **Baseball SID:** Matt Zircher. **Telephone:** (937) 775-2831. **Fax:** (937) 775-2368.
Home Field: Nischwitz Stadium. **Seating Capacity:** 750. **Outfield Dimension:** LF—330, CF—400, RF—370. **Press Box Telephone:** (937) 602-0326.

XAVIER MUSKETEERS

Conference: Atlantic 10.
Mailing Address: 3800 Victory Parkway, Cincinnati, OH 45207. **Website:** www.goxavier.com.
Head Coach: Scott Googins. **Assistant Coach:** Nick Otte. **Telephone:** (513) 745-3727. **Baseball SID:** Jason Ashcraft. **Telephone:** (513) 745-3388. **Fax:** (513) 745-2825.
Home Field: Hayden Field. **Seating Capacity:** 500. **Outfield Dimensions:** LF—310, CF—380, RF—310. **Press Box Telephone:** (513) 598-0327.

YALE BULLDOGS

Conference: Ivy League (Rolfe).
Mailing Address: 20 Tower Pkwy, New Haven, CT 06520. **Website:** yalebulldogs.com.
Head Coach: John Stuper. **Assistant Coaches:** *Tucker Frawley, Ray Guarino, Kevin Huber. **Telephone:** (203) 432-1466. **Baseball SID:** Steve Conn. **Telephone:** (203) 432-1445. **Fax:** (203) 432-1454.
Home Field: Yale Field. **Seating Capacity:** 12,000. **Outfield Dimension:** LF—330, CF—405, RF—315.

YOUNGSTOWN STATE PENGUINS

Conference: Horizon.
Mailing Address: One University Plaza, Youngstown, OH 44555. **Website:** www.ysusports.com.
Head Coach: Rich Pasquale. **Assistant Coaches:** Craig Antush, *Dan Lipari. **Telephone:** (330) 941-3485. **Baseball SID:** John Vogel. **Telephone:** (330) 941-1480. **Fax:** (330) 941-3191.
Home Field: Eastwood Field. **Seating Capacity:** 6,000. **Outfield Dimension:** LF—335, CF—405, RF—335. **Press Box Telephone:** (330) 505-0000, ext 229.

AMATEUR & YOUTH

INTERNATIONAL ORGANIZATIONS

INTERNATIONAL BASEBALL FEDERATION

Headquarters: Avenue de Mon Repos 24, Case Postale 6099, 1002 Lausanne, Switzerland. **Telephone:** (+41-21) 318-82-40. **Fax:** (41-21) 318-82-41.

Website: www.ibaf.org. **E-Mail:** ibaf@ibaf.org.

Year Founded: 1938.

President: Riccardo Fraccari.

1st Vice President: Kazuhiro Tawa. **2nd Vice President:** Alonso Perez Gonzalez. **3rd Vice President:** Antonio Castro. **Secretary General:** Israel Roldan. **Treasurer:** Rene Laforce. **Members at Large:** Luis Melero, Tom Peng, Paul Seiler. **Continental VP, Africa:** Ishola Williams. **Continental VP, Americas:** Eduardo De Bello. **Continental VP, Asia:** Kang Seung Kyoo. **Continental VP, Europe:** Martin Miller. **Continental VP, Oceania:** Rob Finlay.

Manager, Media Relations/Project Development: Ian Young. **Media Coordinator:** Joe Favorito. **Manager, Anti-Doping:** Victor Isola. **Marketing/Tournaments:** Masaru Yokoo.

CONTINENTAL ASSOCIATIONS

CONFEDERATION PAN AMERICANA DE BEISBOL (COPABE)

Mailing Address: Calle 3, Francisco Filos, Vista Hermosa, Edificio 74, Planta Baja Local No. 1, Panama City, Panama. **Telephone:** (507) 229-8684. **Fax:** Unavailable. **E-Mail Address:** copabe@sinfo.net.

President: Eduardo De Bello (Panama). **Secretary General:** Hector Pereyra (Dominican Republic).

AFRICAN BASEBALL/SOFTBALL ASSOCIATION

Mailing Address: Paiko Road, Changaga, Minna, Niger State, PMB 150, Nigeria. **Telephone:** (234-66) 224-555. **Fax:** (234-66) 224-555. **E-Mail Address:** absasecretariat@yahoo.com.

President: Ishola Williams (Nigeria). **Executive Director:** Friday Ichide (Nigeria). **Secretary General:** Mabothobile Shebe (Lesotho).

BASEBALL FEDERATION OF ASIA

Mailing Address: No. 946-16 Dogok-Dong, Kangnam-Gu, Seoul, 135-270 Korea. **Telephone:** (82-2) 572-8413. **Fax:** (82-2) 572-8416.

President: Nae-Heun Lee (Korea). **Secretary General:** Kyung-Hoon Minn (Korea).

EUROPEAN BASEBALL CONFEDERATION

Mailing Address: Otto-FleckSchneise 12, D - 60528 Frankfurt, Germany. **Telephone:** +49-69-6700-284. **Fax:** +49-69-67724-212. **E-Mail Address:** office@baseballeurope.com. **Website:** baseballeurope.com.

President: Martin Miller (Germany). **Secretary General:** Samuel Pelter (Israel).

BASEBALL CONFERERATION OF OCEANIA

Mailing Address: 48 Partridge Way, Mooroolbark, Victoria 3138, Australia. **Telephone:** 613 9727 1779. **Fax:** 613 9727 5959. **E-Mail Address:** bcosecgeneral@basebal-loceania.com. **Website:** www.baseballoceania.com.

President: John Ostermeyer (Australia). **Secretary General:** Chet Gray (Australia).

ORGANIZATIONS

INTERNATIONAL GOODWILL SERIES, INC.

Mailing Address: 982 Slate Drive, Santa Rosa, CA 95405. **Telephone:** (707) 538-0777. **E-Mail Address:** bobw.24@goodwillseries.org. **Website:** www.goodwill-series.org.

President, Goodwill Series, Inc.: Bob Williams.

INTERNATIONAL SPORTS GROUP

Mailing Address: 11430 Kestrel Rd., Klamath Falls, OR 97601. **Telephone:** (541) 882-4293. **E-Mail Address:** isg-baseball@yahoo.com. **Website:** www.isgbaseball.com.

President: Jim Jones. **Vice President:** Tom O'Connell. **Secretary/Treasurer:** Randy Town.

NATIONAL ORGANIZATIONS

USA BASEBALL

Mailing Address, Corporate Headquarters: 403 Blackwell St., Durham, NC 27701 **Telephone:** (919) 474-8721. **Fax:** (919) 474-8822. **E-Mail Address:** info@usa-baseball.com. **Website:** www.usabaseball.com.

President: Mike Gaski. **Secretary General:** Ernie Young. **Treasurer:** Jason Dobis.

Executive Director/Chief Executive Officer: Paul Seiler. **Director, Operations/Women's National Team:** Ashley Bratcher. **General Manager, National Teams:** Eric Campbell. **Chief Financial Officer:** Ray Darwin. **Director, Media/Public Relations:** Jake Fehling. **Director, 14U National Team:** Nate Logan. **Chief Operating Officer:** David Perkins. **Coordinator, Operations:** Adrian Pringle. **Director, Development:** Rick Riccobono. **Director, Community Relations:** Lindsay Robertson. **Director, 16U National Team:** Jeff Singer. **Director, 18U National Team & Alumni:** Brant Ust. **Director, Travel Services:** Katie VanLandingham.

National Members: Amateur Athletic Union (AAU), American Amateur Baseball Congress (AABC), American Baseball Coaches Association (ABCA), American Legion Baseball, Babe Ruth Baseball, Dixie Baseball, Little League Baseball, National Amateur Baseball Federation (NABF), National Association of Intercollegiate Athletics (NAIA), National Baseball Congress (NBC), National Collegiate Athletic Association (NCAA), National Federation of State High School Athletic Associations, National High School Baseball Coaches Association (BCA), National Junior College Athletic Association (NJCAA), Police Athletic League (PAL), PONY Baseball, T-Ball USA, United States Specialty Sports Association (USSSA), YMCAs of the USA.

2011 Events

USA Baseball Professional Teams
Unavailable

USA Baseball Collegiate National Team
June 22-July 9 . . . . Collegiate National Team Trials & Training Cary, N.C.
July 3-8 . . . . USA vs. Japan N.C.

USA Baseball 18U National Team
June 22–26 . . . . USA Baseball Tournament of Stars Cary, N.C.
June 27–30 . . . 18U National Team Trials & Training Cary, N.C.
Sept. 12-21 . . . . 18U National Team Training Cary, N.C.

Sept. 23–Oct. 2 . . COPABE Pan Am 'AAA'/18U Championships Cartagena, Colombia

USA Baseball 16U National Team
June 17–25 . . . . . 16U Championships—Peoria, Surprise and Glendale, Ariz.
June 17–25 . . . . 16U Championships— East Palm Beach County, Fla.
Aug. 7-17. . . . 16U National Team Trials & Training, Cary, N.C.
Aug. 19-28. . . . . . IBAF World 'AA'/16U Youth Championships, Lagos de Moreno, Mexico

USA Baseball 14U National Team
June 17–2214U Championships—West Peoria & Surprise, Ariz.
June 17–22 . . . . 14U Championships—East Lee County, Fla.
TBD . . . . 14U National Team Trials & Training, Cary, N.C.
TBD . . . . .COPABE Pan Am "A" Championships, San Felipe, Venezuela

USA Baseball Women's National Team
Aug. 2–7 . Women's International Friendship Series, Cary, N.C.

USA Baseball National Teams Identification Series (NTIS)
Sept. 9–11 . . . . 17U, 15U, 13U NTIS Cary, N.C.

USA Baseball Athlete Development Camps

Other Events
March 26Coaches Spring Training and Player Clinics, Cary, N.C.
April 3. . . . . USAB Parent & Child Clinic,Cary, N.C.
July 8-10 . . . . USA Baseball 16U Cup Cary, N.C.
July 15-17 . . . . USA Baseball 14U Cup Cary, N.C.
Sept. 3–5 . . . . USA Baseball Labor Day Cup, Cary, N.C.
Nov. 5 . . . . Triangle Classic (12U) Cary, N.C.

BASEBALL CANADA

Mailing Address: 2212 Gladwin Cres., Suite A7, Ottawa, Ontario K1B 5N1. **Telephone:** (613) 748-5606. **Fax:** (613) 748-5767. **E-Mail Address:** info@baseball.ca. **Website:** www.baseball.ca.
Director General: Jim Baba. **Head Coach/Director, National Teams:** Greg Hamilton. **Manager, Baseball Operations:** Andre Lachance. **Program Coordinator:** Kelsey McIntosh. **Manager, Media/Public Relations:** Andre Cormier. **Administrative Coordinator:** Denise Thomas.

NATIONAL BASEBALL CONGRESS

Mailing Address: 300 S. Sycamore, Wichita, KS 67213. **Telephone:** (316) 264-6887. **Fax:** (316) 264-2129. **Website:** www.nbcbaseball.com.
Year Founded: 1931.
General Manager: Josh Robertson. **Tournament Director:** Jerry Taylor.

ATHLETES IN ACTION

Mailing Address: 651 Taylor Dr., Xenia, OH 45385. **Telephone:** (937) 352-1000. **Fax:** (937) 352-1245. **E-Mail Address:** baseball@athletesinaction.org. **Website:** www.aiabaseball.org.
Director, AIA Baseball: Jason Lester. **U.S. Teams Director:** Chris Beck. **International Teams Director:** John McLaughlin. **General Manager, Great Lakes:** John Henschen. **Athletic Trainer:** Natalie McLaughlin.

SUMMER COLLEGE LEAGUES

NATIONAL ALLIANCE OF COLLEGE SUMMER BASEBALL

Telephone: (508) 404-7403. **E-Mail Address:** pgalop@comcast.net. **Website:** www.nacsb.org
Executive Director: Jeff Carter (Southern Collegiate Baseball League). **Assistant Executive Directors:** Kim Lance (Great Lakes Summer Collegiate League), David Biery (Valley Baseball League). **Treasurer:** Jim Phillips (Valley Baseball League). **Director, Public Relations/Secretary:** Sara Whiting (Florida Collegiate Summer League). **Director, Publications:** Todd Thompson (Valley Baseball League). **Compliance Officer:** Dave Chamberlain (New York Collegiate Baseball League).
Member Leagues: Atlantic Collegiate Baseball League, Cal Ripken Collegiate Summer League, Cape Cod Baseball League, Florida Collegiate Summer League, Great Lakes Summer Collegiate League, New York Collegiate Baseball League, Southern Collegiate Baseball League, Valley Baseball League.

ALASKA BASEBALL LEAGUE

Mailing Address: 207 East Northern Lights Blvd, #125, Anchorage, AK 99503. **Telephone:** (907) 745-6401. **Fax:** (907) 746-5068. **E-Mail Address:** gmminers@gci.net.
Year Founded: 1974 (reunited, 1998)
President: Jon Dyson (Anchorage Glacier Pilots). **VP, Scheduling:** Don Dennis (Fairbanks Alaska Goldpanners). **VP, Marketing:** Pete Christopher (Mat-Su Miners). **VP, Umpiring:** Shawn Maltby (Peninsula Oilers). **VP, Secretary:** Dennis Mattingly (Anchorage Bucs). **VP, Rules and Membership:** Chris Beck (Athletes In Action). **League Spokesperson:** Mike Baxter. **League Stats:** Dick Lobdell.
Regular Season: 35 league games and approximately 5 non-league games. **2011 Opening Date:** June 7.

Closing Date: August 3
Playoff Format: League champion and second-place finisher qualify for National Baseball Congress World Series.
Roster Limit: 26 plus exemption for Alaska residents. **Player Eligibility:** Open except drafted seniors.

ANCHORAGE BUCS

Mailing Address: PO Box 240061, Anchorage, AK 99524-0061. **Telephone:** (907) 561-2827. **Fax:** (907) 561-2920. **E-Mail Address:** admin@anchoragebucs.com. **Website:** www.anchoragebucs.com. **General Manager:** Dennis Mattingly. **Head Coach:** Tony Cappuccilli (Irvine Valley CC).

ANCHORAGE GLACIER PILOTS

Mailing Address: 207 East Northern Lights Blvd #125, Anchorage, AK 99503. **Telephone:** (907) 274-3627. **Fax:** (907) 274-3628. **E-Mail Address:** gpilots@alaska.net. **Website:** www.glacierpilots.com. **General Manager:** Jon Dyson. **Head Coach:** Yogi Cox (North Cedar HS, Iowa).

ATHLETES IN ACTION

Mailing Address: 651 Taylor Dr, Xenia, OH 45385. **Telephone:** (937) 352-1237. **Fax:** (937) 352-1245. **E-Mail Address:** chris.beck@athletesinaction.org. **Website:** www.aiabaseball.org. **General Manager/Head Coach:** Chris Beck.

FAIRBANKS ALASKA GOLDPANNERS

Mailing Address: PO Box 71154, Fairbanks, AK 99707. **Telephone:** (907) 451-0095, (619) 561-4581. **Fax:** (907) 456-6429, (619) 561-4581. **E-Mail Address:** addennis@cox.net. **Website:** www.goldpanners.com. **General Manager:** Don Dennis. **Assistant GM:** Todd Dennis. **Head Coach:** Jim Dietz.

MAT-SU MINERS

Mailing Address: PO Box 2690, Palmer, AK 99645-2690. **Telephone:** (907) 746-4914; (907) 745-6401. **Fax:** (907) 746-5068. **E-Mail Address:** generalmanager@matsuminers.org. **Website:** www.matsuminers.org. **General Manager:** Pete Christopher. **Assistant GM:** Bob Plumley. **Head Coach:** Brian Yocke (Archbishop Mitty HS, San Jose)

PENINSULA OILERS

Mailing Address: 601 S Main St, Kenai, AK 99611. **Telephone:** (907) 283-7133. **Fax:** (907) 283-3390. **E-Mail Address:** shawn@oilersbaseball.com. **Website:** www.oilersbaseball.com. **General Manager:** Shawn Maltby. **Head Coach:** Dennis Machado (Cal State Bakersfield).

ATLANTIC COLLEGIATE BASEBALL LEAGUE

Mailing Address: 1760 Joanne Drive, Quakertown, PA 18951. **Telephone:** (215) 536-5777. **Fax:** (215) 536-5177. **E-Mail:** tbonekemper@verizon.net. **Website:** www.acbl-online.com.

Year Founded: 1967.

Commissioner: Ralph Addonizio. **President/Acting Secretary:** Tom Bonekemper. **Vice President:** Doug Cinella. **Treasurer:** Bob Hoffman.

Division Structure: Wolff—Jersey, Lehigh Valley, North Jersey, Quakertown. Kaiser—Long Island, New York, Staten Island, Torrington. Hamptons—North Fork, Riverhead, Sag Harbor, Southampton, Westhampton.

Regular Season: 40 games. **2011 Opening Date:** June 1. **Closing Date:** August 8.

Roster Limit: 25 (college-eligible players only).

JERSEY PILOTS

Mailing Address: 401 Timber Dr, Berkeley Heights, NJ 07922. **Telephone:** (908) 464-8042. **E-Mail Address:** bensmookler@aol.com. **President/General Manager:** Ben Smookler. **Field Manager:** Evan Davis.

LEHIGH VALLEY CATZ

Mailing Address: 103 Logan Dr, Easton, PA 18045. **Telephone:** (610) 533-9349. **E-Mail Address:** valleycatz@hotmail.com. **Website:** www.lvcatz.com. **General Manager:** Pat O'Connell. **Field Manager:** Dennis Morgan.

LONG ISLAND COLLEGIANS

Mailing Address: 825 East Gate Blvd, Suite 101, Garden City, NY 11530. **E-Mail Address:** philpursino@gmail.com. **Website:** www.licollegians.com. **General Manager/VP:** Butch Caulfield. **Field Manager:** Chris Rojas.

NEW YORK ROBINS

Website: www.robinsbaseball.com. **General Manager/Field Manager:** Keith Kenny.

NORTH FORK OSPREYS

Operated by: Hamptons Collegiate Baseball. **Telephone:** (631) 680-7870. **Website:** www.hamptonsbaseball.org. **General Manager:** Joe Finora. **Field Manager:** Shawn Epidendio.

NORTH JERSEY EAGLES

Mailing Address: 107 Pleasant Avenue, Upper Saddle River, NJ 07458. **General Manager:** Doug Cinnella. **Field Manager:** Jorge Hernandez.

QUAKERTOWN BLAZERS

Telephone: (215) 536-5777. **E-Mail Address:** batpower44@hotmail.com. **Website:** www.quakertownblazers.com. **General Manager:** Denny Robison. **Field Manager:** Lee Saverio.

RIVERHEAD TOMCATS

Operated by: Hamptons Collegiate Baseball. **Website:** www.hamptonsbaseball.org. **General Manager:** Tony Sammartano. **Field Manager:** Randy Cadin.

SAG HARBOR WHALERS

Operated by: Hamptons Collegiate Baseball. **Website:** www.hamptonsbaseball.org. **General Manager:** Sandi Kruel. **Head Coach:** Jim Buckley.

STATEN ISLAND TIDE

Website: www.statenislandtide.com. **General Manager/Field Manager:** Tommy Weber.

SOUTHAMPTON BREAKERS

Operated by: Hamptons Collegiate Baseball. **Website:** www.hamptonsbaseball.org. **General Managers:** John Venturella, Skip Norsic. **Field Manager:** Rob Cafiero.

TORRINGTON TITANS

Mailing Address: 167 Cherry St, Suite 109, Milford, CT 06460. **E-Mail Address:** info@ourbaseballhaven.com. **Website:** www.torringtontitans.com. **General Manager:** Cheryl Wheeler. **Field Manager:** Gregg Hunt.

WESTHAMPTON AVIATORS

Operated by: Hamptons Collegiate Baseball. **Telephone:** (631) 466-4393. **Website:** www.hamptonsbaseball.org. **General Manager:** Henry Bramwell. **Field Manager:** Jeff Quiros.

CALIFORNIA COLLEGIATE LEAGUE

Mailing Address: 806 W Pedregosa St, Santa Barbara, CA 93101. **Telephone:** (805) 680-1047. **Fax:** (805) 684-8596. **Email Address:** burns@calsummerball.com. **Website:** www.calsummerball.com.

Year Founded: 1993.

President: Pat Burns.

Member Clubs: Conejo Oaks, Glendale Angelenos, MLB Academy Barons, Orange City Pioneers, San Luis Obispo Blues, San Luis Obispo Rattlers, Santa Barbara Foresters, Team Vegas Baseball Club.

Regular Season: 42 games. **2011 Opening Date:** June 3. **Closing Date:** July 31. **Playoff Format:** None.

Roster Limit: 33.

CAL RIPKEN COLLEGIATE LEAGUE

Address: PO Box 22471, Baltimore, MD 21203. **Telephone:** (410) 746-1829. **E-Mail:** info@calripkenleague.org. **Website:** www.ripkensrcollegebaseball.org.

Year Founded: 2005.

Commissioner: Robert Douglas. **Deputy Commissioner:** Jerry Wargo. **Executive Director:** Alex Thompson.

Regular Season: 42 games. **2011 Opening Date:** June 3. **Closing Date:** July 24. **All-Star Game:** Mid-Atlantic Classic, July 11 vs Valley League at Harrisonburg, Va; in-house game, July 19 at Bethesda, Md. **Playoff Format:** Four-team, double-elimination tournament, July 27-31.

Roster Limit: 30 (college-eligible players 22 and under).

ALEXANDRIA ACES

Address: 600 14th Street NW, Suite 400, Washington, DC 20005. **Telephone:** (202) 265-0200. **E-Mail:** ddinan@ralaw.com. **Website:** www.alexandriaaces.org. **President/**

General Manager: Donald Dinan. Head Coach: Corey Haines.

BALTIMORE REDBIRDS

Address: 2208 Pine Hill Farms Lane, Cockeysville, MD 21030. Telephone: (410) 802-2220. Fax: (410) 785-6138. E-Mail: johntcarey@hotmail.com. Website: baltimoreredbirds.pointstreaksites.com. President: John Carey. Head Coach: Dave Funk.

BETHESDA BIG TRAIN

Address: PO Box 30306, Bethesda, MD 20824. Telephone: (301) 983-1006. Fax: (301) 652-0691. E-Mail: faninfo@bigtrain.org. Website: www.bigtrain.org. General Manager: Jordan Henry. Head Coach: Sal Colangelo.

HERNDON BRAVES

Address: 1305 Kelly Court, Herndon, VA 20170-2605. Telephone: (703) 973-4444. Fax: (703) 783-1319. E-Mail: herndonbraves@cox.net. Website: www.herndonbraves. com. General Manager: Chris Smith. Trainer: Lisa Lombardozzi. Head Coach: Unavailable.

ROCKVILLE EXPRESS

Address: PO Box 10188, Rockville, MD 20849. Telephone: (301) 928-6608. E-Mail: info@rockvilleexpress.org. Website: www.rockvilleexpress.org. President/GM: Jim Kazunas. Vice President: Brad Botwin. Head Coach: Angelo Nicolosi.

SILVER SPRING-TAKOMA T-BOLTS

Address: 906 Glaizewood Court, Takoma Park, MD 20912. Telephone: (301) 270-0794. E-Mail: tboltsbaseball@gmail.com. Website: www.tbolts.org. General Manager: David Stinson. Head Coach: Jason Walck.

SOUTHERN MARYLAND NATIONALS

Address: 2243 Garrity Rd, Saint Leonard, MD 20685. Telephone: (301) 751-6299. E-Mail: winegard@erols.com. President/Head Coach: Chuck Winegardner. General Manager: Don Herbert.

VIENNA RIVER DOGS

Address: 12703 Hitchcock Ct, Reston, VA 201919. Telephone: (703) 904-0548. Fax: (703) 904-1723. E--Mail Address: coach @viennariverdogs.org. Website: www. viennariverdogs.org. President/General Manager/Head Coach: Bruce Hall.

YOUSE'S ORIOLES

Address: 3 Oyster Court, Baltimore, MD 21219. Telephone: (410) 477-3764. E-Mail: tnt017@comcast.net. Website: www.youseorioles.org. General Manager/Head Coach: Tim Norris.

CAPE COD LEAGUE

Mailing Address: PO Box 266, Harwich Port, MA 02646. Telephone: (508) 432-6909. E-Mail: info@capecodbaseball.org. Website: www.capecodbaseball.org.

Year Founded: 1885

Commissioner: Paul Galop. President: Judy Walden Scarafile. Senior Vice President: Jim Higgins. Vice Presidents: Peter Ford, Chuck Sturtevant. Deputy Commissioner: Richard Sullivan. Deputy Commissioner/Umpire in Chief: Sol Yas. Secretary: Kim Wolfe. Director, Memorabilia: Dan Dunn. Director, Public Relations/Broadcasting: John Garner Jr. Director, Communications: Jim McGonigle. Director, Publications: Lou Barnicle. Publications

Editor/Senior Writer, Website: Rob Duca.

Division Structure: East—Brewster, Chatham, Harwich, Orleans, Yarmouth-Dennis. West—Bourne, Cotuit, Falmouth, Hyannis, Wareham.

Regular Season: 44 games

2011 Opening Date: June 10. Closing Date: August 15. All-Star Game: July 29. Playoff Format: Top four teams in each division qualify. Three rounds of best-of-three series.

Roster Limit: 25 (college-eligible players only).

BOURNE BRAVES

Mailing Address: PO Box 895, Monument Beach, MA 02553. Telephone: (508) 345-1013. E-Mail Address: bournebravesgm@hotmail.com. Website: www.bournebraves. org. President: Thomas Fink. General Manager: Michael Carrier. Head Coach: Harvey Shapiro.

BREWSTER WHITECAPS

Mailing Address: PO Box 2349, Brewster, MA 02631. Telephone: (508) 896-8500, ext. 147. Fax: (508) 896-9845. E-Mail Address: PABlatz@comcast.net. Website: www. brewsterwhitecaps.com. President: Peter Blatz. General Manager: Ned Monthie. Head Coach: Tom Myers (UC Santa Barbara).

CHATHAM ANGLERS

Mailing Address: PO Box 428, Chatham, MA 02633. Telephone: (508) 241-8382. Fax: (508) 430-8382. Website: www.chathamas.com. President: Doug Grattan. General Manager: Charlie Thoms. Head Coach: John Schiffner.

COTUIT KETTLEERS

Mailing Address: PO Box 411, Cotuit, MA 02635. Telephone: (508) 428-3358. Fax: (508) 420-5584. E-Mail Address: info@kettleers.org. Website: www.kettleers.org. President: Paul Logan. General Manager: Bruce Murphy. Head Coach: Mike Roberts.

FALMOUTH COMMODORES

Mailing Address: PO Box 808 Falmouth, MA 02541. Telephone: (508) 472-7922. Fax: (508) 862-6011. Website: www.falcommodores.org. President: Christine Clark. General Manager: Bob Clark. Head Coach: Jeff Trundy.

HARWICH MARINERS

Mailing Address: PO Box 201, Harwich Port, MA 02646. Telephone: (508) 432-2000. Fax: (508) 432-5357. E-Mail Address: mehendy@comcast.net. Website: www.harwichmariners.org. President: Mary Henderson. General Manager: Ben Layton. Head Coach: Steve Englert (Boston College).

HYANNIS HARBOR HAWKS

Mailing Address: PO Box 852, Hyannis, MA 02601. Telephone: (508) 364-3164. Fax: (508) 534-1270. E-Mail Address: bbussiere@harborhawks.org. Website: www. harborhawks.org. President: Tino DiGiovanni. General Manager: Bill Bussiere. Head Coach: Chad Gassman.

ORLEANS FIREBIRDS

Mailing Address: PO Box 504, Orleans, MA 02653. Telephone: (508) 255-0793. Fax: (508) 255-2237. Website: www.orleansfirebirds.com. President: Don LeSieur. General Manager: Sue Horton. Head Coach: Kelly Nicholson.

WAREHAM GATEMEN

Mailing Address: PO Box 287, Wareham, MA 02571. Telephone: (508) 748-0287. Fax: (508) 880-2602. E-Mail

Address: sheri.gay4gatemen@comcast.net. **Website:** www.gatemen.org. **President/General Manager:** Thomas Gay. **Head Coach:** Cooper Farris.

YARMOUTH-DENNIS RED SOX

Mailing Address: PO Box 814, South Yarmouth, MA 02664. **Telephone:** (508) 394-9387. **Fax:** (508) 398-2239. **E-Mail Address:** jimmartin321@yahoo.com. **Website:** www.ydredsox.org. **President:** Steve Faucher. **General Manager:** Jim Martin. **Head Coach:** Scott Pickler (Cypress, Calif., CC).

COASTAL PLAIN LEAGUE

Mailing Address: 125 Quantum Street, Holly Springs, NC 27540. **Telephone:** (919) 852-1960. **Fax:** (919) 516-0852. **Email Address:** justins@coastalplain.com. **Website:** www.coastalplain.com.
Year Founded: 1997.
Chairman/CEO: Jerry Petitt. **President/Commissioner:** Pete Bock. **Assistant Commissioner:** Justin Sellers. **Director, On-Field Operations:** Jeff Bock.
Division Structure: North—Edenton, Outer Banks, Peninsula, Petersburg, Wilson. South—Columbia, Fayetteville, Florence, Morehead City, Wilmington. West—Asheboro, Forest City, Gastonia, Martinsville, Thomasville.
Regular Season: 56 games (split schedule). **2011 Opening Date:** May 31. **Closing Date:** August 14. **All-Star Game:** July 18. **Playoff Format:** Three rounds, best of three in each round.
Roster Limit: 27 (college-eligible players only).

ASHEBORO COPPERHEADS

Mailing Address: PO Box 4006, Asheboro, NC 27204. **Telephone:** (336) 460-7018. **Fax:** (336) 629-2651. **E-Mail Address:** info@teamcopperhead.com. **Website:** www.teamcopperhead.com. **Owners:** Ronnie Pugh, Steve Pugh, Doug Pugh, Mike Pugh. **General Manager:** David Camp. **Head Coach:** Donnie Wilson (College of the Sequoias, Calif.).

COLUMBIA BLOWFISH

Mailing Address: PO Box 1328, Columbia, SC 29202. **Telephone:** (803) 254-3474. **Fax:** (803) 254-4482. **E-Mail Address:** info@blowfishbaseball.com. **Website:** www.blowfishbaseball.com. **Owner:** HWS Baseball V (Michael Savit, Bill Shanahan). **General Manager:** Skip Anderson. **Head Coach:** Lee Gronkiewicz.

EDENTON STEAMERS

Mailing Address: PO Box 86, Edenton, NC 27932. **Telephone:** (252) 482-4080. **Fax:** (252) 482-1717. **E-Mail Address:** edentonsteamers@hotmail.com. **Website:** www.edentonsteamers.com. **Owner:** Edenton Steamers Inc. **President/General Manager:** Katy Ebersole. **Head Coach:** Dirk Kinney.

FAYETTEVILLE SWAMPDOGS

Mailing Address: PO Box 64691, Fayetteville, NC 28306. **Telephone:** (910) 426-5900. **Fax:** (910) 426-3544. **E-Mail Address:** info@fayettevilleswampdogs.com. **Website:** www.goswampdogs.com. **Owners:** Lew Handelsman, Darrell Handelsman. **Head Coach/General Manager/Director, Operations:** Darrell Handelsman.

FLORENCE REDWOLVES

Mailing Address: PO Box 809, Florence, SC 29503. **Telephone:** (843) 629-0700. **Fax:** (843) 629-0703. **E-Mail Address:** jamie@florenceredwolves.com. **Website:** www.florenceredwolves.com. **Owners:** Kevin Barth, Donna Barth. **General Manager:** Jamie Young. **Head Coach:**

Blake Newsome (UNC Pembroke).

FOREST CITY OWLS

Mailing Address: PO Box 1062, Forest City, NC 28043. **Telephone:** (828) 245-0000. **Fax:** (828) 245-6666. **E-Mail Address:** forestcitybaseball@yahoo.com. **Website:** www.forestcitybaseball.com. **Owner/President:** Ken Silver. **Managing Partner:** Jesse Cole. **General Manager:** Jeremy Boler. **Head Coach:** Matt Hayes (Limestone, S.C.).

GASTONIA GRIZZLIES

Mailing Address: PO Box 177, Gastonia, NC 28053. **Telephone:** (704) 866-8622. **Fax:** (704) 864-6122. **E-Mail Address:** jesse@gastoniagrizzlies.com. **Website:** www.gastoniagrizzlies.com. **President:** Ken Silver. **Managing Partner/General Manager:** Jesse Cole. **Head Coach:** Jason Plourde (Belmont Abbey, N.C.).

MARTINSVILLE MUSTANGS

Mailing Address: PO Box 1112, Martinsville, VA 24114. **Telephone:** (276) 403-5250. **Fax:** (276) 403-5387. **E-Mail Address:** jtaipalus@ci.martinsville.va.us. **Website:** www.martinsvillemustangs.com. **Owner:** City of Martinsville. **General Manager:** Jim Taipalus. **Head Coach:** Jason Sherrer (Mount Olive, N.C.).

MOREHEAD CITY MARLINS

Mailing Address: 1921 Oglesby Road, Morehead City, NC 28557. **Telephone:** (252) 269-9767. **Fax:** (252) 727-9402. **E-Mail Address:** chris@mhcmarlins.com. **Website:** www.mhcmarlins.com. **President:** Sabrina Bengel. **Vice President:** Buddy Bengel. **General Manager:** Chris Marmo. **Head Coach:** Jay Bergman.

OUTER BANKS DAREDEVILS

Mailing Address: PO Box 7596, Kill Devil Hills, NC 27948. **Telephone:** (252) 441-0600. **Fax:** (252) 441-0606. **E-Mail Address:** owen@obxdaredevils.com. **Website:** www.obxdaredevils.com. **Owners:** Marcus Felton, Tim Beacham, Doug Cook. **General Manager:** Owen Hassell. **Head Coach:** Andy Schatzley (Emporia State, Kan.).

PENINSULA PILOTS

Mailing Address: PO Box 7376, Hampton, VA 23666. **Telephone:** (757) 245-2222. **Fax:** (757) 245-8030. **E-Mail Address:** jeffscott@peninsulapilots.com. **Website:** www.peninsulapilots.com. **Owner:** Henry Morgan. **General Manager:** Jeffrey Scott. **Head Coach/Vice President:** Hank Morgan.

PETERSBURG GENERALS

Mailing Address: 1981 Midway Ave, Petersburg, VA 23803. **Telephone:** (804) 722-0141. **Fax:** (804) 733-7370. **E-Mail Address:** petggenerals@earthlink.net. **Website:** www.generals.petersburgsports.com. **Owner:** City of Petersburg. **General Manager:** Kevin Booker. **Head Coach:** Bob Smith.

THOMASVILLE HI-TOMS

Mailing Address: PO Box 3035, Thomasville, NC 27361. **Telephone:** (336) 472-8667. **Fax:** (336) 472-7198. **E-Mail Address:** info@hitoms.com. **Website:** www.hitoms.com. **Owner:** Richard Holland. **President:** Greg Suire. **General Manager:** Jamie Curtis. **Head Coach:** Jeff Steele (Lubbock Christian, Texas).

WILMINGTON SHARKS

Mailing Address: PO Box 15233, Wilmington, NC 28412. **Telephone:** (910) 343-5621. **Fax:** (910) 343-8932. **E-Mail Address:** info@wilmingtonsharks.com. **Website:**

www.wilmingtonsharks.com. **Owner:** Richard Holland. **President:** Greg Suire. **General Manager:** James Wolfe. **Head Coach:** Chris Youngberg (North Florida).

WILSON TOBS

Mailing Address: PO Box 633, Wilson, NC 27894. **Telephone:** (252) 291-8627. **Fax:** (252) 291-1224. **E-Mail Address:** wilsontobs@gmail.com. **Website:** www.wilsontobs.com. **Owner:** Wilson Tobs Baseball, LLC. **President:** Greg Turnage. **General Manager:** Ben Jones. **Head Coach:** Bruce Johnson (Western Carolina).

FLORIDA COLLEGIATE SUMMER LEAGUE

Mailing Address: 1778 N Park Ave, Suite 201, Maitland, FL 32751. **Telephone:** (321) 206-9174. **Fax:** (407) 628-8535. **E-Mail Address:** info@floridaleague.com. **Website:** www.floridaleague.com.
Year Founded: 2004.
CEO: Sara Whiting. **President/COO:** Rob Sitz. **Vice President:** Stefano Foggi. **Public Relations/Marketing:** Kevin Schnacke.
Regular Season: 45 games. **2011 Opening Date:** June 2. **Closing Date:** July 31. **All-Star Game:** July 12. **Playoff Format:** Four teams. First round features two best-of-three series, with winners meeting in winner-take-all championship game.
Roster Limit: 27 (college-eligible players only).

DELAND SUNS

Operated through league office. **E-Mail Address:** delandsuns@floridaleague.com. **Head Coach:** Rick Hall.

LEESBURG LIGHTNING

Mailing Address: 318 South 2nd St, Leesburg, FL 34748. **Telephone:** (352) 728-9885. **E-Mail Address:** leesburglightning@floridaleague.com. **President:** Bruce Ericson. **Head Coach:** Frank Viola.

ORLANDO MAVERICKS

Operated through league office. **E-Mail Address:** orlandomavericks@floridaleague.com. **Head Coach:** Scott Makarewicz.

SANFORD RIVER RATS

Operated through league office. **E-Mail Address:** sanfordriverrats@floridaleague.com. **Head Coach:** Steve Piercefield.

WINTER HAVEN LOGGERHEADS

Operated through league office. **E-Mail Address:** winterhavenloggerheads@floridaleague.com. **Head Coach:** Nick Vera.

WINTER PARK DIAMOND DAWGS

Operated through league office. **E-Mail Address:** winterparkdiamonddawgs@floridaleague.com. **Head Coach:** Mark Leavitt.

FUTURES COLLEGIATE LEAGUE OF NEW ENGLAND

Mailing Address: 46 Chestnut Hill Rd, Chelmsford, MA 01824. **Telephone:** (617) 593-2112. **E-Mail Address:** futuresleague@yahoo.com. **Website:** www.thefuturesleague.com.
Year Founded: 2010.
Commissioner: Chris Hall.
Member Clubs: Martha's Vineyard Sharks, Nashua

Collegiate Baseball, Seacoast Mavericks, TBA.
Regular Season: 44 games. **2011 Opening Date:** June 9. **Closing Date:** Aug. **1. Playoff Format:** Two teams with best overall records meet in best-of-three championship series at team with better record.
Roster Limit: 26. Half must be from New England or play collegiately at a New England college.

GREAT LAKES SUMMER COLLEGIATE LEAGUE

Mailing Address: 133 W Winter St, Delaware, OH 43015. **Telephone:** (740) 368-3527. **Fax:** (740) 368-3999. **E-Mail Address:** kalance@owu.edu. **Website:** www.greatlakesleague.org.
Year Founded: 1986.
President/Commissioner: Kim Lance.
Regular Season: 42 games. **2011 Opening Date:** June 10. **Closing Date:** July 31. **Playoff Format:** Top six teams meet in playoff.
Roster Limit: 30 (college-eligible players only).

CINCINNATI STEAM

Mailing Address: 2745 Anderson Ferry Rd, Cincinnati, OH 45238. **Telephone:** (513) 922-4272. **Website:** www.cincinnatisteam.com. **General Manager:** Max McLeary. **Head Coach:** Joe Regruth.

GRAND LAKE MARINERS

Mailing Address: 1460 James Drive, Celina, OH 45822. **Telephone:** (419) 586-3187. **Website:** www.grandlakemariners.com. **General Manager:** Betty Feliciano. **Head Coach:** Josh Newman.

HAMILTON JOES

Mailing Address: 6218 Greens Way, Hamilton, OH 45011. **E-mail address:** darrelgrissom@fuse.net. **General Manager:** Mike Brennan. **Head Coach:** Darrel Grissom.

LAKE ERIE MONARCHS

Mailing Address: 2220 West Sigler Road, Carleton, MI 48117. **Telephone:** (734) 626-1166. **Website:** www.lakeeriemonarchs.com. **General Manager:** Jim DeSana. **Head Coach:** Mike Montgomery.

LEXINGTON HUSTLERS

Mailing Address: 1999 Richmond Rd, Suite 300, Lexington, KY 40502. **Telephone:** (859) 335-0928. **General Manager:** Adam Revelette. **Head Coach:** Bobby Wright.

LICKING COUNTY SETTLERS

Mailing Address: 958 Camden Dr, Newark, OH 43055. **Telephone:** (740) 344-1063. **Website:** www.settlersbaseball.com. **General Manager:** Sean West. **Head Coach:** Brian Meyer

LIMA LOCOS

Mailing Address: 3588 South Conant Rd, Spencerville, OH 45887. **Telephone:** (419) 647-5242. **Website:** www.limalocos.com. **General Manager:** Steve Meyer. **Head Coach:** Gene Stechshulte.

SOUTHERN OHIO COPPERHEADS

Mailing Address: PO Box 442, Athens, OH 45701. **Telephone:** (740) 541-9284. **Website:** www.copperheadsbaseball.com. **General Manager:** David Palmer. **Head Coach:** Mike Florak.

STARK COUNTY TERRIERS

Mailing Address: 1019 35th St Northwest, Canton, OH,

44709. **Telephone:** (330) 492-9220. **Website:** www.ter-riersbaseballclub.com. **General Manager:** Greg Trbovich. **Head Coach:** Trent McIlvain.

XENIA SCOUTS

Mailing Address: 651 Taylor Dr, Xenia, OH 45385. **Telephone:** (937) 352-1239. **E-Mail Address:** john.henschen@athletesinaction.org Website: www.aiabaseball.org. **General Manager:** John Henschen. **Head Coach:** Josh Hulin.

JAYHAWK LEAGUE

Mailing Address: 865 Fabrique, Wichita, KS 67218
Telephone: (316) 942-6333
Fax: (316) 942-2009
Website: www.jayhawkbaseballleague.org
Year Founded: 1976
Commissioner: Bob Considine
President: J.D. Schneider
Vice President: Frank Leo
Public Relations/Statistician: Gary Karr
Secretary: Cheryl Kastner
Regular Season: 32 games
2011 Opening Date:
Closing Date:
Playoff Format: Top two teams qualify for National Baseball Congress World Series
Roster Limit: 30 to begin season; 28 at midseason.

DERBY TWINS

Mailing Address: 1245 N. Pine Grove, Wichita, KS 67212. **Telephone:** (316) 992-3623. **Fax:** 316-667-2286. **E-mail:** derbytwins@earthlink.net. **Website:** www.derbytwins.com. **General Manager:** Jeff Wells. **Head Coach:** Jason Santangelo.

DODGE CITY A'S

Mailing Address: 2914 Center, Dodge City, KS 67801. **Telephone:** 620-225-0238. **E-mail:** no1teammom@hotmail.com. **General Manager:** Phil Stevenson. **Head Coach:** Jeremy Irlbeck.

EL DORADO BRONCOS

Mailing Address: 865 Fabrique, Wichita, KS 67218. **Telephone:** (316) 687-2309. **Fax:** (316) 942-2009. **Website:** www.eldoradobroncos.org. **General Manager:** Doug Bell. **Head Coach:** Andy Schatzley.

HAYS LARKS

Mailing Address: 2715 Walnut, Hays, KS 67601. **Telephone:** (785) 259-1430. **Fax:** (630) 848-2236. **E-Mail Address:** cbieber@sbcglobal.net. **General Manager:** Frank Leo. **Head Coach:** Frank Leo.

LIBERAL BEEJAYS

Mailing Address: PO Box 793, Liberal, KS 67901. **Telephone:** (620) 629-1162. **Fax:** (620) 624-1906. **General Manager:** Bob Carlisle. **Head Coach:** John Martin.

HAYSVILLE HEAT

Mailing Address: 417 Apple Ct., Haysville, KS 67060. **Telephone:** (316) 239-1221. **General Manager:** Dick "Chief" Twyman.

M.I.N.K. LEAGUE

(Missouri, Iowa, Nebraska, Kansas)
Mailing Address: PO Box 1155, Chillicothe, MO 64601. **Telephone:** (660) 646-2165. **Fax:** (660) 646-6933. **Email Address:** lfechtig@midwestglove.com. **Website:** www.

minkleaguebaseball.com.
Year Founded: 1995.
Commissioner: Bob Steinkamp. **President:** Liz Fechtig. **Vice President:** Jeff Post. **Secretary:** Edwina Rains.
Regular Season: 48 games. **2011 Opening Date:** June 3. **Closing Date:** July 19. **Playoff Format:** Top team qualifies for National Baseball Congress World Series.
Roster Limit: 28.

CHILLICOTHE MUDCATS

Mailing Address: 426 E. Jackson, Chillicothe, MO 64601. **Telephone:** (660) 646-2165. **Fax:** (660) 646-6933. **E-Mail Address:** lfechtig@midwestglove.com. **Website:** www.chillicothemudcats.com. **General Manager:** Liz Fechtig. **Head Coach:** Kirk Kelley.

CLARINDA A'S

Mailing Address: 225 East Lincoln, Clarinda, IA 51632. **Telephone:** (712) 542-4272. **E-Mail Address:** m.everly@mchsi.com. **Website:** www.clarindaiowa-as-baseball.org. **General Manager:** Merle Eberly. **Head Coach:** Ryan Eberly.

JOPLIN OUTLAWS

Mailing Address: 5860 North Pearl, Joplin, MO 64801. **Telephone:** (417) 825-4218. **E-Mail Address:** merains@mchsi.com. **Website:** www.joplinoutlaws.com. **President/General Manager:** Mark Rains. **Head Coach:** Brad Smith.

NEVADA GRIFFONS

Mailing Address: PO Box 601, Nevada, MO 64772. **Telephone:** (417) 667-6159. **E-Mail Address:** jpost@morrisonpost.com. **Website:** www.nevadagriffons.org. **President:** Pedro Claudio. **General Manager/Stats:** Jeff Post. **Head Coach:** Ryan Mansfield.

OMAHA DIAMOND SPIRIT

Mailing Address: 4618 N 135th Ave, Omaha, NE 68164. **Telephone:** (402) 679-0206. **E-Mail Address:** arkaosky@cox.net. **Website:** www.scorebook.com/spirit2006. **General Manager/Head Coach:** Arden Rakosky.

OZARK GENERALS

Mailing Address: 1336 W Farm Road 182, Springfield, MO 65810. **Telephone:** (417) 832-8830. **Fax:** (417) 877-4625. **E-Mail Address:** rda160@yahoo.com. **Website:** www.generalsbaseballclub.com. **General Manager/Head Coach:** Rusty Aton.

ST. JOSEPH MUSTANGS

Mailing Address: 2600 SW Parkway, St. Joseph, MO 64503. **Telephone:** (816) 279-7856. **Fax:** (816) 749-4082. **E-Mail Address:** rmuntean717@gmail.com. **Website:** www.stjoemustangs.com. **President:** Dan Gerson. **General Manager:** Rick Muntean. **Manager/Director, Player Personnel:** Matt Johnson.

SEDALIA BOMBERS

Mailing Address: 2201 S Grand, Sedalia, MO 65301. **Telephone:** (660) 287-4722. **E-Mail Address:** jkindle@knobnoster.k12.mo.us. **Website:** www.sedaliabombers.com. **President/General Manager/Head Coach:** Jud Kindle. **Vice President:** Ross Dey.

MOUNTAIN COLLEGIATE LEAGUE

E-Mail Address: info@mcbl.net. **Website:** www.mcbl.net. **Year Founded:** 2005.
Directors: Kurt Colicchio, Ron Kailey, Gil Carbajal, Nicko Kleppinger. **Director of Umpires:** Gary Weibert.

Regular Season: 42 games. **2011 Opening Date:** June 1. **Closing Date:** July 29. **Playoff Format:** Second- and third-place teams meet in one-game playoff; winner advances to best-of-three championship series against first-place team. **All-Star Game:** Date TBD in Greeley, Colo.

Roster limit: 31 total, 25 active (college-eligible players only).

CHEYENNE GRIZZLIES

Telephone: (307) 631-7337. **E-Mail Address:** rkaide@aol.com. **Website:** www.cheyennegrizzlies.com. **Owner/General Manager:** Ron Kailey. **Head Coach:** Aaron Holley (University of Redlands, Calif.).

FORT COLLINS FOXES

Telephone: (970) 225-9564. **E-Mail Address:** info@fortcollinsfoxes.com. **Website:** www.fortcollinsfoxes.com. **Owner/General Manager:** Kurt Colicchio. **Head Coach:** Brad Averitte.

GREELEY GRAYS

Telephone: (303) 870-2523. **E-Mail Address:** rklesh@earthlink.net. **Website:** www.greeleygrays.com. **Owner:** Gil Carbajal. **General Manager:** Chris Waters. **Head Coach:** John Barnes.

LARAMIE COLTS

Telephone: (307) 760-0544. **E-Mail Address:** laramiecolts@msn.com. **Website:** www.laramiecolts.com. **Owners:** Kent & Nicko Kleppinger. **Head Coach:** Marty Berson.

NEW ENGLAND COLLEGIATE LEAGUE

Mailing Address: 37 Grammar School Dr, Danbury, CT 06811. **Telephone:** (203) 241-9392. **Fax:** (203) 643-2230. **Website:** www.necbl.com.

Year founded: 1993.

Commissioner: Mario Tiani. **Deputy Commissioner:** Everts "Eph" Mangan. **President:** John DeRosa. **Executive President:** Dick Murray. **Treasurer:** Brigid Schaffer. **Secretary:** Richard Rossiter.

Regular Season: 42 games. **2011 Opening Date:** June 10. **Closing Date:** Aug. 1. **All-Star Game:** July 27 at North Shore. **Playoff Format:** Playoffs begin Aug. 3. Top four teams in each division meet in best-of-three quarterfinals; winners meet in best-of-three divisional championship. Winners meet in best-of-three final for league championship.

Roster Limit: 28 (college-eligible players only).

DANBURY WESTERNERS

Mailing Address: 5 Old Hayrake Rd, Danbury, CT 06811. **Telephone:** (203) 797-0897. **Fax:** (203) 792-6177. **E-Mail Address:** westerners1@aol.com. **Website:** www.danburywesterners.com. **President:** Paul Schaffer. **General Manager:** Terry Whalen. **Field Manager:** Jamie Shevchik.

HOLYOKE BLUE SOX

Mailing Address: 19 Cranberry Lane, Dedham, MA 01026. **Telephone:** (413) 652-9014. **E-Mail Address:** barry@wadsworthsports.net. **Website:** www.holyokesox.com. **President:** John Ferrara. **Chairman/CEO:** Karen Wadsworth Rella. **General Manager:** Kirk Fredriksson. **Chief Operating Officer:** Barry Wadsworth. **Head Coach:** Darryl Morhardt.

KEENE SWAMP BATS

Mailing Address: PO Box 160, Keene, NH 03431. **Telephone:** (603) 357-5464. **Fax:** (603) 357-5090. **Website:** www.swampbats.com. **President:** Kevin Watterson. **General Manager:** Vicki Bacon. **Field Manager:** Marty Testo.

LACONIA MUSKRATS

Mailing Address: 134 Stevens Rd, Lebanon, NH 03766. **Telephone:** (864) 380-2873. **E-Mail Address:** noah@laconiamuskrats.com. **Website:** www.laconiamuskrats.com. **General Manager:** Noah Crane. **Field Manager:** Matt Alison.

MYSTIC SCHOONERS

Mailing Address: 6 Forest Park Dr, Farmington, CT 06032. **Telephone:** (860) 558-6870. **General Manager:** Kevin Kelleher. **General Manager:** Jack O'Keefe. **Field Manager:** Ray Ricker.

NEW BEDFORD BAY SOX

Mailing Address: 85 Shady Hill Road, Newton, MCA 02461. **Telephone/Fax:** (508) 742-5180. **E-Mail Address:** accormier@nbbaysox.com. **Website:** www.nbbaysox.com. **President:** Rita M Hubner. **General Manager:** Field Manager: Unavailable.

NEWPORT GULLS

Mailing Address: PO Box 777, Newport, RI 02840. **Telephone:** (401) 845-6832. **Website:** www.newportgulls.com. **General Manager:** Chuck Paiva. **VP, Baseball Operations:** Chris Patsos. **Assistant General Manager:** Sam Glynn. **Field Manager:** Mike Coombs.

NORTH ADAMS STEEPLECATS

Mailing Address: PO Box 540, North Adams, MA 01247. **Telephone:** (413) 652-1031. **E-Mail Address:** steeplecats_gm@roadrunner.com. **Website:** www.steeplecats.com. **General Manager:** Sean McGrath.

NORTH SHORE NAVIGATORS

Mailing Address: 365 Western Ave, PO Box 8188, Lynn MA 01904. **Telephone:** (781) 595-9400. **E-Mail Address:** pdelani@nsnavs.com. **Website:** www.nsnavs.com. **President:** Tim Haley. **General Manager:** Peter Delani. **Manager:** Jeff Waldron.

OLD ORCHARD BEACH RAGINGTIDE

Mailing Address: 45C Elm Street, Franklin, MA 02038. **Telephone:** (774) 248-4595. **Fax:** (978) 251-1211. **E-Mail Address:** dayotte58@verizon.net. **Website:** www.ragingtide.com. **General Manager:** Doug Ayotte. **Field Manager:** Inaki Ormaechea..

SANFORD MAINERS

Mailing Address: PO Box 26, 4 Washington St, Sanford, ME 04073. **Telephone:** (207) 324-0010. **Fax:** (207) 324-2227. **E-Mail Address:** jwebb@nicholswebb.com. **Website:** www.sanfordmainers.com. **General Manager:** John Webb. **Field Manager:** Aaron Izaryk.

VERMONT MOUNTAINEERS

Mailing Address: PO Box 57, East Montpelier, VT 05651. **Telephone:** (802) 223-5224. **E-Mail Address:** gmvtm@comcast.net. **Website:** www.thevermontmountaineers.com. **General Manager:** Brian Gallagher. **Field Manager:** John Russo.

NEW YORK COLLEGIATE BASEBALL LEAGUE

Mailing Address: 4 Creekside Ln, Rochester, NY 14624-1059. **Telephone:** (585) 314-1122. **E-Mail Address:** slehman@nycbl.com. **Website:** www.nycbl.com.
Year founded: 1978.
President/Commissioner/Executive Director: Stan Lehman. **Vice President:** Mark Perlo. **Treasurer:** Dan Russo. **Secretary:** Paul Welker. **Director of Baseball Operations:** Jake Dennstedt. **Franchise Development:** Cal Kern.
Franchises: East—Oneonta Outlaws, Utica Brewers, Rome Thunderbolts, Sherrill Silversmiths, Syracuse Salt Cats, Syracuse Junior Chiefs. West – Geneva Red Wings, Webster Yankees, Niagara Power, Alfred Thunder, Allegany County Nitros, Hornell Dodgers.
Regular season starts: June 3. **Regular season ends:** July 26. **All-Star Game/Scout Day:** July 11 at Damaschke Field, Oneonta, New York. **Playoff Format:** Round 1 is one playoff game between the second and third place teams in each division. Round 2 is a three-game playoff between first place and the winner of Round 1 in each division. The championship is the East Division winner versus the West Division winner
Roster Limit: 30 (college-eligible players only)

NORTHWOODS LEAGUE

Office Address: 2900 4th St. SW, Rochester, MN 55902. **Telephone:** (507) 536-4579. **Fax:** (507) 536-4597. **E-Mail Address:** info@northwoodsleague.com. **Website:** www.northwoodsleague.com.
Year Founded: 1994.
President: Dick Radatz Jr. **Director of Operations:** Curt Carstensen. **Video Production Director:** Jesse Meehl. **Sports Information Director:** Patrick Reilly.
Division Structure: North—Alexandria, Brainerd, Duluth, Mankato, Rochester, St. Cloud, Thunder Bay, Willmar. South—Battle Creek, Eau Claire, Green Bay, La Crosse, Madison, Rochester, Waterloo, Wisconsin, Wisconsin Rapids.
Regular Season: 70 games (split schedule) **2011 Opening Date:** June 1. **Closing Date:** August 14. **All-Star Game:** July 18 at Wisconsin Rapids. **Playoff Format:** First-half and second-half division winners meet in best-of-three series. Winners meet in best-of-three series for league championship.
Roster Limit: 26 (college-eligible players only).

ALEXANDRIA BEETLES

Mailing Address: 1210 Broadway, Suite #100, Alexandria, MN 56308. **Telephone:** (320) 763-8151. **Fax:** (320) 763-8152. **E-Mail Address:** shawn@alexandriabeetles.com, alex@alexandriabeetles.com. **Website:** www.alexandriabeetles.com. **General Manager:** Shawn Reilly. **Assistant General Manager:** Alex Walker. **Field Manager:** Scott Chisholm (Oakland City University, Indiana).

BATTLE CREEK BOMBERS

Mailing Address: 189 Bridge Street, Battle Creek, MI 49017. **Telephone:** (269) 962-0735. **Fax:** (269) 962-0741. **Email Address:** info@battlecreekbombers.com **Website:** www.battlecreekbombers.com. **General Manager:** Brian Colopy. **Field Manager:** Donnie Scott.

BRAINERD LAKES AREA LUNKERS

Mailing Address: PO Box 431, Brainerd, MN 56401. **Telephone:** (218) 824-3474. **Fax:** (320) 255-5228. **E-Mail Address:** info@lunkersbaseball.com. **Website:** www.lunkersbaseball.com. **Owner/General Manager:** Joel Sutherland. **Assistant General Manager:** Dustin Anaas. **Field Manager:** Ryan Levendoski (Wisconsin-Stout).

DULUTH HUSKIES

Mailing Address: 207 W Superior St, Suite 206, Holiday Center Mall, Duluth, MN 55802. **Telephone:** (218) 786-9909. **Fax:** (218) 786-9001. **E-Mail Address:** huskies@duluthhuskies.com. **Website:** www.duluthhuskies.com. **Owner/President:** Bobby McCarthy. **General Manager:** Craig Smith. **Assistant General Manager:** Aaron Benson. **Field Manager:** Daniel Hersey (Central Florida CC).

EAU CLAIRE EXPRESS

Mailing Address: 108 E. Grand Ave, Eau Claire, WI 54701. **Telephone:** (715) 839-7788. **Fax:** (715) 839-7676. **E-Mail Address:** info@eauclaireexpress.com. **Website:** www.eauclaireexpress.com. **Owner:** Bill Rowlett. **General Manager:** Andy Neborak. **Director of Operations/Field Manager:** Dale Varsho.

GREEN BAY BULLFROGS

Mailing Address: 1306 Main Street, Green Bay, WI 54302. **Telephone:** (920) 497-7225. **Fax:** (920) 437-3551. **Email Address:** info@greenbaybullfrogs.com. **Website:** www.greenbaybullfrogs.com. **President:** Jeffrey L Royle. **General Manager:** Matt Bomberg. **Field Manager:** Jordan Bischel (Northwest Missouri State).

LA CROSSE LOGGERS

Mailing Address: 1223 Caledonia St, La Crosse, WI 54603. **Telephone:** (608) 796-9553. **Fax:** (608) 796-9032. **E-Mail Address:** info@lacrosseloggers.com. **Website:** www.lacrosseloggers.com. **Owner:** Dan Kapanke. **General Manager:** Chris Goodell. **Assistant General Manager:** Ben Kapanke. **Field Manager:** Andy McKay (Sacramento CC).

MADISON MALLARDS

Mailing Address: 2920 N Sherman Ave, Madison, WI 53704. **Telephone:** (608) 246-4277. **Fax:** (608) 246-4163. **E-Mail Address:** conor@mankatomoondogs.com. **Website:** www.mallardsbaseball.com. **Owner:** Steve Schmitt. **President:** Vern Stenman. **General Manager:** Conor Caloia. **Field Manager:** Greg Labbe (Eagle's View Academy, Jacksonville).

MANKATO MOONDOGS

Mailing Address: 1221 Caledonia Street, Mankato, MN 56001. **Telephone:** (507) 625-7047. **Fax:** (507) 625-7059. **E-Mail Address:** office@mankatomoondogs.com. **Website:** www.mankatomoondogs.com. **Owner/President:** Joe Schwei. **General Manager:** Kyle Mrozek. **Assistant General Manager:** Jessie Hays. **Field Manager:** Mike Orchard (Central Arizona JC).

ROCHESTER HONKERS

Mailing Address: PO Box 482, Rochester, MN 55903. **Telephone:** (507) 289-1170. **Fax:** (507) 289-1866. **E-Mail Address:** honkers@rochesterhonkers.com. **Website:** www.rochesterhonkers.com. **Owner/General Manager:** Dan Litzinger. **Assistant General Manager:** Elizabeth Smit. **Field Manager:** Ryan Ruiz (Central Arizona JC).

ST. CLOUD RIVER BATS

Mailing Address: PO Box 5059, St. Cloud, MN 56302. **Telephone:** (320) 240-9798. **Fax:** (320) 255-5228. **E-Mail Address:** info@riverbats.com. **Website:** www.riverbats.com. **Owner/General Manager:** Joel Sutherland. **Field Manager:** Ben Quinto (Menlo College, Calif.).

THUNDER BAY BORDER CATS

Mailing Address: PO Box 29105, Thunder Bay, Ontario P7B 6P9. **Telephone:** (807) 766-2287. **Fax:** (807) 345-8299. **E-Mail Address:** baseball@tbaytel.net. **Website:** www.bordercatsbaseball.com. **President/General Manager:** Brad Jorgenson. **Field Manager:** Mike Steed.

WATERLOO BUCKS

Mailing Address: PO Box 4124, Waterloo, IA 50704. **Telephone:** (319) 232-0500. **Fax:** (319) 232-0700. **E-Mail Address:** waterloobucks@waterloobucks.com. **Website:** www.waterloobucks.com. **General Manager:** Dan Corbin. **Field Manager:** Jason Nell (Iowa Lakes CC).

WILLMAR STINGERS

Mailing Address: PO Box 201, Willmar, MN, 56201. **Telephone:** (320) 222-2010. **E-Mail Address:** ryan@willmarstingers.com. **Website:** www.willmarstingers.com. **Owners:** Marc Jerzak, Ryan Voz. **General Manager:** Ryan Voz. **Field Manager:** Matt Hollod (Southern Utah).

WISCONSIN WOODCHUCKS

Mailing Address: PO Box 6157, Wausau, WI 54402. **Telephone:** (715) 845-5055. **Fax:** (715) 845-5015. **E-Mail Address:** info@woodchucks.com. **Website:** www.woodchucks.com. **Owner/President:** Clark Eckhoff. **General Manager:** Ryan Treu. **Field Manager:** George "Guido" Aspeitia.

WISCONSIN RAPIDS

Mailing Address: 521 Lincoln St., Wisconsin Rapids, WI 54494. **Telephone:** (715) 424-5400. **E-Mail Address:** info@rapidsbaseball.com. **Website:** www.rapidsbaseball.com. **Owner/President:** Vern Stenman. **General Manager:** Liz Kern. **Field Manager:** Scott Laverty (University of Redlands, Calif.).

PACIFIC INTERNATIONAL LEAGUE

Mailing Address: 4400 26th Ave W, Seattle, WA 98199. **Telephone:** (206) 623-8844. **Fax:** (206) 623-8361. **E-Mail Address:** spotter@potterprinting.com. **Website:** www.pacificinternationalleague.com.

Year Founded: 1992.

President: Mike MacColloch. **Vice President:** David Laing. **Commissioner:** Brian Gooch. **Secretary:** Steve Potter. **Treasurer:** Mark Dow.

Member Clubs: Northwest Honkers, Burnaby Bulldogs, Coquitlam Angels, Everett Merchants, Kamloops Sundevils, Kelowna Jays, Langley Blaze, Nanaimo Coal Miners, Seattle Studs, Trail (BC) franchise, Burnaby Collegiate.

Regular Season: 20 league games. **2011 Opening Date:** June 1. **Closing Date:** July 31. **Playoff Format:** The top team is invited to NBC World Series.

Roster Limit: 30; 25 eligible for games (players must be at least 18 years old).

PROSPECT LEAGUE

Mailing Address: 9006 Hillman Way Drive, Bartlett, TN 38133. **Telephone:** (901) 218-3386. **Fax:** (901) 937-5607. **E-Mail Address:** commissioner@prospectleague.com. **Website:** www.prospectleague.com.

Year Founded: 1963 as Central Illinois Collegiate League; 2009 as Prospect League.

Commissioner: Dave Chase.

Regular Season: 56 games. **2011 Opening Date:** June 2. **Closing Date:** Aug. 6. **All-Star Game:** July 13 at Linda K. Epling Stadium, Beckley, W.V. **Championship Game:** Aug 12.

Roster Limit: 26

BUTLER BLUESOX

Mailing Address: PO Box 1425, Washington, PA 15301. **Telephone:** (724) 263-9874. **E-Mail Address:** butlerbluesox@ymail.com. **Website:** www.butlerbluesox.net. **Owner/General Manager:** Leo Trich. **Field Manager:** Unavailable.

CHILLICOTHE PAINTS

Mailing Address: 59 North Paint Street, Chillicothe, OH 45601. **Telephone:** (740) 773-8326. **Fax:** (740) 773-7117. **E-Mail Address:** paints@bright.net. **Website:** www.chillicothepaints.com. **General Manager:** Bryan Wickline. **Field Manager:** Unavailable.

DANVILLE DANS

Mailing Address: PO Box 1041, Danville, IL 61832. **Telephone:** (217) 446-5521. **Fax:** (217) 446-9995. **E-Mail Address:** jc@cooketech.net. **Website:** www.danvilledans.com. **General Mangers:** Jeanie Cooke, Rick Kurth. **Field Manager:** Unavailable.

DEKALB COUNTY LINERS

Mailing Address: 164 East Lincoln Highway, Suite 114-A, DeKalb, IL 60115. **Telephone:** (815) 508-3610. **Fax:** (815) 756-5164. **E-mail Address:** linersbaseball@gmail.com. **Website:** www.linersbaseball.com. **General Manager:** Josh Pethoud. **Field Manager:** Unavailable.

DUBOIS COUNTY BOMBERS

Mailing Address: PO Box 332, Huntingburg, IN 47542. **Telephone:** (812) 683-4700. **Fax:** (812) 683-5661. **E-Mail Address:** jabigness@aol.com. **Website:** www.dcbombers.com. **General Manager:** John Bigness. **Field Manager:** Unavailable.

DUPAGE DRAGONS

Mailing Address: PO Box 3076, Lisle, IL 60532. **Telephone:** (630) 241-2255. **Fax:** (708) 784-1468. **Website:** www.dupagedragons.com. **General Manager:** Geoff Steele. **Field Manager:** Unavailable.

HANNIBAL CAVEMEN

Mailing Address: Clemens Field, 403 Warren Barrett Drive, Hannibal, MO 63401. **Telephone:** (573) 221-1010. **Fax:** (573) 221-5296. **E-Mail Address:** hannibalbaseball@sbcglobal.net. **Website:** www.hannibalcavemen.com. **General Manager:** Unavailable. **Field Manager:** Jay Hemond.

LORAIN COUNTY IRONMEN

Mailing Address: 737 Broadway, Lorain, OH 44052. **Telephone:** (440) 522-9549. **Email Address:** info@lcironmentbaseball.com. **Website:** www.lcironmenbaseball.com. **General Manager:** Brian McCrodden. **Field Manager:** Unavailable.

NASHVILLE OUTLAWS

Mailing Address: 201 22nd Avenue North, Suite B, Nashville, TN 37203. **Telephone:** (615) 866-1040. **Fax:** (615) 346-9405. **Email Address:** info@nashvilleoutlaws.com. **Website:** www.nashvilleoutlaws.com. **General Manager:** Brandon Vonderharr. **Field Manager:** Brian Ryman.

QUINCY GEMS

Mailing Address: 300 Civic Center Plaza, Quincy, IL 62301. **Telephone:** (217) 223-1000. **Fax:** (217) 223-1330. **E-Mail Address:** rebbing@quincygems.com. **Website:**

www.quincygems.com. **General Manager:** Rob Ebbing. **Field Manager:** Chris Martin.

RICHMOND RIVERRATS

Mailing Address: McBride Stadium, 201 NW 13th Street, Richmond, IN 47374. **Telephone:** (765) 935-7287. **Fax:** (765) 935-7529. **E-Mail Address:** dbeaman@richmondriverrats.com. **Website:** www.richmondriverrats.com. **General Manager:** Deanna Beaman. **Field Manager:** Tyler Lairson.

SLIPPERY ROCK SLIDERS

Mailing Address: PO Box 496, Slippery Rock, PA 16057. **Telephone:** (724) 333-0355. **Fax:** (724) 458-8831. **E-Mail Address:** mbencic@zoominternet.net. **Website:** www.theslipperyrocksliders.com. **General Manager:** Mike Bencic. **Field Manager:** Andy Chalot.

SPRINGFIELD SLIDERS

Mailing Address: 1415 North Grand Avenue East, Suite B, Springfield, IL 62702. **Telephone:** (217) 679-3511. **Fax:** (217) 679-3512. **E-Mail Address:** jb@springfieldsliders.com. **Website:** www.springfieldsliders.com. **General Manager:** Unavailable. **Head Coach:** Unavailable.

TERRE HAUTE REX

Mailing Address: 320 Gillum Hall, Terre Haute, IN 47809. **Telephone:** (812) 237-3777. **Fax:** (812) 237-7797. **E-mail Address:** rshelton@indstatefoundation.org. **Website:** www.threxbaseball.com. **General Manager:** Roland Shelton. **Field Manager:** Brian Dorsett.

WEST VIRGINIA MINERS

Mailing Address: 476 Ragland Road, Beckley, WV 25801. **Telephone:** (304) 252-7233. **Fax:** (304) 253-1998. **E-mail Address:** mike@wvminersbaseball.com. **Website:** www.wvminersbaseball.com. **General Manager:** Mike Gilligan. **Field Manager:** Tim Epling.

SOUTHERN COLLEGIATE BASEBALL LEAGUE

Mailing Address: 9723 Northcross Center Court, Huntersville, NC 28078. **Telephone:** (704) 635-7126. **Fax:** (704) 635-7371. **E-Mail Address:** SCBLCommissioner@aol.com. **Website:** www.scbl.org.
Year Founded: 1999.
Commissioner: Bill Capps. **President:** Jeff Carter. **Executive Vice President:** Brian Swords. **Secretary:** James Bradley. **Treasurer:** Brenda Templin. **League Historian:** Larry Tremitiere. **Umpire in Chief:** Tom Haight.
Regular Season: 42 games. **2011 Opening Date:** June 6. **Closing Date:** July 30. **Playoff Format:** Division playoffs with two division champions playing best-of-three for championship.
Roster Limit: 30 (College-eligible players only).

ASHEVILLE REDBIRDS

Mailing Address: PO Box 17637, Asheville, NC 28816. **Telephone:** (828) 691-3679. **Email Address:** billstewart210@charter.net. **General Manager:** Bill Stewart. **Head Coach:** Ryan Smith.

CAROLINA CHAOS

Mailing Address: 142 Orchard Drive, Liberty, SC 29657. **Telephone:** (864) 843-3232, (864) 901-4331. **E-Mail Address:** brian_swords@carolinachaos.com. **Website:** www.carolinachaos.com. **General Manager:** Brian Swords (Southern Wesleyan, S.C.). **Head Coach:** Nathan Swords.

CAROLINA STINGERS

Mailing Address: 1443 Wedgefield Drive, Fort Mill, SC 29732. **Telephone:** (803) 517-6626. **E-Mail Address:** ltrem@comporium.net. **General Manager:** Larry Tremitiere.

LAKE NORMAN COPPERHEADS

Mailing Address: PO Box 9723, Northcross Center Court, Huntersville, NC 28078. **Telephone:** (704) 892-1041, (704) 564-9211. **E-Mail Address:** jcarter@copperheadsports.org. **Website:** www.copperheadsports.org. **General Manager:** Jeff Carter. **Head Coach:** Derek Shoe.

MORGANTON AGGIES

Mailing Address: PO Box 3448, Morganton, NC 28680. **Telephone:** (828) 438-5351. **Fax:** (828) 438-5350. **E-mail Address:** gleonhardt@ci.morganton.nc.us. **General Manager:** Gary Leonhardt. **Head Coach:** Travis Howard.

SPARTANBURG BLUE EAGLES

Mailing Address: PO Box 4786, Cowpens, SC 29305. **Telephone:** (864) 444-4348. **E-Mail Address:** markdudley51@gmail.com. **General Manager:** Mark Dudley. **Head Coach:** Ryan Thomas.

STATESVILLE OWLS

Mailing Address: 8680 Shallowford Road, Lewisville, NC 27023. **Telephone:** (336) 408-1516. **E-Mail Address:** hugh.mcbride@statesvilleowls.net. **President:** Jeff May. **General Manager:** Hugh McBride.

TENNESSEE TORNADO

Mailing Address: 1995 Roan Creek Road, Mountain City, TN 37683. **Telephone:** (423) 727-9111. **E-Mail Address:** tdr@maymead.com. **Owner:** Wiley Roark. **General Manager:** Tom Reese. **Head Coach:** Phillip Al-Mateen (East Tennessee State).

TEXAS COLLEGIATE LEAGUE

Mailing Address: 735 Plaza Blvd, Suite 200, Coppell, TX 75019. **Telephone:** (979) 985-5198. **Fax:** (979) 779-2398. **E-Mail Address:** info@tclbaseball.com. **Website:** www.texascollegiateleague.com.
Year Founded: 2004.
President: Uri Geva.
Regular Season: 56 games (split schedule). **2011 Opening Date:** June 1. **Closing Date:** August 15. **Playoff Format:** The first- and second-half champions will be joined in the TCL playoffs by two wild card teams. **Winners of the best-of-three divisional round meet in the three-game TCL Championship Series.**
Roster Limit: 30 (College-eligible players only)

ACADIANA CANE CUTTERS

Telephone: (337) 237-2923. **Website:** www.canecuttersbaseball.com. **Owner/General Manager:** Richard Chalmers. **Head Coach:** Lonny Landry.

ALEXANDRIA ACES

Mailing Address: 1 Babe Ruth Dr, Alexandria, LA 71301. **Telephone:** (318) 473-2273. **Website:** www.myacesbaseball.com. **President/Chief Executive Officer:** Eric Moran. **Head Coach:** Mike Byrnes.

BRAZOS VALLEY BOMBERS

Mailing Address: 405 Mitchell St, Bryan, TX 77801. **Telephone:** (979) 799-7529. **Fax:** (979) 779-2398. **E-Mail Address:** info@bvbombers.com. **Website:** www.bvbombers.com. **Owners:** Uri Geva, Kfir Jackson. **General**

Manager: Chris Clark. **Head Coach:** Brent Alumbaugh.

EAST TEXAS PUMP JACKS

Physical Address: 1100 Stone Rd, Suite 120, Kilgore, TX 75662. **Mailing Address:** PO Box 2369, Kilgore, TX 75663. **Telephone:** (903) 218-4638. **Fax:** (866) 511-5449. **E-mail Address:** info@pumpjacksbaseball.com. **Website:** www.pumpjacksbaseball.com. **General Manager:** Mike Lieberman. **Head Coach:** Stan Phelps.

MCKINNEY MARSHALS

Mailing Address: 6151 Alma Rd, McKinney, TX 75070. **Telephone:** (972) 747-8248. **E-mail Address:** info@tclmarshals.com. **Website:** www.tclmarshals.com. **Director, General Operations:** David Apple. **Director, Finance:** Steve Pratt. **Director, Baseball Operations:** Mike Henneman.

COPPELL COPPERHEADS

Mailing Address: 735 Plaza Blvd, Suite 200, Coppell, TX 75019. **Telephone:** (972) 745-2929. **Fax:** (972) 315-1955. **Website:** www.tclmarshals.com. **General Manager:** Kyleigh Callender. **Director of Baseball Operations:** John Marston. **Head Coach:** Barry Rose.

TEXAS TOMCATS

Mailing Address: 3708 N Navarro St, Suite A, Victoria, TX 77901. **Telephone:** (361) 485-9522. **Fax:** (361) 485-0936. **E-Mail Address:** info@baseballinvictoria.com. **President:** Tracy Young. **General Manager:** Blake Koch.

VICTORIA GENERALS

Mailing Address: 3708 N Navarro St, Suite A, Victoria, TX 77901. **Telephone:** (361) 485-9522. **Fax:** (361) 485-0936. **E-Mail Address:** info@baseballinvictoria.com. **Website:** www.victoriagenerals.com. **President:** Tracy Young. **General Manager:** Blake Koch. **Head Coach:** Chris Clemons.

VALLEY LEAGUE

Mailing Address: Valley Baseball League, 58 Bethel Green Rd, Staunton, VA 24401. **Telephone:** (540) 213-8254. **Fax:** (540) 213-8255. **E-Mail Addresses:** dmbiery@wildblue.net, davidb@fisherautoparts.com. **Website:** www.valleyleaguebaseball.com.

Year Founded: 1961.

President: David Biery. **Executive Vice President:** Bruce Alger. **Media Relations Director:** Scott Musa. **Secretary:** Ken Newman. **Treasurer:** James R Phillips. **Regular Season:** 44 games. **2011 Opening Date:** June 2. **Closing Date:** July 27. **All-Star Game:** North vs South, July 10 at Haymarket; Valley vs Cal Ripken League, July 11 at Harrisonburg. **Playoff Format:** Eight teams; best-of-three quarterfinals and semifinals; best-of-five finals. **Roster Limit:** 28 (college eligible players only)

COVINGTON LUMBERJACKS

Mailing Address: PO Box 30, Covington, VA 24426. **Telephone:** (540) 969-9923, (540) 962-1155. **Fax:** (540) 962-7153. **E-Mail Address:** covingtonlumberjacks@valleyleaguebaseball.com. **Website:** www.lumberjacks-baseball.com. **Owners:** Dizzy Garten. **Head Coach:** Arlan Freeman.

FRONT ROYAL CARDINALS

Mailing Address: 382 Morgans Ridge Road, Front Royal, VA 22630. **Telephone:** (703) 244-6662, (540) 631-9201. **Fax:** (703) 696-0583. **E-Mail Address:** frontroyalcardinals@valleyleaguebaseball.com. **Website:** www.

frontroyalcardinals.com. **President:** Donna Settle. **Head Coach:** Rusty Bennett.

HARRISONBURG TURKS

Mailing Address: 1489 S Main St, Harrisonburg, VA 22801. **Telephone:** (540) 434-5919. **E-Mail Address:** harrisonburgturks@valleyleaguebaseball.com. **Website:** www.harrisonburgturks.com. **Operations Manager:** Teresa Wease. **General Manager/Head Coach:** Bob Wease.

HAYMARKET SENATORS

Mailing Address: 42020 Village Center Plaza, Suite 120-50, Stoneridge, VA 20105. **Telephone:** (703) 542-2110, (703) 989-5009. **Fax:** (703) 327-7435. **E-Mail Address:** haymarketsenators@valleyleaguebaseball.com. **Website:** www.haymarketbaseball.com. **President/General Manager:** Scott Newell. **Head Coach:** Justin Aspegren.

LURAY WRANGLERS

Mailing Address: 1203 E. Main St, Luray, VA 22835. **Telephone:** (540) 743-3338, (540) 743-7560, (540) 843-4472. **Fax:** (540) 743-4251. **E-Mail Address:** luraywranglers@valleyleaguebaseball.com. **Website:** www.luray-wranglers.com. **President:** Bill Turner. **General Manager:** Head Coach: Mike Bocock.

NEW MARKET REBELS

Mailing Address: PO Box 902, New Market, VA 22844. **Telephone:** (540) 740-4247, (540) 435-8453. **Fax:** (540) 740-9486. **E-Mail Address:** newmarketrebels@valleyleaguebaseball.com. **Website:** www.rebelsbaseball.biz. **President/General Manager:** Bruce Alger. **Executive Vice President:** Jim Weissenborn. **Head Coach:** Corey Paluga

ROCKBRIDGE RAPIDS

Mailing Address: P.O Box 600, Lexington, VA 24450. **Telephone:** (540) 460-7502, (540) 463-3686, (540) 462-7521. **E-Mail Address:** rockbridgerapids@valleyleaguebaseball.com. **Website:** www.rockbridgerapids.com. **General Manager:** Ken Newman. **Head Coach:** Greg Keaton.

STAUNTON BRAVES

Mailing Address: 14 Shannon Place, Staunton, VA 24401. **Telephone:** (540) 886-0987, (540) 885-1645. **Fax:** (540) 886-0905. **E-Mail Address:** stauntonbraves@valleyleaguebaseball.com. **Website:** www.stauntonbravesbaseball.com. **General Manager:** Steve Cox. **Head Coach:** Paul LaMarr.

STRASBURG EXPRESS

Mailing Address: PO Box 417, Strasburg, VA 22657. **Telephone:** (540) 325-5677, (540) 459-4041. **Fax:** (540) 459-3398. **E-Mail Address:** neallaw@shentel.net. **Website:** www.strasburgexpress.com.

WAYNESBORO GENERALS

Mailing Address: PO Box 615, Waynesboro VA 22980. **Telephone:** (540) 949-0370, (540) 280-4802. **Fax:** (540) 932-2322. **E-Mail Address:** waynesborogenerals@valleyleaguebaseball.com. **Website:** www.waynesborogenerals.com. **Owner:** Jim Critzer. **Head Coach:** Ronny Palmer.

WINCHESTER ROYALS

Mailing Address: PO Box 2485, Winchester, VA 22604. **Telephone:** (540) 539-8888, (540) 664-3978. **Fax:** (540) 662-1434. **E-Mail Addresses:** winchesterroyals@valleyleaguebaseball.com, jimphill@shentel.net. **Website:** www.winchesterroyals.com. **President:** Todd Thompson. **Head**

Coach: John Lowery Sr.

WOODSTOCK RIVER BANDITS

Mailing Address: 2044 Palmyra Rd, Edinburg, VA 22824. **Telephone:** (540) 481-0525, (540) 570-8001. **Fax:** (540) 459-8227. **E-Mail Address:** woodstockriverbandits@valleyleaguebaseball.com. **Website:** www.woodstock-riverbandits.org. **Owner/President:** Jim Yates. **General Manager:** Robert Bowman. **Head Coach:** Brent Haring.

WEST COAST LEAGUE

Mailing Address: PO Box 8395, Portland, OR 97207. **Telephone:** (503) 764-9510. **E-Mail Address:** wilson@westcoastleague.com. **Website:** www.westcoastleague.com.

Year Founded: 2005.

President: Ken Wilson. **Vice President:** Bobby Brett. **Secretary:** Dan Segel. **Treasurer:** Jim Corcoran. **Supervisor of Umpires:** Dave Perez

Division Structure: East—Bellingham, Kelowna, Walla Walla, Wenatchee. **West—Bend, Corvallis, Cowlitz, Kitsap, Klamath Falls.**

Regular Season: 54 games. **2011 Opening Date:** June 3. **Closing Date:** August 10. **All-Star Game:** July 26 at Corvallis. **Playoff Format:** First- and second-place teams in each division meet in best-of-three semifinal series; winners advance to best-of-three championship series.

Roster Limit: 25 (college-eligible players only).

BELLINGHAM BELLS

Mailing Address: PO Box 28935, Bellingham, WA 98228. **Telephone:** (360) 746-0406. **E-Mail Address:** info@bellinghambells.com. **Website:** www.bellinghambells.com. **Owner:** Eddie Poplawski. **General Manager:** Justin Stottlemyre. **Head Coach:** Gary Hatch

BEND ELKS

Mailing Address: PO Box 9009, Bend, OR 97708. **Telephone:** (541) 312-9259. **E-Mail Address:** richardsj@bendcable.com. **Website:** www.bendelks.com. **Owner/General Manager:** Jim Richards. **Head Coach:** Sean Kinney (Whitman College, Wash.).

CORVALLIS KNIGHTS

Mailing Address: PO Box 1356, Corvallis, OR 97339. **Telephone:** (541) 752-5656. **E-Mail Address:** dan.segel@corvallisknights.com. **Website:** www.corvallisknights.com. **President:** Dan Segel. **General Manager/Head Coach:** Brooke Knight.

COWLITZ BLACK BEARS

Mailing Address: PO Box 1255, Longview, WA 98632. **Telephone:** (360) 703-3195. **E-Mail Address:** gwil-sonagm@gmail.com. **Website:** www.cowlitzblackbears.com. **Owner:** Tony Bonacci. **General Manager:** Grant Wilson. **Head Coach:** Bryson LeBlanc (Oregon)

KELOWNA FALCONS

Mailing Address: 201-1014 Glenmore Dr, Kelowna, BC, V1Y 4P2. **Telephone:** (250) 763-4100. **E-Mail Address:** mark@kelownafalcons.com. **Website:** www.kelownafalcons.com. **Owner:** Dan Nonis. **General Manager:** Mark Nonis. **Head Coach:** Al Cantwell.

KITSAP BLUEJACKETS

Mailing Address: PO Box 68, Silverdale, WA 98383. **Telephone:** (360) 692-5566. **E-Mail Address:** rsmith@kitsapbluejackets.com. **Website:** www.kitsapbluejackets.com. **Managing Partner/General Manager:** Rick Smith. **Head Coach:** Matt Acker (St. Martin's, Wash.).

KLAMATH FALLS GEMS

Mailing Address: 2001 Crest Street, Klamath Falls, Oregon 97603. **Telephone:** (541) 883-GEMS. **Email Address:** chuck@klamathfallsgems.com. **Website:** www.klamathfallsgems.com. **General Manager:** Chuck Heeman. **Head Coach:** Brian Embery.

WALLA WALLA SWEETS

Mailing Address: 109 E Main Street, Walla Walla, WA 99362. **Telephone:** (509) 522-2255. **E-Mail Address:** Zachary.Fraser@pacificbaseballventures.com. **Website:** www.wallawallabaseball.com. **Owner:** Pacific Baseball Ventures, LLC. **General Manager:** Zachary Fraser. **Head Coach:** J.C. Biagi (Walla Walla CC, Wash.)

WENATCHEE APPLESOX

Mailing Address: PO Box 5100, Wenatchee, WA 98807. **Telephone:** (509) 665-6900. **E-Mail Address:** sales@applesox.com. **Website:** www.applesox.com. **Owner/General Manager:** Jim Corcoran. **Head Coach:** Ed Knaggs.

WCL PORTLAND

Mailing Address: 2811 NE Holman, Portland, Oregon 97211. **Telephone:** (503) 280-8691. **E-Mail Address:** rvance@cu-portland.edu. **Website:** www.wccbl.com/portland.

Year Founded: 2009.

Commissioner: Rob Vance.

Regular Season: 25 games. **2011 Opening Date:** June 4. **Closing Date:** August 7. **All-Star Game:** None. **Playoff Format:** First-place team faces fourth-place team and second-place team faces third-place team in first round. Winners advance to championship game.

Roster Limit: 25 (college-eligible players only).

Teams: Bucks, Dukes, Lobos, Ports, Stars, Toros.

HIGH SCHOOL BASEBALL

NATIONAL FEDERATION OF STATE HIGH SCHOOL ASSOCIATIONS

Mailing Address: P.O. Box 690, Indianapolis, IN 46206. **Telephone:** (317) 972-6900. **Fax:** (317) 822-5700. **E-Mail Address:** baseball@nfhs.org. **Website:** www.nfhs.org.

Executive Director: Robert Kanaby. **Chief Operating Officer:** Bob Gardner. **Assistant Director/Baseball Rules Editor:** Elliot Hopkins. **Director, Publications/Communications:** Bruce Howard.

NATIONAL HIGH SCHOOL BASEBALL COACHES ASSOCIATION

Mailing Address: P.O. Box 12843, Tempe, AZ 85284. **Telephone:** (602) 615-0571. **Fax:** (480) 838-7133. **E-Mail Address:** rdavini@cox.net. **Website:** www.baseballcoaches.org. **Executive Director:** Ron Davini. **President:** Steve Mandl (Washington HS, New York). **First Vice President:** Phil Clark (Bartlett, Tenn., HS). **Second Vice President:** Art Griffith (Winslow, Ariz., HS).

2011 National Convention: Dec. 1-3, 2011 at Raleigh, N.C.

NATIONAL TOURNAMENTS

IN-SEASON

HORIZON NATIONAL INVITATIONAL

Mailing Address: Horizon High School, 5653 Sandra Terrace, Scottsdale, AZ 85254. **Telephone:** (602) 867-9003. **E-mail:** huskycoach1@yahoo.com Website: www.horizonbaseball.com

Tournament Director: Eric Kibler.
2011 Tournament: March 28-31.

INTERNATIONAL PAPER CLASSIC

Mailing Address: 4775 Johnson Rd., Georgetown, SC 29440. **Telephone:** (843) 527-9606, (843) 546-3807. **Fax:** (843) 546-8521. **Website:** www.ipclassic.com.

Tournament Director: Alicia Johnson.
2011 Tournament: March 10-13 (eight teams).

LIONS INVITATIONAL

Mailing Address: 3502 Lark St., San Diego CA 92103. **Telephone:** (619) 602-8650. **Fax:** (619) 239-3539. **Website:** www.anaheimlionsbaseball.org.

Tournament Director: Rod Wallace.
2011 Tournament: April 2, 4-6.

NATIONAL CLASSIC BASEBALL TOURNAMENT

Mailing Address: P.O. Box 338, Placentia, CA 92870. **Telephone:** (714) 993-2838. **Fax:** (714) 993-5350. **E-Mail Address:** placentiamustang@aol.com. **Website:** national-classic.com

Tournament Director: Todd Rogers.
2011 Tournament: April 18-21 (16 teams).

USA CLASSIC NATIONAL HIGH SCHOOL INVITATIONAL

Mailing Address: 5900 Walnut Grove Rd., Memphis, TN 38120. **Telephone:** (901) 872-8326. **Fax:** (901) 681-9443. **Email:** jdaigle@bigriver.net Web-site: www.usabaseball-stadium.org.

Tournament Organizers: John Daigle, Buster Kelso.
2011 Tournament: April 6-9 at USA Baseball Stadium, Millington, TN (16 teams).

POSTSEASON

SUNBELT BASEBALL CLASSIC SERIES

Mailing Address: 505 North Blvd., Edmond, OK 73034. **Telephone:** (405) 348-3839. **Fax:** (405) 340-7538

Chairman: John Schwartz.
2011 Senior Series: Norman, OK, June 20-26
2011 Junior Series: McAlester and Wilburton, OK, June 10-15
2011 Sophomore Series: Oklahoma City, OK, June 2-5

ALL-STAR GAMES/AWARDS

AFLAC HIGH SCHOOL ALL-AMERICA CLASSIC

Mailing Address: 1932 Wynnton Road, Columbus, Georgia 31999. **Telephone:** (706) 763-2827. **Fax:** (706) 320-2288. **Event Organizer:** Blue Ridge Sports & Entertainment. **Vice President, Events:** Lou Lacy. **2011 Game:** Unavailable.

UNDER ARMOUR ALL-AMERICA GAME, POWERED BY BASEBALL FACTORY

Mailing Address: 9176 Red Branch Rd., Suite M, Columbia, MD 21045. **Telephone:** 410-715-5080. **E-Mail Address:** jason@baseballfactory.com. **Website:** baseball-factory.com. **Event Organizers:** Baseball Factory, Team One Baseball. **2011 Game:** August.

GATORADE CIRCLE OF CHAMPIONS

(National HS Player of the Year Award)
Mailing Address: The Gatorade Company, 321 N. Clark St., Suite 24-3, Chicago, IL, 60610. **Telephone:** 312-821-1000. **Website:** www.gatorade.com.

SHOWCASE EVENTS

ALL-AMERICAN BASEBALL TALENT SHOWCASES

Mailing Address: 333 Preston Ave., Unit 1, Voorhees, NJ 08043. **Telephone:** (856) 354-0201. **Fax:** (856) 354-0818. **E-Mail Address:** hitdoctor@thehitdoctor.com. **Website:** thehitdoctor.com. **National Director:** Joe Barth.

AREA CODE GAMES

Mailing Address: 23954 Madison Street, Torrance, CA 90505. **Telephone:** (310) 791-1142, ext. 4426. **E-Mail Address:** knepper@studentsports.com. **Website:** www. areacodebaseball.com.

Event Organizer: Andrew Knepper.

2011 Area Code Games: Aug. 5-10 at the MLB Urban Youth Academy in Compton, CA.

ARIZONA FALL CLASSIC

Mailing Address: 6102 W. Maui Lane, Glendale, AZ 85306 **Telephone:** (602) 978-2929. **Fax:** (602) 439-4494. **E-Mail Address:** azbaseballted@msn.com. **Website:** www. azfallclassic.com.

Directors: Ted Heid, Tracy Heid.

2011 Events

Four Corner Classic (Open HS, 16 & under)	Peoria, AZ, June 2-5
Summer National Classic.	Peoria, AZ, July 7-10
Arizona Fall Invitational	Oct. 7-9
AZ Senior Fall Classic (HS seniors)	Peoria, AZ, Oct. 13-16
AZ Junior Fall Classic (HS juniors)	Peoria, AZ, Oct. 20-23
AZ Sophomore Fall Classic.	
(HS sophomore and Under)	Peoria, AZ, Oct. 27-30

BASEBALL FACTORY

Office Address: 9176 Red Branch Rd., Suite M, Columbia, MD 21045. **Telephone:** (800) 641-4487, (410) 715-5080. **Fax:** (410) 715-1975. **E-Mail Address:** info@baseballfactory.com. **Website:** www.baseballfactory.com.

Chief Executive Officer: Steve Sclafani. **President:** Rob Naddelman. **Executive VP, Baseball Operations:** Steve Bernhardt. **Senior VP, Finance:** Matt Frese. **Senior VP, Operations/Marketing:** Jason Budden. **VP, On-Field Events:** Jim Gemler. **VP, Creative:** Matt Kirby. **VP, Player Development:** Dan Forester. **Senior Director, Baseball Operations:** Andy Ferguson. **Senior Director, Instruction:** Matt Schilling. **Senior Director, College Recruiting:** Dan Mooney. **Senior Director, Youth Baseball:** Jeff Brazier. **Senior Multimedia Producer:** Brian Johnson.

Player Development Coordinators: Steve Nagler, Dave Packer, John Perko, Patrick Wuebben, Chris Brown, Adam Darvick, Will Bach, Will Bowers, Rob Onolfi, Ryan Schweikert. **Client Services Coordinator:** Cecile Banas. **Lessons Coordinator:** Joe Lake. **Director, PVP Program/National Tryouts:** Bryan Dunkel. **Director, College Recruiting Operations:** Woody Wingfield.

Under Armour Pre-Season All-America Tournament: January 14-16 in Tucson, AZ (Kino Sports Complex). **Under Armour All-America Game:** August 2011.

2011 Under Armour Baseball Factory National Tryouts & Premium Video Program: Various locations across the country. Year round. Open to high school players, ages 14–18 and a separate division for pre-high school players, ages 12–13. Check www.baseballfactory.com for full schedule.

BLUE-GREY CLASSIC

Mailing address: 68 Norfolk Road, Mills MA 02054. **Telephone:** (508) 376-1250. **E-Mail address:** impact-prospects@comcast.net. **Website:** www.impactprospects.com.

2011 events: Various dates, locations June-Sept. 2011.

BOBBY VALENTINE ALL-AMERICAN CAMPS

Address: 72 Camp Avenue, Stamford, CT 06907. **Telephone:** (203) 517-1277. **Fax:** (203) 517-1377. **Website:** www.allamericanfoundation.com

COLLEGE SELECT BASEBALL

Mailing Address: P.O. Box 783, Manchester, CT 06040. **Telephone:** (800) 645-9854. **E-Mail Address:** TRhit@msn.com. **Website:** www.collegeselect.org.

Consulting Director: Tom Rizzi.

IMPACT BASEBALL

Mailing Address: P.O. Box 47, Sedalia, NC 27342. **E-Mail Address:** andypartin@aol.com. **Website:** impact-baseball.com.

Operator: Andy Partin.

2011 Showcases: Feb. 5-6, Forsyth Country Day; June 13-14, University of North Carolina; Aug. 12-14, Elon University; August 25, North Carolina State University.

EAST COAST PROFESSIONAL SHOWCASE

Mailing Address: 2125 North Lake Avenue, Lakeland, FL 33805. **Telephone:** (863) 686-8075. **Website:** www.eastcoastproshowcase.com.

Tournament Directors: John Castleberry. **Tournament Coordinator:** Shannon Follett.

2011 Showcase: Aug. 1-4, Lakeland, FL.

PACIFIC NORTHWEST CHAMPIONSHIPS

Mailing Address: 42783 Deerhorn Road, Springfield, Or. 97478. **Telephone:** (541) 896-0841. **E-Mail Address:** mckay@baseballnorthwest.com. **Website:** www.baseball-northwest.com. **Tournament Organizer:** Jeff McKay.

PERFECT GAME USA

Mailing Address: 1203 Rockford Road SW, Cedar Rapids, IA 52404. **Telephone:** (319) 298-2923 Fax: (319) 298-2924. **E-Mail Address:** jerry@perfectgame.org. **Website:** www.perfectgameusa.com.

President/Director: Jerry Ford. **Vice Presidents:** Andy Ford, Jason Gerst, Tyson Kimm, Allan Simpson. **International Director:** Kentaro Yasutake. **National Showcase Director:** Jim Arp. **National Tournament Director:** Taylor McCollough. **Scouting Director:** David Rawnsley. **National BCS Director:** Ben Ford. **Iowa League Director:** Steve James. **Northeast Director/Showcase Director:** Dan Kennedy. **West Coast Director:** Mike Spiers. **Scouting Coordinators:** Jeff Simpson, Greg Sabers, Kyle Noesen, Jason Piddington, Anup Sinha. **National Coordinator:** Frank Fulton.

2011 Showcase/Tournament Events: Sites across the United States, Jan. 9-Nov. 7.

PROFESSIONAL BASEBALL INSTRUCTION—BATTERY INVITATIONAL

(for top HS pitchers and catchers)

Mailing Address: 107 Pleasant Avenue, Upper Saddle River NJ 07458. **Telephone:** (800) 282-4638. **Fax:** (201) 760-8720. **E-Mail Address:** info@baseballclinics.com. **Website:** www.baseballclinics.com/batteryinvitational. html.

President: Doug Cinnella.

Senior Staff Administrator: Greg Cinnella. **General Manager/PR/Marketing:** Jim Monaghan.

SELECTFEST BASEBALL

Mailing Address: 60 Franklin Pl., Morris Plains, NJ 07950. **Telephone:** (862) 222-6404. **E-Mail Address:** selectfest@optonline.net. **Website:** www.selectfestbaseball.org. **Camp Directors:** Bruce Shatel.

2011 Showcase: TBA.

TEAM ONE BASEBALL

(A division of Baseball Factory)

Office Address: 1000 Bristol Street North, Box 17285, Newport Beach, CA 92660. **Telephone:** (800) 621-5452, (805) 451-8203. **Fax:** (949) 209-1829. **E-Mail Address:** jroswell@teamonebaseball.com. **Website:** www.teamonebaseball.com.

Senior Director: Justin Roswell. **Executive VP, Baseball Operations:** Steve Bernhardt. **VP, On-Field Events:** Jim Gemler. **National Recruiting Coordinator:** Vince Sacco.

2011 Under Armour Showcases: Team One West: July 9–10 in Costa Mesa, CA (Vanguard University); Team One South: July 15–16 in Atlanta, GA (Emory University); Team One Midwest: July 18–19 in River Forest, IL (Concordia University); Team One Northeast: July 24–25 in Trenton, NJ (Waterfront Park); Team One Futures East: October 1 in Jupiter, FL (Roger Dean Stadium); Team One Fall: October 14 in St. Petersburg, FL (Al Lang Field); Team One Futures West: October 21 in Peoria, AZ (Peoria Stadium); 2011 Under Armour Tournaments: Under Armour Memorial Day Classic: May 27-30 in Jupiter, FL (Roger Dean Sports Complex), Under Armour Southeast Tournament: June 10–14 in Jupiter, FL (Roger Dean Sports Complex), Under Armour Firecracker Classic: July 1–5 in Jupiter, FL (Roger Dean Sports Complex), Under Armour Southwest Tournament: August 1–4 in Azusa, CA (Azusa Pacific University/Citrus College), Under Armour Labor Day Classic: September 2–5 in Jupiter, FL (Roger Dean Sports Complex), Under Armour Fall Classic: September 30–October 2 in Jupiter, FL (Roger Dean Sports Complex), Under Armour Invitational: October 14–16 in St. Petersburg, FL (Naimoli Baseball Complex), Under Armour SoCal Classic: October 28–30 in Azusa, CA (Azusa Pacific University/Citrus College), Jupiter, Fla.; Thanksgiving Classic, Nov. 27-29 at Vanguard University in Costa Mesa, Calif.; Winter Classic, Dec. 27-30 at Kino Sports Complex in Tucson, Ariz.

TOP 96 COLLEGE COACHES CLINICS

Mailing Address: 6 Foley Dr. Southboro, MA 01772. **Telephone:** 508-481-5935.

E-Mail Address: doug.henson@top96.com. **Website:** www.top96.com.

Directors: Doug Henson, Dave Callum.

2011 Clinics: Various clinics throughout the United States; see website for schedule.

YOUTH BASEBALL

ALL AMERICAN AMATEUR BASEBALL ASSOCIATION

Mailing Address: 331 Parkway Dr., Zanesville, OH 43701. **Telephone:** (740) 453-8531. **Fax:** (740) 453-8531. **E-Mail Address:** clw@aol.com. **Website:** www.aaaba.us.
Year Founded: 1944.
President: Doug Pollock. **Executive Director/Secretary:** Bob Wolfe.
2011 Events: Dates unavailable.

AMATEUR ATHLETIC UNION OF THE UNITED STATES, INC.

Mailing Address: P.O. Box 22409, Lake Buena Vista, FL 32830. **Telephone:** (407) 934-7200. **Fax:** (407) 934-7242. **E-Mail Address:** dan@aausports.org, kristy@aausports. org. **Website:** www.aaubaseball.org.
Year Founded: 1982. **Sports Manager, Baseball:** Dan Stanley.

AMERICAN AMATEUR BASEBALL CONGRESS

National Headquarters: 100 West Broadway, Farmington, NM 87401. **Telephone:** (505) 327-3120. **Fax:** (505) 327-3132. **E-Mail Address:** aabc@aabc.us. **Website:** www.aabc.us.
Year Founded: 1935.
President: Richard Neely.

AMERICAN AMATEUR YOUTH BASEBALL ALLIANCE

Mailing Address: 1703 Koala Drive, Wentzville, MO 63385. **Telephone:** (636) 332-7799. **E-Mail Address:** clwjr28@aol.com. **Website:** www.aayba.com.
President, Baseball Operations: Carroll Wood.

AMERICAN LEGION BASEBALL

National Headquarters: American Legion Baseball, 700 N. Pennsylvania St., Indianapolis, IN 46204. **Telephone:** (317) 630-1213. **Fax:** (317) 630-1369. **E-Mail Address:** baseball@legion.org **Website:** www.baseball.legion.org.
Year Founded: 1925.
Program Coordinator: Jim Quinlan.
2011 World Series (19 and under): Aug. 12-16 at Veteran's Field, Shelby, N.C. (8 teams).
2011 Regional Tournaments (Aug. 3-8, 8 teams): Northeast—Old Orchard Beach, Maine; Mid-Atlantic—Boyertown, Pa.; Southeast—Sumter, S.C.; Mid-South—Minden, La; Great Lakes—Midland, Mich.; Central Plains—Dickinson, N.D.; Northwest—Billings, Mont.; Western—Fairfield, Calif.

BABE RUTH BASEBALL

International Headquarters: 1770 Brunswick Pike, P.O. Box 5000, Trenton, NJ 08638. **Telephone:** (609) 695-1434. **Fax:** (609) 695-2505. **E-Mail Address:** info@baberuth-league.org. **Website:** www.baberuthleague.org.
Year Founded: 1951.
President, Chief Executive Officer: Steven Tellefsen.

CONTINENTAL AMATEUR BASEBALL ASSOCIATION

Mailing Address: 1173 French Court, Maineville, Ohio 45039. **Telephone:** (513) 677-1580. **Fax:** 513-677-2586. **E-Mail Address:** lred-wine@cababaseball.com. **Website:** www.cababaseball.com.
Year Founded: 1984.
Executive Director: Larry Redwine. **Commissioner:** John Mocny. **Executive Vice President:** Fran Pell.

DIXIE YOUTH BASEBALL

Mailing Address: P.O. Box 877, Marshall, TX 75671. **Telephone:** (903) 927-2255. **Fax:** (903) 927-1846. **E-Mail Address:** dyb@dixie.org. **Website:** www.dixie.org.
Year Founded: 1955.
Commissioner: Wes Skelton.

DIXIE BOYS BASEBALL

Commissioner/Chief Executive Officer: Sandy Jones, P.O. Box 8263, Dothan, AL 36304. **Telephone:** (334) 793-3331.

DIZZY DEAN BASEBALL

Mailing Address: P.O. Box 856, Hernando, MS 38632. **Telephone:** (662) 429-4365, (423) 596-1353. **E-Mail Address:** dizzydeanbaseball@yahoo.com. **Website:** www.dizzydeanbbinc.org.
Year Founded: 1962.
Commissioner: Danny Phillips. **Presdient:** Jimmy Wahl. **VP:** Bobby Dunn. **Secretary:** Billy Powell. **Treasurer:** Houston Suggs.

HAP DUMONT YOUTH BASEBALL

(A Division of the National Baseball Congress)
Mailing Address: P.O. Box 83, Lexington, OK 73051. **Telephone:** (405) 899-7689. **E-Mail Address:** stevesmith@hapdumontbaseball.com. **Website:** www.hapdumont-baseball.com, www.oabf.net.
Year Founded: 1974.

LITTLE LEAGUE BASEBALL

International Headquarters: P.O. Box 3485, Williamsport, PA 17701. **Telephone:** (570) 326-1921. **Fax:** (570) 326-1074. **E-Mail Address:** headquarters@LL.org. **Website:** www.littleleague.org.
Year Founded: 1939.
Chairman: Dennis Lewin.
President/Chief Executive Officer: Stephen D. Keener. **Chief Financial Officer:** David Houseknecht. **Vice President, Operations:** Patrick Wilson. **Treasurer:** Melissa Singer. **Senior Communications Executive:** Lance Van Auken.

NATIONAL AMATEUR BASEBALL FEDERATION

Mailing Address: P.O. Box 705, Bowie, MD 20718. **Telephone:** (410) 721-4727. **Fax:** (410) 721-4940. **E-Mail Address:** nabf1914@aol.com. **Website:** www.nabf.com.
Year Founded: 1914.
Executive Director: Charles Blackburn.

NATIONAL ASSOCIATION OF POLICE ATHLETIC LEAGUES

Mailing Address: 658 W Indiantown Road #201, Jupiter, FL 33458. **Telephone:** (561) 745-5535. **Fax:** (561) 745-3147. **E-Mail Address:** cop-nkid@nationalpal.org. **Website:** www.nationalpal.org.

Year Founded: 1914.
President: L.B. Scott.

PONY BASEBALL

International Headquarters: P.O. Box 225, Washington, PA 15301. **Telephone:** (724) 225-1060. **Fax:** (724) 225-9852. **E-Mail Address:** info@pony.org. **Website:** www.pony.org.

Year Founded: 1951.
President: Abraham Key.

REVIVING BASEBALL IN INNER CITIES

Mailing Address: 245 Park Ave., New York, NY 10167. **Telephone:** (212) 931-7800. **Fax:** (212) 949-5695. **Year Founded:** 1989. **Director, Reviving Baseball in Inner Cities:** David James (David.James@mlb.com). **Vice President, Community Affairs:** Thomas C. **Brasuell.** **Email:** rbi@mlb.com. **Website:** www.mlb.com/rbi.

SUPER SERIES BASEBALL OF AMERICA

National Headquarters: 3449 East Kael Street., Mesa, AZ 85213-1773. **Telephone:** (480) 664-2998. **Fax:** (480) 664-2997. **E-Mail Address:** info@superseriesbaseball.com. **Website:** www.superseriesbaseball.com.
President: Mark Mathew.

TRIPLE CROWN SPORTS

Mailing Address: 3930 Automation Way, Fort Collins, CO 80525. **Telephone:** (970) 223-6644. **Fax:** (970) 223-3636. **Websites:** www.triplecrownsports.com. **E-Mail:** thad@triplecrownsports.com, sean@triplecrownsports.com. **Director, Baseball Operations:** Thad Anderson.

U.S. AMATEUR BASEBALL ASSOCIATION

Mailing Address: 7101 Lake Ballinger Way, Edmonds, WA 98026. **Telephone/Fax:** (425) 776-7130. **E-Mail Address:** usaba@usaba.com. **Website:** www.usaba.com.
Year Founded: 1969.
Executive Director: Al Rutledge. **Secretary:** Roberta Engelhart.

U.S. AMATEUR BASEBALL FEDERATION

Mailing Address: 389 Bryan Point Dr. Chula Vista, CA 91914. **Telephone:** (619) 934-2551. **Fax:** (619) 271-6659. **E-Mail Address:** usabf@cox.net. **Website:** www.usabf.com.
Year Founded: 1997.
Senior Chief Executive Officer/President: Tim Halbig.

UNITED STATES SPECIALTY SPORTS ASSOCIATION

Executive Vice President, Baseball: Don DeDonatis III, 33600 Mound Rd., Sterling Heights, MI 48310. **Telephone:** (810) 397-6410. **E-Mail Address:** michusssa@aol.com.
Executive Vice President, Baseball Operations: Rick Fortuna, 6324 N. Chatham Ave., #136, Kansas City, MO 64151. **Telephone:** (816) 587-4545. **E-Mail Address:** rick@kcsports.org. **Website:** www.usssabaseball.org. **Year Founded:** 1965/Baseball 1996.

WORLD WOOD BAT ASSOCIATION

(A Division of Perfect Game USA)
Mailing Address: 1203 Rockford Road SW, Cedar Rapids, IA 52404. **Telephone:** (319) 298-2923. **Fax:** (319) 298-2924. **E-Mail Address:** tay-lor@perfectgame.org. **Website:** www.worldwoodbat.com.
Year Founded: 1997.
President: Andy Ford. **National Director:** Taylor McCollough. **Scouting Director:** David Rawnsley.

BASEBALL USA

Mailing Address: 2626 W. Sam Houston Pkwy. N., Houston, TX 77043. **Telephone:** (713) 690-5055. **Fax:** (713) 690-9448. **E-Mail Address:** info@baseballusa.com. **Website:** www.baseballusa.com.
President: Phil Cross. **Tournament Director:** Steve Olson

CALIFORNIA COMPETITIVE YOUTH BASEBALL

Mailing Address: P.O. Box 338, Placentia, CA 92870. **Telephone:** (714) 993-2838. **Fax:** (714) 961-6078. **E-Mail Address:** ccybnet@aol.com. **Website:** www.ccyb.net.
Tournament Director: Todd Rogers.

COCOA EXPO SPORTS CENTER

Mailing Address: 500 Friday Road, Cocoa, FL 32926. **Telephone:** (321) 639-3976. **Fax:** (321) 639-0598. **E-Mail Address:** athleticdirector@cocoaexpo.com. **Website:** www.cocoaexpo.com.
Athletic Director: Matt Yurish.
Activities: Spring training program, instructional camps, team training camps, youth tournaments.

COOPERSTOWN BASEBALL WORLD

Mailing Address: P.O. Box 530, Brick, NJ 08723. **Telephone:** (888) CBW-8750. **Fax:** (888) CBW-8720. **E-Mail:** cbw@cooperstownbaseballworld.com. **Website:** www.cooperstownbaseballworld.com.
Complex Address: Cooperstown Baseball World, SUNY-Oneonta, Ravine Parkway, Oneonta, NY 13820.
President/Chairman: Eddie Einhorn. **Vice President:** Debra Sirianni.
2011 Tournaments (15 Teams Per Week): Open to 11U, 12U, 13U, 14U, 15U, 16U from July 4 through August 14.

COOPERSTOWN DREAMS PARK
Mailing Address: 330 S. Main St., Salisbury, NC 28144. **Telephone:** (704) 630-0050. **Fax:** (704) 630-0737. **E-Mail Address:** info@cooperstowndreamspark.com. **Website:** www.cooperstowndreamspark.com.
Complex Address: 4550 State Highway 28, Cooperstown, NY 13807.
Chief Executive Officer: Lou Presutti. **Program Director:** Geoff Davis.
2011 Tournaments: Weekly June 4–Aug. 27.

COOPERSTOWN ALL STAR VILLAGE
Mailing Address: 4158 State Highway 23, Oneonta, N.Y. **13820. Telephone:** (800) 327-6790. **Fax:** (607) 432-1076. **E-Mail Address:** info@cooperstownallstarvillage.com. **Website:** www.cooperstownallstarvillage.com.
Team Registrations: Jim Rudloff. **Hotel Room Reservations:** Shelly Yager. **Presidents:** Martin and Brenda Patton.

DISNEY'S WIDE WORLD OF SPORTS
Mailing Address: P.O. BOX 470847, Celebration, Fl 34747. **Telephone:** (407) 938-3802. **Fax:** (407) 938-3442. **E-mail address:** wdw.sports.baseball@disneysports.com. **Website:** www.disneybaseball.com.
Manager, Sports Events: Scott St George. **Sports Manager:** Emily Moak. **Tournament Director:** Al Schlazer. **Sales Manager, Baseball:** Kyle Cantrell.

KC SPORTS TOURNAMENTS
Mailing Address: KC Sports, 6324 N. Chatham Ave., No. 136, Kansas City, MO 64151.
Telephone: (816) 587-4545. **Fax:** (816) 587-4549.
E-Mail Address: info@kcsports.org. **Website:** www.kcsports.org.
Activities: USSSA Youth tournaments (ages 6-18).

U.S. AMATEUR BASEBALL FEDERATION
Mailing Address: P.O. Box 531216, San Diego, CA 92153. **Telephone:** (619) 934-2151. **Fax:** (619) 271-6659. **E-Mail Address:** usabf@cox.net. **Website:** www.usabf.com.
Year Founded: 1997. **Senior Chief Executive Officer/President:** Tim Halbig.

INSTRUCTIONAL SCHOOLS/
PRIVATE CAMPS

ACADEMY OF PRO PLAYERS
Mailing Address: 140 5th Avenue, Hawthorne, NJ 07506. **Telephone:** (973) 772-3355. **Fax:** (973) 772-4839. **E-Mail Address:** proplayer@nji.com. **Website:** www.academypro.com. **Camp Director:** Dan Gilligan.

ALL-STAR BASEBALL ACADEMY
Mailing Addresses: 650 South Parkway Blvd., Broomall, PA 19008; 52 Penn Oaks Dr., West Chester, PA 19382. **Telephone:** (610) 355-2411, (610) 399-8050. **Fax:** (610) 355-2414. **E-Mail Address:** basba@allstarbaseballacademy.com. **Website:** www.allstarbaseballacademy.com. **Directors:** Mike Manning, Jim Freeman.

AMERICAN BASEBALL FOUNDATION
Mailing Address: 2660 10th Ave. South, Suite 620, Birmingham, AL 35205. **Telephone:** (205) 558-4235. **Fax:** (205) 918-0800. **E-Mail Address:** abf@asmi.org. **Website:** www.americanbaseball.org. **Executive Director:** David Osinski. **Chairman of the Board:** James R. Andrews, M.D.

THE BASEBALL ACADEMY
Mailing Address: IMG Academies, 5500 34th St. W., Bradenton, FL 34210. **Telephone:** (800) 872-6425. **Fax:** (941) 739-7484. **Website:** www.imgacademies.com.

AMERICA'S BASEBALL CAMPS
Mailing Address: Ben Boulware, 3020 ISSQ. Pine Lake Road #12, Sammamish, WA 98075. **Telephone:** (800) 222-8152. **Fax:** (888)-751-8989. **E-Mail Address:** info@baseballcamps.com. **Website:** www.baseballcamps.com.

BUCKY DENT'S BASEBALL SCHOOL
Mailing Address: 490 Dotterel Road, Delray Beach, FL 33444. **Telephone:** (561) 265-0280. **Fax:** (561) 278-6679. **E-Mail Address:** staff@dentbaseball.com. **Website:** www.buckydentbaseballschool.com. **VP/GM:** Larry Hoskin.

CHAMPIONS BASEBALL ACADEMY
Mailing Address: Champions Baseball Academy, 1306 US 50, Milford, OH 45150. **Telephone:** (513) 831-8873. **Fax:** (513) 247-0040. **E-Mail Address:** toddmontgomery@championsbaseball.net. **Website:** www.championsbaseball.net.

DOYLE BASEBALL ACADEMY
Mailing Address: P.O. Box 9156, Winter Haven, FL 33883. **Telephone:** (863) 439-1000. **Fax:** (863) 294-8607. **E-Mail Address:** info@doylebaseball.com. **Website:** www.doylebaseball.com. **President:** Denny Doyle. **Director:** Blake Doyle.

FROZEN ROPES TRAINING CENTERS
Mailing Address: 24 Old Black Meadow Rd., Chester, NY 10918. **Telephone:** (845) 469-7331. **Fax:** (845) 469-6742. **E-Mail Address:** info@frozenropes.com. **Website:** www.frozenropes.com. **Corporate Director:** Tony Abbatine.

MARK CRESSE BASEBALL SCHOOL
Mailing Address: 58 Fulmar Lane, Aliso Viego, CA 92656. **Telephone:** (714) 892-6145. **Fax:** (714) 892-1881. **E-Mail Address:** info@markcresse.com. **Website:** www.markcresse.com. **Owner/Founder:** Mark Cresse. **Executive Director:** Jeff Sears.

US SPORTS CAMPS
Mailing Address: Mike de Surville, 750 Lindaro Street, Suite 220, San Rafael, CA 94901. **Telephone:** (415) 479-6060. **Fax:** (415) 479-6061. **E-Mail Address:** baseball@ussportscamps.com. **Website:** www.ussportscamps.com.

MOUNTAIN WEST BASEBALL ACADEMY
Mailing Address: 389 West 10000 South, South Jordan, UT 84095. **Telephone:** (801) 561-1700. **Fax:** (801) 561-1762. **E-Mail Address:** kent@utahbaseballacademy.com. **Website:** www.mountainwestbaseball.com. **Director:** Bob Keyes

NORTH CAROLINA BASEBALL ACADEMY
Mailing Address: 1137 Pleasant Ridge Road, Greensboro, NC 27409. **Telephone:** (336) 931-1118. **E-Mail Address:** info@ncbaseball.com. **Website:** www.ncbaseball.com.
Owner/Director: Scott Bankhead.

PENNSYLVANIA DIAMOND BUCKS
Mailing Address: 2320 Whitetail Court, Hellertown, PA 18055. **Telephone:** (610) 838-1219, (610) 442-6998. **E-Mail Address:** janciganick@yahoo.com. **Camp Director:** Jan Ciganick. **Head of Instruction:** Chuck Ciganick.

PROFESSIONAL BASEBALL INSTRUCTION

Mailing Address: 107 Pleasant Ave., Upper Saddle River, NJ 07458. **Telephone:** (800) 282-4638 (NY/NJ), (877) 448-2220 (rest of U.S.). **Fax:** (201) 760-8820. **E-Mail Address:** info@baseballclinics.com. **Website:** www.baseballclinics.com. **President:** Doug Cinnella.

RIPKEN BASEBALL CAMPS

Mailing Address: 1427 Clarkview Rd., Suite 100, Baltimore, MD 21209. **Telephone:** (410) 823-0808. **Fax:** (410) 823-0850. **E-Mail Address:** information@ripken-baseball.com. **Website:** www.ripkenbaseball.com.

SHO-ME BASEBALL CAMP

Mailing Address: P.O. Box 2270, Branson West, MO 65737. **Telephone:** (800) 993-2267, (417) 338-5838. **Fax:** (417) 338-2610. **E-Mail Address:** info@shomebaseball.com. **Website:** www.shomebaseball.com. **Camp Director:** Christopher Schroeder. **Head of Instruction:** Dick Birmingham.

COLLEGE CAMPS

Almost all of the elite college baseball programs have summer/holiday instructional camps. Please consult the college section for listings.

SENIOR BASEBALL

MEN'S SENIOR BASEBALL LEAGUE

(25 and Over, 35 and Over, 45 and Over, 55 and Over)
Mailing Address: One Huntington Quadrangle, Suite 3N07, Melville, NY 11747. **Telephone:** (631) 753-6725. **Fax:** (631) 753-4031.
President: Steve Sigler. **Vice President:** Gary D'Ambrisi.
E-Mail Address: info@msblnational.com. **Website:** www.msblnational.com.

MEN'S ADULT BASEBALL LEAGUE

(18 and Over)
Mailing Address: One Huntington Quadrangle, Suite 3N07, Melville, NY 11747. **Telephone:** (631) 753-6725. **Fax:** (631) 753-4031.
E-Mail Address: info@msblnational.com. **Website:** www.msblnational.com.
President: Steve Sigler. **Vice President:** Gary D'Ambrisi.

NATIONAL ADULT BASEBALL ASSOCIATION

Mailing Address: 3609 S. **Wadsworth Blvd., Suite** 135, Lakewood, CO 80235. **Telephone:** (800) 621-6479. **Fax:** (303) 639-6605. **E-Mail:** nabanational@aol.com. **Website:** www.dugout.org.
President: Shane Fugita.

NATIONAL AMATEUR BASEBALL FEDERATION

Mailing Address: P.O. Box 705, Bowie, MD 20718. **Telephone:** (301) 464-5460. **Fax:** (301) 352-0214. **E-Mail Address:** nabf1914@aol.com. **Website:** www.nabf.com.
Year Founded: 1914.
Executive Director: Charles Blackburn.

ROY HOBBS BASEBALL

Open (28-over), Veterans (38-over), Masters (48-over), Legends (55-over); Family Affairs Division, Classics (60-over), Seniors (65-over), Women's open.
Mailing Address: 2048 Akron Peninsula Rd., **Akron, OH 44313. Telephone:** (330) 923-3400. **Fax:** (330) 923-1967. **E-Mail Address:** rhbb@royhobbs.com. **Website:** www.royhobbs.com.
President: Tom Giffen. **Vice President:** Ellen Giffen.

DIRECTORIES

- **AGENT**
- **SERVICE**

AGENT DIRECTORY

ACES, INC.
Seth Levinson, Esq.
Sam Levinson
Keith Miller
Peter Pedalino, Esq.
Mike Zimmerman
Brandon O'Hearn
Jamie Appel
Robert Withers
188 Montague Street, 6th Floor
Brooklyn, NY 11201
Phone: 718-237-2900
Fax: 718-522-3906
aces@acesinc1.com

DOUBLE DIAMOND SPORTS MANAGEMENT
Joshua Kusnick
1 E. Broward Blvd.
Suite 1400
Ft. Lauderdale, FL 33301
Phone: 954-472-1047
Fax: 954-523-7009
Joshuakusnick@aol.com

FRANK A. BLANDINO, LLC ATTORNEY AT LAW
Frank Blandino
204 Towne Centre Dr
Hillsborough, NJ 08844
Phone: 908-217-3226
Fax: 908-281-0596
Frank@blandinolaw.com

METIS SPORTS MANAGEMENT, LLC
Storm T. Kirschenbaum, Esq. (Storm@metis-sports.com)
Hector Faneytt (Hector@metissports.com)
132 North Old Woodward Ave.
Birmingham, MI 48009
Phone: 248-594-1070
Fax: 248-281-5150
www.metissports.com

OAK SPORTS MANAGEMENT
Michael Bonanno
Jeffrey Cordova
41 Mortan Ave. East
Brantford, ON N3R 7J5
Phone: 905-462-3001
Fax: 519-753-9495
www.oaksportsmanagement.com
info@oaksportsmanagement.com

PETER E. GREENBERG &ASSOCIATES LTD.
Peter E. Greenberg, Esq.
Edward L. Greenberg
Chris Leible
200 Madison Ave.
Suite 2225
New York, NY 10016
Phone: 212-334-6880
Fax: 212-334-6895
www.petergreenbergsports.com

PRO AGENTS INC.
David P. Pepe
Bill Martin Jr.
90 Woodbridge Center Dr
Woodbridge, NJ 07095
Phone: 800-795-3454
Fax: 732-726-6688
Pepeda@wilentz.com

PRO STAR MANAGEMENT, INC.
Joe Bick, President
Brett Bick, Executive Vice President
Ryan Bick, Vice President
1600 Scripps Center
312 Walnut St
Cincinnati, OH 45202
Phone: 513-762-7676
Fax: 513-721-46283
www.prostarmanagement.com
prostar@fuse.net

SOSNICK COBBE SPORTS
Matt Sosnick
Paul Cobbe
Matt Hofer
Tripper Johnson
Adam Karon
Jonathan Pridie
712 Bancroft Rd, #510
Walnut Creek, CA 94598
Phone: 925-890-5283
Fax: 925-476-0130
www.SosnickCobbeSports.com
MattSoz@aol.com, PaulCobbe@me.com

THE SPARTA GROUP, INC.
Michael Nicotera
Gene Casaleggio
Sohail Shahpari, Esq.
140 Littleton Road
Suite 100
Parsippany, NJ 07054
Phone: 973-335-0550
Fax: 973-335-2148
www.thespartagroup.com
frontdesk@thespartagroup.com

VERRILL DANA SPORTS LAW GROUP
David S. Abramson, Esq.
One Portland Square
Portland, ME 04101
Phone: 207-774-4000
Fax: 207-774-7499
www.verrilldana.com
dabramson@verrilldana.com

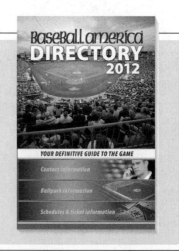

YOUR NAME HERE.
Make sure the baseball community can find you in 2012

Call (919) 682-9635 x124

or e-mail
advertising@baseballamerica.com

BaseBall america
DIRECTORY 2012
YOUR DEFINITIVE GUIDE TO THE GAME
Contact information
Ballpark information
Schedules & ticket information

SERVICE DIRECTORY

ACCESSORIES

WILSON SPORTING GOODS
8750 West Bryn Mawr Ave.
13th Floor
Chicago, IL 60631
Phone: 800-333-8326
Fax: 773-714-4565
www.wilson.com
askwilson@wilson.com

APPAREL

ALL PRO SPORTS
5341 Derry Ave.
Suite P
Agoura Hills, CA 91301
Phone: 818-707-3180
Fax: 818-707-3180
www.allprosports.net/store
win@allprosports.net

MINOR LEAGUES, MAJOR DREAMS
P.O. Box 6098
Anaheim, CA 92816
Phone: 800-345-2421
Fax: 714-939-0655
www.minorleagues.com
mlmd@minorleagues.com

MV SPORT
88 Spence St
Bay Shore, NY 11706-7171
Phone: 800-367-7900
Fax: 631-435-8018
www.mvsport.com
terry@wpmv.com

UNDER ARMOUR
1020 Hull Street
Baltimore, MD 21230
Phone: 888-4-ARMOUR
baseball.underarmour.com

BAGS

DIAMOND BASEBALL COMPANY
11130 Warland Dr
Cypress, CA 90630
Phone: 800-366-2999
Fax: 888-870-7555

GERRY COSBY AND COMPANY
11 Pennsylvania Plaza
New York, NY 10001
Phone: 877-563-6464
Fax: 212-967-0876
www.cosbysports.com
gcsmsg@cosbysports.com

LOUISVILLE SLUGGER
800 Main St.
Louisville, KY 40202
Phone: 800-282-2287
Fax: 502-585-1179
www.slugger.com
customer.service@slugger.com

MV SPORT
88 Spence St
Bay Shore, NY 11706-7171
Phone: 800-367-7900
Fax: 631-435-8018
www.mvsport.com
terry@wpmv.com

SCHUTT SPORTS
710 S. Industrial Dr.
Litchfield, IL 62025
Phone: 217-324-2712
www.schuttsports.com
sales@schutt-sports.com

WILSON SPORTING GOODS
8750 West Bryn Mawr Ave.
13th Floor
Chicago, IL 60631
Phone: 800-333-8326
Fax: 773-714-4565
www.wilson.com
askwilson@wilson.com

BASEBALL BACKSTOP

L.A. STEELCRAFT PRODUCTS, INC.
1975 Lincoln Ave.
Pasadena, CA 91103
Phone: 800-371-2438
Fax: 626-798-1482
www.lasteelcraft.com
info@lasteelcraft.com

BASEBALLS

C&H BASEBALL, INC.
10615 Technology Terrace
Bradenton, FL 34211
Phone: 941-727-1533
Fax: 941-727-0588
www.chbaseball.com
info@chbaseball.com

DIAMOND BASEBALL COMPANY
11130 Warland Dr
Cypress, CA 90630
Phone: 800-333-8326
Fax: 733-714-4565

WILSON SPORTING GOODS
8750 West Bryn Mawr Ave
13th Floor
Chicago, IL 60631
www.wilson.com
askwilson@wilson.com

BASES

C&H BASEBALL, INC.
10615 Technology Terrace
Bradenton, FL 34211
Phone: 941-727-1533
Fax: 941-727-0588
www.chbaseball.com
info@chbaseball.com

BATS

A-BAT BY SUPERIOR BAT COMPANY
11 E 1st St
Jamestown, WY 14701
Phone: 716-499-6887
www.promaplebats.com
stevet@promaplebats.com

B45 BATS
281 Edward-Assh
Ste-Catherine-de-la-Jacques-Cartier,
QC Canada G3N 1A3
Phone: 1-888-669-0145
www.b45online.com
info@b45online.com
*Pro/MLB Contact – Rick Kramer
301-346-1046
rkramer@b45online.com

BRETT BROS. SPORTS
East 9516 Montgomery Street
Building #14
Phone: 509-891-6435
Fax: 509-891-4156
www.brettbros.com
brettbats@aol.com

BWP BATS, LLC
80 Womeldorf Lane
Brookville, PA 15825
Phone: 814-849-0089
Fax: 814-849-8584
www.bwpbats.com
sales@bwpbats.com

DEMARINI
6435 NW Croeni Rd.
Hillsboro, OR 97124
Phone: 800-937-BATS (2287)
Fax: 503-531-5506
www.demarini.com

DIAMOND BASEBALL COMPANY
11130 Warland Dr
Cypress, CA 90630
Phone: 800-366-2999
Fax: 888-870-7555

EASTON
7855 Haskell Ave, Suite 200
Van Nuys, CA 91406
Phone: 800-632-7866
www.eastonbaseball.com

LOUISVILLE SLUGGER
800 Main St.
Louisville, KY 40202
Phone: 800-282-2287
Fax: 502-585-1179
www.slugger.com
customer.service@slugger.com

MATTINGLY SPORTS
2 Enterprise Drive
Suite 407
Shelton, CT 06484
Phone: 866-627-2287
Fax: 203-944-0284
www.mattinglysports.com
marketing@mattinglybaseball.com

OLD HICKORY BAT COMPANY
PO Box 588
White House, TN 37188
Phone: 866-PRO-BATS
Fax: 615-285-0512
www.oldhickorybats.com
copley@oldhickorybats.com

NIKE
One Bowerman Drive
Beaverton, OR 97005
Phone: 800-806-6453
www.nikebaseball.com

RAWLINGS
510 Maryville University Drive
St. Louis, MO 63141
www.rawlings.com

SAM BAT – THE ORIGINAL MAPLE BAT CORPORATION

54 Beech Street
Ottawa, ON K2H 5V4
Phone: 888-SAM BATS
613-724-2421
Fax: 613-725-3299
www.sambat.com
bats@sambat.com

BATTING CAGES

BEACON ATHLETICS

8233 Forsythia St
Suite 120
Middleton, WI 53562
Phone: 800-747-5985
Fax: 608-836-0724
www.beaconathletics.com
info@beaconathletics.com

C&H BASEBALL, INC.

10615 Technology Terrace
Bradenton, FL 34211
Phone: 941-727-1533
Fax: 941-727-0588
www.chbaseball.com
info@chbaseball.com

DIAMOND BASEBALL COMPANY

11130 Warland Dr
Cypress, CA 90630
Phone: 800-366-2999
Fax: 888-870-7555

GOLF RANGE NETTING

40351 US HWY 19 N
#303
Tarpon Springs, FL 34687
Phone: 727-938-4448
Fax: 727-938-4135
www.golfrangenetting.com
info@golfrangenetting.com

JUGS SPORTS

11885 SW Herman Rd
Tualatin, OR 97062
Phone: 1-800-547-6843
Fax: 503-691-1100
www.jugssports.com
stevec@jugssports.com

MASTER PITCHING MACHINE, INC.

4200 NE Birmingham Rd.
Kansas City, MO 64117
Phone: 800-878-8228
Fax: 816-452-7581
www.masterpitch.com
joeg@masterpitch.com

NATIONAL SPORTS PRODUCTS

3441 S 11th Ave
Eldridge, IA 52748
Phone: 800-478-6497
Fax: 800-443-8907
www.nationalsportsproducts.com
sales@nationalsportsproducts.com

WEST COAST NETTING

5075 Flightline Dr
Kingman, AZ 86401
Phone: 928-692-1144
Fax: 928-692-1501
www.westcoastnetting.com
info@westcoastnetting.com

BATTING HELMETS

SCHUTT SPORTS

710 S. Industrial Dr.
Litchfield, IL 62025
Phone: 217-324-2712
www.schuttsports.com
sales@schutt-sports.com

CAMPS/SCHOOLS

BE THE BEST YOU ARE BASEBALL COACHES CLINIC

PO Box 570
Brielle, NJ 08730
Phone: 732-528-5392
Fax: 732-528-4843
www.bethebest.com
bethebest@bytheshore.com

PROFESSIONAL BASEBALL INSTRUCTION

107 Pleasant Ave.
Uppers Saddle River, NJ 07458
Phone: 800-282-4638
Fax: 201-760-8820
www.baseballclinics.com
info@baseballclinics.com

SCORE INTERNATIONAL

P.O. Box 9994
Chattanooga, TN 37412
Phone: 423-894-7111
Fax: 423-894-7303
www.scoreinternational.org
info@scoreinternational.org

CAPS/HEADWEAR

MINOR LEAGUES, MAJOR DREAMS

P.O. Box 6098
Anaheim, CA 92816
Phone: 800-345-2421
Fax: 714-939-0655
www.minorleagues.com
mlmd@minorleagues.com

CARTS AND KIOSKS

B-R CARTS AND KIOSKS

1360 County Road #8
P.O. Box 25338
Farmington, NY 14425
Phone: 585-398-2190
Fax: 585-398-2143
www.brcarts.com
nancyrole@brcarts.com

CLEATS

ALL PRO SPORTS

5341 Derry Ave.
Suite P
Agoura Hills, CA 91301
Phone: 818-707-3180
Fax: 818-707-3180
www.allprosports.net/store
win@allprosports.net

NEW BALANCE

20 Guest Street
Boston, MA 02135
www.newbalance.com

NIKE

One Bowerman Drive
Beaverton, OR 97005
Phone: 800-806-6453
www.nikebaseball.com

REEBOK

1895 JW Foster Blvd
Canton, MA 02021
Phone: 800-934-3566
www.reebok.com

UNDER ARMOUR

1020 Hull Street
Baltimore, MD 21230
Phone: 888-4-ARMOUR
baseball.underarmour.com

COACHES CLINICS

BE THE BEST YOU ARE BASEBALL COACHES CLINIC

PO Box 570
Brielle, NJ 08730
Phone: 732-528-5392
Fax: 732-528-4843
www.bethebest.com
bethebest@bytheshore.com

CONCESSION OPERATIONS

CONCESSION SOLUTIONS INC.

16022-26th Ave NE
Shoreline, WA 98155
Phone: 206-440-9203
Fax: 206-440-9213
www.concessionsolutions.com
theresa@concessionsolutions.com

EMBROIDERED EMBLEMS/ PATCHES

THE EMBLEM SOURCE

4575 Westgrove Dr, #500
Addison, TX 75001
Phone: 972-248-1909
Fax: 972-248-1615
www.theemblemsource.com
info@theemblemsource.com

ENTERTAINMENT

BIRDZERK!

P.O. Box 36061
Louisville, KY 40233
Phone: 800-219-0899/502-458-4020
Fax: 502-458-0867
www.birdzerk.com
dom@birdzerk.com

BREAKIN' BBOY MCCOY

P.O. Box 36061
Louisville, KY 40233
Phone: 800-219-0899/502-458-4020
Fax: 502-458-0867
www.bboymccoy.com
dom@theskillvillegroup.com

COYOTE PROMOTIONS

300 Worthern Blvd, #26
Great Neck, WY 11021
Phone: 800-726-9683
Fax: 516-482-7425
www.coyotepromotions.com
info@coyotepromotions.com

VIRTUS STUNTS, LLC
TED A. BATCHELOR
*Runs the bases on fire
16320 Snyder Rd
Chagrin Falls, OH 44023
Phone: 216-402-8705
Fax: 440-247-1909
www.tedbatchelor.com
stuntma488@aol.com

INFLATAMANIACS
8004 Sycamore Creek
Louisville, KY 40222
Phone: 502-417-8659
Fax: 502-566-1896
www.inflatamaniacs.com
steven@inflatamaniacs.com

MYRON NOODLEMAN
P.O. Box 36061
Louisville, KY 40233
Phone: 800-219-0899/502-458-4020
Fax: 502-458-0867
www.myronnoodleman.com
dom@theskillvillegroup.com

SCOLLON PRODUCTIONS/
SCOLLON LIVE EVENTS
P.O. Box 486
White Rock, SC 29177
Phone: 803-345-3922
Fax: 803-345-9313
www.scollon.com
rick@scollon.com

TOTAL SPORTS
ENTERTAINMENT
2414 State Road
LaCrosse, WI 54601
Phone: 800-962-2471
Fax: 608-782-4655
www.totalsportsentertainment.com
info@totalsportsentertainment.com

ZOOPERSTARS!
P.O. Box 36061
Louisville, KY 40233
Phone: 800-219-0899/502-458-4020
Fax: 502-458-0867
www.zooperstars.com
dom@zooperstars.com

EVENT BADGES

BIG BADGE USA
209 Middlesex Turnpike
Burlington, MA 01803-3316
Phone: 781-993-3350
Fax: 781-272-5950
www.bigbadgeusa.com
info@bigbadgeusa.com

FIELD COVERS/TARPS

BEAM CLAY
Kelsey Park
Great Meadows, NJ 07838
Phone: 800-247-BEAM (2326)
Fax: 908-637-8421
www.beamclay.com
sales@partac.com

See our ad on the insde back cover!

C&H BASEBALL, INC.
10615 Technology Terrace
Bradenton, FL 34211
Phone: 941-727-1533
Fax: 941-727-0588
www.chbaseball.com
info@chbaseball.com

COVERMASTER INC.
100 Westmore Dr, 11-D
Rexdale, ON M9V 5C3
Phone: 800-387-5808
Fax: 416-742-6837
www.covermaster.com
info@covermaster.com

NATIONAL SPORTS PRODUCTS
3441 S 11th Ave
Eldridge, IA 52748
Phone: 800-478-6497
Fax: 800-443-8907
www.nationalsportsproducts.com
sales@nationalsportsproducts.com

REEF INDUSTRIES, INC.
9209 Almeda Genoa Rd.
Houston, TX 77075
Phone: 713-507-4251
Fax: 713-507-4295
www.reefindustries.com
ri@reefindustries.com

FIELD EQUIPMENT

DIAMOND BASEBALL
COMPANY
11130 Warland Dr
Cypress, CA 90630
Phone: 800-366-2999
Fax: 888-870-7555

FIELD WALL PADDING

BEAM CLAY
Kelsey Park
Great Meadows, NJ 07838
Phone: 800-247-BEAM (2326)
Fax: 908-637-8421
www.beamclay.com
sales@partac.com

See our ad on the insde back cover!

BIGSIGNS.COM
22 S. Harbor Dr.
Suite 101
Phone: 800-790-7611
Fax: 800-790-7611
www.bigsigns.com
sales@bigsigns.com

C&H BASEBALL, INC.
10615 Technology Terrace
Bradenton, FL 34211
Phone: 941-727-1533
Fax: 941-727-0588
www.chbaseball.com
info@chbaseball.com

COVERMASTER INC.
100 Westmore Dr, 11-D
Rexdale, ON M9V 5C3
Phone: 800-387-5808
Fax: 416-742-6837
www.covermaster.com
info@covermaster.com

NATIONAL SPORTS PRODUCTS
3441 S 11th Ave
Eldridge, IA 52748
Phone: 800-478-6497
Fax: 800-443-8907
www.nationalsportsproducts.com
sales@nationalsportsproducts.com

WEST COAST NETTING
5075 Flightline Dr
Kingman, AZ 86401
Phone: 928-692-1144
Fax: 928-692-1501
www.westcoastnetting.com
info@westcoastnetting.com

FIREWORKS

PYROTECNICO
P.O. Box 149
New Castle, PA 16103
Phone: 800-854-4705
Fax: 724-652-1288
www.pyrotecnico.com
vlaurenza@pyrotecnico.com

GAME MANAGEMENT
SOFTWARE

TOTAL SPORTS
ENTERTAINMENT
2414 State Road
LaCrosse, WI 54601
Phone: 800-962-2471
Fax: 608-782-4655
www.totalsportsentertainment.com
info@totalsportsentertainment.com

GIVEAWAY ITEMS

COYOTE PROMOTIONS
300 Worthern Blvd, #26
Great Neck, WY 11021
Phone: 800-726-9683
Fax: 516-482-7425
www.coyotepromotions.com
info@coyotepromotions.com

RICO INDUSTRIES, INC/
TAG EXPRESS
7000 N Austin
Niles, IL 60714
Phone: 1-800-423-5856
Fax: 312-427-0190
www.ricoinc.com
jimz@ricoinc.com

GLOVES

ALL PRO SPORTS
5341 Derry Ave.
Suite P
Agoura Hills, CA 91301
Phone: 818-707-3180
Fax: 818-707-3180
www.allprosports.net/store
win@allprosports.net

ALL-STAR DIVISION –
AMPAC ENTERPRISES INC.
P.O. Box 1356
Shirley, MA 01404
Phone: 978-425-6266
Fax: 978-425-4068
www.all-starsports.com
customerservice@all-starsports.com

BRETT BROS. SPORTS
East 9516 Montgomery Street
Building #14
Phone: 509-891-6435
Fax: 509-891-4156
www.brettbros.com
brettbats@aol.com

FRANK'S SPORT SHOP
430 E. Tremont Ave.
Bronx, New York 10457
Phone: 718-299-5223, 212-945
Fax: 718-583-1652
www.frankssportshop.com

See our ad on the insert!

LOUISVILLE SLUGGER
800 Main St.
Louisville, KY 40202
Phone: 800-282-2287
Fax: 502-585-1179
www.slugger.com
customer.service@slugger.com

NIKE
One Bowerman Drive
Beaverton, OR 97005
Phone: 800-806-6453
www.nikebaseball.com

OLD HICKORY BAT COMPANY
PO Box 588
White House, TN 37188
Phone: 866-PRO-BATS
Fax: 615-285-0512
www.oldhickorybats.com
copley@oldhickorybats.com

RAWLINGS
510 Maryville University Drive
St. Louis, MO 63141
www.rawlings.com

REEBOK
1895 JW Foster Blvd
Canton, MA 02021
Phone: 800-934-3566
www.reebok.com

WILSON SPORTING GOODS
8750 West Bryn Mawr Ave.
13th Floor
Chicago, IL 60631
Phone: 800-333-8326
Fax: 773-714-4565
www.wilson.com
askwilson@wilson.com

HIGHER EDUCATION

SAINT LEO UNIVERSITY ONLINE MBA/ SPORTS BUSINESS
33701 State Road 52
P.O. Box 6665/MC2067
Saint Leo, FL 33574
Phone: 352-588-7326
Fax: 352-588-8912
www.saintleo.edu
eric.schwarz@saintleo.edu

INSURANCE

K&K INSURANCE
1712 Magnavox Way
Fort Wayne, IN 46804
Phone: 800-441-3994
Fax: 260-459-5120
www.kandkinsurance.com
kk-sports@kandkinsurance.com

See our ad on the insde front cover!

LIGHTING

GOLF RANGE NETTING
40351 US HWY 19 N
#303
Tarpon Springs, FL 34687
Phone: 727-938-4448
Fax: 727-938-4135
www.golfrangenetting.com
info@golfrangenetting.com

MUSCO LIGHTING, LLC
100 1st Ave W.
P.O. Box 808
Oskaloosa, IA 52577
Phone: 800-825-6020
Fax: 641-673-4740
www.musco.com
rick.sneed@musco.com

MASCOTS

OLYMPUS GROUP (FORMERLY OLYMPUS FLAG & BANNER)
9000 West Heather Ave
Milwaukee, WI 53224
Phone: 414-355-2010
Fax: 414-355-1931
www.olympusgrp.com
sales@olympus-flag.com

SCOLLON PRODUCTIONS/ SCOLLON LIVE EVENTS
P.O. Box 486
White Rock, SC 29177
Phone: 803-345-3922
Fax: 803-345-9313
www.scollon.com
rick@scollon.com

MOBILE APPS

CRITICAL TECHNOLOGIES GROUP, LLC
*iPhone/Android Applications
3508 Overview Drive
Fredericksburg, VA 22408
Phone: 804.657.7268
www.ctgweb.biz
Info@ctgweb.biz

MUSIC/SOUND EFFECTS

SOUND DIRECTOR, INC.
2918 SW Royal Way
Gresham, OR 97080
Phone: 503-665-6869, 888-276-0088
Fax: 503-914-1812
www.SoundDirector.com
JJ@SoundDirector.com

NETTING/POSTS

C&H BASEBALL, INC.
10615 Technology Terrace
Bradenton, FL 34211
Phone: 941-727-1533
Fax: 941-727-0588
www.chbaseball.com
info@chbaseball.com

GOLF RANGE NETTING
40351 US HWY 19 N
#303
Tarpon Springs, FL 34687
Phone: 727-938-4448
Fax: 727-938-4135
www.golfrangenetting.com
info@golfrangenetting.com

L.A. STEELCRAFT PRODUCTS, INC.
1975 Lincoln Ave.
Pasadena, CA 91103
Phone: 800-371-2438
Fax: 626-798-1482
www.lasteelcraft.com
info@lasteelcraft.com

NATIONAL SPORTS PRODUCTS
3441 S 11th Ave
Eldridge, IA 52748
Phone: 800-478-6497
Fax: 800-443-8907
www.nationalsportsproducts.com
sales@nationalsportsproducts.com

WEST COAST NETTING
5075 Flightline Dr
Kingman, AZ 86401
Phone: 928-692-1144
Fax: 928-692-1501
www.westcoastnetting.com
info@westcoastnetting.com

NOVELTY ITEMS

COYOTE PROMOTIONS
300 Worthern Blvd, #26
Great Neck, NY 11021
Phone: 800-726-9683
Fax: 516-482-7425
www.coyotepromotions.com
info@coyotepromotions.com

ON DECK CIRCLES

BIGSIGNS.COM
22 S. Harbor Dr.
Suite 101
Phone: 800-790-7611
Fax: 800-790-7611
www.bigsigns.com
sales@bigsigns.com

PENNANTS, FOAM HANDS AND NOVELTY GIFTS

RICO INDUSTRIES, INC/ TAG EXPRESS
7000 N Austin
Niles, IL 60714
Phone: 1-800-423-5856
Fax: 312-427-0190
www.ricoinc.com
jimz@ricoinc.com

PITCHING AIDS

THROWTHECURVE.COM
107 Pleasant Ave.
Uppers Saddle River, NJ 07458
Phone: 800-282-4638
Fax: 201-760-8820
www.throwthecurve.com

PITCHING MACHINES

ATHLETIC TRAINING EQUIPMENT COMPANY - ATEC
655 Spice Island Dr
Sparks, NV 89431
Phone: (800) 998-ATEC (2832)
Fax: (800) 959-ATEC (2832)
www.atecsports.com
askATEC@wilson.com

C&H BASEBALL, INC.
10615 Technology Terrace
Bradenton, FL 34211
Phone: 941-727-1533
Fax: 941-727-0588
www.chbaseball.com
info@chbaseball.com

JUGS SPORTS
11885 SW Herman Rd
Tualatin, OR 97062
Phone: 1-800-547-6843
Fax: 503-691-1100
www.jugssports.com
stevec@jugssports.com

MASTER PITCHING MACHINE, INC.
4200 NE Birmingham Rd.
Kansas City, MO 64117
Phone: 800-878-8228
Fax: 816-452-7581
www.masterpitch.com
joeg@masterpitch.com

PROBATTER SPORTS
49 Research Dr, Ste A
Milford, CT 06460
Phone: 203-874-2500
Fax: 203-878-9019
www.probatter.com
abattersby@probatter.com

PITCHING TOES

ALL PRO SPORTS
5341 Derry Ave.
Suite P
Agoura Hills, CA 91301
Phone: 818-707-3180
Fax: 818-707-3180
www.allprosports.net/store
win@allprosports.net

PLAYING FIELD PRODUCTS

BEAM CLAY
Kelsey Park
Great Meadows, NJ 07838
Phone: 800-247-BEAM (2326)
Fax: 908-637-8421
www.beamclay.com
sales@partac.com

See our ad on the inside back cover!

C&H BASEBALL, INC.
10615 Technology Terrace
Bradenton, FL 34211
Phone: 941-727-1533
Fax: 941-727-0588
www.chbaseball.com
info@chbaseball.com

DIAMOND PRO
1341 West Mockingbird Lane
Dallas, TX 75247
Phone: 800-228-2987
Fax: 800-640-6735
www.diamondpro.com
diamondpro@txi.com

STALKER RADAR (APPLIED CONCEPTS)
2609 Technology Dr
Plano, TX 75074
Phone: 1-888-STALKER
www.stalkerradar.com
sales@stalkerradar.com

See our ad on page 6!

POINT OF SALE ITEMS

GERRY COSBY AND COMPANY
11 Pennsylvania Plaza
New York, NY 10001
Phone: 877-563-6464
Fax: 212-967-0876
www.cosbysports.com
gcsmsg@cosbysports.com

INTERNATIONAL MICRO SYSTEMS
200 Racoosin Dr
Suite 106
Aston, PA 19014
Phone: 484-482-1600
Fax: 484-482-1601
www.stadis.com
sales-marketing@ims-pos.com

POWDER AND POWDER PRODUCTS

HUPPO BY ITEM X INNOVATIONS, INC.
110 Peaceful Fork Rd
Morehead, KY 40351
Phone: 606-207-1392
www.gotyourhuppo.com
sales@gotyourhuppo.com

PROFESSIONAL SERVICES

GERRY COSBY AND COMPANY
11 Pennsylvania Plaza
New York, NY 10001
Phone: 877-563-6464
Fax: 212-967-0876
www.cosbysports.com
gcsmsg@cosbysports.com

INTERNATIONAL MICRO SYSTEMS
200 Racoosin Dr
Suite 106
Aston, PA 19014
Phone: 484-482-1600
Fax: 484-482-1601
www.stadis.com
sales-marketing@ims-pos.com

PROMOTIONAL ITEMS

BIG BADGE USA
209 Middlesex Turnpike
Burlington, MA 01803-3316
Phone: 781-993-3350
Fax: 781-272-5950
www.bigbadgeusa.com
info@bigbadgeusa.com

COYOTE PROMOTIONS
300 Worthern Blvd, #26
Great Neck, WY 11021
Phone: 800-726-9683
Fax: 516-482-7425
www.coyotepromotions.com
info@coyotepromotions.com

RICO INDUSTRIES, INC/ TAG EXPRESS
7000 N Austin
Niles, IL 60714
Phone: 1-800-423-5856
Fax: 312-427-0190
www.ricoinc.com
jimz@ricoinc.com

PROMOTIONS

COYOTE PROMOTIONS
300 Worthern Blvd, #26
Great Neck, WY 11021
Phone: 800-726-9683
Fax: 516-482-7425
www.coyotepromotions.com
info@coyotepromotions.com

INFLATAMANIACS
8004 Sycamore Creek
Louisville, KY 40222
Phone: 502-417-8659
Fax: 502-566-1896
www.inflatamaniacs.com
steven@inflatamaniacs.com

TOTAL SPORTS ENTERTAINMENT
2414 State Road
LaCrosse, WI 54601
Phone: 800-962-2471
Fax: 608-782-4655
www.totalsportsentertainment.com
info@totalsportsentertainment.com

VIRTUS STUNTS, LLC TED A. BATCHELOR
*Runs the bases on fire
16320 Snyder Rd
Chagrin Falls, OH 44023
Phone: 216-402-8705
Fax: 440-247-1909
www.tedbatchelor.com
stuntma488@aol.com

PROTECTIVE EQUIPMENT

ALL-STAR DIVISION – AMPAC ENTERPRISES INC.
P.O. Box 1356
Shirley, MA 01404
Phone: 978-425-6266
Fax: 978-425-4068
www.all-starsports.com
customerservice@all-starsports.com

DIAMOND BASEBALL COMPANY
11130 Warland Dr
Cypress, CA 90630
Phone: 800-366-2999
Fax: 888-870-7555

EVOSHIELD
300 Commerce Blvd
Bogart, GA 30622
Phone: 770-725-2724
www.evoshield.com

JUGS SPORTS
11885 SW Herman Rd
Tualatin, OR 97062
Phone: 1-800-547-6843
Fax: 503-691-1100
www.jugssports.com
stevec@jugssports.com

LOUISVILLE SLUGGER
800 Main St.
Louisville, KY 40202
Phone: 800-282-2287
Fax: 502-585-1179
www.slugger.com
customer.service@slugger.com

SCHUTT SPORTS
710 S. Industrial Dr.
Litchfield, IL 62025
Phone: 217-324-2712
www.schuttsports.com
sales@schutt-sports.com

WEST COAST NETTING
5075 Flightline Dr
Kingman, AZ 86401
Phone: 928-692-1144
Fax: 928-692-1501
www.westcoastnetting.com
info@westcoastnetting.com

WILSON SPORTING GOODS
8750 West Bryn Mawr Ave.
13th Floor
Chicago, IL 60631
Phone: 800-333-8326
Fax: 773-714-4565
www.wilson.com
askwilson@wilson.com

RADAR EQUIPMENT

JUGS SPORTS
11885 SW Herman Rd
Tualatin, OR 97062
Phone: 1-800-547-6843
Fax: 503-691-1100
www.jugssports.com
stevec@jugssports.com

SPORTS SENSORS INC.
11351 Embassy Dr
Cincinnati, OH 45240
Phone: 888-542-9246
Fax: 513-825-8532
www.sportssensors.com
adilz@cinci.rr.com

STALKER RADAR
(APPLIED CONCEPTS)
2609 Technology Dr
Plano, TX 75074
Phone: 1-888-STALKER
www.stalkerradar.com
sales@stalkerradar.com

See our ad on page 6!

SCOREBOARD

TOTAL SPORTS ENTERTAINMENT
2414 State Road
LaCrosse, WI 54601
Phone: 800-962-2471
Fax: 608-782-4655
www.totalsportsentertainment.com
info@totalsportsentertainment.com

SEATING

CLARIN SEATING
927 North Shore Drive
Lake Bluff, IL 60044
Phone: 508-528-9708
Fax: 508-541-5668
www.clarinseating.com

STURDISTEEL
P.O. Box 2655
Waco, TX 76702
Phone: 800-433-3116
Fax: 254-666-4472
www.sturdisteel.com
rgroppe@sturdisteel.net

SHOES

FRANK'S SPORT SHOP
430 E. Tremont Ave.
Bronx, New York 10457
Phone: 718-299-5223, 212-945
Fax: 718-583-1652
www.frankssportshop.com

See our ad on the insert!

SHOWCASES/PLAYER DEVELOPMENT

PROFESSIONAL BASEBALL INSTRUCTION- BATTERY INVITATIONAL
(pitchers/catchers – early November)
107 Pleasant Avenue
Upper Saddle River, NJ 07458
Phone: 800-282-4638
Fax: 201-760-8820
Greg@baseballclinics.com

SPORTING GOODS

ALL PRO SPORTS
5341 Derry Ave.
Suite P
Agoura Hills, CA 91301
Phone: 818-707-3180
Fax: 818-707-3180
www.allprosports.net/store
win@allprosports.net

JUGHEAD SPORTS
107 Pleasant Avenue
Upper Saddle River, NJ 07458
Phone: 800-282-4638
Fax: 201-760-8820
www.jugheadsports.com

SYNTHETIC TURF

A-TURF
P.O. Box 157
Williamsville, NY 14231
Phone: 888-777-6910
Fax: 716-204-0189
www.aturf.com
info@aturf.com

TICKETS

INDIANA TICKET CO.
P.O. Box 823
Muncie, IN 47308
Phone: 800-428-8640
Fax: 888-428-8640
www.muncienovelty.com
info@muncienovelty.com

NATIONAL TICKET COMPANY
P.O. Box 547
Shamokin, PA 17872
Phone: 800-829-0829
Fax: 800-829-0888
www.nationalticket.com
ticket@nationalticket.com

SPORTS MEDICINE

HUPPO BY ITEM X INNOVATIONS, INC.
110 Peaceful Fork Rd
Morehead, KY 40351
Phone: 606-207-1392
www.gotyourhuppo.com
sales@gotyourhuppo.com

STADIUM ARCHITECTS

360 ARCHITECTURE
Chris Lamberth
300 W 22nd Street
Kansas City, MO 64108
Phone: 816-472-3360
Fax: 816-472-2100
www.360architects.com
clamberth@360architects.com

TRAINING EQUIPMENT

ATHLETIC TRAINING EQUIPMENT COMPANY - ATEC
655 Spice Island Dr
Sparks, NV 89431
Phone: (800) 998-ATEC (2832)
Fax: (800) 959-ATEC (2832)
www.atecsports.com
askATEC@wilson.com

JUGS SPORTS
11885 SW Herman Rd
Tualatin, OR 97062
Phone: 1-800-547-6843
Fax: 503-691-1100
www.jugssports.com
stevec@jugssports.com

LOUISVILLE SLUGGER
800 Main St.
Louisville, KY 40202
Phone: 800-282-2287
Fax: 502-585-1179
www.slugger.com
customer.service@slugger.com

SPORTS SENSORS INC.
11351 Embassy Dr
Cincinnati, OH 45240
Phone: 888-542-9246
Fax: 513-825-8532
www.sportssensors.com
adilz@cinci.rr.com

WEST COAST NETTING
5075 Flightline Dr
Kingman, AZ 86401
Phone: 928-692-1144
Fax: 928-692-1501
www.westcoastnetting.com
info@westcoastnetting.com

TRAVEL

BROACH BASEBALL TOURS
5821 Fairview Rd, Suite 118
Charlotte, NC 28209
Phone: 800-849-6345
Fax: 704-365-3800
www.baseballtoursusa.com
info@broachsportstours.com

SCORE INTERNATIONAL
P.O. Box 9994
Chattanooga, TN 37412
Phone: 423-894-7111
Fax: 423-894-7303
www.scoreinternational.org
info@scoreinternational.org

SPORTS TRAVEL AND TOURS
60 Main St.
P.O. Box 50
Hatfield, MA 01038
Phone: 800-662-4424
Fax: 413-247-5700
www.sportstravelandtours.com
info@sportstravelandtours.com

TURNSTILE ADS

ENTRY MEDIA
127 West Fairbanks Ave.
#417
Winter Park, FL 32788
Phone: 407-078-4446
www.entrymedia.com
martin@entrymedia.com

UNIFORMS

AIS CUSTOM UNIFORM CO.
2202 Anderson St.
Vernon, CA 90058
Phone: 800-666-2733
Fax: 323-582-2831
www.aisathleticuniforms.com
allan@aisuniforms.com

EBBETS FIELD FLANNELS, INC.
PO Box 4858
Seattle, WA 98104
Phone: 206-382-7249
Fax: 206-382-4411
www.ebbets.com
jcohen@ebbets.com

WILSON SPORTING GOODS
8750 West Bryn Mawr Ave.
13th Floor
Chicago, IL 60631
Phone: 800-333-8326
Fax: 773-714-4565
www.wilson.com
askwilson@wilson.com

WINDSCREENS

BEAM CLAY
Kelsey Park
Great Meadows, NJ 07838
Phone: 800-247-BEAM (2326)
Fax: 908-637-8421
www.beamclay.com
sales@partac.com

See our ad on the inside back cover!

COVERMASTER INC.
100 Westmore Dr, 11-D
Rexdale, ON M9V 5C3
Phone: 800-387-5808
Fax: 416-742-6837
www.covermaster.com
info@covermaster.com

GOLF RANGE NETTING
40351 US HWY 19 N
#303
Tarpon Springs, FL 34687
Phone: 727-938-4448
Fax: 727-938-4135
www.golfrangenetting.com
info@golfrangenetting.com

NATIONAL SPORTS PRODUCTS
3441 S 11th Ave
Eldridge, IA 52748
Phone: 800-478-6497
Fax: 800-443-8907
www.nationalsportsproducts.com
sales@nationalsportsproducts.com

WEST COAST NETTING
5075 Flightline Dr
Kingman, AZ 86401
Phone: 928-692-1144
Fax: 928-692-1501
www.westcoastnetting.com
info@westcoastnetting.com

WRISTBANDS

NATIONAL TICKET COMPANY
P.O. Box 547
Shamokin, PA 17872
Phone: 800-829-0829
Fax: 800-829-0888
www.nationalticket.com
ticket@nationalticket.com

**Add your company to the Baseball America
2012 Agent Directory or Service Directory!**

Call 919-682-9635 x298 or email advertising@baseballamerica.com

INDEX

MAJOR LEAGUE TEAMS

Team	Page
Arizona Diamondbacks	16
Atlanta Braves	18
Baltimore Orioles	20
Boston Red Sox	22
Chicago Cubs	24
Chicago White Sox	26
Cincinnati Reds	28
Cleveland Indians	30
Colorado Rockies	32
Detroit Tigers	34
Florida Marlins	36
Houston Astros	38
Kansas City Royals	40
Los Angeles Angels	42
Los Angeles Dodgers	44
Milwaukee Brewers	46
Minnesota Twins	48
New York Mets	50
New York Yankees	52
Oakland Athletics	54
Philadelphia Phillies	56
Pittsburgh Pirates	58
St. Louis Cardinals	60
San Diego Padres	62
San Francisco Giants	64
Seattle Mariners	66
Tampa Bay Devil Rays	68
Texas Rangers	70
Toronto Blue Jays	72
Washington Nationals	74

MINOR LEAGUE TEAMS

Team (League)	Page
Aberdeen (New York-Penn)	156
Akron (Eastern)	109
Albuquerque (Pacific Coast)	100
Altoona (Eastern)	110
Arkansas (Texas)	121
Asheville (South Atlantic)	148
Auburn (New York-Penn)	157
Augusta (South Atlantic)	149
Bakersfield (California)	125
Batavia (New York-Penn)	157
Beloit (Midwest)	140
Billings (Pioneer)	172
Binghamton (Eastern)	110
Birmingham (Southern)	116
Bluefield (Appalachian)	167
Boise (Northwest)	163
Bowie (Eastern)	110
Bowling Green (Midwest)	141
Bradenton (Florida State)	136
Brevard County (Florida State)	136
Bristol (Appalachian)	168
Brooklyn (New York-Penn)	157
Buffalo (International)	92
Burlington (Appalachian)	168
Burlington (Midwest)	141
Carolina (Southern)	117
Casper (Pioneer)	173
Cedar Rapids (Midwest)	142
Charleston (South Atlantic)	149
Charlotte (International)	93
Charlotte (Florida State)	137
Chattanooga (Southern)	117
Clearwater (Florida State)	137
Clinton (Midwest)	142
Colorado Springs (Pacific Coast)	101
Columbus (International)	93
Columbus (South Atlantic)	176
Connecticut (New York-Penn)	158
Corpus Christi (Texas)	122
Danville (Appalachian)	168
Dayton (Midwest)	142
Daytona (Florida State)	138
Delmarva (South Atlantic)	150
Dunedin (Florida State)	138
Durham (International)	94
Elizabethton (Appalachian)	169
Erie (Eastern)	111
Eugene (Northwest)	164
Everett (Northwest)	164
Fort Myers (Florida State)	139
Fort Wayne (Midwest)	143
Frederick (Carolina)	130
Fresno (Pacific Coast)	101
Frisco (Texas)	122
Great Falls (Pioneer)	173
Great Lakes (Midwest)	143
Greeneville (Appalachian)	169
Greensboro (South Atlantic)	150
Greenville (South Atlantic)	151
Gwinnett (International)	94
Hagerstown (South Atlantic)	151
Harrisburg (Eastern)	111
Helena (Pioneer)	173
Hickory (South Atlantic)	152
High Desert (California)	126
Hudson Valley (New York-Penn)	158
Huntsville (Southern)	118
Idaho Falls (Pioneer)	174
Indianapolis (International)	95
Inland Empire (California)	126
Iowa (Pacific Coast)	102
Jackson (Southern)	118
Jacksonville (Southern)	118
Jamestown (New York-Penn)	159
Johnson City (Appalachian)	169
Jupiter (Florida State)	137
Kane County (Midwest)	144
Kannapolis (South Atlantic)	152
Kingsport (Appalachian)	170
Kinston (Carolina)	131
Lake County (Midwest)	144
Lake Elsinore (California)	126
Lakeland (Florida State)	138
Lakewood (South Atlantic)	153
Lancaster (California)	127
Lansing (Midwest)	145
Las Vegas (Pacific Coast)	102
Lehigh Valley (International)	96
Lexington (South Atlantic)	153
Louisville (International)	96
Lowell (New York-Penn)	159
Lynchburg (Carolina)	131
Mahoning Valley (New York-Penn)	159
Memphis (Pacific Coast)	103
Midland (Texas)	122
Mississippi (Southern)	119
Missoula (Pioneer)	174
Mobile (Southern)	119
Modesto (California)	127
Montgomery (Southern)	120
Myrtle Beach (Carolina)	131
Nashville (Pacific Coast)	103
New Britain (Eastern)	112
New Hampshire (Eastern)	112
New Orleans (Pacific Coast)	104
Norfolk (International)	97
Northwest Arkansas (Texas)	123
Ogden (Pioneer)	174
Oklahoma City (Pacific Coast)	104
Omaha (Pacific Coast)	104
Orem (Pioneer)	175
Palm Beach (Florida State)	138
Pawtucket (International)	97
Peoria (Midwest)	145
Portland (Eastern)	113
Portland (Pacific Coast)	107

BaseballAmerica.com

Potomac (Carolina)	132	Newark (Can-Am)	186
Princeton (Appalachian)	170	Normal (Frontier)	191
Pulaski (Appalachian)	171	Pittsfield (Can-Am)	187
Quad Cities (Midwest)	146	Quebec (Can-Am)	187
Rancho Cucamonga (California)	128	Rio Grande Valley (N. American)	196
Reading (Eastern)	113	River City (Frontier)	191
Reno (Pacific Coast)	105	Rockford (North American)	196
Richmond (Eastern)	114	Rockland (Can-Am)	187
Rochester (International)	98	St. Paul (American)	181
Rome (South Atlantic)	154	San Angelo (North American)	196
Round Rock (Pacific Coast)	106	Schaumburg (North American)	196
Sacramento (Pacific Coast)	109	Shreveport-Bossier (American)	181
St. Lucie (Florida State)	138	Sioux City (American)	181
Sacramento (Pacific Coast)	106	Sioux Falls (American)	182
Salem (Carolina)	132	Somerset (Atlantic)	185
Salem-Keizer (Northwest)	164	Southern Illinois (Frontier)	192
Salt Lake (Pacific Coast)	107	Southern Maryland (Atlantic)	185
San Antonio (Texas)	123	Traverse City (Frontier)	192
San Jose (California)	128	Washington (Frontier)	192
Savannah (South Atlantic)	154	Wichita (American)	182
Scranton/Wilkes-Barre (International)	98	Windy City (Frontier)	193
South Bend (Midwest)	146	Winnipeg (American)	182
Spokane (Northwest)	165	Worcester (Can-Am)	188
Springfield (Texas)	124	York (Atlantic)	185
State College (New York-Penn)	160	Yuma (North American)	197
Staten Island (New York-Penn)	160		
Stockton (California)	129		
Syracuse (International)	99		
Tacoma (Pacific Coast)	107		
Tampa (Florida State)	139		
Tennessee (Southern)	120		
Toledo (International)	99		
Trenton (Eastern)	115		
Tri-City (New York-Penn)	165		
Tri-City (Northwest)	167		
Tucson (Pacific Coast)	108		
Tulsa (Texas)	124		
Vancouver (Northwest)	166		
Vermont (New York-Penn)	161		
Vero Beach (Florida State)	166		
Visalia (California)	129		
West Michigan (Midwest)	147		
West Virginia (South Atlantic)	155		
Williamsport (New York-Penn)	162		
Wilmington (Carolina)	133		
Winston-Salem (Carolina)	133		
Wisconsin (Midwest)	147		
Yakima (Northwest)	166		

INDEPENDENT TEAMS

Team (League)	Page
Amarillo (American)	178
Bridgeport (Atlantic)	183
Brockton (Can-Am)	186
Calgary (North American)	194
Camden (Atlantic)	183
Chico (North American)	194
Edinburg (North American)	194
Edmonton (North American)	195
El Paso (American)	178
Evansville (Frontier)	189
Fargo-Moorhead (American)	179
Florence (Frontier)	189
Fort Worth (American)	179
Gary Southshore (American)	179
Gateway (Frontier)	190
Grand Prairie (American)	180
Henderson (North American)	195
Joliet (Frontier)	190
Kalamazoo (Frontier)	190
Kansas City (American)	180
Lake County (North American)	195
Lake Erie (Frontier)	191
Lancaster (Atlantic)	184
Lincoln (American)	180
Long Island (Atlantic)	184
Na Ikaika Koa (North American)	195
New Jersey (Can-Am)	187

OTHER ORGANIZATIONS

Organization	Page
Alaska Baseball League	282
All-American Baseball Talent Showcases	295
America East Conference	251
American Baseball Coaches Association	250
Area Code Games	295
Arizona Fall Classic	295
Association of Professional Ball Players	83
Atlantic 10 Conference	251
Atlantic Coast Conference	251
Atlantic Collegiate Baseball League	283
Atlantic Sun Conference	251
Babe Ruth Birthplace	82
Baseball Assistance Team	84
Baseball Chapel	84
Baseball Factory	295
Baseball Trade Show	84
Baseball Winter Meetings	84
Big East Conference	251
Big South Conference	251
Big Ten Conference	251
Big 12 Conference	251
Big West Conference	251
CBS Sports	80
CNN Sports	80
California Community College Commission on Athletics	250
Canadian Baseball Hall of Fame	82
Colonial Athletic Association	251
Conference USA	252
Cape Cod League	284
Coastal Plain League	285
Donruss/Playoff	84
Elias Sports Bureau	79
ESPN/ESPN 2	79
ESPN Classic/ESPN News	79
ESPN International/Deportes	79
ESPN Radio	80
Field of Dreams Movie Site	82
Florida Collegiate Summer League	286
Fox Sports	79
Fox Sports Net	80
Futures Collegiate League of New England	286
Grandstand Cards	84
Great Lakes Summer Collegiate League	286
Great West Conference	252
HBO Sports	80
Horizon League	252
Ivy League	252
Jayhawk League	287
Jim Evans Academy	82
Little League Baseball Museum	82

INDEX

Louisville Slugger Museum/Factory	83
M.I.N.K. League	287
MLB Advanced Media	79
MLB Advanced Media Multimedia	80
MLB Players Alumni Association	83
MLB Network	79
MLB Players Association	81
MLB Scouting Bureau	81
Metro Atlantic Athletic Conference	252
Mid-American Conference	252
Mid-Eastern Athletic Conference	252
Minor League Baseball Alumni Association	83
Missouri Athletic Conference	83
Mountain Collegiate League	287
Mountain West Conference	252
Multiad Sports	84
NBC Sports	80
National Alliance of Summer College Baseball	282
National Association of Intercollegiate Athletics	250
National Baseball Hall of Fame	83
National Collegiate Athletic Association	250
National Federation of State High School Associations	294
National High School Baseball Coaches Association	294
National Junior College Athletic Association	250
Negro League Baseball Museum	83
New England Collegiate League	288
New York Collegiate Baseball League	289
Nolan Ryan Foundation	83
Northeast Conference	253
Northwest Athletic Association of Community Colleges	250
Northwoods League	289
Ohio Valley Conference	253
Pacific-10 Conference	253
Pacific International League	290
Patriot League	253
Perfect Game USA	295
Professional Baseball Athletic Trainers	82
Professional Baseball Employment Opportunities	84
Professional Baseball Scouts Foundation	81
Professional Baseball Umpire Corp	82
Prospect League	290
Rogers SportsNet	80
Society for American Baseball Research	83
Southeastern Conference	253
Southern Collegiate Baseball League	253
Southern Conference	253
Southland Conference	253
Southwestern Athletic Conference	253
Scout of the Year Foundation	81
Sports Byline USA	80
Sporting News Radio	80
Stats Inc.	79
Summit League	253
Sun Belt Conference	253
Texas Collegiate League	291
The Sports Network	80
The Umpire School	82
Topps	84
Turner Sports	79
Upper Deck	84
Valley League	292
Wendelstedt Umpire School	82
West Coast Conference	253
West Coast League	293
Western Athletic Conference	253
World Umpires Association	82
XM Satellite Radio	80